California

THE ROUGH GUIDE

There are more than one hundred Rough Guide titles
covering destinations from Amsterdam to Zimbabwe

Forthcoming titles include

Chile • Indonesia • New England • New Orleans

Rough Guide Reference Series

Classical Music • European Football • The Internet • Jazz
Opera • Reggae • Rock Music • World Music

Rough Guide Phrasebooks

Czech • Egyptian Arabic • French • German • Greek
Hindi & Urdu • Hungarian • Indonesian • Italian • Japanese
Mandarin Chinese • Mexican Spanish • Polish • Portuguese
Russian • Spanish • Swahili • Thai • Turkish • Vietnamese

Rough Guides on the Internet

www.roughguides.com

ROUGH GUIDE CREDITS

Text editor: Helena Smith
Series editor: Mark Ellingham
Editorial: Martin Dunford, Jonathan Buckley, Samantha Cook, Jo Mead, Kate Berens, Amanda Tomlin, Ann-Marie Shaw, Paul Gray, Sarah Dallas, Chris Schüler, Caroline Osborne, Judith Bamber, Kieran Falconer, Orla Duane, Olivia Eccleshall, Ruth Blackmore, Sophie Martin (UK); Andrew Rosenberg (US)
Production: Susanne Hillen, Andy Hilliard, Judy Pang, Link Hall, Nicola Williamson, Helen Ostick, James Morris

Cartography: Melissa Flack, Maxine Burke, Nichola Goodliffe
Picture research: Eleanor Hill
Online editors: Alan Spicer, Kate Hands (UK); Geronimo Madrid (US)
Finance: John Fisher, Celia Crowley, Neeta Mistry
Marketing & Publicity: Richard Trillo, Simon Carloss, Niki Smith (UK); Jean-Marie Kelly, SoRelle Braun (US)
Administration: Tania Hummel, Alexander Mark Rogers

ACKNOWLEDGEMENTS

Jeff Dickey: I would like to thank my family, especially my wife Brenna; **Edie Jarolim:** thanks to Laurie Armstrong, and to Craig Foltz for research help in San Diego; **Julie Soller:** thanks to the San Francisco Convention & Visitors Bureau; **David Thomsen:** thanks to Helena for patience throughout, the Symons, Dan Weinshenker, Amanda Burke, Adam Wilson, Sibby Ross, Mike Strohecker, Derek Wilson, and my family for support, tips, advice, and laughs.

Thanks, also, to James Morris, Eleanor Hill, Melissa Flack and Jon Bousfield at the Rough Guides, to Russell Walton

for proofreading, to Lisa Pusey for picture research and to Chris Scully for indexing

Extract reprinted by permission of G.P. Putnam's Sons, a division of The Putnam Publishing Group, from *The Joy Luck Club* by Amy Tan. Copyright © by Amy Tan.

Extract from *The Tortilla Curtain* by T. Coraghessan Boyle, copyright © by T. Coraghessan Boyle, used by permission of Viking Penguin, a division of Penguin Putnam Inc., and Bloomsbury Publishing Plc (published by Bloomsbury in 1995).

PUBLISHING INFORMATION

This fifth edition published September 1998 by
  Rough Guides Ltd, 62–70 Shorts Gardens,
  London WC2H 9AB. Reprinted March 1999.
  Distributed by the Penguin Group:
Penguin Books Ltd, 27 Wrights Lane, London W8 5TZ.
Penguin Books USA Inc., 375 Hudson Street, New York
  10014, USA.
Penguin Books Australia Ltd, 487 Maroondah Highway,
  PO Box 257, Ringwood, Victoria 3134, Australia.
Penguin Books Canada Ltd, 10 Alcorn Avenue, Toronto,
  Ontario, Canada M4V 1E4.
Penguin Books (NZ) Ltd, 182–190 Wairau Road,
  Auckland 10, New Zealand.
Typeset in Linotron Univers and Century Old Style to an
  original design by Andrew Oliver.
Printed in England by Clays Ltd, St Ives PLC.
Illustrations in Part One and Part Three by Edward Briant.
Illustration on p.1 by Cathie Felstead and on p.587 by
  Sally Davies.

The publishers and authors have done their best to
  ensure the accuracy and currency of all the information
  in *The Rough Guide to California*; however, they can
  accept no responsibility for any loss, injury, or
  inconvenience sustained by any traveler as a result of
  information or advice contained in the guide.

California

THE ROUGH GUIDE

written and researched by

**Deborah Bosley, Jeff Dickey,
Edie Jarolim, Jamie Jensen, Mick Sinclair,
Julie Soller, David Thomsen, Greg Ward
and Paul Whitfield**

THE ROUGH GUIDES

READERS' LETTERS

Many thanks go to the readers who have taken the time to contact us with comments and suggestions. These include: Geoff and Jane Atkinson, Christoph Bergemann, Adele Brazier, M. Barrett, Dr Kirsteen N. Browning, Bridget Calzaretta, Jan Cross, N.H. Cunnington, K. & J. Douglas-Henry, Marc Dubin, Greta Finer and Kenny Morrison, Liz Forrest, Richard Holt, Angela Katzenmeier, Kevin Kavanagh, Lorenzo and Alida Khan, Graham J. Lawrenson, David Loveless, Rosemary Malihoudis, Tony Mitsak, Simon Poon, Graham Rhind and John Ryne, Marcus Roy, Joanne Rudgely, Matthew Spencer, Mike Stephenson, Jonathan Stewart, Tony Warner, Dylan White and Nicky Hack, Martin Wild, Patrick Wilkes, Sara Withers, Dave Wright and Caroline Smith, and Steve Wright.

CONTENTS

Introduction x

PART THREE CONTEXTS 587

LIST OF MAPS

MAP SYMBOLS

🛡5	Interstate	🏛	Historical house	🪜	Waterfall
101	U.S. Highway	♅	Castle	🌴	Oasis
49	Highway	∴	Ruins	⛳	Golf course
▬▬	Railway	Λ	Campground	🏕	Picnic area
★	BART transport system	◉	Accommodation	(i)	Information office
-----	Path	◖	Cave	⊠	Post office
– – –	Ferry route	▲	Peak	■	Building
———	Waterway	ᴧᴧ	Mountains	⊞	Church (town maps)
– ––	Chapter division boundary	〰	Canyon	⊹⊹	Cemetery
▬▪▬▪	International borders	⬒	Viewpoint	▨	Park
▨ ▪▪	County borders	✕	Airport	▨	National Park
⚓	Church (regional maps)	★	Bus stop	▨	Beach
♀	Museum				

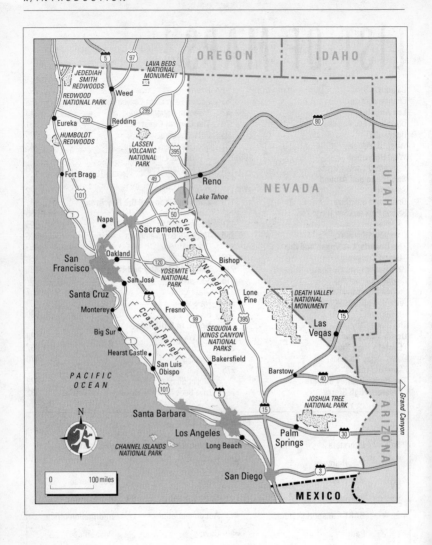

INTRODUCTION

California is America squared. It's the place you go to find more America than you ever thought possible.

What's Wrong with America by Scott Bradfield

No region of the world, perhaps, has been as publicized, and idealized, as **California**, and none lives up to the hype to quite the same degree. A terrestrial paradise of sun, sand, surf and sea, it has a whole lot more besides: high mountain ranges, fast-paced glitzy cities, deep primeval forests, and hot dry deserts.

Having zoomed from the Stone Age to Silicon Valley in little more than a couple of centuries, California doesn't dwell on the past. In some ways this part of America represents the ultimate "now" society, with all that entails – life is lived very much in the fast lane, and conspicuous consumption is emphasized to the exclusion of almost everything else. But this is only one side of the coin; the deeper sense of age here often gets skimmed over. Provided you get out of the cities, it is readily apparent in the landscape: dense groves of ancient trees, primitive rock carvings left by the aboriginal Native American culture, and the eerie ghost towns of the Gold Rush pioneers. A land of superlatives, California really is full of the oldest, the tallest, the largest, the most spectacular, all of which goes far beyond local bravura.

It's important to bear in mind, too, that the supposed "superficiality" of California is largely a myth, an image promoted as much by Americans on the East Coast as by foreigners – even if the area's endeavours to gain cultural credibility can sometimes seem brash. Politically, it's probably the USA's most schizophrenic region, home state of some of its most reactionary figures – Ronald Reagan and Richard Nixon to name just two – yet also the source of some of the country's most progressive political movements. Some of the fiercest protests of the Sixties emanated from here, and in many ways this is still the heart of liberal America. Consider the level of environmental awareness, which puts the smoky East to shame, and the fact that California has set *the* standard for the rest of the US (and the world) regarding gay pride and social permissiveness. Economically, too, the region is crucial, whether it's in the traditionally dominant film industry, the recently ascendant music business, even in the increasingly important financial markets – in which Los Angeles has come to set the pace.

Where to go

California is the third largest state in the US, covering nearly 160,000 square miles: keep in mind that distances between the main destinations can be huge, and that you won't, unless you're here for an extended period, be able to see everything on one trip. In an area so varied it's hard to pick out specific highlights. You may well start off in **Los Angeles**, far and away the biggest and most stimulating city: a maddening collection of freeways and beaches, seedy suburbs and high-gloss neighborhoods and extreme lifestyles that you should see at least once, even if you make a quick exit for more relaxed locales. From Los Angeles you have a number of choices. You can head south to **San Diego** – a smaller, up-and-coming city, with broad, welcoming beaches and a handy position close to the Mexican border, or you could push inland to the Californian **desert** areas, notably **Death Valley** – as its name suggests, a barren inhospitable landscape of volcanic craters and windswept sand dunes that in summer (when you can fry an egg on your car bonnet) becomes the hottest place on earth. It's a logical trip from here across to the **Grand Canyon** via **Las Vegas**; though not in California, we've included these last two in Chapter Three of the guide. An alternative is to make the steady journey up the **Central Coast**, a gorgeous run following the shoreline north through some of the state's most dramatic scenery, and taking in some of its liveliest small towns, notably Santa Barbara and Santa Cruz.

The Central Coast makes the transition from Southern to Northern California – a break that's more than just geographical. **San Francisco**, at the top end, is California's second city, and quite different from LA: the coast's oldest, most European-looking city, it's set compactly over a series of steep hills, with wooden houses tumbling down to water on both sides. San Francisco also gives access to some of the state's most extraordinary scenery, not least in the National Parks to the east, especially **Yosemite**, where powerful waterfalls cascade into a sheer glacial valley that's been immortalized by Ansel Adams and countless others in search of the definitive landscape photograph.

North of San Francisco, the population thins and the physical look changes yet again. The climate is wetter up here, the valleys that much greener, flanked by a jagged coastline shadowed by mighty redwoods, the tallest trees in the world. Though many visitors choose to venture no further than the **Wine Country** and the Russian River Valley on weekend forays from the city, it's well worth taking time out to explore the state's northernmost regions, a volcano-scarred desolation that's as different from the popular image of California as it's possible to be.

When to go

California's climate comes close to its subtropical ideal. In **Southern California** in particular you can count on endless days of sunshine from May to October, and warm dry nights – though **LA**'s notorious smog is at its worst when the temperatures are highest, in August and September.

Right along the **coast** mornings can be hazily overcast, especially in May and June, though you can still get a suntan – or sunburn – even under grayish skies. In winter temperatures drop somewhat, but more importantly it can rain for weeks on end, causing massive mudslides that wipe out roads and hillside homes. Inland, the deserts are warm in winter and unbearably hot (120°F is not unusual) in summer; desert nights can be freezing in winter, when, strangely but beautifully, it can even snow. For serious **snow**, head to the mountains, where hiking trails at the higher elevations are blocked from November to June every year: skiers can take advantage of well-groomed slopes along the Sierra Nevada mountains and around Lake Tahoe.

The coast of Northern California is wetter and cooler than the south, its summers tempered by sea-breezes and fog, and its winters mild but wet. **San Francisco**, because of its exposed position at the tip of a peninsula, can be chilly all year, with summer fogs tending to roll in to ruin what may have started off as a pleasant sunny day. Head a mile inland, and you're back in the sun.

DAYTIME TEMPERATURES (MAX & MIN °F)							
	Jan		April		July		Oct	
San Diego	65	46	68	54	76	63	73	58
Los Angeles	65	47	71	53	83	63	77	57
Fresno	55	36	75	47	99	63	80	48
San Francisco	55	42	64	47	72	54	71	51
Death Valley	65	37	91	61	116	87	91	51

PART ONE

THE
BASICS

GETTING THERE FROM BRITAIN AND EUROPE

Though flying to California from Europe is pretty straightforward, choosing the best route can be more complicated than you might think, with prices fluctuating wildly according to how and when you go. The majority of budget options involve non-stop services from Britain, although many others turn out to be so-called "direct" flights, which can land several times, waiting an hour or so at each stop – a flight is called direct as long as it keeps the same flight number throughout its journey. The first place the plane lands is your point of entry into the US, which means you'll have to collect your bags and go through customs and immigration formalities there, even if you're continuing on to California on the same plane. This can be a real pain after a ten-hour journey, so it's worth finding out before you book a ticket.

FARES, ROUTES AND AGENTS

Although you can fly to the US from any of the regional airports, the only **non-stop flights** from Britain to California are from London. Most of these land at LA, the hub of the region's air travel. Fewer travel non-stop to San Francisco, and you can't fly non-stop at all to San Diego. The non-stop **flight time** is around eleven hours from London to San Francisco or LA; add an hour at least for each intervening stop on direct flights, twice that if you have to change planes. Following winds ensure that return flights are always an hour or two shorter than outward journeys. Because of the time difference between Britain and the West Coast (eight hours almost all year), flights usually leave Britain mid-morning, while flights back from the US tend to arrive in Britain early in the morning.

Britain remains one of the best places in Europe to obtain flight bargains, though **fares** vary widely according to season, availability and the current level of inter-airline competition. The comments that follow can only act as a general guide, so be sure to shop around carefully for the best offers by checking the **travel ads** in the weekend papers, on the **holiday pages** of ITV's *Teletext* and, in London, scouring *Time Out* and the *Evening Standard*. Giveaway magazines aimed at young travelers, like *TNT*, are also useful resources.

Stand-by deals (open-dated tickets which you pay for and then decide later when you want to fly – if there's room on the plane) are few and far between, and don't give great savings: in general you're better off with an **Apex** ticket. The conditions on these are pretty standard whoever

SAMPLE AIR FARES FROM BRITAIN

The prices given below (in £ sterling) are a general indication of the (minimum) transatlantic air fares currently obtainable from specialist companies; remember to add £40–50 airport tax to these figures. Each airline decides the exact dates of its seasons. Prices are for departures from London and Manchester.

	LOW Nov 1–Dec 14, Dec 25–March 28, April 11–30		SHOULDER March 29–Apr 10, May 1–Jun 30, Sept 1–Oct 31		HIGH July 1–Aug 31, Dec 15–24	
	one-way	return	one-way	return	one-way	return
Los Angeles	215	310	215	350	255	490
San Francisco	215	310	215	350	255	490

One word of **warning**: it's not a good idea to buy a **one-way** ticket to the States. Not only are they rarely good value compared to a round-trip ticket, but US immigration officials usually take them as a sign that you aren't planning to go home, and may refuse you entry.

you fly with – seats must be purchased seven days or more in advance, and you must stay for at least one Saturday night; tickets are normally valid for up to six months. Some airlines also do less expensive **Super-Apex** tickets, which fall into two categories: the first are approximately £150 cheaper than an ordinary Apex but must be bought 21 days in advance and require a minimum stay of seven days and a maximum stay of one month, the second are around £100 less than an Apex, must be purchased fourteen days in advance and entail a minimum stay of a week and a maximum stay of two months – such tickets are usually non-refundable or changeable. **"Open-jaw"** tickets can be a good idea, allowing you to fly into LA, for example, and back from San Francisco for little or no extra charge; fares are calculated by halving the return fares to each destination and adding the two figures together. This makes a convenient option for those who want a fly-drive holiday (see below).

Generally, the most expensive time to fly is **high season**, roughly between June and August and around Christmas. May and September are slightly less pricey, and the rest of the year is considered low season and is cheaper still. Keep an eye out for slack season bargains, and, additionally, make sure to check the exact dates of the seasons with your operator or airline; you might be able to make major savings by shifting your departure date by a week – or even a day. **Weekend rates** for all return flights tend to be around £20 more expensive than those in the week.

For an overview of the various offers, and unofficially discounted tickets, go straight to an **agent** specializing in low-cost flights (we've listed some on p.6). Especially if you're under 26 or a student, they may be able to knock up to thirty percent off the regular Apex fares when there are no special airline deals. Agents will usually offer non-stop flights, or "direct" flights via another airport in the USA, although you may be offered other, stranger combinations (London–Los Angeles via Amsterdam, Manchester–Los Angeles via Paris for example) – all worth considering if the price is right.

The same agents also offer cut-price seats on **charter flights**. These are particularly good value if you're traveling from a British city other than London, although they tend to be limited to the summer season, be restricted to so-called "holiday destinations" and have fixed departure and return dates. Brochures are available in most high street travel agents, or contact the specialists direct.

Finally, if you've got a bit more time, or want to see a bit more of the USA, it's often possible to stop over in another city – **New York** especially – and fly on from there for little more than the cost of a direct flight to California. Also, with increased competition on the **London–Los Angeles** route, thanks to Virgin Atlantic among others and price wars between US carriers, the cost of a connecting flight from LA to San Francisco has been brought down to as low as £40. Many airlines also offer **air passes**, which allow foreign travelers to fly between a given number of US cities for one discounted price. For more details on long-distance travel within the US see p.8.

COURIER FLIGHTS

It's still possible, if not as common as it used to be, for those on a very tight budget to travel as **couriers**. Courier firms offer opportunities to travel at discounted rates (as low as £200 return to the West Coast) in return for delivering a package. There'll be someone to check you in and to meet you at your destination, which minimizes any red-tape hassle. However, you'll have to travel light, with only a cabin-bag, and accept tight restrictions on travel dates. For phone numbers, check the *Yellow Pages*, as these businesses come and go.

PACKAGES

Packages – fly-drive, flight/accommodation deals and guided tours (or a combination of all three) – can work out cheaper than arranging the same trip yourself, especially for a short-term stay. The obvious drawbacks are the loss of flexibility and the fact that most schemes use hotels in the mid-range bracket, but there is a wide variety of options available. High-street travel agents have plenty of brochures and information about the various combinations.

FLY-DRIVE

Fly-drive deals, which give cut-rate (sometimes free) car rental when buying a transatlantic ticket, always work out cheaper than renting on the spot and give especially great value if you intend to do a lot of driving. On the other hand, you'll probably have to pay more for the flight than if you booked it through a discount agent. Competition between airlines (especially Northwest and TWA) and tour operators means that it's well worth phoning to check on current special promotions.

Northwest Flydrive offers excellent deals for not much more than an ordinary Apex fare; for example, a return flight to LA or San Francisco and a week's car rental costs around £350 per person in low season. Several of the other companies listed in the box on p.7 offer similar, and sometimes cheaper, packages.

Watch out for hidden extras, such as local taxes, and "drop-off" charges, which can be as much as a week's rental, and Collision Damage Waiver insurance (see p.30). Remember, too, that while you can

drive in the States with a British license, there can be problems renting vehicles if you're under 25. For complete car-rental and driveaway details, see "Getting Around California" (p.29).

FLIGHT AND ACCOMMODATION DEALS

There's really no end of combined **flight and accommodation deals** to California, and although you can often do things cheaper independently, you won't be able to do the *same* things cheaper – in fact, the equivalent room booked separately will normally be a lot more expensive – and you can leave the organizational hassles to someone else. Drawbacks include the loss of flexibility and the fact that you'll probably have to stay in hotels in the mid-range to expensive bracket, even though less expensive accommodation is almost always available.

FLIGHTS FROM BRITAIN

The following carriers operate **non-stop flights** from London to California (all from Heathrow unless otherwise stated):

Air New Zealand, five times a week from Heathrow to Los Angeles.

American Airlines, daily to Los Angeles.

British Airways, daily to Los Angeles and San Francisco; daily to Los Angeles from Gatwick.

United Airlines, daily to Los Angeles and San Francisco.

Virgin Atlantic, daily to Los Angeles and San Francisco.

The following carriers operate **one-stop direct flights** from London to California (all from Gatwick unless otherwise stated):

American Airlines, daily from Heathrow via Dallas, New York or Chicago to San Francisco.

British Airways, five a week from Heathrow in high season via Los Angeles to San Diego.

Continental, daily via Denver, Miami, Houston or Newark to Los Angeles, San Francisco and San Diego.

Delta, daily via Cincinnati or Atlanta to Los Angeles, San Francisco and San Diego.

Northwest, four a week via Detroit or Minneapolis to Los Angeles and San Francisco.

TWA, daily via St Louis to Los Angeles and San Francisco.

The following carriers operate direct flights from **regional airports** to the US:

American Airlines, from Manchester to Chicago and New York, and from Glasgow to Chicago.

British Airways, from Manchester and Glasgow to New York.

Delta, from Manchester to Atlanta.

Northwest, from Glasgow to Boston.

AIRLINES

Air New Zealand ☎0181/741 2299
American Airlines ☎0345/789789
British Airways ☎0345/222111
Continental ☎01293/776464
Delta ☎0800/414767

Northwest ☎01424 /224400
TWA ☎0345/333333
United ☎0181/313 0999
Virgin Atlantic ☎01293/747747

Bridge The World 1–3 Ferdinand St, London NW1 (☎0171/916 0990).

Campus Travel 52 Grosvenor Gardens, London SW1 (☎0171/730 2101); branches nationwide.

Council Travel 28a Poland St, London W1V (☎0171/437 7767).

Destination Group 41–45 Goswell Rd, London EC1 (☎0171/253 9000).

STA Travel 86 Old Brompton Rd, London SW7 (☎0171/361 6262); branches nationwide.

Trailfinders 42–50 Earls Court Rd, London W8 (☎0171/937 5400); branches nationwide.

Travel Bug 597 Cheetham Hill Rd, Manchester M8 5EJ (☎0161/721 4000).

Travel Cuts 295a Regent St, London W1 (☎0171/255 2082).

A handful of tour operators (see below) offer quite deluxe packages, of which Virgin Holidays are about the least expensive: for example, seven nights in San Francisco plus return flight costs around £639–879 per person. Discount agents can set up more basic packages for just over £500 each. Pre-booked accommodation schemes, under which you buy vouchers for use in a specific group of hotels, are not normally good value – see p.36.

TOURING AND ADVENTURE PACKAGES

A simple and exciting way to see a chunk of California's extensive wilderness, without being hassled by too many practical considerations, is to take a specialist **touring and adventure package**, which includes transportation, accommodation, food and a guide. Some of the more adventurous carry small groups around on minibuses and use a combination of budget hotels and camping (equipment, except a sleeping bag, is provided). Most also have a food kitty of around £25 per week, with many meals cooked and eaten communally, although there's plenty of time to leave the group and do your own thing.

TrekAmerica is one UK-based company to offer such deals; a typical package would be ten days in California and the "Wild West" for £425 or so excluding flights. Other operators are listed opposite. If you're interested in **backcountry hiking**, the San Francisco-based Sierra Club (see p.46) offers a range of tours that take you into parts of the state that most people never see.

Both Delta and Aer Lingus fly to California **direct** from Ireland. The **cheapest flights** from Ireland – if you're under 26 or a student – are available from USIT. Student-only return fares to **San Francisco** or **Los Angeles** range from IR£389 to IR£569. Ordinary Apex fares are only marginally higher.

USIT can be contacted at Aston Quay, O'Connell Bridge, Dublin 2 (☎01/677 8117), while Aer Lingus is at 40 O'Connell St, Dublin 1 (☎01/844 4777), and Delta Airlines is at 24 Merrion Square, Dublin 2 (☎01/676 8080 or 1-800/768080).

It is generally far cheaper to fly non-stop to California from London than any other European city. However, for the best deals to New York from Brussels and Paris, contact **Nouvelles Frontières**, 87 boulevard de Grenelle, 75015 Paris (☎41.41.58.58) and 2 boulevard M. Lemonnier, 1000 Brussels (☎02/547 4444). Its London branch is at 2–3 Woodstock St (☎0171/629 7772), although you'll have to go through the Paris or Brussels branch in order to actually book tickets.

Other options are the cut-price charter flights occasionally offered from major European cities; ask at your nearest travel agent for details. In Germany, look for discount **youth fare** deals which United offers (to those under 26 booking 72 hours or less in advance) from Frankfurt, its continental hub (☎069/605020).

SPECIALIST HOLIDAY OPERATORS

Airtours Wavell House, Helmshore, Rossendale, Lancs BB4 4NB (☎01706/240033).
Multi-centre holidays including combinations of Los Angeles, San Francisco and Las Vegas.

American Adventures 64 Mount Pleasant Ave, Tunbridge Wells, Kent TN1 1QY (☎01892/512700).
Small-group touring and adventure holidays on the West Coast.

American Airlines Holidays PO Box 5, 12 Coningsby Rd, Peterborough PE3 8XP (☎0870/605 0506).
Flight plus accommodation and fly-drive deals in Los Angeles, San Diego, San Francisco and Californian beach resorts.

American Connections 10 York Way, Lancaster Rd, High Wycombe, Bucks HP12 3PY (☎01494/473173).
City breaks in Los Angeles and San Francisco.

Bon Voyage 18 Bellevue Rd, Southampton, Hants SO15 2AY (☎01703/330332).
Flight-plus-accommodation deals in San Francisco, Los Angeles and Palm Springs.

Bridge Travel Service Bridge House, Broxbourne, Herts EN10 7DT (☎01992/456101).
Packages to Disneyland California.

British Airways Holidays Astral Towers, Bettsway, London Road, Crawley, West Sussex RH10 2XA (☎01293/723121).
City breaks in Los Angeles, San Diego and San Francisco, and fly-drive deals (including motorhomes).

Contiki Travel Wells House, 15 Elmfield Rd, Bromley, Kent BR1 1LS (☎0181/290 6777).
West Coast coach tours.

Cosmos Tourama House, 17 Homesdale Rd, Bromley, Kent BR2 9LX (☎0181/464 3444).
Packages to Los Angeles/Anaheim and San Diego.

Destination USA 41–45 Goswell Rd, London EC1 (☎0171/253 2000).
Tailor-made accommodation and fly-drive deals.

Explore Worldwide 1 Frederick St, Aldershot, Hants GU11 1LQ (☎01252/319448).
Walking holidays in West Coast National Parks.

Funway 1 Elmfield Park, Bromley, Kent BR1 1LU (☎0181/466 0222).
Package holidays to Los Angeles, San Diego, San Francisco and Palm Springs.

Kuoni Kuoni House, Dorking, Surrey RH5 4AZ (☎01306/742888).
Multi-center flight-plus-accommodation-plus-car deals featuring Los Angeles, San Francisco and San Diego.

North America Travel Service 7 Albion St, Leeds LS1 5ER (☎0113/246 1466).
Also branches in Nottingham, Manchester and Barnsley.

Northwest Flydrive PO Box 45, Bexhill-on-Sea, East Sussex TN40 1PY (☎01424/224400).
Flight-plus-accommodation and fly-drive specials.

Premier Holidays Westbrook, Milton Road, Cambridge CB4 1YQ (☎01223/516516).
Flight-plus-accommodation deals throughout California.

Road Runner 64 Mount Pleasant Ave, Tunbridge Wells, Kent TN1 1QY (☎01892/512700).
Hostelling-based touring and adventure packages.

Travel 4 Hill House, Highgate Hill, London N19 5NA (☎0171/281 7833).
Tailor-made arrangements for Los Angeles, San Diego and San Francisco.

Travelpack 523 High Rd, Wembley HA0 2DH (☎0990/747101).
Escorted tours and tailor-made holidays throughout California.

Top Deck 131 Earls Court Rd, London SW5 (☎0171/370 4555).
Agents for numerous adventure touring specialists.

TrekAmerica Trek House, The Bullring, Deddington, Oxford OX15 0TT (☎01869/338777).
Touring adventure holidays.

United Vacations PO Box 377, Bromley, Kent (☎0181/313 0999).
City breaks, tailor-mades and fly-drives.

Up & Away 19 The Mall, Bromley, Kent BR1 1LY (☎0181/289 5050).
Tailor-mades and fly-drives to Los Angeles and Californian National Parks.

Virgin Holidays The Galleria, Station Road, Crawley, West Sussex RH10 1WW (☎01293/617181).
Packages to a wide range of California destinations.

GETTING THERE FROM NORTH AMERICA

Getting to California from anywhere else in North America is never a problem; the region is well served by air, rail and road networks. All the main airlines operate daily scheduled flights to San Francisco and LA from across the country, and there are daily flights from Toronto and Vancouver as well.

Flying remains the best but most expensive way to travel; taking a train comes a slow second. Traveling by bus is the least expensive method, but again is slow, and is much less comfortable than either train or plane.

BY AIR

To Los Angeles, many domestic flights land at the city's international **LAX** airport, as well as the smaller airports at Burbank, Long Beach, Ontario and John Wayne in Orange County. For San Francisco, besides the main **San Francisco International Airport** (known as SFO), two others, both in the Bay Area, may be useful – particularly **Oakland International** (OAK), across the bay but easily accessible. The third Bay Area airport, **San Jose Municipal** (SJO), forty miles south, is a bit out of the way but has good connections with the western US, LA especially. Some carriers also fly to **San Diego**'s Lindburgh airport non-stop.

As airlines tend to match each other's prices, there's generally little difference in the quoted fares. Barring another fare war, round-trip prices start at around $350 from New York, slightly less from Midwest cities and slightly more from Toronto and Montréal. What makes more differ-

AIRLINES IN THE USA AND CANADA

Aer Lingus ☎1-800/223-6537

Aeromexico ☎1-800/237-6639

Air Canada ☎1-800/776-3000; in Canada call directory inquiries for local toll-free number

Air France ☎1-800/237-2747; in Canada ☎1-800/667-2747

Alaska Airlines ☎1-800/426-0333

America West ☎1-800/2FLYAWA

American Airlines ☎1-800/433-7300

British Airways ☎1-800/247-9297; in Canada ☎1-800/668-1059

Canadian ☎1-800/426-7000; in Canada ☎1-800/665-1177

Continental ☎1-800/525-0280

Delta Airlines ☎1-800/221-1212; in Canada, call directory inquiries for local toll-free number

Iberia ☎1-800/772-4642; in Canada ☎1-800/423-7421

Icelandair ☎1-800/223-5500

KLM ☎1-800/374-7747; in Canada ☎1-800/361-5073

Lufthansa ☎1-800/645-3880; in Canada ☎1-800/563-5954

Northwest ☎1-800/225-2525

Reno Air ☎1-800/736-6247

Scandinavian Airlines ☎1-800/221-2350

Southwest ☎1-800/435-9792

Tower Air ☎1-800/221-2500

Trans World Airlines ☎1-800/221-2000

United Airlines ☎1-800/241-6522

US Airways ☎1-800/428-4322

Virgin Atlantic ☎1-800/862-8621

ence than your choice of carrier are the conditions governing the ticket – whether it's fully refundable, the time and day and most importantly the **time of year** you travel. Least expensive of all is a non-summer-season midweek flight, booked and paid for at least three weeks in advance. Also keep in mind that one-way tickets are sometimes more expensive than round-trip tickets. While it's good to call the airlines directly to get a sense of their official fares, it's also worth checking with a reputable **travel agent** to find out about any **special deals** or student/youth fares that may be available.

In addition to the big-name scheduled airlines, a few lesser-known carriers run no-frills flights, which can prove to be very good value, especially if you have a flexible schedule and can put up with a few delays. Tower Air, the New York-based charter operator, has seven flights a week from New York to Los Angeles for about $250 round-trip and five flights from New York to San Francisco for about $300 round-trip. Southwest flies from a host of Midwestern and Western cities at rock-bottom prices; four daily flights leave Salt Lake City for Oakland (they don't go directly to San Francisco) from $138 round-trip ($76 one way). Their lowest fare out of Seattle to Oakland is $126 round-trip ($72 one way), while LA to Oakland goes for $76 round-trip ($61 one way).

Travelers intending to fly from **Canada** are likely to find that, with less competition on these routes (Canadian flies to San Francisco only from Vancouver; most other routes are monopolized by Air Canada), fares are somewhat higher than they are for flights wholly within the US. You may well find that it's worth the effort to get to a US city first, and fly on to California from there.

BY TRAIN

If you have a bit more money and hanker after a few more creature comforts (all the trains have private cabins and dining cars), or simply have the time and inclination to take in some of the rest of the US on your way to California, then an Amtrak **train** may be just the ticket for you. The most spectacular train journey of all has to be the *California Zephyr*, which runs all the way from Chicago to San Francisco (53 hours; departs 3.05pm daily) and comes into its own during the ride through the Rockies west of Denver. After climbing alongside raging rivers through gorgeous **mountain scenery**, the route drops down the

> For all information on **Amtrak fares and schedules**, and to make reservations, use the toll-free number ☎1-800/USA-RAIL. Do not call individual stations.

west flank of the Rockies and races across the Utah and Nevada deserts by night, stopping at Salt Lake City and Reno. The next day the train climbs up and over the mighty Sierra Nevada, following the route of the first transcontinental railroad on its way into Oakland, where you change to a bus for the ride into San Francisco.

The major southern route, the *Sunset Limited*, originates in San Antonio, Texas, and crosses New Mexico and Arizona (connecting buses from Flagstaff head to the Grand Canyon) before eventually arriving in Los Angeles.

Amtrak **fares** are often more expensive than flying, though off-peak discounts and special deals can make the train an economical as well as an aesthetic choice. One-way cross-country fares are around $285, though if you're traveling round-trip you can take advantage of what they call **"Explore America"** fares, which are zone-based and allow three stopovers in between your origin and eventual return. Travel within the West (from Denver to the Pacific) costs $198 between September and May or $228 from June to August; within the West and Midwest (west of Chicago) costs $258/318; and for the entire USA the cost is $318/378. While Amtrak's basic fares are decent value, if you want to travel in a bit more comfort the cost rises quickly. **Sleeping compartments**, which include meals, small toilets and showers, start at around $150 per night for one or two people.

BY BUS

Bus travel is the most tedious and time-consuming way to get to California, and, for all the discomfort, won't really save you much money. **Greyhound** (☎1-800/231-2222) is the sole long-distance operator and has an extensive network of destinations in California. A one-way ticket from New York to San Francisco, bought 21 days in advance, costs $59. Fourteen days in advance, tickets cost $79, while tickets purchased on the day of travel go for $125.

The only reason to go Greyhound is if you're planning to visit a number of other places en route; Greyhound's **Ameripass** is good for unlimited travel within a certain time, and costs $199 for seven days, $299 for fifteen days, $409 for thirty days, and $599 for sixty days. **Foreign visitors** can buy Ameripasses before leaving home; see p.30 for details.

An alternative, in every sense, is the San Francisco-based **Green Tortoise** bus company; see p.34 for details.

BY CAR

Driving your own car gives the greatest freedom and flexibility, but if you don't have one (or don't trust the one you do have), one option worth considering is a **driveaway**. Companies operate in most major cities, and are paid to find drivers to take a customer's car from one place to another – most commonly between California and New York. The company will normally pay for your insurance and your first tank of gas; after that, you'll be expected to drive along the most direct route and to average 400 miles a day. Many driveaway companies are keen to use foreign travelers (German tourists are ideal, it seems), but if you can convince them you are a safe bet they'll take something like a $250 deposit, which you get back after delivering the car in good condition. It makes obvious sense to get in touch in advance, to spare yourself a week's wait for a car to turn up. Look under "Automobile transporters and driveaway companies" in the *Yellow Pages* and

phone around for the latest offers; or try one of the ninety branches of Auto Driveaway, based at 310 S Michigan Ave in Chicago (☎312/341-1900).

Renting a car is the usual story of phoning your local branch of one of the majors (Avis, Hertz, Budget, Thrifty, etc – listed on p.31), of which Thrifty tends to be the cheapest. Most have offices at destination airports, and addresses and phone numbers are comprehensively documented in the *Yellow Pages*.

Also worth considering are **fly-drive deals**, which give cut-rate (and sometimes free) car rental when buying an air ticket. They usually work out cheaper than renting on the spot and are especially good value if you intend to do a lot of driving.

PACKAGE TOURS

Many operators run all-inclusive **packages** which combine plane tickets and hotel accommodation with (for example) sightseeing, wining and dining, or excursions to tourist sites. Even if the "package" aspect doesn't thrill you to pieces, these deals can still be more convenient and sometimes even work out to be more economical than arranging the same thing yourself, providing you don't mind losing a little flexibility. With such a vast range of packages available, it's impossible to give an overview – major travel agents will have brochures detailing what's available.

GETTING THERE FROM AUSTRALIA AND NEW ZEALAND

From Australia and New Zealand there's very little price difference between airlines and no shortage of flights, via the Pacific or Asia, to Los Angeles and San Francisco. Via the Pacific most flights are non-stop, with traveling time between Auckland/Sydney and LA twelve to fourteen hours, though some allow stopovers in Honolulu and a number of the South Pacific Islands. If you go via Asia (a slightly more roundabout route that can work out a little cheaper), you'll usually have to spend a night, or the best part of a day, in the airline's home city.

Various **coupon deals** – available with your international ticket for discounted flights within the US – are good value if California is part of a

SPECIALIST AGENTS AND OPERATORS

If you prefer to have all the arrangements made for you before you leave, then the **specialist agents** below can help you plan your trip. Unfortunately there are few pre-packaged tours that include airfares from Australia and New Zealand, however, most specialist agents will also be able to assist with flight arrangements. In turn many of the tours below can also be arranged through your local travel agent.

Adventure Specialists 69 Liverpool St, Sydney (☎02/9261 2927).
A good selection of adventure treks and tours.

Adventure World 73 Walker St, Sydney (☎02/956 7766); 8 Victoria Ave, Perth (☎09/9221 2300); 101 Great South Rd, Auckland (☎09/524 5118).
Individual and small group exploratory tours and treks.

American Travel Centre Second Floor, 262 Adelaide St, Brisbane (☎07/3221 4788).
All US travel arrangements.

Creative Tours Bookings through travel agents only.
Escorted bus tours, air passes, accommodation and Disneyland packages.

Insight Bookings through travel agents only.
Offers first class city accommodation, Disneyland packages, car rental and bus tours.

Peregrine Adventures 258 Lonsdale St, Melbourne (☎03/9663 8611); offices in Brisbane, Sydney, Adelaide and Perth.

Small group active holidays from short walking camping to longer overland trips through California.

Sydney International Travel Centre 75 King St, Sydney (☎02/9299 8000).
Individually tailored holidays, Disneyland passes, flights, bus and rail tours.

The Surf Travel Co 2/25 Cronulla Plaza, Cronulla Beach, NSW (☎02/9527 4722); 7 Danbury Drive, Torbay, Auckland (☎09/473 8388).
Lake Tahoe shredding and ski trips.

Top Deck Adventure 350 Kent St, Sydney (☎02/9299 8844).
Agents for Exodus's small group adventure trips in California.

Travel Plan 72 Chandos St, St Leonards, Sydney (☎02/9438 1333).
Ski holiday packages in the Lake Tahoe region.

Wiltrans/Maupintour 10/189 Kent St, Sydney (☎02/9255 0899).
Five-star all inclusive escorted Californian sightseeing holidays.

Gay and Lesbian

Pride Travel, 254 Bay St, Brighton, Melbourne (☎1-800/061 427 or 03/9596 3566).

Silke's Travel, 263 Oxford St, Darlinghurst, Sydney (☎02/9380 5835).

AIRLINES

Air New Zealand Australia ☎13 2476; New Zealand ☎09/357 3000
Daily flights to LA from major cities in Australia and New Zealand, via transfers in Auckland, or several times a week via either Auckland and Honolulu/Papeete, or Auckland, Fiji/Tonga and Honolulu.

Air Pacific Australia ☎1-800/230 150 or 02/9957 0150; New Zealand ☎09/379 2404
Once a week to LA from Sydney, Melbourne, Brisbane and major New Zealand cities via a stopover in Nadi (Fiji).

Cathay Pacific Australia ☎13 1747; New Zealand ☎09/379 0861
Daily to LA from major cities in Australia and New Zealand via a transfer or stopover in Hong Kong.

Delta Air Lines Australia ☎1-800/251 878 or 02/9262 1777; New Zealand ☎09/379 3370
Coupons for extended travel in the US.

Garuda Australia ☎1-800/800 873 or 02/9334 9944; New Zealand ☎09/366 1855
Several flights a week to LA from major cities in Australia and New Zealand via either a transfer or overnight stopover in Jakarta/Denpasar.

JAL Japan Airlines, Australia ☎02/9272 1111; New Zealand ☎09/379 9906
Several flights a week to LA from Sydney, Brisbane, Cairns and Auckland with an overnight stopover in either Tokyo or Osaka included in the fare (codeshare with Air New Zealand).

Northwest Airlines Australia ☎02/9231 6333
Coupons for extended travel in the US.

Philippine Airlines Australia ☎02/9262 3333; no New Zealand office
Several flights a week to LA from Sydney and Brisbane via either a transfer or overnight stopover in Manila.

Qantas, Australia ☎13 1211; New Zealand ☎ 0-800/808 767 or 09/357 8900
Daily to LA from major Australian cities, either non-stop or via Honolulu, and daily from Auckland via Sydney.

Singapore Airlines Australia ☎13 1011; New Zealand ☎09/379 3209
Twice a week to LA from major Australian cities and once a week from Auckland via Singapore.

United Airlines Australia ☎13 1777; New Zealand ☎09/379 3800
Daily to LA and San Francisco from Sydney, Melbourne and Auckland either direct or via Honolulu.

DISCOUNT TRAVEL AGENTS

Anywhere Travel, 345 Anzac Parade, Kingsford, Sydney (☎02/9663 0411).

Brisbane Discount Travel, 260 Queen St, Brisbane (☎07/3229 9211).

Budget Travel, 16 Fort St, Auckland, plus branches around the city (☎0800/808 040 or 09/366 006).

Destinations Unlimited, 3 Milford Rd, Auckland (☎09/373 4033).

Flight Centres Australia: 82 Elizabeth St, Sydney; branches nationwide (☎13 1600); New Zealand: 205 Queen St, Auckland (☎09/309 6171), branches nationwide.
Good flight discounts.

Northern Gateway, 22 Cavenagh St, Darwin (☎08/8941 1394).

STA Travel, Australia: 702 Harris St, Ultimo, Sydney; 256 Flinders St, Melbourne; other offices in state capitals and major universities (nearest branch ☎13 1776, fastfare telesales ☎1300/360 960); New Zealand: 10 High St, Auckland (☎09/309 0458, fastfare telesales ☎09/366 6673); branches in Wellington, Christchurch, Dunedin, Palmerston North, Hamilton and at major universities.
Discounts for students and under 26.

Thomas Cook, Australia: 175 Pitt St, Sydney; 257 Collins St, Melbourne; branches in other state capitals (local branch ☎13 1771, Thomas Cook Direct telesales ☎1-800/063 913); New Zealand: 96 Anzac Ave, Auckland (☎09/379 3920).
Rail and bus passes, travelers checks.

Tymtro Travel, Level 8, 130 Pitt St, Sydney (☎02/9223 2211 or 1300/652 969).
Competitive discounts.

wider US trip. A minimum purchase of three coupons usually applies. For example, American Airlines' **Coupon Pass** costs $US330 for the first three, and US$60–100 for subsequent tickets (maximum of ten in total). Tickets purchased direct from the airlines are usually at published rates, which are often more expensive than a RTW fare. Travel agents offer the best deals on fares and have the latest information on limited special offers, such as free stopovers, fly-drive-accommodation and Disney packages. Flight Centres and STA (which offer fare reductions for ISIC card holders and under 26s) generally offer the lowest fares. Airfares vary throughout the year, with seasonal differences generally working out between A/NZ$200–300. For most airlines **low season** is from mid-January to the end of February and October to the end of November; **high season** mid-May to the end of August and December to mid-January; **shoulder seasons** cover the rest of the year. Seat availability on most international flights out of Australia and New Zealand is often limited, so it's best to book several weeks ahead.

Traveling from **Australia**, fares to LA and San Francisco from eastern cities cost the same, while from Perth they're about A$400 more. There are daily non-stop flights from Sydney, to LA and San Francisco on United Airlines and to LA on Qantas for around A$1899 low season.

In addition there are several airlines that fly via Asia, which involves either a transfer or stopover in their home cities. The best deal is on JAL A$1550–1880 which includes a night's stopover accommodation in Tokyo or Osaka in the fare, while Garuda via either Jakarta or Denpasar and Philippine Airlines via Manila, both start around A$1750. If you don't want to spend the night, Cathay Pacific and Singapore Airlines can get you there, via a transfer in the home cities of Hong Kong and Singapore, for around A$1880.

From **New Zealand**, most flights are out of **Auckland** (add about NZ$150 for Christchurch and Wellington departures) with the best deals on Air New Zealand, to Los Angeles either non-stop or via Honolulu, Fiji, Tonga or Papeete – or United Airlines, also non-stop or via Honolulu to LA or San Francisco (both cost around NZ$2099–2499). Air Pacific via Fiji, and Qantas via Sydney both start around NZ$2150. Via Asia, Singapore Airlines offers the best connecting service to LA and San Francisco from NZ$2099, while the best value for money (around NZ$1850–2250) is on JAL via either a transfer or stopover in Tokyo.

If you intend to take in California as part of a world trip, a round-the-world (**RTW**) ticket offers the best value for money. There are any number of airline combinations to choose from, however. The most comprehensive are Cathay Pacific-UA's "Globetrotter", Air New Zealand-KLM-Northwest's "World Navigator" and Qantas-BA's "Global Explorer". All offer six stopovers world-wide, limited backtracking, and additional stopovers (around A/NZ$120 each), from A$2599/$3299 or NZ$3189/$3699. More US-oriented, but only available in Australia, is Singapore-TWA's "Easyworld" fare, allowing unlimited stopovers worldwide, with a maximum of eight within the US, and limited backtracking within the US (flat rate A$3150).

ENTRY REQUIREMENTS FOR FOREIGN VISITORS

PASSPORT

VISAS

Under the **Visa Waiver Scheme**, designed to speed up lengthy immigration procedures, citizens of Andorra, Argentina, Australia, Austria, Belgium, Brunei, Denmark, Finland, France, Germany, Iceland, Ireland, Italy, Japan, Liechtenstein, Luxembourg, Monaco, the Netherlands, New Zealand, Norway, San Marino, Slovenia, Spain, Sweden, Switzerland, and the United Kingdom visiting the United States for a period of less than ninety days only need a **full passport** (UK citizens should note that a British Visitor's Passport is *not* acceptable) and a **visa waiver form**. The latter will be provided either by your travel agency, or by the airline during check-in or on the plane, and must be presented to immigration on arrival. The same form covers entry across the land borders with Canada and Mexico as well as by air. However, those eligible for the scheme must apply for a visa if they intend to work, study, or stay in the country for more than ninety days.

Prospective visitors from parts of the world not mentioned above require a valid passport and a **non-immigrant visitor's visa**. How you'll obtain a visa depends on what country you're in and your status when you apply, so telephone the nearest embassy or consulate (listed on p.15).

In **Britain**, only British or EU citizens, and those from other countries eligible for the visa waiver scheme, can apply by post – fill in the application form available at most travel agents and send it with a full passport and a SAE to the nearest US embassy or consulate. Expect a wait of one to three weeks before your passport is returned. All others must apply in person, making an appointment in advance. Visa application fees in Britain are currently US$20.

Australian and **New Zealand** passport holders staying less than ninety days do not require a visa, providing they arrive on a commercial flight with an onward or return ticket. For longer stays, US multiple entry visas cost A$26. You'll need an application form, available from the US visa information service (☎1902/262682), one signed passport photo and your passport, and either post it or personally lodge it at one of the American embassy or consulate addresses opposite. For postal applications in Australia, payment can be made at any post office (US visa application payment form no.828); you'll also need to include the receipt of payment and a SAE. Processing takes about ten working days for postal applications; personal lodgements take two days – but check details with the consulate first.

Whatever your nationality, visas are not issued to convicted felons and anybody who owns up to being a communist, fascist or drug dealer.

IMMIGRATION CONTROL

The standard immigration regulations apply to all visitors, whether or not they are using the Visa Waiver Scheme. During the flight, you'll be handed an **immigration form** (and a customs declaration; see p.16), which must be given up at

---

Canadian citizens are in a particularly privileged position when it comes to crossing the border into the US. Though it is possible to enter the States without your passport, you should really have it with you on any trip that brings you as far as California. Only if you plan to stay for more than ninety days do you need a visa. Bear in mind that if you cross into the States in your car, trunks and passenger compartments are subject to spot searches by US Customs personnel, though this sort of surveillance is likely to decrease as remaining tariff barriers fall over the next few years. Remember too, that without the proper paperwork, Canadians are legally barred from seeking gainful employment in the US.

US EMBASSY AND CONSULATES IN CANADA

Embassy:

100 Wellington St, Ottawa, ON K1P 5T1 (☎613/238-5335).

Consulates:

Suite 1050, 615 Macleod Trail, Calgary, AB T2G 4T8 (☎403/266-8962).

Suite 910, Cogswell Tower, Scotia Square, Halifax, NS B3J 3K1 (☎902/429-2480).

Complex Desjardins, South Tower, Montréal, PQ H5B 1G1 (☎514/398-9695).

2 Place Terrasse Dufferin, Québec City, PQ G1R 4T9 (☎418/692-2095).

360 University Ave, Toronto, ON M5G 1S4 (☎416/595-1700).

1095 W Pender St, Vancouver, BC V6E 2M6 (☎604/685-4311).

US EMBASSIES AND CONSULATES ELSEWHERE

Australia

Moonah Place, Canberra, ACT 2600 (☎02/6270 5000).

US Consulate, 39 Castlereagh St, Sydney (☎1800/805 924).

Denmark

Dag Hammerskjöld Allé 24, 2100 Copenhagen (☎31/ 42 31 44).

Ireland

42 Elgin Rd, Ballsbridge, Dublin (☎01/668 8777).

Netherlands

Museumplein 19, 1071 DJ Amsterdam (☎020/575 5309).

Lange Voorhout 102,2514 EJ, Den Hague (☎070/310 9209).

New Zealand

29 Fitzherbert Terr, Thorndon, Wellington (☎4/472 2068).

Yorkshire General Building, corner of Shortland and O'Connell Streets, Fourth Floor, Auckland

(☎09/303 2724 or Non-Immigrant Visas, Private Bag 92022, Auckland 1).

Norway

Drammensveien 18, 0244 Oslo (☎47/22 44 85 50).

South Africa

Kine Centre, Commissioner and Kruis streets, 11th Floor PO Box 2155, Johannesburg (☎11/331 1681).

877 Pretorius St, Arcadia 0083, Pretoria (☎12/342 1048).

Broadway Industries Centre, Heerengracht, Foreshore, Capetown (☎21/21 4280).

Sweden

Strandvägan 101, Stockholm (☎08/783 5300).

UK

24/31 Upper Grosvenor Square, London W1A 1AE (☎0171/499 9000; visa hotline ☎0891/200290).

3 Regent Terr, Edinburgh EH7 5BW (☎0131/556 8315).

Queens House, 14 Queen St, Belfast BT1 6EQ (☎01232/241279).

immigration control once you land. The form requires details of where you are staying on your first night (if you don't know, write "touring") and the date you intend to **leave** the US. You

BRITISH CONSULATES IN CALIFORNIA

11766 Wilshire Blvd, Suite 400, Los Angeles, CA 90025 (☎310/477-3322).

1 Sansome St, Suite 850, San Francisco, CA 94101 (☎415/981-3030).

should be able to prove that you have enough money to support yourself while in the US – $300–400 a week is usually considered sufficient – as anyone revealing the slightest intention of working while in the country is likely to be refused admission. You may also experience difficulties if you admit to being HIV positive or having AIDS or TB. Part of the immigration form will be attached to your passport, where it must stay until you leave, when an immigration or airline official will detach it.

CUSTOMS

Customs officers will relieve you of your customs declaration and check whether you're carrying any fresh foods. You'll also be asked if you've visited a farm in the last month: if you have, you may well have your shoes taken away for inspection. The **duty-free allowance** if you're over 17 is 200 cigarettes and 100 cigars (*not* Cuban) and, if you're over 21, a liter of spirits. As well as foods and anything agricultural, it's prohibited to carry into the country any articles from North Korea, Iran, Iraq, Libya, or Cuba, obscene publications, drug paraphernalia, lottery tickets, chocolate liqueurs or pre-Columbian artifacts. Anyone caught carrying drugs into the country will not only face prosecution, but be entered in the records as an undesirable and probably denied entry for all time.

EXTENSIONS AND LEAVING

The date stamped on your passport is the latest you're legally allowed to stay. Leaving a few days later may not matter, especially if you're heading home, but more than a week or so can result in a protracted, rather unpleasant interrogation from officials, which may cause you to miss your flight and be denied entry to the US in the future. Your American hosts and/or employers could also face legal proceedings.

To get an **extension** before your time is up, apply at the nearest **US Immigration and Naturalization Service** (INS) office; the address will be under the Federal Government Offices listings at the front of the phone book. They will automatically assume that you're working illegally and it's up to you to convince them otherwise. Do this by providing evidence of ample finances, and, if you can, bring along an upstanding American citizen to vouch for you. You'll also have to explain why you didn't plan for the extra time initially.

STAYING ON

Anyone planning an extended legal stay in the United States should apply for a special **working**

Foreign students have a slightly better chance of a prolonged stay in California, especially those who can arrange a "year abroad" through their university at home. Otherwise you can apply directly to a university; if they admit you (and you can afford the painfully expensive fees charged to overseas students), it can be a great way to get to know the country, and maybe even learn something useful. The US grants more or less unlimited visas to those enrolled in full-time further education. Another possibility for students is to get onto an **Exchange Visitor Program**, for which participants are given a J-1 visa that entitles them to accept paid summer employment and apply for a social security number. However, most of these visas are issued for jobs in American **summer camps**, which aren't everybody's idea of a good time; they fly you over, and after a summer's work you end up with around $500 and a month to six weeks to blow it in. If you live in Britain and are interested, contact BUNAC (16 Bowling Green Lane, London EC1; ☎0171/251 3472), or Camp America (37 Queens' Gate, London SW7; ☎0171/581 7373).

visa at any American Embassy *before* setting off. Different types of visas are issued, depending on your skills and length of stay, but unless you've got relatives (parents or children over 21) or a prospective employer to sponsor you, your chances are slim at best.

Illegal work is not as easy to find as it used to be, now that the government has introduced fines as high as $10,000 for companies caught employing anyone without a **social security number** (which effectively proves you're part of the legal workforce). Even in the traditionally more casual establishments like restaurants and bars, things have really tightened up, and if you do find work it's likely to be of the less visible, poorly paid kind – dishwasher rather than waiter. Making up a social security number, or borrowing one from somebody else, is of course completely illegal, as are **marriages of convenience**; usually inconvenient for all concerned and with a lower success rate than is claimed.

INSURANCE, HEALTH AND PERSONAL SAFETY

INSURANCE

Though not compulsory, **travel insurance** is essential for **foreign travelers**. The US has no national health system and you can lose an arm and a leg (so to speak) having even minor medical treatment. Bank and credit cards (particularly American Express) often have certain levels of medical or other insurance included, especially if you use them to pay for your trip.

If you plan to participate in water sports, or do some hiking or skiing, you'll probably have to pay an extra premium; check carefully that any insurance policy you are considering will cover you in case of an accident. Note also that very few insurers will arrange on-the-spot payments in the event of a major expense or loss; you will usually

TRAVEL INSURANCE COMPANIES

UK

Columbus Travel Insurance, 17 Devonshire Square, London EC2M 4SQ (☎0171/375 0011). Does an annual multi-trip policy which offers twelve months' cover for £185.

Endsleigh Insurance, 97–107 Southampton Row, London WC1B 4AG (☎0171/436 4451). Generally offers the cheapest deals at around £43 for three weeks to cover life, limb and luggage (with a 25 percent reduction if you choose to forgo luggage insurance).

Australia and New Zealand

Cover More, 9/32 Walker St, North Sydney (☎1-800/251 881 or 02/9202 8000).

Ready Plan, 141 Walker St, Dandenong, Melbourne (☎1-800/337 462 or 03/9791 5077); 10/63 Albert St, Auckland (☎09/379 3208).

US

Access America, 6600 W Broad St, Richmond, VA 23230 (☎1-800/284-8300; www.worldaccess.com). Basic limited plan is $41 for thirty days or less.

Carefree Travel Insurance, PO Box 9366, Garden City, NY 11530 (☎1-800/323-3149; www.astenet.com/get/berkeley). Deluxe comprehensive policy costs $161 for thirty days.

STA Travel, 6560 N Scottsdale Rd, Scottsdale, AZ 85253 (☎1-800/781-4040; www.sta-travel.com). Basic baggage, trip, emergency medical and accidental death coverage offered for $135 for two months plus $35 for each additional month.

Travel Assistance International, 1133 15th St NW, Suite 400, Washington, DC 20077-2166 (☎1-800/821-2828). Costs $2.50 per day to insure baggage and $15 per $250 of trip cancellation coverage.

Travel Guard, 1145 Clark St, Stevens Point, WI 54481 (☎1-800/826-1300; www.noelgroup.com). Offers affordable family plan.

Travel Insurance Services, 2930 Camino Diablo, Suite 200, Walnut Creek, CA 94596 (☎1-800/937-1387; www.travelinsure.com). Low cost, high deductible comprehensive policies.

be reimbursed only after going home. In all cases of loss or theft of goods, you will have to contact the local police to have a report made out so that your insurer can process the claim.

BRITISH COVER

Most **travel agents** and tour operators will offer you insurance when you book your flight or holiday, and some will insist you take it. These policies are usually reasonable value, though as ever, you should check the small print. If you feel the cover is inadequate, or you want to compare prices, any **travel agent, insurance broker** or **bank** should be able to help. If you have a good "all risks" home insurance policy it may well cover your possessions against loss or theft even when overseas, and many private medical schemes also cover you when abroad – make sure you know the procedure and the helpline number. On all policies, read the small print to ensure the cover includes a sensible amount for medical expenses – this should be at least £1,000,000, which will cover the cost of an air ambulance to fly you home in the event of serious injury or hospitalization.

AUSTRALIAN AND NEW ZEALAND COVER

Travel insurance is available from most travel agents, some banks or direct from insurance companies, for periods ranging from a few days to a year or even longer. All are fairly similar in premium and coverage which includes medical expenses, loss of personal property and travelers checks, cancellations and delays, as well as most .adventure sports. If you plan to indulge in high-risk activities such as mountaineering, bungee jumping or scuba diving, check the policy carefully to make sure you'll be covered as it may be necessary to tailor a policy to suit your requirements. Ready Plan and Cover More give the best value coverage. A normal policy for Canada and the US costs around A\$130/NZ\$145 for 2 weeks, A\$190/NZ\$210 for 1 month, A\$280/NZ\$310 for 2 months.

NORTH AMERICAN COVER

Before buying an insurance policy, **North American travelers** should check that they're not already covered for health charges or costs by their current **health insurance**. If you are unable to use a phone or if the practitioner requires immediate payment, save all the **forms** to support a claim for subsequent reimbursement. Remember also that time limits may apply

when making claims after the fact, so promptness in contacting your insurer is highly advisable. Holders of official **student/teacher/youth cards** are entitled to accident coverage and hospital in-patient benefits. **Students** will often find that their student health coverage extends during the vacations and for one term beyond the date of last enrolment.

Not surprisingly, few if any American health insurance plans cover against **theft** while traveling, though **homeowners'** or **renters'** insurance often covers you for up to \$500 while on the road. Conditions and maximum amounts vary from company to company.

After exhausting the possibilities above, you might want to contact a specialist **travel insurance** company; your travel agent can usually recommend one, or see the box on p.17. Policies are comprehensive (accidents, illnesses, delayed or lost luggage, canceled flights and so on), but maximum payouts tend to be meager. Premiums vary, so shop around. The best deals are usually to be had through student/youth travel agencies – ISIS policies, for example. If you're planning to do any "dangerous sports" (like skiing or mountaineering), figure on a surcharge of twenty to fifty percent.

Most North American travel policies apply only to items lost, stolen or damaged while in the custody of an identifiable, responsible third party – hotel porter, airline or luggage consignment. Even in these cases you will have to contact the local police within a certain time limit.

HEALTH ADVICE FOR FOREIGN TRAVELERS

If you have a serious **accident** while in the US, emergency medical services will get to you quickly and charge you later. For emergencies or ambulances, dial ☎**911**, the nationwide emergency number (or whatever variant may be on the information plate of the payphone).

Should you need to see a **doctor**, lists can be found in the *Yellow Pages* under "Clinics" or "Physicians and Surgeons". A basic consultation fee is \$50–100, payable in advance. Medications aren't cheap either – keep all your receipts for later claims on your insurance policy.

Many **minor ailments** can be remedied using the fabulous array of potions and lotions available in **drugstores**. Foreign visitors should bear in mind that many pills available over the counter at home need a prescription in the US – most codeine-based painkillers, for example. Local brand names can be confusing; ask for advice at the **pharmacy** in any drugstore.

Travelers from Europe do not require **inoculations** to enter the US.

CRIME AND PERSONAL SAFETY

No one could pretend that California is trouble-free, although away from the urban centers, crime is often remarkably low-key. Even the lawless reputation of Los Angeles is far in excess of the truth, and most of the city, by day at least, is fairly safe; at night, though, a few areas – notably Compton, Inglewood, and East LA – are completely off limits. Members of the notorious **LA gangs** are a rare sight outside their own territories (which are usually well away from where you're likely to be), and they tend to kill each other rather than tourists. By being careful, planning ahead and taking care of your possessions, you should have few real problems.

MUGGING AND THEFT

The biggest problem for most travelers is the threat of **mugging**. It's impossible to give hard and fast rules about what to do if you're confronted by a mugger. Whether to run, scream or fight depends on the situation – but most locals would just hand over their money.

Of course, the best thing is simply to avoid being mugged, and a few obvious basic rules are worth remembering: don't flash money around; don't peer at your map (or this book) at every street corner, thereby announcing that you're a lost stranger; even if you're terrified or drunk (or both), try not to appear so; avoid dark streets, especially ones you can't see the end of; and in the early hours stick to the roadside edge of the pavement so it's easier to run into the road to attract attention. If you have to ask for directions, choose your target carefully. Another idea is to carry a wad of cash, perhaps $50 or so, separate from the bulk of your holdings so that if you do get confronted you can hand over something of value without it costing you everything.

If the worst happens and your assailant is toting a gun or (more likely) a knife, try to stay calm: remember that he (for this is generally a male pursuit) is probably scared too. Keep still, don't make any sudden movements – and hand over your money. When he's gone, you should, despite your shock, try to find a phone and dial ☎**911**, or hail a cab and ask the driver to take you to the nearest police station. Here, report the theft and get a reference number on the report to claim insurance and travelers' check refunds. If you're in a big city, ring the local Travelers Aid (their numbers are listed in the phone book) for sympathy and practical advice. For specific advice for women in case of mugging or attack, see p.47.

Another potential source of trouble is having your **hotel room burglarized**. Always store valuables in the hotel safe when you go out; when inside keep your door locked and don't open it to anyone you don't trust. If they claim to be hotel staff and you don't believe them, call reception to check.

POLICE AND PASSPORTS

Foreign visitors tend to report that the police are helpful and obliging when things go wrong, although they'll be less sympathetic if they think you brought the trouble on yourself through carelessness. One way non-Americans might accidentally break the law is by **jaywalking**. If you cross the road on a red light or anywhere except an intersection, and are spotted by a cop, you're likely to get a stiff talking-to – and possibly a ticket, leading to a $20 fine. You might also fall foul of America's puritanical **drinking laws** which prohibit drinking in most public places – parks, beaches and the like.

Needless to say, having bags snatched that contain travel documents can be a big headache, none more so than **losing your passport**. If the worst happens, the British consulates in both Los Angeles and San Francisco (see p.15) will issue emergency passports, provided you have sufficient ID, for $17. The process takes about thirty minutes (longer if you have trouble establishing your identity), but the resulting emergency passport is only a one-way travel document, good for return home. In non-emergency situations, the only way to get a new passport is through the British Embassy in Washington, DC (☎202/588-7800). If you aren't near one of the consulates in California, call and give an address where they can mail you an application form. When you return the filled out application, you'll need to include a notarized (ie specially stamped at any major bank) photocopy of any ID you might still have plus a $38 reissuing fee. The passport issuing process normally takes two weeks, but can take as long as six weeks. If you're in a real hurry, let them know and they will usually be as accommodating as possible.

STOLEN TRAVELERS' CHECKS AND CREDIT CARDS

Keep a record of the numbers of your **travelers' checks** separately from the actual checks; if you lose them, ring the issuing company on the toll-free number below.

They'll ask you for the check numbers, the place you bought them, when and how you lost them and whether it's been reported to the police. All being well, you should get the missing checks reissued within a couple of days – and perhaps an emergency advance to tide you over.

EMERGENCY NUMBERS

American Express (TCs) ☎1-800/221-7282; (credit cards) ☎1-800/528-4800

Diners Club ☎1-800/234-6377

Mastercard (Access) ☎1-800/307-7309

Thomas Cook ☎1-800/223-7373

Visa ☎1-800/227-6811

CAR CRIME

Crimes committed against tourists driving **rental cars** in the US have garnered headlines around the world in recent years. In major urbanized areas, any car you rent should have nothing on it – such as a particular license plate – that makes it easy to spot as a rental car. When driving, under no circumstances stop in any unlit or seemingly deserted urban area – and especially not if someone is waving you down and suggesting that there is something wrong with your car. Similarly, if you are "accidentally" rammed by the driver behind, do not stop immediately but drive on to the nearest well-lit, busy area and **phone ☎911** for assistance. Keep your doors locked and windows never more than slightly open. Do not open your door or window if someone approaches your car on the pretext of asking directions. Hide any valuables out of sight, preferably locked in the trunk or in the glove compartment (any valuables you don't need for your journey should be left in your hotel safe).

COSTS, MONEY AND BANKS

To help with planning your vacation in California, this book contains detailed price information for lodging and eating. Unless otherwise stated, the hotel price codes (explained on p.36) are for the cheapest dou-ble room throughout most of the year, exclusive of any local taxes which may apply, while meal prices include food only and not drinks or tip. For museums and similar attractions, the prices we quote are generally for adults; you can assume that children get in half-price. Naturally, costs will increase slightly overall during the life of this edition, but the relative comparisons should remain valid.

COSTS

Accommodation is likely to be your biggest single expense. Few hotel or motel rooms cost under $30; it's more usual to pay between $40 and $80 for anything halfway decent in a city, and rates in rural areas are not much cheaper. Although hostels offering dorm beds – usually for $12–15 – are reasonably common, they are by no means everywhere, besides which they save little money for two or more people traveling together. Camping, of course, is cheap, ranging from free to about $18 per night, but is rarely practical in or around the big cities.

As for **food**, $15 a day is enough to get an adequate life-support diet, while for a daily total of around $30 you can dine pretty well. Beyond this, everything hinges on how much sightseeing, taxi-taking, drinking and socializing you do. Much of any of these – especially in the major cities – and you're likely to be getting through upwards of $50 a day. With ample spots for eating, drinking, and shopping, San Francisco in particular seems to invite spending and having fun.

The rates for **traveling around**, especially on buses, and to a lesser extent on trains and even planes, may look inexpensive on paper, but the distances involved mean that costs soon mount up. For a group of two or more, **renting a car** can be a very good investment, not least because it enables you to stay in the ubiquitous budget motels along the interstate highways instead of relying on expensive downtown hotels.

Remember that a **sales tax** of 8.5 percent is added to virtually everything you buy in stores except for groceries, but isn't part of the marked price. In addition, a couple of the big cities apply a **hotel tax**; this can add as much as fourteen percent to the total bill.

TRAVELERS' CHECKS AND BANKS

US dollar travelers' checks are the best way to carry money, for both American and foreign visitors; they offer the great security of knowing that lost or stolen checks will be replaced. You should have no problem using the better-known checks, such as American Express and Visa, in the same way as cash in shops, restaurants and gas stations (don't be put off by "no checks" signs, which only refer to personal checks). Be sure to have plenty of the $10 and $20 denominations for everyday transactions.

Banks are generally open from 9am until 5pm Monday to Thursday, and 9am to 6pm on Friday. Most major banks change dollar travelers' checks for their face value (not that there's much point in doing this – and some charge for the privilege, so ask before you do), and **change foreign travelers' checks** and **currency**. Exchange bureau, always found at airports, tend to charge less commission: Thomas Cook or American Express are the biggest names. Rarely, if ever, do hotels change foreign currency. **Emergency phone numbers** to call if your checks and/or credit cards are stolen are on p.20.

To find the nearest bank that sells a particular brand of travelers' check, or to buy checks by phone, call the following numbers: American Express (☎1-800/673-3782), Citicorp (☎1-800/645-6556), Mastercard International/Thomas Cook (☎1-800/223-7373) and Visa (☎1-800/227-6811).

PLASTIC MONEY AND CASH MACHINES

If you don't already have a **credit card**, you should think seriously about getting one before you set off. For many services, it's simply taken for granted that you'll be paying with plastic. When

---

MONEY: A NOTE FOR FOREIGN TRAVELERS

Even when the **exchange rate** is at its least advantageous, most western European visitors find virtually everything – accommodation, food, gas, cameras, clothes and more – to be better value in the US than it is at home. However, if you're used to traveling in the less expensive countries of Europe, let alone in the rest of the world, you shouldn't expect to scrape by on the same minuscule budget once you're in the US.

Regular upheaval in the world money markets causes the relative value of the US dollar against the currencies of the rest of the world to vary considerably. Generally speaking, one pound sterling will buy between $1.40 and $1.80; one Canadian dollar is worth between 70¢ and $1; one Australian dollar is worth between 67¢ and 88¢; and one New Zealand dollar is worth between 55¢ and 72¢.

BILLS AND COINS

US currency comes in bills of $1, $5, $10, $20, $50 and $100, plus various larger (and rarer) denominations. All are the same size and color, making it necessary to check each bill carefully. The dollar is made up of 100 cents with coins of 1 cent (known as a penny), 5 cents (a nickel), 10 cents (a dime) and 25 cents (a quarter). Very occasionally you might come across JFK half-dollars (50¢), Susan B. Anthony dollar coins, or a two-dollar bill. Change (quarters are the most useful) is needed for buses, vending machines, parking meters, and telephones, so always carry plenty.

> Each of the two main networks operates a toll-free line to let customers know the location of their nearest ATM; **Plus System** is ☎1-800/THE-PLUS, **Cirrus** is ☎1-800/4CI-RRUS.

renting a car (or even a bike) or checking into a hotel you may well be asked to show a credit card to establish your creditworthiness – even if you intend to settle the bill in cash. **Visa**, **Mastercard** (known elsewhere as **Access**), **Diners Club**, **American Express** and **Discover** are the most widely used.

With Mastercard or Visa it is also possible to **withdraw cash** at any bank displaying relevant stickers, or from appropriate automatic teller machines (**ATMs**). Diners Club cards can be used to cash personal checks at Citibank branches. American Express cards can only get cash, or buy travelers' checks, at American Express offices (check the *Yellow Pages*) or from the travelers' check dispensers at most major airports. Most **Canadian** credit cards issued by hometown banks are honored in the US.

ATMs are everywhere in California – in addition to banks, many supermarkets, convenience stores, and drug stores now have outlets where you can withdraw cash for a small transaction fee (usually around $2). ATM cards held by visitors from other states usually work in Californian machines – check with your bank before you leave home. This method of financing is safer and more convenient and, if you're visiting from another country, it will usually be slightly cheaper than the commission fees charged by the exchange bureaus.

Most major credit cards issued by **foreign banks** are accepted in the US, as well as cash-dispensing cards linked to international networks such as Cirrus, Plus, and Star – once again, check before you set off, as otherwise the machine may simply gobble up your plastic friend. Overseas vis-itors should also bear in mind that fluctuating exchange rates may result in spending more (or less) than expected when the item eventually shows up on a statement.

FINANCIAL EMERGENCIES

Assuming you know someone who is prepared to send you money in a crisis, the quickest way is to have them take the cash to the nearest **Western Union** office (information on ☎1-800/325-6000 in the US; ☎0800/833833 in the UK; ☎029/223 6633 in Australia; and ☎09/270 050 in New Zealand) and have it instantaneously **wired** to the office nearest you, subject to the deduction of five to ten percent commission: the bigger the transaction the lower the percentage. **American Express Moneygram** (☎1-800/543-4080) offers a similar service.

It's also possible to have money wired directly from a bank in your home country to a bank in the US, although this is somewhat less reliable because it involves two separate institutions. If you go this route, the person wiring the funds to you will need to know the telex number of the bank the funds are being wired to. Having money wired from home is never convenient or cheap, and should be considered a last resort.

If you have a few days' leeway, sending a postal money order, exchangeable at any post office through the mail is a cheaper option. The equivalent for foreign travelers is the **international money order**, for which you need to allow up to seven days in the international air mail before arrival. An ordinary check sent from overseas takes two to three weeks to clear.

Foreign travelers in difficulties have the final option of throwing themselves on the mercy of their nearest national **consulate**, which will – in worst cases only – repatriate you, but will never, under any circumstances, lend you money. See p.15 for the addresses of British consulates in LA and San Francisco.

COMMUNICATIONS, PHONES AND MAIL

Visitors from overseas tend to be impressed by the speed and efficiency of communications in the US. California largely lives up to this high standard, partly at least because its major cities are important business hubs that depend upon reliable links to the East Coast, as well as being able to keep in touch with the many isolated settlements in the state itself. In rural areas you may find it frustrating just getting to the nearest public phone – which may be many miles away – but in general keeping in touch is easy.

TELEPHONES

Californian **telephones** are run by a huge variety of companies, many of which were hived off from the previous Bell System monopoly – the successor to which is the nationwide AT&T network.

Public telephones invariably work, and in cities at any rate can be found everywhere – on street corners, in train and bus stations, hotels, bars and restaurants. They take 5¢, 10¢ and 25¢ coins. The cost of a **local call** from a public phone (generally one within the same area code) varies from a minimum of 20¢, and is usually 25¢; when necessary, a voice comes on the line telling you to pay more.

Some numbers covered by the same area code are considered so far apart that calls between them count as non-local (zone calls) and cost much more. Pricier still are long-distance calls (ie to a different area code, and always preceded by a 1), for which you'll need plenty of change. Non-local

calls and long-distance calls are much less expensive if made between 6pm and 8am – the cheapest rates are after 11pm – and calls from private phones are always much cheaper than those from public phones. Detailed rates are listed at the front of the telephone directory (the *White Pages*, a copious source of information on many matters).

Making telephone calls from **hotel rooms** is usually more expensive than from a payphone, though some budget hotels offer free local calls from rooms – ask when you check in. An increasing number of phones accept **credit cards**, while anyone who has a US billing address can obtain an **AT&T calling card** (information on ☎1-800/451-4341). Foreign visitors will have to make do with **phone cards** – in denominations of $5, $10 and $20 – bought from general stores, some hostels and relatively few 7-Elevens. These provide you with a temporary account (just tap in the number printed on the card), and are a lot cheaper than feeding coins into a payphone, especially if calling abroad.

TELEPHONE AREA CODES

Los Angeles 213

Hollywood and East Los Angeles 323

West Los Angeles 310

East Los Angeles 562

Pasadena and the San Gabriel Valley 626

Burbank and the San Fernando Valley 818

Northern Orange County 714

Southern Orange County 949

San Bernardino & Riverside area 909

San Diego 619

Southeastern California 760

Santa Barbara and San Luis Obispo 805

Monterey and Big Sur 831

San Francisco and Marin County 415

East Bay 510

The Peninsula 650

San Jose 408

Wine Country & North Coast 707

Sacramento 916

Gold Country 209

Lake Tahoe and northeastern California 530

INTERNATIONAL TELEPHONE CALLS

International calls can be dialed direct from private or (more expensively) public phones. You can get assistance from the **international operator** (☎00), who may also interrupt every three minutes asking for more money, and call you back for any money still owed immediately after you hang up. The **lowest rates** for international calls to Europe are between 6pm and 7am, when a direct-dialed three-minute call will cost roughly $5.

In **Britain**, it's possible to obtain a free **BT Chargecard** (☎0800/800838), using which all calls from overseas can be charged to your quarterly domestic account. To use these cards in the US, or to make a **collect call** (to "reverse the charges") using a BT operator, contact the carrier: AT&T ☎1-800/445-5667; MCI ☎1-800/444-2162; or Sprint ☎1-800/800-0008. To avoid the international operator fee, BT credit card calls can be made directly using an automated system: AT&T ☎1-800/445-5688; MCI ☎1-800/854-4826; or Sprint ☎1-800/825-4904.

British visitors who are going to be making a number of calls to the US, and who want to be able to call ☎1-800 numbers, otherwise inaccessible from outside the country, should take advantage of the **Swiftcall** telephone club, for which you need a touch-tone phone. Call your nearest office (see below; daily 8am–midnight), and once you've paid by credit card for however many units you want, you are given a PIN. Any time you want to get an international line, simply dial ☎0171/488-0800, punch in your PIN, and then dial as you would were you in the US, putting a 1 before the area code, followed by the number. Calls to the USA – including ☎1-800 calls – cost about 14p per minute, a **saving** of over fifty percent:

SWIFTCALL NUMBERS
UK ☎0800/769 5555   Ireland ☎0800/409278   USA ☎1-800/513-7325

Telephone cards such as Australia's Telstra Telecard or Optus Calling Card and New Zealand Telecom's Calling Card can be used to make calls abroad, which are charged back to a domestic account or credit card. Apply to Telstra ☎1-800/626008, Optus ☎1300/300300, or NZ Telecom ☎04/382 5818.

The telephone code to dial **TO the US** from the outside world (excluding Canada) is 1.

To make international calls **FROM the US**, dial 011 followed by the country code:

Australia 61	**Denmark** 45	**Germany** 49	**Ireland** 353
Netherlands 31	**New Zealand** 64	**Sweden** 46	**United Kingdom** 44

Many government agencies, car rental firms, hotels and so on have **toll-free numbers**, which always have the prefix ☎1-800 or ☎1-888. Within the US, you can dial any number starting with those digits free of charge, though some numbers only operate inside California: it isn't apparent from the number until you try. Numbers with the prefix ☎1-900 are pay-per-call lines, generally quite expensive and almost always involving either sports, phone psychics or phone sex. Some numbers, particularly those of consumer services, employ letters as part of their number. The letters are on the button, thus for example, ☎1-800/TAXI becomes ☎1-800/8294

California has numerous **area codes** – three-digit numbers which must precede the seven-figure number if you're calling from abroad or from a region with a different area code. In this book, we've included the local area code with every phone number. With an ever increasing number of phones and phone numbers, new area codes in California are popping up every year. If you have trouble getting through, contact the operator or call Pacific Bell at ☎1-800/310-2355 for new area code information.

USEFUL NUMBERS

Emergencies ☎911; ask for the appropriate emergency service: fire, police or ambulance

Directory information ☎411

Directory inquiries for toll-free numbers ☎1-800/555-1212

Long-distance directory information ☎1-(Area Code)/555-1212

MAIL SERVICES

Post offices usually open Monday to Friday from 9am until 5pm, and Saturday from 9am to 4pm, and there are blue **mail boxes** on many street corners. **Ordinary mail** within the US costs 32¢ for letters weighing up to an ounce; addresses must include the **zip code**, and a return address should be written in the upper left corner of the envelope. **Air mail** from California to Europe generally takes about a week. Postcards, aerograms and letters weighing up to half an ounce (a single sheet) cost 60¢.

The last line of the address is made up of the city name, an abbreviation denoting the state (in California "CA") and a five-digit number – the **zip code** – denoting the local post office. (The additional four digits you will sometimes see appended to zip codes are not essential.) Letters which don't carry the zip code are liable to get lost or at least delayed; if you don't know it, phone books carry a list for their service area, and post offices – even in Britain – have directories.

Letters can be sent c/o **General Delivery** (what's known elsewhere as **poste restante**) to the one relevant post office in each city, but must include the zip code and will only be held for thirty days before being returned to sender – so make sure there's a return address on the envelope. If you're receiving mail at someone else's address, it should include "c/o" and the regular occupant's name, or it is likely to be returned.

Rules on sending **parcels** are very rigid: packages must be sealed according to the instructions given at the start of the *Yellow Pages*. To send anything out of the country, you'll need a green customs **declaration form**, available from a post office. **Postal rates** for sending a parcel weighing up to 1lb are $9.75 to Europe and $11.20 to Australia and New Zealand.

TELEGRAMS, FAXES AND EMAIL

To send a **telegram** (also known as a wire), don't go to a post office but to a Western Union office (listed in the *Yellow Pages*). Credit card holders can dictate messages over the phone. **International telegrams** cost slightly less than the cheapest international phone call: one sent in the morning from California should arrive at its destination the following day. For domestic telegrams ask for a **mailgram**, which will be delivered to any address in the country the next morning.

Public **fax** machines, which may require your credit card to be "swiped" through an attached device, are found at photocopy centers and, occasionally, bookstores.

Public access to email and the Internet is increasingly available in California. So-called "Internet cafés", with terminals on each table, can be found in major cities, charging roughly $7/hour for full access to the Web. Additionally, many public libraries have computers available with Internet access. If you don't already have one, you can set up a free email account at *www.rocketmail.com*, *www.hotmail.com*, *www.yahoo.com* or *www.juno.com* before you depart.

INFORMATION, MAPS AND MEDIA

Advance information for a trip to California can be obtained by post from the California Office of Tourism, 801 K St, Suite 1600, Sacramento, CA 95814-3520 (☎1-800/862-2543 or 916/322-2881). Once you've arrived, you'll find most towns have visitor centers of some description – often called the Convention and Visitors Bureau (CVB) or Chamber of Commerce: all are listed in the guide. These will give out detailed information on the local area and can often help with finding accommodation. Free newspapers in most places carry news of events and entertainment.

Most of the tourist offices we've mentioned can supply you with good **maps**, either free or for a small charge, and, supplemented with our own, these should be enough for general sightseeing and touring. Rand McNally produces a decent low-cost ($2.95) map of the state, and its *Road Atlas* ($6.95) covering the whole country plus Mexico and Canada, is a worthwhile investment if you're traveling further afield. For driving or cycling through rural areas, the *Atlas & Gazetteer: Northern California* and *Atlas & Gazetteer: Southern and Central California* (published by DeLorme; $16.95 each) are valuable companions, with detailed city plans, marked campsites and reams of national park and forest information. For something more detailed, say for **hiking** purposes, ranger stations in parks and wilderness areas all sell good-quality local hiking maps for

$1–3, and camping stores generally have a good selection too. The American Automobile Association (☎1-800/272-2155 in Northern CA, ☎1-800/678-3839 in Southern CA), has offices in most large cities and provides excellent free maps and travel assistance to its members, and to British members of the AA and RAC.

Most bookstores will have a range of local trail guides, the best of which we've listed in Contexts, p.618.

THE MEDIA

The only **newspaper** that's read all over California is the *Los Angeles Times*, which gives probably the best coverage of state, national and world events in the country. Otherwise newspapers tend to excel at reporting their own area but generally rely on agencies for their foreign – and even some national – reports. Major newspapers from other parts of the US such as the *New York Times*, and some overseas newspapers, tend to be found in vending machines, news stands and bookstores in major cities.

Every community of any size has at least a few **free newspapers**, found in street distribution bins, in cafés, bars or just lying around in piles. It's a good idea to pick up a full assortment: some simply cover local goings-on, others provide specialist coverage of interests ranging from long-distance cycling to getting ahead in business – and the classified and personal ads can provide hours of entertainment. Many of them are also excellent sources for bar, restaurant and nightlife information; we've mentioned the most useful titles in the guide.

TELEVISION

Californian **TV** is pretty much the standard network barrage of sitcoms, newscasts and talk shows. A number of Spanish-language cable channels serve the state's large Hispanic population; a smaller number are aimed at other, particularly Asian, ethnic groups. PBS, the national public television station, broadcasts a steady stream of interesting documentaries, informative (if slightly dry) news programs, and educational children's television.

There's hardly a motel room in the state that's not hooked up to **cable**, although the number of channels available to guests varies from place to

MAP AND TRAVEL BOOK SUPPLIERS

UK

London

Daunt Books, 83 Marylebone High St, London W1 (☎0171/224 2295).

National Map Centre, 22–24 Caxton St, London SW1 (☎0171/222 4945).

Stanfords, 12–14 Long Acre, London WC2 (☎0171/836 1321); 52 Grosvenor Gardens, London SW1W 0AG; 156 Regent St, London W1R 5TA.

The Travel Bookshop, 13–15 Blenheim Crescent, London W11 (☎0171/229 5260).

Edinburgh

Thomas Nelson & Sons Ltd, 51 York Place, Edinburgh EH1 3JD (☎0131/557 3011).

Glasgow

John Smith and Sons, 57–61 St Vincent St, Glasgow G2 5TB (☎0141/221 7472).

Maps by **mail or phone order** are available from Stanfords; ☎0171/836 1321.

IRELAND

Dublin

Easons Bookshop, 80 Middle Abbey St, Dublin 1 (☎01/873 3811).

Fred Hanna's Bookshop, 27–29 Nassau St, Dublin 2 (☎01/677 1255).

Hodges Figgis Bookshop, 56–58 Dawson St, Dublin 2 (☎01/677 4754).

Belfast

Waterstone's, Queens Building, 8 Royal Ave, Belfast BT1 1DA (☎01232/247355).

US

The Complete Traveler, 199 Madison Ave, New York, NY 10016 (☎212/685-9007); 3207 Fillmore St, San Francisco, CA 92123 (☎415/923- 1511).

Forsyth Travel Library, 226 Westchester Ave, White Plains, NY 10604 (☎1-800/367-7984).

Phileas Fogg's Books & Maps, 87 Stanford Shopping Center, Palo Alto, CA 94304 (☎1-800/533-FOGG).

Rand McNally*, 444 N Michigan Ave, Chicago, IL 60611 (☎312/321-1751); 150 E 52nd St, New York, NY 10022 (☎212/758-7488); 595 Market St, San Francisco, CA 94105 (☎415/777-3131); 10250 Santa Monica Blvd, Suite 681, Los Angeles, CA 90067 (☎310/556-2202).

The Savvy Traveler, 310 S Michigan Ave, Chicago, IL 60604 (☎312/913-9800).

Sierra Club Bookstore, 85 Second St, San Francisco, CA 94105 (☎415/977-5600).

Traveler's Bookstore, 22 W 52nd St, New York, NY 10019 (☎212/664-0995).

*Rand McNally now has 24 stores across the US; call ☎1-800/333-0136 (ext 2111) for the location of your nearest store, or for **direct mail** maps.

CANADA

Open Air Books and Maps, 25 Toronto St, Toronto, ON M5C 2R1 (☎416/363-0719).

Ulysses Travel Bookshop, 4176 St-Denis, Montréal (☎514/843-9447).

World Wide Books and Maps, 736a Granville St, Vancouver, BC V6Z 1G3 (☎604/687-3320).

AUSTRALIA

Adelaide

The Map Shop, 16a Peel St, Adelaide, SA 5000 (☎088/231 2033).

Melbourne

Mapland, 372 Little Bourke St, Melbourne, VIC 3000 (☎039/670 4383).

Sydney

Travel Bookshop, Shop 3, 175 Liverpool St, Sydney (☎02/9261 8200).

US Travel and Tourism, Martin Place, Sydney (☎02/9234 9155).

USA Tourist Service 75 King Street, Sydney (☎02/9299 1222).

Perth

Perth Map Centre, 891 Hay St, Perth, WA 6000 (☎089/322 5733).

NEW ZEALAND

Specialty Maps, 58 Albert St, Auckland (☎09/307 2217).

CALIFORNIA WEB SITES

Travel

California Travel & Tourism
gocalif.ca.gov
Stylishly designed and accessible, California's official travel and tourism site claims to suit you, whether you're traveling for "Family, Romance, Nature, or Recreation".

California Virtual Tourist Listings
www.research.digital.com/SRC/virtual-tourist/final/CaliforniaAlphabetical-N.html
Exhaustive alphabetical listings, linking into a huge variety of Web sites.

Movies

Ain't it Cool News
www.aint-it-cool-news.com
Twenty-stone Texan and self-confessed geek Harry Knowles has attracted huge numbers of readers to his site, which consists of rambling film reviews and Hollywood insider secrets. Harry was credited with changing popular opinion about the film *Titanic*, which had showed every sign of sinking without trace.

E! Online
www.eonline.com
Breathless, gossipy and visually gorgeous, this site has features such as "Celebs Under the Knife", a diary of a genuine striving starlet, and pages of star profiles and movie reviews.

Arts

Los Angeles County Museum of Art
www.lacma.org/
Reviews of current and future shows, such as the 1999 Vincent Van Gogh exhibition – based entirely on the holdings of Amsterdam's Van Gogh Museum.

San Francisco Contemporary Culture
www.YerbaBuenaArts.org/
The Center for the Arts at Yerba Buena Gardens, San Francisco's recent addition to the arts scene, has a high-tech, architecturally-designed Web site: mostly listings and descriptions of the gallery and film exhibits, plus other goings-on at the Center.

Miscellaneous

California Beerpage
www.beerpage.com/index1.html
Nattily designed and accessible guide to California's microbreweries and beer festivals.

Gay Global San Francisco
www.gayglobalsf.com
A great resource for all gay travelers, including an excellent and thorough guide to bars all over the city, not just in the Castro (gay district).

Superlists
www.superlists.com
A series of invaluable "Superlists" on every imaginable San Francisco subject, from pagan groups and movie-extra opportunities to cafés with Internet access and free anonymous HIV testing clinics.

Surf Scene Magazine & Southern California Surf Report
www.surfscene.net/surf/index.html
Hot surfing news for the Southern California counties of Los Angeles and Ventura. There are daily surf reports by a correspondent who's been shootin' tubes for thirty years.

place. Most cable stations are no better than the major networks (ABC, CBS, NBC, and FOX), though some of the more specialized channels are consistently interesting. The ARTS channel broadcasts enjoyable, if po-faced, arts features, imported TV plays and the like. CNN (Cable Network News) offers round-the-clock news, HBO (Home Box Office) shows recent big-bucks movies, AMC (American Movie Channel) shows old black-and-white films, and ESPN exclusively covers sport. Finally, there's MTV (seemingly absent from the menu of most chain hotels), the thirtysomething VH-1 and a number of other music stations.

To watch publicity-hyped pay-per-view events like world heavyweight boxing bouts you may have to pay as much as $40, either to your motel or to a bar that's putting on a live screening. Many larger hotels and motels offer a choice of movies that have just finished their cinema run, for around $7 each.

RADIO

Radio stations are even more abundant than TV channels, and the majority, again, stick to a bland commercial format. Except for news and chat, stations on the **AM** band are best avoided in favor of

FM, in particular the nationally funded public (NPR) and college stations, found between 88 and 92 FM. These provide diverse and listenable programming, be it bizarre underground rock, obscure theater, or BBC newscasts, and they're also good sources for information on local nightlife.

Though the large cities boast good specialist **music** stations – contemporary, jazz and classical – for most of the time you'll probably have to resort to skipping up and down the frequencies,

between re-run Eagles tracks, country and western tunes, fire-and-brimstone Bible thumpers and crazed phone-ins. Driving through rural areas can be frustrating; for hundreds of miles you might only be able to receive one or two (very dull) stations. Finally, **Mexican stations** – many broadcast using very powerful transmitters located south of the border – provide an enjoyable, alternative flavor of Southern California, even if you don't speak Spanish.

GETTING AROUND CALIFORNIA

Although distances can be great, getting around California is seldom much of a problem. Certainly, things are always easier if you have a car, but between the major cities there are good bus links and a reasonable train service. The only regions where things are more difficult using public transportation are the isolated rural areas, though even here, by adroit forward-planning, you can usually get to the main points of interest on local buses and charter services, details of which are in the relevant sections of the guide.

BY CAR

Driving is by far the best way to get around California. Los Angeles, for example, has grown up and assumed its present shape since cars were invented, sprawling for so many miles in all directions that your hotel may be fifteen or twenty miles from the sights you came to see. Away from the cities, many places are almost impossible to reach without your own transportation; most national and state parks are only served by infrequent public transportation as far as the main visitor center, if that. What's more, if you are planning on doing a fair amount of camping, rent-

ing a car can save you money by allowing access to less expensive out-of-the-way campgrounds.

Drivers wishing to **rent** cars are supposed to have held their licenses for at least one year (though this is rarely checked); people under 25 years old may encounter problems, and will probably get lumbered with a higher than normal insurance premium. Car rental companies (listed on p.31) will also expect you to have a credit card; if you don't they may let you leave a hefty **deposit** (at least $200), but don't count on it. The likeliest tactic for getting a good deal is to phone the major firms' toll-free numbers and ask for their best rate – most will try to beat the offers of their competitors, so it's worth haggling.

In general the lowest rates are available at the airport branches – $149 a week for a subcompact is a fairly standard budget rate. Always be sure to get free unlimited mileage, and be aware that leaving the car in a different state to the one in which you rent it will incur a **drop-off charge** that

---

ROAD CONDITIONS

The California Department of Transportation (CalTrans) operates a toll-free **24-hour information line** (☎1-800-427-ROAD) giving up-to-the-minute details of road conditions throughout the state. On a touch-tone phone simply input the number of the road ("5" for I-5, "299" for Hwy-299, etc) and a recorded voice will tell you about any relevant weather conditions, delays, detours, snow closures and so on. From out of state, or without a touch-tone phone, road information is also available on ☎916/445-1534. Nevada Highways has a similar system on ☎702/793-1313.

ADVANCED PLANNING FOR OVERSEAS TRAVELERS

AMTRAK RAIL PASSES

Foreign travelers have a choice of four **rail passes**; including the **Coastal Pass**, which permits unlimited train travel on the east and west coasts, but not between the two.

	15-day (June–Aug)	**15-day** (Sept–May)	**30-day** (June–Aug)	**30-day** (Sept–May)
Far West	$240	$180	$310	$230
West	$310	$195	$395	$250
Coastal	–	–	$275	$215
National	$425	$260	$535	$350

On production of a passport issued outside the US or Canada, the passes can be bought at Amtrak stations in the US. In the **UK**, you can buy them from Destination Marketing, 41–45 Goswell Rd, London SW11 3TW (☎0171/253 9009); in **Ireland**, contact Campus Travel/Eurotrain (☎01/602 1600); in **Australia**, Walshes World (☎029/232 7499); and in **New Zealand**, Atlantic & Pacific (☎09/302 9720).

In addition, **Explore America** fares – available to anyone within a 45 day period – allow up to three stops on a round-trip ticket. See p.000 for details.

GREYHOUND AMERIPASSES

Foreign visitors can buy a **Greyhound Ameripass**, offering unlimited travel within a set time limit, before leaving home: most travel agents can oblige. In the UK, they cost £75 (4-day; Mon–Thurs only), £85 (5-day), £110 (7-day), £140 (10-day), £170 (15-day), £230 (30-day), £260 (45-day) or £340 (60-day). Greyhound's office is at Sussex House, London Road, East Grinstead, West Sussex RH19 1LD (☎01342/317317). No daily extensions are available. The first time you use your pass, it will be dated by the ticket clerk (which becomes the commencement date of the ticket), and your destination is written on a page which the driver will tear out and keep as you board the bus. Repeat this procedure for every subsequent journey.

AIR PASSES

All the main American airlines (and British Airways in conjunction with USAir) offer **air passes** for visitors who plan to fly a lot within the US; these have to be bought in advance, and in the UK are usually sold with the proviso that you cross the Atlantic with the relevant airline. All the deals are broadly similar, involving the purchase of at least three **coupons** (for around £220 and around £60 for each additional coupon), each valid for a flight of any duration in the US.

The **Visit USA** scheme entitles foreign travelers to a thirty percent discount on any full-priced US domestic fare, provided you buy the ticket before you leave home. If you just plan to buy one flight, good low-season fares from New York, Washington and Boston to California are $300–350 round-trip; LA is marginally less expensive than San Francisco.

can be $200 or more – however, many companies do not charge drop-off fees within California itself so check before you book if you plan a one-way drive. Also, don't automatically go for the cheapest rate, as there's a big difference in the quality of cars from company to company; industry leaders like Hertz and Avis tend to have newer, lower-mileage cars, often with air-conditioning and stereo cassette decks as standard equipment – no small consideration on a 2000-mile desert drive.

Alternatively, various **local** companies rent out new – and not so new (try Rent-a-Heap or Rent-a-

Wreck) – vehicles. They are certainly cheaper than the big chains if you just want to spin around a city for a day, but you have to drop them back where you picked them up, and free mileage is seldom included, so they work out far more costly for long-distance travel. Addresses and phone numbers are listed in the *Yellow Pages*.

When you rent a car, read the small print carefully for details on **Collision Damage Waiver (CDW)**, sometimes called Liability Damage Waiver (LDW), a form of insurance which often isn't included in the initial rental charge but is well worth considering. This specifically covers the car that you are driving yourself, as you are in any case insured for damage to other vehicles. At $9–13 a day, it can add substantially to the total cost, but without it you're liable for every scratch to the car – even those that aren't your fault. Some credit card companies offer automatic CDW coverage to anyone using their card; read the fine print beforehand in any case.

You should also check your **third-party liability**. The standard policy often only covers you for the first $15,000 of the third party's claim against you, a paltry sum in litigation-conscious America. Companies strongly advise taking out third-party insurance, which costs a further $10–12 a day but indemnifies the driver for up to $2,000,000.

If you **break down** in a rented car, there'll be an emergency number pinned to the dashboard or tucked away in the glove compartment. You can summon the highway patrol on one of the new emergency phones stationed along freeways (usually at half-mile intervals) and many other remote highways (mostly every two miles) – although as the highway patrol and state police cruise by regularly, you can just sit tight and wait. Raising your car hood is recognized as a call for assistance, although women traveling alone should be wary of doing this.

Another tip, for women especially, is to rent a **mobile telephone** from the car rental agency – you often only have to pay a nominal amount until you actually use it, and in larger cities they increasingly come built into the car. Having a phone can be reassuring at least, and a potential lifesaver should something go terribly wrong.

One variation on renting is a **driveaway**, whereby you drive a car from one place to another on behalf of the owner, paying only for the gas you use. The same rules as for renting apply, but look the car over before you take it, as you'll be lumbered with any repair costs, and a large fuel bill if the vehicle's a big drinker. The most common routes are between California and New York, although there's a fair chance you'll find something that needs shifting up the coast, from Los Angeles to San Francisco. See p.10 for further details.

RENTING AN RV

Besides cars, Recreational Vehicles or **RVs** (camper vans) can be rented for around $500 a week, although outlets are surprisingly rare, as people tend to own their RVs: in LA try El Monte RVs, 12061 E Valley Blvd, El Monte, CA 91732 (☎1-800/367-6511 or 818/443-6158). The Recreational Vehicle Rental Association, 3930 University Drive, Fairfax, VA 22030 (☎1-800/336-0355 or 703/591-7130), publishes a newsletter and a directory of rental firms. Some of the larger companies offering RV rentals are Cruise America (☎1-800/327-7799), Grand Travel RVs (☎1-800/849-9959 or 602/939-6909) and Moturis (☎1-800/566-8874).

CAR RENTAL COMPANIES

IN THE US AND CANADA

Alamo ☎1-800/354-2322

Avis ☎1-800/331-1212

Budget ☎1-800/527-0700

Dollar ☎1-800/421-6868

Enterprise ☎1-800/325-8007

Hertz ☎1-800/654-3131; in Canada ☎416/620-9620

Holiday Autos ☎1-800/422-7737

National ☎1-800/CAR-RENT

Payless ☎1-800/729-5377

Rent-A-Wreck ☎1-800/535-1391

Thrifty ☎1-800/367-2277

IN THE UK

Alamo ☎0990/994000

Avis ☎0171/917 6700

Budget ☎0181/759 2216

Dollar (Eurodollar) ☎01895/233300

Hertz ☎0990/996699

Holiday Autos ☎0171/491 1111

IN AUSTRALIA

Avis ☎1-800/225 533.

Budget ☎1-300/362 848.

Hertz ☎13/3039.

IN NEW ZEALAND

Avis ☎09/379 2650

Budget ☎09/275 3025

Fly and Drive Holidays ☎09/366 0759

Hertz ☎09/309 0989

DRIVING FOR FOREIGN VISITORS

UK nationals can **drive** in the US on a full UK driving license (International Driving Permits are not always regarded as sufficient). Fly-drive deals are good value if you want to **rent a car** (see p.31), though you can save up to sixty percent simply by booking in advance with a major firm. If you choose not to pay until you arrive, be sure you take a written confirmation of the price with you. Remember that it's safer not to rent a car straight off a long transatlantic flight; and that standard rental cars have **automatic transmissions**.

It's also easier and cheaper to book **RVs** in advance from Britain. Most travel agents who specialize in the US can arrange RV rental, and usually do it cheaper if you book a flight through them as well. A price of £1000 for a five-berth van for two weeks is fairly typical. Once you have a vehicle, you'll find that **petrol** (US "gasoline") is fairly cheap; a self-served US gallon (3.8 liters) of **unleaded** – which most cars use – costs between $1.20 and $1.70, depending on the location of the gas station. In California most gas stations are self-service: when removing the nozzle from the pump, remember to lift or turn the lever to activate it. If you insist on having someone else pump your gas, you'll pay for it; full service pumps often charge upwards of $0.30 extra per gallon.

American **miles** are the same as British miles but sometimes **distances** are given in **hours** – the length of time it should take to drive between any two places. There are obviously other differences between driving in the US and in Britain, not least the fact that rules and regulations aren't always nationally fixed. Many foreign travelers have problems at first adjusting to **driving on the right**. This can be remarkably easy to forget – some people draw a cross or tie a ribbon on their right hand to remind them.

There are several **types of road**. The best for covering long distances quickly are the wide, straight and fast **Interstate highways**, usually at least six-lane motorways and always prefixed by "I" (eg I-5) – marked on maps by a red, white and blue shield bearing the number. Even-numbered Interstates usually run east–west and those with odd numbers north–south. Driving on these roads is easier than it first appears, but you need to adapt quickly to the American habit of **changing lanes**: US drivers do this frequently, and overtake on both sides. In California you are also permitted to stay in the fast lane while being overtaken on the inside, although common courtesy dictates that slower drivers stay to the right. All these roads are free: there are none of the turnpikes found in the east. Big overhead signs warn you if the road is about to split towards two different destinations (this happens quite often), or an exit's coming up. Sometimes a lane *must* exit, and if you lose concentration you're liable to leave the Interstate accidentally – no great calamity as it's easy enough to get back on again. **Missing an exit** is more annoying – U-turns are strictly illegal, and you have to continue to the next exit. In urban areas during rush hour, freeway traffic can often slow to a maddening halt. Your best bet is to entirely avoid freeway driving in the Bay Area and Los Angeles in the early morning and evening.

On top of the rental fees, take into account the cost of gas (some RVs do twelve miles to the gallon or less) and any drop-off charges, in case you plan to do a one-way trip across the country. Also, it is rarely legal simply to pull up in an RV and spend the night at the roadside – you are expected to stay in designated parks that cost up to $20 per night.

BY PLANE

A **plane** is obviously the quickest way of getting around California, and much less expensive than you may think; by keeping up to date with the ever-changing deals being offered by airlines – check with your local travel agent or read the ads in local newspapers – you may be able to take advantage of heavily discounted fares.

Airlines with a strong route structure in the state include Alaska, American, Continental, Delta, Northwest, Reno Air, Southwest, TWA and United. Phone the airlines for routes and schedules, then buy your ticket from a travel agent using the computerized Fare Assurance Program, which processes all the available ticket options and searches for the lowest fare, taking into account the special needs of individual travelers. One agent using the service is Travel Avenue (☎1-800/333-3335).

At off-peak times, flights between Los Angeles and San Francisco can cost as little as $50 one-way (only slightly more than the equivalent train fare), though may require a booking to be made 21 days in advance.

A grade down, and broadly similar to British dual carriageways and main roads, are the **State highways** (eg Hwy-1) and the **US highways** (eg US-395). Some major roads in cities are technically state highways but are better known by their local name. Hwy-2 in Los Angeles, for instance, is better known as Santa Monica Boulevard. In rural areas, you'll also find much smaller **County Roads**; their number is preceded by a letter denoting their county. In built-up areas **streets** are arranged on a grid system and labeled at each junction.

Although the law says that drivers must keep up with the flow of traffic, which is often hurtling along at 75mph, the maximum **speed limit** in California is 65mph (it was recently raised from 55mph on most stretches), with lower signposted limits – usually around 25–35mph – in built-up areas. There are no **spot fines** but if given a ticket for **speeding**, your case will come to court and the size of the fine will be at the discretion of the judge; $90 is a rough minimum. If the **police** do flag you down, don't get out of the car, and don't reach into the glove compartment as the cops may think you have a gun. Simply sit still with your hands on the wheel; when questioned, be polite and don't attempt to make jokes.

As for other possible violations, US law requires that any **alcohol** be carried unopened in the boot (trunk) of the car, and it can't be stressed enough that **driving while intoxicated (DWI)** is a very serious offense. If a police officer smells alcohol on your breath or has reason to believe that you are under the influence, he/she is entitled to administer a breath, saliva or urine test. If you fail, you'll be locked up with other inebriates in the drunk tank of the nearest jail until you sober up. Your case will later be heard by a judge, who can fine you as much as $1000, or in extreme (or repeat) cases, imprison you for thirty days. Less serious offenses include making a **U-turn** on an Interstate or anywhere where a single unbroken line runs along the middle of the road; driving in **car pool lanes** with fewer than two people in the vehicle; **parking on a highway**; and front-seat passengers riding without fastened **seatbelts**. At **junctions**, one rule is crucially different from the UK: you can turn right on a red light if there is no traffic approaching from the left; otherwise red means stop. Stopping is also compulsory, in both directions, when you come upon a school bus disgorging passengers with its lights flashing. Blinking red lights should be treated as a stop sign, and blinking yellow lights indicate that you should cross the intersection with caution, but do not need to come to a complete stop.

Once at your destination, you'll find in cities at least that **parking meters** are commonplace. Charges for an hour range from 25¢–$1. **Car parks** (US parking lots) charge up to $15 a day. If you park in the wrong place (such as within 10ft of a fire hydrant) your car is likely to be towed away or **wheel-clamped**; a ticket on the windshield tells you where to pay the $25 fine. Watch out for signs indicating the **street cleaning** schedule, as you mustn't park overnight before an early-morning clean. **Validated parking**, where your fee for parking in, say, a shopping mall's lot is waived if one of the stores has stamped your parking stub (just ask), is common, as is **valet parking** at even quite modest restaurants, for which a small tip is expected.

BY TRAIN

Unlike elsewhere in the US, traveling on the Amtrak **rail** network is a viable way of getting about California, thanks in great measure to the growing number of Amtrak Thruway buses, which bring passengers from the many rail-less parts of the state to the trains. Traveling by train is slightly more expensive than Greyhound, $42 one-way between Los Angeles and San Francisco, for example, but unlike on a bus, a smooth journey with few if any delays is a near certainty. All the major cities are connected and the carriages clean, comfortable, tidy and rarely crowded. Probably the prettiest route is the *Coast Starlight*, which winds along the coast between Santa Barbara and San Luis Obispo, a 100-mile coastline ride during which it's not unusual to see seals, dolphins or even whales in the waters offshore. The other LA-to-SF Amtrak routes head inland, by bus to Bakersfield then by rail north through the dull San Joaquin Valley. Avoid these unless you are making for Yosemite National Park.

Americans can cut **fares** greatly by using one of three **Explore America rail passes**, each of which gives unlimited travel for 45 days; for details see p.9. The coastal pass available to foreign travelers (see p.30) is not sold to US citizens.

For all information on **Amtrak fares** and **schedules** in the US, use the toll-free number ☎1-800/USA-RAIL; do not phone individual stations.

BY BUS

If you're traveling on your own, and making a lot of stops, **buses** are by far the cheapest way to get around. The main long-distance service is **Greyhound**, which links all major cities and many smaller towns. Out in the country, buses are fairly scarce, sometimes appearing only once a day, and here you'll need to plot your route with care. But along the main highways, buses run around the clock to a fairly full timetable, stopping only for meal breaks (almost always fast-food dives) and driver changeovers. Greyhound buses are slightly less uncomfortable than you might expect, too, and it's feasible to save on a night's accommodation by traveling overnight and sleeping on the bus – though you may not feel up to much the next day.

To avoid possible hassle, lone female travelers in particular should take care to sit as near to the driver as possible, and to arrive during daylight hours, as many bus stations are in fairly dodgy areas. It used to be that any sizeable community would have a Greyhound station; in some places the post office or a gas station doubles as the bus stop and ticket office, and in many others the bus service has been canceled altogether. Reservations, either in person at the station or on the toll-free number, are not essential but recommended – if a bus is full you may be forced to wait until the next one, sometimes overnight or longer.

Fares average 10¢ a mile, which can add up quickly; for example, $35 from Los Angeles to San Francisco one-way. For long-trip travel riding the bus costs about the same as the train; considering the time (75 hours coast-to-coast, if you eat and sleep on the bus) it's not that much cheaper than flying. However, the bus is the best deal if you plan to visit a lot of places, and Greyhound's **Ameripasses** for domestic travelers are good for unlimited travel nationwide for 7 days ($199), 15 days ($299), 30 days ($409), and 60 days ($599); the reduced rates for foreign travelers are on p.30.

Greyhound produces a condensed **timetable** of major country-wide routes, but does not distribute it to travelers; to plan your route, pick up the free route-by-route timetables from larger stations.

Greyhound's nationwide toll-free **information service** can give you routes and times, plus phone numbers and addresses of local terminals. You can also make reservations: ☎1-800/231-2222

GREEN TORTOISE

One alternative to Long-Distance Bus Hell is the slightly countercultural **Green Tortoise**, whose buses, furnished with foam cushions, bunks, fridges and rock music, ply the major Californian cities, running between Los Angeles, San Francisco and on into the Pacific Northwest. In summer, they also cross the country to New York and Boston, transcontinental trips which amount to mini-tours of the nation, taking 10–14 days (at a current cost of $299–379, not including contributions to the food fund which amount to around $10 a day), and allowing plenty of stops for hiking, river-rafting and hot springs. Other Green Tortoise trips include excursions to the major national parks (in 16 days for $499), south to Mexico and Central America and north to Alaska.

Main Office: 494 Broadway, San Francisco, CA 94133; ☎1-800/867-8647 or 415/956-7500.

Bear in mind that fair distances can be covered for very little money (if also very slowly) using **local buses**, which connect neighboring districts. It's possible, for example, to travel from San Diego to Los Angeles for $3.50, but it'll take all day and at least three changes of bus to do it. And of course, there's always the hippyish Green Tortoise, which runs between the major Californian cities (see box).

CYCLING

In general, **cycling** is a cheap and healthy method of getting around all the big **cities**, some of which have cycle lanes and local buses equipped to carry bikes – strapped to the outside. In **country areas**, certainly, there's much scenic, and largely level, land, especially around Sacramento and the Wine Country.

Bikes can be **rented** for $25 a day, $90–100 a week from most bike stores; the local visitor center will have details (we've listed rental options where applicable throughout the guide). Apart from the coastal fog, which tends to clear by midday, you'll encounter few **weather** problems (except perhaps sunburn) but remember that the further north you go, the lower the temperatures and the more frequent the rains become.

For **long-distance cycling** you'll need a good quality multi-speed bike (but don't immediately splurge on a mountain bike, unless you are planning a lot of off-road use – good road conditions and trail restrictions in National Parks make a touring bike an equally good or better choice), maps, spare tires, tools, panniers and a helmet (not a legal necessity, but a very good idea). A route avoiding the Interstates (on which cycling is illegal) is essential, and it's also wise to cycle north to south, as the wind blows this way in the summer and can make all the difference between a pleasant trip and acute leg-ache. The main **problem** you'll encounter is traffic: wide, cumbersome recreational vehicles spew unpleasant exhaust in your face and, in Northern California, enormous logging trucks have slipstreams that will pull you towards the middle of the road. Be particularly careful if you're planning to cycle along Hwy-1 on the central coast, since besides heavy traffic, it has tight curves, dangerous precipices, and is prone to fog.

If you're camping as well as cycling, look out for **hiker/biker campgrounds** ($3 per person per night), which are free of cars and campervans,

> ### HITCHING
> The usual advice given to **hitchhikers** is that they should use their common sense; in fact, of course, common sense should tell anyone that hitchhiking in the US is a **bad idea**. We do not recommend it under any circumstances.

dotted across California's state parks and beaches. Many of them were set up in 1976 as part of the **Pacific Coast Bicentennial Bike Route** running 1000 miles from the Mexican to the Oregon border. Sites are allotted on a first-come-first-served basis, and all offer water and toilet facilities but seldom showers. For more information, call ☎1-800/444-7275 or write to Hostelling International – USA (see p.38); Adventure Cycling Association (formerly Bikecentennial), 150 E Pine St, Missoula, MT 59807 (☎406/721-1776); or the Sierra Club (address on p.46).

ACCOMMODATION

Accommodation standards in California – as in the rest of the US – are high, and costs inevitably form a significant proportion of the expenses for any trip to the state. It is possible to haggle, however, especially in the chain motels, and if you're on your own, you can possibly pare costs by sleeping in dormitory-style hostels, where a bed will cost $12–15. However, groups of two or more will find it only a little more expensive to stay in the far more plentiful motels and hotels, where basic rooms away from the major cities typically cost around $30 per night. Many hotels will set up a third single bed for around $5 to $10 on top of the regular

price, reducing costs for three people sharing. By contrast, the lone traveler will have a hard time of it: "singles" are usually double rooms at an only slightly reduced rate. Prices quoted by hotels and motels are almost always for the actual room rather than for each person using it.

Motels are plentiful on the main approach roads to cities, around beaches and by the main road junctions in country areas. High-rise **hotels** predominate along the popular sections of the coast and are sometimes the only accommodation in city centers. In major cities **campgrounds** tend to be on the outskirts, if they exist at all.

Wherever you stay, you'll be expected to **pay in advance**, at least for the first night and perhaps for further nights too, particularly if it's high season and the hotel's expecting to be busy. Payment can be in cash or in dollar travelers' checks, though it's more common to give your credit card number and sign for everything when you leave. **Reservations** are only held until 5pm or 6pm unless you've told them you'll be arriving late. Most of the larger chains have an advance booking form in their brochures and will make reservations at another of their premises for you.

ACCOMMODATION PRICE CODES

Throughout this book, **accommodation** has been price-coded according to the cost of the least expensive **double room** throughout most of the year; we have given individual dollar prices for **hostels** and whole apartments. Expect prices in most places to jump into the next highest category on Friday and Saturday nights.

However, with the exception of the budget interstate motels, there's rarely such a thing as a set rate for a room. A basic motel in a seaside or mountain resort may double its prices according to the season, while a big-city hotel which charges $200 per room during the week will often slash its tariff at the weekend when all the business types have gone home. Particularly in scenic areas, prices might leap into the next higher category at weekends. As the high and low seasons for tourists vary widely across the state, astute planning can save a lot of money. Watch out also for local events, which can raise rates far above normal.

Only where we explicitly say so do these room rates include local taxes.

① up to $30	② $30–45	③ $45–60	④ $60–80	⑤ $80–100
⑥ $100–130	⑦ $130–175	⑧ $175–250	⑨ $250+	

Since cheap accommodation in the cities and on the popular sections of the coast is snapped up fast, **book ahead** whenever possible, using the suggestions in this book.

HOTELS AND MOTELS

Hotels and **motels** are essentially the same thing, although motels tend to be located beside the main roads away from city centers – and thus are much more accessible to drivers. The budget ones are pretty basic affairs, but in general there's a uniform standard of comfort everywhere – double rooms with bathroom, TV and phone – and you don't get a much better deal by paying, say, $50 instead of $35. Over $50, the room and its fittings simply get bigger and more luxurious, and there'll probably be a swimming pool which guests can use for free. Paying over $100 brings you into the realms of the en-suite jacuzzi.

While inexpensive diners may be everywhere, a growing number of Californian hotels are providing a **complimentary breakfast**. Sometimes this will be no more than a cup of coffee and a sticky bun, but increasingly it is a sit-down affair likely to comprise fruit, cereals, muffins and toast. In the pricier places, you may also be offered made-to-order omelets.

In most places you'll be able to find cheap one-off hotels and motels simply by keeping your eyes open – they're usually advertised by enormous roadside signs. Alternatively, there are a number of budget-priced **chains** whose rooms cost $28–45,. such as *Econolodge*, *Days Inn* and *Motel 6*. Mid-priced options include *Best Western*, *Howard Johnson*, *Travelodge* and *Ramada* – though if you can afford to pay this much ($50–100) there's normally somewhere nicer to stay. When it's worth

blowing a hunk of cash on somewhere really atmospheric we've said as much in the guide. Bear in mind the most upscale establishments have all manner of services which may appear to be free but for which you'll be expected to **tip** in a style commensurate with the hotel's status – ie big. For more on tipping see p.42 and p.57.

DISCOUNTS AND RESERVATIONS

During **off-peak periods** many motels and hotels struggle to fill their rooms and it's worth **haggling** to get a few dollars off the asking price. Staying in the same place for more than one night will bring further reductions. Additionally, pick up the many **discount coupons** which fill tourist information offices and look out for the free *Traveler Discount Guide*. Read the small print, though: what appears to be an amazingly cheap room rate sometimes turns out to be a per-person charge for two people sharing, and limited to midweek.

HOTEL DISCOUNT VOUCHERS

For the benefit of overseas travelers, many of the higher-rung hotel chains offer pre-paid **discount vouchers**, which in theory save you money if you're prepared to pay in advance. To take advantage of such schemes, British travelers must purchase the vouchers in the UK, at a usual cost of £30–60 per night for a minimum of two people sharing. However, it's hard to think of a good reason to buy them; you may save a nominal amount on the fixed rates, but better-value accommodation is not exactly difficult to find in the US, and you may well regret the inflexibility imposed upon your travels. Most UK travel agents will have details of the various voucher schemes.

NATIONAL HOTEL, HOSTEL AND MOTEL CHAINS

Most of the hotel and lodging chains listed below publish handy free directories (with maps and illustrations of their properties). Although we have indicated typical room rates (using the codes explained opposite), bear in mind that the location of a particular hotel or motel has a huge impact on price.

Best Western (③–⑥) ☎1-800/528-1234

Comfort Inns (③–⑤) ☎1-800/221-2222

Courtyard by Marriott (④–⑥) ☎1-800/321-2211

Days Inn (③–⑤) ☎1-800/325-2525

Econolodge (①–③) ☎1-800/446-6900

Embassy Suites Hotels (⑥–⑦) ☎1-800/362-2779

Fairfield Inns (③) ☎1-800/228-2800

Friendship Inns (④) ☎1-800/424-4777

Hampton Inns (④–⑤) ☎1-800/426-7866

Hilton Hotels (⑤ and up) ☎1-800/445-8667

Holiday Inns (⑤ and up) ☎1-800/465-4329

Hostelling International – American Youth Hostels ($12–18) ☎202/783-6161

Howard Johnson (②–⑤) ☎1-800/654-2000

Hyatt Hotels (⑧–⑨) ☎1-800/233-1234

ITT Sheraton (⑤ and up) ☎1-800/325-3535

La Quinta Inns (④) ☎1-800/531-5900

Marriott Hotels (⑥ and up) ☎1-800/228-9290

Motel 6 (②–③) ☎1-800/466-8356

Radisson Hotels (⑥) ☎1-800/333-3333

Ramada Inns (④ and up) ☎1-800/272-6232

Red Carpet Inns (②) ☎1-800/251-1962

Red Roof Inns (②–③) ☎1-800/843-7663

Renaissance Hotels (⑧–⑨) ☎1-800/468-3571

Rodeway Inns (④) ☎1-800/228-2000

Scottish Inns (②) ☎1-800/251-1962

Sleep Inns (③) ☎1-800/221-2222

Super 8 Motels (③–④) ☎1-800/800-8000

Travelodge (②–③) ☎1-800/255-3050

YMCA ($12–18) ☎1-800/872-9622

B&B INNS AND HOTELS

Bed and breakfast in California is a luxury – even the mattresses have to conform to a standard of comfort far higher than those in hotels. Typically, the bed-and-breakfast inns, as they're usually known, are restored buildings in the smaller cities and more rural areas – although the big cities also have a few, especially San Francisco. Even the larger establishments – often distinguished by being called B&B Hotels – tend to have no more than ten rooms, without TV and phone but often with plentiful flowers, stuffed cushions and a contrived homey atmosphere; others may just be a couple of furnished rooms in someone's home, or an entire apartment where you won't even see your host. Victorian and Romantic are dominant themes; while selecting the best in that vein, we've also gone out of our way to seek out those which don't conform.

While always including a huge and wholesome breakfast (five courses is not unheard of), prices vary greatly: anything from $70 to $250 depending on location and season. Most fall between $85 and $125 per night for a double, a little more for a whole apartment. Bear in mind, too, that they are often booked well in advance, and even if they're not full, the cheaper rooms which determine our price code may be already taken.

For a list of B&Bs throughout the state and in specific areas, contact one or more of the following:

Bed and Breakfast International, Box 282910, San Francisco, CA 94128-2910 (☎415/696-1690).

California Office of Tourism (see p.26), asking for the brochure *Californian Bed and Breakfast Inns*.

Colby International, 139 Round Hey, Liverpool L28 1RG (☎0151/220 5848 or in the US ☎404/818-5877) for bed-and-breakfast rooms and apartments in the main cities and along the Central Coast.

YS AND HOSTELS

At an average of $12 per night per person, **hostels** are clearly the cheapest accommodation option in California other than camping. There are three main kinds of hostel-type accommodation in the US: YMCA/YWCA hostels (known as "Ys") offering accommodation for both sexes, or in a few cases, women-only accommodation; official HI–AYH hostels; and the growing AAIH (American Association of Independent Hostels) organization.

YOUTH HOSTEL INFORMATION

Local **youth hostel** information can be found at the following HI–AYH council offices:

Central CA Council, PO Box 3645, Merced, CA 95344 (☎209/383-0686).

Golden Gate Council, 425 Divisadero St #307, San Francisco, CA 94117 (☎415/788-2525).

Los Angeles Council, 1434 Second St, Santa Monica, CA 94010 (☎310/393-3413).

San Diego Council, 655 Fourth Ave, San Diego, CA 92101 (☎619/338-9981).

The *Hostel Handbook for the USA and Canada*, produced each May, lists over two hundred hostels and is available for $4 from Jim Williams, *Sugar Hill House International Hostel*, 722 Saint Nicholas Ave, New York, NY 10031 (☎212/926-7030). *Hostelling North America*, the HI guide to hostels in the USA and Canada is available free of charge to any overnight guest at HI-AYH hostels or direct for $2 from the **HI National Office**, 733 15th St NW, Suite 840, Washington DC 20005 (☎202/783-6161).

For **overseas hostellers**, the *International Youth Hostel Handbook* provides a full list of hostels. In Britain, it's available from the Youth Hostel Association headquarters and shop, at 14 Southampton St, London WC2 (☎0171/836 1036), where you can also buy a year's IYHF **membership** for £10 (£5 if you're under 18).

Prices in **YMCA**s range from around $12 for a dormitory bed to $18 for a single or double room. Some Ys are basically health clubs and do not offer accommodation. Those that do are often in older buildings in less than ideal neighborhoods, but facilities can include a gymnasium, a swimming pool, and an inexpensive cafeteria.

You'll find **HI-AYH** hostels (the prefix is usually shortened to HI in listings) in major cities and popular hiking areas, including national and state parks, across California. Most urban hostels have 24-hour access, while rural ones may have a curfew and limited daytime hours. HI also operates a couple of small "home hostels" in the state; though similar to other hostels you need to reserve in advance or there may be no one there to receive you. Rates at HI hostels range from $9 to $18 for HI members; non-members generally pay an additional $3 per night.

Particularly if you're traveling in high season, it's advisable to **book ahead** through one of the specialist travel agents or international youth hostel offices: HI-AYH has a free booking service on ☎202/783-6161. Some HI hostels will allow you to use a **sleeping bag**, though officially they should (and many do) insist on a **sheet sleeping bag**, which can usually be rented at the hostel. The maximum stay at each hostel is technically three days, though this is again a rule which is often ignored if there's space. Few hostels provide meals but most have **cooking** facilities. Alcohol, smoking and, of course, drugs are banned.

The **independent** hostels in the **AAIH** group are usually a little less expensive than their HI counterparts, and have fewer rules. The quality is not as consistent; some can be quite poor, while others, which we've included in this book, are absolutely wonderful. In popular areas, especially LA, San Francisco and San Diego, they compete fiercely for your business with airport and train station pick-ups, free breakfasts and free bike hire. There is often no curfew and, at some, a party atmosphere is encouraged at barbecues and keg parties. Their independent status may be due to a failure to come up to the HI's (fairly rigid) criteria, but often it's simply because the owners prefer not to be tied down by HI regulations.

All the information in this book was accurate at the time of going to press; however, youth hostels are often shoestring organizations, prone to changing address or closing down altogether. Similarly, new ones appear each year; check the noticeboards of other hostels for news.

CAMPING

California campgrounds range from the primitive (a flat piece of ground that may or may not have a water tap) to others which are more like open-air hotels, with shops, restaurants and washing facilities. Naturally enough, prices vary accordingly, ranging from nothing for the most basic plots, up to $20 a night for something comparatively luxurious. There are plenty of campgrounds but often plenty of people intending to use them as well: take care over plotting your route if you're intending to camp in the big National Parks, or anywhere at all during national holidays or the summer, when many

Two private companies oversee a multitude of campgrounds all over California, although these are almost exclusively for RVs. For their brochures and lists contact **California Travel Parks Association**, PO Box 5648, Auburn, CA 95604 (☎916/885-1624) and **Kampgrounds of America (KOA)**, PO Box 30558, Billings, MT 59114 (☎406/248-7444). More tent-friendly sites can be found in the state parks (see p.44). These can be booked ahead (for a $7.50 fee) through a centralized system called **Parknet** (☎1-800/444-7275).

grounds will be either full or very crowded. Vacancies often exist in the grounds outside the parks – where the facilities are usually marginally better – and by contrast, some of the more basic campgrounds in isolated areas will often be empty whatever time of year you're there, and if there's any charge at all you'll need to pay by leaving the money in the bin provided.

Look out too for **hiker/biker campgrounds**, which, at $3 per person per night, are much cheaper than most sites but only available if you are traveling under your own steam (see p.35).

Much of California is in the public domain, and, if you're backpacking, you can **camp rough** pretty much anywhere you want in the gaping **wilderness areas** and **deserts**. However, you must first get a **wilderness permit** (either free or $1), and usually a **campfire permit**, from the nearest park rangers' office. You should also take the proper precautions: carry sufficient food and drink to cover emergencies, inform the park ranger of your travel plans, and watch out for the bears and rattlesnakes, and the effect *your* presence can have on *their* environment; see "Backcountry Camping, Hiking and Wildlife" on

p.44. For more information on these undeveloped regions – which are often protected within either "national parks" or "national forests" – contact the Western Regional Information Office, National Park Service, Fort Mason, Building 201, San Francisco, CA 94123 (☎415/556-0560) or the US Forest Service, 630 Sansome St, San Francisco, CA 94111 (☎415/705-2874).

LONG-TERM ACCOMMODATION

Excluding San Francisco, **apartment-hunting** in California is not the nightmare it is in, say, New York: accommodation is plentiful and not always expensive, although the absence of housing associations and co-ops means that there is very little really cheap accommodation anywhere except in very isolated country areas. Accommodation is almost always rented unfurnished so you'll have to buy furniture; expect to pay at least $700 a month for a studio or one-bedroom apartment and upwards of $1500 per month for two to three bedrooms in Los Angeles or San Francisco. Most landlords will expect one month's rent as a deposit, plus one month in advance.

There is no statewide organization for accommodation so you'll have to check out the options in each place. By far the best way to find somewhere is to ask around – particularly near universities or college campuses, where apartment turnover is unusually frequent. Otherwise rooms for rent are often advertised in the windows of houses and local papers have "Apartments For Rent" sections. In **Los Angeles** the best source is the *LA Weekly*, although you should also scan the *LA Times* classifieds. In **San Francisco** check out the *Chronicle* and the free *Bay Area Guardian*, *East Bay Express* – and, for women, *Bay Area Women's News*.

FOOD AND DRINK

It's not too much of an exaggeration to say that in California – its cities, at least – you can eat whatever you want, whenever you want. On every main street, a mass of restaurants, fast-food places and coffee shops try to outdo one another with bargains and special offers.

California's cornucopia stems largely from its being one of the most agriculturally rich parts of the country. Junk food is as common as anywhere else in the US, but the state also produces its own range of highly nutritious goodies: apples, avocados, dates, grapes, kiwi fruits, melons, oranges and peaches are everywhere, plus abundant fish and seafood and high-quality meat and dairy goods. You'll rarely find anything that's not fresh, be it a bagel or a spinach-in-Mornay-sauce croissant (California's mix'n'match food concoctions can be as anarchic as its architecture), and even fast food won't necessarily be rubbish.

California is also one of the most health-conscious states in the union, and the supermarket shelves are chock-full of products which if not fat-free, are low-fat, low-sodium, caffeine-free and dairy-free. Much the same ethic runs through the menu of most restaurants, though you needn't worry about going hungry: portions are as huge as elsewhere in the States, and what you don't eat can always be "boxed up" for later consumption.

BREAKFAST

For the price, on average $4–7, breakfast is the best-value and most filling meal of the day. Go to a **diner**, or, slightly smarter, a **café** or **coffee shop**, all of which serve breakfast until at least 11am, with some diners serving them all day. There are often special deals at earlier times too, say 6–8am, when the price may be even lower.

The breakfasts themselves are pretty much what you'd find all over the country. **Eggs** are the staple ingredient, and are served in a variety of styles: "sunny side up" (fried on one side, leaving a runny yolk), "over" (flipped over in the pan to stiffen the yolk), "over easy" (flipped for a few seconds giving just a hint of solidity to the yolk), or scrambled (just that). **Omelets** are popular, usually made with three eggs and available with a range of exotic fillings (avocado, for instance). There is usually also some form of **meat** available: ham or bacon, streaky and fried to a crisp; or sausages, skinless and spicy, sometimes shaped as disc-like "sausage patties".

Many breakfasts come with **toast**: rye, white or whole-wheat bread generally, though tangy **sourdough bread** is also common. Alternatives are an **English muffin** (a toasted bread roll) or an **American muffin**, a fruitcake traditionally made with bran and sugar, often flavored with blueberries, poppyseed or chocolate chip. If you wish, you can add **waffles**, **pancakes** or French toast to the combination, consumed swamped in butter with lashings of sickly-sweet syrup, flavored to mimic the more delicate and expensive maple syrup. A concession to California's love of light food is the option of **fruit**: typically apple, banana, orange, pineapple or strawberry, wonderfully styled and served on their own or with pancakes, though costing as much as a full-blown fry-up.

Wherever you eat, a dollar or so will entitle you to wash the meal down with as much **coffee** as you can stomach; **tea** is less common, but isn't hard to find. Be warned, though, that anything called "English tea" will be a poor-quality brew made with weak tea bags or an inferior Earl Grey. Better to try the wide range of **herbal teas** (don't pronounce the "h"): apple and cinnamon, blackcurrant, emperors (a very spicy herb) and ginseng, peppermint and chamomile, and a huge selection of others are available. A cup will cost from 30¢ to $1, and is served straight rather than with milk.

LUNCH AND SNACKS

Most Californian workers take their lunch break between 11.30am and 1.30pm, and during these hours you should look for the low-cost **set menus** on offer – generally excellent value. Chinese restaurants, for example, frequently have help-yourself rice and noodles or dim sum feasts for $5–8, and many Japanese restaurants give you a chance to eat sushi much more cheaply ($8–12) than usual. Most Mexican restaurants are exceptionally well priced all the time: you can get a good-sized lunch for $5–7. In Northern California, watch out for seafood restaurants selling **fish and chips**: the fish is breaded and then fried – a vast improvement on English batter – and the chips are real chipped potatoes rather than the American French fry matchsticks you normally find. A plateful is about $5. Look, too, for **clam chowder**, a thick, creamy shellfish soup served almost everywhere for $3–4, sometimes using a hollowed-out sourdough cottage loaf as a bowl.

As you'd expect, there's also **pizza**, available from chains like *Pizza Hut*, *Round Table* and *Shakey's*, or local, more personalized restaurants. Most are dependable and have a similar range of offerings; count on paying around $10 for a basic two-person pizza. If it's a warm day and you can't face hot food, delis (see below) usually serve a broad range of salads for about $4. Consider also California's favorite healthy fast food: **frozen yogurt**, which is sold in most places by the tub for $2.

For **quick snacks**, you'll find many **delis** do ready-cooked meals for $4–5 as well as a range of **sandwiches "to go"**, which can be meals in themselves: huge French rolls filled with a custom-built combination of meat, cheese, and vegetables. *Subway*, the international chain, makes sandwiches fast-food style, but bear in mind that you'll often pay just as much for lesser quality,

processed ingredients. **Bagels**, also, are everywhere: thick, chewy rolls with a hole in the middle, filled with anything you fancy. **Street stands** sell hot dogs, burgers, tacos, or a slice of pizza for around $1.50 and most shopping malls have ethnic fast-food stalls, often pricier than their equivalent outside, but usually edible and filling. Be a little wary of the grottier **Mexican fast-food** stands if you're buying meat, although they're generally filling, cheap and more authentic than the Tex-Mex outlets. There are chains, too, like *El Pollo Loco*, *Del Taco* and *Taco Bell*, which sell swift tacos and burritos for around $1. And of course the **burger chains** are as ubiquitous here as anywhere in the US: *Wendy's*, *Burger King* and *McDonald's* are the familiar names, along with *Jack-in-the-Box* – a drive-through takeout where you place your order by talking to a plastic clown – and others, all of which now offer more adventurous menus than previously.

Finally, just about any of these places will serve **sodas**. Each brand is available in caffeine-free and sugar-free varieties (though there's even in reaction to this a brand called Jolt, which promises "all the sugar and twice the caffeine"). You can buy sodas from vending machines and in supermarkets for about 65¢ a can, or from a fast-food outlet in three sizes – large, larger and gargantuan – for between 75¢ and $1.50, each with ice added by the shovelful.

RESTAURANTS

Even if it often seems swamped by the more fashionable regional and ethnic cuisines, traditional **American cooking** – juicy burgers, steaks, fries, salads (invariably served before the main dish) and baked potatoes – is found all over California. Cheapest of the food chains is the California-wide *Denny's*, although you'll rarely need to spend more than $10 for a solid blowout anywhere.

By contrast, though, it's **California cuisine**, geared towards health and aesthetics, that's raved about by foodies on the West Coast – and rightly so. Basically a development of French *nouvelle cuisine*, utilizing the wide mix of fresh, locally available ingredients, California cuisine is based on physiological efficiency – eating only what you need to and what your body can process. Vegetables are harvested before maturity and steamed to preserve a high concentration of vitamins, with a strong flavor – and to look better on the plate. Seafood comes from oyster farms

FREE FOOD

Some **bars** are used as much by diners as drinkers, who turn up in droves to fill up on the free **hors d'oeuvres** laid out by a lot of city bars between 5pm and 7pm Monday to Friday – an attempt to nab the commuting classes before they head off to the suburbs. For the price of a drink you can stuff yourself silly on chili, seafood or pasta, though bear in mind that the food is more often than not downright unappetizing until you've had at least three drinks.

and the catches of small-time fishermen, and what little meat there is on the menu tends to come from animals reared on organic farms. The result is small but beautifully presented portions, and high, high prices: it's not unusual to spend $40 a head (or much more) for a full dinner with wine; the minimum you'll need for a sample is $15 which will buy an entree. To whet your appetite, starters include mussels in jalapeño and sesame vinaigrette, snails in puff pastry with mushroom purée, and, among main courses, roasted goat cheese salad with walnuts, swordfish with herb butter and ahi tuna with cactus ratatouille.

Restaurants serving California cuisine build their reputation by word of mouth; if you can, ask a local enthusiast for recommendations, or simply follow our suggestions in the guide, especially in Berkeley, the recognized birthplace of California

cuisine. Of other American regional cooking, **Cajun** remains in vogue. Also known as "Creole", it originated in Louisiana as a way of saving money by cooking up leftovers. It is centered on black beans, rice and seafood, and is always highly spiced. There are a few relatively inexpensive places to find it (charging around $8 per entree), but its cachet has pushed prices up tremendously, and in most places it's not really a budget option.

Although technically ethnic, **Mexican** food is so common that it often seems like (and, historically, often is) an indigenous cuisine, especially in Southern California. What's more, day or night, it's the cheapest type of food to eat: even a full dinner with a few drinks will rarely be over $12 anywhere except in the most upmarket establishments. In the main, Mexican food here is different from what you'll find in Mexico, making more use of fresh vegetables and fruit, but the essentials are the same: lots of rice and pinto beans, often served refried (ie boiled, mashed and fried), with variations on the **tortilla**, a thin maize or flour dough pancake. You can eat it as an accompaniment to your main dish; wrapped around the food and eaten by hand (a **burrito**); filled and folded (a **taco**); rolled, filled and baked (an **enchilada**); or fried flat and topped with a stack of food (a **tostada**). One of the few options for vegetarians in this meat-oriented cuisine is the **chile relleno**, a green pepper stuffed with cheese, dipped in egg batter and fried. Veggie burritos, filled with beans, rice, lettuce, avocado, cheese and sour cream are another prevalent option for those averse to meat.

MEXICAN SPECIALITIES

Burritos	Refried beans, meat, and grated cheese wrapped in a flour tortilla	*Nachos*	Tortilla chips topped with melted cheese
Chiles rellenos	Green chilies stuffed with cheese and fried in egg batter	*Quesadilla*	Folded soft tortilla containing melted cheese
Enchiladas	Soft tortillas filled with meat and cheese or chili and baked	*Salsa*	Diced chilies, tomato, onion and cilantro
Fajitas	Like tacos but a soft flour tortilla stuffed with shrimp, chicken, beef and grilled onions	*Tacos*	Folded corn tortillas, stuffed with chicken, beef or (occasionally) cow's brains
Frijoles	Beans, either regular or mashed and fried	*Tamales*	Corn meal dough with meat and chili, wrapped in a corn husk and baked
Guacamole	Thick sauce made from avocado, garlic, onion and chili, used as a topping	*Tortillas*	Corn or wheat flour pancakes
Mariscos	Seafood	*Tostada*	Fried, flat tortillas, smothered with meat and vegetables

Other ethnic cuisines are plentiful too. **Chinese** food is everywhere, and during lunchtime can often be as cheap as Mexican. **Japanese** is more expensive and fashionable – sushi is worshipped by some Californians. **Italian** food is very popular, but can be expensive once you leave the simple pizzas and pastas to explore the specialist Italian regional cooking that's fast catching on. **French** food, too, is widely available, though always pricey, the cuisine of social climbers and power-lunchers and rarely found outside the larger cities. **Thai**, **Korean**, **Vietnamese** and **Indonesian** food is similarly city-based, though usually cheaper; **Indian** restaurants, on the other hand, are thin on the ground just about everywhere and often very expensive – although as Indian cuisine catches on the situation is gradually changing for the better, with a sprinkling of moderately priced Southern Indian food outlets.

DRINKING

While typically American **bars** and **cocktail lounges** do exist in California – long dimly lit counters with a few punters perched on stools before a bartender-cum-guru, and tables and booths for those who don't want to join in the drunken bar-side debates – in freeway-dominated Los Angeles, the traditional neighborhood bar is as rare as the traditional neighborhood. There are exceptions, but LA bars tend to be either extremely pretentious or extremely seedy, neither good for long bouts of social drinking. On the other hand, San Francisco is the consummate boozing town, still with a strong contingent of old-fashioned, get-drunk bars that are fun to spend an evening in even if you don't plan to get legless.

To **buy and consume alcohol** in California you need to be 21, and could well be asked for ID even if you look much older. **Licensing laws** and **drinking hours** are, however, among the most liberal in the country (though laws on drinking and driving are not; see p.33). Alcohol can be bought and drunk any time between 6am and 2am, seven days a week; and, as well as bars, nightclubs and restaurants are nearly always fully licensed. In addition, it is permitted by California law to take your own bottled wine into a restaurant, where the corkage fee will be $5–10. You can buy beer, wine or spirits more cheaply and easily in supermarkets, many delis, and, of course, liquor stores.

American **beers** fall into two diametrically opposite categories: wonderful and tasteless. You'll probably be familiar with the latter, which are found everywhere: light, fizzy brands such as Budweiser, Miller, Schlitz and Michelob, the only nationally sold variety likely to find fans among British beer drinkers. The alternative is a fabulous range of **"microbrewed" beers**, the product of a wave of backyard and in-house operations that swelled about ten years ago and has now matured to the point that many pump out over 150,000 barrels a year and are classed as "regional breweries". Head for one of the **brewpubs** (many are listed in the guide along with breweries you can visit; see also the California Beerpage Web site listed on p.28) and you'll find handcrafted beers such as crisp pilsners, wheat beers and stouts on tap, at prices only marginally above those of the national brews. Bottled microbrews, like Chico's hoppy Sierra Nevada Pale Ale and the full-bodied, San Francisco-brewed Anchor Steam Beer are sold throughout the state, while Red Tail Ale is found throughout Northern California.

Alternatively, do what many locals do and stick to **imported** beers, especially the Mexican brands Bohemia, Corona, Dos Equis, and Tecate. Expect to fork out $3 for a glass of draught beer, about the same for a bottle of imported beer. Taste aside, imported beers gain advocates for their comparative alcoholic strength.

Don't forget that in all but the most pretentious bars, several people can save money by buying a (quart or half-gallon) **"pitcher"** of beer for $6–8. If bar prices are a problem, you can stock up with **six-packs** from a supermarket ($3–5 for domestic, $5–8 for imported brews).

If you're partial to the internationally known Californian **wines**, like Gallo and Paul Masson, you may be surprised to learn that they are held in low regard on the West Coast, and produced in plants resembling oil refineries. Most people prefer the produce of California's innumerable, and invariably good, smaller wineries. The Napa and Sonoma Valleys – which produce predominantly dry wines made from French-strain grapes – are widely, and rightly, regarded as the cradle of the Californian wine industry. Wines are categorized by grape-type rather than place of origin: Cabernet Sauvignon is probably the most popular, a fruity and palatable red. Also widespread are the heavier reds – Burgundy, Merlot and Pinot Noir. Among the whites, Chardonnay is very dry and flavorful, and generally preferred to Sauvignon Blanc or

Fumé Blanc, though these have their devotees. The most unusual is the strongly flavored Zinfandel, which comes in white (mocked by wine snobs, but popular nonetheless), red or rosé.

You can learn a lot about Californian wine by taking a **winery tour**, mostly including free tastings (although some charge $4–5 for a full glass or two), a number of which we've mentioned in the guide. Alternately, the visitor centers in popular wine-producing areas produce informative regional directories. The best lesson of all, of course, is simply to buy the stuff. It's fairly inexpensive: a decent glass of wine in a bar or restaurant costs about $4, a bottle $10–20. Buying from a supermarket is better still – a quality bottle can be purchased for as little as $7.

Cocktails are extremely popular, especially during **happy hours** (usually any time between 5pm and 7pm) when drinks are half-price and there's often a buffet thrown in. Varieties are innumerable, sometimes specific to a single bar or cocktail lounge, and they cost anything between $3 and $6.

An increasing alternative to drinking dens, **coffee shops** (look out for any joint with "Java" in the title) play a vibrant part in California's social scene, and are havens of high-quality coffee far removed from the stuff served in diners and convenience stores. In larger towns and cities, cafés will boast of the quality of the roast, and offer specialties such as espresso with lemon peel (which accentuates the bitterness wonderfully) as well as a full array of cappuccinos, lattes and the like, served straight, iced, organic or flavored with syrups. Herbal teas and light snacks are often also on the menu.

BACKCOUNTRY CAMPING, HIKING AND WILDLIFE

California has some fabulous backcountry and wilderness areas, coated by dense forests and capped by great mountains. Unfortunately, while still immensely rewarding – and it's one of *the* compelling reasons for coming to California – it isn't all as wild as it once was, thanks to the thousands who tramp through each year. If you're intending to do the same, you can help preserve the special qualities of the environment by observing a few simple rules. For practical information on traveling through the deserts, see the box on p.212.

The US's protected backcountry areas fall into a number of potentially confusing categories. Most numerous are **state parks**, owned and operated by the individual states. Some 275 in all, they include state beaches, state historic parks and state recreational areas, often around sites of geological or historical importance and not necessarily in rural areas. Daily fees are usually $4–6, though a $75 **annual pass** gives free access to most sites for a year.

National Parks – such as Yosemite and Death Valley – are large, federally controlled and preserved areas of great natural beauty comprising several different features or ecosystems; entry is usually $5. These are supplemented by the smaller **national monuments** ($3–4), like Devil's Postpile and Lava Beds, with just one major feature, and **national seashores**. If you plan to visit a few of these, invest in a **Golden Eagle Passport** ($50 cash from any National Park entrance), which grants both driver and passengers (or if cycling or hiking, the holder's immediate family) access to all California's National Parks for a calendar year. Excellent free **ranger programs** – such as guided walks or slide shows – are held throughout the year. The federal government also operates **national recreation areas**, often huge hydro dams where you can jetski or windsurf free from the necessarily restrictive laws of the national parks. Campgrounds and equipment-rental outlets are always abundant.

California's eighteen **national forests** cover twenty percent of the state's surface area. Most of them border the national parks, and are also federally administered (by the US Forest Service), but with much less protection. More roads run through national forests, and often there is some limited logging and other land-based industry operated on a sustainable basis.

All the above forms of protected land can contain **wilderness areas**, which aim to protect natural resources in their most native state. In practice this means there's no commercial activity at all;

BACKCOUNTRY DANGERS AND WILDLIFE

You're likely to meet many kinds of **wildlife** and come upon unexpected **hazards** on your travels through the wilderness, but only a few are likely to cause problems. With due care, many potential difficulties can be avoided.

Hiking in the **foothills** should not be problematic but you should check your clothes frequently for **ticks** – pesky bloodsucking burrowing insects which are known to carry Lyme disease. If you have been bitten, and especially if you get flu-like symptoms, get advice from a park ranger. Also annoying around water are **mosquitoes**; carry candles scented with citronella or insect repellent to keep them at bay.

Other than in a National Park, you're highly unlikely to encounter a **bear**. Even there, it's rare to stumble across one in the wilderness. Reduce the likelihood by making noise (carrying bells in your pack isn't a bad idea) as you walk. If you meet one, keep calm, lie slowly down on the ground and stay there without moving. The bear will get bored and move away. If a bear visits your camp, scare it off by banging pots and pans – if it doesn't go, you should. Leave backpacks open and lying on the ground so a bear can examine the contents without tearing them apart. It will be after your food, which should be stored in airtight containers when camping. Some campgrounds are equipped with **bear lockers**, which you are obliged to use to store food when not preparing or eating it. Camp stores in Yosemite, Kings Canyon and Sequoia National Parks rent hard plastic **bear-resistant canisters** ($3 a day) which can be carried on wilderness trips. Elsewhere, you should hang both food and garbage from a high branch (too weak to support the weight of a bear) some distance from your camp. Never feed a bear: it'll make the bear dependent on humans for food. Bears within state and National parks are protected, but if they spend too much time around people the park rangers are, depressingly, left with no option but to shoot them. Finally, never get between a mother and her cubs. Young animals are cute; irate mothers are not.

Rattlesnakes, which live in the desert areas and drier foothills up to around 7000ft, seldom attack unless provoked: do not tease or try to handle them. Rattlesnake bites are rarely fatal but you might suffer severe tissue damage (see p.213 for advice on what to do if bitten).

Mountain lions (cougars, panthers or pumas) are being hard hit by increasing urban expansion into former habitats (from deserts to coastal and subalpine forests). Sightings are rare in the newly suburbanized areas, and there have been few attacks on pedestrians, but to reduce the already slim chance of an unwanted encounter, avoid walking by yourself, especially after dark, when lions tend to hunt. Make noise as you walk, wield a stick and keep children close to you. If you encounter one, face the lion, try to appear larger by raising your arms or holding your coat above you and it will probably back away. If not, throw rocks and sticks in its vicinity.

Campsite critters – ground squirrels, chipmunks and raccoons – are usually just a nuisance though they tend to carry diseases and you should avoid contact. Only the **marmot** is a real pest, as it likes to chew through radiator hoses and car electrics to reach a warm engine on a cold night. Before setting off in the morning, check the motor for gnawed components, otherwise you might find yourself with a seized engine and a cooked or, at best, terrified marmot as a passenger. Boots and rucksacks also come in for marmot scrutiny.

Poison oak is one thing that isn't going to come and get you, though you may come up against it. Recognized by its shiny configuration of three dark-green veined leaves (turning red or yellow in autumn) which secrete an oily juice, this twiggy shrub or climbing vine is found in open woods or along stream banks throughout much of California. It's highly allergenic, so avoid touching it. If you do, washing with strong soap, taking frequent dips in the sea and applying cortisone cream usually helps relieve the symptoms in mild cases; in extreme cases, see a doctor.

In the mountains, your biggest dangers have nothing to do with the flora or fauna. Late **snows** are common, giving rise to the possibility of avalanches and meltwaters, which make otherwise simple stream crossings hazardous. **Drowning** in fast-flowing meltwater rivers is the single biggest cause of death in the Kings Canyon and Sequoia National Parks. The riverbanks are strewn with large, slippery boulders – keep well clear unless you are specifically there for river activities.

With much of the High Sierra above 10,000ft, **Acute Mountain Sickness** (aka altitude sickness) is always a possibility. Only those planning to bag one of the 14,000-foot peaks are likely to have to contend with much more than a slight headache, but it pays to be on the alert and to acclimatize slowly. Try to limit your exertions for the first day or so, drink plenty of fluids, eat little and often, and note any nausea, headaches or double vision. If you experience any of these symptoms, the only solution is to descend until they ease, then ascend more gradually.

For more on the hazards of snakes and spiders, see Chapter Three, p.213, and for more on Californian wildlife generally, see p.596 of Contexts.

buildings, motorized vehicles and bicycles are not permitted, nor are firearms and pets. Overnight camping is allowed, but **wilderness permits** (free–$1) must be obtained in advance from the land management agency responsible. In California, Lava Beds, Lassen, Death Valley, Sequoia-Kings Canyon, Joshua Tree, Pinnacles, Point Reyes and Yosemite all have large wilderness areas – 94 percent of Yosemite – with only the regions near roads, visitor centers and buildings designated as less stringently regulated "front country".

CAMPING

When **camping rough**, check that fires are permitted before you start one; if they are, use a stove in preference to local materials – in some places firewood is scarce, although you may be allowed to use deadwood. No open fires are allowed in wilderness areas, where you should also try to camp on previously used sites. Where there are no toilets, **bury human waste** at least four inches into the ground and a hundred feet from the nearest water supply and camp. **Burn rubbish**, and what you can't burn, carry away. A growing problem is Giardia, a water-borne protozoan causing an intestinal disease, symptoms of which are chronic diarrhea, abdominal cramps, fatigue and loss of weight, that requires treatment. To avoid catching it, **never drink** from rivers and streams, however clear and inviting they may look (you never know what unspeakable acts people – or animals – further upstream have performed in them). Before you drink it, **water** that isn't from taps should be boiled for at least five minutes, or cleansed with an iodine-based purifier (such as Potable Aqua) or a Giardia-rated filter, available from camping or sports shops.

Finally, don't use ordinary soaps or detergents in lakes and streams; you can buy special ecological soap for such a purpose.

HIKING

Wilderness areas start close to the main areas of National Parks. There is normally no problem entering the wilderness for day walks, but overnight trips require **wilderness permits** (see above). In peak periods, a quota system operates for the most popular paths, so if there's a hike you specifically want to do, obtain your permit well ahead of time (at least two weeks, more for popular hikes). When completing the form for your permit, be sure to ask a park ranger for weather conditions and general information about the hike you're undertaking.

Hikes covered in the guide (usually appearing in boxes) are given with length and estimated walking time for a healthy but not especially fit adult. **State parks** have graded trails designed for people who drive to the corner store, so anyone used to walking and with a moderate degree of fitness will find these ratings very conservative.

ESSENTIAL EQUIPMENT AND BOOKING AHEAD

Choose your tent wisely. Many Sierra sites are on rock with only a thin covering of soil so driving pegs in can be a problem. Free-standing **dome-style tents** are therefore preferable. Go for one with a large area of **mosquito netting** and a removable fly sheet; tents designed for harsh European winters can get horribly sweaty once the sun rises.

Most developed campgrounds are equipped with fire rings with some form of grill for cooking, but many people prefer a **Coleman stove**, powered by white gas, a kind of super-clean gasoline. Both stoves and white gas (also used for MSR backcountry stoves) are widely available in camping stores. Other camping stoves are less common. Equipment using butane and propane – Camping Gaz and, to a lesser extent, EPI gas, Scorpion and Optimus – is on the rise, though outside of major camping areas you'll be pushed to find supplies; stock up when you can. If you need methylated spirits for your Trangia, go to a hardware store and ask for denatured alcohol.

To reserve campgrounds in **National Parks** – highly advisable during the summer – contact the booking agency on ☎1-800/365-2267. Reserving sites in **state parks** means phoning **Parknet** on ☎1-800/444-7275. A charge of $7.50 per reservation is levied. Generally you can reserve up to eight weeks in advance but not less than two days before you arrive. To reserve campgrounds in **national forests** contact Biospherics on ☎1-800/280-2267.

In California, the **Sierra Club**, c/o Outings Dept, 85 Second St, San Francisco, CA 94105 (☎415/977-5500), offers a range of backcountry hikes into otherwise barely accessible parts of the High Sierra wilderness, with food and guide provided. The tours are summer-only, cost around $300 for a fortnight and are heavily subscribed, making it essential to book at least three months in advance. You'll also have to pay $35 to join the club.

WOMEN TRAVELERS

Practically speaking, though a woman traveling alone is certainly not the attention-grabbing spectacle in California that she might be elsewhere in the world (or even elsewhere in the US), you're likely to come across some sort of harassment. More serious than the odd offensive comment, rape statistics in the US are high, and it goes without saying that, even more than anyone else, women should never hitch alone – this is widely interpreted as an invitation for trouble, and there's no shortage of weirdos to give it. Similarly, if you have a car, be careful whom you pick up: just because you're in the driving seat doesn't mean you're safe. If you can, avoid traveling at night by public transportation – deserted bus stations, while not necessarily threatening, will do little to make you feel secure, and where possible you should team up with another woman. On Greyhound buses, follow the example of other lone women and sit as near to the front – and the driver – as possible.

Californian **cities**, especially San Francisco, can feel surprisingly safe, and **mugging** is nowhere near the problem it is in New York. But as with anywhere, particular care has to be taken at night, and a modicum of common sense can often avert disasters. Walking through unlit, empty streets is never a good idea, and you should take cabs wherever possible. The advice that women who look confident tend not to encounter trouble is, like all home truths, grounded in fact but not written in stone; those who stand around looking lost and a bit scared are prime targets, but nobody is immune. Provided you listen to advice, though, and stick to the better parts of a town, going into **bars** and **clubs** alone should pose no problems, especially in San Francisco and LA, where there's generally a pretty healthy attitude towards women who choose to do so and whose privacy will be respected – only extremely unevolved specimens will assume you're available. If in doubt, gay and lesbian bars are usually a trouble-free alternative.

Small towns in rural areas are not blessed with the same liberal attitudes toward lone women travelers that you'll find in the cities. If you have a **vehicle breakdown** in a country area, walk to the nearest house or town for help; don't wait by the vehicle in the middle of nowhere hoping for somebody to stop – they will, but it may not be the kind of help you're looking for. Should disaster strike, all major towns have some kind of rape counseling service available; if not, the local sheriff's office will make adequate arrangements for you to get help, counseling, and, if necessary, get you home.

The **National Organization for Women** is a women's issues group whose lobbying has done much to affect positive legislation. NOW branches, listed in local phone directories, can provide referrals for specific concerns such as rape crisis centers and counseling services, feminist bookstores and lesbian bars. Further back-up material can be found in **Women's' Travel in Your Pocket** ($16; Ferrari Publications, PO Box 37887, Phoenix, AZ 85069; ☎602/863-2408), an annual guide for women travelers. Specific **women's contacts** are listed where applicable in the city sections of the guide.

TRAVELERS WITH DISABILITIES

Travelers with mobility problems or other physical disabilities are likely to find California – as with the US in general – to be much more in tune with their needs than anywhere else in the world. All public buildings must be wheelchair-accessible and have suitable toilets; most city street corners have dropped curbs; subways have elevators, and most city buses are able to kneel to make access easier and are built with space and handgrips for wheelchair users. Most hotels, restaurants and theaters (certainly any built in the last ten years or so) have excellent wheelchair access.

GETTING TO AND FROM CALIFORNIA

Most **airlines**, transatlantic and within the US, do whatever they can to ease your journey, and will usually let attendants of people with serious disabilities accompany them at no extra charge. The Americans with Disabilities Act of 1990 obliged all air carriers to make the majority of their services accessible to travelers with disabilities within five to nine years.

Almost every **Amtrak train** includes one or more coaches with accommodation for disabled passengers. Guide dogs travel free, and Amtrak will provide wheelchair assistance at its train stations, adapted seating on board and a fifteen percent discount on the regular fare, all provided 24 hours' notice is given. Passengers with hearing impairment can get information on ☎1-800/523-6590.

Traveling by **Greyhound** and **Amtrak Thruway** buses, however, is not to be recommended. Buses are not equipped with lifts for wheelchairs, though staff will assist with boarding (intercity carriers are required by law to do this), and the "Helping Hand" scheme offers two-for-the-price-of-one tickets to passengers unable to travel alone (carry a doctor's certificate).

The major **car rental** firms can, given sufficient notice, provide vehicles with hand controls (though these are usually only available on the more expensive models, and you'll need to reserve well in advance). The American Automobile Association (see p.26) produces the *Handicapped Driver's Mobility Guide* for **drivers with disabilities** (available free from AAA, Traffic Safety Dept, 150 Van Ness Ave, San Francisco, CA 94102;

☎415/565-2012). There are no longer differences in state **parking regulations** for disabled motorists; the Department of Transportation has decreed that all state licenses issued to disabled persons must carry a three-inch square international access symbol, and each state must provide placards bearing this symbol to be hung from the rear-view mirror – the placards are blue for permanent disabilities, red for temporary (maximum of six months). More information can be obtained from your state motor vehicle office.

As in other parts of the world, the rise of the **self-service gas station** is unwelcome for many disabled drivers. The state of California has addressed this by changing its laws so that most service stations are required to provide full service to disabled drivers at self-service prices.

INFORMATION

The California Office of Tourism's free 200-page *California Travel Planning Guide* lists "handicap facilities" at places of accommodation and attractions (though some attractions which do have facilities for disabled visitors, such as San Diego Zoo, are not listed as accessible). The *San Francisco Lodging Guide* (free from the San Francisco CVB, PO Box 429097, San Francisco, CA 94142; ☎415/974-6900) lists many "wheelchair-accessible" properties – hotels, motels, apartments, B&Bs, hostels, RV parks – in the city and surrounding counties; as always, travelers should call to confirm details. The Center for Independent Living, 2539 Telegraph Ave in Berkeley (☎510/841-4776) has long been one of the most effective disabled people's organizations in the world; it has a variety of counseling services.

National organizations facilitating travel for people with disabilities include **SATH**, the **Society for the Advancement of Travel for the Handicapped** (347 Fifth Ave, Suite 610, New York, NY 10016; ☎212/447-7284), a nonprofit travel-industry grouping which includes travel agents, tour operators, hotel and airline management for people with disabilities. They will pass on any inquiry to the appropriate member; allow plenty of time for a response. **Mobility International USA** (PO Box 10767, Eugene, OR 97440; ☎541/343-1284) answers transportation queries and operates an exchange program for disabled people. This is the US branch of an international organization, whose main office is at 18 Boulevard Baudouin, B-1000, Brussels, Belgium (☎32 2/201 5608). **Travelin' Talk** (130 Hillcrest Drive, Clarksville, TN 37043; ☎931/552-6670), the brainchild of Rick Crowder, energetic Disabled American of the Year 1991, is a network to assist travelers with disabilities, on the principle that the most reliable information and advice comes from another disabled person. Extensive listings of services for travelers with disabilities are disseminated in a quarterly newsletter (available in large print, or on cassette).

Other useful resources are *Travel for the Disabled*, *Wheelchair Vagabond* and *Directory for Travel Agencies for the Disabled*, all produced by **Twin Peaks Press**, PO Box 129, Vancouver, WA 98666 (☎1-800/637-2256 or 360/694-2462).

ACCOMMODATION

The big motel and hotel chains are often the safest bet for accessible **accommodation**; there are plenty of excellent local alternatives, of course, but with a chain at least you'll know what to expect. At the higher end of the scale *Embassy Suites* (☎1-800/362-2779, voice; 1-800/458-4708, TDD) have been working to implement new standards of access which meet and exceed ADA requirements, involving both new construction and the retrofitting of their one hundred existing hotels, and providing special training to all employees. Although the President of **Hyatt International Corporation** (☎1-800/233-1234) summed up the hotel industry's initial reaction to the ADA as "the end of the world as we know it", Hyatt has also committed itself to extensive redesign to improve accessibility.

THE GREAT OUTDOORS

Citizens or permanent residents of the US who have been "medically determined to be blind or permanently disabled" can obtain the **Golden Access Passport**, a free lifetime entrance pass to those federally operated parks, monuments, historic sites, recreation areas and wildlife refuges which charge entrance fees. The pass must be picked up in person, from the areas described, and it also provides a fifty percent discount on fees charged for facilities such as camping, boat launching and parking. The **Golden Bear Pass** (free to the disabled) offers similar concessions to state-run parks, beaches and historic sites.

For visitors to **National Parks** the somewhat outdated *Access America Guide: An Atlas of the National Parks* costs $44.95, from Northern Cartographic (Suite 131, 4050 Williston Rd, South Burlington, VT 05403; ☎802/860-2886). The guide contains useful information for visitors with mobility impairments, or hearing, visual, or developmental disabilities, and is spiral-bound for ease of handling, with large-print text. Access evaluations are based on national and federal standards and cover campgrounds, lodging, transportation, visitor centers and adventure tours. Some accounts by visitors with disabilities are also included.

The **Disabled Outdoors Foundation** (2052 W 23rd St, Chicago, IL 60608; ☎773/667-7313) is a clearing house for information for the disabled person looking for recreational facilities and adaptive recreational gear. The *Disabled Outdoors Magazine* is the Foundation's quarterly magazine covering outdoor activities for sportspersons with disabilities (US $10, Can $16 yearly). Also useful is *Easy Access to National Parks*, by Wendy Roth and Michael Tompane ($15), a detailed guide to all US National Parks for people with disabilities, senior citizens, and families with young children, published by the **Sierra Club** (85 Second St, San Francisco, CA 94105; ☎415/977-5500, voice; ☎415/977-5780, TDD).

Yosemite National Park (PO Box 577, Yosemite, CA 95389; ☎209/372-0515, voice; 209/372-4726, TDD) can supply general information direct, but an invaluable guide is *Access Yosemite National Park* ($7.95), a one-park excerpt from its parent publication, above.

The **state parks** service also offers reduced rates for permanently disabled people who apply by mail for a Disabled Discount Pass ($3.50 once-only payment) to Department of Parks and Recreation, Disabled Discount Pass Program, 1416 Ninth St, Sacramento, CA 95814. Call ☎916/653-4000 for the required application. The pass gives a fifty percent discount on all parking and camping fees above $3, except at Hearst Castle.

PACKAGES

Many US **tour companies** cater for disabled travelers or specialize in organizing disabled group tours. State tourist departments should be able to provide lists of such companies; failing that, ask the National Tour Association, 546 E Main St, PO Box 3071, Lexington, KY 40596 (☎1-800/755-8687 or 606/226-4444). They can put you in touch with operators whose tours match your needs.

TRAVELING WITH CHILDREN

Traveling with kids in California is rela- tively problem-free; children are readily accepted – indeed welcomed – in public places everywhere. Hotels and motels are well used to them (although some bed and breakfasts have a minimum age requirement of twelve – ask when making reservations), most state and national parks organize chil- dren's activities, every town or city has clean and safe playgrounds, and of course LA's Disneyland is the ultimate in kids' entertainment. Restaurants make consider- able efforts to encourage parents to bring their offspring. All the national chains offer bolster chairs and a special kids' menu, packed with huge, excellent-value (though not necessarily healthy) meals – cheese- burger and fries for $2, and so on.

Local tourist offices (see p.26) can provide spe- cific information on what California has to offer children, and various **guidebooks** have been writ- ten for parents traveling with children – as *California With Kids* ($18), in the Frommer's Family Guides list, and the very helpful *Trouble Free Travel with Children* ($6.95), available through Publishers Group West. John Muir Publications puts out a series of books for children, called *Kidding Around*, which tell about the history and describe the vari- ous sights of major US cities.

GETTING AROUND

Most families choose to travel **by car**, and while this is the least problematic way to get around it's worth planning ahead to assure a pleasant trip. Don't set yourself unrealistic targets if you're hoping to enjoy a driving vacation with your kids – those long, boring journeys on the Interstate can be disastrous. If you're on a fly-drive vaca- tion, note that when **renting a car** the company is legally obliged to provide free car seats for kids. RVs are also a good option for family travel, combining the convenience of built-in kitchens and bedrooms with freedom of the road (see Getting Around on p.31 for details).

Children under two years old **fly** free on domestic routes, and for ten percent of the adult fare on international flights – though that doesn't mean they get a seat, let alone frequent-flier miles. When aged from two to twelve they are usually entitled to half-price tickets.

Traveling **by bus** may be the cheapest way to go, but it's also the most uncomfortable for kids. Under-twos travel (on your lap) for free; ages two to four are charged ten percent of the adult fare, as are any toddlers who take up a seat. Children under twelve years old are charged half the standard fare.

Taking the train is by far the best option for long journeys – not only does everyone get to enjoy the scenery, but you can get up and walk around, relieving pent-up energy. Most cross- country trains have sleeping compartments, which may be quite expensive but are likely to be seen as a great adventure. On Amtrak, two chil- dren aged between two and fifteen can travel at half fare with each adult passenger.

SENIOR TRAVELERS

For many senior citizens, retirement brings the opportunity to explore the world in a style and at a pace that is the envy of younger travelers. As well as the obvious advantages of being free to travel for longer periods during the quieter, more congenial and less expensive seasons, anyone over the age of 62 can enjoy the tremendous variety of discounts, but must produce suitable ID. Both Amtrak and Greyhound, for example, and many US airlines, offer (smallish) percentage reductions on fares to older passengers.

Any US citizen or permanent resident aged 62 or over is entitled to free admission for life to all National Parks, monuments and historic sites using a **Golden Age Passport**, for which a once-only $10 fee is charged; it can be issued at any such site. This free entry also applies to any accompanying car passengers in their car or, for those hiking or cycling, the passport-holder's immediate family. It also gives a fifty percent reduction on fees for camping, parking and boat launching.

The **Golden Bear Pass** ($5 to seniors) offers a fifty percent discount on admission to state-run parks, beaches and historic sites, subject to a means test. There is also a Senior Citizen Discount (based on proof of age only) giving $1 off parking and $2 off family camping except where the fee is less than $3.

Museums, art galleries and even **hotels** offer small discounts, and since the definition of Senior can drop as low as 55, it is always worth asking.

The **American Association of Retired Persons**, 601 E St NW, Washington DC 20049 (☎1-800/424-3410 or 202/434-2277), membership of which is open to US residents aged fifty or over for an annual fee of $8, organizes group travel for senior citizens and can provide discounts on accommodation and vehicle rental.

GAY AND LESBIAN CALIFORNIA

The gay scene in California is huge, albeit heavily concentrated in the major cities. San Francisco, where anything between a quarter and a third of the voting population is reckoned to be gay or lesbian, is the premier gay city of the world; Los Angeles comes a close second, and up and down the coast gay men and women enjoy the kind of visibility and influence those in other places can only dream about. Gay politicians, and even police officers, are more than a novelty here and representation at every level is for real. Resources, places, facilities and organizations are endless.

In Los Angeles, the gay population has been growing steadily since the earliest days of the movie industry – a job which gave considerably greater freedom of lifestyle than most others at the time. Later, during World War II, the military purged suspected homosexuals at their point of embarkation. For those expecting to serve in the Pacific war zone, this meant they got off in San Francisco – where, unable to face the stigma of a return home, many remained, their ranks later swelled by gays who lost their government jobs during McCarthy's swipes of the 1950s.

In both these cities, the activism of the 1960s succeeded in highlighting gay issues, but they only developed into fully mainstream topics during the 1970s, when, particularly in San Francisco, gays organized themselves into the largest and most influential minority group in the city. Politicians realized that the gay vote was the difference between winning and losing and quickly got on the case. In 1977 San Francisco got its first city official on the Board of Supervisors, the openly gay Harvey Milk. Milk's hero status was assured forever when, in 1978, he was assassinated by another councilor, the conservative Dan White.

Since the heady Seventies, however, and in the face of the AIDS crisis, the energies of gay men and women have been directed to the protection of existing rights and helping victims of the disease. California has lost many to AIDS, but the state, perhaps more than anywhere else, has responded quickly and with compassion and intelligence: public health programs have had hitherto unheard of sums of money pumped into them, and attitudes across the board are broad-minded and supportive.

Ghettoization, then, is no longer a problem for Californian gays, although there are sizeable, predominantly gay areas in almost all the major cities – San Diego's **Hillcrest**, Los Angeles' **West Hollywood**, San Francisco's **Castro** district – and both Guerneville and Palm Springs have earned gay resort status. However, although tolerance is high everywhere, the liberal attitudes of the major cities are not always reflected in the more isolated areas. For a complete rundown on local **resources**, **bars** and **clubs**, see the relevant city chapters of the guide.

SPORTS

Nowhere in the country do the various forms of athletic activity and competition have a higher profile than in California. The big cities generally have at least one team in each of the major professional sports – football (though LA lost its last football team to Oakland in 1995), baseball and basketball – as well as supporting teams in soccer, volleyball, ice hockey, wrestling and even roller derby.

AMERICAN SPORTS FOR OVERSEAS VISITORS

For foreign visitors, American sports can appear something of a mystery, not least the passion for **intercollegiate sports** – college and university teams, competing against one another in the Pacific-10 Conference, usually with an enthusiasm fueled by passionate local rivalries. In Los Angeles, USC and UCLA have an intense and high-powered sporting enmity, with fans on each side as vociferous as any European soccer crowd, and in the San Francisco Bay Area, the rivalry between UC Berkeley and Stanford is akin to that of Britain's Oxford and Cambridge.

FOOTBALL

Football in America attracts the most obsessive and devoted fans of any sport, perhaps because there are fewer games played – only sixteen in a season, which lasts throughout the fall. With many quick skirmishes and military-like movements up and down the field, it's ideal for television, and nowhere is this more apparent than during the **televised games** which are a feature of many bars on Monday nights – though most games are played on Sundays.

THE RULES OF FOOTBALL

The rules of **American football** are fairly simple: the **field** is 100 yards long by 40 yards wide, plus two **endzones** at each end; there are two teams of eleven men. The game begins with a **kickoff**, after which the team in possession of the ball tries to move downfield to score a **touchdown**, while the opposing team tries to stop them. The attacking team has four chances to move the ball forward ten yards and gain a **first down**; otherwise they forfeit possession to the opposition. After the kickoff the **quarterback**, the leader of the attack, either hands the ball off to a **running back**, or throws the ball through the air downfield to a **receiver**. Play ends when the man with the ball is tackled to the ground (or runs out of bounds), or if the pass attempt falls incomplete.

A **touchdown**, worth six points, is made when a player crosses into the defending team's endzone carrying the ball; unlike in rugby, no actual touching down is necessary, it is enough just to carry the ball over the line. After a touchdown, the scoring team has one attempt at an "extra point" by either kicking a field goal (1 point) or crossing into the endzone (2 points) from three yards out. A regular **field goal**, worth three points, is scored when the **place-kicker** – always the smallest man on the team and usually the lone foreigner – kicks the ball, as in rugby, through the **goalposts** that stand in the endzone. If the attacking team has failed to move the ball within scoring range, and seems unlikely to gain the required ten yards for another first down, they can elect to **punt** the ball, kicking it to the other team.

A change of possession can also occur if the opposition players manage to **intercept** an attempted pass.

THE RULES OF BASEBALL

The setup for **baseball** looks like the English game of rounders, with four **bases** set at the corners of a 90-foot diamond. The base at the bottom corner is called **home plate**, and serves much the same purpose as do the stumps in cricket. Play begins when the **pitcher**, standing on a pitcher's mound in the middle of the diamond, throws the ball at upwards of a hundred miles an hour, making it curve and bend as it travels towards the **catcher**, who crouches behind home plate; seven other defensive players take up **positions**, one at each base and the others spread out around the field of play.

A **batter** from the opposing team stands beside home plate and tries to hit the ball. If the batter swings and misses, or if the pitched ball crosses the plate above the batter's knees and below his chest, it counts as a **strike**; if he doesn't swing and the ball passes outside this **strike zone**, it counts as a **ball** – equivalent to a "no ball" in cricket. If the batter gets **three strikes** against him he is **out**; four balls and he gets a free **walk**, and takes his place as a runner on first base. Foul balls, hit out of the field of play count as a strike, but a player cannot strike out (get a third strike) on a foul ball.

If he succeeds in hitting the pitched ball into **fair territory** (the wedge between the first and third bases), the batter runs toward first base; if the opposing players catch the ball before it hits the ground, the batter is **out**. Otherwise they field the ball and attempt to relay it to first base before the batter gets there; if they fail he is **safe** – and stays there, being moved along by subsequent batters until he makes a complete circuit and scores a **run**. The most exciting moment in baseball is the **home run**, when a batter hits the ball over the outfield fences, a boundary some 400 feet away from home plate; he and any runners on base when he hits the ball each score a run. If there are runners on all three bases it's called a **grand slam**, and earns four runs.

The nine players per side bat in rotation; each side gets three outs per innings, and there are nine innings per game – the "top" of the innings is when the first team (usually the visiting team) is batting, or is about to bat; the "bottom" of the innings is during the second team's turn. Games normally last two to three hours, and are never tied; if the scores are level after nine innings, extra innings are played until one side pulls ahead and wins.

The game lasts for four fifteen-minute quarters, with a fifteen-minute break at half-time. But since time is only counted when play is in progress, matches can take up to three hours to complete, mainly due to interruptions for TV advertising. Commentators will discuss the game throughout to help your comprehension, though they use such a barrage of statistics to illustrate their remarks that you may feel hopelessly confused. Not that it matters – the spectacle of American football is fun to experience, even if you haven't a clue what's going on. Players tend to be huge, averaging about six foot five and weighing upwards of three hundred pounds; they look even bigger when they're suited up for battle in shoulder pads and helmets. The best players become nationally known celebrities, raking in millions of dollars in fees for product endorsements on top of astronomical salaries.

Teams and tickets

All major teams play in the **National Football League** (NFL), the sport's governing body, which divides the teams into two conferences of equal stature, the **National Football Conference** (NFC) and the **American Football Conference** (AFC). In turn, each conference is split into three divisions, East, Central and West. For the end of season playoffs, the best team in each of the six divisions plus a second-place wildcard from each conference fight it out for the title.

The Californian **teams** are the San Francisco **49ers**, the Oakland **Raiders** – both always near the top of the NFL – and the San Diego **Chargers**. There are no second division equivalents, though the **college teams**, particularly USC and UCLA, serve as a training ground for future NFL stars.

Tickets cost $20–80 for professional games, $5–10 for college games. To book tickets call:

NFL	☎212/450-2000
San Diego Chargers	☎619/280-2121
San Francisco 49ers	☎415/468-2249
Oakland Raiders	☎1-800/949-2626

BASEBALL

Baseball, much like cricket in its relaxed, summertime pace and seemingly Byzantine rules, is often called "America's pastime", though its image was tarnished by the bitter strike by players which shortened the 1994 season and saw the unthinkable canceling of the World Series.

Games are played – 162 each full season– all over the US almost every day from April to September, with the league championships and the World Series, the final best-of-seven playoff, lasting through October. Watching a game, even if you don't understand what's going on, can be at the least a pleasant day out, drinking beer and eating hot dogs in the bleachers and unshaded benches beyond the outfield; tickets are cheap ($5–10) and the crowds usually friendly and sociable.

Teams and tickets

All Major League baseball teams play in either the **National League** or the **American League**, each of equal stature and split into three divisions, East, Central and West. For the end of season playoffs and the World Series, the best team in each of the six divisions plus a second-place wild-

card from each conference fight it out for the title.

California's Major League clubs are the **Oakland A's**, **Los Angeles Dodgers**, **San Diego Padres**, **Anaheim Angels** and the **San Francisco Giants**. In addition, there are also numerous **minor league** clubs, known as **farm teams** because they supply the top clubs with talent. Details are included in relevant chapters of the guide.

Tickets for games cost $5–25 per seat, and are generally available on the day of the game. To book tickets call:

Major League	☎212/339-7800
National League	☎212/339-7700
American League	☎212/339-7600
Los Angeles Dodgers	☎213/224-1448
San Diego Padres	☎619/283-4494
San Francisco Giants	☎415/468-3700
Anaheim Angels	☎714/634-2000
Oakland Athletics (A's)	☎510/638-0500

BASKETBALL

Basketball is one of the few professional sports that is also actually played by many ordinary Americans, since all you need is a ball and a hoop. It's a particularly popular sport in low-income inner-city areas, where school playgrounds are packed with young hopefuls.

The professional game is played by athletes of phenomenal agility, seven-foot-tall giants who float through the air over a wall of equally tall defenders, seeming to change direction in mid-flight before slam-dunking the ball (smashing it through the hoop which such force that the backboard sometimes shatters) to score two points. Games last for an exhausting 48 minutes of playing time, around two hours total.

Teams and tickets

California's basketball clubs, including the **Los Angeles Lakers**, who play in front of a crowd of celebrities (actor Jack Nicholson, for example, has a season-long front court seat), haven't met with much success in the 1990s. Other pro teams include the Golden State **Warriors** (who play in Oakland), the Sacramento **Kings** and the Los Angeles **Clippers**. LA's **UCLA** dominated the college game, winning national championships throughout the 1960s; they emerged to win again in 1995. Stanford, UC Berkeley, and USC also field perpetually competitive intercollegiate teams.

Tickets cost $15–60 for professional games, $4–10 for college games. To book tickets call:

National Basketball Association (NBA)
☎212/407-8000

Golden State Warriors	☎510/986-2200
Los Angeles Clippers	☎213/745-0400
Los Angeles Lakers	☎310/419-3865
Sacramento Kings	☎916/928-0000

WOMEN'S BASKETBALL

Two **women's basketball** leagues, the **WNBA** and the **ABL** (American Basketball League) were launched amidst a media blitz in late 1996. Both leagues enjoyed considerable success in their inaugural seasons, although their long-term viability has yet to be determined. With financial and marketing support from the NBA, the WNBA drew more fans, although the two leagues still compete fiercely for the world's top players.

Teams and tickets

Starting at about $8, **tickets** are much more reasonable than their NBA counterparts, and if you don't mind rooting for a bunch of talented players who you've probably never heard of, the action can be quite exciting. The WNBA's season takes place in the summer, while the ABL's eight teams play during the fall and winter.

WNBA:

General Information	☎212/688-WNBA
Los Angeles Sparks	☎310/330-2434
Sacramento Monarchs	☎916/928-3650

ABL:

General Information	☎650/856-3225
Long Beach Stingrays	☎562/951-7297
San Jose Lasers	☎408/271-1500

HOCKEY

Despite California's sun and sand reputation, **hockey** enjoys considerable popularity in the state, although most of the players are imported from more traditionally hockey-centric regions in Canada, Eastern Europe and Scandinavia. A considerable rivalry has developed over the years between players from the United States and Canada, owing largely to Canada's fear of losing their longtime claim as the world's premier hockey nation. As heavy favorites in the 1998 Winter Olympics, however, the over-confident US and Canadian national teams were both humiliated by the Czech Republic, Russia, and Finland.

Teams and tickets

California boasts three **NHL** (National Hockey League) teams, and although all are mediocre, they still manage to draw considerable crowds; the **San Jose Sharks** sell out nearly every game. **Tickets** start at about $15. Call on the following numbers:

NHL	☎212/789-2000
San Jose Sharks	☎408/287-7070
Los Angeles Kings	☎310/419-3160
Mighty Ducks of Anaheim	☎714/704-2700

PARTICIPANT SPORTS

Surfing is probably the best-known Californian pastime, immortalized in the songs of the Beach Boys and Frankie Avalon. The Southern California coast up to San Francisco is dotted with excellent surfing beaches. Some of the finest places to catch a wave, with or without a board, are at **Tourmaline Beach** near San Diego, **Huntington Beach** and **Malibu** in Los Angeles, along the coast north of **Santa Barbara**, and at **Santa Cruz** – where there's a small but worthy surfing museum.

Cycling is an extremely popular sport, with California home to some highly competitive, world-class road races, particularly around the Wine Country. The heavy-duty, all-terrain **mountain bike** was invented here, designed to tackle the slopes of Mount Tamalpais in Marin County. Weekend enthusiasts now put their knobby tires to use on the countless trails that weave throughout California's beautiful wilderness areas. Special mountain bike parks, most of them operating in summer only, exploit the groomed snow-free runs of the Sierra ski bowls of Lake Tahoe and Mammoth. In such places, and throughout California, you can rent bikes for $20–30 a day; see "Getting Around", p.34, for more on general cycling.

Skiing is the biggest mass-market participant sport, with downhill resorts all over eastern California – where, believe it or not, it snows heavily most winters. In fact, the Sierra Nevada mountains offer some of the best skiing in the US, particularly around Lake Tahoe, where the 1960 Winter Olympics were held (see p.000). You can rent equipment for about $40 a weekend, plus another $35 to $50 a day for lift tickets.

A cheaper option is **cross-country skiing**, or ski-touring. A number of backcountry ski lodges in the Sierra Nevada offer a range of rustic accommodation, equipment rental and lessons, from as little as $20 a day for skis, boots and poles, up to about $200 for an all-inclusive weekend tour.

All these, and other sporting outlets and facilities, are detailed in the relevant chapters of the guide.

FESTIVALS AND PUBLIC HOLIDAYS

Someone, somewhere is always celebrating something in California, although apart from national holidays, few festivities are shared throughout the entire state. Instead, there is a disparate multitude of local events: art and craft shows, county fairs, ethnic celebrations, music festivals, rodeos, sandcastle building competitions, and many others of every hue and shade.

Among California's major annual events are the **gay and lesbian freedom** parades held in June in LA and, particularly, San Francisco; the **Academy Awards** in LA in March, and the world-class **Monterey Jazz Festival** in September. These and other local highlights are covered in the text. In addition, California tourist offices can provide full lists, or you can just phone the visitor center in a particular region ahead of your arrival and ask what's coming up.

PUBLIC HOLIDAYS

The biggest and most all-American of the **national festivals and holidays** is **Independence Day** on the Fourth of July, when the entire country grinds to a standstill as people get drunk, salute the flag and take part in firework displays, marches, beauty pageants and more, all in commemoration of the signing of the Declaration of Independence in 1776. **Halloween** (October 31) lacks any such patriotic overtones, and is not a public holiday despite being one of the most popular yearly flings. Traditionally, kids run around the streets banging on doors demanding "trick or treat", and being given pieces of candy. These days that sort of activity is mostly confined to rural and suburban areas, while in bigger cities Halloween has grown into a massive gay celebration: in West Hollywood in LA and San Francisco's Castro district, the night is marked by mass cross-dressing, huge block parties and general licentiousness. More sedate is **Thanksgiving Day**, on the last Thursday in November. The third big event of the year is essentially a domestic affair, when relatives return to the familial nest to stuff themselves with roast turkey, and (supposedly) fondly recall the first harvest of the Pilgrims in Massachusetts – though in fact Thanksgiving was already a national holiday before anyone thought to make that connection.

On the national **public holidays** listed below, shops, banks and offices are liable to be closed all day. Many states also have their own additional holidays, and in some places Good Friday is a half-day holiday. The traditional **summer season** for tourism runs from **Memorial Day to Labor Day**; some tourist attractions are only open during that period.

January 1 **New Year's Day**

January 15 **Martin Luther King Jr's Birthday**

Third Monday in February **Presidents' Day**

Easter Monday

Last Monday in May **Memorial Day**

July 4 **Independence Day**

First Monday in September **Labor Day**

Second Monday in October **Columbus Day**

November 11 **Veterans' Day**

Last Thursday in November **Thanksgiving Day**

December 25 **Christmas Day**

DIRECTORY FOR OVERSEAS VISITORS

ADDRESSES Though initially confusing for overseas visitors, American addresses are masterpieces of logical thinking. Generally speaking, roads in built-up areas are laid out to a grid system, creating "blocks" of buildings: addresses of buildings refer to the block, which will be numbered in sequence, from a central point usually downtown; for example, 620 S Cedar will be six blocks south of downtown. In small towns, and parts of larger cities, "streets" and "avenues" often run north–south and east–west respectively; streets are usually named (sometimes alphabetically), avenues generally numbered.

CIGARETTES AND SMOKING Smoking is a much-frowned-upon activity in the US, and especially so in California which recently banned smoking in all indoor public places, including bars and restaurants. In fact, it's quite possible to spend a month in the States without ever smelling tobacco. Cigarettes are sold in virtually any food shop, drugstore or bar, and also from vending machines. A packet of twenty costs around $2.50 – much cheaper than in Britain – though many smokers buy cigarettes by the carton for around $18.

DEPARTURE TAX All airport, customs and security taxes are included in the price of your ticket.

DRUGS Possession of under an ounce of the widely consumed marijuana is a misdemeanor in California, and the worst you'll get is a $200 fine. Being caught with more than an ounce, however, means facing a criminal charge for dealing, and a possible prison sentence – stiffer if caught anywhere near a school. Other drugs are, of course, completely illegal and it's a much more serious offense if you're caught with any.

ELECTRICITY 110V AC. The insubstantial two-pronged plugs have now largely been replaced by a more sturdy three-pronged affair. Some travel plug adapters don't fit American sockets.

FLOORS In the US, what would be the ground floor in Britain is the first floor, the first floor the second floor and so on.

ID Should be carried at all times. Two pieces should diffuse any suspicion, one of which should have a photo: driving license, passport and credit card(s) are your best bets.

MEASUREMENTS AND SIZES The US has yet to go metric, so measurements are in inches, feet, yards and miles; weight in ounces, pounds and tons. American pints and gallons are about four-fifths of Imperial ones. Clothing sizes are always two figures less what they would be in Britain – a British women's size 12 is a US size 10 – while British shoe sizes are half a size below American ones for women, and one size below for men.

TIME California runs on Pacific Standard Time (PST), eight hours behind GMT in winter and three hours behind the East Coast. British Summer Time runs almost concurrent with US Daylight Saving Time – implemented from the last Sunday in April to the last Sunday in October – causing a seven-hour time difference for two weeks of the year.

TIPPING You really shouldn't leave a bar or restaurant without leaving a tip of at least fifteen percent (unless the service is utterly disgusting); it causes a lot of embarrassment and nasty looks, and a short paypacket for the waiter/waitress at the end of the week. About the same should be added to taxi fares, and rounded up to the nearest 50¢ or dollar. A hotel porter should get roughly $1 for each bag carried to your room. When paying by credit card you're expected to add the tip to the total bill before filling in the amount and signing.

VIDEOS The standard format used for video cassettes in the US is different from that used in Britain. You cannot buy videos in the US compatible with a video camera bought in Britain.

WHALE-WATCHING During November and December, Californian gray whales migrate from the Arctic to their breeding grounds off the coast of Baja California, making their return journey during February and March. Along the coast in these months you'll often find open-air whale-themed events, generally with a display or talk about the whales, and with food, drink and even music supplied, as people peer out to the ocean hoping for (and usually getting) a glimpse of the great creatures.

PART TWO

THE

GUIDE

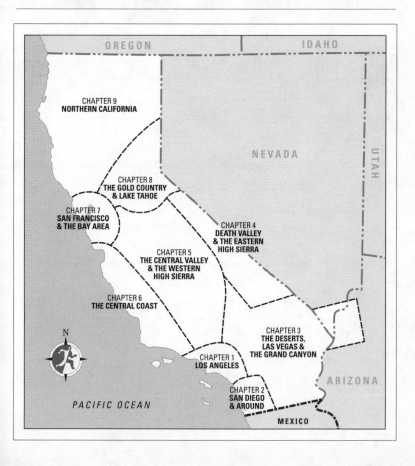

CHAPTER ONE

LOS ANGELES

The rambling metropolis of **LOS ANGELES** sprawls across the floor of a great desert basin in a colorful jangle of fast-food joints, shopping malls, palm trees and swimming pools, bounded by snowcapped mountains and the Pacific Ocean, and held together by an intricate network of high-speed freeways rising above a thousand square miles of architectural anarchy. It's an extremely visual, often voyeuristic, city, and famously hard to make sense of – understandable, in F. Scott Fitzgerald's phrase, "only dimly, and in flashes".

For all that, LA can surprise you with a powerful sense of familiarity. The entertainment industry has been popularizing the city ever since film-makers arrived in the 1910s, attracted by a climate which allowed them to film outdoors year-round, plenty of cheap open land on which to build elaborate sets, and nearby landscapes varied enough to form an imaginary backdrop to just about anywhere in the world. Since then, the money and glamor of Hollywood have enticed countless thousands of would-be actors, writers, designers and, more recently, rock stars. The myth of overnight success is very much part of the LA mind-set, but so is the reality of sudden disaster: floods, fires and earthquakes are facts of life here, and the co-existence of both extremes lends an on-the-edge, almost unhinged personality to the city. LA, certainly, is like nowhere else on earth. Mud-wrestling venues and porn cinemas stand next door to quality bookstores and trendy restaurants, in a relentless but strangely addictive assault on the senses that can make everywhere else you go afterwards somehow tame and predictable.

Originally settled by Chumash and Tongva native tribes a thousand years before the arrival of eighteenth-century Spanish settlers, the LA region soon became a staging ground for part of Junipero Serra's string of 21 Franciscan missions. Later subdivided into Mexican "ranchos" and usurped by the expanding United States, until just over a century ago LA was a multicultural community of white American immigrants, poor Chinese laborers and wealthy Mexican ranchers, with a population of under fifty thousand. Only on completion of the transcontinental railroad in the 1880s did the city really begin to grow, consistently doubling in population every ten years. Hundreds of thousands descended upon the basin, lured by the prospect of living in a subtropical paradise. Ranches were subdivided into innumerable suburban lots and scores of new towns, and land speculators marketed an enduring image of Los Angeles, epitomized by the family-sized suburban house (with swimming pool and two-car garage) set amid the orange groves in a glorious land of sunshine. The boom years came after World War II when many of the veterans who'd passed through on their way to the South Pacific came back to stay, buying government-subsidized houses and finding well-paid work in the mushrooming aeronautics industry.

In the late 1980s though, Southern California was hit very hard by post-Cold War cutbacks, particularly in the aeronautics industry. Unemployment reached a peak of ten percent, with crime rocketing as a result. Unemployment is now back down around five percent in the region, but the conservative suburb of Orange County, also known as the Orange Curtain, is still in a state of shock nicknamed White Fright. Its residents have become so scared of LA's crime that they have retreated into "gated communities", housing estates with boundary fences and roads patrolled by private security forces. Safely locked in, they voted in 1994 for Proposition 187, a state law denying access to health and education services to illegal immigrants, particularly the Mexican

> Because Los Angeles has five telephone **area codes** – ☎213, ☎310,
> ☎626, ☎714 and ☎818 – we have included the code in each number we list.

"wetbacks" they perceive as responsible for the city's problems. Nevertheless, Latino immigration to Orange County has recently begun to increase dramatically, especially in Santa Ana and Garden Grove, and once-entrenched suburbanites now seek new refuges in distant "edge cities" like Rancho Cucamonga and San Juan Capistrano.

In LA proper, numerous glossy museums, built during the 1980s, mean that Los Angeles is still an international center of visual art, and the forest of downtown skyscrapers is proof of its key position as the high-finance gateway between America and the Far East. But the extent of the contradictions involved in dwelling in – and visiting – a metropolis that contains at least one hundred thousand homeless alongside some of the highest standards of living in the world are never far away. Race rioting has been as much a part of LA history as film-making. Six years on in South Central, the Rebuild LA program has yet to make much of a dent in the devastation caused by 1992's riots and is generally regarded as a noble failure. Empty lots stand where there were once supermarkets, and it's still easier to buy a quart of whisky than to buy groceries. The psychological scars go much deeper.

When he chose to play the so-called "race card" in the 1995 double murder trial of fallen football hero O.J. Simpson, lead defence attorney Johnnie Cochran tapped into questions and emotions that are at the core of the city and, some would say, of contemporary America. Although "The Trial of the Century" is now long past, its legacy continues in the form of abiding racial animosities and outright hostility. Unwilling to let go of historical prejudices, and its geographical, political, social and economic ghettos, Los Angeles may be in for more trouble, though in a city whose dynamism seems forever intertwined with internal strife, perhaps this is to be expected.

Arrival and information

Arriving in LA is potentially one of the most nerve-wracking experiences you're ever likely to have. However you get to the city, and especially if you're not driving, you're faced with an urban sprawl that can be a source of bewilderment even for people who've lived in it for years. Provided you don't panic, however, the city is far from the savage beast it first appears.

By plane

All European and many domestic **flights** use Los Angeles International Airport – always known as **LAX** – sixteen miles southwest of downtown LA (☎310/646-5252). If you're on a budget, and not planning to rent a car (in which case see "Driving and car rental" on p.66), the cheapest option is to take the free **"C" shuttle bus** (not "A" or "B", which serve the parking lots), running 24 hours a day from each terminal, to the LAX Transit Center at Vicksburg Avenue and 96th Street. From here, local **buses** (the MTA and others) leave for different parts of LA – see "City transportation" on p.66 for more details.

The most convenient way into town is to ride a minibus service such as **Airport Shuttle** (☎1-800/545-7745) or **SuperShuttle** (☎1-800/554-3146 or 310/782-6600), which run to downtown, Hollywood, West LA and Santa Monica (the SuperShuttle also goes to Long Beach and Disneyland) and deliver you to your door; most have flashing signs on their fronts, advertising their general destination. If you're heading for the Santa Monica area, or the South Bay, another possibility is the **Coast Shuttle** (☎310/417-3988). Fares vary depending on your destination, but are generally around $20. The shuttles run around the clock from outside the baggage reclaim areas, and you should never have to wait more than fifteen or twenty minutes; pay the fare when you board.

Taxis from the airport are always expensive: reckon on at least $25 to downtown, $30 to Hollywood and $90 to Disneyland. Unlicensed taxi operators may approach you and offer flat fares to your destination; generally, such offers are best avoided. Don't even consider using the **Metro** system to get to your destination from LAX. The first train stops miles from the airport, and the overall journey involves three time-consuming transfers (very difficult with luggage) before you even arrive in downtown Los Angeles. Other destinations are completely inaccessible by rail.

The vast majority of flights into LA use LAX, but if you're arriving from elsewhere in the US, or Mexico, you may land at one of the **other airports** in the LA area – at Burbank, Long Beach, Ontario or Orange County's John Wayne Airport. These are similarly well served by car rental firms; if you want to use public transportation phone the MTA Regional Information Network on arrival (Mon–Fri 6am–7pm, Sat 8am–6pm; ☎ 1-800/COMMUTE (outside LA 1-800/2LA-RIDE) or 213/626-4455), and tell them where you are and where you want to go.

By bus

The main **Greyhound** bus terminal, at 1716 E Seventh St, is in a seedy section of downtown – though access is restricted to ticket holders and it's safe enough inside. There are other Greyhound terminals elsewhere in LA, which handle fewer services: in Hollywood at 1409 Vine St; in Pasadena at 645 E Walnut St; in North Hollywood at 11239 Magnolia Blvd; in Santa Monica at 1433 Fifth St; and in Anaheim at 1711 S Manchester Blvd. Only the downtown terminal is open round the clock; all have toilets and left luggage lockers.

Green Tortoise offers $30 one-way fares to LA from San Francisco and stops in Hollywood at *McDonald's* on Vine Street, a block south of Sunset Boulevard, and in Santa Monica at the HI-LA/Santa Monica, 1434 Second St at Santa Monica Boulevard.

By train

Arriving in LA by **train**, you'll be greeted with the expansive architecture of Union Station, on the north side of downtown at 800 N Alameda St (you can also access the recently constructed Gateway Transit Center, from which you can connect to bus lines). Amtrak trains also stop at outlying stations in the LA area; for all listings call Amtrak (☎1-800/USA-RAIL).

By car

The main routes by **car** into Los Angeles are the interstate highways, all of which pass through downtown. From the east, I-10, the San Bernardino Freeway, has replaced the more sonorous Route 66. Of the non-interstate routes into the city, US-101, the scenic route from San Francisco, cuts across the San Fernando Valley and Hollywood into downtown; Hwy-1, which follows the entire coast of California, is also known as Pacific Coast Highway (PCH) and takes surface streets through Santa Monica, the South Bay and Orange County.

Information

For free maps, accommodation suggestions and general information, the **CVB (Convention and Visitors Bureau)** operates two **visitor centers**: downtown at 685 S Figueroa St (Mon–Fri 8am–5pm, Sat 8.30am–5pm; ☎213/689-8822), and in Hollywood at the Janes House, 6541 Hollywood Blvd (Mon–Fri 9am–5pm; ☎213/236-2331). You can also call toll-free for information on ☎1-800/228-2452.

Other LA suburbs have their own bureaux: in Santa Monica at 1400 Ocean Ave (daily 10am–4pm; ☎310/393-7593); Anaheim near Disneyland at 800 W Katella Ave (daily 9am–5pm; ☎714/999-8999); Beverly Hills, 239 S Beverly Drive (☎1-800/345-2210 or 310/271-8174); and Long Beach, 1 World Trade Center, Suite 300 (☎310/436-3645).

All the centers offer free **maps** of their area, but you'd do better to purchase Gousha Publications' fully indexed *Los Angeles and Hollywood Street Map*, available from vending machines in visitor centers and most hotel lobbies. If you're in LA for a considerable period of time, the fully indexed *LA County Thomas Guide* is the definitive **road atlas**. It's no good if you're absolutely lost and have no idea of the city compass (use a freeway map, local streetguides and ring ahead to your destination for directions instead), but for a meticulous, up-to-date guide of hard-to-find streets, every driver in this city should have one.

Newspapers and magazines

LA has just one **daily newspaper** of consequence: the *Los Angeles Times*, available from street corner racks all over Southern California (25¢). The Sunday edition is huge, and its *Calendar* section contains the most complete listings of what's on and where, as well as reviews and gossip of the city's arts and entertainment worlds. Of the city's many **free papers**, much the fullest and most useful is the free *LA Weekly*, with over a hundred pages of trendier-than-thou news, reviews and listings. A more grown-up second is the smaller and harder-to-find *LA Reader*, with well-informed reviews and comment, and the less established *LA Village View* is also worth a look. Copies of the free papers are available all over LA, especially at cafés and record- and bookstores.

To get a sense of how style-conscious LA sees itself, thumb through a copy of the monthly *Los Angeles* magazine ($3) or the younger and hipper *Buzz* ($4). Both are packed with gossipy news and profiles of local movers and shakers, as well as reviews of the city's trendiest restaurants and clubs. There are also dozens of less glossy, more erratic 'zines – including *Spunk*, *Planet Homo* and *The Edge* – focusing on LA's diverse gay and lesbian culture and nightclubs.

City transportation

The only certainty when it comes to **getting around** LA is that wherever and however you're going, you should allow plenty of time to get there. Obviously, this is partly due to the sheer size of the city, but the confusing entanglements of freeways and the tailbacks common during rush hours can make car trips lengthy undertakings – and the fact that most local buses stop on every corner hardly makes bus travel a speedy alternative.

Driving and car rental

The best way to get around LA – though by no means the only way – is to **drive**. Despite the traffic being bumper-to-bumper much of the day, the **freeways** are the only way to

---

MTA OFFICES AND INFORMATION

For **MTA route and transfer information**, phone ☎1-800-COMMUTE or 213/626-4455 (Mon–Fri 6am–8.30pm, Sat 8am–6pm); be prepared to wait, and be ready to give precise details of where you are and where you want to go. Otherwise, you can go in person to Gateway Transit Center (Mon–Fri 6am–6.30pm) or to three other centrally located offices: at 515 S Flower St, on level C of Arco Plaza (Mon–Fri 7.30am–3.30pm); at 5301 Wilshire Blvd (Mon–Fri 9am–5pm); or in Hollywood at 6249 Hollywood Blvd (Mon–Fri 10am–6pm).

cover long distances quickly. The system, however, can be confusing, especially since each stretch can have two or three names (often derived from their eventual destination, however far away) as well as a number. Four major freeways fan out from downtown: the Hollywood Freeway (a section of US-101) heads northwest through Hollywood into the San Fernando Valley; the Santa Monica Freeway (I-10) crosses West LA to Santa Monica; the Harbor Freeway (I-110) runs south to San Pedro – heading northeast it's called the Pasadena Freeway; and the Santa Ana Freeway (I-5) passes Disneyland and continues through Orange County. **Other freeways** include the San Diego Freeway (I-405), which roughly follows the coast through West LA and the South Bay; the Ventura Freeway (Hwy-134), which links Burbank, Glendale and Pasadena to US-101 in the San Fernando Valley; and the Long Beach Freeway (I-710), which connects East LA and Long Beach. For **shorter journeys**, especially between Hollywood and West LA, the wide avenues and boulevards are a better option (sometimes the only option), not least because you get to see more of the city.

All the major **car rental** firms have branches all over the city (simply look in the phone book for the nearest office or call one of the toll-free numbers listed in Basics on p.31), and most have their main office close to LAX, linked to each terminal by a free shuttle bus. A number of smaller rental companies specialize in everything from Gremlins to Bentleys. Rent-a-Wreck, 12333 W Pico Blvd (☎310/478-0676), has mid-Sixties Mustang convertibles and other, less appealing, vehicles; Dream Boats, 2929 Pico Blvd, Santa Monica (☎310/828-3014), also deals in Mustangs, as well as pink Cadillacs. Expect to pay in the region of $50 per day.

Parking is a particular problem downtown, along Melrose Avenue's trendy Westside shopping streets, and in Beverly Hills and Westwood. Anywhere else is less troublesome, but watch out for restrictions – some lampposts boast as many as four placards listing dos and don'ts. Sometimes it's better to shell out $5 for valet parking than get stuck with a $30 ticket for parking in a residential zone.

Public transportation

The bulk of LA's public transportation is operated by the LA County Metropolitan Transit Authority (**MTA** or **"Metro"**), which is still sometimes abbreviated to its old name, the RTD. Its brand-new, massive **Gateway Transit Center**, to the east of Union Station on Vignes Street, may eventually serve 100,000 commuters a day traveling by Metrorail, light rail, commuter rail, Amtrak and the regional bus systems. The Center comprises **Patsaouras Transit Plaza**, from which you can hop on a bus; the glass-domed **East Portal**, through which you can connect to a train; and the 26-story **Gateway Tower**, at which you can find an MTA customer service office on the ground floor.

Metrorail

Hampered by a series of construction scandals and budget difficulties, LA's **Metrorail** system is beginning to come into at least partial use. A light rail network that may one day cover the whole of Los Angeles county, it is currently made up of three lines. The underground **Red Line** as yet reaches only from the Transit Center west to the intersection of Wilshire and Western Avenues, but it will soon cut through Hollywood and Universal City, eventually reaching the San Fernando Valley and, its planners hope, becoming the city's central transportation line in the next century. Of more use to residents than tourists, the **Green Line** runs between industrial El Segundo and colorless Norwalk, along the middle of the Century Freeway. Tantalizingly close to LAX, but in practical terms absolutely useless if you are in a hurry, the placing of the line has attracted much just criticism. Currently the most complete route, the **Blue Line** leaves downtown and heads overground through South Central to Long Beach. It's a safe journey through some of the most economically depressed areas of the city, and highlights the normality of everyday commuters' lives rather than the gangs and guns of media repute. A trolley line from downtown to Pasadena is also under construction, though MTA has yet to announce an estimated due date. **Fares** on all journeys are $1.35 one way. Peak-hour trains run at five- to six-minute intervals, at other times every ten to fifteen minutes. Don't bring takeaway refreshments on the trains – the fine is $250.

Buses

Car-less Angelenos are still most at ease with **buses**. Although initially bewildering, the gist of the MTA bus network is quite simple: the main routes run east–west (ie between downtown and the coast) and north–south (between downtown and the South Bay). Establishing the best transfer point if you need to change buses can be difficult, but with a bit of planning you should have few real problems – though you must always allow plenty of time.

Area brochures are available free from MTA offices, and you can pick up diagrams and timetables for individual bus routes, as well as regional bus maps showing larger sections of the metropolis. Buses on the major arteries between downtown and the coast run roughly every fifteen minutes between 5am and 2am; other routes, and the **all-night**

MTA BUS ROUTES

MTA's **buses** fall into six categories, as outlined below. Some of the routes can be characterized by their passengers; the early morning east–west route along Wilshire Boulevard is full of Latin American service workers traveling to the homes of their Westside employers, whereas tourists dominate the route west along Santa Monica Boulevard to the beach and pier. The drivers add to the atmosphere too; some deliver a chirpy running commentary, others are sour and abrupt. Whatever bus you're on, if traveling alone, especially at night, sit up front near the driver. Try and sit near a ventilation hatch, too, as the air conditioning can emit a rather sickly-sweet odour.

#1–99 – local routes to and from downtown.

#100–299 – local routes to other areas.

#300–399 – limited-stop routes (usually rush hours only).

#400–499 – express routes to and from downtown.

#500–599 – express routes, other areas.

#600–699 – special service routes (for sports events and the like).

MAJOR LA BUS SERVICES

From LAX to:

Downtown #42, #439.

Long Beach #232.

San Pedro #225.

West Hollywood #220 (for Hollywood change to #4 along Santa Monica Boulevard).

To and from downtown:

Along Hollywood Blvd #1.

Along Sunset Blvd #2, #3, #302.

Along Santa Monica Blvd #4, #304.

Along Melrose Ave #10, #11.

Along Wilshire Blvd #20, #21, #22, #320.

From downtown to:

Santa Monica #22, #434.

Venice #33, #333, #436.

Forest Lawn Cemetery, Glendale #90, #91.

Exposition Park #38, #81.

Huntington Library #79.

Burbank Studios #96.

San Pedro #445, #446, #447, transfer to LADOT #142 for Catalina.

Manhattan Beach/Hermosa Beach/Redondo Beach #439.

Palos Verdes #444.

Long Beach #60.

Orange County, Knott's Berry Farm, Disneyland #460.

services along the major thoroughfares, are less frequent, usually every thirty minutes or hourly. At night be careful not to get stranded downtown waiting for connecting buses.

The standard **one-way fare** is $1.35; **transfers**, which can be used in one direction within the time marked on the ticket (usually three hours), cost 25¢ more; **express buses** (a limited commuter service), and any others using a freeway, are usually $1.85, but can be as much as $3.85. Put the correct money (coins or notes) into the slot when getting on. If you're staying a while, you can save some money with a **monthly pass**, which costs $42 (slightly more to include express buses) and also gives reductions at selected shops and travel agents. If you're staying about two weeks, consider a **semi-monthly pass**, which is sold for $21.

There are also the mini **DASH** buses, which operate as LADOT lines, with a flat fare of 25¢. Several lines ply a circuit around Hollywood, and five routes through the center of downtown roughly every ten minutes between 6.30am and 6pm on weekdays, every fifteen minutes between 10am and 5pm on Saturday, but not at all on Sunday. Other DASH routes travel through the mid-Wilshire area, Pacific Palisades, Venice and several sections of South Central LA.

Other **local bus services** include: Orange County (OCTD) ☎714/636-7433; Long Beach (LBTD) ☎310/591-2301; Culver City ☎310/253-6500; and Santa Monica ☎310/451-5444.

Taxis

You can find **taxis** at most terminals and major hotels. Otherwise phone – among the more reliable companies are Independent Cab Co (☎1-800/521-8294), LA Taxi (☎310/859-0111) and United Independent Taxi (☎1-800/822-TAXI or 213/653-5050). The typical fare is $2, plus $1.60 for each mile: the driver won't know every street in LA but will know the major ones; ask for the nearest junction and give directions from there.

Cycling

Cycling in LA may sound perverse, but in some areas it can be one of the better ways of getting around. There are beach bike paths between Santa Monica and Redondo Beach, and from Long Beach to Newport Beach, and many equally enjoyable inland routes, notably around Griffith Park and the grand mansions of Pasadena. Contact the AAA (☎213/741-3686) or the LA Department of Transportation (☎213/485-3051) for maps and information.

The best place to **rent a bike** for the beaches is on Washington Street around Venice Pier, where numerous outlets include Spokes'n'Stuff (☎310/306-3332); in summer bike rental stands line the beach. For Griffith Park, use Woody's Bicycle World, 3157 Los Feliz Blvd (☎213/661-6665). Prices range from $8 a day for a clunker to $15 a day or more for a ten-speed. For similar cost, many beachside stores also rent **roller skates** and **blades**.

Walking and hiking

Although some people are surprised to find sidewalks in LA, let alone pedestrians, **walking** is in fact the best way to see much of downtown and a number of other districts. You can structure your stroll by taking a **guided walking tour**, the best of which are organized by the Los Angeles Conservancy (☎213/623-CITY), whose treks around downtown's battered but still beating heart is full of heyday Art Deco movie palaces, once-opulent financial monuments and architectural gems like the Bradbury Building (see p.83). Among many alternatives, it runs downtown tours every Saturday, leaving the *Biltmore Hotel* on Olive Street at 10am (reservations required; $5). See the box overleaf for details of other tour operators. You can also take guided **hikes** through the

GUIDED TOURS OF LA

One quick and easy way to see something of LA is from the window of a **guided bus tour**. These vary greatly in cost and quality. The **mainstream tours** carrying large bus-loads around the major sights are only worth considering if you're very pushed for time – none covers anything that you couldn't see for yourself at less cost. **Specialist tours** tailored to suit particular interests, which usually carry smaller groups of people, are often better value. **Studio tours** of film and TV production areas are covered on day trips by most of the mainstream operators, though again you'll save money by turning up independently.

MAINSTREAM TOURS

By far the most popular of the mainstream tours is the half-day **"stars' homes"** jaunt. Usually including the Farmer's Market, Sunset Strip, Rodeo Drive, the Hollywood Bowl and Chinese Theater, as well as, of course, the "stars' homes", this is much less tempting than it sounds – frequently no more than a view of the gate at the end of the drive-way of the house of some TV or celluloid celebrity. These tours are typically the most visible to newcomers, and the area around the Chinese Theater is thick with tourists queueing for their tickets. Other programs include tours around the Westside at night, to the beach areas, the *Queen Mary*, day-long excursions to Disneyland and shopping trips to the Mexican border city of Tijuana.

   Costs are $30 minimum per person; assorted leaflets are strewn over hotel lobbies and visitor centers. You can make reservations at, and be picked up from, most hotels. Otherwise contact one of the following booking offices:

Casablanca Tours, at the *Hollywood Roosevelt*, 7000 Hollywood Blvd (☎213/461-0156).

Hollywood Tours, 6328 Hollywood Blvd (☎1-800/523-8864 or 213/957-2480).

Starline Tours, at the Janes House, 6541 Hollywood Blvd (☎213/463-3333).

Hollywood Fantasy Tours, 6715 Hollywood Blvd (☎213/469-8184).

SPECIALIST TOURS

The typical specialist tours listed are also generally $30 plus per person. For more suggestions, pick up the free *LA Visitors Guide* from hotels and visitor centers.

Black LA Tours, 3420 W 43rd St, STE 108 (☎213/750-9267). Black historical and entertainment tours.

The California Native, 6701 W 87th Place (☎310/642-1140). Sea kayaking and adventure hikes. Tour uninhabited islands off the coast of California for $99 and up.

Googie Tours (☎213/980-3480). Pilgrimages to Southern California's remaining space-age glass and formica diners. Choose between the six-hour "San Gabriel Valley" and "Behind the Orange Curtain" tours, the three hour "Coffee Shop Modern & More" jaunt, or the four-hour, night-time "Cocktails 'n' Coffee Shops" trip.

Grave Line Tours, PO Box 931694, Hollywood (☎213/469-4149). Two-and-a-half hours in the back of a 1969 Cadillac hearse pausing at the scene of many, though by no means all, of the eventful deaths, scandals, perverted sex acts and drugs orgies that have tainted Hollywood and the surrounding area. Leaves Tuesday through Sunday at 9.30am from the corner of Hollywood Boulevard and Orchid Avenue with overflow cortege running at 12.30pm and 3.30pm.

SPARC tours: the Murals of LA, 685 Venice Blvd, Venice (☎310/822-9560). Public art in LA is alive and well in the tradition of Diego Rivera, and this is a thoroughly enlightening tour of the "mural capital of the world".

STUDIO TOURS

For some small insight into how a film or TV show is made, or just to admire the special effects, there are guided tours costing $7–36 at Warner Bros Studios, NBC Television Studios, Universal Studios, all in or near Burbank; see p.138. If you want to be part of the **audience** in a TV show, the street just outside the Chinese Theater is the major solicitation spot: TV company reps regularly appear handing out free tickets, and they'll bus you to the studio and back. All you have to do, once there, is laugh and clap on cue.

wilds of the Santa Monica Mountains and Hollywood Hills free of charge every week-end with a variety of organizations, including the Sierra Club (☎213/387-4287), the State Parks Department (☎818/880-0350) and the Santa Monica Mountains National Recreation Area (☎818/597-1036).

Accommodation

Since LA has 100,000-plus rooms, finding **accommodation** is easy. Whether you're looking for a budget place to rest your head, or a world-class hotel where you can hob-nob with Hollywood stars and entertainment industry tycoons, LA has something for everyone, even though prices have been rising with LA's recent economic recovery.

That said, however, finding somewhere that's low-priced and well-located is more dif-ficult, though not impossible. If you're driving, of course, you needn't worry about stay-ing in a less than ideal location – a freeway is never far away. Otherwise you'll need to be a sight more choosy about the district you plump for, as getting across town can be a time-consuming business.

Motels and the lower-range hotels start at around $40 for a double, but many are sit-uated in seedy or out-of-the-way areas and often you'll find you gain by paying a little more for a decent location in any of a number of other, non-chain mid-range hotels. **Bed and breakfast inns** are rare in LA, and tend to be quite expensive and frequently fully booked. For those on a tight budget, **hostels** are dotted all over the city, many in good locations, though at some stays are limited to a few nights. Camping, perhaps surpris-ingly, is also an option: there are a few **campgrounds** on the edge of the metropolitan area – along the beach north of Malibu, and in the San Gabriel mountains, for example – but you'll need a car to get to them. Hostels and campgrounds are listed at the end of this section. **College rooms** are also sometimes available for rent during student vaca-tion time: contact **UCLA** Interfraternity Council (☎310/825-7878) or **USC**'s off-campus housing office (☎1-800/USC-4632) for information.

LA is so big that if you want to see it all without constantly having to cross huge expanses, it makes sense to divide your stay between several districts. Prices – and options – vary by area. Downtown has expensive and mid-range hotels; Hollywood has similar options, but with motels providing cheaper accommodation; more salubrious West LA, Santa Monica, Venice and Malibu are predominantly mid-to-upper-range ter-ritory. Among options further out, the South Bay and Harbor area, well connected with other parts of town, carry a good selection of low- to mid-range hotels (and a hostel) strung mostly along the Pacific Coast Highway. It's only worth staying in Orange County, thirty miles southeast of downtown, if you're aiming for Disneyland or are trav-eling along the coast: hotels under $70 a night are a rarity and you must book at least a week in advance, especially if a convention is in town. Unfortunately many of the plen-tiful rooms along Katella Avenue and Harbor Boulevard in Anaheim are decrepit and depressing, even though they charge up to $100 a night. By far a better alternative are the hostels and coastal campgrounds in easy reach.

Since there are no **booking agencies**, and visitor centers don't make accommoda-tion reservations (though they will offer information and advice), you can only book a room through a travel agent or by phoning the hotel directly. Ask if there are special weekend or midweek rates. Especially at the lower end of the price scale, hotels are cheaper if booked by the week than the night, and don't be afraid to **haggle**.

Hotels are listed below by neighborhood, with specific accommodation options for gay and lesbian travelers listed in a special section on p.161. In case you're arriving on a late flight, or leaving on an early one, we've also listed a few places to stay near the airport: hotels near LAX are blandly similar and generally around $60, but most have complimentary limo service to and from the terminals.

ACCOMMODATION PRICE CODES

All accommodation prices in this book have been coded using the symbols below; prices are for the least expensive **double rooms** in each establishment. For a full explanation see p.36 in Basics. Bear in mind that in Los Angeles all quoted room rates are subject to a **room tax** – currently fourteen percent on top of your total bill. Individual rates rather than price codes are given for **hostels**.

① up to $30   ④ $60–80   ⑦ $130–175
② $30–45   ⑤ $80–100   ⑧ $175–250
③ $45–60   ⑥ $100–130   ⑨ $250+

Downtown and around

See the map on p.79 for the locations of these hotels.

Biltmore Hotel, 506 S Grand Ave at Fifth (☎1-800/245-8673 or 213/624-1011). Classical architecture combined with modern luxury to make your head swim. ⑧.

City Center Motel, 1135 W Seventh St at Lucas (☎213/628-7141). Bare but clean Sixties-style decor, with free continental breakfast and airport shuttle bus. ②.

Figueroa Hotel, 939 S Figueroa St at Olympic (☎1-800/421-9092 or 213/627-8971). Mid-range hotel on the south side of downtown, with a jacuzzi-equipped pool and 24-hour coffee shop. ④.

Holiday Inn Downtown, 750 Garland Ave at Eighth (☎1-800/628-5240 or 213/628-5242). On the western fringe of downtown beside the Harbor Freeway. ⑤.

Hotel Inter-Continental, 251 S Olive St at Fourth (☎1-800/442-5251or 213/617-3300). New Bunker Hill hotel, home to financial kingpins and Academy Award attendees. Very plush, adjacent to MOCA and the Music Center. ⑧.

Kawada Hotel, 200 S Hill St at Second (☎1-800/752-9232 or 213/621-4455). Comfortable and clean if drab rooms in recently renovated, medium-sized hotel near the Civic Center. Popular with value-oriented business travelers. ④.

Nutel Motel, 1906 W Third St at Bonnie Brae (☎213/483-6681). A few blocks from MacArthur Park (dicey for pedestrians at night), a mile from downtown. ③.

Orchid Hotel, 819 S Flower St at Eighth (☎1-800/874-5855 or 213/624-5855). The best deal in the heart of downtown, near the Seventh and Flower Metrorail station. Clean, comfortable and safe. Weekly rates. ②.

Park Plaza, 607 S Park View St, between Sixth and Wilshire (☎213/384-5281). Facing MacArthur Park, with a marble floor and sumptuous lobby popular with filmmakers – but ordinary rooms. ④.

Westin Bonaventure, 404 S Figueroa St, between Fourth and Fifth (☎1-800/228-3000 or 213/624-1000). Luxury post-modern masterpiece or oversized nightmare depending on your point of view. Five glass towers, six-story lobby with a "lake". Breathtaking exterior elevator – featured in the climax of Clint Eastwood's *In the Line of Fire* – to a rotating cocktail lounge which averages seven proposals of marriage a week. ⑦.

Hollywood

Best Western Hollywood Hills, 6141 Franklin Ave, between Gower and Vine (☎213/464-5181). Part of the nationwide chain, with cable TV and pool, at the foot of the Hollywood Hills. ④.

Dunes Sunset Motel, 5625 Sunset Blvd (☎1-800/452-3863 or 213/467-5171). On the dingy eastern side of Hollywood, but far enough away from the weirdness of Hollywood Boulevard to feel safe; also good for reaching downtown. ③.

Holiday Inn Hollywood, 1755 N Highland Ave (☎1-800/465-4329 or 213/462-7181). Massive, but perfectly placed. The price becomes reasonable with triple occupancy. ⑤.

Hollywood Metropolitan Hotel, 5825 Sunset Blvd (☎1-800/962-5800 or 213/962-5800). Sleek high-rise in central Hollywood. Good value for the area. ④.

Hollywood Roosevelt, 7000 Hollywood Blvd, between Highland and La Brea (☎1-800/423-8262). The first hotel built for the movie greats, now in the Clarion chain. The rooms are plain, but the place has been lately revamped and reeks atmosphere. ⑤.

Hollywood Towne House Hotel, 6055 Sunset Blvd at Gower (☎213/462-3221). Hotel with decayed exterior and 1920s-era phones that connect to the front desk only. The rooms themselves are clean and comfortable enough. ③.

Saharan Motor Hotel, 7212 Sunset Blvd at Poinsetta (☎213/874-6700). Unexciting but functional, and comparatively good value, considering its central location. ③.

Sunset 8 Motel, 6516 Sunset Blvd between Wilcox and Highland (☎213/461-2748). Many of the rooms on this strip rent by the hour, vibrating bed included. This place, though downtrodden, is a cut above; if you see a clean room grab it for a brief stay near Hollywood's traditional sights. Across from the former Hollywood Athletic Club and a coin-op laundromat. ②.

West LA

Beverly Hills Hotel, 9641 Sunset Blvd (☎310/276-2251). Painted bold pink and green and surrounded by its own exotic gardens, this famous hotel to the stars is pretty hard to miss. Marilyn Monroe once stayed here, and one of the bungalows is decorated in her honor. ⑨.

Beverly Laurel Motor Hotel, 8018 Beverly Blvd at Laurel (☎213/651-2441). The hotel coffee shop, *Swingers* (see p.141), attracts the most attention here, primarily as a hang-out for locals and inquisitive tourists. Stylish, reasonable and friendly, with a good location. ④.

Bevonshire Lodge Motel, 7575 Beverly Blvd at Curson (☎213/936-6154). Well situated for both West LA and Hollywood. All of the functionally decorated rooms come with a refrigerator, and for a few dollars more you can have a kitchenette. ③.

Chateau Marmont, 8221 Sunset Blvd at Crescent Heights (☎213/626-1010). Exclusive French-style hotel – one-time haunt of John and Yoko; earlier saw the likes of Boris Karloff, Greta Garbo, Errol Flynn, Jean Harlow and, tragically, John Belushi. ⑧.

Claremont Hotel, 1044 Tiverton Ave (☎310/208-5957). Cheerful and inexpensive small hotel very close to UCLA and Westwood Village. ③.

Hotel Bel Air, 701 Stone Canyon Rd (☎1-800/648-1097 or 310/472-1211). LA's nicest hotel bar none, and the only hotel in Bel Air, in a lushly overgrown canyon above Beverly Hills. Go for a beautiful brunch by the Swan pond if you can't afford the rooms which reach a dizzying $435 a night. ⑨.

Hotel Del Flores, 409 N Crescent Drive at Little Santa Monica (☎310/274-5115). Three blocks from Rodeo Drive, this place is small, pleasant and excellent value. ④.

Le Montrose, 900 Hammond St (☎310/855-1115). West Hollywood hotel with Art Nouveau stylings, featuring rooftop tennis courts, pool and jacuzzi. Most rooms are suites with full amenities. ⑧.

Le Parc, 733 N West Knoll (☎1-800/578-4837 or 310/855-8888). Apartment hotel with studios, one- and two-bedroom suites, rooftop pool and jacuzzi with view of the hills. A British rock star hangout. ⑦.

Le Reve Hotel, 8822 Cynthia St (☎1-800/835-7997 or 310/854-1111). Gay friendly place a few blocks north of Santa Monica Blvd, in residential West Hollywood. Elegant suites in the style of a French provincial inn. ⑥.

AIRPORT HOTELS

Days Inn, 901 W Manchester Blvd (☎1-800/231-2508 or 310/649-0800). Outdoor pool, free parking, free LAX shuttle. ③.

Howard Johnson, 8620 Airport Blvd (☎310/645-7700). A mile northeast of LAX, with a swimming pool and complimentary airport shuttle. ③.

Quality Inn, 5249 W Century Blvd (☎1-800/228-5151 or 310/645-2200). Featuring ten floors of comfortable, well-equipped rooms and a restaurant and bar, this motel also offers free LAX shuttles every fifteen minutes. ③.

Travelodge LAX South, 1804 E Sycamore Ave (☎310/615-1073). Just five minutes south of LAX; convenient for the South Bay. Rates include use of the pool and free tea, coffee and breakfast. ③.

Santa Monica, Venice and Malibu

Bayside Hotel, 2001 Ocean Ave at Bay (☎310/396-6000). Just a block from Santa Monica beach and the Sixties-style café scene of Main Street, to which the original psychedelic bathroom tiles pay tribute. Bland exterior and no phones, but generally comfortable, with ocean views from the more expensive rooms. ③.

Cadillac Hotel, 8 Dudley Ave at Rose (☎310/399-8876). Stylishly restored Art Deco hotel/hostel on the Venice Boardwalk. Its private rooms are spartan and have few amenities, but given the location and price, there are few better deals in town. Nine additional dorm rooms cost only a third as much as private rooms. Sundeck, pool, gym and sauna. ④.

Channel Road Inn, 219 W Channel Rd at PCH (☎310/459-1920). Fourteen rooms in a romantic getaway nestled in lower Santa Monica Canyon, with ocean views, a hot tub and free bike rental. Eat free grapes and sip champagne in the sumptuous rooms, each priced according to its view. ⑥.

Hotel Carmel, 201 Broadway at Second (☎310/451-2469). The best budget bet for lodging near Santa Monica beach, with the ocean two blocks away. ⑤.

Loew's Santa Monica Beach Hotel, 1700 Ocean Ave at Pico (☎310/458-6700). One of Santa Monica's newest hotels: a deluxe affair overlooking the ocean and the Santa Monica pier, often in demand as a film set. The best rooms top $400. ⑧.

Malibu Riviera Motel, 28920 PCH (☎310/457-9503). Quiet place outside town, less than a mile from the beach, with a sundeck and jacuzzi. Fairly isolated from the rest of the city. ④.

Malibu Surfer Motel, 22541 PCH (☎310/456-6169). Frightful decor, but located across from the beach and boasting kingsize beds, refrigerators and TVs. Sufficient parking also. ④.

Pacific Shore Hotel, 1819 Ocean Ave at Pico, Santa Monica (☎310/451-8711). A popular stop for package-tour Europeans, with great bay views. ⑤.

Santa Monica-Pico Blvd Travelodge, 3102 Pico Blvd at 31st (☎1-800/231-7679 or 310/450-5766). At the eastern edge of Santa Monica, a mile from the beach. ④.

Santa Monica Travelodge, 1525 Ocean Ave (☎1-800/255-3050 or 310/451-0761). Another of the reliable nationwide chain. ⑤.

The South Bay and Harbor Area

Hotel Hermosa, 2515 PCH (☎310/318-6000). Plush hotel at moderate prices, a short walk to the beach. ④.

Palos Verdes Inn, 1700 S PCH, Palos Verdes (☎1-800/421-9241 or 310/316-4200). Reasonable luxury on the edge of Redondo Beach on a busy highway stretch; not far from the beach. ⑤.

Rodeway Inn, 50 Atlantic Ave at Ocean (☎310/435-8369). Safe bet a block from the beach, a serviceable base for exploring Long Beach and vicinity. Free in-room movies. ③.

Seahorse Inn, 233 N Sepulveda Blvd, Manhattan Beach (☎1-800/233-8050 or 310/376-7951). Faded pastel exterior but clean and simple rooms. Further from the beach than others, but with a pool. ②.

Sea Sprite Ocean Front Apartment Motel, 1016 Strand (☎310/376-6933). Right next to the beach along a popular strip. Ask the manager what's available as there are several different room options with varying prices. ④.

Around Disneyland

Best Western Stovall's Inn, 1110 W Katella Ave (☎714/778-1880). Along with *Pavilions* at 1176 W Katella Ave (☎714/776-0140) and *Park Place Inn* at 1544 S Harbor Blvd (☎714/776-4800), a reliable member of the nationwide chain. ④.

Desert Palm Inn and Suites, 631 W Katella Ave, Anaheim (☎1-800/521-6420). Very comfortable and spacious rooms with refrigerators, microwaves, VCRs and continental breakfast. Conventions in town make prices jump. ③.

Disneyland Hotel, 1150 W Cerritos Ave at West St, Anaheim (☎714/778-6600). The place to go for a pricey Disney-themed wedding with Mickey in attendance. A bit overpriced (theme park admission is separate), but the Disneyland monorail does stop right outside. ⑦.

Motel 6, 100 W Freedman Way, Anaheim (☎714/520-9696). Given the surrounding options, the best bargain in the area. ②.

The Orange County Coast

Hotel Laguna, 425 S Coast Hwy at Laguna (☎714/494-1151). If you have the cash, this is the place to spend it; atmospheric and comfortable, and nearly every room has a sea view. In the center of Laguna Beach. ⑤.

Mission Inn, 26891 Ortega Hwy at I-5 (☎714/493-1151). Rooms at this reasonably priced place come with use of jacuzzi and pool. Located in distant San Juan Capistrano. ③.

Ocean View Motel, 16196 PCH, Huntington Beach (☎310/592-2700). Family-run establishment with clean rooms. Get a jacuzzi in your room for an extra $15. ②.

Sail-Inn Motel, 2627 Newport Blvd (☎714/675-1841). Fairly basic rooms on a busy strip, but the motel is the least costly you're likely to find in the Newport area. Close to Balboa Peninsula. ④.

Seacliff Motel, 1661 S Coast Hwy (☎714/494-9717). Right on the ocean near Laguna Beach. ④.

Seal Beach Inn and Gardens, 212 Fifth St, Seal Beach (☎310/493-2416). Bed-and-breakfast establishment offering sumptuous furnishings two blocks from the sands. ⑥.

The San Gabriel and San Fernando Valleys

Best Western Colorado Inn, 2156 E Colorado Blvd, Pasadena (☎818/793-9339). Affordable accommodation just north of San Marino's Huntington Museum. ④.

Ritz-Carlton Huntington Hotel, 1401 S Knoll, Pasadena (☎818/568-3900). Utterly luxurious and refurbished landmark 1906 hotel, discreetly tucked away in residential southern Pasadena. Suites start at $350. Rooms ⑨.

Sheraton Universal, 333 Universal Terrace, Burbank (☎1-800/325-3535 or 818/980-1212). With the neighboring *Universal City Hilton*, 555 Universal Terrace (☎818/506-2500), a large and luxurious hotel on the Universal Studios lot, with health club and elegant restaurant. Both ⑧.

Vagabond Inn Hotel, 1203 E Colorado Blvd at Michigan, Pasadena (☎818/449-3170). Friendly budget chain motel, usefully placed for exploring Pasadena. Other *Vagabond Inns* are at 2863 E Colorado Blvd (☎1-800/468-2251 or 818/578-9791) and 20157 Ventura Blvd, Woodland Hills (☎818/347-8080), the latter with a large heated pool. ③.

Hostels

Banana Bungalow-Hollywood Hotel, 2775 Cahuenga Blvd West, in Cahuenga Pass (☎1-800/446-7835 or 213/851-1129). Popular large hostel near Universal City and US-101, with free airport shuttles, city tours to Venice Beach and Magic Mountain, and a relaxed atmosphere. Outdoor pool, free parking, and as much beer as you can drink every second night for $3. Dorms $15–18, and more expensive private doubles.

HI-Anaheim/Fullerton, 1700 N Harbor Blvd at Brea, Fullerton (☎714/738-3721). Convenient and comfortable, five miles north of Disneyland on the site of a former dairy farm. The hostel's excellent facilities include a grass volleyball court, golf driving range and picnic area. There are only 22 beds, so reservations are a must. Summer check-in 5–11pm, rest of year 4–10pm. Mornings open 7.10–10.30am. OCTA bus #43 stops outside. Members $14, others $17.

HI-LA/Santa Monica, 1436 Second St at Broadway, Santa Monica (☎310/393-9913). A few blocks from the beach and pier, the building was LA's Town Hall from 1887 to 1889, and retains its historic charm, with a pleasant inner courtyard, ivy-covered walls and a skylight. Members $16, others $20 – the price includes laundry machines and huge kitchens. Smoking and drinking are prohibited. Reservations essential in summer; open 24hr.

HI-LA/South Bay, 3601 S Gaffey St, building no. 613, San Pedro (☎310/831-8109). Sixty beds in old US Army barracks, with a panoramic view of the Pacific. Ideal for seeing San Pedro, Palos Verdes and the whole Harbor area. Open 7–11am and 4pm–midnight. $11 members, $14 others; private rooms $27 per person. MTA bus #446 passes close by, but it's a two-hour journey from downtown. You can also take the SuperShuttle from LAX.

Hostel California, 2221 Lincoln Blvd at Venice, Venice (☎310/305-0250). Twelve six-bed dorms with kitchens, pool table, big-screen TV, linen and parking. Cheap shuttle bus to and from LAX. $12 members, $14 others, or $84 a week.

Huntington Beach Colonial Hostel, 421 Eighth St at Pecan, Huntington Beach (☎714/536-3315). Four blocks from the beach and mostly double rooms. Sleeping bags allowed. Open 8am–11pm. Key rental after 1pm, $1 (plus $20 deposit). Dorms $12, private rooms $16.50 per person.

LA AREA CAMPGROUNDS

A company called Parknet (☎1-800/444-7275) processes reservations at many of the **campgrounds** listed below and can look for an alternative if your chosen site is full. It charges a $6.75 fee per reservation per night up to a maximum of eight people per site, including one vehicle.

Bolsa Chica Campground (☎714/846-3460). Facing the ocean in Huntington Beach, near a wildlife sanctuary and bird-watchers' paradise. $14 for campers with a self-contained vehicle. No tent camping.

Chilao Flat, on Hwy-2 twenty miles northeast of Pasadena (☎818/574-1613). The only campground in the San Gabriel Mountains reachable by car, though there are many others accessible on foot. For more details contact the Angeles National Forest Ranger Station at 701 N Santa Anita Ave, Arcadia (☎818/574-1613). $17.

Dockweiler Beach County Park (☎310/305-9545 or via Parknet on ☎1-800/444-7275). On a noisy stretch of Vista del Mar, almost at the western end of the LAX runways. Mainly for RVs, tent sites cost $17–25.

Doheny State Beach Campground, Dana Point (☎714/496-6171 or via Parknet on ☎1-800/444-7275). Often packed with families, especially at weekends. Located at southern end of Orange County. $16–21 per site.

Leo Carrillo State Beach Park, Malibu (☎818/706-1310 or via Parknet on ☎1-800/444-7275). Near one of LA's best beaches, 25 miles northwest of Santa Monica on Pacific Coast Hwy, and served twice an hour in summer by MTA bus #434. $16.

Malibu Creek State Park 1925 Las Virgenes Rd, fifteen minutes from the center of the San Fernando Valley (☎818/706-8809). A rustic campground in a park which can become crowded at times. Sixty sites in the shade of huge oak trees, almost all with fire pits, solar heated showers and flush toilets. One-time filming location for TV show *M*A*S*H*. $19.

San Clemente State Beach Campground, two miles south of San Clemente (☎714/492-7146 or via Parknet on ☎1-800/444-7275). $20 hook-up sites, $16 others.

Jim's at the Beach, 17 Brooks Ave at Speedway, Venice (☎310/399-4018). Disorganized hostel near beach. Dorm accommodation on production of a passport. $17 per night or $120 per week, including free breakfast.

Share-Tel Apartments, 20 Brooks Ave at Speedway, Venice (☎310/392-0325). Apartments, each with 6–8 people sharing facilities and bedrooms. $15, including breakfast and dinner Mon–Fri.

Orientation

Spilling over a vast flat basin and often lacking well-defined divisions, LA is not a city in the usual sense. Instead, it's a massive conglomeration of interconnected districts, not all of which have that much in common. Traveling from one side to the other takes you through virtually every social extreme imaginable, from mind-boggling beachside luxury to the most severe inner-city poverty anywhere in the US – both a result of the city's dizzying growth within a confined area. With the basin bordered by desert to the east, mountains to the north and ocean to the west, the millions of new arrivals who have poured in have had to fill the spaces between what were once geographically quite isolated and small communities, creating a metropolis on the most mammoth scale.

If LA has a heart, however, it's **downtown**, in the center of the basin, its towering office blocks punctuating what's for the most part a very low and level skyline. With everything from avant-garde art to the abject dereliction of Skid Row, downtown offers a taste of almost everything you'll find elsewhere around the city, compressed (unusually for LA) into an area of small, easily walkable blocks. It's a good place to get your initial bearings, and, usefully, the hub of the transportation network.

Around downtown, a serviceable label for a hotchpotch of areas with little in common except for being adjacent to or fanning out from downtown, demonstrates still more of LA's diversity: from the decaying Victorian relics of the turn-of-the-century suburbs, and the later Art Deco buildings that characterized the city in the Twenties, to the center of LA's enormous Hispanic population, home to some rare sights of enjoyable street life, and the sprawl of dull and desperate neighborhoods that make up South Central LA.

Away from downtown, you'll probably spend most of your time in the broad corridor that runs 25 miles west to the coast. Here are LA's best-known and most interesting districts, the first of which, **Hollywood**, has streets caked with movie legend – even if the genuine glamor is long gone. Tourists flock here, and it's also where some of LA's most eccentric street people choose to parade themselves. Neighboring **West LA**, on the other hand, is home to the city's newest money, shown off in the incredibly expensive shops of Beverly Hills and the posey restaurants and nightspots of the Sunset Strip, and on its western edge merges into **Santa Monica** and **Venice** – the quintessential coastal LA of palm trees, white sands, and laid-back living. The coastline itself is perhaps the major draw, stretching north from here twenty miles to the northern edge of LA and **Malibu**, noted for its celebrity residences and their keenly guarded privacy – and for the wildfires that have destroyed many of those residences.

South along the coast from Venice, the three **South Bay beach cities** – Manhattan Beach, Hermosa Beach, and Redondo Beach – are quieter, lived in by middle-class commuters, and a long way in spirit from the more bustling and fad-conscious portions of the city. The beaches are the sole focus of attention here, their bluffs and coves leading

LA'S MUSEUMS

Aerospace Building p.88
Armand Hammer Museum p.113
Beit HaShoa Museum of Tolerance p.111
Burbank Studios p.138
Cabrillo Marine Museum p.122
California African-American Museum p.88
California Heritage Museum p.117
Carol and Barry Kaye Museum of Miniatures p.106
Children's Museum p.80
Fantasy Foundation p.97
Forest Lawn Museum p.137
Geffen Contemporary p.84
Gene Autry Western Heritage Museum p.102
George C. Page Museum p.106
Getty Center p.113
Hall of Economics and Finance p.88
Hall of Health p.88
Hollywood Bowl Museum p.103
Hollywood Entertainment Museum p.99
Hollywood Wax Museum p.98
Huntington Library and Gardens p.135
Japanese American National Museum p.84
La Brea Tar Pits p.106

LA County Museum of Art p.105
Laguna Beach Museum of Art p.131
Long Beach Museum of Art p.123
Maritime Museum (San Pedro) p.122
Movieland Wax Museum p.127
Museum of Flying p.116
Municipal Art Gallery p.97
Museum of Contemporary Art (MOCA) p.81
Museum of Neon Art p.83
Museum of Science and Industry p.88
Museum of Television and Radio p.110
Natural History Museum of LA County p.88
Newport Harbor Art Museum p.130
Norton Simon Museum p.134
Pacific Asia Museum p.134
Peterson Automotive Museum p.106
Richard Nixon Library and Birthplace p.127
Skirball Cultural Center p.113
Southwest Museum p.93
Universal Studios p.138
Wells Fargo Museum p.82
Will Rogers Museum p.118

on to the **Harbor Area** – though, again, despite recent facelifts and some mildly enjoyable resort areas, there's nothing to detain you for more than half a day.

Orange County, east of the Harbor Area, is mainly lifeless suburban sprawl, and the only reason most people come here is to visit **Disneyland**, the city's biggest single tourist attraction and the granddaddy of all theme parks. If you're not keen on seeing "the happiest place on Earth" – as Disneyland calls itself – it's best to hug the coast and continue south, along the **Orange County Coast**, whose string of surprisingly individualistic communities provides for a few days' exploration on the way to San Diego.

In the opposite direction, LA has also grown on the other side of the hills that make up the northern wall of the basin to the **San Gabriel** and **San Fernando Valleys**, which stretch east and west until LA fades into desert, mountains and ocean. The valleys are distanced from mainstream LA life socially as well as geographically, their inhabitants the butt of most Angeleno hick jokes and constantly threatening to secede from the city. On the whole there is no reason to venture here. The few honorable exceptions include a number of worthwhile art collections and a couple of working (and tourable) film studios, as well as the most famous of LA's cemeteries.

Downtown LA

From the homeless families on the steps of City Hall to the phallic towers of multinational finance, nowhere else do the social, economic and ethnic divisions of LA clash quite as loudly and visibly as in the square mile that makes up **DOWNTOWN LA**. In the space of a few short blocks, adobe buildings and Mexican market stalls give way to Japanese-style shopping plazas and avant-garde art galleries, and you're as likely to rub shoulders with a high-flying yuppie as with a down-and-out drunk. Though it's long been the commercial focus of the city, and always the seat of local government, as businesses spread out across the basin in the postwar boom years, so the area became more dilapidated. Things picked up in the 1980s, when revitalization initiatives created museums, theaters and a rash of plush new condos for young professionals, but these have ultimately only served to intensify the extremes, and despite the development money that flows freely from city coffers, downtown is unlikely to usurp the Westside as the focus of tourism or cultural activity. Despite all this, it remains the city's most changed – and changing – neighborhood.

Each part of downtown has its own share of history, museums and architecture, and it makes most sense to divide the area into simple geographic segments and see it on foot, starting with LA's historic and governmental heart at the **Civic Center**, crossing into the brasher and more modern corporate-tower-dominated **Bunker Hill**, continuing through the chaotic streets and historic movie theaters of **Broadway**, and finally stepping into the strange combination of street people (an estimated 15,000 homeless live on downtown's streets), warehouses and diminishing experimental art galleries that makes up the **Eastside**.

Downtown can easily be seen in a day, and if your feet get tired you can hop aboard the **DASH buses** which run every ten minutes on five loop systems through key areas (look for the silver-signed bus stops). Parking is expensive on weekdays (around $5 per hour), but on weekends is quite affordable (a flat $3–8); in any case, downtown is the hub of the MTA networks and easily accessible by public transportation.

Civic Center Area

Although the bland municipal buildings of LA government form the focus of the **Civic Center**, the general area also includes **Chinatown** to the north and **Union Station** to the northeast. Just across US-101 from the current seat of local government, you can

△ Chinatown

SUNSET BOULEVARD
HOLLYWOOD FREEWAY

Union
Station

El Pueblo de
Los Angeles

SANTA ANA FREEWAY

LA River

1ST STREET

Ahmanson
Theatre

Mark Taper
Forum

TEMPLE STREET

LA Children's
Museum

City
Hall

The Geffen
Contemporary

Dorothy
Chandler
Pavilion

BEAUDRY AVENUE

MAIN STREET

2ND STREET

MOCA

Japanese American
Cultural and
Community Center

Angels Flight
Railway

LITTLE
TOKYO

9

Park Plaza

BUNKER
HILL

OLIVE STREET

3RD STREET

Bradbury
Building

4TH STREET

SKID ROW

Grand
Central
Market

CENTRAL AVENUE

Central
Library

1

PERSHING
SQUARE

5TH STREET

SAN PEDRO STREET

6TH STREET

WILSHIRE BOULEVARD

ACCOMMODATION

i

Red Line Metrorail

3

1 Biltmore
2 Bonaventure Hotel
3 City Center Motel
4 Figueroa Hotel
5 Holiday Inn Downtown
6 Hotel Inter-Continental
7 Kawada Hotel
8 Orchid Hotel
9 Nutel Motel

7TH STREET

2

8

GARMENT
DISTRICT

Flower
Markets

MAIN STREET

8TH STREET

HARBOR FREEWAY

4

Blue Line Metrorail

Cooper
Building

9TH STREET

5

Metro Stations
Dash Mini-Bus Routes

Museum of
Neon Art

HOPE STREET
GRAND AVENUE

OLYMPIC BOULEVARD

BROADWAY

0   500 yds

FIGUEROA STREET

12TH STREET

LOS ANGELES STREET

SAN PEDRO STREET

DOWNTOWN
LOS ANGELES

LA
Convention
Center

PICO BOULEVARD

VENICE

get a glimpse of LA's earlier days. **El Pueblo de Los Angeles**, off Alameda Street, was the site of the original late-eighteenth-century Mexican settlement of Los Angeles, and the few very early buildings that remain evoke a strong sense of LA's Spanish and Mexican origins. The **plaza church** is the city's oldest and has long served as a sanctuary for illegal Central American refugees (with immigration again becoming a potent political issue). Try and squeeze in during one of the Mariachi Masses (Sun 11.30am & 4.30pm), held completely in Spanish and accompanied by a six-piece Mariachi band.

You can also see the city's first **firehouse**, with a small but intriguing roomful of firefighting gear, and the exterior of the handsome mission-style **Pico House**, LA's most luxurious hotel when it opened in 1870, but now closed to the public. **Olvera Street**, which runs north from the plaza, is a less successful restoration, contrived in part as a pseudo-Mexican village market. Taken over for numerous festivals throughout the year, like November's Day of the Dead, when Mexicans traditionally honor the spirits of the departed (see p.157), the street is at its best on such communal occasions.

Like other historic districts around the country, especially Virginia's Williamsburg, Olvera Street is not simply a charming remnant that just happened to thwart ruin. Rather, its re-emergence was the work of one Christine Sterling, who, with other powerful citizens and help from the city government, tore down the slum she found here in 1926 and built much of what you see today, incorporating some of the salvageable historic structures. For the next twenty years she organized fiestas and worked to popularize the city's Mexican heritage while living in the early nineteenth-century **Avila Adobe** at 10 Olvera St – touted as the oldest structure in Los Angeles, although almost entirely rebuilt out of reinforced concrete following the 1971 Sylmar earthquake. Inside the house are two **museums** (Tues–Sun 10am–3pm; free): one featuring an idealized view of pueblo-era domestic life; the other, across the landscaped courtyard, telling the sanitized official version of how the LA authorities connived to get a secure supply of water for the city (for the real story, see p.138).

Across the street, a **visitor center** (Mon–Sat 10am–3pm, closed on holidays; ☎213/628-1274) offers the usual information, and shows an informative free film (Mon–Sat 11am & 2pm) on the history of Los Angeles. For a more detailed look at the pueblo area, there are also free **guided walking tours** (on the hour Tues–Sat 10am–1pm) from the building next to the firehouse.

Union Station, across Alameda from Olvera Street, echoes LA's roots in a rather different way: it is a magnificent example of monumental mission-style municipal architecture, finished in 1939. It is also the site of the original **Chinatown**, whose residents were forced to relocate when construction on the station began. Currently, the country's national rail system has been crippled by budget cuts and mismanagement, and the building is no longer the evocative point of arrival and departure it once was. However, the structure itself is in fine condition, with a spacious vaulted lobby, heavy wooden benches and intact Art Deco signs, surrounded by courtyards planted in informal combinations of fig trees and jacarandas. Once thronged with passengers, it now sees just a few trains each day, although the new **Gateway Transit Center** (see p.67) has been built with the intention of somehow bringing back the crowds.

What's now **CHINATOWN** was established by 1938 along North Broadway and North Spring streets. It's not the bustling affair you'll find in a number of other US cities, however, and unless it's Chinese New Year, when there's a parade of dragons and firework celebrations, there's little point in turning up here except to eat in one of the restaurants. (To get a truer sense of contemporary Chinese culture, visit **Alhambra** or **Monterey Park**, both bustling ethnic suburbs located just beyond LA's eastern boundary.)

Across the channel of the Santa Ana Freeway from Olvera Street, the central part of the **Civic Center** is a collection of plodding bureaucratic office buildings around a lifeless plaza. The exception to this, the Art Deco **City Hall**, known to the world through LA cop badges seen in TV shows ever since *Dragnet*, was until 1960 the city's tallest structure. The building's crown is as close as most visitors will ever get to seeing the Mausoleum at Halicarnassus, one of the ancient wonders of the world, which provided a curious, only-in-LA architectural inspiration. Though its 28th-story 360° observation deck is closed for seismic renovations, you can still get a good look at the inside of the building on the free tours (daily 10am & 11am; reserve on ☎213/485-4423).

Northeast of City Hall, at 310 N Main St, the **Children's Museum** (summer Tues–Fri 9.15am–1pm, Sat & Sun 10am–5pm; rest of year varied weekday hours, Sat & Sun 10am–5pm; $5, children $3, free for all weekdays in winter; ☎213/687-8801) is largely uninspired, but does offer mildly interesting science exhibits and high-tech toys for the kids. More edifying, on the south side of the Civic Center plaza, are the free tours of the **Los Angeles Times** building (Mon–Fri 11.15am; ☎213/237-5757) which show how the West Coast's biggest newspaper is put together.

Bunker Hill

Up until a century ago the area south of the Civic Center, **BUNKER HILL**, was LA's most elegant neighborhood, its elaborate mansions and houses connected by funicular railroad to the growing business district down below on Spring Street. As with all of downtown, though, the population soon moved to stylish new suburbs and many of the old homes were converted to rooming houses, later providing the seedy *film noir* back-drop for detective films, notably *Kiss Me Deadly*.

The **Angel's Flight** funicular, removed in 1969 but newly restored and repainted, is a bright and colorful memory of a long-departed era. Hop aboard one of the two trains near the corner of Hill and Fourth streets and, for a mere 25¢, ascend to the top of Bunker Hill and be dwarfed by office blocks, which have in the last three decades taken the place of the old Victorians. Once you arrive, the **FINANCIAL DISTRICT** looms above you with sleek modernity. Most of the fifty-story towers have a concourse of shops and restaurants at their base, high-style shopping malls designed to provide a synthetic street life for the brokers and traders, jaded from the day-to-day routine of set-ting up mega-buck deals.

The Museum of Contemporary Art

The largest and most ambitious development in the district is the **California Plaza** on Grand Avenue, a billion-dollar complex of offices and luxury condos centering on the **Museum of Contemporary Art (MOCA)** (Tues–Wed & Sat–Sun 11am–5pm, Thurs–Fri 11am–8pm; $6, students $4, free Thurs 5–8pm). Funded by a one-percent tax on the value of all new downtown construction, MOCA opened at the end of 1986 in an effort to raise the cultural stature of the area, and of the whole city. Designed by show-man architect Arata Isozaki as a "small village in the valley of the skyscrapers", it justi-fies a visit for the building alone, its playful exterior a welcome splash of color among the dour downtown skyscrapers. You may recognize its geometric red shapes from the occasional television commercials that are filmed here.

A barrel-vaulted entrance pavilion on Grand Avenue opens on to an outdoor sculp-ture plaza, off which are the ticket booth, the **museum store** and the entrance to the administration wing, covered in diamond-shaped green aluminum panels with bright pink joints. Stairs lead down from the upper plaza to a smaller courtyard, between the café and the main entrance to the galleries.

The brainchild of the high-rollers of the LA art world, MOCA was put together as a gesture of goodwill – and, cynics say, to raise the value of the works they loan for dis-play. Much of the gallery is used for temporary exhibitions, and the bulk of the per-manent collection is from the Abstract Expressionist period, including work by Franz Kline and Mark Rothko. You'll also find plenty of Pop Art, in Robert Rauschenberg's urban junk and Claes Oldenburg's papier-mâché representations of hamburgers and gaudy fast foods. Don't be surprised to find a few minimalist creations, either, such as Donald Judd's mind-numbing, machine-produced metallic boxes.

Unfortunately, there are few singularly great pieces among the established names, and most of the compelling ideas are expressed amid the paintings and sculpture of the rising stars in the stock bequeathed by collector Barry Lowen. Hard to categorize, these are something of a greatest hits collection of work by artists you're likely to come across in the trendier city galleries – Jennifer Bartlett, David Salle, Anselm Keifer and Eric Fischl, to name a famous few. The museum is also strong on photography, and has recently acquired the two-thousand-print collection of New York dealer Robert Freidhaus, featuring the work of Diane Arbus, Larry Clark, Robert Frank, Lee Freidlander, John Pfahl and Gerry Winograd, among many others.

The theater on the lower floor of MOCA hosts some bizarre multimedia shows and performances, as well as the more standard lectures and seminars (☎213/621-2766 for details). The best time to visit MOCA is on a Thursday evening in summer, when entry is free, and concerts, usually jazz or classical and also free, are laid on. At other times, a ticket to MOCA also entitles you to same-day entrance to the Geffen Contemporary (see p.84), the museum's warehouse-like exhibition space on the east side of downtown.

Around MOCA

The shallow but amusing **Wells Fargo Museum** (Mon–Fri 9am–4pm; free) at the base of the shiny towers of the Wells Fargo Center provides relief from the rigors of MOCA's modern art. It tells the history of Wells Fargo & Co, the bank of Gold Rush California, with among other things a two-pound nugget of gold, some mining equipment and a simulated stagecoach journey from St Louis to San Francisco.

A block away, the shining glass tubes of the **Westin Bonaventure Hotel** (see "Accommodation", p.72) have become one of LA's most unusual landmarks. Although it is the only LA building by modernist architect John Portman, it doesn't fully live up to its billing. The disappointing interior doubles as a shopping mall and office complex – an M.C. Escher-style labyrinth of spiralling ramps and balconies that is disorientating enough to make it necessary to consult a color-coded map every twenty yards or so. But brace yourself and step inside for a ride in the glass elevators that run up and down the outside of the building, giving views over much of downtown and beyond (be careful venturing outside – the area around the building may be LA's most pedestrian-unfriendly space).

From the *Bonaventure*'s rotating skyline bar you'll get a bird's-eye view of one of LA's finest buildings, the Los Angeles **Central Library** across the street, restored after an arson attack many years back. The concrete walls and piers of the lower floors, enlivened by Lee Laurie's figurative sculptures symbolizing the "Virtues of Philosophy" and the "Arts", form a pedestal for the squat central tower, which is topped by a brilliantly colored pyramid roof. The library, built in 1926, was the last work of architect Bertram Goodhue, and its pared-down, angular lines set the tone for many LA buildings, most obviously the City Hall. Keep in mind that not all the interior design is original to Goodhue, especially the grand atrium added by the renovators, which seems to appear out of nowhere after you step off the escalators to the upper floors.

In exchange for planning permission and air rights, the developers of the **Library Tower** across Fifth Street – the tallest building west of Chicago – agreed to pay some fifty million dollars toward the restoration of the library. Now owned by Wells Fargo, the tower features Lawrence Halprin's huge staircase, modelled after the Spanish Steps in Rome, which curves up to Bunker Hill between a series of terraces with outdoor cafés and boutiques. Not wildly thrilling, but as good a way to ascend the hill as any.

Broadway and Pershing Square

Though it's hard to picture now, **Broadway** once formed the core of Los Angeles' most fashionable shopping and entertainment district, lively with movie palaces and department stores. Today it's largely taken over by the clothing and jewelery stores of a bustling Hispanic community, a cash-rich hustle and bustle where as many pesos change hands as dollars, all to a salsa soundtrack blaring from ghetto blasters nailed to the walls. The most vivid taste of the area is to be had amid the pickled pigs' feet, sheep's brains and other delicacies inside the **Grand Central Market**, on Broadway between Third and Fourth. It's a real scrum but without doubt the best place (at least for carnivores) to enter the spirit of things.

The **Bradbury Building** (Mon–Sat 9am–5pm; free) across the street makes for a break from the mayhem of the market, its magnificent sunlit atrium surrounded by wrought-iron balconies, and open-cage elevators alternating up and down on opposite sides of the narrow court, with elaborate open staircases at either end. The whole place is an art director's dream – not surprisingly, most of the income for this 1893 office building is generated by film shoots: *Blade Runner* and *Citizen Kane* were both filmed here. Tourists are now only permitted in the lobby, but it's a great view up. (Los Angeles Conservancy tours often begin here; see p.69 for more information.)

Aside from the street life, the best things about Broadway are the great movie palaces of the **THEATER DISTRICT**, some of whose "enchanted realms" still function today, if not exactly as their builders intended. Two are especially noteworthy: next to the Grand Central Market, the opulent 1918 **Million Dollar Theater**, its whimsical terracotta facade mixing buffalo heads with bald eagles in typical Hollywood Spanish Baroque style, is a theatrical icon and was originally built by theater magnate Sid Grauman, who went on to build the Egyptian and Chinese theaters in Hollywood (see p.98). It's now a South American-style evangelical meeting hall and entry is of course, free to all. The **Los Angeles Theater**, at 615 S Broadway, is even more extravagant, built in ninety days for the world premiere of Charlie Chaplin's *City Lights* in 1931, and crowning what had become the largest concentration of movie palaces in the world. The plush lobby behind the triumphal arch facade is lined by marble columns supporting an intricate mosaic ceiling, while the 1800-seat auditorium is enveloped by trompe l'oeil murals and lighting effects. Many think this theater to be the era's finest in LA, if not the West Coast altogether. In June, a program called Last Remaining Seats draws huge crowds to this and the nearby **Orpheum Theater** to watch revivals of classic Hollywood films, many from the silent era. If you're in town at the time, don't miss it.

With the advent of TV, the rise of the car and LA's drift to the suburbs, the movie palaces lost their customers and fell into decline. An underground parking lot was built in **Pershing Square** in an attempt to bring the punters back – a task for which it failed, and many of the movie houses are these days showing exploitation and Spanish-language films to sadly depleted numbers. Pershing Square itself, however, is a generally amenable place, benefiting somewhat from a recent overhaul. Inspired by the work of Mexican architect Luis Barragan, it features brightly painted concrete elements, including a massive bell tower that chimes on the hour.

Some of the buildings around the square have – albeit after years of neglect – emerged in fine form. The most prominent of these, the **Biltmore Hotel**, stands over the west side of the square, its three brick towers rising from a Renaissance Revival arcade along Olive Street. Inside, the grand old lobby that was the original main entrance has an intricately painted Spanish-beamed ceiling that you can admire over a pricey glass of wine. A block south, at 617 S Olive St, the Art Deco **Oviatt Building** is another sumptuous survivor. The ground floor housed LA's most elegant haberdashery, catering to dapper types such as Clark Gable and John Barrymore, and has since been converted into the exquisite (and outrageously expensive) *Rex Il Restaurante* (see p.146). If you can't afford a $100-a-head meal, the elevators, which open on to the street level exterior lobby, are still worth a look, featuring hand-carved oak panelling, designed and executed by Parisian craftsman René Lalique. If you don't wish to go inside, marvel at the intricate 1928 design of the structure's exterior, especially the building's grand sign and its looming clock above. Finally, four blocks to the south at 501 W Olympic Blvd, you can find the adulterated visage of Mona Lisa smiling at you through blue-and-yellow tubing at the **Museum of Neon Art** (Tues–Sun 11am–6pm; $3.50). Recently relocated next to the pleasant **Grand Hope Park**, the museum offers a small exhibition space featuring classic neon signs, more modern interpretations of the noble gas and a range of bizarre kinetic art.

The Eastside

A block east of Broadway, take a daring step into LA's old financial district along **Spring Street** between Fourth and Seventh Streets. Once at the center of the city's commerce and banking, the area has since been reduced to a virtual ghost town, with barren Neoclassical facades and shuttered entrances. Its only denizens are either homeless or mentally ill, or both. Despite the decay, the street is definitely worth a look for its departed glory.

Nearby, downtown takes a further downturn in LA's **SKID ROW**: a shabby, down-trodden area around Los Angeles Street south from City Hall that has a more than slightly threatening air. A seedy neighborhood for decades, Skid Row has the dubiously arty associations to match. The Doors posed here for the cover of their album, *Morrison Hotel*, and Charles Bukowski is just one luminary of the booze 'n' broads school of writers who've used the bars and poolrooms as a source of inspiration. At the new **Union Rescue Mission**, 545 S San Pedro St (call ☎213/347-6300 to arrange a visit), a public art project, "The Voice of the Homeless" designed by R.B. Krivaneck, is the new face of the Skid Art movement. Consisting of two parts, "Orientation Rotunda" and "Electronic Statement", the piece was created around interviews with the local dispossessed. Their words in English and Spanish have been applied to the rotunda – nouns in the top tier, adjectives in the middle, verbs at the bottom – with negative and positive attributes placed at 180° angles from one another, allowing anyone standing in the middle to create a variety of sentences. An additional interactive element may shortly allow local people to create statements of their own through a computer connected to an electronic message board, 18 feet above San Julian Street on the mission's west wall.

To the south of Skid Row, the lively **GARMENT DISTRICT**, with its Mexican food wagons and cut-rate shops, is a respite from the bleak streets and attracts a lively multiethnic crowd. The **Cooper Building**, which takes up most of the Ninth Street block between Santee and Los Angeles streets, is famous for its infrequent designer sample sales. It also houses at least fifty stores where you'll find big markdowns on outfits that may normally be out of your price range. At the atmospheric early-morning **Flower Market** (Mon, Wed & Fri 8–11am, Tues, Thurs & Sat 6–11am, closed Sun) on Wall Street between Seventh and Eighth Streets, you can mingle with the wholesalers and buy flowers for a fraction of the high street prices.

Over the last ten years, the northern boundaries of Skid Row have been pushed back by the sanitized shopping precincts of **LITTLE TOKYO** – the clearest evidence of the Japanese money that accounted for most of the new construction in LA during the 1980s. If you feel like a quick taste of this, head for the **Japanese American Cultural and Community Center**, 244 S San Pedro St, whose **Doizaki Gallery** (Tues–Fri noon–5pm, Sat & Sun 11am–4pm; free), shows traditional and contemporary Japanese art and calligraphy. The center also includes the **Japan America Theater**, which regularly hosts Kabuki theater groups. Improbably shoehorned between the two and easy to miss, the stunning **James Irvine Garden**, with a 170-foot stream running along its sloping hillside, is a real inner-city treasure. Though named after its biggest financial contributor, it really owes its existence to the efforts of two hundred Japanese-American volunteers who gave up their Sundays to carve the space out of a flat lot.

From the cultural center, a zigzagging pathway takes you through the Shoji screens, sushi bars, shops and Zen rock gardens of **Village Plaza** and along to the new **Japanese American National Museum** at First and Central (Tues–Sun 10am–5pm, Thurs closes at 8pm; $4, students $3), a converted Buddhist temple now housing exhibits on everything from origami to the internment of Japanese-Americans during World War II. A replica internment hut stands out front.

Across the street from Little Tokyo is the **Geffen Contemporary** at 152 N Central Ave (hours and prices as for MOCA, to which a ticket also entitles same-day entrance, see p.81) – an exhibition space in a converted police garage that shows works by contemporary artists other LA museums won't touch. Designed by local maverick Frank Gehry, the museum was initially developed as the temporary home of the Museum of Contemporary Art, but the success of the gallery was such that it was kept on as an alternative exhibition space to the more refined main building. The giant south side of the building, which once displayed a huge Barbara Kruger slogan, is now disappearing behind new construction for Little Tokyo.

Around downtown

When you leave downtown you enter the LA sprawl, the diverse environs of which tend to be forgotten quarters, scythed by freeways, and with large distances separating their few points of interest. Added together, however, there's quite a bit worth seeing, in areas either on the perimeter of downtown or simply beginning here and continuing for many miles south or east. The districts immediately northwest of downtown, around **Angelino Heights** and **Echo Park**, are where the upper crust of LA society luxuriously relocated itself at the turn of the century in groupings of wooden Victorian houses (now mostly in impressive states of preservation), vivid indicators of the prosperity of their time, just as the nondescript drabness surrounding them now evidences the blight which later befell the area. Much the same applies to the streets around **MacArthur Park**, though they still contain some of the impressive commercial architecture that set the stylistic tone for the city in the 1920s.

The other areas that surround downtown are too far apart for it to make sense to try to see them consecutively; each is a ten- to thirty-minute drive away from the next. Directly south of downtown, the long succession of unimaginative low-rent housing developments is interrupted only by the contrast of the **USC campus**, populated by conservative, well-coddled students, and the neighboring **Exposition Park**, with acres of gardens and several museums, a couple of which merit going out of your way to see. Beyond here, the deprivation resumes, leading into one of LA's most depressed areas – the vast urban nightmare of **South Central LA**. A chilling counterpoint to the commercial vibrancy of downtown, this surrounds the main route (I-110) between downtown and the Harbor Area, and, while it's certainly a place to stop only with caution or with someone who knows the area, it does give a picture of the grim reality behind LA's glamorous myths. More appealing is the Hispanic-dominated **East LA**, the largest Mexican city outside Mexico, and a buzzing district of markets, shops and street-corner music that gives a tangible insight into the other, relatively unacknowledged, side of LA. More recent arrivals, many of them from Central America, often end up in the **Temple-Beaudry** and **Pico-Union** barrios, located to the immediate west of downtown. These areas have a reputation as LA's most dangerous, but as long as you stick to the main thoroughfares and travel during daylight, you're unlikely to encounter any trouble. It's less hectic northeast of downtown, where, amid the preserved homes of the **Highland Park** district, the **Southwest Museum** holds a fine and extremely comprehensive collection of Native American artifacts.

Angelino Heights and Echo Park

Long before there was a Malibu or a Beverly Hills, some of the most desirable addresses in Los Angeles were in **ANGELINO HEIGHTS**, LA's first suburb, laid out in the flush of a property boom at the end of the 1880s on a hilltop a little way northwest of downtown. Though the boom soon went bust, the elaborate houses that were built here, especially along **Carroll Avenue**, have survived and been recently restored as reminders of the optimism and energy of the city's early years. There's a dozen or so in all, and most repay a look for their catalog of late-Victorian details – wraparound verandahs, turrets and pediments, set oddly against the downtown skyline; one, with a weird Great Pyramid roof, was used as the set for the haunted house in Michael Jackson's *Thriller* video. Neighboring **Kellam Avenue** has fewer appealing structures, many of them in severe disrepair. All the homes are private, and not generally open to visitors, though the Angelino Heights Community Organization (☎213/413-8756) sometimes offers tours.

At the foot of the hill, to the west of Angelino Heights, **Echo Park** is a tiny park of palm trees set around a lake. In the large white **Angelus Temple** on the northern side of the lake, the evangelist **Aimee Semple McPherson** used to preach fire and brimstone sermons to five thousand people, with thousands more listening in on the radio. The first in a long line of media evangelists, "Sister Aimee" died in mysterious circumstances in 1944, but the building is still used for services by her Four Square Gospel ministry, who dunk converts in the huge water tank during mass baptisms. A more typical reflection of life in Echo Park appears in Alison Anders' 1994 *Mi Vida Loca* (*My Crazy Life*), a semi-fictional film based on the street life of local girl gangs, some scenes of which were shot here. Roman Polanski's *Chinatown* also pays homage to the park by having detective Jake Gittes follow the town water boss to clandestine meetings amid the palms and lotuses.

MacArthur Park and around

Wilshire Boulevard leaves downtown between Sixth and Seventh as the main surface route across 25 miles of Los Angeles to the Santa Monica beaches. It was named by and for entrepreneur Gaylord Wilshire, who made a fortune selling an electrical device that claimed to restore greying hair to its original color. Wilshire used the proceeds from this and other ventures to buy up a large plot of land west of Westlake Park, later renamed **MacArthur Park**, through the center of which he ran the wide thoroughfare. When the property market collapsed in 1888, Gaylord discovered politics, ran for Congress (and lost), and later moved to England, where he made friends with George Bernard Shaw and the Fabian Socialists. The park has since fallen into disrepair and, despite police efforts, remains a venue for drug deals after dark, but the new Red Line Metrorail connection has turned its patches of green and large lake into the nearest relief from the sidewalks of downtown. Don't miss the overhead sign for the Westlake Theater, which proudly advertises a classic moviehouse that has since become a grungy swap meet (flea market).

Half a mile west, the **Bullocks Wilshire** department store is a seminal building of Art Deco Los Angeles, the most complete and unaltered example of late-1920s architecture in the city. Built in 1929, in what was then a beanfield in the suburbs, Bullocks was the first department store in LA to be built outside downtown, and the first to build its main entrance at the back of the structure adjacent to the parking lot – catering for the automobile in a way that was to become the norm in this car-obsessed city. Transportation was the spirit of the time, and throughout the building mural and mosaic images of planes and ocean liners glow with activity in a studied celebration of the modern world. The building was badly vandalized during the 1992 riots, and was closed for five years. It has since reopened as the law library of adjacent **Southwestern University**, but is still off-limits to the general public, unless you can get someone to give you an impromptu tour.

The **Ambassador Hotel**, just past Vermont Avenue at 3400 Wilshire Blvd, is another landmark of the boulevard's golden age. From the early 1920s to the late 1940s, when the hotel was the winter home of transient Hollywood celebrities, its *Cocoanut Grove* club was a favorite LA nightspot. The large ballroom hosted some of the early Academy Award ceremonies, and was featured in the first two versions of *A Star is*

Born – though the hotel's most notorious event occurred on June 5, 1968, when **Bobby Kennedy** was fatally shot in the hotel kitchen while trying to avoid the press after winning the California Presidential Primary. Converted into a film location and closed to public view, billboards now advertise the ballroom to location hunters. Across the street, another of LA's landmarks has been bizarrely reconstructed. The **Brown Derby** restaurant, once the city's prime example of programmatic architecture (or buildings shaped like objects – in this case a hat), has now been relocated to the roof of a Korean mini-mall. Brimless and painted silver, it has become a curious nightclub called *Xcess*.

From the *Ambassador* you can either continue west up the so-called "Miracle Mile" (see p.105) or, two blocks south of Wilshire, between Vermont and Western, look in on **KOREATOWN**, the largest concentration of Koreans outside Korea and five times bigger than Chinatown and Little Tokyo combined. In reality, the comparison is unfair, for Koreatown is an active residential and commercial district, not just a tourist site. The more fruitful comparison would be with the vibrant enclave of **Monterey Park**, east of LA, which is the focus of regional Chinese culture just as surely as Koreatown is of Korean culture. However, it's by no means without its tensions; the area has its share of LA's inter-racial violence – TV images of heavily armed Koreans "defending" their property against rioters filled screens during the 1992 riots. Yet, as those images recede, residents have made Koreatown into a thriving place and an area as fundamental to LA's cultural mosaic as any.

The USC Campus

The **USC** (University of Southern California) **CAMPUS**, a few minutes south of downtown, is an enclave of wealth in one of the city's poorer neighborhoods. USC or "University of Spoiled Children" is one of the most expensive universities in the country, its undergraduates thought of as more likely to have rich parents than fertile brains. Indeed, the stereotype is often borne out, both by their easy-going, suntanned, beach-bumming nature, and by the fact that USC is more famous for its sporting prowess than academic achievement. Alumni include O.J. Simpson who collected college football's highest honor, the Heisman Trophy, when he played for USC. There have been attempts to integrate the campus population more closely with the local community, but for the moment at least USC is something of an elitist island, right down to its own fast-food outlet, and its students are cheerfully oblivious to the blight around them.

Though sizeable, the campus is reasonably easy to get around. If you do want to visit, however, you might find it easiest to take the free hour-long **walking tour** (Mon–Fri 10am–2pm by appointment; ☎213/743-2183). Without a guide, a good place to start is in the **Doheny Library** (during academic year Mon–Thurs 8.30am–10pm, Fri 8.30am–5pm, Sat 9am–5pm, Sun 1–10pm; free), where you can pick up a campus map and pass an hour or so investigating the large stock of overseas newspapers and magazines on the second floor, although they tend to be at least three weeks behind the times and UCLA (see p.112) has a better selection. Another place for general information is the **Student Union** building, just across from the library and straight out of *Beverly Hills 90210*. Food is priced to make the college money, and the **bar** is an underused and claustrophobic room with mirrored walls and terrible beer. A café under the Wolfgang Puck banner provides some respite, however.

Of things to see, USC's art collection is housed in the **Fisher Gallery** on Exposition Boulevard (during academic year Tues–Fri noon–5pm, Sat 11am–3pm; free), which stages several major international exhibitions each year, and has a broad permanent stock. Elsewhere in the building, you can see smaller shows of students' creative efforts in the **Helen Lindhurst Architecture Gallery** (Mon–Fri noon–6pm, Sat noon–5pm; free) and **Helen Lindhurst Fine Arts Gallery** (Mon–Fri 9am–5pm; free).

The campus is also home to the **George Lucas Film School**, named after the producer who studied here, which is a decidedly mainstream rival to the UCLA film school in Westwood. Ironically, **Steven Spielberg**, one of the biggest box-office directors in the history of film, couldn't get in to USC when he applied as an aspiring director. Now, his name is hallowed here, and writ large on the wall of the large and expensive cinema-and-TV-school sound mixing center he later funded. A short walk away, the **Arnold Schoenberg Institute** (Mon–Fri 9am–5pm; free) is a study center devoted to the pioneering composer whose wide influence on modern musical thought – largely through his experiments with atonal and twelve-tone structures – is even more remarkable when you consider that he had no formal training. Schoenberg, born in Austria in 1871, came to the US to escape the Nazis, and spent the fourteen years before his death in 1951 in LA. The reception area holds a mock-up of his studio, while the small auditorium displays his personal mementoes. During the academic year, students often give free lunchtime concerts of the great man's music.

Between USC and Exposition Park, sports fans may want to stop at the **Coliseum** on Hoover Boulevard. The site of the 1932 and 1984 Olympic Games has fallen on hard times lately, with the Los Angeles Raiders relocating to Oakland and possible new American football franchises insisting on a brand-new venue with fancy "skyboxes" to create maximum profit. However, USC home games are still played here, and the imposing grand arch on the facade and muscular commemorative statues create enough visual interest to make the place worth a look.

Exposition Park

Across Exposition Boulevard from the campus, **EXPOSITION PARK** is, given the grim nature of the surrounding area, one of the most appreciated parks in LA, incorporating lush landscaped gardens, a sports stadium and a number of decent museums.

It's large by any standards, but the park retains a sense of community – a feeling bolstered by its function as a favorite lunchtime picnic place for schoolkids. After eating, their number one spot tends to be the **California Museum of Science and Industry**, set among a cluster of **museums** off Figueroa Street (unless otherwise stated all daily 10am–5pm; free); though largely uncritical, it has scores of working models and thousands of pressable buttons. Just outside, the **Hall of Health** includes a replica "classic" American diner carrying displays on what not to eat if you want to stay healthy. There's more fun and games at the neighboring **Hall of Economics and Finance**, where with the aid of a few machines you can wreck the American economy – though all the simulations are, again, irritatingly lightweight and geared for children rather than adults.

In the vicinity, an **IMAX Theater** plays a range of eye-popping documentaries on a gigantic curved screen. Because of the general lack of storytelling in many of the films, one screening (most are around 30min) is usually enough to get a sense of the unusual moviehouse. The **Aerospace Building** marked by the DC10 parked outside, is rather bland: a few models and displays pertaining to space and weather prediction. The building itself is something of a landmark, designed by Frank Gehry and prefiguring some of his later, better work. Nearby, head for the stimulating **California African-American Museum**, which has diverse, temporary exhibitions on the history, art and culture of black people in the Americas.

The **Natural History Museum of Los Angeles County** (Tues–Sun 10am–5pm; $6, students $3.50) has much appeal. Apart from housing the biggest collection, it's also the nicest building in the park – an explosion of Spanish Revival with echoing domes, travertine columns and a marble floor. Foremost among the exhibits is a tremendous stock of dinosaur bones and fossils, and some individually imposing skeletons (usually casts) including the crested "duck-billed" dinosaur, the skull of a Tyrannosaurus Rex, and the astonishing frame of a Diatryma – a huge bird incapable of flight. But there's a lot beyond strictly natural history in the museum, and you should allow several hours at least for a comprehensive look around. In the fascinating pre-Columbian Hall are Mayan pyramid murals and the complete contents of a Mexican tomb (albeit a reconstruction), while the Californian history sections usefully document the early (white) settlement of the region during the Gold Rush era and after, with some amazing photos of Los Angeles in the 1920s. Topping the whole place off is the gem collection: several breathtaking roomfuls of crystals, their qualities enhanced by special lighting. On a sunny day, spare some time for walking through Exposition Park's **Rose Garden** (daily 9am–5pm; free). The flowers are at their most fragrant in April and May, when the bulk of the 45,000 annual visitors come by to admire the 16,000 rose bushes and the downright prettiness of their setting.

South Central LA

Lacking the scenic splendor of the coast, the glamor of West LA and the history of downtown, **SOUTH CENTRAL LA** hardly ranks on the tourist circuit – especially since it burst onto the world's TV screens as the focal point of the April 1992 **riots** (see box below). However much wealthy white LA would like to pretend South Central doesn't exist, it's an integral part of the city, if only in terms of size: a big, roughly circular chunk reaching from the southern edge of downtown to the northern fringe of the Harbor Area. The population was once mostly black, but is increasingly Hispanic and Asian, interspersed here and there by bottom-of-the-heap working-class whites. The dislocations occasioned by immigration have made for surprising trends and not a little racial hostility. **Watts**, for example, once overwhelmingly black, is now equally divided between blacks and Hispanics. As a whole, South Central doesn't look so terribly rundown at first sight, mostly made up of detached bungalows enjoying their own patch of

---

THE LA RIOTS

The unexpected acquittal in 1992 of five white Los Angeles police officers, charged with using excessive force after they were videotaped kicking and beating black motorist Rodney King, could almost have been calculated to provoke a **violent backlash** in LA's poverty-stricken ghettos. What few predicted, however, was the sheer scale of the response to the verdict. The violence and anger far surpassed the Watts Riots of 1965 (see overleaf), beginning in South Central LA with motorists being pulled from their cars and attacked, and quickly escalating into a chaos of arson, shooting and looting that spread across the city from Long Beach to Hollywood. Downtown police headquarters were surrounded by a mixed crowd of blacks, Hispanics and whites, chanting "No Justice, No Peace", as state governor Pete Wilson appealed for calm on live TV. It took the imposition of a four-day dusk-to-dawn curfew, and the presence on LA's streets of several thousand well-armed US National Guard troops, to restore calm – whereupon the full extent of the rioting became apparent. The worst urban violence seen in the US this century had left 58 dead, nearly 2000 injured, and caused an estimated $1 billion worth of damage. With much of the devastation in the city's poorest areas, a relief operation of Third World dimensions was mounted to feed and clothe those most severely affected by the carnage. A second trial, on charges that the officers violated Mr King's civil rights, resulted in prison sentences for two of the officers.

Though ignited by a single incident, the riots were a very real indication of the **tensions** in a city whose controllers (and affluent inhabitants) have traditionally been all too ready to turn a blind eye to social problems. Prompted by the Rodney King case, the Christopher Commission was set up to investigate racial prejudice within the LAPD. Sadly, its recommendations had all too blatantly not been implemented by the time of the O.J. Simpson trial in 1995, when the world was once again reminded that race is always an issue in Los Angeles.

palm-shaded lawn. But this picture is deceptive, and doesn't conceal for long the fact that just about all the people around here are very poor, get an abysmal deal at school and at work, and have little chance of climbing the social ladder and escaping to the more affluent parts of the city – unless they become sportsmen or rap artists, a long shot for most.

What will immediately strike you in South Central LA is the sheer monotony of the place: every block for twenty-odd miles looks much like the last, enlivened periodically by fast-food outlets, dingy liquor stores and uninviting factory sites. You'll see a lot of this by driving past on the Harbor Freeway (I-110), which links downtown to the Harbor Area.

Watts

The district of **WATTS**, on the southernmost fringe of downtown, achieved notoriety as the scene of the six-day **Watts Riot** of August 1965. The arrest of a 21-year-old unemployed black man, Marquette Frye, on suspicion of drunken driving, gave rise to charges of police brutality and led to bricks, bottles and slabs of concrete being hurled at police and passing motorists during the night. The situation had calmed by the next morning, but the following evening both young and old black people were on the streets, giving vent to an anger generated by years of what they felt to be less than even-handed treatment by the police and other white-dominated institutions. Weapons were looted from stores and many buildings set alight (though few residential buildings, black-owned businesses or community services, such as libraries and schools, were touched); street barricades were erected, and the events took a more serious turn. By the fifth day the insurgents were approaching downtown, which – along with the fear spreading through white LA – led to the call-out of the National Guard: 13,000 troops arrived, set up machine-gun placements and road blocks, and imposed an 8pm to dawn curfew, which caused the rebellion to subside.

In the aftermath of the uprising, which left 36 dead, one German reporter said of Watts, "it looks like Germany during the last months of World War II". Much of it still does – Watts is by far the ugliest part of South Central LA. The promises of investment made after 1965 never amounted to much; indeed any forward strides made during the 1970s have long since been wiped out by wider economic decline, and eclipsed by the events of 1992. Although city politicians continue to pontificate about helping out the area, and business leaders occasionally promise to build a supermarket here or a bank there, this is still LA's economic ground zero.

Watts hit the headlines in 1975 when members of the Symbionese Liberation Army (SLA), who had kidnapped publishing heiress Patti Hearst, fought a lengthy – and televised – gun battle with police until the house they were trapped in burned to the ground. The site of the battle, at 1466 E 54th St, is now a vacant lot, though the surrounding houses are still riddled with bullet holes, visible reminders of another unpleasant chapter in local history.

The one valid reason to come here is to see the Gaudi-esque **Watts Towers**, sometimes called the Rodia Towers, at 1765 E 107th St. Constructed from iron, stainless steel, old bedsteads and cement, and decorated with fragments of bottles and around 70,000 crushed seashells, these striking pieces of street art are surrounded by more than a little mystery. Their maker, Simon Rodia, had no artistic background or training at all, but labored over the towers' construction from 1921 to 1954, refusing offers of help and unable to explain either their meaning or why on earth he was building them. Once finished, Rodia left the area, refused to talk about the towers, and faded into complete obscurity. The towers managed to stave off bureaucratic hostility and structural condemnation for many decades; finally, they were declared a cultural landmark. However, 1994's earthquake left the towers shrouded in scaffolding, and the bandages have not yet been removed; call the adjacent Watts Tower Arts Center, 1727 E 107th St (☎213/847-4646) to check on their condition.

The **Dunbar Hotel** at 4225 S Central Ave marks the first US hotel built specifically for blacks and patronized by almost every prominent African-American during the 1930s through the 1950s. Unfortunately, you can only see the hotel's restored lobby and facade, as it is now a home for the elderly. For information call the Dunbar Hotel Economic Development Corporation at ☎213/234-7882.

Compton, Inglewood and Gardena

Between Watts and the Harbor Area, only a few districts are of passing interest. Despite its fame as the home of many of LA's rappers – NWA, for example, sang venomously of its ills on their album *Straight Outta Compton* – **COMPTON** is not a place where strangers should attempt to sniff out the local music scene. History buffs secure in their cars, however, might fancy a stop at the **Dominguez Ranch Adobe**, 18127 S Alameda St (Tues & Wed 1–4pm, second & third Sun of each month 1–4pm; free conducted tour ☎213/636-3030), now restored to chronicle the social ascent of its founder, Juan Jose Dominguez – one of the soldiers who left Mexico with Padre Serra's expedition to found the California missions, whose long military service was acknowledged in 1782 by the granting of these 75,000 acres of land. As the importance of the area grew, so did the influence of Dominguez's descendants, who became powerful in local politics.

On the other side of the Harbor Freeway, west of Watts, **INGLEWOOD**, unenticing in itself, is home to the **Hollywood Park Racetrack**, a landscaped track with lagoons and tropical vegetation, and a state-of-the-art computer-operated screen to give punters a view of the otherwise obscured back straight. Next door are the white pillars which ring **The Forum**, the 17,000-seat stadium that is the headquarters of both the LA Lakers (basketball) and the LA Kings (hockey), and is also a major concert venue; see "Listings" on p.166 for more.

One of the safer segments of South Central LA, **GARDENA**, a few miles south, is best known for its large Japanese population and, more importantly, a city ordinance which permits gambling – rare in California. As with Monterey Park and Chinatown for Chinese-Americans, Gardena is an authentic center for Japanese culture, as opposed to the more touristy Little Tokyo. Along Vermont and Western avenues, half a dozen or so clubs devoted to poker are combined with restaurants and cocktail lounges, which charge a half-hourly rental on seats ($1–25). Food and drink are served round the clock, though the bars are separate from the tables. Slightly tacky perhaps, but if you're desperate for a flutter . . .

Crenshaw

As a general rule it's not a good idea to venture into South Central looking for entertainment, unless you are with a local. The **CRENSHAW** district and adjacent **Leimert Park**, on its western fringe, may be an exception. Where the old center of African-American culture was once along Central Avenue, the location of many nightclubs and the focus of a thriving big-name jazz scene, it is now here. Crenshaw and Leimert Park feature a number of restaurants and book and record stores, as well as the B, a multimillion dollar shopping mall created with community redevelopment money and acting as the real commercial center of the area. Beyond Crenshaw, the black upper-middle class resides in **BALDWIN HILLS**, a picturesque district marred by a slew of nearby oil wells.

East LA

You can't visit LA without being made aware of the Hispanic influence on the city's demography and culture, whether it be through the thousands of Mexican restaurants, the innumerable Spanish street names, or, most obviously, through the sheer volume of Spanish spoken by people on the streets. None of this is surprising given

THE GANGS OF LOS ANGELES

South Central LA is the heartland of the city's infamous **gangs**, said to number over one hundred thousand members between them. The gangs have existed for over forty years and often encompass several generations of a family. The black gangs known as Crips and Bloods have many Hispanic counterparts and are often organized by regional chapters. For example, the "Shoreline Gangster Crips" denotes a local gang active in the central ghetto of Venice.

Each new wave of immigration adds to the roster of gangs which usually, though not always, organize themselves by ethnicity, but it's only recently, with the massive influx of drug money, that violence has escalated and automatic weaponry (not least Uzi machine guns) has become commonplace. Although most fatalities (there are about 350 a year) are a direct result of drug-trade rivalry, in recent years there's been an increase in "drive-by shootings", the vast majority of which take place in established gangland areas and typically involve the death of bystanders, often children. It was indicative of LA's entrenched racial and social divisions that it wasn't until the death of a white professional woman during a shoot-out in West LA in 1987 that a gang-related death caused widespread publicity and led to major anti-gang initiatives on the part of the police. The resulting clampdowns have seen a thousand arrests made on a single night, but on the whole have made little real headway in tackling the problem – and seem unlikely to do so until the outlook for people in LA's poorer sections improves.

Despite the violence, an outsider is unlikely to see much evidence of the gangs beyond the occasional blue or red scarf (the colors of the Crips and Bloods) tied around a street sign to denote "territory" and, in some areas, the widespread graffiti consisting of various letters and symbols and almost always indecipherable. Don't expect to witness any inter-gang warfare, unless you do something foolish like cruising down Central Avenue on a Saturday night. As for personal danger, driving through South Central LA by day is generally safe, but be wary of delays at traffic lights, and avoid the area after dusk unless you're with people who know their way around.

LA's proximity to Mexico, but equally apparent are the clear distinctions between the Latino community and white LA. As a rule it's the former who do the menial jobs for the latter, and, although a great number live in the US lawfully, they're also the people who suffer most from the repeated drives against illegal immigration. During the 1992 riots, there were charges of brutality and racism against Immigration and Naturalization Service agents, who may have used the chaos as an opportunity to hunt down undocumented foreign workers.

Of the many Hispanic neighborhoods all over LA, the key one is **EAST LA**, which begins two miles east of downtown, across the concrete-clad dribble of the Los Angeles river. There was a Mexican population here long before the white settlers arrived, and from the late nineteenth century onward millions more arrived, coming here chiefly to work on the land. As the white inhabitants gradually moved west towards the coast, the Mexicans stayed, creating a vast Spanish-speaking community that's more like a Hispanic barrio than part of a North American city.

Activity in East LA (commonly abbreviated to "ELA" or "East Los") tends to be outdoors, in cluttered markets and busy shops. Non-Hispanic visitors are comparatively thin on the ground, but you are unlikely to meet any hostility on the streets during the day – though you should steer clear of the rough and very male-dominated bars, and avoid the whole area after dark.

Guadalupe, the Mexican image of the mother of god, appears in mural art all over East LA, nowhere better than at the junction of Mednik and Cesar Chavez avenues. When a housing project across the street was demolished in the early 1970s, one wall, bearing a particularly remarkable image of the Blessed Mother surrounded by a rich band of rainbow colors, was saved from the wrecking ball and reinstated across the street. Lined with blue tile, it now forms an unofficial shrine where worshippers place fresh flowers and candles.

Other than the street life and murals, there are few specific "sights" in East LA. The best plan is just to turn up on a Saturday afternoon (the liveliest part of the week) and stroll along **Cesar Chavez Avenue**, formerly Brooklyn Avenue, going eastward from Indiana Street and look at the wild pet shops, with free-roaming parrots and cases of boa constrictors, and at the **botanicas shops**, which cater to practitioners of Santeria – a religion that is equal parts voodoo and Catholicism. Browse amid the shark's teeth, dried devil fish and plastic statuettes of Catholic saints and buy magical herbs, ointments or candles after consulting the shopkeeper and explaining (in Spanish) what ails you. Only slightly less exotic fare can be found in **El Mercado de Los Angeles**, 3425 E First St, an indoor market not unlike Olvera Street (see p.79) but much more authentic.

Afterwards, head through the LA district of **Boyle Heights**, which through the 1940s was a center for Jewish culture but has since become a solid Hispanic enclave. Go to the junction of **Soto** and **Cesar Chavez**, where at 5pm each afternoon, *Norteños* combos (upright bass, accordion, guitar and banjo sexto) showcase their talents for free, hoping to be booked for weddings; failing that, listen to the mariachi bands that strike up at 6.30pm outside the Olympic Donut Shop, at First and Boyle, four blocks south of Cesar Chavez Avenue.

Highland Park

North of downtown, the **Pasadena Freeway** curves its way along a dry riverbed towards the foothill community whose name it bears. The freeway, LA's first, was completed in 1940 as the Arroyo Seco Parkway. Highway engineers have since learned their lessons, but be aware that this antiquated roadway has "stop" signs on the on-ramps and exit curves so sharp that the speed limit is 5mph.

Beside the freeway, two miles from downtown, **HIGHLAND PARK** has a number of exuberantly detailed Victorian houses brought together from around the city to form **Heritage Square**, a fenced-off ten-acre park at 3800 Homer St (Fri 10am–3pm, Sat & Sun 11.30am–3pm; $5). Just beyond the next freeway exit, at 200 E Ave 43, the **Lummis House** (Fri–Sun 12–4pm) is the well-preserved home of Charles F. Lummis, a publicist who was at the heart of LA's nineteenth-century boom. Unlike many of the real-estate speculators and journalists who did little more than publicize and glorify aspects of the Southern Californian good life, Lummis did some genuinely good deeds: he was an early champion of civil rights for Native Americans, and worked to save and preserve many of the missions, which were then in ruin. His house was a cultural center of turn-of-the-century Los Angeles, where the literati of the day would meet to discuss poetry and the art and architecture of the Southwest. Lummis built this house for himself in an ad hoc mixture of mission and medieval styles, naming it *El Alisal* after the many large sycamore trees (*Alisal* in Spanish) that shade the gardens. He constructed the thick walls out of rounded granite boulders taken from the nearby riverbed, and the beams over the living room of old telephone poles. The solid wooden front doors are similarly built to last, reinforced with iron and weighing tons, while the plaster-and-tile interior is rustically kitted out with hand-cut timber ceilings and home-made furniture.

The Southwest Museum

Although people in LA scarcely know about it, the **Southwest Museum** (Tues–Sun 11am–5pm; $5, $3 students), which rises castle-like below Mount Washington, was Charles F. Lummis' most enduring achievement and is well worth an afternoon's visit. Half a mile north of the Lummis House (take the #81 or #83 bus from downtown), the recently renovated museum is the oldest in Los Angeles, founded in 1907. Its name is a bit deceptive – there are displays of Native American artifacts from all over North America, with exhibits of pre-Columbian pottery, coastal Chumash rock art and a full-size Plains Indian Cheyenne tepee. The museum also hosts traveling exhibitions, and its educational program of lectures, films and theatrical events have made it an international center for indigenous American cultures. The Braun Research Library has an unmatched collection of recordings and photographs of Native Americans from the Bering Straits to Mexico, and the museum shop features Navajo rugs, kachina dolls and turquoise jewelery, as well as an extensive selection of books and specialist publications.

Nearby, the **Casa de Adobe**, administered by the museum, is a 1917 attempt to recreate a Mexican hacienda. It contains a small museum of its own detailing LA history into the nineteenth century. Call 213/221-2163 for more information.

Hollywood

The violet hush of twilight was descending over Los Angeles as my hostess, Violet Hush, and I left its suburbs headed towards Hollywood. In the distance a glow of huge piles of burning motion-picture scripts lit up the sky. The crisp tang of frying writers and directors whetted my appetite. How good it was to be alive, I thought, inhaling deep lungfuls of carbon monoxide.

S.J. Perelman

If a single place name epitomizes the LA dream of glamor, money and overnight success, it's **HOLLYWOOD**. Ever since American movies, and their stars, became the international symbols of the good life, Hollywood has been a magnet to millions of tourists on once-in-a-lifetime pilgrimages and an equally massive assortment of hopefuls drawn by the thought of riches and glory. Even if the real prospects of success were one in a million, enough people were taken in by the dream to make Hollywood what it is today – a weird combination of insatiable optimism and total despair. It may be a cliché, but Hollywood really does blur the edges of fact and fiction, simply because so much seems possible here – and yet so little, for most residents, actually is.

The truth is that Hollywood was more a center of corruption and scandal than the city of dreams the studio-made legend suggests. Successful Hollywoodites actually spent little time here – they left as soon as they could afford to for the privacy of the hills or coast. Although the area continues to be a secondary center for the film business, with technical service companies like prop shops and equipment suppliers in residence, the big film companies relocated long ago, leaving Hollywood in isolation, with prostitution, drug dealing and seedy adult bookstores becoming the reality behind the fantasy. Things have brightened up a little in the last few years, but the district can still be dangerous on occasion – though not to the extent that you should think twice about coming.

Orientation

Approaching from downtown, **East Hollywood** is the first taste of the district, a ramshackle and grubby area of cheap housing and low-rent businesses where shop signs are often in Spanish. Things pick up in **Central Hollywood**, a compact area that's the real movie history territory, swarmed around by an eccentric street mix of social derelicts and starstruck tourists. Whether the memories have been hammed-up into bizarre shrines, or forgotten and turned into parking lots, Central Hollywood has them in quantity, and you'd have to be avidly uninterested in filmlore to find the place dull. Protecting Hollywood from the outside world, the rising slopes of the Santa Monica Mountains contain **Griffith Park** – several thousand acres of nature offering rugged hiking trails

Hollywood Memorial Cemetery & Paramount Studios ▽

and busy sports and picnic grounds, which forms a scenic northern edge to the area. Beyond the park, the more southerly of the slopes form the high ground known as the **Hollywood Hills**: exclusive homes perched on snaking driveways that are the most tangible reminders of the wealth generated in the city – and the incredible roll call of household names which has sprung from it. A small intermediary area between the park and East Hollywood, **Los Feliz Village** has become a trendy place to live and socialize, so much so that several pop stars have opened small boutiques here.

East Hollywood

By night extremely seedy, by day tattily vibrant, **EAST HOLLYWOOD** is mostly inhabited by Hispanic immigrants who have yet to fulfil the American dream. The area between downtown and Central Hollywood can be particularly unpleasant: this end of Sunset Boulevard is a notorious red-light strip, along whose length Hugh Grant famously encountered Divine Brown in 1995. But as ever in Los Angeles, where perimeter neighborhoods bordering the hills are highly sought after, the streets around Beachwood Avenue, and at the foot of Griffith Park, have evolved into downbeat but popular places to live and hang out, and Mediterranean-style homes now litter the hillside.

Four blocks north of Sunset Boulevard, the **SILVERLAKE** neighborhood was home to some of Hollywood's first studios, now largely converted into trendy restaurants and galleries. Walt Disney opened his first studio at 2719 Hyperion Ave in 1926 (it's now a grocery store); and the Keystone Kops were dreamt up in Mack Sennett's studio at 1712 Glendale Blvd, where just a single sound studio now remains. Another faded bit of movie history can be found in the vicinity of 930 Vendome Street, where a lengthy stairway was a location for Laurel and Hardy's 1932 flick *The Music Box*, in which the

A HISTORY OF HOLLYWOOD

Given its racy character, it's odd to think that Hollywood started life as a **temperance colony**, intended to provide a sober God-fearing alternative to raunchy downtown LA, eight miles away by rough country road. Purchased and named by a pair of devout Methodists in 1887, the district remained autonomous until 1911, when they were forced, in return for a regular water supply, to affiliate their own city to LA as a suburb. The film industry, meanwhile, gathering momentum on the East Coast, needed somewhere with guaranteed sunshine and a diverse assortment of natural backdrops to enable pictures to be made quickly, and somewhere to dodge patent laws that had restricted film-making in the east. Southern California, with its climate, scenery and isolation, was the perfect spot. A few offices affiliated to eastern film companies appeared downtown from 1906 and the first true studios opened in nearby Silverlake, but independent hopefuls soon discovered the cheaper rents on offer in Hollywood. Soon, the first **Hollywood studio** opened in 1911, and within three years the place was packed with filmmakers – many of them, like **Cecil B. DeMille** who shared his barn-converted office space with a horse, destined to be the big names of the future.

The ramshackle industry expanded fast, bringing instant profits and instant fame, and the hopefuls who arrived eager for a slice of both soon swamped the original inhabitants, outraging them with their hedonistic lifestyles. Yet movie-making was far from being a financially secure business, and it wasn't until the release of D.W. Griffith's **The Birth of a Nation** in 1915 that the power of film was demonstrated. The film's right-wing and racist account of the Civil War caused riots outside cinemas and months of critical debate in the newspapers (President Woodrow Wilson described it as "writing history with lightning"), and for the first time drew the middle classes to moviehouses – despite the exorbitant $2 ticket price. It was also the movie which first experimented with the narrative style and production techniques that gradually became standard in classic Hollywood cinema.

Modern Hollywood took shape from the 1920s on, when film production grew more specialized and many small companies either went bust or were incorporated into one of the handful of bigger studios that came to dominate film-making. The **Golden Age** of the studio system was at its peak from the 1930s through the early 1950s, when a Supreme Court ruling put an end to studio monopolies controlling their exhibitors. Despite lean years from the later 1950s until the 1970s, and the onslaught of competition from television, Hollywood's enduring success is in making slick, pleasurable movies that sell – from the hard-bitten *film noir* of the 1940s to the new creativity of filmmakers such as Francis Ford Coppola, Martin Scorsese, David Lynch and Quentin Tarantino. Ultimately, though, it's been big names, big bucks and conservatism that have kept Hollywood alive. With its profits gnawed into by TV and rock music, the film industry today rarely even thinks about taking artistic risks, even as it regularly takes unnecessary financial ones.

lads tried to haul a piano up the many steps, to humorous effect. This is the only point of interest in an otherwise decrepit and unappealing neighborhood.

Nearby **LOS FELIZ VILLAGE** is home to many different communities, with fair-sized Hispanic and gay contingents. On busy summer nights its bars are full of students from the local **American Film Institute** campus, USC party animals, and slumming arty types from the Hollywood Hills. Johnny Depp's *Ed Wood* was partly shot, and premiered, at the architecturally impressive **Vista** movie theater, just off Hollywood Boulevard near Virgil.

Hollyhock House, on a small hill close to the junction of Hollywood Boulevard and Vermont Avenue (Tues–Sun noon–3pm; $2), was the first of architect Frank Lloyd Wright's contributions to LA and was largely supervised by his student, Rudolph Schindler, later one of LA's pre-eminent architects. Completed in 1921, covered with Mayan motifs and imbued with an Art Deco fervour, it's an intriguingly obsessive dwelling, whose original furniture (now replaced by detailed reconstructions) continued the conceptual flow. The bizarre quality of the building was obviously too much for its oil heiress owner, Aline Barnsdall, who lived here only for a short time before donating both the house and the surrounding land to the city authorities for use as a cultural center. In keeping with this wish, the grounds of the house became known as **Barnsdall Art Park**, in which the **Municipal Art Gallery** (Wed–Sun 12.30–5pm, Fri until 8.30pm; $1.50) was erected to give exposure to new Southern Californian artists. If you've no interest in art or architecture, the park is still worth a visit as one of the few quiet spots around here to enjoy a view: the Hollywood Hills in one direction, all of downtown and beyond in the other.

Another Wright building, the 1924 **Ennis-Brown House**, looms over Los Feliz on Glendower Avenue. One of four of his local structures to feature "textile" concrete block, its ominous, pre-Columbian appearance has added atmosphere to over sixty movies, from Vincent Price horror flicks to *Blade Runner*. At 2495 Glendower, the **Fantasy Foundation** (daily 10am–4pm; free) boasts a truly amazing hoard of more than 300,000 items of horror, fantasy and sci-fi memorabilia. Forrest J. Ackerman, former editor of *Famous Monsters of Filmland* magazine and winner of science fiction's first Hugo award, has filled eighteen rooms of the "Ackermansion" with such delights as the fake breasts worn by Jane Fonda in *Barbarella*, the robot from *Metropolis* and the life masks of Boris Karloff, Bella Lugosi and Lon Chaney. Sixty-nine years in the making, this is a unique collection enhanced by the draw of the man himself: numerous personal anecdotes and odds and ends of gossip make his one-on-one tour a must.

Central Hollywood

The myths, magic, fable and fantasy splattered throughout the few short blocks of **CENTRAL HOLLYWOOD** would put a medieval fairytale to shame. With the densest concentration of faded glamor and film mythology in the world, a pervasive sense of nostalgia makes the area deeply appealing in a way no measure of commercialism can diminish. Although you're much more likely to find a porno theater than spot a star (no bona fide "somebody" would be seen dead here these days), the decline that blighted the area from the early 1960s is slowly receding in the face of prolonged efforts by local authorities – including repaving Hollywood Boulevard with a special glass-laden tarmac that sparkles in the streetlights. Nevertheless the place still gets hairy after dark, when the effects of homelessness, drug addiction and prostitution are more evident, Hispanic adolescents cruise Hollywood Boulevard in flashy customized cars and petty thieves go hunting for the odd purse or wallet.

Along Hollywood Boulevard

Following Hollywood Boulevard west, you'll come to the junction of **Hollywood and Vine**, a juxtaposition of street names that still tingles the spines of dedicated Hollywoodphiles, some of whom can be spotted standing in respectful silence before crossing the road. During the golden years the rumour spread that any budding star had only to parade around this junction to be "spotted" by big-shot film directors (the major studios were in those days all concentrated nearby), who nursed coffees behind the windows of neighboring restaurants. In typical Hollywood style the whole tale was blown wildly out of proportion, and while many real stars did pass by, it was only briefly on their way to and from work, and the crossing did nothing but earn a fabulous reputation. The only thing marking the legend today, apart from disappointed tourists, is a small plaque on the wall of the *New York Pizza Express*.

A block on, at Hollywood and Ivar, the ominous **L. Ron Hubbard Life Exhibit** (9.30am–10pm, tours at 10am, 1.30pm, 3.30pm, 5.30pm & 8pm; $5) is the latest manifestation of the Hubbardization of Hollywood, home to the world's highest concentration of Scientologists, including celebrities such as John Travolta. It details Hubbard's early career as a teenage explorer and B-movie and comic book writer, lays out the tenets of Scientology, and culminates in a *Wizard of Oz*-style presentation in which a ten-foot image of Ron dispenses recorded advice at the push of a button. Further along Hollywood Boulevard at no. 6741, the Church's walk-in **Dianetics Testing Center** (read "recruitment office") gives personality tests to people who fear they have "occasional twitches of the muscles when there is no need for it".

The bulky **Knickerbocker Hotel**, 1714 Ivar Ave, is now an old people's retirement center, but was also where the widow of legendary escapologist, Harry Houdini, conducted a rooftop seance in an attempt to assist her late spouse in his greatest escape of all. During the 1930s and 1940s, the hotel had a reputation for rooming some of Hollywood's more unstable characters, and a number of lesser-name suicides plunged from its high windows. At 1817 Ivar St is the flea-bag rooming house where author and screenwriter **Nathanael West** lived during the 1930s, after coming west to revive his flagging financial situation. Gazing over the street's parade of extras, hustlers and make-believe cowboys, West penned the classic satirical portrait of Hollywood, *The Day of the Locust*, the apocalyptic finale of which was inspired by Hollywood Hills wildfires in the summer of 1935.

Back on Hollywood Boulevard, at no. 6608, the purple-and-pink **Frederick's of Hollywood** is a Hollywood landmark. Opened in 1947, it has been (under-)clothing Hollywood's sex goddesses ever since, and many more mortal bodies all over the world through its mail-order outlet. Inside, the **lingerie museum** (Mon–Thurs & Sat 10am–6pm, Fri 10am–9pm, Sun 12–5pm; free) displays some of the company's best corsets, bras and panties, donated by a host of happy big-name wearers, ranging from Liz Taylor and Lana Turner to Cher and Madonna.

A little further on, at no. 6708, the very first Hollywood premiere (*Robin Hood*, an epic swashbuckler starring Douglas Fairbanks Sr), took place in 1922 at the **Egyptian Theater**. Financed by impresario Sid Grauman, in its heyday the Egyptian was a glorious fantasy, modestly seeking to re-create the Temple of Thebes, its usherettes dressed as Cleopatra. This great old building was shattered in the 1994 earthquake, has been bought by the city, and is currently being renovated to become a film study center.

The **Hollywood Wax Museum**, 6767 Hollywood Blvd (Sun–Thurs 10am–midnight, Fri & Sat 10am–2am; $8.25), is a tawdry selection of over two hundred charmless dummies. Besides Spock's ears, Marilyn's backside and Dolly's breasts, there's a replica of Leonardo da Vinci's *The Last Supper* and other "greatest hits" of the art world, like Michelangelo's *Pietà*.

Much of the pavement along this stretch of Hollywood Boulevard is marked by the brass name plates that make up the **Walk of Fame** (officially beginning at Hollywood and Vine). The laying of the plates began in 1960, instigated by the local Chamber of Commerce which thought that by enshrining the big names in radio, television, movies, music and theater, it could somehow restore the boulevard's faded glamor and boost tourism. However, oversights have often been made; the Rolling Stones, for example, took decades to gain a star, long after they were past their prime. Selected stars have to part with several thousand dollars for the privilege of being included: among them are Marlon Brando (1717 Vine St), Marlene Dietrich (6400 Hollywood Blvd), Michael Jackson (6927 Hollywood Blvd), Elvis Presley (6777 Hollywood Blvd) and Ronald Reagan (6374 Hollywood Blvd).

Nothing as vulgar as money can taint the appeal of the foot- and handprints embedded in the concrete concourse of **Mann's Chinese Theatre** at 6925 Hollywood Blvd, opened in 1927 as a lavish setting for premieres of swanky new productions. Through the halcyon decades, this was *the* spot for movie first-nights, and the public crowded behind the rope barriers in their thousands to watch the movie aristocrats arriving for the screenings. The foot-and-hand-prints-in-concrete idea came about when actress

Norma Talmadge accidentally (though some say it was a deliberate publicity stunt) trod in wet cement while visiting the construction site with the owner Sid Grauman. The first formally to leave their marks were Mary Pickford and Douglas Fairbanks Sr, who ceremoniously dipped their digits when arriving for the opening of *King of Kings*, and the practice continues today – Al Pacino was a recent inductee. It's certainly fun to work out the actual dimensions of your favorite film stars, and to discover if your hands are smaller than Julie Andrews' or your feet are bigger than Rock Hudson's (or both). As for the building, it's an odd version of a classical Chinese temple, replete with dodgy Chinese motifs and upturned dragon tail flanks. Try to catch a movie here when a spectacle isn't taking place out front; the Art Deco splendor of the lobby and the grand chinoiserie of the auditorium make for interesting viewing.

To catch a movie in the making, cross the road to the **Motion Picture Production Office**, Room 602, 6922 Hollywood Blvd (Mon–Fri 8am–5pm), which issues a free "shoot sheet" every weekday from 10.30am, detailing exactly what's being filmed around town that day. Most film shoots hire a couple of off-duty LAPD officers for "security", but not all sets are impenetrable.

A few doors down, 7000 Hollywood Blvd, the **Hollywood Roosevelt** was movieland's first luxury hotel. Opened in the same year as the Chinese Theatre, it fast became the meeting place of top actors and screenwriters, its *Cinegrill* restaurant feeding and watering the likes of W.C. Fields, Ernest Hemingway and F. Scott Fitzgerald, not to mention legions of hangers-on. In 1929 the first Oscars were presented here, beginning the long tradition of Hollywood rewarding itself in the absence of honors from elsewhere. Look inside for a view of the splashing fountains and elegantly weighty wrought-iron chandeliers of its marble-floored lobby, and for the intelligently compiled pictorial **History of Hollywood** on the second floor. The place is thick with legend: on the staircase from the lobby to the mezzanine Bill "Bojangles" Robinson taught Shirley Temple to dance; and the ghost of Montgomery Clift (who stayed here while filming *From Here to Eternity*) apparently haunts the place, announcing his presence by blowing a bugle. Surviving lounge divas like Eartha Kitt still put on the occasional show at the *Cinegrill*.

Across the street, the **Hollywood Entertainment Museum**, 7021 Hollywood Blvd (Tues–Sun 10am–6pm; $7.50, students $4.50) is a newly opened site that occupies a lower level of the Hollywood Galaxy theater building. Although it contains the full set of the TV show *Cheers* and of the bridge of the Enterprise from *Star Trek*, along with rotating exhibitions and various antiques and curios from Hollywood history, the museum's real jewel is the **Max Factor Collection**, a display of beauty artifacts from Hollywood's Golden Age which was formerly housed in its own building on Highland Avenue. The famous kissing machine, used to test the endurance of Factor's potions, and the calibration machine, invented to determine which features needed equalizing, are both on show.

Along Sunset Boulevard

There's more Hollywood nostalgia directly south of the central section of Hollywood Boulevard, on and around the less touristy **Sunset Boulevard**, which runs parallel. You might start your explorations at the corner of Sunset Boulevard and **Gower Street**. During the industry's formative years, when unemployed movie extras hopeful of a few days' work with one of the small local B-movie studios would hang around here, the junction earned the nicknames "Gower gulch" and "poverty row".

The delectable Spanish Revival-style building at 6525 Sunset Blvd was, from the 1920s until the 1950s, known as the **Hollywood Athletic Club**. Another of Hollywood's legendary watering holes, the likes of Charlie Chaplin, Clark Gable and Tarzan himself lounged beside its Olympic-sized pool, while Johns Barrymore and Wayne held drinking parties in the apartment levels above. After standing empty for 25 years, the building re-opened in 1990 as a billiards club, bar and restaurant.

The grouping of shops at the **Crossroads of the World**, 6672 Sunset Blvd, isn't much to look at now, but when finished in 1936 this was one of LA's major tourist attractions. The central plaza supposedly resembles a ship, surrounded by shops designed with Tudor, French, Italian and Spanish motifs – the idea being that the shops are the ports into which the shopper would sail. Oddly enough, time has been kind to this place, and considering the more recent and far brasher architecture found in the city, this has a definite, if muted, charm. However, it can be seen in its full glory in the 1997 cop film *LA Confidential*, which also uses the nearby *Formosa Café* (see p.151) and *Frolic Room* as period emblems of 1950s LA swagger.

The Hollywood Memorial Cemetery
Despite the beliefs of some of their loopiest fans, even the biggest Hollywood stars are mortal, and the many LA cemeteries that hold their tombs get at least as many visitors as the city's museums. One of the least heralded and least dramatically landscaped of them, though with more than its fair share of big names, is the **Hollywood Memorial Cemetery** (daily 8am–5pm; free), close to the junction of Santa Monica Boulevard and Gower Street and overlooked by the famous water tower of the neighboring Paramount Studios (whose even more famous gates are just around the corner on Santa Monica Boulevard).

In the southeastern corner of the cemetery, the cathedral mausoleum sets the tone for the place, a solemn collection of tombs that includes, at no. 1205, the resting place of **Rudolph Valentino**. In 1926 10,000 people packed the cemetery when the celebrated screen lover died aged just 31, and to this day on each anniversary of his passing (23 August), at least one "Lady in Black" will likely be found mourning – a tradition that started as a publicity stunt in 1931 (the first weeping damsel claimed to be a former paramour of Valentino's but was exposed as a hired actress) and has continued ever since. While here, spare a thought for the more contemporary screen star, Peter Finch, who died in 1977. His crypt is opposite Valentino's and tourists often lean their rears unknowingly against it while photographing Rudolph's marker.

Fittingly, outside the mausoleum, the most pompous grave in the cemetery belongs to **Douglas Fairbanks Sr** who, with his wife Mary Pickford, did much to introduce social snobbery to Hollywood. Even in death Fairbanks keeps a snooty distance from the pack, his ostentatious memorial, complete with sculptured pond, only reachable by a shrubbery-lined path from the mausoleum. In quite a different vein, one of the cemetery's more recent arrivals was **Mel Blanc**, "the man of a thousand voices" – among them Bugs Bunny, Porky Pig, Tweety Pie and Sylvester – whose epitaph simply reads "That's All, Folks".

Despite its morbid glamor, the cemetery also has a contemporary function. As you enter, you will notice the many tightly packed rows of glossy black headstones with Orthodox crosses and Cyrillic lettering. These mark the resting places of Russian and Armenian immigrants, who increasingly populate the graveyard just as their living counterparts populate Central Hollywood.

Griffith Park

Vast **GRIFFITH PARK**, between Hollywood and the San Fernando Valley (daily 5am–10.30pm, mountain roads close at dusk; free), is a combination of gentle greenery and rugged mountain slopes that makes a welcome escape from the mind-numbing hubbub almost everywhere else in the city. The largest municipal park in the country, it's also one of the few places where LA's multitude of racial and social groups at least go through the motions of mixing together. Above the landscaped flat sections, where the crowds assemble to picnic, play sports or visit the fixed attractions, the hillsides are rough and wild, marked only by foot and bridle paths, leading into desolate but appealingly unspoilt terrain that gives great views over the LA basin and out towards the ocean. Bear in mind, though, that while the park is safe by day, its reputation for after-dark violence is well founded.

Around the park

There are four **main entrances** to Griffith Park. Western Canyon Road, north of Los Feliz Boulevard, enters the park through **the Ferndell** – as the name suggests, a lush glade of ferns, from which numerous trails run deeper into the park – continuing up to the **Observatory** (summer daily 12.30–10pm; rest of year Tues–Fri 2–10pm, Sat & Sun 12.30–10pm; free), familiar from its use as a backdrop in *Rebel Without A Cause* and numerous low-budget sci-fi flicks, and with moderately interesting science displays and shows in the Planetarium (Tues–Fri 3pm & 7.30pm, Sat & Sun 1.30–7.30pm; $4) and Laserium (Sun–Thurs 6pm & 8.45pm, Fri–Sat & various holidays 6pm, 8.45pm & 9.45pm; $6.50). More enticingly, on clear nights there are brilliant views of the cosmos through the powerful **telescope** mounted on the roof (daily 7–10pm; free). One Saturday a month, the LA Astronomical Society gathers on the front lawn. Thirty or forty telescopes and their knowledgeable owners set up at 1pm to see the sun through filters and stay until the area closes, happy to discuss the planets and stars with passers-by.

Descending from the observatory by way of Vermont Canyon Road (effectively the continuation of Western Canyon Road) brings you to the small **bird sanctuary**, set within a modest-sized wooded canyon. Various species have been encouraged to nest here, but as the birds aren't in captivity you might not see them. Across the road is the **Greek Theatre**, an open-air amphitheater that seats nearly five thousand beneath its Greek-style columns – though if you're not going in for a show (the *Greek* is a venue for big-name rock, jazz and country music concerts during summer) you'll see just the bland exterior.

Opposite the entrance to the park on the corner of Riverside Drive and Los Feliz Boulevard is the **William Mulholland Memorial Fountain**, whose cascades are a reminder of the man credited with building the aqueduct that gave the city its first reliable supply of water in 1913, a feat that's part of a long saga laced with scandal and corruption (see p.138). His reputation was ultimately ruined when his St Francis dam gave way in 1928 and killed 450 people.

Crystal Springs Drive, off Riverside Drive, takes you to the ranger station, and the **northern end** of the park, over the hills in the San Fernando Valley, is best reached directly by car from the Golden State Freeway, although you can take the park roads (or explore the labyrinth of hiking trails) that climb the park's hilly core. At the end of the journey, don't bother with the cramped **LA Zoo** (summer daily 10am–6pm; rest of year daily 10am–5pm; $8.25) or the unkempt old locomotives of **Travel Town** (Mon–Fri 10am–5pm, Sat & Sun 10am–6pm; free).

HIKING AND BIKING IN GRIFFITH PARK

The steeper parts of **Griffith Park**, which blend into the foothills of the Santa Monica Mountains, are the focus of a variety of **hikes**. You can get maps from the **ranger station**, at 4730 Crystal Springs Rd (☎213/655-5188) – also the starting point for guided hikes and atmospheric evening hikes, held whenever there's a full moon. The rangers also have maps for drivers that detail the best vantage points for views over the whole of Los Angeles, not least from the highest place in the park – the summit of Mount Hollywood. The park is also a great place for **cycling**; the closest place to rent a bike is Woody's Bicycle World, 3157 Los Feliz Blvd (☎213/661-6665), located across I-5 in Atwater Village.

The Gene Autry Western Heritage Museum

Sharing a parking lot with the zoo, the **Gene Autry Western Heritage Museum** (Tues–Sun 10am–5pm; $7, students $5), at the northeastern corner of Griffith Park near the junction of the Ventura and Golden State freeways, bears the name of the "singing cowboy" who cut over six hundred discs from 1929, starred in blockbusting Hollywood Westerns during the 1930s and 1940s, and became even more of a household name through his TV show in the 1950s.

Autry fans hoping for a shrine to the man who pined the immortal *That Silver-Haired Daddy of Mine*, are in for a shock, however: the **collection** – from buckskin jackets and branding irons to Frederic Remington's sculptures of turn-of-the-century Western life and the truth about the shoot-out at the OK Corral – is a serious and very credible attempt to explore the mind-set and concerns of those who participated in the US's colonization of the West. It also contains a nod to Hollywood, with a sizeable collection of movie artifacts, posters and assorted memorabilia, much of it also discussed in an analytical, non-jingoistic fashion.

The Hollywood Hills

Quite apart from giving the chance to appreciate how flat the LA basin is, the views from the **Hollywood Hills** feature perhaps the oddest, most opulent, selection of properties to be found anywhere. Around these canyons and slopes, which run from Hollywood itself into Benedict Canyon above Beverly Hills, mansions are so commonplace that only the half-dozen fully blown castles (at least, Hollywood-style castles) really stand out.

Mulholland Drive, which runs along the crest, passes some of the most notorious abodes – Rudolph Valentino's extravagant **Falcon Lair**; Errol Flynn's **Mulholland House**; the former home of actress Sharon Tate, where some of the Manson family killings took place; and a number of run-of-the-mill million-dollar residences belonging to an assortment of luminaries, visionaries, former politicians and movie moguls, some of whom have helped forge LA's reputation for ostentatious and utterly decadent living.

Unfortunately, though, most of the houses are hidden away, and there's no real way to explore in depth without your own car and a knowledgeable friend to help pinpoint

THE°HOLLYWOOD SIGN

One thing you can see from more or less anywhere in Hollywood is the **Hollywood Sign**, erected to spell "Hollywoodland" in 1923 as a promotional device to sell property at the foot of the hills. The "land" part was removed in 1949, leaving the rest as a world-renowned symbol of the entertainment industry here. It has also (unjustifiably) gained a reputation as a suicide spot, ever since would-be movie star Peg Entwhistle terminated her career and life here in 1932, aged 24. It was no mean feat – the sign being as difficult to reach then as it is now: from the end of Beachwood Drive she picked a path slowly upward through the thick bushes and climbed the fifty-foot-high "H", eventually leaping from it to her death. Stories that this act led to a line of failed starlets desperate to make their final exit from Tinseltown's best known marker are untrue however – though many troubled souls may have died of exhaustion while trying to get to it. Less fatal mischief has been practiced by students of nearby Caltech, who on one occasion tried to rename the sign for their school. More unsavory acts of sign desecration have also occurred, most of them too juvenile and numerous to mention. Because of this history, there's no public road to the sign (Beachwood Drive comes nearest, but ends at a closed gate) and you'll incur minor cuts and bruises while scrambling to get anywhere near. In any case, infrared cameras and radar-activated zoom lenses have been installed to catch graffiti writers, and innocent tourists who can't resist a close look are also liable for the $103 fine. It's simply not worth the bother.

the sights, spread widely across every hillside. You could use one of the guided tours (see p.70), but for the most part you're better off doing your own exploring, preferably with a copy of the latest *Thomas Guide* map and, if possible, a detailed and updated guide to LA architecture.

Lake Hollywood

Hemmed in among the hills between Griffith Park and the Hollywood Freeway, **Lake Hollywood** feels like a piece of open country in the heart of the city. The clear, calm waters, actually a reservoir intended to lubricate the whole of LA in times of drought, make a delightful spot, surrounded by clumps of pines in which squirrels, lizards and a few scurrying skunks and coyotes easily outnumber humans. You can't get too near the water, as metal fences protect it from the general public, but the footpaths that encircle it are pleasant for a stroll. There's no social kudos associated with being seen trotting around the footpath – which may explain why so few Angelenos deem it worthy of their presence. Nevertheless, the lake has figured in a few Hollywood films, notably the disaster epic *Earthquake*, which showed the dam bursting and flooding the basin to devastating effect. Of course, apocalypse is a constant theme in stories about LA.

You can only reach the lake by car. Although opening and closing times vary widely throughout the year, the lake **access road** is generally open from 7am until noon and 2pm until 7pm on weekdays, and 7am until 7.30pm on weekends: to get to it, go north on Cahuenga Boulevard past Franklin Avenue and turn right onto Dix Street, left into Holly Drive and climb to Deep Dell Place; from there it's a sharp left on Weidlake Drive. Follow the winding little street to the main gate.

The Hollywood Bowl

Where Highland Avenue hits the Hollywood Freeway, the **Hollywood Bowl** is an open-air auditorium opened in 1921, which has since gained more fame than it deserves. The Beatles played here in the mid-1960s, but the Bowl's principal function is as home to the Los Angeles Philharmonic, which gives evening concerts from July to September. These are far less highbrow than you might imagine, many of them featuring pop pieces like *Victory at Sea* and the *1812 Overture*. It's long been the done thing to eat a picnic in the grounds before making the climb to your seat, and nowadays the consumption tends to continue throughout the show, often rendering the music barely audible above the crunching of popcorn and fried chicken, and the clink of empty wine bottles rolling down the steps. It's probably not a choice spot for lovers of fine music, but can be fun nonetheless, and ticket prices start at $1. If you're really broke, come to the Bowl Tuesday through Friday between 9.30am and noon to listen to rehearsals for free.

More about the Bowl's history can be gleaned from the video show inside the **Hollywood Bowl Museum** (summer 10am–8.30pm; rest of year Tues–Sat 10am–4pm; free) near the entrance, which has recently been refurbished. It's not an essential stop by any means, but is worth a visit if you have any affection for the grand old concrete shell. With a collection of musical instruments from around the world, the museum also features recordings of notable symphonic moments in the Bowl's history and architectural drawings by Lloyd Wright, Frank's son (more famous for his Wayfarer's Chapel; see p.121).

West LA

LA's Westside begins immediately beyond Hollywood in **WEST LA**, which contains some of the city's most expensive neighborhoods. Bordered by the foothills of the Santa Monica Mountains to the north and the Santa Monica Freeway to the south, West LA is fashionable LA, and perhaps closer than anywhere else to embodying the stylish images that the city projects to the outside world. Actually, once you're there, the reality is often less dazzling: away from the showcase streets are the usual long, residential blocks, only marginally less drab than normal with their better tended lawns, swisher supermarkets, cleaner gas stations – and a higher class of fast-food stand.

The single best reason to come to West LA is the engrossing collection of the **LA County Museum of Art**, on the eastern perimeter of the area in the still firmly Jewish **Fairfax** district. It's not until you cross west of Fairfax Avenue and north of Beverly Boulevard that West LA truly reveals itself in **West Hollywood** – known for its art and design, clogged by posey restaurants and boutiques, and surprisingly small-scale, except for a giant design center at its core. **Beverly Hills**, a little way west, is less gregarious but more affluent: you may need an expense account to buy a sandwich but it's a matchless place to indulge in upscale window shopping on the way to the more roundly appealing **Westwood Village**. The main business in this low-rise, Spanish Revival, near-pedestrianized area has always been movies – seeing them rather than making them. The original Art Deco palaces still remain, a short way from the **UCLA Campus** – the second of LA's university sites, home to a number of galleries and museums and altogether more appealing for visitors than the fortress atmosphere of USC. The **Sepulveda Pass** forms the western edge of West LA and leads the visitor to two museums that have recently relocated to the area: the **Getty Center** and the **Skirball Cultural Center**, both positioned high above the basin's turmoil.

The Fairfax District and the LA County Museum of Art

The West LA section of **Fairfax Avenue**, between Santa Monica and Wilshire, is the backbone of the city's Jewish culture. Apart from countless temples, yeshivas, kosher butcher shops and delicatessens there's little actually to see here, but by local standards it's a refreshingly vibrant neighborhood, and easily explored on foot. Fairfax continues down to the lacklustre wooden structures of **Farmer's Market**, at the junction with Third Street (June–Sept Mon–Sat 9am–8pm; Oct–May Mon–Sat 9am–6.30pm, Sun 10am–5pm; free). The market is a rabbit warren of food stalls and produce stands, the former offering greasy treats and the latter more natural delights. To the east on Third Street, **Pan Pacific Park** once featured the wondrous Streamline Moderne Pan Pacific Auditorium, a masterpiece of late Art Deco architecture. However, the structure burned in a 1989 fire, and only a pleasant park of the same name remains. Further on, the May Company department store on Wilshire Boulevard was built in 1934 and has been compared to an oversized perfume bottle ever since. The store was placed here to announce the western entrance to the premier property development of the time, **Miracle Mile**, as it was named, which stretched along Wilshire eastward to La Brea Avenue and is still lined with Art Deco monuments. The department stores have long since closed, but an unprecedented number of museums, including LACMA, now create an impressive "Museum Mile" in their place. Although many of the office blocks are empty, look out for the old site of **Desmond's**, a former department store at no. 5514 consisting of a Zigzag Moderne tower stepping up from a streamlined two-story pedestal, and, just east of La Brea Avenue, the 1929 black-and-gold **Security Pacific Bank**. The bank gives you a hint of what LA's greatest Art Deco structure, the **Richfield Building** downtown, must have looked like before it was summarily destroyed in 1968.

LACMA, the La Brea Tar Pits and Peterson Automotive Museum
Oddly enough, the **LA County Museum of Art** or **LACMA** (Mon–Tues & Thurs noon–8pm, Fri noon–9pm, Sat & Sun 11am–8pm; $6, students $4) is an unimpressive series of buildings along Miracle Mile that was plopped down in 1965 in a fit of municipal-mindedness that has never really taken root. The buildings aside, some of the collections of applied art here are among the best in the world, and despite the loss of Armand Hammer's stock of paintings to his own museum in Westwood (see p.112), it justifies a lengthy visit. If you arrive on a Wednesday before 1pm, check out the schedule of films playing in the **Leo S. Bing Theater**, where you can see anything from a Hitchcock classic to a screwball comedy for only $2.

LACMA is enormous, and there's no way you could see the lot in one go; you're best off either focusing on the contemporary art and traveling exhibitions in the **Anderson Building** or diving into the fine selection of Old Masters and world art in the **Ahmanson Building**. Get a **map** of the complex from the information desk in the central courtyard. Alongside many excellent collections of Southeast Asian sculpture and Middle Eastern decorative arts in the Ahmanson Building, the **Fearing Collection** consists of funeral masks and sculpted guardian figures from the ancient civilizations of pre-Columbian Mexico. Where the museum really excels, however, is in its specializations, notably the prints and drawings in the **Robert Gore Rifkind Center for German Expressionist Studies**, which includes a library of magazines and tracts from Weimar Germany, and the **Pavilion for Japanese Art**. This is a recent addition to the museum and the only effective building on the site; it was created by iconoclastic architect Bruce Goff and built to resemble the effects of traditional *shoji* screens, filtering varying levels and qualities of light through to the interior. Displays include painted screens and scrolls, ceramics, and lacquerware, rivalling the collection of the late Emperor Hirohito as the most extensive in the world.

The roof combs of the pavilion make a playful reference to the tusks of a model mastodon sinking slowly into the adjacent **La Brea Tar Pits**, a large pool of smelly tar (*"la brea"* is Spanish for tar) surrounded by full-size models of mastodons and sabretooth tigers. In prehistoric times, such creatures tried to drink from the thin layer of water covering the tar in the pits, only to become stuck fast and preserved for modern science. Millions of bones belonging to the animals (and one set of human bones) have been found here and reconstructed in the adjacent **George C. Page Discovery Center** (Tues–Sat 10am–5pm; $6, students $3.50). Tar still seeps from the ground, but most of the sticky goo is kept out of range behind chain link fences.

At 6060 Wilshire Blvd, the **Peterson Automotive Museum** (daily 10am–6pm; Fri until 9pm; $7). The baby of media mogul Robert Peterson, its three floors pay sumptuous if superficial homage to the automobile, with special exhibits of movie stars' cars, customized lowriders and vintage footage of land-speed record attempts in the desert. It fails to explain the reasons behind the collapse of LA's early public transportation system and is not critical by any means, but it has enough mint-condition classic models to render the car-crazy delirious with joy.

The next museum along the road is the curious **Carol and Barry Kaye Museum of Miniatures**, 5900 Wilshire Blvd (Tues–Sat 10am–5pm, Sun 11am–5pm; $7.50, students $5), housing the world's most comprehensive collection of miniatures. Exhibits include a Victorian mansion, medieval palace, Japanese garden and Hollywood Bowl, complete with pint-sized Ella, Satchmo and Dizzy.

St Elmo's Village

Not far from the art works on display in the County Museum, **St Elmo's Village** at 4836 St Elmo Drive, a mile south of Wilshire (☎213/931-3409), is a popular version of community art-in-action. An arts project now more than twenty years old, the colorful murals and sculptures here grew out of efforts to foster a constructive and supportive environment for local youth. It's now also the site of the **Festival of the Art of Survival**, an annual celebration of hippy-flavoured folk and popular art and music held each Memorial Day.

West Hollywood

Between Fairfax Avenue and Beverly Hills, **WEST HOLLYWOOD** is the newest of LA's constituent cities. Thanks to various legal technicalities, it was for many years a separate administrative entity from the rest of Los Angeles, notorious for its after-hours vice clubs and general debauchery. Things changed in 1983, however, when the autonomous city of West Hollywood was established, partly to clean up the place and partly to represent the interests of the predominantly gay community. There are still sleazy rent-boy areas around La Brea Avenue in the east, but much of the rest has smartened up considerably, from the new sculpture garden down the center of **Santa Monica Boulevard**, the district's main drag, to the flashy dance clubs and designer clothes stores appearing over the rest of the neighborhood. In front of the **Tomkat Theater**, beneath a marquee that has proclaimed everything from *Deep Throat* to *In Thrust We Trust*, the alternative **Porno Walk of Fame** is devoted entirely to X-rated film stars. By way of contrast, the eastern end of the boulevard has recently become home to a large and growing contingent of Russians, not all of whom mesh well with the affluent gay scene around them.

Melrose Avenue, LA's trendiest shopping street, runs parallel to Santa Monica Boulevard three blocks south, a streetscape that at times resembles nothing more than a low-budget 1950s sci-fi feature: neon and Art Deco abound among a fluorescent rash of designer and second-hand boutiques, exotic antique shops, avant-garde galleries, record shops and high-fashion restaurants. The west end of Melrose is more upmarket, with furniture shops and art galleries spread out around the hulking, bright blue glass mass of the **Pacific Design Center**, a furniture marketplace near San Vicente Boulevard known as the "Blue Whale" for the way it dwarfs its low-rise neighbors.

The stylistic extremes of Melrose Avenue are also reflected in the area's domestic architecture. Three blocks east of La Cienega Boulevard, the 1922 **Schindler House**, 835 N King's Rd (tours Sat & Sun 1–5pm, and by appointment; ☎213/651-1510; $5 donation), was for years the blueprint of California Modernist architecture, with sliding canvas panels designed to be removed in summer, exposed roof rafters, and open-plan rooms facing onto outdoor terraces – banal in replication but compelling in the original. Coming from his native Austria via Frank Lloyd Wright's studio to work on the Hollyhock House (p.96), Schindler was so pleased with the California climate that he built this house without any bedrooms, romantically planning to sleep outdoors year-round in covered sleeping baskets on the roof; he misjudged the weather, however, and soon moved inside.

Four blocks west, **La Cienega Boulevard** divides West Hollywood roughly down the middle, separating the next-wave trendies on the Hollywood side from the establishment couturiers on the Beverly Hills border. La Cienega ("the swamp" in Spanish) holds a mixture of LA's best and most expensive restaurants and art galleries, and continues south, passing the huge **Beverly Center** shopping mall at Beverly Boulevard – a nightmarish fortress of brown plaster that was thrown up in 1982 on top of the fun-but-faded **Beverlyland** amusement park. Another landmark structure, and one that managed to survive the wrecker's ball by some adroit repositioning, is the **Tail o' the Pup**, the world-famous hot-dog stand shaped like a (mostly bun) hot dog, which was moved a block away from La Cienega to 329 San Vicente Blvd to make way for the garish *Sofitel* hotel.

Further south, right on the Beverly Hills border at 333 S La Cienega, the Academy of Motion Picture Arts and Sciences' **Margaret Herrick Library** (Mon–Tues & Thurs–Fri 10am–6pm) is a research library that holds a huge hoard of film memorabilia and scripts inside a Moorish-style building that used to be a water treatment plant.

Sunset Strip

Above western Hollywood, on either side of La Cienega Boulevard, the roughly two-mile long conglomeration of restaurants, plush hotels and nightclubs on Sunset Boulevard has long been known as **Sunset Strip**. These establishments first began to appear during the early 1920s, along what was then a dusty dirt road serving as the main route between the Hollywood movie studios and the West LA "homes of the stars". F. Scott Fitzgerald and friends spent many leisurely afternoons over drinks here, around the swimming pool of the long-demolished *Garden of Allah* hotel, and the nearby *Ciro's* nightclub was *the* place to be seen in the swinging 1940s, surviving today as the original *Comedy Store*. With the rise of TV the Strip declined, only reviving in the 1960s when a scene developed around the landmark *Whisky-a-Go-Go* club, which featured seminal psychedelic rock bands such as Love and Buffalo Springfield during the heyday of West Coast flower power. Since the incorporation of West Hollywood, the striptease clubs and "head shops" have been phased out, and this fashionable area now rivals Beverly Hills for entertainment-industry executives per square foot.

WEST HOLLYWOOD

0   500 yds

Beverly Hills
Library/Civic Center

Pacific
Design
Center

Cedars-Sinai
Hospital

Beverly
Center

RESTAURANTS

1 Barefoot
2 Barney's Beanery
3 Ca' Brea
4 Canter's Deli
5 Cava
6 Chianti
7 Chin Chin
8 Citrus
9 Duke's
10 East India Grill
11 Eat A Pita
12 Ed Debevic's
13 El Coyote
14 Erewhon
15 Figs
16 French Market Place
17 Georgia
18 The Gumbo Pot
19 Hard Rock Café
20 Inaka
21 India's Oven
22 Jerry's Famous Deli
23 Johnie's
24 Kate Mantilini
25 La Masia
26 Locanda Veneta
27 L'Orangerie
28 Mark's
29 Mishima
30 Noura
31 Spago
32 Swingers
33 Tail o' the Pup
34 Tommy Tang's

BARS AND NIGHTCLUBS

35 Billboard Live
36 Café Largo
37 Coconut Teaszer
38 Doug Weston's Troubador
39 Formosa Café
40 Girl Bar
41 Klub Banshee
42 Lunapark
43 Molly Malone's
44 The Palms
45 Rage
46 The Roxy
47 7969
48 Union
49 The Viper Room
50 Whisky-a-Go-Go

For reviews of all the above places, see "Eating", "Drinking: bars, pubs and cafés" and "Nightlife" listings starting on p 139.

Some tourists come to the strip just to see the enormous **billboards**. The ruddy-faced and reassuring Marlboro Man is now a fixture, but there are many more along the strip that consistently re-invent the medium: fantastic commercial murals animated with eye-catching gimmicks, movie ads with names like "Schwarzenegger" in gargantuan letters and self-promotions for unknown actors whose dream is to loom over Tinseltown in day-glo splendor.

Greta Garbo was only one of many stars and starlets to appreciate the quirky character of the huge Norman castle that is the **Chateau Marmont Hotel**, towering over the east end of Sunset Strip at no. 8221. Built in 1927 as luxury apartments, this stodgy block of white concrete has long been a Hollywood favorite. Howard Hughes used to rent the entire penthouse so he could keep an eye on the bathing beauties around the pool below, and the hotel made the headlines in 1982 when comedian John Belushi died of a heroin overdose in the hotel bungalow that he used as his LA home. Belushi's spirit lives on across the street at no. 8430: the **House of Blues**, in which his estate and one-time partner Dan Aykroyd are prime investors, is a bar in the *Hard Rock Café/Planet Hollywood* mould (see p.156), and plays much of the man's music.

Beverly Hills and Century City

Probably the most famous small city in the world, **BEVERLY HILLS** has over the years sucked in more than its fair share of wealthy residents (the local pawnbrokers have an Oscar and a Ferrari for sale). It's not a particularly welcoming place, especially if your clothes don't match the elegant attire of the residents – the pets in Beverly Hills are better dressed and groomed than some of the people elsewhere in LA. It can be fun, though, to stroll the designer stores of Rodeo Drive and, if driving, take a spin by the mansions up in the canyons before the police (and Beverly Hills has more police per capita than anywhere else in the US) ask for your ID.

Beverly Hills divides into two distinct halves, separated by the old train line down Santa Monica Boulevard. Below the tracks are the flatlands of modest houses on rectangular blocks, set around the "Golden Triangle" business district that fills the wedge between Santa Monica and Wilshire Boulevards. **Rodeo Drive** cuts through the triangle in a two-block-long concentrated showcase of the most expensive names in international fashion. It's an intimidatingly stylish area, each boutique trying to outshine the rest: none as yet charges for admission, though some require an invitation. Presumably by virtue of their impeccable movie star credentials, the owners of **Planet Hollywood** have opened a massive food and merchandising operation right next to an exclusive shopping area adjacent to Rodeo on Wilshire – a coup beyond the dreams of *McDonald's* or *Burger King*. Look out for the tourist trap of **Two Rodeo** nearby, a *faux* European shopping alley that is the height of pretentious kitsch. Much more worthwhile is the newly opened **Museum of Television and Radio** at 465 N Beverly Drive (Wed–Sun noon–5pm, Thurs until 9pm; $6, students $4), which features a collection of more than 75,000 TV and radio programs and is LA's first real attempt at providing a media museum of scholarly value. The city still awaits a decent film museum, however.

Above Santa Monica Boulevard is the upmarket part of residential Beverly Hills, its gently curving drives converging on the gorgeous and gauche pink plaster **Beverly Hills Hotel**, on Sunset and Rodeo. Built in 1913 to attract wealthy settlers to what was then a town of just five hundred people, and currently owned by the Sultan of Brunei, the hotel's social cachet makes its *Polo Lounge* a prime spot for movie execs to power-lunch.

In the verdant canyons and foothills above Sunset a number of palatial estates lie hidden away behind landscaped security gates. **Benedict Canyon Drive** climbs from the hotel up past many of them, beginning with the first and most famous: the site of the lavish **PickFair** mansion at 1143 Summit Drive, built for Mary Pickford and Douglas Fairbanks in 1919 and demolished by Pia Zadora in the 1980s. Further up Benedict Canyon, Harold Lloyd's **Green Acres**, where he lived for forty years, with its secret passageways and large private screening room, survives intact, though the grounds, which contained a waterfall and a nine-hole golf course, have since been broken up into smaller lots.

The grounds of the biggest house in Beverly Hills, Greystone Mansion, are now maintained as a public park by the city, which uses it to disguise a massive underground reservoir. Though the fifty-thousand-square-foot manor house is rarely open, you can visit the sixteen-acre **Greystone Park** (daily 10am–5pm) at 905 Loma Vista, which affords fine views of the LA sprawl and its attendant pollution. Up the hill are the fabulously expensive tract homes of **Trousdale Estates**, a late-Fifties exercise in ostentatious banality, with two sub-repro Greek columns per stucco shed and, as a bonus, a panoramic view.

Century City

The gleaming boxes of **CENTURY CITY**, just west of Beverly Hills, were erected during the Sixties on the backlot of the 20th Century-Fox film studios. The plate-glass office towers aren't at all inviting, rising sharply and inhospitably skywards from sidewalks that have never been used – a perhaps typically Sixties disaster, planned at a time when pedestrian concerns were considered irrelevant. The massive **ABC Entertainment Center** complex, on Avenue of the Stars, might conceivably bring you here – its *Shubert Theater* (see p.160) is one of LA's leading live theaters, specializing in touring productions of the latest Andrew Lloyd Webber hit.

Along the south edge of Century City, **Pico Boulevard** is quintessential LA: mile after mile of single-story shop fronts, auto parts stores and delis, with a mini-mall on every other corner. To the west, look through the front gates of the still-working **20th Century-Fox** film and TV studios to catch a glimpse of the intact New York City street set used for the production of *Hello Dolly!*.

Less frivolously, just east of Century City, below Beverly Hills, an inauspicious white building houses the **Simon Wiesenthal Center for Holocaust Studies** at 9786 West Pico Blvd. The US headquarters of the organization devoted to tracking down ex-Nazis, the center has an extensive library of Holocaust-related documents, photographs and accounts – but the main draw for visitors is the affecting **Beit HaShoa Museum of Tolerance** (Mon–Thurs 10am–4pm, Fri 10am–3pm, Sun 11am–4pm; $8), an extraordinary interactive resource center aimed at exposing the lies of revisionist historians. The most technologically advanced institution of its kind, it uses videotaped interviews to provide LA's frankest examination of the 1992 riots, and leads the visitor through re-enactments outlining the rise of Nazism to a harrowing conclusion in a replica gas chamber.

Westwood Village, UCLA and the Sepulveda Pass

Just west of Beverly Hills, on the north side of Wilshire Boulevard, **WESTWOOD VILLAGE** is one of LA's more user-friendly neighborhoods, a grouping of low-slung red-brick buildings that went up in the late 1920s, along with the nearby campus of the nascent University of California at Los Angeles (UCLA). It's an area that's easily explored on foot, and one very much shaped by the proximity of the university campus, which is really the lifeblood of the area. Because of its ease for pedestrians, the neighborhood has limited parking; for minimum frustration, find a cheap parking lot and dump your vehicle there for a few hours while you explore.

Broxton Avenue, the main strip of Westwood Village, was for many years the weekend cruising strip of choice for Westside teenagers. Following a gang-related shooting outside on Broxton in the late-1980s, the popularity of the area waned, although it still attracts students making the circuit of record stores, video parlours and diners. It's also a big movie-going district, with thirty or so cinema screens within a quarter-mile radius.

Much of the original Spanish Revival design has survived the intervening years of less imaginative construction, though the ordinary businesses of the old days have been replaced by fancy boutiques and designer novelty shops. The tower at the end of the street belongs to the 1931 **Fox Westwood Village**, which, together with the neon-signed Bruin across the street, is sometimes used by movie studios for "sneak" previews of films to gauge audience reaction, and is now part of the Mann theater chain.

South of the village, Westwood Boulevard has more cinemas, a few interesting shops and a number of specialist bookstores below Wilshire Boulevard. This section of Wilshire exploded in the 1970s with oil-rich high-rise developments, leading to a change of scale that would seem bizarre anywhere outside of LA. Modest detached houses sit next to twenty-story condo towers in which penthouse apartments with private heliports sell for upwards of $12 million.

Inside one of the towers, on the corner with Westwood Boulevard, the **Armand Hammer Museum of Art and Culture Center** (Tues–Wed & Fri–Sat 11am–7pm, Thurs 11am–9pm, Sun 11am–5pm; $4.50, students $3, Thurs 6–9pm free) is one of the city's most debated art stashes, amassed over seven decades by the flamboyant and ultra-wealthy boss of the Occidental Petroleum Corporation. Art critic Robert Hughes called the paintings here "a mishmash of second or third-rate works by famous names", but while the Rembrandts and Rubens may be less than stunning, the nine-teenth-century pieces like Van Gogh's intense and radiant *Hospital at Saint Remy* more than make amends.

Across Wilshire from the museum, at the end of the driveway behind the tiny Avco cinema, you'll find Hammer's speckled marble tomb, sharing the tiny cemetery of **Westwood Memorial Park** with the likes of movie stars Peter Lorre and Natalie Wood, wildman jazz drummer Buddy Rich, and, to the left of the entrance in the far northeast corner, the lipstick-covered plaque that marks the resting place of **Marilyn Monroe**.

The UCLA campus

The **UCLA campus** is the dominant feature in Westwood, a grouping of Italianate buildings spread generously over well-landscaped grounds. It's worth a wander if you've time to kill, particularly for a couple of good exhibition spaces. The student union building, at the north end of Westwood Boulevard, half a mile north of the village, has a bowling alley, a good bookstore and a "rideboard" offering shared-expense car rides, and there's also a decent coffeehouse, in Kerckhoff Hall just behind.

Before embarking on your exploration, pick up a **map** from various information kiosks scattered around campus. Of things to see, the spacious rotunda of the **Powell Library**, on one side of the central quadrangle, was where Aldous Huxley put in long hours at the card catalogs in the late 1930s, researching his novel *After Many a Summer*, based on the life and legend of William Randolph Hearst. At the northern end of campus – fronted by the large Franklin D. Murphy **Sculpture Garden** (always open; free) which contains work by Rodin, Maillol, Moore and other modern artists, shaded by jacaranda trees – the **Wight Art Gallery** holds a variety of top-quality visiting exhibitions (Tues–Fri 11am–5pm, Sat & Sun 1–5pm; free).

Nearby, UCLA's **film school** is less mainstream and industry-oriented than USC's film school, and has produced offbeat film-makers like Francis Ford Coppola, Alison Anders and Alex Cox; it also has one of the most extensive collections of old films and TV programs in the world, examples of which are shown daily, often for free, in the large auditorium in **Melnitz Hall**. Check the bulletin board in the lobby or phone ☎310/206-FILM for the current schedule.

The Sepulveda Pass

The gap through the Santa Monica Mountains known as the **Sepulveda Pass** was, like the boulevard and nearby community, named for Mexican soldier Francisco Sepúlveda, who gained ownership in 1839 of the Rancho San Vicente y Santa Monica, which once encompassed the surrounding area. Now, the pass is best known for the 405 freeway that cuts through it, but it also contains part of Sepulveda Boulevard, the longest road in the city or county of Los Angeles, which leads from Long Beach into the San Fernando Valley. Recently, the pass has become more important as it connects several key museums in the area.

Starting at Sunset Boulevard just northwest of UCLA, you can follow the pass as it divides several of LA's most exclusive residential zones. **Brentwood** to the west is an insular enclave best known for being the former home of O.J. Simpson; to the east, **Bel Air** is a hillside community that is similarly well-heeled and boasts a particularly fine hotel, the Bel Air (see p.73). A short distance away is Getty Center Drive, which leads up to the monumental **Getty Center** (Tues–Wed 11am–7pm, Thurs–Fri 11am–9pm, Sat & Sun 10am–6pm; free), a gleaming complex that towers over the city as oil titan J. Paul Getty once towered over his competitors. You cannot stop at the Center on a whim, however. Reservations for parking, which costs $5, are always made in advance and are difficult to get on weekends or holidays. However, if you arrive by cab or bus (the #561 line, which you can pick up at LAX), you are assured entry.

Designed by arch-modernist Richard Meier, the center was built for around $1 billion and was five years in the making. Originally, Meier planned for the whole museum complex to be constructed from white metallic panels – his signature style – but protests from the Brentwood neighbors below forced him to re-design part of it in travertine, in the end a good aesthetic choice. Although the Getty foundation plunked down a ten-figure sum for the Center, it still has billions in reserve and must, by law, spend hundreds of millions each year from its endowment. Thus, it plays an elephantine role on the international art scene and can freely outbid its competitors for anything it wants. If he were still around, J. Paul would have been proud.

Getty started building his massive collection in the 1930s, storing much of it in his house until the Getty Museum opened in 1974, on a bluff overlooking the Pacific Ocean. That site is now closed, but will reopen in the next century as a showcase for the foundation's antiquities, few of which will then be shown here. As the collection is, not surprisingly, determined by the enthusiasms of Getty himself, there's a formidable array of ornate furniture and decorative arts, with clocks, chandeliers, tapestries and gilt-edged commodes, designed for the French nobility from the reign of Louis XIV, filling several overwhelmingly opulent rooms. Getty was much less interested in painting – although he did scoop up a very fine stash from the Renaissance and Baroque periods, including works by Rembrandt, Rubens, La Tour and more – but a large collection has been amassed since his death, featuring all the major names from the thirteenth century to the present: drawings by Raphael and Bernini, paintings of the Dutch Golden Age and a handful of French Impressionists, to name just a few. By contrast, there's also an extensive and highly absorbing collection of photographs by Man Ray, Laszlo Moholy-Nagy and notable others.

From the museum, continue up the Sepulveda Pass until you come to the **Skirball Cultural Center** at 2701 N Sepulveda Blvd (Tues–Fri 10am–4pm, Sat noon–5pm, Sun 10am–5pm; $7, students $5). The Center has in recent years taken the same step as the Getty Museum and relocated to a more isolated setting, removing itself from the limited confines of **Hebrew Union College** near USC. Devoting its attention to describing some of the history, beliefs and rituals of Judaism, the Center concentrates on the more mystical elements of the faith and is fairly absorbing. It also hosts a range of exhibitions and lectures designed to illuminate the American Jewish experience and offers a good, incisive overview of Judaic history and culture.

Santa Monica, Venice and Malibu

Set along an unbroken, twenty-mile strand of clean, white-sand beaches, and home to a diverse assortment of LA's finest stores, restaurants and art galleries, the small, self-contained communities that line the **Santa Monica Bay** feature some of the best of what Los Angeles has to offer, with none of the smog or searing heat that can make the rest of the metropolis unbearable. The entire area is well served by public transportation, near (but not too near) the airport, and there's a wide selection of accommodation, making the area an ideal base for seeing the rest of LA.

Santa Monica, set on palm-tree-shaded bluffs above the blue Pacific, is the oldest, biggest and best-known of the resort areas. Once a wild beachfront playground, and the memorable location for many scenes from the underworld stories of Raymond Chandler, it's now a self-consciously healthy and liberal community, which has enticed a large expatriate British community of writers and rock stars, ranging from Rod Stewart to John Lydon. In recent years, however, once-liberal policies towards homeless people have become more severe, as have rent-control laws, courtesy of a state effort to keep landlords and property owners happy. Directly south, **Venice**'s once-expansive network of canals and the beachfront boardwalk bring together a lively mixture of street performers, roller skaters and casual voyeurs.

North from Santa Monica along the Pacific Coast Highway, **Pacific Palisades** is a gathering of hugely expensive suburban houses clinging to the lower foothills of the nearby mountains. Aside from some pioneering postwar architecture, however, there's nothing much to see, though you could push a few miles inland to **Will Rogers State Park**, home and museum of one of the legends of the American West, and with some rewarding hiking paths leading into the neighboring canyons. A few miles further along the coastal road, **Topanga Canyon** has more hiking, its reputation as haven of back-to-nature hippydom gone, but still with a surprisingly wild set of trails leading into the deep, wooded canyons and sculptured rock outcrops of the Santa Monica Mountains.

Malibu, at the top of the bay, twenty miles from Santa Monica and the northern- and westernmost edge of LA, is a whole other world, studded with beach colony houses owned by those who are famous enough to need privacy and rich enough to afford it, despite the constant threat of hillside wildfires. However, you don't have to be a millionaire to enjoy its fine surfing beaches, or the birds, seals – and, in migrating season, whales – for which this part of the coast is noted.

Santa Monica

As little as a century ago, most of the land between **SANTA MONICA** and what was then Los Angeles was covered by beanfields and citrus groves, interrupted by the occasional outposts of Hollywood and Beverly Hills. Like so much of the state, the land was owned by the Southern Pacific Railroad, who tried – and failed – to make Santa Monica into the port of Los Angeles, losing out to other interests who dredged the harbor at Wilmington, near Long Beach. The linking of the beachfront with the rest of Los Angeles by the suburban streetcar system meant the town instead grew into one of LA's premier resorts – a giant funfair city that was the inspiration for Raymond Chandler's anything-goes "Bay City", described in *Farewell My Lovely*. Today Chandler wouldn't recognize the place: changes in the gaming laws and the advent of the private swimming pool have led to the removal of the offshore gambling ships and many of the bathing clubs, and Santa Monica is among the city's more elegant seaside towns. It's also well known for its rent control and stringent planning and development regulations, for which perceived infractions, local right-wingers refer sneeringly to the city as the "People's Republic".

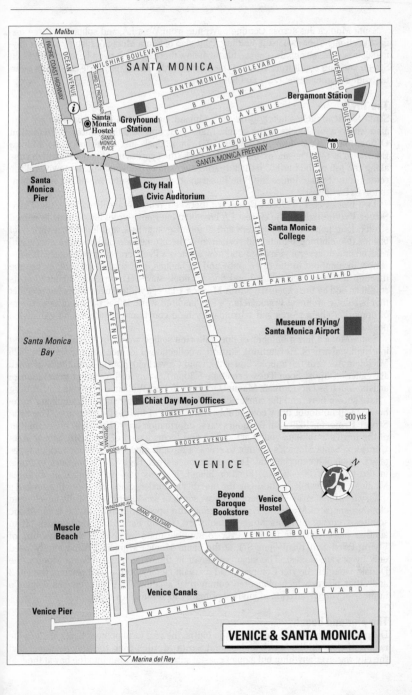

Santa Monica lies across Centinela Avenue from West LA, and splits into three distinct portions. The town itself, holding a fair slab of Santa Monica's history and its day-to-day business, sits on the coastal bluffs; below there's the pier and beach; while Main Street, running south from close to the pier towards Venice, is a style-conscious quarter, with designer restaurants and fancy shops.

The Town

Santa Monica reaches nearly three miles inland, but most things of interest are situated within a few blocks of the beach. Make your first stop the **Visitor Information Office** (daily 10am–4pm; ☎310/393-7593), in a kiosk just south of Santa Monica Boulevard at 1400 Ocean Ave in Palisades Park (the cypress-tree-lined strip which runs along the top of the bluffs). Its handy free map shows the whole of the town and the routes of the Santa Monica Big Blue Bus transit system, a useful Westside complement to the MTA network.

Two blocks east of Ocean Boulevard, between Wilshire and Broadway, the **Third Street Promenade** is the closest LA comes to energetic street life. A pedestrianized stretch long popular with buskers and itinerant evangelists, and lined by a variety of fashionable clothing outlets and restaurants, the promenade underwent a successful refurbishment several years ago and now attracts a lively crowd of characters. It's fun simply to hang out in the cafés, pubs and nightclubs, play a game of pool, or browse through the many secondhand and fine-art book shops. The mall is anchored at its southern end by the expensive **Santa Monica Place**, a white stucco shopping precinct that is among architect Frank Gehry's less inspired work. It has the usual assortment of upmarket chain stores and a mandatory food court, all executed in an exhausted postmodern idiom.

Santa Monica has a number of fine **galleries** selling works by emerging local and international artists. **Bergamont Station**, a collection of former tramcar sheds at 2525 Michigan Ave near the intersection of 26th and Cloverfield, houses a multitude of small art galleries (most open Tues–Fri 11am–5.30pm). Many of LA's latest generation of artists – such as Lari Pittman, Manuel Ocampo, Robert Williams and Erika Rothenberg – have shown here, and the construction of two small theater stages in adjoining warehouses will no doubt draw comparably rising stars of the performing arts. The **Side Street Projects**, 1629 18th St (hours vary; information on ☎310/829-0779) is another of the town's ambitious young art spaces and forms a part of the **18th Street Arts Complex**, Santa Monica's attempt to create a hip and modern center for various types of art, much of it experimental. The performance space Highways is one such example in the complex (see p.159). Further inland, it's less easy to stumble upon Santa Monica's worthwhile sights. On the northern border, **San Vicente Boulevard**'s grassy tree-lined strip is a joggers' freeway; south of San Vicente, the flashy novelty and clothing shops of **Montana Avenue** reflect the upward mobility of the area. At the southeast corner of Santa Monica Boulevard, Ocean Park Boulevard spears off to another place you'd be unlikely ever to stumble upon by chance, the **Museum of Flying** (Wed–Sun 10am–5pm; $7), at the Santa Monica Municipal Airport (now used only by private planes). The major employer in the early years of Santa Monica, the Donald Douglas Aircraft Company, had its main factory here – birthplace of the DC-3 and other planes which pioneered commercial aviation. The old premises display a number of vintage aircraft, of interest primarily to aeronautics buffs.

The pier and beach

Despite the many features on top of the bluffs, the real focal point of Santa Monica life is down below, on the **beach** and around **Santa Monica pier**, the only reminder that the city was ever anything but a quiet coastal suburb. Jutting out into the bay at the foot of Colorado Avenue, the pier is a great example of its kind, recently having cleaned up its grungy appearance with new rides, a giant helter-skelter and a restored 1922 wooden **carousel** (daily 9am–6pm; 50¢ a ride). The pier has also opened a new carnival center, **Pacific Park**, featuring a roller coaster and various other thrill rides designed to attract the family crowd back from the suburbs.

The grand beach houses just north of the pier were known as the "Gold Coast", because of the many Hollywood personalities who lived in them. The largest, now the **Sand and Sea** beach club, was built as the servants' quarters of a massive 120-room house, now demolished, that belonged to William Randolph Hearst. MGM boss Louis B. Mayer owned the adjacent Mediterranean-style villa, where the Kennedy brothers were later rumored to have had their liaisons with Marilyn Monroe. If you're not intending to stretch out on the sands, you can follow the **bike path**, which begins at the pier, twenty miles south to Palos Verdes. Or, on foot, wander south along the beach to Pico Boulevard and head two blocks inland to Main Street.

Main Street

Santa Monica underwent a major change following completion of the Santa Monica Freeway in 1965, which brought the beachfront homes within a fifteen-minute drive of downtown and isolated the bulk of the town from **Main Street**, five minutes' walk from the pier – where the collection of novelty shops, kite stores and classy restaurants is now one of the popular shopping districts on the Westside.

Beyond shopping, eating and drinking, though, there's not much to do or see. **California Heritage Museum** on Main Street at Ocean Park Boulevard (Wed–Sat 11am–4pm, Sun noon–4pm; $3) is the city's effort to preserve some of its architectural past in the face of new money. Two houses were moved here to escape demolition. One hosts temporary displays on Californian cultural topics like the reign of the Dodgers, and has several rooms restored to variously evoke the years 1890–1930. The other is known as the *Victorian Restaurant* and serves tea on its patio at weekends (reserve on ☎310/392-8537). Not all of Santa Monica has been so lucky, however. Ocean Park Boulevard was one of the main routes to the coast via the old streetcars of the Pacific Electric, and the entire beachfront between here and the Venice border, now overshadowed by massive gray condominiums, used to be the site of the largest and wildest of the amusement piers, the fantastic **Pacific Ocean Park**. "P-O-P", as it was known, had a huge roller coaster, a giant funhouse and a boisterous midway arcade, described by architectural historian Reyner Banham as a "fantasy in stucco and every known style of architecture and human ecology". Sadly, not a trace remains.

Venice

Immediately south of Santa Monica, **VENICE** was laid out in the marshlands of Ballona Creek in 1905 by developer Abbot Kinney as a romantic replica of the northern Italian city. Intended to attract artsy folk from Los Angeles to sample its sub-European Bohemian air, this twenty-mile network of canals, lined by sham palazzos and waterfront homes, never really caught on, and the coming of the automobile finished it off altogether. Many of the canals were filled in, and the area, now annexed by the city of Los Angeles, fell into disrepair, with most of the home sites being taken over by oil wells – an era that features in Orson Welles' film *Touch of Evil*, in which derelict Venice stars as a seedy Mexican border town.

Kinney was, however, ahead of his time. A fair bit of the original plan survives, and the pseudo-European atmosphere has since proved just right for pulling in the artistic community he was aiming at, making Venice one of the coast's trendier spots. Main Street, for instance, is home to the offices of advertising firm **Chiat Day Mojo**. Marked by Claes Oldenburg's huge pair of binoculars at the entrance, the Frank Gehry-designed offices have no assigned desks, leaving employees to roam free with laptops and mobile phones, through spartan rooms lined with original modern art. Just to the north, the frightening *Ballerina Clown*, a gargantuan sculpture by Jonathan Borofsky, looms over a nearby intersection, its clown face and tutu creating one of the most disturbing pieces of public art in recent memory. Elsewhere, a strong alternative arts scene centers around the **Beyond Baroque Literary Arts Center and Bookshop** in the old City Hall at 681 Venice Blvd (Tues–Fri 10am–5pm, Sat noon–5pm; ☎310/822-3006), which holds regular readings and workshops of poetry, prose and drama.

Windward Avenue is the town's main artery, running from the beach into what was the Grand Circle of the canal system, now paved over and ringed by a number of galleries and the Venice post office, inside which a mural depicts the early layout. Leading to the beach, the original Romanesque **arcade**, around the intersection with Pacific Avenue, is alive with health-food shops, used-record stores and roller skate rental stands, but sadly, less and less of it remains with passing years. Here and there colorful and portentous giant **murals** cover the whitewashed walls of the original hotels, and of the Venice Pavilion on the beach. The few remaining **canals** are just a few blocks south (enter on Dell Avenue westward from Washington Boulevard), where the original quaint little bridges survive, and you can sit and watch the ducks paddle around in the still waters.

It's **Venice Beach** that draws most people to the town. Nowhere else does LA parade itself quite so openly and as sensuously as it does along the **Venice Boardwalk**, a wide pathway also known as Ocean Front Walk. Year-round at weekends and every day in summer it is packed with people and people-watchers, jugglers, fire-eaters, Hare Krishnas and roller-skating guitar players. You can buy anything you might need to look like a local without ever leaving the beach: cheap sunglasses, T-shirts, personal stereos and tennis shoes. South of Windward is **Muscle Beach**, a now legendary outdoor weightlifting center where serious-looking hunks of muscle drive some serious iron, and high-flying gymnasts swing on the adjacent rings and bars.

Incidentally, be warned that Venice Beach at **night** is a dangerous place, taken over by street gangs, drug dealers and assorted psychos. Even walking on the beach after dark is illegal, and anywhere in the immediate vicinity you should take great care.

Pacific Palisades and Will Rogers State Park

The district of **PACIFIC PALISADES**, which rises on the bluffs two miles north of Santa Monica pier, is slowly but very surely falling away into the bay, most noticeably on the point above Chautauqua Boulevard and Pacific Coast Highway, otherwise known as "PCH". With each winter's rains, a little bit more of the bluffs gets washed away in mud slides, blocking traffic on PCH, and gradually shrinking the back yards of the clifftop homes. There are few places of interest among the suburban ranch houses, although some of the most influential buildings of post-war LA were constructed here – the **Eames house**, for example, at 203 Chautauqua St, was fashioned out of prefabricated industrial parts in 1947 and is now generally inaccessible to the public.

In complete contrast, a mile east along Sunset Boulevard from the top of Chautauqua is the **Will Rogers State Historic Park** (summer daily 8am–7pm; rest of year daily 8am–6pm; free, parking $5), a steep climb from the MTA bus (#2, #302, #576) stop. This was the home and ranch of the Depression-era cowboy philosopher and journalist Will Rogers, one of America's most popular figures of the time – after his death in a plane crash in 1935, there was a nationwide thirty-minute silence. He was renowned for his down-home, common-sense thinking, and the saying that he "never met a man he didn't like". The overgrown ranch-style house serves as an informal **museum** (daily 10am–5pm; free), filled to overflowing with cowboy gear and Native American art; and the 200-acre park has miles of foot and bridle paths, one of which leads up to the top of

Topanga Canyon. Just north of Sunset Boulevard's intersection with Pacific Coast Highway, the **Getty Villa** sits on a picturesque bluff overlooking the ocean. Once the site of the Getty Museum (now in West LA; see p.113), the villa is closed to the public but is due to reopen as an antiquities center in 2001.

Topanga Canyon

In complete and surprising contrast to the turmoil of LA, **Topanga Canyon** provides an excellent natural refuge. With hillsides covered in golden poppies and wildflowers, a hundred and fifty thousand acres of these mountains and the seashore have been protected as the Santa Monica Mountains National Recreation Area, but as yet very few people take advantage of the fine views and fresh air, thus missing out on the sight of the deer, coyotes and the odd mountain lion that still live here. Like LA itself, the area is not without its element of danger, especially in winter and early spring, when mud slides threaten houses and waterfalls cascade down the cliffs. Park rangers offer free guided hikes throughout the mountains most weekends (information and reservations ☎818/597-9192), and there are self-guided trails through the canyon's Topanga State Park, off Old Topanga Canyon Road at the crest of the mountains, with spectacular views out over the Pacific.

Beyond Topanga Canyon, the beaches and ocean-views are blocked off by mile after mile of private homes all the way to Malibu. There are a few signposted beach-access points, but most of the rock stars and others who can afford to live here treat the sands and seas as their own. Although any bit of land below the high-tide line is legally in the public domain, you're sure to feel like a trespasser.

Malibu

Everyone has heard of **MALIBU**; the very name conjures up images of beautiful people sunbathing on a palm-fringed beach and lazily consuming cocktails. And the image is not so very far from the truth – even though you might not think so on arrival. As you enter the small town, the succession of ramshackle surf shops and fast-food stands scattered along both sides of PCH around the graceful Malibu Pier don't exactly reek of money, but the secluded estates just inland are as valuable as any in the entire US, even though many are subject to being battered by hillside wildfires that destroy anything in their path.

The south-facing beach next to the pier, Surfrider Beach, was the surfing capital of the world in the 1950s and early 1960s, popularized by the many Beach Blanket Bingo movies filmed here, starring the likes of Annette Funicello and Frankie Avalon. It's still a big surfing spot: the waves are best in late summer, when storms off Mexico cause them to reach upwards of eight feet. Just beyond is **Malibu Lagoon State Park** (parking $6), a nature reserve and bird refuge; birdwatching walks around the lagoon are offered some weekends, and there's a small **museum** (Wed–Sat 11am–3pm; $2), detailing the history of the area.

Most Malibu residents live in the houses and small ranches that hide away in the narrow canyons on the edges of the town, together forming a well-off, insular community with a long-established dread of outsiders. Up until the 1920s all of Malibu was owned by one **May K. Rindge**, who hired armed guards and dynamited roads to keep travelers from crossing her land on their way to and from Santa Monica. Rindge fought for years to prevent the state from building the Pacific Coast Highway across her property, but lost her legal battle in the State Supreme Court, and her money in the Depression. Her son took over the ranch and quickly sold much of the land, establishing the **Malibu Colony** at the mouth of Malibu Canyon as a haven for movie stars. Robert Altman's film *The Long Goodbye* provides a sharply critical view of the colony as a home to washed-up artists and moral slackers. There's very little to see here except the garage doors of the rich and famous; if you must get a glimpse of the elite, visit the **Malibu Colony Plaza**, near the area's gated entrance – good for star-spotting and stocking up on food and drink before a day on the sands.

Much of **Malibu Creek State Park**, at the crest of Malibu Canyon Road along Mulholland Drive, used to belong to 20th Century-Fox studios, who filmed many Tarzan pictures here and used the chaparral-covered hillsides to simulate South Korea for the TV show *M*A*S*H*. The 4000-acre park includes a large lake, some waterfalls, and nearly fifteen miles of hiking trails. Nearby **Paramount Ranch**, near Mulholland Drive on Cornell Road, is another old studio backlot, with an intact Western movie set used for, among other things, the interminable TV drama *Dr. Quinn Medicine Woman*.

The beaches

Five miles along the coast from Malibu Pier, **Zuma Beach** is the largest of the Los Angeles County beaches, popular with San Fernando Valley high-school kids, who drive over Kanan-Dume road to escape the sweltering inland summer heat. Adjacent **Point Dume State Beach**, below the bluffs, is a lot more relaxed, especially up and over the rocks at its southern tip, where **Pirate's Cove** is used by nudists. The rocks here are also a good place to look out for seals and migrating gray whales in winter, as the point juts out into the Pacific at the northern lip of Santa Monica Bay.

El Matador State Beach, about 25 miles up the coast from Santa Monica, is about as close as an ordinary Joe can get to the private-beach seclusion enjoyed by the stars. Thanks to its northern location and an easily missable turn off PCH, its rocky coved sands are a recluse's dream. Another five miles along PCH, where Mulholland Drive reaches the ocean, **Leo Carrillo State Beach Park** marks the northwestern border of LA County and the end of the MTA bus route (#434). The mile-long sandy beach is divided by Sequit Point, a small bluff that has underwater caves and a tunnel you can pass through at low tide. Leo Carrillo is also the nearest and most accessible **campground** for the rest of LA (see p.76). Five miles further on, at **Point Mugu State Park**, there are some very good walks through mountain canyons, and campsites right on the beach. Point Mugu is also the site of the US Navy's Pacific Missile Test Center, which takes up most of the five miles of coast south of Ventura (see p.332), at the southern edge of the Central Coast.

The South Bay and Harbor Area

South of Venice, Marina del Rey and the faded resort town of Playa del Rey, the coast is dominated by the runways of LAX, a huge Chevron Oil refinery, and LA's main sewage treatment plant. Beyond this industrial zone, however, is an eight-mile strip of beach towns – **Manhattan Beach**, **Hermosa Beach** and **Redondo Beach** – collectively known as the South Bay. These are more modest (though far from poor), quieter, more suburban and smaller than the Westside beach communities. Along their shared beach-side bike path the joggers and roller skaters are more likely to be locals than poseurs from other parts of LA, and all three can make a refreshing break if you like your beaches without pretentious packaging. Each has a beckoning strip of white sand, and Manhattan and Hermosa especially are well equipped for surfing and beachsports. They're also well connected to the rest of the city – within easy reach of LAX and connected by regular buses to downtown LA.

Visible all along this stretch of the coast, the large vegetated peninsula of **Palos Verdes** looks more tempting than it really is, much of it an upmarket residential area, although the comparatively rough-hewn little district of **San Pedro** is a worthwhile destination around the far side (not least for the local youth hostel, the area's cheapest accommodation by a long way; see p.75) sited on the LA harbor, the busiest cargo port in the world and still growing. On the other side of the harbor, **Long Beach**, connected to downtown by bus #60, is best known as the resting place of the *Queen Mary*, even though it is also the region's second largest city with nearly half a million people.

Perhaps the most enticing, and certainly the strangest, place in the area is **Santa Catalina Island**, twenty miles offshore and easily reached by ferry. It's almost completely conserved wildland, with many unique forms of plant and animal life and just one small center of population.

Manhattan Beach, Hermosa Beach and Redondo Beach

Accessible along the bike path from Venice, or by car along Pacific Coast Highway, **MANHATTAN BEACH** is a likeable place with a healthy well-to-do air, home mainly to white-collar workers whose middle-class stucco homes tumble towards the beach, uncluttered by high-rise hotels. There's not much to see or do away from the beach, but then that's the main reason for coming. Surfing is a major local pastime, there's a two-week international surf festival each August, and the city is a major center for beach volleyball, evidenced by the profusion of nets across the sands. If you can, call at the **historical center** in the post office building at 1601 Manhattan Beach Blvd (Sat & Sun noon–3pm; free), for its entertaining collection of photos and oddments from the city's earliest days. If these whet your appetite, you can purchase (for $1) a map that describes a history-oriented **walking tour**.

HERMOSA BEACH, across Longfellow Boulevard, is more down-at-heel than Manhattan Beach, its houses smaller and less showy. The center, near the foot of the pier around Hermosa and Pier avenues, is an unlikely setting for one of the South Bay's best-known nightspots, *The Lighthouse* (see p.155). Again, there's little of note except the beach, though you should take a look in the **Either/Or** bookshop, 124 Pier Ave (see p.165), once a haunt of writer Thomas Pynchon.

Despite some good strips of sand, and fine views of Palos Verdes' stunning greenery, **REDONDO BEACH**, situated south of Hermosa, is less inviting. Condos and large hotels line the beachfront, and the eateries around the yacht-lined King's Harbor are off limits to impecunious visitors.

Palos Verdes

A great green hump marking LA's southwest corner, **PALOS VERDES** isn't of special interest, but it can be enjoyable to explore the bluffs and coves along the protected coastline. **Malaga Beach**, by Torrance County Beach just south of Redondo, is a popular scuba-diving spot; **Abalone Cove**, reached from the parking lot on Berkentine Road, off Palos Verdes Drive, boasts rock and tide pools, and offshore kelp beds alive with rock scallops, sea urchins and, of course, abalone. A couple of miles east at the end of a path off Peppertree Drive, Smugglers Cove is a renowned **nudist beach**.

While you're in the area, don't miss **Wayfarer's Chapel**, at 5755 Palos Verdes Drive. Designed by Frank Lloyd Wright's son, Lloyd, it's a tribute to the eighteenth-century Swedish scientist and mystic Emanuel Swedenborg. The ultimate aim is for the redwood grove around the chapel to grow and entangle itself around the glass-framed structure – a fusing of human handiwork with the forces of nature of which Swedenborg would have been proud. A few miles further on, just before the end of Palos Verdes Drive, **Point Fermin Park** is a small tip of land prodding into the ocean. In the park is a curious little wooden lighthouse dating from 1874 (no admittance), and a whale-watching station where you can read up on the winter migrations. Bottle-nosed dolphins can often be seen during their fall departure and spring return, and there's also the less seasonally dependent thrill of spotting hang-gliders swooping down off the cliffs.

From the park, it's an easy stroll along Bluff Place and down the 29th Street stairway to Cabrillo Beach and the excellent **Cabrillo Marine Museum**, at 3720 Stephen White Drive (Tues–Fri noon–5pm, Sat & Sun 10am–5pm; free, parking $6.50, $5.50 in winter). A diverse collection of marine life has been imaginatively and instructively assembled: everything from predator snails and the curious "sarcastic fringehead" to larger displays on otters, seals and whales.

San Pedro and around

About three miles further on along Bluff Place, the scruffy harbor city of **SAN PEDRO** is in stark contrast to the affluence of the rest of Palos Verdes. It was a small fishing community until the late nineteenth century, when the construction of the LA harbor nearby brought a huge influx of labor, much of it drawn from the migrants who arrived on the ships, chiefly from Portugal, Greece and Yugoslavia. Many of these, and their descendants, never left the place, lending a striking racial mix to the town, manifest around the narrow sloping central streets in one of LA's densest groupings of ethnic groceries.

Some of this history is revealed in the **Maritime Museum**, on the harbor's edge at the foot of Sixth Street (Tues–Sun 10am–5pm; free), while the **Bloody Thursday Monument**, on the corner of Sixth and Beacon close to the City Hall, is another reminder of the city's gritty past. It marks the 1934 strike by local waterfront workers, commemorating the two who were killed when police and private guards opened fire. A fifteen-minute walk along the shore from the museum will bring you to the over-rated **Ports O'Call Village** – a dismal batch of wooden and corrugated iron huts supposedly capturing the flavor of exotic seaports around the world. Don't bother to visit.

Between San Pedro and Long Beach (connected by LADOT bus #142) soar two tall road bridges, giving aerial views of oil wells and docks, and the vast Naval Supplies Center. Just inland, the community of **WILMINGTON** is home to the Greek-style **Banning House** at 401 E Main St (guided tours hourly Tues–Thurs 12.30–2.30pm, Sat & Sun 3.30pm; $2). A mid-nineteenth-century entrepreneur, Phineas Banning, made his fortune when the value of his land increased astronomically as the harbor was developed. Through his promoting of the rail link between the harbor and central LA he also became known as "the father of Los Angeles transportation" – no mean accolade at a time when the local transportation system was one of the best in the world.

Long Beach

With San Pedro, **LONG BEACH** is home to the world's third-largest port, and biggest outside of China. Once the stamping ground of off-duty naval personnel, the city's porn shops and sleazy bars made the place just the wrong side of seedy. The last decade or so, however, saw a billion-dollar cash injection into the town that has led – in the downtown area at least – to a spate of glossy office buildings, a convention center, new hotels, a swanky shopping mall and a clean-up campaign that has restored some of the best turn-of-the-century buildings on the coast. Inland from downtown, however, it's a different story – grim, uninviting housing developments on the perimeter of the impoverished district of South Central LA (see p.89).

Downtown Long Beach is clearly the place to spend most of your time, with, especially along Pine Avenue, the best of Long Beach's rescued architecture and numerous thrift stores, antique/junk emporiums and bookstores. Nearby, on Third Street, is **"The Mural"**, whose depiction of the Long Beach population appears to be contemporary but was in fact painted in the 1930s under Roosevelt's New Deal, unwittingly predicting the racial mixture that Long Beach attained much later. From the mural, the pedestrianized Promenade leads towards the sea, passing the concrete open-air auditorium – often the site of free art and music events – and crosses the busy Ocean Beach

Boulevard into **Shoreline Village**, a waterfront entertainment belt. It's a bit contrived but fine for a quick look, especially at weekends when Long Beach youth is on parade.

Ocean Boulevard leads away from Shoreline Village down to **Breakers Hotel**: twelve stories of Spanish Revival pinkness topped by a green copper roof. A mile further on, 2300 Ocean Blvd was once owned by Fatty Arbuckle and now houses the **Long Beach Museum of Art** (Wed–Thurs & Sat–Sun 10am–5pm, Fri 10am–8pm; $2), fringed by a sculpture garden and featuring a good collection of contemporary Southern Californian art and some experimental work in a video annexe. Another mile in this direction, the **Belmont Shores** area was built by old – and is maintained by new – money. Its main thoroughfare, Second Street, a collection of designer shops and yuppie-frequented cafés, sustains the affluent style of the surrounding avenues, where many of the wealthy Long Beachers of the 1920s had their homes.

Between November and March, more than fifteen thousand whales cruise the "Whale Freeway" past Long Beach on their annual migration to and return from winter breeding and berthing grounds in Baja California. Shoreline Village Cruises (☎310/495-5884) and Star Party Cruises (☎562/799-7000) operate good whale-watching trips for around $10.

The Queen Mary

Long Beach's most famous attraction is not indigenous at all. The mighty ocean liner, the **Queen Mary** (daily 10am–6pm; $11 guided tours, self tour free), was acquired by the local authorities with the specific aim of bolstering tourism, and has generally succeeded in doing so. The *Queen Mary* lies across the bay, opposite Shoreline Village, and is easily accessible either by a lengthy walk or free Long Beach Transit shuttle from downtown. Now kitted out as a luxury hotel, the ship is as tangible a testament to the hypocrisy of the British class system as you'll find. The suggestion is that all who sailed on the vessel – the flagship of the Cunard Line from the 1930s until the 1960s – enjoyed the extravagantly furnished lounges and the luxurious cabins, all carefully restored and kept sparkling. But a glance at the spartan third-class cabins reveals something of the real story, and the tough conditions experienced by the impoverished migrants who left Europe on the ship hoping to start a new life in the USA. The red British telephone kiosks around the decks and the hammy theatrical displays in the engine room and wheelhouse – closer to *Star Trek* than anything nautical – don't help, but it's nonetheless a marvellous ship, well worth a look.

Santa Catalina Island

Though it's overlooked by many foreign visitors, **SANTA CATALINA ISLAND**, a mix of uncluttered beaches and wild hills twenty miles off the coast, is favored by Californians in the know. Claimed by the Portuguese in 1542 as San Salvador, and renamed by the Spanish in 1602, it has somehow stayed firmly outside the historical mainstream. Since 1811, when the indigenous Gabrileño Indian population was forced to resettle on the mainland, the island has been in private ownership, and has over the years grown to be something of a resort – a process hastened by businessman William Wrigley Jr (part of the Chicago-based chewing gum dynasty), who financed the construction of the Art Deco *Avalon Casino*, still the island's major landmark, in the 1920s.

Occupying mostly incorporated county territory, the island has become a popular destination for boaters and nature lovers, and its small marina overflows with luxury yachts and cruise ships in summer. Even so, tourism has been held largely at bay: the hotels are unobtrusive among the whimsical architecture and cars are a rarity, as there's a ten-year waiting list to bring one over from the mainland. Consequently most of the 3,000 islanders walk, ride bikes or drive electrically powered golf carts or mokes.

Arrival and accommodation

Depending on the season, a round-trip **ferry** from San Pedro or Long Beach to Catalina Island's one town, **Avalon**, costs between $20 and $30. Catalina Cruises (☎1-800/228-2546) and Catalina Express (☎310/519-1212) run several services daily. From Newport Beach (see p.130) to Avalon, the Catalina Passenger Service (☎714/673-5245) runs a daily round-trip for about $30. Alternatively, a catamaran day excursion from San Diego with SeaJet will set you back $70, (☎619/696-0088). If you get seasick or feel extravagant, **helicopter** services to Avalon, costing around $100 round-trip, are offered by Island Express (☎310/510-2525) from Long Beach and San Pedro.

Be warned that the price of hotel **accommodation** in Avalon hovers upwards of $85, and most beds are booked up throughout the summer and at weekends. The most interesting **hotel** is the *Zane Grey Pueblo Hotel* (☎1-800/446-0271 or 310/510-0966; ③), detailed below, but the cheapest is usually the *Atwater*, on Sumner Avenue (☎1-800/4-AVALON; ③). The *Bayview Hotel*, on Whittley Avenue (☎310/510-7070; ③), is also reasonable. The only budget option is **camping** (around $8 per person). *Hermit Gulch* (☎310/510-8368) is the closest site to Avalon and thus the busiest. Three other sites – *Blackjack*, *Little Harbor* and *Two Harbors* – in Catalina's interior, all bookable on ☎888/510-7979, are usually roomier. For **eating**, *Catalina Cantina*, 313 Crescent Ave (☎310/510-0100), is the best, offering tasty and affordable Mexican staples washed down with margaritas, and live music at weekends.

Transportation and trips

Catalina Safari Shuttle Bus runs between Avalon and Two Harbors for $29 round-trip. Catalina Island Company (☎1-800/851-0217 or 310/510-2500) offers **tours** of the island, ranging from whistle-stop town jaunts and short voyages in glass-bottomed boats ($7) to a fuller four-hour affair ($23) – the only way to see the interior of Catalina without hiking. **Golf carts**, for which you need a driver's license, and **bikes** (both banned from the rough roads outside Avalon) can be rented for $30 a day from the stand opposite the *Busy Bee* restaurant on Bay Shore Drive.

The waters around the island are rich in yellowtail, calico bass, barracuda and sharks. Catalina Mako (☎1-800/296-MAKO or 310/510-2720) runs **charter fishing trips** for around $100 an hour (although you can fish for free from the pleasure pier), and snorkel and scuba gear is available for rent at **Catalina Divers Supply** (☎1-800/353-0330 or 310/510-0330).

Avalon

AVALON can be fully explored on foot in an hour, with maps issued by the **Chamber of Commerce** at the foot of the ferry pier (☎310/510-1520). The best place to begin is at the **Avalon Casino**, a 1920s structure with mermaid murals, gold-leaf ceiling motifs, an Art Deco ballroom, and a small **museum** (daily 10.30am–4pm; $1.50) displaying Native American artifacts from Catalina's past.

On the slopes above the casino, the **Zane Grey Pueblo Hotel** (see above) is the former home of the Western author, who visited Catalina with a film crew to shoot *The Vanishing American* and liked the place so much he never left, building for himself this pueblo-style house, complete with a beamed ceiling and thick wooden front door. It's now a hotel, with rooms themed after his books and a pool shaped like an arrowhead, and offers good views of Avalon and the bay.

The interior

If possible, venture into the **interior** of Catalina. You can take a tour (see above) if time is short; if it isn't, get a free **wilderness permit**, which allows you to hike and camp, from the Chamber of Commerce or the **Parks and Recreation office**

(☎310/510-0688), both in Avalon. Mountain biking requires a $50 permit from the **Catalina Island Conservancy**, 125 Calressa Ave, Avalon (☎310/510-1421) or the *Two Harbors* campsite.

The carefully conserved wilderness of the interior holds a wide variety of flora and fauna, some of it unique. Keep a sharp eye out for the Catalina Shrew, so rare it's only been sighted twice, and the Catalina Mouse, bigger and healthier than its mainland counterpart thanks to abundant food and lack of natural enemies. There are also buffalo, descended from a smattering of fourteen left behind by a Hollywood film crew and now a sizeable herd that wanders freely about the island.

Anaheim: Disneyland and around

Life in Anaheim, California, was a commercial for itself, endlessly replayed. Nothing changed; it just spread farther and farther in the form of neon ooze. What there was always more of had been congealed into permanence long ago, as if the automatic factory that cranked out these objects had jammed into the on position.

Philip K. Dick, *A Scanner Darkly*

In the early 1950s, illustrator/film-maker Walt Disney conceived a theme park where his cartoon characters – Mickey Mouse, Donald Duck, Goofy and the rest, already indelibly imprinted on the American mind – would come to life, and his fabulously successful company would rake in even more money from them.

Disneyland opened in 1955, in anticipation of the acres of orange groves thirty miles southeast of downtown – at **ANAHEIM** and, inland, in **Orange County** – becoming the nexus of population growth in Southern California. The area around Anaheim is pure Eisenhower era – staunchly conservative suburbs made up of mile after mile of unvarying residential plots and still one of the US's fastest growing areas, if not expanding exactly the way the area's original white suburbanites would prefer. Hispanics and Asians are increasingly populating areas like Anaheim, Garden Grove, Santa Ana and Westminster (the latter being a key center for Vietnamese expatriates), to the chagrin of old-time Orange County dwellers, many of whom have left the center of the county in "white fright" to find more distant digs in Irvine, Dana Point and San Juan Capistrano.

Certainly Disneyland utterly dominates the Anaheim area and contributes to its commercial growth, and the boom doesn't look like slowing. If you're not coming to see Disneyland, you may as well give the place a miss: it hasn't an ounce of interest in itself. But if you do come, or are staying in one of Anaheim's many hotels, the creakier rides at **Knott's Berry Farm** go some way to restoring antique notions of what amusement parks used to be like; the **Movieland Wax Museum** is occasionally entertaining; and, on an entirely different note, the **Crystal Cathedral** is an imposing reminder of the potency of the evangelical movement. If you're a sports fan, note that baseball's Anaheim Angels play at Anaheim Stadium and hockey's Mighty Ducks play at Arrowhead Pond; the latter team is owned by the town's mouse-in-chief.

Disneyland

It's hard to think of anything that comes closer to demonstrating the wishful thinking of the modern US than **DISNEYLAND** (summer daily 8am–1am; rest of year Mon–Fri 10am–6pm, Sat 9am–midnight, Sun 9am–10pm; $36 adults, $30 kids, parking $6; ☎714/781-4565), the most famous, most carefully constructed, most influential theme park anywhere. Disneyland is a phenomenon, the ultimate fantasy, with the emphasis strongly on family fun. While it has been known for people to cruise around Disneyland on LSD, it is not a good idea; the authorities take a dim view of anything remotely anti-social, and anyone acting out of order will be thrown out; in any case the place is sur-real enough without the need for mind-expanding drugs.

Bear in mind, too, that Disneyland is not LA's only large-scale amusement park; the whirlwind rides at Magic Mountain, for example (see p.139), are always much better.

Practicalities

Disneyland is at 1313 Harbor Blvd, Anaheim, about 45 minutes by **car** from downtown using the Santa Ana Freeway. By **train** from downtown (there are nine a day), make the thirty-minute journey to Fullerton, from where OCTD buses will drop you at Disneyland or Knotts Berry Farm. By **bus**, use MTA #460 from downtown, which takes about ninety minutes, or the quicker Greyhound service, which runs thirteen times a day, and takes 45 minutes to Anaheim, from where it's an easy walk to the park.

As for **accommodation**, most people try to visit Disneyland just for the day and spend the night somewhere else, or at home. It's not a very appealing area, and anyway most of the hotels and motels close to Disneyland cost well in excess of $70 per night; still, the park is at its least crowded first thing after opening, so staying nearby can help avoid the crowds. If you must stay, the *HI-Anaheim/Fullerton* hostel (☎714/738-3721; members $14, others $17) is by far the best bet; see p.74 for further recommendations.

A massive central kitchen produces all the **food** that's eaten in the park (you're not permitted to bring your own), unloading popcorn, hot dogs, hamburgers and other all-American produce from the many stands by the ton. For anything healthier or more substantial, you'll need to leave the park and travel a fair way. The "Eating" listings on p.142 suggest some options.

The park

The only way to enjoy Disneyland is to jump into it with both feet: don't think twice about anything and go on every ride you can. The admission price includes them all, although during peak periods you might have to wait in line for hours – lines are short-est when the park opens, so choose a few top rides and get to them very early.

From the front gates, **Main Street** leads through a scaled-down, camped-up replica of a turn-of-the-century Midwestern town, filled with small souvenir shops, food stands and penny arcades, to Sleeping Beauty's Castle, a pseudo-Rhineland palace at the heart of the park. **New Orleans Square**, nearby, contains two of the best rides in the park: the "Pirates of the Caribbean", a boat trip through underground caverns, singing along with drunken pirates, and the "Haunted Mansion", a riotous "doom buggy" tour in the company of the house spooks. In **Adventureland**, you may, or may not, wish to spend time on the drearily antiquated "Jungle Cruise" listening to your "tour guides" make crude puns about the fake animatronic beasts lurking amid the trees.

Over four hundred "Imagineers" worked to create the **Indiana Jones Adventure**, Disney's biggest opening in years. Two hours of queuing are built into the ride, with an interactive archeological dig and 1930s-style newsreel show leading up to the main fea-ture – a giddy journey along 2500ft of skull-encrusted corridors in which you face fire-balls, burning rubble, venomous snakes and inevitably, a rolling-boulder finale.

Less fun is **Frontierland**, the smallest and most all-American of the various theme-lands, taking its cues from the Wild West and the tales of Mark Twain, with the less savory and more complex elements of each carefully deleted.

Fantasyland, across the drawbridge from Main Street, shows off the cleverest but also the most sentimental aspects of the Disney imagination: "Mr Toad's Wild Ride" through Victorian England, "Peter Pan" flying over London, and "It's a Small World", a tour of the world's continents in which animated dolls warble the same cloying song over and over again.

There's only one spot in the park where you can actually see the outside world: by looking over the boundary walls when riding the Skyway cars that travel via a dangling cable from Fantasyland into **Tomorrowland**. This is Disney's vision of the future, where the Space Mountain roller coaster zips through the pitch-blackness of outer space, silly scientists dabble with 3-D trickery in *Honey, I Shrunk the Audience*, and R2D2 pilots a runaway space cruiser through George Lucas' *Star Tours* galaxy of Luke Skywalker and Darth Vader.

In addition to these fixed attractions, over-the-top **firework displays** explode every summer night at 9pm, and all manner of parades and special events celebrate important occasions – such as Mickey Mouse's birthday.

Around Disneyland

It's hard to escape the clutches of Disneyland even when you leave: everything in the surrounding area seems to have been designed to service the needs of its visitors. A few places within easy reach offer a chance to forget, at least temporarily, its existence, but if Disneyland has given you a taste for distortions of reality, there's always the **Richard Nixon Library and Birthplace** to enjoy in Yorba Linda.

Knott's Berry Farm and the Movieland Wax Museum

If you're a bit fazed by the excesses of Disneyland, you might prefer the more tradit-ional **Knott's Berry Farm**, four miles northwest off the Santa Ana Freeway at 8039 Beach Blvd (summer Sun–Thurs 9am–11pm, Fri–Sat 9am–midnight; rest of year Mon–Fri 10am–6pm, Sat 10am–10pm, Sun 10am–7pm; $30, kids $20). This relaxed, rough-at-the-edges park was born during the Depression when people began queuing up for the fried chicken dinners prepared by Mrs Knott, a local farmer's wife. To amuse the children while they waited for their food, Mr Knott reconstructed a Wild West ghost town and added amusements until the park had grown into the sprawling carnival of roller coasters and thrilling rides that stands today, albeit in the shadow of the Mouse.

Across the street at 7711 Beach Blvd, the **Movieland Wax Museum** (summer daily 9am–7pm; $13; kids $7), is a Madame Tussaud's for the Hollywood set, displaying a col-lection of wax dummies posed in scenes from favorite films and TV shows. The Marx Brothers, Captain Kirk and the crew from the *Starship Enterprise*, and Arnold Schwarzenegger may not be essential viewing, but they're good for a laugh, provided you haven't had the same experience in Hollywood (see p.98). Both attractions are on the MTA #460 route from downtown.

The Crystal Cathedral

The giant **Crystal Cathedral**, on the other side of Disneyland just off the Santa Ana Freeway on Chapman Avenue (daily 9am–4pm; free), is a Philip Johnson design of tubu-lar space frames and plate glass walls that forms part of the vision of evangelist Robert Schuller, who, not content with owning the world's first drive-in church (next door to the cathedral), commissioned this dramatic prop to boost the ratings of his televised Sunday sermons. These shows reach their climax with the special Christmas production, using live animals in biblical roles and people disguised as angels suspended on ropes. Schuller raised $1.5 million for the construction of the building during one Sunday ser-vice alone – a statistic worth pondering as you wander the cavernous interior.

The Richard Nixon Library and Birthplace

Mickey Mouse may be its most famous resident, but conservative Orange County's favorite son is former US president Richard Milhouse Nixon, born in 1913 in what is now the freeway-caged **YORBA LINDA**, about eight miles northeast of Disneyland. Here,

RICHARD M. NIXON: A LIFE IN POLITICS

Qualified as a lawyer and fresh from wartime (non-combat) service in the US Navy, **Richard Milhouse Nixon** entered politics as a Republican Congressman in 1946, without so much as a civilian suit to his name. A journalist of the time observed that Nixon employed "the half-truth, the misleading quotation, the loose-joined logic" to cast doubts on his rival – traits he would perfect in the years to come.

Shortly after arriving in Washington, the fresh-faced Nixon joined the **House Un-American Activities Committee** (HUAC), a group of reds-under-the-bed scaremongers led by the fanatical Joseph McCarthy. Through the now notorious anti-Communist "witch trials", McCarthy and Nixon wrecked the lives and careers of many Americans and, in the process, launched Nixon to national prominence, culminating in his becoming Eisenhower's vice president in 1953, aged just 39. Seven years later, Nixon was defeated in his own bid for the nation's top job by the even younger John F. Kennedy, a loss which led him into the **"wilderness years"**. Staying out of the public spotlight, he took several highly lucrative posts and wrote *Six Crises*, a book whose deep introspection came as a surprise – and convinced many of the author's paranoia. Seeking a power base for the next presidential campaign, Nixon contested the governorship of California in 1962. His humiliating defeat prompted a short-lived "retirement" and did nothing to suggest that six years later he would beat Ronald Reagan to the Republican nomination and be **elected president** in 1969.

Nixon had attained his dream, but the country he inherited was more divided than at any time since the Civil War. The **Vietnam conflict** was at its height, and his large-scale illegal bombing of Cambodia earned him worldwide opprobrium. Nixon was not, however, a conservative by modern standards. By breaking with his own party's right wing, he was able to re-establish diplomatic relations with China, begin arms reduction talks with the Soviet Union, create the Environmental Protection Agency, impose wage and price controls over an unruly economy and quietly oversee the implementation of court-ordering bussing to alleviate racial segregation. Nixon's actions surprised many and contributed, at least in part, to his winning re-election in 1972.

Despite his huge victory over George McGovern, Nixon's second term was ended prematurely by the cataclysmic **Watergate Affair**. In January 1973, seven men were tried for breaking into and bugging the headquarters of the Democratic Party in the Watergate building in Washington, an act that was discovered to have been financed with money allocated to the Campaign to Re-elect the President (CREEP). Nixon may not have sanctioned the actual bugging operation, but there was ample evidence to suggest that he participated in the cover-up. Ironically, his insistence on taping all White House conversations in order to ease the writing of his future memoirs was to be the major stumbling block to his surviving the crisis. Facing the threat of impeachment, President Nixon **resigned** in 1974.

The full **pardon** granted to Nixon by his successor, Gerald Ford (appointed to the vice-presidency during Watergate – some allege, on the condition of such a pardon being given) did little to arrest a widespread public disillusionment with the country's political machine, which has only deepened since the 1970s. The rose-tinted faith, long held by many Americans, in the unflinching goodness of the President *per se* seemed irredeemably shattered. Remarkably, however, the years since Richard Nixon's ignoble demise saw him quietly seek to establish elder-statesman credentials, opining on world and national affairs through books and newspaper columns. He died in 1994 and was buried at Yorba Linda.

the **Richard Nixon Library and Birthplace**, 18001 Yorba Linda Blvd (Mon–Sat 10am–5pm, Sun 11am–5pm; $5), is an unrelentingly hagiographic library/museum that features oversized gifts from world leaders, amusing campaign memorabilia, and a collection of obsequious letters written by and to Nixon (including one he despatched to the boss of *McDonald's* proclaiming the fast-food chain's hamburgers to be "one of the finest food buys in America"). But it's in the constantly running archive radio and TV recordings that the distinctive Nixon persona really shines through.

Although famously embarrassed in 1960s live TV debates with John F. Kennedy (refusing to wear make-up, and with a visible growth of beard, Nixon perspired freely under the TV lights and was seen as the embodiment of sleaze), Nixon had earlier used the medium to save his political life. In 1952, the discovery of undeclared income precipitated the "fund crisis", which cast doubts over Nixon's honesty. Incredibly, his **"Checkers speech"** convinced 58 million viewers of his integrity, with a broadcast to rival the worst soap opera; his performance climaxed with the statement that, regardless of the damage it may do to his career, he would not be returning the cocker spaniel dog (Checkers) given to him as a gift and now a family pet. Throughout the museum, Nixon's face leers down in Orwellian fashion from almost every wall, but only inside the **Presidential Auditorium** (at the end of the corridor packed with notes attesting to the president's innocence in the Watergate Affair) do you get the chance to ask him a question. Many possibilities spring to mind, but the choice is limited to those already programmed into a computer. Ten or so minutes after making your selection, Nixon's gaunt features will fill the overlarge screen and provide the stock reply – as endearingly and believably as ever.

The Orange County Coast

As Disneyland grew, so did the rest of Orange County. Besides providing tourist services, the region become a major center for light industry and home to many of the millions who poured into Southern California during the Sixties and Seventies – its population density is even greater than that of neighboring, more metropolitan, Los Angeles County. But it was expansion without style, and those who could afford to soon left the anonymous inland sprawl for the more characterful coast. As a result, the **ORANGE COUNTY COAST**, a string of towns stretching from the edge of the Harbor Area to the borders of San Diego County 35 miles south, is suburbia with a shoreline: swanky beachside houses line the sands, the general ambience is easy-going, affluent, and conservative or libertarian depending on the area.

As the names of the main towns suggest – **Huntington Beach**, **Newport Beach** and **Laguna Beach** – there's no real reason beyond sea and sand to go there. But they do provide something of a counterpart to LA's more cosmopolitan side, and, despite the destructive bushfires of 1993 they do form appealing stopovers on a leisurely journey south. You might even spy a bit of countryside: unlike most of the city's other districts, the communities here don't stand shoulder-to-shoulder but are a few miles apart, in many instances divided by an ugly power station but sometimes by a piece of undeveloped coast. The one place which genuinely merits a stop is just inland at **San Juan Capistrano**, site of the best kept of all the Californian missions. Further on, there's little to see before you reach adjoining San Diego County, but the campground at **San Clemente** provides the only cheap accommodation along the southern part of the coast.

If you're in a rush to get from LA to San Diego, you can skip the coast by passing through Orange County on the inland San Diego Freeway. The coastal cities, though, are linked by the more adventurous Pacific Coast Highway (PCH), part of Hwy-1, which you can pick up from Long Beach (or from the end of Beach Boulevard, coming from Anaheim), though it's often heaving in summer.

OCTD bus #1 rumbles along PCH roughly hourly throughout the day. Greyhound connections aren't so good: San Clemente gets nine buses a day and two early morning buses go to San Juan Capistrano, but there are none to Huntington, Laguna or Newport Beach. Most Greyhound buses bound for San Diego use the freeway. Amtrak is a good way to get from downtown LA (or Disneyland) to San Juan Capistrano, but one point to remember is that you can travel all the way along the coast from LA to San Diego using local buses for about $4 – though you should allow a full day for the journey.

Huntington Beach

HUNTINGTON BEACH is the first place of any interest on the Orange County coast, the wildest of the beach communities and one that you don't need a fortune to enjoy. It's a compact little place composed of engagingly ramshackle single-story cafés and beach stores grouped around the foot of a long pier. The beach is the sole focus: it was here that Californian **surfing** began – imported from Hawaii in 1907 to encourage curious day-trippers to visit on the Pacific Electric Railway. Top surfers still flock to Huntington Beach for the annual **OP Pro Surfing Championship**, a world-class televised event held each June. In October, the largely blonde and suntanned locals celebrate a plausible **Oktoberfest**, with German food and music. Otherwise, once you've exhausted the beach and the local shops, there's not much else, although Huntington Beach is a good place to be based for a while, with Orange County's cheapest beds in the **youth hostel** at 421 Eighth St, three blocks from the pier (see p.75 for details).

Newport Beach and Corona Del Mar

Ten miles south from Huntington, **NEWPORT BEACH** could hardly provide a greater contrast. With ten yacht clubs and ten thousand yachts, this is upmarket even by Orange County standards, a chic image-conscious town that people visit to acquire a tan they can show off on the long stretches of sand or in the bars alongside. You'll need a pocketful of credit cards and a presentable physique to join them, but the sheer exclusivity of the place may be an attraction in itself.

Newport Beach is spread around a natural bay that cuts several miles inland, but *the* place to hang out is on the thin **Balboa Peninsula**, along which runs the three-mile-long beach. The most youthful and boisterous section is about halfway along, around Newport Pier at the end of 20th Street. North of here, beachfront homes restrict access; to the south the wide sands are occupied by a sporty crowd and, further along, around the second of Newport's two piers, the **Balboa Pier** is claimed by seasiding families. Balboa Pier is the most touristy part of Newport, but it does hold a marina from which you can escape to Catalina Island (see p.123), or take a boat ride on the *Pavilion Queen* (summer daily, hourly cruises 11am–7pm; rest of year daily 11am–3pm; $6–8) around Newport's own, much smaller, islands.

On the peninsula there's little in the way of conventional sights, but you might cast an eye over the exterior (there's no public access) of the modernist **Lovell House** on 13th Street, designed by Rudolph Schindler and finished in 1926. Raised on five concrete legs, its living quarters jutting out toward the sidewalk, the house formed the basis of the architect's international reputation. Away from the peninsula, Newport Beach is home to the much-hyped **Newport Harbor Art Museum** at 850 San Clemente Drive (Tues–Sun 11am–5pm; $5, free Tues), another of Southern California's important art museums, which stages occasionally brilliant exhibitions of contemporary work.

Just a few miles along PCH from Newport, **CORONA DEL MAR** is a much less ostentatious place, worth a short stop for its good beach and the **Sherman Foundation Center**, devoted to the horticulture of the American Southwest and rais-

LAGUNA'S FESTIVALS

Laguna hosts a number of large summer **art festivals** over a six-week period during July and August. The best-known, and most bizarre, is the **Pageant of the Masters**, a kind of great paintings charade in which the participants pose in front of a painted backdrop to portray a famous work of art. It might sound ridiculous, but it's actually quite impressive, and takes a great deal of preparation – something reflected in the prices: $15 for the cheapest tickets for shows which sell out months in advance, though you may be able to pick up cancellations on the night. The idea for the pageant was hatched during the Depression as a way to raise money for local artists, and the action takes place at the Irving Bowl, close to where Broadway meets Laguna Canyon Road, a walkable distance from the Laguna Beach bus station. The pageant is combined with the **Festival of the Arts** held at the same venue during daylight hours.

The excitement of both festivals waned in the Sixties, when a group of hippies created the alternative **Sawdust Festival**, in which local artists and craftspeople set up makeshift studios to demonstrate their skills – now just as established but a lot cheaper and easier to get into than the other two. It takes place at 935 Laguna Canyon Rd, and admission is around $5.

ing many vivid blooms in its **botanical gardens**. Between here and Laguna Beach lies an invitingly unspoilt three-mile-long hunk of coastline, protected as **Crystal Coves State Park**. It's perfect to explore on foot, far from the crowds. OCTD bus #1 stops alongside.

Laguna Beach

Six miles further south, and nestling among the crags around a small sandy beach, **LAGUNA BEACH** grew up late in the nineteenth century as a community of artists, drawn by the beauty of the location. You need a few million dollars to live here nowadays, but there's a relaxed and tolerant feel among the inhabitants, who span everything from rich industrialists to leftovers from the 1960s when Laguna became a hippy haven – even Timothy Leary was known to hang out at the *Taco Bell* on PCH. The scenery is still the great attraction, and despite the massive growth in population Laguna remains relatively unspoilt, with a still flourishing minor arts scene manifest in the many galleries crammed into the narrow streets.

PCH passes right through the center of Laguna, a few steps from the small main **beach**. From the beach's north side, an elevated wooden walkway twists around the coastline above a conserved **ecological area**, enabling you to peer down on the ocean and, when the tide's out, scamper over the rocks to observe the tide-pool activity. From the end of the walkway, make your way through the legions of posh beachside homes and head down the hill back to the center. You'll pass the **Laguna Beach Museum of Art** (summer Tues–Sun 11am–5pm; $5), which has changing exhibitions from its stock of Southern Californian art from the 1900s to the present day. A few miles along is less-touristy **SOUTH LAGUNA**, where the wonderfully secluded Victoria and Aliso beaches are among several below the bluffs.

Dana Point

From Laguna it's often possible to see **Dana Point**, a town and promontory jutting into the ocean about four miles south. It was named after sailor and author Richard Henry Dana Jr, whose *Two Years Before the Mast*, a novel of life on the high seas in the early days of California, described how cattle hides were flung over these cliffs to trading ships waiting below. He ended his voyaging career here in 1830, and there's a statue of him and a replica of his vessel, *The Pilgrim*, at the edge of the harbor. These days, Southern Californians mostly know the town as a place where a postal worker went berserk a few years ago and killed several people.

San Juan Capistrano and San Clemente

Three miles inland from Dana Point along the I-5 freeway, most of the small town of **SAN JUAN CAPISTRANO** is built in a Spanish Colonial style derived from the **Mission San Juan Capistrano** on Camino Capistrano in the center of town (daily 8.30am–5pm; $4), a short walk from the Amtrak stop. The seventh in California's chain of missions, this was founded by Junipero Serra in 1776, and within three years was so well populated that it outgrew the original chapel. Soon after, the **Stone Church** was erected, the ruins of which are the first thing you see as you walk in. The enormous structure had seven domes and a bell tower but was destroyed by an earthquake soon after its completion in 1812. For an idea of how it might have looked, visit the full-sized reconstruction – now a working church – just northwest of the mission.

The rest of the mission is in an above-average state of repair, due to an ongoing restoration program. The **chapel** is small and narrow, decorated with Indian drawings and Spanish artifacts from its earliest days, and is set off by a sixteenth-century altar from Barcelona. In a side room is the chapel of St Pereguin; during the 1970s, a woman suffering from cancer prayed for six months to the saint asking to be cured, and afterwards her doctor declared that the cancer had indeed disappeared. Now the tiny room is kept warm by the heat from the dozens of candles lit by hopeful pilgrims who arrive here from all over the US and Mexico.

The other restored buildings reflect the mission's practical role during the Indian period: the kitchen, the smelter, and the workshops used for dyeing, weaving and candle-making. There's also a rather predictable **museum**, which gives a broad historical outline of the Spanish progress through California and displays odds and ends from the mission's past. The mission is also noted for its **swallows**, popularly thought to return here from their winter migration on March 19. They sometimes do arrive on this day – along with large numbers of tourists – but the birds are much more likely to show up as soon as the weather is warm enough, and when there are enough insects on the ground to provide a decent homecoming banquet.

San Clemente
Five miles south of San Juan Capistrano down I-5, the town of **SAN CLEMENTE** is a pretty little place, its streets contoured around the hills, lending an almost Mediterranean air. Because of its proximity to one of the largest military bases in the state, **Camp Pendleton**, it's a popular weekend retreat for military personnel. It's also predominantly a retirement town which had a brief moment of fame during the 1970s, when President Nixon convened his Western White House here. The 25-acre estate and house are visible from the beach, which is clean and virtually deserted, and there's a decent campground (see p.76), but little else of interest.

The San Gabriel and San Fernando Valleys

The northern limit of LA is defined by two long, wide valleys lying beyond the hills from the central basin, starting close to one another a few miles north of downtown and spanning outwards in opposite directions – east to the deserts around Palm Springs, west to Ventura on the Central Coast.

Sunset Boulevard

Century City

Getty Centre Museum

Watts Towers

Malibu shores

Coronado Bay Bridge, San Diego

Seaworld in San Diego

Balboa Park, San Diego

"It's a Small World", Disneyland

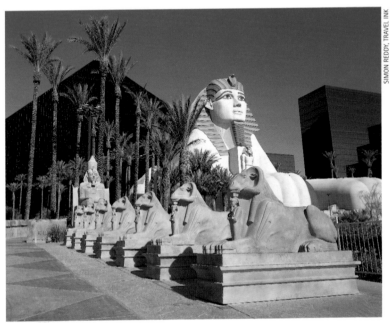

The Luxor Hotel, Las Vegas

The **San Gabriel Valley** was settled by farmers and cattle ranchers who set up small towns on the lands of the eighteenth-century Mission San Gabriel. The foothill communities grew into prime resort towns, luring many here around the turn of the century. **Pasadena**, the largest of the foothill communities, holds many elegant period houses, as well as the brilliant but underpublicized **Norton Simon Museum**, and has lately become an increasingly popular spot for dining, shopping and a range of cultural activities. Above Pasadena, the slopes of the San Gabriel Mountains are littered with explorable remains from the resort days, and make great spots for hiking and rough camping, although you'll nearly always need a car to get to the trailheads. The areas around Pasadena are generally less absorbing, although, to the south, WASP-ish **San Marino** is dominated by the **Huntington Library**, a stash of art and literature ringed by botanical gardens that itself makes the journey into the valley worthwhile.

The **San Fernando Valley**, spreading west, is *the* valley to most Angelenos: a sprawl of tract homes, mini-malls, fast-food drive-ins and auto-parts stores. It has more of a middle-American feel than anywhere else in LA and is culturally, if not economically, similar to much of inland Orange County. There are a few isolated sights, notably **Forest Lawn Cemetery** – a prime example of graveyard kitsch that's hard to imagine anywhere except in LA – but otherwise, beyond a couple of minor historical sites, it's the **movies** that bring people out here. Rising land values in the 1930s pushed many studios out of Hollywood and over the hills to **Burbank**, an anodyne community now overpowered by several major film and TV companies, several of which are open to the public.

At the far west end, the ultra-conservative suburb of **Simi Valley** is known for two things: finding five police officers "not guilty" of beating Rodney King in April 1992 (see p.89), and providing a home for the **Ronald Reagan Presidential Library** (daily 10am–5pm; $4, kids free), a federal library containing all the papers pertaining to the Reagan administration.

EARTHQUAKE CITY: THE SAN FERNANDO VALLEY

The devastating 6.7 magnitude **earthquake** that shook LA on the morning of January 17, 1994 was one of the most destructive disasters in US history. Fifty-five people were killed, two hundred more suffered critical injuries, and the economic cost has been estimated at some $8 billion (by way of comparison, the construction of the Channel Tunnel between Britain and France cost around $4 billion). One can only guess how much higher these totals would have been had the quake hit during the day, when the many collapsed stores would have been crowded with shoppers and the roads and freeways full of commuters.

As it is, the tremor toppled chimneys and shattered windows all over Southern California, with the worst damage concentrated at the epicenter in the San Fernando Valley community of **Northridge**, where a dozen people were killed when an apartment building collapsed. At the northern edge of the valley, the vital I-5/Hwy-14 interchange was destroyed, killing just one motorist but snarling traffic for at least a year, while in West LA, the Santa Monica Freeway overpass collapsed onto La Cienega Boulevard at one of LA's busiest intersections. The Northridge event just eclipsed LA's previous worst earthquake, the 6.6 magnitude tremor of February 9, 1971, which had its epicenter in Sylmar.

Small earthquakes happen all the time in LA, usually doing no more than rattling supermarket shelves and making dogs howl. In the unlikely event a sizeable earthquake strikes when you're in LA, try to protect yourself under something sturdy, such as a heavy table or a door frame, and well away from windows or anything made of glass. Afterwards, don't use telephones or electricity unless you have to, as this may overload the systems. In theory, all the city's new buildings are "quake-safe"; the extent of the crisis in January 1994, however, has given the city the chance to rebuild and reinforce buildings on a scale not previously imagined. Yet, when the inevitable "Big One", a quake in the 8.0 range, arrives, no one knows exactly what will be left standing.

Pasadena

Marking the entrance to the San Gabriel Valley, **PASADENA** is as much the home of the *grandes dames* of Los Angeles society as it is to the "little old lady from Pasadena" of the Jan and Dean song. In the 1880s, wealthy East Coast tourists who came to California looking for the good life found it in this foothill resort ten miles north of Los Angeles, where luxury hotels were built and railways cut into the nearby San Gabriel mountains to lead up to taverns and astronomical observatories on the mile-high crest. Many of the early, well-to-do visitors stayed on, building the rustically sprawling houses that remain, but as LA grew so Pasadena suffered, mainly from the smog which the mountains collect. The downtown area underwent a major renovation in the 1980s, with modern shopping centers being slipped in behind 1920s facades, but the historic parts of town have not been forgotten. Maps and booklets detailing self-guided tours of Pasadena architecture and history are available from the **Pasadena CVB** at 171 S Los Robles Ave (Mon–Fri 8am–5pm, Sat 10am–4pm; ☎818/795-9311). If you're around at the right time, watch out also for the New Year's Day **Tournament of Roses**, which began in 1890 to celebrate and publicize the mild Southern California winters, and now attracts over a million visitors every year to watch its marching bands and elaborate flower-emblazoned floats (see box on pp.156–157).

A block north of Colorado Boulevard, a replica Chinese Imperial Palace houses the **Pacific Asia Museum** at 46 N Los Robles Ave (Wed–Sun 10am–5pm; $4, students $2), which has a wide range of objects from Japan, China and Thailand – though if you have even the slightest interest in the art of South East Asia, your time would be better spent at the collection of the Norton Simon Museum.

The Norton Simon Museum

You may not have heard of the **Norton Simon Museum**, but its collections, housed in a modern building at 411 W Colorado Blvd (Thurs–Sun noon–6pm; $4, students $2), are at least as good as the County or Getty museums. Established and overseen by the eponymous industrialist until his death in 1993, the museum, perhaps because of its unfashionable location, sidesteps the hype of the LA art world to concentrate on the quality of its presentation. You could easily spend a whole afternoon, or day, wandering through the spacious galleries.

The core of the collection is Western European painting from the Renaissance to the modern period. It's a massive collection, much of it rotated, but most of the major pieces are on view constantly. You'll see Dutch paintings of the seventeenth century – notably Rembrandt's vivacious *Titus, Portrait of a Boy* and Frans Hals' quietly aggressive *Portrait of a Man* – and Italian Renaissance work from Pietro Longhi and Guido Reni. Among more modern works, there's a good sprinkling of French Impressionists and post-Impressionists: Monet's *Mouth of the Seine at Honfleur*, Manet's *Ragpicker* and a Degas capturing the extended yawn of a washerwoman in *The Ironers*, plus works by Cézanne, Gauguin, Van Gogh and Picasso. As a counterpoint to the Western art, the museum has a fine collection of **Asian sculpture** and many highly polished Buddhist and Hindu figures, a mixture of the contemplative and the erotic, some inlaid with precious stones.

Arroyo Seco

Although many outsiders may not realize it, the residential pocket northwest of the junction of the 134 and 210 freeways should be, according to architecture critic David Gebhard, "declared a national monument". The area known as **ARROYO SECO**, or "dry riverbed" in Spanish, boasts some of the region's best architecture and features some of the Valley's key attractions that visitors should by no means miss. Orange Grove

Avenue leads you into the neighborhood from central Pasadena and takes you to the **Pasadena Historical Society** on Walnut and Orange Grove (Thurs–Sun 1–4pm; $4), which is decorated with its original 1905 furnishings and paintings, and has fine displays on Pasadena's history. The building was once the Finnish Consulate, and much of the folk art on display comes from Pasadena's "twin town" of Jarvenpää in Finland.

But it's the **Gamble House**, 4 Westmoreland Place (hour-long tours Thurs–Sun noon–3pm; $4), which brings people out here. Built in 1908, and one of the master-pieces of Southern Californian Craftsman architecture, it's a style you'll see replicated all over the state, at once relaxed and refined, freely combining elements from Swiss chalets and Japanese temples in a romantic, sprawling shingled house. Broad eaves shelter outdoor sleeping porches, which in turn shade terraces on the ground floor, leading out to the spacious lawn. The interior was crafted with the same attention to detail, and all the carpets, cabinetry and lighting fixtures, designed specifically for the house, remain in excellent condition. The area around the Gamble House is filled with at least eight other **houses** by the two brothers (the firm of "Greene & Greene") who designed it, including Charles Greene's own house at 368 Arroyo Terrace. A quarter of a mile north of the Gamble House is a small, concrete block house by Frank Lloyd Wright, *La Miniatura*, which you can glimpse through the gate opposite 585 Rosemont Ave. Also in the vicinity are houses by noted architects Gregory Ain, Craig Ellwood and Richard Neutra, but the area most rewards casual driving through its hilly concourses and serene setting. Almost incongruously, the 104,000-seat **Rose Bowl** is just to the north, out of use for most of the year but home to a very popular **flea market** on the second Sunday of each month and, in the autumn, the place where the UCLA football team plays its home games. The other football was also played here in 1994, when the site hosted the World Cup Final.

Into the foothills

On the other side of the Foothill Freeway, **Descanso Gardens** (daily 9am–4.30pm; $5, students $3) in the city of La Cañada Flintridge, concentrates all the plants you might see in the mountains into 155 acres of landscaped park. The gardens are especially bril-liant during the spring, when all the wild flowers are in bloom. From La Cañada, the **Angeles Crest Highway** (Hwy-2) heads up into the mountains above Pasadena. This area was once dotted with resort hotels and wilderness camps, and today you can hike up any number of nearby canyons and come across the ruins of old lodges that either burned down or were washed away towards the end of the hiking era in the 1930s, when automobiles became popular. One of the most interesting of these trails, a five-mile round trip, follows the route of the Mount Lowe Railway, once one of LA's biggest tourist attractions, from the top of Lake Avenue up to the old railway and the founda-tions of **"White City"** – formerly a mountaintop resort of two hotels, a zoo and an observatory. Today a brass plaque embedded in concrete is the only reminder of the resort, and even this is slowly becoming overgrown with pine trees and incense cedars. The Crest Highway passes through the **Angeles National Forest**, where you can hike and camp most of the year and ski in winter to Mount Wilson, high enough to be the major siting spot for TV broadcast antennae, and with a small **museum** (daily 10am–3pm; $1) near the 100-inch telescope of the 1904 Mount Wilson Observatory.

Around Pasadena: San Marino, Arcadia and Sierra Madre

South of Pasadena, **SAN MARINO** is a dull, upper-crust suburb with little of interest beyond the **Huntington Library, Art Collections and Botanical Gardens**, off Huntington Drive at 1151 Oxford Rd (Tues–Fri 1–4.30pm, Sat & Sun 10am–4.30pm; $7.50, students $4). Part of this comprises the collections of Henry Huntington, the nephew of the childless multimillionaire Collis P. Huntington, who owned and operated the Southern Pacific Railroad – which in the nineteenth century had a virtual monopoly on transportation in California. Henry, groomed to take over the company from his uncle, was dethroned by the board of directors and took his sizeable inheritance to Los Angeles, where he bought up the existing streetcar routes and combined them as the Pacific Electric Railway Company. It was a shrewd investment: the company's "Redcars" soon became the largest network in the world, and Huntington the largest landowner in the state, buying up farmland and extending the streetcar system at a huge profit. He retired in 1910, moving to the manor house he had built in San Marino, devoting himself full time to buying rare books and manuscripts, and marrying his uncle's widow Arabella and acquiring her collection of English portraits.

You can pick up a self-guided walking tour of each of the three main sections from the bookstore and information desk in the covered pavilion. The **Library**, right off the main entrance, is a good first stop, its two-story exhibition hall containing numerous manuscripts and rare books, among them a Gutenberg Bible, a folio edition of Shakespeare's plays, and the **Ellesmere Chaucer**, a c.1410 illuminated manuscript of the *Canterbury Tales*. Displays around the walls trace the history of printing and of the English language from medieval manuscripts to a King James Bible, through Milton's *Paradise Lost* and Blake's *Songs of Innocence* and *Experience*, to first editions of Swift, Coleridge, Dickens, Woolf and Joyce.

To decorate the **main house**, a grand mansion done out in Louis XIV carpets and later French tapestries, the Huntingtons traveled to England and returned laden with the finest art money could buy; most of it still hangs on the walls. Unless you're a real fan of eighteenth-century English portraiture, head through to the back extension, added when the gallery opened in 1934, which displays, as well as works by Turner, van Dyck and Constable, the stars of the whole collection – Gainsborough's *Blue Boy* and Reynolds' *Mrs Siddons as the Tragic Muse*.

You'll find paintings by Edward Hopper and Mary Cassatt, and a range of Wild West drawings and sculpture, in the **Scott Gallery for American Art**. For all the art and literature, though, it's the grounds that make the Huntington really special, and the acres of beautiful themed **gardens** surrounding the buildings include a Zen Rock Garden, complete with authentically constructed Buddhist Temple and Tea House. The Desert Garden has the world's largest collection of desert plants, including twelve acres of cactuses in an artful setting. While strolling through these botanical splendors, you might also call in on the Huntingtons themselves, buried in a neo-Palladian mausoleum at the northwest corner of the estate, beyond the rows of an orange grove.

Foothill Boulevard, parallel to the Foothill Freeway (I-210), was once best known as part of **Route 66**, formerly the main route across the US: "from Chicago to LA, more than three thousand miles all the way". The freeway stole Route 66's traffic, and following Foothill Boulevard out of Pasadena nowadays leads to the adjacent town of **ARCADIA**, whose **State and County Arboretum** on Baldwin Avenue (daily 9am–4.30pm; $5, students $3) has forests of trees arranged according to their native continent. The site was once the 127-acre ranch home of "Lucky" Baldwin, who made his millions in the silver mines of the Comstock in the 1870s. He settled here in 1875, and built a fanciful white palace along a palm-treed lagoon, later used in the TV show *Fantasy Island*, on the site of the 1839 Rancho Santa Anita. He also bred horses, and raced them on a neighboring track that has since grown into the **Santa Anita Racetrack** (racing Oct to early Nov & late Dec to late April, Wed–Sun, post time 12.30pm or 1pm; $3–8), still the most glamorous racetrack in California.

The district of **SIERRA MADRE**, on the northern edge of town, lies directly beneath Mount Wilson and is worth a visit if you're a hiker. A seven-mile round-trip trail up to the summit has recently been restored and is now one of the best hikes in the range. (The trailhead is 150 yards up the private Mount Wilson Road.) South of Sierra Madre stands the valley's original settlement, the church and grounds of

Mission San Gabriel Arcangel (daily 9am–4.30pm; $3). Still standing at the corner of Mission and Serra in the heart of the small town of **San Gabriel**, the mission was established here in 1771 by Junipero Serra. Though still partially covered in scaffolding following decades of damage by earthquakes and the elements, the church and grounds have recently been reopened, its grapevine-filled gardens giving some sense of mission-era life.

Glendale and Forest Lawn Cemetery

GLENDALE, eight miles north of downtown and the gateway to the San Fernando Valley, was once a fashionable suburb of LA. Now it's a nondescript bedroom community, and the only reason to come here is to visit the Glendale branch of **Forest Lawn Cemetery** at 1712 S Glendale Ave (daily 9am–5pm; free) – immortalized with biting satire by Evelyn Waugh in *The Loved One*, and at the vanguard of the American way of death for decades. Founded in 1917 by a Dr Hubert Eaton, this fast became *the* place to be seen dead, its pompous landscaping and pious artworks attracting celebrities by the dozen to buy their own little piece of heaven.

It's best to climb the hill and see the cemetery in reverse from the **Forest Lawn Museum**, whose hotchpotch of old artifacts from around the world includes coins from ancient Rome, Viking oddments, medieval armour, and a mysterious sculpted Easter Island figure, discovered being used as ballast in a fishing boat in the days when the statues could still be removed from the island. How it ended up here is another mystery, but it is the only one on view in the US. Next door to the museum, the grandiose **Resurrection and Crucifixion Hall** houses the biggest piece of religious art in the world, *The Crucifixion* by Jan Styka – though you're only allowed to see it during the ceremonial unveiling every hour on the hour (and you'll be charged $1 for an eyeful). Besides this, Eaton owned a stained glass re-creation of da Vinci's *Last Supper* and, realizing that he only needed one piece to complete his set of "the three greatest moments in the life of Christ", he commissioned American artist Robert Clark to produce *The Resurrection* – an effort which is also only viewable when unveiled, though this happens on the half-hour. If you can't be bothered to stick around for the showings (with both, in any case, the size is the only aspect that's impressive), you can get a good idea of what you're missing from the scaled-down replicas just inside the entrance.

From the museum, walk down through the terrace gardens – loaded with sculptures modelled on the greats of classical European art – to the **Freedom Mausoleum**, where you'll find a handful of the cemetery's better-known graves. Just outside the mausoleum's doors, Errol Flynn lies in an unspectacular plot (unmarked until 1979), rumored to have been buried with six bottles of whiskey at his side, while a few strides away is the grave of Walt Disney, who is not cryogenically preserved as urban legend would have it. Inside the mausoleum itself you'll find Clara Bow, Nat King Cole, Jeanette MacDonald and Alan Ladd handily placed close to each other on the first floor. Downstairs are Chico Marx, and his brother Gummo, the Marx Brothers' agent and business manager. To the left, heading back down the hill, the **Great Mausoleum** is chiefly noted for the tombs of Clark Gable (next to Carole Lombard, who died in a plane crash just three years after marrying him), and Jean Harlow, in a marble-lined room which cost over $25,000, paid for by fiancé William Powell.

A number of other **Forest Lawn cemeteries** continue the style of the Glendale site, to a much less spectacular degree. There's a Hollywood Hills branch in Burbank (6300 Forest Hills Drive, close to Griffith Park) which has a formidable roll call of ex-stars – Buster Keaton, Stan Laurel, Liberace, Charles Laughton and Marvin Gaye – but little else to warrant a visit. The others, Covina Hills, Cypress Beach and Long Beach, also hold limited appeal.

Burbank and the studios

Although Hollywood is the name that's synonymous with the movie industry, in reality many of the big studios moved out of Tinseltown long ago, and much of the nitty-gritty business of actually making films goes on over the hills in otherwise boring **BUR-BANK**, the perennial butt of Johnny Carson's jokes. Hot, smoggy and in some places downright ugly, Burbank nonetheless has a media district bustling with production activity, thanks to the explosion in demand from overseas markets, cable TV and broadcast networks. Disney recently constructed a curious new building to house over seven hundred animators, and **Warner Brothers** is planning an $800 million expansion to its premises over the next twenty years. The latter studio, located at Warner Blvd and Hollywood Way, offers "insider" tours of its facilities (Mon–Fri 9am–4pm; $27; ☎818/972-TOUR), as does **NBC**, at 3000 W Alameda St (Mon–Fri 9am–3pm; $7; ☎818/840-3537). With a frank and interesting ninety-minute tour of the largest production facility in the US, the studio offers the chance to be in the audience for the taping of a program (phone ahead for free tickets). It's worth the price of admission just to see *Tonight Show* host Jay Leno in action.

The largest of the old backlots belongs to **Universal Studios**, whose tours (summer daily 8am–10pm; rest of year daily 9am–7pm; $36; ☎818/508-9600) are firmly tourist-oriented, four hours long and, with high-tech interactive rides, more like a trip around an amusement park than a film studio. The first half features a tram ride through a make-believe set where you can experience the fading magic of the parting of the Red Sea and a collapsing bridge; the second takes place inside the corny Entertainment Center, where unemployed actors and stuntmen engage in Wild West shoot-outs and stunt shows based on the latest movies. You never actually get to see any filming.

The **Universal Amphitheater**, which hosts pop concerts in summer, is also part of the complex, as is a twenty-screen movie theater complex, with a lobby reminiscent of 1920s movie palaces. **Universal CityWalk**, also on the same lot, is a few square blocks of neon-lit themed restaurants, free to all who pay the $5 parking (redeemable at the cinemas), where rock bands churn out MOR covers, street performers warble slick set pieces, and giant TV screens run ads for the latest Universal release. After Thanksgiving, an open-air ice-rink adds to the merriment.

Los Encinos State Historic Park and northwards

At the western end of the San Fernando Valley, the Ventura Freeway (US-101) passes below the increasingly expensive hillside homes of **Sherman Oaks** and **Encino**, close to which the **Los Encinos State Historic Park**, on Balboa Boulevard (Wed–Sun

---

THE LA AQUEDUCT

Just beyond the Mission San Fernando, I-5 runs past two of LA's main reservoirs, the water in which has been brought hundreds of miles through the **California Aqueduct** from the Sacramento Delta, and through the **LA Aqueduct** from the Owens Valley and Mono Lake on the eastern slopes of the Sierra Nevada mountains. However, with all due respect to the engineering expertise involved, the legality of the arrangements by which Los Angeles gained control of such a distant supply of water is still disputed. Agents of the city, masquerading as rich cattle-barons interested in establishing ranches in the Owens Valley, bought up most of the land along the Owens River before selling it on, at personal profit, to the City of Los Angeles. These cunning tactics provided the inspiration for Roman Polanski's 1974 movie *Chinatown*.

For more on Mono Lake and the Owens Valley, see p.279 and p.270.

10am–5pm, tours 1–4pm; grounds free, tours $2), is all that remains of the original Native American settlement and later Mexican hacienda that were here. The high-ceilinged rooms of the 1849 adobe house open out onto porches, shaded by oak trees (in Spanish, "encinos") and kept cool by the two-foot-thick walls.

West of Encino, Topanga Canyon Boulevard crosses the Ventura Freeway, leading south towards Malibu (p.119) or north to **Stony Point**, a bizarre outcrop of sandstone that has been used for countless budget Western shoot-outs, and in recent years as a popular venue for LA's contingent of lycra-clad rock climbers. The area, though crossed by both Amtrak and Metrorail coastal trains, certainly has a desolate spooki-ness about it, and it comes as little surprise to learn that during the late 1960s the Charles Manson "family" lived for a time at the **Spahn Ranch**, just west at 12000 Santa Susana Pass.

Mission San Fernando and Magic Mountain

At the north end of the Valley, the San Diego, Golden State and Foothill freeways join together at I-5, the quickest route north to San Francisco. Standing near the junction at 15151 San Fernando Mission Blvd, the church and many of the buildings of **Mission San Fernando Rey De España** (daily 9am–5pm; $4) had to be completely rebuilt fol-lowing the 1971 earthquake. It's hard to imagine now, walking through the nicely land-scaped courtyards and gardens, but eighty-odd years ago, director D.W. Griffith used the then-dilapidated mission as a film site for movies such as *Our Silent Paths*, his tale of the Gold Rush. Another twenty miles north, Hwy-14 splits off east to the Mojave desert, while I-5 continues north past Valencia and **Magic Mountain** (summer daily 10am–10pm; rest of year Sat & Sun only 10am–8pm; $33, $5 parking), a three-hundred-acre complex that has some of the wildest roller coasters and rides in the world – a hun-dred times more thrilling than anything at Disneyland.

Eating

LA's **restaurants** cover every extreme: whatever you want to eat and however much you want to spend, you're spoilt for choice. **Budget food** is as plentiful as in any other US city, ranging from good sit-down meals in street-corner coffee shops and cafés to big franchise burgers. Almost as common, and just as cheap, is **Mexican food**. This is the closest thing you'll get to an indigenous LA cuisine – most notably in the burrito, a filled tortilla that's rarely seen in Mexico and is available everywhere, both from street vendors and comfortable restaurants. If you simply want to load up quickly and cheaply, the options are almost endless, and include free food available for the price of a drink at **happy hours**.

However, you should also try to take at least a few meals in one of LA's **top-notch restaurants**, which serve superb food in consciously cultured surroundings – if only to watch the city's many self-appointed food snobs going through their paces. Scores of restaurants whack up their prices on the back of a good review, and get away with it because they know the place will be packed with first-timers trying to impress their cohorts by claiming that they've been eating there for years.

Catering appears to be the movie stars' sideline of choice these days, and LA is lit-tered with **celebrity-owned** outfits – like Steven Spielberg's submarine-shaped sand-wich store *Dive!* and the brand-new *Planet Hollywood* in Beverly Hills (where displays include Forrest Gump's box of chocolates) – but the food is usually so unremarkable we haven't listed them.

Budget food: coffee shops, delis, diners and drive-ins

Budget food is everywhere in LA, at its best in the many small and stylish **coffee shops**, **delis** and **diners** that serve wholesome soups, omelets, sandwiches and so forth; it's easy to exist entirely this way and never have to spend much more than $6 for a full meal. There are of course the internationally franchised fast-food places on every street and locally based chains of **hamburger stands**, most open 24 hours a day; *Fatburger*, originally at San Vicente and La Cienega on the border of Beverly Hills has branches everywhere.

Sadly but surely, the best of the 1950s **drive-ins** such as *Tiny Naylors* in Hollywood have been torn down. So too have some of the classic googie-style **diners** met their demise; the venerable *Ships* franchise now comprises only a boarded-up ruin in Culver City and a pair of leftover boomerang signs near a gas station in West LA.

Downtown and around

Cassell's Hamburgers, 3266 W Sixth St (☎213/387-5502). No-frills, lunch-only takeout hamburger stand that some swear by.

Clifton's Cafeteria, 648 S Broadway (☎213/627-1673). Classic 1930s cafeteria, but with bizarre decor: redwood trees, waterfall and mini-chapel. The food is traditional meat-and-potatoes American, and cheap too.

Grand Central Market, 317 S Broadway (☎213/624-2378). Choose from dozens of market stalls selling tacos, deli sandwiches and cheap Chinese food – and 24 fresh fruit and vegetable drinks from *Geraldine's* at the Hill Street entrance.

Langer's Deli, 704 S Alvarado St (☎213/483-8050). "When in doubt, eat hot pastrami" says the sign, though you still have to choose from over twenty ways of having it, and a huge deli selection. Half a block south of the MacArthur Park Metrorail station.

Original Pantry, 877 S Figueroa St (☎213/972-9279). There's always a queue for the hearty portions of very meaty American cooking – chops and steaks, mostly – in this 24-hr diner owned by Mayor Riordan. Ask for one of the restaurant's creative and informative brochures.

Philippe's Famous French Dip Sandwiches, 1001 N Alameda St (☎213/628-3781). Sawdust café, a block north of Union Station. Long communal tables and a decor unchanged since 1908.

Shabbazz Restaurant and Bakery, 3405 W 43rd St, Leimert Park, South Central (☎213/299-8688). Jazz greats waft out of the speakers, Malcolm X and Muhammed Ali grace the walls, and the chili and bean pie delights your palate.

The Yorkshire Grill, 610 W Sixth St (☎213/629-3020). Big sandwiches and friendly service for under $10. Lunchtime is crowded; get there early.

Hollywood

Alex Donut, 6211 Franklin Ave (☎213/464-6148). Classic American doughnuts served in a freeway-side strip mall. Try the foot-long cinnamon twist if you are up to it.

Hampton's, 1342 N Highland Ave (☎213/469-1090). Gourmet hamburgers with a choice of over fifty toppings, plus an excellent salad bar.

Johnny Rockets, 7507 Melrose Ave (☎213/651-3361). Chrome-and-glass, Fifties-derived hamburger joint, open until 2am at weekends. Three other Westside locations.

Maurice's Snack 'n' Chat, 5549 W Pico Blvd (☎213/931-3877). Everything here is cooked to order: spoon bread or baked chicken requires a call two hours ahead, though you can just call in for fried chicken, pork chops, grits or salmon croquettes. Autographed pictures of celebrity diners – from Sammy Davis Jr to Ted Kennedy – line the walls.

Pink's Hot Dogs, 711 N La Brea Ave (☎213/931-4223). The quintessence of chili dogs. Depending on your taste, these monster hot dogs are life-savers or gut bombs.

Village Coffee Shop, 2695 Beachwood Drive (☎213/467-5398). A classic coffee shop in the hills below the Hollywood sign, and a good spot for relaxing.

Yukon Mining Co, 7328 Santa Monica Blvd (☎213/851-8833). Excellent 24-hr coffee shop with a curious clientele – don't be surprised to see a crowd of newly arrived Russians, neighborhood pensioners and glammed-up drag queens.

West LA

The Apple Pan, 10801 W Pico Blvd (☎ 310/475-3585). Grab a spot at the counter and enjoy freshly baked apple pie and what some consider the best hamburgers in the world. Fans of *Beverly Hills 90210* take note, the *Peach Pit* was shamelessly copied from this landmark restaurant.

Barney's Beanery, 8447 Santa Monica Blvd (☎213/654-2287). Two hundred bottled beers and hot dogs, hamburgers and bowls of chili served in a hip, grungy environment.

Canter's Deli, 419 N Fairfax Ave (☎213/651-2030). Huge sandwiches for around $7, excellent kosher soups served by waitresses in pink uniforms and running shoes. Open 24-hr.

Duke's, 8909 Sunset Blvd (☎310/652-9411). A favorite haunt of rock stars, this place attracts a motley crew of night owls and bleary-eyed locals; open until 4am.

Ed Debevic's, 134 N La Cienega Blvd (☎310/659-1952). Fifties-style diner with singing waitresses and pricey beer.

Hard Rock Café, in the Beverly Center, Beverly Blvd at San Vicente (☎310/276-7605). Rock 'n' roll decor and loud music are the attractions; the greasy food is an afterthought.

Jerry's Famous Deli, 8701 Beverly Blvd (☎310/289-1811). One of several Jerry's locations in LA, this place features a sizeable menu and is open late. Occasionally, celebrities stop in to nosh.

Johnie's, across from May's department store on Fairfax and Wilshire (☎213/938-3521). Tasteless food and a drafty atmosphere, but this landmark café has been home to many a film shoot.

John o' Groats, 10516 W Pico Blvd (☎310/204-0692). Excellent cheap breakfasts and lunches, but come at an off hour; the morning crowd can cause a headache.

Kate Mantilini, 9101 Wilshire Blvd (☎310/278-3699). Well-prepared versions of classic American diner food, served up in one of LA's most stylish interiors. Open late on weekends.

Nate 'n' Al's, 414 N Beverly Drive (☎310/274-0101). The best-known deli in Beverly Hills, popular with movie people and one of the few reasonable places in the vicinity.

Swingers, *Beverly Laurel Motor Lodge*, 8018 Beverly Blvd at Laurel (☎213/651-2441). Basic and cheap American food served in a strangely trendy motel environment.

Tail o' the Pup, 329 N San Vicente Blvd (☎310/652-4517). Worth a visit for the roadside pop architecture alone, though the dogs and burgers are good too.

Santa Monica, Venice and Malibu

Bicycle Shop Café, 12217 Wilshire Blvd, Santa Monica (☎310/826-7831). Pseudo-bistro serving light meals and salads that's also a good place to drink.

Café 50s, 838 Lincoln Blvd, Venice (☎310/399-1955). No doubts about this place: Ritchie Valens on the jukebox, burgers on the tables.

Café Montana, 1534 Montana Ave, Santa Monica (☎310/829-3990). Good breakfasts and excellent salads and grilled fish in upmarket Santa Monica.

Gilliland's, 2424 Main St, Santa Monica (☎310/392-3901). Highly eclectic menu of good and hearty foods, from tangy samosas to a thick Irish stew.

Norm's, 1601 Lincoln Blvd, Santa Monica (☎310/450-0074). One of the last remaining classic diners, this local chain has several other Westside branches and serves $2 breakfasts and similarly cheap lunches. Great googie architecture, too.

Rae's Diner, 2901 Pico Blvd, Santa Monica (☎310/828-7937). Classic 1950s diner behind a turquoise-blue facade. Popular with the late-night crowd; open 6am–10.30pm.

Reel Inn, 18661 Pacific Coast Highway, Malibu (☎310/456-8221). Seafood diner by the beach, with appealing prices and a good atmosphere. Also at 1220 W Third St, Santa Monica (☎310/395-5538).

The Sidewalk Café, 1401 Ocean Front Walk, Venice (☎310/399-5547). Breakfast on the beach, and watch the daily parade of beach people. Live music most evenings.

The South Bay and Harbor Area

East Coast Bagel Company, 5753 E PCH, Long Beach (☎310/985-0933) Located in a dreary mini-mall, but with an excellent wide selection of bagels, ranging from New York staples to California hybrids like the jalapeno-cheddar bagel stuffed with cream cheese.

Hof's Hut, 4823 E Second St, Long Beach (☎310/439-4775). One bite of the Hut's juicy Hofburger and you know you've found the real deal.

Johnnie's Broiler, 7447 Firestone Blvd, Downey (☎310/927-3383). Decent food in a rather bleak corner of LA. On Wednesday nights, Fifties-car fanatics park outside in their Chevys and Fords and are waited upon by perky, roller-skating teens.

The Local Yolk, 3414 Highland Ave, Manhattan Beach (☎310/546-4407). As the name suggests, everything done with eggs, plus muffins and pancakes.

Ocean View Café, 229 13th St, Manhattan Beach, (☎310/545-6770). Light breakfasts and soup and baguettes for around $4, all in a pleasant hillside location.

Pier Bakery, 100-M Fisherman's Wharf, Redondo Beach (☎310/376-9582). A small but satisfying menu featuring the likes of jalapeno cheese bread and cinnamon rolls. Probably the best food in this touristy area.

Russell's, 5656 E Second St, Long Beach (☎310/434-0226). Worth a trip to sample the great burgers and fresh pies. Also at 4306 Atlantic Ave (☎310/427-6869).

Tony's Famous French Dip Sandwiches, 701 Long Beach Blvd, Long Beach (☎310/435-6238). The name says it all, but alongside the dips is a beckoning array of soups and salads.

Disneyland and around

Angelo's, 511 S State College Blvd, Anaheim (☎714/533-1401). Straight out of *Happy Days*, a drive-in complete with roller-skating car-hops, neon signs, vintage cars and, incidentally, good burgers. Open until 2am on weekends.

Belisle's, 12001 Harbor Blvd, Garden Grove (☎714/750-6560). Open late for filling sandwiches, meat pies and a variety of things baked. Known as much for quantity as quality.

Knott's Berry Farm, 8039 Beach Blvd, Buena Park (☎714/827-1776). People flocked here for the delicious fried chicken dinners long before Disneyland was around, and they still do. Look out for the steep entry fee, though.

Mimi's Café, 18342 Imperial Highway (☎714/996-3650). Huge servings, low prices and a relaxing atmosphere just down the street from the Nixon Library in Yorba Linda.

Orange County Coast

C'est Si Bon, 149 Riverside Ave off PCH, Newport Beach (☎714/645-0447). Small seaside café serving croissants, baguettes, and French cheese, paté and coffee.

Ruby's, Balboa Pier, Newport Beach (☎714/675-RUBY). The first, and one of the finest, of the retro-streamline 1940s diners that have popped up all over LA – in a great location at the end of Newport's popular pier.

The San Gabriel and San Fernando Valleys

Dr Hogly-Wogly's Tyler Texas Bar-B-Q, 8136 Sepulveda Blvd, Van Nuys (☎818/780-6701). Long lines for some of the best chicken, sausages, ribs and beans in LA, despite the depressing surroundings.

24-HR EATS

This is just a brief checklist of places to satisfy hunger at all hours. For full restaurant reviews, see the appropriate sections.

Downtown
Pacific Dining Car, 1310 W Sixth St (☎213/483-6000).
Original Pantry, 877 S Figueroa St (☎213/972-9279).

Hollywood
Yukon Mining Co, 7328 Santa Monica Blvd (☎213/851-8833).

West LA
Canter's Deli, 419 N Fairfax Ave (☎213/651-2030).

Fair Oaks Pharmacy and Soda Fountain, 1526 Mission St, South Pasadena (☎818/799-1414). A run-of-the-mill corner store transformed into a fabulous old-fashioned soda fountain.

Goldstein's Bagel Bakery, 86 W Colorado Blvd, Pasadena (☎818/792-2435). If money's tight, feast here on day-old 15¢ bagels; otherwise enjoy fresh pastries, coffees and teas. Two other area locations in La Cañada and Arcadia.

The Hat, 491 N Lake Ave, San Gabriel (☎818/449-1844). Very popular roadside stand selling good burgers and French-dip sandwiches at this and four other nearby locations.

Hidden Springs Café, 23255 Angeles Forest Hwy, Angeles National Forest (☎818/792-9663). The only restaurant on the Angeles Forest Highway. Filling portions are served in open stone rooms with real fires and rustic decor as eclectic as the clientele, which includes Hell's Angels, fly-fishers, gold-miners and tourists.

Pie 'n' Burger, 913 E California Blvd, Pasadena (☎818/795-1123). Classic coffee shop, with good burgers and excellent fresh pies.

Portos Bakery, 315 Brand Blvd, Glendale (☎818/956-5996). Popular and cheap café serving Cuban flaky pastries, cheesecakes soaked in rum, as well as more standard muffins, danishes, croissants, tort, and cheap cappuccino.

Rose Tree Cottage, 824 E California Blvd, Pasadena (☎818/793-3337). Cream or high tea in a country home setting so thoroughly English that it's the West Coast HQ of the British Tourist Board. Reservations are essential.

Mexican and Latin American

LA's **Mexican** restaurants are the city's best – and most plentiful – eating standby, serving tasty, healthy and filling food for as little as $5 a head, including the requisite ice-cold bottle of Bohemia or Corona beer. They're at their finest and most authentic in East LA, although there's a good selection of more Americanized examples all over the city. Aside from restaurants, there are far less enticing but even cheaper Mexican fast-food outlets like *Taco Bell*, *Pollo Pollo*, *Pollo Rico* and *El Pollo Loco* just about everywhere. **Caribbean** food is less visible but, when sought out, can be quite rewarding.

Downtown and around

Ciro's Mexican Food, 705 N Evereny Ave, East LA (☎213/269-5104). A split-level cave of a dining room, serving enormous platters of shrimp and mole specials. The *flautas* bannered prominently across the menu are the main draw, and every meal comes with guacomole.

El Cholo, 1121 S Western Ave (☎213/734-2773). One of LA's first big Mexican restaurants and still one of the best, despite the drunken frat-rats from USC.

King Taco Warehouse, 4504 E Third St 4027, East LA (☎213/264-4067 or 4661). More like a mini-mall than a restaurant, with every kind of taco imaginable.

Luminarias, 3500 Ramona Blvd, Monterey Park (☎213/268-4177). Slightly sanitized and with some unappealing views: two freeways and a women's prison. Also live salsa music; see p.157.

Hollywood

Burrito King, 2109 W Sunset Blvd at Alvarado (☎213/413-9444). Excellent burritos and tasty tostadas from this small stand; open until 2am.

Casa Carnitas, 4067 Beverly Blvd (☎213/667-9953). Tasty Mexican food from the Yucatán: the dishes are inspired by Cuban and Caribbean cooking – lots of fine seafood, too.

Mario's Peruvian Seafood Restaurant, 5786 Melrose Ave (☎213/466-4181). The chefs look Asian but this is authentic Peruvian fare, the result of an influx of Japanese into Brazil and Peru in the 1920s. Supremely tender squid, and a hint of soy sauce in some dishes.

Mexico City, 2121 N Hillhurst Ave (☎213/661-7227). Spinach enchiladas and other Californian versions of Mexican standards served in a decent corner of East Hollywood.

Yuca's Hut, 2056 N Hillhurst Ave (☎213/662-1214). Tasty al fresco burritos opposite *Mexico City*.

West LA

El Coyote, 7312 Beverly Blvd (☎213/939-2255). Labyrinthine restaurant serving hearty Mexican food, and lots of it. But cheap and lethal margaritas are the primary draw to this gloomy setting.

El Mexicano Deli & Restaurant, 1601 Sawtelle Blvd (☎310/473-8056). Cozy combo deli and restaurant; the deli section is like an old-fashioned general store, selling fruit, vegetables and canned products from south of the border.

La Salsa, 11075 W Pico Blvd at Sepulveda (☎310/479-0919). A pilgrimage spot for Spike Jones fans (he immortalized the road junction in his hit, *Pico and Sepulveda*), and for lovers of well-crafted soft tacos and burritos.

Versailles, 10319 Venice Blvd (☎310/558-3168). Busy and noisy Cuban restaurant with a wealth of hearty fare, including fried plantains, paella and black beans and rice. Also at 1415 S La Cienega Blvd, a short distance away (☎310/289-0392).

Santa Monica and Venice and Malibu

La Cabana, 738 Rose Ave, Venice (☎310/392-7973). Corn tortillas as thick as pancakes, and interesting stuffed *quesadillas*. Busy on weekends.

Mariasol, 401 Santa Monica Pier, Santa Monica (☎310/917-5050). *Cervezas* with a view, hidden away at the end of the pier. On weekend afternoons, the small rooftop deck affords a sweeping panorama from Malibu to Venice.

Marix Tex-Mex Playa, 118 Entrada Drive, Pacific Palisades (☎310/459-8596). Flavourful fajitas and massive margaritas in this rowdy but stylish beachfront cantina.

The South Bay and Harbor Area

Cha Cha Cha, 762 Pacific Ave, Long Beach (☎310/436-3900). Paella, black pepper shrimp and jerk chicken are but a few of the tasty Caribbean treats you can find at this very popular restaurant. Also located at 656 N Virgil Ave in Hollywood (☎213/664-7723).

Pancho's, 3615 Highland Ave, Manhattan Beach (☎310/545-6670). Big portions, comparatively cheap for the area.

The San Gabriel and San Fernando Valleys

Don Cuco's, 3911 Riverside Drive, Burbank (☎818/842-1123). Good local place with a great Sunday brunch.

El Tepayac, 800 S Palm, Alhambra (☎818/281-3366). Huge burritos and very hot salsa – be prepared to wait in line.

Merida, 20 E Colorado Blvd, Pasadena (☎818/792-7371). Unusual Mexican restaurant, featuring dishes from the Yucatán; try the spicy pork wrapped up and steamed in banana leaves.

Señor Fish, 4803 Eagle Rock Blvd, Eagle Rock (☎818/257-7167) The best fish tacos this side of Rosarita, with charbroiled halibut for under $10, in a converted house with patio.

Wolfe Burger, 46 N Lake St, Pasadena (☎818/792-7292). Praised by the *LA Weekly* and *LA Times* for its chili, tamales and burgers. *Huevos rancheros* are served for breakfast.

American, California cuisine and Cajun

Down-to-earth **American** cuisine, with its steaks, ribs, baked potatoes and mountainous salads, has a deceptively low profile in faddish LA, although it's available almost everywhere and usually won't cost more than $10 for a comparative blow-out. Much more prominent – and more expensive, at upwards of $15 – is **California cuisine**, based on fresh local ingredients, more likely grilled than fried, and stylishly presented with a nod to nouvelle French cuisine. Another rage is for spicy, fish-based **Cajun** cooking, still available in authentic form and relatively inexpensive.

Downtown and around

Bernard's, 506 S Grand Ave in the *Biltmore Hotel* (☎213/612-1580). Beautifully preserved, lushly decorated dining room in this landmark hotel, serving contemporary versions of classic American meat and fish dishes.

B 'n' Bar-B-Que, 1958 W Florence Ave (☎213/671-8190) and 10303 Avalon Blvd in Watts. Slabs of LA's best ribs, smothered in your choice of barbecue sauce, served with baked beans and a sweet potato tart.

Checkers Restaurant, 535 S Grand Ave in the *Checkers Kempinski Hotel* (☎213/624-0000). One of the most elegant downtown restaurants, serving top-rated California cuisine all day.

Engine Co 28, 644 S Figueroa St (☎213/624-6996). All-American grilled steaks and seafood, served in a renovated 1912 fire station. Great French fries and an excellent wine list.

McCormick and Schmicks, 633 W Fifth St (☎213/629-1929). Swank seafood joint for business types known for a great weekend dinner special – call for details.

Pacific Dining Car, 1310 W Sixth St (☎213/483-6000). Would-be English supper club housed inside an old railroad carriage. Open 24hr for (very expensive) steaks. Breakfast is the best value.

Café Pinot, 700 W Fifth St (☎213/239-6500). Located next to the LA Public Library, this elegant restaurant offers a mix of California and French cuisines at less exorbitant prices than you might expect.

Hollywood

Musso and Frank Grill, 6667 Hollywood Blvd (☎213/467-7788). Since it opened in 1919, anyone who's anyone in Hollywood has been seen in the dark-panelled dining room, though at $15 for bacon and eggs you pay for the atmosphere. Better stick to the bar (see p.151).

Patina, 5955 Melrose Ave (☎213/467-1108). The height of the culinary elite, this ultra-chic place delivers exquisite California cuisine, satisfying the palate while depriving the wallet.

Pinot Hollywood's Restaurant and Martini Bar, 1448 Gower St (☎213/461-8800). Upmarket American food in a spacious environment, plus 24 types of martini and Polish potato vodka.

West LA

Barefoot, 8722 W Third St (☎310/276-6223). Good pastas, pizzas and seafood between Beverly Hills and the Beverly Center. Considering the location, very affordable.

Ca' Brea, 346 S La Brea Ave (☎213/938-2863). Hip California-cuisine restaurant in a trendy part of town. Popular because of the delicious risotto and despite the difficulty of getting a table.

Citrus, 6703 Melrose Ave (☎213/857-0034). The trendiest and best of the newer upmarket restaurants, serving California cuisine in an outdoor-style setting indoors, and at garish prices.

Georgia, 7250 Melrose Ave (☎213/633-8420). Down-home Southern cooking served in a mahogany dining room for about $25 a plate. Part-owned by a small team of celebrities including Denzel Washington.

The Gumbo Pot, 6333 W Third St in the Farmer's Market (☎213/933-0358). Delicious and dirt-cheap Cajun cooking in a busy, chaotic setting; try the *gumbo yaya* of chicken, shrimp and sausage, and the fruit-and-potato salad.

L'Orangerie, 903 N La Cienega Blvd (☎310/652-9770). Nouvelle California-style French cuisine; if you haven't got the $150 it takes to sit down, enjoy the view from the bar.

Spago, 1114 Horn Ave above Sunset Blvd (☎310/652-4025). Perhaps LA's most famous restaurant, both for its chef Wolfgang Puck, the inventor of "designer pizza", and for its star-studded clientele. Recent expansion to Beverly Hills hasn't drawn away the crowds. Reservations are essential.

Santa Monica, Venice and Malibu

Gladstone's 4 Fish, 17300 Pacific Coast Highway (☎310/454-3474). Located near the junction of Sunset Boulevard, this restaurant is known more for its excellent beachfront location than for its seafood, most of which is fairly good, though heavily fried.

Michael's, 1147 Third St, Santa Monica (☎310/451-0843). California cuisine served amid modern art. This venerable establishment always attracts the crowds – reservations are essential.

17th Street Café, 1610 Montana, Santa Monica (☎310/453-2771). Seafood, pasta and burgers at moderate prices in a chic section of town. Also serves breakfast.

Italian, Spanish, Greek and pizza

After years of having nothing more exotic than the established takeout pizza chains – *Pizza Hut* and *Shakey's* are among the more widespread names – LA has woken up to the delights of regional **Italian** cuisine, and there is a growing number of specialist restaurants, especially around the Westside, serving more refined and varied Italian food. Another recent phenomenon is the **designer pizza**, invented at Hollywood's *Spago* restaurant and made to a traditional formula but topped with duck, shiitake mushrooms and other exotic ingredients. The problem with all this is that it doesn't come cheap: even a pasta dish in the average Italian restaurant can cost upwards of $8, and the least elaborate designer pizza will set you back around $15. **Spanish** food and tapas bars have similarly become a swish night out for LA's Westside thirtysomethings. In contrast, if you're looking for **Greek** food, you'll have to look hard – restaurants are good but uncommon.

Downtown

California Pizza Kitchen, 330 S Hope St (☎213/626-2616). Inventive pizzas; not cheap but worth the extravagance, if you don't mind the crowds. Two branches in West LA and one downtown.

La Bella Cucina, 949 S Figueroa St (☎213/623-0014). Fabulous pizzas and homemade pastas, with the accent on northern and rural Italian cuisine.

Rex il Ristorante, 617 S Olive St (☎213/627-2300). Exorbitant prices at this elegant restaurant in downtown LA, housed in a René Lalique-crafted one-time haberdashery.

Hollywood

Campanile, 624 S La Brea Ave (☎213/938-1447). Incredible but extremely expensive northern Italian dishes; if you can't afford a full dinner, just try the dessert or pick up some of the best bread in Los Angeles at the adjacent *La Brea Bakery*.

Palermo, 1858 N Vermont Ave (☎213/663-1178). As old as Hollywood, and with as many devoted fans, who flock here for the stodgy pizzas and gallons of cheapish red wine.

West LA

Cava, 8384 W Third St (☎213/658-8898). Latin and Iberian dishes appear on the menu, but the main attraction is tasty tapas accompanied by shots of prime sherry.

Chianti, 7383 Melrose Ave (☎213/653-8333). A welcome respite: good Italian food served at the center of LA's chaotic Melrose shopping district.

La Masia, 9077 Santa Monica Blvd (☎310/273-7066). Upscale Castilian dining, after which you can hit the dancefloor and enjoy a spot of salsa and merengue.

Locanda Veneta, 8638 W Third St (☎310/274-1893). Located in the shadow of the Beverly Center, this Italian restaurant serves tasty ravioli and risotto and is one of the city's quiet culinary joys.

Mario's, 1001 Broxton Ave, Westwood Village (☎310/208-7077). Far and away the best pizza in West LA; serves a wide range of pasta dishes too. Also at 1444 Third Street Promenade, Santa Monica (☎310/576-7799).

Santa Monica, Venice and Malibu

Abbot's Pizza Company, 1407 Abbot Kinney Blvd, Venice (☎310/396-7334). Owned by former New Yorkers, the rock 'n' roll Shiffer brothers, this home of the bagel crust pizza tops them with your choice of seeds, tangy sweet citrus sauce or shiitake and wild mushroom sauce.

Boston Wildflour Pizza, 2807 Main St, Santa Monica (☎310/392-3300). A cheese slice is $2 in the *LA Times*-nominated "Best Thin Pizza" house.

Wolfgang Puck Express, 1315 Third Street Promenade, Santa Monica (☎310/576-4770). On the second floor of an anodyne food mall, but the cheap pizzas and Chinois chicken and Caesar salads are justly famous.

The South Bay and Harbor Area

Alegria Café & Tapas Bar, 115 Pine Ave, Long Beach (☎310/436-3388). Tapas, gazpacho and a variety of *platos principales* served with sangria on the patio, and to the beat of live flamenco at weekends. Good location downtown near the harbor.

Giovanni's Salerno Beach Restaurant, 193 Culver Blvd, Playa Del Rey (☎310/821-0018). The tasty southern Italian food takes second place to the decor: this 31-year-old eatery is a riot of Christmas decorations, inflatable toys, live birds and fish, maps of Italy and photos. It all began when the owners didn't get around to taking the Christmas decorations down one year . . .

Mangiamo, 128 Manhattan Beach Blvd, Manhattan Beach (☎310/318-3434). Fairly pricey but worth it for the specialist northern Italian seafood.

Santorini's, 2529 Pacific Coast Highway, Torrance, South Bay (☎310/534-8898). As good as Greek food gets in the South Bay. Rough retsina, *tzatziki* and good fresh bread add to the authenticity, despite the faceless mini-mall location.

The San Gabriel and San Fernando Valleys

La Scala Presto, 3821 Riverside Drive, Burbank (☎818/846-6800). Stylish and tasty antipasti, pizza and fresh pasta.

Market City Caffé, 33 S Fair Oaks Ave, Pasadena (☎818/568-0203). Southern Italian cuisine featuring fine pizzas and seafood.

Chinese, Japanese, Thai and Korean

LA's most fashionable districts offer high-style sushi bars and dim sum restaurants, favored by Far East businessmen and fast-lane yuppies alike, in which you can easily eat your way through more than $20. Lower priced and much less pretentious outlets tend, not surprisingly, to be downtown, in **Little Tokyo** and **Chinatown**, where you can get a fair-sized meal for around $10. Thai and Korean food – for which you can expect to pay around $15 per meal – are popular, although the latter has as yet to spread beyond the confines of **Koreatown**.

Downtown and around

Buffet Palace, 3014 Olympic Blvd, Koreatown (☎213/388-9292). Korean restaurant off busy thoroughfare; especially strong on spicy barbecued beef.

Dong Il Jang, 3455 W Eighth St, Koreatown (☎213/383-5757). A cozy Korean restaurant where the meat is grilled at your table.

Grand Star Restaurant, 934 Sun Mun Way, Chinatown (☎213/626-2285). Go late as there's video karaoke from 8pm–1am at this Chinese place on Sunday, Tuesday and Wednesday.

Mandarin Deli, 727 N Broadway (☎213/623-6054). Very edible and very cheap noodles, dumplings, and other hearty staples in the middle of Broadway's riot of activity.

Mitsuru Café, 117 Japanese Village Blvd, Little Tokyo (☎213/613-1028). On a hot day nothing beats the snow cones at *Mitsuru*, in such exotic flavours as *kintoki* (azuki-bean paste) or *milk kintoki* (sweet custard). On a cold day, try the *imagawayaki* – azuki beans baked in a bun.

Mon Kee, 679 N Spring St, Chinatown (☎213/628-6717). Long-standing favorite for fresh fish.

Ocean Seafood, 750 N Hill (☎213/687-3088). Cavernous but often busy restaurant serving cheap and excellent food that's well worth the wait; due to renovation, call first.

Restaurant Horikawa, 111 S San Pedro St, Little Tokyo (☎213/680-9355). Upmarket Japanese restaurant, popular with business types.

Shibucho, 333 S Alameda St, Little Tokyo (☎213/626-1184). Excellent sushi bar in the heart of Little Tokyo; go with someone who knows what to order, as the waiters don't speak English.

Hollywood

Chan Dara, 1511 N Cahuenga Blvd (☎213/464-8585). Terrific Thai food, and the locals know it. If you can't get in here, there are other Westside locations at 310 N Larchmont Blvd (☎213/467-1052) and 11940 W Pico Blvd (☎310/479-4461).

Katsu, 1972 N Hillhurst Ave (☎213/665-1891). Minimalist sushi bar for the cyberpunk brigade; the only splash of color is in the artfully presented bits of fish on your plate.

West LA

Chin Chin, 8618 Sunset Blvd (☎310/652-1818). Flashy but not overpriced dim sum café, open till midnight.

Chung King, 11538 W Pico Blvd (☎310/477-4917). The best neighborhood Chinese restaurant in LA, serving spicy Szechuan food: don't miss out on the *bum-bum* chicken and other house specialties.

Mishima, 8474 W Third St (☎213/782-0181). *Udon* and *soba* are quickly replacing sushi as the Japanese dish of choice in west LA. *Mishima* is the reason: bright and spacious, it serves bowls of hot and cold noodles for about what you'd pay at your local burger chain drive-thru.

The Sushi House, 12013 W Pico Blvd (☎310/479-1507). Reggae and sushi coalesce in a hole in the wall bar with only limited seating. Try the "Superman", a rainbow-colored roll of salmon, yellowtail, whitefish and avocado.

Tommy Tang's, 7313 Melrose Ave (☎213/937-5733). Excellent, very chic Thai restaurant and the incongruous setting for occasional full drag nights.

Santa Monica, Venice and Malibu

Chaya, 110 Navy St, Venice (☎310/396-1179). Elegant cultural crossroads serving Japanese and Mediterranean foods to a smart clientele.

Chinois on Main, 2709 Main St, Santa Monica (☎310/392-9025). Wolfgang Puck, the man who created designer pizza at *Spago* (see p.146) afterwards turned his sights across the Pacific to China and opened this enduringly popular restaurant, a mix of nouvelle French and Chinese cuisine designed to go with the green-and-black decor. Very expensive, but worth it for a splurge.

Flower of Siam, 2553 Lincoln Blvd, Venice (☎310/827-0050). Thai food guaranteed to set your tastebuds on fire and your eyes watering.

Lighthouse Buffet, 201 Arizona Ave, Santa Monica (☎310/451-2076). All-you-can-eat sushi; indulge to your heart's content for under $10 at lunchtime or $18 in the evening.

The San Gabriel and San Fernando Valleys

Genmai-Sushi, 4454 Van Nuys Blvd, Sherman Oaks (☎818/986-7060). *Genmai* is Japanese for brown rice, but you can still get soft shell crabs in ponzu sauce along with the sushi and seasonal macrobiotic dishes and the eponymous staple.

Saladang, 363 S Fair Oaks Ave, Pasadena (☎818/793-8123). *Pad thai* and Saladang spicy noodles that would pass muster anywhere.

Sea Star, 2000 W Main St, Alhambra (☎818/282-8833). Dim sum at its best: pork *baos*, potstickers and dumplings, and delicious sweets.

Indian, Sri Lankan, Middle Eastern and Ethiopian

Indian restaurants are on the increase in LA, as Indian food is enjoying an upsurge in popularity – with restaurant menus often embracing uniquely Californian dishes. **Artesia** is home to a recognizable community of Indian shops and food stores along Pioneer Boulevard. **Middle Eastern** places in LA are few, and tend to be fairly basic, as do the city's even fewer **Ethiopian** food outlets. Most of the Indian and Middle Eastern restaurants in Hollywood or West LA fall into a fairly mid-range price bracket – around $10 for a full meal, less for a vegetarian Indian dish.

Hollywood

Addis Ababa, 6263 Leland Way, a block south of Sunset Blvd (☎213/463-9788). Unpretentious Ethiopian food served with fresh *injera* bread in a quiet setting.

Chamika Catering, 1717 N Wilcox Ave (☎213/466-8960). Inexpensive papadums, *rotis* (garlic and coconut stuffed pancakes) and chicken, beef or lamb curries, marinated in special Sri Lankan sauces. Strawberry or mango delight washes the food down.

India Inn, 1638 N Cahuenga Blvd (☎213/461-3774). Good, low-cost Indian restaurant.

Shamshiry, 5229 Hollywood Blvd (☎213/469-8434). The best of Hollywood's Iranian restaurants, offering kebabs, pilafs and exotic sauces.

West LA

East India Grill, 345 N La Brea Ave (☎213/936-8844). Southern Indian cuisine given the California treatment: impressive specialities include spinach curry and curried pasta.

Eat A Pita, 465 N Fairfax Ave (☎213/651-0188). Open-air stand serving cheap, cheerful and filling falafel, hummus and vegetable juice drinks popular with locals.

India's Oven, 7231 Beverly Blvd (☎213/936-1000). Bring your own bottle to this friendly, award-winning Indian restaurant.

Koutoubia, 2116 Westwood Blvd (☎310/475-0729). Rich Moroccan food with especially good lamb, couscous and seafood.

Noura Cafe, 8479 Melrose Ave (☎213/651-4581). Moderately priced Middle Eastern specialities. At night the leafy crowded patio is lit by a central circular sandpit. For beginners, the "taster's delight" plate – hummus, *baba ganoush*, tabouli, falafel, fried eggplant, zucchini and stuffed grape leaf – is a good, filling bet.

Vegetarian and wholefood

It's small wonder that mind- and body-fixated LA has a wide variety of **wholefood** and **vegetarian** restaurants, and even less of a shock that the bulk of them are found on the consciousness-raised Westside. Some vegetarian places can be very good value ($5 or so), but watch out for the ones that flaunt themselves as a New Age experience and include music – these can be three times as dear. Otherwise for a picnic try the local *Trader Joe's* chain – which started as a liquor store with a sideline in unusual food, but now supplies imported cheeses, breads and canned foods to the Europeans who crave them most – or the area's frequent **Farmer's Markets**, heaving with organic produce, advertised in the press. Healthfood stores are listed in "Shopping".

Hollywood

The Bodhi Garden Restaurant, 1498 Sunset Blvd (☎213/250-9023). Vegetarian Vietnamese food, including fancy dishes like sweet and sour walnuts, bean curd and black moss. The crowd is eclectic, and the decor features chubby Buddhas resting alongside offerings of fruit. Closed Tues.

Inaka, 131 S La Brea Ave (☎213/936-9353). Located in newly trendy La Brea district, featuring vegetarian and macrobiotic food with a strong Japanese theme. Live music at weekends.

Santa Monica, Venice and Malibu

Figtree's Café, 429 Ocean Front Walk, Venice (☎310/392-4937). Tasty veggie food and grilled fresh fish on a sunny patio just off the Boardwalk.

Inn of the Seventh Ray, 128 Old Topanga Rd, Topanga Canyon (☎310/455-1311). The ultimate New Age restaurant, serving vegetarian and other wholefood meals in a relatively secluded environment.

Shambala Café, 607 Colorado Ave (☎310/395-2160). Apart from organic chicken, the menu is meat-free, with shrimp, pasta, tofu, eggplant and some interesting seaweed dishes.

The South Bay and Harbor Area

The Spot, 110 Second St, Hermosa Beach (☎310/376-2355). A staggering array of vegetarian dishes, based on Mexican and other international cuisines and free of refined sugar or any animal products. Purified water, too.

Drinking: bars, pubs and coffee bars

Social **drinking** in LA is far less popular than it is up the coast in San Francisco. Many bars are simply places to pose while waiting to meet friends, before heading off to pose again somewhere more exotic. However, it is possible to have a good time, provided you don't smoke, a practice now banned in most establishments under recent Californian law. You should be able to get a drink almost anywhere, and for serious, uninterrupted drinking there are bars and cocktail lounges on every other corner – just look for the neon signs. In fickle Los Angeles, bar styles go in and out of fashion like nobody's business, often according to music and showbiz trends.

The recommendations below have a little more character than most: enjoyable places either for an entire evening's socializing or a quick splash on the way to somewhere else. As you'd expect, they reflect their locality: a clash of beatnik artists and financial whiz kids downtown; the legacy of the movies and the subsequent arrival of leather-clad rock fans in Hollywood; the cleaner-cut trendiness of West LA; a batch of jukebox and dartboard-furnished bars in Santa Monica, evidence of the British contingent in the area; and the less fashionable, more hedonistic beachside bars of the South Bay. A few hard-bitten bars are open the legal maximum hours (from 6am until 2am daily), though you're liable to be drinking alone if you arrive for an early liquid breakfast; busiest hours are between 9pm and midnight. If you want something of the bar atmosphere without the alcohol, present yourself at one of the fast-growing band of gregarious **coffee bars**; lately they've become the places to be seen, not least because they won't leave a hardened socialite too drunk to drive home – a crime that carries harsh penalties in LA.

Downtown

Al's Bar, 305 S Hewitt St (☎213/687-3558). At the heart of the trendy Loft District art scene, in the middle of a grimy industrial area; drink cans of cheap beer in post-apocalyptic-looking, smoke-filled rooms, with a pool table and frequent live acts. Be prepared for homeless people to offer to watch your car for $1.

HAPPY HOURS

Many bars and some restaurants have **happy hours**, usually from 5pm until 7pm, when drinks are cheap, sometimes half-price, and there'll be a selection of help-yourself snacks: taco dips, chips or popcorn. A few offer piles of free food that you can attack once you've bought a drink – and thereby save you the cost of dinner later on.

Bona Vista, at the *Westin Bonaventure*, 404 S Figueroa St (☎213/624-1000). Thirty-five floors up, this constantly rotating cocktail lounge spins faster after a few of the expensive drinks, and offers an unparalleled view of the sun setting over the city.

Casey's Bar, 613 S Grand Ave (☎213/629-2353). White floors, dark wood-panelled walls and nightly piano music; something of a local institution.

Hollywood

Bar Deluxe, 1710 N Las Palmas St (☎213/469-1991). Enjoy sake, beer and rockabilly in a bare-bones crimson-lit bar popular with young poseurs.

Barragan Café, 1538 W Sunset Blvd (☎213/250-4256). Actually a Mexican restaurant, but reputedly producing the most alcoholic margarita in LA.

Boardners, 1652 N Cherokee Ave (☎213/462-9621). A likeably unkempt neighborhood bar in the middle of Hollywood's prime tourist territory.

Cat N' Fiddle, 6530 Sunset Blvd (☎213/468-3800). A boisterous but comfortable pub with expensive English beers on draught and live jazz on Saturdays. See also "Live Music", p.156.

The Dresden Room, 1760 N Vermont Ave (☎213/665-4298). Wednesday night is open mike, otherwise the resident husband-and-wife lounge act takes requests from the crowd of old-timers and goatee-wearing hipsters.

Formosa Café, 7156 Santa Monica Blvd (☎213/850-9050). Tiny ex-silent-era film studio done out in pillar-box red Chinese style (à la Mann's Chinese Theatre), better for its drink than its food.

The Garage, 4519 Santa Monica Blvd (☎213/683-3447). With a funky lounge and a pool room, this Silverlake bar and club offers live music after 9pm.

Jack's Sugar Shack, 1707 N Vine St (☎213/466-7005). Eat and drink near a famous Hollywood intersection and hear various rock and blues bands belt out tunes nightly.

Musso and Frank Grill, 6667 Hollywood Blvd (☎213/467-7788). If you haven't had a drink in this 1940s landmark bar, you haven't been to Hollywood. It also serves food (see "Eating", p.145).

Pinot Hollywood's Restaurant and Martini Bar, 1448 Gower St (☎213/461-8800). Twenty-four types of martini and Polish potato vodka, served in airy surroundings. See also "Eating", p.145.

The Power House, 1714 N Highland Ave (☎213/463-9438). Enjoyable heavy rockers' watering hole just off Hollywood Boulevard; few people get here much before midnight.

Tiki Ti, 4427 W Sunset Blvd (☎213/669-9381). Tiny grass-skirted cocktail bar straight out of *Hawaii-Five-O* on the edge of Hollywood.

West LA

Barney's Beanery, 8447 Santa Monica Blvd (☎310/654-2287). Well-worn poolroom bar, stocking over 200 beers. It also serves food, of sorts (see "Eating", p.155).

Crooked Bar, 8121 Sunset Blvd (☎213/654-4773). Wedged underneath the *Coconut Teaszer* club (see "Nightlife", p.153), this place features live acoustic tunes most nights of the week.

Molly Malone's Irish Pub, 575 S Fairfax Ave (☎213/935-1577). Self-consciously authentic Irish bar, from the music to the shamrocks in the foaming Guinness (see also "Live Music", p.155).

Tom Bergin's, 840 S Fairfax Ave (☎213/936-7151). Great place for Irish Coffee, less rough and ready than *Molly Malone's* down the road.

Santa Monica, Venice and Malibu

14 Below, 1348 14th St, Santa Monica (☎310/451-5040). At this casual bar, pool tables and a fireplace compete for your attention with rock, folk and blues performers.

The Oarhouse, 2941 Main St, Santa Monica (☎310/396-4725). Studenty bar which gets suitably rowdy on a Friday.

Red Setter Irish Pub, 2615 Wilshire Blvd, Santa Monica (☎310/449-1811). Formerly *McGinty's*, this pub features plenty of darts and beer, plus "Lobster Friday," in which you get a pound of the crustacean for under $10.

Ye Olde King's Head, 116 Santa Monica Blvd (☎310/451-1402). Jukebox, dartboards and signed photos of all your favorite rock dinosaurs; popular with local British expatriates.

The San Gabriel and San Fernando Valleys

Blue Saloon, 4657 Lankershim Blvd (☎818/766-4644). This valley bar is enlivened by a wide range of live music, including rock, country, blues and reggae.

The Colorado, 2640 E Colorado Blvd (☎818/449-3485). A bright spot along a bleak Pasadena stretch. Salty bartenders, cheap drinks and a couple of pool tables amid a decor based around hunting.

Coffee bars

All-Star Theater Café, 1714 N Ivar Ave, Hollywood (☎213/962-8898). Antiques store/café/cumpool hall with a 1920s feel and comfortably overstuffed armchairs, near Nathanael West's former stomping ground. Never opens until 7pm.

Anastasia's Asylum, 1028 Wilshire Blvd, Santa Monica (☎310/394-7113). Comfortable place with strong coffee and tea; also with nightly entertainment, of varying quality.

Bourgeois Pig, 5931 Franklin Ave, Hollywood (☎213/962-6366). Hip environment and outrageously overpriced cappuccinos, though fun for people-watching.

Cobalt Café, 22047 Sherman Way, Canoga Park (☎818/348-3789). A somewhat grungy but hip coffeehouse in the Valley, with coffee, food and live music.

Highland Grounds, 742 N Highland Ave, Hollywood (☎213/466-1507). The poshest and posiest of LA's coffee bars, serving iced latté and whole pancakes. At night it's a club, with poetry readings and anonymous bands.

Hot House Café, 12123 Riverside Drive, North Hollywood (☎818/506-7058). Ultra-caffeinated java in a Valley joint with art, books and music on the weekend.

Java Man, 157 Pier Ave, Hermosa Beach (☎310/379-7209). Tables lit by halogen lamps, and a rotating display of work from local artists. Not far from the beach.

King's Road Espresso House, 8361 Beverly Blvd, West Hollywood (☎213/655-9044). Sidewalk café with the usual beautiful staff. Popular day and night with the *nuovo* beatnik crowd and, increasingly, out-of-towners.

The Novel Café, 212 Pier Ave, Santa Monica (☎310/396-8566). Used books and high-backed wooden chairs set the tone; this place has good coffees, teas and pastries.

Sacred Grounds, 399 W Sixth St, San Pedro (☎310/514-0800). Combination coffeehouse and club with a sizeable stage, located not far from the harbor.

The World Café, 2820 Main St, Santa Monica (☎310/392-1661; *www.worldcafe.la.com*). Surf the Net with other technophiles on the patio, or drag yourself away and drink in the dark café/bar. Often crowded and always touristy.

Nightlife: clubs and discos

Like most things in LA, **nightlife** here is very style-conscious, and LA's clubs are probably the wildest in the country. Ranging from absurdly faddish hangouts to industrial noise cellars, even the more image-conscious joints are often more like singles bars, with plenty of dressing-up, eyeing-up and picking-up (and sometimes not much else) going on, and everybody claiming to be either a rock star or in the movies. If you don't fall for the make-believe, the city's nightlife jungle can be great fun to explore, if only to eavesdrop on the vapid chat. Nowadays, many of the more interesting and unusual clubs are homeless, especially those catering to the house, ambient and rave scene. As a result, the trendier side of the club scene is hard to pin down, and you should always check the *LA Weekly* before setting out.

Not surprisingly, Friday and Saturday are the busiest nights, but during the week things are often cheaper, and though less crowded, rarely any less enjoyable.

Everywhere, between 11pm and midnight is the best time to turn up. There's nearly always a cover charge, usually from $6 to $10, and a minimum age of 21 (it's normal for ID to be checked, so bring your passport or other photo ID), and you should obviously dress with some sensitivity to the club's style. That said, prohibitive dress codes are a rarity, and although you may be more welcome if you look completely outrageous, most places won't exclude you solely on account of your clothes.

Most of the top-name clubs are either in Hollywood or along a ten-block stretch of West Hollywood, in West LA. Downtown is home to a number of transient clubs operating above and below board, while the San Fernando Valley has its own version of a scene – usually confined to the weekends.

Downtown

Glam Slam, 333 S Boylston St (☎213/482-6626). Very glam but not posey club, owned and inspired by the artist formerly known as Prince – hence the purple dance floor.

Mayan, 1038 S Hill St (☎213/746-4287). Convince the doorman that you deserve to be allowed in and your reward is a place among the cool and most fashionable of LA, eager to shake a leg in gorgeous and historic surrounds. Fri and Sat; $12, no sneakers.

Hollywood

Arena, 6655 Santa Monica Blvd (☎213/462-0714). Work up a sweat to funk, hip-hop and house sounds on a massive dance floor inside a former ice factory; $8.

Club Lingerie, 6507 Sunset Blvd (☎213/891-2775). Long-established, stylish modern dance club with intimate bar and hip-hop, dance and R&B music; $5–10. See also "Live Music", p.154.

The Derby, 4500 Los Feliz Blvd (☎213/663-8979). Restored supper club with gorgeous high wooden ceilings and round bar that has become the epicenter of LA's swingdancing craze.

Dragonfly, 6510 Santa Monica Blvd (☎213/466-6111). Unusual decor, two large dance rooms, an "eye-contact" bar and club nights that are continually buzzing.

Florentine Gardens, 5951 Hollywood Blvd (☎213/464-0706). Stuck between the Salvation Army and a porno theater, but very popular with the faddish LA crowd. Cover $8.

Probe, 836 N Highland Ave (☎213/461-8301). Ultra-trendy club with gothic, industrial and techno beats. If you like the scene, this is one of LA's more enjoyable clubs; cover $8–10.

West LA

Bar One, 9229 Sunset Blvd (☎310/271-8355). Bring plenty of attitude to this club frequented by actual and would-be celebrities. Fancy outfits and reservations required.

Billboard Live, 9039 Sunset Blvd (☎310/274-5800). The newest kid on the club scene, this tri-level operation features live and recorded music leaning heavily toward dance, hip-hop and rock. $10 cover.

Coconut Teaszer, 8117 Sunset Blvd (☎213/654-4773). Poseurs, rockers and voyeurs mix uneventfully on the two dance floors. No cover before 9pm, otherwise $5.

7969, 7969 Santa Monica Blvd (☎213/654-0280). West Hollywood's longest running gay and lesbian disco. Cover varies; over 18s only. See also "Gay and lesbian bars and clubs", p.162.

Union, 8210 Sunset Blvd (☎213/654-1001). Relaxed supper club with funk, soul and R&B groove room. Frequented by the young actor crowd on Tuesdays.

Viper Room, 8852 Sunset Blvd (☎310/358-1880). Stellar live acts, a famous owner and a headline-hitting past. Unpredictable schedule means anyone might show up onstage. See also "Live Music", p.155.

The San Gabriel and San Fernando Valleys

Aftershock, 11345 Ventura Blvd, Studio City (☎818/752-9833). Disco and dance music reign supreme at this Valley club with four bars and three high-tech rooms. Wed–Sun.

The Muse, 54 E Colorado Blvd (☎626/793-0608). Old Town Pasadena is the site where dance, funk and hip-hop tunes collide in one tri-level club with no less than eleven pool tables. Thurs–Sun.

Live Music

LA has a near-overwhelming choice if you're looking for **live music**. Because new bands haven't broken through until they've won over an LA crowd, there's seldom an evening without something exciting going on. Since the nihilistic punk bands of a decade or so ago drew the city away from its spaced-out slacker image, LA's **rock music** scene has been second to none, to the extent that it has replaced the film industry as the quick route to riches and fame. There's a proto-rock star at every corner, and the guitar case is in some districts (notably Hollywood) an almost *de rigueur* accessory. The old punk phenomenon has, of course, long since been overtaken, and nowadays the trend is for industrial noise, practiced with verve by the likes of Trent Reznor, and neo-punk, in the Green Day mold. The influence and popularity of South Central's **hip-hop** and **rap** music is spotty elsewhere and found mostly in dance clubs. Avoid hunting down the local rappers in their home territory – see "South Central LA" on p.89 for why you should stay clear.

In addition to local talent there are always plenty of British and European names in town, from major artists to independents. There's an enormous choice of **venues**, and inevitably it's a constantly changing scene, but the clubs we've listed are pretty well established. Most open at 8pm or 9pm; headline bands are usually onstage between 11pm and 1am. Admission ranges from $10 to $20 and you should phone ahead to check set times and whether the gig is likely to sell out. As with discos, you'll need to be 21 and will almost certainly be asked for ID. As ever, *LA Weekly* is the best source of **listings**.

In an entirely different category, **country music** is fairly prevalent, at least away from trendy Hollywood, and the Valleys are hotbeds of bluegrass and swing. There's **jazz**, too, played in a few genuinely authentic downbeat dives, though more commonly found in diluted form to improve the atmosphere of a restaurant. The lively Latin dance music of **salsa**, immensely popular among LA's Hispanic population, was promoted heavily by record companies in the city during the mid-1970s. At the time it failed to cross over into the mainstream, though this is now changing. Even so, it's still found mostly in the bars of East LA, though it's worth saying that these are very male-oriented gathering places and visitors may well feel out of place – though they're rarely dangerous. Finally there's a small live **reggae** scene, occasionally featuring biggish names but more often sticking to the increasingly numerous local bands.

The big performance venues

Greek Theater, in Griffith Park (☎213/665-1927). Outdoor, summer-only venue with a broad range of big-name musical acts.

Hollywood Palladium, 6215 Sunset Blvd, Hollywood (☎213/962-7600). Once a big-band dance hall, with an authentic 1940s interior.

LA Sports Arena, 3939 S Figueroa St, Downtown (☎213/480-3232). Cavernous with no atmosphere at all, perfect for mega metal bands and dinosaur rockers.

Pantages Theater, 6233 Hollywood Blvd, Hollywood (☎213/468-1770). An exquisite, atmospheric Art Deco theater, in the heart of historic Hollywood.

Universal Amphitheater, Universal Studios, Burbank (☎818/622-4440). A huge but acoustically excellent auditorium with regular rock shows.

Rock venues

anti-club, 4658 Melrose Ave, Hollywood (☎213/661-3913). Occasionally great, but far fewer worthwhile bands play here now than used to. Leans toward punk and thrash music.

Café Largo, 432 N Fairfax Ave, West LA (☎213/852-1073). Intimate cabaret venue that often features LA's more unusual live bands. Free–$10.

Club Lingerie, 6507 Sunset Blvd, West LA (☎213/891-2775). Wide-ranging venue that's always at the forefront of what's new; $3–8. See also "Nightlife: clubs and discos", p.153.

WHAT'S ON AND TICKETS

Apart from the radio stations listed below, which carry details, previews and sometimes free tickets for forthcoming events, the best sources of **what's on information** are the *LA Weekly* and *LA Reader*, and the "Calendar" section of the Sunday *Los Angeles Times*. You can buy seats for concerts or sports events from **Ticketmaster**, which has branches in Tower Records stores, and charge-by-phone numbers (☎213/480-3232 or 714/740-2000). A quick way through the maze of LA's **theaters** is to phone **Theatrix** (☎213/466-1767 or 888-8023), which handles reservations and provides details on what's playing at several of the smaller venues.

RADIO STATIONS

KCRW 89.9 FM Has interesting new music and transatlantic imports, and one of the few good sources of world news. Great evening music programs leaning toward trance, dub and eclectic tunes.

KCSN 85.9 FM Latino classics and salsa.

KFWB 980 AM Frequent local news, plus talk shows.

KLSX 97.1 FM Rock music and, in the morning, NY shock-jock Howard Stern.

KNX 1070 News with half-hourly sports reports.

KPCC 89.3 FM Jazz and blues concerts, plus arty talk radio.

KPFK 90.7 FM Up-to-the-minute opinions, politics, news and music, from activists and angry sceptics with a leftish perspective.

KROQ 106.7 FM Rock music with a touch of grunge.

KRTH 101.1 FM Nothing but oldies, advertised incessantly around town.

KUSC 91.5 FM Classical, jazz, world music.

KXLU 88.9 FM Underground hip-hop and performer interviews on Saturday night.

Doug Weston's Troubadour, 9081 Santa Monica Blvd, West Hollywood (☎310/276-6168). The best-known club for the heaviest riffs and shaggiest manes.

The Lighthouse, 30 Pier Ave, Hermosa Beach (☎310/372-6911). Adjacent to the beach, this club has a broad booking policy which spans rock, jazz, reggae and more; cover varies.

Lunapark, 665 N Robertson Blvd, Hollywood (☎310/652-0611). Eclectic musical mix upstairs at this West Hollywood club; downstairs, there's a cabaret. Cover $3–20.

The Roxy, 9009 Sunset Blvd, West LA (☎310/276-2222). The showcase of the music industry's new signings, intimate and with a great sound system; cover varies.

The Viper Room, 8852 Sunset Blvd, West LA (☎310/358-1880). Less trendy than many clubs, though it has gained a certain notoriety since River Phoenix overdosed here in late 1993. Cover $3–6. See also "Nightlife: clubs and discos", p.153.

Whisky-a-Go-Go, 8901 Sunset Blvd, West LA (☎310/535-0579). Another critical spot for LA's rising music stars; mainly hard rock; $10-15.

Country and folk venues

Crazy Jack's, 4311 W Magnolia Blvd, Burbank (☎818/845-1121). Before the music starts at 9pm, this place offers free dance lessons Tues & Thurs–Sat.

The Foothill Club, 1922 Cherry Ave, Signal Hill (☎310/494-5196). A glorious dance hall from the days when hillbilly was cool, complete with mural showing life-on-the-range. $8.

McCabe's, 3103 W Pico Blvd, Santa Monica (☎310/828-4403). LA's premier acoustic guitar shop; long the scene of some excellent and unusual shows; $10–20.

Molly Malone's Irish Pub, 575 S Fairfax Ave, West LA (☎213/935-1577). Traditional Irish music, American folk, rock and R&B; see also "Drinking: bars, pubs and coffee bars", p.151. $5.

The Silver Bullet, 3321 South St, Long Beach. A riotous Country and Western talent competition is held here every Tuesday, and dance lessons most other nights; free–$3.

LA'S FESTIVALS

January

1 Tournament of Roses in Pasadena. A parade of floral floats and marching bands along a five-mile stretch of Colorado Boulevard.

9 Martin Luther King Parade and Celebration. The civil rights hero is honored with spirited activities at King Park and Baldwin Hills-Crenshaw Mall.

February

14–15 Queen Mary Scottish Festival. All the haggis you can stand at this two-day Long Beach celebration, along with highland dancing and bagpipes.

First full moon after 21 Chinese New Year. Three days of dragon-float street parades and cultural programs, based in Chinatown.

March

17 St Patrick's Day. Parade along Colorado Boulevard in Old Town Pasadena. No parade but freely flowing green beer in the "Irish" bars along Fairfax Avenue.

End The Academy Awards are presented at the Shrine Auditorium or Dorothy Chandler Pavilion. Bleacher seats are available to watch the limousines draw up and the stars emerge for the ceremony.

April

Early The Blessing of the Animals. A long-established ceremony, Mexican in origin. Locals arrive in Olvera Street to have their pets blessed, then watch the attendant parade.

Weekend nearest 13 Thai New Year. Focus of activity at North Hollywood's Wat Thai Temple.

May

5 Cinco de Mayo. A day-long party to commemorate the Mexican victory at the Battle of Puebla (not Mexican Independence Day as many Californians think). Spirited parade in Olvera Street, and several blocks downtown blocked off for Chicano and Hispanic music performances. There are also celebrations in most LA parks.

Late Valley Jewish Festival. The largest such event west of the Mississippi. Activities begin at Pierce College, in the San Fernando Valley district of Woodland Hills.

June

Second weekend Irish Fair and Music Festival. Spirited celebration held at Santa Anita racetrack in Arcadia.

Late Gay Pride. Parade on Santa Monica Boulevard in West Hollywood. Carnival atmosphere, 250 vendors and an all-male drag football cheerleading team.

Jazz venues

The Baked Potato, 3787 Cahuenga Blvd, North Hollywood (☎818/980-1615). A small but near-legendary contemporary jazz spot, where many reputations have been forged; $8, $5 on Thurs.

BB King's Blues Club, 1000 Universal Center Drive, Burbank (☎818/6-BBKING). Has a garish Universal CityWalk exterior, but *Lucilles*, the club room, features acoustic blues on weekends. Low cover.

Catalina Bar & Grill, 1640 N Cahuenga Blvd, Hollywood (☎213/466-2210). Newly reopened, this Hollywood jazz institution offers plenty of style and atmosphere, for $10–20.

Cat N' Fiddle Pub, 6530 Sunset Blvd, Hollywood (☎213/468-3800). This pseudo-English pub has jazz, usually a dual-sax quintet, on Sunday from 7pm until 11pm; no cover. See also "Drinking: bars, pubs and coffee bars", p.151.

House of Blues, 8430 Sunset Blvd, West Hollywood (☎213/650-1451). Over-commercialized mock sugar shack, with good but pricey live acts. Very popular with tourists and heavily influenced by the life and legend of John Belushi, whose estate has a business interest.

Jazz Bakery, 3233 Helms Ave, Culver City (☎310/271-9039). More performance space than club, the brainchild of singer Ruth Price. The best local musicians play alongside big-name visitors.

July

4 Independence Day. *Queen Mary* in Long Beach hosts particularly large fireworks display, as well as colorful entertainment.

August

First two weeks Culmination of the South Bay's International Surf Festival.

10–14 Nisei Week in Little Tokyo. A celebration of Japanese America, with martial arts demonstrations, karaoke, Japanese brush painting, baby shows and performance.

September

4 LA's birthday. A civic ceremony and assorted street entertainment around El Pueblo de Los Angeles to mark the founding of the original pueblo in 1781.

18–21 Koreatown Multicultural Festival. Dancing, parading and Tae Kwon Do exhibitions.

Last two weeks Los Angeles County Fair in Pomona, in the San Gabriel Valley. The biggest County Fair in the country, with livestock shows, eating contests and fairground rides.

Late Watts Jazz Festival. Two days of free music with the Watts Towers as a backdrop.

October

Early Scandinavian Festival. Folk dancing with assorted food and art. Held at MGM Plaza in Santa Monica.

Early Greek Festival. Food and music celebration at St Katherine Greek Orthodox Church in Redondo Beach.

Second weekend LA Street Scene. Free rock music, theater and comedy on downtown streets. At the same time as West Hollywood Street Festival, a display of handmade arts and crafts.

31 Halloween Parade. More West Hollywood frolicking

November

3 Dia de Los Muertos (Day of the Dead) celebrated throughout East Los Angeles and for the tourists on Olvera Street. Mexican traditions, such as picnicking on the family burial spot, are upheld.

Saturday after Thanksgiving Doo-dah Parade. Quintessential LA event featuring absurd or bizarre characters marching through Pasadena. Surprisingly popular.

End Hollywood Christmas Parade. The first and best of the many Yuletide events, with a cavalcade of mind-boggling floats.

World Stage, 4344 Degnan Blvd, Crenshaw (☎213/293-2451). Informal, bare-bones rehearsal space that attracts top-name players like drummers Billy Higgins and Max Roach. Thursday jams, Friday and Saturday gigs.

Salsa venues

La Bamba, 61 N Raymond Ave, Pasadena (☎818/584-9771). Terrific Latin performers nightly at this Caribbean/South American restaurant. Weekend cover $5.

La Cita, 336 S Hill St, Downtown (☎213/972-9785). Traditional Hispanic music played nightly at 9pm in this authentic downtown bar at the foot of Bunker Hill. Cheap drinks, no cover.

Luminarias, 3500 Ramona Blvd, Monterey Park, East LA (☎213/268-4177). Hilltop restaurant (see p.143) with live salsa reckoned to be as good as its Mexican food; no cover.

Zabumba, 10717 Venice Blvd, Culver City (☎310/841-6525). In a colorful building amid drab surroundings, this venue is more bossa nova Brazilian than straight salsa, but it's still great.

Reggae venues

Golden Sails Hotel, 6285 E Pacific Coast Highway, Long Beach (☎310/498-0091). Some of the best reggae bands from LA and beyond on Friday and Saturday; $8.

Kingston 12, 814 Broadway, Santa Monica (☎310/451-4423). Santa Monica's top venue for reggae music. Small and comfortable; $10–12.

Classical music, opera and dance

Considering its size and stature in the other arts, LA has very few outlets for **classical music**. The Los Angeles Philharmonic (☎213/850-2000), the only major name in the city, performs regularly during the year, and the Los Angeles Chamber Orchestra (☎213/622-7001) appears sporadically at different venues; also, occasionally during the semester, students of the Schoenberg Institute give **free lunchtime concerts** on the USC campus. Otherwise, attractions are thin. Watch the press, especially the *LA Times*, for details, and expect to pay from $10 to $40 for most concerts, much more for really big names.

As for **opera**, the Music Center Opera (☎213/972-7211) stages productions between September and June, as does Orange County's Opera Pacific (☎213/480-3232 or 714/740-2000), which performs both grand opera and operettas. Prices can be anything from $10 to $120. **Dance** in LA is not to be dismissed, either. The big event of the year is the **Dance Kaleidoscope**, held over two weeks in July at the John Anson Ford Theater and organized by the Los Angeles Area Dance Alliance (LAADA; ☎213/343-5120) – a co-operative supported by LA's smaller dance companies that provides a central source of information on events. Otherwise check for performances at the **universities**, where some of the most exciting new names in dance have residencies.

Major venues

The Dorothy Chandler Pavilion, in the Music Center, 135 N Grand Ave, Downtown (☎213/972-7211 or 7460). Home to the LA Philharmonic from October until May. Also used by the Music Center Opera and other top names. Hosts Oscars on alternate years with The Shrine Auditorium (see below).

The Hollywood Bowl, 2301 N Highland Ave, Hollywood (☎213/850-2000). The LA Philharmonic gives open-air concerts here (July–Sept Tues–Sat evenings; see p.103 for more on the Bowl).

Japan America Theater, 244 S San Pedro St, Little Tokyo (☎213/680-3700). Dance and performance works drawn from Japan and the Far East.

John Anson Ford Theater, 2850 Cahuenga Blvd, Hollywood (☎213/974-1343). Besides the summer Dance Kaleidoscope, this open-air venue also has eclectic productions by local groups.

Orange County Performing Arts Center, 600 Town Center Drive, Costa Mesa (☎714/556-ARTS). Home of the Pacific Symphony Orchestra and Opera Pacific.

The Pacific Amphitheater, 100 Fair Drive, Costa Mesa (☎310/410-1062). A big open-air venue, Orange County's answer to the Hollywood Bowl.

Royce Hall, on the UCLA campus (☎310/825-9261 or 2101). Classical concerts often involving big names throughout the college year.

The Shrine Auditorium, 665 W Jefferson, South Central LA (☎213/749-5123), box office at 655 S Hill St (☎213/749-5123). Hosts Oscars and regular performances by choral gospel groups.

UCLA Center for the Performing Arts, 10920 Wilshire Blvd, Westwood (☎310/825-4401). Hosts a wide range of touring companies, and runs an "Art of Dance" series with an experimental emphasis between September and June.

Comedy

Gags are cracked every night all over LA at a range of **comedy clubs** across the city. Although rising stars and hopeless beginners can be spotted on the "underground", open-mike scene, the vast majority of famous and soon-to-be-famous comedians, both stand-up and improvisational, appear at the more established clubs, most of them in

Hollywood or West LA. These venues usually have a bar, charge a cover of $10–12, and put on two shows each evening, generally starting at 8pm and 10.30pm – the later one is generally more popular. The better-known places are open every night, but are often solidly booked on Friday and at weekends.

Comedy venues

Acme Comedy Theater, 135 N La Brea Ave, Hollywood (☎213/525-0202). A fancy new theater with sketch and improvised comedy, as well as variety shows.

Bang Theater, 457 N Fairfax Ave, Hollywood (☎213/653-6886). One-person shows and long-form improvisation are the specialties at this recently opened theater/comedy club.

Comedy & Magic Club, 1018 Hermosa Ave, Hermosa Beach (☎310/372-1193). Strange couplings of magic and comedy. Jay Leno sometimes tests material here.

The Comedy Store, 8433 W Sunset Blvd, West LA (☎213/656-6225). LA's comedy showcase and popular enough to be spread over three rooms – which means there's usually space, even at weekends. Always a good line-up too.

Groundlings Theater, 7307 Melrose Ave, West LA (☎213/934-9700). Another pioneering improvisational venue where only the gifted survive.

HBO Workspace, 733 N Seward St, Hollywood (☎213/993-6099). If you're in the mood for free experimental comedy, this is the place. HBO runs it as a proving ground for risky acts.

The Ice House, 24 N Mentor Ave, Pasadena (☎626/577-1895). The comedy mainstay of the Valley, very established and fairly safe.

The Improvisation, 8162 Melrose Ave, West LA (☎213/651-2583). Known for hosting some of the best acts working in the area, this is one of LA's top comedy spots – so book ahead.

LA Cabaret Comedy Club, 17271 Ventura Blvd, Encino (☎818/501-3737). Stand-up comics of mixed worth.

LA Connection, 13442 Ventura Blvd, Sherman Oaks (☎818/784-1868). An improvisation showcase for highly rated obnoxiousness specialists. Seldom less than memorable.

The Laugh Factory, 8001 Sunset Blvd, West Hollywood (☎213/656-1336). Stand-ups of varying standards and reputations, with the odd big name.

Theater

LA has a very active **theater** scene. While the bigger venues host a predictable array of clapped-out old musicals and classics starring a crowd-pulling line-up of big film names, there are over a hundred "Equity waiver" theaters with fewer than a hundred seats, enabling non-Equity-cardholders to perform; and a vast network of fringe writers, actors and directors. A number of alternative theaters have sprung up in Hollywood west of Cahuenga Boulevard, revolving around **The Complex**, a group of six small theaters at 6470/6 Santa Monica Blvd (☎213/466-1767). Tickets are less expensive than you might expect: a big show will set you back upwards of $25 (matinees are cheaper), smaller shows around $10 to $20, and you should always book ahead.

Fringe theaters

Cast-At-The-Circle, 804 N El Centro Ave, Hollywood (☎213/462-0265). Small Hollywood theater hosting a variety of smaller productions.

Highways, 1651 18th St, Santa Monica (☎213/660-8587). Located in an arts complex, this adventurous performance space offers a range of topical drama and one-person shows.

Odyssey Theater Ensemble, 2055 S Sepulveda Blvd, Westside (☎310/477-2055). Well-respected Westside theater company, relocated in new home.

You can get **information** and book theater **tickets** through **Theatrix** (☎213/466-1767).

Powerhouse Theater, 3116 Second St, Santa Monica (☎310/396-3680). Adventurous and risk-taking experimental shows.

Major theaters

Coronet Theater, 366 N La Cienega Blvd, West Hollywood (☎310/657-7377). Home of the LA Public Theater, whose productions include the odd famous name, and also home to the Youth Academy of Dramatic Arts.

Geffen Playhouse, 10886 Le Conte Ave, Westwood (☎310/208-5454). One of the smaller of the major theaters, often with one-person shows. Hollywood connection.

Mark Taper Forum, 135 N Grand Ave, Downtown (☎213/628-2772). Theater in the three-quarter round, frequently innovative new plays.

Shubert Theater, ABC Entertainment Center, Century City (☎1-800/447-7400). A rare reason to visit Century City is to ogle the razzamatazz Andrew Lloyd Webber musicals, among others.

Film

It's no shock to find that many major feature **films** are released in LA months (sometimes years) before they play anywhere else in the world, and a huge number of cinemas show both the new releases and the classic favorites – with fewer screens showing independent and foreign movies. Depending on where you go and what you see, a ticket will be around $8.

For **mainstream cinema**, though less popular than it used to be, Westwood still has a high concentration of movie houses, as does Santa Monica promenade. Of the multi-screen facilities, the eighteen-screen Cineplex Odeon, at Universal Studios (☎818/508-0588), is a plush complex that includes a pair of pseudo-Parisian cafés. Despite all the screens, only six or seven films are typically shown in the multiple theaters. Another more enterprisingly programmed venue is the Beverly Cineplex (☎310/652-7760) in the Beverly Center mall (see p.163), which has fourteen tiny screens featuring artsy independent film programs and first-run blockbusters.

For **cheap** and **free films**, the places to hit are the Bing Theater at the County Art Museum, 5905 Wilshire Blvd (☎213/857-6010), which has afternoon screenings of many neglected Hollywood classics and charges just $2; the USC and UCLA campuses also often have interesting free screenings aimed at film students, announced on campus notice boards. Otherwise, the best places to find **art-house** and **cult films** are the New Beverly Cinema, 7165 Beverly Blvd (☎213/938-4038), especially strong on imaginative double bills, and the Nuart Theater, 11272 Santa Monica Blvd (☎310/478-6379), which runs rarely seen classics, documentaries and foreign-language films. (Be prepared to wait in a lengthy queue outside, though.) The Los Feliz Theater, 1822 N Vermont Ave, resisted a descent into the porn movie market in the 1960s; its three small screens still show international and low-budget American independent movies.

If you're looking for a golden-age-of-film **atmosphere**, you'll need either to take in an action triple bill in one of the historic downtown movie palaces (described on p.83), where the delirious furnishings may captivate your attention longer than the triple-bills, or visit one of the Hollywood landmarks. The Chinese Theatre, 6925 Hollywood Blvd (☎213/468-8111), with its large screen, six-track stereo sound and wild chinoiserie interior, shows relentlessly mainstream films, but the first-night audience's loud participation is entertainment in itself. If this doesn't appeal, you could always indulge in the Cinerama Dome's near-wraparound screen, at 6360 Sunset Blvd (☎213/466-3401), which is said to be the biggest in California.

Gay and lesbian LA

Although nowhere near as big as that of San Francisco, the **gay scene** in LA is far from invisible, and gay people are out and prominent in workplaces and environments right across the city. Of a number of specific areas where gay people tend to locate, the best known is the autonomous city of **West Hollywood**, which has become synonymous with the (affluent, white) gay lifestyle, not just in LA but all over California. The section of West Hollywood on Santa Monica Boulevard east of Doheny Drive has restaurants, shops and bars primarily aimed at gay men. Another established community is **Silverlake**, home to the gay-oriented bars and restaurants on Hyperion Boulevard.

Gay couples will find themselves readily accepted at just about any LA **hotel**, but there are a few that cater especially to gay travelers and can also be useful sources of information on the LA gay scene generally. We've also listed below a few restaurants that cater specifically to gay men and lesbians. For up-to-date (if ad-packed), gay-oriented publications, see "Information" on p.66.

Gay resources

AIDS Project Los Angeles, 1313 Vine St, Hollywood (☎213/993-1600). Sponsors fund-raisers throughout the year and a well-attended annual walkathon.

A Different Light, 8853 Santa Monica Blvd, West Hollywood (☎213/668-0629). The city's best-known gay and lesbian bookshop, with monthly art shows, readings, women's music events and comfortable chairs for lounging.

Gay and Lesbian Community Services Center, 1625 N Schrader Blvd, Hollywood (☎213/993-7400). Counselling, health-testing and information in Hollywood. It publishes *The Center News*, a useful bi-monthly magazine.

Gay Community Yellow Pages, 1604 Vista Del Mar Ave, Hollywood (☎213/469-4454). Gay businesses, publications, services and gathering places listed yearly; available all over LA.

Gay hotels

Coral Sands Motel, 1730 N Western Ave, Hollywood (☎1-800/367-7263). Exclusively geared towards gay men. All rooms face the inner courtyard pool. Basically very cruisy. ④.

Holloway Motel, 8465 Santa Monica Blvd, West Hollywood (☎213/654-2454). Typical clean roadside motel, if rather dreary looking. ③.

Ramada 8585 Santa Monica Blvd, West Hollywood (☎1-800/845-8585 or 310/652-6400). Very gay-friendly, modern place with brand-new rooms, in the center of the community. ④.

Gay and lesbian restaurants

Figs, 7929 Santa Monica Blvd, West Hollywood (☎213/654-0780). Highly recommended all-American down-home cooking.

French Market Place, 7985 Santa Monica Blvd, West Hollywood (☎310/654-0898). Theme restaurant that's at least as much fun as Disneyland.

Gloria's Café, 3603 W Sunset Blvd (☎213/664-5732). Popular local hangout near Silverlake that's a great spot for dinner, especially Cajun.

Mark's Restaurant, 861 N La Cienega, West Hollywood (☎310/652-5252). High-end establishment serving California cuisine.

Gay and lesbian bars and clubs

Arena, 6655 Santa Monica Blvd (☎213/462-0714). Many clubs under one huge roof, large dance floors throbbing to funk, Latin and hi-NRG grooves, and sometimes live bands. **Club 6655** is another name for the place, used when it becomes a dance, house and hip-hop club. **Circus** is yet another variation it becomes when hosting dance, disco and drag parties.

Detour, 1087 Manzanita, Silverlake (☎213/664-1189). A friendly and quite cheap denim and leather bar in a faceless section of town.

Girl Bar, 657 N Robertson Blvd, West Hollywood (☎310/659-0471). Madonna's been here and Chastity Bono once worked behind the bar. The cavernous dance floor warms up eventually with the help of girl go-go dancers.

Jewel's Catch One, 4067 W Pico Blvd, Mid-City (☎213/734-8849). Sweaty barn catering to a mixed crowd, both on two wild dance floors. Cover varies.

Klub Banshee, 8512 Santa Monica Blvd, West Hollywood (☎310/288-1601). Weekend dance club for women, with international and funk beats.

Le Bar, 2375 Glendale Blvd, Silverlake (☎213/660-7595). Quiet and welcoming bar in a bland section of Silverlake.

The Palms, 8572 Santa Monica Blvd, West Hollywood (☎310/652-6188). Mostly house and dance nights at West Hollywood's most established lesbian bar.

Probe, 836 N Highland Ave, Hollywood (☎213/461-8301). LA's longest-running gay men's disco, playing all the Euro Pop dance hits, but with a dark touch of gothic on Wednesdays.

Rage, 8911 Santa Monica Blvd, West Hollywood (☎310/652-7055). Very flash gay men's club playing the latest hi-NRG. Also with drag comedy. Drinks are cheap, the cover varies.

7969, 7969 Santa Monica Blvd, West Hollywood (☎213/654-0280). Formerly called *Peanuts*, West Hollywood's oldest mixed gay and lesbian disco has drag shows and topless girl dancers, and clubs *Fetish* and *Fuck!* on the weekend. Call for details; cover varies.

Women's LA

It's hardly surprising that a city as big as LA should have such an organized **women's** network, with many resource centers, bookstores, publications and clubs. Women travelers are unlikely to encounter any problems which aren't applicable to all the West Coast (for more on which see Basics, p.47), but the resources here are much more developed.

There are many good sources of general and detailed information on the local women's movement, though there's an inevitable crossover with the city's sizeable lesbian community – see "Gay and Lesbian LA", above. *LA Woman*, Los Angeles' largest women's magazine, profiling local personalities and providing a calendar of events, is available from most newsstands and bookstores – notably the Sisterhood Bookstore, at 1351 Westwood Blvd (☎310/477-7300), a Westside landmark south of Westwood Village, that sells books, music, cards, jewelery and literature pertaining to the women's movement. The *Women's Yellow Pages* (☎310/398-5761), another good resource, is a yearly listing of over 1400 women-owned businesses and services. Call for a copy.

Shopping

Shopping in LA is an art. The level of disposable income in the wealthy parts of the city is astronomical, and touring the more outrageous stores can be a great insight into LA life – revealing who's got the money and what they're capable of wasting it on. Whether you want to pop out for a new light bulb or pair of socks, lay waste to a wad or simply be a voyeur in the orgy of acquisition, there are, besides the run-of-the-mill retailers you'll find anywhere, big **department stores**, mega-sized **malls** – where most of the serious shopping goes on – and **Rodeo Drive**, three blocks of the world's most exclusive and expensive shopping. The trendiest shops line **Melrose Avenue**, between La Brea and Fairfax in West Hollywood. **Old Town Pasadena** boasts a few of the more upmarket chains, while the few blocks above Prospect on N Vermont Avenue in Los Feliz Village are home to some of the underground's trendier boutiques.

RODEO DRIVE

The black hole for expense accounts is **Rodeo Drive** in Beverly Hills, a solid line of exclusive stores to which you might be drawn by sheer curiosity. One store worth looking into is Fred Hayman, at 273 N, one of the first stores on Rodeo Drive and housing the autographed photos of a number of Hollywood celebs alongside its mostly Italian designer-menswear. Another is Ralph Lauren, 444 N, which caters to well-heeled WASPS who fancy themselves as canine-fixated English gentry. Besides thousand-dollar suits and monogrammed Wellingtons, there are exquisitely carved walking sticks and mounted game heads, and a huge assortment of wooden dogs, bronze dogs and paintings of dogs. At the foot of Rodeo Drive are LA's premier department stores, including Barney's and, most famously, Neiman-Marcus, 9700 Wilshire Blvd, who sell everything from $5 Swiss truffles to his 'n' hers leopard skins. Nearby, **Two Rodeo**, the area's mock-European tourist trap, also competes for buyers' attention, though in a much cruder and less appealing fashion.

The city also has a good assortment of specialist stores, sporting extensive selections of **books** and **records**. There's an equally diverse assortment of **food stores**, from corner delis and supermarkets to fancy cake stores and gourmet markets. You'll also find several stores selling perfect LA souvenirs, like the **LA County Coroner Gift Shop** at 1104 N Mission Rd (☎213/343-0760), which sells everything from skeleton-decorated beach towels and T-shirts to toe-tag key chains – all typical LA merchandise.

Department stores and malls

Each of LA's neighborhoods has a collection of ordinary stores and mini-malls. You'll find much the best sources of cheap toiletries and staples at places such as K-Mart and Target. A step up from these in price and quality, though still good for general shopping, are **department stores**, which more often than not are included within massive **malls**, often resembling self-contained city suburbs, around which Angelenos do the bulk of their serious buying.

The malls

Beverly Center, Beverly and La Cienega Blvd, West Hollywood. Chic shopping at its best: seven acres of boutiques, a Bullocks department store, a multiplex cinema and a *Hard Rock Café*, all in one complex that resembles a giant brown concrete bunker – trimmed in hideous green and purple.

Century City Marketplace, 10250 Santa Monica Blvd, Century City. Outdoor mall with a hundred upscale shops, including a branch of New York's Metropolitan Museum gift shop. The place to come to see stars do their shopping, and to catch a first-run movie in excellent surrounds.

Santa Monica Place, Broadway and Second St, Santa Monica. Sunny, skylit mall with three tiers of shops. The Third Street Promenade, which runs north from the mall, is one of the most popular shopping and nightlife precincts in LA, and all the more enjoyable for being outdoors.

Seventh Street Marketplace, Seventh and Figueroa streets, Downtown. Anchored by Macy's department store, at the foot of the Citicorp office towers.

Westside Pavilion, Pico and Westwood Blvd, West LA. Postmodern shopping complex centered on the Nordstrom department store, a clothes, shoes, jewelery and cosmetics store that provides regular customers with a personal "shopper" (ie an employee who does all the legwork around the store and comes back with a choice of goods).

Food and drink

Since eating out in LA is so common, you may never have to shop for **food** at all. But if you're preparing a picnic, or want to indulge in a spot of home cooking, there are plenty of places to stock up. **Delis**, many open round the clock, are found on more or less every corner in LA; **supermarkets** are almost as common, some open 24 hours, or at least until 10pm – Lucky's, Alpha-Beta, Pavilions, Ralphs and Trader Joe's are the names to look out for. There are also **ethnic groceries** and **markets**, and – although much more expensive – the **gourmet markets** and **stores**, not to mention a bizarre collection of one-off outlets for all kinds of food oddities, mainly clustered in fashionable West LA. To buy **drink** you need go no further than the nearest supermarket – Trader Joe's is the cheapest and best.

Pastries and cakes

The Cheese Store, 419 N Beverly Drive, Beverly Hills (☎310/278-2855). Over four hundred types of cheese from all over the world, including every kind produced in the US.

Mousse Fantasy, 2130 Sawtelle Blvd, West LA (☎310/479-6665). A Japanese version of a French patisserie, though in a crowded strip mall. The green tea mousse cake is a taste of heaven.

Mrs Field's Cookies, 907 Westwood Blvd, Westwood (☎310/208-0096). Chewy, sweet cookies, made to a "secret recipe" that has plenty of devoted fans – and branches all over the US, including eight others in LA alone.

Viktor Benes Continental Pastries, 8718 W Third St, West LA (☎310/276-0488). The place for freshly baked bread, coffee cakes and Danish pastries. Three other area locations.

Delis and groceries

Bay Cities Importing, 1517 Lincoln Blvd, Santa Monica (☎310/395-8279). Like a gigantic deli, with piles of fresh pasta, spices, meats, sauces and many French and Middle Eastern imports.

Claro's Italian Market, 1003 E Valley Blvd, San Gabriel (☎818/288-2026). A compact but well-stocked haven of Italian wines, chocolate, crackers and own-brand frozen meals. A second room houses a deli and bakery with at least forty varieties of cookies. Worth a trip to distant San Gabriel.

Erewhon, 7660 Beverly Blvd, West LA (☎213/937-0777). Next door to the CBS studios, selling pricey health food and all the wheatgrass you can swallow. The epitome of self/health-obsessed LA.

Full o' Life, 2525 W Magnolia Blvd, Burbank (☎818/845-8343). This mother of all health food stores dates back to 1959. It offers an organic market, deli, dairy, restaurant and book department, and there are two nutritionists and a naturopathic doctor on the premises daily.

La Canasta in El Mercado, 3425 E First St, East LA (☎213/269-2953). Three floors of authentic Mexican food and Central American food: chilis, chayotes and mouthwatering desserts.

Standard Sweets and Snacks, 18600 Pioneer Blvd, Artesia (☎310/860-6364). A good Indian finger food joint selling vegetarian dosas (pancakes) and delicious sweets.

Wild Oats Community Market, 603 S Lake Ave, Pasadena (☎818/792-1778). The best selection of organic wine in LA in a pleasantly European market atmosphere.

Books

There are almost as many bookstores in LA as there are people. Of the ubiquitous **discount chains** that have spread across the US in the last few years, Crown offer the latest hardbacks and blockbusters plus many more (and magazines) at knock-down prices. On the pricier side, Barnes and Noble and Borders provide standardized branches that are ubiquitous across the US. The city is also exceptionally well served by a wide range of **specialist bookstores** and many **secondhand bookstores**, worthy of several hours' browsing along the miles of dusty shelves.

Specialist bookstores

A Different Light, 8853 Santa Monica Blvd, West Hollywood (☎310/854-6601). The city's best known gay and lesbian bookstore, with monthly art shows, readings, and women's music events.

Amok Books, 1764 N Vermont Ave, Los Feliz (☎213/655-0956). Mayhem, true crimes, fanzines and paranoid conspiracy rants; the extremes of information in print. A small shop with a large mail order clientele favored by tabloid TV researchers. Now publishing its own authors.

Bodhi Tree, 8585 Melrose Ave, West Hollywood (☎310/659-1733). New Age, occult and all things spiritually trendy.

Book Soup, 8818 W Sunset Blvd, West LA (☎310/659-3110). Great selection, right on Sunset Strip, open daily until midnight. Narrow, winding aisles packed pell-mell with books.

Either/Or, 124 Pier Ave, Hermosa Beach (☎310/374-2060). A voluminous fiction selection and a wide variety of New Age tomes, with free publications littering the floor. Open till 11pm.

Hennessey and Ingalls, 1254 Third St Promenade, Santa Monica (☎310/458-9074). An impressive range of art and architecture books makes this bookstore the best in LA in its field; also sells rare posters and catalogs and hard-to-find books.

Larry Edmunds Book Shop, 6644 Hollywood Blvd, Hollywood (☎213/463-3273). Stacks of books, many of them out of print, on every aspect of film and theater, with movie stills and posters.

Midnight Special, 1318 Third St Promenade, Santa Monica (☎310/393-2923). A large general bookstore, with eccentrically filled shelves and a broad focus on lefty politics and social sciences.

Norton Simon Museum Bookstore, 411 W Colorado Blvd, Pasadena. Prices in this museum-attached store are lower than in any other art bookstore in LA, and the stock is superb.

Secondhand books

Acres of Books, 240 Long Beach Blvd, Long Beach (☎310/437-6980). Worth a trip down the Blue Line Metrorail just to wallow in LA's largest, and most disorganized, secondhand collection.

Book City, 6627 Hollywood Blvd (☎213/466-2525). Tightly packed from floor to ceiling with eclectic titles, many of which are physically well out of reach.

Wilshire Books, 3018 Wilshire Blvd, Santa Monica (☎310/828-3115). Without question the best used bookstore in LA for its size. Mid-sized collection of tomes on art, politics, religion, music, science and other such categories, all coherently organized.

Music

If anything, **record stores** are even more plentiful than bookstores in LA. With the rise of the CD, the number of stores selling LPs has dropped, though the plunge has stopped for the moment, if only because of the demand of die-hard vinyl fans. Most of the stores below carry used LPs, along with CDs and cassettes.

Aron's Records, 1150 N Highland Ave (☎213/469-4700). Secondhand discs – all styles, all prices, huge stock.

Moby Disc, 28 W Colorado (☎818/449-9975) and 3731 E Colorado (☎818/793-3475), both in Pasadena. Secondhand and deletion stocklist.

Music and Memories, 5057 Lankershim Blvd, North Hollywood (☎818/761-9827). Three hundred Sinatra LPs, and myriad others that sound like he should be on them.

Penny Lane, 12 W Colorado Blvd, Pasadena (☎818/564-0161). New and used records at reasonable prices; this local chain features massive listening stations from which you can sample up to a hundred discs. Also branches in Venice and Westwood.

Poo-Bah Records, 1101 E Walnut Ave, Pasadena (☎818/449-3359). American and imported New Wave sounds.

Record Surplus, 11609 W Pico Blvd, West LA (☎310/478-4217). Massive LP collection of surf music, ancient rock 'n' roll, 60s soundtracks and unintentionally hilarious spoken-word recordings.

Rhino Records, 1720 Westwood Blvd (☎310/474-8685). The biggest selection of international independent releases.

Vinyl Fetish, 7305 Melrose Ave, West Hollywood (☎213/935-1300). Besides the punk and post-punk merchandise, a good place to discover what's new on the LA music scene and buy a cheesy Gen-X T-shirt or two.

Listings

Airport Information Hollywood/Burbank ☎213/840-8847; John Wayne/Orange County ☎714/834-2400; LAX ☎310/646-5252; Long Beach ☎310/421-8293; Ontario ☎714/785-8838.

Automobile Club of Southern California, 2601 S Figueroa St, South Central LA (☎213/741-3686). For maps, guides and other motoring information.

Beach Information Weather conditions ☎310/457-9701; surfers' weather ☎213/379-8471.

Coastguard Search and Rescue ☎562/980-4444.

Consulates UK, 11766 Wilshire Blvd, West LA (☎310/477-3322); Australia, 11895 Wilshire Blvd, West LA (☎310/444-9310); New Zealand, 10960 Wilshire Blvd, Westwood (☎310/207-1605).

Currency Exchange Outside of banking hours daily at LAX until 11.30pm.

Dental Treatment The cheapest place is the USC School of Dentistry (☎213/743-2800), on the USC Campus, costing $20–200. Turn up and be prepared to wait all day.

Directory Enquiries Local ☎411 (this is a free call at pay phones); Long distance 1, then area code, then 555-1212.

Emergencies ☎911. For less urgent needs: ambulance ☎213/483-6721; fire ☎213/384-3131 or 213/262-2111; paramedics ☎213/262-2111; police ☎213/625-3311; poison control center ☎1-800/777-6476; earthquake tips ☎818/787-3737.

Hospitals The following have 24-hr emergency departments: Cedars-Sinai Medical Center, 8700 Beverly Blvd, Beverly Hills (☎310/855-6517); Good Samaritan Hospital, 616 Witmer St, Downtown (☎213/397-2121); UCLA Medical Center, Tiverton (☎310/825-8611) or Le Conte in Westwood (☎310/825-2111).

International Newspapers Both the USC and UCLA campuses have libraries holding recent overseas newspapers for browsing. Day-old English and European papers are on sale at Universal News Agency, 1655 N Las Palmas (daily 7am–midnight), and World Book and News, 1652 N Cahuenga Blvd (24-hr).

Left Luggage At Greyhound stations and LAX for $1 a day ($2 for larger lockers).

Mexican Tourist Office, Suite 224, 10100 Santa Monica Blvd, Century City (☎310/203-8151). Call for general information or pick up a tourist card – necessary if you're crossing the border. Mon–Fri 9am–5pm.

Pharmacies 24-hr pharmacy at Kaiser Permanente in the LA Medical Center, 4867 Sunset Blvd, Hollywood (☎213/667-8301)and various Thrifty drugstores downtown.

Post Office The main downtown post office is at 900 N Alameda St (☎213/617-4543), next to Union Station. Zip Code is 90086; pick up letters Mon–Fri 8am–3pm.

Smog Like many other things in the city, LA's smog is more hype than reality, yet the air quality *is* often very poor and, especially in the Valleys in late summer, can sometimes be quite dangerous. An air-quality index is published daily, and if the air is really bad, warnings are issued on TV, radio and in the press.

Sports Baseball: the LA Dodgers (☎213/224-1500) play at Dodger Stadium near downtown, seats $5–15; Anaheim Angels (☎714/634-2000) at Anaheim Stadium in Orange County, seats $6–15. Basketball: the LA Lakers (☎310/419-3100) at the Forum, in Inglewood, seats $21–70; the less flashy LA Clippers (☎213/748-8000) at the ugly LA Sports Arena near Exposition Park, seats $10–50. Football: Los Angeles currently has no professional football teams, but Pasadena's 102,000-capacity Rose Bowl is used for the annual New Year's Day Rose Bowl football game and is the home field for UCLA's football team. Hockey: LA Kings are also based at the Forum (☎310/419-3160), seats $11–80.

Traffic Check the AM radio news channels for frequent updates on what freeways are suffering from gridlock or congestion; if a highway section is particularly immobile, a "Sig-Alert" will be issued, meaning "avoid at all costs".

travel details

Trains

Los Angeles to: Anaheim (7 daily; 45min); Fullerton (for Disneyland) (9 daily; 35min); Glendale (7 daily; 33min); Oxnard (5 daily; 1hr 37min); Palm Springs (1 daily; 2hr 22min); Sacramento (1 daily; 14hr 12min); San Bernardino (1 daily; 1hr 40min); San Clemente (1 daily; 1hr 30min); San Diego (8 daily; 2hr 45min); San Francisco (1 daily; 12hr 40min); San Juan Capistrano (8 daily; 1hr 13min); Santa Barbara (5 daily; 2hr 45min); Tucson (1 daily; 8hr 50min); Van Nuys (5 daily; 35min); Ventura (4 daily; 1hr 50min).

Buses

Los Angeles to: Las Vegas (10–15 daily; 5hr 30min); Palm Springs (6–11 daily; 3hr); Phoenix (5–10 daily; 8hr 50min); Portland (4–6 daily; 23hr); Salt Lake City (2–3 daily; 17hr 15min); San Diego (18–30 daily; 2hr 45min); San Francisco (12–18 daily; 8hr); Seattle (3–5 daily; 27hr); Tijuana, Mexico (15–21 daily; 3hr 30min); Tucson (5–9 daily; 11hr 20min).

CHAPTER TWO

SAN DIEGO AND AROUND

Relatively free from smog, jungle-like entwinements of freeways, and shocking extremes of wealth and poverty, **San Diego** and much of its surrounding county represent the acceptable face of Southern California. Pipped by Los Angeles in the race to become *the* Southern Californian city, San Diego was for a long time considered an insignificant spot between Los Angeles and Mexico, but is now exacting revenge on its overgrown rival 125 miles to the north. Built on a gracefully curving bay, San Diego is not only scenically inviting, but also boasts a range of museums that is among the nation's most impressive, an evocative and nowadays well-tended history, several major tourist attractions, and much to discover away from the usual visitors' points of call.

Not surprisingly, the city is very much the social and commercial hub of San Diego County, and things change as you travel out from the metropolis. The **North County** divides into two quite different sections: the small and often enticing beach communities strung along the coast from the northern edge of San Diego itself to the rugged chaparral of the Camp Pendleton marine base; and, inland, the vineyards and avocado groves of a large agricultural area that reaches east towards much wilder and more mountainous land. Most settlements away from the coast are tiny and insular, and some have barely changed since the Gold Rush: a number of deep forests and several state parks are ideal for exploration by hiking and taking obscure back roads.

South from San Diego, there's little between the city and Mexico. **Tijuana**, just 25 miles from downtown, is an obvious jumping-off point for explorations of **Baja California**, and while it may not be the most appealing destination in Mexico, it's an entertaining enough place to spend a few hours – as thousands of Californians do each weekend. And since most of the border formalities are waived for anyone traveling less than twenty miles or so into Mexico, day-trips to the party-time beach town of Rosarito and the more enticing Ensenada are perfectly viable.

Of course, there is also heavy traffic in the other direction, as hordes of Mexicans, both legal and undocumented, flood into Southern California. Most are hotel and restaurant workers, but first- and especially second-generation migrants are gradually becoming integrated into less menial levels of the workforce. However, Mexicans in San Diego County are largely ghettoized, their presence resented by those born-and-bred Californians who can't see beyond the evident strain on the social welfare and the healthcare system. Such prejudices eased the passage, in 1994, of "Proposition 187", which denies illegals access to all manner of social services.

ACCOMMODATION PRICE CODES

All accommodation prices in this book have been coded using the symbols below; prices are for the least expensive **double rooms** in each establishment. For a full explanation see p.36 in Basics. Individual rates rather than price codes are given for **hostels**.

① up to $30	④ $60–80	⑦ $130–175
② $30–45	⑤ $80–100	⑧ $175–250
③ $45–60	⑥ $100–130	⑨ $250+

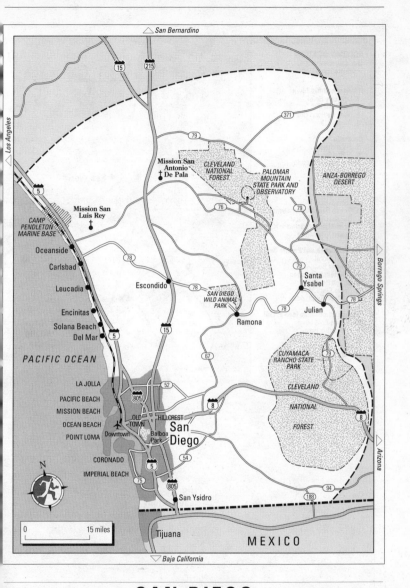

SAN DIEGO

Basking in almost constant sunshine and with its humidity tempered by the proximity of the ocean, **SAN DIEGO**, the second largest city in the state, is a near-perfect holiday resort. Anyone can enjoy idling on its varied beaches and viewing the obvious sights: San Diego Zoo, Sea World and the museums and sculptured greenery of Balboa

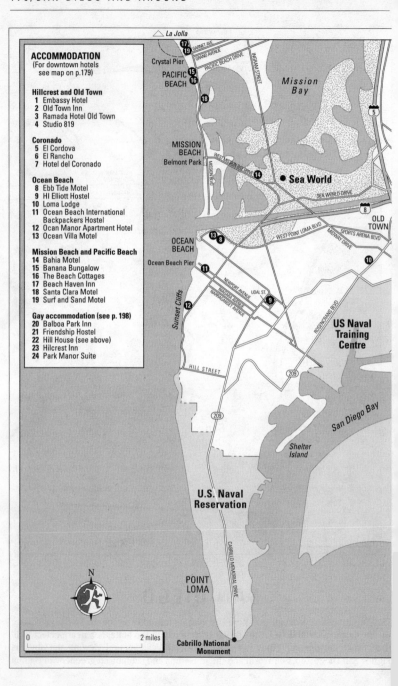

ACCOMMODATION
(For downtown hotels
see map on p.179)

Hillcrest and Old Town
1 Embassy Hotel
2 Old Town Inn
3 Ramada Hotel Old Town
4 Studio 819

Coronado
5 El Cordova
6 El Rancho
7 Hotel del Coronado

Ocean Beach
8 Ebb Tide Motel
9 HI Elliott Hostel
10 Loma Lodge
11 Ocean Beach International
   Backpackers Hostel
12 Ocan Manor Apartment Hotel
13 Ocean Villa Motel

Mission Beach and Pacific Beach
14 Bahia Motel
15 Banana Bungalow
16 The Beach Cottages
17 Beach Haven Inn
18 Santa Clara Motel
19 Surf and Sand Motel

Gay accommodation (see p. 198)
20 Balboa Park Inn
21 Friendship Hostel
22 Hill House (see above)
23 Hilcrest Inn
24 Park Manor Suite

△ La Jolla

GARNET AVE.
GRAND AVENUE

Crystal Pier

PACIFIC
BEACH

PACIFIC BEACH DRIVE

INGRAM STREET

*Mission
Bay*

5

MISSION
BEACH
Belmont Park

WEST MISSION BAY DRIVE

MISSION BLVD

14 ● **Sea World**

SEA WORLD DRIVE

8

OLD
TOWN

WEST POINT LOMA BLVD

SPORTS ARENA BLVD

MIDWAY DRIVE

OCEAN
BEACH

13 8

Ocean Beach Pier

11

NEWPORT AVENUE

UDAL ST.

VOLTAIRE AVENUE

NARRAGANSETT AVENUE

9

ROSECRANS BLVD

**US Naval
Training
Centre**

12

Sunset Cliffs

HILL STREET

209

San Diego Bay

*Shelter
Island*

**U.S. Naval
Reservation**

CABRILLO MEMORIAL DRIVE

**POINT
LOMA**

N

0   2 miles

**Cabrillo National
Monument**

Park. But at least as important as these is the recent expensive facelift given to the downtown area, restoring a sense of the city's real history and character.

The national image of San Diegans as healthy, affluent and conservative is true to a large extent – San Diego is certainly cleaner, and cleaner-cut, than Los Angeles or San Francisco. Yet it's also an extremely amiable and easy-going place. Increasing numbers of aspirant young professionals – the embodiment of the comfortable Southern Californian lifestyle – have swept away the reputation for dull smugness that San Diego acquired through the Sixties and Seventies, and given the city quite a different face. The presence of three college campuses (SDSU, UCSD, and USD) also keeps the cobwebs away – and helps sustain the image of a city that's on the up-and-up.

The first European to land on Californian soil, the Portuguese adventurer Juan Rodríguez Cabrillo (in the employ of the Spanish), put ashore at Point Loma, a spot about ten miles from the center of present-day San Diego, in 1542. White settlement didn't begin until two centuries later, however, with the building of a mission – the first in California – and a garrison, on a site overlooking San Diego Bay. Conflict between *Californios* and the fresh waves of settlers from the east led to the raising of the Stars and Stripes over San Diego in 1847, an event closely followed by the transference of the Mexican provinces to the US. But San Diego missed out on the new mail route to the west and was plagued by a series of droughts through the 1860s, causing many bankruptcies. Although the transcontinental Santa Fe railroad link was short-lived – repeated flooding led the terminus to be moved north to Los Angeles and San Bernardino, and to this day there's no direct rail service to San Diego from the east – its establishment resulted in an economic boom through the 1880s. A few decades later came the first of two international expositions in Balboa Park, which were to establish San Diego (and the park itself) nationwide.

In part because it lacks a train connection to the east, the city has long played second fiddle to Los Angeles in terms of major trade and significance, but it has used its strategic seaside location to establish an economically important military presence. During World War II, the US Navy took advantage of the numerous sheltered bays and made San Diego its Pacific Command Center – a function it retains to the present day. The military still dominates the local economy, although tourism is gaining ground.

Arrival and information

Drivers will find it simple to reach the city center from any of the three interstate highways: I-5 is the main link from Los Angeles and passes through the northern parts of the central city; from the east, I-8 runs through Hotel Circle before concluding in Ocean Beach; and I-15, the main route from inland San Diego County, cuts through the city's eastern suburbs. **Parking lots** are scattered around downtown, and there's plenty of metered parking – free overnight, but not allowed on evenings when the streets are being cleaned.

All forms of **public transportation** drop you in the heart of downtown San Diego: **trains** use the Santa Fe Depot, close to the western end of Broadway, while the **Greyhound** terminal is even more central at Broadway and First Avenue. Lindbergh Field **airport** is only two miles from downtown, so low-flying jets are a feature of the city. There are two terminals, East and West, connected with downtown by bus #2 ($1.50), the service starting around 6am and finishing just after midnight. Obviously, given the distance, **taxis** into downtown aren't expensive, and quite a few hotels – even some of the budget ones – offer guests a free **airport limo** service. All the main **car rental** firms have desks at the airport (see "Listings" on p.198).

Information

A good first stop in the city is the **International Visitor Information Center**, 11 Horton Plaza, Downtown at F Street and First Avenue (June–Aug Mon–Sat 8.30am–5pm, Sun 11am–5pm; Sept–May Mon–Sat 8.30am–5pm; ☎619/236-1212), which has maps, the useful *Official Visitors Guide*, and all kinds of information on the area including accommodation. Another useful source is the HI-AYH office inside the hostel foyer at 521 Market St (☎619/525-1531) – outside business hours a recorded message gives local hostel information. For eating and entertainment information, scan the free weekly *San Diego Reader* and *Metropolitan*, which can be found in many shops, bars and clubs; you could also try the tourist-oriented *In San Diego Today* and Thursday's *San Diego Union-Tribune*.

City transportation

Despite its size, **getting around** San Diego without a car is slow but not terribly difficult, whether you use buses, the tram-like trolley or a rented bike. Taxis are also an option: the average fare is $2 for the first mile and $1.40 for each mile thereafter. Traveling can be harder at night, with most routes closing down around 11pm or midnight. The transportation system won't break anyone's budget, but a number of cut-rate tickets and passes can reduce costs over a few days or weeks.

Buses

Of the seven companies that operate **buses** in the San Diego area, by far the most common is San Diego Transit (☎619/233-3004), which covers much of the city. There's a flat-rate fare of $1.75 (or $2 on the few express routes), transfers are free, and you should pay the exact fare when boarding (dollar bills are accepted). In general, the service is reliable and frequent, with even comparatively far-flung spots connected to downtown – known on route maps and timetables as "Center City" – at least twice an hour.

If you have any **queries** about San Diego's local buses, call into **The Transit Store**, 102 Broadway (Mon–Sat 8.30am–5.30pm; ☎619/234-1060) for detailed timetables, the free *Regional Transit Guide*, the Day Tripper Transit Pass, and monthly passes. If you know your point of departure and destination, you can get automated bus information by phoning ☎619/685-4900.

The Trolley

Complementing bus travel around the city is the **San Diego Trolley**, often called the "Tijuana Trolley" because it runs on the sixteen miles of track from the Santa Fe Depot (departures from C Street) to the US–Mexico border at San Ysidro. Fares are $1–1.75, depending on how long you stay on. Tickets should be bought from the machines at trolley stops, and occasionally an inspector may appear and demand proof of payment.

USEFUL SAN DIEGO BUS ROUTES

The following buses connect **downtown San Diego** with the surrounding area:

Balboa Park #7, #16, #25	Imperial Beach #901
Hillcrest #3, #11, #25	Ocean Beach #35
Mission Beach #34	East San Diego #1, #15
Old Town #5, #34	La Jolla #34
Coronado #19, #903, #904	Pacific Beach #30, #34

CUT-RATE TICKETS AND PASSES

If you intend to use public transportation a lot, buy the **Day Tripper Transit Pass**, which lasts one or four consecutive days ($5 or $15 respectively) and is valid on any San Diego Transit bus, as well as the trolley and the San Diego Bay ferry (which sails between Broadway Pier downtown and Coronado; $2 each way, 50¢ for bicycles – see p.187 for more details). If you're around for a few weeks and using buses regularly, get a **Monthly Pass**, giving unlimited rides throughout one calendar month for $49, or the half-price, two-week version which goes on sale midway through each month.

Apart from being a cheap way to reach Mexico, the trolley is a link to the southern San Diego communities of National City, Chula Vista and Palm City, and from the "transfer station" at Imperial and 12th its Euclid Avenue line makes much of southeastern San Diego easily accessible. Additionally, a new section of the network runs to Old Town San Diego, where a transit center links the trolley to ten bus lines as well as with the North County Coaster. Trolleys leave every fifteen minutes during the day; the last service back from San Ysidro leaves at 1am (and there's one an hour through Saturday night), so an evening of south-of-the-border revelry and a return to San Diego the same night is quite possible.

The Coaster
North County San Diego has recently been linked to downtown via a light rail system called **The Coaster**, which starts out at Oceanside and stops at Carlsbad, Encintas, Solana Beach, Sorrento Valley, and Old Town along the way. Fares range from $2.75 to $5 one way, $5 to $7 for a round-trip.

Cycling
San Diego has many miles of **bike paths** as well as some fine park and coastal rides, and is a good city for cycling. **Rental** shops are easy to find, especially prevalent around bike-friendly areas; many such outlets also rent out rollerblades and surfboards. Three reliable outlets are: Bikes & Beyond, at the Ferry Landing, 1201 First St, Coronado (☎619/435-7180); Rent-a-Bike, First Avenue and Harbor Drive, Downtown (☎619/232-4700), offering free delivery and pickup; and Hamel's Action Sport Center, 704 Ventura Place, Mission Beach (☎619/488-5050). You can carry bikes on several city bus routes; board at any bus stop displaying a bike sign and tack your machine securely (they're known to fall off) to the back of the bus. The Transit Store has copies of an explanatory leaflet entitled *How To Take Your Bike For a Ride*, and hands out free passes that allow you to take your bike on the trolley.

OLD TOWN TROLLEY TOURS

Not to be confused with the San Diego Trolley, the **Old Town Trolley Tour** is a two-hour narrated trip around San Diego's most interesting areas, including downtown, Balboa Park, the Old Town and Coronado, aboard an open-sided motor-driven carriage. A single ticket ($20) lasts all day and you can board and reboard the trolley at any of its stops. If you're short of time in San Diego, the tour is a good way to cover a lot of ground quickly, and the driver's commentary is often corny but fairly informative. Leaflets detailing the route are found in hotel lobbies and at tourist information offices; alternatively call ☎619/298-8687.

Accommodation

Accommodation is plentiful throughout San Diego, at prices to suit all pockets. Hotels and motels are abundant, and there's also a decent selection of hostels and B&Bs – only travelers with tents are likely to feel restricted, with just a couple of inconveniently located and comparatively expensive campgrounds to choose from.

The restoration of downtown – the best base if you're without a car and want to do more than idle by the ocean – has given rise to two hostels and a batch of surprisingly inexpensive hotels in renovated buildings. Sleeping is marginally more expensive at the many beach motels, though both Ocean Beach and Pacific Beach have hostels. There's another group of motels in a freeway maze called Hotel Circle close to Old Town (useful if you're driving or just staying for a night while seeing the immediate area), and budget motels line the approach roads to the city.

Bed and breakfast accommodation is in ever increasing supply, especially in the Hillcrest district. Contact the downtown visitor center (see p.173), or send $3.95 for the *Bed & Breakfast Directory for San Diego*, PO Box 3292, San Diego, CA 92163 (☎1-800/619-7666).

Wherever you're staying, especially if you're arriving in summer, it's wise to **book in advance** – where this is essential, we've said as much below – though again, the downtown visitor center has a large stock of accommodation leaflets (many of which carry discount vouchers) and will phone around hotels, motels or hostels on your behalf for free. **Gay** travelers are unlikely to encounter hostility wherever they choose to stay in San Diego, and several hotels and bed and breakfast inns are particularly noted for their friendliness to gay guests (see "Gay and Lesbian San Diego", p.197).

Hostels

Banana Bungalow, 707 Reed Ave, Pacific Beach (☎1-800/5-HOSTEL or 619/273-3060). Who cares about poky, scruffy rooms when you can party all night and sleep all day on the beach immediately outside? A free buffet breakfast, keg nights, barbecues, a communal kitchen and a good rides board flesh out the package. Six-person dorms run to $18, and it's $7 for floor space, when there's nothing else. Turn off Mission Boulevard at no.4250, or take bus #34.

Grand Pacific Hostel, 726 Fifth Ave between F and G streets, Downtown (☎1-800/438-8622 or 619/232-3100). Well placed hostel on the edge of the Gaslamp District. Beds in six- to eight-bed rooms with sheets and continental breakfast for $15–18, depending on the season; doubles available for $40. Free bike use, organized tours to Tijuana, and a handy shuttle to LA make this the best of the city hostels.

HI-Elliott Hostel, 3790 Udall St, Ocean Beach (☎1-800/909-4776 or 619/223-4778). Well-run, friendly and minus the relentless party-time atmosphere that prevails at the other hostels. However, it's a couple of miles back from the beach and, at six miles from downtown (on bus #35), awkward for getting about the rest of San Diego. Eight-bed (or smaller) dorms ($12) and double rooms ($15); non-members $3 extra.

HI-Metropolitan Hostel, 521 Market St at Fifth, Downtown (☎1-800/909-4776 or 619/525-1530). Convenient for the Gaslamp District and Horton Plaza. $14–$16 for HI members, $19 for others, and more expensive private doubles. Free coffee and bagels. No curfew.

Ocean Beach International Backpackers Hostel, 4961 Newport Ave, Ocean Beach (☎1-800/339-7263 or 619/223-7873). New, predominantly fun-oriented place a block from the beach. Bikes and boards are available for rent, and videos are shown every night. Space in a four-bed dorm $14, double rooms $18, all with sheets, showers and continental breakfast.

Downtown

Golden West Hotel, 720 Fourth Ave (☎619/233-7596). A little seedy, but with a great historic lobby and hard-to-beat location in the Gaslamp District at rock-bottom rates. Ask to see your room first. ①.

Horton Grand, 311 Island Ave at Third (☎1-800/542-1886 or 619/544-1886). Classy, modernized amalgam of two century-old hotels, with fireplaces in most rooms, and staff dressed in Victorian-era costumes. ⑥.

J Street Inn, 222 J St between Third and Fourth (☎619/696-6922). A winner. Close to the Gaslamp District, Greyhound station and waterfront, this little-known bargain has units with microwaves and refrigerators (downtown's largest supermarket is nearby, too); weekly and monthly rates available. ②.

La Pensione, 1700 India St, Little Italy (☎619/236-8000). Great value small hotel in a quiet area within walking distance of the city center. The rooms, around a central court, are smallish but tastefully done out and equipped with microwave and fridge. ③.

The Maryland Hotel, 630 F St (☎619/239-9243). Amenable restored hotel, if somewhat lacking in frills, in a good downtown location. ①.

Pickwick Hotel, 132 W Broadway at First (☎1-800/675-7122 or 619/234-9200). Though large and characterless, this shares a building with the Greyhound station, making it a convenient, inexpensive place to flop down after a long bus journey. ②.

The US Grant, 326 Broadway between Third and Fourth (☎1-800/237-5029 or 619/232-3121). Directly across the street from Horton Plaza, this has been downtown's poshest address since 1910, and has hosted presidents and celebrities. ⑦.

Village Lodge, 600 G St at Seventh (☎619/238-4100). Pleasant, modern hotel, with cable TV, cooking facilities and fridges in each room. ②.

Hillcrest, Balboa Park, and Old Town

For Hillcrest, see also Gay and Lesbian San Diego, p.197.

Hotel del Coronado, 1500 Orange Ave (☎1-800/468-3533 or 619/522-8000). The place that put Coronado on the map and which is still the area's major tourist sight (see p.187) – it's been pampering wealthy guests for over a century. ⑦.

Embassy Hotel, 3645 Park Blvd, Balboa Park (☎619/296-3141). Nothing to write home about, but close to Balboa Park and with all the amenities (free in-room movies and local phone calls) for low rates. ②.

El Cordova, 1351 Orange Ave (☎1-800/229-2032 or 619/435-4131). The best deal in Coronado, but no secret so you'll need to reserve at least six months ahead. Lovely rooms in hacienda-style buildings ranged around lovely gardens. There's the obligatory pool, and some rooms have kitchenettes. ⑤.

El Rancho, 370 Orange Ave (☎619/435-2251). Tiny but attractive motel with relaxing decor, one of the cheapest on this side of the water. Rooms come equipped with microwave ovens and fridges, and there's a jacuzzi for guests' use. ④.

Old Town Inn, 4444 Pacific Hwy, Old Town (☎1-800/225-9610). Serviceable base within a few strides of the Old Town's liveliest areas. ③.

Ramada Hotel Old Town, 2435 Jefferson St, Old Town (☎1-800/260-8500). An attractive exterior conceals average rooms and facilities, though it does offer a great location, free evening cocktails and a complimentary, albeit skimpy, breakfast. ⑥.

Studio 819, 819 University Ave, Hillcrest (☎619/542-0819). Standard but safe budget accommodation in the heart of the Hillcrest action. ②.

Ocean Beach

Ebb Tide Motel, 5082 W Point Loma Blvd (☎619/224-9339). Modest-sized motel that's handy for the beach and has rooms with kitchenettes and cable. ②.

Loma Lodge, 3202 Rosecrans St (☎1-800/266-0511 or 619/222-0511). Among the best value in the district, with a beckoning pool and complimentary breakfast; good for exploring the peninsula though not close to the beach. ②.

Ocean Manor Apartment Motel, 1370 Sunset Cliffs Blvd (☎619/222-7901). A bit of a Fifties throwback, this place has a loyal clientele who book year after year. The kitchen suites are especially popular – reserve them far ahead. ③.

Ocean Villa Motel, 5142 W Point Loma Blvd (☎1-800/759-0012 or 619/224-3481). Usefully placed for the sands; the ocean-view rooms have kitchenettes and there's a pool. ③.

Mission Beach and Pacific Beach

Bahia Hotel, 998 W Mission Bay Drive, Mission Beach (☎1-800/288-0770 or 619/488-0551). Sprawling pleasure complex curling around the waters of Mission Bay – a watersport fan's delight. ⑥.

The Beach Cottages, 4255 Ocean Blvd, Mission Beach (☎619/483-7440). Beside the beach and *Banana Bungalow*, three blocks south of the pier, but away from the crush – a relaxing place for a few days of quiet tanning. ④.

Beach Haven Inn, 4740 Mission Blvd, Pacific Beach (☎1-800/831-6323 or 619/272-3812). Comfortable, tastefully decorated rooms around heated pool; continental breakfast included. One of the nicest places to unwind at the beach. ⑤.

Santa Clara Motel, 839 Santa Clara Place, Mission Beach (☎619/488-1193). No-frills rooms with kitchenettes an easy walk from the hectic Mission Beach sands, and a good half-mile north of Belmont Park. ④.

Surf & Sand Motel, 4666 Mission Blvd, Pacific Beach (☎619/483-7420). Cozy motel close to the beach. ③.

La Jolla

Colonial Inn, 910 Prospect St (☎1-800/832-5525 or 619/454-2181). A Twenties landmark sited in the heart of La Jolla and a short walk from the cove; various package deals, especially in winter, bring significant savings on the regular rate. ⑧.

La Jolla Cove Suites, 1155 Coast Blvd (☎1-800/248-2683 or 619/459-2621). Kitchen-equipped rooms and suites right by the sea – better value for three or four people sharing the $160 two-bedroom suites. ⑥.

La Valencia Hotel, 1132 Prospect St (☎1-800/451-0772 or 619/454-0771). Within these radiant pink walls Hollywood celebs enjoyed themselves in the 1920s; today the place is less glamorous but no less plush, with beautiful public areas and sea views. No reductions. ⑧.

Prospect Park Inn, 1110 Prospect St (☎1-800/433-1609 or 619/454-0133). Well priced for the area, with views over the ocean and complimentary breakfast and afternoon tea. Studios and a range of rooms. ⑦.

Campgrounds

Of the city's half-dozen **campgrounds**, only two accept tents. The best-placed of these is *Campland on the Bay*, 2211 Pacific Beach Drive (☎1-800/BAY FUN or 619/581-4200), linked to downtown by bus #30; the alternative, *San Diego Metro KOA*, 111 N Second Ave (☎1-800/762-CAMP), is fifteen miles south in Chula Vista – from downtown, take bus #29 or the trolley to 24th Street. Both charge over $20 for the most basic sites, making **Silver Strand State Park** (☎619/435-5184; $14), a couple of miles south of Coronado on bus #901(see p.188), a reasonable option, if inconvenient for the city.

The City

You never feel under pressure in San Diego to do anything other than enjoy yourself. Though the work-hard-play-hard ethic is as prevalent here as anywhere else in Southern California, the accent is very strongly on the second part of the equation. Indeed, the city, with its easily managed central area, scenic bays, lively beaches, plentiful parks and commendable museums, is hard not to like from the moment you arrive – even New York homeless people are known to migrate to San Diego for the winter.

The city divides into several fairly easily defined sections. You'll probably spend at least some of your time **downtown**, where anonymous high-rise bank buildings stand shoulder-to-shoulder with more personable structures from San Diego's earlier boom days, in what's now the café- and bar-choked **Gaslamp District**, bestowing a mood more welcoming than is usual in American city centers. Besides being the nucleus of the public transportation network, downtown contains a fair chunk of the city's nightlife, and has much inexpensive accommodation. A few miles northeast, the well-maintained parkland of massive **Balboa Park** not only has San Diego's major museums and the highly rated San Diego Zoo, but is perfectly suited for strolls and picnics beside the walkways that cut around the many acres of carefully nurtured plant life. A similar distance northwest of downtown is where the city really got started, the first white settlement growing up beneath the hill that was site of the original San Diego mission, an area now fastidiously sanitized as **Old Town San Diego**. The sense of history here is often powerfully evoked and quite believable, despite the inevitable Mexican-themed shops and restaurants which strain credibility – though not to the extent that you should be put off visiting, especially since the trolley now stops here. A couple of other districts close to downtown don't have any points of interest as such, but can be worth a call for different reasons. You might find yourself in **East San Diego**, whose large college campus livens up what is an otherwise featureless sprawl, while **Hillcrest**'s eclectic mix of trendy young professionals, gays, bohemians and would-be artists make it one of the city's best areas for ethnic eating and intellectually slanted nightlife.

More appealing for pure relaxation are the **beach** communities, all within easy reach of downtown and good for a half-day trip – or longer, if bronzing beside the ocean is your main reason for being in San Diego (see p.187 for details).

Downtown San Diego

Always vibrant and active, **DOWNTOWN** is the urban heart of San Diego, and is much the best place to start a tour of the city. Improvement initiatives begun in the late 1970s have restored many of the city's older buildings, resulting in several blocks of stylishly renovated turn-of-the-century architecture, while the more recent, sleek bank buildings symbolize the city's growing economic importance on the Pacific Rim. Though downtown is largely safe by day, at night it can be an unwelcoming place, and you should confine your after-dark visits to the restaurants and clubs of the comparatively well-lit and well-policed Gaslamp District.

Along Broadway

One of the most memorable first impressions of San Diego is that received by travelers arriving by train at the **Santa Fe Railroad Depot**, whose tall Moorish archways were built to welcome visitors to the 1915 Panama-California Exposition in Balboa Park. The architecture of the depot provides a dramatic contrast to the postmodern contours of the neighboring **American Plaza**, a combination of high-rise offices and glass-roofed public areas, which began as a symbol of San Diego's pre-eminence in international finance in the mid-1980s but found its development stunted by the economic slump of the early 1990s. Nonetheless, the plaza succeeds in throwing a sheltering canopy over the main terminal of the San Diego Trolley, and over the entrance to the downtown branch of the **Museum of Contemporary Art** (Tues–Sat 10am–5pm, Sun noon–5pm; $4, free first Tues & Sun of month), which frequently stages compelling temporary shows.

American Plaza marks the western end of **Broadway**, a busy main drag which slices through the center of downtown. The most hectic portion of Broadway is the block between Fourth and Fifth Avenues, where the pedestrian traffic is a broad mix: shoppers, sailors, yuppies, homeless people and others, some lingering around the fountains on the square outside **Horton Plaza** (summer & holidays Mon–Sat 10am–9pm, Sun 11am–6pm; rest of year Mon–Fri 10am–9pm, Sat 10am–6pm, Sun 11am–6pm), completed in 1985 for a cool $140 million and a great contributor to the resurgence of San Diego's downtown; its almost instant success caused real estate prices to soar and condo development to surge. Additionally, the complex's whimsical, colorful style, with lots of updated Art Deco features, influenced the architecture of the surrounding area. A major tourist draw and a posing platform for the city's spoilt young things, Horton

**DOWNTOWN
SAN DIEGO**

ACCOMMODATION
1 Golden West Hotel
2 Grand Pacific Hostel
3 The Metropolitan Hostel
4 Horton Grand
5 J Street Inn
6 Maryland Hotel
7 La Pensione
8 Pickwick Hotel
9 U.S. Grant
10 Village Lodge

CEDAR STREET

Firehouse
Museum

BEECH STREET

San Diego County
Administration Center

ASH STREET

A STREET

Maritime
Museum

San Diego Bay
Ferry Docking
Stage

Museum of
Contemporary
Art

Santa Fe
Railroad Depot
& American Plaza

B STREET

Tramline

C STREET

Greyhound Station

BROADWAY

Transit
Store

Library

Horton
Plaza

E STREET

F STREET

i

Newtown
Park

G STREET

GAS LAMP
DISTRICT

MARKET STREET

Tramline

EMBARCADERO

William Heath
Davis House

ISLAND AVENUE

J STREET

Seaport
Village

HARBOR DRIVE

San Diego
Convention
Center

K STREET

0   200 yds

Embarcadero
Marina Park

▽ East San Diego & Coronado

Balboa Park

Coronado

NORTH HARBOR DRIVE

PACIFIC HIGHWAY

KETTNER BOULEVARD

INDIA STREET

COLUMBIA STREET

STATE STREET

UNION STREET

FRONT STREET

FIRST AVENUE

THIRD AVENUE

FOURTH AVENUE

FIFTH AVENUE

SEVENTH AVE

EIGHTH AVENUE

N

Plaza has no roof, making the most of the region's sunny climate. If you don't want to join the conspicuous consumers, the top level, with its open-air eating places, is the one to make for. You'll find an array of ethnic fast food – not especially sophisticated, but not overly expensive, either – and it's fun to sit over a coffee or snack and watch the parade go by, especially on Saturday when the suburban mall rats are out in force. All the typical American department stores and specialty shops (including the world's largest Sam Goody's record store) are represented, and don't miss the 21-foot-tall **Jessop Clock**, on level one, made for the California State Fair of 1907.

Further along Broadway things begin to get tatty and dull, but walk a couple of blocks or so for the secondhand bookstores (such as Wahrenbrock's Book House, 726 Broadway) and the **library**, 820 E St (Mon–Thurs 10am–9pm, Fri & Sat 9.30am–5.30pm), which has book sales on Friday and Saturday and an extensive reference section where you can pore over Californian magazines and newspapers. Tucked away on an upper floor of the library, the **Wangenheim Room** (Mon–Sat 1.30–4.30pm) holds the obsessive collection of local turn-of-the-century bigwig Julius Wangenheim, including Babylonian clay tablets, palm-leaf books from India, silk scrolls from China and many more transglobal curios documenting the history of the printed word – worth a stop for its oddity value.

Less quirky, but a useful time-passer, the **Firehouse Museum**, six blocks north of Broadway at 1572 Columbia St (Thurs–Fri 10am–2pm, Sat & Sun 10am–4pm; $1), maintains firefighting appliances and outfits and has photographs vividly recalling some of San Diego's most horrific fires – and the men, horses and equipment who tackled them.

The Gaslamp District

South of Broadway, the **Gaslamp District** occupies a sixteen-block area running south to K Street, bordered by Fourth and Seventh avenues. This was the heart of San Diego when it was still a frontier town, and was, according to local opinion, full of "whore-houses, opium dens and guys getting rolled". The area remained at the core of local carnality for years: street prostitution, though illegal from 1916, flourished here until the late 1970s, when a revitalization operation cleaned things up – and the city's flesh-for-sale moved to the erotic-dance bars near the Sports Arena, a couple of miles northwest.

The few remaining adult emporia are incongruities on the smart streets lined with cafés, antique stores, art galleries – and ersatz "gaslamps", powered by electricity. This is now the heart of the city's nightlife, though its Friday and Saturday night bustle was unimaginable just a decade ago. There's also a relatively high police profile designed to keep the area clean and safe. A tad artificial it may be, but the Gaslamp District is intriguing to explore, not least for the scores of late nineteenth-century buildings in various stages of renovation. They're best discovered – and the area's general history gleaned – during the two-hour **walking tour** (Sat 11am; $5, includes admission to the William Heath Davis House) which begins from the small cobbled square at the corner of Fourth and Island avenues.

The square is within the grounds of the **William Heath Davis House** (variable hours, call ☎619/233-4691; $2) included in the walking tour, though also visitable on your own. It was William Davis who founded "New Town" San Diego in 1850, believing that a waterfront location (the fledgling city had previously been located a few miles inland and to the north – the site of Old Town San Diego; see p.184) would stimulate growth. It didn't, at least not for some time, and Davis left the city before long, eventually dying penniless. He, and the more influential Alonzo Horton, whose later efforts to stimulate waterfront growth were ultimately successful, are remembered in the house through photographs, while the fittings and furnishings recreate something of the mood of their times.

Even without the walking tour, there's a lot to be enjoyed around this area simply by keeping your eyes open. One of the finest interiors in the whole city is in *Johnny M's 801* (see also p.193), a seafood restaurant at 801 Fourth Ave, restored in the style of the tavern which opened here in 1907. Diners stuff themselves with crabs' legs beneath an epic stained-glass dome and on a tiled floor once described as "the handsomest floor in the state" – even if you're not hungry, drop in for a look. Also worth a peek is the **Horton Grand Hotel** opposite the William Davis House, created in the mid-1980s by cobbling together two historic hotels, the *Grand Hotel* and the *Kahle Saddlery*, both dating back to the 1880s; they were painstakingly dismantled and moved about four blocks from their original sites. A small museum with Chinese artifacts is a reminder of the once-thriving Chinatown area, where railroad laborers and their families crowded together. If you fancy staying here, see "Accommodation" on p.176.

The Embarcadero, Seaport Village and around

Over the last few years, the once-shabby streets south of the Gaslamp District have been transformed by the arrival of elegant, expensive condos – providing a fitting setting for the San Diego Convention Center, a $165-million boost to civic pride that opened in 1989 and is booked solidly into the twenty-first century. For non-convention-going visitors, the most interesting facet of the building is the sail-like roof imitating the yachts tethered in the marina just beyond, which also indicates the beginning of the **Embarcadero**, a pathway that continues for a mile or so along the bayside, curling around to the western end of downtown.

The path is favored by San Diegan strollers, joggers and kite-flyers, and most out-of-towners get no further along than **Seaport Village**, a twee but mildly enjoyable collection of souvenir shops and restaurants, often with free clown and puppet shows laid on for kids. You should, however, make a point of strolling the full length of the Embarcadero, as it makes an enjoyable route to the trio of historic ships moored beside Harbor Drive, which is also the departure point for the ferry to Coronado (see p.187).

The three vintage sailing craft, just north of the B Street Pier, make up the **Maritime Museum** (daily 9am–8pm; $5). The most interesting of them is the *Star of India*, built in 1863 and now the world's oldest iron sailing ship still afloat. The *Berkeley*, alongside, which served for sixty years as a ferry on San Francisco Bay, is of lesser appeal, and the *Medea*, a small steam-powered yacht, has no special displays.

Landlubbers nonplussed by the Maritime Museum should explore the **San Diego County Administration Center** (Mon–Fri 8.30am–5pm; free), one of the most distinctive public buildings in California: a rich burst of Spanish colonial with a beaux-arts arrangement of gold and azure tiles. It's one of the unsung beauties of San Diego, and from Harbor Drive you can walk right through the foyer to the main entrance, on the way viewing the *Guardian of Water* statue (on the Harbor Drive side) and the three interior murals.

Balboa Park and San Diego Zoo

The fourteen hundred sumptuous acres of **BALBOA PARK** contain one of the largest groupings of museums in the US. Yet its real charm is simply itself: its trees, gardens, traffic-free promenades – and a great concentration of Spanish colonial-style buildings.

Balboa Park was a wasteland inhabited by cactuses, rattlesnakes and lizards until 1898, when a local woman, Kate Sessions, began cultivating nurseries and planting trees there in lieu of rent. The first buildings were erected for the 1915 Panama-California International Exposition, held to celebrate the opening of the canal. The memories of its success lingered well into the Depression, and in 1935 another building program was undertaken for the California-Pacific International Exposition.

Along El Prado

Most of the major museums flank **El Prado**, the park's pedestrianized east–west axis which bulges out to form a plaza at the heart of the park. Here you'll find the **Timkin Museum of Art** (Tues–Sat 10am–4.30pm, Sun 1.30–4.30pm; Sept closed; free), representing a sufficient number of European masters to make the stiflingly formal atmosphere and the evangelical zeal of the attendants worth enduring. Works from the early Renaissance to the nineteenth century include minor pieces by Rembrandt and El Greco, as well as a stirring collection of Russian icons.

THE BALBOA PARK MUSEUMS: PRACTICALITIES

Ideally, you should come to Balboa Park on the first Tuesday of the month when admission to almost all the museums is free; don't come on a Monday, when the bigger collections are closed. None of the museums is essential viewing but at least three – the Museum of Man, the Museum of Photographic Arts and the Museum of Art – could collectively keep you engrossed for a few hours. The cheapest way to see them is to buy the $21 **Balboa Park Passport**, which allows admission to the park's twelve museums and is valid for a week, although you can visit each museum once only. The passport is available at all the museums and at the **visitor center** (daily 9am–4pm; ☎619/239-0512), located in the newly – and gorgeously – refurbished **House of Hospitality** on the Prado.

The park, within easy reach of downtown on **buses** #7, #16 or #25, is large but fairly easy to get around on foot – if you tire, the free **Balboa Park tram** runs frequently between the main museum groupings and the parking lots.

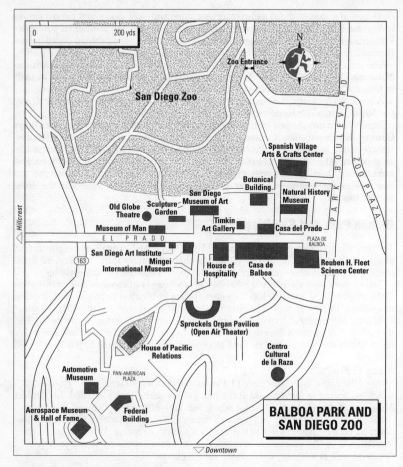

The following labels appear on the map:

0   200 yds

N

Zoo Entrance

San Diego Zoo

Spanish Village
Arts & Crafts Center

PARK BOULEVARD

ZOO PLAZA

Botanical
Building

Natural History
Museum

San Diego
Museum of Art

Old Globe   Sculpture
Theatre   Garden

Timkin
Art Gallery

Casa del Prado

Museum of Man

EL PRADO

PLAZA DE
BALBOA

Hillcrest

163

San Diego Art Institute

Mingei
International Museum

House of
Hospitality

Casa de
Balboa

Reuben H. Fleet
Science Center

Spreckels Organ Pavilion
(Open Air Theater)

House of Pacific
Relations

Centro
Cultural
de la Raza

Automotive
Museum

PAN-AMERICAN
PLAZA

Aerospace Museum
& Hall of Fame

Federal
Building

BALBOA PARK AND
SAN DIEGO ZOO

Downtown

The nearby **San Diego Museum of Art** (Tues–Sun 10am–4.30pm; $7.50) has few individually striking items in its permanent collection, but is the main venue for any shows that come through town. There's a solid stock of European paintings from the Renaissance through to the nineteenth-century "Europe in Transition" canvases, matched by a fairly uninspiring US selection from the same century, and finally some welcome bright rooms of moderns, especially strong on California artists. The biggest surprises, perhaps, are amid the exquisitely crafted pieces within the Asian section, mainly from China and Japan but with smaller representations from India and Korea. The Interactive Multimedia Art Gallery Explorer (IMAGE) lets you browse the collection without wearing out any shoe leather – and take home copies of your favorite pieces. It's one of the first – and finest – such interactive museum computer systems in the US. Outside, don't miss the **Sculpture Court and Garden**, which you can walk into free at any time, with a number of important works, most notably those by Henry Moore and Alexander Calder. There's a pleasant, if somewhat pricey, restaurant here.

Just across El Prado, the **Mingei International Museum** (Tues–Sun 10am–4pm; $5) has settled into its new home; it used to be in La Jolla. Its appealing collection of folk art is one of the most important in the country, featuring everything from weather vanes and carousels to furniture made from bottle caps. None of the exhibits are permanent, so you'll never know what you'll encounter. Next door, the **San Diego Art Institute** (Tues–Sat 10am–4pm, Sun noon–4pm; $3) is a venue for the works of its artist members, some more talented than others.

The contents of the **Museum of Man** (daily 10am–4.30pm; $4), which straddles El Prado, veer from the banal to the excellent – and into the truly bizarre. The demonstrations of tortilla-making and Mexican loom-weaving are labored, while the large number of replicas – particularly the huge "Mayan" stones that dominate the ground level – would better be replaced by photographs of the real thing. But there's much to see and be fascinated by, not least the Native American displays. The temporary shows, too, can be absorbing.

The Casa de Balboa between the House of Hospitality and the Space Theater (see below) was built for the 1915 Expo to display the latest gadgetry and now houses three museums. Only two of them are likely to occupy you for more than a few minutes: the recently expanded **Museum of Photographic Arts** (daily 10am–5pm; $4), with a fine permanent collection dating back to the daguerreotype and including all the modern masters, as well as challenging temporary shows; and the **Museum of San Diego History** (Wed–Sun 10am–4.30pm; $4) virtually next door, which cleverly charts the booms and busts that have turned San Diego from uninviting scrubland into the sixth biggest city in the US within 150 years. Only the craftsmanship put into creating scaled-down versions of large chunks of the US, and the tracks crossing them, make the third occupant of the building, the **Model Railroad Museum** (Tues–Fri 11am–4pm, Sat & Sun 11am–5pm; $3), viewable.

The **Reuben H. Fleet Science Center** (Mon–Tues 9.30am–6pm, Wed–Sun 9.30am–9pm; Science Center $4, Science Center and theater or simulator $8, all three $11), close to the Park Boulevard end of El Prado, is one of the more recent and most hyped features of Balboa Park. The Science Center has a batch of child-oriented exhibits, but more impressive sensations are induced by the **Space Theater**'s dome-shaped tilting screen and 152 loudspeakers, which take you on stomach-churning trips into volcanoes, over waterfalls and through outer space. The complex is undergoing a multi-million dollar expansion and the newest addition, a high-tech motion simulator, should be even more nausea-inducing.

Across the plaza, the worthy **Natural History Museum** (daily 9.30am–4.30pm; $6) has a great collection of fossils, a comprehensive if somewhat unappetizing array of stuffed creatures, an entertaining hands-on mineral section, and an affecting section called "On The Edge", dealing with endangered wildlife. A short walk behind the Natural History building, the **Spanish Village Arts and Crafts Center** (daily 11am–4pm; free) dates from the 1935 Expo and, as its name suggests, was designed in the style of a Spanish village. Some 42 craftspeople now have their workshops here and you can watch them practice their skills, including painting, sculpture, photography, pottery and glass-working. It's fun to walk through, though you'd have to be pretty loaded to buy any of the original works.

The rest of the park

The fifteen-minute walk to the Aerospace Museum, the major collection away from El Prado, takes you past several spots of varying interest. There's a **puppet theater** (shows at 11am, 1pm & also 3.30pm at weekends; $1.50, children $1), in the Pacific Palisades building; the **Spreckels Organ Pavilion** (free Sunday concerts) is home to the world's largest pipe organ; and the series of cottages comprising the **House of**

Pacific Relations (Sun 12.30–4pm; free) contains extremely kitsch collections from countries all over the world – enjoy the proffered tea, coffee and cakes but don't expect any multicultural education.

All but the most technically minded could find a better place to pass an hour than in the **Aerospace Museum and International Aerospace Hall of Fame** (daily 10am–4.30pm; $6). If you're really keen to see a replica of *The Spirit of St Louis* (Charles Lindbergh began the journey that was to make him the first solo pilot to cross the Atlantic in San Diego), you can do so quickly and for nothing because it's in the entrance hall. Otherwise, on the paying side of the turnstiles, there's a numbing mass of portraits of everyone who was ever anyone in aviation, and a fairly tedious collection of model planes, real planes and plane-related artifacts from the Wright brothers to the Space Shuttle.

Next to the Aerospace building, the **Automotive Museum** (daily 10am–4.30pm; $6) continues the technological theme, with a host of cars, bikes and other internal-combustion contraptions. The most curious item, however, is the *Lincoln Continental* which carried President Reagan to a would-be assassin's bullet in 1981.

About to be installed nearby in the interesting Federal Building, with its pseudo-Mayan bas reliefs on the front, is the **Hall of Champions**. Devoted to American sports in general and San Diegan athletic achievers in particular, the building will open in the summer of 1999.

San Diego Zoo

The **San Diego Zoo** (daily mid-June to early Sept 9am–10pm; early Sept to mid-June 9am–5pm; $15), immediately north of the main museums, is one of the city's biggest and best-known attractions. As zoos go, it's undoubtedly one of the world's finest, with a wide selection of animals, among them very rare Chinese pheasants, Mhorr gazelles and a freak-of-nature two-headed corn snake – as well as some pioneering techniques for keeping them in captivity: animals are restrained in "psychological cages", with moats or ridges rather than bars. It's an enormous place, and you can easily spend a full day here; take a bus tour early on to get a general idea of the layout, or survey the scene on the vertiginous Skyfari overhead tramway. Bear in mind, though, that many of the creatures get sleepy in the midday heat and retire behind bushes to take a nap; the much-hyped pair of visiting Chinese **pandas** spend a lot of time sleeping or off being prodded by biologists who are trying to get them to breed. There's a children's zoo as well, with walk-through bird cages and an animal nursery.

The $15 **admission** only covers entry to the main zoo and the children's zoo; to add a 35-minute bus tour and a round-trip ticket on Skyfari, you'll need the $21 Deluxe Ticket Package. A $32 ticket also admits you to the San Diego Wild Animal Park (near Escondido; see p.203) within a five-day period.

Centro Cultural de la Raza

Visiting all the museums in Balboa Park, or spending hours threading through the crowds at the zoo, could well leave you too jaded even to notice the unassuming round building on the edge of the park beside Park Boulevard. This, the **Centro Cultural de la Raza** (Thurs–Sun noon–5pm; free), mounts strong temporary exhibits on Native American and Hispanic life in an atmosphere altogether less stuffy than the showpiece museums of the park – make time for it.

Old Town

In 1769, Spanish settlers chose what's now Presidio Hill as the site of the first of California's missions. As the soldiers began to leave the mission and the *presidio* (fortress), they settled at the foot of the hill. This was the birthplace of San Diego, later to be dominated by Mexican officials and afterwards the early arrivals from the eastern US, and the area is now preserved as **Old Town State Historic Park** (locally referred to as "Old Town"), a state historical park that holds a number of original **adobe dwellings**, together with the inevitable souvenir shops. Although undoubtedly touristy, it's a good place to get a sense of the city's Hispanic roots, dolled up though they may be; it's still frequented by many of the city's Mexican-Americans.

To get to Old Town, take bus #5 or the trolley from downtown; by car, take I-5 and exit on Old Town Avenue, following the signs. Alternatively, from I-8 turn off onto Taylor Street and head left on Juan Street; new signs should prevent any confusion. Most things in the park which aren't historical – the shops and restaurants – open around 10am and close at 10pm (though a number of the restaurants do business until midnight or later), but the best time to be around is during the afternoon, when you can learn something of the general history of the area and enter the more interesting of the adobes (including several which are otherwise kept locked) with the excellent **free walking tour**, which leaves at 2pm from outside the Seeley Stable, just off the central plaza. You can get details on this, and other aspects of the park, inside the stable, which serves, for the time being, as the **visitor center** (daily 10am–5pm; ☎619/220-5422).

Exploring Old Town

Many of the old structures in the state park are thoughtfully preserved and contain a lot of their original furnishings, giving a good indication of early San Diegan life. A good walking-tour book is available at the visitor center. Most of the houses are open daily from 10am–4pm; admission is free. Of the historic buildings, one of the more significant is the **Casa de Estudillo** on Mason Street, built by the commander of the *presidio*, José Mariá de Estudillo, in 1827. The chapel in this poshest of the original adobes was claimed to be the setting for the wedding in Helen Hunt Jackson's overblown romance about early California, *Ramona*. When the house was bought in 1910 by sugar baron J.D. Spreckels, he advertised it as "Ramona's Marriage Place." Next door, the **Casa de Bandini** was the home of the politician and writer Juan Bandini and was the social center of San Diego during the mid-nineteenth century. Following the switch of ownership of California, the house became the *Cosmopolitan Hotel*, considered among the finest in the state; some of the elegant features of that period can still be seen in the dining room. You can wander through the rest of the building freely, and reward yourself with a lavish Mexican lunch in the courtyard restaurant. Of moderate interest are the **San Diego Union Building**, where the city's newspaper began in 1868, and **Seeley Stable**, filled with Old West memorabilia.

An idealized recreation of an eighteenth-century Mexican street market, **Bazaar del Mundo** abuts the state park. Though rife with gift shops, it's enjoyable enough on a Sunday afternoon, when there's free music and folk dancing in its tree-shaded courtyard. It's also a fair place to **eat**: stands serve fresh tortillas, *La Panaderia* sells Mexican pastries for a dollar, and the two sit-down Mexican restaurants are decent enough if you can grab an outside seat.

Just beyond the park gates on San Diego Avenue, the **Thomas Whaley Museum** (daily 10am–5pm; closed Tues in winter; $4) was the first brick house in California. Once the home of Thomas Whaley, an early San Diego luminary, it displays furniture and photos from his time, and a reconstruction of the courtroom held here from 1869. Many people come, however, because of the house's supposed current occupants – the place has been officially stamped by the US Department of Commerce as haunted, possibly by one of the occupants of the neighboring **El Campo Santo Cemetery**. Once the site of public executions (Antonio Garra, leader of an uprising by the San Luis Rey Indians, was forced to dig his own grave here before he was killed), the inscriptions on its tombs read like a *Who's Who* of late nineteenth-century San Diego.

Modest though it is, the cemetery makes a better stop than **Heritage Park**, just north on Juan Street, where several Victorian buildings have been gathered from around the city – to be inhabited at weekends by period-attired history fanatics. They're now shops and offices and, in one case, a B&B. It's more productive to walk along Conde Street and peer into the atmospheric, sculpture-filled interior of the **Old Adobe Chapel**, dating from the 1850s and used as a place of worship until 1917.

Presidio Hill: the Serra Museum – and the San Diego Mission

The Spanish-style building that now sits atop Presidio Hill is only a rough approximation of the original mission – moved in 1774 – but contains the intriguing **Junípero Serra Museum** (Tues–Sat 10am–4.30pm, Sun noon–4.30pm; $3), a collection of Spanish furniture, weapons, diaries and historical documents pertaining to the man who led the Spanish colonization of California, and an acerbic commentary on the struggles of a few devoted historians to preserve anything of San Diego's Spanish past against the wishes of dollar-crazed developers.

Outside the museum, pause by the **Serra Cross**, a modern marker on the site of the original mission. To find the actual mission, you'll need to travel six miles north to 10818 San Diego Mission Rd, where the **Mission Basilica San Diego de Alcalá** (daily 9am–5pm; $2), was relocated to be near a water source and fertile soils – and to be further from the likelihood of attack by rebellious Indians. This was wishful thinking: Padre Luis Jayme, California's first Christian martyr, was clubbed to death here by Native Americans in 1775. The present building (take bus #43 from downtown), the fifth to be constructed on this site, is still a working parish church (mass daily 7am & 5pm). Walk through the dark and echoey church – the fourteenth-century stalls and altar were imported from Spain – to the garden, where two small crosses mark the graves of Native American neophytes, making this California's oldest cemetery. A small **museum** holds a collection of Native American craft objects and historical articles from the mission, including the crucifix held by Junípero Serra at his death in 1834. Despite accusations that the missionary campaign was one of kidnapping, forced baptisms, and treatment of natives as virtual slaves, Serra was beatified during 1988 in a ceremony at the Vatican, the Pope declaring him a "shining example of Christian virtue and the missionary spirit".

East San Diego and Hillcrest

Scruffy **EAST SAN DIEGO** is largely suburban sprawl, only really of interest if you want to venture into its western fringes as far as 1925 K St, the site of **Villa Montezuma** (Fri–Sun noon–4.30pm; also open Thurs in Dec; $3). Ignored by the majority of visitors to San Diego, possibly due to its location, the villa is a florid show of Victoriana, with a rich variety of domes and all manner of loopy eccentricities. Local kids know the villa simply as the "haunted house", a nickname that doesn't seem unreasonable when you see the place. It was built for Jesse Shepard – English-born but noted in the US as a composer, pianist, author and all-round aesthete – and paid for by a group of culturally aspirant San Diegans in the 1880s. The glorious stock of furniture remains, as do many ornaments and oddments and the dramatic stained-glass windows. It's a house which well reflects Shepard's introspective nature and interest in spiritualism, both of which must have been entirely out of step with brash San Diego through the boom years. To get to the villa without a car, you can either make the long walk (about 45min) from downtown, take bus #3, #5 or #16, each stopping within about five blocks, or use the trolley, transferring to the Euclid Avenue line and getting off near 20th Street.

North of downtown and on the northwest edge of Balboa Park, **Hillcrest** is an increasingly lively and artsy area, thanks to the wealthy liberals who've moved into the district in recent years. It's also the center of the city's **gay community** and home to a couple of gay hotels (see "Gay and Lesbian San Diego", p.197). The streets around

University and Fifth, easily reached from downtown on bus #3 or #11, hold a selection of interesting cafés and restaurants (see "Eating", p.193) and a fine gathering of Victorian homes.

The beaches

San Diego undeniably excels with its fine array of museums and historic sites, but thousands are happy to trade time spent in Balboa Park for a few days on the city's **beaches**. In most cases, they're not strong on seclusion, but they're fine for sunbathing and swimming, and opportunities abound to rent rollerblades or a boogieboard and enter into the spirit of Southern California.

Directly south of downtown across the bay, **Coronado** is a plush and well-manicured settlement, reflecting the wholesome nature of the large naval base to which it's home. Traditionally, Coronado's visitors have been wealthy health-seekers, here for its sea breezes, palm trees and famous (and expensive) hotel. Just beyond, and much less upscale, **Imperial Beach**'s chief draw is simply the quiet of a seldom crowded stretch of sand, and, if you're into such things, the horse-riding trails nearby.

Across the bay to the north, the rugged **Point Loma** peninsula forms the western wall of San Diego Bay, with trees along its spine and a craggy shoreline often marked by explorable tidepools – though offering little opportunity for sunbathing. **Ocean Beach**, at the western edge of the peninsula, is extremely lively, but the exclusive and wealthy community that's developed a little way inland is tempering its reputation for all-out partying. These days much of Ocean Beach's former youthful vitality has moved to **Mission Beach**, eight miles northwest of downtown, and the adjoining, and slightly more salubrious, **Pacific Beach** – "PB" – linked by a beachside walkway which, on any weekend, is where you'll find San Diego at its most exuberant. The city is at its most chic, however, a few miles further north up the coast in stunning **La Jolla**, whose coastline of perfect caves and coves is matched on land by short, litter-free streets lined by small coffee bars and art galleries, and a stylishly designed modern art museum.

Coronado and Imperial Beach

Across San Diego Bay from downtown, the bulbous isthmus of **CORONADO** is a well-scrubbed resort community with a major naval station at its western end. The many saltbox-style houses give the town an incongruous New England air, and make it pleasant to stroll around. Otherwise, Coronado is of limited interest, save for a historic hotel and the long and thin streak of sands – a natural breakwater for the bay – that runs south. The simplest way to get here is on the **San Diego Bay ferry** ($2 each way) which leaves Broadway Pier daily on the hour between 9am and 9pm (10pm Fri & Sat), returning on the half hour. From the ferry landing on First Street, shuttle bus #904 (Mon & Tues hourly, Wed–Sun half-hourly; 50c) runs the mile up Coronado's main street, Orange Avenue, to the *Hotel del Coronado*. Alternatively use bus #901 (or #19, though this only goes as far as the naval station) from downtown. By road, you cross the **Coronado Bridge** (southbound drivers without passengers have to pay a $1 toll), its struts decorated with enormous murals depicting daily Hispanic life, best seen from the community park beneath the bridge in the district of Barrio Logan.

The town of Coronado grew up around the **Hotel del Coronado**, a whirl of turrets and towers erected as a health resort in 1888. Using Chinese laborers who worked in round-the-clock shifts, the aim was to lure the ailing rich from all parts of the US – a plan in which it succeeds to this day, although the hotel and its elaborate architecture have lost much of their charm, dwarfed by newer high-rises, including the hotel's new tower. Nevertheless, if you're passing, the place is certainly worth dropping into, if only for its glamorous history. Through the lobby and courtyard a small basement **museum** (free) records the hotel's past. It was at the "del", as it's locally known, that Edward VIII (then Prince of Wales) met Mrs Simpson (then a Coronado housewife) in 1920 – a contact which eventually led to their marriage and his abdication from the British throne, and which is remembered here by an unintentionally hilarious cardboard head stuck on top of a dinner suit. More thrilling is the tablecloth signed by Marilyn Monroe and the rest of the cast who filmed *Some Like It Hot* at the hotel in 1958. Outside, past the tennis courts occasionally graced by world champions but more commonly by moneyed guests, are the sands and palms on and around which much of the movie's action took place. A guided, hour-long **historical tour** (Thurs–Sat 10am & 11am; $10) wends its way around the hotel, beginning in the lobby.

A less grandiose place to explore Coronado's past is at the **Coronado Beach Historical Museum**, 1126 Loma Ave (Wed–Sun 10am–4pm; free), where photos and knick-knacks recall the community's early pioneers and some of its first naval aviators. Nearby, the **Coronado Visitor Information Center**, 1047 B Ave, just off Orange Ave (Mon–Fri 9am–5pm, Sat 10am–5pm, Sun 11am–4pm; ☎1-800/622-8300 or 619/437-8788) carries reams of practical information on the area.

Silver Strand and Imperial Beach

For a little isolation, follow Silver Strand Boulevard along the glistening sands south of the *Hotel del Coronado* (bus #901). Here you'll find plenty of good spots to stretch out and relax – though no food and drink facilities at all – foremost among them **Silver Strand State Beach** (daily 8am–dusk; $4 per vehicle) where you can camp (see p.177). At the end of Silver Strand Boulevard, down-at-heel **IMPERIAL BEACH** is a contrast to smart Coronado, but does have a pleasant and fairly quiet beach, disturbed only by the helicopters periodically buzzing in and out of the naval air station. Also peaceful is nearby **Border Field State Park**, a flat area noted for its horse trails, right by the Mexican border and reached by car along Tia Juana Street from San Ysidro.

To return directly to San Diego from Imperial Beach, take bus #934 to the trolley and head north through dreary Chula Vista and National City.

Ocean Beach and Point Loma

Once ruled by a drug-running chapter of Hell's Angels, **OCEAN BEACH**, six miles northwest of downtown and accessible from there on bus #35, is now one of the more sought-after addresses in San Diego. Vacant plots with a sea view regularly change hands for half a million dollars, and the single-story adobe dwellings that have been home to several generations of Portuguese fishing families and characterized the area as recently as a decade ago, have virtually disappeared – the few that remain look like dinky-sized outhouses beside the opulent newer structures. The new money is less in evidence at the main beach, half a mile south by the pier; **Newport Street** here, rife with the trappings of beach culture, is where most young backpackers spend their time, amid rows of cheap snack bars, T-shirt stalls and surf and skate rental shops. The beach itself can be good fun – especially at weekends, when you really shouldn't bother coming unless you're in the mood to party.

Further south from the pier – and the best of the beaches – rise the dramatic **Sunset Cliffs**, a great vantage point for watching the sun go down, and the grandstand of choice during the San Diego Yacht Club's defence of the America's Cup title in 1995. Be warned, though, that the cliffs are notoriously unstable and more than a few people have tumbled over the edge following an afternoon of excess on the beach.

Beyond here, you're into the hilly and very green peninsula of **POINT LOMA** – most of it owned by the navy, which has been beneficial in keeping some of the more attractive parts of the coastline unspoilt and accessible to the public. You can get here direct from downtown by taking the trolley to Old Town, where you can pick up bus #26, but there's little to see until you get past the naval base to the southern extremity, and the **Cabrillo National Monument** (daily 9am–5.15pm; seven-day pass $5 per vehicle, $2 per pedestrian or cyclist). It was here that Cabrillo and crew became the first Europeans to land in California in the sixteenth century, though that's as far as the historical interest goes, for they quickly reboarded their vessel and sailed away. The startling views from this high spot, however, across San Diego Bay to the downtown skyline and right along the coast to Mexico, easily repay the journey here, and there's ample opportunity for discovering the marine life in the numerous tidepools around the shoreline, reached on a clearly marked **nature walk** beginning close to the monument.

Also nearby, a **visitor center** informs on what creatures you might spot and when the tides are most willing to reveal them (obviously the pools are flooded at high tide). If your timing is wrong, climb the hill to the **Old Point Loma Lighthouse** and take a quick tour of the interior (usually daily 9am–5pm). As it happens, the structure led an unfulfilled life: soon after it was built it was realized that the beacon would be obscured by fog, and another lighthouse was erected at a lower elevation.

Facing the Pacific, a mile or two from the monument, a platform makes it easy to view the November to March **whale migration**, when scores of gray whales pass by on their journey between the Arctic Ocean and their breeding grounds off Baja California.

Mission Bay and Sea World

Heading northwest from downtown towards the coast, you pass through the unredeemed area surrounding the Sports Arena – frequented by military personnel for its topless bars and by unfussy tourists for its low-priced, spartan hotels – before reaching **MISSION BAY**, whose mud flats quickly become a landscaped expanse of lagoons and grassy flatlands usually crowded with watersports fanatics. From Ocean Beach, only a couple of miles away, you need to cross the San Diego River on Sunset Cliffs Boulevard.

Mission Bay is also the setting for San Diego's most popular tourist attraction, **SEA WORLD** (daily 9am–dusk; $32.95, children $22.95, parking $5) – take Sea World Drive off I-5, or bus #9 from downtown. It's really only worth visiting if you have kids, and the outrageously high entry price dictates that you allow a whole day to make it worthwhile (better still, shell out a few more dollars for the next-day return pass). Highly regimented, Sea World has a large number of exhibits and timetabled events (get the day's schedule as you enter), ranging from "performances" by killer whales and dolphins, designed to demonstrate the creatures' intelligence and skills, to the eerie sight of the heads of hundreds of moray eels protruding from the hollow rocks of the Forbidden Reef display. Of the rest, two features in particular draw the crowds: the Shark House, where all manner of sharks circle menacingly, although none of them is as violent or as demonstrative as the infamous Great White, an eat-anything monster that Sea World hopes one day to raise and keep in captivity (ironically, as they claim to be eco-conscious); and the Penguin Exhibit – a mock Antarctica behind glass, where hundreds of the birds noisily jump around on ice and dive into the water.

Mission Beach and Pacific Beach

Anyone of a nervous disposition, or lacking a tanned, toned physique, might well find **MISSION BEACH**, the peninsula that separates Mission Bay from the Pacific Ocean, too hot to handle. On the other hand, the raver-packed sands, scantily clad torsos and surfboard-clutching hunks might be precisely what you've come to California for.

In summer bumper-to-bumper traffic fills Mission Boulevard, the sole through-road; at such times the fastest way to get about is by bike or blade (see p.174 for rental outlets) along Ocean Front Walk, the concrete boardwalk running the length of the beach.

First impressions may suggest otherwise, but the city authorities have made major endeavours to limit the anarchic hedonism long associated with this classic example of Southern California beachlife, including approving the revitalization of the once derelict **Belmont Park**, by the southern end of Ocean Front Walk. The roller coaster, one of the few of its era still left in the US, and the pool, once the largest saltwater plunge in the world and the setting for famous celluloid swimmers Johnny Weissmuller and Esther Williams, both opened in 1925. These days the two main attractions are supplemented by a collection of swimwear stores, a pricey fitness center, and lots of seaside snack stalls. The funfair has encouraged more families to use the area but, so far, has made little impact on the beach's freewheeling character.

By following Mission Boulevard north you cross from the social inferno of Mission Beach into the more sedate **PACIFIC BEACH**. Here, expensive oceanside homes with tidy lawns set a refined tone, although there's still plenty to enjoy: a more than serviceable beach around Crystal Pier, and Garnet Avenue running inland from the pier, lined by funky eating places and nightspots. Adept surfers are no strangers to Pacific Beach either – a mile north of the pier, **Tourmaline City Surf Park**, regularly pounded by promising waves, is reserved exclusively for their use.

La Jolla and around

"A nice place – for old people and their parents", wrote Raymond Chandler of **LA JOLLA** (pronounced "La Hoya") in the 1950s, though that didn't stop him moving here (his former house is at 6005 Camino de la Costa) and setting much of his final novel *Playback* in the town, renaming it "Esmeralda". Since Philip Marlowe concluded his last case, La Jolla has been infused with new money and fresh vitality, and its opulence is now less stuffy and more welcoming. The main section, around Prospect Street and Girard Avenue, has spotless sidewalks flanked by tidy grassy verges, and numerous chic art galleries sit side-by-side with equally chic cafés.

This means it's pretty expensive, but it's worth coming at least to savor the town's unique (if clearly contrived) elegance, which includes the ornate pink **La Valencia Hotel**, 1132 Prospect St, frequented by Hollywood's elite in the Thirties and Forties. On a quieter section of the same thoroughfare, the newly expanded La Jolla site of the **Museum of Contemporary Art**, 700 Prospect St (Tues & Thurs–Sat 10am–5pm, Wed 10am–8pm, Sun noon–5pm; $4, free first Tues & Sun of the month), has a huge – and regularly changing – stock of paintings and sculptures from 1955 onwards. Minimal, Pop and California schools are in evidence, bolstered by a strong range of temporary shows, and there are fabulous views of the Pacific surf crashing against the rocks immediately below the building's huge windows. The museum also has exhibition space downtown; see p.178.

The building was once the home of Ellen Scripps, a prominent local philanthropist whose seemingly endless reserves of wealth were injected into La Jolla through the first half of the century. It was she who commissioned architect Irving Gill (who raised several distinctive public buildings in La Jolla) to design her house, and even today the Scripps name is almost everywhere, not least in the small, neat and exquisitely tasteful **Ellen Scripps Browning Park**, on the seaward side of the museum. Where the park meets the coast is the start of **La Jolla Cove**, much of it an ecological reserve, with an underwater park whose clear waters make it perfect for snorkeling (if you can ever find a parking space nearby).

Further along the coast

North of the cove, upmarket residential neighborhoods stretch from the clifftops to the main route, Torrey Pines Road. Following this thoroughfare and then La Jolla Shores Drive, which soon branches left, you'll find nothing of interest for several miles until

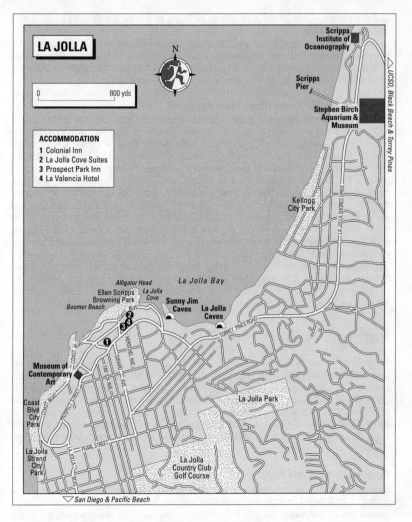

LA JOLLA

N

0   800 yds

ACCOMMODATION
1 Colonial Inn
2 La Jolla Cove Suites
3 Prospect Park Inn
4 La Valencia Hotel

Scripps
Institute of
Oceanography

Scripps
Pier

Stephen Birch
Aquarium &
Museum

△ UCSD, Black Beach & Torrey Pines

Kellogg
City Park

LA JOLLA SHORES DRIVE

La Jolla Bay

Alligator Head
Ellen Scripps   *La Jolla*
Browning Park   *Cove*
Boomer Beach

COAST BLVD

Sunny Jim
Caves

La Jolla
Caves

TORREY PINES ROAD

HERSCHEL AVE.

GIRARD AVE.

FAY AVE.

IVANHOE AVE.

**Museum of
Contemporary
Art**

Coast
Blvd
City
Park

PROSPECT STREET

La Jolla
Strand
City
Park

LA JOLLA BLVD

PEARL STREET

La Jolla Park

La Jolla
Country Club
Golf Course

▽ San Diego & Pacific Beach

you reach the **Stephen Birch Aquarium and Museum** (daily 9am–5pm; $7.50, parking $3), part of the Scripps Institute of Oceanography, which provides entertaining up-close views of captive marine life, informative displays on the earth's ecology, and exhibits detailing the marine exploration work carried out by the Institute.

On a hillside setting above the museum and also reached from Torrey Pines Road, the **University of California at San Diego (UCSD)** campus is a huge, fairly bland affair, only meriting a call if you fancy trekking around to locate the various specially commissioned works scattered about the 1200-acre grounds, which constitute the **Stuart Collection of Sculpture**. The first acquisition, in 1983, has yet to be bettered: Niki de Saint Phalle's *Sun God*, a large colorful bird whose outstretched wings welcome visitors to the parking lot opposite Peterson Hall. To find the rest, pick up a leaflet from the office in the Visual Arts Building or one of the campus's two visitor information booths.

Without the benefit of a car, you can reach the campus on bus #34 or express #30 from downtown, which end their routes a mile or two away at a spick-and-span shopping mall called University Towne Square. The Mingei International Museum, once the main reason to come, has now moved to Balboa Park (see p.183).

Beyond La Jolla: Torrey Pines State Preserve

As it leaves the campus area, La Jolla Shores Drive meets North Torrey Pines Road. A mile north of the junction, Torrey Pines Scenic Drive, branching left, provides the only access (via a steep path) to **Torrey Pines City Beach Park** – almost always called **Blacks Beach** – the region's premier, clothing optional, gay-friendly beach. This lies within the southern confines of the **Torrey Pines State Preserve** (daily 8am–sunset; parking $4), best entered a few miles further north, which preserves the country's rarest species of pine, the Torrey Pine – one of two surviving stands. Though scarce, the pines are not especially distinctive, although thanks to salty conditions and stiff ocean breezes, they do manage to contort their ten-foot frames into a variety of tortured, twisted shapes best viewed at close quarters from the half-mile **Guy Fleming trail**, which starts near the beachside parking lot. The small **museum and interpretive center** (daily 9am–5pm; free) will tell you more than you need to know about Torrey Pines, especially if your visit coincides with a **guided nature tour** (Sat & Sun 11.30am & 1.30pm). The less scenic short **beach trail** leads from the interpretive center down to Flat Rock and a popular beach. Beyond the preserve you're into the North County community of Del Mar (see p.199).

Eating

Wherever you are in San Diego, you'll have few problems finding somewhere to eat **good food** at good value. Everything from crusty coffee shops to stylish ethnic restaurants are in copious supply, and, unsurprisingly, Mexican food is much in evidence, especially in **Old Town**. The **Gaslamp District**, which has the greatest concentration of hip restaurants and bars, explodes on Friday and Saturday nights. The ascendant **Little Italy**, on the northern fringes of downtown, is still too small a quarter to challenge the bohemian hegemony of **Hillcrest**, the most appealing area to simply hang out and eat.

Downtown and Little Italy

Anthony's Fish Grotto, 1360 Harbor Drive (☎619/232-5103). Cut-rate offshoot of a local seafood institution, justly famed for its freshly caught fish. Right by the Maritime Museum.

Athens Market Taverna, 109 W F St (☎619/234-1955). Popular Greek restaurant with fine food at affordable prices – and belly dancers gyrating between the tables at weekends.

Caffe Italia, 1704 India St at Date, Little Italy (☎619/234-6767). Sandwiches, salads, cakes, gelati and coffee served in a sleek modern interior or out on the sidewalk. There's a nice *frittata* bar brunch on Sunday.

Café 222, 222 Island Ave at Second (☎619/236-9902). Industrial-looking café serving some of the city's best breakfasts and lunches, with inventive twists on traditional sandwiches and burgers (including vegetarian), at reasonable prices. Open 7am–2pm.

California Café, Top Floor, Horton Plaza (☎619/238-5440). A good place to sample California cuisine without breaking your budget. It's not cheap, but lunch dishes can be had for $8–11.

The Cheese Shop, 401 G St (☎619/232-2303). A good spot for inexpensive deli sandwiches and espresso near Horton Plaza.

Croce's Restaurant & Jazz Bar, 802 Fifth Ave (☎619/233-4355). Pricey but excellent range of pastas and salads; the Sunday jazz brunch is the talk of the town. See also "Nightlife", p.196.

Filippi's Pizza Grotto, 1747 India St at Date, Little Italy (☎619/232-5094). Thick, chewy pizzas and a handful of pasta dishes served in a small room at the back of an Italian grocery. A winner.

Fio's Cucina Italiana, 801 Fifth St at F (☎619/234-3467). Very classy, fairly expensive Italian place serving the likes of lobster ravioli and gnocchi in rabbit sauce. Invent a special occasion.

Galaxy Grill, 522 Horton Plaza (☎619/234-7211). A Fifties-style diner that's the prime location in this upscale shopping mall to munch a burger and watch the well-groomed crowds go by.

Grand Central Café, 500 Broadway (☎619/234-2233). The youth hostel it adjoined is no longer around, but the café still serves wholesome, inexpensive dishes throughout the day. Breakfast only on Sunday.

Johnny M's 801, 801 Fourth Ave (☎619/233-1131). Quantity takes precedence over quality, though the piles of seafood are still very edible and the restaurant has one of downtown's most impressive historic interiors (see p.180).

Olé Madrid Café, 755 Fifth St (☎619/557-0146). Enjoyable mid-priced Spanish restaurant, with an informal ambience and flamenco dancers midweek. After dinner at weekends, it becomes a very popular funk and dance venue – see "Nightlife", p.196.

Sushi Deli, 828 Broadway (☎619/231-9597). Tasty and beautifully arranged sushi at reasonable prices in a relaxed atmosphere.

Hillcrest

Cafe on the Park, 3831 Park Blvd (☎619/293-7375). Eclectic American grill with large portions, reasonable prices, and a chic San Francisco-style interior. No dinner Sun & Mon.

Chilango's Mexican Grill, 142 University Ave (☎619/294-8646). Gourmet Mexican food for under $8; large veggie selection, too.

The Good Egg, 7947 Balboa Ave (☎619/565-4244). Until 9am, as much coffee as you can drink for 5¢, provided you buy a breakfast: the gigantic pancakes created from various mouthwatering ingredients are a wise choice. On the northern edge of Hillcrest.

Ichiban, 1449 University Ave (☎619/299-7203). There are few better places in which to enjoy quality Japanese cuisine than this unpretentious and simple restaurant. The combination platters are extremely well priced, and you can eat your fill for under $10.

Monsoon, 3975 Fifth Ave (☎619/298-3155). Hillcrest's newer vegetarian place, with a modern feel and a menu dominated by soups, sandwiches and burgers for around $6.

Taste of Thai, 527 University Ave (☎619/291-7525). Terrific Thai for reasonable prices in the center of Hillcrest; expect a wait on weekends.

The Vegetarian Zone, 2949 Fifth Ave (☎619/298-7302). Decent though unspectacular homespun vegetarian cuisine in a non-smoking environment. Mains $8–10.

Old Town

Berta's, 3928 Twiggs St (☎619/295-2343). A far cry from the area's many touristy Mexican restaurants, offering low-priced, authentic cooking from all over Latin America. One of the best-kept secrets in town.

Cafe Pacifica, 2414 San Diego Ave (☎619/291-666). A bit pricey but worth it for a winning California cuisine/seafood mix. A good wine list too.

Garden House, 2480 San Diego Ave (☎619/220-0723). Tea, coffee and muffins beside a shady lawn, an oasis in bustling Old Town.

Old Town Mexican Café y Cantina, 2489 San Diego Ave (☎619/297-4330). Lively and informal Mexican diner; only at breakfast are you unlikely to have to wait for a table.

Old Town Thai Restaurant, 2540 Congress St (☎619/291-6720). Simply decorated place a block away from most of the restaurants and serving an extensive array of Thai dishes. Excellent lunches for $5 and plenty of vegetarian dishes. Closed Mon.

Village Kitchen, 2497 San Diego Ave (☎619/294-4180). Good-sized portions of Mexican and American food cooked and presented in a wholesome, unpretentious style.

Coronado

Kensington Coffee Company, 1106 First St (☎619/437-8506). Aromatic coffees, imported teas and pastries that make for a tasty snack close to the landing stage.

Mexican Village Restaurant, 120 Orange Ave (☎619/435-1822). Long-standing Mexican diner of ballroom dimensions, patronized as much for its margaritas and music as for its food.

Miguel's Cocina, 1351 Orange Ave (☎619/437-4237). Brilliant fish tacos and a full range of other Mexican choices. Worth seeking out.

Stretch's, 943 Orange Ave (☎619/435-8886). For the health-conscious, extremely nutritious meals, with fresh natural ingredients.

Ocean Beach and Point Loma

Old Venice Italian Restaurant Caffe and Bar, 2910 Canon Ave, Point Loma (☎619/222-5888). Upscale and hip atmosphere at moderate prices. Great for pizza, pasta, seafood and salads.

Point Loma Seafoods, 2805 Emerson St (☎619/223-1109). Fast, inexpensive counter where you can get San Diego's freshest fish in a basket with fries or in an oversized sandwich. This justly popular place is packed on weekends; it's not easy to find a parking spot nearby.

Rancho Mexican and Vegetarian Cafe, 1830 Sunset Cliffs Blvd, Ocean Beach (☎619/226-7619). Come to this healthy Tex-Mex restaurant for tasty dishes like *mahi-mahi* tacos or eggplant burritos. Daily seafood and veggie specials.

The Venetian, 3663 Voltaire St, Ocean Beach (☎619/223-8197). Excellently priced pizzas and pasta, very welcome after a hard day on the beach.

Mission Beach and Pacific Beach

The Eggery, 4130 Mission Blvd, Mission Beach (☎619/274-3122). A coffee shop with imagination, serving breakfast – omelets, pancakes and so on – until 2pm.

Luigi's Italian Restaurant, 3210 Mission Blvd, Mission Beach (☎619/488-2818). Enormous pizzas and a rowdy beachside atmosphere, bolstered by competing TV sets.

Mission Cafe, 3795 Mission Blvd, Mission Beach (☎619/488-9060). Eclectic Chino-Latino breakfast and lunch menu, very fairly priced. A good way to jump-start your day.

Saska's, 3768 Mission Blvd, Pacific Beach (☎619/488-5754). Laid-back dining place where substantial breakfasts are served all day and (nearly) all night, alongside the usual selection of main meals.

La Jolla

Ashoka, 8008 Girard Ave (☎619/454-6263). Slightly pretentious Indian restaurant, but the combination lunchtime deals for under $10 are unmatched.

John's Waffle Shop, 7906 Girard Ave (☎619/454-7331). This hole-in-the-wall place surrounded by designer clothing stores has been perfecting the art of the waffle since the 1950s – the long lines outside (especially on Sunday) are proof of its success. Other diner favorites fill out the menu.

Ocean Terrace at George's on the Cove, 1250 Prospect St (☎619/454-2214). If you can't afford the stuffier downstairs restaurant, head up to the roof for an only mildly overpriced lunch and an unbeatable ocean view.

Star of India, 1025 Prospect St (☎619/459-3355). Mostly northern Indian cuisine, with good vegetarian and tandoori choices. Most mains $13–15.

Sushi on the Rock, 1277 Prospect St (☎619/456-1138). Tempting array of inexpensive sushi combination plates served to a soundtrack of rock and reggae.

Nightlife

San Diego's arch-conservatism is apparent even in the city's **nightlife**: money is lavished on pursuits such as theater and opera, but the crowds flock to the much-of-a-muchness beachside discos and boozy live music venues – or spend the evening in a

MAJOR VENUES

Any big name in contemporary music visiting San Diego is likely to appear at one of the following **major venues**:

Belly Up Tavern, 143 S Cedros Ave, Solana Beach (☎619/481-9022; see p.199).

Centro de Arte Reina Sofía: Sat after 2.30pm & Sun 10am–2.30pm.

Copley Symphony Hall, 750 B St, Downtown (☎619/699-4205).

4th and B, 345 B St, Downtown (☎619/231-4343).

Humphrey's, 2241 Shelter Island Drive (☎619/523-1010).

The New Bacchanal, 8022 Claremont Mesa Blvd (☎619/277-7326).

San Diego Convention Center, 111 W Harbor Drive, Downtown (☎619/525-5000).

San Diego Sports Arena, 3500 Sports Arena Blvd (☎619/220-TIXS).

TICKETS

Assuming they're available, **half-price tickets** for theater and classical music events for that evening can be bought at Times Arts Tix, 28 Horton Plaza at Broadway Circle (Tues–Thurs 11am–6pm, Fri & Sat 10am–6pm; ☎619/497-5000), which also handles full-price advance sales. On Saturday, half-price tickets are available for Sunday performances.

Otherwise, tickets for all major shows can be had from the venue or through Ticketmaster (☎619/220-TIXS). The **SRH Info Hotline** (☎619/973-9269) has a select list of alternative events.

coffee bar. It may be narrow in scope, but at least there's plenty going on. For full listings, pick up the free *San Diego Reader*, buy the Thursday edition of the *San Diego Union-Tribune*, or seek out the youth-lifestyle-oriented *Slamm* at some of the places listed below. **Cover** charges at live music venues range from $2 to $8, unless someone big is playing.

Coffee bars

Café Lulu, 419 F St, Downtown, (☎619/238-0144). A good selection of coffees and what may be downtown's latest food orders (2am) make this a popular scene.

Gas Haus, 640 F St, Downtown (☎619/232-5866). Alcohol-free, eclectically decorated café where rollerblading teenagers, students and ageing hippies co-exist on deep couches, and take each other on at pool.

Gelato Vero Caffe, 3753 India St, just at the foot of Hillcrest (☎619/295-9269). Enjoy good espresso and gelato while getting clued in to local events by staff and regulars.

Newbreak Coffee Co, 523 University Ave, Hillcrest (☎619/295-1600). Linger over a coffee while reading overseas newspapers or viewing the small-scale art exhibitions. A good place to seek out listings and gay-interest free papers.

Upstart Crow, Seaport Village, Downtown (☎619/232-4855). Coffee bar fused with a bookstore which makes for a lively cross section of customers – and a surfeit of reading material.

Zanzibar, 976 Garnet Ave, Pacific Beach (☎619/272-4762). Relatively serene retreat from the brash bars along this strip. Coffees, sandwiches and muffins served until 2am, or 4am at weekends.

Bars

The Daily Planet, 1200 Garnet Ave, Pacific Beach (☎619/272-6066). Sizeable sports bar with a 3–6pm happy hour, and cut-rate drinks offered through the evening. Dancing at weekends, Karaoke Sunday, and Monday night football in season.

Karl Strauss Old Columbia Brewery, 1157 Columbia St at B, Downtown (☎619/234-2739). Where discerning beer hunters enjoy ales and lagers brewed on the premises.

La Jolla Brewing Company, 7536 Fay Ave, La Jolla (☎619/456-2739). Currently the liveliest evening rendezvous in La Jolla, where a youngish crowd quaffs the home-brewed beers and makes merry beneath vintage surfboards and photos of historic San Diego.

Live Wire, 2103 El Cajon Blvd, just east of Hillcrest (☎619/291-7450). The local indie rockers gather here to sample the twenty microbrews on tap. There's a loud jukebox and a pool table.

Olé Madrid Café, 755 Fifth St, Downtown (☎619/557-0146). Spanish restaurant that on weekends becomes a very popular funk and dance club. Arrive before 11pm if you want to get in. See also "Eating", p.193.

Pac Shores, 4927 Newport St, Ocean Beach (☎619/233-7549). Easy-going local dive that's been around forever. Check out the giant clam over the bar.

Red Fox Room, 2223 El Cajon Blvd, just east of Hillcrest (☎619/297-1313). Makes a popular tandem nightcrawl with *Live Wire*, one block away. An old style piano bar and good steaks draw nostalgia buffs of all ages.

Live music venues

Blind Melons, 710 Garnet Ave, Pacific Beach (☎619/483-7844). Earthy, live blues croaked out nightly from 9pm, in a spot right by the pier.

Brick by Brick, 1130 Buenos Ave, Mission Bay (☎619/276-3993). Tends to attract nationally known alternative, blues, and hard rock acts.

The Casbah, 2501 Kettner Blvd, Downtown (☎619/232-4355). Varying roster of blues, rock and indie bands.

Croce's Top Hat, 805 Fifth Ave, Downtown (☎619/233-4355). Classy jazz in the back room of a pricey restaurant; has a jazz brunch on Sundays. See also "Eating", p.193.

Island Saloon, 104 Orange Ave, Coronado (☎619/435-3456). Standard bar which rocks to local R&B groups on Friday and Saturday.

Patrick's II, 428 F St, Downtown (☎619/233-3077). No-frills bar with matching R&B bands most nights. Occasional jazz and blues; $3 cover at weekends.

Winston's Beach Club, 1921 Bacon St, Ocean Beach (☎619/222-6822). Rock bands most nights, reggae on Thursday. Close to the pier.

Clubs and discos

Blue Tattoo, 835 Fifth Ave, Downtown (☎619/238-7191). If you want to experience foam dancing, this is the place to come.

Cafe Sevilla, 555 Fourth Ave, Downtown (☎619/233-5979). Traditional Spanish cuisine upstairs, hip Latin American-flavored club downstairs. Attracts a European crowd.

Emerald City, 945 Garnet Ave, Pacific Beach (☎619/483-9920). Lively disco with drink specials at weekends, and the "Underworld" industrial and Gothic night on Sunday.

Theater

There's a thriving **theater** scene in San Diego, with several mid-sized venues and many smaller fringe venues putting on quality shows. Tickets are $20–25 for a major production, $10–15 for a night on the fringe. The *San Diego Reader* carries full listings. The main **venues** are the Lyceum Stage in Horton Plaza (☎619/235-8025), the Old Globe Theater, part of the Simon Edison Complex for the Performing Arts in Balboa Park (☎619/239-2255), the Civic Theater at Third and B streets (☎619/236-6510), and the La Jolla Playhouse at the Mandell Weiss Center on the UCSD campus (☎619/551-1010). The alternative theatrics at **Sushi Performance and Visual Art**, 3201 11th Ave, Downtown (☎619/235-8466) are sometimes pretentious but rarely boring.

Comedy

The **comedy** scene in San Diego has been distinctly unfunny lately, with most of the major clubs closing down. If you want to catch some of the acts bound for the more glamorous venues of LA or New York, you might try 4th & B (see the box on p.195).

Film

San Diego has many **cinemas**, most of them offering the latest Hollywood block-busters. Scan the newspapers for full listings; admission is usually $5–8, a few dollars less for most matinée shows. For more adventurous programs – foreign-language films, monochrome classics or cult favorites – look for the afternoon screenings (Mon–Sat) at the San Diego Public Library, 820 E St, Downtown (☎619/236-5489). After dark, The Ken, 4061 Adams Ave (☎619/283-5909), in the up-and-coming Kensington area, is the most popular venue for art and revival films, changing its offerings almost every evening. The Guild, Park, and Hillcrest cinemas, all in Hillcrest, can also be relied on to eschew the usual popular pap.

Classical music and opera

San Diego's symphony recently fell on hard times and went under. These days, local culture vultures mostly rely on the jazz, classical, and chamber music series held at the Museum of Contemporary Art's Sherwood Auditorium in La Jolla (☎619/454-2594). Still thriving is the **San Diego Opera**, frequently boasting top international guest per-formers during its January to May season; it's based at the Civic Theater (see p.196).

Gay and Lesbian San Diego

Mostly centered on the Hillcrest area, San Diego's **gay and lesbian** population makes its presence felt through a number of publications and resource centers, and a network of gay bars and clubs. Also, several hotels and bed and breakfast inns are noted for their friendliness towards gay and lesbian travelers – several being all but exclusively gay. For sun-worshippers, the place to go is **Blacks Beach** (see p.192) north of La Jolla.

Publications and resource centers

The primary source of gay and lesbian news, views and upcoming events is the free *Gay & Lesbian Times*, which appears weekly and is distributed through gay bars and clubs, many of the city's coffee bars, and most gay-run businesses. Look out, too, for the newsy *Update* with its *Etcetera* insert full of personals, classifieds and a "what's on" bul-letin board. The LA-based *Edge* also makes its way down here. You can learn more by calling at the **Lesbian and Gay Men's Community Center**, 3916 Normal St (☎619/692-2077).

Bars and clubs

Bourbon Street, 4612 Park Blvd, University Heights (☎619/291-0173). A smart gay crowd gathers around the piano bar at this elegant New Orleans-style club north of Hillcrest.

Caliph, 3102 Fifth Ave, Downtown (☎619/298-9495). Piano bar with live music aimed mainly at an older gay clientele.

The Flame, 3780 Park Blvd, Hillcrest (☎619/295-4163). The city's premier lesbian club, open for dancing, pool and occasional live acts from early evening to early morning. Tuesday is a no-holds-barred "Boys Night".

Montage, 2028 Hancock St, Old Town (☎619/295-3724). A three-floor disco very popular with a gay and straight crowd. Mainly under-25s.

Number One Fifth Avenue, 3845 Fifth Ave, Hillcrest (☎619/299-1911). A fairly casual neighbor-hood bar with a pleasant patio. DJs play requests some nights, mainly Fifties through Seventies.

Rich's, 1051 University Ave, Hillcrest (☎619/295-0750). Popular club with heavy dance grooves on Friday and Saturday, and "Hedonism" night on Thursday when the hat-check even accepts T-shirts and jeans, so you can dance in your Calvin Kleins. Cover charge most nights.

Gay accommodation

Balboa Park Inn, 3402 Park Blvd, Hillcrest (☎1-800/938-8181 or 619/298-0823). Elegant B&B in a Spanish colonial-style building, within walking distance of Balboa Park and its museums and popular with gay, lesbian and straight guests. Some rooms have kitchenettes and there's a jacuzzi. ⑤.

Friendship Hotel, 3942 Eighth Ave, Hillcrest (☎619/298-9898). One of the least expensive hotels in the area, but still with TVs and refrigerators in rooms. Mostly gay and lesbian. ②.

Hillcrest Inn, 3754 Fifth Ave, Hillcrest (☎1-800/258-2280 or 619/293-7078). Predominantly gay hotel right in the heart of Hillcrest. The fairly basic, mostly non-smoking rooms all have bath, refrigerator and microwave. It's a little characterless but has a friendly atmosphere. ③.

Park Manor Suites, 525 Spruce St, near Balboa Park (☎1-800/874-2649 or 619/291-0999). The rooms – all with kitchens and nice, large sitting areas – are not quite as posh as the lobby of this residential-style inn would suggest, but then neither are the prices. Continental breakfast is included. ⑤.

Listings

American Express Main branches are at 258 Broadway (☎619/234-4455) and 1020 Prospect St in La Jolla (☎619/459-4161). Both open Mon–Fri 9am–5pm.

Amtrak recorded schedule information ☎619/239-9021.

Beach and surf conditions ☎619/221-8884.

Car Rental Alamo, 2942 Kettner Blvd (☎619/297-0311); Avis, 3180 N Harbor Drive (☎1-800/331-1212); Budget, 2535 Pacific Highway (☎1-800/283-4382); Hertz, 3202 N Harbor Drive (☎1-800/654-3131); Rent-a-Wreck, 1904 Hotel Circle North (☎619/223-3300); Thrifty, 1120 W Laurel (☎619/294-7500).

Disabled assistance Accessible San Diego, 1010 Second Ave, Suite 1630, San Diego 92101 (☎619/279-0704); Access Center of San Diego, 1295 University Ave, Suite 10, San Diego 92013 (☎619/293-3500, TDD 293-7757).

Flea Market The huge Kobey's Swap Meet takes place at the Sports Arena, 3500 Sports Arena Blvd; Thurs–Sun 7am–3pm.

Hospitals For non-urgent treatment, the cheapest place is the Beach Area Family Health Center, 3705 Mission Blvd, Mission Beach (☎619/488-0644).

Left Luggage At the Greyhound terminal ($2 for 6hr, $4 for 24hr) and, for ticketed travelers, at the Santa Fe Depot ($1.50 for 24hr).

Pharmacy 24-hour pharmacy at Sharp Cabrillo Hospital, 3457 Kenyon St, between downtown and Ocean Beach (☎619/221-3400).

Post Offices The downtown post office is at 815 E St (Mon–Fri 8.30am–5pm, Sat 8.30am–noon), but for *poste restante* (general delivery) use the main office at 2535 Midway Drive, between downtown and Mission Beach (Mon–Fri 8.30am–5pm, Sat 8.30am–4.40pm; zip code 92138; ☎619/293-5410).

Rape Crisis Center/Hotline 4508 Mission Bay Drive (☎619/233-3088).

Sport Baseball: the San Diego Padres play in the same stadium as the Chargers, tickets from the stadium office or Ticketron (☎619/283-4494). Football: the San Diego Chargers play in the Jack Murphy Stadium in Mission Valley (☎619/563-8281).

Ticketmaster Call ☎619/220-TIXS for the nearest branch, or look in the phone book.

Traveler's Aid At the airport, daily 9am–10pm (☎619/231-7361), and at Santa Fe Depot (☎619/234-5191).

Weather Recorded information ☎619/289-1212.

Victims of Crime Resource Center ☎619/842-8467.

Western Union ☎1-800/325-6000.

What's On A recorded rundown of what's on and what's open: ☎619/239-9696.

AROUND SAN DIEGO

San Diego County lies largely north of the city, and runs from small, sleepy suburban communities to completely open – and rugged – country. Passing through at least some of it is unavoidable, though how much time you actually spend in the region depends on whether you want to allow several days to camp out and follow forest and desert hikes, or simply to dash along the coast as fast as possible to Los Angeles.

To the south there's Mexico, or more accurately the Mexican border city of **Tijuana**. To be honest this isn't up to much, giving the merest hint of how Mexico really is and a much stronger taste of the comparative affluence of the US – most visitors are shoppers and it's hard to avoid the tensions that arise from that. However, it is at least a different country, and is extremely easy to reach from San Diego.

Transportation around the region is straightforward. By car, I-5, skirting along the coast, and I-15, a little deeper inland, are the main links with the north, while I-8 heads east from San Diego towards the southern part of the Anza-Borrego Desert (see p.229). The area east of I-15, around the scattered rural communities, is covered by a simple network of smaller roads. Public transportation is no problem between San Diego and the North County coast, with frequent Greyhound buses and Amtrak trains between LA and San Diego calling at most communities, though only a skeletal bus service penetrates inland. In contrast, you're spoilt for choice on ways of getting to the Mexican border.

The North County Coast

The towns of the **North County Coast** stretch forty miles north from San Diego in a pretty much unbroken line as far as the Camp Pendleton marine base, which divides the county from the outskirts of Los Angeles. The communities tend to get less upmarket the farther they are from San Diego and the closer they are to military bases, but generally tend to mix slick San Diego commuters, beach bums, and crewcuts. The main attraction is the coast itself: miles of fine sandy beaches with great opportunities for swimming and surfing.

Del Mar

The tall bluff that marks the northern edge of the city of San Diego and holds Torrey Pines State Preserve (see p.192) forms the southern boundary of **DEL MAR**, a smart and pleasant little town whose **fairgrounds** are famous for the **racetrack** where the rich and famous gather between early July and early September for one of the most fashionable meets in California. The fairgrounds are also the address for the **Southern California State Exposition**, held for twenty days just before the racing season begins. It's largely an old-fashioned event, with barbecues and livestock shows, though it's mixed with a fair amount of contemporary arts and music events. Otherwise, Del Mar is a place to eat well and shop well – at a price. Additionally, the train station is just a pebble's throw from an inviting beach.

Solana Beach

SOLANA BEACH, the next town north from Del Mar, makes a better place for an overnight stop. Motels line the coast road, there's some decent nightlife – the *Belly Up*

Tavern, 143 S Cedros Ave (☎760/481-9022), is one of the major mid-sized music venues in the area (see the box on p.195 for details) – and striking views over the ocean from the Solana Beach County Park. If you're driving, take a quick detour inland along Hwy-8, passing the rolling Fairbanks Ranch (built by the film star, Douglas Fairbanks Jr) to **Rancho Santa Fe**, a small but extremely rich community shaded by trees and given its distinctive Spanish architectural flavor through the 1920s and 1930s. It got a great deal of unwelcome attention in 1997 as home to the Heaven's Gate cult, which committed mass suicide on the appearance of the Hale-Bopp comet.

Encinitas and Leucadia

ENCINITAS is a major flower-growing center, its abundant blooms at their best during the spring, when soft waves of color from the flowers cast a calm and collected air over the whole place. It's no surprise that an Indian guru chose the town as the HQ of the Self-Realization Fellowship, near the Sea Cliff Roadside Park, a popular surfing beach dubbed "Swami's" by the locals. The Fellowship's serene **Meditation Gardens**, around the corner at 216 K St (Tues–Sun 11am–5pm; free), are open to all, and there's further flower power nearby at the **Quail Botanical Gardens**, 230 Quail Gardens Drive (daily 9am–5pm; $3). For more local information call at the **visitor center**, 138 Encinitas Blvd (☎760/753-6041). Encinitas, and the adjoining community of **LEUCADIA** three miles to the north, both offer reasonably priced **accommodation**, such as the *Moonlight Beach Motel*, 233 Second St, Encinitas (☎1-800/323-1259 or 760/753-0623; ③), nicely located for the beach with kitchenettes in all rooms. Otherwise, there's the landscaped **campground** at San Elijo Beach State Park (☎760/642-4200 or Parknet ☎1-800/444-7275; $17–23), near **Cardiff-by-the-Sea** just to the south, whose name – the whim of its founder's British wife, which also explains the presence of Manchester and Birmingham avenues – is its only interesting feature.

Carlsbad

Surfers constitute the major element of **South Carlsbad State Beach** (with a busy cliff-top campground; ☎760/438-3143 or Parknet ☎1-800/444-7275; $17–25), marking the edge of **CARLSBAD**, one of the few coastal communities with a past worth shouting about, though it is manifested in lots of cutesy pseudo-Teutonic structures. During the early 1880s, water from a local spring was deemed to have the same invigorating qualities as the waters of Karlsbad, a European spa town in what was then Bohemia (now part of the Czech Republic). Carlsbad thus acquired its name and a money-spinning reputation as a health resort, ably promoted by pioneer-settler turned entrepreneur John Frazier, whose bronze image overlooks the (now dry) original springs.

The springs and most things you'll need are close to the junction of Carlsbad Boulevard (the coast road) and Carlsbad Village Drive; along the latter, inside the train station, the **visitor center** (Mon–Fri 9am–5pm, Sat 10am–4pm, Sun 10am–3pm; ☎1-800/227-5722 or 760/434-6093) will give you a sense of the town's history.

Other than the campground, the best **accommodation** is at the *Ocean Palms Beach Resort*, 2950 Ocean St (☎760/729-2493; ④), overlooking the water but with its own pool and rooms with kitchenettes. Two well-priced places to **eat** are *Pollos Maria*, 3055 Harding St (☎760/729-4858), for fast, tasty Mexican food, and, out from the center but easy to find thanks to its "Danish windmill", a branch of *Pea Soup Andersen's*, 850 Palomar Airport Rd (☎760/930-3880), with an all-American menu of sandwiches and salads, and a chunky pea soup famous since the 1920s, though it's hard to say why.

Oceanside, Mission San Luis Rey and around

The most northerly town on the San Diego county coast, **OCEANSIDE** is dominated by the huge **Camp Pendleton marine base** and has little charm. But, for those without a car, it's a major transportation center (Amtrak, Greyhound and local bus services all pass through) and the easiest place from which to reach Mission San Luis Rey (see below).

If you find yourself having to **stay** here, the *Beechwood Motel*, 210 Surfrider St (☎760/722-3866; ②), is tolerable and cheap. For **eating**, *The Hill Street Coffee House*, 524 S Hill St (☎760/966-0985), is a real find in Oceanside's fast food wasteland. It's an old house with bohemian leanings, with great coffee, cakes, sandwiches and salads, and live music on Saturday nights. For a surfeit of entertainment, you could take a look at the lagoon-centered **Buena Vista Audubon Nature Center**, 2202 S Hill St (Tues–Sat 10am–4pm, Sun 1–4pm; free).

Four miles inland from Oceanside along Hwy-76 and accessible on local bus #313, **Mission San Luis Rey**, 4050 Mission Ave (Mon–Sat 10am–4.30pm, Sun 11.30–4.30pm; $3), is the largest of the Californian missions, founded in 1798 by Padre Laséun and once home to three thousand Native Americans. Franciscan monks keep the impressively restored mission's spiritual function alive and there's a **museum** and a serene candle-lit **chapel**. Even if you don't go inside, look around the foundations of the guards barracks immediately outside the main building, and, across the road, the remains of the mission's ornate **sunken gardens** (daily 9am–4.30pm; free), once *lavanderías*, where the mission's inhabitants did their washing.

The strong sense of history at the mission is fast being diluted by new property developments all around, the commercial spillover from Oceanside that is creeping into the community of **San Luis Rey** itself. To escape, push on another four miles beyond San Luis Rey to the **Rancho Guajome Regional Park** (9.30am to an hour before dusk; $2 per vehicle), with its centerpiece, the ranch, a twenty-room adobe building erected in the mid-eighteenth century as home for the newly married Cave Couts and Ysidora Bandini, who turned the place into a major social gathering spot. Among the many celebrities entertained at the ranch were Ulysses S. Wright and Helen Hunt Jackson, who, according to legend, based the central character of *Ramona*, her sentimental tale of Indian life during the mission era, on Ysidora's maid. After Cout's death in 1874, Ysidora fought to maintain the upkeep of the place but over the years it became dilapidated, until it was bought and restored by the county authorities. There are **guided tours** of the house (11am & 2pm Sat & Sun; $2).

Highway 76 continues inland to Mission Asistencia San Antonio de Pala, and to the Palomar Observatory, both described overleaf. Along the coast beyond Oceanside, the **military** has kept its territory in a raw state, creating a vivid impression of how stark the land was before industrialization took hold. When manoeuvres aren't in progress, it's possible to pitch a tent in the lower parts of the camp area, close to the uncluttered **beach**. The northern part of the camp, around the San Onofre Nuclear Plant, is popular with surfers because the plant's by-products apparently keep the water warm – though you might prefer to steer clear.

The North County inland

Inland, the North County is quite different from the coastal strip, given over to farming as far as the terrain allows and with no sizeable towns, the outlook one of thick forests, deep valleys and mile-high mountain ranges. Besides a few reminders of the ancient indigenous cultures, remnants from the mission era and a few tiny settlements

– some of which can comfortably consume an hour or two of your time – it's best to make for the area's state parks and enjoy some leisurely countryside walks, or venture east to the dramatic Anza-Borrego desert (see p.229).

Escondido

About forty miles north of San Diego on I-15, the unhurried dormitory town of **ESCONDIDO** sits in a quiet valley. The town is accessible on bus #20 from downtown San Diego; you're dropped seven miles out at the North County Fair shopping mall, but bus #382 or #384 will get you into town. The extremely well-informed **CVB**, 720 N Broadway (Mon–Fri 8.30am–5pm, Sat 10am–4pm; ☎ 1-800/848-3336 or 760/745-4741) provides information for the entire north San Diego County area.

In Escondido itself, the main focus of visitor attention is **Heritage Walk** in Grape Day Park, which leads into and around several restored Victorian buildings (Thurs–Sat 1–4pm; free) and to a 1925 railroad car that holds an elaborate scale model of the railroad which once linked Escondido to Oceanside. The **California Center for the Arts**, 340 N Escondido Blvd (Tues–Sat 10am–5pm, Sun 12pm–5pm; $4) features a good contemporary art museum, as well as two theaters that are the focus of a variety of high-tone music and dance performances. The **Orfila Winery**, 13455 San Pasqual Valley Rd (daily 10am–6pm), five miles south of the Escondido town center and set in stunning scenery, offers tastings of wines produced by a former Napa Valley vintner, while six miles north of town, the **Deer Park Vintage Cars and Wine**, 29013 Champagne Blvd (daily 10am–5pm), also shows off a sizeable collection of vintage cars to anyone who turns up to sample the produce of its vines.

To most Americans over 65, however, Escondido is best known for the **Lawrence Welk Resort**, a thousand-acre vacation complex of golf courses, guest villas and the Welk Dinner Theater, eight miles north of the town off I-15 (no public transportation). Welk himself rose from accordion-playing obscurity to become an adored band leader, TV celebrity and inventor of an anodyne sound known as "champagne music". Even if you don't consider Welk a role model for aspiring composers, there's something to be said for taking a look at the hagiographic account of his life displayed around the lobby of the theater, and for gorging yourself on the $10 lunch buffet laid out in the nearby restaurant (Tues–Thurs & Sun).

North from Escondido

Hwy-S6 leads fifteen miles north from Escondido to **Mission San Antonio de Pala** (Tues–Sun 10am–3pm; $2), close to the junction with Hwy-76 from Oceanside. Built as an outpost of Mission San Luis Rey, this lay in ruins until the Cupa Indians were ousted from their tribal home (to make room for the building of Warner Hot Springs) and moved to this area, where the mission was revived to serve as their church. The buildings here now are rarely used and are all reconstructions of the originals, but they're not without atmosphere, with a breeze whispering through the gaping windows and an eerie silence hanging over the cemetery. The gardens here are lovely, and a single-room museum contains artifacts created by the Pala Indians and dating back to the days of the original mission. There's a small basic **campground** opposite the mission.

Continuing east, Hwy-76 runs into **Cleveland National Forest** and a good sprinkling of **campgrounds** (both state- and federal-run). The enormous forest stretches south from here almost to the Mexican border, although less-than-hardcore backpackers tend to prefer the **Palomar Mountain State Park** (☎760/742-3462), on Hwy-S7, for its cooler, higher altitude (some parts rise above 5000ft) and enjoyable, fairly easy

---

THE NORTH EAST RURAL BUS SYSTEM

The only **bus service** through the sparsely populated northeastern section of the county is the reliable but infrequent **North East Rural Bus System** (☎760/767-4287; calls answered Mon–Sat 7am–noon & 2–5pm) that links San Diego with Escondido, Ramona, Santa Ysabel, Julian, and the Anza-Borrego desert (see p.229) and runs Monday to Saturday.

The departure point in San Diego is the Grossmont Center near El Cajon, roughly ten miles east of downtown (get there with city bus #15). It's strongly advisable to phone at least a day in advance to check schedules – and you must phone ahead if you want to be collected from Cuyamaca State Park. Board the buses either at marked stops or, where there are none, simply flag the vehicle down. A consolation for the scarcity of buses are the low **fares**: just $2.50 from San Diego to Julian, for example. Bicycles are carried free of charge but, again, you need to reserve in advance.

---

hiking trails. **Camping** at the Doane Valley site costs $14 (reserve through Parknet on ☎1-800/444-7275) and supplies are available at the well-stocked Palomar Mountain General Store at the junction of routes S6 and S7.

Capable of seeing a billion light years into the cosmos, the two-hundred-inch telescope of the **Palomar Observatory** on Hwy-S6 (daily 9am–4pm; free) is something of a legend in astronomy circles. As a visitor, it's not possible to view the distant galaxies directly, but look in on the observatory's impressive collection of deep-space photographs taken using the powerful telescope.

East from Escondido

Ten miles east from Escondido on Hwy-78 (bus #307; Mon–Sat) and thirty miles north of San Diego (bus #878 or #879 from the Grossmont Center; Tues–Sat), the **San Diego Wild Animal Park** on San Pasqual Valley Road (mid-June to Sept Mon–Wed 9am–5pm, Thurs–Sun 9am–8pm; rest of year daily 9am–4pm; $18.95, combined ticket with San Diego Zoo $32) is the major tourist target in the area: a 2100-acre enclosure that's well worth a day's visit. It's obviously a place for kids, and attractions include a sizeable aviary, noisy with the massed squawks of tropical birds; mock-African Bush; a Kilimanjaro hiking trail; not to mention elephant rides and various films and exhibitions. Admission includes a fifty-minute ride on the **Wgasa Bush Line Monorail**, which skirts through the outer reaches of the park, where the animals – including lions, tigers, cheetahs, deer and monkeys – roam in relative freedom.

In contrast to the crowded coast, the population – and the landscapes – become increasingly sparse as you press further east along Hwy-78, into a region that's a near-impossible nut to crack without personal transportation (see the box above). If you're coming this way by car directly from San Diego, use Hwy-67 and join Hwy-78 at **Ramona**, eighteen miles from Escondido, and continue east for sixteen miles to **SANTA YSABEL**, a tiny crossroads community enlivened by two things. Right on Hwy-78 just before its junction with Hwy-79 you can't miss **Dudley's Bakery**, famous far and wide for its homebaked breads and pastries at giveaway prices – the date, nut and raisin loaf is justly a popular line. A mile and a half north of town on Hwy-79, the tiny **Mission Santa Ysabel** (daily 8am–4pm; $1), a 1924 replacement of an 1818 original, sits in moody isolation. There's a small chapel and, around the side, a one-room **museum** (same hours; $1) detailing the history of the mission. Outside is an Indian burial ground, and the church continues to serve several local Native American communities.

Julian

A different atmosphere prevails in **JULIAN**, seven miles southeast of Santa Ysabel on Hwy-78, and surrounded by pines – a sure sign that you're entering the foothills of the mountains that divide the coastal side of the county from the desert. Indeed, you're some 4000ft up, and even in summer it can get a bit brisk. Hard as it may be to believe today, the discovery of gold here in 1869 turned Julian into the second-biggest town in the San Diego area. Since then, the local population has stayed constant at around 1500, and has earned more from harvesting apples than from precious metal; the cider and apple pies produced here bring thousands of weekend visitors. You might also consider using Julian as a temperate base from which to make forays into the Anza-Borrego desert (see p.229) less than ten miles to the east.

With its little buildings and carefully nurtured down-home charms, Julian is immediately appealing, but a short stroll reveals little of consequence beyond the shops, realty stores and restaurants grouped along Main Street. The *Julian Café*, 2112 Main St (☎760/765-2712), has the best atmosphere and good-value, basic **food**, including the ubiquitous apple pie. As its name suggests, *Baily Barbecue*, 2307 Main St (☎760/765-9957) features grilled meat, served fall-off-the-bone tender in a down-home setting. The **Chamber of Commerce**, 2129 Main St (daily 10am–4pm; ☎760/765-1857), has details of the town's many **B&Bs**. Among these, the *Julian Hotel*, at the junction of Main and B (☎1-800/734-5854 or 760/765-0201; ⑤), is the oldest functioning hotel in the state, opened in 1897 by a freed slave; rates include afternoon tea and a full breakfast. The *Julian Lodge*, Fourth and C streets (☎1-800/542-1420 or 760/765-1420; ④) is only a replica of a historic hotel, but has a similar country cozy atmosphere; breakfast is buffet-style continental. A less expensive option is to **camp** in the Cuyamaca Rancho State Park (see opposite).

If you find yourself with a few spare hours in Julian, take a look at the absorbing clutter inside the **Julian Pioneer Museum** on Hwy-78 just off Main Street (April–Nov Tues–Sun 10am–4pm; Dec–March Sat & Sun & holidays 10am–4pm; $1). Alternatively, wander half a mile up C Street to the **Eagle Mining Company** (daily 10am–3pm, weather permitting; $7), where hour-long tours of the old gold mine give an inkling of the subterranean perils faced by the town's early settlers.

HIKES IN THE CUYAMACA MOUNTAINS

Widely considered a four-season **hiking** area, the trails in the **Cuyamaca Mountains** seldom fall below 4500ft. Outside the summer months snow is always a possibility, and even in summer, nights are cool and thunderstorms common.

Cuyamaca Peak Trail (6 miles; 4hr; 1600ft ascent). Despite following the vehicle-free, paved Cuyamaca Peak Fire Road, this is the most rewarding of all the park's trails; a steep climb from either the *Paso Picacho* campsite (day-use fee) to a 6512-foot summit giving views east to the desert and west to the Pacific Ocean.

Harvey Moore Trail (12 miles; 7–8hr; 1000ft ascent). This well-signposted loop trail is relatively flat and winds through several ecological zones – prairie, oak woodland, meadowland and chaparral – all perfect territory for a cowboy such as Harvey Moore, the park's first superintendent in the 1930s. Starts a mile south of the park HQ.

Middle Peak (6 miles; 4hr; 1000ft ascent). There are several routes to Middle Peak, all easier than the Cuyamaca Peak Trail. The most direct is Sugar Pine Trail, named after the tall pines which bear the world's longest cones. The trail starts at the *Boy Scout* camp, ten miles south of Julian where the road turns sharply east at the end of the dammed Cuyamaca Lake.

Cuyamaca Rancho State Park

You could spend at least a few hours among the oaks, willows, sycamores, Ponderosa and Jeffrey pines that fill the **Cuyamaca Rancho State Park** (unrestricted entry), which starts nine miles south of Julian along Hwy-79. Even if you stay for days, you won't see everything: from lush sub-alpine meadows to stark mountain peaks, the park spans more than 25,000 acres, much of it designated wilderness area and only criss-crossed by a hundred miles of hiking trails (see box opposite), many of them hugging the 5000-foot contour.

Pick up information and maps, from the **park headquarters** (Mon–Fri 8am–5pm; ☎760/765-0755), sixteen miles south of Julian beside Hwy-79 in the heart of the park. At the same place, check the latest on the park's **campgrounds** strung along Hwy-79 (reservation through Parknet ☎1-800/444-7275; $12–16), chiefly *Paso Picacho*, twelve miles south of Julian, and *Green Valley*, five miles further south. These sites (where a $5 day-use fee is charged) are the only accommodation on offer unless you are prepared to hike into the $3 backcountry sites: *Arroyo Seco* is a mile and a half northwest of *Green Valley*, and *Granite Spring* is almost five miles east.

For some historical back-up to the scenery, drop into the excellent **museum** (Mon–Fri 10am–4pm, Sat & Sun 10am–2pm; free) in the park HQ, which details the formidable resistance of the local Native Americans to Spanish attempts to cut down the area's forests; this group also strongly resisted the arrival of settlers from the eastern US and was one of the last to be forced onto reservations. For more on the native peoples, take a stroll along the nature trails at Paso Picacho and at the park headquarters.

Tijuana and northern Baja California

TIJUANA has the odd distinction of being both one of the least culturally interesting places in Mexico, and one of the most visited cities in the world. Twenty million people a year cross the border here, most of them Californians and tourists on day-long shopping expeditions seeking somewhere cheap and colorful to spend money. And they find it: blankets, pottery, cigarettes, tequila, dentistry or car repair – everything is lower-priced in Tijuana than in the US (though more expensive than in the rest of Mexico), and all of it is hawked with enthusiasm.

What's most dramatic about Tijuana for first-time arrivals is the abrupt realization of the vast economic gulf separating the two countries. Crossing the *frontera*, or border, takes you past beggars crouched in corners and dirty children scuffling for change thrown by tourists. It's both a depressing and revealing experience. For regular visitors, however, it's a shock that soon fades; it's also unrepresentative of Tijuana itself which is, in fact, one of the wealthiest Mexican cities, thanks to the influx of well-heeled residents from Mexico City and the large number of international manufacturing companies who operate *maquiladoras* (factories) here to get a cheaper workforce.

Whatever its faults, Tijuana is, at least, quite unique, and you could hardly find a more intriguing day-trip out from San Diego. However, it's not typically Mexico, and if you want a proper taste of the country you'd do well to hurry on through. Things are much safer these days than was the case decades ago when Tijuana lived up to its rough border town image. Then prostitution was rife and the streets extremely creepy after dark; these days the red-light area is limited to the easily avoided blocks around the junction of Avenida Artícula and Mutualismo. Provided you take the usual amount of care there's little danger in most parts of town.

The main streets and shopping areas are a few blocks from the border in **downtown**, where the major thoroughfare is Avenida Revolución, lined with street vendors and people trying to hustle you into the shopping emporia. Stroll up and down for a while to get the mood and then retire to one of the plentiful bars and watch the throng in the

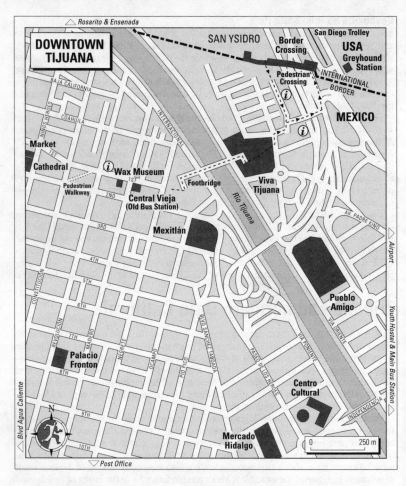

company of a sizeable margarita (in the bigger bars expect to pay $2.50 for a large one, $2 for a tequila and about $1.50 for a beer). At night, the action mostly consists of inebriated North American youths dancing themselves silly in flashy discos and rowdy rock 'n' roll bars – not hard to find around the main streets.

As a break from shopping or drinking, visit the **Centro Cultural**, sitting like a huge golf ball amid high-rise office towers on the corner of Paseo de los Héroes and Mina. The museum's permanent and rotating exhibits (daily 9am–8pm; $1) give strong accounts of Mexico's history and culture; films in the Omnimax Theater ($3.50, including museum admission) focus on Mexican landscapes and cityscapes.

Lesser attractions include **Mexitlán**, Avenida Ocampo between Calles 2 and 3 (Wed–Sun 9am–4pm; $4.50), a miniature Mexican theme park with models of famous Mexican buildings; a very tacky **wax museum** at Madero and First (don't waste your money); and lively *jai alai* – a Basque game similar to handball – at the Moorish-style Palacio Fronton on Avenida Revolucion at Calle 8 (Tues–Sun 8pm; $5).

Practicalities

Getting to Tijuana from San Diego could hardly be easier. The San Diego Trolley (see p.173) ends its route close to the elevated concrete walkway which leads over the border, as does bus #932 from the Santa Fe Depot in downtown San Diego. Mexicoach operates a bus service from the US side of the border to Avenida Revolucion in Tijuana.

Crossing into Mexico, **border formalities** are minimal: simply negotiate a turnstile and you're there. Customs and immigration checks are only carried out twenty miles or so inside the country, so you only need to be carrying a Mexican Tourist Card if you're continuing on from Tijuana. These are available free from any Mexican consulate in the US – see the phone book for the one nearest you – and also at the Mexican customs office just inside the Tijuana side of the border. Returning to the US, however, the formalities are as stringent as anywhere (see Basics, p.14). Even if you've just traveled down for the day, you will need to satisfy the usual entry requirements. Dollars are accepted as readily as pesos everywhere in Tijuana, but although you can **change money** at any of the banks along Avenida Revolución or at the *casas de cambio* on both sides of the border, it's only worth doing so if you're traveling further into Mexico. That said, you'll get marginally better prices if you do pay in pesos. Bánamex and the *casas de cambio* will change travelers' checks.

If you do want to sample Tijuana's discos into the small hours and stay overnight, the **accommodation** options are fairly good, if basic. You'll spend much less here for a **hotel** room than you would north of the border, and many passable lodgings can be found close to the central streets. At the lowest end of the price scale are *Hotel Nelson*, Avenida Revolucion 503 (☎66/85-43-03; ①), and *Hotel Caesar*, Avenida Revolucion at Calle 8 (☎66/85-16-06; ②). Slightly more upmarket, *La Villa de Zaragoza*, Avenida Madero 1120 (☎66/85-18-37; ③), has clean rooms with air-conditioning and cable TV.

Into Mexico

As for traveling further **into Mexico**, on the whole the northwest of the country has fewer cultural attractions than the mainland, and many people head straight for Mexico City and the regions beyond. A closer option, though, is the peninsula of **Baja California**, which has miles of unspoilt coast and a few moderately sized cities. The only sensible destinations within easy reach of Tijuana are **Rosarito**, *the* south-of-the-border party beach, and the sizeable town of **Ensenada**, your best introduction to more typical Mexican life. Both are briefly described overleaf, and for full details, pick up the *Rough Guide to Mexico*, most easily available in San Diego from Le Travel Store, 745 Fourth Ave (☎760/544-0005).

GETTING TO, AND AROUND, NORTHERN BAJA

Customs formalities present no problems for a quick trip to **northern Baja**: visitors to Tijuana, Rosarito and Ensenada staying for up to 72 hours need only their passports and are not required to obtain tourist cards. **Vehicle permits** are not required in Baja but most US rental agencies don't allow their vehicles into Mexico, so you'll need to approach companies such as Fuller Auto Rentals, 560 Auto Park Drive, Chula Vista (☎760/656-3370) who allow their cars to be taken as far south as Ensenada. With your own vehicle ensure you get **Mexican insurance**, easily obtainable from numerous companies whose fliers are all over San Ysidro: try Oscar Padilla's Drive-Thru, 110 Calle Primero (☎760/428-2221), or "Instant" Mexico, 223 Via de San Ysidro (☎1-800/345-4701 or 760/428-4717). All things considered, it's probably easier to get the bus.

Rosarito

Forty-five minutes south of Tijuana, on buses from Central Vieja bus terminal at First and Madero, the old coast road hits the sea at **ROSARITO** which boasts much the best beach in these parts. It is much more restful here than in Tijuana, but at weekends it has all-pervasive frat-house atmosphere. The town's landmark is the smart and once elegant *Rosarito Beach Hotel* (☎66/12-01-44; ④), to which Hollywood's Prohibition refugees fled for a little of the hard stuff in the Thirties. For cheaper **accommodation**, try *Cupalas del Mar* on Calle Victoria (☎66/12-24-90; ②), between Boulevard Juarez and the beach. There's no shortage of reasonable taco stands and inexpensive **restaurants**, many specializing in fish dishes: just wander along and gauge which seems currently the most popular. The weekend bonhomie is particularly frenzied at the beachside *Papas and Beer,* a bohemia-and-beach-volleyball bar.

Ensenada

Venturing to **ENSENADA**, two hours south from Tijuana's Central Vieja, brings a taste of the real Mexico. Cruise ships from San Diego dock here, and at weekends the bars are thronged with Americans, but otherwise Ensenada ticks by, gently milking dollars from *norteños* who have wised up to the town's superiority over Tijuana. On Avenida Mateos you'll find the majority of the bars, restaurants, souvenir shops and places organizing **fishing** trips. Drag yourself away for a little while to tour and taste the products of the Bodegas de Santo Tomás **winery** (tours Mon–Sat 11am, 1pm & 3pm, Sun 11am & 1pm; $1; ☎61/78-33-33) at Miramar 666 between Calle 6 and Calle 7. Sadly, most vintages aren't a patch on even run-of-the-mill offerings from north of the border. *La Esquina de Bodegas*, across the street from the winery, is a pleasant café/gallery and wine-shop annex. The other famous local attraction is **La Bufadora**, a natural blowhole six miles south of Ensenada, which occasionally spouts up to eighty feet, though thirty is more common. Buses leave roughly hourly from the Tres Cabezas park on the coast road at the bottom of Avenida Riveroll.

The pick of the **accommodation** (book at weekends) is the *San Nicolas*, Mateos at Guadalupe (☎61/76-49-30; ④); though *Motel America*, Mateos 1309 at Espinoza (☎61/76-13-33; ①), is decent. For **eating**, *Hussongs Cantina*, Ruiz 113 – famous throughout Southern California – has managed to maintain its rumbustious reputation and heaves at weekends. Soak up the beer with fish tacos from the **fish market** by the harbor, or the straightforward Mexican dishes at *El Charro*, Mateos 475.

travel details

Trains

San Diego to: Anaheim (9 daily; 2hr); Solana Beach (nr Del Mar; 10 daily; 30–40 min); Los Angeles downtown (10 daily; 2hr 45min to 3 hr 20min); Oceanside (10 daily; 45min to 1hr); San Clemente (1 daily; 1hr 15min); San Juan Capistrano (9 daily; 1hr 15min to 2hr).

Buses

San Diego downtown to: Anaheim (8 daily; 2hr 30min); Long Beach (7 daily; 2hr 30min); Los Angeles downtown (26 daily; 2hr); Oceanside (16 daily; 55min); San Clemente (6 daily; 1hr 30min).

San Diego, Grossmont Center to: Cumacaca (6 monthly; 2hr 30min); Julian (1 weekly; 2hr); Ramona (1 daily; 45min); Santa Ysabel (1 daily; 1hr 30min).

International buses

San Diego to: Tijuana (21 daily; 50min).

CHAPTER THREE

THE DESERTS, LAS VEGAS AND THE GRAND CANYON

T he **deserts** of Southern California represent only a fraction of the half a million square miles of North American Desert that stretch away eastwards into another four states and cross the border into Mexico in the south. Contrary to the monotonous landscape you might expect, California's deserts are a varied and ever-changing kaleidoscope, dotted with everything from harsh settlements to posh resorts. The one thing you can rely on is that, for a large part of the year, they will be uniformly hot and dry – though desert rainfall is highly irregular, and a whole year's average of three or four inches may fall in a single storm.

Most of the 25 million acres that make up the desert are protected in state and national parks, but not all are entirely unspoiled. Three million acres are used by the US Government as military bases for training and weapons testing, and when underground nuclear explosions aren't shaking up the desert's fragile ecosystem, the region's many fans flock here to do their damage.

In spite of this, most of the desert remains a wilderness, and with a little foresight
could be the undisputed highlight of your trip. Occupying a quarter of the state,
California's desert divides into two distinct regions: the **Colorado** or **Low Desert** in
the south, stretching down to the Mexican border and east into Arizona where it's an
extension of the Sonoran Desert, and the **Mojave** or **High Desert**, which covers the
south-central part of the state. The Low Desert is the most easily reached from LA, with
the extravagantly wealthy **Palm Springs** serving as an access point – though, pulling
in the likes of Donald Trump for events like the Bob Hope Chrysler Classic Golf
Tournament, it's the kind of town where it helps to have a bankroll for optimum enjoyment. The hiking trails around **Joshua Tree** are the big attraction for serious desert
people, bridging the divide between Low and High Desert in a vast silent area of craggy trees. In contrast, **Imperial Valley** to the south – agricultural land, though you could
pass through without realizing anyone lived there – and the **Salton Sea** beyond, are
undiluted Low Desert. There's no reason to visit them except that they lead into the
vast expanse of the **Anza-Borrego Desert**, the largest state park in the country, boasting multifarious varieties of vegetation and geological quirks which can, with a little
effort, be as rewarding as the better-known deserts to the north.

Interstate 10 crosses the Low Desert from east to west and carries a considerable flow
of traffic. This includes packs of bikers heading out for a long weekend ride and some
high jinks in the popular gambling resorts, like **Lake Havasu City**, that dot the stunning **Colorado River** region on the California/Arizona border. I-15 cuts north from I-10
at **Barstow**, often a first stop for those heading into the High Desert, where the **Mojave
National Preserve** makes a worthwhile natural detour en route to the unnatural neon
oasis of **Las Vegas**, just across the border in Nevada, where gambling is legal. Once
you've got that far, a day's drive east (or a thirty-minute flight) takes you to the magnificent **Grand Canyon** in Arizona. Afterwards you can loop back into California by way of
Death Valley, part of the desert region but covered in Chapter Four.

Desert practicalities

Public transportation in the desert is poor to non-existent: Los Angeles connects
easily with the major points – Palm Springs, Barstow, Las Vegas – and the Anza-
Borrego is an easy trip from San Diego, but on arrival you're stuck without your own
vehicle. If you do have a car, it will need to be in very good working order – don't rely
on the Thunderbird you picked up in LA for $250 to get you through the worst of the
desert. Three major interstate highways cross the desert from east to west: I-15 cuts
directly through the middle of the Mojave on its way from Los Angeles to Las Vegas,
joined at Barstow by I-40, which then heads eastwards to the Grand Canyon, while I-
10 takes you from LA through the Palm Springs and Joshua Tree area, heading into
Arizona. Some fast, empty, secondary roads can get you safely to all but the most

remote areas of the desert, but be wary of using the lower-grade roads in between, which are likely to be unmaintained and are often only passable by four-wheel drive. Other than in the Palm Springs area, **motels** in the California deserts are low in price, and you can generally budget for under $40 per night. However, even if cost is no object, you'll get a greatly heightened sense of the desert experience by spending some time **camping** out.

THE LOW DESERT

Despite the **Low Desert**'s hundreds of miles of beauty and empty highways, most visitors to the region have no intention of getting away from it all. They're heading for where it's at, **Palm Springs**, a few square miles overrun with the famous, the starstruck, the ageing and the aspirational. It is said, not completely in jest, that the average age and average temperature of Palm Springs are about the same – a steady 88. This is a town that fines home owners who don't maintain their property to what local officials deem to be a suitable standard. But it's got a prime location, and you'll find it hard to avoid: it's the first stopping point east from LA on I-10, and hub of a resort area – the **Coachella Valley** – that stretches out for miles around, along Hwy-111. The valley's farming communities have the distinction of forming part of the most productive irrigated agricultural center in the world, growing dates, oranges, lemons and grapefruit in vast quantities, though sadly they're steadily giving way to the condos and complexes that comprise Palm Springs' ever-growing industry.

Fortunately you don't have to travel impossible distances to see the desert at its natural best. **Joshua Tree**, one of the most startling of California's National Parks, lies one hour's drive east of Palm Springs, three and a half from LA. A day-trip in a fast car would give you a taste, but you really need a couple of days to get to grips with Joshua Tree's sublime landscape, taking in the sunsets and the howl of coyotes at twilight. The desert east of the park, to the Colorado River and Nevada, and south to the Mexican border, is arid and uncomfortable, with only the highly saline **Salton Sea** to break the monotony. A drive in this direction is rewarded, however, by the **Anza-Borrego desert**, southwest of Joshua Tree, whose starkly beautiful vistas are punctuated by several oases and unusual vegetation.

Palm Springs and around

With its manicured golf courses, condominium complexes and some seven hundred millionaires in residence, **PALM SPRINGS** does not conform to any typical image of the desert. Purpose-built for luxury and leisure, it tends to attract conspicuous consumers and comfort seekers rather than the scruffier desert rats and low-rent retirees of less geographically desirable areas. But though it may seem harder to find the natural attractions and reasonably priced essentials among the glitz, they do exist.

Palm Springs and its adjacent resort towns sit in the lushest agricultural area of the Colorado Desert, with the massive bulk of the San Jacintos and neighboring mountain ranges looming over its low-level buildings, casting an instantaneous and welcome shadow over the area in the late afternoon. Since Hollywood stars were spotted enjoying a bit of mineral rejuvenation out here in the 1930s, it has taken on a celebrity status all its own, a symbol of good LA living away from the amorphous, smoggy city. In recent years it has also become a major **gay** resort, with many exclusively gay – and generally expensive – hotels, bars and restaurants. Every Easter weekend twenty thousand

DESERT SURVIVAL

To survive the rigors of the desert, you have to be cool in more ways than one. Don't let adventure get the better of you and go charging off into the wilderness without heeding the warnings. The desert is rarely conquered by a pioneering spirit alone and every year people die here. **Hikers** are particularly vulnerable, especially those who venture beyond the designated areas of the National Parks, but **drivers** too should not be blasé and should take considerable precautions whatever their destination. On the highways, extra water and as full a tank of gas as possible should be all the precautions you need, but anything more adventurous requires planning. Above all, think. Tell somebody where you are going, and your expected time of return. Carry an extra two days' **food** and **water** and never go anywhere without a **map**. Only the well-prepared can enjoy the desert with any sense of security.

CLIMATE AND WATER

First and most obviously you're up against a pretty formidable **climate**. This varies from region to region, but the basic safety procedures remain the same: not only are you doing battle with incredible heat, but at high elevations at night you should be prepared for below-freezing temperatures too. Between May and September, when daytime temperatures frequently exceed 120°F, you really shouldn't come at all (although, of course, people do).

Outside of the summer months, the daytime temperature is more manageable, ranging between the mid-sixties and low nineties. At any time of year, you'll stay cooler during the day if you wear full-length sleeves and trousers, though you'll look incongruous among the bare legs and torsos. Also, a wide-brimmed hat and a pair of good sunglasses will spare you the blinding headaches that can result from the desert light.

You can never drink enough **liquid** in the desert: the body loses up to a gallon each day and even when you're not thirsty you are continually dehydrating and should keep drinking. Before setting off on any expedition, whether on foot or in a car, two gallons of water per person should be prepared; one is an absolute minimum, and don't save it for the walk back, drink it as you need it. Waiting for thirst, dizziness, nausea or other signs of dehydration before doing anything can be dangerous. If you notice any of these symptoms, or feel weak and have stopped sweating, it's time to get to the doctor. Watch your alcohol intake too: if you must booze during the day, compensate heavily with pints of water between each drink. Any activity in this heat can be exhausting so you also need to **eat** well, packing in the carbohydrates.

Campers need to take particular heed of these warnings, especially if backpacking away from the main roads. In summer, ventures of more than one night are all but impossible as you end up having to carry more water than is comfortable. In the valleys, you may also have to contend with **flash floods**, which can appear from nowhere: an innocent-looking dark cloud can turn a dry wash into a raging river. Never camp in a dry wash and don't attempt to cross flooded areas until the water has receded.

ROADS: ON WHEELS AND ON FOOT

Roads and **highways** across much of the desert are not maintained, and in an area where it's often a challenge to make it across existing dirt roads, trailblazing your own path through the desert is insanity. Of course you'll be tempted – if you must, rent a dune buggy or four-wheel drive and tear about one of the off-road driving areas specifically designated for this purpose.

Even sticking to the main highways, you stand a good chance of getting an **overheated engine**. If your car's temperature needle rises alarmingly, most likely when negotiating steep gradients, turn the air-conditioning off and the heater on full-blast to cool the engine quickly. If this fails and the engine blows, stop with the car facing into the wind and the engine running, pour water over the radiator grille and top up the water reservoir. In an **emergency**, never leave the car: you'll be harder to find wandering around alone.

Among other things you might consider taking along, an **emergency pack** with flares, a first aid and **snakebite kit** (see below), matches and a compass, a shovel, a tyre pump and extra gas are always a good idea. A few white towels to drape over the dashboard, steering wheel and back ledge will save you a lot of discomfort when you get back in your car after leaving it parked for a few hours.

When **hiking**, try and cover most of your ground in the early morning: the midday heat is too debilitating, and you shouldn't even think about it when the mercury goes over 90°F. Almost all parks will require you to register with them – this is very wise, especially for those who are hiking alone. If you get lost, find some shade and wait. So long as you've registered, the rangers will eventually come and fetch you. However, they'll have a lot of trouble if you've fallen down an old mine shaft, so watch your footing and keep your eyes peeled for unexploded artillery.

DESERT WILDLIFE

Most people's biggest fear of the desert is of encountering **poisonous creatures**. If you do, you'll be far better served by strong boots and long trousers than sports sandals and shorts. Not only do they offer some protection in case of attack, but firm footfalls send vibrations through the ground giving ample warning of your approach. Walk heavily and you're unlikely to see anything you don't want to.

Of all the **snakes** in the California desert, only the rattlesnake is poisonous. You might not be able to tell a rattler from any other kind of snake; in fact many rattlers don't rattle at all. If in doubt, assume it is one. When it's hot, snakes lurk in shaded areas under bushes, around wood debris, old mining shafts and piles of rocks. When it's cooler, they sun themselves out in the open, but they won't be expecting you and if disturbed will attack. While **black widow spiders** and **scorpions** are non-aggressive, they are extremely venomous and easily disturbed. A bite from any of the above is initially like a sharp pin-prick, but within hours the pain becomes severe, usually accompanied by swelling and acute nausea. Forget any misconceptions you may harbor about sucking the poison out; it doesn't work and even tends to hasten the spread of venom. Since this travels mainly through the lymph system just under the skin, the best way of inhibiting the diffusion is to wrap the whole limb firmly, but not in a tourniquet, then contact a ranger or doctor as soon as possible. Do all you can to keep calm – a slower pulse rate limits the spread of the venom. Keep in mind that even if you do get bitten by a snake, about fifty percent of the time it's a dry – or non-venomous – strike. Snakes don't want to waste their venom on something too large to eat. However, it's a wise precaution to carry a **snakebite kit**, available for a couple of dollars from most sports and camping stores.

Tarantulas are not at all dangerous. A leg span of up to seven inches means they're pretty easy to spot, but if you're unlucky and get bitten don't panic – cleansing with antiseptic is usually sufficient treatment once you've got over the initial pain.

Nasty critters aren't the only things to avoid. Most **cactuses** present few problems, but you should keep an eye out for the eight-foot *cholla* (pronounced choya), or jumping cholla as they're called because of the way segments seem to jump off and attach themselves to you if you brush past. Don't use your hands to get them off, you'll just spear all your fingers; instead use a stick or comb to flick off the largest piece and remove the remaining spines with tweezers. The large pancake pads of prickly pear cactus are also worth avoiding: as well as the larger spines they have thousands of tiny, hair-like stickers that are almost impossible to remove. You should expect a day of painful irritation before they begin to wear away. For more on the delights of desert flora and fauna, see Contexts, p.596.

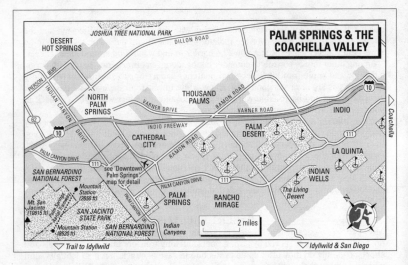

gay men flock here for the "White Party", four days of hedonism centered on the *Wyndham* and *Marquis* hotels in downtown Palm Springs. **Lesbians** get their turn a couple of weeks earlier during the Nabisco Dinah Shore women's golf tournament.

For years, high-school kids arrived in their thousands, too, for the drunken revelry of Spring Break (around the end of March and beginning of April). Local antipathy finally persuaded the city council, under the leadership of the late Sonny Bono, to ban the annual invasion in 1993, and the inebriated youth promptly decamped east to Lake Havasu City (see p.237). The alcoholically inclined still flock to Palm Springs, but not to get drunk: the **Betty Ford Center**, smack in the middle of the valley at Rancho Mirage, draws a star-studded patient list to its booze- and drug-free environment, attempting to undo a lifetime's behavioural disorders in a $11,000 month-long stay.

The town's siting is superb, surrounded by the beautiful Indian Canyons with the snowcapped mountains behind. Meteorologists have noted changes in the humidity of the desert climate around the town which they attribute to the moisture absorbed from the hundreds of swimming pools – the consummate condo accoutrement, and the only place you're likely to want to be during the day if you come in the hotter months. When scarce water supplies aren't being used to fill the pools or nourish the nearby orchards, each of Palm Springs' vast golf-course complexes receives around a million gallons daily to maintain their rolling green pastures.

Palm Springs wasn't always like this. Before the wealthy settlers moved in it was the domain of the **Cahuilla**, who lived and hunted around the San Jacinto Mountains, to escape the heat of the desert floor. They still own much of the town, and via an odd checkerboard system of land allotment, every other square mile of Palm Springs is theirs and forms part of the **Agua Caliente Indian Reservation** – a Spanish name which means "hot water", referring to the ancient mineral springs on which the city rests. The land was allocated to the tribe in the 1890s, but exact zoning was never settled until the 1940s, by which time the development of hotels and leisure complexes was well under way. The Cahuilla, finding their land built upon, were left with no option but to charge rent, a system that has made them the second richest of the native tribes in America – worth, by the latest estimates, more than $2 billion. If anything, it looks like their purses will be growing fatter still: they recently opened Palm Springs' first casino in the spa whose underground waters originally gave the town its name.

THE WINDMILLS OF PALM SPRINGS

After trawling through the dull eastern suburbs of Los Angeles, I-10 throws you a surprise at the San Gorgonio Pass just before Palm Springs. Over four thousand **wind turbines** dot the valley, their glinting steel arms sending shimmering patterns across the desert floor. This is the largest concentration of windmills in the country, generating enough electricity to service a small city, and the conditions are perfect. The sun beating down on the desert creates a low pressure zone which sucks air up from the cooler coastal valleys, funnelling it through the San Gorgonio Pass, the only break between two 10,000-foot-plus ranges of mountains. Strong winds often howl for days in spring and early summer, reaching an average speed of between fourteen and twenty miles per hour. You'll learn more than you ever wanted to know about these structures and about alternative energy in general if you book one of the surprisingly interesting ninety-minute **Windfarm Tours** (☎760/251-1997), conducted via wind-powered golf cart ($20). Even if you don't do the tour, stop in at the new windfarm visitors center (get off I-10 at the Indian Road exit; it's on the north frontage road, one mile west of Indian Road) to see all kinds of unusual electric vehicles.

Arrival, information and getting around

Palm Springs lies 110 miles east of Los Angeles along the Hwy-111 turn-off from I-10. Arriving by **car**, you drive into town on N Palm Canyon Drive (Hwy-111), the main thoroughfare. Coming by **bus**, you'll arrive at the Greyhound terminus at 311 N Indian Canyon Drive, linked with LA ten times daily – a three-hour journey. **Trains** from LA stop in Indio (at Jackson and Railroad Avenue) and Palm Springs (N Indian Avenue, just south of I-10) on Tuesday, Friday, and Sunday, unfortunately in the middle of the night. You can also **fly**, but this can be expensive – you'll land at the Palm Springs Regional Airport, 3400 E Tahquitz-McCallum Way (☎760/323-8161), from where you take bus #21 into town.

The very helpful **visitor center**, 2781 N Palm Canyon Drive (daily 9am–5pm; ☎760/778-8418), can offer accommodation deals and has an exhaustive selection of maps – including one that details the homes of the famous ($5) – and brochures, plus various "what's on" guides.

Travel to the resorts around Palm Springs – **Cathedral City**, **Desert Hot Springs**, **Rancho Mirage**, **Palm Desert**, **Indio**, **Indian Wells**, **La Quinta** – is possible with the Sun Bus (☎760/343-3456), which operates daily from 6am to 8pm (until 11pm on some routes) and charges 75¢ to get around town, plus 25¢ for each additional zone beyond; a day pass costs $3. It's unlikely that you'll need to use the bus to get around Palm Springs itself: downtown is no more than several blocks long and wide, and except in the summer heat, walking is easy. For a **taxi**, call Checker Cabs (☎760/325-2868).To get the absolute best out of Palm Springs and the surrounding towns though, you might think about **car rental**. Aztec Rent-A-Car, 477 S Palm Canyon Drive (☎760/325-2294) has cars for as little as $30 per day ($150 a week), while Foxy Wheels, 440 S El Cielo Rd (☎760/321-1234), also has good deals.

Accommodation

Palm Springs was designed for the rich, and big luxury **resorts** are abundant there and in most of the Coachella Valley's other towns. If you want to take a shot at seeing how the other half lives, consider visiting in summer when temperatures rise and prices drop dramatically. Many of the bigger hotels slash their prices by up to seventy percent, and even the smaller concerns give twenty to thirty percent off. The visitor center (see above) also offers special deals. If you couldn't care less about cachet, Motel 6 (five of them) and other **low-priced chains** are represented.

CENTRAL PALM SPRINGS

ACCOMMODATION
1 Avanti Resort
2 Bee Charmer Inn
3 Budget Host Inn
4 Casa Cody
5 Casa Rosa
6 Desert Lodge
7 Ingleside Inn
8 Mira Loma
9 Motel 6
10 Palm Court Inn
11 Quality Inn
12 Vagabond Inn
13 Villa Hotel
14 Villa Royale
15 The Willows

LITTLE TUSCANY

Palm Springs Visitor Center

O'Donnell Golf Course

Palm Springs Desert Museum

Greyhound Station

Spa Hotel, Casino & Mineral Springs

Adagio Gallery

Palm Springs Swim Center

Palm Springs Regional Airport

Moorten's Botanical Gardens

Smoke Tree Stables

Canyon Golf Club

Palm Springs Aerial Tramway

Oasis Water Park

13 & Cathedral City

Indian Canyons

SAN RAFAEL
FRANCIS DRIVE
VERONA
RACQUET CLUB ROAD
VISTA CHINO WAY
WEST VEREDA SUR
TACHEVAH ROAD
TAMARISK ROAD
ALEJO ROAD
AMADO ROAD
TAHQUITZ CANYON WAY
BARISTO ROAD
RAMON RD
WARM SANDS DRIVE
SUNNY DUNES ROAD
MESQUITE AVENUE
SONORA ROAD
EAST PALM CANYON DRIVE
LAVERNE WAY
MURRAY CANYON DRIVE

NORTH PALM CANYON DRIVE
INDIAN CANYON DRIVE
PALM CANYON DRIVE
AVENIDA CABALLEROS
SUNRISE WAY
FARRELL DRIVE
SOUTH CAHUILLA RD
CALLE EL SEGUNDO
CALLE ENCILIA
GRENFALL ROAD
EL CIELO
SOUTH PALM CANYON DRIVE
SOUTH PALM CANYON TRAIL
TOLEDO AVENUE

N

0   1 mile

The north end of town along Hwy-111 holds the most affordable places, in the main perfectly acceptable and all with pools. **Bed and breakfast** inns are becoming more common, and with double room rates at around $80 per night are the best bargains. If you're traveling in a group, it may work out cheaper to rent an **apartment**: many of the homes in Palm Springs are used only for a brief spell and are let out for the rest of the year. Again summer is the best time to look, but there is generally a good supply throughout the year. The Coachella Valley's daily paper, the *Desert Sun*, has rental information in its classified pages, and many rental agencies operate around town – the visitor center will be able to point you to the more affordable ones. **Camping** is not really a viable option, unless you have an RV; the only tent site is *Lake Cahuilla* (☎1-800/234-PARK or 760/564-4712) in La Quinta, some six miles east of central Palm Springs. Otherwise, tent-carriers will have a better time exploring Joshua Tree or Borrego.

Listed below are some of the more reasonable and/or interesting options, with summer rates quoted; in the popular October to April period, when you should also book in advance, you can expect the rates to be hiked up by a price bracket – or two or three. Some historical quirk of snobbery on the part of the city council dictates that accommodation can't be referred to as a motel, though some of the places listed obviously are.

Palm Springs now claims to have taken over from Key West as America's largest gay resort and has around 35 exclusively **gay hotels**, most of them in the Warm Sands district, half a mile southwest of downtown. However, such is the power of the pink dollar in Palm Springs that virtually all hotels here are gay-friendly.

Hotels, motels and B&Bs

Budget Host Inn, 1277 S Palm Canyon Drive (☎1-800/829-8099 or 760/325-5574). The cheapest place in town but still with clean, pleasant rooms, cable and a pool. ②.

Casa Cody, 175 S Cahuilla Rd, downtown (☎1-800/231-2639 or 760/320-9346). Built in the 1920s by glamorous Hollywood pioneer Harriet Cody, this is the town's second oldest hotel, offering tastefully furnished Southwestern-style rooms, a shady garden, great pool and wonderful breakfasts in a good location two blocks from downtown. Large kitchen suites also available. ⑤.

Desert Lodge, 1177 S Palm Canyon Drive (☎1-800/385-6343 or 760/325-1356). Spacious motel-style place with free continental breakfast and in-room movies. ②.

Ingleside Inn, 200 W Ramon Rd, downtown (☎760/325-0046). Expensive, but with real class, having attracted such guests as Garbo, Dali and Brando over the years. Built on a private estate, each room has a personal steam bath and individual whirlpool. The restaurant still lures the glitterati. ⑥.

Mira Loma, 1420 N Indian Canyon Drive (☎760/320-1178). Small, welcoming hotel with well-appointed rooms around a central pool where breakfast is served at weekends. In 1949 Marilyn Monroe stayed in Room 3 while awaiting her big break. ④.

Motel 6, 660 S Palm Canyon Drive (☎760/327-4200). The most central of the budget motels, with a good pool. ②.

Palm Court Inn, 1983 N Palm Canyon Drive (☎1-800/667-7918 or 760/416-2333). On four nicely landscaped acres, so it doesn't feel like a faceless motel. There's a jacuzzi as well as a nice size pool, and continental breakfast is included in the room rate. ③.

Quality Inn, 1269 E Palm Canyon Drive (☎1-800/288-5151 or 760/323-2775). Modern motel with spacious grounds and restaurant. ②.

The Willows, 412 W Tahquitz Canyon (☎760/320-0771). The former estate of a US Secretary of State whose friends – among them Clark Gable, Carole Lombard, and Albert Einstein – holed up here during the 1930s. Opulently decorated rooms, gorgeous lush grounds, a stunning San Jacinto Mountain backdrop, and an ideal downtown location make this worth the splurge. ⑦.

Vagabond Inn, 1699 S Palm Canyon Drive (☎1-800/522-1555 or 760/325-7211). Well-run three-story motel halfway between downtown Palm Springs and Cathedral City with its own reasonably priced coffee shop. ②.

Villa Royale, 1620 S Indian Trail (☎1-800/245-2314 or 760/327-2314). Beautiful inn with individually designed and exquisitely furnished rooms and suites, most with jacuzzi, ranged around a pool. In the winter season meals and drinks are served from the bougainvillea-draped restaurant. ④.

Exclusively gay accommodation

Avanti Resort, 715 San Lorenzo Rd (☎1-800/572-2779 or 760/325-9723). One of the least costly of the Warm Sands hotels, with an emphasis on fun. ③.

Bee Charmer Inn, 1600 E Palm Canyon Drive (☎760/778-5883). Lesbian motel a mile or so south of downtown, offering continental breakfast and pool. ④.

Casa Rosa, 589 Grenfall Rd (☎1-800/322-4151 or 760/322-4143). Oddly decorated but comfortable suites ranged around the pool where "natural sunbathing" is encouraged. Breakfast served poolside or in your room. ④.

The Villa Hotel, 67-670 Carey Rd, Cathedral City (☎1-800/845-5265 or 760/328-7211). The area's largest gay resort, attracting an older, less party-oriented crowd. Rooms are spacious. ③.

Palm Springs

Downtown Palm Springs stretches for about half a mile along Palm Canyon Drive, a wide, bright and modern strip full of boutiques and restaurants that's engulfed the town's original Spanish village-style structures. Shops run the gamut from Saks Fifth Avenue to shlocky T-shirt emporia and bookstores devoted exclusively to Hollywood stars. Ditto restaurants, which range from casual sports bars to overdressed Continental eateries with jacked-up prices. Should your budget not run to the conventional extravagance of a luxury stay in Palm Springs, there are a handful of things to do that won't break the bank. The attractive **Palm Springs Desert Museum**, 101 Museum Drive (Tues–Sat 10am–5pm, Sun noon–5pm; $7.50), is a part-art, part-natural history collection that's especially strong on Native American and Southwestern art – its holdings are so large, in fact, that despite the enormous exhibition space, only a small part can be shown at any given time. The only permanent display is the late actor William Holden's collection of Asian and African art. The natural science exhibits focus on the variety of animal and plant life in the desert, proving that it's not all sandstorms and rattlesnakes. Also inside the museum, the Annenberg Theater has a seasonal program of shows, films and classical concerts (10am–4pm; ☎760/325-4490).

The concentration of wealth in Palm Springs has fostered a disproportionate number of **art galleries**, not all of them good, along and around Palm Canyon Drive. The Adagio Gallery, 193 S Palm Canyon Drive (☎760/320-2239), is perhaps the most impressive, with the largest collection of Latino and Southwest art on the coast.

Downtown's most anarchic piece of landscape gardening can be seen at **Moorten Botanical Garden**, 1701 S Palm Canyon Drive (Mon–Sat 9am–4.30pm, Sun 10am–4pm; $2), a bizarre cornucopia of every desert plant and cactus, lumped together in no particular order, but interesting for those who won't be venturing beyond town to see them in their natural habitat.

Knowing that they're in the thick of a megastar refugee camp, few can resist the opportunity to see the homes and country clubs of the international elite on a **celebrity tour**. As tacky as they are, these tours have some voyeuristic appeal, allowing you to spy on places like Bob Hope's enormous home, and the star-studded area known as **Little Tuscany** – Palm Spring's prettiest quarter, where the famous keep their weekend homes. The best part of the tour is not the houses, but the fascinating trivia about the lives of those who live in them. Several companies offer these excursions, the best of them being Palm Springs Celebrity Tours, 4751 E Palm Canyon Drive (☎760/770-2700), which conducts one-hour jaunts for $12 and longer excursions around the country clubs and the Sinatra estate (where Frank used to bring Ava Gardner) for $17. Of course if you've got a car, you can do it yourself with a $5 map of the stars' homes from the visitor center (see p.215), but you'll miss the sharp anecdotal commentary that makes it such fun.

One reason people come here is to enjoy the Californian obsession with all things physical, and get fit. The **mineral spring** that the Cahuilla discovered on the desert floor over a century ago has grown into the elaborate *Spa Hotel and Casino and Mineral Springs* complex, 100 N Indian Ave (daily 8am–7pm; ☎1-800/854-1279 or 760/325-1461). The "basic spa experience" is $19.55, an all-day pass that includes use of the pool and eucalyptus room, although you're encouraged to spend a lot more at the on-site casino. Just as therapeutic is a swim in the **Olympic-sized pool** in the Palm Springs Swim Center, Sunrise Way at Ramon Road (daily 11am–5pm, later in summer; $3; ☎760/323-8278), a good alternative to the often crowded, and generally small hotel pools. Lots more water gets used up at the 22-acre playground **Oasis Waterpark**, at 1500 Gene Autry Trail between Ramon Road and E Palm Canyon Drive (daily 11am till dusk March 14–Labor Day; 11am till dusk weekends through Oct 19; ☎760/327-0499) where, for $18, you can surf on its one-acre wavepool and mess around on its eight adult waterslides. For a seriously sybaritic experience, check out one of Palm Springs' **day spas**. The Guest House, 246 N Palm Canyon Drive (☎760/320-3366) offers everything from reflexology massages ($30) to the Twin Palms Salt Glow ($100), where two masseuses pummel and soothe you simultaneously.

A hard core of desert enthusiasts visit Palm Springs for the **hiking** and **riding** opportunities in the **Indian Canyons** (daily: spring & summer 8am–6pm; fall & winter 8am–5pm; $5), on part of the **Agua Caliente Indian Reservation** that lies to the east of downtown. Centuries ago, ancestors of the Cahuilla tribe settled in the canyons and developed extensive communities, made possible by the good water supply and animal stock. Crops of melons, squash, beans and corn were grown, animals hunted and plants and seeds gathered for food and medicines. Evidence of this remains, and despite the near extinction of some breeds, mountain sheep and wild ponies still roam the remoter areas. To reach the best of them, follow S Palm Canyon Drive about three miles southeast to the clearly signposted entrance. Of the three canyons here, **Palm Canyon** and **Andreas Canyon** are very beautiful and have the easiest hiking trails. About fifteen miles long, they're surprisingly lush oases of waterfalls, rocky gorges and palm trees, easily toured by car, although to appreciate them at their best, you should get out and walk for at least a few miles. A tiny trading post at Palm Canyon sells hiking maps, refreshments, and even raccoon hats, though to indulge in real Wild West fantasy you should see things on **horseback**. The Smoke Tree Stables, 2500 Toledo Ave (☎760/327-1372), offer scheduled one- and two-hour riding tours of the Canyons at $25 per hour – well worth it, especially if you go early morning (tours start from 7am) to escape the midday heat. Longer rides are available by advance arrangement.

Sections of the canyons and surrounding land are set aside for the specific lunacy of **trailblazing** in jeeps and four-wheel drives. If you're a good, experienced driver with nerves of steel (or know one), you should rent your own from OffRoad Rentals, 59755 Hwy-111 (Sept–June only; ☎760/325-0376), about four miles north of the Palm Springs tram ($25 per hour, including instruction on manoeuvring). For those who can't face the driving and want to learn something about the area while zooming through it, the **guided jeep adventure** is probably nearer the mark: Desert Adventures, 67-555 E Palm Canyon Drive, Cathedral City (☎760/324-JEEP), offer excellent tours of the Santa Rosa mountains for around $70 for two hours, or $100 for half a day. One of its most popular tours takes you across the desert floor and two thousand feet up through bighorn sheep preserves, spectacular cliffs and steep-walled canyons. It's a bit expensive, but brilliant fun for the fearless.

The other Coachella Valley cities

Many visitors to the area think of the Coachella Valley towns strung along Hwy-111 as a single sprawling resort named Palm Springs. The towns are initially somewhat hard to distinguish from each other – not all the boundaries between them are clearly marked and, on their main drags, they tend to share faceless low-slung architecture – but differences become evident to those who have time to explore.

About twelve miles north of Palm Springs – the only one of the towns that's on the other side of I-10, separated by a fault line – the city of **DESERT HOT SPRINGS** was chosen in a national competition as having the best-tasting water in the country. The underground wells for which the town is named supply water for the multitude of swimming pools as well as for drinking. A good jumping-off point for Joshua Tree, it's somewhat more casual than the other communities.

Adjacent to Palm Springs, about five miles east along Hwy-111, is **Cathedral City** ("Cat City"), named for soaring rock formations that are now, sadly, obscured by development. There are further changes slated for this town, which should be getting an **IMAX theater**, a **sports complex** with three stadiums, and a valley-wide **visitors center** in the next few years. Although it's fairly family-oriented during the day, it comes out at night with a **gay scene** that's second only to the one in Palm Springs itself.

Next in line, the generally more staid **RANCHO MIRAGE** tends to attract dignitaries – and high-profile substance abusers. Home to former President Gerald Ford and his wife, it's also host to the latter's upscale drunk tank, the **Betty Ford Center**.

PALM DESERT, directly east along Hwy-111, is the safest place to witness the animal life that flourishes despite the inhospitable climate. Here, the **Living Desert**, 47-900 Portola Ave (Sept to mid-June daily 9am–5pm; $7), is home to coyotes, foxes, bighorn sheep, snakes, gazelles and eagles, on view around a series of trails that cover the 1200-acre park. There's also a **botanical garden**, but this is only worth a look in spring when the desert is in bloom. You can glimpse a different species of local creature on **El Paseo**, the Rodeo Drive of the desert, a long strip of **trendy restaurants** and **shops** looping south of Hwy-111. And come November, the non-indigenous but increasingly populous species *homo golfus* turns out en masse for the nation's only **golf cart parade**.

Adjacent **INDIAN WELLS** has the largest per capita income in the US, as well as the largest concentration of the Coachella Valley's grand **resorts**. It's known for its four-day New Year **Jazz Festival**, its high profile **tennis tournaments**, and its prestigious Desert Town Hall **lecture series**, four or five talks that run into spring (Margaret Thatcher took part in January 1998 and Princess Di was scheduled to have spoken in 1997).

Next comes **LA QUINTA**, named for the Valley's first **exclusive resort**, built in 1927 and thriving during the Depression, when Hollywood's escapist popularity rose as the country's income fell. Director Frank Capra wrote the script for multiple Academy Award winner *It Happened One Night* here in 1934, and considered the place so lucky he kept coming back, bringing the likes of Greta Garbo in his wake. It's still so posh

THE AERIAL TRAMWAY

When the desert heat becomes simply too much to bear, you can travel through five climatic zones from the arid desert floor to snow-covered alpine hiking trails on top of Mount San Jacinto on the **Palm Springs Aerial Tramway** on Tramway Drive, just off Hwy-111 north of Palm Springs (Mon–Fri 10am–8pm, Sat & Sun 8am–8pm; $17.65). Every thirty minutes large cable cars grind and sway over nearly six thousand feet to the Mountain Station near the 10,815ft summit. Literally breathtaking, it's well worth the nerve-wracking fourteen-minute ascent for both the view, some 75 miles all the way to the Salton Sea, and the welcome change from the blistering heat to temperatures that drop an average of 30°F. Cinder trails stretch for a couple of miles around, leading into the 13,000-acre Mt San Jacinto Park, a wilderness area through which, in a few hours, you can reach Idyllwild (on the Devil's Slide; see opposite). From November 15 through April 15, snow conditions permitting, the **Nordic Ski Center** operates. There's a **bar** and **restaurant** at the Mountain Station where, for a $4 voucher, you can eat as much as you want.

that it's not marked on the main road (take Washington Street south to Eisenhower to find it). The Santa Rosa Mountain backdrop is stunning, and the rich no longer get very duded up, so you won't feel out of place if you come for a drink at the piano lounge.

In stark contrast is neighboring **INDIO**, a low-key town whose agricultural roots show in its many date and citrus outlets (take 50th Avenue east from behind La Quinta Resort to get here and you'll pass so many date groves you'll think you're in Saudi Arabia – in fact, the town of Mecca is not far away). Stop in at **Shields** on Hwy-111, built in 1924 but fixed in the 1950s, for a date shake at the original soda fountain and a look at the kitschy free film *The Romance and Sex Life of the Date*. The town's huge February **Date Festival** draws people from as far as LA to its wonderfully goofy camel and ostrich races. More serious animal lovers might want to stop in at the **Wild Bird Center**, 46-500 Van Buren St (☎760/347-2647), where injured owls, hawks, and other desert avians are cared for and, if feasible, released back into the wild.

Idyllwild

Fifty miles from Palm Springs and five thousand feet up the opposite side of Mount San Jacinto, **IDYLLWILD** is the perfect antidote to in-your-face success. Fresh, cool and snow-covered in winter, this small alpine town of about two thousand inhabitants has only a few chalet-style restaurants and hotels, but it's a great place to slow up the cash drain that inevitably occurs on a visit to Palm Springs. It is accessible by heading twenty miles west along I-10 to Banning, then taking the exit for Hwy-243 which sweeps you up the mountain on a sharply curved road.

Idyllwild attracts visitors who want to walk on magnificent trails away from the searing heat of the desert basin below. **Mount San Jacinto State Park** surrounds the town and has numerous trails, ranging from a gentle meander along beautiful **Strawberry Creek** to a more strenuous trek along **Deer Springs Trail** to the stunning Suicide Rock and San Jacinto Peak, and the moderately difficult **Devil's Slide** to the Aerial Tramway (see opposite).

The **Forest Service Ranger Station**, 54270 Pine Crest Ave (daily 8am–4.30pm; ☎909/659-2117), has stacks of information about hiking and camping in the area and hands out the free **permits** required for all wilderness sites. You can set up **camp** anywhere over two hundred feet away from trails and streams, or in designated Yellow Post Sites ($5 per day, $30 a year with an Adventure Pass parking permit) with fire rings but no water. There are also drive-in campgrounds run by the Forest Service ($7–10; ☎1-800/280-CAMP), the state park ($9–14; ☎MISTIX) and the county park ($15, ☎1-800/234-PARK).

Otherwise, you can stay in **chalets** and **log cabins**, most of which cost from $60–90 and usually sleep four or more people. The cheapest rooms are the little red-and-white chalets of *Singing Wood Lodge*, 25525 Hwy-243, half a mile north of the ranger station (☎909/659-2201; ②), while *The Fireside Inn* at 54540 North Circle Drive, about half a mile east is considerably more appealing with cozy wood-panelled rooms (☎909/659-2966; ③). The *Strawberry Creek Inn*, 26370 Hwy-243 (☎1-800/262-8969 or 909/659-3202; ⑤), a few hundred yards south, is a B&B-style place for those craving real luxury.

Eating, drinking and nightlife

Palm Springs restaurants run the gamut, from super posh to fast food, with some reasonable ethnic options in between. **Nightlife** tends to the retro side, although there are some hipper options, especially for the gay crowd and concentrated in Cathedral City. The visitor center (see p. 215) has details of **what's on** around town, and stocks the seasonal *Palm Springs Visitors Guide* and the gay bi-monthly *The Bottom Line*.

Restaurants

If you come off season, the desert sun may squelch your appetite sufficiently that you go without eating most of the day and find yourself ravenous at dusk. Although most of the more famous **restaurants** in Palm Springs are ultra-expensive, more reasonable options can be found with a little effort. For the really budget-conscious, supermarket shopping is the best bet: Von's in the Palm Springs shopping mall, is open from early morning until around 11pm for basics.

El Gallito, 68820 Grove St, Cathedral City (☎760/328-7794). A busy Mexican cantina that has the best food for miles and lines to prove it – get there around 6pm to avoid the crowds.

John Henry's Café, 1785 Tahquitz Canyon Way at Sunrise Way (☎760/327-7667). Large portions of eclectic American fare, from rack of lamb to imaginative fish, perfectly served and at half the price you'd expect. Dinner is around $15; reserve after 2pm. Closed June–Sept.

Las Casuelas, 368 N Palm Canyon Drive (☎760/325-3213). Opened in 1958, the original of what has become a string of Valley Mexican restaurants, all owned by the same family. This one is still the most popular with locals, but the others are also good and reasonably priced.

Louise's Pantry, 124 S Palm Canyon Drive (☎760/325-5124). Original 1950s diner with low(ish) prices and huge servings. Especially good for breakfast. Closes 2.30pm.

Mykonos, 139 E Andreas Road (☎760/322-0223). A family-run Greek place just off Palm Canyon Drive with friendly service, large portions of excellent, unpretentious food, and low prices.

Nates, 100 S Indian Canyon Drive. Good, large portions of fair-priced deli food right in the center of town. An enormous variety of burgers and sandwiches through the day and full meals in the evening.

The Red Tomato, 65-751 Grove St at Hwy-111, Cathedral City (☎760/328-7518). Terrific pizza, especially the garlicky "white" pies.

Shame on the Moon, 69-950 Frank Sinatra Drive at Hwy-111, Rancho Mirage (☎760/324-5515). Long-standing bistro with California cuisine and an intimate bar, attracting a loyal gay crowd.

Thai Smile, 653 N Palm Canyon Drive (☎760/320-5503). Few points for decor or ambience but great, authentic Thai green curries and the odd Szechuan dish for around $10.

Le Vallauris, 385 W Tahquitz Canyon Way (☎760/325-5059, reservations only). Palm Springs' best restaurant does not exactly hide its light under a bushel, describing itself as "*the* restaurant where the Stars entertain their friends"; you are indeed likely to run into one or two once-renowned artistes. Even if star-gazing is not your style, the Californian/French/Italian cuisine is excellent, and the service impeccable. The price, however, is around $80 per head.

Wheel-Inn Eat, 16 miles west on I-10 at the Cabazon exit (marked by two fifty-foot concrete dinosaurs). Humble, 24-hour desert truck stop with a burly clientele and enormous portions – so unpretentious you'd think they'd never heard of Palm Springs. One of the dinosaurs houses a wonderfully kitsch gift shop.

The Wild Goose, 67-938 E Palm Canyon Drive, Cathedral City (☎760/328-5775). An antique-crammed award-winning restaurant serving great food for around $40 per head.

Bars and clubs

If you're not a member of one of the exclusive country clubs, or disco-crazy, you'll have to work a little to find good nightlife. If you're not looking for anything raucous, stop in at one of the resort **piano lounges**, where, if you shell out for an (over)priced drink, you can sometimes catch surprisingly good jazz. Lots of people just sit out at one of the **coffeehouses** like *Starbucks*, on downtown's main drag. The area is especially crowded on Thursday evenings, when the surprisingly funky Village Fest **street fair** along N Palm Canyon Drive draws equal numbers of tourists and young locals to booths selling everything from fresh baked bread to tacky souvenirs. A few venues lay on music, and you may find a trailer hosting a live alligator, $1 for a look.

CCC Construction, 1775 E Palm Canyon Drive (☎760/778-1234). A devoted gay crowd followed when this one-time Cathedral City club moved to Palm Springs. Disco at weekends, pool and big-screen videos during the week.

Gumbo Joe's, Hwy 111 and Painter's Path, Palm Desert (☎760/341-8333). Good house bands play from Wednesday through Saturday, everything from R&B to Cajun blues. The food's fine, too.

Harley's Café, 168 N Palm Canyon Drive (☎760/325-5350). Café and smart beer-bar populated by twentysomethings here for the occasional live jazz and blues. Decent meals by day.

Peabody's Coffee Bar & Jazz Studio, 134 S Palm Canyon Drive (☎760/322-1877). Spend the evening sipping an espresso, reading a slightly off-beat publication, and surveying the crowd. Poetry readings on Tuesday and jazz on Friday.

Pompeii, 67-399 E Palm Canyon Drive (☎760/770-1001) A garish new place to quench your Saturday Night Fever. Attracts a GenX and older crowd.

Zelda's, 169 N Indian Canyon Drive (☎760/325-2375). Pick-up joint for teeny-boppers.

Listings

Bookstore Super Crown Books, 332 S Palm Canyon Drive (☎760/325-1265). Travel guides, paperback fiction, maps, etc.

Cinema Courtyard 10, 777 Tahquitz Canyon Way (☎760/322-3456).

Dry Cleaning American Cleaners and Laundry, 364 S Indian Ave (☎760/320-8414).

Hospital Desert Hospital, 1150 N Indian Canyon Drive (☎760/323-6511).

Left Luggage at Greyhound station, 311 N Indian Canyon Drive

Pharmacy Thrifty Drug and Discount Store, 366 S Palm Canyon Drive.

Police ☎760/323-8116 in Palm Springs; ☎760/321-0111 in Cathedral City.

Post Office 333 E Amado Rd (Mon–Fri 8.30am–5pm; ☎760/325-9631).

Travel Agency Las Palmas Travel, 403 N Palm Canyon Drive (☎760/325-6311).

Joshua Tree National Park

In a unique transitional area where the high Mojave meets the lower Colorado desert, 800,000 acres of freaky trees, their branches ragged and gnarled, flourish in an otherwise sparsely vegetated landscape, making **JOSHUA TREE NATIONAL PARK** one of the most unusual, and fascinating of California's national parks. In recognition of its uniqueness, and the need for its preservation, the national park system took the area under its jurisdiction as a national monument in 1936 and has vigilantly maintained its beauty ever since. It lost some of the original area to mining interests in the 1950s, but that was more than compensated for in 1994 when it was promoted to a National Park, with the addition of 234,000 acres. If you're staying in Palm Springs, there's no excuse not to visit; if you've further to come, make the effort anyway.

The grotesque trees, which can reach forty feet or more in height, have to contend with extreme aridity and rocky soil and, with the exception of springtime, when creamy white blossom clusters on the tips of the branches, the strain of their struggle to survive is evident. Complementary to the trees, which can only be seen in certain parts of the park, are great rockpiles, heaps of boulders pushed up from the earth by the movements of the Pinto Mountain fault, which runs directly below. Often as high as a hundred feet, their edges are rounded and smooth from thousands of years of flash floods and winds.

In all it's a mystical, even unearthly, landscape, best appreciated at sunrise or sunset when the whole desert floor is bathed in red light; at noon it can feel like an alien and threatening furnace, with temperatures often reaching 125°F in summer, though dropping to a more bearable 70°F in winter. If you're visiting between May and October you must stick to the higher elevations to enjoy Joshua Tree with any semblance of comfort. In the Low Desert part of the park, the Joshua trees thin out and the temperature rises as you descend below three thousand feet. Over eighty percent of the park is designated wilderness – get out of the car at least once or twice and absorb the silence.

JOSHUA TREE NATIONAL PARK

Some history

"Joshua Tree" may be a familiar name nowadays, thanks to U2, but previously it was almost unknown. Unlike the vast bulk of the state, nobody, save a few Native Americans, prospectors and cowboys, has had the chance to spoil it. Despite receiving less than four inches of annual rainfall, the area is surprisingly lush, and although craggy trees and rockpiles are what define Joshua Tree today, it was grass that attracted the first significant pioneers. Early cattlemen heard rumours of good pastures from the forty-niners who hurried through on their way to the Sierra Nevada gold fields. The natural corrals made perfect sites for cattle rustlers to brand their illegitimate herds before moving them out to the coast for sale. Ambushes and gunfights were common. Seeking refuge in the mountains, rustlers, by chance, discovered small traces of gold and sparked vigorous mining operations that continued until the 1940s. To the Mormons who traveled through here in the 1850s, the area signified something entirely different; they saw the craggy branches of the trees as the arms of Joshua leading them to the promised land – hence the name.

Practicalities

About an hour's drive northeast from Palm Springs, Joshua Tree National Park (always open; $10 per vehicle for 7 days, $5 per cyclist or hiker) is best approached from Hwy-62, which branches off I-10. You can enter the park via the west entrance at the town of **Joshua Tree**, or the northern entrance at **Twentynine Palms**, where you'll also find the **Oasis Visitor Center** (daily: Feb–Sept 8am–5pm; Oct–Jan 8am–4.30pm; ☎760/367-7511) and several good **motels**. Alternatively, if you're coming from the south, there is an entrance and the **Cottonwood Visitor Center** (Mon–Thurs & Sun 8am–4pm, Fri–Sat 9am–5pm) seven miles north of I-10 on the Cottonwood Spring Road exit. It's worth stopping at one of the visitor centers to collect **maps** and the free *Joshua Tree Journal*.

Visiting the park using **public transportation** is not really an option. Morongo Basin Transit Authority (☎1-800/794-6282 or 760/367-7433) runs a regular service (1 daily; $9 one-way, $14 round-trip) between Palm Springs and the towns of Joshua Tree and Twentynine Palms, but not into the park itself. At best, you're looking at a ten-mile desert walk to get to anything very interesting. **Cyclists** are restricted to roads open to motor vehicles, so don't expect any off-road action: the nearest you'll get are the dirt surfaces of Geology Tour Road and the Covington Flats road. There is no bike rental anywhere near the park.

Twentynine Palms and Joshua Tree

The appealing desert settlement of **TWENTYNINE PALMS** is a small, serviceable place that enjoys good weather and low-key living. It is also home to the Marine Corps Air Ground Combat Center, the world's largest marine base. Apart from the boom of gunfire that can be heard for miles around, Twentynine Palms is a pleasant place to visit. Just two minutes' drive from the park, it's a fairly busy town by desert standards, stretching for about a mile along Hwy-62 with a fair selection of places to eat, drink and bed down. The climate has been considered perfect for convalescents ever since physicians sent World War I poison gas victims here for treatment of their respiratory illnesses; development of health spas and real estate offices has been considerable. The town is now billing itself as an "Oasis of Murals"; you can get a map of these interesting hyperrealistic historical artworks – there's one of the Dirty Sock Camp (named for method used by miners to filter out gold), as well as other **information** at the Twentynine Palms Chamber of Commerce, 6455 Mesquite Ave (☎760/367-3445).

CAMPING IN JOSHUA TREE

Joshua Tree National Park has nine **campgrounds**, all concentrated in the northwest except for one at Cottonwood by the southern entrance. All have wooden tables, places for fires (bring your own wood) and pit toilets, but only two (*Black Rock Canyon* and *Cottonwood*) have water supplies and flush toilets. These cost $10 and $8 respectively; there's a fee for *Indian Cove* ($10), but all the rest are free. You can reserve sites at Black Rock and Indian Cove by phoning ☎1-800/365-2267; the rest are on a first-come-first-served basis with no facility for reservations, unless you're traveling with a group.

Each campground has its merits, but for relative solitude and a great, central location, the *Belle* (often closed in summer) and *White Tank* sites are perfect. The much larger *Jumbo Rocks* site is one of the highest, at 4400ft, and is therefore a little cooler, while for the winter months you may prefer the lower altitude of *Cottonwood* in the south. *Black Rock Canyon* and *Indian Cove* cannot be reached from within the park; if you've entered, you have to retrace your steps to the entrances on Hwy-62. The lack of showers, electrical and sewage hook-ups at any of the sites keeps the majority of RVers at bay, but in the popular winter months the place fills up quickly, especially at weekends. Each campsite is good for up to six people and two vehicles.

Backcountry camping is permitted provided you register before you head out. Twelve backcountry boards are dotted through the park at the start of most trails. Here you can self-register, leave your vehicle and study the regulations which include prohibition of camping within a mile of a road, five hundred feet of a trail and 440 yards of a water source.

The best place in town to **stay** is the *Twentynine Palms Inn*, 73950 Inn Ave off National Monument Drive (☎760/367-3505; ④), where an array of characterful adobe bungalows and wood frame cabins are set around attractively arid grounds and gardens, and a central pool area contains a restaurant and bar. Owned by the same large family since 1928, the inn was built on the Oasis of Mara, the only privately owned oasis in the High Desert, and (like the rest of the town) has several fault lines – including the Pinto Mountain fault – running beneath it.

Among the cheaper options nearby are the *29 Palms Motel*, 71487 Twentynine Palms Hwy (☎760/367-2833; ②), and the *El Rancho Dolores Motel*, along the road at no. 73352 (☎760/367-3528; ①). Both have perfectly acceptable pools and good rooms, but are nowhere near as much fun as the inn, which is also the best place to **eat**, with excellent $12–15 meals including soup and salad. For less pricey Mexican, check out *Ramona's*, 72115 Twentynine Palms Hwy (☎760/367-1929); *Don's American BBQ*, 72183 Twentynine Palms Hwy (☎760/367-0301) draws the seriously carnivorous crowd. Alternatively, head fifteen miles west to **JOSHUA TREE** town, and sink into a worn-out sofa at *Jeremy's Cappuccino Bar and Beer Haus*, 61597 Twentynine Palms Hwy (☎760/336-9799), which enjoys great coffee, snacks, beer and breakfast, and occasional live music at weekends. They recently added a cyber café (*www.joshua-tree.com*). The town is also home to the Joshua Tree Rock Climbing School; if you're interested in doing mountain-goat manoeuvres in the National Park, call ☎1-800/890-4745 or 760/366-4745 for details.

Exploring the park

The best way to enjoy the park is to be selective. As with any desert area, you'll find the heat punishing and an ambitious schedule impossible in the hotter months. Casual observers will find a day-trip plenty, though it's a nice idea to camp out for a couple of nights, and serious rock-climbers and experienced hikers may want to take advantage of the park's excellent if strenuous trails. The rangers and staff at the visitor centers will be able to recommend the most enjoyable itineraries, tailored to your requirements and abilities.

Never venture anywhere without a **map**: either the *Topographic Trail Map* ($8) or the *Recreation Map* ($7), both available at the visitor centers. Many of the roads are unmarked, hard to negotiate and restricted to four-wheel-drive use. If a road is marked as such, don't think about taking a normal car – you'll soon come to a grinding halt, and it could be quite a few panic-stricken hours before anybody finds you. Of course, maps are even more essential if you are planning to explore the park's **hiking trails** (see box below).

Starting in the north of the park, quartz boulders tower around the *Indian Cove* camping area, and a trail from the eastern branch of the campground road leads to **Rattlesnake Canyon** – its streams and waterfalls (depending on rainfall) breaking an otherwise eerie silence among the monoliths. The **Fortynine Palms Oasis** to the east can only be visited on foot.

HIKING IN JOSHUA TREE NATIONAL PARK

To get a real feel for the majesty of the desert you'll need to leave the main roads behind and hike. But **stick to the trails**: Joshua Tree is full of abandoned gold mines and although the rangers are fencing them as quickly as possible, they don't have the funds to take care of all of them. Watch for loose gravel around openings, undercut edges, never trust ladders or timber, and bear in mind that the rangers rarely check mines for casualties. Some of the shafts contain water and poisonous fumes, and even if you survive a fall, you'll still have to contend with snakes, scorpions and spiders.

Most of the trails listed below are all in the slightly cooler and higher Mojave Desert. There's tougher stuff on the eastern side of the park around **Pinto Basin**, a notorious danger zone when the flash floods strike. To cover it on foot, it's essential that you **register** at one of the visitor centers first and check the trail conditions with the rangers. You'll need to be well armed with maps and water supplies, and on the whole it's unwise even to attempt it unless you're a very experienced hiker or are traveling as part of a group. If you do reach here, you'll find no Joshua trees and few other signs of life. Even on the easier trails allow around an hour per mile: there's very little shade and you'll tire quickly.

SOME HIKES

These are listed northwest to southeast through the park.

Fortynine Palms Oasis (3 miles; 2hr). Moderately strenuous, this leaves the badly signposted Canyon Road six miles west of the visitor center at Twentynine Palms. A barren rocky trail leads to this densely clustered and partly fire-blackened oasis which, since it was named, seems to have flourished on the seepage down the canyon. There's not enough water to swim in, nor are you allowed to camp (the oasis is officially closed 8pm–7am), but a late afternoon or evening visit presents the best wildlife rewards.

Lost Horse Mine (4 miles; 3hr). Another moderately strenuous trail climbs 450ft to the mine which in the 1890s made an average of $20,000 a week. The hike takes you through abandoned mining sites, with building foundations and equipment still intact, to the top of Lost Horse Mountain. The trail starts a mile east of Keys View Road.

Ryan Mountain (3 miles; 2hr). Some of the best views in the park are from the top of Ryan Mountain (5461ft), seven hundred strenuous feet above the desert floor. Start at the parking area near the *Sheep Pass* campground and follow the trail past the Indian Cave, which contains bedrock mortars once used by the Cahuilla and Serrano.

Mastodon Peak (3 miles; 2hr). Another peak climb, less strenuous but with great views, especially south to the Salton Sea. Start from the *Cottonwood* campground.

Lost Palms Oasis (7.5 miles; 5hr). This moderate trail leads across desert washes, past palo verde, cottonwood and ironwood trees to the largest stand of palms in the park, and presents possible scrambling side trips to Victory Palms and Munsen Canyon. There's little surface water, but often enough to lure bighorn sheep. Start from the *Cottonwood* campground.

Moving south into the main section of the park, you drive through the **Wonderland of Rocks** area comprising giant, rounded granite boulders that draw **rock-climbers** from all over the world. The various clusters flank the road for about ten miles giving plenty of opportunity to stop for a little "bouldering" or, for those suitably equipped and skilled, to try more adventurous routes. Pick up a *Climber Ethics* leaflet from the visitor centers. Well-signposted nature trails lead to **Hidden Valley** (1 mile), where cattle rustlers used to hide out, and to the rain-fed **Barker Dam** (1 mile) to the east: this is Joshua Tree's crucial water supply, built around the turn of the century by cattlemen (and rustlers) to prevent the poor beasts expiring halfway across the park. The route back passes a number of petroglyphs.

If you're **driving**, you can reach **Key's View** from here. This 5185-foot-high spot was named after Bill Keys, an eccentric miner who raised his family in this inhospitable landscape until he was locked away in 1943 for shooting one of his neighbors over a right-of-way argument (the mystery writer Erle Stanley Gardner helped him get paroled). He was revered for being a tough desert rat and indefatigable miner, who dug on long after less hardy men had abandoned the arid wasteland. The best views in the whole park can be had from up here, on a good day as far as the Salton Sea and beyond to Mexico – a brilliant desert panorama of badlands and mountains.

The road then passes the start of the Ryan Mountain hike and the turn-off for Geology Tour Road, which leads down through the best of Joshua Tree's **rock formations**. A little further on, the Jumbo Rocks campground is the start of a loop (1.7 miles) through boulders and desert washes to **Skull Rock**.

Almost at the transition zone between the Colorado and Mojave deserts and on the fringes of the Pinto Basin, the **Cholla Cactus Garden** is a quarter-mile loop through an astonishing concentration of the "jumping" cholla cactus (see box on p.213) for which it is named, as well as creosote bushes, jojoba and several other cactus species. Come at dusk or dawn for the best chance of seeing the mainly nocturnal desert wood rat.

Around Joshua Tree

Just west of Joshua Tree Village is the rather more developed **Yucca Valley**. The town's **Hi-Desert Nature Museum**, 57117 Twentynine Palms Hwy (Tues–Sun 10–5pm; free), holds a largely poor collection of paintings and tacky souvenirs, but some commendable catches of snakes and scorpions; the **Desert Christ Park**, at no. 57090 (dawn–dusk; free), has 37 of local sculptor Antone Martin's massive fifteen-foot concrete figures depicting tales from the Bible – a fittingly bizarre addition to the region. Finally, **Pioneertown** is an old West town created in the 1940s for the filming of movies and TV serials; today it's a residential settlement with full eating amenities – a nice bit of synthetic cowboy country when the real thing gets too much.

If you've got a good car that can handle bad roads and mountain passes, then **back road driving** on the way back from Yucca Valley to LA via the Morongo Valley is a fun way to get a sense of the Wild West. Arm yourself with a San Bernardino County map and explore the Lucerne Valley and the small towns of **Big Bear City** or **Fawnskin**.

The Imperial Valley and Salton Sea

The patch of the Colorado desert **south** of Joshua Tree and Palm Springs is the least friendly of all the Californian desert regions and its foreboding aspect discourages exploration. It's best not to come in summer, when intense heat makes journeys uncomfortable and services are greatly reduced.

Sandwiched between Hwy-111 and Hwy-86, which branch off I-10 soon after Palm Springs and the Coachella Valley, the area from the **Salton Sea** down to the furnace-like migrant-worker towns of the agricultural **Imperial Valley** lies in the two-thousand-square-mile Salton Basin: aside from a small spot in Death Valley, the largest area of dry land below sea level in the western hemisphere. Hwy-86, for what it's worth, was California's most notorious two-lane highway, with a staggering record of deaths and accidents, though it's now being widened into four lanes. There's not a lot to come here for unless you're heading for the Anza-Borrego desert or the Mexican border.

Created accidentally in 1904, when engineers tried to divert the Colorado River to get water to the Imperial Valley, the Salton Sea and its shores were once extremely toney, attracting the likes of Frank Sinatra and Dean Martin to its yacht clubs; in its 1940s heyday, the sea was a bigger tourist draw than Yosemite National Park. A series of mid-1970s storms caused the sea to rise and swallow shoreline developments, but more serious damage to tourism was due to fact that the Salton Sea, without a natural outlet (it is 235 feet below sea level), has over the years become grossly polluted – plagued by agricultural runoff and toxic wastes carried in by two rivers from Mexico – and excessively saline. Fish carry a consumption warning, and people rarely swim and waterski here these days. There's an effort underway, however, to change all that: before his death, Palm Springs Congressional representative Sonny Bono was spear-heading an effort to replace the Salton Sea's contaminated brine with ocean water pumped in from Mexico's Gulf of California, pricetag $2 billion.

In the meantime, the Salton Sea remains an important wintering area for shore birds and waterfowl. Brown pelicans come by in summer and terns and cormorants nest here. The best place to see them is the **National Wildlife Refuge** (daily dawn–dusk; free) at the sea's southern tip. By the informative **visitor center** (April–Sept Mon–Fri 7am–3.30pm; Oct–March daily 7am–3.30pm) there's a viewing platform, or you can take the twenty-minute Rock Hill Trail to the water's edge for a closer look. To get to the refuge, take the poorly signposted backroads off Hwy-111 south of **Niland** or off Hwy-86 at **Westmorland**; both run past fields of alfalfa, can-taloupe, tomatoes and other crops – proof that just about anything will grow in this fertile land provided it is suitably irrigated.

Although you probably wouldn't want to spend the night there, if you've come this far it's worth turning east on the main street of Niland and traveling three miles to see **Slab City**, a huge settlement of squatters that swells in size in winter when Canadian RVers come down for warmth – and free city water. At the entrance to the town, **Salvation Mountain** is a fantastic work of religious folk art, incorporating for example an abandoned motorboat, to represent Noah's Ark.

The only other reasons you might stop are to **camp** at one of several lakeside sites on the eastern side of the Salton Sea ($7–8) or to eat some authentic **Mexican food**. Agricultural work brings thousands of Mexicans north of the border, and the restaurants generally cater to them: practise your Spanish.

The Anza-Borrego desert

Southwest of the Salton Sea, though usually approached from San Diego (see Chapter Two), the **ANZA-BORREGO DESERT** is the largest state park in the country, covering 600,000 acres and, in contrast to the Imperial Valley, offering a diverse variety of plant and animal life as well as a legend-strewn history spanning Native American tribes, the first white trailfinders and Gold Rush times. It takes its double-barrelled name from Juan Baptista de Anza, a Spanish explorer who crossed the region in 1774, and the Spanish for the native bighorn sheep, *borrego cimarron*, which eats the brittle-

ANZA-BORREGO DESERT
STATE PARK

N

Anza

PACIFIC CREST TRAIL

Coyote Canyon

Desert Gardens
Picnic Area

COYOTE MOUNTAIN

SANTA ROSA MOUNTAINS

Borrego Palm
Canyon

Borrego Springs
Chamber of Commerce

Peg Leg Smith
Monument

S22

Culp Valley

Borrego
Springs

Font's
Point

Borrego
Badlands

San Diego

S22

PINYON
MOUNTAINS

S2

78 & Salton Sea

OCOTILLO WELLS
STATE VEHICULAR
RECREATION AREA

S3

Yaqui
Flat

Aqui Pass

Ocotillo
Wells

78 & Salton Sea

San Diego

Tamarisk Grove

Scissors
Crossing

78

Julian

Banner

Harper
Flat

78

VALLECITO
MOUNTAINS

Cuyamaca
Reservoir

Blair
Valley

CUYAMACA
RANCHO
STATE
PARK

79

Vallecito Stage
Station

Palm Spring

Carrizo
Impact
Area
(Restricted Zone)

San Diego

8

S1

IN-KO-PA
MOUNTAINS

Bow Willow

S2

El Centro

San Diego & Imperial
Valley Railroad

Ocotillo

8

Anza-Borrego
Boundary

Southern Emigrant
Trail Historic Route

0   5 miles

brush and agave found here. Some of Anza-Borrego can be covered by car (confidence on gravel roads is handy), although you'll need four-wheel drive for the more obscure – and most interesting – routes, and there are over five hundred miles of hiking trails where vehicles are not permitted at all.

During the fiercely hot summer months, the place is best left to the lizards, although most campgrounds stay open all year. The desert **blooming season**, between March and May, is popular, when scarlet octillo, orange poppies, white lilies and purple verbena and other peacock-like wildflowers are a memorable – and fragrant – sight.

As well as taking the usual desert precautions (see box on p.212), you should read the comments in Basics on p.45 – this is mountain lion territory.

Practicalities

Anza-Borrego State Park is served by **public transportation**; from San Diego, the Northeast Rural Bus System (see p.203) makes daily trips to **BORREGO SPRINGS**, the park's one sizeable settlement, at the northern end of Hwy-S3. There's not much happening in Borrego Springs, but it's one of the most pleasant of all the desert towns, self-contained but remarkably uncommercialized; the lack of development is in part due to the efforts of San Diego's Copley family, conservative newspaper magnates who want to keep it a pristine escape for the rich. If you're camping out it's the place to gather (expensive) supplies – no big supermarket chains here – or to use the **Chamber of Commerce**, 622 Palm Canyon Drive (daily June–Sept 10am–2pm; Oct–May 10am–4pm; ☎760/767-5555), for details of motels and restaurants. Though the Chamber of Commerce doesn't like to mention it, the town of Borrego Springs is three miles southwest of the most seismically active area in the western hemisphere, Clark's Dry Lake, where some ten thousand earthquakes a year are registered. For information on this phenomenon, as well as on desert hiking, camping, flora and fauna, head two miles west to the excellent **Visitor Information Center**, 200 Palm Canyon Drive (June–Sept Sat, Sun & holidays 9am–5pm; Oct–May daily 9am–5pm; ☎760/767-5311), where you can also pick up an informative free newspaper and a detailed map of the park. The center is landscaped into the desert floor so you barely notice it as you wander through the short **Desert Plant Trail** (it's a bit confusing; don't take the dirt Visitor Center Loop but the paved path to enter). When the center is closed, the administration office (Mon–Fri 9am–5pm) fills in.

If you're not feeling adventurous enough to camp (see below), there are a handful of **motels** in Borrego Springs, though only *Oasis*, at 366 W Palm Drive (☎760/767-5409; ②), with available kitchenettes, and *Hacienda del Sol* (☎760/767-5442; ②), near the Chamber of Commerce, are at all affordable. For plain but decent diner **meals**, make for *Bailey's Café* (☎760/767-3491), almost opposite the Chamber of Commerce. More upscale and far more interesting is the new *Krazy Coyote Saloon & Grille*, 2220 Hoberg Road (☎760/767-7788), the local favorite with a good bar, terrific desert setting, and tasty American/Continental fare. Just outside the eastern park boundary, **OCOTILLO WELLS** has basic facilities and the attractively located *Desert Ironwoods Motel*, 4875 Hwy-78 (☎760/767-5670; ③).

Recreational opportunities in the park are strictly controlled to preserve the fragile ecosystem. The main exception to this rule is the **Ocotillo Wells State Vehicular Recreational Area**, to the east of the park, a region mapped out for dune buggies and the like. Owners drive like demons in a maelstrom of tossed sand and engine noise; if you're tempted to join them, call Recreation Headquarters (daily 8am–5pm; ☎760/767-5391) for information or contact Desert Rat Tours (☎760/767-3755) in Borrego Springs ($40 for an hour-long accompanied spin); otherwise stay well clear. **Mountain biking** is permitted but only on paved and dirt roads; the hiking trails are off limits. Bikes can be rented ($7 for the first hour, $5 for each additional hour) from Carrizo Bikes, 648

CAMPING IN ANZA-BORREGO

Two developed and nine primitive campgrounds exist within the Anza-Borrego Desert State Park, but this is one of the few parks which allows **open camping**, giving you the freedom to pitch a tent pretty much anywhere without a permit, although it's advisable to let a park ranger know your plans. The few provisos are that you don't drive off-road, don't camp near water holes, camp away from developed campgrounds, light fires only in fire rings or metal containers, collect no firewood, and leave the place as you found it, or cleaner.

The largest site, and the only one with RV hook-ups, is the *Borrego Palm Canyon* campground ($16 per tent site, $10 in summer) a mile from the visitor center. *Tamarisk Grove* (tent sites $16/$10), thirteen miles south on Hwy-S3, is the only other developed site. Both have hiker/biker sites for $3 each and charge $5 for day use of the facilities. Both also organize **guided hikes** and have regular discussion and activity evenings led by a park ranger. Places can be reserved through Parknet on ☎1-800/444-7275 (essential for holidays and weekends, and in the March–May blooming season). The other, primitive, campgrounds fill on a first-come-first-served basis; those in the backcountry always have space. All are accessible by road vehicles and are free, except for *Bow Willow* which charges $9 and is the only one with drinking water. Most sites are below 1500ft which is fine in winter, but in the hotter months you might try *Culp Valley*, ten miles southwest of Borrego Springs, at a blissfully cool 3400ft. There is spring water here but you're better off bringing your own.

Palm Canyon Drive (☎760/767-3872), behind the Chamber of Commerce. For guided excursions into the park, contact Desert Jeep Tours (☎1-888/BY-JEEPS); rates start at $49 for a two-hour tour of the badlands and go up to $79 for half-day jaunts that cover Indian ruins and mudcaves.

The park

Coming from the San Diego area through Julian (see p.204), you'll first hit the western section of the park which contains some of the more interesting historical debris. At Scissors Crossing, Hwy-78 intersects Hwy-S2 which follows the line of the old **Butterfield Stage Route**, the first regular line of communication between the eastern states and the newly settled West, which began service from 1857.

From Scissors Crossing, Hwy-S2 heads towards the park's southeast corner, traversing **Blair Valley**, with a primitive campground, and **Box Canyon**, where the Mormon Battalion of 1847, following what is now known as the **Southern Emigrant Trail Historic Route**, forced a passage along the desert wash. It isn't especially spectacular, but makes for some safe desert walking, never more than a couple of hundred yards from the road. Nine miles further on, the **Vallecito Stage Station** is an old adobe stage rest stop that gives a good indication of the comforts – or lack of them – of early desert travel. To the south lies the least-visited portion of Anza-Borrego, good for isolated exploration and undisturbed views around Imperial Valley, where there's a vivid and spectacular clash as gray rock rises from the edges of the red desert floor, and a cool oasis at Palm Spring.

Northwest of Scissors Crossing, Hwy-S2 meets Hwy-S22, which descends tortuously through fields of popcorn-shaped rock formations to Borrego Springs. Six miles further east is a memorial marker to Peg Leg Smith, an infamous local spinner of yarns from the Gold Rush days who is further celebrated by a festival of tall stories – the **Peg Leg Liars Contest** – which takes place at this spot on the first Saturday in April; anybody can get up before the judges and fib their hearts out, the most outrageous tales earning a modest prize. Roughly four miles further on, a fairly tough dirt road leads to **Font's Point** and a view over the **Borrego Badlands** – a long sweeping plain devoid of vegetation whose strange, stark charms are oddly inspiring. Sunset is the best time to fully appreciate the layered alluvial banding.

In the north of the park, the campground at Borrego Palm Canyon marks the start of the **Borrego Palm Canyon Trail** (3 miles; 2hr; 350ft ascent), one of the most popular paths in the park. It follows a detailed nature trail to a dense concentration of desert palms – the only palms native to California.

THE HIGH DESERT

Desolate, lifeless and silent, the **Mojave Desert**, mythic badland of the west, has no equal when it comes to hardship. Called the High Desert because it averages a height of around two thousand feet above sea level, the Mojave is very dry and for the most part deadly flat, dotted here and there with the prickly bulbs of a Joshua tree and an occasional abandoned miner's shed. For most, it's the barrier between LA and Las Vegas, an obstacle to get over before they reach either city; and, short on attractions as it is, you may want to follow their example. But you should linger a little just to see – and smell – what a desert is really like: a vast, impersonal, extreme environment, sharp with its own peculiar fragrance, and alive in spring with acres of fiery orange poppies – the state flower of California – and other brightly coloured wildflowers.

You will have relatively little company. If LA is the home of the sports car, the Mojave is the land of huge dust-covered trucks, carrying goods across the state to Nevada. Other signs of life include the grim military subculture marooned on huge weapons-testing sites. There is also a hard-core group of desert fans: backdrop for the legion of road movies spawned by the underground film culture in the late 1960s and early 1970s, the Mojave is a favorite with bikers and hippies drawn by the barren panorama of sand dunes and mountain ranges. Members of the California Sierra Club and other savvy in-state nature lovers light out for the less barren beauties of the Mojave National Preserve. But otherwise visitors are thin on the ground, and for most of the year you can rely on being in sparse company.

I-15 cuts through the heart of the Mojave, dividing it into two distinct regions. To the north is **Death Valley** (which, because of its unique character and proximity to the Owens Valley, is covered in Chapter Four), and to the south **Barstow**, the lacklustre capital of the Mojave, redeemed only by its location halfway between LA and **Las Vegas** on I-15, which makes it both a potential stopover between the two points and a good base for the surrounding attractions, explorable by dune buggy, on horseback or even on foot.

If Barstow isn't exactly alluring, the huge **Mojave National Preserve**, which lies just south of the road to LasVegas, is. Here you can see spectacular sand dunes, striking rock formations, and a huge variety of plant life, including large concentrations of Joshua Trees. Much of the preserve rises to about 4000 feet, so it also offers respite from the harshest of the area's heat. South and east of here, close to the Nevada and Arizona borders, the desert is at its most demanding, largely empty, inhospitable and potentially miserable, and the only reason you might find yourself in the region is if you're driving through on the way to the **Grand Canyon**.

Barstow

Just a few hours from LA along the thundering, seemingly endless I-15, **BARSTOW** looms up out of the desert, providing a welcome opportunity to get out of the car. Though capital of the Mojave and the crossroads of three major thoroughfares (I-40 and Hwy-58 also run through here) it's a small town, consisting of just one main road lined with a selection of motels and restaurants that make an overnight stop possible.

This main street was once part of the famed **Route 66**, so fans of neon will enjoy some classic examples, and two nearby **outlet malls** attract area bargain hunters. There, however, the town's appeal ends. For many months of the year, the relentless sun manages to keep people in their air-conditioned homes for a good part of the day; in summer Barstow can seem more like a ghost town.

Practicalities

Near the junction of Barstow Road and I-15, the **California Desert Information Center** (daily 9am–5pm; ☎760/252-6060) has a good selection of maps of the surrounding area, lodging and restaurant guides and various flyers on local attractions.

If you're arriving by bus or train, you'll be dropped at the combined Greyhound and Amtrak station on First Street. A few blocks away, Main Street is the best place to look for a **motel**. All are of a similar standard and price, generally only distinguished by the condition of the neon sign outside. Cruise up and down until you find the best deal, but among those you might try are: *Desert Inn Motel*, 1100 E Main St (☎760/256-2146; ②), and the *Astro Motel*, 1271 E Main St (☎760/256-2204; ①). For a little more comfort, try the corporate-style *Holiday Inn*, 1511 E Main St (☎760/256-5673; ④). You can **camp** eight miles north of Barstow in the simple *Owl Canyon Campground* ($6) at Rainbow Basin (see opposite), or if you need more facilities, at **CALICO**, a re-created ghost town (detailed below) with shaded canyons where you can pitch a tent ($18) or hook-up campers for $22 per night including showers.

Food in Barstow, though far from exotic, is plentiful and cheap. Restaurants sit snugly between the many hotels on Main Street and are usually of the rib and steak variety (*Idle Spurs Steak House*, 29557 Hwy-58, is tops in that mode) although you can get good Mexican food at *Rosita's*, 540 W Main St, or a reasonable Chinese meal at the *Golden Dragon*, 1231 E Main St. Evening **entertainment** comes in the form of a few grubby bars frequented by bike gangs, the least threatening of which is the *Katz*, 127 W Main Street at First, open from 6am to 2am.

Around Barstow

Most people who stop in Barstow are not here to enjoy the desert, but to visit the contrived **Calico Ghost Town** (daily 9am–5pm; $6), ten miles east along I-15. In the late nineteenth century Calico produced millions of dollars worth of silver and borax and supported a population of almost four thousand. Attractively set in the color-streaked Calico Hills, but subject to the extreme heat of the Mojave, the town was quickly deserted when the silver ran out. It's since been rather cynically – and insensitively – restored, with souvenir shops and hot-dog stands, and a main thoroughfare lined with ersatz saloons, an old school house, a vaudeville playhouse, and shops kitted out in period styles. However, should you so desire, there are miles of mining shafts and tunnels open to crawl around in – until claustrophobia forces you up for air.

Calico is brightened by its festivals, held throughout the year. The best of these is the **Hullabaloo** (Palm Sunday weekend), which features the World Tobacco Spitting Championships. Huge beast-like men gather to chew the wad and direct streams of saliva and tobacco juice at an iron post, cheered on by rowdy crowds who take their sport seriously and their drink in large quantities.

Primitive males also feature five miles northeast of Calico along I-15. The **Calico Early Man Site** (visit by guided tour only Wed & Thurs 1.30pm & 3.30pm, Fri–Sun 9.30am–4pm; $1), more popularly known as the "Calico Dig", has become one of the most important archeological sites in North America since it was excavated in 1964, its findings of old tools and primitive shelter (which some have suggested are around 200,000 years old) having dated mankind's presence to far earlier than was previously thought. Pick up details of the tour from the small caravan that serves as an information office.

Of equal prehistoric importance, but far more vivid, the **Rainbow Basin** (unrestricted access), eight miles north of town along Fort Irwin Road, is a rock formation that after thirty million years of wind erosion has been exposed as a myriad of almost electric colors. You'll see plenty of fossilized animal and insect remains, but most visitors will probably be content to weave the car through the tricky four-mile loop road around the canyon and marvel at the prettiness of it all. You can camp here (see "Practicalities" opposite) at minimally-equipped sites.

Heading some eight miles east on the other main highway out of Barstow, I-40, just past Dagget, the original Department of Energy's Solar One Power Plant has been replaced by the **SEGS II Solar Power Plant**, which, marked by a hundred-acre field of mirrors, is a surreal example of how California is putting its deserts to use. Anyone who has seen the film *Bagdad Café* will remember the light reflections the mirrors give off for miles around.

Two designated **off-road recreational areas** lie south of Barstow: **Rasor** and **Stoddard Valley**. If you didn't bring your own dune buggy, you're out of luck – there's nowhere to rent them in Barstow – but you can always travel out to the dunes and get friendly with someone there. Camping is permitted in much of Stoddard Valley, a pretty area of rolling hills but one that's dotted with abandoned mineshafts. Watch where you lay down your backpack.

If you're heading out from here to Palm Springs or Joshua Tree National Park (see above), consider the scenic Apple Valley back route via **VICTORVILLE**, some 34 miles south of Barstow on I-15. Take the Roy Rogers exit and drive down Civic Street to reach the **Roy Rogers-Dale Evans Museum** (daily 9am–5pm; $7), a repository of the Hollywood cowboy couple's memorabilia, some of it extremely bizarre – including Trigger and Buttermilk, the horses they rode in many of their films, preserved by an expert taxidermist. Also dedicated to American myth, the small **California Route 66 Museum**, on D Street between Fifth and Sixth streets (Thurs–Mon 10am–4pm; free), has displays relating to the westernmost strip of the Mother Road.

Baker and the Eastern Mojave

Once you get past Barstow and off the main roads, you'll be amazed to discover that some of the most spectacular – and undervisited – scenery in the state lies in the **Eastern Mojave**, where 1.4 million acres of land between I-15 and I-40 were set aside by the 1994 Desert Protection Act to create the **Mojave National Preserve**. Those heading for Las Vegas would be far better off spending some extra hours here than devoting them to the gaming tables.

Driving west from Barstow, take the Afton Road turn off I-15 to get to **Afton Canyon**, outside of the preserve proper and dubbed the "Grand Canyon of the Mojave". It's not quite as impressive as the Arizona original, but it's striking nevertheless, with multicolored strata formed by erosion from an extinct lake. The lake may be gone, but Afton Canyon is one of the three places where the Mojave River flows above-ground throughout the year, making this a marshy mecca for almost two hundred types of birds and desert creatures. There's camping here; to book call the Bureau of Land Management in Barstow (☎760/252-6060; $6).

You'll next come to the road leading four miles south to the western edge of the preserve and the oasis of **Zzyzx**, a former health resort that's now home to the Soda Springs Desert Studies Center, run jointly by the National Park Service and the California State University system. If there are no happy-to-be-distracted researchers around, go to the unmanned visitor center to learn about the area's colorful history.

BAKER is the main supply source for the immediate region. The town's claim to fame is the world's tallest functioning thermometer, rising to 134 feet to commemorate the highest temperature ever recorded in Death Valley, which lies directly to the north via Hwy-127. You can pick up **information** on the national park and other desert recreation areas at the Mojave Desert Information Center, located at the base of the thermometer (daily 9am–5pm; ☎760/733-4040). If you're looking for **lodging**, the *Bun Boy* (☎760/733-4363; ②) and *Wills* (sic) *Fargo* (☎760/733-4477; ②) motels are owned by the same people, so the prices are exactly the same (the latter has a pool and slightly more characterful rooms). The supplies at the town's **general store** aren't cheap, but this is your last chance to stock up. If you buy a lottery ticket here, you may never have to worry about such matters again: the place has produced the most jackpot winners in the state of California. Standing out from the fast food joints, the *Bun Boy* **restaurant** has good diner food, though it's not as interesting inside as its Twenties facade would suggest.

West of Baker, a series of roads lead south from I-15 into the main part of the **Mojave National Preserve**. Kelbaker Road, the farthest west, shoots past a series of dramatic black-red **cinder cones**, created relatively recently (a thousand years ago), before reaching the graceful Spanish-style **Kelso depot**, built in 1924 for workers on the Union Pacific Railroad. Closed in 1985, the building is in the process of being restored, perhaps to serve as a visitor center for the preserve. Visible to the south of the depot are the spectacular **Kelso Dunes**, a golden five-mile stretch of sand reaching up as high as seven hundred feet. The faint booming sound you might hear is caused by dry sand cascading down the steep upper slopes.

Turn northeast at Kelso to get to the small town of **CIMA** (there's a little store here, but no gas) and the adjacent **Cima Dome**, a perfectly formed batholith rising some 1500ft above the desert floor. Cloaked in Joshua trees, parts of it can be visited on foot. To the southeast, along Black Canyon Road, you'll see a turnoff for the **Mid Hills Campground**, beautifully sited in pinyon-juniper woodland; from here a moderately difficult eight-mile trail winds through Wild Horse Canyon and ends up at the park's other developed campground, **Hole-in-the-Wall** (both cost $10). Named by Bob Hollimon, a member of the Butch Cassidy gang, because it reminded him of his former hideout in Wyoming, Hole-in-the-Wall sits in at an elevation of 4500 feet among striking volcanic rock formations. If you've driven here and don't want to take a long hike, an interpreted nature trail leads from the **visitor center** (May–Oct Sat & Sun approximately 10.30am–3.30pm; Nov–April daily approximately 10.30am–3.30pm; ☎760/928-2572). In the off-season, you'll still find someone at the visitor center for the 5900-acre **Providence Mountain State Recreation** area ($5 per day, free for those taking cave tours), a further ten miles south, then six miles west. Vegetation here changes from scrubby bushes at lower desert elevations to the pinyon pines that grow along rocky Fountain Peak (6996 feet) and Edgar Peak (7171 feet). Some people come to camp at the small campground (six spaces only; $12), but most are here to tour **Mitchell Caverns** (mid-Sept to mid-June tours Mon–Fri 1.30pm, Sat & Sun 10am, 1.30pm & 3pm; rest of the year call ☎760/928-2586 for reservations & tour times; $6), used by the Chemehuevi Indians for almost five hundred years. There's one brief claustrophobia-inducing part, but otherwise this ninety-minute walk through stalactites and stalagmites and rarer limestone formations is superb.

The Colorado River area

While you'd be well advised to steer clear of the Eastern Mojave, the eastern portion of the **Colorado Desert** is not so bleak. In recent years small resorts have sprung up along the **Colorado River**. The strength of the river, over a thousand miles long, has by this southern stage of its course been sapped by a succession of dams (though even in the Grand Canyon there are white-water rapids), until here it proceeds towards the Gulf of California in a stately flow, marking its western border as it goes.

If you're not heading east to the Grand Canyon itself – or if you're looking for an overnight stop en route – the stretch between Needles, the small border town on I-40, and Blythe a hundred miles south where I-10 meets Hwy-95, and especially **Lake Havasu City** in between the two, is marginally the most interesting area. Most of the small waterfront settlements that dot its course are dependent on watersports, though some, such as **Laughlin** in Nevada, right on the border with California and Arizona, have taken advantage of Arizona's restrictions on gambling and turned themselves into mini-Vegases, enjoying considerable popularity with packs of bikers who make a week-end of driving across the desert, spending all their money on gambling and drink and then riding back again.

Lake Havasu City

Ten miles east of the California state line on I-40, a twenty-mile detour south on Hwy-95 brings you to the most incongruous sight of the Southwestern deserts. At **LAKE HAVASU CITY**, the old gray stones of **London Bridge** reach out across the stagnant waters of the dammed Colorado River.

Californian chainsaw manufacturer **Robert P. McCulloch** moved his factory to this unlikely spot – occupied by a disused military airstrip – in 1964, so he could try out his new sideline in outboard motors on the waters of Lake Havasu. Three years later, he heard Johnny Carson mention that London Bridge was up for sale; in the words of the nursery rhyme, it really was falling down, unable to cope with all those new-fangled automobiles. McCulloch bought it for $2,460,000, and painstakingly shipped ten thousand numbered blocks of granite across the Atlantic. Lacking anything for the bridge to span, he dug a channel that turned a riverbank promontory into the island of Pittsburg Point. Despite the jibes that McCulloch thought he was buying picturesque Tower Bridge – the turreted one that opens in the middle – instead of merely the latest in a long line of London Bridges, dating only from 1831, his investment paid off handsomely. The bridge now ranks second among Arizona's tourist attractions, after the Grand Canyon, and Lake Havasu City has become a major vacation resort and retirement center, with a population of thirty thousand.

That said, it's not often you see anything quite as boring in Arizona as London Bridge. Lake Havasu City is one of those places with an undeniable attraction for the parched urbanites of cities such as Phoenix, who flock to fish on the lake or charge up and down in motorboats and on jet-skis, but holds minimal appeal for travelers from further afield.

Only when you cross the bridge onto the island and then look back, do you appreciate how large Lake Havasu City has grown, sprawling up the gentle slope away from the river. Most of those broad hillside streets are lined with condo blocks and minor malls; the only place tourists bother to visit is the **English Village**, a mock-Tudor shopping mall, which also holds a handful of riverview restaurants, at the base of the bridge. Out on the island, if you head south from the bridge past the *Island Inn Resort*, you'll soon come to **London Bridge Beach**. The "beach" is more grit than sand, and few people swim from it. With its bizarre fringe of date palms, however, and its panorama of weird desert buttes and the Chemehuevi Mountains, it does at least linger in the memory.

Practicalities

The local **visitor center** is up from the river at 1930 Mesquite Ave (Mon–Fri 9am–5pm; ☎1-800/242-8278 or 520/453-3444); there's also an information kiosk at 420 English Village (daily 10am–4pm; ☎520/855-5655).

Several operators, such as Blue Water Charters (☎520/855-7171) and Dixie Belle Cruises (☎520/453-6776), offer short **river cruises** from the quayside of the English Village, charging around $12 for an hour-long trip focusing on the bridge, or $20 for a two-hour excursion to see rock formations upriver. Companies renting **jet-skis** (at around $40 per hour) and the like, include Arizona Jet Ski (☎1-800/393-5558 or 520/453-5558), and Fun Time Boat Rentals (☎1-800/680-1003 or 520/680-1003).

Lake Havasu City has a good 25 or so **motels**, though relatively few of them are immediately obvious from Hwy-95. They range from the perfectly adequate *Windsor Inn Motel*, 451 London Bridge Rd (☎1-800/245-4135 or 520/855-4135; ②), by way of the fancier, all-suite *Pioneer Hotel*, 271 S Lake Havasu Ave (☎1-800/528-5169 or 520/855-5169; ③), to the frankly ridiculous riverfront *London Bridge Resort*, 1477 Queen's Bay Rd (☎1-800/624-7939 or 520/855-0888; ④), where everything has a British-royalty theme.

As for **nightlife**, most of Lake Havasu City seems to be tucked up in bed by 9pm. For a night out, the **Island Fashion Mall**, at the island end of London Bridge, is your best bet. The dining room at *Shugrue's* here (☎520/453-1400) looks out over the bridge, and serves fresh fish (even sushi), salads and pasta, and a new **microbrewery** was due to open as this book went to press.

Las Vegas

Little emphasis is placed on the gambling clubs and divorce facilities – though they are attractions to many visitors – and much is being done to build up the cultural attractions. No cheap and easily parodied slogans have been adopted to publicize the city, no attempt has been made to introduce pseudo-romantic architectural themes or to give artificial glamor or gaiety. Las Vegas is itself – natural and therefore very appealing to people with a wide variety of interests.

WPA Guidebook to Nevada, 1940

Shimmering from the desert haze of Nevada like a latter-day El Dorado, **LAS VEGAS** is the most dynamic, spectacular city on earth. At the start of the twentieth century, it didn't even exist; now it's home to over one million people, with enough newcomers arriving all the time to need a new school every month. Boasting nine of the world's ten largest hotels, it's a monument to architectural exuberance, whose flamboyant, no-expense-spared **casinos** lure in thirty million tourists each year. Las Vegas has been stockpiling superlatives since the 1950s, but never rests on its laurels for a moment. Long before they lose their sparkle, yesterday's showpieces are blasted into rubble, to make way for ever more extravagant replacements. A few years ago, when the fashion was for fantasy, Arthurian castles and Egyptian pyramids mushroomed along the legendary Strip; now Vegas demands nothing less than entire cities, and has already acquired pocket versions of New York, Paris, Monte Carlo and Venice.

While Las Vegas has certainly cleaned up its act since the early days of Mob domination, there's little truth in the notion that it's become a family destination. In fact, for kids, it's not a patch on Orlando. Several casinos have added theme parks or fun rides to fill those odd non-gambling moments, but only five percent of visitors bring children, and the crowds that cluster around the exploding volcanoes and pirate battles along the Strip remain almost exclusively adult. Neither is Vegas as consistently cheap as it used to be. It's still possible to find good, inexpensive rooms, and the all-you-can-eat buffets offer unbeatable value, but the casino owners have finally discovered that high-rollers happy to lose hundreds of dollars per night don't mind paying premium prices to eat at top-quality restaurants, and some of the latest developments are budgeting on room rates of $300 rather than $30 per night.

Your first hours in Las Vegas are like entering another world, where the religion is luck, the language is money, and time is measured by revolutions of a roulette wheel. Once you're acclimatized, the whole spectacle can be absolutely exhilarating – assuming you haven't pinned your hopes, and your savings, on the pursuit of a fortune. Las Vegas is an unmissable destination, but one that palls for most visitors after a couple of (hectic) days.

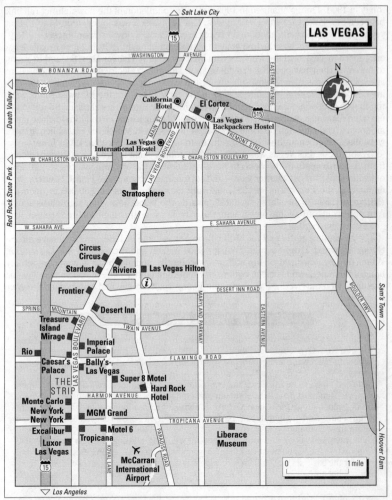

If you've come solely to **gamble**, there's not much to say beyond the fact that all the casinos are free, and open 24 hours per day, with acres of floor space packed with ways to lose money: million-dollar slots, video poker, blackjack, craps, roulette wheels, and much much more. The casinos will just love it if you try to play a system; with the odds stacked against you, your best hope of a large win is to bet your entire stake on one single play, and then stop, win or lose.

Some history

The name *Las Vegas* – Spanish for "the meadows" – was originally applied to a group of natural springs that served as a way-station for travelers on the Old Spanish Trail from 1829 onwards. For the rest of the nineteenth century, the Paiute Indians shared the region with a handful of Mormon ranchers, and the valley had a population of just thirty in 1900. Things changed in 1905, with the completion of the now-defunct rail link between Salt Lake City and Los Angeles. Las Vegas itself was founded on May 15 that year, when the railroads auctioned off lots around what's now Fremont Street.

Ironically, Nevada was the first state to outlaw gambling, in 1909, but it was made legal once more in 1931, and the workers who built the nearby Hoover Dam flocked to Vegas to bet away their pay-packets. Providing abundant cheap electricity and water, the dam amounted to a massive federal subsidy for the infant city. Hotel-casinos such as the daring 65-room *El Rancho* began to appear in the early 1940s, but the Midwest Mafia were the first to appreciate the potential for profit. Mobster Bugsy Siegel raised $7 million to open the *Flamingo* on the Strip in December 1946; early losses forced him to close again in January, and although he swiftly managed to re-open in March his erstwhile partners were dissatisfied enough with their returns to have him murdered in LA in June.

By the 1950s, Las Vegas was booming. The military had arrived – mushroom clouds from **A-bomb tests** in the deserts were visible from the city and visitors would drive out with picnics to get a better view – and so, too, had big guns like **Frank Sinatra**, who debuted at the *Desert Inn* in 1951, and **Liberace**, who received $50,000 to open the *Riviera* in 1955. As the stars gravitated towards the Vegas honeypot, nightclubs across America went out of business, and the city became the nation's undisputed live-entertainment capital.

The beginning of the end for Mob rule in Vegas came in 1966, after reclusive airline tycoon **Howard Hughes** sold TWA for $500 million and moved into the *Desert Inn*. When the owners tired of his stingy – specifically non-gambling – ways, he simply bought the hotel, and his clean-cut image encouraged other entrepreneurs to follow his example. **Elvis** arrived a little later; the young rock'n'roller had bombed at the *New*

GETTING MARRIED IN LAS VEGAS

Second only to making your fortune as a reason to visit Las Vegas is the prospect of **getting married**. Over a hundred thousand weddings are performed here each year, many so informal that bride and groom just wind down the window of their car during the ceremony; a Vegas wedding has become a byword for tongue-in-cheek chic.

You don't have to be a resident to get wed here, and you don't need a blood test, either. However, you must be at least eighteen years old and not already married, and purchase a $35 license from the Clark County Marriage License Bureau at 200 S Third St (Mon–Thurs 8am–midnight, 8am on Fri to midnight on Sun; ☎702/455-3156) any time before the ceremony.

The city phone book lists fourteen pages of **wedding chapels**, with an inconceivable range of trappings, and most casinos also have their own facilities. Prices start at around $100 for the basic service, and the sky is literally the limit – you can get spliced while floating in a hot-air balloon, or parachuting out of a plane. Las Vegas Weddings and Rooms (☎1-800/488-6283) offer all-inclusive wedding packages, or contact the chapels direct.

Graceland Wedding Chapel, 619 S Las Vegas Blvd; ☎1-800/824-5732 or 702/474-6655. Home of the King – an Elvis impersonator will act as best man, give the bride away or serenade you, but unfortunately he can't perform the service.

Little Church of the West, 3960 S Las Vegas Blvd; ☎1-800/821-2452 or 702/739-7971. On the National Register of Historic Places, this fifty-year-old chapel is among the more peaceful and quiet places – if that's really what you want – to exchange your Vegas vows.

Little White Chapel, 1301 S Las Vegas Blvd; ☎1-800/545-8111 or 702/382-5943. Where Bruce Willis and Demi Moore married each other, and Michael Jordan and Joan Collins married other people. Open all day every day, with "The One & Only 24hr Drive-Up Wedding Window", if you're in a major hurry.

Stratosphere, 2000 S Las Vegas Blvd; ☎1-800/789-9IDO or 702/380-7777. The three highest wedding chapels in the world, 700 feet up.

Frontier in 1956, but started a triumphant five-year stint as a karate-kicking lounge lizard at the *International* (now the *Las Vegas Hilton*) in 1969. He married Priscilla at the *Aladdin* on May 1, 1967, nine months to the day before the birth of Lisa Marie, and just eight years before Michael Jackson met Lisa Marie at a Jackson Five gig in Vegas.

Endless federal swoops and stings drove the Mob out of sight by the 1980s, in time for Vegas to re-invent itself on a surge of junk-bond megadollars. The success of Steve Wynn's *Mirage* in enticing a new generation of visitors, from 1989 onwards, spawned a host of imitators. The long-established *Circus Circus* crew swiftly erected the *Excalibur* and the amazing *Luxor*, the *Hard Rock* arrived and *Planet Hollywood* is on its way, the *Stratosphere* appeared from nowhere to tower over the city, and Wynn himself built *Treasure Island* and will soon open the $1.2 billion *Bellagio*. Beneath the glitz, however, **gambling** remains the bedrock, and Las Vegas' pre-eminence seems little dented by the spread of casinos elsewhere in the US. City boosters point out that only fifteen percent of Americans have so far seen Vegas, and they're confidently expecting the rest to turn up any day now.

Arrival, information and getting around

Las Vegas' busy **McCarran International Airport** (☎702/261-5743) is a mile southeast of the Strip, and four miles from downtown. Some hotels run free shuttle buses for guests, while Bell Trans (☎702/739-7990) run a minibus service to the Strip ($3.50) and downtown ($5), and a **cab** to the Strip costs around $12.

If you plan to see more of Vegas than the Strip – and even there, it's too hot to walk more than a couple of blocks in the daytime – a **car** is invaluable. All the big rental companies have outlets at the airport; Allstate (☎1-800/634-6186) is an inexpensive local alternative. **Public transportation** does exist, however. The oak-veneered streetcars of the Las Vegas Strip Trolley (☎702/382-1404) ply the Strip between Hacienda Avenue (south of the *Luxor*) and Sahara Avenue, for a flat fare of $1.30, but don't go downtown. CAT **buses** (☎702/228-7433; $1.50) serve the whole city; #301 connects the Strip to downtown. **Greyhound**'s long-distance buses use a terminal at 200 S Main St, downtown, though arriving buses also stop on the Strip, outside the *Stardust*, 3000 N Las Vegas Blvd. Amtrak **trains** no longer serve Las Vegas, but Amtrak run connecting buses to Vegas from LA and Bakersfield in California.

Any number of freesheets and magazines – usually bursting with discount vouchers, plus details of accommodation, buffets and the latest shows – provide local **information**. There are also **visitor centers** at 3150 Paradise Rd (daily 8am–5pm; ☎702/892-0711), near the Strip and next to the vast Convention Center, and 711 E Desert Inn Rd (Mon–Fri 8am–5pm; ☎702/735-1616). There can be no easier city in which to **change money**: the casinos gladly convert almost any currency, and their walls are festooned with every conceivable ATM machine.

Accommodation

Although Las Vegas has well over 100,000 motel and hotel **rooms** (most of them hitched to casinos), it's best to book accommodation ahead if you're on a tight budget, or arriving on Friday or Saturday; upwards of 200,000 people descend upon the city every weekend. Rooms can be very inexpensive, but be sure to get the rate confirmed for the duration of your stay – that $25 room you found on Thursday may cost $100 on Friday, and if a championship fight or other special event is on, room rates hit the roof. The CVB runs a **reservation service** on ☎1-800/332-5333.

If you're planning a trip from elsewhere in North America, check local newspaper advertisements for the latest Vegas bargains – virtually all hotels and motels offer discounts and food vouchers.

Caesar's Palace, 3570 S Las Vegas Blvd (☎1-800/634-6661 or 702/731-7110). Right in the heart of the Strip, this epitome of 1960s luxury has recently trebled in size, and offers the last word in pseudo-Roman splendor, with top-class restaurants and shops. ⑥.

California Hotel, 12 Ogden Ave at First St (☎1-800/634-6255 or 702/385-1222). Mid-range down-town casino, with a mere 800 rooms, where the guests are mostly Hawaiian, and Hawaiian food and drink dominates the bars and restaurants. ③.

Circus Circus, 2880 S Las Vegas Blvd (☎1-800/634-3450 or 702/734-0410). Venerable Strip hotel that's a big hit with kids, with circus acts performing live above the casino floor. ③.

Desert Inn, 3145 Las Vegas Blvd (☎1-800/634-6906 or 702/733-4444). The classiest and most expensive of the Strip hotels, with its own golf course and spa, and big-name entertainment. ⑦.

El Cortez Hotel, 600 E Fremont St (☎1-800/634-6703 or 702/385-5200). Long-standing downtown hotel, charging bargain rates for reasonable rooms; suites cost just a little extra. ①.

Excalibur, 3850 S Las Vegas Blvd (☎1-800/937-7777 or 702/597-7777). Arthurian legend built larger than life, with plenty to amuse the kids while the adults gamble away their college funds. Four thousand rooms plus assorted drawbridges, turrets and nightly jousting matches; staff have to call guests M'Lord and M'Lady. ④.

Hard Rock Hotel, 4455 Paradise Rd (☎1-800/473-7625 or 702/693-5000). "The world's only rock-'n'roll casino", over a mile east of the Strip, is a pale imitation of Las Vegas' showcase giants, but the guest rooms are above average, and there's a great pool. ⑦.

Las Vegas Backpackers Hostel, 1322 Fremont St (☎702/385-1150). Clean, very well equipped pri-vate hostel, a short walk east of downtown, with dorms from $12 plus en-suite doubles, on-site bar and restaurant, pool and jacuzzi, and a full program of tours and activities.

Las Vegas International Hostel, 1208 S Las Vegas Blvd (☎702/385-9955). Friendly, bare-bones AAIH hostel north of the Strip, which arranges tours to state and national parks. Dorm beds cost $14, rooms with shared baths under $30 – little cheaper than some Strip hotels.

Luxor, 3900 S Las Vegas Blvd (☎1-800/288-1000 or 702/262-4000). Vast smoked-glass pyramid, where guests sail Nile barges to the elevators up to their desert-view rooms. All that plus seven restaurants, virtual reality experiences, and the obligatory casino. ⑤.

MGM Grand, 3799 S Las Vegas Blvd (☎1-800/929-1111 or 702/891-1111). The world's largest hotel, with 5005 rooms, is home to the world's largest casino, several of Las Vegas' finest restaurants, a vast events arena, an amusement park and a model of Oz's Emerald City. ④.

Mirage, 3400 S Las Vegas Blvd (☎1-800/627-6667 or 702/791-7111). Glitzy casino, with its own vol-cano, rainforest, and coral reef, some good restaurants and surprisingly tranquil rooms. ⑦.

Motel 6 – Tropicana, 195 E Tropicana Ave (☎702/798-0728). At 880 rooms, the largest Motel 6 in the country; a ten-minute walk off the Strip from the MGM Grand. ③.

New York New York, 3790 S Las Vegas Blvd (☎1-800/NYFORME or 702/740-6969). Mock Manhattan, looped by a high-speed roller-coaster and a riot of neon at night; the 2000 rooms are plush by usual Strip standards. ⑦.

Sam's Town, 5111 Boulder Hwy (☎1-800/634-6371 or 702/456-7777). Old-style Western-themed casino over six miles east of the Strip that's popular with older visitors. ④.

Stratosphere, 2000 S Las Vegas Blvd (☎1-800/99-TOWER or 702/380-7777). Hundred-story tower just north of the Strip, with amazing views, nauseating thrill-rides, good restaurants, and the world's three highest wedding chapels. ④.

Super 8, 4250 Koval Lane (☎1-800/800-8000 or 702/794-0888). The closest of Vegas' three *Super 8*s to the Strip has its own little casino and a reasonable restaurant. ③.

Treasure Island, 3300 S Las Vegas Blvd (☎1-800/944-7444 or 702/894-7111). Sister hotel to the neighboring *Mirage*, where an endless pirate battle plays to the passing crowds on the Strip, the restaurants within are swathed with rigging, and one TV channel shows the movie *Treasure Island* non-stop. ⑦.

Tropicana, 3801 S Las Vegas Blvd (☎1-800/634-4000 or 702/739-2222). Jungle-themed casino, recently spruced up to compete with its giant neighbors, but still offering swim-up gaming tables around the world's largest indoor-outdoor swimming pool. ④.

The City

Though the Las Vegas sprawl measures fifteen miles wide by fifteen miles long, most tourists stick to the six-mile stretch of Las Vegas Boulevard that includes the **Strip**, home to the major casinos, and **downtown**, slightly southeast of the intersection of I-15 and US-95. In between the two lie two somewhat seedy miles of gas stations, fast-food drive-ins and wedding chapels, while the rest of town is largely residential, and need barely concern you.

The Strip

For its razor-edge finesse in harnessing sheer, magnificent excess to the deadly serious business of making money, there's no place like the **Las Vegas Strip**. It's hard to imagine a time when Las Vegas was an ordinary city, and Las Vegas Boulevard a dusty thoroughfare scattered with the usual edge-of-town motels. After five decades of capitalism run riot, with every new casino-hotel setting out to surpass anything its neighbors ever dreamed of, the Strip seems to be locked into a hyper-active craving for thrills and glamor, forever discarding its latest toy in its frenzy for the next jackpot.

Each casino is a self-contained fantasyland of high camp and genuine excitement. Almost against your will, huge moving walkways sweep you in from the sidewalk; once inside, it can be almost impossible to find your way out. The action keeps going day and night, and in this sealed and windowless environment you rapidly lose track of which is which. Even if you do manage to get back onto the streets during the day, the scorching heat is liable to drive you straight back in again; night is the best time to venture out, when the blazing neon is at its brightest.

As the Strip pushes deeper into the desert, the newest casinos tend to rise at its southern end, not far west of the airport. The procession kicks off with the 36-story bronze and glass pyramid of the **Luxor**, which opened in 1993. From the palm-fringed avenue of sphinxes guarding the entrance to the reconstruction of Tutankhamun's tomb inside, the whole building plays endless variations on the theme of Egyptian archeology. In Las Vegas' closest approximation to Disneyland, three separate simulator rides and 3-D movies combine to reveal the "Secrets of the Luxor Pyramid", a confusing saga of derring-do that's overpriced at $13. Meanwhile, the most powerful artificial light beam ever created shines up from the pyramid's apex; visible from planes circling over LA, 250 miles west, it supposedly pays tribute to the ancient Egyptian belief that the soul of a dead Pharaoh would rise directly into the skies.

The *Luxor*'s architect, Veldon Simpson, had previously designed the **Excalibur**, immediately north. A less sophisticated mock-up of a medieval castle, complete with drawbridge, crenellated towers, and a basement stuffed with fairground-style sideshows for the kids, it's usually packed out with low-budget tour groups. Its brief reign as the world's largest hotel, from 1990 to 1993, ended when the five-thousand-room **MGM Grand Hotel and Theme Park** – another Simpson creation – opened across the street. Entered beneath the gaping jaws of MGM's trademark lion, it has become the most prestigious big-fight venue in town, and offers the Strip's finest selection of restaurants. Turnover in its casino is so phenomenal that when the crowds after the Holyfield–Tyson debacle in June 1997 mistook the popping of champagne corks for gunfire and the resulting panic forced the tables to close down for two hours, the loss was estimated in millions of dollars. **MGM Grand Adventures** (daily 10am–6pm; unlimited rides $17), a 33-acre theme park behind the hotel, is however disappointingly thrill-free for adults.

Excalibur and the *MGM Grand* are not the only giants facing off across the intersection of Las Vegas Boulevard and Tropicana Avenue. The northwest corner, diagonally opposite the veteran **Tropicana**, is now occupied by a brash newcomer, **New York**

New York. Fronted of course by the Statue of Liberty, and approached across a 300-foot Brooklyn Bridge, this miniature Manhattan boasts a skyline featuring twelve separate skyscrapers, while the interior depicts Central Park at dusk (not perhaps somewhere you'd choose to be in real life). The one respect in which it surpasses New York itself is that for $5 you can swoop around the whole thing at 65mph on the hair-raising Manhattan Express roller coaster.

A couple of blocks north – which in Vegas means almost a mile – and just beyond the intersection where rapper Tupac Shakur was gunned down in 1996, the long-established **Caesar's Palace** still encapsulates Las Vegas at its best. Here the walkway delivers you past grand marble staircases that lead nowhere, and full-sized replicas of Michaelangelo's *David*, into a vast labyrinth of slots and green baize, peopled by strutting half-naked Roman centurions and Cleopatra-cropped waitresses. Above the stores and restaurants of the extraordinary **Forum**, the blue-domed ceiling dims and glows as it endlessly cycles from dawn to dusk and back again.

Night-time crowds jostle for space on the sidewalk outside the glittering **Mirage**, beyond *Caesar's Palace*, to watch the somewhat half-hearted volcano that erupts every fifteen minutes, spewing water and fire into the lagoon below. Next door, a pirate galleon and a British frigate, crewed by actors, do noisy battle outside **Treasure Island** (shows every ninety minutes; daily 4–11pm). The family-oriented **Circus Circus**, another mile north, uses live circus acts to pull in the punters – a trapeze artist here, a fire-eater there – and also has an indoor water-oriented theme park, **Grand Slam Canyon**, vaguely modelled on the Grand Canyon, where you pay separately for each roller coaster or river-ride. If you really want to cool off, you'd do better to head on to the flumes and chutes of Vegas' one purpose-built water park, **Wet'n'Wild**, 2601 S Las Vegas Blvd (summer daily 10am–8pm; $22). Alternatively, the **Las Vegas Hilton** – off the Strip at 3000 Paradise Rd, half a mile east of *Circus Circus* – offers the Star Trek Experience, in which visitors pay $10 to dress up as their favorite Star Trek character and take a virtual-reality trip aboard the Enterprise.

Circus Circus has traditionally marked the northern limit of the Strip, but the 1996 opening of the **Stratosphere Tower**, half a mile towards downtown, may change that. At 1149 feet, the *Stratosphere* is the tallest building west of the Mississippi, and the outdoor deck and indoor viewing chamber in the sphere near the summit offer amazing panoramas across the city ($5). Two utterly demented thrill rides can take you even closer to heaven; the **world's highest roller coaster** swirls around the outside of the sphere, while the ludicrous Big Shot shunts you to the very top of an additional 160-foot spire, from which you free-fall back down again ($5 each). Financial difficulties are said to have delayed plans to build a King-Kong-shaped elevator that would climb the exterior of the tower.

Downtown and the Liberace Museum

As the Strip has gone from strength to strength, **downtown Las Vegas**, the city's original core, has by comparison been neglected. Long known as "Glitter Gulch", and consisting of a few compact blocks of lower-key casinos, it has recently embarked upon a revival. Between Main Street and Las Vegas Boulevard, five entire blocks of Fremont Street, its principal thoroughfare, have been roofed with an open-air mesh to create the **Fremont Street Experience**. This "Celestial Vault" is studded with neon, choreographed in dazzling nightly displays of color, and shelters a mall of bars, restaurants and souvenir stores as well as several rapidly expanding casinos. However, there's still a long way to go before it can really compete with the Strip.

Almost all Las Vegas' handful of museums are eminently missable, with one unarguable exception: the **Liberace Museum**, two miles east of the Strip at 1775 E Tropicana Ave (Mon–Sat 10am–5pm, Sun 1–5pm; $6.50). Popularly remembered as a beaming buffoon who knocked out torpid toe-tappers, Liberace, who died in 1987, started out playing piano in the rough bars of Milwaukee during the 1940s. A decade later, he was being mobbed by screaming adolescents and ruthlessly hounded by the scandal-hungry press. All this is recalled by a yellowing collection of cuttings and family photos, along with electric candelabra, bejewelled quail eggs with inlaid pianos, rhinestone-covered fur coats, glittering cars and more. The music, piped into the scented toilets, may not have improved with age, but the museum is a satisfying attempt to answer the seminal question "how does a great performer top himself on stage?".

Red Rock Canyon

For a blast of sunlight and fresh air away from the casinos, and a sample of some classic Southwestern canyon scenery, head twenty miles west of the Strip along Charleston Boulevard to the **Red Rock Canyon National Conservation Area**. This BLM-run park consists of a cactus-strewn desert basin surrounded by stark red cliffs that are pierced repeatedly by narrow canyons accessible only on foot.

Red Rock Canyon's **visitor center**, which has displays about the canyon and a viewing window overlooking its main features (daily 8am–5pm; free), stands just before the start of the **Scenic Drive** (daily 7am–dusk). As this thirteen-mile loop road meanders around the edge of the basin, it passes trailheads like the one for the cool, slender **Ice Box Canyon** (a 2.5-mile round-trip hike), and the three-mile **Pine Creek Trail**, which follows a flower-lined creek beyond a ruined homesite towards a towering red-capped monolith.

Lake Mead and the Hoover Dam

Almost as many people as go to Las Vegas visit **LAKE MEAD**, the vast reservoir thirty miles southeast of the city that was created by the construction of the Hoover Dam. A bizarre spectacle, its blue waters a vivid counterpoint to the surrounding desert, it gets excruciatingly crowded all year round.

Though the **Lake Mead National Recreation Area** straddles the border between Nevada and Arizona, the best views come from the Nevada side. Even if you don't need details of how to sail, scuba-dive, water-ski or fish from the marinas along the five-hundred-mile shoreline, call in at the **Alan Bible visitor center** (daily 8.30am–4.30pm; ☎702/293-8990), four miles northeast of Boulder City on US-93, to enjoy a sweeping prospect of the whole thing.

Eight miles on, beyond the rocky ridges of the Black Mountains, US-93 reaches the **Hoover Dam** itself, completed in 1935. Designed to block the Colorado River and provide low-cost electricity for the cities of the Southwest, it's among the tallest dams ever built (760ft high), and used enough concrete to build a two-lane highway from the West Coast to New York. Informative thirty-minute guided tours of the dam leave from the new **Hoover Dam Visitor Center** on the Nevada side of the river (daily 8.30am–5.45pm; $5; ☎702/293-1824). Five-hour, $23 **bus tours** to the dam from Las Vegas are run by Gray Line (☎702/384-1234).

Eating and drinking

Eating is one of the real treats of Las Vegas. Keen to entice visitors onto their premises – and keep them there – all the casinos offer good-value round-the-clock **buffets**. Even when the food isn't that great – the buffets at the *MGM Grand* and the *Excalibur* spring to mind – you're bound to find something you can keep down. Breakfast typically costs between $3 and $6 – or is even free with a voucher; lunch, served until 3pm or 4pm, is more like $4 to $7, and dinner is anything from $5 up to $15. Between 6pm and 9pm, the lines at the larger casinos can be endless.

Each casino has in addition at least one top-quality conventional **restaurant**, and though there are plenty of dining places away from the Strip, only a small proportion of eccentric tourists bother to venture off in search of them. **Drinks** – beer, wine, spirits and cocktails – are freely available in all the casinos to anyone gambling, and are very cheap for anyone else.

Buffets

Bally's Big Kitchen Buffet, *Bally's Casino*, 3645 S Las Vegas Blvd (☎702/739-4930). The best of the Strip buffets; a quite phenomenal spread of fresh seafood, meats and salads (7.30am–2pm $9; 4.30–10pm $13). *Bally's* Champagne Sterling Brunch, served in a separate room (Sun 9.30am–2.30pm), is magnificent – as it should be for $50.

Golden Nugget Buffet, *Golden Nugget*, 129 E Fremont St (☎702/385-7111). Downtown's classiest buffet, with full carvery and a fine spread of salads; ranges from $6 for breakfast up to $10.50 for dinner.

Rio's Carnival World Buffet, *Rio Hotel*, 3700 W Flamingo Rd (☎702/252-7777). Superb, albeit meat-heavy buffet, with a lush array of desserts (Mon–Fri breakfasts $4 & lunches $6; Sat & Sun all day $8.

Sam's Town – The Great Buffet, *Sam's Town*, 5111 Boulder Hwy; (☎702/456-7777). Unassuming, inexpensive but top-quality buffet, a few miles east of the Strip. Prices only exceed $8 for the $12 Friday-night seafood extravaganza, and there's live country music and dancing with no cover charge.

Restaurants

Coyote Cafe, *MGM Grand*, 3799 S Las Vegas Blvd (☎702/891-7349). Outpost of Mark Miller's definitive "Modern Southwestern" restaurant, with entrees priced at up to $30 in the dinner-only *Grill Room* and under $20 in the adjoining *Cafe*, open from 9am daily.

Emeril's New Orleans Fish House, *MGM Grand*, 3799 S Las Vegas Blvd (☎702/891-7374). Excellent seafood, most but not all with spicy Cajun flavorings. Crispy baby calamari, steamed bass, crabmeat fishcakes and lobster at $20 and up per entree, plus an oyster bar.

Spago's, *Caesar's Palace*, 3570 S Las Vegas Blvd (☎702/369-6300). Surreal Californian restaurant that's Vegas' premier site for star-spotting, with a space-age decor to complement Caesar's blue-domed *Forum*. Entrees at up to $30 in the dinner-only *Dining Room*, half that in the all-day *Cafe*.

Top of the World, *Stratosphere*, 2000 S Las Vegas Blvd (☎702/380-7711). The food at this 106th-floor revolving restaurant is little more than ordinary – though the Asian-influenced dinners, at up to $30, are a cut above lunch-time's salads and sandwiches – but the amazing views make up for it.

Nightlife and entertainment

The days of the big-budget Vegas **"spectacular"** are far from over, though as the great names of the past fade from view few stars can now carry an extended-run show, and the tendency these days is to rely on lavish stunts and effects. The illusionist-magicians Siegfried and Roy rule the roost at the *Mirage* (Fri–Tues 7.30pm & 11pm; $84), while the *MGM Grand* offers David Cassidy in a show called "EFX" (Mon, Fri & Sat 7.30pm & 10.30pm, Tues, Wed & Sun 7.30pm; $70). There's a more contemporary feel at *Treasure Island*, where the postmodern Cirque du Soleil are in long-term residency (Wed–Sun 7.30pm & 10.30pm; $60, under-12s $30). If only **Elvis** will do, he's one of several performers impersonated in the "Legends in Concert" show at the Imperial Palace, 3535 S Las Vegas Blvd (Mon–Sat 7.30pm & 10.30pm; $30, under-13s $15).

Entertainment schedules are of course subject to change without notice; for full details of what's coming up, consult papers like the *Las Vegas New Times*, or call casinos such as the *Hard Rock* – the best bet for big-name touring acts – ahead of time.

The Grand Canyon

The **GRAND CANYON OF THE COLORADO** in Arizona, three hundred long and featureless driving miles from Las Vegas, is one of those sights that you really *have* to see once in your life, and once you've ventured east of the California state line it would be a real shame to exclude it from your itinerary.

Although three million people come to see the Grand Canyon every year, it remains beyond the grasp of the human imagination. No photograph, no set of statistics, can prepare you for such vastness. At more than one mile deep, it's an inconceivable abyss; at from four to eighteen miles wide it's an endless expanse of bewildering shapes and colors, glaring desert brightness and impenetrable shadow, stark promontories and soaring never-to-be-climbed sandstone pinnacles. Somehow it's so impassive, so remote – you could never call it a disappointment, but at the same time many visitors are left feeling peculiarly flat. In a sense, none of the available activities can quite live up to that first stunning sight of the chasm. The **overlooks** along the rim all offer views that shift and change unceasingly from dawn to dusk; you can **hike** down into the depths on foot or by mule, hover above in a **helicopter** or raft through the **whitewater rapids** of the river itself; you can spend a night at **Phantom Ranch** on the canyon floor, or swim in the waterfalls of the idyllic **Havasupai Reservation**; and yet that distance always remains – the Grand Canyon stands apart.

The vast majority of visitors come to the **South Rim**, which you'll find described in full on the next few pages – it's the most accessible part of the canyon, there are far more facilities (mainly at **Grand Canyon Village**), and it's open year-round. There's another lodge and campground at the **North Rim**, which by virtue of its isolation can be a whole lot more evocative (for accommodation reservations, see p.249), but at one thousand feet higher this is usually closed by snow from mid-October until May. An even less eventful drive from Las Vegas brings you here via St George in southern Utah. Few people visit both rims; to get from one to the other demands either a two-day hike down one side of the canyon and up the other, or a 215-mile drive by road. Until the 1920s, the average visitor would stay for two or three weeks; these days it's more like two or three hours – of which forty minutes are spent actually looking at the canyon.

Finally, there's a definite risk that on the day you come the Grand Canyon will be invisible beneath a layer of **fog**; many people blame the 250 tons of sulphurous emissions pumped out every day by the Navajo Generating Station, seventy miles upriver at Page.

Admission prices to the park, valid for seven days on either rim, are $20 per vehicle, or $10 per pedestrian or cyclist.

Practicalities

The most usual approach to the South Rim of the Grand Canyon is by **road**, turning north off I-17 at **Williams** to drive the last 56 miles on Hwy-64, or detouring further east via the larger town of **Flagstaff** and then following Hwy-180 past the San Francisco mountains. The two roads join twenty miles before the canyon, at Valle. Most of this stretch is through thick ponderosa pine forests, so the ride up from Williams on the restored **steam trains** of the Grand Canyon Railway is not especially scenic (departs Williams 9.30am: daily late March to Oct; rest of year weekends only; $55 round-trip; ☎1-800/THE-TRAIN or 520/773-1976). Passengers who arrive on Flagstaff's two daily Amtrak **trains** can reach Grand Canyon Village on connecting Nava-Hopi **buses** (☎1-800/892-8687 or 520/774-5003; $12.50); one leaves Flagstaff at 8am, calls at Williams at 8.50am, and arrives at the canyon at 10.10am, the other runs straight from Flagstaff to the canyon, departing at 2.45pm and arriving 4.40pm. Return trips leave

THE GRAND CANYON

25 miles

0

Bright Angel Lodge at 10.30am – a direct service to Flagstaff, arriving at 12.30pm – and 5pm, reaching Williams at 6.15pm and Flagstaff at 7pm.

The small **airport** at Tusayan – just outside the park boundary, and used primarily by "flight-seeing" tour companies (see box, p.252) – also welcomes scheduled services, especially from Las Vegas, with operators such as Scenic Airlines (from $60 one-way; ☎1-800/634-6801 or 702/739-1900).

During high season (roughly May–Sept) free **shuttle buses** operate every fifteen minutes within Grand Canyon Village, and along the West Rim Drive (which at those times is barred to motorists), stopping at the main overlooks.

Grand Canyon Village

GRAND CANYON VILLAGE is not a very stimulating place to spend any time. However, in the absence of significantly cheaper accommodation within fifty miles (for example, in **Tusayan** at the park entrance), there's little option but to stay here. The centerpiece is the magnificent **terrace** in front of *Bright Angel Lodge* (usually the liveliest spot in town) and the black-beamed 1905 *El Tovar Hotel*, which gives many visitors their only look at the canyon – though the Colorado itself is too deep in the Inner Gorge to be seen from here. Further back are more lodges and gift shops, and employee housing, while about a mile east through the woods are the informative **visitor center** (daily 8am–6pm; ☎520/638-7888), the **post office**, the **general store** and the **campground**.

Grand Canyon accommodation

All the "lodges" in the village charge similar prices, with no budget alternative. To see the canyon, it makes little difference where in the village you stay. Even in the "rim-edge" places – *El Tovar Hotel* (⑥) and the *Bright Angel* (rooms ③, rim-side cabins ⑤), *Thunderbird* and *Kachina* lodges (both with ordinary rooms ⑤, canyon view ⑥) – few rooms offer much of a view, and in any case it's always dark by 8pm. Further back are the *Maswik Lodge* (group cabins ③, rooms ④), *Yavapai Lodge* near the visitor center (⑤), and *Moqui Lodge* at the park entrance (mid-Feb to Nov; ④).

Camping facilities (and a laundry) are available at the *Mather* campground and RV park ($12) near the visitor center, at least one section of which is open year-round. If you arrive on foot, you don't need a reservation; all vehicles should, however, check in well in advance (you can book on☎1-800/365-2267). The summer-only *Desert View* campground, 26 miles east, is first-come-first-served, and has no hook-ups. It's also possible to camp inside the canyon itself, if you first obtain a free permit from the **Backcountry Reservations Office** near the *Mather* campground (daily 8am–noon; phone enquiries Mon–Fri 1–5pm ☎520/638-7875); indeed you can camp anywhere in Kaibab National Forest so long as you're more than 200 yards from a roadway.

If all the park accommodation is full, the nearest alternative is the underwhelming service village of **TUSAYAN**, just over a mile south of the park entrance. *Seven Mile Lodge* (☎520/638-2291; ④) offers the least expensive rooms; *Red Feather Lodge* (☎520/638-2414; ⑥) is a little more comfortable. Much the most popular of the commercial **campgrounds** outside the park – with families, at least – is *Flintstone's Bedrock City* (mid-March to Oct; ☎520/635-2600; $12–16), 22 miles south at the junction of Hwy-64 and Hwy-180, which has its own prehistoric theme park.

All in-park **accommodation reservations** – for the lodges on both the South and the North rims, as well as *Phantom Ranch* (see p.252) and RV camping – are handled by Amfac Parks & Resorts, 14001 East Iliff, #600, Aurora, CO 80014 (same-day ☎520/638-2631; advance ☎303/297-2757). The best rooms are often booked as much as a year ahead, and your chances of turning up without a reservation and finding a place in summer are minimal.

Grand Canyon eating

Thanks to the canyon's remoteness and lack of water, **food prices** tend to be well above average; if you're on a tight budget, bring your own. However, *Yavapai* and *Maswik* lodges have reasonable basic cafeterias, open until 10pm. *Bright Angel Lodge* has its own restaurant as well as the *Arizona Steakhouse*, both also open until 10pm, and both costing $15–30. At *El Tovar*, where the dining room looks right out over the canyon, the sumptuous menu is enormously expensive. Breakfast is the most affordable meal; lunch and dinner can easily cost upwards of $40. In **Tusayan**, *We Cook Pizza* (☎520/638-2278) is good but pricey.

Along the South Rim

It's possible to walk along the South Rim for several miles in either direction from the village, the first few of them on railed and concreted pathways. The most obvious short excursions are to see the sun rise and set. At or near the village, the giant wall that reaches out in the west overshadows much of the evening view. If, however, you walk right out to **Hopi Point** at its end, looking down as you go onto the Bright Angel Trail as it winds across the Tonto Plateau, you may well see a magical **sunset**, with the Colorado – 350ft wide at this point – visible way below.

The best place within walking distance to watch the **dawn** is **Mather Point**, a mile east of the visitor center. Nearby, if you can tear your eyes away from its panoramic bay windows, the **Yavapai Geologic Museum** (summer daily 9am–7pm; free) has illuminating displays on how the canyon may have been formed.

Further dramatic views are available along the **East Rim Drive** – although unless you take an excursion you'll need your own vehicle to see them. **Desert View**, 23 miles out from the village, is at 7500ft the highest point on the South Rim. Visible to the east

GEOLOGY AND HISTORY OF THE CANYON

Layer upon layer of different rocks, readily distinguished by color and each with its own **fossil record**, recede down into the Grand Canyon and back through time, until the strata at the river bed are among the oldest exposed rocks on earth. And yet how the canyon was formed is a mystery. Satellite photos show that the Colorado actually runs through the heart of an enormous hill (what the Indians called the *Kaibab*, the mountain with no peak); experts cannot agree on how this could happen. Studies show that the canyon still deepens, at the slow rate of 50ft per million years. Its fantastic sandstone and limestone formations were not literally carved by the river, however; they're the result of erosion by wind and extreme cycles of heat and cold. These features were named – **Brahma Temple**, **Vishnu Temple**, and so on – by Clarence Dutton, a student of comparative religion who wrote the first Geological Survey report on the canyon in 1881.

It may look forbidding, but the Grand Canyon is not a dead place. All sorts of desert **wildlife** survive here – sheep and rabbits, eagles and vultures, mountain lions, and, of course, spiders, scorpions, and snakes. The **human** presence has never been on any great scale, but signs have been found of habitation as early as 2000 BC, and the **Anasazi** were certainly here later on. A party of **Spaniards** passed through in 1540 – less than twenty years after Cortes conquered the Aztecs – searching for cities of gold, and one Father Garcés spent some time with the Havasupai in 1776. **John Wesley Powell**'s expeditions along the fearsome and uncharted waters of the Colorado in 1869 and 1871–72 were what really brought the canyon to public attention. A few abortive attempts were made to mine different areas, but facilities for tourism were swiftly realized to be a far more lucrative investment. With the exception of the Indian reservations, the Grand Canyon is now run exclusively for the benefit of visitors; although even as recently as 1963 there were proposals to dam the Colorado and flood 150 miles of the Canyon, and the Glen Canyon dam has seriously affected the ecology downstream.

are the vast flatlands of the **Navajo Nation**; to the northeast, **Vermillion and Echo Cliffs**, and the gray bulk of **Navajo Mountain** ninety miles away; to the west, the gigantic peaks of **Vishnu** and **Buddha temples**. Through the plains comes the narrow gorge of the **Little Colorado**; somewhere in the depths, before it meets the Colorado itself, is the *sipapu*, the hole through which the Hopi believe that men first entered the world, the Third World. The odd-looking construction on the very lip of the canyon is **Desert View Watchtower**, built by Fred Harvey in 1932 in a conglomeration of Native American styles (though a steel frame props it all up) and decorated with Hopi pictographs. It contains a gift shop, as does the general store a few yards away. Groups of tarantulas are often seen in the evenings at Desert View, scuttling back into the warmth of the canyon for the night.

Tusayan Ruin, three miles west of Desert View (and not to be confused with modern Tusayan) is a genuine Anasazi pueblo, though not comparable in scale to the relics elsewhere in this region.

Into the Canyon

Hiking any of the trails that descend into the Grand Canyon offers something more than just another view of the same thing. Instead you pass through a sequence of utterly different landscapes, each with its own distinct climate, wildlife and topography. However, while the canyon can offer a wonderful wilderness experience, it's essential to remember that it can be a hostile and very unforgiving environment, gruelling even for expert hikers.

The South Rim is 7000 feet above sea level, an altitude which for most people is fatiguing in itself. Furthermore, all hikes start with a long, steep descent – which can come as a shock to the knees – and unless you camp overnight you'll have to climb all the way back up again when you're hotter and wearier.

If you're day-hiking, the golden rule is to keep track of how much time you spend hiking down, and allow twice that much to get back up again. Average summer temperatures inside the canyon exceed 100°F (38°C); to hike for eight hours in that sort of heat, you have to drink an incredible thirty pints of water. Always carry at least a quart per person, and much more if there are no water sources along your chosen trail. You must have food as well, as drinking large quantities without also eating can cause water intoxication.

There's only space here to detail the most popular trail, the **Bright Angel**. Many of the others, such as the **Hermit**, date from the days prior to 1928, when the obstreperous Ralph Cameron controlled access to the Bright Angel and many other rim-edge sites by means of spurious mining claims, and the Fred Harvey company had to find other ways to get its customers down to the Colorado. These other trails tend to be overgrown now, or partially blocked by landslides; check before setting out.

Bright Angel Trail

The **Bright Angel Trail**, followed on foot or mule by thousands of visitors each year, starts from the wooden shack in the village which was once the Kolb photographic studio. It takes 9.6 miles to switchback down to **Phantom Ranch** beside the river, but park rangers have a simple message for all would-be hikers: don't try to hike down and back in a single day. It might not look far on the map, but it's harder than running a marathon. The longest feasible day-hike is to go instead as far as **Plateau Point** on the edge of the arid Tonto Plateau, an overlook above the Inner Gorge from which it is not possible to descend any further – a twelve-mile round trip that will probably take you at least eight hours. In summer, water can be obtained along the way.

The first section of the trail was laid out by miners a century ago, along an old Havasupai route, and has two short tunnels in its first mile. After another mile, the **wildlife** starts to increase (deer, rodents and the ubiquitous ravens), and there are a few **pictographs** which have been all but obscured by graffiti.

At the lush **Indian Gardens** almost five miles down, where you'll find a ranger station and campground with water, the trails split, to Plateau Point or down to the river via the **Devil's Corkscrew**. The latter route leads through sand dunes scattered with cactuses and down beside **Garden Creek** to the Colorado, which you then follow for more than a mile to get to Phantom Ranch.

Phantom Ranch

It's a real thrill to spend a night at the very bottom of the canyon, at the 1922 **Phantom Ranch**. The cabins are reserved exclusively for the use of excursionists on Fred Harvey two-day mule trips ($252 per person for one night, $353 for the winter-only two-night trips). Beds in the four ten-bunk **dorms** ($22) are usually reserved way in advance, through Amfac (see p.249), but it's worth checking for cancellations at the Bright Angel transportation desk as soon as you reach the South Rim. Do not hike down without a reservation, and even if you do have one, re-confirm it the day before you set off. All supplies reach Phantom Ranch the same way you do (an all-day hike on foot or mule), so **meals** are expensive, a minimum of $12 for breakfast and $17 for dinner.

The **suspension bridge** here was set in place in 1928 (hanging from twin cables carried down on the shoulders of 42 Havasupai). The delta of **Bright Angel Creek**, named by Powell to contrast with the muddy **Dirty Devil** upriver in Utah, is several hundred feet wide here, and strewn with boulders. All the water used on the South Rim now comes by pipeline from the North Rim, and crosses the river on the 1960s Silver Bridge nearby.

The Havasupai Reservation

The **Havasupai Reservation** really is another world. A 1930s anthropologist called it "the only spot in the United States where native culture has remained in anything like its pristine condition"; things have changed a little since then, but the sheer magic of its turquoise waterfalls and canyon scenery make this a very special place. Traditionally, the Havasupai would spend summer on the canyon floor and winter on the plateau above. However, when the reservation was created in 1882, they were only granted land at the bottom of the canyon, and not until 1975 did the concession of another 251,000 acres up above make it possible for them to resume their ancient lifestyle.

GRAND CANYON TOURS

The Fred Harvey Company (contact the "transportation desks" in the South Rim lodges, or call ℅520/638-2401) runs at least two short daily coach tours along the rim to the west ($11) and east ($17) of the village, a sunset trip to Yavapai Point ($7.50), and mule rides to Phantom Ranch (from $252; see above). It also operates a five-hour Smooth Water River Raft Excursion through Marble Canyon ($80); whitewater rafting trips in the canyon proper, such as those run by Wilderness River Adventures (Box 717, Page, AZ 86040; ℅1-800/528-6154 or 520/645-3279) are booked up literally years in advance, so this is probably your only chance of a trip along the river at short notice.

Airplane tours cost from around $65 for thirty minutes ($30 child), up to as long as you like for as much as you've got. Operators include Air Grand Canyon (℅1-800/AIR-GRAND or 520/638-2686) and Grand Canyon Airlines (℅1-800/528-2413 or 520/638-2307). Helicopter tours, from $90 for thirty minutes, are offered by AirStar Helicopters (℅520/638-2622) and Papillon Helicopters (℅520/638-2419), who also operate $440 day-trips to the Havasupai Reservation. Unless otherwise specified, all the companies are in Tusayan, at or near the airport.

Havasu Canyon is a side canyon of the Grand Canyon, about 35 miles west of Grand Canyon Village as the raven flies, but almost two hundred miles by road. Turn off the interstate at Seligman or Kingman, onto AZ-66, which curves north between the two, stock up with food, water and gas, and then turn on to Arrowhead Hwy-18. Plans to build a road – or even a tramway – down into Havasu Canyon have always been rejected, in part because much of the income of the five or six hundred Havasupai comes from guiding visitors on foot, mule or horseback. Instead, the road ends at **Hualapai Hilltop**, from where an eight-mile trail zigzags down a bluff and leads through the stunning waterless Hualapai Canyon to the village of **SUPAI**. Riding down costs $50 one way, $80 for a round-trip, while hiking is free; all visitors, however, pay a $15 entry fee on arrival at Supai.

Beyond Supai the trail becomes more difficult, but leads to a succession of spectacular waterfalls, including **Havasu Falls**, one of the best for swimming, and **Mooney Falls**, which was named after an unfortunate prospector who dangled here for three days in the 1890s, at the end of a snagged rope, before falling to his death.

A **campground** (☎520/448-2141) stretches between Havasu and Mooney Falls, and Supai itself holds the motel-like *Havasupai Lodge* (☎520/448-2111; ⑤), along with a café, a general store, and the only post office in the US still to receive its mail by pack train. From time to time Supai is hit by freak floods which can result in the temporary closure of the campground and hotel.

Flagstaff

As the nearest town of any size to the canyon, seventy miles northwest, **FLAGSTAFF** remains the major junction for road and rail passengers heading for the Grand Canyon. Although some of its old streets are still charmingly redolent of the Wild West – its main thoroughfare, Santa Fe Avenue, was once part of Route 66, and before that, the pioneer trail west – there's not all that much of interest in the town itself. However, the exceptional **Museum of Northern Arizona** (daily 9am–5pm; $5), three miles northwest on Hwy-180 (and not on a local bus route), provides a good introduction to Arizona's native American cultures, past and present. At all times there are pots, rugs and kachina dolls on display, but *the* time to come is for the Indian Craftsmen Exhibitions each summer. The **Zuni** show lasts for five days around Memorial Day weekend in late May; the **Hopi** one is on the weekend closest to July 4, and the nine-day **Navajo** event is at the end of July and the start of August, with every item for sale.

Practicalities

Two Amtrak **trains** still pull in each day – the 6.44am to Albuquerque and the 9.14pm to Los Angeles – at the wooden station house right in the heart of town, a minute's walk from the helpful **visitor center** at 101 W Santa Fe Ave (summer Mon–Sat 8am–7pm, Sun 8am–5pm; rest of year Mon–Sat 8am–6pm, Sun 8am–5pm; ☎1-800/842-7293 or 520/774-9541). Connecting buses to the Grand Canyon's South Rim, run for Amtrak by Nava-Hopi, 114 W Route 66 (☎1-800/892-8687 or 520/774-5003), are detailed on p.247. The least expensive **car rental**, which shared between a group should cost less than the bus, is Budget Rent-a-Car at 100 N Humphreys St (☎520/779-0307). Cosmic Cycles, 113 S San Francisco St (☎520/779-1092), rent out **mountain bikes** for $20 per day, $75 per week.

Nava-Hopi also operate a wide range of one-day **tours**, not only of the Grand Canyon ($38 by bus, $64 for a combination bus-and-train tour via Williams), but also to the nearby towns of Sedona and Jerome ($38), and northeast to stunning Monument Valley ($74). Greyhound, a few blocks south of downtown at 399 S Malpais Lane (☎1-800/231-2222 or 520/774-4573), run **buses** south to Phoenix, west to Las Vegas and LA, and east towards Albuquerque.

Several basic central **hostels** offer dorm beds for around $12 and private rooms for more like $30. Both the *Motel du Beau International Hostel*, 19 W Phoenix Ave (☎1-800/398-7112 or 520/773-1656; ①) and the *Downtowner*, 19 S San Francisco St (☎520/774-8461; ①) run their own excursions up to the Grand Canyon, while the HI-AYH-approved *Weatherford Hotel*, 23 N Leroux St (☎520/774-2731; ①) offers inexpensive accommodation. The *Monte Vista*, 100 N San Francisco St (☎520/779-6971; ④) is a very pleasant little **hotel** that in addition to dorm beds has some much more comfortable rooms, each named after a movie star, and budget **motels** like the *Super 8*, 3725 Kasper Ave (☎1-800/800-8000 or 520/526-0818; ④), abound just off the interstate further east. The best **campground** is three miles south on US-89A, at *Fort Tuthill County Park* (☎520/774-5139).

For **food**, *Charly's Pub and Grill* in the *Weatherford Hotel* makes a classy if unlikely contrast with the hostel rooms upstairs, serving good cheap food accompanied by live music (cocktail piano at lunch, bands at night). The area around San Francisco Street, south of the tracks and near the university, has largely been taken over by the alternative student crowd. The *Mad Italian* at no. 101 (☎520/779-1820) is a highly sociable **bar** with several pool tables, while *Hassib's* at no. 211 (☎520/774-1037) does a variety of mid-Eastern and European dishes, but closes early. The Museum Club, 3404 E Route 66 (☎520/526-9434), is a real oddity: a 1930s log-cabin taxidermy museum that somehow transmogrified into a classic Route 66 roadhouse, saloon and country music venue, and became a second home to hordes of dancing cowboys.

The Western Mojave

The **western expanse** of the Mojave Desert spreads out on the north side of the San Gabriel Mountains, fifty miles from Los Angeles via Hwy-14, a barren plain that drivers have to cross to reach the alpine peaks of the eastern Sierra Nevada mountains or Death Valley, at the Mojave's northern edge. The few towns that have grown up in this stretch of desert over the past couple of decades are populated in the main by two sorts of people: retired couples who value the dry, clean air, and aerospace workers employed in one of the many military bases or aircraft factories. **Lancaster**, near Edwards Air Force Base, is the largest town and one of the few places to pick up supplies; **Mojave**, thirty miles north, is a main desert crossroads that caters mainly to drive-by tourists. **Tehachapi**, twenty miles west and a few thousand feet higher, offers a cool retreat. Hwy-14 joins up with US-395 another forty miles north, just west of the huge naval air base at **China Lake** and the faceless town of **Ridgecrest**, a good jumping off point for some interesting attractions.

Lancaster and the Antelope Valley

From the north end of LA's San Fernando Valley, Hwy-14 cuts off from I-5 and heads east around the foothills of the San Gabriel Mountains, passing **Placerita Canyon**, site of an early gold discovery that's been preserved as a nature reserve (daily 9am–5pm; free). Ten miles further on stands the massive sandstone outcrop of the 700-acre **Vasquez Rocks County Park** (daily 8am–sunset; $3 per vehicle) once a hiding place for frontier bandits and bank robbers, and later used by Hollywood movie studios as the backdrop for a variety of TV shows and films. Beyond here Hwy-138 cuts off east, heading up to the ski resorts and lakes along the crest of the San Gabriel Mountains, while Hwy-14 continues north across the sparsely settled flatlands of the Mojave Desert.

The biggest place for miles is the twin town of **LANCASTER**, a soulless sprawling community of retirees and RV parks whose economy is wholly based on designing, building and testing aeroplanes, from B-1 bombers for the military to the record-setting

Voyager, which flew non-stop around the globe in 1987. The **Blackbird Airpark**, at 25th Street, three miles west along Avenue P (Fri–Sun 10am–5pm; free; ☎760/277-8050), comprises just two sinister-looking black planes standing by the roadside. These are in fact the fastest and highest-flying planes ever created. The A-12 was designed in the 1950s as prototype for the SR-71 – the *Blackbird* – a reconnaissance plane which could reach 2100 miles per hour at 85,000ft. Unless you strike one of the infrequent "open cockpit" days (call for details), all you can do is circle the planes admiring the sleek lines and astonishing statistics.

If you're not a military buff, there's little else to draw you into Lancaster except a need for a bed or supplies. The **Chamber of Commerce** at 544 Lancaster Blvd (Mon–Fri 9am–5pm; ☎805/948-4518) has information on **accommodation** – at motels such as the *Tropical* (☎805/945-7831; ②) at 43145 Sierra Hwy, on the east side of town, and the *All-Star Inn* (☎805/948-0435; ②) at 43540 W 17th St, just off Hwy-14.

Unlikely as it may seem at first glance, there are some things to see in the surrounding area, known as the **Antelope Valley**, where the **California Poppy Reserve** ($5 per vehicle), fifteen miles west of Hwy-14 on Lancaster Road, is in full bloom in the spring with the state flower, the Golden Poppy. Depending upon the amount and timing of the winter rains, the flowers peak between March and May, when the reserve is covered in bright orange blossom; in season, the **visitor center** (Mon–Fri 9am–4pm, Sat & Sun 9am–5pm; ☎805/924-0662) has interpretive displays of desert flora and fauna. The building itself is proof that passive-solar, underground architecture works: built into the side of a hill, it keeps cool naturally and is powered entirely by an adjacent windmill generator.

Saddleback Butte State Park, seventeen miles east of Lancaster at the junction of Avenue J and 170th St (daily dawn–dusk; ☎805/942-0662; $5 per vehicle), centers on a smallish hill whose slopes are home to a splendid collection of Joshua trees. It's also a likely spot to catch a glimpse of the Desert Tortoise, for whom the park provides a refuge from the motorcyclists and dune buggy enthusiasts who tear around the region. There's a **visitor center** (Feb–May & Oct–Nov only), a half-mile nature trail, and under-used **campgrounds** ($10). The visitor center runs a campfire program on Saturday evenings and nature hikes the following morning. Three miles southwest, the **Antelope Valley Indian Museum** on Avenue M (mid Sept–mid-June Sat & Sun 10am–4pm; $3), housed in a mock Swiss chalet painted with Native American motifs, contains an extensive collection of ethnographic material from all over the state.

The desert and dry lake beds north of Lancaster make up **Edwards Air Force Base**, the US military testing ground for experimental, high-speed and high-altitude aircraft (such as the *Blackbird*; see above). Ninety-minute **tours** of NASA's Dryden Flight Research Facility (Mon–Fri 10.15am & 1.15pm; free; reserve at least a day in advance on ☎805/258-3446) include a short film (a jingoistic cross between *The Right Stuff* and *Top Gun*) and a look at hangars full of unique aeroplanes, including the missile-like *X-15*. The base is currently a backup landing spot for the Space Shuttle, though in the past, when it was on the regular route, thousands of people made the journey out here to welcome the astronauts home. (Note: the Dryden Flight Research Facility can be reached from the north via the Rocket Site exit of Hwy-58, between Mojave and Boron.)

Mojave and Tehachapi

MOJAVE, strung out along the highway thirty miles north of Lancaster, is a major junction on the interstate train network, though it's used solely by goods trains. The town itself – mostly a mile-long highway strip of gas stations, $25-a-night motels and franchised fast-food restaurants, open around the clock – is a good place to fill up on food and gas before continuing north into the Owens Valley or Death Valley.

About twenty miles west from Mojave, Hwy-58 rises to the rolling hillsides of **TEHACHAPI**, an apple-growing center which, at an elevation of around 4000 feet, offers a nice respite from the Mojave's heat. In addition to its pretty setting, the town has a couple of minor claims to fame. Some 5100 **wind generators** – both familiar three-bladed windmills and more unusual egg-beater-style Darreius turbines – make the Tehachapi Wind Resource Area, ranked along Cameron Ridge to the east, one of the world's most productive renewable energy stations. Train enthusiasts, meanwhile, cross states to see groaning Santa Fe diesels hauling their mile-long string of boxcars around the **Tehachapi Loop**, eight miles west of town. Built in the 1870s as the only means of scaling the steep slopes of the region, the tracks cleave to the rockface, doubling back on themselves to make a complete 360° loop. The sight of a train twisting around a mountain, its front end 77ft above its tail, is awesome. You can't see it properly from Hwy-58, so follow the signs three miles from the Keene exit to a roadside plaque commemorating the loop's engineers. For **information** about these and other local attractions, ranging from pick-your-own-fruit orchards and antiques shops to ostrich farms, stop in at the **Chamber of Commerce**, 209 E Tehachapi Blvd (☎805/822-4180). You can also find out about **accommodation**, including the *Santa Fe Motel*, 120 W Tehachapi Blvd (☎805/822-3184; ②) and the *Ranch Motel*, 507 S Curry St (☎805/822-4233; ②). Eight miles southwest of town, there's **camping** ($8) at a refreshing 5500 to 7000 feet in Tehachapi Mountain Park (☎805/861-2345). Popular local **restaurants** include the *Apple Shed*, 333 E Tehachapi Blvd (☎805/823-8333), good for country-style breakfasts or apple-pie breaks, and *Domingo's*, 201416 Valley Blvd (☎805/822-7611), a family-owned Mexican place in the newer section of town.

Randsberg and Ridgecrest

Northeast from Mojave, along Hwy-14, the desert is virtually uninhabited, the landscape only marked by the bald ridges of the foothills of the Sierra Nevada mountains that rise to the west, though you might see the odd ghostly sign of the prospectors who once roamed the region in search of gold and less precious minerals. Twenty miles north of Mojave, Hwy-14 passes through **Red Rock Canyon**, where brilliantly colored rock formations have been eroded into a miniature version of Utah's Bryce Canyon; the highway passes right through the center of the most impressive section, though if you walk just a hundred yards from the road you're more likely to see an eagle or coyote than another visitor. There's a **state park** (day use $5 per vehicle) with a **visitor center** (open spring & fall Fri–Sun) and a fairly primitive but beautifully sited **campground** ($7–$10).

Continuing north of Red Rock Canyon, Hwy-14 merges into US-395 for the run into the Owens Valley (see Chapter Four). But a worthwhile detour cuts fifteen miles east to **RANDSBERG**, a near ghost town of two bars and a dozen shops, its lifeblood provided by the Rand gold deposit of the Yellow Aster and Baltic mines, the last to be worked commercially in California. The **Desert Museum**, 161 Butte Ave (Sat & Sun 10am–5pm; free), has displays on the glory days of the 1890s, when upwards of three thousand people lived in the town, mining gold, silver and tungsten out of the arid, rocky hills. The nearby **General Store**, almost always open (unlike the rest of the town which pretty much shuts down during the week), is a good source of local **information**. The restored *Cottage Hotel B&B*, 130 Butte Ave (☎760/374-2258; ③), offers unexpectedly civilized **accommodation** in this generally disheveled town. In neighboring Johannesburg, the *HI-Death Valley Hostel* (☎760/374-2323) has twelve beds ($12 members, $15 non-members) and one private family/couples room.

Twenty miles north of Randsberg Hwy-178 cuts east towards Death Valley to the sprawling desert community of **RIDGECREST**, dominated by the huge China Lake Naval Weapons Center. Jet fighters scream past overhead, taking target practice on land that's chock-full of ancient **petroglyphs**. Though access to the sites is strictly controlled, you can get some idea of the native culture of the Mojave Desert by visiting the **Maturango Museum**, off China Lake Boulevard at 100 E Las Flores Ave (Wed–Sun 10am–5pm; $2), which as well as acting as regional **visitor center**, has exhibits on both the natural and cultural history of the region, including examples of the rock-cut figures. To get out and see the figures and designs in their natural surroundings, plan ahead and join one of the volunteer-led five-hour **tours** (spring and fall only; $20) by contacting the museum (Ridgecrest, CA 93555; ☎760/375-6900, fax ☎375-0479) well in advance. You can check out some more recent inhabitants of the desert at the **wild horse** and **burro corrals** run by the Bureau of Land Management three miles east of town on Hwy-178. The animals are waiting for adoption, but even if you're not prepared to take one home, you can arrange to see them (Mon–Fri 7.30am–4pm; ☎760/446-6064). To ensure an enthusiastic reception, bring along some apples or carrots.

Twenty miles east along Hwy-178 from Ridgecrest, an eight-mile dirt road (passable except after rain) leads to the **Pinnacles National Natural Landmark**, where five hundred tufa spires stretch up to 140ft. They were considered extra-terrestrial enough to form a backdrop for parts of *Star Trek V*. Visit them on a half-mile nature trail near a primitive, free **campground**.

Take Hwy-178 west to Hwy-395 north, and turn off at Cinder Rock Road to reach **Fossil Falls**, another rather unearthly formation some 27 miles northwest of Ridgecrest. Relatively recent volcanic eruptions (about 20,000 years ago) drove lava through one of this region's dry river channels, creating what looks like a petrified cataract. Some remaining petroglyphs as well as various small artifacts and polished indentations in the rocks, used for grinding grain, attest to widespread human habitation in this area.

travel details

Trains

LA to: Barstow (1 daily; 3hr); Flagstaff (1 daily; 10hr); Palm Springs (3 weekly; 2hr 20 min).

Buses

All buses are Greyhound unless otherwise stated.
Grand Canyon to: Flagstaff (2 Nava-Hopi daily; 2hr).
Las Vegas to: Barstow (7 daily & 1 Amtrak Thruway daily; 3hr); Flagstaff (1 daily; 5hr).

LA to: Barstow (8 daily; 3hr); Las Vegas (12 daily & 2 Amtrak Thruway; 4hr/6hr); Palm Springs (11 daily; 3hr).

Palm Springs to: Bakersfield (1 Amtrak Thruway daily; 5hr 45min); Joshua Tree (1 Morongo Basin Transit Authority daily; 55 min).

San Diego to: Borrego Springs (1 Northeast Rural Bus System daily; 2hr 50min).

CHAPTER FOUR

DEATH VALLEY AND THE EASTERN HIGH SIERRA

The far eastern edge of California, rising up from the Mojave and cleaving to the border with Nevada, is a long narrow strip as scenically dramatic as anywhere else in the state, veering from blistering desert to ski country, much of it in the lee of the mighty High Sierra. It's a region devoid of Interstates, scarcely populated and, but for the scant reminders of gold-hungry pioneers, developed in only the most tentative way.

At the region's base, technically forming the Mojave's northern reach but more usually visited along with the Owens Valley, is **Death Valley**. With the highest average summer temperatures on earth and so remote that it's almost a region unto itself, this vast National Park is a distillation of the classic desert landscape: an arid, otherworld terrain of brilliantly colored, bizarrely eroded rocks, mountains and sand dunes, 150 miles from the nearest town.

The towering **eastern** peaks of the High Sierra drop abruptly to the largely desert – and deserted – landscape of the Owens Valley far below. Seen from the eastern side, the mountains are perfectly described by their Spanish name, **Sierra Nevada**, which literally translates as "snowcapped saw". Virtually the entire range is preserved as wilderness, and hikers and mountaineers can get higher much more quickly here than almost anywhere else in California: well-maintained roads lead to trailheads at over ten thousand feet, providing quick access to spires, glaciers and clear mountain lakes. **Mount Whitney** the highest point in the continental US at almost 14,500ft, marks the southernmost point of the chain, which continues north for an uninterrupted 150 miles to the backcountry of Yosemite National Park.

The five-mile-wide **Owens Valley** starts at the foot of Mount Whitney, hemmed in to the east by the **White Mountains**, nearly as high but drier and less hospitable than the High Sierra, and home to the gnarled **bristlecone pines**, the oldest living things on earth. In between, US-395 runs the length of the Valley, which has few signs of settlement at all beyond the sporadic roadside towns and the larger **Bishop**. Just a few miles further on, **Mammoth Lakes** is the region's busiest resort, thick with skiers in winter and fishing enthusiasts in summer. Finally, at the far northern tip of the Valley, the placid blue waters of ancient **Mono Lake** (once the subject of a fierce battle between environmentalists and the City of Los Angeles) are set in a bizarre desert basin of volcanoes and steaming hot pools. Beyond, and far enough out of most people's way to deter the crowds, is the wonderful ghost town of **Bodie**, which preserves a palpable sense of gold-town life eight thousand feet up in a parched, windswept valley.

Getting around

US-395 is the lifeline of the Owens Valley, and pretty much the only access to the area from within California. Once north of Mojave, where Hwy-58 branches west to Bakersfield, no road crosses the Sierra Nevada until Hwy-120, a spur over the 10,000-foot Tioga Pass into Yosemite. To the east Hwy-190 cuts through the Panamint Range into Death Valley.

US-395 is traveled once daily by Greyhound between LA and Reno in Nevada (note that this bus is best used when traveling from north to south; otherwise most arrivals and departures are in the early hours of the morning) and has plenty of cheap motels along its length and campgrounds in the nearby foothills. Access to Death Valley without your own wheels is all but impossible: **no public transportation** whatsoever runs into the park.

Inyo Trailhead Transportation (☎760/876-5518) runs minivans out of Lone Pine to the main lower Owens Valley trailheads, picking up passengers from Greyhound

---

ACCOMMODATION PRICE CODES

All accommodation prices in this book have been coded using the symbols below; prices are for the least expensive **double rooms** in each establishment. For a full explanation see p.36 in Basics. Individual rates rather than price codes are given for **hostels** and whole **apartments**.

① up to $30	④ $60–80	⑦ $130–175
② $30–45	⑤ $80–100	⑧ $175–250
③ $45–60	⑥ $100–130	⑨ $250+

---

stations and other points in the Owens Valley; make arrangements well in advance and be prepared to send a deposit. A similar service to the more northern trails and ski slopes is run by Country Corners (☎760/872-4411) in Bishop.

Death Valley National Park

DEATH VALLEY is an inhuman environment: barren and monotonous, burning hot and almost entirely without shade, much less water. At first sight it seems impossible that the landscape could support any kind of life, yet it is home to a great variety of living creatures, from snakes and giant eagles to tiny fishes and bighorn sheep. But it's the rocks that you come to see: deeply shadowed, eroded crevices at the foot of sharply silhouetted hills, whose exotic mineral content turns million-year-old mud flats into rainbows of sunlit phosphorescence.

Throughout the summer, the air temperature in Death Valley averages 112°F – with a recorded high of 134°F – and the ground can reach near boiling point; it's best to stay away at this time unless you're a real glutton for sweaty, potentially fatal punishment. It's better to come during the spring, especially March and early April, when the wild flowers are in bloom and daytime temperatures average a manageable 83°F, dropping to the mid-fifties at night. Any time between October and May it's generally mild and dry, with occasional rainfall on the surrounding mountains causing flash floods through otherwise bone-dry gullies and washes.

The central north–south valley, after which the park is named, holds the park's two main outposts for provisions and accommodation: **Stovepipe Wells** and **Furnace Creek**. It is surrounded by many more, equally inhospitable desert valleys, punctuated with the remains of mine workings. High above stand the less visited but far cooler peaks of the Panamint Range – from where you can see both the highest (Mount Whitney) and the lowest (near Badwater) points in the continental United States.

Geology and history

The sculpted rock layers exposed in Death Valley, tinted by oxidized traces of various **mineral deposits**, comprise a nearly complete record of the earth's past, from 500 million-year-old mountains to the relatively young **fossils** of marine animals left on the valley floors by the Ice Age lakes, which covered most of the park's low-lying areas. There's also dramatic evidence of volcanic activity, as at the massive **Ubehebe Crater** on the north side of the park.

Humans have lived in and around Death Valley for thousands of years, beginning about ten thousand years ago when the valley was still filled by a massive lake; the climate was then quite mild and wild game was plentiful. Later, wandering tribes of desert **Shoshone** wintered near perennial freshwater springs in the warm valley, spending the long, hot summers at cooler, higher elevations in the surrounding mountains; there is still a small, inhabited Shoshone village near the *Furnace Creek Inn*.

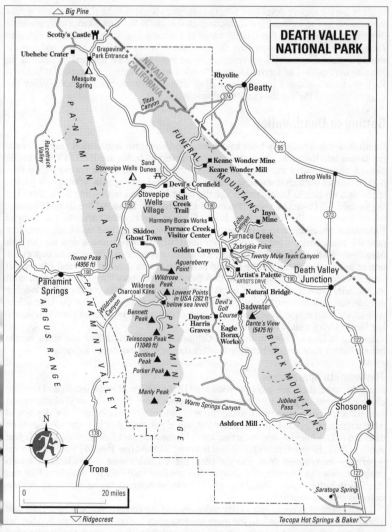

The first whites passed through in 1849, looking for a short cut to the Gold Rush towns on the other side of the Sierra Nevada; they ran out of food and water but managed to survive, and gave Death Valley its name. For the next 75 years the only people willing to brave the hardships of the desert were miners, who searched for and found deposits of gold, silver and copper. The most successful mining endeavours were centered on **borates**, a harsh alkaline used in detergent soaps (and, eventually, in a variety of industries – everything from cosmetics to nuclear reactors). In the late nineteenth

For advice on **desert survival**, see the box on p.212.

century borate miners developed twenty-mule-team wagons to haul the powders across the deserts to the railroad line at Mojave. In the 1920s the first tourist facilities were developed, and in 1927 the mining camp at Furnace Creek was converted into the *Furnace Creek Inn*. Six years later the two million acres of Death Valley and around were purchased by the US government, to be preserved as a national monument. In 1994, as part of the **California Desert Protection Act**, Congress accorded it National Park status and added a further 1.3 million acres to its area, making Death Valley the largest National Park in the country outside Alaska.

Getting to Death Valley

Death Valley is a long way from anywhere, and there's **no scheduled public transportation** into the park. The nearest places served by buses are **BEATTY**, just inside Nevada and 35 miles from Furnace Creek, and Lone Pine in the Owens Valley (see p.270); neither is much use unless you have a bicycle. **Las Vegas** in Nevada (see p.238), is the nearest city to Death Valley. For the most direct and interesting route from Las Vegas, take US-95 or Las Vegas Boulevard south to Blue Diamond Rte (Hwy-160 west), which leads past the scenic **Red Rock Canyon Recreation Area** to the town of **Pahrump**; the Smith's supermarket there is a good spot to load up on supplies. Just past the town, make a left at Bella Vista Road, where there's also a sign for the **Ash Meadows National Wildlife Refuge**, a desert oasis worth a detour for its concentration of indigenous species – the second largest in North America. Beyond the turnoff for the refuge, at **Death Valley Junction** (see opposite), take Hwy-190 west into Death Valley. Alternatively, if you want to take advantage of the cheap (and cooler) lodging outside the park in Beatty, take US-95 past Nellis Air Force Base and the US nuclear weapons testing range; from Beatty, you'll coast down into the park on Hwy-374, watching Death Valley unfold from above.

Driving to Death Valley from within California, you should follow one of the routes below. Fill up your vehicle before you enter the park, as gas inside is pricey.

The western approaches

From the west, there are two routes towards Death Valley, of equal length and running along either side of the China Lake Naval Weapons Base. Five miles west of Ridgecrest (see p.256), US-395 runs north along the west side of China Lake up to the dry bed of what used to be Owens Lake; the water that would naturally flow in to the lake has been diverted to Los Angeles, and is carried south by the aqueduct that parallels US-395. Just south of here, Hwy-190 cuts off due east to Hwy-136, the Lone Pine to Death Valley road – perhaps the prettiest drive into the park. Fifteen miles west of this junction a loop peels southeast to **Darwin**, and shortly after another road cuts north to **Lee Flat** and the **Saline Valley** – see p.267. At nearby **Panamint Springs** are an expensive gas station and a motel (see p.264).

The less-traveled route loops sixty miles around the eastern side of China Lake and allows the quickest access into the more mountainous backcountry of Death Valley, an area once home to Charles Manson and his "family". Wildrose Road, the continuation of Hwy-178 beyond Ridgecrest, curves through the chemical plants of **Trona** past the gold-mining town of **Ballarat** – whose eroded adobe ruins still stand in the foothills three miles east of the highway – before joining Hwy-190 for the final fifteen miles east to the entrance to Death Valley. What makes this route worthwhile is the possibility of following the steep Mahogany Flat Road, which cuts off Wildrose Road thirteen miles south of Hwy-190, up the Panamint Mountains to **Telescope Peak** (see p.267), the highest and coolest part of the park. The road is well maintained, but although there is excellent free **camping** (see box on p.264), the nearest food, drinking water or gas are

25 miles away at Stovepipe Wells village. Another potential side trip is to the **Skidoo Ghost Town** (see p.267) a few miles to the north.

The southern approaches

Hwy-127 branches off I-15 at Baker (see p.235) – the last stop for supplies on the southern route into Death Valley – and cuts across fifty miles of desolate Mojave landscape before reaching any civilization. A couple of miles east of Hwy-127 two dilapidated settlements of scrappy trailer homes make unexpectedly decent places to stop off. The settlement of **Tecopa Hot Springs** has become a popular winter retreat, thanks to its natural hot springs always open to the public and bequeathed in perpetuity by a local chief provided they remain free. Many people stay across the road at the bleak campground ($6.50), though the hostel in nearby **TECOPA** is a better bet (see below).

The hamlet of **SHOSHONE**, eight miles north of Tecopa, wouldn't really rate a mention but for a decent motel (see below) within striking distance of the park. **Death Valley Junction**, a further thirty miles north, offers no fuel, but its *Amargosa Hotel* (see below) houses the **Amargosa Opera House**, the creation of Marta Becket, a New York dancer and artist who settled here in the late 1960s. The inside of the theater is painted with trompe l'oeil balconies peopled by sixteenth-century Spanish nobles and revellers. Ballet-pantomimes, in which Ms Becket takes almost all the parts herself, are staged here between October and May ($10; ☎760/852-4441). An ice cream parlor and pizza place were recently opened in the theater complex.

Entrance and information

Entrance to the park is $10 per vehicle, or $5 if you are walking or cycling. For that you get unrestricted entry for seven days, an excellent map and a copy of the biannual *Death Valley National Park* newspaper with up-to-date details on campgrounds and visitor services.

Most visitor facilities are concentrated in two settlements, both comprised solely of gas stations, motels and grocery stores. The busiest of the two, **FURNACE CREEK**, is right in the center of the Valley and has an excellent **visitor center** (winter daily 8am–7pm; ☎760/786-2331) with a small but interesting **museum** (same hours; free). **STOVEPIPE WELLS**, 25 miles to the northwest, is slightly smaller. More information is available from the **ranger stations** close to the park boundaries. The main ones are on the west side at *Wildrose Campground* on Hwy-178 and on the northern edge of the park at Scotty's Castle.

Accommodation and eating

To get the full impact of a desert visit you really need to **camp** out. For most of the year you don't even need a tent – it isn't going to rain – though a sleeping bag is a good idea. Camping is also much the cheapest way to stay in Death Valley: all the campgrounds are operated by the National Park Service and most cost $10 a night, while sites without a water supply are free. If camping isn't an option you are limited to fairly expensive **hotels** and **motels** inside the park, or lower-cost possibilities on the fringes. Reservations should be made as early as possible, especially during peak holiday periods. The following listings cover all the rooms in the park and the settlements nearby, but also see Lone Pine (p.270) for accommodation slightly further afield.

Hotels, motels and hostels

Amargosa Hotel, Death Valley Junction (☎760/852-4441). Pleasantly run-down adobe hotel built by the Pacific Coast Borax Company in 1924. It has no TVs or phones, but boasts an attached opera

CAMPING IN DEATH VALLEY

Most sites cannot be reserved and stays are limited to thirty days (so that people don't move in for the winter). Take note of the **altitude** listed for each, as this indicates the kind of temperatures you can expect.

The main sites are at **Furnace Creek** ($16; open all year, reservable Oct–April ☎760/786-2331; -196ft) which fills up very early each day in winter; the enormous **Sunset** ($10; Oct–April; -190ft) and the designated "quiet" **Texas Spring** ($6; Oct–April; sea level), both close to Furnace Creek; and at **Stovepipe Wells** ($10; Oct–April; sea level) – though the smaller and relatively shady site at **Mesquite Spring** ($10; all year; 1800ft), near Scotty's Castle on the north side of the park, is much more pleasant. There is one free site with water, **Emigrant** (April–Oct; 2100ft), eight miles west of Stovepipe Wells. This is on the way to the only place with guaranteed shade, the canyons on the forested slopes of Telescope Peak, on the western edge of the park. Here there are three free sites, **Wildrose** (all year, water available April–Nov; 4100ft), **Thorndike** (open March–Nov; 7400ft) and **Mahogany Flat** (March–Nov; 8200ft), just off the mostly paved Wildrose Road. The upper two are (just) accessible in ordinary cars, but high clearance or four-wheel-drive vehicles are better. **Fires** are allowed in all sites except *Sunset*, *Stovepipe Wells* and *Emigrant*, but designated fireplaces must be used and no collecting of firewood is allowed.

Free **backcountry camping** is allowed in most areas of the park provided you keep two miles away from any roads (paved or otherwise) and a quarter of a mile from water sources. No permits are required, but voluntary backcountry **registration** is recommended.

house (see above). Ask to see a few rooms before choosing as they vary enormously – there's a trompe l'oeil wardrobe in the Jezebel room and cherubs in the Baroque. ③.

Exchange Club Motel, Junction of US-95 and Hwy-374, Beatty (☎702/553-2333). Nice rooms with refrigerators, adjoining a casino (its 1906 bar dates back to the days when miners used to exchange gold nuggets for cash – thus the name) with a decent coffee shop. ②.

Furnace Creek Inn, Furnace Creek (☎760/786-2345). *The* place to stay if you're in the Valley with money to burn. Beautifully sited amid palms, with great views and plush rooms. ⑥.

Furnace Creek Ranch, Furnace Creek (☎760/786-2345). Cheaper than the *Inn*, but redolent of a holiday camp and with no sense of being in a desert. The comfortable but ordinary motel rooms are rather overpriced. ⑥.

HI-Desertaire Hostel, Old Spanish Trail, Tecopa (☎760/852-4580). A relaxed hostel an hour south of Furnace Creek. There are only ten beds, but you can sleep outside in the warm desert air in a wooden tower with commanding views of the surrounding desert. Book the first night by phone or in writing: PO Box 306, Tecopa, CA 92389. ①.

Panamint Springs Motel, Panamint Springs (☎702/482-7680). Basic motel 35 miles west of Stovepipe Wells at a mountain pass. No pool, though one is planned. ③.

Phoenix Motel. First St, Beatty (☎1-800/845-7401). On a quiet side street, and one of the few Beatty motels not in or attached to a casino. ②.

Shoshone Inn, Shoshone (☎760/852-4335). Reasonable motel with pool an hour south of Furnace Creek on Hwy-127 and near Tecopa Hot Springs. ③.

Stovepipe Wells Motel, Stovepipe Wells (☎760/786-2387). The best-priced option inside the park, offering comfortable rooms and a mineral-water pool. ③.

Eating

There's not a great variety of **eating places** in Death Valley – you're limited to the hotel dining rooms and restaurants at Furnace Creek and Stovepipe Wells, all of which are fairly pricey. *Furnace Creek Ranch* is the only place with any choice: *The Ranch Restaurant*, an upgraded coffee shop, and *The Wrangler Steakhouse* (unless you're dying for a big slab of meat, you're better off at the similarly steep but more interesting restaurant at the *Furnace Creek Inn*). Beatty, with restaurants attached to all-night casinos, offers a number of inexpensive diners, though you wouldn't want to drive there and back to the park after dark.

To quench a **thirst** after a day in the sun, do as the few locals do and head to the *Corkscrew Saloon*, also at *Furnace Creek Ranch* and open until 1am. There's also an expensive grocery store here, and another at Stovepipe Wells.

Exploring Death Valley

You can get an unforgettable feel for Death Valley just by passing through, and you could quite easily see almost everything in a day. If you have the time, though, aim to spend at least a night here, if possible camped out somewhere far from the main centers of activity. Even if you've got your own car, the best way to experience the huge and empty spaces and the unique landforms of Death Valley is to leave the roads and crowds behind and wander off – taking care to remember the way back. Sunrise and sunset are the best times to experience the color that's bleached out by the midday sun, and they're also the most likely times for seeing the **wildlife**, mostly lizards, snakes and small rodents, which hide out through the heat of the day.

Along the Badwater road

Many of the park's most unusual sights are located south of Furnace Creek along the road to Badwater, which forks off Hwy-190 by the *Furnace Creek Inn*. Pick up a self-guided tour booklet (50¢) from a box at the junction. A good first stop, two miles along, is **Golden Canyon**. Periodic rainstorms over the centuries have washed a slot-shaped gully through the clay and silt here, revealing golden-hued walls that are particularly vibrant in the early evening. A three-quarter-mile-long interpretive trail winds into the U-shaped upper canyon, and a hike to Zabriskie Point (see box on p.268) continues from there.

Five miles further on, signs point to **Artists Drive**, a tortuous one-way loop road, perhaps best left until the drive back, especially if this means catching the afternoon sun on the **Artists Palette**, an evocatively eroded hillside covered in an intensely colored mosaic of reds, golds, blacks and greens.

A couple of miles further south, a dirt road leads a mile to the **Devil's Golf Course**, a weird field of salt pinnacles and hummocks protruding a couple of feet from the

---

PARK ACTIVITIES

Besides hiking and sightseeing, Death Valley offers ample opportunities for **mountain biking**. Only roads open to road vehicles are accessible to cyclists (hiking trails are off limits) but this still leaves plenty to go at for those who bring their machine along: there are no rentals available. The map provided with your entry ticket shows the major four-wheel-drive routes: Echo Canyon into the Funeral Mountains and the Inyo Mine, Cottonwood Canyon from Stovepipe Wells, and the Warm Springs Canyon/Butte Valley road in the south of the park are all worthwhile. Topographical maps are available at Furnace Creek visitor center.

Horse-riding is laid on by the *Furnace Creek Ranch* for $20 an hour, $35 for two and, when the phase of the moon is right, $30 for an hour-long evening ride. Also departing from *Furnace Creek Ranch*, the Fred Harvey Transportation Company offers a series of **bus tours**. These range from $12 for a two-hour Lower Valley tour, to $30 for a full-day excursion to Titus Canyon.

After a day in the desert, **swimming** in a tepid pool is an ideal way to enjoy a balmy evening. The pools at the *Furnace Creek Ranch* and the *Stovepipe Wells Motel* are open to the public for a $2 fee.

desert floor. Capillary action draws saline solutions from below the surface where alternate layers of salt and alluvial deposits from ancient lakes have been laid down over the millennia. As the occasional rainfall evaporates, the salt accretes to form a landscape as little like a golf course as you could imagine.

It is another four miles south to **Badwater**, an unpalatable but non-poisonous thirty-foot-wide pool of water, loaded with chloride and sulphates, that's also the only home of the endangered, soft-bodied Death Valley snail and a species of tiny fish. Notice how much hotter it feels in the humid air beside the water. From the pool two rather uninteresting hikes, both around four miles long, lead across the hot, flat valley floor to the two **lowest points in the western hemisphere**, both at 282ft below sea level.

Zabriskie Point and Dante's View

The badlands around **Zabriskie Point**, overlooking Badwater and the Artist's Palette off Hwy-190, four miles south of Furnace Creek, were the inspiration for Antonioni's eponymous 1970 movie. Even so, its sculpted spires of banded rock are less interesting than **Dante's View**, a further 21 miles south off Hwy-190 and then ten miles on a very steep (and very hot) road. At a point almost six thousand feet above the blinding white saltpan of Badwater, the valley floor does indeed look infernal. The view is best during the early morning, when the pink and gold Panamint Mountains across the Valley are highlighted by the rising sun.

North from Furnace Creek

In the township of Furnace Creek you could spend a few minutes in the **Borax Museum** (Mon–Fri 9am–4.30pm; free), which rather ploddingly tells the story of the mineral and its excavation, but you are better advised to head two miles north to the old **Harmony Borax Works** (unrestricted entry) where a quarter-mile interpretive trail tells of the mine and processing plant.

Twelve miles to the north, the **Keane Wonder Mine** and **Keane Wonder Mill** (unrestricted entry to both) were indeed wonderful during their heyday between 1904, when the mine was discovered by Jack Keane, and 1916. Gold and silver worth $1.1 million was extracted at the mountainside mine and worked at in the valley-floor mill, where it was carried down a three-quarter-mile-long aerial tramway which is still more or less intact. From the parking lot by the remains of the mill, a very steep path climbs alongside the thirteen tramway towers to the lowest of the mineshafts. It is only a mile but seems a lot more in the noonday heat. Don't be tempted to seek shelter in the adits and shafts leading off the path; all are dangerous and most unfenced.

Near Stovepipe Wells on the western side of the park spread the most extensive of the Valley's **sand dunes**, some fifteen rippled and contoured square miles of ever changing dunes, just north of Hwy-190 to the east of the campground and ranger station. On the opposite side of Hwy-190 stands the **Devil's Cornfield**, an expanse of tufted grasses quite out of character with its surroundings.

West of the campground, at the end of a ten-mile dirt road, stand the sheer black walls of **Marble Canyon**, on which are scratched ancient and mysterious petroglyph figures.

Scotty's Castle

On the north edge of the park (45 miles from the visitor center) and thus well out of the way of most of the rest of the tourist attractions, **Scotty's Castle** (tours daily 9am–5pm; $8) is nevertheless the most popular single stop in the park; hordes of overheated tourists wait in long lines for the chance to wander through the surreal attraction of this unfinished but still luxurious mansion. Executed in extravagant Spanish Revival style, the castle was built during the 1920s as the desert retreat of wealthy

Chicago insurance broker Albert Johnson, but was known and named after the cowboy, prospector and publicity hound, "Death Valley" Scotty, who managed the construction, and claimed the house was his own, financed by his hidden gold mine. The $2 million house features intricately carved wooden ceilings, waterfalls in the living room and, most entertaining of all, a remote-controlled player piano. In winter, you may have to wait as long as three hours for a place on one of the fifty-minute-long **tours** of the opulently furnished house, left pretty much as it was when Johnson died in 1948. Scotty himself lived here until 1954, and is buried on the hill just behind the house: a good place to wander while waiting for your tour.

Ubehebe Crater, Racetrack Valley and the Eureka Sand Dunes

Eight miles northwest of Scotty's Castle – though it might as well be five hundred miles for all the people who venture a look – gapes the half-mile wide **Ubehebe Crater**, the rust-colored result of a massive volcanic explosion; a half-mile south sits its thousand-year-old younger brother, **Little Hebe**. Beyond the craters the road (high clearance vehicles recommended) continues west for another 27 dusty miles to **Racetrack Valley**, a two-and-a-half-mile-long mud flat across which giant boulders seem slowly to be racing, leaving faint trails in their wake. Scientists believe that the boulders are pushed along the sometimes icy surface by very high winds; sit and watch (but don't hold your breath) from the rock outcrop at the northern end, known as the **Grandstand**.

The extension of Death Valley into a national park claimed several features formerly outside its boundaries. The **Eureka Sand Dunes**, forty miles northwest of Scotty's Castle, are the most exciting. Far more extensive than those around Stovepipe Wells, these stand up to seven hundred feet above the surrounding land, making them the highest in California and a dramatic place to witness sunrise or sunset. While here, keep your eyes open for the Eureka Dunes grass and evening primrose, both indigenous to the area and federally protected.

Skidoo Ghost Town, Wildrose Charcoal Kilns and Telescope Peak

To escape the heat and dust of the desert floor, head up Emigrant Canyon Road, off Hwy-190 in the west, into the Panamint Mountains. Ten miles up the canyon, a nine-mile dirt track turns off to the east toward **Skidoo Ghost Town**. Only a few ruins – and a number of roaming wild burros – remain of what in 1915 was a gold-mining camp of seven hundred people watered by snowmelt from Telescope Peak, 23 miles away, and kept informed by telegraph from Rhyolite. Well above the valley floor, it is tolerably cool but otherwise there's not much going for it.

The main road leads for another, very steep, fifteen miles over Emigrant Pass and down to the Wildrose ranger station and campground. To the right the road leads to Trona and Ridgecrest (see p.256), while a left turn carries you steeply up into the Panamint range, initially on tarmac, then on gravel. Five miles beyond the ranger station the **Wildrose Charcoal Kilns** loom into view. This series of ten massive, beehive-shaped stone kilns some 25 feet high was used in the 1880s to make charcoal for use in the smelters of local silver mines. The road continues through juniper and pine forests past the free Thorndike campground to its end at Mahogany Flat, where there's another free campground and the trailhead for the strenuous hike up **Telescope Peak**, which at 11,049ft is the highest – and coolest – point in the park (see box, p.268).

Darwin Falls, Lee Flat and Saline Valley

A mile west of Panamint Springs along Hwy-190, a dirt road leads south to the tumble-down wooden ruins of **DARWIN**, a ghost of a mining town (though forty people still live here) that was built in the 1870s by prospectors searching for seams of silver,

---

HIKES IN AND AROUND DEATH VALLEY

Anything more than a short stroll in the desert heat can become an ordeal. This is less true of the Telescope Peak and Wildrose Peak walks in the Panamint Range, but you still need to carry all your **water** with you. Always register your intended route at the visitor center or any of the ranger stations and for anything a little more adventurous than the walks listed here, get yourself a **topographic map** from the visitor center. All listed distances and times are for the round trip.

Golden Canyon to Zabriskie Point (5 miles; 3hr; 500ft ascent). Start at Golden Canyon and follow the interpretive trail, continuing on an unmaintained, moderately strenuous trail to Zabriskie Point. Done in reverse it is all downhill.

Mosaic Canyon (4 miles; 2hr; 300ft ascent). A rough three-mile access road just west of Stovepipe Wells leads to the trailhead for a relatively easy hike through this water-smoothed canyon. There's some scrambling at the upper end.

Telescope Peak (14 miles; 8hr; 3000ft ascent). The easy-to-follow but moderately strenuous trail climbs from the trailhead by Mahogany Flat campground, skirting a pair of 10,000-foot peaks, through bristlecone pines to the summit and its grand panorama of Death Valley and across to Mount Whitney and the eastern face of the Sierra Nevada mountains. Sign the summit register while you admire the view. There's no water en route except for snowmelt (often well into June) which should be treated. Crampons and ice axes may be required in harsh winters, and at all times you should self-register in the book a short way along the trail.

Wildrose Peak (8 miles; 5hr; 2000ft ascent). If winter conditions or your own level of fitness rule out Telescope Peak, this hike makes a perfect, easier alternative. Start by the Charcoal Kilns on Wildrose Canyon Road and wind up through piñon pines and juniper to a stunning summit panorama.

---

inspired by tales of an Indian who repaired an explorer's rifle by fashioning a gunsight out of solid silver. Nearby, and more interesting, are the thirty-foot, spring-fed **Darwin Falls**, reached by following a quarter-mile creekside trail up a small canyon.

You might not expect to see Joshua trees in Death Valley, but **Lee Flat**, a dozen miles west of Panamint Springs, has a whole forest of them on its higher slopes. At this point a dirt road leads north to Saline Valley. The main forest starts eight miles along at lower Lee Flat; a side road branches left to the densest section.

In **Saline Valley** in the far northwest corner of the park, old mine workings and the remains of a dilapidated salt tramway can be seen on your way to the generally clothing-free **hot springs** at Lower Warm Spring and Palm Spring. It's about a fifty-mile trek out here, so be prepared to camp out at the primitive site nearby, mercifully equipped with showers and toilets.

Outside the park

As ghost towns go, **RHYOLITE**, up a side road three miles west of Beatty, Nevada, is one of the more appealing. Rhyolite was a gold mining town whose mines were prematurely closed after just six boom years in 1912, due to a combination of mismanagement and lack of technological know-how (the working Bullfrog Mine just outside the town attests to the area's continuing mineral wealth). By then the town had spread over the hillside (made of the rock which gave the town its name) and had its own train station. The station is still the dominant structure, but the remains of other buildings, including a jail, schoolhouse and bank, still stand, as does a **bottle house** built of some fifty thousand beer and spirit bottles in 1906. A more recent attraction is the distinctly off-beam roadside **sculpture garden** (unrestricted access), complete with structures built from car parts and an arresting series of white fibreglass figures arranged in imitation of *The Last Supper*. As you enter town you'll be greeted by the most conspicuous piece, installed not long ago: a huge metal miner accompanied by a similarly proportioned penguin. Visiting Rhyolite before Scotty's Castle (see p.266) gives you the opportunity to explore the one-way Titus Canyon road which winds past several crumbling lead mines. High-clearance or four-wheel drive vehicles are recommended.

Mount Whitney

Rising out of the northern reaches of the Mojave Desert, the Sierra Nevada Mountains announce themselves with a bang two hundred miles north of Los Angeles at **Mount Whitney**, the highest point on a silver-gray knifelike ridge of pinnacles that forms a nearly sheer wall of granite, eleven thousand feet above the Valley below.

Mount Whitney lies on the eastern border of Sequoia National Park, and its sharply pointed peaks dominate the small roadside town of **Lone Pine** at its feet. The view of the High Sierra summits from the town is fantastic, captured by photographer Ansel Adams in a much-reproduced shot of the full moon suspended above stark cliffs.

CLIMBING MOUNT WHITNEY AND BACKCOUNTRY PERMITS

Climbing up to the 14,494-foot **summit** of Mount Whitney is a real challenge: it's a very strenuous, 22-mile round trip, made especially difficult by the lack of oxygen in the rarefied air of what is the highest point in the lower 48 states. Vigorous hikers starting before dawn from the 8000-foot trailhead can be up and back before dark, but a couple of days spent acclimatizing up here is advisable. The trail gains over a mile in elevation, cutting up past alpine lakes to boulder-strewn Trail Crest Pass – the southern end of the 220-mile John Muir Trail that heads north to Yosemite. From the pass it climbs along the clifftops, finally reaching the rounded hump of the summit itself, where a **stone cabin** serves as an emergency shelter.

If a full-on slog to the summit doesn't appeal, make the relatively easy five-mile hike to Lone Pine Lake, for which no permit is required.

Most people **camp** near the trailhead at the easily accessible *Whitney Portal* campground (mid-May to mid-Oct; $12; ☎1-800/280-2267), thirteen miles west of Lone Pine, which has a combined restaurant and camping-cum-general store, plus showers – or at the nearby *Whitney Trailhead Walk-in* (mid-May to mid-Oct; $6), which has water and toilets. Shuttle service to the campgrounds is always available; Inyo Trailhead Transportation (☎760/876-5518) is the current concessionaire but that frequently changes. Check with the helpful Mount Whitney Ranger Station (see below) for the latest information.

Between May 22 and October 15 – the only time the trail is normally free of snow – you can book permits to hike the mountain by contacting **Inyo National Forest Wilderness Reservation Service** (PO Box 430, Big Pine, CA 93513; ☎888/374-3733 or 760/938-1136, fax 938-1137; *www.sierrawilderness.com*). The various other sections of the 78,000-acre wilderness area detailed in this chapter are also covered by this service. An overnight permit costs $4 per person, a day-use permit $2. For Mount Whitney, you can – and should – book up to six months in advance of the day you'd like to come; permits are limited and get snapped up quickly. In addition, a few permits are also handed out on a first-come-first-served basis at the **Mount Whitney Ranger Station** (☎760/876-6200) on the main street of Lone Pine.

Day-use permits are not required for the rest of the Inyo wilderness area, but permission is needed if you want to spend the night; inquire at the Eastern Sierra Interagency Visitor Center (see p. 270) for the ranger station nearest the region you'd like to hike. Out of season (Sept 16 through the last Thursday in June) self-issue permits are available at the various trailheads.

Lone Pine and around

Straddling the desert and the mountains, the town of **LONE PINE** has a funky, low-key appeal, though it appears to be little more than a string of motels and gas stations straggling along US-395. It makes a good base for exploring the area, particularly if you're not prepared to camp out, and is also a final supply post for eastbound travelers approaching Death Valley (see p.260).

For information on hiking or camping, stop by the **Eastern Sierra Interagency Visitor Center** (daily: June–Aug 8am–6.50pm; Sept–May 8am–5.50pm; ☎760/876-6222), a mile south of town on US-395 at the junction of Hwy-136, the Death Valley road. The center has practical and historical information on the whole of eastern California – including the High Sierra, Owens Valley, White Mountains, Death Valley – and the latest on mountain and high pass conditions. Most of the region is protected within the massive **Inyo National Forest**, and if you're planning to spend any amount of time in the area, pick up the very helpful **map** ($4), which covers everything between Mount Whitney and Yosemite National Park, including all hiking routes and campgrounds. Interestingly, this is the only map that makes clear the extent of the City of Los Angeles' holdings in the Owens Valley – basically the entire Valley floor.

Many early Westerns, and the epic *Gunga Din*, were filmed in the **Alabama Hills** immediately west of Lone Pine, a rugged expanse of sedimentary rock that's been sculpted into bizarre shapes by 160 million years of erosive winds and rains. Some of the oddest formations are linked by the **Picture Rocks Circle**, a paved road that loops around from Whitney Portal Road, passing rocks shaped like bullfrogs, walruses and baboons; the 100-foot rock faces make it a popular place for rock-climbers to hone their skills. In celebration of its movie heritage, the town now hosts the **Lone Pine Film Festival**, usually in early October, showing only films made in the area. Contact the Chamber of Commerce (see below) for details.

Practicalities

Greyhound buses stop once a day at 1452 S Main St. If you're looking for a **motel**, try the *Dow Villa Motel/Historic Dow Hotel* (☎1-800/824-9317 or 760/876-5521; ②) at 310 S Main St, built in 1923 to house movie industry visitors (John Wayne always requested Room 20); the *Best Western Frontier Motel* (☎1-800/528-1234 or 760/876-5571; ③), 1008 S Main St; or the *Alabama Hills Inn* (☎1-800/800-6468 or 760/876-8700; ③), 1920 S Main St. Decent **restaurants** along the highway include the *Pizza Factory*, 301 S Main St (☎760/876-4707) and *PJ's*, a 24-hour coffee shop (☎760/876-5796). For great coffee and cinnamon buns, go for *Caffeine Hannah's*, also on Main Street. In summer, the **swimming pool** at the high school opposite is open daily ($2); after a week in the mountains, you can get cleaned up at Kirk's Sierra Barber Shop, 104 N Main St, where you can take a **hot shower** for $3. For more **information** on local services, contact the **Chamber of Commerce** at 126 S Main St (Mon–Fri 8am–4pm; ☎760/876-4444).

The Owens Valley

The **OWENS VALLEY** – stretching from Lone Pine north beyond Bishop – is hot, dry and numinously thrilling: a desolate desert landscape, bordered by parallel ridges of 14,000-foot peaks. It is almost entirely unpopulated outside of the few towns along the highway, though a few solitary souls live in old sheds and caravans off the many dirt roads and tracks that cross the floor of the Valley. Years ago the area was a prime spot for growing apples and pears, but since 1913 its plentiful natural water supply, fed by the many streams which run down from the Sierra Nevada, has been drained away to fill the swimming pools of Los Angeles.

Manzanar National Historic Site and Independence

Just west of US-395, ten miles north of Lone Pine, on the site of the most productive of the Owens Valley orchards, stand the concrete foundations of the **Manzanar Relocation Camp**, where more than ten thousand Americans of Japanese descent were corralled during World War II. Considering them a threat to national security, the US government uprooted whole families and confiscated all their property; they were released at the end of the war, though claims for compensation were only settled in 1988, when the government agreed to pay damages amounting to millions of dollars, and finally offered an official apology. The camp was once ringed by barbed wire and filled with row upon row of wooden barracks; now only a couple of guardhouses and a small cemetery remain. As the bronze plaque on the guardhouse says: "May the injustices and humiliation suffered here as a result of hysteria, racism and economic exploitation never emerge again". The remains of the camp have been designated a national historic site (daytime access only; free), and funds were recently allocated to install a visitor center and restore some of the barracks and one of the guard towers. Some of the former internees return each year, on the last Saturday in April, in a kind of pilgrimage.

An evocative and affecting exhibit about Manzanar, detailing the experiences of many of the young children who were held there, is on display inside the **Eastern California Museum** at 155 N Grant St (Wed–Mon 10am–4pm; donation), three blocks west of the porticoed County Courthouse in the sleepy town of **INDEPENDENCE**, six miles further north. The cinder-block museum also has displays on the natural environment of the Owens Valley, including the bighorn sheep that live in the mountains west of town, and exhibits on the region's history, from native Paiute basketry to old mining and farming equipment. There's also a reconstructed pioneer village behind the museum, made up of old buildings from all over the Owens Valley that have been brought together and restored here.

Independence takes its heroic name not from any great libertarian tradition but from a Civil War fort that was founded north of the town on the Fourth of July, 1862; every year on that day there's a parade down Main Street followed by a mass barbecue and fireworks show in **Dehy Park**, along tree-shaded Independence Creek on the north side of town. The park is marked by a large steam locomotive, which once ran from here to Nevada on narrow gauge tracks and is now being gussied up again.

Practicalities

To **stay** here, try the inexpensive *Independence Courthouse Motel* at 157 N Edwards St (☎1-800/801-0703 or 760/878-2732; ②), or the much more atmospheric 1920s *Winnedumah Hotel*, 211 N Edwards St (☎760/878-2040; ③), once a film-star haven. There's a small **campground** ($5) half a mile west of town, reached by following Market Street beside the creek. For **food** stop by *Mair's Market*, or (before 9pm), enjoy sandwiches, salads or full meals at the *Whistle Stop*. There's also a new Chinese restaurant that locals recommend, *The Asian Cookhouse*. All are on the central Edwards Street.

Onwards from Independence

The minor Onion Valley Road leads beyond Independence's campground, twisting up the mountains to **Onion Valley**, ten miles west, where there's the *Onion Valley* **campground** (June to mid-Sept; $11; ☎760/876-6200) and the trailhead for **hiking** across the Sierra Nevada into Kings Canyon National Park, sixteen miles over Kearsarge Pass to Cedar Grove (see p.308). This is the easiest and shortest route across the Sierra; you can get the required **wilderness permit** from the Inyo National Forest Wilderness Reservation Service (see box on p.269) or, off-season, at the trailhead.

The slopes of Mount Williamson, south of Onion Valley, and of Mount Baxter to the north are the protected home of the increasingly rare **California bighorn sheep**: nimble creatures that roam around the steep, rocky slopes and sport massive, curling horns. Far more common these days, however, are **black bears**; many of the local campgrounds require you to have bear-resistant food containers (you can buy or rent them at area sporting goods stores). The **Winnedumah Monument**, a giant boulder standing on the flat ridge of the Inyo Mountains, six miles east of Independence and clearly visible from US-395, resembles nothing so much as the monolith from the movie *2001*. Local legends tell of how members of the Paiute tribe would hide behind the smaller boulders at its base and ambush wild game that had been chased up from the hills below. There are lots of abandoned mineshafts and poorly marked tunnels at the foot of the mountains, so watch your step.

Ten miles north of Independence is the actual start of the **LA Aqueduct**. Follow any of the dirt tracks that head east from US-395 and you can't fail to spot the traces of the railroads built to haul in the material needed to construct the great ditch – which Space Shuttle astronauts claim to have seen while orbiting the globe.

Two-thirds of the way to Big Pine (see below), the **Tinnemaha Wildlife Viewpoint** warrants a brief pause to see if you can spot any of the five-hundred-strong herd of Tule Elk, now-protected California natives which were nearly wiped out by the end of the nineteenth century.

Big Pine and the White Mountains

The town of **BIG PINE**, thirty miles north, is slightly larger than Independence but doesn't have much more in the way of services. There are a few gas stations, Greyhound buses stop once a day in each direction, and there are a couple of serviceable **motels** along US-395 – the *Big Pine Motel*, 370 S Main St (☎760/938-2282; ②), and the *Starlight Motel*, 511 S Main St (☎760/938-2011; ②). There is also the *Triangle* **campground** ($6) half a mile north of town at the junction of Hwy-168, several more up Glacier Lodge Road (see below), and reasonable **food** at *Rula's Ice Cream and Pizza*, which is right next door to the recently established **visitor center** at 126 S Main St (daily 8am–4.30pm; ☎760/938-2114). Big Pine is, however, the gateway to two of the most unusual natural phenomena in California: the **Palisade Glacier** in the Sierra Nevada, west of the town, and the ancient Bristlecone Pine Forest in the barren **White Mountains** to the east. It is also a jumping off point for the northern section of Death Valley, in particular the Eureka Sand Dunes (see p.267) and the hot springs of the Saline Valley (see p.268).

The Palisade Glacier

The southernmost glacier in the US, the **Palisade Glacier** sits at the foot of the impressive Palisade Crest, center of one of the greatest concentrations of enjoyably climbable (though only for the experienced) peaks in the Eastern Sierra. To the south is Norman Clyde Peak, named after California's most prolific early mountaineer; Thunderbolt Peak and Mount Agassiz are highlights of the Inconsolable Range to the north of the glacier, itself an excellent introduction to snow and ice-climbing, while in the center the immense bulk of Temple Crag offers a range of routes unparalleled outside of Yosemite Valley. The trailhead for all of these climbs, and the many local hikes, is ten miles west of Big Pine, at the end of Glacier Lodge Road, along which there are three, three-season, $10-a-night **campgrounds** – *Sage Flat, Upper Sage Flat* and *Big Pine Creek* – all above 7000ft and with water and toilets; and a free site at 8300ft, a mile from the trailhead. *Glacier Lodge* (☎760/938-2837; ④), right at the end of the road, is a more luxurious option, with a restaurant and general store.

The imposing glacier is nine miles from the end of the road on a well-marked trail along the north fork of Big Pine Creek, past a number of alpine lakes. Before heading off into the wilderness, get a backcountry camping **permit** (see box on p.269).

The White Mountains

Big Pine is also the gateway to the intimidating **White Mountains**, a bald, dry, unwelcoming range, made up of some of the oldest, fossil-filled rock in California (hundreds of millions of years older than the Sierra), which acts as the eastern wall of the Owens Valley. The mountains are accessible only by car (or bike) via Hwy-168. Be sure to fill up on gas and **drinking water**, both of which are unavailable east of US-395. The highest point in the range, White Mountain, rises to a height of 14,246ft. Near the summit, a strenuous fifteen-mile hike from the end of a long dusty road, a research station (closed to the public) studies the physiology of high-altitude plant and animal life, which is in many ways similar to that of the arctic regions.

The gnarled trees that are the prime reason for coming here stand on the lower slopes in the ancient **Bristlecone Pine Forest**, but snow renders them inaccessible for all but three or four months in the summer. **Schulman Grove**, named after Dr Edmund Schulman who discovered and dated the trees in the mid-1950s, is the most accessible collection, at the end of the paved road that twists up from Hwy-168. The grove is split up into two self-guided nature trails. One, the mile-long Discovery Trail, passes by a number of splendid examples; the other, longer Methuselah Trail loops around past the oldest tree, the 4700-year-old Methuselah, and the newly enlarged **visitor center**. **Patriarch Grove**, eleven miles further on, along a dusty dirt road that gives spectacular views of the Sierra Nevada to the west and the Great Basin ranges of the deserts to the east, contains the Patriarch Tree, the largest of the bristlecone pines.

Three miles beyond here, a gate prevents unauthorized vehicles from getting to the research station on the summit; hikers and all-terrain **mountain bikes** are permitted to continue. In fact, the steep canyons running down from the ridge are tailor-made for thrill-seekers, who race down the steep washes at incredibly high speed. **Silver Canyon**, descending from just beyond Schulman Grove, is the route taken by the **Plumline Outback**, a rigorous mountain bike race held each July; cyclists begin in Bishop, race up to the ridge and career back down again.

BRISTLECONE PINES

Bristlecone pines (*pinus longaeva*) are the oldest known living things on earth. Some of them have been alive for over 4500 years (1500 years more than any sequoia), earning them a place in the *Guinness Book of Records*. The oldest examples cling to thin alkaline soils (predominantly dolomite) between 10,000 and 11,000 feet, where the low precipitation keeps the growing season to only 45 days a year. But such conditions, which limit the trees' girth expansion to an inch every hundred years, promotes the dense resin-rich and rot-resistant wood that lasts for millennia. Battered and beaten by the harsh environment into bizarrely beautiful shapes and forms, they look like nothing so much as twenty-foot lumps of driftwood. The most photogenic examples comprise mostly **dead wood**, the live section often sustained by a thin ribbon of bark. Even when dead, the wind-scoured trunks and twisted limbs hang on without decaying for upwards of another thousand-odd years, slowly being eroded by wind-driven ice and sand.

Bristlecones can thrive at lower altitudes and richer soils than those described in the preceding paragraph, but they don't live as long as the specimens subjected to the harsher conditions and they're hardly recognizable as bristlecone pines because they grow tall and wide, though the five-needle bundles and the egg-shaped, barbed cone which lends the tree its name give the game away.

There is **camping** available, but no water; the only campground is 8600ft up at *Grandview* (May–Oct; free), two miles south of Schulman Grove. Backcountry camping is not permitted in the ancient Bristlecone Pine Forest, but elsewhere backpackers will need to obtain a wilderness permit (see box on p.269). The ranger station in Bishop can provide you with first-come, first-served permits, and also tell you which springs and small creeks (if any) are flowing.

Bishop

BISHOP, to a Californian, means **outdoor pursuits**. The largest town (population 3500) in the Owens Valley, it's an excellent base from which to explore the mountains that surround it. If you want to try rock-climbing, hang-gliding, cross-country skiing or fly-fishing, there's no better place to be, with some of the world's best mountaineers offering their services through lessons and guided trips.

Bishop's best feature is its proximity to the wilderness, but there's also a laid-back ambience to the town which is worth hanging around to enjoy. It's an easy place to get to, with Greyhound calling at the station at 201 S Warren St (☎760/872-2721) and Country Corners (☎760/872-4411) to get you out to the trailheads.

Finding **accommodation** is no problem either. The **visitor center** at 690 N Main St (Mon–Fri 9am–5pm, Sat & Sun 10am–4pm; ☎760/873-8405) on the north side of town has a visitor guide listing accommodation, most of it within a block of US-395 (Main Street through the town). The best budget options are the *El Rancho Motel*, 274 W Lagoon St on the south side of town (☎760/872-9251; ②), and the *Thunderbird Motel*, 190 W Pine St (☎760/873-4215; ②); the more upmarket *Best Western Creekside Inn*, 725 N Main St (☎760/872-3044; ③) offers large rooms and complimentary breakfast.

With a 24-hour Vons store at 174 S Main St, and a number of cafés and diners, Bishop is a good spot to buy **food** and **supplies**. *Jack's Waffle Shop*, 437 N Main St, is open seven fluorescent-lit days a week for breakfasts and burgers. For good espresso and pastries, head to the pseudo-Dutch *Erick Schat's Bakkerij*, 736 N Main St (☎760/873-7156). For lunch or dinner try *Bar-B-Q Bill's* at 187 S Main St (☎760/872-5535), *Amigo's Mexican Restaurant*, 285 Main St (☎760/872-2189), or *Whiskey Creek*, 524 N Main St (☎760/873-7174), which also has a lively **bar** open till 2am.

For information on **hiking** and **camping** in the area, contact the White Mountain Ranger Station at 798 N Main St (July to mid-Sept daily 8am–4.30pm; rest of year Mon–Fri 8am–4.30pm; ☎760/873-2500), which also issues the first-come, first-served wilderness permits. Another place worth a stop is Wilson's East Side Sports, an excellent mountaineering and sporting goods supply shop at 206 N Main St. Hikers and backcountry campers in need of a **shower** can get one at the Bishop City Pool, 688 N Main St (Mon–Sat 7am–8pm; $1) from Memorial Day through Labor Day, or year-round at Sierra Bodies Gym, 192 E Pine St (Mon–Sat 6am–9pm, Sat & Sun 8am–6pm; $3).

Around Bishop

US-6 heads north and east from Bishop into Nevada, passing by the **Laws Railroad Museum** (daily 10am–4pm; donation), a restoration of the old town of **Laws**, five miles off US-395, with some old buildings and a slender black narrow-gauge train that used to run along the eastern edge of the Owens Valley. It's worth a quick look on your way to see the **Red Rock Canyon Petroglyphs**, four miles west of US-6; the rock carvings have been terribly vandalized, but enough remains of the spacey figures to justify a trip. Obtain a free permit from the Bureau of Lands Management, Suite E, 785 N Main St in Bishop (☎760/872-4881).

There are petroglyphs all over the Owens Valley – about the only sign of the Paiute peoples that once roamed the area, hunting and gathering and living off the land. Their descendants have been gathered in reservations outside each of the Valley towns, the largest just west of Bishop along Hwy-168, where they've established the **Paiute Shoshone Indian Cultural Center** (Mon–Fri 9am–5pm, Sat & Sun 9am–4pm; donation) at 2300 W Line St. Here they put on displays of basketry and weaving, food gathering and processing, and of traditional ways of building; they also run a good bookstore.

Further west along this road, which runs up into the foothills of the Sierra Nevada, there are a number of **campgrounds** between 7500 and 9000 feet up – almost all with water and costing $11 a night. The shady *Sabrina* site, right by the lake of the same name, is perhaps the best.

A number of **hiking routes** set off up into the High Sierra wilderness from the end of the road. The trail from South Lake over Bishop Pass heads into Dusy Basin, where you can see the effects of centuries of glaciation in the bowl-like cirques and giant "erratic" boulders left by receding glaciers. Another path follows the northern fork of Bishop Creek under the rusty cliffs of the Paiute Crags, before climbing over Paiute Pass into the Desolation Lakes area of the John Muir Wilderness.

North towards Mammoth

North of Bishop US-395 climbs out of the Owens Valley up Sherwin Grade onto the 6500-feet-high **Mono Basin**. Eighteen miles north of Bishop, at the foot of the climb, Gorge Road leads west into the 1000-feet deep **Owens River Gorge**, one of the best climbing spots on this side of the Sierra.

Much more of the money that flows into Bishop comes from the brigades of fishing enthusiasts, who spend their summer vacations angling for rainbow trout placed in the streams and lakes by the state government. The largest assembly of fisherfolk gather on the last Saturday in April around **Lake Crowley**, an artificial reservoir built to hold water diverted from Mono Lake, thirty miles north of town.

Just east of US-395, a mile south of the exit for Mammoth Lakes, is one of the more pleasurable and easily accessible examples of the region's volcanic activity in the hot springs that bubble up at **Hot Creek** (daily dawn–dusk; free). Jets of boiling water mix with the otherwise chilly, snow-melt water to form pools ranging from tepid to scalding; you have to search to find a happy medium, and it's a bit of a challenge since the flows are ever-changing (note, too, that the US Forest Service discourages bathing, as chemicals are sometimes produced in the springs – not that anyone takes any notice). Paths and wooden steps lead down to the most likely spots, but wear shoes, because idiots have shattered bottles under the water. This is one of the best, and best known, springs in the region; details of others appear in George William's *Hot Springs of the Eastern Sierra*, found in the area's bookshops and visitor centers.

Mammoth Lakes and around

During winter, masses of weekend skiers speed through the Owens Valley from LA on their way to the slopes of Mammoth Mountain, forty miles north along US-395 from Bishop then five miles west on Hwy-203, above the resort town of **MAMMOTH LAKES**. Outside the Lake Tahoe basin, this is the state's premier ski mountain, and it is for this and the summer fishing that Mammoth is traditionally known, although it now also hosts an increasing number of on- and off-road bike races. Mammoth is unbeatable for outdoor activities and is scenically as dramatic as just about anywhere in the Sierra, but unless you're a serious jock, you're likely to find the testosterone overload oppressive and the town overpriced.

With one of the longest Californian seasons (often stretching well into June), 2200 vertical feet of skiing and more than its fair share of deep powder, **Mammoth Mountain** is understandably popular. Pick up **lift tickets** ($47 per day) from the Main Lodge on Minaret Road, where you can also rent **equipment** ($20 for basic skis, boots

MAMMOTH LAKES

△ 395 (2 miles)

SAWMILL ROAD

MERIDIAN BOULEVARD

SHERWIN CREEK ROAD

US Forest Service/
Visitor Center

RV Park

Greyhound
stop

Minaret Village Mall

OLD MAMMOTH ROAD

Mammoth Gateway Mall

Sierra Center Mall

CHATEAU ROAD

MAIN STREET

BOULEVARD

MERIDIAN ROAD

MINARET ROAD

MINARET

LAKEVIEW

CANYON BOULEVARD

MINARET ROAD

OLD MAMMOTH ROAD

N

0   800 yds

Scenic loop to 395 & June Lake △

Lake Mary, Lake George & Horseshoe Lake (Summer only) ▷

Twin Lakes

Upper Twin

LAKE MARY ROAD

Chair lift

MAMMOTH MOUNTAIN
SKI AREA

Climbing Rock

Mammoth Mountain
Bike Park
(Summer only)

Main
Lodge

▲ Mammoth Mountain
(11,053 ft)

Devil's Postpile National Monument (Summer only) ▷

ACCOMMODATION
1 Davison St Guesthouse
2 Mammoth Mountain Inn
3 Snowcreek Resort
4 Snow Goose Inn
5 Tamarack Lodge Resort
6 Ullr Lodge
7 White Stag Inn

and poles), and book **lessons** ($32 per half-day). Without a ski pass, a cable car ride to the 11,053-foot summit will set you back $10.

In summer, fifty miles of snow-free ski slopes transform themselves into the 3500-acre **Mammoth Mountain Bike Park** ($18 a day for trail access, $23 for trails and the cable car, $35 a day for bike rental), likely to give sensation-seeking mountain bikers the thrill of their lives. The season's highlight is the massive World Cup event held over the Fourth of July weekend, which features the **kamikaze**, the ultimate downhill race, with speeds hitting sixty miles per hour. August sees the family-oriented **Adventure Week** (☎1-800/367-6572 or 760/934-3068 for information) with guided tours, night rides and special children's events. There's also a 32-foot artificial **climbing rock** in front of the *Mammoth Mountain Inn*; details of this and further sporting activities appear in the box below. On a less energetic but equally lively note, the annual Jazz Jubilee, held in the second week in July (details on ☎760/934-2478), also packs the town out with trad-jazz types.

The daily Greyhound stops in the *McDonald's* parking lot on Hwy-203. During the ski season, get around on the four-line Mammoth Shuttle (☎760/934-3030). In summer, **rent a bike** (see box).

The best source of practical information for the area is the combined US Forest Service and Mammoth Lakes **visitor center** (daily 9am–5pm; ☎760/924-5500) on the main highway half a mile east of the town center.

Devil's Postpile National Monument

The evocatively named **Devil's Postpile National Monument** (free), twelve miles west of town, is accessible when there's no snow on the roads. In the height of the summer

---

ADVENTURE TRAVEL SPECIALISTS

Ballooning High Sierra Ballooning ☎760/934-7118.

Cross-country skiing *Tamarack Lodge Resort* (see Accommodation, p.278) offers ski packages, including instruction, tours, and rentals. For day rentals and instruction only, contact Sierra Meadow Ranch (☎760/934-2442) at Old Mammoth Road in Mammoth.

Kayaking Caldera Kayaks (☎760/935-4942) based at Crowley Lake Marina runs guided kayak trips on Mono and Crowley lakes ($55) and rents out gear for $30–45 a day.

Mountain bike tours and rental Cindy Whitehead's Sierra Bike Rentals (☎760/924-2955) leads off-road treks and runs instruction clinics; they'll deliver bikes to your door.

Mountaineering and rock-climbing guides For expert instruction or guided trips in the High Sierra backcountry, contact Tim Villanueva (☎760/872-4413), John Fischer (☎760/873-5037), or Todd Vogel (☎760/873-8526), all in Bishop, or the Mammoth Mountaineering School (☎760/924-9100). All cover rock climbing, alpine climbing and ski mountaineering. Mammoth High Adventures (☎760/924-5683) operates Mammoth's **climbing rock** ($13 per hour, $20 per day, group discounts) and rents sticky boots for $3. The rock is first-come-first-served, but reservations are recommended for ropes and orienteering courses.

Pack mules If you want to enjoy the wilderness without the burden of a heavy backpack, for around $65 per day you can join a mule train and let the animals carry your load. Try Pine Creek Pack Trains (☎760/387-2797) in Bishop, Red's Meadow Pack Station (☎1-800/292-7758 or 760/934-2345) and Mammoth Lakes Pack Outfit (☎760/934-2434).

Snowmobiling If you prefer a motorized approach to the white stuff, you can rent equipment (rates start at $38 per hour) and clothing from Mammoth Snowmobile Adven-Tours, which has self-guided tours, private tours, and lessons.

season, unless you're camping in the area, you must go via the Mammoth Shuttle bus ($8) leaving every thirty minutes from *Mammoth Mountain Inn*; if the shuttle has stopped but the road is still open, you can drive there along Minaret Road. A collection of slender, blue-gray basalt columns, some as tall as sixty feet, the Postpile was formed as lava from the eruption of Mammoth Mountain (really a volcano) cooled and fractured into multi-sided forms. The highlight of the monument is **Rainbow Falls**, reached by a two-mile hike through Red's Meadow and along the Middle Fork of the San Joaquin River, which drops over a hundred feet into a deep pool, the spray reflecting and refracting, especially at midday, to earn its name. The adjacent **Minarets Peaks** are a spiky volcanic ridge just south of pointed Mount Ritter – one of the Sierra's most enticing high peaks.

June Lake

The freneticism and crowding of Mammoth Lakes sends some skiers and summer visitors a few miles further north to the relative solitude of **June Lake** and its neighbors, Grant, Silver and Gull lakes. Reached by way of the seventeen-mile **June Lake Loop** road, which branches off US-395 thirteen miles north of the Mammoth turning, this region of high-altitude lakes is some of the most striking in these parts, and offers Mammoth's attractions on a more manageable scale.

Accommodation

Mammoth offers so many **accommodation** opportunities, including three hostels, that beds are at a premium only during peak-season weekends. Winter prices are highest, summer rates (quoted here) come next, and in between some relative bargains can be found. Campers should head for any of a number of the **campgrounds** close to the Devil's Postpile National Monument or in the Red's Meadow area. All have water and cost from $8 to $11. There's also excellent camping and backpacking in the Minarets Wilderness.

Davison St Guesthouse, 19 Davison St, off Main St (☎760/924-2188). Wooden A-frame chalet with mountain views. Four-bed rooms for $45 and dorm space from $18, with a kitchen available for guests' use.

Mammoth Mountain Inn, Mammoth Mountain (☎1-800/228-4947 or 760/934-2581). *The* place to stay – right where the action is at the foot of the ski tows, adjacent to the bike park and overlooking the climbing rock. It's a touch sterile but you'll be well looked after. ⑤.

Snowcreek Resort, Old Mammoth Rd, by the golf course (☎1-800/544-6007 or 760/934-3333). Well-appointed condos with a two-night minimum stay, spring and fall discounts (three nights for two), and use of the pool, spa and tennis club. Especially good value for groups. ⑥.

Snow Goose Inn, 57 Forest Trail (☎1-800/874-7368 or 760/934-2660). Relatively reasonable rates and generous morning and late afternoon spreads help compensate for the typical bed and breakfast cutesineness. ④.

Tamarack Lodge Resort, Lake Mary Rd (☎1-800/237-6879 or 760/934-2442). Lodge rooms ($70–105) or rustic cabins ($80–115) with fully-equipped kitchens, beautifully situated beside Twin Lake right on the edge of a cross-country ski area.

SIERRA PASS CLOSURES

After coming through the Mojave or Death Valley it seems hard to imagine that many of the passes across the Sierra Nevada can remain closed well into June. Theoretically, Memorial Day is the date for the **Tioga Pass** (into Yosemite) just below Mono Lake to open, but harsh winters frequently leave it closed until early July. Passes to the north of here, Hwy-108 and Hwy-4, tend to open a couple of weeks earlier, in mid-May; Hwy-88, yet further north, stays open all year. All close again with the first heavy snowfall, perhaps around mid-October. For information on the state of the highways call CalTrans on ☎1-800/427-ROAD (see box on p.29).

ULLR Lodge, 5920 Minaret Rd (☎760/934-2454). Private rooms from $20 midweek in summer, and popular 4-bed dorms with lockers for $13. Showers are available to non-residents for $4 (it's an extra $1 if you don't have your own towel).

White Stag Inn, corner of Main and Minaret (☎760/934-7507). Pleasant, centrally located motel; some rooms with kitchenettes. ③.

Eating, drinking and nightlife

Restaurants are plentiful here, and they're less pricey than at many ski resorts, though the snack bars actually on the mountain are less competitive. To stock up on **groceries**, head for Vons, in the Minaret Village Mall. A couple of good **bars**, some with live **music**, provide entertainment after a day's activity.

Angel's, Main St at Sierra Blvd (☎760/934-7427). The menu has a Southwestern kick at this friendly place, popular with families and couples alike; good salads and fish tacos.

Cervino's, 3752 Viewpoint Rd (☎760/934-4734). Pricey but excellent northern Italian fare, good for a splurge.

Giovanni's, Minaret Village Mall, Old Mammoth Rd (☎760/934-7563). The favorite local stop for pasta and pizza, with great lunchtime deals.

Grumpy's, Old Mammoth Rd, just off Main St (☎760/934-8587). Non-smoking sports bar with pool table, video games, and a good grill.

The Lakefront Restaurant, *Tamarack Lodge* (☎760/934-3534). Superb lake views – for a price. But the food is fine, and nothing in Mammoth is very formal.

Looney Bean Coffee Roasting Co., Main St (☎760/934-1345). Come here for the scene; the coffee's better at other places in town (try World Cup Coffee if it's the java you're after). Open until 11pm at weekends, later in the ski season.

Schat's Bakery & Café, 3305 Main St (☎760/934-6055). Easily the best baked goods in town.

The Stove, 644 Old Mammoth Rd, opposite the Sherwin Plaza (☎760/934-2821). Long-standing Mammoth favorite, serving egg, waffle and pancake breakfasts, sandwiches and full meals later on – all served in massive portions.

Whiskey Creek, Main St and Minaret Rd (☎760/934-2555). One of the town's liveliest bars and restaurants, with its own good microbrews. Bands Wed–Sun in winter; Thurs–Sat in summer.

Mono Lake

The blue expanse of **Mono Lake** sits in the middle of a volcanic, desert tableland, its sixty square miles reflecting the statuesque, snowcapped mass of the eastern Sierra Nevada. At close on a million years old, it's an ancient lake, one of the oldest in North America, with two large volcanic islands, the light-colored **Pahoa** and the black **Negit**, surrounded by salty, alkaline water. It resembles nothing more than a science-fiction landscape, with great towers and spires formed by mineral deposits ringing the shores; hot springs surround the lake, and all around the basin are signs of lava flows and volcanic activity, especially in the cones of the Mono Craters, just to the south.

The lake's most distinctive feature, the strange, sandcastle-like **tufa** formations, have been increasingly exposed over the past fifty years or so since the City of Los Angeles began draining away the waters that flow into the lake (see box overleaf). The towers of tufa were formed underwater, where calcium-bearing freshwater springs well up through the carbonate-rich lake water; the calcium and carbonate combine and sink to the bottom as limestone, slowly growing into the weird formations you can see today. Before striking out for a close look at the lake and its tufa, call in at the excellent **Mono Basin Scenic Area Visitor Center**, a mile north of Lee Vining beside US-395 (May–Sept daily 9am–4:45pm; Oct–April Thurs–Mon 9am–4.45pm; ☎760/647-3044). Here exhibits and a good short film detail the lake's geology, and rangers give talks on various aspects of its ecology. The center is also the place to check the **guided walks**

THE BATTLE FOR MONO LAKE

At around a million years old, **Mono Lake** is one of the oldest bodies of water on the continent. It has survived several ice ages and all the volcanic activity that the area can throw at it, but the lake's biggest threat has been the City of Los Angeles, which owns the riparian rights to Mono Lake's catchment. In 1941, the Los Angeles Department of Water and Power diverted four of the five streams that fed the lake into its Owens Valley Aqueduct, which drains the Mono Basin through an eleven-mile tunnel. This was an engineering marvel, dug through the volcanically active Mono Craters, but it's been overshadowed by the legal battle surrounding the depletion of the lake itself, long one of the biggest **environmental controversies** raging in California.

The **water level** in Mono Lake has dropped over forty feet since 1941, a disaster not only because of the lake's unique beauty, but also because Mono Lake is the primary nesting ground for California gulls and a prime stopover point for thousands of migratory geese, ducks and swans. The lake is now roughly half its natural size, and as the levels dropped, the islands in the middle of the lake where the gulls lay their eggs became peninsulas, and the colonies fell prey to coyotes and other mainland predators. Also, as less fresh water reached the lake, the landlocked water became increasingly saline, threatening the unique local ecosystem. Brine shrimp and alkali flies are about all that will thrive in the harsh conditions, but these are critical to the birdlife. Humans are not immune to the harmful effects: winds blowing across the salt pans left behind by the receding lake create clouds containing selenium and arsenic, both contributors to lung disease.

Seemingly oblivious to the plight of the lake, the City of Los Angeles built a second aqueduct in 1970 and the water level dropped even faster, sometimes falling eighteen inches. Prompted by scientific reports of an impending ecological disaster, a small group of activists set up the Mono Lake Committee in 1978, fighting for the preservation of this unique ecosystem partly through publicity campaigns – "Save Mono Lake" bumper stickers were once *de rigueur* for concerned citizens – and partly through the courts. Though the California Supreme Court declared in 1983 that Mono Lake must be saved, it wasn't until 1991 that emergency action was taken. A target water height of 6377ft above sea level (later raised to 6392ft) was grudgingly agreed to make Negit Island once again safe for nesting birds. Streams dry for decades are now flowing again, but target levels won't be reached for another twenty to thirty years.

(July to early Sept daily 10am, 1pm & 6pm) which leave from the **South Tufa Reserve** ($2), one of the best places to look at the tufa spires, five miles east of US-395 via Hwy-120. Also here is **Navy Beach**, where you can float in salty water three times as buoyant as sea water. Adjacent to the south shore of the lake stands the **Panum Crater**, a 640-year-old volcano riddled with deep fissures and fifty-foot towers of lava, visited on two short and fairly easy trails, the **Plug Trail** and **Rim Trail**.

On the north shore of the lake, three miles along US-395, stands **Mono County Park**, where a guided boardwalk trail leads down to the lakefront and the best examples of mushroom-shaped tufa towers. Accessible by trail from the county park, or by a two-mile dirt road off Hwy-167, **Black Point** is the result of a massive eruption of molten lava some thirteen thousand years ago. As the lava cooled and contracted, cracks and fissures formed on the top, some only a few feet wide but as much as fifty feet deep.

Regular **canoe trips** (mid-June to mid-Sept Sat & Sun 8am, 9.30am & 11am; $15; reservations recommended ☎760/647-6595) give a closer look at what the lake has to offer.

Lee Vining

Within easy walking distance of Mono Lake, the appealing small town of **LEE VINING** offers the usual range of visitor services along either side of US-395, and not a great deal more. Greyhound buses stop here daily at 11am (there's no terminal in town, so simply flag the bus down from outside the Lee Vining Supermarket). The town's **Mono Lake Committee Information Center** (daily 9am–5pm; ☎760/647-6595) is partly the showcase for the committee's battle for Mono Lake, but also has helpful staff, many books on the Eastern Sierra, and a nice gift shop. There are several **motels** along US-395 including *El Mono Motel* (☎760/647-6310; ②) and *Murphey's* (☎1-800/334-6316 or 760/647-6316; ②). More expensive but more characterful are the recently refurbished cabins at the 1918 *Tioga Lodge* (☎1-800/647-6423 or 760/647-6423; ⑤), just up Hwy-395 and overlooking the lake. A number of **campgrounds** lie along Lee Vining Creek off Tioga Pass Road, Hwy-120. **Eat** breakfast at *Nicely's Restaurant* on US-395 (☎760/647-6477), a great Fifties vinyl palace that opens at 6am. For dinner, the newly reopened *Mono Inn Restaurant*, 55620 Hwy-395 (☎760/647-6581), owned by Ansel Adams' grand-daughter, serves up primo yuppie fare and has a superb lake view.

Bodie Ghost Town and Bridgeport

In the 1870s the gold-mining town of **BODIE** boasted three breweries, some sixty saloons and dance halls and a population of ten thousand, with a well-earned reputation as the raunchiest and most lawless mining camp in the West. Contemporary accounts describe a town that ended each day with a shootout on Main Street, and church bells, rung once for every year of a murdered man's life, that seemed never to stop sounding. The town boomed for less than ten years, from 1877, when a fairly poor existing mine collapsed exposing an enormously rich vein. Within four years this was the second largest town in the state after San Francisco, even supporting its own Chinatown. By 1885, the population was down to three thousand, and the gold and silver – now valued at over $750 million – was all but mined out. A series of fires progressively destroyed the town, and it was evacuated and closed down in 1942. What remains has been turned into the **Bodie Ghost Town and State Park** ($2, $1 for a good tour booklet; ☎760/647-6445), thirteen miles (three of them dirt) along Hwy-270, which branches off US-395 eighteen miles north of Lee Vining. The park is open throughout the year (8am to an hour before sunset), but phone for the road conditions if you're going off season, as snow often prevents access between December and April. If you can get in during that time, bundle up: Bodie is often cited on the national weather report as having the lowest temperature in the US.

There are over 150 wooden buildings – about six percent of the original town – surviving in a state of arrested decay around the intact town center. Some buildings have been re-roofed and others supported in some way, but it is by and large a faithful preservation: even the dirty dishes are much as they were in the 1940s, little damaged by fifty years of weathering. The **Miner's Union Building** on Main Street was the center of the town's social life; founded in 1877, the union was one of the first in California, organized by workers at the Standard and Midnight mines. The building now houses a small **museum** (free), which paints a graphic picture of mining life. Various **tours** depart from here in the summer, including one of the stamp mill ($3) and one detailing the mining works ($5). Other highlights of the town include the **Methodist church** with its intact pipe organ, the **general store** with its beautiful pressed-steel ceiling, and the **saloon**.

Its many remaining structures and freedom from theme park-type tampering give Bodie an authentically eerie atmosphere absent from other US ghost towns. The place should keep you entertained for a few hours, so remember to bring all you need; there's no food available out here.

Bridgeport

Six miles further north is the mountain hamlet of **BRIDGEPORT** – an isolated village that provided the new start in life for fugitive Robert Mitchum in the *film noir* masterpiece *Out of the Past*. The gas station he owned in the film is long gone, though the place is otherwise little changed, a pretty little community of ranchers and fishermen, worth stopping at for a look at the dainty white 1880 **County Courthouse** and the small local history **museum** (Memorial Day to Sept daily 10am–5pm; $1), behind the pleasant town park in a restored old schoolhouse. Bridgeport **accommodation** ranges from a beautifully furnished B&B, *The Cain House*, 340 Main St (☎1-800/433-CAIN or 760/932-7040; ⑤), through decent motels such as the *Silver Maple Inn*, 310 Main St (☎1-800/688-3351 or 760/932-7383; ④) to the decidedly decrepit *Victoria House* across the street (☎760/932-7020; ②), a building which, like several in Bridgeport, is said to have been transported here from Bodie. All are closed October through April; the *Best Western Ruby Inn*, 333 Main St (☎760/932-7241; ④), is one of the only lodgings that stays open year round. For **eating**, *Hays Street Café*, on the southern approach to town, does the best breakfasts and lunches.

From Bridgeport, US-395 continues north into Nevada, through the capital Carson City and the gambling city of Reno, both described fully in Chapter Eight.

travel details

Buses

Los Angeles to: Bishop (1 daily; 7hr 55min); Bridgeport (1 daily; 10hr 15min); Lee Vining (1 daily; 9hr 20min); Lone Pine (1 daily; 6hr 45min); Mammoth Lakes (1 daily; 8hr 50min); Reno (1 daily; 13hr 10min). Note that this one bus leaves LA in the late afternoon and arrives at most of these destinations in the middle of the night.

Reno to: Bishop (1 daily; 6hr); Bridgeport (1 daily; 2hr 55min); Lee Vining (1 daily; 3hr 30min); Lone Pine (1 daily; 7hr 15min); Los Angeles (1 daily; 13hr 25min); Mammoth Lakes (1 daily; 4hr 15min). This bus leaves Reno in the morning and arrives at most of these destinations at midday.

CHAPTER FIVE

THE CENTRAL VALLEY AND THE WESTERN HIGH SIERRA

The vast **interior** of California – stretching three hundred miles from the edges of the Mojave Desert in the south right up to the Gold Country and northern California – comprises the wide floor of the agricultural Central Valley (also known as the San Joaquin Valley) flanked on the east by the massive Sierra Nevada mountains. It's a region of unparalleled beauty, yet the ninety percent of Californians who live on the coast are barely aware of the area, encountering it only while driving between LA and San Francisco on the admittedly tedious I-5, and consider it the height of hicksville.

The **Central Valley** is radically different to anywhere else in the state. During the 1940s, this arid land was made super-fertile by a massive program of aqueduct building, using water flowing from the mountains to irrigate the area. The valley, as flat as a pancake, now almost totally comprises farmland, periodically enlivened by scattered cities that offer a taste of ordinary Californian life away from the glitz of LA and San Francisco. More than anywhere else in the state, the abundance of low-paying agricultural jobs has encouraged decades of immigration from south of the border, and there are now towns in the Central Valley where Spanish is the first language and *taquerias* outnumber burger joints ten to one. Fertile land and cheap labor has brought relative wealth to large numbers of Central Valley residents, who have responded by becoming increasingly mobile. This, and town planning which dictates that everyone must drive everywhere, has created a dense photochemical haze – trapped by mountains on both flanks – which is now so thick that the pristine peaks once visible throughout the year are now seldom seen.

The only reason most coastal Californians head through the Central Valley is to reach the **National Parks** that cover the foothills and upper reaches of the Sierra

ACCOMMODATION PRICE CODES

All accommodation prices in this book have been coded using the symbols below; prices are for the least expensive **double rooms** in each establishment. For a full explanation see p.36 in Basics. Individual rates rather than price codes are given for **hostels** and whole **apartments**.

① up to $30	④ $60–80	⑦ $130–175
② $30–45	⑤ $80–100	⑧ $175–250
③ $45–60	⑥ $100–130	⑨ $250+

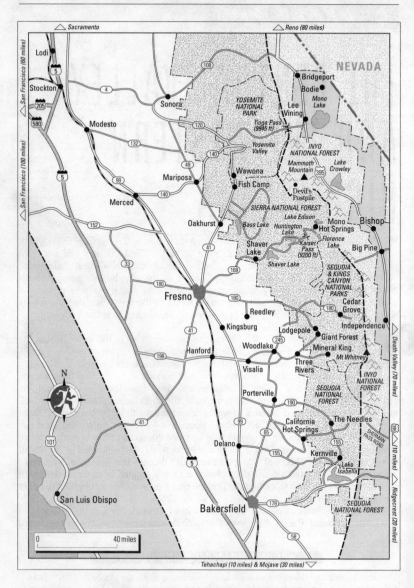

Nevada Mountains. From the valley, a gentle ascent through rolling, grassy foothills takes you into dense forests of huge pine and fir trees, interspersed with tranquil lakes and cut by deep rocky canyons. The most impressive sections are protected within three National Parks. **Sequoia** is home to the last few stands of huge prehistoric trees, giant sequoias (see Wildlife, p.599) which form the centerpiece of a rich natural landscape. **Kings Canyon** shares a common border with Sequoia – together they make up one huge park – and presents a similar, though even wilder, array of Sierra wonders, not least of them the miles of backcountry hiking trails. **Yosemite**, with its towering walls of silvery granite artfully sculpted by Ice Age glaciers, is the most famous of the parks and one of the absolute must-sees in California. Only a few narrow, twisting roads penetrate the hundred miles of wilderness in between the parks, but the entire region is crisscrossed by hiking trails leading up into the pristine alpine backcountry of the western **High Sierra**, which contains the glistening summits of some of the highest mountains in the country.

Getting around

Drivers who aren't particularly interested in exploring the wilds can simply barrel through on I-5, an arrow-straight interstate through the western edge of the Central Valley that's the quickest route between LA and San Francisco. Four daily **trains** and frequent Greyhound **buses** run through the Valley, stopping at the larger cities and towns along Hwy-99 – two of which, Merced and Fresno, have bus connections to Yosemite. Otherwise, getting to the mountains is all but impossible without a car, though with a bit of advance planning, you might be able to join one of the many camping trips organized by the Sierra Club, the California-based environmentalist group (see p.46).

THE CENTRAL VALLEY

The **Central Valley** grows more fruit and vegetables than any other agricultural region of its size – a fact that touches the lives, in one way or another, of its every inhabitant. The area is much more conservative and midwestern in feel than the rest of California, but even if the nightlife begins and ends with the local ice-cream parlour, after the big cities of the coast it can all be refreshingly small-scale and enjoyable. Admittedly, nowhere has the energy to detain you long and, between the settlements, the drab hundred-mile vistas of almond groves and vineyards can be sheer torture, as can the weather – summers in the Central Valley are frequently scorching.

Bakersfield, the first town you come to across the rocky peaks north of Los Angeles, is hardly the valley's most prepossessing destination, but in recent years its **country music** scene has burgeoned into the best in the state, and there can be few better places on this side of the Atlantic to sample Basque cuisine. It also offers a museum recording the beginnings of the local population, and the chance to mess about on the Kern River. Greater rewards lie further on: **Visalia** is a likeable community, near which are two well-restored turn-of-the-century towns, **Hanford** and **Reedley**, plus the bizarre would-be Swedish village of **Kingsburg**.

In many ways the region's linchpin, **Fresno** is the closest thing to a bustling urban center the Valley has – and it's just about impossible to avoid. Though thriving economically, it's frequently voted the least desirable place to live in the US, and on arrival it's easy to see why . Its redeeming features, such as they are, take a bit of time to discover, though you shouldn't pass up the opportunity to visit the bizarre labyrinth of Forrestiere Underground Gardens.

Beyond Fresno, in the northern reaches of the Valley, lie sedate **Merced** and slightly more boisterous **Modesto**, the inspiration for George Lucas' movie *American Graffiti*. At the top end of the Valley **Stockton** is scenically improved by the delta that connects the city to the sea, but is otherwise a place of few pleasures, though you may have to pass through on your way from San Francisco to the Gold Country or the National Parks.

Bakersfield and around

An unappealing vision behind a forest of oil derricks, **BAKERSFIELD**'s flat and featureless look does nothing to suggest that this is one of the nation's liveliest country music communities, with a batch of venues where locally- and nationally-rated musicians will blow your socks off. Before you hit some of the venues listed (see box below), be sure to taste Basque cuisine – at its best in one of the specialist restaurants run by descendants of sheep-herders who migrated to the San Joaquin Valley in the early twentieth century.

Beyond these two draws, however, there's little reason to be here: the town owes its existence to the fertile soil around the Kern River – once the longest river in the state but now dammed to form Lake Isabella (see p.288) – and to the discovery of local oil and gas deposits. The **Kern County Museum & Pioneer Village**, a couple of miles

---

COUNTRY MUSIC IN BAKERSFIELD

The main reason to dally for more than a few hours in Bakersfield is to hear **country music** – on any weekend the town's numerous honky-tonks reverberate to the sounds of the best country musicians in the US, many of them local residents.

The **roots** of Bakersfield's country music scene are with the midwestern farmers who arrived in the Central Valley during the Depression, bringing their hillbilly instruments and campfire songs with them. This rustic entertainment quickly broadened into more contemporary styles, developed in the bars and clubs that began to appear in the town, where future legends such as Merle Haggard and Buck Owens (who now owns the local country radio station, KUZZ 107.9 FM) cut their teeth. A failed attempt to turn Bakersfield into "Nashville West" during the 1960s, and bring the major country music record labels here from their traditional base, has left the town eager to promote the distinctive "Bakersfield Sound": a far less slick and commercial affair than its Tennessee counterpart. You can gain an inkling of the Bakersfield Sound from the 1988 hit *Streets of Bakersfield*, a duet by Buck Owens and Dwight Yoakam, but you really need to get out and listen to some live music.

Venues

To find out **what's on**, read the Friday edition of the *Bakersfield Californian*, check the flyers at the tourist offices mentioned below, or phone one of the venues we've listed. Fridays and Saturdays are the liveliest nights, although there's often something to enjoy during the week, even if it's only the free **country dancing lessons** offered at many of the town's bars. There's never a cover charge for someone spinning platters, and seldom one for live sets – usually entailing one band playing for four or five hours from around 8pm and taking a fifteen-minute break every hour – though big names might demand $3–5 a head. Stetson hats and flouncy skirts are the sartorial order of the day, and audiences span generations.

Most **venues** are hotel lounges or restaurant backrooms, though there are a couple which don't fit the mold: one not to be missed is *Trouts*, 805 N Chester Ave (☎805/399-6700), a country music bar a couple of miles north of downtown that's been in business for over forty years. Closer to town, *Buck Owens Crystal Palace*, 2800 Pierce Rd (☎805/328-7560; $5), represents the latest addition to the country music master's ever-expanding empire, combining a burgers-and-grills restaurant, a museum of Buck Owens memorabilia (5pm onwards; free to customers) and a club with local bands midweek and Buck himself doing a turn on Friday and Saturday nights. The other hotspot to add to your itinerary is the younger and more clubby *Rockin' Rodeo*, 3745 Rosedale Hwy (☎805/323-6617) with a New Country/Rock DJ every night and a Texas-style oval dancefloor.

north of downtown at 3801 Chester Ave (Mon–Fri 8am–5pm, Sat 10am–5pm, Sun noon–5pm; $5), documents Bakersfield's development with an impressive collection of over fifty (mostly) restored buildings, many of them dating from the late-nineteenth or early twentieth century. Presumably unintentionally, the cumulative effect is to emphasize how comparatively boring the place is today. There is some hope, though, and in the last couple of years the moribund downtown area – which resembles an Edward Hopper painting – has seen something of a renaissance, with half a dozen new bars opening up.

Practicalities

Bakersfield is an important public transportation hub, and the downtown area – roughly four blocks each way from the junction of 19th and J streets – is home to both the southern terminus of Amtrak's San Joaquin route from San Francisco (connections to LA via Thruway bus) and the bus station. Traveling by Greyhound (1820 18th St) you may need to change routes here – although overnight stops are rarely necessary. The best source of information is the **Kern County Board of Trade**, 2101 Oak St (Mon–Fri 8am–5pm; ☎1-800/500-KERN or 805/861-2367, fax 861-2017), though the **Chamber of Commerce**, 1033 Truxtun St (Mon 9am–5pm Tues–Fri 8am–5pm; ☎805/327-4421, fax 327-8751), is handier for downtown. Both provide essential free maps of town.

Bakersfield is full of cheap **motels**, grouped together in two main clusters: at the junction of Pierce and 24th streets, and a couple of miles north around the Olive Drive exit off Hwy-99. At the former, the pool-equipped *EZ-8*, 2604 Pierce Rd (☎1-800/326-6835 or 805/322-1901, fax 323-9013; ②) marginally edges out the *Roadrunner Motel*, 2760 Pierce Rd (☎ & fax 805/323-3727; ②), though the latter is cheaper if you are traveling alone. Around Olive Avenue the *Economy Motel*, 6100 Knudsen Drive (☎805/392-1800, fax 392-1612; ②), and *Motel 6*, 5241 Olive Tree Crescent (☎805/392-9700, fax 392-0223; ②), both have pools and are quite adequate. The best bets in the center are *Downtowner Inn*, 1301 Chester Ave (☎1-800/251-3057 or 805/327-7122, fax 327-8350; ②), and the *Padre Hotel*, 1813 H St (☎805/322-1419; ①), a relic of yesteryear that's just hanging on with engagingly dingy yet comfortable rooms, many with original fittings and ancient plumbing in the en-suite bathrooms.

Don't pass Bakersfield without **eating** Basque food. The most authentic experience is at the turn-of-the-century *Noriega Hotel*, 525 Summer St, just east of downtown (☎805/322-8419), where louvered shutters and ceiling fans cool diners seated at long tables and served an all-you-can-eat set menu of soup, salad, beans, pasta, a meat dish, cheese to finish and jug wine. There are three sittings ($7 breakfast from 7am to 9am, $8 lunch at noon sharp and $15 dinner at 7pm); reservations are recommended for dinner. *Pyrenees*, 601 Sumner St (☎805/323-0053) and *Wool Growers*, 620 E 19th St (☎805/327-9584) both have a similar set-up.

If Basque doesn't appeal, the *24th Street Café*, 1415 24th St, does top-rate breakfasts; *Joseph's*, hidden back off the road at 3013 F St, serves huge, very impressive calzone and jalapeño beef piccata to dedicated regulars, while closer to downtown, *The Garden Spot*, 3320 Truxton Ave makes healthy eating a pleasure with a great salad bar and outdoor seating. To stay in tune with Bakersfield's country-music persona, eat at *Zingo's*, 2625 Pierce Rd, a truck stop whose frilly-aproned waitresses deliver plates of diner staples.

Nightlife now extends beyond slide-guitar and torch songs with a number of places downtown offering local rock bands several nights a week, usually with no cover charge. Stroll 19th Street and see what turns up, but you could kick off at the cocktail bar in the *Hotel Padre* and move across the road to *Guthrie's Alley Cat*, 1525 Wall St, tucked down an alley parallel to 18th and 19th streets.

Lake Isabella and the Kern River

After a night spent in Bakersfield's smoky honky-tonks, you might like to clear your head by driving forty-five miles east to the mile-wide **Lake Isabella**, typically alive with windsurfers, jet skiers and anglers. Mountain-biking and rock-climbing are also popular activities here, and the place is heaving in the summer. Information on activities and rental outlets are available from the lakeside **visitor center** (mid-May to Oct daily 8am–5pm; Nov to mid-May Mon–Fri 8am–4.30pm; ☎760/379-5646, fax 379-8597) half a mile north of Hwy-178 along Hwy-155. Developed though barely shaded **campgrounds** ring the dry, scrubby lakeside, almost all costing $14 a pitch: there are always first-come-first-served sites or you can reserve at least a week in advance (☎1-800/280-2267).

Lake Isabella is fed by the **Kern River** which churns down from the slopes of Mount Whitney and spills into the lake at the appealing community of **KERNVILLE** on its northern shore, the sort of town where anyone without aquatic paraphernalia looks out of place. Most people come to ride the Kern which ranks as one of the steepest rivers in the United States, dropping over 12,000ft along 150 miles, and producing some of the world's most exhilarating whitewater opportunities. The tougher stuff is generally left to the experts, but during the season, which runs from May until mid-August or longer if there has been a heavy winter, commercial rafting operators vie for custom (see box).

Only campers will find cheap **accommodation** in Kernville. Central motels start at around $60 with *The Kernville Inn*, 11042 Kernville Rd (☎760/376-2206; ③), right in the center and with a pool, and range up through the *Kern River Inn B&B*, 119 Kern River Drive (☎1-800/986-4382; ④) to the luxurious *Whispering Pines Lodge*, 13745 Sierra Way (☎760/376-3733, fax 376-3735; ⑥), a mile north of town, with a nice pool and balconies overlooking the river. The cheapest rooms lie over two miles north at *Falling Waters*, 15729 Sierra Way (☎1-888/376-2242 or 760/376 2242; ②), a rambling array of motel-style rooms most with self-catering facilities and barbecue areas out front. There are several **restaurants** around town including the reliable *That's Italian* by the central park. If for some reason you can't find all this yourself, consult the central **Chamber of Commerce**, 11447 Kernville Rd (☎1-800/350-7393 or 760/376-2629, fax 376-4371), and for information on the wooded country to the north call in at the **Sequoia Forest Ranger Station**, 105 Whitney Rd (mid-May to Oct daily 8am–5pm, Nov to mid-May Mon–Fri 8am–4.30pm; ☎760/376-3781, fax 376-3795), tucked away behind the park.

RIDING THE KERN – RAFTING AND KAYAKING FROM KERNVILLE

Three main sections of the Kern River are regularly rafted: the **Lower Kern**, downstream of Lake Isabella and classed III–IV (fairly rugged); the **Upper Kern**, immediately upstream of Kernville and classed II–IV; and **The Forks**, fifteen miles upstream of Kernville, which is Class V (wild). By far the most popular section is the Upper Kern, the site for the **Lickety-Split** rafting trip – one for the first-timer, with some long, rough rapids.

A one-hour Lickety-Split excursion to the Upper Kern (including the bus ride to the put-in) costs $18. Half-day runs cost around $50–60 ($60–70 at weekends), day-trips run close to the $100 mark ($120 at weekends), and three-day backcountry trips on The Forks can range up to $600. Wetsuits (essential early in the season and for the longer trips) are extra. Within this basic framework there are any number of permutations involving kayaking, eskimo-rolling, river rescue and even rock-climbing on the nearby Kernville Slab. Generally there is little need to reserve ahead – the Lickety-Split is run throughout the day – except for the longer expeditions.

Of the many competitive operators in Kernville, two of the biggest are Sierra South, 11300 Kernville Rd (☎1-800/457-2082 or 760/376-3745), and Chuck Richards' Whitewater, right next door at no. 11200 (☎1-800/624-5950 or 760/379-4444). If you have the equipment for private rafting or kayaking expeditions, you'll still need a free **permit** from any of the area's Forest Service offices.

The Sequoia National Forest

Wedged between Lake Isabella and its National Park namesake, the **Sequoia National Forest** is a vast canopy of pine trees punctuated by massive, glacier-polished domes and gleaming granite spires. Much of it is untouched wilderness that's barely less stunning than the National Parks to the north, and it boasts just as many sequoias. But it is less rigidly controlled and far less visited, making it perfect if you're really seeking solitude; hiking trails run everywhere. Backcountry camping only requires a free permit for your stove or fire, available from the Sequoia Forest Ranger Stations which are dotted around the perimeter of the forest and which also have details of the scores of drive-in campgrounds which stud the forest – some free, others up to $12 a pitch.

There's **no public transportation** through here; the roads are in good shape, though subject to **snow-closure** in winter. The best access is along Sierra Way from Lake Isabella, which passes through Kernville and follows the Upper Kern River past numerous $14 campgrounds to Johnsondale Bridge, fifteen miles north of Kernville, where the Sherman Pass Road cuts east to Hwy-395 and the Owens Valley. From the Johnsondale Bridge, Sierra Way turns west and starts climbing seven miles to a junction signed straight ahead to **California Hot Springs**, 42177 Hot Springs Drive (☎805/548-6582), where $7 buys you a long soak. The popular *Leavis Flat* campground ($10 pitch) is just across the road.

North from the road junction you're on the twisting and narrow **Western Divide Highway** (Hwy-190) which, after a couple of miles, passes the **Trail of a Hundred Giants**, a shaded interpretive trail around the second most southerly stand of giant trees, easily covered in thirty minutes. Among more sequoias across the road is the *Redwood Meadow* campground ($10 a pitch).

Continuing north, you catch glimpses of magnificent sierra vistas as the road climbs above the 7000-foot mark, but for the best views it is worth pressing on five miles to the 7200-foot exfoliated scalp of **Dome Rock**, just half a mile off the highway, or **The Needles**, a further three miles on. This series of tall pinnacles – the Magician, the Wizard, the Warlock and more – present some of America's fiercest and most demanding crack climbs, but can be visited on the moderate, undulating hiking-and-biking **Needles Lookout Trail** (5-mile round trip; 2hrs), which starts three miles off the highway. The final switchback leads to a fire lookout station (May–Oct Wed–Sun 9am–6pm), precariously perched on a rock pinnacle with supreme views over the Kern Valley and across to Mount Whitney. Nearby **accommodation** extends to the *Quaking Aspen* campground (mid-May to mid-Nov; $12) half a mile to the north of the Needles, the rustic *Mountain Top B&B* half a mile to the south (☎209/542-2639, fax 542-1318; ④), and the adjacent *Ponderosa Lodge* (☎209/542-2579; ④) with pleasant motel rooms, a restaurant, bar, grocery store and expensive gas.

The **Western Divide Highway** then executes endless twists and turns forty miles down to the valley town of Porterville.

Visalia and Tulare County

As you leave Bakersfield heading north on Hwy-99, the oil wells fade into full-blown agricultural territory. You can turn east onto Hwy-190 at Tipton for the Sequoia National Forest (see above). Otherwise, nowhere merits a stop until you reach **Tulare County**, some seventy miles north of Bakersfield, where several small communities repay quick visits and make viable bases for day-trips into the Sequoia and King's Canyon National Parks.

Visalia

The first and largest of the towns north of Bakersfield is **VISALIA**, just east of Hwy-99 on Hwy-198. Due to a large oak forest that offered both shade and timber for home-building, Visalia was the first place in the Central Valley to be settled. Although the forest is gone, large numbers of oaks and eucalyptus are still planted around the city, and local people put an extraordinary amount of care into the upkeep of parks and gardens. In short, it's a pretty place, with a calm and restful air – if you're seeking anything more active you'll be disappointed.

Visalia is best seen on foot: self-guided walking tours of its older parts can be obtained free from the **Chamber of Commerce** (see below), or you could visit the **Tulare County Museum**, Mooney Grove Park, about two miles from the city center at the end of South Mooney Boulevard. The museum (Mon & Thurs–Sat 10am–4pm; $2) has a hotchpotch of local historical curios, and in the park you'll find the *End of the Trail* statue, originally made for the 1915 Panama-Pacific Exhibition in San Francisco, which portrays the defeat of the Indians at the hands of advancing white settlers. Intentionally gloomy, the statue became well known throughout the West, and still inspires a host of copies and numerous snap-happy tourists.

Practicalities

Greyhound buses and Orange Belt Stages from Hanford, arrive at the **bus station** at 1927 E Mineral King Ave, inconveniently distant from either downtown, or the **Chamber of Commerce**, 720 W Mineral King Ave (Mon–Fri 8.30am–5pm; ☎209/734-5876, fax 734-7478).

As the closest town to the southern entrance of the Sequoia National Park – less than an hour's drive away along Hwy-198 – Visalia makes a comfortable base for exploring this raw wilderness. The most sumptuous **accommodation** is at the pool- and spa-equipped *Ben Maddox House B&B*, 601 N Encina St (☎1-800/401-9800 or 209/739-0721, fax 625-0420; ⑤), a large redwood house built in 1876 for Ben Maddox, the man who brought hydro-electricity to the Central Valley. South Mooney Boulevard has the densest concentration of **motels**: *Mooney Motel* at no. 2120 (☎209/733-2666; ②) is very reasonable with a pool, while *Econolodge* at no. 1400 (☎209/732-6641; ②) is a good standby for a few bucks more.

Visalia also has some of the best places to **eat** for miles around: try the under-$5 Chinese lunch buffet at *Mooney*, 2332 S Mooney Blvd (☎209/734-1688), *Merle's* Fifties-style drive-in diner down the street at no. 604, or the inexpensive American-style breakfasts and lunches at *Bea's Kafé*, 215 N Giddings Ave (☎209/732-9036). *Little Italy*, 303 W Main St, dishes up some excellent wood-fired pizzas and a good line in veal and chicken main courses for around $12, while upscale diners are catered for at the *Vintage Press*, 216 N Willis St (☎209/733-3033), where you could have wild mushrooms sautéed in cognac followed by red snapper with toasted almonds and capers, dessert and coffee for around $40 a head – much more if you explore the vast and wonderful wine list.

Hanford

HANFORD, twenty miles west of Visalia on Hwy-198, was named after James Hanford, a paymaster on the Southern Pacific Railroad who became popular with his employees when he took to paying them in gold. The town formed part of a spur on the railroad and became a major stopover on the route between Los Angeles and San Francisco, which it remains.

The Town

The Visitor Agency (see opposite) can give you a map of the center of town detailing the now spotless and spruced-up buildings around Courthouse Square which were the core of local life at the turn of the century. The honey-colored **Courthouse** (Mon–Sat 10am–6pm, Sun 10am–5pm; free) retains many of its Neoclassical features – not least a magnificent staircase – and has, more recently, been occupied by shops and galleries. As you'd expect, the old Hanford **jail**, rather pretentiously modelled on the Paris Bastille, is only a ball-and-chain's throw away. It was used until 1968 and is now restored as a restaurant (*The Bastille*, see below), although you can wander through to see the old cells – now and again used for secluded dining.

Much less ostentatiously, rows of two-story porched dwellings, four blocks east of the square, mark the district that was home to most of the eight hundred or so Chinese families who came to Hanford to work on the railroad. At the center of the community was the **Taoist Temple** on China Alley (groups of 6–20 only and by appointment, more details from the Visitor Agency; $2.50 per person). Built in 1893, the temple served a social as well as a spiritual function, providing free lodging to work-seeking Chinese travelers, and was used as a Chinese school during the early 1920s. Everything inside is original, from the teak burl figurines to the marble chairs, and it's a shame that entry is so restricted. You can, however, take a look at another institution of Hanford's Chinese community: the **Imperial Dynasty Restaurant**, two doors along from the temple, still run by the family who opened it fifty years ago. The interior is simple and modest, but the fame of the cooking – oddly French, not Chinese – has spread far and wide and prices have risen as a result.

Mildly absorbing oddments from Hanford's past are gathered at the **Carnegie Museum**, 109 E Eighth St (Tues–Fri noon–3pm, Sat noon–4pm; $1), filling part of the interior of the town's elegant 1905 library – one of many small-town libraries financed by the altruistic millionaire industrialist Andrew Carnegie. The only other item of possible interest is the **Kings Art Center**, 605 N Douty St (Tues–Sun noon–3pm; free), with its temporary displays of contemporary painting, sculpture and photography.

Practicalities

Orange Belt Stages (☎1-800/266-7433) provide twice-daily **bus** links to Visalia and the Greyhound station at Goshen Junction (for connections to Los Angeles and San Francisco), and also run a service across to San Luis Obispo on the coast. The town's **Visitor Agency** (Mon–Fri 9am–5pm; ☎1-800/722-1114 or 209/582-5024) is conveniently located inside the handsomely restored Amtrak depot at 200 Santa Fe Ave. If you decide to **stay** in Hanford your choice is limited to the *Irwin St Inn*, 522 N Irwin St (☎209/583-8000; ④) and a couple of motels, the cheapest and most central being the *Downtown Motel*, 101 N Redington (☎209/582-9036; ②). For **eating**, the most atmospheric place is *The Bastille*, 113 Court St, which does fine deep dish pizzas, mountainous lean burgers and sandwiches until late, followed by *Wired Angels*, 700 N Irwin St, a good café (with Internet access) in a Victorian house a couple of blocks north of the center. During the day, don't miss the rich creaminess of the made-on-the-premises ice cream at *Superior Dairy*, 325 N Douty St just across from *The Bastille*.

Kingsburg and Reedley

Over half the inhabitants of **KINGSBURG**, twenty miles north of Visalia on Hwy-99, are of Swedish descent, but it's only in the last thirty years that they've sought to exploit their roots, converting the town's buildings to Swedish-style architecture and plastering their windows and walls with tributes to the Swedish royal family and the Dana Horse (an object traditionally carved by woodcutters from the Dalarna district of Sweden). Save for such peculiarities, it hardly warrants a call, except perhaps on the third Saturday in May when it stages – predictably – a Swedish festival. Compared to Kingsburg, **REEDLEY**, five miles northeast, is a metropolis, though beyond its main thoroughfare – G Street – it's just as quiet, and the only attraction is the **Mennonite**

Quilting Center, 1012 G St (Mon–Fri 9.30am–4.30pm, Sat 10am–2pm; free), essentially a shop selling Amish quilts ($500–900) from Pennsylvania. Quilters can be seen working away on local versions until 3pm on Mondays.

Fresno

Almost classic in its ugliness, **FRESNO** is very much the hub of business in the Central Valley. Caught between being a farming town and a fully blown commercial city, Fresno seems to have missed out on the restoration programs that have improved similar communities elsewhere in California, while its solution to traffic congestion has been to insert a freeway plumb through its center. It's probably significant too, that the indoor shopping mall was first seen here. For all that, Fresno does have its good points (not least a daily bus service to Yosemite), the main draw being the fascinating Forestiere Underground Gardens which lie outwith the center.

The Town and around

The one place which turns Fresno into a destination in its own right is **Forestiere Underground Gardens**, 5021 W Shaw Ave (tours on the hour: June to early Sept Wed–Sun 10am–4pm; early Sept to Nov Sat & Sun noon–3pm; $5), seven miles northwest of the center, a block east of the Shaw Ave exit off Hwy-99. A subterranean labyrinth of over fifty rooms, the gardens were constructed by Sicilian emigré and former Boston and New York subway tunneler Baldasare Forestiere, who came to Fresno in 1905. In a fanatical attempt to stay cool and protect his crops, Forestiere put his digging know-how to work, building underground living quarters and skylit orchards with just a shovel and wheelbarrow. He gradually improved techniques for maximizing his yield but wasn't above playful twists like a glass-bottomed underground aquarium and a subterranean bathtub fed by water heated in the midday sun. He died in 1946, his forty years of work producing a vast earth honeycomb, part of which was destroyed by the construction of Hwy-99 next door, while another section awaits restoration. Wandering around the remainder of what he achieved is a fascinating way to pass an hour out of the heat of the day, enlivened by the tour guide's homespun anecdotes.

With more time to spare, head seven miles west from downtown along Kearney Boulevard, a long, straight and exotically planted thoroughfare that was once the private driveway through the huge Kearney Park ($3 per car; free with Mansion entry) to the **Kearney Mansion** (Fri–Sun tours 1pm 2pm & 3pm; $4). It was built for M. Theo Kearney, an English-born turn-of-the-century agricultural pioneer and raisin mogul, who maintained it in the opulent French Renaissance style to which he seemed addicted. He had even grander plans to grace Fresno with a French chateau, the mind-boggling designs for which are displayed here. Regarded locally as something of a mystery man, Kearney apparently led a pacey social life on both sides of the Atlantic, which may explain why he died following a heart attack during an ocean crossing.

Once you've seen these attractions, you've really seen the best of the town. **Downtown Fresno** is the business heart, with not much to view except the **Metropolitan Museum**, 1555 Van Ness Ave (daily 11am–5pm; $4), which covers a bit of (almost) everything, mainly with temporary exhibitions. The best features are the re-creations of earthquakes, tornadoes and floods. The **Fresno Art Museum**, 2233 N First St at Clinton, in Radio Park (Tues–Fri 10am–5pm, Sat & Sun noon–5pm; $2, Tues free), has a worthy but slightly desperate selection of paintings, sculpture and lithographs; there's more compelling stuff in the **Meux Home Museum** (guided tours Feb–Dec Fri–Sun noon–3.30pm; $3) at the corner of Tulare and R streets, just behind the Amtrak station. Built for what in the late nineteenth century was the staggering sum of $12,000, this was the home of a doctor who arrived from the Deep South, bringing with him the novelty of a two-story house and a plethora of trendy Victorian features. What isn't original is a convincing reconstruction, and the turrets, arches, and octagonal master bedroom help make the place stylish and absorbing – quite out of synch with the Fresno that has sprawled up around it.

In a town with a tradition of almond-growing and cattle-rustling, Fresno's **Tower District**, three miles north of downtown at the junction of Wishon and Olive avenues, comes as a pleasant surprise. Proximity to the City College campus made the area something of a hippy hangout during the Sixties; today it has a well-scrubbed liberal feel, plus several blocks of antique stores and bookstores, ethnic restaurants and coffee bars to fill a few hours of idle browsing.

Over the rail tracks at the end of Olive Avenue on the Tower District's western edge, the tree-filled **Roeding Park** (Feb–Oct $1 per car, Nov–Jan free) boasts the **Chaffee Zoological Gardens** (daily 9am–5pm; $4.50), a couple of amusement parks and a lake. This is where Fresnoites come to convince themselves that the city is a nice place to live, and strolling here on a day that's not totally baking, you could almost believe them.

Practicalities

You can check details on everything in and around the city (and transportation to and from the National Parks) at the **CVB**, 808 M St (Mon–Fri 8am–5pm; ☎1-800/788-0836 or 209/233-0836, fax 445-0122). The **bus** and **train** terminals are both downtown: Greyhound at 1033 H St and Amtrak at Tulare and Q. **Traveling onwards**, Fresno has in Hwy-41 a direct road link to Yosemite National Park (see p.312); and Hwy-180 goes to Kings Canyon National Park (see p.305). To get to **Yosemite** by bus, catch the VIA Yosemite Connection service ($20 each way, $38 round-trip; 4hr; ☎1-800/369-7275 or

209/384-1315) from the Fresno Air Terminal; tickets include park entry. To get to the air terminal, use the Fresno Area Express (☎209/498-1122) route #26, which runs hourly from downtown.

For those who want to enjoy the Tower District's nightlife, scores of inexpensive **motels**, all with pools, are clustered together near the junction of Olive Avenue (the district's main drag) and Hwy-99. Some charge rock-bottom rates for rooms that are well below par, so the best deals here are the *Ramada*, 1804 W Olive Ave (☎209/442-1082; ③), and *Economy Inns*, 2570 S East St (☎209/486-1188; ②). You might save a few dollars, however, by using *Thrifty Lodge* at 777 N Parkway Drive (☎209/237-2175; ②), or *Motel 6*, along the road at no. 933 (☎209/233-3913; ②).

To pick up fresh, good **food**, head for the **outdoor produce market**, at Merced and N (Tues, Thurs & Sat 7am–3pm). Otherwise, the Tower District, centered on the Tower Theater at the junction of Olive and Wishon avenues, is very much the place to eat and drink. You'll get good-value lunches and dinners, and excellent home-brewed beers, at the *Butterfield Brewing Company Bar & Grill*, 777 E Olive Ave (☎209/264-5521); the relaxed *Java Café*, 805 E Olive Ave, presents soups, salads and mugs of very fine coffee with beans roasted on the premises, and the *Daily Planet*, 1211 N Wishon Ave (☎209/266-4259), serves a fixed-price four-course dinner (usually under $20) in Art Deco surroundings. For some very fine traditional Mexican food – chicken mole, *ceviche* and so on – cross the road to *Mexiphilia*, 1153 N Fulton Ave. Step next door to *Jax House*, 1145 N Fulton Ave (Wed–Sun; $2–10; ☎209/268-4289), for regular DJs and live bands, when they can coax anyone worthwhile to these parts. For less fraught entertainment try *Java Café* which puts on comedy, jazz, folk and blues from Thursday to Saturday evenings.

The free monthly *Talk of the Tower District* lists upcoming events, gigs and the Tuesday night outdoor movies shown on the back wall of the Tower Theater (June–Aug only).

Continuing north: Merced and Modesto

The best thing about sluggish **MERCED**, fifty miles north of Fresno, is its courthouse, a gem of a building in the main square that's maintained as the **County Courthouse Museum** (Wed–Sun 1–4pm; free). The striking Italian Renaissance-style structure, with columns, elaborately sculptured window frames and a cupola topped by a statue of the Goddess of Justice (minus her customary blindfold), was raised in 1875, dominating the town then as it does now. Impressively restored in period style, the courtroom retained a legal function until 1951, while the equally sumptuous offices were vacated in the 1970s, leaving the place to serve as storage space for local memorabilia – the most exotic item being a Taoist shrine, found by chance in the back room of a Chinese restaurant.

Six miles out of Merced, close to the dormitory community of **ATWATER**, the **Castle Air Museum** (daily 9am–5pm; $5), displays forty-odd military aircraft – mostly bulky bombers with a few fighters thrown in, including the world's fastest plane, the SR-71 – and a slightly less militaristic collection of aviation paraphernalia.

Practicalities

Neither of the sights are much of a reason to visit, though the convenient **bus links** to Yosemite are Greyhound buses from Bakersfield, Sacramento and San Francisco stop at the station on W 16th St at N St where you'll find the **Chamber of Commerce**, 690 W 16th St (Mon–Fri 8.30am–5pm; ☎1-800/446-5353 or 209/384-3333, fax 384-8472). The Amtrak station is at 24th and K streets, about ten blocks away on the opposite side of the town center. Both stations are stops for the Yosemite VIA Connection ($38 round-trip, $20 one-way; 2hr 30min; ☎1-800/369-7275 or 209/384-1315) which makes the trip to Yosemite Village, via Mariposa, three times daily (currently 6.45am, 10.15am & 3.15pm) and includes the park entry fee.

The Mariposa exit from Hwy-99 leaves you right by two good **places to stay**: the *Holiday Inn Express*, 730 Motel Drive (☎1-800/337-0333 or 209/283-0333; ④), and the bargain *Happy Inn*, 740 Motel Drive (☎209/722-6291; ②), both with pool and continental breakfast. A third option is the reservations-only *HI–Merced Home Hostel* (☎209/725-0407; ①), which organizes bargain car rental (around $20 a day) through a local agency.

Modesto

Forty miles further along Hwy-99, **MODESTO**, the childhood home of movie director George Lucas, became the inspiration (though not the location) for his movie *American Graffiti*, the classic portrayal of growing up in small-town America during the late 1950s. The movie contains a number of references to local people, particularly the teachers who rubbed Lucas up the wrong way in his formative years. Sadly, local ordinances (enacted in 1992 after several years of bad behaviour) have put an end to both the fine art of **cruising**, and the annual festival which saw dozens of classic cars from all over the state and beyond dusted off and cruised through the city. Pretty much the only reminders of those heady days now are the *A&W Root Beer Drive-In*, 1404 G St, which has roller-skating waitresses in celebration of the celluloid connection, and a rather token duck-tail, bobby-sox and '57 Chevy statue at the corner of J St and McHenry Avenue.

It may seem hard to believe, but as a fairly typical Valley town, Modesto does have a history stretching back beyond the Fifties. Its (comparatively) distant past is encapsulated by the shabbily grand **Modesto Arch** – erected in 1912 over Ninth and I to attract attention to the city's expanding economy – and, more imposingly, the Victorian **McHenry Mansion** at 906 15th St (Tues–Thurs & Sun 1–4pm; free), which is jam-packed with the fixtures, fittings and personal features of a family whose fate was linked with Modesto's for years. Robert McHenry was a successful wheat-rancher who did much to bring about a general uplift in the agricultural well-being of the area. Surprisingly, his luxurious dwelling was still being rented out as apartments, at quite low rates, as recently as the early 1970s.

A few minutes' walk from the mansion, the **McHenry Museum**, 1402 I St (Tues–Sun noon–4pm; free), originally financed by the McHenry family, sports mock-ups of a doctor's office, blacksmith's shop, dentist's surgery and gathering of cattle brands, revealing something of the past, but lacking the period atmosphere of the mansion. Adjoining the museum, the **Central California Art League Gallery** (Mon–Sat 10am–4pm; free) displays a show of regional painting and sculpture that should consume no more than a few minutes.

To find out more and to pick up maps and general information about the various food factory tours that draw in the tour groups – including the massive Hershey's chocolate factory in nearby Oakdale – contact Modesto's **CVB**, 1114 J St (Mon–Fri 8.30am–5pm; ☎1-800/266-4282, fax 209/571-6486). The Greyhound station is at J St and Ninth.

Stockton and around

Perched at the far northern limit of the Central Valley, the immediately striking thing about **STOCKTON** is the sight of ocean-going freighters so far inland. The San Joaquin and Sacramento rivers converge here, creating a vast delta with thousands of inlets and bays, and a man-made deep-water channel enables vessels to carry the produce of the Valley's farms past San Francisco and directly out to sea. But the geography that aided commerce also saddled Stockton with the image of being a grim place to live and a tough city to work in. During the Gold Rush it was a supply stop on the route to the gold mines, and it became a gigantic flophouse for broken and dispirited ex-miners who gave up their dreams of fortune and returned here to toil on the waterfront. Though valiant efforts have been made to shed this reputation and beautify the less attractive quarters, it's still primarily a hard-working, sleeves-rolled-up city.

A scattering of buildings downtown evoke the early decades of the century, thanks to which Stockton is often in demand as a film set. John Huston's downbeat boxing picture, *Fat City*, for example, was shot here.

Marginally more appealing are the blocks bordered by Harding Way and Park Street, and El Dorado and California, a short way north of the center, which have been preserved as the **Magnolia Historical District**, with sixteen intriguing specimens of domestic architecture spanning seven decades from the 1860s. To find them all, pick up the free leaflet from the **San Joaquin CVB**, downtown at 46 W Fremont St (Mon–Fri 8am–5pm; ☎1-800/888-8016).

Roughly a mile west of the Magnolia district, in Victory Park alongside Pershing Avenue, Stockton gathers totems of its past in the varied and large stock of the **Haggin Museum**, 1201 N Pershing Ave (Tues–Sun 1.30–5pm; donation requested). Not surprisingly, much is given over to agriculture, including the city's finest moment: the invention by local farmers of a caterpillar tread to enable tractors to travel over muddy ground, adapted by the British for use on tanks and standard use since for the military everywhere. In tremendous contrast, the museum also contains a batch of nineteenth-century French paintings, including works by Renoir and Gauguin, as well as Bouguereau's monumental *Nymphs Bathing*.

Practicalities

Stockton's **Greyhound station** is at 121 S Center St; **Amtrak** at 735 S San Joaquin St. Even traveling by public transportation doesn't mean you have to stay overnight in Stockton – connections both onwards to San Francisco and south down the Valley are plentiful – but it can be worth stopping here to **eat**, ethnic restaurants being in good supply. For genuine, inexpensive Mexican food try *Arroyo's*, 324 S Center St (closed Mon) and for Chinese there's *On Lock Sam*, 333 S Sutter St (☎209/466-4561), in Stockton since the last century, or *Dave Wong's*, 5602 N Pershing Ave. For something lighter go for the stuffed sandwiches at the *Fox Café*, in the foyer of the newly restored Fox Theater at 220 Main St; *Java on the Run*, 200 Main St; and later on sample the microbrews at the *Valley Brewing Company*, 157 West Adams St.

There's a **campground** eight miles south of Stockton – *Dos Reis Park* (☎209/953-8800), just off I-5 – or you can stay in the city in one of the plentiful mid-range chain **hotels**. The pick of these are *Days Inn*, 33 N Center St (☎209/948-6151; ③) close to the Greyhound station, and *The Holiday Inn*, 111 E March Lane (☎1-800/633-3737 or 209/474-3301; ⑤), about three miles north of downtown. There are budget **motels** near the Waterloo Road exit off Hwy-99.

Micke Grove Park and Lodi

If Stockton begins to pall, or it's simply too nice a day to spend in a city, venture five miles north to the Armstrong Road exit off Hwy-99 for the pastoral relief – at least outside weekends and holidays – of the **Micke Grove Park** (daily 8am–dusk; parking $4 weekends, $2 midweek), an oak grove which holds a Rose Garden, a Japanese Garden and a zoo. It also features the **San Joaquin Historical Museum** (Wed–Sun 1–4.45pm; $1), recording the evolution of the local agricultural industry and, more revealingly, the social history that accompanied it. Don't miss the Stockton clamshell dredge bucket, a tool used in the reclamation of the delta and restored and displayed like a major work of art.

Beyond the park, on the way north to Sacramento, the state capital (see p.496), sits **LODI**, a small country town immortalized in song by Creedence Clearwater Revival ("oh Lord, stuck in Lodi again"), though these days it's best known for its mass-market **wineries**, several of which offer daily tours and tastings. You can get a full list from the **Chamber of Commerce**, 215 W Oak St (Mon–Fri 8.30am–4.30pm; ☎209/334-4773), or the San Joaquin CVB Visitors' Bureau in Stockton.

SEQUOIA AND KINGS CANYON NATIONAL PARKS

Separate parks but jointly run and with a long common border, the Sequoia and Kings Canyon National Parks contain an immense variety of geology, flora and fauna. **Sequoia National Park**, as you might expect from its name, contains the thickest concentration – and the biggest individual specimens – of giant sequoia trees to be found anywhere. These ancient trees tend to outshine (and certainly outgrow) the other features of the park – an assortment of meadows, peaks, canyons and caves. Notwithstanding a few notable exceptions, **Kings Canyon National Park** doesn't have the big trees, but compensates with a gaping canyon gored out of the rock by the Kings River, which cascades in torrents down from the High Sierra during the snow-melt period. There's less of a package tourism feel here than in Yosemite: the few established sights (like the drive-on Auto Log) of both parks are near the main roads and concentrate the crowds, leaving the vast majority of the landscape untrammelled and unspoilt, but well within reach for willing hikers.

To the north lies the even more vast and almost equally spectacular **Sierra National Forest**, which is bound by fewer of the National Park-style restrictions on hunting and the use of motorized playthings. Consequently there is greater potential for disturbance, though this is counteracted by the sheer immensity of the region.

The best time to come is in late **summer** and **fall**, when the days are still warm, the nights are getting chilly at altitude, the roads remain free of snow and most visitors have left. Bear in mind that although most roads are kept open through the winter, snow blocks Hwy-180 into Kings Canyon and the road into Mineral King (see "Winter in the parks" box on p.299).

Some history
The land now encompassed by the Sequoia and Kings Canyon National Parks was once the domain of **Yokut sub-tribes** – the Monache, Potwisha and Kaweah peoples – who made summer forays into the high country from their permanent settlements in the lowlands, especially along the Marble Fork of the Kaweah River. The first real European contact came with the 1849 California **gold rush**, when prospectors penetrated the area in search of pasture and a direct route through the mountains. Word of abundant lumber soon got out and loggers came to stake their claim in the lowlands. The high country was widely ignored until, in 1858, local Indians led Hale Tharp, a cattleman from Three Rivers, up to the sequoias around Moro Rock. Tharp spent the next thirty summers up there in his log home where he was occasionally visited by John Muir (see p.314), who wrote about the area and brought it to the attention of the general public and the loggers. Before long, narrow gauge railways and log flumes littered the area, mainly for clearing fir and pine rather than the sequoias which tended to shatter when felled. Nonetheless, Visalia conservationist George Stewart, campaigned in Washington for some degree of **preservation** for the big trees and, in 1890, four square miles around Grant Grove became the country's second National Park after Yellowstone. In 1940 this was incorporated into the newly formed Kings Canyon National Park.

SEQUOIA AND
KINGS CANYON
NATIONAL PARKS

△ Yosemite (60 miles)

Bishop (5 miles) △

0   5 miles

N

JOHN MUIR WILDERNESS

■ McClure
Meadow
9600 ft

JOHN MUIR TRAIL AND PACIFIC CREST TRAIL

INYO NATIONAL FOREST

Muir Pass
11955 ft

Bishop Pass
11972 ft

JOHN MUIR WILDERNESS

LeConte
Canyon

Big Pine ●

SIERRA NATIONAL FOREST

▲ Spanish Mountain
10051 ft

KINGS CANYON
NATIONAL PARK

395

Rae
Lakes

Independence ●

Monarch
Wilderness
Area

△ Kings Canyon
Lodge

Kings Canyon
180

Cedar
Grove

JOHN MUIR TRAIL

Princess

Hume
Lake

Boyden Cave

△ Hume Lake

Charlotte
Lake

Grant
Grove

SEQUOIA NATIONAL FOREST

Buck
Rock

△ Cedar Grove

Kings-Kern Divide

Lone Pine (15 miles) △

Grant Grove
■ Big Stump

△ Big Meadows

Big Stump
Entrance

245

Montecito-
Sequoia Lodge

△ Stony Creek

Badger ●

Stony Creek

Dorst △

GENERALS
HIGHWAY

198

△ Lodgepole

Crystal Cave ■

Lodgepole ■

Giant Forest

Wolverton Ski Touring Center
General Sherman Giant Sequoia

Crescent
Meadow

Bearpaw
Meadow

Great Western

HIGH SIERRA TRAIL

Mt Whitney ▲

Whitney
Portal ●

JOHN MUIR TRAIL

PACIFIC CREST TRAIL

Hospital Rock △
Potwisha △

Moro Rock ■
Buckeye Flat

Ash Mountain
Entrance

ℹ Foothill Visitor Center

Three Rivers ●

Mineral King ●

Visalia (25 miles) △

Fresno (50 miles) △

Lake
Kaweah

198

Lookout Point
Entrance Station

Atwell
Mill

Cold
Springs

Lemon
Cove

SEQUOIA NATIONAL PARK

△ South Fork

Golden Trout
Wilderness Area

INYO
NATIONAL
FOREST

SEQUOIA NATIONAL FOREST

Giant Forest is a big tourist draw, with the greatest accessible concentration of giant sequoias, though in recent years it has been recognized that the huge numbers of visitors are irreparably damaging the Giant Forest ecosystem. The authorities have begun removing facilities, so that by the end of the 1997 season over a thousand rooms had been demolished, leaving only a hundred for the 1998 season. These, along with the Giant Forest restaurant, will then be cleared and the whole area re-seeded.

Arrival and information

Although easy to reach by **car** – a fifty mile drive along the tortuous Hwy-198 from Visalia or a slightly longer but faster journey from Fresno on Hwy-180 – Sequoia and Kings Canyon are not served by public transportation. Once in Sequoia, reduce traffic congestion and your own parking problems by using the **shuttle bus** (mid-June to early Sept daily 8am–5pm, every 40min; $1 a ride, $4 all day, $6 all-day family ticket) which runs between Lodgepole, the Sherman Tree, Giant Forest Village, Moro Rock and Crescent Meadow. There is currently no gas in the parks, so drivers should fill up with cheap gas in Visalia or Fresno, or slightly pricier stuff at Three Rivers. If you're desperate, you can get expensive gas at the *Hume Lake Christian Camp*, see p.301. There are no banks in either park, but travelers' checks are widely accepted and there are **ATMs** at Grant Grove, Lodgepole and Giant Forest.

The parks are always open: **park entry** costs $10 per car, or $5 per hiker or biker and is valid for seven days. This will be collected at the entrance stations, where you'll be given an excellent map and a copy of the free newspaper, *The Sequoia Bark*, which has details on the numerous **guided hikes** and other interpretive activities, as well as general information on the parks.

There are currently four **visitor centers** in the two parks: the Park Headquarters at Foothills, a mile north of the southern (Hwy-198) entrance to the park (daily 8am–5pm); and others at Lodgepole, Grant Grove Village and Cedar Grove Village (see the relevant

---

WINTER IN THE PARKS

The high country of both parks is covered in a blanket of **snow**, usually from November until April or May, and while this limits a great deal of sightseeing and walking, it does open up opportunities for some superb cross-country skiing. With chains, access is seldom much of a problem. Both main roads into the parks – Hwy-198 to Giant Forest and Hwy-180 to Grant Grove – are kept open all year, except for exceptional circumstances when it is still cleared quickly. The General's Highway is usually open as far north as Lodgepole and as far south as the *Montecito-Sequoia Lodge*, but the stretch in between is often left until no further snowfalls are expected, then cleared: it's best then to choose one section of the parks as a base. The Cedar Grove section of Kings Canyon is off limits to cars from late September to early May, but Grant Grove stays open all year. Facilities are restricted and camping is only available at snow-free lowland sites.

The big activity up here is **cross-country skiing** and **snowshoeing**. The northern highway gives access to two places at the hub of miles of marked trails: the Grant Grove Ski Touring Center at Grant Grove (Nov–April; ☎209/335-2314) where there's ski and snowshoe rental, guided naturalist snowshoe walks at weekends, restaurants and accommodation; and the *Montecito-Sequoia Lodge* (see "Accommodation", p.300), a resort with its own groomed trails, also open to visitors for around $10 a day. Nearby, the mile-long Big Meadows Nordic Ski Trail is perfect beginner's terrain. To the south, the Sequoia Ski Touring Center at Wolverton, just over two miles south of Lodgepole (Nov–April; ☎209/565-3435), has excellent day-use facilities with rentals, lessons and a retail shop but, unless you're a super-hardy camper, you'll need to return to Three Rivers for somewhere to stay.

accounts for details). There is also a useful **ranger station** at Mineral King and a new visitor facility is planned for Giant Forest, due to open for the 2000 summer season. For details of hikes and campgrounds in the surrounding Sequoia National Forest, visit the **Hume Lake Ranger District Office**, 35860 Hwy-180, at Clingan's Junction, seventeen miles west of the Big Stump entrance (Mon–Fri 8am–4.30pm; ☎209/338-2251).

In addition there is a comprehensive 24-hour recorded information line (☎209/565-3341), with details of weather and road conditions, as well as the facility to order information by mail; check out a stack more stuff on the parks' **website**: *www.nps.gov/seki*.

Accommodation

Inside the parks, all facilities, including accommodation, are managed by **Kings Canyon Park Services** (KCPS ☎209/335-5500, fax 335-2498), though with the demolition underway at Giant Forest, there isn't much accommodation to manage, and what remains is fairly expensive. Space is at a premium during the summer when booking a couple of months in advance is advisable, although you can occasionally pick up cancellations on the day.

Outside the parks, the most reasonably priced **accommodation** is in the motels lining the approach roads, a few miles from the entrances. The best selection is in the south at Three Rivers, where booking ahead is advised at weekends through the summer and holidays.

Under the first two headings below, all available roofed accommodation has been included, with just a selection of the best places to stay under the final two headings. For **camping**, see the box opposite).

In the parks

Bearpaw Meadow Camp (mid-June to mid-Sept; call KCPS). Soft beds, fluffy towels, hot showers and hearty meals served up in magnificent wilderness are the trump cards for this cluster of wooden-floored permanent tents on the High Sierra Trail, eleven miles walk east of Giant Forest Village: just follow the High Sierra Trail from Crescent Meadow. There's no electricity, everything is helicoptered in for the season and all meals are included in the $135 per person price tag. Bookings are accepted from January 2 when most weekends and holidays are taken, though you've a reasonable chance of an on-spec place on weeknights in June and September. Meals are also served to passing hikers, at a price. ⑨.

Cedar Grove (May–Sept; call KCPS). Cozy lodge with private bathroom and air conditioning, right by the Kings River and in the same block as the restaurant and shops. ⑤.

Grant Grove (all year; call KCPS). The widest selection of ways of sleeping under a roof, most options accommodating up to four people. The most basic are the kerosene lamp-lit tent cabins (②) which are too cold for winter use, rising through the more solid rustic cabins (③) with cooking stove, to comfortable standard cabins (④) with baths.

In Sequoia National Forest

Kings Canyon Lodge (☎209/335-2405). Pleasant enough rooms with an associated bar and small restaurant located midway between Grant Grove and Cedar Grove. ③.

Montecito-Sequoia Lodge (☎1-800/227-9900 or 650/967-8612, fax 967-8612), on the Generals Highway (Hwy-198) between Grant Grove Village and Giant Forest. Large but low-key and informal resort with the emphasis on fun for all the family; a communal atmosphere prevails around the huge fireplaces. It's tastefully set next to an artificial lake and has all manner of activity programs: canoeing, tennis, swimming, volleyball in summer; and snowshoeing, skating and cross-country skiing in winter (see box, p.299). Several all-inclusive packages invite multi-day stays but outside peak times you can stay for just a night or two in rustic cabins (③) or lodge rooms with private bath (④), with breakfast and dinner included.

CAMPING IN KINGS CANYON AND SEQUOIA

Except during public holidays, there is always plenty of **camping space** in the parks and the surrounding National Forest. All sites operate on a first-come-first-served basis except for *Lodgepole* and *Dorst* which can be reserved on ☎1-800/365-2267. RV drivers won't find any hook-ups but there are dump stations at Potwisha, Lodgepole, Dorst, Grant Grove and Cedar Grove. Collecting firewood is prohibited in the National Park but permitted in the National Forest. For **backcountry** camping see the "Hiking" box on p.306. There are coin-operated public **showers** at Lodgepole, Grant Grove Village and Cedar Grove Village.

Campgrounds are listed south to north. Take note of the **altitude** listed for each, as this indicates the kind of temperatures you can expect.

South Fork (all year; $6 mid-May to Oct, free rest of year; 3600ft). Trailer-free site thirteen miles east of Lake Kaweah on the very southwestern tip of the park. Water available during fee period.

Cold Springs, Mineral King (April to mid-Nov; $6; 7500ft). Excellent shaded riverside site 25 miles west of Hwy-198, with some very quiet walk-in sites. Gathering of dead wood permitted. Water available.

Atwell Mill, Mineral King (April to mid-Nov; $6; 6650ft). Slightly less appealing than *Cold Springs*, but still quiet and pleasant, and five miles closer to the highway. Some tent-only sites. Water available.

Potwisha (all year; $12; 2100ft). Smallish, RV-dominated site close to Hwy-198 three miles northeast of the park's southern entrance and beside the Marble Fork of the Kaweah River. Water available.

Buckeye Flat (mid-April to mid-Oct; $12; 2800ft). Peaceful, trailer-free site six miles east of Hwy-198 close to the park's southern entrance and beside the Middle Fork of the Kaweah River. Water available.

Lodgepole (all year; $14 mid-May to Sept, $12 rest of year when water is turned off, free after heavy snow; 6700ft). The largest and busiest of the sites, four miles north of Giant Forest Village and close to the highway. Reserve through Parknet (☎1-800/444-7275) in the high season, when there are pay showers, a camp store, water and flush toilets.

Dorst (late May to Sept; $14, rest of year $12; 6800ft). Another large site, twelve miles north of Giant Forest Village, with flush toilets and water during the season. In summer reserve through Parknet (☎1-800/444-7275).

Buck Rock (all year; free; 6300ft). Excellent and under-utilized National Forest site three miles west of the highway, midway between Lodgepole and Grant Grove Village. No water.

Big Meadows (all year; free; 6500ft). Similar site to *Buck Rock*, a mile further west, among exfoliated granite domes. No water.

Princess (May–Sept; $12; 6000ft). National Forest campground with water and toilets, handily sited on the way into Kings Canyon.

Hume Lake (all year; $14; 5200ft; ☎1-800/280-CAMP). Reservable National Forest site with water, toilets and lake swimming for the brave.

Sunset, **Azalea** & **Crystal Spring**, Grant Grove Village. (*Azalea* year-round, others late May to mid-Sept; $12; 6500ft). Comparable large sites all within a few hundred yards of the Grant Grove visitor center.

Sheep Creek, **Sentinel**, **Canyon View** & **Moraine**, Cedar Grove Village (mid-May to Sept; $12; 4600ft). A series of all-but contiguous forest sites around the Cedar Grove visitor center. *Canyon View* is tents-only.

Stony Creek (June–Sept; ☎209/561-3314). Plain, comfortable motel-style rooms with showers in a block with a good restaurant and a grocery store. ⑤.

Along Hwy-198: Lemon Cove and Three Rivers

Buckeye Tree Lodge, 46000 Hwy-198, Three Rivers (☎209/561-5900, fax 561-4611). Small but comfortable modern rooms with TV, video and private bathrooms, and a five-berth cottage (⑥), all located right by the park entrance and equipped with a pool. ④.

Gateway Lodge, 45978 Hwy-198, Three Rivers (☎209/561-4133, fax 561-3656). Spartan but perfectly functional motel-style rooms and a large house sleeping six with self-catering facilities (⑦). It is located right by the park entrance and beside the Kaweah River. ④.

Mesa Verde Plantation B&B, 33038 Hwy-198, Lemon Cove (☎1-800/240-1466 or 209/597-2555, fax 598-2551). Luxurious B&B with heated pool and spa, and gourmet breakfasts, located on a citrus orchard seventeen miles from the park entrance. Rooms follow a *Gone with the Wind* theme to the extent that the Belle Watling room comes bordello-hued with a mirrored bedstead.

Sierra Lodge, 43175 Hwy-198 (☎209/561-3681). Spacious lodge with large, modern rooms with bathrooms and many with decks, plus the use of a pool. ④.

Three Rivers Trailer Park, 43365 Hwy-198 (☎209/561-4413). RV-only site with a few ageing and very basic cabins at the lowest prices for miles around. ③.

Along Hwy-180

Sierra Inn Motel, 37692 Hwy-180, Dunlap (☎209/338-2144). Small and functional motel rooms with TV and air-conditioning, located fourteen miles west of the Big Stump entrance and next to a sandwiches-and-steaks restaurant and bar. ③.

Snowline Lodge, 44138 Hwy-180, Dunlap (☎209/336-2300). Woodsy collection of spartan but appealing rooms, some with a verandah that catches the morning sun, located seven miles west of the Big Stump entrance. Straightforward meals are available in the great rustic bar and restaurant. ③.

Eating

There are **food** markets and fairly basic cafeterias at Lodgepole (the most extensive), Stony Creek and Cedar Grove Village, though none is spectacular and prices will be higher than places outside the park, such as Three Rivers. Much the same applies to restaurants, with Three Rivers offering the best local selection at reasonable prices.

In the parks and surrounding National Forest

Grant Grove Coffee Shop, Grant Grove. Basic diner fare – burgers, sandwiches and breakfasts – at tolerable prices.

Lodgepole Deli, Lodgepole. The best of the parks' budget eating places, with respectable low-cost breakfasts, sandwiches and pizza.

Montecito-Sequoia Lodge. Resort which also serves nutritious meals to non-residents. Hearty breakfasts ($7), lunches ($8) and buffet dinners ($15) are all served communally at large tables, and a bar operates until 9pm.

Three Rivers

The Bakery, Hwy-198. A good and friendly stop for breakfast, especially for the freshly baked cakes and pastries.

Gateway Restaurant, 45978 Hwy-198. Superbly set restaurant with a sunny deck overlooking the Kaweah River. Burgers, sandwiches and pasta dishes go for $8–10, meat and fish main courses for around $15. Closed Mon.

Noisy Water Café, 41775 Hwy-198. Cozy, friendly and locally-popular family restaurant with an extensive menu of American staples.

Sequoia National Park

The main center in **SEQUOIA NATIONAL PARK** is **Lodgepole** – the accommodation base and starting point for many of the hiking trails. To the south there's also the more isolated Mineral King area. While trees are seldom scarce – patches where the giant sequoias can't grow are thickly swathed with pine and fir – the scenery varies throughout the park: sometimes subtly, sometimes abruptly. Everywhere paths lead through deep forests and around meadows; longer treks rise above the tree line to reveal the barren peaks and gorgeous sights of the High Sierra.

The history of the park is laced with political intrigue. In the 1880s the Giant Forest area was bought by the Co-operative Land Purchase and Colonization Association, a group of individuals known as the **Kaweah Colony** that had the idea of forming a workers' colony here. They began what became the four-year task of building a road from the Central Valley up to Giant Forest, intending to start commercial logging of the huge trees there. Due to legal technicalities, however, their rights to the area were disputed, and in 1890 a bill (probably instigated by a combination of agricultural and railroad interests) was passed by the Senate which effected the preservation of all sequoia groves. The colony lost everything, and received no compensation for the road, which remained in use for thirty years – although decades later the ex-leader of the colony acknowledged that the eventual outcome was of far greater benefit to society as a whole than his own scheme would have been.

Three Rivers, Kaweah and Mineral King

Approaching the park from the south, you pass through **THREE RIVERS**, a lowland community strung out for seven miles along Hwy-198 and providing the greatest concentration of accommodation and places to eat anywhere near the park. As you approach the center of town a sign directs you three miles west to what remains of the Kaweah Colony, essentially just the **Kaweah Post Office**, which must be one of the smallest still operating in the country. Little more than a shed, it still has the original brass-and-glass private boxes, and, even outside normal opening times, the tiny lobby acts as the local secondhand book exchange.

A couple of miles north of Three Rivers, the century-old, twisting Mineral King Road branches east into the southern section of the park to **Mineral King**, sitting in a scalloped bowl at 7800ft surrounded by snowy peaks and glacial lakes. This is the only part of the high country accessible by car and makes a superb hiking base when you can reach it – essentially from June to September, or a little longer if the snows hold off. Eager prospectors built the thoroughfare hoping the area would yield silver. It didn't, the mines were abandoned and the region was left in peace until the mid-1960s when Disney threatened to build a huge ski resort here, only to be defeated by the conservation lobby which campaigned for the region's inclusion in the Sequoia National Park, something finally achieved in 1978. Now there's just a couple of basic campgrounds and near-complete tranquility. Having negotiated the seven-hundred-odd twists and turns from the highway, you can relax by the river before hiking up over steep Sawtooth Pass and into the alpine bowls of the glaciated basins beyond. There's also a gentler introduction to the flora and fauna of Mineral King by way of a short **nature trail** from the *Cold Springs* campground.

Pick up practical information and wilderness permits from the **ranger station** (late May to Sept daily 7am–3.30pm) opposite the *Cold Springs* campground. Permits are required year round and are in great demand in certain areas in July and August. Reservations can be made in advance from March 1 (☎209/565-3708) and some permits are offered on a first-come-first-served basis. The *Silver City Resort* (☎209/561-3223; rustic cabins ③, deluxe chalets ⑤) near the *Atwell* campground is the only place you'll find food; it has limited provisions, a café/restaurant and decent cabins.

Giant Forest and around

Entering the park on **Hwy-180 from Visalia**, you pass **Hospital Rock**, easily spotted by the side of the road and decorated with rock drawings and grain grinding holes from an ancient Monache settlement. The rock got its name from a trapper who accidentally shot himself in the leg and was treated by the local tribe – who are further remembered by a small outdoor exhibition telling something of their evolution and culture. The road opposite leads to the small and appealing *Buckeye Flat* campground.

From Hospital Rock, the road soon becomes the **Generals Highway** and twists rapidly uphill into the densely forested section of the park, the aptly labelled **Giant Forest**. GIANT FOREST VILLAGE near the junction with Crescent Meadow Road, will cease to offer food and lodging by the 1999 season, but for the moment makes a good base for exploring the features of the area. It is quite feasible to do a long, but gentle, day walk taking in Moro Rock, Crescent Meadow, Tharp's Log and the General Sherman Tree (see all below).

Along Crescent Meadow Road

A spur off the main highway, **Crescent Meadow Road** provides easy access to a host of photo opportunities. The first attraction is the **Auto Log**, a fallen trunk chiselled flat enough to enable motorists to nose up onto it. Beyond here, a side loop leads to the dramatic **Moro Rock** (also accessible on a three-mile trail from the village), a granite monolith streaking wildly upward from the green hillside. Views from its remarkably level top can stretch 150 miles across the Central Valley and, in the other direction, to the towering Sierra (incidentally, the top is also reputed to make a good platform for feeling vibrations of distant earthquakes). Thanks to a concrete staircase, it's a comparatively easy climb up the rock, although at nearly 7000ft the altitude can be a strain.

Back on the road, you pass under the **Tunnel Log**: a tree that fell across the road in 1937 and has since had a vehicle-sized hole cut through its lower half. Further on, **Crescent Meadow** is, like other grassy fields in the area, more accurately a marsh, and too wet for the sequoias that form an impressive boundary around. Looking across the meadow gives the best opportunity to appreciate the changing shape of the ageing sequoia. The mainly flat trail circling its perimeter (1.5 miles; 1hr) leads to **Log Meadow**, to which a farmer, Hale Tharp, searching for a summer grazing ground for his sheep, was led by local Native Americans in 1856. He became one of the first white men to see the giant sequoias, and the first to actually live in one – a hollowed-out specimen which still exists, remembered as **Tharp's Log**. Climb inside to appreciate the hewn-out shelves. From here the loop presses on to the still living **Chimney Tree**, its center completely burnt out so that the sky is visible from its hollow base. Hardy backpackers can pick up the John Muir Trail here and hike the 74 miles to Mount Whitney (the tallest mountain in the continental US; see p.269). Several less demanding trails cover the couple of miles back to Giant Forest Village.

The big trees and Crystal Cave

Just north of Giant Forest on the Generals Highway (and reachable on foot by various connecting trails) is the biggest sequoia of them all. The three-thousand-year-old **General Sherman Tree** is 275ft high, with a base diameter of 36ft (and was, for a time, renamed the Karl Marx Tree by the Kaweah Colony). While it's certainly a thrill to be face-to-bark with what is widely held to be the largest living thing on earth, its extraordinary dimensions are hard to grasp alongside the almost equally monstrous sequoias around, and the other tremendous batch that can be seen on the **Congress Trail** (2 miles; 1–2hr; negligible ascent), which starts from here.

When you've had your fill of the magnificent trees, you might consider a trip nine miles from Giant Forest Village along a minor road to **Crystal Cave** (50min guided tours: mid-May to mid-June & Sept Fri–Mon 11am–4pm; mid-June to Aug daily 11am–4pm; $5) which has a mildly diverting batch of stalagmites and stalactites. Tickets can only be purchased at the Lodgepole and Foothill visitor centers at least a couple of hours beforehand. The early morning tours are not usually full. Remember to take a jacket.

Lodgepole and around

Whatever your plans, you should stop at **LODGEPOLE VILLAGE** – four miles along the Generals Highway from Giant Forest Village – for the geological exhibits, film shows and general information at the **visitor center** (daily: mid-May to Aug 8am–6pm; rest of year 8am–5pm, may be closed in the depths of winter). Lodgepole is at one end of the Tokopah Valley, a glacially formed canyon (not unlike the much larger Yosemite Valley) that's a piece of cake to explore on a number of hiking trails (see the box on p.306). Foremost among them is the **Tokopah Valley Trail** – leading from Lodgepole through the valley to the base of Tokopah Falls, beneath the 1600-foot **Watchtower** cliff. The top of the Watchtower, and its great view of the valley, are accessible by way of the **Lakes Trail**, or try the sharpest ascent of all the Lodgepole hikes, the **Alta Peak and Alta Meadows Trail**, which rises four thousand feet over seven miles.

Kings Canyon National Park

KINGS CANYON NATIONAL PARK is wilder and less visited than Sequoia, with just two small settlements containing the park's main visitor facilities: Grant Grove lies close to the Big Stump entrance, and Cedar Grove huddles in the bottom of the canyon some 25 miles to the east at the start of most of the marked hikes. The one real road (closed in winter, usually Oct–May) links the two, spectacularly skirting the colossal canyon. Away from these two places, you're on your own. The vast untamed park has a maze of canyons and a sprinkling of isolated lakes – the perfect environment for careful self-guided exploration.

Grant Grove, the Big Stump Area and Hume Lake

Confusingly, **GRANT GROVE** is an enclave of Kings Canyon National Park within the Sequoia National Forest, but unless you're planning a major backcountry hike across the parks' boundaries you'll have to pass through here before reaching Kings Canyon proper. Grant Grove has the largest concentration of visitor facilities in the Kings Canyon National Park, with accommodation, post office, restaurant and a useful **visitor center** (daily: mid-May to Aug 8am–6pm; rest of year 8am–5pm) with all the background information you'll need.

This concentrated stand of sequoias, sugar pines, incense cedar, black oak and mountain dogwood is named after the **General Grant** tree, which, along with the **Robert E. Lee** tree (also here), rivals the General Sherman for bulk. A half-mile trail (guides $1) wends its way amongst these and other giants, calling in at the **Fallen Monarch**, which you can walk through, and the **Gamlin Cabin**, where Israel and Thomas Gamlin lived while exploiting their timber claim until 1878. The massive stump of one tree had a slice cut and shipped off to the 1876 Centennial Exhibition in Philadelphia – an attempt to convince cynical easterners that such enormous organisms really existed.

HIKING IN SEQUOIA AND KINGS CANYON

The trails in Kings Canyon and Sequoia see far less traffic than those in Yosemite, but can still get busy in high summer. There are no restrictions on day-walks, but a quota system applies if you are planning to camp in the back country. Numbers are severely limited, but around half the places are offered on a first-come-first-served basis and provided you are fairly flexible you should be able to land something by turning up at the ranger station nearest your proposed trailhead after 1pm on the day before you wish to start. To reserve free **wilderness permits**, write or fax in advance to Wilderness Permit Reservations, Sequoia & King's Canyon National Park, Three Rivers, CA 93271 (fax 209/565-3797) stating entry and exit dates, desired route with an alternative, number of people and estimated camping spots. Reservations are accepted after March 1 and at least fifteen days before your start date. More details are available in the free *Backcountry Basics* leaflet available in the park and from the above address. The visitor centers also sell a series of trail guides ($1.50 each) with route descriptions of most of the short trails.

Remember that this is **bear country**: read the box on p.45. Bear canisters can be rented ($3 a day and $75 deposit) from the ranger station in Mineral King and camp stores at Cedar Grove, Grant Grove and Lodgepole.

FROM MINERAL KING, SEQUOIA

Eagle Lake Trail (7 miles; 6–8hr; 2200ft ascent). Starting from the parking area a mile beyond the ranger station, this trail starts gently but gets tougher towards Eagle Lake. Highlights include the Eagle Sink Hole (where the river vanishes) and some fantastic views.

Groundhog Meadow Trail (2 miles; 1–2hr; 900ft ascent). Starting a quarter of a mile back from the road beyond the ranger station. A short but demanding trail which switchbacks up to Groundhog Meadow, from where there's a great view of Sawtooth Ridge.

Mosquito Lakes No. 1 Trail (7 miles; 6hr; 1150ft ascent). Follows the first half of the Eagle Lake Trail, then branches left to the lowest of the Mosquito Lakes at 9000ft.

Mosquito Lakes No. 5 Trail (10 miles; 8hr; 2300ft ascent). As above plus a bit, bringing you to the uppermost lake at over 10,000ft. Stupendous views.

Paradise Peak via Paradise Ridge Trail (9 miles; 9hr; 2800ft ascent). Superb walk starting opposite the *Atwell Mill* campground and climbing steeply to Paradise Ridge, which affords views of Moro Rock. From there it is a fairly flat stroll to the 9300-foot Paradise Peak.

Two miles south of Grant Grove, the **Big Stump Area** unsurprisingly gets its name from the gargantuan stumps that litter the place – remnants from early logging of sequoias carried out during the 1880s. A mile-long trail (almost meaningless without the leaflet from the Grant Grove visitor center; $1.50) leads through this scene of devastation to the Mark Twain Stump, the headstone of another monster killed to impress: a sliver of this one resides in the American Museum of Natural History and another was sent to London's British Museum.

Hume Lake and around

About eight miles north of Grant Grove, a minor road spurs off three miles to **Hume Lake**, actually a reservoir built in 1908 to provide water for logging flumes, and now forming the heart of an underpopulated area of the Sequoia National Forest. It's a delightful spot to swim or launch your canoe, is handily placed for the local hiking trails and makes a good place to spend a night beside the lake at the comparatively large *Hume Lake* campground (see p.301). At the head of the lake, the facilities of the *Hume Lake Christian Camp* provide expensive gas, groceries, a post office and a coffee shop.

FROM GIANT FOREST AND LODGEPOLE, SEQUOIA

Alta Peak and Alta Meadows Trail (14 miles; 8–10hr; 4000ft ascent). Starting a mile or so south of Lodgepole, this strenuous but rewarding trail rises four thousand feet over seven miles. The trail splits after three miles: there's an easy, level walk to Alta Meadow and its fine views of the surrounding peaks (and a four-mile trail to the desolate Moose Lake), or the daunting near-vertical hike to the stunning Alta Peak.

Lakes Trail (13 miles; 6–8hr; 2300ft ascent). Starting a mile or so south of Lodgepole, this popular if fatiguing trail leads past three lakes. The two furthest lakes, Emerald Lake and Pear Lake, have campgrounds and, for the really adventurous (and experienced), make good starting points for self-guided trekking into the mountains.

Little Baldy Trail (3 miles; 2–3hr; 700ft ascent). Starting from Little Baldy Saddle, six miles north of Lodgepole, this loop trail leads to the rocky summit of Little Baldy.

Moro Rock via Soldiers Trail (4.5 miles; 3–4hr; 300ft ascent). Starting at Giant Forest, this fairly easy self-guided trail leads through meadow and forest, calling at Hanging Rock, Moro Rock and Tunnel Log.

Tokopah Trail (3 miles; 2–3hr; negligible ascent). Starting from the Lodgepole visitor center, this is a valley walk beside the Marble Fork of the Kaweah River, leading to impressive granite cliffs and the Tokopah Falls.

FROM KINGS CANYON

Cedar Grove Overlook Trail (5 miles; 3–4hr; 1200ft ascent). Starting half a mile north of Cedar Grove Village on Pack Station Road, this switchback trail rises through forest and chaparral to a viewpoint overlooking Kings Canyon.

Don Cecil Trail to Lookout Peak (13 miles; 6–8hr; 4000ft ascent). Starting 400 yards east of Cedar Grove Village, a strenuous trail which largely follows the pre-highway road route. After two miles you reach the shady glen of Sheep Creek Cascade before pressing on up the canyon to the wonderfully panoramic summit.

Hotel Creek–Lewis Creek Loop Trail (8 miles; 5hr; 1200ft ascent). Follows the first two miles of the Cedar Grove Overlook Trail, before branching downhill and returning to Cedar Grove through some extensively fire-damaged forest.

Mist Falls Trail (8 miles; 4–5hr; 600ft ascent). An easy sandy trail starts from Road's End, eventually climbing steeply to Mist Falls, one of the largest waterfalls in the twin parks.

Kings Canyon Highway

For most, Hume Lake doesn't even warrant a diversion from the northern park's main attraction, Kings Canyon, which some measurements make the deepest canyon in the US, at some 7900ft. Whatever the facts, its wall sections of granite and gleaming blue marble and the yellow pockmarks of yucca plants are visually outstanding: this is especially true from Junction View as Hwy-180 winds its way down to the riverside. A vast area of the wilderness beyond is drained by the South Fork of the Kings River, a raging torrent during the springtime snowmelt spate, and perilous for wading at any time: people have been swept away even when paddling close to the bank in a seemingly placid section.

Near the foot of the canyon, the road passes the less diverting of the region's two show caves, the **Boyden Cave** (summer daily 10am–5pm, 45min tours on the hour; $6), whose interior has a number of bizarre formations grown out of the forty-thousand-year-old rock, their impact intensified by the stillness and coolness inside. The cave stays at a constant 55°F, causing the numerous snakes and small animals who tumble in through the hole in the roof to enter instant hibernation.

Cedar Grove

Once properly into the National Park, the canyon sheds its V-shape and gains a floor, where the settlement of **Cedar Grove** sprawls among incense cedars. With a lodge, a food store and snack bar, several campgrounds and, across the river, a **ranger station** (June–Aug daily 9am–5pm; May, Sept & Oct hours reduced), this is as close to a built-up area as the park gets.

Three miles east are the **Roaring River Falls** which, when in spate, undoubtedly merit their name. Apart from the obvious appeal of the scenery, the main things to see around here are the **flowers** – leopard lilies, shooting stars, violets, Indian paintbrush, lupines and others – and a variety of bird life. The longer hikes through the creeks, many of them seven or eight miles long (see box on p.306), are fairly stiff challenges and you should carry drinking water. An easy alternative, however, is to potter along the **nature trail** (1.5 miles; 1–2hr; flat) around the edge of **Zumwalt Meadow**, a beckoning green carpet a mile beyond the falls and a short walk from the road, beneath the forbidding gray walls of Grand Sentinel and North Dome mountains. The meadow boasts a collection of big-leaf maple, cat's-tails and creek dogwood, and there's often a chance of an eyeful of animal life.

Just a mile further, Kings Canyon Road comes to an end at **Copper Creek**. Thirty years ago it was sensibly decided not to allow vehicles to penetrate further. Instead the multitude of canyons and peaks that constitute the Kings River Sierra are networked by **hiking paths**, all accessible from here and almost all best enjoyed armed with a tent and some provisions. To obtain **wilderness permits** in this area, call at the Road's End Wilderness Permit Station (June to mid-Sept daily 7am–2pm; rest of Sept Fri & Sat 7am–2pm) at the end of Hwy-180. The less ambitious only need to venture a hundred yards riverward to **Muir Rock**, to see where John Muir (see box on p.314) conducted early meetings of the Sierra Club. On the way back down the valley, cut right and follow the **Motor Nature Trail** (westbound only) along the north side of the river back to Cedar Grove.

The Sierra National Forest

Consuming the entire gaping tract of land between Kings Canyon and Yosemite, the **SIERRA NATIONAL FOREST** boasts some of the Californian interior's most beautiful mountain scenery, though it is less well known – and less visited – than either of its National Park neighbors. A federally run area that lacks the environmental protection given to the parks, many of the rivers here have been dammed and much of the forest developed into resort areas that are better for fishing and boating than hiking. Central Valley residents stream up here at weekends through the summer. That said, there are far fewer people and any number of remote corners to explore, not least the rugged, unspoilt terrain of the vast **John Muir Wilderness** and the neighboring **Ansel Adams Wilderness** which contain some of the starkest peaks and lushest alpine meadows of the High Sierra. If you want to discover complete solitude and hike and camp in isolation, this is the place to do it – the sheer challenge of the environment can make the National Parks look like holiday camps. But don't try any lone exploration without thorough planning and accurate maps, and don't expect buses to pick you up if you're tired – public transportation is virtually nonexistent. We haven't highlighted walks in this area; there are hundreds of them, and any of the **ranger stations** can suggest suitable hikes, supply permits (necessary for any overnight hikes into most of the forest) and sell you the detailed *Sierra National Forest Map* ($3.25), useful even if you are driving. **Dispersed camping** is allowed in most areas of the forest, provided you keep a hundred feet away from any stream; a free campfire permit is needed even for a portable stove.

The paltry network of roads effectively divides the forest into three main areas: the more southerly **Pineridge** district, accessible by way of Hwy-168; the **Bass Lake** and the Mariposa district in the north, just off Hwy-41 between Fresno and Yosemite, and the **Minarets Loop**, which reaches out into the Sierra to the southeast of Yosemite. Call ☎209/855-5360 for road information.

The Pineridge District and the John Muir Wilderness

A forty-mile drive from Fresno along Hwy-168 through a parched and knobbly land-scape dotted with blue, live and scrub oak soon brings you to the best place for adventurous hiking, the **Pineridge** district. Around the **Kaiser Pass**, which scrapes 9200ft, you'll find isolated alpine landscapes, served by decent campgrounds, a couple of hotels and even some hot springs. The western section of the district is dominated by the weekend boating and fishing playgrounds of Huntington and Shaver lakes, while the east, up and over the Kaiser Pass, is bigtime hiking territory.

Hwy-168 – aka The Sierra Heritage National Scenic Byway – penetrates seventy miles into the forest among the snow-capped peaks of the **John Muir Wilderness**. It's a drive of at least four hours even in good weather – and this is an area prone to bad weather and road closure, although you can always get to the lakes. The best-placed source of information is the **Pineridge Ranger Station** (daily 8am–4.30pm; ☎209/855-5360), located along Hwy-168 at Prather, five miles west of the forest entrance.

Shaver and Huntington lakes

From the ranger station, Hwy-168 climbs rapidly over eighteen miles from undulating foothills studded with oaks to **Shaver Lake**, a mile-high community amongst the pines. If you fancy an afternoon dodging the jetskiers out on the lake, drop in at Shaver Lake Watersports, Shaver Lake Lodge Marina (☎209/841-8222) to rent windsurfers ($45 a day), kayaks ($7 an hour) and canoes ($15 an hour). Otherwise, there's little reason to stop except for groceries, gas, meals at one of the half-dozen restaurants, or perhaps to stay at either *Musick Creek Inn & Chalets* (☎209/841-3323; ③), which has motel units and A-frames, or *Shaver Lake Village* (☎1-800/695-7368 or 209/841-7183; ④), with hotel rooms and studio cabins. There are a couple of decent **campgrounds** hereabouts: *Dorabelle*, near the lake on Dorabelle Road (June to mid-Sept; reserve with CLM ☎1-800/280-CAMP; $12), which has water; and *Swanson Meadow*, two miles east on Dinkey Creek Road ($8), both at around 5500ft.

Beyond Shaver Lake, Hwy-168 climbs the 7500-foot Tamarack Ridge that effectively separates **Huntington Lake**, twenty miles east, from the Central Valley. This lake is more isolated than its neighbor over the hill but is almost equally popular; again watersports and angling are the pastimes of choice. There's a restaurant, bar, gas station, post office and general store all a few yards from the lake, while *Lakeside Resort* (☎209/893-3193; ③) provides sheltered shorefront accommodation, with rustic knotty pine cabins sleeping four (bedlinen extra). From here on, the lakeshore is almost entirely taken up by campgrounds, all costing $12, bookable through CLM and with piped water. The useful **Eastwood ranger station** beside Huntington Lake (late May to early Sept daily 8am–5pm; ☎209/893-6611) has details. East off Hwy-168, just before the lake, the mile-long **Rancheria Falls Trail** (350ft ascent; 1hr round trip) is a wood-land route to the 150-foot Rancheria Falls.

If you crave solitude, head to the lake's western end, where a winding, forty-mile, partly-gravel road skirts the whole of the **Kaiser Wilderness**, passing a couple of free, primitive campgrounds, before rejoining Kaiser Pass Road on the east side. It's a trek, but once here you'll feel a million miles from anywhere.

Beyond Kaiser Pass: Mono Hot Springs and around

Beyond the Eastwood ranger station (see overleaf) you're into the wild country climbing Kaiser Pass on a rapidly deteriorating road up to 9200 feet, passing the *Badger Flat* campground ($8; no water) along the way. Eight miles from Eastwood, a side road leads to **White Bark Vista** with one of the best mountain views in these parts. Over the pass is a vast basin, draining the south fork of the San Joaquin River. The road drops past the *Portal Forebay* campground ($8; no water), one of the best in the region, before reaching the **High Sierra Ranger Station** (late May to early Sept daily 7.30am–5pm; ☎209/877-7173). A mile east the road splits into two narrow and winding seven-mile routes: north to Lake Edison, its approach marred by a huge earth dam, and west to the more appealing Florence Lake. Both boast splendid scenery and hiking, fishing and camping opportunities, but don't hold enough to make a prolonged stay worthwhile.

Mono Hot Springs, two miles north of the junction on the road to Lake Edison, is the best thing about the region; a place to relax or clean up after hikes. For the full experience head for the modest *Mono Hot Springs Resort*, right on the banks of the San Joaquin River (mid-May to mid-Oct ☎209/449-9054; winter 209/325-1710; ②), which offers individual mineral baths ($5), showers ($4), and massages for $32 per half-hour. Outside there's a chlorinated spa filled with spring water, costing $4 for an all-day pass. Accommodation ranges from simple cabins with communal ablutions and no linen to attractive modern suites with kitchen; reserve at weekends. The resort also has a small restaurant, an understocked general store, gas, and a large but decent campground ($10; water). Better still, across the river there's a five-foot-deep **natural pool** (unrestricted access), perfect for soaking your bones while stargazing. This is just one of many such pools (mostly more secluded) on this side of the river; ask around.

Bass Lake and the Mariposa district

The northern reaches of the Sierra National Forest are most easily reached from **Oakhurst** (see "Approaching Yosemite" on p.314), the center of the Mariposa district and just seven miles west of much the biggest tourist attraction in the area – the pine-fringed **BASS LAKE**. A stamping ground of Hell's Angels in the 1960s – the leather and licentiousness memorably described in Hunter S. Thompson's book *Hell's Angels* – Bass Lake is nowadays a family resort, crowded with boaters and anglers in summer, but a good spot to rest for a day or two. For detailed campground and hiking information, consult the **Oakhurst Ranger Station** (☎209/683-4665).

Road 222 runs right around the lake, though not always within sight of it. At the main settlement, **Pines Village**, you can buy groceries, eat moderately well and **spend the night** at *The Pines* (☎1-800/350-7463 or 209/642-3121; ⑦) in luxurious two-story chalets with kitchens or even more palatial lakeside suites. By the southwestern tip of the lake, *Miller's Landing Resort*, 37976 Road 222 (☎209/642-3633), offers cabins without bathrooms for $30 right up to fancy chalets and suites (②–⑦). *Miller's Landing* is also the best place to rent aquatic equipment – **canoes** and **fishing boats** are $25 and $60 a day respectively, while **jetskis** are $55 an hour – and they have public showers and laundry.

The western side of Bass Lake is slung with $16-a-night family **campgrounds**, most oriented towards long stays beside your camper. In summer, book well in advance (call CLM on ☎1-800/280-CAMP), though no-shows are sometimes available at the California Land Management Office, 39900 Road 222 on the southwest side (late May to early Sept Mon–Fri 8am–8pm Sat & Sun 8am–9pm; ☎209/642-3212). For tent campers, the best site is *Lupine*, just north of *Miller's Landing*.

The Minarets Loop

If Bass Lake is too commercial and overcrowded for you, the antidote starts immediately to the north. The Sierra Vista Scenic Byway, more succinctly known as the **Minarets Loop**, makes a ninety-mile circuit west of Hwy-41 topping out at the Clover Meadow Station (7000ft), trailhead for much of the magnificent **Ansel Adams Wilderness**. Apart from a lot of trailheads and campgrounds, there's not a great deal to it, though the views are fantastic and people scarce. A straight circuit (snow-free June–Oct at best) takes five hours. Stock up on supplies before you start: there are a few stores and gas stations dotted along the loop but, as ever, they're not cheap and the range is limited. Accommodation is largely restricted to campgrounds all (except two free sites) costing $10–15.

The north side

Immediately north of Bass Lake is Beasore Road, but a better start for the circuit is Sky Ranch Road, which cuts east four miles north of Oakhurst. First stop, after seven miles, is the **Nelder Grove Historical Area** (unrestricted entry), a couple of miles north along a dirt road. Over a hundred giant sequoias are scattered through the forest here, though the overall impression is of devastation evidenced by enormous stumps amongst the second-growth sugar pine, white fir and cedar. The mile-long "Shadow of the Giants" interpretive walk explains the logging activities which took place here in the 1880s and early 1890s and, with its low visitor count, offers a more serene communion with these majestic trees than do any of the National Parks. A second interpretive trail leads from the attractive but mosquito-ridden *Nelder Grove Campsite* (free; 5500ft; stream water) to **Bull Buck Tree**, once a serious contender for the world's largest tree. Several $10 campgrounds, most without running water, are dotted either side of the road. At 6400ft, the *Fresno Dome* site ($10; no water) is particularly pleasant and acts as a base for a moderately strenuous walk to the top of its exfoliated granite namesake.

Sky Ranch Road joins Beasore Road at Cold Springs Meadow and continues to **Beasore Meadow**, where the summer-only Jones Store has supplied groceries, gas and meals for the best part of a century, and offers showers to hikers. The large **Globe Rock** heralds the end of asphalt for the next five miles, making *Minarets Pack Station* (June–Sept; ☎209/868-3405; ①), the return to tarmac, all the more welcome. As well as a general store and reasonable meals, the station offers simple lodging and horseback trips from $45 a day. It's a great base for wilderness trips, many of which start by the Clover Meadow Ranger Station, a couple of miles up a spur road (June–Oct daily 9am–5pm). Nearby are two free and wonderfully sited campgrounds, *Clover Meadow* and *Granite Creek*, the former with potable water.

The south side

From *Minarets Pack Station*, the loop starts to descend, passing a small ranger outpost (daily 8am–4.30pm; ☎209/877-2218) en route to the rather disappointing **Arch Rock**, where the earth under a slab of granite has been undermined to leave a kind of bridge. It's better to push on to the eight-mile side road to the dammed **Mammoth Pool**, where summer anglers boat on the lake and smoke their catch at one of four campgrounds. The quietest of them are *Sweetwater* ($10; 3800ft) and *Placer* ($10; 4100ft), away from the pool but by streams.

Back on the loop road, continue to **Mile High Vista** for endless views of mountain ranges and granite domes stretching back to Mammoth Mountain (see p.275). There's little to stop for on the last 25 miles back to civilization, except for the mildly diverting **Sierra Mono Indian Museum** (Mon–Sat 9am–4pm; $2) at the hamlet of North Fork.

YOSEMITE NATIONAL PARK

No temple made with hands can compare with the Yosemite. Every rock in its walls seems to glow with life. Some lean back in majestic repose; others, absolutely sheer or nearly so for thousands of feet, advance beyond their companions in thoughtful attitudes, giving welcome to storms and calms alike, seemingly aware, yet heedless, of everything going on about them.

John Muir, *The Yosemite*

More gushing adjectives have been thrown at **YOSEMITE NATIONAL PARK** than at any other part of California. But however excessive the hyperbole may seem, once you enter the park and turn the corner which reveals Yosemite Valley – only a small part of the park but the one at which most of the verbiage is aimed – you realize it's actually an understatement. For many, **Yosemite Valley** is, very simply, the single most dramatic piece of geology to be found anywhere in the world. Just seven miles long and one mile across at its widest point, it's walled by near-vertical, mile-high cliffs whose sides are streaked by cascading waterfalls and whose tops, a variety of domes and pinnacles, form a jagged silhouette against the sky. At ground level, too, the sights can be staggeringly impressive. Grassy meadows are framed by oak, cedar, maple and fir trees, with a variety of wild flowers and wildlife – deer, coyotes and even black bears are not uncommon. As if that wasn't enough, in the southern reaches of the park near Wawona, sequoias grow almost as densely and to as vast dimensions as those in the Sequioa National Park.

Perhaps understandably, tourists are even more common. Each year Yosemite has to cope with four million visitors, and if you're looking for a little peace it's advisable to avoid the valley and Wawona on weekends and holidays. That said, the whole park is diverse and massive enough to endure the crowds: you can visit at any time of year, even in winter when the waterfalls turn to ice and the trails are blocked by snow, and out of high summer even the valley itself resists getting crammed. Further-flung reaches of the park, especially around the crisp alpine Tuolumne Meadows (pronounced Too-ol-uh-me), and the completely wild backcountry accessible beyond them, are much less busy all year round – nature in just about the most peaceful and elemental setting you could imagine. Everywhere you go, it is, of course, essential to be careful not to cause ecological damage or upset the wildlife population (see pp.596–601 of Basics for advice).

Some history

Yosemite Valley was created over thousands of years by glaciers gouging through and enlarging the canyon of the Merced River; the ice scraped away much of the softer portions of granite but only scarred the harder sections, which became the present cliffs. As the glaciers melted a lake formed, filling the valley, and eventually silting up to create the present valley floor.

The Awahneechee people occupied the area quite peaceably for some 4000 years until the mid-nineteenth century, when the increasingly threatening presence of white Gold Rush settlers in the Central Valley led the tribes here to launch raiding parties to the nearest encampments. In 1851 Major James Savage led a force, the Mariposa Battalion, in pursuit of the Native Americans, trailing them into the foothills and beyond, and becoming the first white men to set foot in Yosemite Valley. It wasn't long before the two groups clashed properly, and the original population was moved out to white settlements to make way for farmers, foresters and, soon after, tourists (the first group of sightseers arriving in 1855). Moves were quickly afoot to conserve the natural beauty of the area: in 1864 Yosemite Valley and Mariposa Grove were preserved as

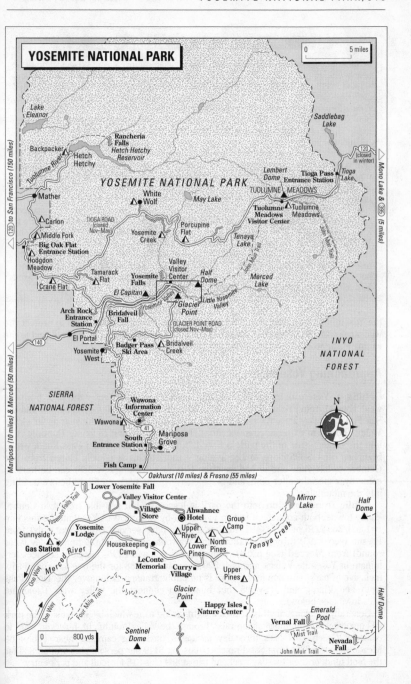

YOSEMITE NATIONAL PARK

0   5 miles

Lake Eleanor

Saddlebag Lake

Backpacker

Rancheria Falls

Hetch Hetchy

Hetch Hetchy Reservoir

120 (closed in winter)

Tuolumne River

120 to San Francisco (150 miles)

Mono Lake & 395 (5 miles)

YOSEMITE NATIONAL PARK

Mather

White Wolf

May Lake

Lembert Dome

Tioga Pass Entrance Station

Tioga Lake

TUOLUMNE MEADOWS

Carlon

Middle Fork

Tuolumne Meadows Visitor Center

Tuolumne Meadows

Big Oak Flat Entrance Station

TIOGA ROAD (closed Nov–May)

Porcupine Flat

Hodgdon Meadow

Yosemite Creek

Tenaya Lake

John Muir Trail

Tamarack Flat

Crane Flat

Yosemite Falls

Valley Visitor Center

Half Dome

Merced Lake

El Capitan

Yosemite Valley

Glacier Point

Little Yosemite Valley

Arch Rock Entrance Station

Bridalveil Fall

GLACIER POINT ROAD (closed Nov–May)

El Portal

140

Yosemite West

Badger Pass Ski Area

Bridalveil Creek

INYO NATIONAL FOREST

SIERRA NATIONAL FOREST

Wawona Information Center

Wawona

41

Mariposa Grove

N

South Entrance Station

Mariposa (10 miles) & Merced (50 miles)

Fish Camp

▽Oakhurst (10 miles) & Fresno (55 miles)

Lower Yosemite Fall

Yosemite Falls Trail

Valley Visitor Center

Mirror Lake

Half Dome

Village Store

Ahwahnee Hotel

Group Camp

Sunnyside

Yosemite Lodge

Gas Station

Upper River

North Pines

Tenaya Creek

Housekeeping Camp

Lower Pines

Merced River

One Way

LeConte Memorial

Curry Village

Upper Pines

One Way

Four Mile Trail

Glacier Point

Happy Isles Nature Center

Emerald Pool

Vernal Fall

Half Dome

Sentinel Dome

Mist Trail

Nevada Fall

John Muir Trail

0   800 yds

JOHN MUIR AND THE SIERRA CLUB

Scottish immigrant **John Muir** worked as a mechanical inventor in Wisconsin until he nearly lost an eye in an accident. Discouraged, he set off in search of adventure and walked, via the Gulf of Mexico, to San Francisco. Arriving in 1868, he immediately asked directions for "anywhere that's wild" and began months of camping and exploration, reputedly carrying no more than a notebook, a tin cup and a supply of tea. His diary was published a year later as *My First Summer in the Sierra* and was an instant hit, becoming a classic of American geographical writing.

Muir was so taken with the Sierra, and Yosemite in particular, that he made it his home. Over the years, appalled by the destruction he saw taking place around him, he campaigned for the preservation of the Sierra Nevada range, and is credited with having prompted Congress to create Yosemite National Park in 1890. In 1892, he set up the **Sierra Club**, an organization whose motto – "take only photographs; leave only footprints" – has become a model for like-minded groups around the world.

In 1913, the construction of the Hetch Hetchy dam (see p.327) in the northern reaches of Yosemite to provide water for San Francisco was a setback in the struggle to keep Yosemite free of development (many think the struggle to prevent it led to John Muir's death the following year), but the publicity actually aided the formation of the present National Park Service in 1916, which promised – and has since provided – greater protection. Muir's name crops up throughout California in memorials to his inspiration, not least in the 212-mile John Muir Trail which twists through his favorite scenery from Yosemite Valley south to Mount Whitney.

the Yosemite Land Grant, the nation's first region specifically set aside to protect the wilderness. In 1890 it became America's third National Park, thanks in great part to the campaigning work of Scottish naturalist John Muir (see box).

Approaching Yosemite

Getting to Yosemite by car is straightforward. Three roads enter the park from the west: Hwy-41 from Fresno, Hwy-140 from Merced and Hwy-120 from Stockton and the San Francisco Bay area. All are generally kept open throughout the year as far as the Valley, though in extreme circumstances Hwy-140 is the first to close. The only road into the eastern side of the park is Hwy-120, the 10,000-foot Tioga Pass Road, which branches off US-395 close to Lee Vining – though this is usually closed from late October to late June and in bad weather. **Gas** (see "Listings", p.328) can be hard to come by, especially after 6pm, and is expensive in the park, so fill up before heading into the mountains.

Public transportation into the park is less easy, but possible from two Central Valley towns, both connected to San Francisco by Amtrak. VIA Yosemite Connection (☎1-800/369-7275 or 209/384-1315) has a twice daily service (April–Sept only) from Fresno (see p.293) through Oakhurst and Wawona, and runs three times a day (year round) from **Merced** (see p.294) through Mariposa and El Portal. Both services terminate in Yosemite Village and cost $20 one-way and $38 for the one-day round-trip, inclusive of park entrance fees. There is no public transportation over the Tioga Pass from Lee Vining and Hwy-395, but buses do connect the valley with Tuolumne Meadows (see below).

Generally speaking, anything called a **sightseeing tour** which begins outside the park will involve you in an unsatisfying race through the Valley. You might, however, want to consider Green Tortoise's three-day packages (including camping near Tuolumne Meadows; see p.325) from San Francisco, costing $119 per person, plus around $30 for the food fund, or their two-day weekend trip at $69 plus $16 for food and park entry.

The hinterland towns

The heavy demand for accommodation within the park drives many to consider staying in one of the small, mostly former gold-mining towns along the main access roads. These are increasingly gearing themselves to park-bound tourists and do a reasonable job offering both lodging and food, though they are a poor substitute for actually staying in the park.

If approaching from the east and US-395 you could stop at **Lee Vining** (see p.280) and visit Tuolumne Meadows from there, but you are a long way from the Yosemite Valley heartland. Better bets are the eastern towns, particularly tiny **Groveland**, forty miles from the Valley on Hwy-120, which retains verandahed wooden sidewalks and exudes a liberal air.

Further south, Hwy-140 runs through bustling **MARIPOSA**, 45 miles from the Valley, another former gold town which celebrates its heritage in the **History Center and Museum**, corner of Jesse and 12th streets (March–Oct daily 10am–4.30pm; Feb, Nov & Dec Sat & Sun 10am–4pm; donations welcome), mildly diverting for its mock-up of a gold-era store and the large-scale mining paraphernalia scattered outside. In truth, you're better off at the **California State Mining and Mineral Museum**, two miles south on Hwy-49 (May–Sept daily except Tues 10am–6pm; Oct–April Wed–Sun 10am–4pm; $3.50), which revels in the glory days of the mid-nineteenth century with realistic reconstructions of a mine and stamp mill plus a vault where, among the assorted treasures, lies the largest single nugget ever uncovered in California, a thirteen-pound chunk valued at over $1 million. There's a useful **visitor center** at 5158 Hwy-140 (mid-May to mid-Sept Mon–Sat 8am–9pm, Sun 10am–6pm; mid-Sept to mid-May Mon–Sat 8am–5pm; ☎1-800/208-2434 or 209/966-2456, fax 966-6168) with all you need to know about Yosemite and around.

Yosemite visitors arriving from the south will come through **Oakhurst**, fifteen miles south of the southern park entrance and fifty miles south of the Valley proper, a growing huddle of malls and sky-high signs for chain hotels and fast food joints. Nonetheless, it makes a handy base for the southern section of the park, and, with your own transportation, day-trips into the Valley are by no means out of the question. Make use of the **Southern Yosemite Sierra Visitors Bureau**, 41729 Hwy-41, two miles north of Oakhurst (Mon–Sat 9am–5pm, Sun 9am–4pm; ☎209/683-4636, fax 683-5697) which, as well as armloads of bumf on Yosemite, stocks the misleadingly titled Yosemite Sierra Visitor's Guide, concentrating on Bass Lake and environs (see p.310). The tiny huddle of hotels which makes up **Fish Camp** lies ten miles north of Oakhurst, handy for Wawona, the Mariposa Grove and something to keep the kids quiet – The Logger, 56001 Hwy-41 (☎209/683-7273; $10), an oil-burning train which plys a two-mile track into the forest from where hewn timber was once carted. In the height of summer several trains run each day, giving you the option of spending some time at the picnic area in the woods at the far end.

Arrival and information

Yosemite is always open: **park entry** costs $20 per vehicle including passengers, $10 for each cyclist, hiker or bus passenger, and is valid for seven days. Pay at the ranger stations when you enter, or if they're closed, at the visitor center in the valley, or when you leave. If you're just passing through and over the Tioga Pass, there's a $5 transit ticket allowing a two-hour passage (three hours from the South Entrance).

On arrival at any of the park entrances you'll be given an excellent map of the park and the pertinent, quarterly *Yosemite Guide* which covers pretty much everything you need to know. If you have more specific enquiries, try the park's most useful **visitor center** at **Yosemite Village** (daily: mid-June to early Sept 8am–7pm; early Sept to May

WINTER IN YOSEMITE

From December to April, those prepared to cope with blocked roads – the Tioga Pass is always closed in winter – and below-freezing temperatures are amply rewarded at Yosemite – thick snow, frozen waterfalls and far fewer people make for almost unimaginable beauty and silence. **Accommodation** is cheaper at these times too, and much easier to obtain, though weekends can still get pretty full. Many low-country **campgrounds** are open, and restrictions on backcountry camping are eased – you'll want a good sleeping bag and tent.

Much of Yosemite is fabulous **skiing** country. Lessons, equipment rental and forty-five miles of groomed trails are available at the **Badger Pass Ski Area**, on the road to Glacier Point, accessible via free shuttle from the Valley. All-day lift tickets cost $28 at weekends and $22 midweek. Daily equipment rental will set you back $18 for downhill, $15 for cross-country and $30 for snowboards; lessons start from $40. There are also various special deals offered from Sunday through Thursday between January and March when guests at *Yosemite Lodge*, *The Ahwahnee* and the *Wawona Hotel* get a **free ski pass** for the following day. This deal also gives you free entry to the open-air Curry Village **ice skating** rink (normally $5, plus $2 skate rental).

If you want someone to take you out on Badger Pass's groomed trails, contact Yosemite Cross Country Ski School (☎209/372-8444) who run all manner of beginners, improvers, Telemark and skating lessons, and lead overnight ski tours.

Be aware if driving into the park that chains are recommended from November to April and can be rented in towns approaching the park. Inside the park they are only available for sale.

9am–5pm; ☎209/372-0299), where you can pick up information and maps, including a topographic map ($6), essential for any adventurous walks. There are other visitor centers at **Tuolumne Meadows** (July to mid-Oct daily 8am–7pm; ☎209/372-0263), at the **Big Oak Flat** entrance (July–Sept daily 8am–6pm), and **Wawona** (all year daily 8am–5pm). For **free** hiking permits, the *Keep it Wild* guide to planning wilderness trips, and all the route planning help you could ask for, pop next door to the **Wilderness Center** (mid-June to early Sept Sun–Fri 7.30am–7.30pm, Sat 6.30am–7.30pm; early Sept to Oct daily 8am–5pm): wilderness permits are self-issued once the Wilderness Center closes.

Useful **phone numbers** and **Web sites** are covered in the box opposite, and all manner of other services are including in the Listings (see p.328).

Getting around

The three roads from the Central Valley end up at **Yosemite Valley**, roughly in the center of the park's 1200 square miles, and featuring its most dramatic scenery. At the southern edge of the park Hwy-41 passes the **Mariposa Grove** and **Wawona**; from here it's 27 miles further to the Valley. **Tuolumne Meadows** is in the high country, sixty-odd miles northeast of the Valley, close to the Tioga Pass entrance (Hwy-120) on the eastern side of the park.

Free and frequent **shuttle buses** operate on the valley floor, running anticlockwise on a loop that passes through, or close to, all the main points of interest, trailheads and accommodation areas. In high season they run every twenty minutes between 7am and 10pm to most sections of the Valley, with slightly reduced hours at other times. The summer-only **Tuolumne Bus** makes the two-and-a-half hour run to Tuolumne Meadows ($10 one-way), leaving Yosemite at 9.15am and departing Tuolumne at 2.45pm. There's also a **hikers' bus** running up to Glacier Point three times daily through the summer ($10 one-way; ☎209/372-1240), and as far as the Badger Point ski area in winter.

   Cars spoil everybody's fun on the valley floor; if you're driving in just for the day, leave your vehicle in the day-use parking lot at Curry Village. In any case, **cycling** is the best way to get around: a number of good bicycle paths cross the valley floor, but bike rental is limited to the outlets at *Yosemite Lodge* and *Curry Village* (April–Nov only) which charge $5 per hour or $20 per day. Bikes are basic machines but since cycling is only allowed on asphalt surfaces, that's all you need: leave your mountain bike at home.

   Failing that, there are always **guided tours** (☎209/372-1240), which range from the rather dull two-hour valley floor spin, costing $17, to the all-day Mariposa and Glacier Point Grand Tour (June–Nov) at $45; all bookable from accommodation reception areas.

Accommodation

Once in the park, **accommodation** can be a problem; it's almost essential to book well in advance, and anything other than camping can be surprisingly expensive. Even tents cost what you would pay for a reasonable motel elsewhere. All accommodation in the National Park – the majority of it right in the Valley – is operated by **Yosemite Concession Services** (YCS; 5410 East Home, Fresno, CA 93727; ☎209/252-4848) and can be reserved up to a year and a day in advance, though a few weeks is adequate at most times. Places generally reduce their charges in winter, though weekend prices remain close to high season levels. One solution to the problem is to stay just outside the park (see "Approaching Yosemite" on p.314) and commute into it daily.

   If you are really well organized you might also want to consider the High Sierra vacations (see "Listings", p.328).

In the Valley

Ahwahnee Hotel, a short distance from Yosemite Village at shuttle stop 4. Unless you strike lucky, you'll need to book months in advance to stay in this wonderfully grand but surprisingly low-key hotel (see p.324), though it is well worth popping in for a look around, a coffee or a meal. ⑨.

Curry Village, a mile from Yosemite Village at shuttle stops 1 & 14. A large area dotted mostly with canvas tent cabins each fitted with four beds an a wooden plinth. There are also cramped solid-walled cabins and spacious motel-style rooms. Tents ③, cabins ④, rooms ⑤.

Housekeeping Camp, half a mile from Yosemite Village at shuttle stop 12. Ranks of simple canvas tent cabins with beds on sleeping platforms and the use of a fire grate and picnic table. Mid-March to late Oct only. ③.

Yosemite Lodge, half a mile west of Yosemite Village. Sprawling site popular with tour groups, its proximity to half-decent restaurants and grocery shops making it perhaps the most convenient accommodation in the valley. It has reasonable wooden huts with and without bath, and much nicer regular rooms, though all need to be booked well in advance for most of the year. ③.

USEFUL CONTACTS

Campground reservations
(from North America) ☎1-800/436-7275

Hotel reservations ☎209/252-4848

Other enquiries (daily 8am–4.30pm)
☎1-800/454-YOSE

Recorded general park information
☎209/372-0200

Road and weather information
☎209/372-0200

Web sites

Park Service Web site *www.nps.gov/yose*

Yosemite Association Web site with visitor information, a bookstore, weather forecast and video Valley tour
http://yosemite.org

Yosemite Fund Web site with details of current conservation projects in the park
www.connect.net/yosemite

ROCK-CLIMBING

Rock-climbers the world over flock to Yosemite, drawn by the challenge of inching up mile-high walls of sheer granite which soar skyward under the California sun. Quite simply, the Valley is seen as the pinnacle of climbing aspiration, the acres of superb, clean rock, easily accessible world-class routes and reliable summer weather drawing a vibrant climbing community bubbling over with campfire tales.

The best place to marvel at climbers' antics is **El Cap Meadows**, always dotted with tourists craning their necks and training binoculars on the biggest slab of granite of them all, El Capitan. The apparently featureless face hides hairline crack systems a thousand feet long, seemingly insurmountable overhangs and gargantuan towers topped with narrow ledges only given any sense of scale by the flea-like figures of climbers. If you can't spot them, look for their huge haul sacks; or come out here after dark, when the light from head torches and the faint, distant chatter give the game away.

The routes are highly convoluted, but the single most famous climb in the world, **The Nose** route of El Capitan, lies straight ahead, tracing a line up the prow of the cliff and passing the relative luxury of El Cap Towers. This twenty-foot by six-foot patio, over 1500 feet above the valley floor, is used as a bivvy spot by climbers who typically spend two or three nights on the route. "In-a-day" attempts usually involve 24 hours of continuous climbing, though the current record stands at an astounding four hours and twenty minutes. The famous **North American Wall** route lies to the right, passing directly through a massive stain on the rock which looks remarkably like a map of North America.

BATHOOKS AND BUGABOOS

Many of the most celebrated routes in Yosemite are what's known as "Big Wall" routes, tackled by **aid climbing**, where bits of metal are hammered into cracks and hauled on to acheive upward movement. The demands of ever harder climbs have pushed the development of an extensive armory that's totally baffling to the uninitiated: bathooks, birdbeaks, bongs, bugaboos, circleheads, fifi hooks, a funkness device, lost arrows and RURPs are all employed either to grapple a ledge or wedge into cracks of different sizes. The scale of Yosemite's walls is such that few cracks can be followed from top to bottom and to get from one crack to another, climbers set up death-defying **pendulums**, and repeatedly sweep across the face, gaining momentum until they can lunge out at a tiny flake or fingertip hold. All this nailing and swinging takes time and most Big Wallers are forced to spent nights slung in a kind of lightweight camp bed known as a **portaledge**. Food, gallons of water, sleeping bags, warm clothing and wet weather gear must all be lugged up in haul sacks, along with a boombox and a rack of cassettes deviously strapped and arranged so they can't be dropped – after all it can get a bit tedious hammering away up there for hours on end. As Yosemite veteran John Long writes: "Climbing a wall can be a monumental pain in the ass. No one could pay you enough to do it. A thousand dollars would be too little by far. But you wouldn't sell the least of the memories for ten times than sum".

SOME HISTORY

Yosemite has long captured the imagination of climbers, but technical rock-climbing didn't kick off here until 1933, when four Bay Area climbers reached what is now known as the Lunch Ledge, 1000 feet up Washington Column - the tower opposite Half Dome – using hemp ropes to afford meagre protection in case of a fall. With the aid of heavy steel **pitons** for driving into cracks, and equally weighty **carabiners** for attaching the ropes to the pitons, climbers began to knock off climbs such as the fifteen-pitch **Royal Arches** route which weaves its way up the ledges and slabs behind the *Ahwahnee Hotel*.

After World War II, demobbed climbers employed newly developed, tough nylon ropes and lightweight safety equipment to push standards to new levels, and pipe dreams became realistic propositions. An early conquest, in 1947, was **Lost Arrow Spire**, which rises to the right of Yosemite Falls and is easy to spot in the early morning and late afternoon light when the spire casts a shadow on the wall nearby. This was the first route intentionally approached as a multi-day ascent, much of the groundwork being laid by Swiss-born blacksmith **John Salathé**. He was at the cutting edge of climbing, putting up technically demanding aid routes through the late 1940s and early 1950s, and even fashioning his own tougher carbon-steel pitons from the axles of a Model A Ford.

For the next twenty years Salathé's mantle was assumed by classical purist **Royal Robbins** and **Warren Harding**, who was prepared to bang in a piton just about anywhere if it would help him get up something new. Little love was lost between them but, in 1957, they formed the backbone of a team which scaled the face of **Half Dome**, a magnificent effort which ranked as the hardest climb in North America at the time. Yosemite became an international forcing ground for aid climbing, and Americans were suddenly matching, and even surpassing, the achievements of previously dominant Europeans.

Now even the mighty El Cap seemed possible. **The Nose** was the most obvious line but refused to submit for seventeen months, even after Warren Harding fashioned four massive pitons from stove legs scavenged from the Berkeley city dump, and drove them into what are still known as the Stoveleg Cracks. Harding and two colleagues finally topped out in 1958 after a single thirteen-day push, the culmination of 47 days work on the route.

With these critical ascents completed, the 1960s became the **Golden Age** of climbing in the Yosemite Valley, when it drew a motley collection of dropouts and misfits, many ranking among the world's finest climbers. Almost all the major walls and hundreds of minor routes were completed at this time, as Yosemite led the world. Purists at the top of their sport became disenchanted with the artificiality of aid ascents and began to "free" pitches. The culmination of years of cutting edge climbing, and months of route-specific training was Lynn Hill's free ascent of The Nose in 1993, praised and admired by all, if ruefully by some, in Yosemite's traditionally macho climbing community.

PRACTICALITIES

The **best months** for climbing in the Yosemite Valley are April, May, September and October. In summer, the climbs on the domes around Tuolumne Meadows are cooler and usually considered a better bet. Some areas, notably the southeast face of El Capitan, are occasionally off limits to protect the nesting sites of peregrine falcons. Whatever type of climbing you do, follow the guidelines for **"minimum impact climbing"** – never chip holds or add bolts to existing routes, and remove all litter, including human waste.

Everyone stays at the bohemian **Camp 4** (aka *Sunnyside Walk-In* campground), near *Yosemite Lodge*, a trampled, dusty and often noisy site often entirely taken over by climbers. It is relatively cheap, with a great sense of camaraderie, and an excellent **bulletin board** for teaming up with climbing partners, selling gear, organizing a ride or just meeting friends. Normally you can only stay for seven nights at a stretch, but after the end of September you're allowed to settle in for a month.

For a more organized introduction to the climber's craft or to brush up on a few skills, engage the services of the **Yosemite Mountaineering School** which is based at Tuolumne Meadows in summer (June–August, ☎209/372-8435) and in Yosemite Valley in spring and autumn (☎209/372-8444). Experts run daily courses ranging from the one-day beginners' classes ($80–100) through various intermediate classes to private full-day guided climbs (one person $220, two people $155 each). Rock-climbing **gear** is available from the Mountain Shop in Tuolumne Meadows (summer only), and the well-stocked and competitively-priced Mountain Shop, Curry Village (daily 8am-6pm).

The essential guide **books** to local climbs are Don Reid's *Yosemite: Free Climbs* and *Yosemite: Big Walls*, published by Chockstone Press. To catch something of the spirit of the scene read *Camp 4: Recollections of a Yosemite Rockclimber* (The Mountaineers) by Yosemite veteran Steve Roper, and *The Vertical World of Yosemite* (Wilderness Press), a collection of inspiring stories on the Valley, both available in the Ansel Adams Gallery. You can also get a sense of what it is all about by checking out the rock-climbing **exhibition** in the *Ahwahnee Hotel* Cocktail Bar and the additional displays in the Winter Club Room and the Indian Room, both off the Great Hall.

The rest of the park

Tuolumne Meadows Lodge, Tuolumne Meadows. A large cluster of canvas tent cabins each with four beds and a stove but no electricity, located at nearly 9000ft and perfect for the first or last night of a long hiking trip. Only available late April to October; meals served. ③.

Wawona Hotel, Wawona. An elegant hotel, parts of which date from 1879. Rooms are comfortable though smallish and over-modernized, but the marvellous public areas and distinctive wooden verandah with white wicker chairs make it all worthwhile. There's a pool, tennis courts and a nine-hole golf course in the grounds. Worth a splurge if you can afford it. ④.

White Wolf Lodge, about halfway from the Valley to Tuolumne Meadows. Four cabins with bath and several primitive tent cabins perfectly sited for day hikes to Lukens and Harden Lakes, and the Grand Canyon of the Tuolumne River. Cabins ④, tents ③.

Hwy-120: Groveland

Groveland Hotel, 18767 Hwy-120, Groveland (☎1-800/273-3314 or 209/962-4000, fax 962-6674). Gorgeous mining-era hotel with luxurious individually-styled antique-filled rooms mostly with deep baths. Suites (⑧) feature spa tubs and real fires. ⑥.

Groveland Motel, 18933 Hwy-120, Groveland (☎209/962-7865). Woodsy air-conditioned cabins with TV at what for these parts are bargain rates. ④.

CAMPING IN YOSEMITE

As with any National Park, **camping** is the best way to really feel part of your surroundings, though this is perhaps less true in Yosemite Valley where the campgrounds are large and crowded. You can, and should, book beforehand (Parknet ☎1-800/444-7275; from outside the US or Canada ☎619/452-8787): reservations open in one month chunks, four months in advance, so to book for the month beginning July 15 you can, and should, call from March 15 (after 7am Pacific time). Otherwise you'll need to show up at the Curry Village Reservations Office very early in the morning and hope for cancellations. Other than the *Sunnyside Walk-In*, all sites cost $15 and none have **showers** or **laundry** facilities (see Listings, p.328). Camping in the Valley is restricted to a month in any calendar year, but between May and mid-September a week is the maximum stay.

In addition to the main campgrounds there are **backpacker campgrounds** in Yosemite Valley, Tuolumne Meadows and Hetch Hetchy, designed for hikers and cyclists and costing $3 per night. People with vehicles who are planning a wilderness trip can stay at these sites for one night at the beginning and end of the trip. Camping outside recognized sites in the Valley is strictly forbidden.

Finally, with enough time you really should get out to one of the many **primitive campgrounds** in the backcountry. Designed specifically for hikers, these have fire rings and some form of water source, which must be treated. To use them, or to camp elsewhere in the backcountry, you must get a **wilderness permit** (see "Hiking" box, p.327) – as ever, you must camp a mile from any road, four miles from a populated area, and at least a hundred yards from water sources and trails. Remember to carry a stove and fuel, as indiscriminate use of trees could jeopardize future freedom to camp in the backcountry. Camping on the summit of Half Dome is not permitted.

IN THE VALLEY

North Pines, **Upper Pines**, **Lower Pines** (April–Oct, *Upper Pines* April–Nov; $15; 4000ft). Largely indistinguishable, pine-shrouded sites, all with toilets, water and fire rings. Popular with RV users. Reservations essential.

Sunnyside Walk-In (all year; $3 per person; 4000ft). West of and away from the other Valley sites, and very popular with rock-climbers who know it as Camp 4. Each plot is just a few yards from the inadequate parking spaces. The campground is non-reservable and often full by 9am in summer, so join the line early.

Yosemite Lakes Resort, 31191 Hwy-120, eighteen miles east of Groveland (☎1-800/533-1001 or 209/962-0121). Combined hostel (with limited self-catering facilities), campground and RV site in the middle of nowhere. Simple double rooms (①), cabins (②) and four-berth tent-cabins equipped with satellite TV (④) are scattered around among the $16 tent sites. Not especially appealing but close to the park.

Hwy-140: Mariposa and Midpines

5th Street Inn, corner of Fifth and Bullion streets, Mariposa (☎1-800/567-8584 or 209/966-6048). Luxurious B&B with a nice sunny verandah and air-conditioned rooms all equipped with cable TV, and some with a kitchenette. ④.

Mariposa Lodge, 5052 Hwy-140, Mariposa (☎1-800/341-8000 or 209/966-3607, fax 742-7038). Good value motel right on Mariposa's main street with outdoor pool, spa and spacious rooms equipped with coffee filters, HBO and VCRs. ④.

Sierra View Motel, 4993 Seventh St, Mariposa (☎1-800/627-8439 or 209/966-5793, fax 742-5669). Peaceful, welcoming and good value motel just off Mariposa's main drag offering continental breakfast with smallish air-conditioned rooms and larger suites. Both ④.

Yosemite Bug Hostel, 6979 Hwy-140, Midpines, ten miles east of Mariposa (☎209/966-6666, fax 966-6667). Numerous buildings scattered through the woods operate as a HI-AYH hostel without the usual limitations. Individually-decorated rooms come with kitsch artwork, dorms ($12 each) are

---

OUTSIDE THE VALLEY

Bridalveil Creek (June–Sept; $10; 7200ft). High country first-come-first-served site off Glacier Point Road, with good access to wilderness trails.

Carlon (April–Nov; free; 4400ft). Just outside the park boundary in the surrounding Stanislaus National Forest; spacious sites with vault toilets but no water. Take Evergreen Road north for a mile and a half.

Crane Flat (June–Oct; $15; 6200ft). Northwest of the Valley, at the start of Hwy-120 and close to a stand of sequoias. Reservations required.

Hodgdon Meadow (all year; $15; 4900ft). Relatively quiet site right on the park's western boundary just off Hwy-120. Take Old Big Oak Flat Road for half a mile. Reservations required May–Oct, first-come-first-served at other times.

Middle Fork (all year; free; 4300ft). Half a mile south of and similar to the *Carlon* site.

Porcupine Flat (June–early Sept; $6; 8100ft). Attractive and small RV-free site near the road to Tuolumne Meadows, nearly forty miles from the Valley. Stream water.

Tamarack Flat (June–early Sept; $6; 6300ft). Small site two miles off the Hwy-120 Tioga road, 23 miles from the Valley and with only limited RV access. Stream water.

Tuolumne Meadows (mid-June–Sept; $15; 8600ft). A streamside site in a sub-alpine meadow. It's popular with backpackers and car-campers alike, but you'll probably find a place. Several walk-in sites are reserved for hikers who wish to camp away from vehicles. Showers ($2) are available nearby.

Wawona (all year; $15; 4000ft). The only site in the southern sector of the park, approximately a mile or so north of the *Wawona Hotel*. Some walk-in sites are reserved for car-free campers. Reservations required May–Oct.

White Wolf (June–early Sept; $10; 8000ft). Tent and RV site a mile north of Hwy-120 midway between the Valley and Tuolumne Meadows.

Yosemite Creek (June to early Sept; $6; 7600ft). First-come-first-served tent-only site ideal for escaping the crowds, though it can fill up very quickly in the summer. Inconveniently sited five miles off Hwy-120, but almost equidistant between the Valley and Tuolumne Meadows. Stream water.

clean and comfortable, and there are on-site tents ($17 for two) ground to pitch your own ($12 per tent), and private rooms (②). As well as self-catering facilities there's the licensed *Recovery Café* (see "Eating" opposite) with low-cost Internet access. Its location, thirty-five miles west of the Valley and well placed on the VIA Yosemite Connection bus route from Merced, makes it the handiest budget lodgings near Yosemite, and in summer they even organize a shuttle from the San Francisco hostels ($20 each way).

Yosemite View Lodge, 11136 Hwy-140, one mile east of El Portal (☎1-800/321 5261 or 209/379-2681, fax 379-2704). Vast, luxurious and slightly soulless complex beside the Merced River featuring rooms, all with kitchenettes and some with riverside balconies and whirlpool baths. This is about as close to the park as you can get without being in it. ⑤.

Hwy-41: Oakhurst and Fish Camp

Hounds Tooth Inn, 42071 Hwy-41, almost three miles north of Oakhurst (☎209/642-6600, fax 658-2946). Brand new and luxurious bed and breakfast with a dozen individually-decorated rooms most with either a fireplace or a spa bath and all air-conditioned. Complimentary wine served each evening and there are delicious buffet breakfasts. ④.

Ramada, 48800 Royal Oaks Drive, Oakhurst (☎1-800/658-2888 or 209/658-5500, fax 658-5505). Brand new and slightly soulless chain hotel but with large airy rooms, cable TV, outdoor pool and spa, and a complimentary breakfast. ⑤.

Tenaya Lodge, 1122 Hwy-41, Fish Camp (☎1-800/635-5807 or 209/683-6555, fax 683-8684). Extensive establishment that's a cross between a conference hotel and a holiday camp with over two hundred modern comfortable rooms, three on-site restaurants open to all-comers, including a good deli and coffee shop, indoor and outdoor pools, free sauna, hot tubs and gym, and all sorts of outdoor activities like mountain biking, horse riding and guided hiking. ⑧.

Owl's Nest B&B, 1235 Hwy-41, Fish Camp (☎209/683-3484). About the best deal on the southern side of the park, with guest rooms for two (④) and self-contained cabins (⑥) which will sleep up to eight ($15 per extra person). Nicely decorated, friendly and right by a stream.

Snowline Lodge, 42150 Hwy-140, three miles north of Oakhurst (☎209/683-5854). Small, cozy cabins with bathrooms and TV, plus an outdoor pool. Great value. ③.

White Chief Mountain Lodge, 7776 White Chief Mountain Rd, Fish Camp (☎209/683-5444). Basic and functional motel units for two (④) and nicer cabins for up to four (⑥). Just 300yd off Hwy-41. Closed in winter.

Yosemite Fish Camp B&B, Hwy-140, Fish Camp (☎209/683-7426). Attractive and homey B&B with a couple of bargain rooms sharing a bathroom (③) and one bathroom-equipped room. Continental breakfast is served. ④.

Eating, drinking and entertainment

With the notable exception of the *Ahwahnee Dining Room* (see opposite), **eating** in Yosemite is a function rather than a pleasure. Food, whether in restaurants or in the grocery stores around Yosemite Village (where there's a well-stocked supermarket), Curry Village, Wawona and Tuolumne Meadows, is much more expensive inside the park than out. **Outside the Valley** the choice is considerably better with plenty of good restaurants and a smattering of bars in the gateway towns of Groveland, Mariposa and Oakhurst.

Yosemite Village is the center of the park's **evening entertainment**, in the form of talks, photographic shows and even theatrical productions. The *Yosemite Guide* has the full program (and see "Listings" on p.328). *Yosemite Lodge* and the *Ahwahnee Hotel* have the valley's liveliest **bars**.

In the valley

Awahnee Cocktail Lounge, *Awahnee Hotel* (noon–10.30pm). Inappropriately-named but a real find, this admirable café and bar serves good coffee, beer and the likes of chicken *quesedilla* and chocolate espresso torte in dark wood and stone surroundings at much the same prices you pay elsewhere in the park for inferior goods.

Ahwahnee Dining Room, *Awahnee Hotel* (☎209/372-1489; reserve well in advance). Quite simply one of the most beautiful restaurants in the US, in baronial style and serving by far the best food in Yosemite – especially in winter when it brings in top chefs for weekend gourmandizing. À la carte dining on say crab and avocado cocktail followed by roast duckling, costs around $50 for three courses with wine. Jacket and tie preferred though not essential; breakfast and lunch are more casual and appreciably cheaper.

Curry Village. The cafeteria serves reasonable breakfasts and sandwiches, tolerable pizza is served up on the terrace and there's a bar with TV lounge.

Degnan's Deli, Yosemite Village (daily 7am–10pm). Some of the best snacking in the Valley with massive sandwiches, burritos and salads at under $5; or go upstairs to the *Pasta Place*, where you can fill up with salad, pasta and a drink for around $10.

Yosemite Lodge, Yosemite Village. Casual dining in the *Garden Terrace* where an $8 pasta and salad bar operates from noon to 9pm with meat from the carvery an extra $4. There's also the fairly pricey, evening-only à la carte *Mountain Room Restaurant*, which serves grilled trout and rack of lamb for around $20, a downbeat cafeteria and a lively bar.

The rest of the park

Tuolumne Meadows Lodge, Tuolumne Meadows (☎209/372-1313). Family-style breakfasts and dinners at moderate prices served in tents beside the Tuolumne River.

Wawona Hotel Dining Room at the *Wawona Hotel* (☎209/375-6556). Relatively formal dining in a grand room with white linen tablecloths. Expect to fork out $40 for an evening meal of smoked trout or roast corn chowder followed by ribeye steak. The buffet lunch goes for $8.

White Wolf Lodge, Just off Hwy-120 on the way to Tuolumne (☎209/252-4848). Large portions of good value American food in rustic surroundings.

Hwy-120: Groveland

Cocina Michoacana, 13955 Hwy-120. Excellent, authentic and low-priced Mexican specializing in dishes from immediately west of Mexico City.

Groveland Hotel, 18767 Hwy-120, (☎1-800/273-3314). Lovely restaurant in keeping with the rest of the hotel serving the likes of crab cakes with *cilantro* and caper sauce, and poached salmon. Expect to pay $40–50 for three courses.

PJ's Café, 18986 Hwy-120. Good-value diner serving burgers and sandwiches all day and pizza from 4pm.

Hwy-140:Mariposa, Midpines and El Portal

Castillo's, 4995 Fifth Street, Mariposa. Small Mexican restaurant offering a cozy atmosphere with good portions of decent home-cooked meals at around $10, fajitas for around $12 and juicy steaks for a little more.

Meadows Ranch Café, 5027 Hwy-140, Mariposa. Excellent all-day combination of family restaurant (delectable sandwiches, burgers and grills), juice bar and café, with a bakery and a very good microbrewery.

Parkline Restaurant, 11174 Hwy-140, El Portal. Hotel restaurant close to the park entrance serving hearty dinners for under $20 and some of the best vegetarian lasagne ever.

Recovery Café, at Yosemite Bug Hostel, Midpines. Superb value and wholesome breakfasts and dinners served to all-comers, not just hostel guests.

Hwy-41: Oakhurst and Fish Camp

Castillo's, 49271 Golden Oak Loop, Oakhurst. Larger sister restaurant to the Mariposa establishment and equally good.

El Cid, 41939 Hwy-41. Reasonable Tex-Mex belly-filler with a strong line in frosty margaritas.

The Narrow Gauge Inn, 48571 Hwy-41, Fish Camp (☎209/683-6446). Fine dining in an olde worlde setting where you can start by dipping sourdough into a rich fondue and continue with charbroiled swordfish or filet mignon. Expect to pay $40–50 each, more with wine.

Yosemite Coffee Roasting Company, 40879 Hwy-41, a mile north of Oakhurst. Local java joint with toothsome muffins, sandwiches and cakes.

Yosemite Valley

Even the most evocative photography can only hint at the pleasure to be found in simply gazing at **Yosemite Valley**. From massive hunks of granite rising five thousand feet up from the four-thousand-foot valley floor to the subtle colorings of wildflowers, the variations in the valley can be both enormous and discreet. Aside from just looking, there are many easy walks around the lush fields to waterfalls and lakes, and much tougher treks up the enormous cliffs (see box, p.327). Whichever way you decide to see it, the valley's concentration of natural grandeur is quite memorable. If there is any drawback, it's that this part of Yosemite is the busiest, and you're rarely far from other visitors or the park's commercial trappings: a couple of days exploring the Valley leaves you more than ready to press on to the park's less populated regions.

Yosemite Village

Very much the heart of things in the Valley, **YOSEMITE VILLAGE** has shops, restaurants, banking facilities, a post office (see "Listings" for the last two) and one of the park's **visitor centers** (see pp.315–316). Beside the visitor center, the small but interesting **Indian Cultural Museum** (daily: June–Aug 8am–5.30pm; Sept–May 8am–4.30pm; free), comprises a roomful of artifacts from the local Native Americans (including some very fine basketwork) and, outside, a self-guided trail around a reconstructed group of their buildings. There's something of the more recent past to be found in the nearby **cemetery**, which holds the unkempt graves of some of the early white settlers who attempted to farm the valley, and often perished in its isolation. By contrast, and worth a quick look even if you don't intend to stay or eat there (if you do, see p.317 and p.323), is the **Ahwahnee Hotel**, a short signposted walk from Yosemite Village. It was built in grand style in 1927 from local rock, and is decorated with Native American motifs and some wonderful rugs and carpets. It was intended to blend into its surroundings and attract the richer type of tourist and still does both fairly effortlessly – pop in for a few minutes to sink into the deep sofas, view the collection of paintings of Yosemite's early days, or browse the rock-climbing and skiing exhibitions in the Cocktail Bar and the Winter Club Room off the Great Hall.

The Valley floor

There's little around the village to divert attention from Yosemite's beckoning natural features for long. It's true that you'll never be alone on the valley floor, but most of the crowds can easily be left behind. The more strenuous hikes are detailed in the box on p.327.

One of the more popular easy strolls is to **Lower Yosemite Falls** (shuttle bus stop 7) just a few minutes' walk from *Yosemite Lodge*, at the western end of the Valley. Come towards the end of summer and the falls disappear altogether, but in spring ice-cold meltwater thunders down three hundred feet, drenching onlookers in spray. If this inspires you, consider the walk to the far more impressive **Upper Yosemite Falls**, which crash down almost 1500ft in a single cascade. Together with the cataracts in between, the two drop the Yosemite River two thousand five hundred feet, constituting the highest fall in North America.

Three other waterfalls can be easily reached from the Valley. One of the more sensual is the 600-foot **Bridalveil Falls**, a slender ribbon at the Valley's western end which in Ahwahneechee goes by the name of *Pohono*, "spirit of the puffing wind". The base of the falls is at the end of a quarter-mile trail from a parking lot four miles west of the village and is not on the shuttle route. More rugged routes head up Little Yosemite Valley to the 300-foot **Vernal Falls** and the 600-foot **Nevada Falls** beyond – the only two cascades guaranteed to be still active in September and October.

Joshua Tree National Monument

Carmel

Grand Canyon

The ghost town of Bodie

Death Valley

Sequoia National Forest

Blue Jay, Yosemite National Park

Sequoia trunks

Yosemite Valley

Neptune Pool, Hearst Castle

Cannery Row, Monterey

Big Sur

Perhaps one of the most rewarding of the easy trails leads from shuttle stop 17 around the edge of the valley floor to **Mirror Lake** (2 miles; 1hr; 100ft ascent). This compellingly calm lake lies beneath the great bulk of Half Dome (see below), the rising cliff reflected on the lake's surface, and is best seen in the early morning, before too many others arrive. The lake is a microcosm of the whole Yosemite Valley, its meditative stillness due in part to the fact that it's slowly silting up as the valley floor has done since the last Ice Age: already the lake dries up by summer's end but re-emerges each spring. From Mirror Lake, trails continue around the lake (1 mile), to Tenaya Lake (11 miles) and to Tuolumne Meadows (21 miles). Most visitors to Mirror Lake follow the traffic-free paved road from the shuttle stop, but several easily found diversions steer you clear of the asphalt and the crowds.

The big cliffs: El Capitan and Half Dome

Of the two major peaks that you can see from the valley, **El Capitan**, rising some 3600ft above the floor, is the biggest piece of exposed granite in the world. Though undoubtedly a domineering presence, its enormous size isn't really apparent until you join the slack-jawed tourists craning their necks and pointing binoculars and cameras at rock-climbers on the face. Eventually you'll pick out flea-sized specks inching up what is the holy grail of rock-climbing worldwide (see box on pp.318–19)

Much the same applies to **Half Dome**, the sheerest cliff in North America, only seven degrees off the vertical and topping out at 8842 feet, almost 5000 feet above the valley floor. A true sense of its bulk, and the amazingly sheer face, is best appreciated from Glacier Point (see below) but better still, you can hike to its top from the far end of Little Yosemite Valley. The final 400 feet of ascent is by way of a steel staircase hooked on to its curving whale back which leaves you at the nearly-flat summit, where the brave or foolish can inch out along a finger of rock projecting out from the lip. The steps and cable supports stay in place throughout the summer (May to mid-Oct) and the cables remain all year, making a winter ascent difficult but possible.

Views of the valley: Glacier Point

The most spectacular views of Yosemite Valley are from **Glacier Point**, the top of a 3200-foot almost sheer cliff, 32 miles by road (usually open mid-May to late Oct) from the Valley. It's possible to get there on foot using the very steep four-mile track (see the box on p.327) which begins at the western end of the valley, beside Hwy-41, though you can use the bus (see p.316) to go up and take the trail down. The valley floor lies directly beneath the viewing point, and there are tremendous views across to Half Dome (easy from here to see how it got its name) and to the distant snowcapped summits of the High Sierra. In winter, one of the best **cross-country ski** trips is the eight miles here from the Badger Pass ski area.

Outside the Valley

However crowded the Valley might be, the rest of the park sees very few tourists. Even places you can get to by car, like **Wawona** and **Mariposa Grove** on the park's southern edge, remain peaceful most of the time, and if you're willing to hike a few miles and camp out overnight, you've got the 99 percent of Yosemite that's untouched by road – acres of pristine scenery, especially around **Tuolumne Meadows** on the park's eastern border.

Tuolumne Meadows

On the eastern edge of the park, the alpine **Tuolumne Meadows** have an atmosphere quite different from the Valley. Here, at 8500ft, it is much more open; you almost seem to be level with the tops of the surrounding snow-covered mountains, and the air always has a fresh, crisp bite. That said, there can still be good-sized blasts of carbon monoxide at peak times in the vicinity of the campground and lodge – the only accommodation base in the area and within easy reach of the park's eastern entrance at Tioga Pass (Hwy-120). But it's a better starting point than the Valley for backcountry hiking into the High Sierra, where seven hundred-odd miles of trails, both long and short, crisscross their way along the Sierra Nevada ridge. Also, because the growing season is short so high up, early summer in Tuolumne reveals a plethora of colorful wild blossoms. If you haven't the time for a long hike from here, at least stroll the half-mile trail to the naturally carbonated **Soda Springs**, starting from the foot of the distinctive smooth granite of Lembert Dome.

Between July and mid-August, a bus links Tuolumne and Yosemite Valley ($10 each way; ☎209/372-1240), and a free shuttle service also links Tuolumne to Tenaya Lake (July to early Sept 7am–6pm). Alternatively, it's possible to hike between the two settlements using part of the **John Muir Trail**, a distance of roughly twenty miles from the Happy Isles trailhead. The Pacific Crest Trail, stretching from Mexico right up to Canada, also passes through Tuolumne, and there are innumerable other paths into the canyons and valleys in the area. One of the best hikes leads north and west through the Grand Canyon of the Tuolumne River; get the full details from the **visitor center** at the Tuolumne campground.

Hwy-120 from the valley to Tuolumne Meadows passes as a mile-long walking trail to the **Tuolumne Grove** of giant sequoias, nowhere near as spectacular as the Mariposa Grove (see below) but more convenient.

Note that vehicles are not allowed to stay overnight at Tioga Pass Road trailheads (including Tuolumne Meadows) after mid-October, even if the road is open, effectively ruling out overnight hikes in this region.

Wawona and the Mariposa Grove

Driving to Yosemite from Fresno, you'll probably pass through **WAWONA**, 27 miles west of the Valley on Hwy-41, whose landmark is the *Wawona Hotel* (see p.320), surrounded by a nine-hole golf course where $22 will get you a full eighteen-hole round (plus $9 for club rental, if needed), and tennis courts ($2.50 per hour). Close by, the **Pioneer Yosemite History Center** (mid-June to early Sept daily 9am–5pm; free) is a collection of buildings culled from the early times of white habitation. The jail, homesteads, covered bridge and the like are good for a scoot around, and, once you're away from the main road, the area makes a quiet spot for a picnic.

Mariposa Grove, three miles east of Hwy-41 on a small road which cuts off just past the park's southern entrance, is the biggest and best of Yosemite's groves of giant sequoia trees. To get to the towering growths, walk the two-and-a-half mile loop trail from the parking lot at the end of the road, which is also served by a tram from the entrance (9am–6pm; $8).

Trails around sequoia groves call first at the **Fallen Monarch**, familiar from the 1899 photo, widely reproduced on postcards, in which cavalry officers and their horses stand atop the prostrate tree. The most renowned of the grouping, well marked along the route, is the **Grizzly Giant**, thought to be 2700 years old and with a lower branch thicker than the trunk of any non-sequoia in the grove. Other highlights include the now-fallen **Wawona Tunnel Tree** through which people drove their cars until it fell in 1969, the similarly bored **California Tunnel Tree**, which you can walk through, and all manner of trees which have grown together, split apart, been struck by lightning, or are simply staggeringly large. It's also worth dropping into the **Mariposa Grove Museum** (daily 9am–5.30pm; free), towards the top end of the trail, which has modest displays and photos of the mighty trees. For more on the life of the sequoia, see p.599 of Contexts.

Hetch Hetchy

John Muir's passion for Yosemite Valley was matched, if not exceeded, by his desire to preserve the beauty of **Hetch Hetchy**, eighteen miles north of the Valley, five miles west of the Oak Flat Entrance. When it came under threat from power and water supply interests in San Francisco, he battled for 25 years, eventually losing in 1913 to a federal bill which paved the way for the Tuolumne River to be blocked by the O'Shaughnessey Dam, thereby creating the slender Hetch Hetchy reservoir. This drowned a valley which some claim rivalled Yosemite Valley for scenic splendor. It is certainly no match now, but the view of granite domes and waterfalls from the path which crosses the dam gives some sense of what it must have been like. It is barely worth the trip though, unless you plan on using the backpacker campground

---

HIKING IN YOSEMITE

To camp out overnight in most of Yosemite's designated wilderness you need a free **wilderness permit**. Popular trails – Merced River Trail up to Little Yosemite or Tuolumne Meadows to Lyle Fort – fill up quickly, but with flexibility you should be able to get something, even in high summer. Don't despair if you have trouble landing the trail you want: paths are so numerous that you may start at a less popular trailhead but end up doing largely the same hike. Between May and October a quota system is in operation, half of which can be reserved up to 24 weeks in advance ($3 per person) by contacting Wilderness Reservations, PO Box 545, Yosemite, CA 95389 (☎209/372-0740), stating your requirements, the size of your party and your desired itinerary with alternatives. The other half is offered on a first-come-first-served basis and is available the day before you plan to start: line up at one of the park's ranger stations – at Yosemite Village, Wawona, Big Oak Flat, Hetch Hetchy and Tuolumne – early in the day. From November to April when demand is lowest, permits are self-issued at trailheads.

Camping gear can be rented quite reasonably from Yosemite Mountaineering School (see p.319), as can bear-resistant canisters ($3 a day plus $75 deposit), which you'll also find in Yosemite's stores.

Four-mile Trail (10 miles; 5–6hr; 3200ft ascent). The asphalt path from the valley floor to Glacier Point doesn't give much of a sense of being in the wilderness, but the magnificent views make this one of the Valley's more popular day walks. Closed in winter.

Half Dome (17 miles; 10–12hr; 4800ft ascent). Probably the Valley's finest, if most arduous, walk. The route starts by following the Vernal and Nevada Falls Trail (below) and continues around the back of Half Dome. The final 400ft ascent is over the huge, smooth, humped back aided by a pair of steel cables and wooden steps which are partly removed in winter (Nov–May) to discourage ascent: gloves to grip the cables are a good idea at any time. Even with a head for heights, the near vertical 5000-foot drop from the top can induce vertigo. If you plan a one-day assault, you'll need to start at the crack of dawn.

Tuolumne Meadows to Yosemite Valley (20 miles; 2 days; strenuous in parts; 10,000ft ascent). Several routes, all quite popular, leave from Yosemite to Tuolumne. All can be done fairly easily in two days if you're in reasonably good shape, less if done in reverse using the Tuolumne Shuttle. One of the best routes (reserve your permits early) follows the **John Muir Trail** up Little Yosemite Valley past Vernal and Nevada Falls and the base of the final climb up Half Dome.

Upper Yosemite Falls (7 miles; 4hr; 2700ft ascent). A fairly strenuous walk, the almost continuous ascent sapping on the leg muscles, but with fine views and, during the meltwater period at least, a chance to appreciate the power and volume of the water at the end. Start just by the *Sunnyside* campground (shuttle stop 7).

Vernal and Nevada Falls (7 miles; 6hr; 1900ft ascent) The trail begins at the southeastern side of the Valley (shuttle bus stop 16).The route is steep and can be wet and slippery – it's not referred to as the "mist trail" for nothing – but otherwise is not especially tough, and the visual rewards of reaching either or both falls are tremendous.

(wilderness permit required) as a base for trekking through the little-visited northern reaches of the park. A short and mostly flat alternative crosses the dam, passes through a short tunnel and follows the north bank of the reservoir to Wapama Falls (five miles round-trip) and on to Rancheria Falls (a further four miles each way).

Listings

Activity programs The park service operates an extensive and worthwhile range of mostly free walks, talks films and slide shows, for both adults and kids, usually in the Valley but also at Glacier Point, Tuolumne Meadows and at the Tuolumne Grove. Consult the Yosemite Guide for details and look out especially for the Yosemite Theater program which presents the admirable "Conversations with a Tramp" ($5), which evokes the spirit of John Muir.

Banks The Bank of America in Yosemite Village is open daily from 8am to 4pm and operates a 24-hr ATM. There is no provision for foreign currency exchange.

Bike rental Bikes are only allowed on the Valley's flat, paved roads and bikeways, so the basic single-speed bikes ($20 per day) available at *Yosemite Lodge* (all year) and *Curry Village* (summer only) are quite adequate. Child carriers are not available.

Books The Yosemite Village Visitor Center has a good selection of Yosemite-related books and maps; the Ansel Adams Gallery specializes in photography and nature publications and the Mountain Shop at Curry Village stocks climbing guides.

Campfires Summertime air quality restrictions exist which limit campfires to 5pm to 10pm from May to mid-October. For ecological reasons, firewood must not be gathered in the Valley or above 9600ft, but is available for sale at the Yosemite Store.

Camping equipment Camping gear can be rented from the Yosemite Mountaineering School at Curry Village (expect to pay $10 for a sleeping bag, $8 for a pack and comparable rates for tents, bear canisters, snowshoes and so on) and bought from the Village Sport Shop in Yosemite Village, or better from the Mountain Shop in Curry Village. The store in Tuolumne Meadows also stocks camping equipment, climbing gear and lightweight food.

Gas Available at good prices in Oakhurst, moderate prices in Mariposa and Groveland and expensively in the park, year-round at Wawona and seasonally at Tuolumne Meadows and Crane Flat. The Valley currently has no gas.

Guided trips Southern Yosemite Mountain Guides, PO Box 301, Bass Lake, CA 93604 (☎1-800/231-4575 or 209/658-8735, fax 658-8734) run High Sierra backpacking trips (four-day $265, ten-day $985), seven-day horseback trips ($1345), weekend and week-long mountain biking trips ($225/$945), five-day rock-climbing camps ($395) and more, all based in the south of Yosemite.

High Sierra vacations Visitors organized enough to enter a lottery before the end of November can apply for July to September stays in a series of five dormitory-style tent cabin complexes – complete with proper beds, hot showers and meals cooked for you – dotted around the Yosemite high country. Most combine them in a circuit, either the seven-day guided hike with one rest day, the six-day mule-back saddle trip or the four-day saddle trip. Prices are $93 a night per person and include a delicious breakfast and dinner. Merced Lake, the largest of the camps, sometimes has spare short-notice spaces for those willing to hike the thirteen miles for Yosemite Valley or the fifteen miles from Tuolumne Meadows, and all camps will serve meals to passing hikers if you reserve in advance. Write for an application form to Yosemite Reservations, 5410 East Home Avenue, Fresno, CA 93727.

Horseback riding Recent floods put the Yosemite Valley and Wawona stables out of action leaving only those at Tuolumne Meadows (July to mid-Sept; ☎209/372-8427) where rides last two hours ($35), or half a day ($45).

Laundry There's a coin-op affair at *Housekeeping Camp* (7am–10pm).

Library A public research library (usually Tues–Fri 8am–5pm) is situated upstairs from the museum entrance in Yosemite Village and contains all manner of Yosemite, backcountry and climbing information including recent magazines and daily papers.

Lost property ☎209/379-1001 (Mon–Fri 8am–4pm).

Medical assistance Yosemite Medical Clinic, between Yosemite Village and the *Ahwahnee Hotel* (☎209/372-4637) have 24-hour emergency care and accept appointments (Mon–Fri 8am–5pm, Sat & Sun 9am–noon). Dental treatment (Mon–Fri 8am–4.30pm; ☎209/372-4200) is also available.

Photography The Ansel Adams Studio in Yosemite Village stocks slide and professional as well as ordinary print film at reasonable prices. They also run free two-hour guided photography walks at noon on weekends and the *Ahwahnee Hotel* runs free morning photography walks open to all-comers (Mon & Wed 7.30am).

Post office Located in Yosemite Village (Mon–Fri 8.30am–5pm) and accepting general delivery (aka poste restante). Also year-round services at *Yosemite Lodge* and Wawona and summer-only service at *Curry Village* and Tuolumne Meadows.

Rafting Inside the park itself, *Yosemite Lodge* rents guideless six-berth rafts ($12.50 per person; min two; June & July only) allowing you to float gently along a relatively serene section of the Merced River – the cost includes a return bus ride. Outside the park, from April to June, far more rugged one-day stretches (Class III–IV) are run in the traditional guided fashion by Mariah Wilderness Expeditions (☎1-800/462-7424 or contact the *Yosemite Bug Hostel*, p.321), Ahwahnee Whitewater Expeditions (☎1-800/359-9790), Whitewater Voyages (☎1-800/488-RAFT) and others, all charging around $100 midweek and $130 at weekends.

Recycling Glass, aluminium, newspapers and plastic are recycled at Yosemite Village, and beverage containers may be returned for deposits at all retail outlets.

RVs Campers can use all the main campgrounds but there are no hook-ups in Yosemite. Dump stations are in Yosemite Valley, Wawona and Tuolumne Meadows (summer only).

Showers In the valley the best showers are at Curry Village (24-hr; $2), though there are also showers at *Housekeeping Camp* (7am–10pm; $2); both include use of a towel.

travel details

Trains

The four-times-daily San Joaquin service runs between Bakersfield and Oakland, the terminus for San Francisco. Amtrak Thruway bus connections from **Los Angeles** (Union Station, LAX, UCLA, Santa Monica, Long Beach and Glendale) link with the train at Bakersfield.

Bakersfield to: Fresno (2hr); Hanford (1hr 20min); Merced (2hr 50min); Oakland (6hr); Stockton (4hr).

Buses

Buses are either Greyhound, Amtrak Thruway or Orange Belt Stages (☎209/584-6957) which often use Amtrak stations as hubs for their network.

Bakersfield to: Merced (12 daily; 4–5hr).

Fresno to: Merced (15 daily; 1hr 10min); Modesto (17 daily; 2hr 10min); Stockton (9 daily; 3hr); Yosemite (1 daily; 3hr 30min).

Hanford to: San Luis Obispo (1 daily; 3hr).

Los Angeles to: Bakersfield (18 daily; 1hr 25min); Fresno (16 daily; 6hr 45min); Merced (9 daily; 6–8hr); Modesto (12 daily; 8hr 25min); Stockton (11 daily; 6hr 45min); Visalia (6 daily; 6hr 15min).

Merced to: Los Angeles (13 daily; 6–8hr); Modesto (6 daily; 1hr); Sacramento (8 daily; 3hr); San Francisco (6–7 daily; 4–5hr); Yosemite (3–5 daily; 2hr 45min).

San Francisco to: Bakersfield (7 daily; 7hr 20min); Fresno (9 daily; 4hr 40min); Merced (8 daily; 3hr 30min–5hr); Modesto (8 daily; 2hr 10min); Stockton (3 daily; 1hr 30min); Visalia (2 daily; 5hr).

Stockton to: Lodi (5 daily; 30min); Merced (6–7 daily; 2hr); Sacramento (11 daily; 1hr).

Visalia to: Hanford (2 daily; 1hr 30min); Reedley (1 daily; 40min).

CHAPTER SIX

THE CENTRAL COAST

After the hustle of LA and San Francisco, the four hundred miles of coastline in between – the **Central Coast** – can seem like the land that time forgot: sparsely populated outside the few medium-sized towns, and lined by clean, sandy beaches that are often little disturbed by modern life. Indeed, first-time visitors, and those who rarely set foot out of the cities, may be surprised to find just how much of the region survives in its natural state. The mountain ranges that separate the shore from the farmlands of the inland valleys are for the most part pristine wilderness, sometimes covered in thick forests of tall and slender redwood trees, while, in winter especially, fast-flowing rivers and streams course down valleys to the sea. All along the shore, sea otters and seals play in the waves, and endangered gray whales pass close by on their annual migration from Alaska to Mexico.

Big Sur, where the brooding Santa Lucia mountains rise steeply out of the thundering Pacific surf, is the heart of the region, and the best place to experience this untouched environment at its most dramatic. Nature aside, though, the Central Coast also marks the gradual transition from Southern to Northern California. The two largest towns here, **Santa Barbara** and **Santa Cruz**, are poles apart: Santa Barbara, a hundred miles north of Los Angeles, is a conservative, wealthy resort; in Santa Cruz, 75 miles south of San Francisco, long hair and tie-dye are very much the order of the day. What they have in common is miles of broad clean **beaches**, with chilly waters but excellent surf, and a branch of the University of California energizing the local nightlife. In between, the small town of **San Luis Obispo** provides a languorous contrast to them both, and is a feasible base for the Central Coast's biggest tourist attraction, **Hearst Castle**, the opulent hilltop palace of publishing magnate William Randolph "Citizen Kane" Hearst.

The Central Coast is also one of the most historic parts of the state, and contains the bulk and the best of the late-eighteenth-century Spanish colonial **missions** – the first European settlements on the West Coast, set up to convert the natives to Christianity while co-opting their labor. Almost all of the towns that exist today grew up around the adobe walls and red-tiled roofs of these Catholic colonies, strung out along the Pacific, each deliberately sited a long day's walk from the next and typically composed of a church and a cloistered monastery, enclosed within thick walls to prevent attacks by Indian tribes. **Monterey**, a hundred miles south of San Francisco, was the capital of California under Spain, and later, Mexico, and today retains more of its early nine-

---

ACCOMMODATION PRICE CODES

All accommodation prices in this book have been coded using the symbols below; prices are for the least expensive **double rooms** in each establishment. For a full explanation see p.36 in Basics. Individual rates rather than price codes are given for **hostels** and whole **apartments**.

① up to $30	④ $60–80	⑦ $130–175
② $30–45	⑤ $80–100	⑧ $175–250
③ $45–60	⑥ $100–130	⑨ $250+

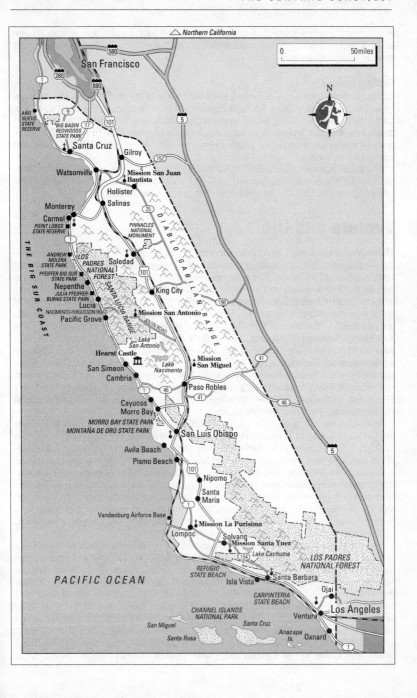

△ *Northern California*

0   50 miles

N

San Francisco

AÑO
NUEVO
STATE
RESERVE

BIG BASIN
REDWOODS
STATE PARK

Santa Cruz

Gilroy

Watsonville

Mission San Juan
Bautista

Hollister

Monterey

Salinas

Carmel

POINT LOBOS
STATE RESERVE

DIABLO GABILAN RANGE

PINNACLES
NATIONAL
MONUMENT

THE BIG SUR COAST

ANDREW
MOLERA
STATE PARK

LOS
PADRES
NATIONAL
FOREST

Soledad

PFEIFFER BIG SUR
STATE PARK

Nepenthe

JULIA PFEIFFER
BURNS STATE PARK

SANTA LUCIA RANGE

King City

Lucia

NACIMENTO-FERGUSSON ROAD

Pacific Grove

Mission San Antonio

Lake
San Antonio

JOLON ROAD

Hearst Castle

Mission
San Miguel

Lake
Nacimento

San Simeon

Cambria

Paso Robles

Cayucos

Morro Bay

MORRO BAY STATE PARK
MONTAÑA DE ORO STATE PARK

San Luis Obispo

Avila Beach

Pismo Beach

Nipomo

Santa
Maria

Vandenburg Airforce Base

Mission La Purisima

Lompoc

Solvang

Mission Santa Ynez

Lake Cachuma

LOS PADRES
NATIONAL
FOREST

REFUGIO
STATE BEACH

Isla Vista

Santa Barbara

Ojai

PACIFIC OCEAN

CARPINTERIA
STATE BEACH

Ventura

Los Angeles

CHANNEL ISLANDS
NATIONAL PARK

San Miguel

Santa Cruz

Santa
Rosa

Anacapa
Is.

Oxnard

teenth-century architecture than any other city in the state; it's also a good base for one of the most beautiful of the missions, which stands three miles south in the uppercrust seaside resort of **Carmel**.

Getting around

Getting around is easy by Californian standards: some of the best views in the state can be had from Amtrak's Coast Starlight train, which runs right along the coast up to San Luis Obispo before cutting inland north to San Francisco. Greyhound buses stop at most of the towns, particularly those along the main highway, US-101 – though a better route, if you've got a car, is the smaller Hwy-1, which follows the coast all the way but takes twice as long.

   Places to stay are easy to find, at least outside summer weekends when otherwise quiet towns and beaches are packed solid with vacationing families. Opportunities for **camping** are plentiful, too, in a string of state parks, beaches and forests.

Ventura and Ojai

The valleys of suburban Los Angeles meet the Pacific coast at **VENTURA**, a long-standing farming and fishing community that's slowly being submerged beneath fast-food restaurants and mini-malls. The only real reason to stop, besides buying fresh strawberries or other seasonal produce from the many roadside stalls, is to catch a boat out to the offshore Channel Islands (see opposite) from the harbor four miles southwest of town. If you've got more time to spare, look in on the seemingly time-warped town center, just north of the intersection of US-101 and Hwy-1, around the restored church of **San Buena Ventura Mission** at 211 E Main St (daily 10am–5pm; $1), founded in 1782. Also on Main Street are two small but reasonably engaging museums: the **Albinger Archaeological Museum**, at no. 113 (Wed–Sun 10am–4pm; free), has exhibits explaining 3500 years of local history, from ancient Native American cultures to the mission era; while across the street the **Ventura County Museum of History and Art** (Tues–Sun 10am–5pm; $3) takes up where the former leaves off, with exhibits on local pioneer families and their farming equipment.

   Amtrak trains pull in near Harbor Boulevard and Figueroa Street, three blocks from the Greyhound stop at Thomson Boulevard and Palm Street. The **CVB** at 89 California St (Mon–Fri 8.30am–5pm, Sat 9am–4pm, Sun 10am–4pm; ☎ 1-800/333-2989 or 805/648-2075) can help with accommodation and has local bus maps. As Ventura is a springboard for visiting the Channel Islands there is a **Channel Islands National Park visitor center** (daily 8am–5pm; ☎805/658-5730), next to the ferry landing in Ventura Harbor, which has well-presented displays on the geology and the native plant and animal life of the islands, including seals, sea lions, pelican rookeries and giant kelp forests. It also has up-to-date information on arranging trips, and a tower from which, on fine days, you can view the islands.

   Nestled in the hills above Ventura, the small town of **OJAI** (pronounced "O-hi") is a wealthy resort community, and center for the exclusive health spas and tennis clubs that dot the surrounding countryside. It's also headquarters of the Krishnamurti Society, which spreads the word of the theosophist who lived and lectured here during the 1920s, considering the Ojai Valley "a vessel of comprehension, intelligence and truth." The **Krishnamurti Library**, several miles northeast of town at 1130 McAndrew Rd (Wed 1–9pm, Thurs–Sun 1–5pm; ☎805/646-4948), has details on his teachings. Otherwise, about the only place in town worth stopping at is Bart's Books, an outdoor bookstore at Cañada and Matilija, with an excellent selection of secondhand books. The **Chamber of Commerce**, 150 W Ojai Ave (Mon-Fri 9am–4.30pm, Sat &

Sun 10am–4pm; ☎805/646-8126), has information on the town's numerous B&B **inns**. The friendly *Farm Hostel*, on a country farm ten minutes from downtown (☎805/646-0311), offers free pickup from the Greyhound and Amtrak stations in Ventura and dorm beds for $12. Nearby is the massive **Los Padres National Forest**, with some good hiking and several **campgrounds** – call ☎805/646-4348 for more information.

The Channel Islands National Park

Stretching north from Catalina Island off the coast of Los Angeles, a chain of little-known desert islands has been protected in its natural state as the **CHANNEL ISLANDS NATIONAL PARK** (free entry), offering excellent hiking and close-up views of sea lions, as well as fishing and skindiving through the many shipwrecks in the crystal-clear Pacific waters. All five of the main islands are accessible, though it is the closest, Anacapa, some fourteen miles south of Ventura, which sees the most traffic.

Tiny **Anacapa** is actually two islets. West Anacapa is mostly a refuge for nesting brown pelicans, although Frenchy's Cove is a great beach and base for scuba or snorkeling expeditions. More happens on East Anacapa where there's a small visitor center and a mile-and-a-half-long nature trail. There are no beaches, but there's swimming in the cove where the boats dock. West of Anacapa, **Santa Cruz** is the largest and highest of the islands, and the only one with some private ownership, at its eastern end. **Santa Rosa**, with its grasslands, is less rugged but still has its share of steep ravines. Hiking inland requires a permit. The most distant island, windswept **San Miguel** – fifty miles offshore – is thought to be the burial place of sixteenth-century Spanish explorer Juan Cabrillo. No grave has been found but a monument has been erected at Cuyler Harbor on the eastern end. For many years San Miguel was used by the military as a bombing and missile range, so stick to the trails and keep your eyes skinned for unexploded bombs.

South of the main group lies **Santa Barbara** Island, named by Sebastian Vizcaino who dropped by on Saint Barbara's Day (December 4) in 1602. The island's appeal these days is largely ornithological, as kestrels, larks and meadowlarks can all be seen on land gradually recovering its native flora after years of destruction by now extinct rabbits.

Practicalities

Anacapa Island is served by several tours run by Island Packers, 1867 Spinnaker Drive in Ventura Harbor, three miles west of US-101 and a mile south of town (☎805/642-7688 for 24hr recorded information; ☎805/642-1393 for reservations 9am–5pm). Trips range from half-day excursions ($32), through full-day trips to East or West Anacapa ($37), to overnight stays ($48). The fifteen-mile trip takes ninety minutes each way, and there's a free, very basic **campground** a half-mile walk from the landing cove. Bring plenty of **food** and especially **water**, as none is available on the boat or on the island. Permits are required for camping. Boats don't run every day and often fill up, so call at least a couple of days ahead.

The **other islands** are more difficult to visit, though Island Packers run boats, less frequently, to them all. Day-trips to the western end of Santa Cruz (3hr each way) are $49, overnight excursions to the eastern end are $54. Visits to Santa Rosa (5hr one way; $62 for the day, $80 including camping) are often combined with a stop (or camp) on San Miguel for the same price. Santa Barbara trips are a fraction cheaper.

An alternative way to reach Santa Rosa island is to **fly** with Channel Islands Aviation (☎805/987-1301) which runs day-trips and weekend excursions ($85 & $150 respectively) from Camarillo Airport off Hwy-101, twenty miles south of Ventura. Santa Cruz is also the venue for **kayak** trips from Santa Barbara (see p.337).

Perhaps the best time of all to visit any of the islands is between February and April when there's the chance of **whale-watching**. During these months, three trips daily from Santa Barbara Harbor are organized by Sea Landing Sportfishing, 301 W Cabrillo Blvd (☎805/963-3564), aboard the *Condor* – these cost $24, and take about three hours.

The **Channel Islands National Park visitor center** in Ventura (see p.332) can help with trips, and has lots of information on the islands' flora and fauna.

Santa Barbara

The six-lane freeway that races past the oil wells and offshore drilling platforms along the coast beyond Ventura slows to a more leisurely pace a hundred miles north of Los Angeles at **SANTA BARBARA**, a moneyed seaside resort that for years has been known as the "home of the newly wed and the nearly dead" – a not entirely inaccurate summary. Despite the recent completion of the vast modern El Paseo Nuevo shopping mall in the center of town and a growing selection of budget hotels and fast food joints on its outskirts, Santa Barbara has managed to maintain its quaintly upscale, yet relaxed character. With its sunny beaches and bustling nightlife, it's a lively, fun place to visit – what Southern California is meant to be.

Home to Ronald Reagan, and weekend escape for much of the old money of Los Angeles, it's a conservative town, but is undeniably beautifully sited. Rising on gently sloping hills above the Pacific, the insistent red-tiled roofs and white stucco walls of the low-rise buildings form a background to some fine examples of Spanish Revival architecture, while the golden beaches are wide and clean, lined by palm trees along a gently curving bay. Locals look tanned and healthy, playing volleyball, surfing, or cycling along the shore.

Arrival, information and transportation

Getting to Santa Barbara is easy. Greyhound **buses** arrive from LA and San Francisco every couple of hours stopping downtown at 34 W Carrillo St; Amtrak **trains** stop at the old Southern Pacific station at 209 State St, a block west of US-101. Santa Barbara **airport** (☎805/683-4011), eight miles from the town center (near the University of California at Santa Barbara) at 515 Marxmiller Drive in Goleta, has a limited and very expensive scheduled service to other Californian cities. Carriers include American Eagle (☎1-800/433-7300) and United.

For more **information** on Santa Barbara, or for help with finding a place to stay, contact either the **Visitor Information Office** on East Beach at 1 Santa Barbara St (Mon–Sat 9am–5pm, Sun 10am–5pm; ☎805/965-3021) or Hot Spots, 36 State St (24hrs; ☎1-800/793-7666 or 805/564-1637), tucked in behind the café of the same name and very helpful. The **US Forest Service** office in Goleta, near UCSB at 6144 Calle Real (☎805/683-6711), has information on **hiking** in the vicinity of Santa Barbara, and the many good trails easily accessible from downtown.

Getting around Santa Barbara is simple: your feet can take you most places and there's a quarter-a-ride shuttle bus which loops between downtown and the beach on a ten- to fifteen-minute schedule, and along the waterfront to the zoo every thirty minutes until 5.30pm, and 8pm on Friday and Saturday. The outlying areas are covered by Santa Barbara Metropolitan Transit District buses (☎805/683-3702). If you want to **rent a car**, the best value is U-Save Auto Rental, 510 Anacapa St (☎805/963-3499), which rents late-model cars for as little as $24 a day including one hundred free miles. The chain offices are Budget (☎805/963-6651) and Hertz (☎805/967-0411), both at the airport.

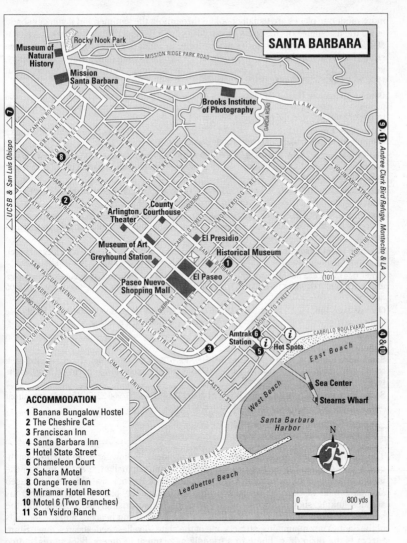

SANTA BARBARA

Museum of Natural History
Rocky Nook Park
MISSION RIDGE PARK ROAD
Mission Santa Barbara
ALAMEDA
Brooks Institute of Photography
ALAMEDA
GARCIA ROAD
CANYON ROAD
PADRE STREET
SANTA BARBARA STREET
GARDEN STREET
ANACAPA STREET
ANAPAMU STREET
CANYON PERDIDO STREET
VOLUNTARIO STREET
MASON STREET
UCSB & San Luis Obispo
CHAPALA STREET
DE LA VINA STREET
BATH STREET
TERRACE STREET
MITCHELTOREA STREET
CHINO STREET
SAN ANDRES AVENUE
SAN PASCUAL AVENUE
VICTORIA STREET
CARRILLO STREET
LOMA ALTA DRIVE
County Courthouse
Arlington Theater
Museum of Art
Greyhound Station
Paseo Nuevo Shopping Mall
El Presidio
Historical Museum
El Paseo
FIGUEROA STREET
CARRILLO STREET
SAN BARBARA STREET
CASTILLO STREET
DE LA GUERRA ST
ORTEGA STREET
COTA STREET
HALEY STREET
GUTIERREZ STREET
MONTECITO STREET
Amtrak Station
Hot Spots
CABRILLO BOULEVARD
101
East Beach
Sea Center
Stearns Wharf
West Beach
Santa Barbara Harbor
SHORELINE DRIVE
Leadbetter Beach
N
0   800 yds

Andree Clark Bird Refuge, Montecito & LA

ACCOMMODATION
1 Banana Bungalow Hostel
2 The Cheshire Cat
3 Franciscan Inn
4 Santa Barbara Inn
5 Hotel State Street
6 Chameleon Court
7 Sahara Motel
8 Orange Tree Inn
9 Miramar Hotel Resort
10 Motel 6 (Two Branches)
11 San Ysidro Ranch

Accommodation

Home to some of the West Coast's most deluxe resorts – it's the sort of place movie stars go to get married or to honeymoon – Santa Barbara is among the most expensive places to **stay**, with rooms averaging over $110 a night. However, there is a hostel, and with a bit of advance planning, finding somewhere good shouldn't take too big a bite out of your budget – especially if you are willing to stay in one of the junkier chain motels along the western stretch of State St. The least expensive as well as most of the more moderate places are usually booked throughout the summer, but if you get stuck, enlist the assistance of Hot Spots (see p.334) or the Passport Reservation Service (☎1-800/289-6255). Also, while there's no **camping** in Santa Barbara proper, there are several grounds along the coast to the north. In the mountains of the Santa Ynez Valley, you might try the *Los Prietos Campground*, nineteen miles northwest of the city off of Hwy-154 (☎805/967-3481; $8).

Banana Bungalow Hostel, 210 E Ortega St (☎805/963-0154). Newly converted from commercial premises and catering to raucous backpackers. A party atmosphere pervades, engendered as much by the 2.30am curfew as the occasional keg parties. $12–15 a night.

Chameleon Court, 1011b State St (☎805/962-1054). Small new travelers hostel right in the center of town with helpful owners and comfortable dorm beds. $15.

The Cheshire Cat, 36 W Valerio St (☎805/569-1610). Tastefully decorated B&B with hot tub and bikes for guests' use. Complimentary wine on arrival and breakfast under a palm tree. Ten minutes' walk from the restaurant zone. ⑥.

Franciscan Inn, 109 Bath St (☎805/963-8845). Comfortable, quiet and very clean motel just a block from the beach, with a pool, spa and complimentary breakfast. ④.

Hotel State Street, 121 State St (☎805/966-6586). Near the wharf and beach in a characterful old mission-style building, though with some noise from the nearby railway. Reasonable rates include breakfast. Communal bathrooms. ②.

Miramar Hotel Resort, 1555 S Jameson Lane (☎805/969-2203). Slightly faded, once elegant beach resort with (higher priced) seaview rooms, and the only place in town with a private strand. ⑤.

Motel 6, 443 Corona del Mar (☎1-800/466-8356 or 805/564-1392). Inexpensive but extremely popular beachfront lodging in no-frills chain motel. There's another north of the town center at 3505 State St (☎805/687-5400). Both ③.

Orange Tree Inn, 1920 State St (☎1-800/536-6764 or 805/569-1521). Good value, basic hotel close to the center of town with a pool and complimentary pastries in the morning. ④.

Sahara Motel, 2800 State St (☎805/687-2500). As basic as they get, but also as cheap as they get in Santa Barbara. ②.

San Ysidro Ranch, 900 San Ysidro Lane (☎1-800/368-6788 or 805/969-5046). Gorgeous, ultra-posh resort with private cottages in lovely gardens (Jackie and JFK spent their honeymoon here), in the hills ten minutes' drive south of town. ⑧.

Santa Barbara Inn, 901 E Cabrillo Blvd (☎1-800/231-0431 or 805/966-2285). Upscale oceanfront motel with large pool, lovely views, and renovated rooms. ⑥.

The Town

The mission-era feel of Santa Barbara is no accident. Following a devastating earthquake in 1925, the city authorities decided to rebuild virtually the entire town in the image of an apocryphal Spanish Colonial past – even the massive "historic" El Paseo shopping mall is covered in pseudo-whitewashed adobe plaster – with numerous arcades linking shops, offices, and restaurants. It's surprisingly successful, and the square-mile town center, squeezing between the south-facing beaches and the foothills of the Santa Ynez mountains, attracts one of the state's liveliest pedestrian scenes. **State Street** is the main drag, home to a friendly assortment of diners, bookstores, coffee bars and nightclubs catering to the needs of the locals – and the twenty thousand students at the nearby UCSB – as much as to visitors.

The town's few remaining, genuine mission-era structures are preserved as **El Presidio** (daily 10.30am–4.30pm; donation), in the center of which are the two-hundred-year-old barracks of the old fortress, **El Cuartel**, standing two blocks east of State Street on Canon Perdido Street. The second-oldest building in California, this now houses historical exhibits and a scale model of the small Spanish colony. The more recent past is recounted in the **Santa Barbara Historical Museum** (Tues–Sat 10am–5pm, Sun noon–5pm; donation), a block away at 136 E de la Guerra St.

On the corner of State and Anapamu streets, the **Museum of Art** (Tues–Wed & Fri–Sat 11am–5pm, Thurs 11am–9pm, Sun noon–5pm; $3) is of more interest, a refreshingly accessible small museum with some fine classical Greek and Egyptian statuary and a fairly comprehensive collection of American painting, as well as some French Impressionists. Just east of here, on Anacapa Street, the **County Courthouse** is the one first-rate piece of Spanish Revival architecture in Santa Barbara, an idiosyncratic variation on the mission theme that has been widely praised as one of the finest public buildings in the US. Take a break in the sunken gardens, explore the quirky staircases, or climb the seventy-foot-high **clocktower** (Mon–Fri 8.30am–5pm, Sat & Sun 10am–5pm; free) for a view out over the town. Two blocks up State Street the landmark **Arlington Theater** is an intact and still-functioning 1930s movie palace and performance venue, whose trompe l'oeil interior simulates a Mexican village plaza.

The beaches and around

Half a mile down State Street from the town center, Cabrillo Boulevard runs along the south-facing shore, a long, clean strand stretching from the yacht and fishing harbor beyond palm-lined **West Beach** to the volleyball courts and golden sands of **East Beach**, which hosts an outdoor arts and crafts market every Sunday. At the foot of State Street take a stroll among the pelicans on **Stearns Wharf**, the oldest wooden pier in the state, built in 1872 and recently restored, with seafood restaurants, ice cream stalls and a fish market at the far end. Also on the wharf is the **Sea Center** (daily 10am–5pm; $2), an annex of the natural history museum in the foothills above town. Just west of the pier, world-class athletes keep in shape in the Los Baños open-air fifty-meter swimming pool ($2.25), while **windsurfers** can be rented from beachfront stalls. **Kayaks** are available from Paddle Sports, 100 State St ($20 for two hours, $40 a day; ☎805/899-4925),which also conducts lessons and runs all-inclusive paddling and snorkeling trips out to Santa Cruz Island ($150). Beach Rentals, 22 State St (☎805/966-6733), offers **bicycles** for around $30 a day, and provides a map of Santa Barbara's extensive system of bike paths; the longest and most satisfying leads west along the bluffs all the way to Isla Vista and UCSB, and passes a mile or so back from the rarely crowded, creekside **Arroyo Burro Beach** (locally known as "Hendry's"), four miles west of the wharf at the end of Las Positas Road. Alternatively head along the beachfront bike path two miles east past the Santa Barbara **zoo** (daily 10am–5pm; $5), and cycle around the **Andree Clark Bird Refuge** (unrestricted access) just beyond, an enclosed saltwater marsh where you can see a variety of seabirds, including egrets, herons and cormorants.

The foothills: the Mission and the museums

One sight that's worth leaving the beach for is in the hills above the town on the upper end of Laguna Street: **Mission Santa Barbara** (daily 9am–5pm; $3), the so-called "Queen of the Missions," whose colorful twin-towered front makes it the most beautiful and impressive of all the California missions, sitting majestically in well-landscaped gardens overlooking the city and the ocean. The present structure was finished and dedicated in 1820, built of local sandstone to replace a series of three adobe churches that had been destroyed by earthquakes; a small **museum** displays historical artifacts from the mission archives. Get there by SBMTD bus, or walk or ride the half-mile from State Street up Mission Street and Mission Canyon.

Just beyond the mission at 2559 Puesta del Sol Rd, the **Museum of Natural History** (Mon–Sat 9am–5pm, Sun 10am–5pm; $5) has intriguing and informative displays on the plants and animals of the ecosystems of Southern California, and an entrance constructed out of the skeleton of a Blue Whale. Across the road, **Rocky Nook Park** is a great place to picnic or wander among the trees and, half a mile east of the mission, the

Brooks Institute of Photography, at 1321 Alameda Padre Serra (daily 10am–4pm; free), displays over a thousand antique cameras and, more interestingly, mounts changing exhibitions of works by some of the world's best contemporary photographers.

Eating

Because of its status as a prime resort area, Santa Barbara has a number of very good and very expensive **restaurants**, but it also has numerous more affordable options that offer a range of good food. Since it's right on the Pacific, you'll find a lot of seafood (and sushi); Mexican places are also numerous and of a very high standard. Smoothies – blended fruit and yogurt milkshakes – are everywhere, a welcome snack on a hot summer day.

Cuvée, 26 W Anapamu St (☎805/730-1766). Eclectic international cuisine in a dimly-lit atmosphere. Entrees go for about $15.

Enterprise Fish Company, 225 State St (☎805/962-3313). Lively, moderately priced fish spot popular with locals and tourists alike.

Esau's Coffee Shop, 403 State St (☎805/965-4416). Ancient-looking café serving Santa Barbara's most popular greasy-spoon breakfasts. Open until 1pm daily; additional hours for the drinking crowd from Fri & Sat 9pm–3am.

Joe's Café, 536 State St (☎805/966-4638). Long-established bar and grill. A great place to stop off for a burger and a beer, more or less midway between the beach and the downtown museums.

La Super-Rica Taqueria, 622 N Milpas St (☎805/963-4940). Some of the finest Yucatan cuisine to be found in these parts. Casual outdoor dining at a price.

Palazzio Trattoria Italiana, 1151 Coast Village Rd, Montecito (☎805/969-8565). Trattoria of choice for the region's smart set, though by no means intimidating. The portions are huge, the prices moderate, and the tiramisu divine. Ten minutes' drive south of town.

Paradise Café, 702 Anacapa St (☎805/962-4416). Stylish, slightly upmarket 1940s era indoor/outdoor grill, with good steaks and ultra-fresh seafood.

Pascicci, 811 State St, in Paseo Nuevo (☎805/963-8123). Cheap and delicious pastas, gourmet pizzas, and panini served in a small, chic dining room or outside among the beautiful shoppers.

RG's Giant Hamburgers, 922 State St (☎805/963-1654). The burgers here, meatless ones included, are regularly voted the biggest and best in Santa Barbara. Good salads too, and breakfast daily from 7am.

Something's Fishy, 502 State St (☎805/966-6607). Skip a couple of meals before you tackle their $16 all-you-can-eat sushi deal. Try the delicious Tokyo Roll.

World Café, 1208 State St (☎805/962-5352). A wide range of affordable salads, sandwiches and healthy international food served in sunny, smoke-free surroundings.

Zia Cafe, 532 State St (☎805/962-5391). Upscale but not expensive Santa Fe-style Mexican restaurant, with subtle variations on the tacos-and-burritos theme: try the fried chillies stuffed with pine nuts and melted cheese, or the Hopi blue-corn tortillas.

Drinking and nightlife

There are quite a few **cafés**, **bars** and **clubs** along the entire length of State Street, especially in the downtown strip; for the most up-to-date nightlife listings, check out a copy of the free weekly *Santa Barbara Independent*, available at area bookstores, record stores and convenience stores.

Earthling Books, 1137 State St (☎805/965-0926). Late-night café in Santa Barbara's biggest and best bookstore, with signings, talks and films at 7pm most evenings.

Espresso Roma, 728 State St (☎805/962-7241). Excellent coffee, and lively from early morning until late every night.

Madhouse Martini Lounge, 434 State St (☎805/962-5516). Drink classic martinis and exotic cocktails in a swanky, slightly contrived bar full of Santa Barbara's "hipsters."

Matty's Lounge, 26 W Anapamu St (☎805/963-6788). Friendly new jazz club with music nightly. Downstairs from *Cuvée*, a delicious but expensive gourmet restaurant (see "Eating" opposite).

O'Malley's, 523 State St (☎805/564-8904). Frequently State Street's wildest bar, with nightly drink specials, sports on TV, and lots of college students.

Sojourner Coffee House, 134 E Cañon Perdido (☎805/965-7922). Coffee, beer, wine, and a range of vegetarian food, in a friendly, hippyish setting, with live music some nights.

Zelo, 630 State St (☎805/966-5792). One of Santa Barbara's more fashionable bars and restaurants, which evolves into a dance club as the night wears on, offering alternative dance, Latin, retro and such throughout the week. Closed Mon.

On from Santa Barbara

Continuing north from Santa Barbara you can either cut inland through the wine region of the Santa Ynez Valley (see below) or continue along the coast where, a few miles along from Santa Barbara, you'll pass the forty-year-old campus of the University of California at Santa Barbara – **UCSB** for short – whose solid academic record is often overshadowed by its strong sporty reputation. The characterless, though decidedly wild town of **Isla Vista** – the most populated city per square mile in the United States – borders the campus on the west, and staircases lead down the bluffs to a sandy **beach** that has some good tidepools and, at the west end, a popular surfing area at Coal Oil Point ("Devereux" to locals); the estuary nearby has been preserved as a botanical study center and nature refuge.

All along this part of the coast the **beaches** face almost due south, so the surf is very lively, and in winter the sun both rises and sets over the Pacific. About twenty miles out from Santa Barbara, **El Capitan State Beach** is a popular surfing beach, while **Refugio State Beach**, another three miles along, is one of the prettiest in California, with stands of palm trees dotting the sands at the mouth of a small creek. Inland on Refugio Road, up the canyon high in the hills, stands Rancho El Cielo, the one-time Western White House of retired President **Ronald Reagan**. Ten miles west, **Gaviota State Beach** is not as pretty, but there's a fishing pier and a large wooden railway viaduct that bridges the mouth of the canyon. All the state beaches have **campgrounds** (☎805/968-3294 or Parknet ☎1-800/444-7275; $18), and parking is $5.

Just beyond Gaviota the highways split, US-101 heading inland and the more spectacular Hwy-1 branching off nearer the coast. Half a mile off the highway, but a world away from the speeding traffic, is the small **Las Cruces hot spring** (daylight hours; parking $2), a pool of 95°F mineral water set in a shady, peaceful ravine. Take the turn-off for Hwy-1, but stay on the east side of the freeway and double back onto a small road a quarter of a mile to the parking lot at the end. Walk half a mile or so up the trail until you smell the sulphur.

The Santa Ynez Valley

An alternative to the coastal route out of Santa Barbara is to take Hwy-154 up and over the very steep **San Marcos Pass** through the **Santa Ynez Valley**, a pleasant route through a prime wine-growing region that's popular with leather-clad bikers and masochistic cyclists.

Three miles out of Santa Barbara, the walls of the **Chumash Painted Cave**, on Painted Caves Road, are daubed with pre-conquest Native American art, but are only just visible as you can't actually enter the cave. On the other side of the San Marcos

Pass the *Cold Springs Tavern*, under the massive concrete arch bridge at 5995 Stagecoach Rd (☎805/967-0066), is a good place to stop for a beer and a bite to eat.

Two miles beyond the San Marcos Pass, Paradise Road follows the Santa Ynez River up to **Red Rocks**, an excellent swimming area amidst the stony outcrops. **Lake Cachuma**, six miles further along Hwy-154, is a popular recreation area with a large **campground** (☎805/686-5054; $14); it's not actually a lake but a massive reservoir that holds the over-stretched water supply for Santa Barbara.

Beyond the lake, Hwy-246 cuts off to Solvang, while Hwy-154 continues on through the vineyards around **LOS OLIVOS**, where wineries like Firestone, 5017 Zaca Station Rd, offer free tours and tastings (daily 11am–4pm; ☎805/688-3940).

Solvang and around

It is difficult to imagine anyone falling for the sham windmills and plastic storks that fill the town of **SOLVANG**, but people come by the busload to see the community, which was established in 1911 by a group of Danes looking for a place to found a Danish folk school. Nowadays the town, three miles off US-101 on Hwy-246, lives off tourism, and locals dress up in "traditional" costume to entertain visitors. Of the plethora of all things Danish sold just about everywhere, the only things that make the town worth a stop are the fresh coffee and pastries.

There's marginal interest in the **Mission Santa Ines** (June–Sept daily 9am–7pm; Oct–May daily 9.30am–5.30pm; donation, tours $2) on the eastern edge of town, founded by Spanish friars a century before the Danes arrived. The mission itself is unremarkable, but worth a look for its curious plaques thanking the Franciscan fathers for improving the lives of the native Chumash, and a gift shop with an obsessive assortment of crucifixes and devotional items. If this doesn't grab you either, you'd really do better to give it all a miss and stop by **Nojoqui Falls County Park**, six miles from Solvang off US-101, where a gentle ten-minute walk brings you to a 75-foot waterfall. The route to the park is in any case gorgeous, winding along Alisal Road under thick garlands of Spanish moss that dangle from a canopy of oak trees.

Lompoc

Hwy-1 splits off US-101 near Gaviota on a marvelous route through the inland valleys of the Santa Ynez mountains. **LOMPOC**, the only town for miles, calls itself the "flower seed-growing capital of the world", and claims to produce as much as three-quarters of the flower seeds sold on earth, the products of which during summer form a thick carpet of color over the gently rolling landscape of the surrounding countryside. For a leaflet detailing where particular species have been planted this season, contact the **Lompoc Valley Chamber of Commerce**, 111 South I St (Mon–Fri 9am–5pm; ☎805/736-4567), where you can also find out about the **murals** which, in recent years, have sprung up to beautify an otherwise faceless downtown.

Lompoc Museum, 200 South H St (Tues–Fri 1–5pm, Sat & Sun 1–4pm; $2 donation), is strong on Chumash and other Native American artifacts, and also has material on the town's **original mission site**, the scant remains of which can be found three blocks to the south on F Street off Locust Avenue.

Lompoc is also the home of **Vandenburg Air Force Base**, sprawled along the western side of town, where various new missiles and guidance systems get put through their paces over the Pacific Ocean. Their vapor trails are visible for miles, particularly at sunset, though the only way to see any of it up close is by the Amtrak Coast Starlight **train**, which runs along the coast. The route was writer **Jack Kerouac**'s favorite rail journey: he worked for a while as a brakeman on the train and subsequently used the

"Midnight Ghost" for a free ride between LA and the Bay area. Aerospace enthusiasts who plan at least a week ahead can visit the air base on four-hour **tours** (Wed 10am–2pm; reservations required ☎805/734-8232; free) which visit launch pads and a missile silo.

The **beaches** along this section of coast are secluded and undeveloped, and nearly inaccessible much of the year, either because of bad weather or impending missile launches. **Jalama Beach** at the end of Jalama Road, twisting fourteen miles off Hwy-1, spreads beneath coastal bluffs where you can camp overnight; the large sand dunes of **Ocean Beach**, a broad strand at the mouth of the Santa Ynez River ten miles west of Lompoc, are the nesting grounds of many seabirds.

La Purisima Mission

Four miles east of Lompoc and signposted off Hwy-246, **La Purisima Mission State Park** (June–Aug daily 8am–6pm; Sept–May daily 9am–5pm; $5 per car) is the most complete and authentic reconstruction of any of the 21 Spanish missions in California, and one of the best places to get an idea of what life might have been like in these early colonial settlements. La Mission la Purisima Concepcion de Maria Santisima, as it's called, was founded in 1787 on a site three miles north of here, and by 1804 had converted around 1500 Chumash, five hundred of whom died in a smallpox epidemic over the next two years. In 1812 an earthquake destroyed all the buildings, and the fathers decided to move to the present site. The complex did not last long, however, after the missions were secularized in 1834, and over the next hundred years they were all but abandoned, pillaged by treasure-hunters and used as stables.

The buildings that stand here today were rebuilt on the ruins of the mission as part of a Depression-era project for the unemployed. From 1933 to 1940 over two hundred men lived and worked on the site, studying the remaining ruins and rebuilding the church and outbuildings using period tools and methods. Workers cavorted in puddles of mud to mix in the straw to make the adobe bricks, roof timbers were shaped with handtools, and even the colors of the paints were made from native plants.

The focus of the mission is a narrow church, furnished as it would have been in the 1820s; nearby, at the entrance, small but engaging displays of documents and artifacts from the mission era and photographs of the reconstruction are housed in the old wagon house that serves as a **museum** and gift shop. On summer weekends you might catch a "living history day," when volunteers dress up as padres and Indians, and hold a traditional Mass, along with craft demonstrations – fun if you like that kind of thing.

Pismo Beach and Avila Beach

Most of the land along the Santa Maria River, 75 miles north of Santa Barbara, is given over to farming, and both Hwy-1 and US-101 pass through a number of small agriculture-based towns and villages. Some seem hardly to have changed since the 1930s, when thousands of Okies, as they were known, fled to the region from the Dustbowl of the Midwest – an era portrayed in John Steinbeck's novel and John Ford's movie, *The Grapes of Wrath*. They were notoriously poor: just off US-101, the little town of **NIPOMO** was the site of **Dorothea Lange's** famous 1936 photograph of a migrant mother who had just been forced to sell the tires off her truck. Twenty-five miles north of Lompoc, Hwy-1 passes through the center of **GUADALUPE**, a small farming village where Spanish signs and advertisements far outnumber those in English, and ramshackle saloons, cafés and vegetable stalls line the dusty streets. At the mouth of the river, five miles west of the highway at the end of Main Street, large **sand dunes** surround wetlands that are an essential habitat for endangered seabirds.

Pismo Beach

The dunes stretch ten miles up the coast, reaching as far as two miles inland and ending just south of the loud and characterless yet mildly entertaining holiday town of **PISMO BEACH**, where the two highways merge. The southern portion of the dunes, three miles south of the town, is open to off-road vehicle enthusiasts, who excite themselves flying up and over the sandpiles of the **Pismo Dunes State Vehicle Recreation Area** in dune buggies and four-wheel drives, motoring along the beach to reach them. Inland from the gray beach, the northern quarter of the dunes is protected as a **nature reserve**, a good place to hike around and play Lawrence of Arabia.

North from the nature reserve, between the town and the dune buggy area, a number of beach-front **campgrounds** line Hwy-1; mostly RV-packed, they all charge around $20 a site. The **Pismo Beach State Park** has hot showers and beach camping for $18, and is a good place to see the black and orange Monarch butterflies that winter in the eucalyptus trees here and leave before the summer crowds. The once-plentiful **Pismo clams** that gave the town its name, however (from the local Indian word *pismu*, or "blobs of tar" that the shells resemble), have been so depleted that any you might dig up nowadays are probably under the four-and-a-half inch legal minimum size.

Most of the town's commercial activity happens at the junction where Pomeroy Avenue crosses Hwy-1. The **Chamber of Commerce**, 581 Dolliver St (Mon–Sat 9am–5pm, Sun 10am–4pm; ☎ 1-800/443-7778 or 805/773-4382), is near the junction, as are a number of **motels** (②) and the shambolic but charming *El Pismo Inn*, 230 Pomeroy Ave (☎805/773-4529; ③), a faded former bolthole for movie stars on location. For something a little classier try the beachfront *Edgewater*, 280 Wadsworth Ave (☎1-800/634-5858 or 805/773-4811; ④), with heated pool, hot tubs and some rooms with kitchens. The cozy *Black Pearl Coffeehouse*, 230 Pomeroy Ave, serves gourmet coffee and espresso, and the cheap but popular *Splash Cafe*, down the street at no. 197 (☎805/773-4653), dishes out reputable clam chowder. The only **public transportation** is Greyhound, which stops downtown five times a day in each direction.

Avila Beach

North of Pismo Beach the coastline becomes more rugged and interesting, with caves and tidepools below ever-eroding bluffs, and sea lions in the many coves. The three-mile-long strand in front of the summer resort town of **AVILA BEACH** is the last outpost of Southern California beach life, with a high concentration of tumble-down burger stands and one good budget **motel**, the *Inn at Avila Beach*, 256 Front St (☎805/595-2300; ③). On the road into town, *Sycamore Mineral Springs*, at 1215 Avila Rd (☎1-800/234-5831 or 805/595-7302; ⑥), boasts rooms with their own private mineral baths.

Teenagers on the loose from their families cruise the Avila Beach boardwalk, while anyone old enough takes refuge in **bars** like *Mr Rick's*, at 480 Front St. The party atmosphere continues all summer long, and no one seems to mind the presence of nearby oil refineries and the **Diablo Canyon Nuclear Plant**, which straddles an earthquake fault six miles up the coast (for what it's worth, three long bursts of a loud siren indicate catastrophe). The scenic route north from here to San Luis Obispo, **See Canyon Road**, cuts off north a mile from US-101, climbing gradually up the narrow, overgrown canyon between sharply profiled volcanic cones, with great views out over the Pacific.

San Luis Obispo

SAN LUIS OBISPO, ten miles northeast of Avila Beach and almost exactly halfway between LA and San Francisco, is a main stop-off for both Amtrak and Greyhound, and, although a few miles inland, makes the best base for exploring the nearby coast. It's still primarily an agricultural town, and a market center for the farmers and ranchers of the surrounding countryside, something which contributes to its Middle American feeling – though the 16,000 students at the adjacent Cal Poly campus help keep things reasonably active. On the whole it is an appealing place to pass a night or two, with a town center boasting some of the Central Coast's best architecture, from turreted Victorian

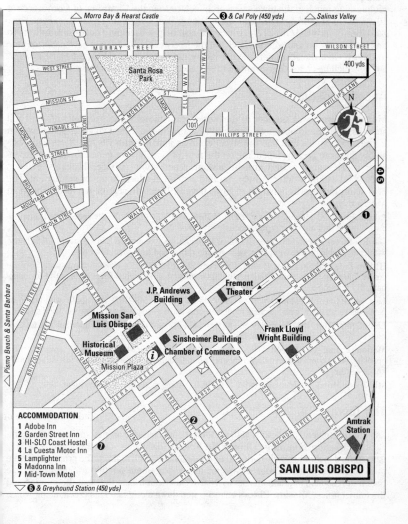

ACCOMMODATION
1 Adobe Inn
2 Garden Street Inn
3 HI-SLO Coast Hostel
4 La Cuesta Motor Inn
5 Lamplighter
6 Madonna Inn
7 Mid-Town Motel

SAN LUIS OBISPO

residences along Buchon Street south of the town center to some fine commercial buildings, not to mention any number of good places to eat, a couple of pubs and night-clubs, and – outside summer holiday weekends – places to stay for the asking.

Arrival and information

The Greyhound terminal is at 150 South St, half a mile down Higuera Street from the center of town near US-101, and there are regular bus connections with both LA and San Francisco. Amtrak trains stop once a day in each direction at the end of Santa Rosa Street, half a mile south of the business district, and a daily Amtrak Thruway bus arrives from Hanford in the Central Valley (see p.290). You can pick up a free walking-tour map highlighting much of the town's best architecture from the **Chamber of Commerce** at 1039 Chorro St (Sun & Mon 10am–5pm, Tues & Wed 8am–5pm, Thurs & Fri 8am–8pm, Sat 10am–8pm; ☎805/781-2777), which will also help with finding **accommodation**. To find out **what's on** and where, check out the free weekly *New Times* newspaper or tune to the excellent non-commercial community radio station KOTR 94.9 FM (☎805/927-5021), which has telephone events hotlines and is happy to play requests.

Accommodation

Monterey Street was the site of the world's first **motel** – the *Milestone Motel* – still standing and due to open again soon after a long hiatus. Meanwhile, its spirit lives on in the other motels that line the street up to its junction with US-101. Rates and avail-ability fluctuate greatly depending on the time of year, but are generally quite inexpen-sive; there's also a **bed-and-breakfast** reservation service, Megan's Friends (☎805/544-4406), which can help you find a room in a local home or nearby inn. The best **camping** nearby is south of town beyond Pismo Beach, or north off Hwy-1 in Morro Bay.

Adobe Inn, 1473 Monterey St (☎1-800/676-1588 or 805/549-0321). Newly redecorated, English-owned motel with nice rooms; rates include breakfast. ③.

Garden Street Inn, 1212 Garden St (☎805/545-9802). Very central B&B in a restored 1880s house with comfortable rooms, complimentary wine on arrival and tasty breakfasts. ⑥.

HI-San Luis Obispo Coast Hostel, 1292 Foothill Blvd (☎805/544-4678). A 20min walk from the center following Santa Rosa Street north, this comfortable hostel has dorm beds at $14 for mem-bers, $17 for others.

La Cuesta Inn, 2074 Monterey St (☎1-800/543-2777 or 805/543-2777). As popular with business-people as vacationers, with spacious modern rooms and a good-sized swimming pool and spa. ④.

Lamplighter Inn, 1604 Monterey St (☎1-800/547-7787 or 805/547-7777). Older but comfortable motel with a pool. Popular with families. ③.

Madonna Inn, 100 Madonna Rd (☎1-800/543-9666 or 805/543-3000). Local landmark (see opposite) set in over 2000 acres, offering over a hundred theme-decorated rooms in a stupendously kitsch setting. ⑤.

Mid-Town Motel, 475 Marsh St (☎805/543-4533). Simple motel but excellent value. ②.

The Town

San Luis is eminently walkable, with a compact core centered around the late eighteenth-century **Mission San Luis Obispo de Tolosa** (daily June–Dec 9am–5pm; Jan–May 9am–4pm; donation), a fairly dark and unremarkable church that was the prototype for the now ubiquitous red-tiled roof, developed as a replacement for the original, flammable thatch in response to arson attacks by Native American tribes. Between the mission and the tourist office, **Mission Plaza**'s terraces step down along San Luis creek, along which footpaths meander, crisscrossed by bridges every hundred feet and overlooked by a number of stores and outdoor restaurants on the south bank. Downstream, across a small park, the San Luis Obispo County **Historical Museum** (Wed–Sun 10am–4pm; free) holds a low-key collection of local artifacts tending toward the domestic, housed in the richly detailed 1904 Carnegie Library building. The main drag, **Higuera Street** (pronounced "Hi-Geara"), a block south of Mission Plaza, springs to life every Thursday afternoon and evening for the **Farmer's Market**, when the street is closed to cars and filled with vegetable stalls, mobile barbecues and street-corner musicians. All of San Luis comes out to sample the foods and entertainment of this weekly county fair.

Monterey Street, which leads up the hill from Mission Plaza, holds some of the best of the town's commercial buildings, notably the 1884 **Sinsheimer Building** at no. 849, which has California's only surviving cast-iron facade; the **J.P. Andrews Building**, a block or so up, with its elaborately detailed frontage of granite and terracotta; and, a block further on, the Art Deco **Fremont Theater**. Many other distinguished buildings lie south of the business district, some of which – along Marsh Street above Santa Rosa Street – were built for railroad workers and their families, a reminder of the days when San Luis was a bustling railroad town.

Standing out from the many turn-of-the-century houses, built for middle-class families in a variety of exuberant late-Victorian styles with turrets and towers and other exotic touches, is a doctor's surgery on the corner of Santa Rosa and Pacific streets designed by **Frank Lloyd Wright** in 1955, at the end of his career. Wright's confident experimentation with forms and materials is as bold here as ever, most visibly in the abstracted images of the local volcanic landscape, cut out of plywood to form a frieze of windows and the clerestory above the waiting room – complete with signature hearth. The building isn't open for visits but during work hours you can pop in for a quick look.

If you have neither the time nor the inclination to sample the small-town charms of San Luis, at least stop to look at the now famous **Madonna Inn** (see "Accommodation" opposite), a shocking-pink behemoth along the highway just south of town that is the ultimate in kitsch, with a laser-activated waterfall to flush the gents' urinals (which look like whale mouths) and rooms decorated on a variety of themes from fairy-tale princesses to Stone Age cavemen. A very different sort of place is the **Shakespeare Press Museum** on the Cal Poly campus (Mon–Fri by appointment; ☎805/756-1108) – nothing to do with the Bard, but a great collection of old printing presses and lead typefaces, collected mainly from the frontier newspapers of California's Gold Rush towns.

Eating and drinking

Higuera Street is the place to head to **eat**, especially during the Thursday afternoon Farmer's Market, when barbecues and food stalls set up amidst the jostling crowds. You'll also find a couple of popular **bars** and **cafés** on and just off Higuera, around the Mission Plaza area.

Big Sky Café, 1121 Broad St (☎805/545-5401). An airy, modern place with an emphasis on Cajun and Creole food. $7 dishes and an assortment of coffees.

Buona Tavola, 1037 Monterey St (☎805/545-8000). Small and stylish bistro with good range of moderately priced northern Italian food and wine.

Cafe Roma, 1819 Osos St (☎805/541-6800). Extremely popular family-owned Italian restaurant with excellent pasta dishes served in a romantic setting for around $10.

The Graduate, 990 Industrial Way (☎805/541-0969). A mile east of the center but worth a trip for the low-priced beer and huge piles of food (all-you-can-eat specials before 9pm). Dancing nightly until 2am, popular with Cal Poly students.

Hudson's Grill, 1005 Monterey St (☎805/541-5999). Lively collegiate beer-and-burger bar open until midnight.

Linnaea's Café, 1110 Garden St, off Higuera (☎805/541-5888). A very successful small café, serving up good espresso and top-notch breakfasts, sandwiches, pastries, pies and cakes. There's occasionally live music at night, too.

Rhythm Creekside Café, 1040 Broad St, across from the Historical Museum beside the river (☎805/541-4048). Good, healthy, expensive food served on a waterfront terrace.

Spike's, 570 Higuera St (☎805/544-7157). This place has one of the best beer selections on the California Coast. Join its "Drink your way around the world" club and get a free beer for every dozen you sample – nobody minds if the burgers aren't that special.

Thai Classic, 1011 Higuera St (☎805/541-2025). Ignore the decor, the food's great – lots of traditional Thai cuisine at reasonable prices, with $4 weekday lunch specials. Closed Mon.

Tio Alberto's, 1131 Broad St (☎805/546-9646). San Luis Obispo's best burritos in a small windowed storefront a block off of Higuera – stuff yourself for less than $5.

Tortilla Flats, 1051 Nipomo St at Higuera (☎805/544-7575). Raucous, neon-lit Mexican restaurant, better known for copious margaritas than great food, but with free happy hour nachos and dancing from 9pm.

Woodstock's Pizza, 1000 Higuera St, (☎805/541-4420). Appetizing pizza and pitchers of beer served in this SLO institution. Sun–Thurs until 1am, Fri & Sat until 2am.

Morro Bay and the coast to Cambria

North of San Luis Obispo the highways diverge again, US-101 – and the trains and buses – speeding up through the Salinas Valley (see p.350), while Hwy-1 takes the scenic route along the coast. The first dozen miles of Hwy-1 follow the line of a ridge-back string of hills, a series of plugs from extinct volcanoes the most prominent of which have been dubbed the **Seven Sisters**. Two more continue the chain; the last is invisible under the sea, while the eighth is the coastal **Morro Rock** which, according to local lore, was named by the sixteenth-century explorer Juan Cabrillo, who thought it looked like the Moorish turbans in southern Spain. Nowadays it's off limits to the public in order to protect the nesting areas of the endangered peregrine falcons; in any case it's most impressive from a distance, dominating the fine harbor at **MORRO BAY**, where the local fishing boats unload their catches to sell in the many fish markets along the waterfront.

The adjacent easy-paced resort town is accessible from San Luis Obispo via CCAT **bus** #7 (6 times daily; ☎805/541-CCAT), though apart from the many seafood restaurants the only places worth coming here for are spread out around the bay, miles from public transportation. You get one of the best views of the rock and surrounding coastline from the top of **Cerro Alto**, eight miles east of Morro Bay off Hwy-41, a 2620-foot volcanic cone with good hiking and camping.

Closer in, on a point above the bay a mile south of town at the end of Main Street but providing a good view of Morro Rock, there's a small **Museum of Natural History** (daily 10am–5pm; $2); the **campground** across the street in **Morro Bay State Park** (reserve through Parknet ☎1-800/444-7275) costs $18 a night and has hot showers. Across the bay, the thin sandy peninsula that protects the harbor is hard to reach except by boat – it's entirely undeveloped and about the only place where you stand a chance of finding any Pismo clams. You can rent **kayaks**, which cost $6 per hour, from the likes of Kayaks of Morro Bay, 699 Embarcadero #9 (☎805/772-1119), or hike the two miles out there from Los Osos Valley Road.

Montaña de Oro State Park (☎805/528-0513; free), four miles south at the end of Los Osos Valley Road, is much more primitive than the Morro Bay park, and has some excellent tidepools. The windswept promontory stands solidly against the crashing sea, offering excellent hiking along the shore and through the sagebrush and eucalyptus trees of the upland hillsides, which in spring are covered in golden poppies.

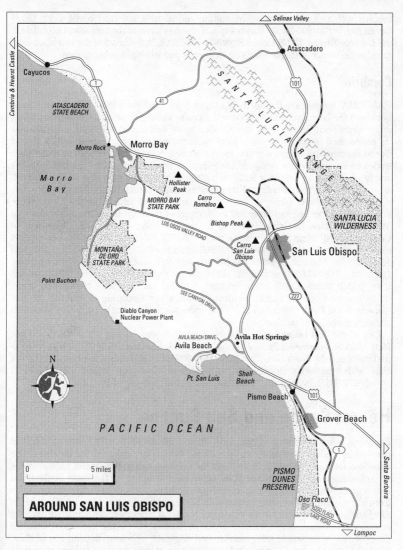

AROUND SAN LUIS OBISPO

There are $9 **campgrounds** in the park, and numerous reasonably priced **motels** in town, including a recently improved *Motel 6*, 298 Atascadero Rd (☎805/772-5641; ②), close to the beach. For **eating** try *Hofbrau Der Albatross*, 571 Embarcadero (☎805/772-2411), essentially a classy burger and sandwich joint but with added bratwurst and sauerkraut. The **Chamber of Commerce** is at 880 Main St (Mon–Fri 8am–5pm, Sat 10am–3pm; ☎ 1-800/231-0592 or 805/772-4467).

The next town north is **CAYUCOS**, four miles along Hwy-1, originally a small port built by Englishman James Cass in the 1870s, and now a sleepy place ranged along sandy beaches with a nice pier. For coffee, muffins and pastries, you can't beat *Kelley's*, 155 N Ocean Ave (☎805/995-2980). Surprisingly, it also has some of the area's best **nightlife** in the *Cayucos Tavern*, 130 N Ocean St (☎805/995-3209), in the heart of the two-block-long ramshackle center, with live bands on weekends and late-night poker games.

Cambria

CAMBRIA, ten miles to the north, is a touch pricey and more than a little pretentious, but about the best place to base yourself if you're visiting Hearst Castle, another seven miles further on. Hidden away in a wooded valley half a mile off Hwy-1, Cambria was an established town serving the local ranchers and fishermen long before Hearst Castle became the region's prime tourist attraction, and to some extent these days trades on its past, with a synthetic Olde English quarter along the highway. Skip this and head directly to the older and much nicer section half a mile east on Main Street, where the stores, restaurants and art galleries cater as much for locals as visitors.

There's not a lot to see or do in Cambria, but for **food and drink** the town excels. For details of the bed-and-breakfast inns, many of them on the picturesque seafront **Moonstone Beach Drive** (starting at around $70), contact the **Chamber of Commerce**, 767 Main St (daily 9am–5pm; ☎805/927-3624). Otherwise, the best **places to stay** are the *Cambria Palms Motel*, 2662 Main St (☎805/927-4485; ②), the *Bluebird Motel* at 1880 Main St (☎1-800/552-5434 or 805/927-4634; ③), or the *Cambria Pines Lodge* (☎1-800/445-6868 or 805/927-4200; ④) on Burton Drive on the hill above the town, which caters mostly to conferences, but also has very large rooms, and sometimes live music in its rustic, comfortable main bar. **Camping** is available at **San Simeon State Park** (☎805/927-2035) two miles north along the coast, where sites with showers cost $14, $7 without.

One of the best **breakfasts** this side of anywhere can be had at the *Redwood Café*, 2094 Main St, *Lombardi's Pasta Familia*, 4158 Bridge St (☎805/927-0777), lays on plentiful pasta and the *Sow's Ear*, 2248 Main St (☎805/927-4865), attracts locals and visitors alike with reasonably priced American dinners. *Camozzi's Saloon*, 2262 Main St (☎805/927-8941), is a rumbustious cowboy bar with occasional live bands.

Hearst Castle and San Simeon

Forty-five miles northwest of San Luis Obispo, **HEARST CASTLE** sits on a hilltop overlooking rolling ranchlands and the Pacific Ocean. Far and away the biggest single attraction for miles, bringing in over a million visitors a year, the former holiday home of publishing magnate **William Randolph Hearst** is one of the most opulent and extravagant houses in the world. Its interior combines walls, floors and ceilings stolen from European churches and castles with Gothic fireplaces and Moorish tiles, and is filled to overflowing with Greek vases and medieval tapestries. It's actually more of a complex of buildings than a "castle." Three guesthouses circle the hundred-room main *Casa Grande* – the whole thing surrounded originally by a free-roaming zoo of lions, tigers, bears and zebras – in which Hearst held court over the most famous politicians and movie stars of the 1920s and 1930s. Winston Churchill, Charlie Chaplin, George Bernard Shaw and Charles Lindbergh were just a few who accepted Hearst's invitation to come and stay for as long as they liked.

Hearst Castle, which Hearst himself referred to as "the ranch" (the official name is now "Hearst San Simeon State Historic Monument"), manifests all the subtlety and lightness of touch one would expect from the man whose domination of the national media inspired Orson Welles' classic film *Citizen Kane*. Construction began after his mother's death in 1919, on the southern edge of the 250,000-acre ranch he inherited. The work, managed by architect Julia Morgan, was never actually completed: rooms would often be torn out as soon as they were finished in order to accommodate some bits and pieces of old buildings Hearst had just acquired, and much of the structure's rough reinforced concrete is still exposed. The main facade, a twin-towered copy of a Mudejar cathedral, stands at the top of steps that curve up from an expansive swimming pool of pure spring water, lined by a Greek colonnade and marble statues. Inside the house, ketchup and mustard bottles complete the place-settings of fine crystal and china on the long dark oak table of the baronial dining hall, festooned with banners from Siena's Palio.

Practicalities

To see Hearst Castle you must take one of the guided **tours** (daily 8am–4pm; $14). Tour One, comprising a short film, an introductory spin around a guesthouse and the main rooms of the *Casa Grande*, is best for the first visit. If you're coming back, or are simply fascinated (and rich) enough to stay for a whole day, there are three other tours: Tour Two takes in the upper floors of the main house, including Hearst's library and bedroom suite, which occupies an entire floor; Tour Three concentrates on one of the guesthouses; Tour Four (summer only) is of the grounds and gardens. Special evening tours ($25) visit the house and grounds at sunset. For more information, or to arrange for a wheelchair – there are lots of stairs – phone ☎805/927-2020.

All tours take about two hours, including the fifteen-minute-each-way bus ride up and down the hill, and leave from the parking lot and visitor center on Hwy-1 where you buy tickets. **Reservations**, always a good idea and necessary in summer when tours sell out hours in advance, can be made through Parknet on ☎1-800/444-4445. While waiting for the tour bus, find out more about Hearst and his castle from the excellent **museum** (daily 9am–5pm; free) in the rear half of the visitor center, beyond the point where you board the buses.

W.R. HEARST – CITIZEN KANE

It would be quite easy to portray **William Randolph Hearst** (or "W.R.") as a power-mad monster, but in retrospect he seems more like a very rich, over-indulged little boy. Born in 1863, the only son of a multi-millionaire mining engineer, he was avidly devoted to his mother, Phoebe Apperson Hearst, one of California's most sincere and generous philanthropists, a founder of the University of California and the Traveler's Aid society.

Hearst learned his trade in New York City working for the inventor of inflammatory **"Yellow Journalism"**, Joseph Pulitzer, who had four rules for how to sell newspapers: one – emphasize the sensational; two – elaborate on the facts; three – manufacture the news; four – use games and contests. When he published his own newspaper, Hearst took this advice to heart, his *Morning Journal* fanning the flames of American imperialism to ignite the Spanish-American War of 1898. As he told his correspondents in Cuba: "You provide the pictures, and I'll provide the war." Hearst eventually controlled an empire that at its peak during the 1930s sold 25 percent of the newspapers in the entire country, including two other New York papers, the *Washington Times*, and the *Detroit News* – as well as *Cosmopolitan* and *Good Housekeeping* magazines. In California Hearst's power was even more pronounced, with his San Francisco and Los Angeles papers controlling over sixty percent of the total market.

Somewhat surprisingly, considering his warmongering and extreme nationalism, Hearst was fairly middle-of-the-road politically, a lifelong Democrat who served two terms in the House of Representatives but failed in bids to be elected Mayor of New York and President of the US. Besides his many newspapers, Hearst owned eleven radio stations and two movie studios, in which he made his mistress Marion Davies a star. He was forced to sell off most of his holdings by the end of the Depression, but continued to exert power and influence until his death in 1951 aged 88.

San Simeon and north

The boarded-up pier of **SAN SIMEON**, an all-but-abandoned harbor town along the coast just north of Hearst Castle, is where all of Hearst's treasures were unloaded, as were the many tons of concrete and steel that went into the building of the house. Before the Hearsts bought up the land, San Simeon was a whaling and shipping port, of which all that remains is a one-room schoolhouse and the 1852 Sebastian's Store, a combination post office, café and souvenir shop. The beach south of the pier is protected by San Simeon Point, which hooks out into the Pacific, making the beach safe for swimming. Along the highway three miles south there's a concentrated blot of gas stations, fast-food restaurants and **motels**, mostly overpriced but for a *Motel 6*, 9070 Castillo Rd (☎805/927-8691; ②). There's **camping** four miles south along the beach at San Simeon State Park (see p.348).

North of Hearst Castle the **coastline** is mostly rolling grasslands and cattle ranches still owned and run by the Hearst family, with few buildings on the distant hills. About three miles past San Simeon, a small strip of sand provides a resting point for a large colony of seals in the fall and early winter; illegal trails lead past a barbed wire fence down to the beach, where you can watch the huge piles of blubber cuddle one another and frolic in the waves. Beyond here the highway seems to drop off in mid-air, marking the southern edge of Big Sur (see p.354), probably the most dramatic stretch of coastline in America.

The Salinas Valley and Steinbeck Country

If you're in a hurry, US-101 through the **Salinas Valley** takes four hours to cover the 220 miles between San Luis Obispo and San Francisco, compared to the full day it takes to drive the more scenic coast along Hwy-1 through Big Sur. In any case, as both Greyhound and Amtrak take the inland route, you may not have the choice; of the two Greyhound is for once the better option, as its local buses stop at all the small rural towns. The four-lane freeway closely follows the path of El Camino Real, the trail that linked the 21 Spanish **missions** – each a day's travel from its neighbor – through the miles of farmland along the Salinas River that are some of the most fertile in the nation.

This region is also popularly known as **Steinbeck Country** for having nurtured the imagination of Nobel Prize-winning writer John Steinbeck, whose naturalistic stories and novels, including the epic *East of Eden*, were set in and around the valley.

The Salinas Valley

North of San Luis Obispo over the steep Cuesta Pass, US-101 drops down into the **Salinas Valley**, and, before long, **ATASCADERO**: a small town laid out to a curiously grand plan in 1914 that centers on its Palladian **City Hall**, a huge red-brick edifice whose domed rotunda now houses a small **museum** (Mon–Sat 1–4pm; free) describing the area's history.

PASO ROBLES, eight miles north, is a thriving little town surrounded by horse ranches, nut farms and a number of small, family-operated **wineries** that are among the finest in the state. Take a free and friendly tour (daily 10am–4pm) of the Arciero or Meridian wineries, five miles east of town on Hwy-46. Another ten miles east, past the junction of Hwy-41 near Cholame, pay your respects at the stainless steel monument near the site where **James Dean** met his maker in a silver Porsche Speedster on September 30, 1955.

Even if you're racing up US-101, it's worth taking a break from your journey to have a look at the most intact and authentic of California's Spanish missions, **Mission San**

Miguel Arcangel (daily 9.30am–4.30pm; donation), just off the freeway in the small town of **SAN MIGUEL**. Built in 1816, it's the only mission in the chain not to have suffered the revisionist tendencies of a restoration. It was actually used for a while as a saloon and dance hall, though the chapel has been left pretty much unscathed, with colorful painted decoration and a marvelous sunburst reredos, complete with a striking Eye of God. The other buildings are interesting too, in their rough imprecision, with irregularly arched openings and unplastered walls forming a courtyard around a cactus garden. The *Western States Inn*, right off Hwy 101 on Tenth St (☎805/467-3674; ②), is the only hotel in town and has surprisingly comfortable rooms.

There's a second mission, accessible only by car, twenty miles west of US-101 along the Jolon Road (G-18), which splits off the highway twelve miles north of San Miguel. The **Mission San Antonio de Padua** (Mon–Sat 9.30am–4.30pm, Sun 11am–5pm; donation) is a rarely visited restoration of the 1771 settlement, less sanitized than some of the other California missions and giving a very good idea of what life might have been like for the missionaries and their converts. This mission was among the most prosperous of the entire chain, and around the extensive grounds, in a wide valley of oak trees and tall grasses, a number of scattered exhibits describe the work that went on in the long-abandoned vineyard, tannery and gristmill. There's a monastic peace to Mission San Antonio these days, and the brown-robed Franciscan friars who live here are rarely disturbed, despite being in the middle of the Hunter Liggett Army Base; indeed the only sign of the military is at the gates of the base, five miles east of the mission, where you'll have to show your passport or some other form of ID. The large house across the valley from the mission used to belong to W.R. Hearst, who sold it and most of the land between here and Hearst Castle to the government in 1940 to help clear a $120 million debt. The **Nacimiento-Fergusson Road** leads from the mission on a tortuous but picturesque journey over the mountains, past a couple of enticing $10 National Forest **campgrounds**, to Big Sur (see p.354).

Nearby **JOLON** has a market and gas station, and the washed-out ruins of an 1840s stagecoach stop at the **Old Dutton Hotel**. The San Antonio Reservoir, five miles southeast, has swimming, **camping** and showers along the west shore, as does the Nacimiento Reservoir further south.

The Jolon Road loops back to US-101 at **KING CITY**: "the most metropolitan cow town in the West," as it likes to be known. On the town's western edge, just off US-101, San Lorenzo Park is the site of the **Agricultural and Rural Life Museum** (daily 9am–5pm; free, parking $3, Sat & Sun $5), a collection of old barns, farmhouses and a one-room schoolhouse, all gathered here from various sites in Monterey county. The park also has a **campground** ($13) with hot showers, along the Salinas River. Backpacking permits for the **Ventana Wilderness** in the Santa Lucia Mountains, which divide the Salinas Valley from the Big Sur coast, are handled by the **US Forest Service** office, off the freeway at 406 S Mildred Ave (Mon–Fri 8am–4.30pm; ☎831/385-5434).

The Pinnacles National Monument and around

From King City, you have a choice of approaches to the bizarre rock formations of the **Pinnacles National Monument** ($5 per vehicle); either follow G-13 and Hwy-25 to the eastern entrance and the **visitor center** (daily 8am–5pm; ☎831/389-4485), or continue up Hwy-101 to Soledad (see overleaf) and turn onto Hwy-146 to the more spectacular western side. Contrary to what appears on some maps, no road goes right through the monument, but the place is small and it is quite possible to hike from one side to the other and back in a day.

This region of grotesque volcanic spires, brilliant reds and golds against the blue sky, is best visited in the spring, when the air is still cool and the chaparral hillsides are covered in wildflowers, in particular the orange California poppy and deep-lilac Owl's

Clover. Its many **trails** include a four mile loop around the high peaks on the **Juniper Canyon Trail**, and the two-mile **Balconies Trail** to the multicolored, 600-foot face of the **Balconies** outcrop – good for **rock-climbing** (register at the visitor center and use only brown chalk) – and a nearby series of talus **caves** (take a flashlight), formed by huge boulders that have become wedged between the walls of the narrow canyons. These pitch-black caves were popular with bandits who would hide out here after robbing stagecoaches.

The trails are exposed so avoid hiking in the middle of the day in summer, and remember to carry plenty of **water**. There are nineteen walk-in **campgrounds** ($10), each of which only accommodates six people, and the commercial, swimming pool-equipped *Pinnacles Campground Inc* ($6 per person), just outside the park. All are first-come-first-served.

Soledad, Mission Soledad and Paraiso hot springs

The nearest town to the Pinnacles is **SOLEDAD**, a quiet farming community twelve miles west of the western entrance. It has a definite Mexican flavor, its *panaderias* selling cakes and fresh tortillas – a good place to stock up on food and drink for a trip to the monument. The only other reason to stop is for a visit to **Mission Nuestra Señora de la Soledad** (daily except Tues 10am–4pm; donation), three miles west of US-101 on the south side of town, which lay neglected for over a hundred years until there was little left but a pile of mud. The mission was never a great success (perhaps because of its full name, which translates as the "most sorrowful mystery of the solitude"), suffering through a history of epidemics, floods and crop failures. Parts have been dutifully restored and now contain a museum on mission life, but the **ruins** adjacent to the rebuilt church are the most evocative section.

More hedonistically you could head out to **Paraiso Hot Springs** (daily 8am–5pm; ☎831/678-2882), seven miles further west, high above Soledad in the foothills of the Santa Lucia Mountains: a palm-treed oasis looking out across the Salinas Valley to the Gabilan Mountains and the Pinnacles National Monument. The natural hot springs were popular with the local Native Americans for their healing properties, and have been operated as a commercial venture since 1895. The series of pools costs $25 a day to enter, and you can **camp** here overnight for a further $5.

While you pamper yourself in the steamy water, it's worth remembering that most Californians know Soledad for one thing only: as the site of the **Soledad State Penitentiary** – a grim building looming alongside US-101 two miles north of town where black militant "Soledad Brother" George Jackson was imprisoned for many years.

Salinas and around

The second-largest city between LA and San Francisco and the seat of Monterey County, **SALINAS**, twenty miles north, is a sprawling agricultural town of 120,000 people. It's best known as the birthplace of John Steinbeck, and for the **California Rodeo** the biggest in the state, held here during the third week in July. These attractions aside you may well find yourself here anyway: Salinas is a main stop for Greyhound buses and the Coast Starlight train, and makes an excellent and inexpensive base for exploring the perhaps more obvious attractions of the **Monterey Peninsula**, twenty miles away over the Santa Lucia mountains, with the MST bus #21 making the 55-minute trip every hour from the Transit Center on Salinas Street.

Salinas and the agricultural valley to the south are often bracketed together as Steinbeck Country. The writer **John Steinbeck** was born and raised in Salinas, though there's not a lot left to remind you of his presence: he left the town in his mid-twenties to live in Monterey and later in New York City. His childhood home at 132 Central Ave has been turned into an English-style tearoom; head instead for the **Steinbeck Room**

THE NOVELS OF JOHN STEINBECK

John Steinbeck's novels and stories are as valuable and interesting for their historical content as for their narratives. **The Grapes of Wrath**, his best-known work, was made into a film starring Henry Fonda while still at the top of the bestseller lists, having captured the popular imagination for its portrayal of the miseries of the Joad family on their migration to California from the Dust Bowl. *Cannery Row* followed in 1945, a nostalgic portrait of the Monterey fisheries, which ironically went into steep decline the year the book was published. Steinbeck spent the next four years writing *East of Eden*, an allegorical retelling of the biblical story of Cain and Abel against the landscape of the Salinas Valley, in which he expresses many of the values that underlie the rest of his work. Much of Steinbeck's writing is concerned with the dignity of labor, and with the inequalities of an economic system that "allows children to go hungry in the midst of rotting plenty". Although he was circumspect about his own political stance, when *The Grapes of Wrath* became a bestseller in 1939 there was a violent backlash against Steinbeck in Salinas for what were seen as his Communist sympathies.

of the public library two blocks away at 110 W San Luis St (daily 10am–6pm; free), which displays a variety of manuscripts and memorabilia.

Today as much as in Steinbeck's day, Salinas is a hotbed of labor disputes, with the gap between the wealthy owners and agribusiness empires that run the giant farms and the low-paid manual laborers who pick the produce still unbridged. In the 1960s and early 1970s the United Farm Workers union, under the leadership of Cesar Chavez and Dolores Huerta, had great success in organizing and demanding better pay and conditions for the almost exclusively Latino workforce, most notably masterminding a very effective boycott of the valley's main product, lettuce. But workers are once again under siege, with wages less than half of what they were fifteen years ago amidst increasing worries about the dangers of exposure to pesticides and agricultural chemicals.

Salinas is not the sort of place where you'd expect to find a large public sculpture by a major avant-garde artist, but **Claus Oldenburg's** *Hat in Three Stages of Landing* is just that: a triad of giant yellow steel cowboy hats floating above the grass between the Salinas Community Art Gallery and the Rodeo Grounds, at 940 N Main St. On the outskirts of town, at the end of West Laurel Drive a mile west of US-101, the **Boronda Adobe** lies in the middle of rich farmland, virtually unaltered since its construction in 1848, alongside other historic structures that have been brought to the site as part of an expanding regional history center.

Between Salinas and the Monterey Peninsula, twenty miles distant via Hwy-68, are a couple of other places of divergent interest. **SPRECKELS**, five miles southwest, is a small factory town with an arts-and-crafts feel, built in 1898 for employees of the Spreckels sugar factory, at the time the largest in the world: the small torchlike wooden objects on the gable ends of the many workers' cottages are supposed to represent sugar beets. Parts of the movie *East of Eden* were filmed here, including the famous scene when James Dean – playing Cal – hurls blocks of ice down a chute to get his father's attention.

Along Hwy-68 halfway to Monterey you'll come to **Laguna Seca Raceway** (☎831/373-1811), where race driver and part-time actor Paul Newman keeps in practice on the two-mile road course; races are held throughout the summer, and there's also **camping**.

Practicalities

Hourly Greyhound buses between LA and San Francisco stop in the center of town at 19 W Gabilan St near Salinas Street, while Amtrak trains leave once a day in each direction, two blocks away at 40 Railroad Ave. For a handy **place to stay** try the *Traveler's Hotel* at 16 E Gabilan St (☎831/758-1198; ①), which is convenient, if seedy; if you're driving choose from the many $45-a-night **motels** along Main Street on either side of US-101. For help with finding a place to stay, and for a free **map** and guide to the places that Steinbeck wrote about, contact the **Chamber of Commerce** at 119 E Alisal St (Mon 9am–5pm, Tues–Fri 8.30am–5pm, Sat 9am–3pm; ☎831/424-7611). There are quite a few good **Mexican restaurants** around the city, the best, oldest and most central being *Rosita's Armory Café*, 231 Salinas St (☎831/424-7039), open daily from 9am until midnight for fine food and stiff margaritas.

The Big Sur Coast

The California coastline is at its most spectacular along the ninety miles of rocky cliffs and crashing sea known as **BIG SUR**. This is not the lazy beachfront of Southern California, but a sublime landscape at the edge of a continent, where redwood groves line river canyons and the Santa Lucia mountains rise straight out of the blue Pacific. Named by the Spanish *El Pais Grande del Sur*, the "big country to the south" (of their colony at Monterey), it's still a wild and undeveloped region except for occasional outposts along the narrow **Hwy-1**, the dramatic coast road that follows a tortuous, exhilarating route carved out of bedrock cliffs five hundred feet above the Pacific Ocean, passing by mile after mile of rocky coves and steep, narrow canyons.

Before the highway was completed in 1937, the few inhabitants of Big Sur had to be almost entirely self-sufficient: farming, raising cattle and trapping sea otters for their furs. The only connections with the rest of the world were by infrequent steamship to Monterey, or by a nearly impassable trail over the mountains to the Salinas Valley. Perhaps surprisingly, even fewer people live in the area today than a hundred years ago, and most of the land is still owned by a handful of families, many of whom are descendants of Big Sur's original pioneers. Locals have banded together to fight US government plans to allow offshore oil-drilling, and to protect the land from obtrusive development. If you'd like to know more about Big Sur's history and the contentious present, an excellent free **guide** to the area, *El Sur Grande*, is available at ranger stations and the Big Sur post office.

The coast is also the protected habitat of the sea otter, and gray whales pass by close to the shore on their annual winter migration. Visit in April or May to see the vibrant wildflowers and lilac-colored ceanothus bushes, though the sun shines longest, without the morning coastal fog, in early autumn through until November. Hardly anyone braves the turbulent winters, when violent storms drop most of the eighty inches of rain that fall each year, often taking sections of the highway with it into the sea. Summer weekends, however, see the roads and campgrounds packed to overflowing – though even in peak season, if you're willing to walk a mile or two, it's still easy to get away from it all.

The best way to see Big Sur is slowly, leaving the car behind to wander through the many parks and wilderness preserves, where a ten-minute walk takes you from any sign of the rest of the world. The only **public transportation** is by the summer-only MST bus #22 from Monterey (see p.362) running as far south as Nepenthe, four times a day in each direction, though the narrow Hwy-1 is a perennial favorite with cyclists.

Much the most interesting, and most developed, stretch of Big Sur is the northern end, ranged along the wide and clear Big Sur River, 25 miles south of Monterey and focusing on **Pfeiffer Big Sur State Park**, where you can swim among giant boulders, hike up redwood canyons to a waterfall or sunbathe on a fine sandy beach. There is no Big Sur village as such, just a ten-mile string of grocery stores, gas stations and places to eat and drink dotted at roughly one-mile intervals on either side of the park. The main concentrations are by the post office two miles south of the Pfeiffer Big Sur State Park, at Fernwood, a mile north of the park entrance and, confusingly, at The Village a further mile and a half north. Almost everything you may need to know is in the free *El Sur Grande* newspaper, but you could also call the **Chamber of Commerce** (☎831/667-2100) or the **park headquarters** (☎831/667-2315).

We've gathered all our **accommodation**, **camping** and **eating** recommendations for the Big Sur area into comprehensive listings starting on p.357.

Southern Big Sur

The southern coastline of Big Sur is the region at its most gentle – not unlike Portugal's Algarve, with sandy beaches hidden away below eroding yellow-ochre cliffs. The landscape grows more extreme the further north you go. Twenty miles north of Hearst Castle, a steep trail leads down along Salmon Creek to a coastal waterfall, while the chaparral-covered hills above were booming during the 1880s with the gold mines of the **Los Burros Mining District**.

Another ten miles north, the cliffs get steeper and the road more perilous around the vista point at **Willow Creek**, where you can watch the surfers and the sea otters playing in the waves. **Jade Cove**, a mile north, takes its name from the translucent California jade stones that are sometimes found here, mainly by scuba divers offshore. The rocky cove is a ten-minute walk from the highway, along a trail marked by a wooden stile in the cattle fence.

Just beyond the Plaskett Creek **campground**, half a mile to the north, **Sand Dollar Beach** is a good place to enjoy the surf or watch for **hang gliders**, launched from sites in the mountains off the one-lane Plaskett Ridge Road. This steep road is good fun on a mountain bike, and passes by a number of free basic campgrounds along the ridge, ending at the paved Nacimiento-Fergusson Road. Check at the **Pacific Valley ranger station** (☎805/927-4211; irregular hours) for up-to-date information on backcountry camping, since some areas may be closed in summer during the peak of the fire season. The station also handles the 25 permits a day allowed to people wanting to hang-glide, ten of which are given out on a first-come-first-served basis on the day. **Pacific Valley Center**, a mile north, has an expensive gas station, a grocery store and a good coffee shop, open from 8am until dark.

Kirk Creek to Julia Pfeiffer Burns State Park

The coastal **campground** at **Kirk Creek** (see p.357) sits at the foot of the **Nacimiento-Fergusson Road**, which twists over the Santa Lucia mountains to the Salinas Valley. The road passes the excellent Mission San Antonio de Padua (see p.351), but it would be a shame to break the continuity of the drive up the coast, and in any case the views are better coming over the hills in the other direction. Two miles north of here, **Limekiln Creek** is named after the hundred-year-old kilns that survive in good condition along the creek behind the privately owned **campground**. In the 1880s local limestone was burned in these kilns to extract lime powder for use as cement, then carried on a complex aerial tramway to be loaded onto ships at Rockland Landing. The ships that carried the lime to Monterey brought in most of the supplies to this isolated area.

ESALEN, ten miles further north, is named after the local Native Americans, the first tribe in California to be made culturally extinct. Before they were wiped out, they frequented the healing waters of the natural **hot spring** here (nightly 1–3am; $10; must reserve on ☎831/667-3047), at the top of a cliff two hundred feet above the raging Pacific surf – now owned and operated by the Esalen Institute. Since the 1960s, when all sorts of people came to Big Sur to smoke dope and get back to nature, Esalen has been at the forefront of the "New Age" human potential movement. Today's devotees tend to arrive in BMWs on Friday nights for the expensive, reservation-only massage treatments, yoga workshops and seminars on Eastern religion and philosophy; phone ☎831/667-3000 for information on classes and workshops.

Julia Pfeiffer Burns State Park (daily dawn–dusk; $6 parking), three miles north of Esalen along McWay Creek, has some of the best day hikes in the Big Sur area: a ten-minute walk from the parking area leads under the highway along the edge of the cliff to an overlook of McWay Falls, which crash onto a beach below Saddle Rock. A less-traveled path leads down from Hwy-1 two miles north of the waterfall (at milepost 37.85) through a two-hundred-foot-long tunnel to the wave-washed remains of a small wharf at **Partington Cove**, one of the few places in Big Sur where you can get to the sea.

Nepenthe and Pfeiffer Beach

Big Sur's commercial development starts in earnest with **NEPENTHE**, a complex of restaurants and stores named after the mythical drug that induces forgetfulness of grief. It stands atop the hilltop site where star-crossed lovers Orson Welles and Rita Hayworth once shared a cabin. The excellent restaurant here has been run since the 1960s by the family of master knitter and painter Kaffe Fassett, who grew up in Big Sur – though *Café Kevah* (see p.358), on a rooftop terrace just down the hill, is more afford-able and has arguably more impressive views. Downstairs there's an outdoor sculpture gallery and a decent bookstore, including works by, among others, Henry Miller, who lived in the area on and off until the 1960s. The **Henry Miller Library** across Hwy-1 (daily hours vary, ☎831/667-2574; donation) displays an informal collection of first-edi-tion books and mementos of the writer's life in the house of Miller's old friend Emil White. The library has also evolved into a popular performance and exhibit space, fea-turing weekly poetry readings, writing workshops, and works by local artists; call for a current schedule.

Two miles north along Hwy-1, the unmarked Sycamore Canyon Road leads a mile west to Big Sur's best beach, **Pfeiffer Beach** (open until dusk), a sometimes windy, white-sand stretch dominated by a charismatic hump of rock whose color varies from brown to red to orange in the changing light. Park where you can at the end of the road, and walk through an archway of cypress trees along the lagoon to the sands.

The Big Sur River Valley

Two miles north of Pfeiffer Beach, and 65 miles north of Hearst Castle, Hwy-1 drops down behind a coastal ridge into the valley of the Big Sur River, where most of the accommodation and eating options are located.

The first stop should be the US Forest Service **ranger station** (daily 8am–6pm; ☎831/667-2423) which handles the camping permits for the Ventana Wilderness in the mountains above. A popular hike leads steeply up from the Pine Ridge trailhead behind the station, six miles into the mountains to **Sykes Hot Springs** (unrestricted entry), just downstream from the free **campground** at Sykes Camp along the Big Sur River, continuing fifteen miles over the Santa Lucia mountains to the **Tassajara Zen Buddhist Center**, where you can reward yourself with a dip in the natural hot springs (May–Sept; reservations required ☎415/431-3771; $12).

Plumb in the middle of the valley, the **Pfeiffer Big Sur State Park** ($6 per vehicle) is one of the most beautiful and enjoyable parks in California, with miles of hiking trails and excellent swimming along the Big Sur River – which in late spring and summer has deep swimming holes among the large boulders in the bottom of the narrow steep-walled gorge. The water is clean and clear, nude sunbathing is tolerated (except on National Holidays, when the park tends to be overrun with swarms of screaming chil-dren) and, since it's sheltered a mile or so inland, the weather is warmer and sunnier than elsewhere along the coast. This is also the center for information on all the other parks in the area, and the main **campground** in the entire Big Sur region.

The most popular hiking trail in the park leads to the sixty-foot **Pfeiffer Falls**, half a mile up a narrow canyon shaded by redwood trees from a trailhead opposite the entrance. The thoroughly functional bridges over the river have an understated grace, as does the nearby amphitheater – built by the Civilian Conservation Corps during the Depression – where rangers give excellent campfire talks and slide shows about Big Sur.

Accommodation

In keeping with Big Sur's backwoodsy qualities, most of the available **accommodation** is in rustic (but rarely inexpensive) mountain lodges, and the very few rooms on offer are full most nights throughout the summer, especially on weekends. Mid-range accommodation is limited to a few cabins and motels, usually adjoining a privately oper-

---

CAMPING IN BIG SUR

Public campgrounds are dotted all along the Big Sur coast, in addition to a few less developed ones in the Santa Lucia mountains above, where you can also see deer, bobcats and (rarely) mountain lions. Sites along the coast are popular year-round, and all, unless otherwise stated, are available for around $15 a night (a rare few with $3 per person hiker/biker sites) on a first-come-first-served basis, so get there early in the day to ensure a space. Reservations are, however, taken at Pfeiffer Big Sur State Park, through Parknet ☎1-800/444-7275. For further **information** on camping in Big Sur phone the State Parks (☎831/667-2315) or the Los Padres National Forest office in King City (☎831/385-5434). The following campgrounds are listed south to north:

Plaskett Creek. Thirty miles north of Hearst Castle and a mile south of Pacific Valley. Across the highway from the ocean with some hiker/biker sites. $17.

Kirk Creek. Three miles north of Pacific Valley and more exposed, but right on the ocean and with hiker/biker sites.

Nacimiento. Shaded, streamside site in the Santa Lucia mountains, 11 miles inland along the Nacimiento-Fergusson Road. $5.

Ponderosa. Two miles further inland from the Nacimiento site and equally appealing. $5.

Limekiln State Park (☎831/667-2403). Two miles south of Lucia, with hot showers, general store, and developed trail to the limekilns. $22.

Julia Pfeiffer Burns State Park. Has two campgrounds, beautifully situated overlooking the Pacific at the end of the Overlook Trail. There's no water, the toilets are primitive, and the area is often windy and chilly even in summer. $14.

Pfeiffer Big Sur State Park. This is the main campground in the area, with spacious and well-shaded sites, many among the redwoods. Hot showers, a well-stocked store, a laundrette and some (officially) biker-only sites. $17.

Andrew Molera State Park. The only walk-in site around. A vast meadow, half a mile from the beach, with water and latrines. First-come-first-served basis, so show up early. Camping payment waives day-use fee. $3.

Bottcher's Gap. Eight miles inland from Hwy-1 on Palo Colorado Road, eighteen miles north of Pfeiffer Big Sur State Park. A good base for exploring the Ventana Wilderness. No water and no fee.

There are also four commercially operated **campgrounds** in the Big Sur Valley: *Ventana* (☎831/667-2688), *Fernwood* (☎831/667-2422), *Riverside* (☎831/667-2414), and *Big Sur* (☎831/667-2322). All charge about $24 a night for two people, offer deluxe facilities, and accept reservations; they also rent out **cabins** (see "Big Sur accommodation", above). By Californian standards, all are fairly crowded, and all but *Riverside* mix tents with RVs.

ated campground or right along the highway, and not really ideal for getting the total Big Sur experience. If you're having trouble, Big Sur Reservations (☎831/667-2929), will help you find a room to fit your tastes.

Big Sur Campgrounds and Cabins, a mile north of Pfeiffer Big Sur State Park (☎831/667-2322). Campground with the best of the cabins: wooden tent affairs sleeping up to three for $40 and fancier places from $65. ②.

Big Sur Lodge, in Pfeiffer Big Sur State Park (☎1-800/424-4787 or 831/667-3100). Good-sized modern cabins arranged around a large swimming pool; popular with families. ④.

Deetjen's Big Sur Inn, on Hwy-1 seven miles north of Julia Pfeiffer Burns State Park (☎831/667-2377). The southernmost, oldest and perhaps nicest of the Big Sur lodges, with twenty very different rooms hand-crafted from thick redwood planks, all with fireplaces. ④.

Glen Oaks Motel, just over a mile north of Pfeiffer Big Sur State Park (☎831/667-2105). Tidy simple rooms with baths, close to the highway. ④.

River Inn Resort, two and a half miles north of Pfeiffer Big Sur State Park (☎1-800/548-3610 or 831/667-2700). Woodsy lodge with a handful of very nice (if pricey) rooms overlooking the river, and more basic motel-style rooms across Hwy-1. ④.

Eating and drinking

Most of the places to **eat and drink** in Big Sur are attached to the inns and resorts listed above. Many of these are fairly basic burger-and-beer bars right along the highway, but there are a few special ones worth searching out, some for their good food and others for their views of the Pacific. Because of its isolation, prices anywhere in Big Sur are around 25 percent higher than you'd pay in town.

Café Kevah, Nepenthe (☎831/667-2344). Subtly prepared wholefood concoctions served up on a sunny, outdoor terrace. Big Sur's best views and a dozen healthy and flavorful variations on Eggs Benedict, plus a range of coffees and ice-cold bottles of Red Tail Ale. March–Dec 9am–4pm.

Deetjen's Big Sur Inn, on Hwy-1 seven miles north of Julia Pfeiffer Burns State Park (☎831/667-2377). Excellent, unhurried breakfasts ($8) and a variety of top-quality fish and vegetarian dinners ($13–25) in a snug, redwood-paneled room.

Fernwood Burgers, Hwy-1 a mile north of Pfeiffer Big Sur State Park (☎831/667-2422). For burgers or fish-and-chips, this budget diner is the place. There's a small grocery store/deli in the same building if you want to pick up supplies for a picnic.

Glen Oaks Restaurant, Hwy-1 in The Village (☎831/667-2264). Gourmet California cuisine – mostly fresh fish and pasta dishes, with some vegetarian options – in a cozy, flower-filled cottage. $12–16.

Nepenthe, Nepenthe (☎831/667-2345). Up the hill from the *Café Kevah*, this steak-and-seafood place has raging fires, an amazing view, and a James Bond-ish après-ski atmosphere.

River Inn Resort, at the north end of The Village (☎1-800/548-3610 or 831/625-5255). Tasty range of sautéed and grilled seafood starters and hearty main dishes, served in a spacious, redwood-log dining room. In summer you can linger over lunch or an evening drink in the lovely riverside garden, or on the sunny terrace; in winter, the fireplace attracts locals and visitors in about equal numbers. Also offers accommodation (see above) and presents some kind of entertainment on the weekend.

North to Monterey

Though it's rarely visited, **Andrew Molera State Park** (daily dawn–dusk; parking $4), five miles north of Pfeiffer Big Sur State Park is the largest park in Big Sur with two and a half miles of rocky oceanfront reached by a mile-long trail. It occupies the site of what was the El Sur Ranch, one of the earliest and most successful Big Sur cattle ranches, initially run by Juan Bautista Alvarado, who later became California governor, and later by English sea captain Roger Cooper, whose cabin is preserved here. You can reach it on some of the fifteen miles of hiking trails also used for guided two-hour

horseback rides from the stables ($25–55; ☎ 1-800/942-5486 or 831/625-5486). There is also walk-in **camping** (see box on p.357).

From the north end of the park the Old Coast Road takes off inland from Hwy-1 up over the steep hills, affording panoramic views out over miles of coastline. The part-paved, roughly ten-mile road winds over wide-open ranch lands and through deep, slender canyons until it rejoins the main highway at **Bixby Creek Bridge**, fifteen miles south of Carmel. When constructed in 1932 this was the longest single-span concrete bridge in the world, and is the most impressive (and photogenic) engineering feat of the Coast Road project.

A mile and a half north, beyond the **Point Sur Light Station** (tours Sat 10am & 2pm, Sun 10am $5; ☎831/625-4419), a paved road turns off up **Palo Colorado Canyon**, past a number of houses and the remains of an old lumber mill obscured behind the redwood trees, finishing up eventually at Bottcher's Gap campground on the edge of the Ventana Wilderness. On the coast at the foot of the road, the derelict buildings at **Notley's Landing** were once part of a bustling port community. The northernmost stop on the wild Big Sur coast is at **Garrapata State Park** (daily dawn-dusk), three miles south of Point Lobos and the Monterey Peninsula. A mile-long trail leads from Hwy-1 out to the tip of **Soberanes Point**, about ten miles south of Carmel – a good place to watch for sea otters and gray whales.

The Monterey Peninsula

Waves which lap quietly about the jetties of Monterey grow louder and larger in the distance . . . and from all around, even in quiet weather, the low, distant, thrilling roar of the Pacific hangs over the coast and the adjacent country like smoke from a battle.

Robert Louis Stevenson, *The Old Pacific Capital.*

The dramatic headlands of the **Monterey Peninsula** mark the northern edge of the spectacular Big Sur coast, a rocky promontory where gnarled cypress trees amplify the collision between the cliffs and the thundering sea. The towns here thrive on the tourist trade, though each has a character very much its own. **Monterey**, the largest of the three and a lively harbor town, was the capital of California under the Spanish and Mexicans, and retains many old adobe houses and places of genuine historic appeal alongside some overstated attractions. **Carmel-by-the-Sea**, on the other hand, three miles to the south, is a contrivedly quaint village of million-dollar holiday homes, best known for the many golf courses that line the coast nearby. Smallest of the trio, **Pacific Grove**, at the very tip of the peninsula amid its most arresting scenery, is far enough off the beaten track to preserve its Victorian seaside character reasonably intact.

Arrival, information and getting around

The Monterey Peninsula juts out into the Pacific to form the Monterey Bay, a hundred miles south of San Francisco; coastal Hwy-1 cuts across its neck, and Hwy-68 links up with US-101 at Salinas, twenty miles east. Greyhound **buses** (three daily in each direction between LA and San Francisco) stop at the Exxon station, 1042 Del Monte Ave, along the Monterey waterfront. Amtrak **trains** stop in Salinas, connecting with local bus #21 for the 55-minute trip (every hour) to Monterey.

The Monterey Chamber of Commerce **tourist office** at 380 Alvarado St (Mon–Fri 8.30am–5pm; ☎831/649-1770) has fairly comprehensive accommodation listings, but you might find it easier to stop by the town's **visitor center**, 401 Camino El Estero (April–Oct Mon–Sat 9am–6pm, Sun 9am–5pm; Nov–March Mon–Sat 9am–5pm, Sun

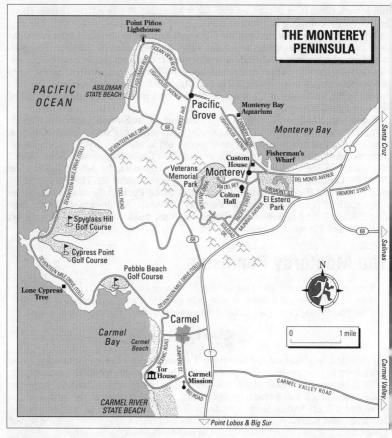

THE MONTEREY PENINSULA

Point Piños Lighthouse

PACIFIC OCEAN

ASILOMAR STATE BEACH

OCEAN VIEW BLVD

ASILOMAR BLVD

LIGHTHOUSE AVENUE

FOREST AVE

Pacific Grove

Monterey Bay Aquarium

Monterey Bay

68

SEVENTEEN MILE DRIVE

LIGHTHOUSE AVENUE

CANNERY ROW

Custom House

Fisherman's Wharf

Veterans Memorial Park

Monterey

DEL MONTE AVENUE

TOLL ROAD

SKYLINE DRIVE

VIA DEL REY

PACIFIC STREET

FREMONT ST.

FREMONT STREET

Colton Hall

El Estero Park

Spyglass Hill Golf Course

MUNRAS AVENUE

SOLEDAD DR.

68

SEVENTEEN MILE DRIVE (TOLL)

Cypress Point Golf Course

Pebble Beach Golf Course

SEVENTEEN MILE DRIVE (TOLL)

Lone Cypress Tree

N

0   1 mile

Carmel

Carmel Bay

Carmel Beach

SCENIC ROAD

JUNIPERO ST.

1

Santa Cruz

Salinas

68

Carmel Valley

Tor House

Carmel Mission

RIO ROAD

CARMEL VALLEY ROAD

CARMEL RIVER STATE BEACH

▽ Point Lobos & Big Sur

10am–5pm; no phone): park outside for free and walk the six blocks into town. The **Monterey County Travel and Tourism Alliance**, 137 Crossroads Blvd, in Carmel (daily 9.30am–6pm; ☎831/626-1424) has extensive information on the entire peninsula and will help with hotel reservations. The **Carmel Business Association** (Mon–Fri 9am–5pm; ☎831/624-2522), hidden away upstairs on San Carlos Street above the *Hog's Breath Inn*, midway between Fifth and Sixth, is another possible source of rooms but has little other information, while the Pacific Grove **Chamber of Commerce** (Mon–Fri 9am–5pm, Sat 11am–3pm; ☎831/373-3304), across from the Natural History Museum at Forest and Central, has walking tour maps of the town's historic buildings and can help find a room in the many local bed and breakfast inns. The best guides to **what's on** in the area are the widely available freebies *Go!*, *The Coast Weekly* and *Peninsula*, all with listings of movies, music and art galleries.

Getting around is surprisingly easy: Monterey–Salinas Transit (MST) buses (☎831/899-2555) run between 7am and 6pm (11pm on some routes), radiating out from Transit Plaza in the historic core of Monterey, and covering the entire region from Nepenthe on the Big Sur coast north to Watsonville near Santa Cruz and inland to the agricultural heartland of the Salinas Valley. The region is divided into four zones: the peninsula, Salinas, Big Sur and the north coast; fares are $1.50 per zone, $3 for an all-day, single zone pass, and $6 for an all routes, all zones day pass. The most useful routes are buses #4 and #5, which link Monterey with Carmel; #21, which runs between Monterey and Salinas; and #1, which runs along Lighthouse Avenue out to Pacific Grove; there's also the WAVE shuttle bus which runs every ten minutes from downtown to the Monterey Bay Aquarium on Cannery Row, and from Cannery Row to Pacific Grove, costing $1.25 but free if you can present an MST receipt for that day. The only way to get to the Big Sur coast on public transportation is on bus #22, which leaves four times a day, in summer only.

Another option is to **rent a bike** for $24 a day: in Monterey, try Adventures by the Sea, 201 Alvarado Mall (☎831/372-1807) outside the Maritime Museum, or Bay Sports, 640 Wave St (☎831/646-9090) on Cannery Row; there's also a branch in Carmel (☎831/625-BIKE) on Lincoln between Fifth and Sixth. For more leisurely riding, Monterey Mopeds (☎831/373-2696) at 1250 Del Monte north of the Wharf rents mopeds for $20 per hour and $50 per day.

Accommodation

What Santa Barbara is to southern California, the Monterey Peninsula is to the north, making it among the most exclusive and expensive resort areas in California, with **hotel** and **bed and breakfast** room rates averaging $120 a night. This may tempt you to stay elsewhere – in Santa Cruz, or in agricultural Salinas – and come here on day-trips; the other budget option is to avail yourself of one of the many **motels** along Fremont Street, half a mile north of the center of Monterey via MST bus #9 (last bus back at 11.45pm) or #10.

The only **camping** within walking distance is in Veteran's Memorial Park, site of Steinbeck's fictional Tortilla Flat, at the top of Jefferson Street in the hills above town; it's only $3 a night if you're on foot or bike, or $15 per car, and is operated on a first-come-first-served basis.

Motels

Bayside Inn, 2055 N Fremont St, Monterey (☎831/372-8071). Rooms with breakfast and use of a pool for $40. ②.

Bide-a-Wee Motel, 221 Asilomar Blvd, Pacific Grove (☎831/372-2330). Excellent value, no-frills rooms, including a few with kitchenettes. A two-minute walk to the ocean. ③.

Carmel River Inn, Rio Road at Hwy-1, Carmel (☎831/624-1575). Clean, pleasant and functional motel that was the model for Brian Moore's novel *The Great Victorian Collection*. Right on the banks of the Carmel River, near the beach and Carmel Mission. ③.

Driftwood Motel, 2362 N Fremont St, Monterey (☎831/372-5059). Among the best-value places on northern Monterey's motel row. ②.

Motel 6, 2124 N Fremont St, Monterey (☎831/646-8585). Basic motel, but you'll have to reserve a room months in advance. ③.

Pacific Grove Motel, Lighthouse Avenue at Grove Acre, Pacific Grove (☎1-800/858-8997 or 831/372-3218). Simple, small motel in marvelous setting, 100 yards from the sea. Rates rise in summer and at weekends. ③.

Hotels and B&B Inns

Del Monte Beach, 1110 Del Monte Ave, Monterey (☎831/649-4410). A bargain B&B close to the center of Monterey. All the usual trappings for half the normal cost. ③.

Green Gables Inn, 104 Fifth St, Pacific Grove (☎831/375-2095). Plush doubles in one of the prettiest houses in a town of fine homes, on the waterfront just a few blocks from the Monterey Bay Aquarium. ⑥.

Homestead, Eighth & Lincoln, Carmel (☎831/624-4119). The least expensive accommodation in Carmel. Centrally placed, with rooms and cottages in attractive gardens. ④.

Horizon Inn, Third & Junipero, Carmel (☎1-800/350-7723 or 831/624-5327). Comfy bed and breakfast place with a pool. ⑤.

Monterey Marriott, 350 Calle Principal, Monterey (☎831/649-4234). Luxurious modern hotel right at the heart of historic Monterey, with views out over the bay and peninsula. Pricey, but in winter and spring the good-value "Aquarium Package" includes two tickets to the Monterey Bay Aquarium. ⑤.

Pacific Grove Inn, 581 Pine Ave at Forest, Pacific Grove (☎831/375-2825). Thoughtfully modernized 1904 mansion with spacious rooms, five blocks from the shore. ④.

Seven Gables Inn, 555 Ocean View Blvd, Pacific Grove (☎831/372-4341). Great views out over the beautiful coast from this immaculately restored, antique-filled Victorian mansion. Rates include full breakfast and afternoon tea and scones. ⑥.

Monterey

The town of **MONTEREY** rests in a quiet niche along the bay formed by the forested Monterey Peninsula, proudly proclaiming itself the most historic city in California, a boast which, for once, may be true. Its compact town center features some of the best vernacular **buildings** of California's Spanish and Mexican colonial past, most of which stand unassumingly within a few blocks of the tourist-thronged waterfront. The single best stop, though, not to be missed if you've got an afternoon to spare, is the **Monterey Bay Aquarium**, a mile west of town, at the end of the Steinbeck-memorializing Cannery Row.

Monterey was named by the Spanish merchant and explorer Vizcaino, who landed in 1602 to find an abundant supply of fresh water and wild game after a seven-month voyage from Mexico. Despite Vizcaino's enthusiasm for the site, the area was not colonized until 1770, although it played a pre-eminent role in the development of California thereafter. Under the Spanish the *Presidio de Monterey* was the military headquarters for the whole of Alta California, and thereafter Monterey continued to be the leading administrative and commercial center of a territory that extended east to the Rocky Mountains and north to Canada, but had a total population, excluding Native Americans, of less than seven thousand.

American interest in Monterey was at first purely commercial, until 1842 when an American naval commodore received a false report that the US and Mexico were at war, and that the English were poised to take California. Commodore Catesby Jones anchored at Monterey and demanded the peaceful surrender of the port. Two days later the American flag was raised, though the armed but cordial US occupation lasted only until Jones examined the official documents closely, and realized he'd got it all wrong. When the Mexican-American War began in earnest in 1846 the United States took possession of Monterey without resistance. The discovery of gold in the Sierra Nevada foothills soon focused attention upon San Francisco, and Monterey became something of a backwater, hardly affected by the waves of immigration which followed.

Old Monterey

Many of Monterey's wonderful old buildings have survived in pristine condition, and can be found, now preserved as the **Monterey State Historic Park**, scattered throughout the quarter-mile square of the modern city. A loosely organized, roughly mile-and-a-half-long **Path of History** connects the 37 sites. Most can't be entered unless you're part of a guided historic **walking tour** (daily every hour 10am–3pm; ☎831/649-7118; $5), leaving from the Maritime Museum, near the waterfront at the foot of the main drag, Alvarado Street. The Customs House and the First Brick House are open free of charge.

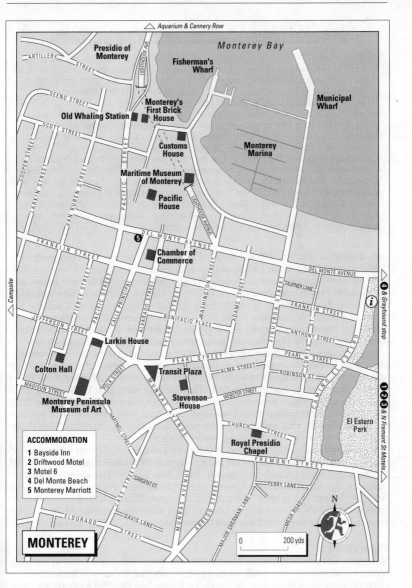

△ Aquarium & Cannery Row

Monterey Bay

Presidio of Monterey

ARTILLERY STREET

LIGHTHOUSE AVE

SEENO STREET

Monterey's First Brick House

Old Whaling Station

SCOTT STREET

COOPER STREET

LARKIN STREET

VAN BUREN STREET

PACIFIC STREET

Fisherman's Wharf

Municipal Wharf

Customs House

Maritime Museum of Monterey

Pacific House

Monterey Marina

DEL MONTE AVENUE

FRANKLIN STREET

⑤

Chamber of Commerce

PIERCE STREET

PACIFIC STREET

CALLE PRINCIPAL

ALVARADO STREET

WASHINGTON STREET

BONIFACIO PLACE

ADAMS STREET

TYLER STREET

FIGUEROA STREET

DEL MONTE AVENUE

TAUFNER LANE

FRANKLIN STREET

ANTHONY STREET

□ Campsite

JEFFERSON STREET

Larkin House

PEARL STREET

PEARL STREET

ALMA STREET

ROBINSON ST.

WEBSTER STREET

CAMINO EL ESTERO

▷ ④ & Greyhound stop

ⓘ

Colton Hall

POLK STREET

MADISON STREET

Transit Plaza

MUNRAS AVENUE

Stevenson House

Monterey Peninsula Museum of Art

HARTNELL STREET

CHURCH STREET

Royal Presidio Chapel

FREMONT STREET

El Estero Park

▷ ① ② ③ & N Fremont St Motels ▷

ACCOMMODATION

1 Bayside Inn
2 Driftwood Motel
3 Motel 6
4 Del Monte Beach
5 Monterey Marriott

CASS STREET

SARGENT CT.

ELDORADO

DAVIS LANE

STREET

MUNRAS AVENUE

ABREGO STREET

MAJOR SHERMAN LANE

PERRY LANE

MESA ROAD

N

0   200 yds

MONTEREY

The best place to get a feel for life in old Monterey is at the **Larkin House** (entered only as part of walking tour – you can join one as it enters if you don't want to take the whole tour, but you still have to pay $5), on Jefferson Street a block south of Alvarado, home of the first and only American Consul to California and successful entrepreneur, Thomas Larkin. New England-born Larkin, the wealthy owner of a general store and redwood lumber business, was one of the most important and influential figures in

ROBERT LOUIS STEVENSON AND MONTEREY

The Gold Rush of 1849 bypassed Monterey for San Francisco, leaving the community little more than a somnolent Mexican fishing village – which was pretty much how the town looked when a 29-year-old, feverishly ill Scotsman arrived by stagecoach, flat broke and desperately in love with a married woman. **Robert Louis Stevenson** came to Monterey in the fall of 1879 looking for Fanny Osbourne, whom he had met while traveling in France two years before. He stayed here for three months, writing occasional articles for the local newspaper and telling stories in exchange for his meals at Jules Simoneau's restaurant behind what is now the **Stevenson House**, halfway between the Larkin House and the Royal Presidio Chapel (see below).

Stevenson witnessed Monterey (no longer politically important but not yet a tourist attraction) in transition, something he wrote about in his essay *The Old and New Pacific Capitals*. He foresaw that the lifestyle that had endured since the Mexican era was no match for the "Yankee craft" of the "millionaire vulgarians of the Big Bonanza," such as Charles Crocker, whose lavish *Hotel Del Monte* which opened a year later (the site is now the Naval Postgraduate School, east of downtown), turned the sleepy town into a seaside resort of international renown almost overnight.

early California. He was actively involved in efforts to attract American settlers to California, and lobbied the Californians to turn towards the United States and away from the erratic government of Mexico. Through his designs for his own house, and the Customs House near Fisherman's Wharf, Larkin is credited with developing the now-familiar Monterey style of architecture, combining local adobe walls and the balconies of a Southern plantation home with a puritan Yankee's taste in ornament. The house, the first two-story adobe in California, is filled with many millions of dollars' worth of antiques and is surrounded by gorgeous gardens which are open all day.

Larkin, as unhappy with the American military government as he had been with the Mexicans, helped to organize the Constitutional Convention that convened in Monterey in 1849 to draft the terms by which California could be admitted to the US as the 31st state – which happened in 1850. The meetings were held in the grand white stone building across the street from his house, the then newly completed **Colton Hall**, now an engaging **museum** (daily 10am–noon & 1–4pm; free) furnished as it was during the convention, with quill pens on the tables and an early map of the West Coast, used to draw up the boundaries of the nascent state.

Stevenson House, at 530 Houston St (daily; see Larkin House for entry fee), is an old rooming house now filled with Robert Louis Stevenson memorabilia, much of it collected by the writer on his travels around the South Sea Islands. The oldest building in Monterey, the **Royal Presidio Chapel** (daily 8.30am–6pm; free), stands on Church Street at the top of Figueroa Street, half a mile east. This small and much-restored Spanish colonial church was built in 1795 as part of a mission founded here by Junipero Serra in 1770, the rest of which was soon removed to a better site along the Carmel River.

The waterfront

Nowadays, catering to visitors is Monterey's main livelihood. A good deal of the trade is concentrated along the waterfront, around the tacky **Fisherman's Wharf**, where the catch-of-the-day is more likely to be families from San Jose than the formerly abundant sardines. Most of the commercial fishermen moved out long ago, leaving the old wharves and canneries as relics of a once-prosperous industry; fat sea lions float in the dirty water under the piers.

The most prominent building near the wharf, at the foot of Pacific Street, is the modern **Maritime Museum of Monterey** (daily 9am–5pm; $5) with well-displayed but essentially mundane collections of ships in glass cases enlivened by interesting background on the town's defunct sardine industry. If none of this appeals, you should still pop in for the free, fourteen-minute film on Monterey history in preparation for the **Pacific House** (daily 10am–5pm; free), across the plaza, which since its construction in 1847 has been a courthouse, a rooming house and a dance hall. It is now the best of the local **museums**, with displays on Monterey history and a fair collection of Native American artifacts. While in the area, wander by the **Customs House** (daily 10am–5pm; free). This is the oldest governmental building on the West Coast, portions of which were built by Spain in 1814, Mexico in 1827 and the US in 1846. The balconied building has been restored and now displays 150-year-old crates of confiscated coffee and liquor in a small museum inside. A block west, look out for the unusual whalebone pavement in front of the period-furnished **Old Whaling Station** (now a residence and office – if you're curious, knock and they'll let you take a peek) and, next door, Monterey's **First Brick House** (daily 10am–5pm; free), the first house in the state constructed of brick, built in 1847 and now decked out as a restaurant, one of its previous incarnations.

Cannery Row and the Monterey Bay Aquarium

A waterfront **bike path** runs from the wharf along the disused railroad two miles out to Pacific Grove, following the one-time Ocean View Avenue, renamed **Cannery Row** after John Steinbeck's evocative portrait of the rough-and-ready men and women who worked in and around the thirty-odd fish canneries here. During World War II Monterey was the sardine capital of the Western world, catching and canning some 200,000 tons of the fish each year. However, overfishing meant that by 1945 the fish were more or less all gone, and the canneries were abandoned, falling into disrepair until the 1970s, when they were rebuilt, redecorated and converted into shopping malls and flashy restaurants. Many have adopted names from Steinbeck's tales, and now pack in the tourists by the bus-load. It's all rather phony, best visited in the early evening to take advantage of the low-priced food and drinks on offer during the many Happy Hours.

Ride, walk or take the WAVE shuttle from Fisherman's Wharf to the end of Cannery Row to visit its one (very) worthwhile feature: the engaging **Monterey Bay Aquarium** (daily 10am–6pm; $14.75; ☎ 1-800/756-3737 or 831/648-4888 for advance tickets). Arrive early to avoid the summer lines or call to reserve; you pay a $3 fee for any number of tickets. Built upon the foundations of an old sardine cannery, and housed in modernist buildings that blend a sense of adventure with pleasant promenades along Monterey Bay, the acclaimed aquarium and study center exhibits over five thousand marine creatures in innovative replicas of their natural habitats. Sharks and octopuses roam around behind two-foot-thick sheets of transparent acrylic, there's a 300,000 gallon Kelp Forest tank, and a touch pool where you can pet your favorite bat rays. The recently installed jellyfish exhibit is a highlight not to be missed. Try also to catch the sea otters at feeding time (usually 11am, 2pm & 4.30pm); the playful critters were hunted nearly to extinction for their fur – said, with some one million hairs per square inch, to be the softest in the world.

Pacific Grove

PACIFIC GROVE – or "Butterfly Town USA," as it likes to call itself – stands curiously apart from the rest of the peninsula, less known but more impressively sited than its two famous neighbors. The town began as a campground and Methodist retreat in 1875, a summertime tent city for revivalist Christians in which strong drink, naked flesh and reading the Sunday papers were firmly prohibited. The Methodists have long since gone, but otherwise the town is little changed. Its quiet streets, lined by pine trees and grand old Victorian wooden houses, are enlivened each year by hundreds of thousands of golden **monarch butterflies**, which come here from all over the western US and Canada to escape the winter chill. Forming soft orange and black blankets on the trees near the lighthouse at the very tip of the peninsula, the butterflies are the town's main tourist attraction, protected by local law – in fact, there's a $1000 fine for molesting a monarch.

Downtown Pacific Grove centers upon the intersection of Forest Street and Lighthouse Avenue, two miles northwest of central Monterey. Two blocks north at 667 Lighthouse Ave, the **Bookworks** bookstore and café (Sun–Thurs 9am–10pm, Fri & Sat 9am–11pm; ☎831/372-2242), is the place to pick up more detailed guides to the local area, or just stop for a cup of coffee and a pastry. A block down Forest Street, on the corner of Central Avenue, the **Pacific Grove Museum of Natural History** (Tues–Sun 10am–5pm; free) has an interesting collection of local wildlife, including lots of butterflies, over four hundred stuffed birds, a relief model of the undersea topography and exhibits on the ways of life of the aboriginal Costanoan and Salinan Indians. Across the park, the **Chautauqua Hall** was for a time in the 1880s the focus of town life, as the West Coast headquarters of the instructional and populist Chautauqua Movement, a left-leaning, traveling university which reached thousands of Americans long before there was any accessible form of higher education. Nowadays the plain white building is used as a dance hall, with a three-piece band playing favorites from the Thirties and Forties every Saturday night, and square dancing on Thursday.

About the only reminder of the fundamentalist camp meetings are the intricately detailed, tiny wooden **cottages**, along 16th and 17th streets, which date from the revival days; in some cases wooden boards were simply nailed over the frames of canvas tents to make them habitable year-round. Down Central Avenue at 12th, at the top of a small wooded park overlooking the ocean, stands the deep-red Gothic wooden church of **Saint Mary's By-The-Sea**, Pacific Grove's first substantial church, built in 1887, with a simple interior of redwood beams polished to a shimmering glow, and an authentic signed Tiffany stained-glass window, nearest the altar on the left.

Ocean View Boulevard, which runs between the church and the ocean, circles along the coast around the town, passing the headland of **Lovers Point** – originally called Lovers of Jesus Point – where preachers used to hold sunrise services. Surrounded in early summer by the colorful red and purple blankets of blooming ice plant, it's one of the peninsula's best **beaches**, where you can lounge around and swim from the intimate, protected strand, or rent a glass-bottomed boat and explore the sheltered cove. Ocean View Boulevard runs another mile along the coast out to the tip of the peninsula, where the 150-year-old **Point Piños Lighthouse** (Thurs–Sun 1–4pm; free), is the oldest operating lighthouse on the California coast.

Around the point, the name of the coastal road changes to Sunset Drive – which will make obvious sense if you're here at that time of day – and leads on to **Asilomar State Beach**, a wilder stretch with more dramatic surf, too dangerous for swimming, though the rocky shore provides homes for all sorts of tidepool life. The **Butterfly Trees**, where the monarchs congregate, are on Ridge Road, a quarter of a mile inland along Lighthouse Avenue. Hwy-68 from the end of Sunset Drive takes the inland route over the hills, joining Hwy-1 just north of Carmel, while the **Seventeen Mile Drive** ($7.25 per car), a privately owned, scenic toll road, loops from Pacific Grove along the coast south to Carmel and back again, passing by the golf courses and country clubs of Pebble Beach. Halfway along stands the trussed-up figure of the **Lone Cypress**, subject of many a postcard, and there are enough beautiful vistas of the rugged coastline to make it almost worth braving the hordes who pack the road on holiday weekends.

Carmel

Set on gently rising headlands above a sculpted, rocky shore, **CARMEL**'s reputation as a rich resort belies its origins. There was nothing much here until the San Francisco earthquake and fire of 1906 led a number of artists and writers from the city to take refuge in the area, forming a bohemian colony on the wild and uninhabited slopes that soon became notorious throughout the state. Figurehead of the group was the poet George Stirling, and part-time members included Jack London, Mary Austin and the young Sinclair Lewis. But it was a short-lived alliance, and by the 1920s the group had broken up and an influx of wealthy San Franciscans had put Carmel well on its way to becoming the exclusive corner it is today.

Certainly, there's little about the town to welcome travelers of modest means and low credit-rating; Carmel instead often seems the very epitome of parochial snobbishness. Local laws, enacted to preserve the rustic character of the town, prohibit parking meters, street addresses and postal deliveries (all mail is picked up in person from the post office); planning permission is required to cut down any tree, so they sprout everywhere, even in the middle of streets; and franchise stores or restaurants are banned outright within the city limits. For these aspects alone Carmel is probably worth a look at least, and the chance to catch a rare glimpse of ex-mayor Clint Eastwood may make the pretentious atmosphere worth bearing for an hour or so; but without a doubt the town's best feature is the largely untouched nearby coastline, among the most beautiful in California.

Carmel's center, fifteen minutes south of Monterey on MST bus #4 or #5, doesn't have much to recommend it – it's largely designer-shopping territory, in which Armani and Ralph Lauren rub shoulders with mock-Tudor tearooms and a number of **art galleries**, concentrated along Dolores Street between Fifth and Sixth, filled with uninspired watercolor renderings of golf scenes and local seascapes. The Weston Gallery on Sixth Street between Dolores and Lincoln is worth a look, however, hosting regular shows of the best contemporary photographers and with a permanent display of works by Fox Talbot, Ansel Adams and Edward Weston – who lived in Carmel for most of his life. To get the lowdown on the other galleries, check out the free, widely available *Carmel Gallery Guide*.

Fortunately, the contrivedness of the town center doesn't extend to the gorgeous, unspoiled coastline. **Carmel Beach**, down the hill at the end of Ocean Avenue, is a tranquil cove of emerald blue water bordered by soft white sand and cypress-covered cliffs, though the tides here are deceptively strong and dangerous – be careful if you chance a swim. A mile south from Carmel Beach along Carmel Bay, **Tor House** was, when built in 1919, the only building on a then treeless headland. The poet Robinson Jeffers (whose very long, starkly tragic narrative poems were far more popular in his time than they are today) built the small cottage and adjacent tower by hand, out of granite boulders he carried up from the cove below. Hourly guided **tours** of the house and gardens (Fri & Sat 10am–3pm; $7; reservations essential on ☎831/624-1840) include a rather obsequious account of the writer's life and work.

Another quarter of a mile along Scenic Road, around the tip of Carmel Point, the mile-long **Carmel River State Beach** is less visited than the city beach, and includes a bird sanctuary on a freshwater lagoon that offers safe and sometimes warm swimming. Again, if you brave the waves, beware of the strong tides and currents, especially at the south end of the beach, where the sand falls away at a very steep angle, causing big and potentially hazardous surf.

Carmel Mission

Half a mile or so up the Carmel River from the beach, also reachable by following Junipero Avenue from downtown, **Carmel Mission** (daily 10.30am–4.30pm; donation) – La Misión San Carlos Borromeo del Rio Carmelo – was founded in 1770 by Junipero Serra as the second of the California missions and the headquarters of the chain. Father Serra never got to see the finished church – he died before its completion and is buried under the floor in front of the altar. Finally completed by Father Lasuén in 1797, the sandstone church has since been well restored. The facade is unexpectedly exotic and whimsical; flourishes on the central pediment resemble cattle horns, and the interior walls curve gently into a vaulted ceiling to interesting effect. Some three thousand local Native Americans are buried in the adjacent **cemetery**, and three small **museums** in the mission compound recount the history of the missionary effort alongside ornate silver candle-holders, decorated vestments and relics of the life of Father Serra.

Point Lobos State Reserve

Two miles south of the mission along Hwy-1, accessible in summer on MST bus #22, the **Point Lobos State Reserve** (daily: summer 9am–6.30pm; spring & fall 9am–5.30pm; winter 9am–4.30pm; $7 parking) gives some of the best undisturbed views of the ocean and a chance to see everybody's favorite furry creature, the sea otter, in its natural habitat. The park, named after the *lobos marinos* – the noisy, barking sea lions that group on the rocks off the reserve's tip – protects some of the few remaining Monterey cypress trees on its knife-edged headland, despite being buffeted by relentless winds. Craggy granite pinnacles, landforms which inspired Robert Louis Stevenson's *Treasure Island*, reach out of jagged blue coves below, close to which sea lions and otters play in the crashing surf.

A number of **hiking trails** loop around the reserve, giving good views down into deep coves. The sea here is one of the richest underwater habitats in the state, and California gray whales are often seen offshore, migrating south in January and returning with young calves in April and early May. Because the point juts so far out into the ocean, you have a good chance of seeing them from surprisingly close, often as little as a hundred yards away.

Except for a small parking lot, the reserve is closed to cars, so lines sometimes form along the highway to wait for a parking space. A worthwhile **guide** and **map** is included in the admission fee.

Eating and drinking

There are many excellent **eating places** all over the peninsula, though because it's a holiday resort, be prepared to spend a bit more than you'd have to elsewhere. By and large the offerings are pretty standard, mostly steaks and seafood, with pricey Mexican places playing off the Hispanic heritage. For a full list of the hundreds of eating options in the area, check out a copy of the free, weekly and widely available *Go!* or *Coast Weekly*. If you're on anything like a tight budget, the best eats are on the north side of Monterey along Fremont Street, and in the shopping malls along Hwy-1 south of Carmel.

Budget food

Chutney's Gourmet Café, 230 Crossroads Blvd, Crossroads Mall, Hwy-1, Carmel (☎831/624-4785). Soups, salads, sandwiches and burgers in eccentric combinations in a lively, unpretentious café setting.

Little Swiss Cafe, Sixth Ave between Lincoln and San Carlos, Carmel (☎831/624-5007). The name says it all at this straightforward breakfast and lunch spot. Reasonable salads and sandwiches, and for breakfast, try the Eggs Benedict.

Mediterranean Market, Ocean Ave and Mission St, Carmel (☎831/624-2022). Perfect for packing a picnic basket for a day on the sands; full of fine cheeses, deli meats, bread and wine.

Mom's Home Cookin', 1988 Fremont St, Seaside, Monterey (☎831/394-9191). Great BBQ ribs and chicken, plus cornbread, collard greens and all the trimmings.

Old Monterey Café, 489 Alvarado St, Monterey (☎831/646-1021). More-than-you-can-eat breakfasts, with great omelets and buckwheat pancakes, plus tasty sandwiches; daily except Tues 7am–2.30pm.

Papa Chano's Taqueria, 462 Alvarado St, Monterey (☎831/646-9587). Delicious and cheap Mexican food, featuring great burritos. The chicken rotisserie of the same name, two doors down at 470 Alvarado, serves roasted chicken, also cheap.

Moderate to expensive food

La Boheme, Dolores Street between Ocean and Seventh, Carmel (☎831/624-7500). Fine dining the Carmel way – in a scaled-down replica of a French country hotel courtyard, complete with whitewashed walls and hanging laundry. Multi-course, *prix-fixe* meals for about $20 plus wine and service.

Café Fina, middle of Fisherman's Wharf, Monterey (☎831/372-5200). Pastas, wood-oven pizzas, and, of course, grilled fresh fish in the Wharf's most style-conscious setting.

Fishwife at Asilomar Beach, 1996 Sunset Drive at Asilomar, Pacific Grove (☎831/375-7107). Long-standing local favorite, serving great food at reasonable prices – king prawns sautéed in red peppers and lime juice with rice and steamed vegetables for $10 – in cozy, unpretentious surroundings.

Pasta Mia Trattoria, 481 Lighthouse, Pacific Grove (☎831/375-7709). Tasty homemade pastas, grilled seafood, and veal in a rustic, homey setting. Pasta entrées for about $11.

Pepper's Mexicali Café, 170 Forest Ave, Pacific Grove (☎831/373-6892). Gourmet Mexican seafood Californified into healthy, high-style dishes at reasonable prices.

Rosine's, 434 Alvarado St, Monterey (☎831/375-1400). The huge menu at this popular high-ceilinged establishment right in the center of town features sandwiches, pastas, salads, and burgers. Also serves breakfast.

Toot's Lagoon, on Dolores Street below Seventh, Carmel (☎831/625-1915). Good-sized portions on a wide-ranging menu – pizzas, salads, steaks, burgers, fresh fish and famous BBQ ribs – popular with families and for birthday outings.

Triples, 220 Oliver St, Monterey (☎831/372-4744). Light and healthy California cuisine, fresh fish and great salads, on a sunny outdoor patio or inside historic Duarte's Store. Behind the Pacific House in the Monterey State Historic Park.

Tuck Box Tearoom, Dolores Street between Ocean and Seventh, Carmel (☎831/624-6365). Breakfast, lunch and afternoon tea in half-timbered mock-Tudor Olde Englande setting; costly and kitsch but fun.

Drinking and nightlife

A number of clubs on the Monterey Peninsula feature a fairly sedate range of live and canned music, though things do pick up a bit in September, when it hosts the world-class **Monterey Jazz Festival** at the County Fairgrounds east of town; phone ☎831/373-3366 for more information. Besides the places listed below, most restaurants have a bar or cocktail lounge, generally filled with golfers.

After Dark, 214 Lighthouse Ave, Monterey (☎831/373-7828). Mainly gay dance club with a more mixed clientele on Thursdays.

Bay Books, 316 Alvarado St, Monterey (☎831/375-1855). Sip coffee until 10pm (11pm at weekends) while browsing in one of Monterey's better book shops.

The Club of Monterey, Alvarado and Del Monte (☎831/646-9244). DJ-dance club with a fairly young, upscale crowd; darts and pool tables downstairs. Cover $1–8, with the odd live act.

Doc Ricket's Lab, 95 Prescott St, Cannery Row (☎831/649-4241). Popular drinking venue with occasional live acts, and disco most evenings.

Morgan's Coffee & Tea, 498 Washington St, Monterey (☎831/655-6804). Environmentally conscious coffeehouse with live folk music every weekend.

The Mucky Duck, 479 Alvarado St, Monterey (☎831/655-3031). The menu at this friendly and popular Tudor-style bar/restaurant features British food with a California flair. Occasional live music.

Planet Gemini, 625 Cannery Row (☎831/373-1449). Mixed music and comedy venue usually with a $5 cover. Closed Mon.

North from Monterey

The landscape around the **Monterey Bay**, between the peninsula and the beach town of Santa Cruz, 45 miles north, is almost entirely given over to agriculture. **Castroville**, ten miles north along Hwy-1, is surrounded by farmland which grows more than 85 percent of the nation's artichokes (try them deep-fried in one of the local cafés), while the wide **Pajaro Valley**, five miles further north, is covered with apple orchards, blossoming white in the spring. The marshlands that ring the bay at the mouths of the Salinas and Pajaro rivers are habitats for many of California's endangered species of coastal wildlife and migratory birds. At **Elkhorn Slough Estuarine Sanctuary** (Wed–Sun 9am–5pm; $2.50; free guided tours Sat & Sun 10am & 1pm) near the lively fishing port of **Moss Landing** – a good place to stop for seafood – you may spot a falcon or an eagle among the many pelicans that call it home. The **beaches** along the bay are often windy and not very exciting, though they're lined by sand dunes into which you can disappear for hours on end.

- **Sunset State Beach**, fifteen miles south of Santa Cruz, has $18-a-night **campgrounds** (book through Parknet ☎1-800/444-7275; information only ☎831/763-7062) along a seven-mile strand. Four miles inland, east of Hwy-1, the earthquake-devastated town of **Watsonville** was more or less the epicenter of the October 1989 Loma Prieta tremor that rattled San Francisco. Its once-quaint downtown of ornate Victorian houses and 1930s brick structures was virtually flattened, and more recently the area economy has been hard-hit by closure of its Green Giant vegetable-packing plant, once one of the largest in the country. Like many American cities, the place is saturated with fast-food restaurants and outlet malls and there isn't a lot of interest for travelers, but Watsonville is still the main transfer point between the Monterey and Santa Cruz bus systems, so you may well have to pass through.

San Juan Bautista

Inland from the Monterey Bay area, on US-101 between Salinas and San Francisco, **SAN JUAN BAUTISTA** is about the only place worth making for: an old Mexican town that, but for a modest scattering of craft shops, has hardly changed since it was bypassed by the railroad in 1876. The early nineteenth-century **Mission San Juan Bautista** (daily 9.30am–5pm; donation), largest of the Californian mission churches – and still the parish church of San Juan Bautista – stands on the north side of the town's central plaza, its original bells still ringing out from the bell tower; the arcaded monastery wing that stretches out to the left of the church contains relics and historical exhibits. If it all looks a bit familiar, you may have seen it before – the climactic stairway chase scene in Alfred Hitchcock's *Vertigo* was filmed here. In front of the church are explanatory panels on the **San Andreas Fault** which runs just a few yards away.

Most of the town that grew up around the mission has been preserved as a **state park** (daily 10am–4.30pm; $2), with sporadic exhibits interpreting the restored buildings. On the west side of the plaza, the two-story, balconied adobe **Plaza Hotel** was a popular stopping place on the stagecoach route between San Francisco and Los Angeles; next door, the 1840 **Castro-Breen Adobe**, administrative headquarters of Mexican California, later belonged to the Breen family – survivors of the ill-fated Donner Party (see p.528) – who made a small fortune in the Gold Rush.

Across from the mission, the large **Plaza Hall** was built to serve as the seat of the emergent county government, but when the county seat was awarded instead to Hollister (a small farming community eight miles east, and scene of a motorcycle gang's rampage that inspired the movie *The Wild One*), the building was turned into a dance hall and saloon. The adjacent stables display a range of old stagecoaches and wagons, and explain how to decipher an array of cattle brands, from "lazy H" to "rockin double B". The commercial center of San Juan Bautista, a block south of the plaza, lines Third Street in a row of evocatively decaying facades. If you're hungry, the best of the half-dozen **places to eat** is the *Mission Café*, on the corner of Mariposa Street: for more information contact the **Chamber of Commerce**, 402a Third St (☎831/623-2454).

Santa Cruz

> *Santa Cruz is part of the post-orgy world, the world left behind after the great social and sexual convulsions. The refugees from the orgy – the orgy of sex, political violence, the Vietnam War, the Woodstock crusade – are all there, jogging along in their tribalism.*

Jean Baudrillard, America

Seventy-five miles south of San Francisco, **SANTA CRUZ** is a hard place to pin down. In many ways it's the ideal Californian coastal town, a heady mix of intellect and pure pleasure that's perfect for a few days' stopover on your way north or south. And there are any number of things to occupy you, from surfing or sunning along the many miles of beaches, or hiking around the surrounding mountaintop forests, to riding the Big Dipper – the largest and wildest wooden roller coaster on the West Coast. But there's another side to Santa Cruz: the town has grown unwieldy over the last couple of decades fueled largely by its role as a dormitory suburb for San Jose and Silicon Valley. In spite of a reputation for Sixties liberalism, there's a long-term town-versus-gown split between the locals and the students from UCSC, and some of the town's suburbs have a redneck feel more akin to the Central Valley than the laid-back languid coast. Only rarely do you get the impression of a resort totally at ease with itself, and the underlying conflicts are one of the many reasons why the town has been so slow to rebuild following the destruction wreaked by the 1989 earthquake.

The town has an enduring reputation as a holdout from the 1960s, which is only fitting since this is where it all began. Ken Kesey and his Merry Pranksters turned the local youth on to the wonders of LSD years before it defined a generation, a mission recorded by Tom Wolfe in *The Electric Koolaid Acid Test*, and the area is still considered among the most politically and socially progressive in California. One upshot of this is that Santa Cruz has, in recent years, become to lesbians what San Francisco is to gay men, although the scene is, as yet, small.

The town is also surprisingly untouristy: no hotels spoil the miles of wave-beaten coastline – in fact, most of the surrounding land is used for growing fruit and vegetables, and roadside stalls are more likely to be selling apples or sprouts than postcards and souvenirs. Places to stay are for once good value and easy to find, and the town sports a range of bookstores and coffeehouses, as well as some lively bars and nightclubs where the music varies from hard-core surf-punk to longtime local Neil Young and friends.

Arrival, information and city transportation

By **car**, Santa Cruz is on Hwy-1, 45 miles north of Monterey; Hwy-17 runs over the mountains, 33 miles from San Jose and US-101. **Greyhound buses** (☎831/423-1800) stop five times a day in each direction at 425 Front St in the center of town, with connecting services to all the major cities in the state. Amtrak Thruway buses connect the town with San Jose four times daily; there's also a weekly Green Tortoise. Coming from the Monterey peninsula, local MST and SCMTD buses link up in Watsonville.

The **Santa Cruz Visitors' Council** at 701 Front St (Mon–Sat 9am–5pm, Sun 10am–4pm; ☎ 1-800/833-3494 or 831/425-1234) has lots of handy information on places to stay, and sells a detailed map of Santa Cruz's historic districts for $1.50. To find out

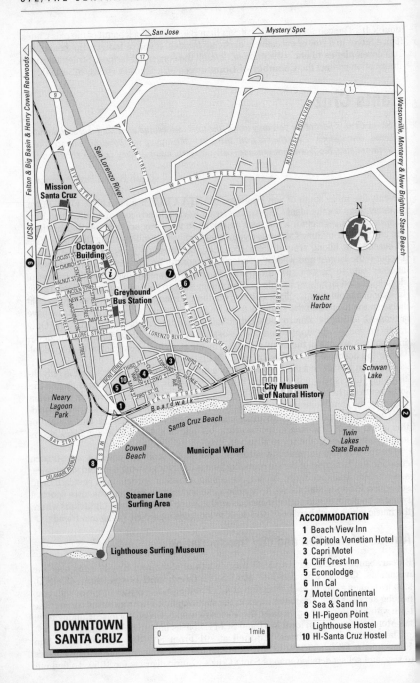

△ San Jose   △ Mystery Spot

◁ Felton & Big Basin & Henry Cowell Redwoods

▷ Watsonville, Monterey & New Brighton State Beach

17

9

1

N

Mission Santa Cruz

OCEAN STREET

WATER STREET

San Lorenzo River

RIVER STREET

Octagon Building

LOCUST

CHURCH

WALNUT STREET

LINCOLN STREET

NEW ST

CHESTNUT STREET

ELM ST

MAPLE ST

WASHINGTON ST

LAUREL STREET

i

SOQUEL   AVENUE

BROADWAY

Greyhound Bus Station

OCEAN STREET

SEABRIGHT AVENUE

7

6

San Lorenzo Blvd

EAST CLIFF DR

MURRAY STREET

EATON ST

Yacht Harbor

Schwan Lake

LAKE AVENUE

THIRD ST

SECOND ST

FIRST ST

FRONT STREET

THIRD STREET

LORENZO AVE

RIVERSIDE AVE

3

4

10

5

1

City Museum of Natural History

Neary Lagoon Park

BEACH STREET

Boardwalk

Santa Cruz Beach

Twin Lakes State Beach

BAY STREET

DELAWARE AVENUE

WEST CLIFF DRIVE

Cowell Beach

Municipal Wharf

2

Steamer Lane Surfing Area

● **Lighthouse Surfing Museum**

9

UCSC

9

8

2

DOWNTOWN SANTA CRUZ

0   1mile

ACCOMMODATION

1 Beach View Inn
2 Capitola Venetian Hotel
3 Capri Motel
4 Cliff Crest Inn
5 Econolodge
6 Inn Cal
7 Motel Continental
8 Sea & Sand Inn
9 HI-Pigeon Point
   Lighthouse Hostel
10 HI-Santa Cruz Hostel

what's on in the area, check out the free magazine rack at the **Bookshop Santa Cruz**, 1520 Pacific Ave (☎831/423-0900), where you'll find generally useful weeklies like the *Good Times* and the *Santa Cruz Metro*.

Santa Cruz has an excellent **public transportation** system, based around the Metro Center wedged between Front Street and Pacific Ave, and operated by the Santa Cruz Metropolitan Transit District or SCMTD (information Mon–Fri 8am–5pm; ☎831/425-8600), which publishes *Headways*, a free bilingual guide to getting around the area. The basic fare is $1 and an all-day pass costs $3. Some of the most useful routes are: #1, which runs up the hill to UCSC; #71 to Watsonville; #67 along the eastern beaches; and #3 to the western beaches. Route #35, which runs up Hwy-9 into the mountains to Big Basin Redwoods State Park, is equipped with bike racks.

Though there are buses to most of the beaches, you might find it easier to get around by **bicycle**: Mission Street Cyclery, 1211 Mission St (☎831/426-7299), or The Dutchman, 3961 Portola Ave at 46th Ave (☎831/476-9555), rent bikes from $25 a day, while the waterfront Go-Skate, 601 Beach St (☎831/425-8578) also rents out roller skates and surfboards. You can get ocean-going **kayaks** for $15 an hour or $30 a day from Venture Quest on the wharf and at 125 Beach St (summer daily 8am–8pm, rest of year Sat 9am–4pm, Sun 11am–4pm, call during the week; ☎831/427-2267).

Accommodation

Compared to most California beach resorts, **accommodation** in Santa Cruz is inexpensive and easy to come by, especially during the week or outside of summer. Most of the establishments we've listed offer good-value weekly rates. **Camping** opportunities in and around Santa Cruz are abundant and varied, from beaches to forests and points in between; **reservations** for all state park campgrounds are handled through Parknet ☎1-800/444-7275.

Hotels, motels and B&Bs

Beach View Inn, 50 Front St (☎831/426-3575). Clean, recently refurbished budget motel near the boardwalk. ③.

Capitola Venetian Hotel, 1500 Wharf Rd, Capitola (☎1-800/332-2780 or 831/476-6471). Quirky, ageing beachfront hotel just across the bridge from Capitola's lively esplanade. All rooms have kitchens, some are two-bedroom suites; rates increase at weekends when there's a two-night minimum. Weekly rental begins at $325. ⑦.

Capri Motel, 337 Riverside Ave (☎831/426-4611). The cheapest of a dozen or so budget motels near the beach and the boardwalk. ②.

Cliff Crest Inn, 407 Cliff St (☎831/427-2609). Nicely furnished 1887 Queen Anne-style Victorian home set in lovely gardens at the top of Beach Hill. Rates include a full breakfast and afternoon sherry. ⑤.

Econolodge, 550 Second St (☎831/426-3626). The most salubrious of the beachfront motels, with a heated pool and continental breakfast. On Beach Hill: take Front Street from the boardwalk and then first right. ②.

Inn Cal, 370 Ocean St (☎1-800/550-0055 or 831/458-9220). Across the river from the center of town, with clean, no-frills double rooms. A winter bargain and very popular in summer. ③.

Motel Continental, 414 Ocean St (☎831/429-1221). Top value for an off-the-bottom-rung motel. Comfortable, tastefully decorated rooms an easy walk to everything. ③.

Sea and Sand Inn, 201 West Cliff Drive (☎831/427-3400). Small and well-placed hotel with great views over the bay, beaches and Steamer Lane surfers. Complimentary breakfast. ⑤.

Hostels

HI–Pigeon Point Lighthouse Hostel, Pescadero (☎650/879-0633). Located some 25 miles north of town, near Año Nuevo State Park, but well worth the effort for a chance to bunk down in the old lighthouse keeper's quarters right on the point. Dorm beds $12–14 per person, plus $3 for non-HI members; more expensive private doubles, and there's an excellent hot tub ($6 per half-hour) hanging out over the thundering surf.

HI–Santa Cruz Hostel, 321 Main St (☎831/423-8304). Well-sited hostel in a set of cottages just a couple of blocks from the beach. The atmosphere is informal but the place is closed during the day and is often booked up in advance. Members $13–15.

Campgrounds

Big Basin Redwoods State Park, Hwy-236, Boulder Creek (☎408/338-8860). High up in the hills; sites with showers for $18, and numerous backcountry sites for hikers and mountain bikers.

Henry Cowell Redwoods State Park, Graham Hill Rd (☎831/335-4598). In the hills above town and UC Santa Cruz, in a redwood grove along the San Lorenzo River. Bus # 35 serves the park, and sites cost $18 a night.

New Brighton State Beach, 1500 Park Avenue, Capitola (☎831/429-2850). Three miles south of Santa Cruz on the edge of the beachfront village of Capitola, set on bluffs above a lengthy strand. Sites cost $16 a night, including hot showers.

The Town

After the overcharged tourism of the Monterey Peninsula across the bay, Santa Cruz – a quiet, easy-going community of 45,000 residents plus some 10,000 students – comes as a welcome surprise, spread out at the foot of thickly wooded mountains along a clean, sandy shore. There's not a lot to see in the town, almost all of which is within a ten-minute walk of the beach, apart from the many blocks of Victorian wooden houses.

The sluggish San Lorenzo river wraps around the town center, two blocks east of **Pacific Garden Mall**, a landscaped, prettified and pedestrianized stretch of Pacific Avenue that has recovered from the devastation of the earthquake and is once again Santa Cruz's main street, lined with bookstores, record stores, beachwear shops and cafés, and home to some of the town's chic denizens as well as the fossilized fallout from the 1960s.

One place that survived the tremor is the ornate brick-and-stone **Octagon Building**, 118 Cooper St, at the north end of Pacific Avenue. Completed in 1882 as the Santa Cruz Hall of Records, it now houses a **museum** of local history (Tues–Sun 11am–4pm; free), with exhibits that dwell on the Victorian era. Three blocks away, at 126 High St, fragments dating from the region's earlier Spanish colonial days are shown off in a restored army barracks, next to a scaled-down copy of **Mission Santa Cruz** (daily 9am–5pm; donation). The original adobe church was destroyed by an earthquake in the mid-nineteenth century; the replica that stands on its site today is dwarfed by a large Gothic Revival church next door.

Between the town center and the beach, **Beach Hill** rises at the foot of Pacific Avenue, its slopes lined with some of Santa Cruz's finest turn-of-the-century homes, such as the striking Queen Anne-style house at 417 Cliff St, and the slightly odd structure around the corner at 912 Third St, constructed out of the remains of a shipwreck.

The boardwalk and around

Standing out at the foot of the low-rise town, the **Santa Cruz Boardwalk** (summer daily 11am–10pm; rest of year Sat & Sun only; $1.50–$3 per ride, unlimited rides $11.95) stretches half a mile along the sands, one of the last surviving beachfront amusement parks on the West Coast. Packed solid on weekends with teenagers on the prowl, most of the time it's a friendly funfair where barefoot hippies mix with mushroom farmers and their families. First opened in 1907 as a gambling casino, the elegant *Coconut Grove* at the west end has recently been restored, and the grand ballroom now hosts 1940s swing bands and salsa and R&B combos which offer a change of pace from the raucous string of bumper cars, shooting galleries, log flume rides and ferris wheels that line up beside the wide beach, filled in with every sort of arcade game and test of skill. The star attraction is the **Giant Dipper**, a wild and wooden roller coaster that's listed on the National Register of Historic Places and often doubles for a Coney Island attraction in the movies.

Half a mile west of the boardwalk, the hundred-year-old wooden **Municipal Pier** juts out into the bay, crammed with fresh fish shops, burger joints and seafood restaurants, at the end of which people fish for crabs – you don't need a license, and can rent tackle from one of the many bait shops. Just east of the boardwalk, across the river, the small **Santa Cruz City Museum of Natural History**, 1305 East Cliff Drive (Tues–Fri 10am–5pm, Sat & Sun 11am–4pm; $2), marked by a concrete whale, has concise displays describing local animals and sea creatures, and a brief description of the local Native American culture.

The beaches

The **beach** closest to town, along the boardwalk, is wide and sandy, with lots of volleyball courts and water that, in August and September at least, is easily warm enough for swimming. However, not surprisingly it can get crowded and somewhat rowdy (and dirty), so for a bit more peace and quiet, or to catch the largest waves, simply follow the coastline east or west of town to one of the smaller beaches hidden away at the foot of the cliffs: most are undeveloped and easily accessible.

From the City Museum, **East Cliff Drive** winds along the top of the bluffs, past many coves and estuaries. The nearest of the two coastal lagoons that border the volleyball courts of **Twin Lakes State Beach**, half a mile east, was dredged and converted into a marina in the 1960s; the other, **Schwan Lake** is still intact, its marshy wetlands serving as a refuge for sea birds and migrating waterfowl. Beyond Twin Lakes there's another long strand of beach, with good tidepools at Corcoran Lagoon, a half mile on.

East Cliff Drive continues past popular surfing spots off rocky **Pleasure Point**, to the small beach-front resort of **CAPITOLA**. The town, three miles east of central Santa Cruz, began as a fishing village, living off the many giant tuna that populated the Monterey Bay, but soon became popular as a holiday spot, with its own railway line. The large wooden trestle of the now-disused railroad still dominates what is now a moneyed town, rising over the soft and peaceful sands of **Hooper Beach**, west of the small fishing pier.

Capitola is especially attractive in late summer, when the hundreds of begonias – the town's main produce – are in bloom. Any time of year, stop by *Mr Toots*, upstairs from 221 Esplanade (see "Drinking and Nightlife", p.377), a café and bakery with great views out over the bay and live music most nights.

The beaches west of the Santa Cruz Boardwalk, along **West Cliff Drive**, see some of the biggest waves in California, not least at **Steamer Lane**, off the tip of Lighthouse Point beyond the Municipal Pier. Cowell Beach, just north of the municipal pier, is the best place to give surfing a try; Club Ed, in the parking lot, will rent boards and assist with lessons. The ghosts of surfers past, and the risks of shark attack, are animated at the **Surfing Museum** (daily except Tues noon–4pm; donation), housed in the old lighthouse on the point, which holds surfboards ranging from twelve-foot redwood planks used by the early pioneers to modern, high-tech, multi-finned cutters. A clifftop bicycle path runs two miles out from here to **Natural Bridges State Park** (8am–dusk; $6 per car), where waves have cut holes through the coastal cliffs, forming delicate arches in the remaining stone; three of the four bridges after which the park was named have since collapsed, leaving large stacks of stone sticking out of the surf. The park is also famous – like Pacific Grove further south – for its annual gathering of **monarch butterflies**, thousands of whom return each winter.

Above Santa Cruz: UCSC and the mountains

The **University of California Santa Cruz**, on the hills above the town (served by SCMTD bus #1), is very much a product of the 1960s: students don't take exams or get grades, and the academic program stresses individual exploration of topics rather than rote learning. Architecturally, too, it's deliberately different, its 2000-acre park-like campus divided into small, autonomous colleges, where deer stroll among the redwood trees overlooking Monterey Bay – a decentralized plan, drawn up under the then-Governor Ronald Reagan, that cynics claim was intended as much to diffuse protests as to provide a peaceful backdrop for study. You can judge for yourself by taking one of the guided tours that start from the **visitor center** at the foot of campus (☎831/459-0111); be sure to keep an eye out for signs of the major expansion that's in the works, which will enable UCSC to absorb the overflow from overcrowded UC campuses elsewhere.

On the south side of the San Lorenzo River, three miles up Branciforte Drive from the center of town, there's a point within the woods where normal laws of gravity no longer apply: trees grow at odd angles, balls roll uphill and bright yellow stickers appear on the bumpers of cars that pass too close to the **Mystery Spot** (frequent 40-min tours; daily 9am–7.15pm; $4). Many explanations are offered – including its being an extraterrestrial signaling device that's wreaking havoc with local physics – but most of the disorientation is caused by the not-quite-square corners and perspective tricks used in the various exhibits, spread out around the cool forest.

High up in the mountains that separate Santa Cruz from Silicon Valley and the San Francisco Bay Area, SCMTD bus #35 runs to the village of **FELTON**, six miles north of Santa Cruz on Hwy-9, where the hundred-year-old **Roaring Camp and Big Trees Narrow Gauge Railroad** (summer daily 11am–3pm; rest of year most weekdays 11am, Sat & Sun noon–3pm, departing approximately every 90min; $13; ☎831/335-4484), steams on a six-mile loop amongst the massive trees that cover the slopes of the **Henry Cowell Redwoods State Park** (9am–dusk; $6 per car; ☎831/335-4598) along the San Lorenzo River gorge. From the same station the 1920s-era **Santa Cruz Big Trees and Pacific Railway Company** (early June to early Sept daily; late May to early June & early Sept to Oct Sat & Sun; $15 round trip; ☎831/335-4484) powers down to the boardwalk and back (or you can board there and ride up) in around two and a half hours. **Felton Covered Bridge** out on the same road a mile east of town is also worth a look, if you've got a car; it spans the river between heavily wooded slopes.

Buses continue further up the mountains to the **Big Basin Redwoods State Park** ($5 per vehicle; ☎408/338-8860), an hour's ride from Santa Cruz, where acres of three-hundred-foot-tall redwood trees cover some 25 square miles of untouched wilderness, with excellent hiking and camping. A popular "Skyline-to-the-Sea" backpacking **trail** steps down through cool, moist canyons ten miles to the coast at **Waddell Creek Beach** – fifteen miles north of Santa Cruz and a favorite spot for watching world-class windsurfers negotiate the waves – from where SCMTD bus #40 (twice daily) will take you back to town.

Eating

Restaurants in Santa Cruz run to two extremes: health-conscious, tofu-fired vegetarian places, and all-American burger-and-beer bars. In between there are bakeries and sandwich shops, and good seafood from a number of establishments on the wharf. The Wednesday afternoon **Farmer's Market** downtown, popular with local hippies, is a good place to pick up fresh produce.

Budget food

The Bagelry, 320a Cedar St (☎831/429-8049). Spacious, but usually packed, bakery selling coffees and cakes and an infinite range of filled bagels. Open 6.30am–5.30pm.

Dharma's Natural Foods, 4250 Capitola (☎831/462-1717). A little way south of central Santa Cruz. Low-priced, healthy fast food; used to be called *McDharma's* before they got sued (guess who by?) for breach of trademark. Claims to be the oldest completely vegetarian restaurant in the country.

El Paisano, 609 Beach St at Riverside (☎831/426-2382). Very good and inexpensive Mexican place with great *tamales* a specialty. Two blocks from the boardwalk and beach.

Taqueria Vallarta, 608 Soquel Ave at Ocean (☎831/457-8226). Don't be put off by the fast-food ambiance, the food is authentically Mexican and abundant, and can be washed down with rice or tamarind drinks.

Zoccoli's Deli, 1534 Pacific Ave at Water St (☎831/423-1711). Great old Italian deli, displaced by the earthquake but still serving up great food, including a minestrone that's a meal in itself.

Moderate to expensive food

Bittersweet Bistro, 787 Rio Del Mar Blvd, Rio Del Mar (☎831/662-9799). Delicately prepared gourmet fish and pasta dishes for $15–20. Don't miss the beautifully presented desserts. A few miles east of Santa Cruz along Hwy-1 but worth the trip.

Clouds Downtown, 110 Church St (☎831/429-2000). Well seasoned meats and Cal-Italian dishes in a pleasantly upbeat environment. The stuffed portabello mushrooms are especially good. Entrees go for $10–20.

Gabriella Café, 910 Cedar St (☎831/457-1677). Elegant without being snooty, this place is gaining quite a reputation for its California cuisine.

Margaritaville, 221 Esplanade, Capitola (☎831/476-2263). One of many good restaurants lined up along the beach, offering sunset cocktails and huge plates of Mexican food.

Miramar, 45 Municipal Wharf (☎831/423-4441). Long-established, family-owned seafood restaurant, with gorgeous views – especially at sunset – of the Pacific and seafront homes. Modern menu and reasonable prices.

Shadowbrook, 1750 Wharf Rd, Capitola (☎831/475-1511). Very romantic steak and seafood place, stepping down along the banks of a creek.

Drinking and nightlife

Santa Cruz has the Central Coast's best nightlife, with a number of unpretentious and unthreatening **bars and nightclubs** where the music varies from heavy-duty surf-thrash through lilting reggae to the rock of local resident Neil Young. For drinking, your best bet is the range of **espresso bars** and **coffeehouses** that rival those in any big city. For details of the lesbian and gay scene, contact the Santa Cruz Lesbian, Gay, Bisexual & Transgendered Community Center, 1332 Commerce St (☎831/425-5422).

The Catalyst, 1011 Pacific Ave (☎831/423-1336). The main venue for big-name touring artists and up-and-coming locals, this medium-sized club has something happening nearly every night. Usually 21 and over only; cover varies.

Herland, 902 Center St (☎831/429-6636). Café with light food and an attached feminist and lesbian bookstore. Closes 6pm Mon–Fri, 7pm Sat & Sun.

Kuumbwa Jazz Center, 320 Cedar St (☎831/427-2227). The Santa Cruz showcase for traditional and modern jazz, friendly and intimate with cover ranging from $1–15.

Palookaville, 1133 Pacific Ave (☎831/454-0600). Touring bands and local talent play here. Cover varies widely.

Caffe Pergolesi, 418a Cedar St (☎831/426-1775). Great coffeehouse in an old wooden house with a garden. Open until around midnight.

Mr Toots Coffee House, 221a Esplanade (upstairs), Capitola (☎831/475-3679). Bustling tea-and-coffee café overlooking the beach and wharf, with live music most nights; open 8am until midnight (at least) every day.

Red Room, 1003 Cedar St (☎831/426-2994). Hip spot for cocktails and conversation.

Santa Cruz Café and Roasting Co, 1330 Pacific Ave (☎831/459-0100). Just the place to start the day, with an excellent range of coffees, by the bean or by the cup.

The coast north to San Francisco

The **Año Nuevo State Reserve** (8am–sunset; parking $5), twenty-five miles north of Santa Cruz, was named by the explorer Vizcaino, who sailed past on New Year's Day 1603. It's a beautiful spot to visit at any time of year, and in winter you shouldn't miss the chance to see one of nature's most bizarre spectacles – the mating rituals of the Northern Elephant Seal. These massive, ungainly creatures, fifteen feet long and weighing up to three tons, gather on the rocks and sand dunes to fight for a mate. The male's distinctive, pendulous nostrils aid him in his noisy honking, which is how he attracts the females; their blubbery forms are capable of diving deeper than any other mammal, to depths of over 4500ft. Obligatory three-hour **tours** (☎650/879-0227 for information; $4; reserve through Parknet ☎1-800/444-7275) are organized during the breeding season; throughout the year you're likely to see at least a few, dozing in the sands. See Contexts, p.598 for more on the elephant seal's mating habits, and on other coastal creatures.

Five miles north of Año Nuevo, Gazos Creek Road heads inland three miles to **Butano State Park** ($5 per car; ☎650/879-2040), which has five square miles of redwood trees, views out over the Pacific and **camping** amongst the redwoods for $16 ($3 for hiker/biker sites). Another two miles north along Hwy-1, and fifty miles south of the Golden Gate Bridge, the beginning of the San Francisco Peninsula is marked by the **Pigeon Point Lighthouse** and the adjacent **hostel** (see p.373), where you can spend the night in the old lighthouse keeper's quarters and relax in a hot tub, cantilevered out over the rocks. Pigeon Point took its name from the clipper ship, *Carrier Pigeon*, that broke up on the rocks off the point, one of many shipwrecks that led to the construction of the lighthouse in the late nineteenth century.

The cargo of one of these wrecked ships inspired residents of the nearby fishing village of **PESCADERO**, a mile inland on Pescadero Road, literally to "paint the town," using the hundreds of pots of white paint that were washed up on the shore. The two streets of the small village are still lined with white wooden buildings, and the descendants of the Portuguese whalers who founded the town keep up another tradition, celebrating the **Festival of the Holy Ghost** every year, six weeks after Easter, with a lively and highly ritualized parade. Pescadero is also well known as one of the better places to **eat** on the entire coast, with an excellent restaurant, *Duarte's*, 202 Stage Rd (☎650/879-0464), serving moderately priced fish dinners and fresh fruit pies, the sporadically open *Tony's*, 1956 Pescadero Creek Rd (☎650/879-0106), with tasty fried artichoke hearts amongst the Greek, Chinese and American food, and *Los Amigos*, a celebrated fast-food Mexican restaurant in the gas station on the corner.

Half Moon Bay is the next place of note north along the coast, and is covered in the San Francisco and the Bay Area chapter on p.477.

travel details

Trains

LA to: Amtrak's Coast Starlight leaves at 9.30am for Oakland (1 daily; 10hr 45min; a shuttle bus connects to San Francisco); Salinas (1 daily; 8hr 15min); San Jose (1 daily; 9hr 50min); San Luis Obispo (3 daily; 5hr 20min); Santa Barbara (1 daily; 2hr 30min); and continues on through Sacramento, Chico, Redding, through Oregon to Seattle.

One train a day leaves Oakland at 9.35am on the return route.

Long-distance buses

All buses are Greyhound unless otherwise stated.

LA to: Salinas (8 daily; 8hr); San Francisco (17 daily; 8–12hr; also one Green Tortoise per week in each direction along the coast); San Luis Obispo (7 daily; 4hr 45min); Santa Barbara (11 daily; 3hr 10min), Santa Cruz (6 daily; 10hr 30min).

Oakland to: Santa Cruz (4 daily; 2 hr).

San Francisco to: LA (19 daily; 8–12hr); Monterey (4 daily; 4hr); Salinas (9 daily; 2hr 45min); San Luis Obispo (5 daily; 6hr); Santa Barbara (5 daily; 7hr); Santa Cruz (4 daily; 2hr 40min); San Jose (13 daily; 1hr 30min); Sacramento (17 daily; 2hr 20min).

San Jose to: Santa Cruz (4 daily; 1hr).

CHAPTER SEVEN

SAN FRANCISCO AND THE BAY AREA

The Bay Area is so beautiful, I hesitate to preach about heaven while I'm here.

Billy Graham

Americas favorite city sits at the edge of the Western world, a position which lends even greater romantic currency to its legend. Arguably the most beautiful, certainly the most liberal city in the US, and one which has had more platitudes heaped upon it than any other, **SAN FRANCISCO** is in serious danger of being clichéd to death. But in the last twenty-five years the city has undergone a steady transition away from – or maybe out of – the iconoclasm which made it famous, to become a swanky, high-end town with a palpable air of widespread affluence. One by one the central neighborhoods have been smartened up, with poorer families edged out into the suburbs, leaving only a couple of areas that could still be considered transitional. Interestingly, this gentrification is a by-product of the city's willingness to embrace all comers – the now wealthy and influential gay and singles communities, and the peculiarly eccentric entrepreneurism that has flourished here, are at the root of the city's steady growth.

For all the change, though, San Francisco remains a funky, individualistic, surprisingly small city whose people pride themselves on being the cultured counterparts to their cousins in LA – the last bastion of civilization on the lunatic fringe of America. A steadfast rivalry exists between the two cities. San Franciscans like to think of themselves as less obsessed with money, less riddled with status than those in the south – a rare kind of inverted snobbery that you'll come across almost immediately. But San Francisco has its own element of narcissism, rooted in the sheer physical aspect of the place. Downtown streets lean upwards on impossible gradients to reveal stunning views of the city, the bay and beyond. It has a romantic weather pattern, blanket fogs roll in unexpectedly to envelop the city in mist, adding a surreal quality to an already unique appearance. It's a compact and approachable place, one of the few US centers in which you can comfortably survive without a car. (In fact, finding parking is so time-consuming and expensive that it's *easier* to survive without one.) This is not, however, the California of monotonous blue skies and slothful warmth – the temperatures rarely exceed the seventies, and even during summer can drop much lower, when consistent and heavy fogs muscle in on the city and the area as a whole.

San Francisco proper occupies just 48 hilly square miles at the tip of a slender peninsula, almost perfectly centered along the California coast. But its metropolitan area sprawls out far beyond these narrow confines, east and north across to the far sides of the bay, and south back down the coastal strip. This is the **Bay Area**, one of the most rapidly growing regions in the US: less than 730,000 people live in the city, but there are six million in the Bay Area as a whole. It's something of a mixed bag. In the **East Bay**, across one of the two great bridges that connect San Francisco with its

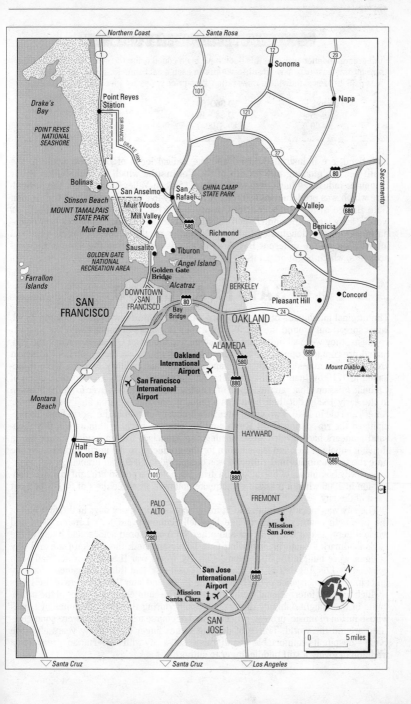

ACCOMMODATION PRICE CODES

All accommodation prices in this book have been coded using the symbols below; prices are for the least expensive **double rooms** in each establishment. For a full explanation see p.36 in Basics. Individual rates rather than price codes are given for **hostels**.

① up to $30	④ $60–80	⑦ $130–175
② $30–45	⑤ $80–100	⑧ $175–250
③ $45–60	⑥ $100–130	⑨ $250+

---

hinterland, are industrial Oakland and the radical locus of Berkeley, while to the south lies the gloating new wealth of the **Peninsula**, which its multi-billion dollar computer industries have earned the tag of "Silicon Valley," wiping out the agriculture which was predominant as recently as twenty-five years ago. Across the Golden Gate Bridge to the north, **Marin County** is the Bay Area's wealthiest suburb, its woody, leafy landscape and rugged coastline a bucolic – though in places *very* chic – harbinger of the delights of California's earthy northern coast. Specific practical information on the different Bay Area locales is given within the various regional accounts, which begin on p.448.

SAN FRANCISCO

The original inhabitants of San Francisco were the **Ohlone**, who lived in some 35 villages spread out around the bay. Within a very few years of contact with the Spanish colonists, they were all but wiped out – some five thousand Ohlone, over half the estimated pre-contact population, are buried in mass graves on the grounds of **Mission Dolores**. The mission, which still stands, and a small military *presidio*, were established in 1776 by Juan Bautista de Anza as the sixth in the colonial Spanish chain of Catholic missions that ran the length of the state. Mexicans took over from the Spanish in the early 1820s, but their hold was a tenuous one and the area finally came under American rule in 1846. Two years later the discovery of gold in the Sierra foothills precipitated the rip-roaring **Gold Rush**, and the city was born. Within a year, fifty thousand pioneers had traveled west, turning San Francisco from a muddy village into a thriving supply center and transit town for the goldfields to the north and east. By the time the **transcontinental railroad** was completed in 1869, San Francisco was a lawless, rowdy boomtown of bordellos and drinking holes – a period brought to a swift conclusion in 1906 when a massive earthquake, followed by three days of fire, wiped out most of the city.

The city was quickly rebuilt, and in many ways saw its glory days in the first half of the twentieth century – writers like Dashiell Hammett and Jack London lived and worked here, as did Diego Rivera and other WPA-sponsored artists, and many of the city's landmark structures, including Coit Tower and both the Golden Gate and Bay bridges, were built in the 1920s and 1930s. By World War II San Francisco had been eclipsed by Los Angeles as the main West Coast city, and things remained relatively quiet until the emergence of the Beats in the 1950s, and later the hippy era of the 1960s – which brought international media attention to the counterculture antics of the inhabitants of the Haight-Ashbury district, especially during the 1967 "Summer of Love," whose fusion of music, protest, rebellion, and of course a lot of drugs, were soon emulated around the world. Traces of dropout values linger some thirty years after the event – despite its comfortable wealth, this is still a city with a libertarian streak and a tradition of giving a stiff middle finger to authority.

San Francisco is the heart of one of the largest metropolitan areas in the country, but it retains a parochial air, and chooses its heroes with care. When the pope came to visit in 1987, the city's traffic was re-routed to cope with an expected crowd of one and a half million. Only a very sorry-looking fifty thousand turned out. That same year the fiftieth anniversary of the Golden Gate Bridge, supposedly a small civil affair, brought five times that number of partying Bay Area residents onto the bridge in celebration of their cherished city – only a gay pride march could have matched the numbers. Similarly, the earthquake of October 1989 that literally rocked the city brought the best out of San Francisco: once the casualties had been taken care of and before electricity was restored, a party atmosphere took hold as people barbecued, stuck beers in ice boxes and rounded up neighbors in a show of community spirit and indifference to disaster.

The city's reputation as a politically liberal oasis was dented in the early 1990s when the then mayor, Frank Jordan, displayed a bully-boy approach to its growing homelessness problem. Nonetheless, the entire Bay Area is a firm Democrat stronghold, now back on course with a new, more progressive city mayor, Willie Brown. The significant **gay** community is influential, too, with clever politicians and businessmen well aware of the power of the pink dollar. Freedom is still the key word, and for all its failings, San Francisco remains one of the least prejudiced and most proudly distinct cities on earth.

Arrival and information

All international and most domestic flights arrive at **San Francisco International Airport** (SFO; ☎415/876-2377), about fifteen miles south of the city. There are several ways of getting into town from here, each of which is clearly signed from the baggage reclaim areas. The least expensive is to take a San Mateo County Transit (SamTrans) **bus**, leaving from the airport's upper level. The #7F express takes around twenty-five minutes to reach downtown (every 30min; $2.50), the slower #7B stops everywhere and takes over an hour (every 30min; $1), Bear in mind, though, that you're only allowed as much luggage as you can carry on your lap on the express route. To transfer to the BART system, catch the #3B which runs every hour to Daly City BART ($1) or the #3X express, which runs more frequently and at extended hours to Colma BART ($1). The SFO **Airporter** bus ($10) picks up from outside each baggage claim area every fifteen minutes (5am–11pm) and travels to the downtown areas of Union Square and the Financial District. The blue **Supershuttle** and the **Yellow Airport Shuttle** minibuses cost a little more and are much quicker; they pick up every five minutes from outside the baggage claim area and will take you and up to five other passengers to any city-center destination for around $12–15 per head.

Taxis from the airport cost $25–35 (plus tip) for any city location, more for East Bay and Marin County, and are good value if you're in a group or too tired to care. If you're planning to drive, there's the usual clutch of **car rental** agencies at the airport, all of which operate shuttle buses that circle the top departure level of the airport road and take you to their depot free of charge. Drive into town on either US-101 or the prettier I-280, a journey of about thirty minutes.

A number of domestic airlines (Southwest and United are two) fly into **Oakland International Airport** (OAK; see p.450 for details), across the bay. This airport is actually closer to downtown San Francisco than SFO, and is efficiently connected with the city by the $2 AirBART shuttle bus from the Coliseum BART station. The third Bay Area airport, **San Jose Municipal** (SJO), also serves domestic arrivals, but is only worth considering if flights into the other two are booked up, or if you're going to be spending much time in the Silicon Valley.

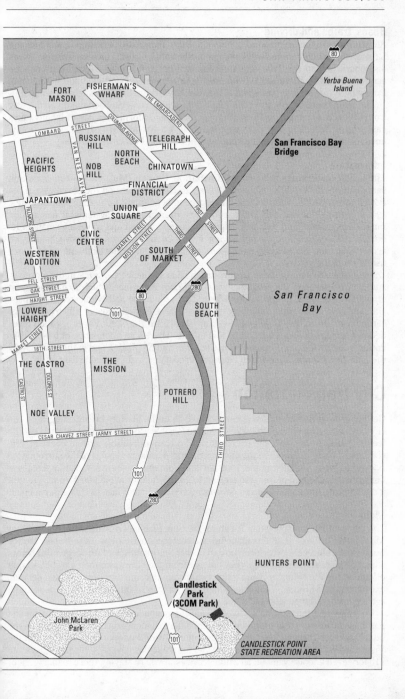

FORT MASON

FISHERMAN'S WHARF

THE EMBARCADERO

Yerba Buena Island

LOMBARD STREET

COLUMBUS AVENUE

RUSSIAN HILL

TELEGRAPH HILL

San Francisco Bay Bridge

PACIFIC HEIGHTS

VAN NESS AVENUE

NOB HILL

NORTH BEACH

CHINATOWN

JAPANTOWN

FILLMORE STREET

UNION SQUARE

FINANCIAL DISTRICT

FIRST STREET

CIVIC CENTER

MARKET STREET

THIRD STREET

WESTERN ADDITION

MISSION STREET

SOUTH OF MARKET

San Francisco Bay

FELL STREET

OAK STREET

HAIGHT STREET

280

80

LOWER HAIGHT

101

MARKET STREET

SOUTH BEACH

16TH STREET

THE CASTRO

CASTRO ST

DOLORES ST

THE MISSION

POTRERO HILL

NOE VALLEY

THIRD STREET

CESAR CHAVEZ STREET (ARMY STREET)

101

280

HUNTERS POINT

John McLaren Park

Candlestick Park (3COM Park)

101

CANDLESTICK POINT STATE RECREATION AREA

Buses, trains and driving

All San Francisco's **Greyhound** services use the **Transbay Terminal** at 425 Mission St, near the Embarcadero BART station in the SoMa district. **Green Tortoise** buses disembark behind the Transbay Terminal on First and Natoma. **Amtrak** trains stop across the bay in **Richmond** (with easy BART transfers) and continue to Oakland, from where free shuttle buses run across the Bay Bridge to the Transbay Terminal.

The main route **by car** from the east is I-80, which runs via Sacramento all the way from Chicago. The main north–south route through California, I-5, passes by fifty miles east, and is linked to the Bay Area by I-580. US-101 and Hwy-1, the more scenic north–south routes, pass right through downtown San Francisco.

Information

The main **San Francisco Visitor Information Center** (Mon–Sat 8.30am–5pm, Sun 9am–3pm; ☎415/391-2000; *www.sfvisitor.org*) in Hallidie Plaza on the concourse of the Powell Street BART/Muni station, makes a good benchmark for getting your bearings, as it's centrally located and at the hub of city transportation systems. It has a good range of free maps, and staff will help with accommodation and travel information. Its useful free booklet, known as the *San Francisco Book*, gives extensive listings on accommodation, sightseeing, exhibitions, restaurants and entertainment, as well as a useful shopping guide.

San Francisco's major **daily papers** are the *San Francisco Chronicle* in the morning, and in the afternoon the revamped *San Francisco Examiner*, which is making great efforts to capture the liberal market with in-depth reporting and syndicated columnists. On Sundays the two papers combine into a very large edition, most of which can be discarded apart from the "Datebook" section (also called the "Pink Pages"), which gives detailed listings of arts, clubs, films and events. There's an abundance of **free publications**, led by the *San Francisco Bay Guardian* and *SF Weekly*, and in the East Bay by the *East Bay Express*, all of which have lively reporting and invaluable listings.

City transportation

Getting around San Francisco is simple. In spite of the literally breathtaking hills, the city center is small enough to make walking a feasible way to see the sights and get the feel of things. In addition, the excellent **public transportation** system is cheap, efficient and easy to use, both in the city and the more urbanized parts of the surrounding Bay Area. We've detailed public transportation options in the relevant Bay Area sections towards the end of this chapter, but to go any further afield you'd do well to rent a car. **Cycling** is a good option too, though you'll need stout legs to tackle those hills.

Muni

The city's public transportation is run by the **San Francisco Municipal Railway**, or Muni (☎415/673-6864), and is made up of a comprehensive network of **buses**, **trolley buses** and **cable cars**, which run up and over the city's hills, and **underground trains** which become **streetcars** when they emerge from the downtown metro system to split off and serve the suburbs. Muni trains run throughout the night on a limited service, except on the M-Ocean View line, which stops around 1am; buses, too, run at night, again greatly reduced after midnight.

On buses and trains there's a flat **fare** of $1; on cable cars $2. With trains, you must purchase tickets to get through the barriers before descending to the platforms; on the buses, correct change is required on boarding. **Muni Passports**, available from the Visitor Information Center (above), cost $6 for a one-day pass, $10 for three days and $15 for seven and are valid on all Muni services. If you're staying more than a week or

USEFUL BUS ROUTES

#38 From Geary Street via Civic Center, west to the ocean along Geary Boulevard.

#5 From the Transbay Terminal, west along the north side of Golden Gate Park to the ocean.

#7 From the Ferry Terminal (Market Street) to the end of Haight Street and to Golden Gate Park.

#24 From Castro Street north along Divisadero Street to Pacific Heights and the Marina.

#37 From Market at Church Street to Twin Peaks.

#30 From the Caltrain depot in SoMa (Third Street), north to Ghirardelli Square, via Chinatown and North Beach, and out to Chestnut Street in the yuppie Marina district.

#22 From the Mission along Fillmore Street north to Pacific Heights and the Marina district.

#15 From Third Street (SoMa) to Pier 39, Fisherman's Wharf, via the Financial District and North Beach.

#20 (on Golden Gate Transit) From Civic Center to the Golden Gate Bridge.

#44 From the Muni N-Judah train line or from buses #5 and #38, you can connect to bus #44 which goes by the De Young Museum, Asian Art Museum, Japanese Tea Garden, California Academy of Sciences and Steinhart Aquarium in Golden Gate Park.

MUNI TRAIN LINES

Muni J-Church Line From downtown to Mission and the edge of the Castro.

Muni K-Ingleside Line From downtown to Balboa Park.

Muni L-Taraval Line From downtown west to the zoo and Ocean Beach.

Muni M-Ocean View From downtown west to Ocean Beach, via the Stonestown Galleria (shopping center) and San Francisco State University.

Muni N-Judah Line From downtown west to Ocean Beach, via the outer Haight.

CABLE CAR ROUTES

Powell–Hyde From Powell Street along Hyde through Russian Hill to Fisherman's Wharf.

Powell–Mason From Powell Street along Mason via Chinatown and North Beach to Fisherman's Wharf.

California Street From the foot of California Street in the Financial District through Nob Hill to Polk Street.

so and need to rely heavily on public transportation, get a **Fast Pass**, which costs $35 and is valid for unlimited travel on the Muni and BART systems within the city limits for a full calendar month. Note that Fast Passes are not available from Muni or BART stations; you can buy them at most supermarkets and newsagents.

For more detailed information pick up the handy Muni map ($2.17) from the Visitor Information Center or bookstores, though it's unlikely that you'll need to be familiar with more than a few of the major bus routes, the most important of which are listed above.

Other public transportation

A number of **other public transportation networks** run into San Francisco, though these are most useful to connect with the rest of the Bay Area. Along Market Street downtown, Muni shares the station concourses with **BART**, the ultra-modern Bay Area Rapid Transit system, linking major points in San Francisco with the East Bay and outer suburbs. The **Caltrain** commuter railroad (its depot is at Fourth and Townsend, South of Market) connects San Francisco with points along the Peninsula south to San Jose. **Golden Gate Ferry** boats leave from the Ferry Building on the Embarcadero, crossing the bay past Alcatraz to Marin County. **Red and White** and **Blue and Gold** ferries leave Fisherman's Wharf for Alcatraz and Angel islands and the cities of Tiburon, Sausalito and Larkspur (also in Marin). For more details see the various Bay Area accounts later in this chapter.

Driving: taxis and cars

Taxis, as in most American cities, don't trawl the streets in San Francisco the way they do in some cities. Reputedly there are three thousand licensed taxis in the city, but if you want one and you're not in a busy part of town or near a big hotel you'll probably have to phone: try Veterans (☎415/552-1300) or Yellow Cab (☎415/626-2345). Fares within the city are $1.70 for the first mile, $1.80 for each additional mile and the customary fifteen percent tip, plus charges for time spent sitting in traffic. A classier alternative to taxis is TownCar USA (☎415/334-9200), a fleet of luxury cars with courteous drivers. You must call ahead for a car and the flat rate into town from the airport is $35, otherwise fares are $4.50 for the first mile and $2.50 per mile thereafter, plus tip. Not a bad deal, especially on nights when the taxis are all full and you're traveling in a group.

You don't need a **car** to get around San Francisco, but if you're staying some way out from the center, it can make life easier – especially if you want to see something of the Bay Area while you're here. Special rules for **driving** in the city are designed to contend with its often very steep gradients: you are obliged to turn your wheels to the curb when parking on hills. It can be maddeningly difficult to find a place to leave the car, but don't lose your cool: **parking** restrictions in San Francisco are strictly enforced, and traffic officers will cheerfully ticket you – or tow your car away – in a matter of seconds. A number of **parking lots** in the South of Market industrial area charge $5 per day; more central garages charge that much per hour. Of these, the best deals are to be had in the multistory garage at Sutter and Stockton, Stockton and O'Farrell (most handy for Macy's) and the parking lots under Union Square downtown, under Portsmouth Square in Chinatown, and at Ghirardelli Square near Fisherman's Wharf.

Cycling

In general, **cycling** is an economical and healthy method of getting around San Francisco and the Bay Area, some parts of which have cycle lanes, and local buses are often equipped to carry bikes strapped to the outside. Good-value city **rental shops** include Park Cyclery, 1749 Waller St (☎415/221-3777), which offers mountain bikes for $5 per hour or $25 per day. Golden Gate Park has some wonderful routes, as does Angel Island (see p.488).

Organized tours

If you've just arrived, you may want to orient yourself by taking an **organized tour**. Gray Line Tours (☎415/558-9400) will take you around the city in three and a half fairly tedious hours, stopping at Twin Peaks and the Cliff House, for around $28 a head. Skip it unless you're really pushed for time and want to get a general idea of the city's layout with minimal effort.

Excruciatingly expensive but spectacular **aerial tours** of the city and Bay Area in light aircraft are available from several operators: San Francisco Helicopter Tours (☎1-800/400-2404) and Scenic Air Tours (☎1-800/957-2364) will fly you over the sights for around $100. Mile High Airlines (☎510/713-2359) specializes in fantasy flights for couples determined to enjoy each other as well as the sights. The bashful might prefer one of the more leisurely **bay cruises** offered by both the Red and White and Blue and Gold fleets (☎415/705-5555 or 705-5444) from piers 43^1/$_2$ and 41 – though at $16 and up these don't come cheap either, and in any case everything may be shrouded in fog.

WALKING TOURS

There are some excellent personalized **walking tours** available in San Francisco. The better ones usually permit no more than five people to a group and can often make an informative and efficient way to get to know a particular area of town. The Visitor Information Center can give you a full list, but among those you might like to try are:

All About Chinatown, 812 Clay St (☎415/982-8839). Three-hour, $35 tour conducted by Chinatown native Linda Lee, including all the sights, history and anecdotes you can absorb and a *dim sum* lunch.

City Guides (☎415/557-4266). The most extensive range of guided walks, sponsored by the San Francisco Public Library and all free.

Cruisin' the Castro, 375 Lexington St (☎415/550-8110). The Supreme Champion of the walking tour circuit in San Francisco, Trevor Hailey, a resident of San Francisco's premier gay district for twenty years, takes you on a fascinating tour of this small area. Her knowledge includes everything from politics to the best parties and she embellishes her three-and-a-half-hour tour with funny stories. A tour costs $35 per person includes brunch – worth every cent. Reservations required.

Flower Power Haight-Ashbury Walking Tour (☎415/863-1621). As well as reliving the Summer of Love and learning about important hippies, this two-hour tour will show you the Haight's past as a Victorian resort destination.

Friends of Recreation and Parks, MacLaren Lodge, Stanyan and Fell (☎415/263-0991). Tour Golden Gate Park with trained guides pointing out the park's flora, fauna and history. Free tours weekends and some weekdays (call for times).

Victorian Home Walk, 2226 15th St (☎415/252-9485). Learn about the architecture, lifestyle and history of the Victorian era in San Francisco. The group size is small and the pace leisurely – walking is level or downhill. Tours depart daily, year-round and cost $20 per person for two and a half hours.

Accommodation

With over 30,000 hotel rooms, San Francisco isn't short on **accommodation**. Visitors are the city's number one business, and even during the peak summer months failure to phone ahead needn't find you stuck for a place to sleep. Since room rates average around $100 per night, accommodation may prove to be the major expense of your stay, but fortunately there are enough options in all price ranges – from youth hostels to five-star luxury hotels – to be able to find something to suit both your taste and your bank balance.

Hotels in the slightly seedy SoMa and Tenderloin areas start at around $30 per night, $120 per week – though they tend to be of the welfare variety and you shouldn't expect a private bath or even a toilet for that amount – while in the glitzier areas around Union Square or atop Nob Hill it's hard to find anything at all for under $125 a night. Try Hwy-101 coming in from the bridge for pleasant, if rather bland, **motels**. Wherever you stay, during the off season rates can drop considerably, and special deals are often available for guests who stay for longer periods. Always ask about reductions, as hoteliers generally won't volunteer the information if they think they can sell you a room at full price.

The city's **bed and breakfast** inns can be pricey, usually not less than $80 a night, but are generally cozier than a hotel and offer sumptuous breakfasts to boot. A dorm bed in a **hostel** is as cheap as you can get in San Francisco; **camping** is not really an option, as there are no sites within an hour's drive of the city.

If you do have trouble finding a place to stay, try contacting the ultra-efficient and friendly **San Francisco Reservations** (☎1-800/677-1500), which will find you a place without fail, though you should expect to spend upwards of $80 per night. They also have their own Web site – *www.hotelres.com* – which allows you to browse through pictures of hotels and check their locations on a map before you make reservations.

Hotels and B&Bs are listed below by neighborhood, with hostels listed separately. In case you're arriving on a late flight, or leaving on an early one, we've also listed a few places to stay near the **airport**. Specifically **gay** and **women-only** accommodation options listed in special sections on p.439 and p.442.

Downtown

Beresford Arms, 701 Post St at Jones (☎415/673-2600). Luxury B&B in the heart of town, well worth the few extra dollars. ⑥.

Campton Place, 340 Stockton St at Sutter (☎415/781-5555). Smallish Union Square hotel that draws in a quietly moneyed crowd. Luxurious but not showy, with a first class restaurant. ⑨.

Cartwright, 524 Sutter St at Powell (☎1-800/227-3844 or 415/421-2865). Distinguishes itself from its rivals with little touches such as fresh flowers, afternoon tea and bend-over-backwards courtesy. Good location one block north of Union Square. ⑦.

Clarion-Bedford, 761 Post St at Leavenworth (☎415/673-6040). Excellent-value hotel with a high degree of personalized service. When you want to be looked after but don't have a top dollar budget, alight here. ⑥.

Commodore International, 825 Sutter St at Jones (☎415/923-6800). Classic Art Deco structure a couple of blocks from Union Square with spacious, affordable rooms and a great atmosphere. ④.

Dakota, 606 Post St at Taylor (☎415/931-7475). Recently converted 1920s hotel near Union Square. Low rates, thanks to the lack of luxury trimmings or fancy service, but all rooms have antique baths. ④.

David, 480 Geary St (☎1-800/524-1888 or 415/771-1600). By no means the least expensive place in town, but a great Theater District location above San Francisco's largest and best Jewish deli. You get an all-you-can-eat breakfast, and free transportation from the airport if you stay two nights or more. ⑤.

Fairmont, 950 Mason St at Sacramento (☎415/772-5000). Most famous of San Francisco's top-notch hotels, the *Fairmont* is an excessively decorated palace with four restaurants and four lounges, and fantastic views from the rooms. ⑨.

Gates, 140 Ellis St at Powell (☎415/781-0430). Super-cheap downtown location, with rooms of a predictable standard. ②.

Grant Plaza, 465 Grant Ave at Pine (☎415/434-3883). Newly renovated hotel with clean rooms in the middle of Chinatown. ③.

Harbor Court, 165 Steuart St between Mission and Howard (☎1-800/346-0555 or 415/882-1300). Plush rooms, some of which offer the best bay views of any hotel in the city, and guests have free use of the excellent YMCA health club next door. Next door to the fashionable *Harry Denton's* in the up-and-coming Embarcadero district. ⑧.

Huntington, 1075 California St at Taylor (☎415/474-5400). Understated and quietly elegant compared to its Nob Hill compatriots, this is the hotel for the wealthy who don't need to flash it about. The only large hotel in town that is still family-run, its bars are neither rooftop, nor revolving, but instead opt for simple dark-wood furnishing, a piano player and a very intimate atmosphere. There are fax machines in all the rooms and a limousine service. ⑧.

Nob Hill Pensione, 835 Hyde St at Bush (☎415/885-2987). On the Tenderloin/Nob Hill border, this hotel offers relatively inexpensive accommodation. Small, clean and comfortable rooms with shared bath, though rooms with private bath available. ③.

Mandarin Oriental, 222 Sansome St at California (☎415/885-0999). You'll need silly amounts of money – rooms *start* at $325 – if you want to stay in what are reputedly San Francisco's most luxurious hotel rooms, but the views from said rooms, which start on the 38th floor of this impressive building, across the Financial District are pretty cool. Amenities include valet, concierge and 24hr room service. ⑨.

Monaco, 501 Geary St at Taylor (☎1-800/214-4220 or 415/292-0100). Best of the new wave of San Francisco hotels, offering great style and decor – though prices have gone up in recent years. Next door to the sumptuous but reasonable *Grand Café*. ⑧.

Petite Auberge, 863 Bush St at Taylor (☎415/928-6000). One of two opulent B&Bs, next to one another on Bush Street. This one offers complimentary afternoon tea, wine and hors d'oeuvres as well as full breakfast. ⑥.

Prescott, 545 Post St between Taylor and Mason (☎1-800/283-7322 or 415/563-0303). The flagship of hotelier Bill Kimpton's San Francisco properties, this small Union Square hotel offers understated luxury, four-star comfort – and preferred seating at the city's most popular restaurant, *Postrio*, with which it shares space. ⑧.

Ritz-Carlton, 600 Stockton St at California (☎1-800/241-3333 or 415/296-7465). The most luxurious hotel in San Francisco perched on the stylish slope of Nob Hill with gorgeously appointed rooms, a swimming pool, multi-million dollar art collection and one of the city's best hotel restaurants, the *Dining Room*. ⑨.

Sir Francis Drake, 450 Powell St at Post (☎415/227-5480). Don't be put off by the Beefeaters outside, this is a colonial California hotel whose greatest attraction is *Harry Denton's Starlight Room* (see "Drinking: bars and cafés", p.426) on the 21st floor. ⑦.

Triton, 342 Grant Ave at Bush (☎1-800/433-6611 or 415/394-0500). Very stylish, very comfortable and very central hotel, catering to design professionals and weekend shoppers. Across the street from the Chinatown Gateway, two blocks from Union Square. ⑧.

Westin St Francis, 335 Powell St at Post (☎1-800/228-3000 or 415/397-7000). Truly grand hotel with a sumptuous lobby, five restaurants, an elegant bar and disappointingly plain rooms. Its reputation far outstrips the reality of a stay here, but as long as you don't mind the throngs of tourists who pour in to gape at the lobby, you'll be happy. ⑦.

White Swan Inn, 845 Bush St between Taylor and Mason (☎415/775-1755). The other Bush Street B&B, this one with a convincing English manor-house theme: raging fires, oak-paneled rooms and afternoon tea. ⑦.

York, 940 Sutter St at Hyde (☎1-800/808-YORK or 415/885-6800). Quiet, older hotel on the western edge of downtown. An essential stop for Hitchcock fans, this is where the dramatic stairway scenes in *Vertigo* were filmed. ⑥.

North Beach and the northern waterfront

Art Center Bed and Breakfast, 1902 Filbert St at Laguna (☎415/567-1526). Quirky little inn that's a real home away from home. ⑥.

Bed and Breakfast Inn, 4 Charlton Court off Union Street (☎415/921-9784). One of the first B&Bs to be established in the city, this lovely, sun-drenched Victorian house, tucked away down a quiet side street, offers some of San Francisco's most pleasant accommodation. ④.

Bel Aire Travelodge, 3201 Steiner St at Greenwich (☎415/921-5162). Good-value motel, one block from Lombard Street. ④.

Edward II, 3155 Scott St at Lombard (☎415/922-3000). Large and comfortable inn-style accommodation with free breakfast and afternoon sherry. ④.

Holiday Lodge, 1901 Van Ness Ave at Washington (☎1-800/367-8504 or 415/776-4469). Good family hotel with pool and free parking close to Pacific Heights and Fisherman's Wharf. Landscaped grounds and bungalows give it a resort feel. Comfortable and secure. ⑤.

Marina Inn, 3110 Octavia St at Lombard (☎415/928-1000). Comfortable, homey set-up, six blocks from the curvy part of Lombard Street. ③.

San Remo Hotel, 2237 Mason St at Francisco (☎1-800/352-7366 or 415/776-8688). Pleasant, old-fashioned rooms in nicely preserved North Beach house. Friendly staff and the best bargain in the area, though you'll have to share a bathroom. ④

Tuscan Inn, 425 North Point at Mason (☎1-800/648-4626 or 415/561-1100). The most upmarket hotel on the waterfront, with afternoon wine reception and free limo downtown in the mornings. ⑥.

Washington Square Inn, 1660 Stockton St at Filbert (☎415/981-4220). Cozy B&B smack dab on North Beach's lovely main square. Non-smokers only. ⑥.

Civic Center, South of Market and the Mission

Abigail Hotel 246 McAllister at Larkin (☎415/861-9728). Comfortable, stylish and affordable, this hip Civic Center hotel caters mainly to revelers performing at the nearby arts centers and sports an excellent (believe it or not) vegan restaurant, *Millennium*, in its basement. Weekly and monthly rates available. ⑤.

Albion House Inn, 135 Gough St at Oak (☎415/621-0896). Small and comfortable B&B above a fine restaurant. ⑤.

Amsterdam Hotel, 749 Taylor St at Bush (☎1-800/637-3444 or 415/673-3277). On Nob Hill, but actually closer to the Tenderloin, with good-value clean and pleasant rooms. ④.

Atherton, 685 Ellis St (☎415/474-5720). Cozy, clean, good-value hotel four blocks from Civic Center. ④.

Bay Bridge Inn, 966 Harrison St at Sixth (☎415/397-0657). Basic and somewhat noisy but perfectly sited for late nights in SoMa's clubland. ④.

Golden City Inn, 1554 Howard St at 12th (☎415/255-1110). Best of the inexpensive SoMa hotels, smack in the middle of the district's nightlife scene. Unbelievably good value. ①.

Inn at the Opera, 333 Fulton St between Franklin and Gough (☎415/863-8400). Deluxe boutique hotel with free continental breakfast and complimentary shuttle to Union Square. Stay here if you want to bump into visiting divas. ⑦.

Pensione San Francisco, 1668 Market St at Franklin (☎415/864-1271). A good base near the Civic Center, within walking distance of SoMa and the Castro. ③.

Phoenix Hotel, 601 Eddy St at Polk (☎415/776-1380). Marginal neighborhood on the edge of the Tenderloin but the hip music-biz crowd who lounge around the pool drinking cocktails don't seem to mind. Next door to the retro *Backflip* bar. ⑤.

Renoir Hotel, 45 McAllister St at Market (☎415/626-5200). Convenient location, three blocks from the Civic Center and Union Square. Classic Victorian lobby and large, comfy rooms. Great deals to be had in winter, always ask about special offers and flash your *Rough Guide*. ⑤.

Sherman House, 2160 Green St between Webster and Fillmore (☎415/563-3600). Rated the best in San Francisco by *Zagat* readers' guide, this small Pacific Heights hotel is one of the city's lesser-known jewels, but carries a whopper of a tariff; rooms start at $325. ⑨.

The central neighborhoods

Alamo Square Inn, 719 Scott St at Fulton (☎415/922-2055). A beautifully restored Victorian building. The rates are par for the course for a B&B, and guests get the use of a handsome dwelling, some rooms complete with fireplace and one with jacuzzi. ⑤.

AIRPORT HOTELS

Best Western Grosvenor Hotel, 380 South Airport Blvd (☎415/873-3200). Large comfortable hotel with pool and free shuttle service to the airport. ⑥.

Goose & Turrets Bed and Breakfast, 835 George Street, Montara (☎650/728-5451). Twenty minutes west of the airport, in the seaside hamlet of Montara, this is a more restful and intimate B&B alternative to the other airport accommodation. Close to the beaches and hiking trails, this is a perfect place to unwind either before or after a long trip. ⑤.

Hilton at San Francisco Airport, San Francisco Airport (☎415/589-0770). Actually on top of the airport, this is both easy to find and a guarantee that you won't miss your flight. Basic, business-class accommodation. ⑧.

Motel 6, 1101 Shoreway Road, Belmont (☎415/591-1471). A no-frills motel which is good preparation for a long and uncomfortable journey. ④.

Radisson Hotel San Francisco Airport, 1177 Airport Blvd (☎415/342-9200). Great facilities include restaurant, pool, jacuzzi, live music and a free shuttle to the airport. ⑥.

Super 8 Lodge, 111 Mitchell Ave (☎415/877-0770). Plain, motel-style accommodation with free airport shuttle (6–11am). ④.

Archbishop's Mansion, 1000 Fulton St at Steiner (☎415/563-7872). Deluxe, grandly-camp mansion that has been everything, from its namesake, to a school for wayward Catholic boys, and now a really quirky bed and breakfast. Attentive personal service and a variety of packages offering everything from getting fit to getting decked out by a professional image consultant. Home to Noel Coward's piano, this place is a riot. ⑥.

Best Western Miyako, 1800 Sutter St at Buchanan (☎1-800/528-1234 or 415/921-4000). Immaculate Japan Center hotel, with quiet rooms. ⑤.

Grove Inn, 890 Grove St at Fillmore (☎415/929-0780). Nothing fancy (some shared baths), but good value and a fine location on Alamo Square. ⑤.

Jackson Court, 2198 Jackson Street (☎415/992-7670). Pacific Heights converted mansion, offering luxury B&B service. Very nice indeed. ⑦.

The Mansions, 2220 Sacramento St at Laguna (☎415/929-9444). Luxury-swaddled Victorian mansion, perched high up in the fancy reaches of Pacific Heights. ⑤.

The Red Victorian Bed, Breakfast and Art (aka the Peace Center), 1665 Haight St at Cole (☎415/864-1978). Smack dab in the middle of the Haight-Ashbury, a time-warped B&B with hippy art gallery and rooms with New Agey themes, courtesy of owner Sami Sunchild. ⑤.

Golden Gate Park, the beaches and outlying areas

Beach Motel, 4211 Judah St (☎415/681-6618). Very average motel in a good spot by the edge of the park and Ocean beach. ④.

Ocean Park Motel, 2690 46th Ave (☎415/566-7020). A fair way from downtown (25min by Muni), this is nonetheless a great Art Deco motel (San Francisco's first), opposite the zoo and the beach. Outdoor hot tub and jacuzzi, and a play area for children. ③.

Stanyan Park Hotel, 750 Stanyan St at Waller (☎415/751-1000). Gorgeous, small Victorian hotel in a great setting across from Golden Gate Park, with friendly staff and free continental breakfast. ⑤.

Sunset Motel, 821 Taraval St (☎415/681-3306). One of the finest little motels in San Francisco – clean, friendly and safe. ③.

Hostels

Green Tortoise Hostel, 494 Broadway at Kearny (☎415/834-1000). Funky North Beach hostel with complimentary breakfast. From $29 per night single, $39 double, dorm $18.

HI-San Francisco Youth Hostel, Building 240, Fort Mason (☎415/771-7277). On the waterfront between the Golden Gate Bridge and Fisherman's Wharf. One of the most comfortable and convenient hostels around, with 150 beds and free parking. $16 per person and no day membership necessary because it's built on federal land. No curfew either.

HI-San Francisco at Union Square, 312 Mason St at O'Farrell (☎415/788-5604). Large new downtown hostel with dorm beds for $14–16 a night. No curfew. HI members only; day memberships cost $3.

Interclub/Globe Hostel, 10 Hallam Place, between Seventh and Eighth off Folsom (☎415/431-0540). Lively, recently redecorated SoMa hostel with no curfew. $14–17 per person; doubles $38.

San Francisco International Guest House, 2976 23rd St at Douglass (☎415/641-1411). Very popular with European travelers. Four-to-a-room dorms in the Mission plus a few private rooms. $13 daily – five-day minimum stay; for stays of 28 days or longer, $11 daily. Two kitchens; no curfew.

YMCA Central Branch, 220 Golden Gate Ave (☎415/885-0460). Well-equipped and centrally located, two blocks from the Civic Center. Singles $29, doubles $39, price includes a free continental breakfast and use of the gym, swimming pool and sauna.

The City

The first and most obvious thing that strikes the visitor is that San Francisco is a city of hills. Becoming familiar with these forty-odd hills is not just a good way to get your bearings, it will also give you a real insight into the city's class distinctions. As a general rule, geographical elevation is a stout indicator of wealth – the higher you live, the better off you are. Commercial square-footage is surprisingly small and mostly confined to the downtown area, and the rest of the city is made up of distinct, primarily residential neighborhoods, most of which are very easily explored on foot. Armed with a good map you could plough through three a day, but frankly, the best way to get to know San Francisco is to dawdle, unbound by itineraries: the most interesting districts, certainly, merit at least half a day each of just hanging about.

The top right-hand corner of the Peninsula, bordered by I-80 to the south, US-101 to the west, and the water, makes up the part of the city known as **downtown**, though really the neighborhoods themselves make the best orientation points. The core of downtown, mainly north of the city's main artery, **Market Street** – the wide thoroughfare, lined with stores and office buildings, that bisects the city center and is a main reference point for your wanderings – is signalled by the bay-front buildings of the **Embarcadero** and the corporate high-rises of the **Financial District**. Just beyond are the department stores and hotels that make up the city's busiest shopping district around **Union Square**, while above the lot, swanky **Nob Hill**, with its mansions and grand hotels, sits snootily on its quiet hilltop perch. A few blocks away, Nob Hill's borders merge with the neon intensity of **Chinatown**, easily the densest part of town and a good bet for great food.

At the northernmost tip of the city, **Fisherman's Wharf** and the waterfront has been carefully crafted with the visitor in mind – and pulls them in by the tour-bus-load. At night the area improves, but it's generally best to glimpse it in passing and make a beeline for the livelier old Italian enclave of **North Beach**, which, though chichi in places, still harbors a vaguely literary bohemian population that's a holdover from the days of the Beats in the Fifties. Above here, the very desirable neighborhoods of **Russian Hill** and **Telegraph Hill** flank North Beach on either side, affording fabulous views of the shimmering bay; just west, the truly rich enjoy similar vistas from the sumptuous homes of **Pacific Heights**.

Not a million miles from this rampant affluence, the slums of the **Tenderloin** form an often alarming quarter that begins a few blocks west of Union Square and runs south for a six-block stretch of dilapidated urban sleaze all the way to Market Street, home to a good many of the city's dispossessed. Crossing over Market Street, **South of Market** (or **SoMa**) used to be one of the city center's few industrial enclaves, until the arty, nightclubbing crowd discovered it. However, the area is now caught up in the wave of unstoppable gentrification, and is beginning to host some smart buildings – foremost among them the new San Francisco Museum of Art – so it's only a matter of time before more bulldozers move in and the artists move out. **Civic Center**, a little way west, is San Francisco's municipal – and arts – nucleus and site of some of the city's more grandiose architecture, rather awkward among the stagnating slums that surround it.

Walk much further south or west from Civic Center and you're out of downtown and in the more staunchly residential neighborhoods that enclose the city center. A lengthy stroll or short bus ride southwest, the garrulous Hispanic district of **The Mission**, San Francisco's largest neighborhood, is a good first choice for a trip further afield, filled with cheap restaurants, bars and clubs, and with a street life that's about as nonstop as San Francisco gets. **The Castro**, just beyond, has long been the city's primary gay district and makes no bones about it: refurbished for and by the gay community, and although to some extent tempered by the post-AIDS years, there's still an emphasis on cute shops and vigorous nightlife. West of downtown, the **Haight-Ashbury** district was once San Francisco's radical focus and tries hard to hold on to its countercultural traditions, with a caucus of left-wing bookstores, some tastefully tatty café-society and a smattering of residents still flying a slightly limp freak flag. At the end of Haight Street, **Golden Gate Park** is the antidote to all this: San Francisco's main city park and a sublime piece of landscape design, stretching west to the Pacific Shore and city beaches.

Downtown: the Financial District

With its plate-glass-and-steel skyscrapers soaring dramatically into the sky to form San Francisco's only real high-rise district, casting long shadows where thirty years ago there were none, the **FINANCIAL DISTRICT** is the city's most dynamic neighborhood – a Manhattan in miniature that's a symbol of San Francisco's enduring wealth and prosperity. Sharp-suited workers clog the streets in well-mannered rush-hour

ACCOMMODATION

1	Abigail Hotel	8	David
2	Beresford Arms Hotel	9	Fairmont Hotel
3	Cartwright	10	Gates
4	Clarion-Bedford	11	Grant Plaza
5	Commodore International Hotel	12	Green Tortoise & Guest House
6	Compton Place	13	Harbor Court Hotel
7	Dakota	14	HI-Hostel at Union Square
		15	Huntington Hotel
		16	Mandarin Oriental
		17	Hotel Monaco
		18	Nob Hill Pensione
		19	Petite Auberge
		20	Phoenix
		21	Prescott
		22	Renoir Hotel
		23	Ritz-Carlton
		24	San Remo Hotel
		25	Sir Francis Drake
		26	Hotel Triton
		27	Tuscan Inn
		28	Westin St Francis
		29	White Swan Inn
		30	York Hotel

DOWNTOWN SAN FRANCISCO

0   500 yds

droves, racing between their offices and the Montgomery BART/Muni station on Market Street. Originally, the center of the city's financial dealings was entirely to the north of Market Street, where the old low-rise banking halls are now flanked by newer, larger structures of corporate power. But to avert the complete demolition of the area for more profitable towers, the city is nowadays directing new development to South of Market (see p.409).

The Financial District comprises a veritable hodgepodge of architectural styles and periods, from Palladian piles to postmodern redoubts. Scattered between the banks and bars are the copy centers and computer boutiques that serve the offices above, with an occasional restaurant of note; the people are as dressed up as they come in this casual town, though they're still largely a testament to comfort before style. San Francisco's movers and shakers distinguish themselves from the rest of the American financial community on the last business day of the year, when local custom dictates that office workers throw their desk calendar pages out of the window. Standing on the street and looking skywards, the scene is reminiscent of a ticker-tape parade – not to be missed if you're in town for Christmas and New Year. Otherwise, there's not a lot to come for here, although on Friday evenings the bars buzz with relieved workers. On weekends it's deserted, save for the odd tourist.

Still, there are gems to be discovered in the Financial District, best reached by a dramatic plunge downhill on the California Street cable car. Once cut off from the rest of San Francisco by the double-decker Embarcadero Freeway – which was damaged in the 1989 earthquake, and finally torn down in 1992 – the **Ferry Building**, at the foot of Market Street, was modeled on the cathedral tower in Seville, Spain, and before the bridges were built in the 1930s, was the main point of arrival for fifty thousand crossbay commuters daily. A few ferry boats still arrive here, but the characterless office units inside do little to suggest its former importance. A lively **farmer's market** on Saturdays at the Ferry Plaza across the way attracts crowds of food lovers to the beautifully-presented produce, much of it organic, and makes a good starting point for a stroll. Facing downtown is the **Embarcadero** or **City Front District**, which has experienced quite a renaissance since the freeway was pulled down. Although dominated by the vast **Embarcadero Center** – a modern and rather unimaginative complex of offices, stores and cafés which stretches for several blocks west from **Justin Herman Plaza** – this little pocket of the city is nonetheless developing charm. Some very stylish hotels and the city's smartest new restaurants now sit along its bayview streets, and smart new residential blocks are springing up in unexpected corners. Tucked discreetly into a nondescript building at 121 Steuart St is the little-known **Jewish Museum San Francisco** (Sun–Wed noon–5pm, Thurs noon–8pm; $5, free first Mon of the month), which, far from being the sombre trudge through history its name suggests, has an impressive collection of contemporary work by Jewish artists.

From the Embarcadero, it's a few blocks down Market to **Montgomery Street** and the Financial District proper, where the grand pillared entrances and banking halls of the post-1906-earthquake construction era jostle for attention with the mixed bag of modern towers that is gradually moving in. For a real hands-on grasp of the dynamics of modern finance, the **World of Economics Gallery** in the **Federal Reserve Bank Building**, 101 Market St (Mon–Fri 9am–6pm), is unbeatable: computer games allow you to engineer your own stock-market disasters, while gallery exhibits detail recent scandals and triumphs in the financial world. The **Wells Fargo History Museum**, 420 Montgomery St (Mon–Fri 9am–5pm), details the origins of San Francisco's banking and financial boom with engaging exhibits from the days of the Gold Rush. Mining equipment, gold nuggets, photographs, and even a genuine stagecoach show the far-from-slick roots of San Francisco's big money. You'll find a drier collection of clippings and gold dust of the era in the **Museum of American Money from the West** in the **Union Bank of California**, a Corinthian-columned temple at 400 California St (Mon–Fri 9am–5pm).

The city's second tallest tower, the **Bank of America** building on Kearny and California, is a plate-glass and marble beast that the bank had to sell off after some overzealous lending to developing countries. The great lump of black marble in the entryway is known by locals as the "banker's heart," and the prices in the *Carnelian Room* rooftop restaurant are equally uncharitable. Skip the food and simply take the elevator up for cocktails and an unforgettable view.

Jackson Square and the Barbary Coast

A century or so ago, the northern flank of what is now the Financial District was part of the so-called **Barbary Coast**, a rough-and-tumble waterfront district packed with saloons and brothels where hapless young male visitors were given "Mickey Finns" and "Shanghaied" into involuntary servitude on merchant ships. Its wicked reputation made it off limits for military personnel up until World War II, and many of the old dives died an inevitable death. During the 1930s, the Barbary Coast became a low-rent district that attracted writers and artists including Diego Rivera, who had a studio on Gold Street at the height of his fame as the "communist painter sought after by the world's biggest capitalists." Most of these old structures have since been done up and preserved as the **Jackson Square Historic District** – not in fact a square, but a rectangle formed by Jackson, Montgomery, Gold and Sansome streets, making up a dense few blocks of low-rise, mostly brick buildings that now house the offices of advertising agencies and design firms, as well as the requisite cafés and watering holes.

The **Transamerica Pyramid**, at the foot of diagonal Columbus Avenue, is San Francisco's most unmistakable (some would say unfortunate) landmark and the city's tallest building, marking the edge of the Financial District and the beginning of North Beach. There was something of a rumpus when this went up, and it earned the name "Pereira's Prick" after its LA-based architect William Pereira, but since then it's become institutionalized as almost a symbol of San Francisco and figures on a great deal of the city's tourist and promotional literature. The original building on this site was the Montgomery Block, the city's first office building of any significance, but known more for the important names that moved in when the businesses moved off to alternative premises. Rudyard Kipling, Bret Harte, Robert Louis Stevenson, Mark Twain and William Randolph Hearst all rented office space in the building and regularly hung around the notorious "Bank Exchange" bar within. Legend also has it that Sun Yat-Sen – whose statue is in Chinatown, three blocks away (see p.399) – wrote the Chinese constitution and devised the successful overthrow of the Manchu Dynasty from his second-floor office here.

Union Square

West of Kearny Street, around **Union Square**, the skyscrapers thin out and are replaced by the bright lights and window displays of San Francisco's **shopping district**: a collection of boutiques, specialty and department stores which stretches for several blocks in all directions. Limousines are bumper-to-bumper here, as the well-heeled pop in and out of their favorite emporia; by contrast, bums and winos sprawl across the green lawns of Union Square, having drifted in from the Tenderloin to do a brisker trade from passing shoppers. The square takes it name from the mass meetings held here on the eve of the Civil War by Northerners demonstrating their loyalty to the Union, but these days it's remembered more for the attempted assassination of President Gerald Ford outside the St Francis Hotel in 1975. It was also the location of Francis Ford Coppola's *The Conversation*, where eavesdropper Gene Hackman spied on strolling lovers. The hotel played a similar role in many of **Dashiell Hammett's** detective stories, as well as in his own life – in the 1920s he worked there as an operative for the Pinkerton detective agency, investigating the notorious rape and murder case against the silent movie star Fatty Arbuckle.

On Geary Street, west of the square, the optimistically named **Theater District** is a pint-sized Broadway of restaurants, tourist hotels, serious and "adult" theaters – as in New York's Broadway or London's Soho, the Theater District of San Francisco shares space with less rarefied institutions. Also part of this district, just north of the Square along Post and Sutter are downtown's least visible landmarks: some fourteen private clubs hidden behind discreet facades. Money isn't the only criteria for membership to these highly esteemed institutions, though being *somebody* usually is. Most notorious is the **Bohemian Club** at Post and Taylor. Better known for its *Bohemian Grove* retreat at the Russian River, where ex-presidents and corporate giants get together for masonic rituals and schoolboy larks, the San Francisco chapter is housed in a Lewis Hobart Moderne-style building. Organized in the late 1880s by newspaper men and artists, it evolved into a businessmen's club with an arty slant, including Frank Norris, Ambrose Bierce and Jack London among its members. On the eastern side of the square you'll find still more stores and **Maiden Lane**, a chic little urban walkway that before the 1906 earthquake and fire was one of the city's roughest areas, where prostitutes solicited openly and homicides averaged around ten a month. Nowadays, aside from some prohibitively expensive boutiques, its main feature is San Francisco's only **Frank Lloyd Wright** building (now occupied by the **Folk Art International/Xanadu** ethnic art gallery), an intriguing circular space which was a try-out for the Guggenheim museum in New York.

If you're heading back up to the waterfront, **cable cars** run along Powell Street but are usually too packed to board at their Market Street origin. Move a few blocks up the hill where there are fewer people trying to get on, and climb to palatial Nob Hill before descending once more to the water's edge.

Nob Hill

Nob Hill, the hill of palaces, must certainly be counted the best part of San Francisco. It is there that the millionaires gather together, vying with each other in display. From thence, looking down upon the business wards of the city, we can decry a building with a little belfry, and that is the stock exchange, the heart of San Francisco; a great pump we might call it, continually pumping up the savings of the lower quarter to the pockets of the millionaires on the hill.

Robert Louis Stevenson

If the Financial District is representative of new money in the city, the posh hotels and masonic institutions of **NOB HILL**, just above it, exemplify San Francisco's old wealth; it is, as Joan Didion wrote, "the symbolic nexus of all old California money and power." Perhaps San Francisco's most revered address, it's worth the stiff climb (though the wise will take the cable car) to view the mansions, hotels and elitist restaurants that serve those who come closest to being San Francisco gentry. There are very few sights as such, but nosing around is pleasant enough, taking in the aura of luxury that distinguishes the neighborhood, and enjoying the views over the city and beyond.

Originally called the California Street Hill, the area became known as Nob Hill after robber-baron industrialists such as Leland Stanford and Charles Crocker came to the area to construct the Central Pacific Railroad, and built their mansions here. Only one of these ostentatious piles survived the 1906 fire – the brownstone mansion of James C. Flood, which cost a cool $1 million in 1886 and is now the Pacific Union Club, a private retreat for the ultra-rich. Other, later residences have given way to hotels, the most elaborate of which is the **Fairmont Hotel** on California and Mason, until recently San Francisco's classiest joint and setting for the television soap opera *Hotel*. One block west on California stands one of the biggest hunks of sham-Gothic architecture in the

US, **Grace Cathedral**. Construction began soon after the 1906 earthquake, though most of it was built, of faintly disguised reinforced concrete, in the early 1960s. One part that's worth a look is the entrance, adorned with faithful replicas of the fifteenth-century Ghiberti doors of the Florence Baptistery.

But the invention that made high-society life on the hills possible and practical – the **cable car** (the sort that runs along the ground, not swings precipitously from mountainsides) – is Nob Hill's dominant feature. Since 1873 when Scotsman Andrew Hallidie piloted the first of these little trolleys up the Clay Street hill to Portsmouth Square, they have been an integral part of San Francisco life. At their peak, just before the earthquake, over six hundred cable cars traveled 110 miles of track throughout the city, though by 1955 their usage had dwindled to such an extent that nostalgic citizens voted to preserve the remaining seventeen miles of track (now just ten) as a moving historic landmark. Today there are three lines: two run from Powell Street to Fisherman's Wharf and the oldest climbs Nob Hill along California Street from the Embarcadero, rattling past the fanciest hotels in the city. The Powell & Hyde line is the steepest, reaching a hair-raising 21-degree grade between Lombard and Chestnut streets. The cars fasten onto a moving two-inch cable which runs beneath the streets, gripping on the ascent then releasing at the top and gliding down the other side. You can see the huge motors which power these cables in the **Cable Car Museum and Powerhouse**, at 1201 Mason at Washington Street (daily 10am–5pm; free).

Chinatown

Completely distinct from any other neighborhood in the city, **CHINATOWN** comprises 24 square blocks of seeming chaos smack in the middle of town, its main thoroughfare running from the ornamental Chinese gate on Bush along Grant to Broadway. Dense, noisy, smelly, colorful and overcrowded, the second largest Chinese community outside Asia manages to be almost entirely autonomous, with its own schools, banks and newspapers. In among the brightly lit streets of restaurants, groceries and souvenir stores, however, the occasional dark and gloomy alleyway reminds you that commercial enterprise has not brought prosperity to all of the city's Chinese population.

The first Chinese arrived in Northern California in the late 1840s, many of them fleeing famine and the opium wars at home and seeking the easy fortunes of the Gold Rush. Later, in the 1860s, thousands more were shipped across to build the Transcontinental Railroad. At first the Chinese, or "coolies" as they were called (taken from the words *ku li*, meaning "bitter toil"), were accepted as hard-working laborers, but as the railroad neared completion and unemployment rose, many moved to San Francisco, to join what was already a sizeable community. The city didn't extend much of a welcome: jingoistic sentiment turned quickly into a tide of racial hatred, manifest in sometimes vicious attacks that bound the Chinese defensively into a solid, tight-knit community. The population stagnated until the 1960s, when the lifting of anti-Chinese immigration restrictions swelled the area's numbers to close on 160,000. Nowadays, the Chinese families that do well tend to move out to the more spacious districts of the Sunset and Richmond (see p.417), coming back on Sundays to shop and eat. The population is still massive, however, and now includes Vietnamese, Koreans, Thais and

---

CHINESE NEW YEAR

If you're visiting at the end of January or early February, make an effort to catch the celebration of **Chinese New Year**, when the streets almost self-combust with energy and noise. Floats and papier-mâché dragons trundle past as people hang off balconies, out of windows and shimmy up lampposts until there isn't an inch of space left.

Laotians. By day the area seethes with activity and congestion, by night the traffic moves a little easier, but the blaze of neon and marauding diners gives you the feeling that it just never lets up. Overcrowding is compounded by a brisk tourist trade and sadly, though fish can still be found hanging from washing lines, Chinatown boasts some of the most egregiously tacky stores and facades in the city. Genuine snatches of ethnicity are sullied by pseudo-Chinese Americana at every turn.

You can approach Chinatown from many directions: as well as Nob and Russian Hills, North Beach blends into its northern edges, and if you're coming from the south, Union Square is just a few blocks away. It is from this direction that you'll encounter the large dragon-clad archway (a gift from the Government of Taiwan, and, judging by the look of it, not one that broke the bank) that crosses the intersection of Bush Street and **Grant Avenue**, a long, narrow street, crowded with gold-ornamented portals and brightly painted balconies perched above the souvenir stores and restaurants. Chirping mechanical crickets, cloisonné "health balls," and wooden noisemakers assault the eye and ear from every doorway. Before the days of all-consuming tourism, Grant Avenue was known as Dupont Street, a wicked ensemble of opium dens, bordellos and gambling huts policed and frequently terrorized by Tong hatchet men – gangs who took it upon themselves to police and protect their district in any (usually extremely violent) way they saw fit. Their original purpose was to retaliate against the racial hooliganism, but they developed quickly into Mafia-style family feuding – as bloody as any of the Chicago gangster wars. These days there isn't much trace of them on the streets, but the mob continues to operate, battling for a slice of the lucrative West Coast drug trade.

Parallel to Grant, **Stockton Street** is closer to the real thing – Chinatown's main street, crammed with exotic fish and produce markets, bakeries and herbalists. Your dollar will go further here than anywhere else in the neighborhood, and your search for the authentic face of Chinatown will be better rewarded. Inside the **Ellison Herb Shop** at 805 Stockton St, Chinatown's most well-stocked herbal pharmacy, you'll find clerks filling orders the old-fashioned way – with hand-held scales and abacuses – from cases filled with dried bark and roots, sharks' fins, cicadas, ginseng and other staples of Chinese medicine. Tucked away in little Ross Alley (between Grant Street and Waverly Place), the **Golden Gate Fortune Cookie Factory** is a hole-in-the-wall where you can watch the cookies being made on two ancient-looking iron presses, then folded by hand. These crisp wafers end up in restaurants all over the city and the bakers will even insert your own custom-written fortunes, or sell you a bag of cookies with racy messages inside. Three blocks down, at California and Grant, **St Mary's Square** holds a sculpture of Sun Yat-Sen, founder of the Chinese Republic; its little old men and pastoral ambiance a far cry from the days when this was the area's red light district.

Chinatown's history is well documented in the **Chinese Historical Society of America** at 650 Commercial St (Tues–Fri, 10am–4pm; donations), which traces the beginnings of the Chinese community in the US and has a small but worthy collection of photographs, paintings and artifacts from the pioneering days of the last century. But to really get the measure of Chinatown, you should wander its alleys with their hidden temples and family clubs and organizations. Waverly Place is particularly good; in the late nineteenth century it was lined with brothels, but the earthquake helped clean up the area. There are three opulently decorated but skilfully hidden temples (nos 109, 125 and 146), their interiors a riot of black, gold and vermilion. They're still in use and open to visitors, but the erratic opening times mean you'll need luck to get in. More accessible is **Buddha's Universal Church** at 720 Washington St, where America's largest Zen sect gives free tours on the second and fourth Sunday of each month, the only time it's open to the public. This five-story building was painstakingly built by the sect's members from an exotic collection of polished woods, adorned everywhere by the mosaic images of Buddha. Not as rich with history, the **Chinese Cultural Center**, inside the *Holiday Inn* at 750 Kearny St (Tues–Sun 10am–4pm), does nonetheless host a sporadic program of art shows, mostly contemporary, that go some way to dispelling the popular myth that Chinese art is all pastel colors and oblique images.

The best of Chinatown's very few **bars** is **Li Po's**, at 916 Grant Ave, a dimly lit retreat from the confusion of the surrounding streets, named after the Chinese poet, and something of a hangout for the small contingent of Chinese writers in the city. However, you are more likely to have come here to **eat** in one of over a hundred restaurants (see p.421). Some are historical landmarks in themselves, none less so than **Sam Woh**, 813 Washington St, cheap and churlish ex-haunt of the Beats where Gary Snyder taught Jack Kerouac to eat with chopsticks, and had them both thrown out for his loud and passionate interpretation of Zen poetry.

Half a block east, **Portsmouth Square**, now best known as the roof of a multistory garage, was originally the first port of entry, and the place where Sam Brannan announced the discovery of gold – an event which transformed San Francisco from a sleepy Spanish pueblo into a rowdy frontier city. Fresh off the boat and in search of riches from "Gold Mountain," their name for San Francisco, the arriving Chinese sailors banded together and founded what became known as Chinatown in the streets and alleys surrounding the port. Though not the most attractive of parks, Portsmouth Square is nonetheless an oasis in a very cramped part of town, and serves as an "outdoor living room" for people without even an indoor one. Old men come to play chess, while younger ones fly past on skateboards; in the northwest corner there's a monument to Robert Louis Stevenson, who, it's claimed, used to come here to write. More recently, sculptor Thomas Marsh's bronze, *The Goddess of Democracy*, was erected here after an unsuccessful stay in Tiananmen Square, Beijing in the spring of 1989.

North Beach

Resting in the hollow between Russian and Telegraph Hills, and split down the middle by Columbus Avenue, **NORTH BEACH** likes to think of itself as the happening district of San Francisco. While not cutting-edge contemporary, North Beach's charm has endured several incarnations and fashion waves to remain one of the most consistently interesting areas of town. Originally the city's Italian quarter, since the 1950s – when the more prominent figures of the Beat movement gathered here – it has been among the sought-after neighborhoods for anyone vaguely alternative. The place still has an Italian flavor, somehow resisting the encroaching neon of the strip joints and sex clubs on Broadway, and is home to some of the most loyally-patronized bars and restaurants in the city. Rocketing real estate prices leveled off in the 1980s, and the die-hard freethinkers have just about managed to maintain their territory amid the sharp-suited young professionals slumming it in North Beach's traditionally scruffy cafés. Consequently, it is still a most likeable neighborhood, inhabited by a solid core of people who remember what bohemia was really like. The anecdotes connected with North Beach are legion – get chatting to any barfly over fifty, they seem to know them all.

San Francisco's most visible landmark, the **Transamerica Pyramid** on Montgomery and Columbus, marks the southern edge of North Beach and the beginning of the more corporate identity of the Financial District. A little further up Columbus Avenue, the green flatiron **Columbus Tower** looks somewhat surreal against the backdrop of the downtown skyline. Developers have been trying to knock it down for years, but the efforts of its owner, film-maker Francis Ford Coppola, have so far ensured its survival. Across Columbus, the *Purple Onion* nightclub and the *Hungry i* down Jackson Street hosted some of the biggest names of the Fifties San Francisco scene. Politically conscious comedians such as Lenny Bruce (who made himself a name in the area for regular doped-out attempts to throw himself from the upper windows) and Mort Sahl performed here, and even though these places have now closed or changed beyond recognition, the district continues to trade on a reputation earned decades ago.

THE BEATS IN NORTH BEACH

North Beach has always been something of a literary hangout: it was home to Mark Twain and Jack London for a while, among other boomtown writers. But it was the **Beat generation** in the late 1950s that really put the place on the map, focusing media attention on the area – and the **City Lights Bookstore** (see below) – as literary capital of California. The first Beat writings had emerged a decade earlier in New York's Lower East Side from Jack Kerouac, Allen Ginsberg and William Burroughs, who, like many writers of the time, were frustrated by the conservative political climate, and whose lifestyle and values emphasized libertarian beliefs that America wasn't perhaps ready for. Nothing really crystallized, however, until a number of the writers moved out West, most of them settling in North Beach and forming an esoteric cluster of writers, poets, musicians and inevitable hangers-on around the City Lights. It wasn't long before the Beats were making news. In 1957 a storm of controversy rose up when police moved in to prevent the sale of Ginsberg's poem **Howl** under charges of obscenity – an episode the press latched onto immediately, inadvertently hyping the Beats to national notoriety, as much for their hedonistic antics as for the literary merits of their work. Within six months, Jack Kerouac's **On the Road**, inspired by his friend Neal Cassady's benzedrine monologues and recorded in a marathon two-week session in New York six years earlier – previously rejected by all the publishers he had taken it to – shot to the top of the bestseller lists.

As well as developing a new, more personal style of fiction and poetry, the Beats eschewed most social conventions of the time, and North Beach soon became almost a symbol across the nation of a wild and subversive lifestyle. The road trips and riotous partying, the drug-taking and embrace of Eastern spiritualism were revered and emulated nationwide. Whether the Beat message was an important one is a moot point; in any case, the Beats became more of an industry than a literary movement, and tourists poured into North Beach for "Beatnik Tours" and the like. The more enterprising fringes of bohemia responded in kind with "The Squaresville Tour" of the Financial District, dressed in Bermuda shorts and carrying plaques that read "Hi, Squares." The legend has yet to die, not least in North Beach itself, where Ferlinghetti has had his wish granted by City Hall and many of the city's streets have been renamed as a tribute to the famous figures who have graced the neighborhood; indeed the small alley which runs down the side of the City Lights store has been called "Jack Kerouac Lane."

Further along Columbus at Broadway, amid the flashing neon and sleazy clubs, the **City Lights Bookstore** was the first paperback bookstore in the US, established in 1953, and still owned by poet and novelist Lawrence Ferlinghetti. The vast collection of avant-garde, contemporary and Beat works is open for business and browsing until midnight, seven days a week. Next to the bookstore, across the narrow Kerouac Alley, **Vesuvio's** is an old North Beach bar where most of the local writers hung out at some point. The likes of Dylan Thomas and Jack Kerouac regularly got loaded here, and while times have changed considerably since then, it remains a haven for the lesser-known to get sloshed with impunity and pontificate on the state of the arts. Assuming you leave *Vesuvio's* with your brain intact, you'll find yourself at the crossroads of **Columbus and Broadway**, where poetry meets porn in a raucous assembly of strip joints, coffeehouses and drag bars. Most famous, the *Condor Club* was where Carol Doda's infamous revelation of her silicone-implanted breasts started the topless waitress phenomenon. Now reopened as the (fully-clothed) *Condor Sports Bar*, the landmark site still preserves her neon nipples, once immortalized above the door, in their museum, along with photos and clippings from the *Condor Club's* heyday. Nowadays the sex business seems a bit limp along the strip as scantily-clad ladies try to lure you through their darkened doorways. **Finocchio's** at 506 Broadway, now home to polished drag-acts (see p.436), was a famous speakeasy during prohibition.

As you continue north on Columbus, the bright lights fade and you enter the heart of the old **Italian neighborhood**, an enclave of restaurants, cafés, delicatessens and offbeat stores set against a background of narrow streets and leafy enclosures. A quick diversion along any of the side streets will lead you to small landmarks such as the **Café Trieste**, at 601 Vallejo, a literary waking-up spot since the days of the Beats and still a reminder of more romantic times: the jukebox blasts out opera classics to a heavy-duty art crowd toying with their cappuccinos and browsing slim volumes of poetry.

A couple of hundred yards further along Columbus Avenue, **Washington Square Park** isn't, with five sides, much of a square; neither, due to urban overcrowding, is it much of a park. However, it's big and green enough for the elder Italians to rest on the benches and the neighboring Chinese to do their Tai Chi routines on a Sunday morning, and is lined with stylish restaurants, where serious media people and politicos come to power-lunch. On the Columbus Avenue side of the park is one of old San Francisco pioneer Lily Coit's many tributes to her fascination with firemen; a big, bronze macho monument with men holding hoses. On the north side of the park the lacy spires of the **Church of St Peter and Paul**, where baseball hero Joe DiMaggio married Marilyn Monroe, dominate the center of the neighborhood. Inside this stately Romanesque testament to local Italian pride (it also has a school built around it) is *La Madre del Lume*, a wonderful painting of a Madonna, child on hip, reaching into the inferno to pull out a sinner by his arm. Not quite so holy is the art at the **Tattoo Museum**, 841 Columbus Ave – actually a working tattoo parlor – where you can wonder at Lyle Tuttle's bizarre photographs of the flesh canvases who have submitted to his needle.

Two steep hills dwarf the area. To the east of Columbus Avenue, **TELEGRAPH HILL** is a neighborhood of small alleys and houses perched on 45-degree inclines. It was once an extension of the wilder North Beach territory, but is now firmly rich country, its elegant homes dangling precipitously on the steep hills below **Coit Tower** (daily 10am–6.30pm; $3) – a monument to the firefighters who doused the flames of 1906, decorated with WPA murals depicting muscle-bound Californians working the land. Built with $100,000 bequeathed by Lily Coit in 1929, the 210-foot, simple concrete column is an attractive component of the city's skyline, but the greatest reward for the trudge uphill is to take the elevator up to the tower's observation deck – the swooping panorama takes in the bay and the famous Golden Gate Bridge in the north, to the more seductively simple Bay Bridge in the east.

To the west of Columbus, **RUSSIAN HILL** is an elegant neighborhood named after the Russian sailors who died on an expedition here in the early 1800s and were buried on its southeastern tip. The neighborhood today draws a steady stream of visitors, who come to drive down **Lombard Street**: a narrow, tightly curving street with a 5mph speed limit and long line of cars waiting to get onto it. Surrounded by palatial dwellings and herbaceous borders, Lombard is featured as often as the Golden Gate Bridge in San Francisco publicity shots, and at night when the tourists leave and the city lights twinkle below, it makes for a thrilling drive. But even without a car it's worth the journey up here for a visit to the **San Francisco Art Institute**, 800 Chestnut St (Tues–Sat 10am–5pm; free). The oldest art school in the West, the Institute has been central in the development of the arts in the Bay Area, and has four excellent galleries, three dedicated to painting and one to surrealist photography. The remarkably high standard of work puts some of San Francisco's galleries proper in a very shady second place. But the highlight of the institute is unquestionably the **Diego Rivera Gallery**, which has an outstanding mural executed by the painter in 1931 at the height of his fame. A small **cafeteria** at the back of the building offers cheap refreshments and great views of North Beach, Telegraph Hill and the bay.

From the western edge of Russian Hill along Union Street all the way to the *presidio*, runs an area known as **COW HOLLOW**. Originally a small valley of pastures and dairies in the post-Gold Rush years, Cow Hollow languished until the 1950s when enterprising merchants decided its old clapboard dwellings had possibilities. Gorgeous old Victorian houses have had their faces lifted, and the stretch of Union between Van Ness and Divisadero now holds some very cutesy boutiques and cafés. Best seen on foot because of all the little alleyways and tucked-away basements, it's an excellent place to use up any excess dollars.

Fisherman's Wharf, Alcatraz and the northern waterfront

San Francisco doesn't go dramatically out of its way to please the tourist on the whole, but with **Fisherman's Wharf** and the nearby waterfront district, it makes a rare exception. An inventive use of statistics allows the area to proclaim itself the most visited tourist attraction in the entire country; in fact this crowded and hideous ensemble of waterfront kitsch and fast-food stands make for a sad and rather misleading introduction to the city. Hard to believe now, but this was originally a serious fishing port, trawling in real crabs and not the frozen sort now masquerading as fresh on the stalls; the few fishermen that can afford the exorbitant mooring charges are usually finished by early morning and get out before the tourists arrive. The most charming sight here is the large colony of boisterous sea lions (no feeding allowed) that have taken over a number of floating platforms between piers 39 and 41. For some reason, these wild ani-

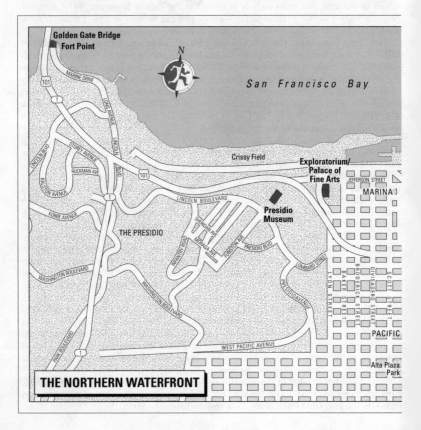

mals have made the wharf their home for over eight years and, protected by the Marine Mammal Act, live undisturbed and free to come and go as they please.

Almost directly opposite, the **Cannery**, on Leavenworth Street, is a one-time fruit-packing factory that has experienced similar refurbishment. And at the far eastern end of the wharf, about half a mile away, **Pier 39** is another shopping complex, contrived to look like San Francisco of old, but failing rather miserably and charging heavily for the privilege. In between the two a cluster of exorbitantly priced museums and exhibitions are designed to relieve you of more money; not one is worth expending time on, unless you're with restless children. Further east, **Ghirardelli Square** at 900 North Point is perhaps a fitting conclusion to this part of the waterfront, a former chocolate factory whose major parts have been transformed into pricey stores and restaurants – although some small-scale production does continue.

Bay cruises depart from piers 39, 41 and 43¹/₂ several times a day. Provided the fogs aren't too heavy, they give good city views (see p.387 for details).

West from the wharf

A little way west of the wharf, beyond Ghirardelli Square, the **Golden Gate National Recreation Area** was established in 1972 to protect much-needed central park space for the city, and now encompasses almost seventy square miles of waterfront property, from the beaches to the south right up to the cliffs of Marin County across the Golden Gate Bridge. Closest to the wharf, the **Aquatic Park** complex of buildings groups around the foot of Hyde Street, at its center the "bathhouse" – a bold, Art Deco piece of architecture now home to the **Maritime Museum** (daily 10am–5pm; free). It's worth dropping by just to see Hilaire Hiler's mural, symbolizing the lost continent of Atlantis in 37 hallucinogenic panels that dominate the main room. The rest of the complex includes a maritime library, and a forgettable collection of ocean-going memorabilia. At the adjacent **Hyde Street Pier**, the museum has restored a number of old wooden ships, including a transbay ferry, the *Eureka* ($4). Another, the *Balclutha* ($4), is the sole survivor of the great sailing ships that journeyed around Cape Horn in the 1800s, and later had bit parts in movies of the Thirties like *Mutiny on the Bounty*.

Fort Mason, half a mile west along the waterfront, sits behind a lovely open park, accessible via Muni bus lines #28 and #30 (stops two blocks away). Originally a Civil War defense installation, now turned over to public use, the old buildings are occupied by around fifty nonprofit groups and include four theaters, two galleries, four museums and a **youth hostel** (see p.393). The acclaimed **Magic Theater** (see p.435) presents first-run plays while Bay Area Theater Sports puts on improvisational shows in the Bayfront Theater. Displays at the **Museo Italo-Americano** (Wed–Sun noon–5pm; free first Wed of the month) relate to the culture and history of the Italian community in the US; the rather better **Mexican Museum** (Wed–Fri noon–5pm, Sat & Sun 11am–5pm; $3, free first Wed of the month and open until 7pm), while awaiting the construction of a new building South of Market, still exhibits its large collection of funky folk art and representational works.

San Francisco's most theatrical piece of architecture lies at Marina Boulevard and Baker Street. **The Palace of Fine Arts** is not the museum its name suggests, but a huge, freely interpreted classical ruin originally built of wood and plaster for the Pan Pacific International Exhibition in 1915 – held to celebrate the rebirth of the city after the 1906 catastrophe. Sentimental San Franciscans saved it from immediate demolition after the exhibition, and it crumbled with dignity until a wealthy resident put up the money for its reconstruction in 1958, making it the sole survivor of the Pan Pacific pageant, surrounded by a swan-filled lagoon and other touches of urban civility. Next door, in what has to be the coolest museum in San Francisco – the **Exploratorium** (summer daily 10am–6pm, Wed until 9.30pm; winter Tues–Sun 10am–5pm, Wed until 9.30pm; $9 adults, free first Wed of the month; ☎415/561-0362 for Tactile Dome reservations) – over 650 hands-on exhibits demonstrate scientific principles of electricity, sound waves, lasers and more. From real traveling flea circuses to a giant, completely dark labyrinth called the "Tactile Dome" (you explore it on hands and knees; reservations required), this place will boggle your mind and keep any kid enthralled for hours. From here the waterfront stretches west through the Presidio National Park to the Golden Gate Bridge and beach area close to the Golden Gate Park (see p.415).

The area around the Palace of Fine Arts has been tagged the **Marina** district by the young, image-conscious, money-no-object sort of professionals who live there. One of the city's greenest districts, the Marina enjoys a prime waterfront location, open spaces and lots of trees. Ironically, though it was built specifically to celebrate the rebirth of the city after the massive earthquake of 1906, the Marina was the worst casualty of the earthquake in 1989 – tremors tore through fragile landfill and a good number of homes collapsed into a smoldering heap. The neighborhood's commercial center runs along **Chestnut Street** between Broderick and Fillmore. As a neighborhood, it has a reputation for being something of a haven for swinging singles; the local watering holes are known as "high intensity breeder bars" and even the local Safeway has been dubbed "The Body Shop" because of the inordinate amount of cruising that goes on in the aisles.

Looming above, wealthy **PACIFIC HEIGHTS** is home to some of the city's most monumental Victorian piles. Among these, the wooden turrets of the **Haas-Lilienthal House** at 2007 Franklin St (Wed & Sun noon–3pm; $5; ☎415/441-3000), with its Tiffany

ALCATRAZ

The rocky little islet of **Alcatraz**, rising out of San Francisco Bay, was originally home to nothing more than the odd pelican (*alcatraz* in Spanish). In the late nineteenth century, the island became a military fortress, and in 1934 it was converted into America's most dreaded **high-security prison**. Surrounded by freezing, impassable water, it was an ideal place for a jail, and safely kept some of America's most wanted criminals behind bars – Al Capone and Machine Gun Kelly were just two of the villains imprisoned here. The conditions were about as inhuman as you'd expect: inmates were sometimes kept in solitary confinement, in cells no larger than five by nine feet, most without light; they were not allowed to eat together, read newspapers, have a game of cards or even talk; relatives were permitted to visit them for only two hours each month. Escape really was impossible. In all, nine men managed to get off the rock, but there is no evidence that they made it to the mainland.

For all its usefulness as a jail, the island turned out to be a fiscal disaster. After years of generating massive running costs, not to mention whipping up a storm of public protest for its role as a prison for petty criminals, it closed in 1963. The remaining prisoners were distributed among decidedly less horrific detention centers, and the island remained abandoned until 1969, when a group of Native Americans staged an occupation as part of a peaceful attempt to claim the island for their people – citing treaties which designated all federal land not in use as automatically reverting to their ownership. Using all the bureaucratic trickery it could muster, the government finally ousted them in 1971, claiming the operative lighthouse qualified it as active.

Nowadays the only people to set foot on the island are the annual 750,000 tourists who participate in the excellent hour-long, self-guided **audio tours** ($5) of the abandoned rows of cells, which include some sharp anecdotal commentary. **Boats** across to Alcatraz leave frequently (schedule depends on season) from pier 41, beginning at 9.30am, with the last boat back at 4.30pm (reserve two weeks ahead in summer; ☎415/705-5555; $11).

art glass and stenciled leather paneling, is a grand symbol of Old California wealth. The **Octagon House**, 2645 Gough at Union (call for visiting times; ☎415/441-7512), is, as the name suggests, a unique octagonal building, built in 1861 and purchased by the National Society of Colonial Dames of America, who have crammed it full of colonial and federal period antiques.

The Tenderloin, Civic Center and South of Market

While much of San Francisco tends to be depicted as an urban utopia – and in some cases, almost lives up to the promise – the adjoining districts of the **Tenderloin**, **Civic Center** and **South of Market** reveal a city of harsh realities. Pretty tree-lined streets, hills and stunning views are conspicuously absent, and for the most part these areas are a gritty blue-collar reminder that not everybody here has it so good. The homeless and disaffected are very much in evidence – the flipside of Californian prosperity is alive and unwell. Sporadic attempts to improve the areas (like the removal of over three hundred homeless people who set up camp outside the offices of the former mayor), are at best well-meaning hit-and-misses or, at worst, patently cosmetic gestures that are bound to fail. Yet these districts are not uninteresting and neither are they as menacing as their LA equivalents, though you shouldn't expect to walk along this section of Market Street without being hassled for money.

The Tenderloin

West of Union Square on the north side of Market, the **TENDERLOIN**, sandwiched between Civic Center and downtown, provides bold contrast with the rest of San

Francisco: a small, uninviting area no more than four blocks by five, it remains the poorest and shabbiest spot in the city. Despite a recent wave of Vietnamese and Laotian immigrants, soup kitchens and flophouses remain the area's major industry, though it is here you'll find San Francisco's best budget accommodation and you may well find yourself staying in one of the numerous low-priced hotels and lodgings. The Tenderloin is at least smack in the middle of town, and you'll be safe as long as you keep your wits about you and don't mind vagrants asking you for money. With common sense you shouldn't find it threatening, though areas you might take care to avoid are those along **Taylor Street** and around the lower part of **Eddy** and **Turk** near Market. Gangs have made this their territory and nonchalantly mooching around is not recommended.

Partly as an attempt to spruce the area up, the city has gone to great lengths to design a "tramp-proof" **park** on Jones and Eddy, replete with every imaginable barrier to dissuade the locals from establishing residence. On a good day, and with heavy patrolling by local police, it can claim to be a success. In addition, the appearance of trendy nightspots and stupefyingly hip restaurants is doing more to make the area safe than any public program has managed so far.

Attempts to dignify **Polk Street** to the west have been less successful. Even the police find this wild stretch hard to control, with cars cruising the strip of dodgy-looking bars for rent boys and prostitutes. Genuinely sleazy after the sometimes tedious charm of other areas in San Francisco, Polk Street is a neon haven of gay bars, affordable small stores, movie theaters and, further up towards Russian Hill, some pretty good restaurants.

Civic Center

Born out of a grand, celebratory architectural scheme, **CIVIC CENTER**, squashed between the quasi-slums of the Tenderloin and industrial SoMa, is an impressive layout of majestic federal and municipal buildings that can't help but look strangely out of synch, both with its immediate neighbors and with San Francisco as a whole. Its grand Beaux Arts structures, flags and fountains are at odds with the quirky wooden architecture that characterizes the rest of the city. It's the city's center for the performing arts, and by night can look quite impressive – beautifully lit, and swarming with dinner suits heading in and out of the ballet, opera and symphony hall. But by day it's much less appealing, populated either by office workers from the various local government departments situated here, or by the homeless who loiter on the grass verges of the elegant central quadrangle.

Emerging from the BART/Muni station, the first thing you see is the **United Nations Plaza**, a memorial to the founding of the UN here in 1949 – though the only sign of life is on Wednesdays when it's the site of San Francisco's largest and cheapest **farmers' market**. Most other days it's a rather dismal location for the dispossessed to beg for small change around the fountains in front of the **City Hall**, at the northern edge of the quadrangle. Modeled on St Peter's in Rome, this huge, green-domed Baroque building of granite and marble is the city's most grandiose structure and forms the nucleus of Civic Center. It was here in 1978 that conservative ex-supervisor Dan White got past security and assassinated Mayor George Moscone and gay supervisor Harvey Milk; later, when White was found guilty of manslaughter (not murder), it was the scene of violent demonstrations as gay protesters set fire to police vehicles and stormed the doors of the building.

Opposite City Hall, at Fulton and Larkin streets, the seven-story, ultra high-tech **New Main Library** opened in 1996 amid much fanfare and controversy – not only because librarians threw out 100,000 books for lack of space in the new building. The New Main is supposed to be a library "for the twenty-first century" providing hookups for your laptop, public Internet computers and towers of CD-ROMs, but the state-of-the-art computerized catalog breaks down with alarming regularity. On the sixth floor, the **San Francisco History Room** contains an extensive collection of books and photographs which, with the help of maps, details the city's evolution. To get a handle on the area's cultural venues, the **San Francisco Performing Arts Library and Museum**, 399 Grove St (Wed 1–7pm, Thurs & Fri 10am–4pm, Sat noon–4pm; free) is not really a museum but a research library, though it does contain a one-room gallery showing exhibits related to performing arts not just in Civic Center, but the Bay Area as a whole. In addition, a number of galleries and smart shops are beginning to group themselves around the district: the **Vorpal Gallery**, 393 Grove St, has earned a reputation for consistently high-class contemporary paintings, while the **Arts Commission Gallery**, 155 Grove St, has both indoor and outdoor exhibitions by emerging Bay Area artists.

Directly behind City Hall are San Francisco's cultural mainstays. The ritzy **War Memorial Opera House**, on Van Ness, is the pride and joy of the city's performing arts institutions – recently reopened after essential earthquake-proofing, this is ornate Beaux-Arts architecture at its finest. In thoroughly modern contrast, the giant aquarium-like **Louise M. Davies Symphony Hall** is home to the highly rated San Francisco Symphony, whose season runs from September to May (see p.434). Less rarefied (but nonetheless well-known) entertainment can be found in the **Mitchell Brothers O'Farrell Theater**, 895 O'Farrell St, unmissable for its facade painted with jungle murals. This San Francisco institution is notorious for its "sexual entertainment" and entered into legend several years ago when one of the Mitchell brothers murdered the other.

South of Market

Although traditionally among San Francisco's least desirable (and most notorious) neighborhoods, the district South of Market, aka **SoMa**, enjoyed a bit of a renaissance in the 1980s and entered the 1990s with an altered reputation. The recent arrival of the new **Museum of Modern Art** highlights its transformation. It's reminiscent in a way of New York's SoHo, and while by day it can seem little more than a bleak expanse of largely deserted warehouse spaces, by night it can fairly claim to be the epicenter of San Franciscan nightlife. The decline of San Francisco's shipping and rail freight industry in the 1950s and 1960s left much of the area desolate, but since the city planners put a stop to all new development in the Financial District there's been a boom in new construction here, highlighted by major projects such as the **Moscone Convention Center**, named after the Mayor who was assassinated along with Harvey Milk. Many of SoMa's abandoned warehouses have been converted into studio space and small art galleries, and the neighborhood is now home to artists, musicians, hep-cat entertainers and a number of trendy restaurants.

Of all the recent buildings, the most talked about has been the new home of the **Museum of Modern Art** (MOMA), 151 Third St (Mon–Tues & Fri–Sun 11am–6pm, Thurs 11am–9pm; $8, Thurs 6–9pm half price, free first Tues of the month) designed by Swiss architect Mario Botta, which has more than doubled the exhibition space the museum had in the Civic Center and will, optimists predict, make San Francisco the foremost center for contemporary art on the West Coast. Major works include paintings by Jackson Pollock, Mark Rothko, Frida Kahlo and Diego Rivera. Georgia O'Keefe, Dali, Matisse and Picasso are also represented, if not at their peak. There is an excellent selection of photography, but the museum's strongest suit is its calendar of temporary exhibitions. Despite these many treasures, the building is arguably far more beautiful than anything inside – flooded with natural light from a soaring, truncated, cylindrical skylight, it's a sight to behold.

Opposite the museum is the other totem of civic pride, the **Yerba Buena Center**, bounded by Third and Fourth streets, Mission and Folsom. A spectacular $44 million project to house the arts, featuring a theater and visual arts center, it aims to provide a forum for the work of San Francisco's diverse artistic and ethnic communities. Much of the work is provincial (naturally) compared to the stuff in the MOMA, and the center's best feature is its setting – five and half acres of lovely gardens with a fifty-foot Sierra granite waterfall memorial to Martin Luther King Jr.

Above all, SoMa is the nucleus of **clubland**, and it's a chance to see the city's wildlife at its best. Folsom Street was once a major gay strip, the center for much lewder goings-on than the now-respectable Castro, but recently the mix has become pretty diverse and you should expect to find anything but the very tame. The kernel of activity is around 11th and Folsom, where the largest grouping of clubs and bars draw crowds who don't mind waiting in line at weekends. Comparatively little traffic uses this intersection during the day, and it comes as a surprise to see the bumper-to-bumper and double-parked vehicles after midnight. If you want to check out the area during the day, head for the block of Folsom Street between Seventh and Ninth. *Brainwash* at 1122 Folsom is the epitome of SoMa, a café where you can also do your laundry.

Nestled between Brannan and Bryant and Second and Third about half a mile away, **South Park** is the sole survivor of what in the 1870s was the city's most upscale district, a small square designed by an English architect to mirror London's fashionable Georgian squares. The construction of the Bay Bridge – which has its western foot just a block away – spelled the end of this as a residential neighborhood, and the smart-set hightailed it to Pacific Heights. Long an industrial district, South Park has recently been rediscovered and increasingly houses the offices of architects and designers, who can be seen lunching at the chic French cafés on the square. Around the corner, where Third Street meets Brannan, a **plaque** marks the birthplace of *Call of the Wild* writer Jack London, though he soon escaped what were then pretty mean streets, enjoying his better days in Oakland and the valleys of Sonoma.

With all the new development, it can be hard to imagine what SoMa looked like before, but the real spirit of blue-collar, industrial San Francisco still exists around the abandoned docks and old shipyards known as **China Basin** and **Mission Rock**. Not much goes on here now, but the site has an isolated, romantic quality suited to desolate walks, stopping off for drinks at the few places that dot the shoreline. The easiest way to reach the area is to follow Third Street south from Market as it curves round to meet the docks at the **switchyards** where the drawbridge crosses China Basin Channel. It was here that **Jack Kerouac** worked as a brakeman in the Fifties, at the same time writing the material that was later to appear in *Lonesome Traveler*, detailing scenes of SoMa's skid row hotels, drunks and whores. A short walk south takes you to the heart of the China Basin, the old water inlet, and Mission Rock – the old Pier 50 that juts out into the bay. This was the focus of the old port where freight ships used to dock from Asia. Occasionally the odd ship will sail by, but today it's more likely to be the military ships from the Oakland Naval Base cruising the bay than the freight liners that used to jam the waterways. A few small boat clubs have sprung up along the waterfront, but most people come to visit the Mission Rock Resort (now closed) or The Ramp – two creaky wooden structures that are local landmarks.

The Mission

Low-rent, colorful, occasionally dangerous and Hispanic working-class, the **MISSION** is claimed by some to be the second-hippest neighborhood in the whole US (after New Orleans' Lower Garden District). Positioned way south of downtown, it is the city's warmest area, avoiding the fogs that blanket most of the Peninsula during the summer. Trendy new restaurants and jukebox joints continue to open on 16th and Valencia streets, drawing crowds from the more well-to-do neighborhoods and creating an inviting mix of cheap and chic. Add to this the fair concentration of lively nightspots, and the Mission is a good base if you're staying in the city for any length of time, easily accessible via the 16th Street or 24th Street BART.

As a first stop for immigrants to the city, the Mission is something of a microcosm of the history of San Francisco. It was first inhabited by Scandinavians and Germans, later the Irish, then the Italians, and now San Francisco's Hispanic population. It is from this that the area gets its marked political edge: this is perhaps the only truly radical pocket left in the city, with its left-wing, feminist and lesbian bookstores, Hispanic labor associations and the requisite bohemian bars and cafés. For the rest, it's a noisy melange of garages, furniture and junk stores, old movie houses and parking lots. The one sight here is the **Levi Strauss & Co** factory at 250 Valencia St (free tours Wed 10am & 1pm; reservations required ☎415/565-9159), where you can see how the world's most famous jeans are made. Tours of the plant include the cutting and sewing operations and how to "stonewash" a pair of jeans and make your new pair look old.

The district takes its name from the old **Mission Dolores**, 16th and Dolores (daily 9am–4pm; $2), the most ancient building to survive the 1906 earthquake and fire. Completed in 1791, it was the sixth in a series of missions built as Spain staked its claim to California, trying to "civilize" the natives with Christianity while utilizing their (cheap) labor. Cruel treatment and neglect, however, led to disease and many natives died; their graves, and those of white pioneers, can be seen in the cemetery next door. During the day tour buses are double parked outside, and if you really want to get the feel for this lovely old Mission, the 7.30am daily mass (Mon–Sat) or the noon service in Spanish (Sunday) is a better bet. **Dolores Park**, a few blocks along at Dolores and 18th, high on a hill at the edge of the neighborhood, is a pretty, quiet space to rest and take in the good views of the city, plagued though it is with defecating dogs and children on BMX bikes. Its southern bank is nicknamed "Dolores Beach" because of the crowds of semi-naked gay men who gather on warm days to work on their tans and eye each other up – it's quite a scene. Avoid it by night, however, when it becomes the local meeting place for the area's crack dealers.

While hipsters, off-duty chefs and slumming yuppies live it up around 16th and Valencia, the underdog heart of Mission life continues along Mission Street east of 24th, stretching as far as Potrero. Here you'll absorb the district's original Latino flavor, with Nicaraguan, Salvadoran, Costa Rican and Mexican stores and restaurants lining the street, along tropical fruit markets and *panaderias* baking traditional pastries.

What really sets the Mission apart from other neighborhoods, however, are its more than two hundred **murals**. Precita Eyes, the community's knowledgeable and starving-artist-promoting mural organization, hosts weekend mural tours by foot, bike or bus (call for times ☎415/285-2287; $4, $10 & $30). If you don't have time for a whole tour, you should at least go and see the brilliant tribute to local hero **Carlos Santana** adorning three buildings where 22nd Street meets South Van Ness. For more controversial subject matter take a walk down **Balmy Alley** between Folsom and Harrison off 24th Street (unquestionably the axis of Latino shopping), where every possible surface is covered with murals depicting the political agonies of Central America.

The Castro

Arguably San Francisco's most progressive, if no longer most celebratory neighborhood, **THE CASTRO** is the city's avowed queer capital and as such, the best barometer for the state of the gay scene. As a district, the Castro occupies a large area that stretches south from Market Street as far as Noe Valley (see p.413), but in terms of visible street life the few blocks from Market to 20th Street contain about all there is to see. People say many things about the changing face of the neighborhood – some insist that it's still the wildest place in town, others reckon that post-AIDS it's a shadow of its former self – but all agree that things are not the same. It is claimed that over 10,000 men in this area alone have been lost to the virus. A walk down the Castro ten, or even five, years ago would have you gaping at the revelry, and while most of the same bars and hangouts still stand, these days they're host to an altogether different, younger and more conservative breed. But while there are no "sights" as such, it is the stories and the history connected with the district that make this area so interesting and give you an idea of just how progressive San Francisco really is. For an insider's view, Trevor Hailey's "Cruisin' The Castro" walking tour (see p.389) is just about unbeatable.

Harvey Milk Plaza, by the Castro Muni station, is as good a place as any to start your wanderings, dedicated to the gay supervisor (or councillor) who before his assassination in 1978 owned a camera store and was a popular figure in the Castro. Milk and Mayor George Moscone's assailant, Dan White, was a disgruntled ex-supervisor who resigned when the liberal policies of Moscone and Milk didn't coincide with his conservative views. He later tried to get his post back but was refused by Moscone, and soon after sauntered into City Hall and shot them both. At the trial, White pleaded temporary insanity caused by harmful additives in his diet of fast food – a plea which came to be known as the "Twinkie defense" (Twinkies are synthetic-cream cakes) – and was sentenced to five years' imprisonment for manslaughter. The gay community reacted angrily to the brevity of White's sentence, and the riots that followed were among the most violent San Francisco has ever witnessed, protesters marching into City Hall turning over and burning police cars as they went. White was released in 1985 and moved to Los Angeles, where he committed suicide shortly after.

Before heading down the hill into the heart of the Castro, take a short walk across Market Street to the Visitor Center of the **Names Project** at no. 2363a (daily 10am–7pm; ☎415/863-1966). The organization was founded in the wake of the AIDS crisis and sponsored the creation of "The Quilt" – a gargantuan blanket composed of panels, each 6ft x 3ft (the size of a gravesite) and bearing the name of a person lost to the disease. Made by their lovers, friends and families, the panels are stitched together and regularly toured around the country; it has been spread a number of times on the Mall in Washington DC to dramatize the epidemic to seemingly indifferent governments. Sections of the quilt, too large to be exhibited in any one place in its entirety, continue to tour the world to raise people's awareness of the tragedy and keep the care programs alive. Inside the showroom, you can see the thousands of panels stored on shelves; some are hung up for display and machinists tackle the endless task of stitching the whole thing together. Those interested in making their own panel can do so at the Quilting Bee held every Wednesday evening from 7–10pm. Next door, **Under One Roof** is another organization raising money for various AIDS welfare agencies, by selling books, T-shirts and gifts.

Back on Castro Street, one of the first things you see is the **Castro Theater**, self-described as "San Francisco's landmark movie palace." It's undeniably one of San Francisco's better movie houses, as popular for its pseudo-Spanish baroque interior as it is for its billing, which includes revivals and twenty-minute performances on a Wurlitzer. A little further down the hill, the junction of **Castro and 18th Street**, known as the "gayest four corners of the earth," marks the Castro's center, cluttered with bookstores, clothing stores, cafés and bars. The side streets offer a slightly more exclusive range of exotic delicatessens, fine wine shops and fancy florists, and enticingly leafy residential territory that keeps a neat distance from the bright lights and noise of the main drag.

Before leaving the Castro, make an effort to go to **Twin Peaks**, about a mile and a half along Market from the Harvey Milk Plaza. (Travel west until you hit Twin Peaks

HALLOWEEN IN THE CASTRO

The Castro is at its best during **Halloween** – a big deal in San Francisco anyway, but here the zenith of the social calendar. Six-foot beauties bedecked in jewels and ballgowns strut noisily between Market Street and the junction of Castro and 20th, stopping off at all the most popular watering holes. Those not in their finery strip down and take their beautifully worked-on pectorals out for a stroll. Police block off roads and turn a blind eye to minor indiscretions. Not to be missed.

Boulevard; the #37 Corbett bus will take you to Park Ridge.) The highest point in the city, this gives a 360-degree view of the Peninsula. Real estate prices in the city are gauged in part by the quality of the views, so it's no surprise that the curving streets that wind around the slopes of Twin Peaks hold some of the city's most outrageously unaffordable homes. During the day, busloads of tourists arrive to point their Pentaxes, and during the summer crowds often build up waiting for the fog to lift. It's better to go at night, picking out landmarks from either side of the shimmering artery of Market Street. If you want to avoid the crowds (and pickpockets), Tank Hill, a small promontory just beneath Twin Peaks – where you'll need a map to find your way through the maze of small streets – is perfect.

You might also consider a quick visit to **NOE VALLEY**, on the far side of the hill. Until a couple of years ago it was remarkable only for its insignificant status in the pantheon of San Francisco neighborhoods, so good was it at failing to capture the imagination that it was fondly tagged "Noewhere Valley." Sitting snugly in a sunny valley, the main vein of which runs along 24th Street, crammed with delicatessens, coffee shops, small boutiques and some excellent lunch venues, it has an air of rugged unfashionableness manifest in clean streets, blue-collar sports bars and a noticeable lack of street crime and vagrancy – all of which can be refreshing, after the sleaze of the Mission and SoMa. Needless to say, discerning professional San Franciscans have discovered it, and it is fast becoming one of the city's most desirable neighborhoods.

Haight-Ashbury

Two miles west of downtown San Francisco, **HAIGHT-ASHBURY** is a neighborhood that lent its name to an era, giving it a fame that far outstrips its size. A small area, spanning no more than eight blocks in length, centered around the junction of Haight and Ashbury Street and bordered by Golden Gate Park at its western edge, "The Haight," as it's known, was a respectable Victorian neighborhood-turned-slum that emerged in the 1960s as the epicenter of the countercultural scene. Since then it's become slightly smartened up, but still retains a collection of radical bookstores, laid-back cafés, record stores, smokestores and thrift stores that recall its era of international celebrity – when to some it was the scene of one of the most significant of Sixties protest movements, to others simply the best acid party in history.

The Haight today has few real sights as such, relying instead on the constant turnover of hip shopping spots to sustain its legend. Two blocks east of the Haight-Ashbury junction, **Buena Vista Park** is a mountainous forest of Monterey pines and California redwoods, used by dogwalkers in the daylight hours, but come nightfall the locale of much sex-in-the-shrubbery. Walk here accompanied by day and not at all at night, unless you're male and looking for some action. The "**Haight-Ashbury Free Clinic**," at 558 Clayton St, is a venerable Sixties hangover: an unusual phenomenon, certainly by American standards, which first began providing free health care when drugs-related illnesses became a big problem in the Haight. It now survives – barely – on contributions, continuing to treat local drug casualties and the poor, both disproportionately large groups in this area of the city. Otherwise, stroll along the Haight and take advantage of what is still one of the best areas in town to **shop**. It shouldn't take more than a couple of hours to update your record collection, dress yourself up and blow money on good books and cold beers. Things get livelier as you move west, the increasing number of street musicians merging eventually into the hardcore hippy guitarists along what is known as the **Panhandle**, a finger-slim strip of greenery that eventually leads into Golden Gate Park.

The funkiest corner of the district lies at the eastern end of Haight Street, around the crossing with Fillmore Street. Known as the **Lower Haight**, and the center of black San Francisco for decades, it briefly emerged a few years ago – thanks to low rents – as the

HIPPIES

The first **hippies** were an offshoot of the Beats, many of whom had moved out of their increasingly expensive North Beach homes to take advantage of the low rents and large spaces in the Victorian houses of the Haight. The post-Beat bohemia that subsequently began to develop here in the early 1960s was initially a small affair, involving drug use and the embrace of Eastern religion and philosophy, together with a marked anti-American political stance and a desire for world peace. Where Beat philosophy had emphasized self-indulgence, the hippies, on the face of it at least, attempted to be more embracing, focusing on self-coined concepts such as "universal truth" and "cosmic awareness." Naturally it took a few big names to get the ball rolling, and characters like **Ken Kesey and his Merry Pranksters** soon set a precedent of wild living, challenging authority and dropping (as they saw it) out of the established norms of society. Drugs were particularly important, and seen as an integral – and positive – part of the movement. **LSD** especially, the effects of which were just being discovered and which at the time was not actually illegal, was claimed as an avant-garde art form, pumped out in private laboratories and distributed by Timothy Leary and his network of supporters with a prescription ("Turn on, tune in, drop out") that galvanized a generation into inactivity. An important group in the Haight at the time was The Diggers, who, famed for their parties and antics, truly believed LSD could be used to increase creativity. Before long life in the Haight began to take on a theatrical quality: Pop Art found mass appeal, light shows became legion, dress flamboyant, and the Grateful Dead, Jefferson Airplane and Janis Joplin made names for themselves. Backed by the business weight of promoter Bill Graham, the **psychedelic music** scene became a genuine force nationwide, and it wasn't long before kids from all over America started turning up in Haight-Ashbury for the free food, free drugs and free love. Money became a dirty word, the hip became "heads," and the rest of the world were "straights."

Other illustrious tenants of the Haight at this time include Kenneth Rexroth, who hosted a popular radio show and wrote for the *San Francisco Examiner*. Hunter S. Thompson, too, spent time here researching and writing his book *Hell's Angels*, and was notorious for inviting Angels round to his apartment on Parnassus Street for noisy, long and occasionally dangerous drinking and drug-taking sessions.

Things inevitably turned sour towards the end of the decade, but during the heady days of the massive "be-in" in Golden Gate Park in 1966 and the so-called **Summer of Love** the following year, this busy little intersection became home to no less than 75,000 transitory pilgrims who saw it as the mecca of alternative culture.

major stomping ground for young hipsters. It flourished for a while with some of the city's grooviest bars, ethnic restaurants and meeting places, but the truth is there just isn't enough money or traffic in the neighborhood to support such trendiness for long. However, given its proximity to downtown, it's a fine place to get a cheap breakfast, browse the bookstores, rake through vintage clothing emporia and drink yourself silly (see "Eating" on p.418 and "Drinking" on p.426 for a few good suggestions).

Ten blocks north of here, up Geary Street, **WESTERN ADDITION** is also firmly black, one of the city's most relentlessly poor neighborhoods – dangerous in parts and certainly not tourist territory. Its boundaries reach to **JAPANTOWN**, something of a misnomer for what is basically a shopping mall with an eastern flavor – the Japan Center – around which only a small percentage of San Francisco's Japanese Americans actually live. Visit only to check out the **Kabuki Hot Springs**, 1750 Geary Blvd (Mon–Fri 10am–10pm, Sat & Sun 9am–10pm; ☎415/922-6000): community baths with shiatsu massage, steam baths and other luxuriating facilities for around $12 per visit, $37 and up for massage. If you're in the area, jump over a few blocks to where Geary Boulevard meets Gough and look at the monumentally elaborate **St Mary's Cathedral**.

Golden Gate Park

Unlike most American cities, San Francisco is not short on green space, and **Golden Gate Park** is its largest, providing a wonderfully bucolic antidote to the center of town. Despite the throngs of joggers, polo players, roller-skaters, cyclists and strollers, it never gets overcrowded, and you can always find a spot to be alone. Designed by Frederick Olmsted (who also created Central Park in New York) in the late nineteenth century, this is one of the most beautiful, and safest, corners of the city, with none of the menace of its New York counterpart. Spreading three miles or so west from the Haight as far as the Pacific shore, it was constructed – on what was then an area of wild sand dunes buffeted by the spray from the nearby ocean – with the help of a dyke to protect the western side from the sea. John McLaren, park superintendent for fifty-odd years, planted around a million trees here, and nowadays it's a peaceful and skilfully crafted spot to relax, with over a thousand acres of gardens, forests, lakes, waterfalls and museums.

Exploration of the whole place could take days of footwork. Among its more mainstream attractions, there's a Japanese Tea Garden, a horticultural museum (modelled on the Palm House at Kew Gardens), a Shakespeare Garden with every flower or plant mentioned in the writer's plays, not to mention the usual contingent of serious joggers, cyclists and roller-skaters. If you're feeling energetic, activities are many and quite cheap: **boat rental** is available on Stow Lake (parallel with 19th Avenue) for $10–14 per hour, and **horse-riding** for around $25 per hour from the Golden Gate Park Stables at John F. Kennedy Drive and 36th Avenue. **Admission** to all park museums and the tea garden is discounted with the $14 Explorer Pass, available from the museums and the TIX Bay Area booth at Union Square (see "Theater", p.435).

Of the park's numerous museums, the **M.H. de Young Museum** (Wed–Sun 9.30am–5pm; $7, $2 off with Muni transfer and free first Wed of each month) is the largest, with San Francisco's most diverse range of painting and sculpture, ranging from the ancient art of Greece and Rome to an outstanding twentieth-century collection in the American Wing – a hundred or so paintings bequeathed by John D. Rockefeller III. Rubens, Rembrandt and seventeenth-century European painters are also well represented; you can get an exhaustive commentary on all with a free "Directors Tour," actually a personal headset that you wear for about an hour. Next door, in the West Wing, the **Asian Art Museum** (same hours) has a rather less impressive, in fact drearily exhaustive, collection of ten thousand paintings, sculptures, ceramics and textiles from all over Asia. Donated by Avery Brundage in 1966, the collection receives much attention for its sheer vastness, but it's only worth seeing if you're an enthusiast.

You'll find another group of museums opposite, in the **California Academy of Sciences** (summer daily 9am–6pm; winter daily 10am–5pm; $8.50, $1 off with Muni transfer and free first Wed of each month) – the perfect place to amuse restless children. There's a natural history museum with a thirty-foot skeleton of a 130 million-year-old dinosaur, and life-size replicas of elephant seals and other California wildlife, and a colony of twenty black-footed penguins. But the show-stealer is the collection of 14,500 specimens of aquatic life in the **Steinhart Aquarium** (daily 10am–5pm; included with Academy admission), the best of which are the alligators and other reptiles lurking in a simulated swamp. Also, if you catch it at the right time, the **Morrison Planetarium** (schedule varies; ☎415/750-7141; $2.50) can be a great experience. Daily skyshows, laser light shows and rock music draw often acid-crazed crowds for evening performances.

Slightly west of the museums is the usually crowded **Japanese Tea Garden** (daily 9am–5.30pm; $2.50). Built in 1894 for the California Midwinter Exposition, the garden was beautifully landscaped by the Japanese Hagiwara family, who were also responsible for the invention of the fortune cookie (despite the prevalent belief that fortune cookies are Chinese). The Hagiwaras looked after the garden until World War II, when along with other Japanese Americans they were sent to internment camps. A massive bronze Buddha dominates the garden, and bridges, footpaths, pools filled with shiny oversized carp, plus bonsai and cherry trees lend the place a peaceful feel – but for the busloads of tourists that pour in regularly throughout the day. The best way to enjoy the garden is to get there around 9am when it first opens and have a breakfast of tea and fortune cookies in the tea house.

Apart from the formal attractions, on Sundays, in the central space near the museums, you can hear free concerts at the **Music Pavilion** bandstand; to enjoy the quieter corners of the park head west through the many flower gardens and eucalyptus groves towards the ocean. Perhaps the most unusual thing about Golden Gate Park is its substantial herd of bison, roaming around the **Buffalo Paddock** off JFK Drive near 38th Avenue; you can get closest to these noble giants in their feeding area at the far west end. Moving towards the edge of the park at Ocean Beach, passing a tulip garden and large windmill, you'll come to the **Beach Chalet** facing the Great Highway. This two-story, white-pillared structure, designed by Willis Polk, is home to some of San Francisco's lesser-known public art. A series of frescoes painted in the 1930s depicts the growth of San Francisco as a city and the creation of Golden Gate Park, while upstairs is a lively brewery-restaurant.

The Golden Gate Bridge

The orange towers of the **Golden Gate Bridge** – probably the most beautiful, certainly the most photographed bridge in the world – are visible from almost every point of elevation in San Francisco. As much an architectural as an engineering feat, the bridge took only 52 months to design and build and was opened in 1937. Designed by Joseph Strauss, it was the first really massive suspension bridge with a span of 4200ft, and until 1959 ranked as the world's longest. Over 5000 gallons of paint are used annually to keep the bridge in good condition. It connects the city at its northwesterly point on the Peninsula to Marin County and Northern California, rendering the hitherto essential ferry crossing redundant, and was designed to stand winds of up to a hundred miles an hour. Handsome on a clear day, the bridge takes on an eerie quality when the thick white fogs pour in and hide it almost completely. Perhaps the best-loved symbol of San Francisco, in 1987 the Golden Gate proved an auspicious place for a sunrise party when crowds gathered to celebrate its fiftieth anniversary. Some quarter of a million people turned up (a third of the city's population); the winds were strong and the huge numbers caused the bridge to buckle, but fortunately not to break.

You can either drive or walk across the bridge. The drive is probably the more thrilling of the two options as you race under the bridge's towers, but the windy, thirty-minute walk across gives you time to take in its enormity and absorb the views of the city behind you and the headlands of Marin County straight ahead. Pause at the midway point and consider the seven or so suicides a month who choose this spot, 220ft up, for jumping off – apparently always facing the city as they do so. In 1995, when the suicide toll had reached almost one thousand, police kept the figures quiet to avoid a rush of would-be-suicides going for the dubious distinction of being the thousandth person to leap.

Standing beneath the bridge is almost as memorable as traveling over it. The **Fort Point National Historic Site**, a brick fortress built in the 1850s to guard the bay, gives a good sense of the place as the westernmost outpost of the nation. Formerly part of the Presidio Army Base (now a National Park), it was to have been demolished to make way for the bridge above, but the redesign of the southern approach – note the additional arch which spans it overhead – left it intact. It's a dramatic site, the surf pounding away beneath the great span of the bridge high above – a view made famous by Kim Novak's suicide attempt in Alfred Hitchcock's *Vertigo*. It is alleged by some that the water here makes for one of the best (if most foolhardy) surfing spots in the area. A small **museum** (Wed–Sun 9am–4pm; free) inside the fort shows some rusty old cannons and artillery, although a far superior military collection can be seen in the **Presidio Army Museum** (Tues–Sun 10am–4pm; free) at Lincoln Blvd and Funston Ave in the Presidio proper, with uniforms, photographs and some detailed documentation of San Francisco's military history.

Beaches and outlying areas

Filling up the western half of the city, and divided by Golden Gate Park, two residential districts – **Richmond** to the north, the **Sunset** to the south – have more in common with typical American suburbs than they do with the rest of San Francisco. Built almost entirely in the years following World War II and populated mainly by families, these neat, clean and terrifically dull neighborhoods are well off the tourist map. Unless you're attracted by the good, cheap restaurants of the thriving Asian neighborhoods along Clement Street in Richmond, or the many Irish bars along Geary Boulevard and throughout the Sunset, you're most likely to visit the area in passing, en route to the breathtaking (but often fog-bound) coastline at its edge.

Partly due to the weather and partly due to the coldness of the ocean water, beach culture doesn't exist in San Francisco the way it does in Southern California, and people here tend to watch the surf rather than ride it. Powerful currents and crashing waves dissuade all but the most fearless swimmers, and as a result the city's beaches remain blissfully uncrowded. Stretching south a mile from the Golden Gate Bridge, **Baker Beach** is San Francisco's prettiest and most popular, drawing a mixed crowd of fishermen and *au naturel* sunbathers, and giving some great views of the soaring red bridge. It's also easy to reach: stairways drop down from Lincoln Avenue, and Muni bus #29 stops at the main parking lot every thirty minutes. A half-mile further southwest at the foot of the ritzy Sea Cliff district, **China Beach** is more protected and better for swimming, and also offers free showers and changing rooms.

Above the beaches, paths stretch south around the Peninsula to **Land's End**: it takes about thirty minutes to get round the cliffs, tricky to negotiate but worth it for the brilliant views of the ocean. A small beach in a rocky cove beneath the cliffside walk is a favorite spot for gay sunbathers. Inland lies **Lincoln Park**, primarily a golf course, but as part of the Point Lobos Headlands it has some striking trails.

The isolated **California Palace of the Legion of Honor** (Tues–Sun 9.30am–5pm; $7, $2 off with Muni transfer and surcharge for special exhibitions) – best reached by taking the #38 bus from Geary Boulevard and transferring to the #18 at the Lincoln Park Golf Course – is arguably San Francisco's best art museum, housing a remarkable collection of fine art. It is probably also its most beautifully located, the romantic setting, graceful architecture and colonnaded courtyard combining to lend a truly elegant impression: a white-pillared twin of the more famous Legion d'Honneur in Paris. Built from a donation from the wealthy San Franciscan Spreckels family, it was erected in 1920 and dedicated on Abraham Lincoln's birthday in 1921. The museum was reopened in 1995 after several years of extensive seismic engineering and a grand facelift, and it now displays the permanent collection to even greater advantage. The **Renaissance** is represented with the works of Titian, El Greco and sculpture from Giambologna, while some great canvases by Rembrandt and Hals, as well as Rubens' magnificent *Tribute Money*, are highlights of the seventeenth-century Dutch and Flemish collection. Among the **Impressionist** and **post-Impressionist** paintings are works by Courbet, Manet, Monet, Renoir, Degas and Cézanne, but the section dedicated to the sculpture of **Rodin** steals the show. One of the world's finest Rodin collections features bronze, porcelain and stone pieces including *The Athlete*, *Fugit Amor*, *The Severed Head of John the Baptist* and a small cast of *The Kiss*.

A rather bigger stop for the tour buses is the **Cliff House**, dangerously balanced on the western tip of the Peninsula above the head of Ocean Beach. There's a **visitor center** here (daily 10am–5pm), with information on the surrounding area and an exhibit on the original Cliff House built by Prussian immigrant Adolph Sutro in the late-nineteenth-century as an exclusive resort for the leisured classes, which burned down long ago. There's also the quirky **Musée Mécanique** (Mon–Fri 11am–7pm, Sat & Sun & holidays 10am–8pm; free), home to 145 antique but functional coin-operated penny arcade machines, dating from the 1800s. The *Cliff House Restaurant* is where most visitors end up, though avoid it unless you want to pay through the nose to sit in a bar with an ocean view (no big deal in a city flanked on three sides by water).

Down by the water you'll find more picturesque ruins – what remains of the **Sutro Baths**. This collection of opulent recreational pools, gardens and elegant sculptures was another of Sutro's creations, sadly destroyed by fire in the 1960s. From here you can explore the ramparts and tunnels of the fortified coastline – a bit frightening at night, when the surf really starts crashing, but there's a certain romance too, and on a rare warm evening it becomes one of the city's favorite snogging spots.

Finally, you might want to visit San Francisco's small but expertly designed **zoo** at Sloat Boulevard and 45th Avenue (daily 10am–5pm; $7, free first Wed of the month). It's not bad as zoos go, thoughtfully crafted to resemble the natural habitat of the animals as closely as possible. It's closer to the beaches than the city though, and unless you've got a car you'll have to backtrack and board the Muni L-Taraval to get here (or call ☎415/753-7080 for bus information).

Eating

With well over three thousand restaurants of every possible ethnicity and style crammed onto the small peninsula, and scores of bars and cafés that are open all day (and some all night), **eating** is *the* culture in this town. San Franciscans gourmandize expertly around the city and most people will have at least four restaurant recommendations up their sleeves. It doesn't have to be expensive either, with **budget places** ranging from the usual array of pizza and burger joints to the **Chinese** restaurants in Chinatown and the **Mexican** places of the Mission – indeed, these are the two cuisines that San Francisco does best, or at least most widely. A little more expensively, **Italian** restaurants are common in North Beach and around much of the rest of downtown; **French** food is a perennial favorite, at least with the power-broking crowd, although nouvelle cuisine is finally beginning to loosen its grip on San Franciscan menus. **California cuisine** nowadays has grown away from its minimalist roots, but still features the freshest food, beautifully presented. **Japanese** food, notably sushi, is also still massively popular though not always affordable. **Thai**, **Korean** and **Indonesian** food is similarly in vogue, and is usually cheaper. Not surprisingly, health-conscious San Francisco also has a wide range of **vegetarian** and **wholefood** restaurants, and it's rare to find anywhere that doesn't have at least one meat-free item on the menu. With the vineyards of Napa and Sonoma Valley on the city's doorstep, quality **wines** are a high-profile feature in most San Francisco restaurants.

Be warned: San Francisco closes up early and you'll be struggling to find places that will serve you much after 10 or 11pm, unless they're of the 24-hour diner variety. And thanks to recent statewide legislation you now cannot **smoke** in any restaurant in the city.

In the listings that follow, the **restaurants** are arranged by cuisine, together with a roundup of where to eat around the clock. However, San Francisco chefs being the innovators that they are, the enduring craze is for combining styles – Chinese/French for example – and it can be difficult to categorize restaurants. So don't take the breakdowns below as set in stone: there's no such thing as a straight anything in this town.

Budget food: breakfasts, burgers and diners

Bagdad Café, 2295 Market St at 16th St. Good, hearty breakfasts and burgers served 24 hours per day.

Brain Wash Laundromat/Café, 1122 Folsom St at Seventh, SoMa. If you don't mind watching people pile their dirties into the machines, this is a surprisingly good venue for well-prepared, simple sandwiches, pizzas and salad. A boisterous SoMa hangout, providing a good opportunity to check out the locals. See also "Drinking: bars and cafés", p.427.

The Grubstake, 1525 Pine St at Polk. Converted 1920s railroad dining car, with some of the city's best late-night burgers.

Hamburger Mary's, 1582 Folsom St at 12th, SoMa. Raucous SoMa burger bar, with punky waiting staff and good range of vegetarian options. Inexpensive, and open late for the club-going crowds.

Mel's Drive-In, 3355 Geary Blvd at Beaumont and 2165 Lombard St at Fillmore. Straight out of *American Graffiti*, with burgers, fries, milkshakes and a lot of rock'n'roll on the jukebox. No longer a drive-in, but open late – after midnight every night, till 3am at weekends.

Orphan Andy's, 3991 17th St at Castro. Favorite Castro hangout, serving burgers, omelets and breakfast 24 hours a day.

The Pine Crest, 401 Geary St at Mason. Every inch the greasy diner, but ideal for getting rid of your spare change and hunger at the same time.

Spaghetti Western, 576 Haight St at Fillmore. Best breakfasts for miles and a lively Lower Haight crowd to look at while you chow down.

Sparky's, 240 Church St at Market. 24hr Castro diner cooking up burgers, pastas and pizzas plus breakfasts including a very good Eggs Florentine on weekends. Beer and wine too.

American and California cuisine

Aqua, 253 California St at Battery (☎415/956-9662). Gorgeously decorated, mainly seafood restaurant that pulls in a discerning Financial District crowd.

Chow, 215 Church at Market (☎415/552-2469). New neighborhood eatery near the Castro serving absolutely wonderful, lovingly-made dishes for cheap. A real find.

Cliff House, 1090 Point Lobos Ave (☎415/386-3330). Much maligned by some as a tourist trap, which the adjacent gift shop suggests, the Cliff House is nevertheless a San Francisco institution – charming, historic and offering unmatched views of the Pacific Ocean. Eat dinner elsewhere; come instead for a drink at sunset, or to sample some of their excellent desserts.

Cypress Club, 500 Jackson St near Columbus (☎415/296-8555). Jackson Square hot spot famed for its delicately presented, inventive California cuisine, served up in one of the most stylish dining rooms to be found in San Francisco – a cross between the *Ritz Carlton* and a Bedouin tent.

Farallon, 450 Post between Mason and Powell (☎415/956-6969). Brand new and sumptuously styled as an undersea grotto, serving small portions of creative seafood dishes. Definitely worth a splurge if you're into elegant dining experiences; if you can't afford it, go for a drink in the fanciful bar that looks like the Octopus' Garden.

Firefly, 4288 24th St at Douglass (☎415/821-7652). Noe Valley restaurant with wide-ranging, innovative menu and a knowing crowd. Very much a neighborhood joint.

Flying Saucer, 1000 Guerrero St at 22nd, Mission (☎415/641-9955). Popular hot spot that has recently expanded into a neighboring storefront, offering exquisitely assembled, adventurous cuisine that mixes fruit with meat and every wacky combination you can think of. Reserve in advance.

42 Degrees, 235 16th St at Third (☎415/777-5558). Fashionable jazz supper club, in a great location down on the old dockyards with a stark modern interior and well-made simple California cuisine.

Hard Rock Café, 1699 Van Ness Ave at Sacramento (☎415/885-1699). Standard *Hard Rock* clone, downtown. Loud music, rock'n'roll decor and the sort of crowd who don't mind waiting in line for hours for the above-average burgers.

Hayes Street Grill, 320 Hayes between Gough and Franklin (☎415/863-5545). Fresh ingredients perfectly prepared and not overwrought. Excellent grilled fish and standard American fare, drawing a conservative crowd at lunch and opera- and theatergoers at dinner.

Indigo, 687 McAllister St at Gough (☎415/673-9369). Stylish without being pretentious, this newcomer to the Cal-cuisine scene delivers generous portions of inventive, seasonally-inspired entrees at moderate prices, accompanied by top-notch service. Recommended.

Julie's Supper Club, 1123 Folsom St at Seventh (☎415/861-0707). The cuisine, both at the bar and in the backroom restaurant, can only be described as eclectic. The decor however, is straight out of a B-52's/Jetsons dream. Worth a look, especially if you can get there before 9pm and escape the $5 cover for the live jazz, R&B, and Seventies retro bands in the evenings. See also "Drinking: bars and cafés", p.428.

Liberty Café, 410 Cortland Ave (☎415/695-8777). Excellent food, beautifully prepared in this Bernal Heights favorite. Best of all, you get dinner for under $20.

Lou's Pier 47, 300 Jefferson St at Taylor (☎415/771-0377). Incongruously placed among the pricey seafood joints on Fisherman's Wharf. Not just one of the best places to hear live R&B in the city, it also serves fresh, inexpensive seafood. A must for dinner, a few beers and great music. See also "Live music", p.433.

LuLu, 816 Folsom St between Fourth and Fifth (☎415/495-5775). Gone downhill in recent years, from stellar to merely satisfying. The loud, high-ceilinged dining room is packed regularly with those who know no nostalgia, chowing down on Cal-cuisine served family-style in large portions.

Maye's Original Oyster House, 1233 Polk St at Sutter (☎415/474-7674). In business since the 1860s, this is one of the city's oldest restaurants, turning out reasonably priced, well-cooked fish dishes in plush surroundings.

Moose's, 1652 Stockton St at Filbert (☎415/987-7800). Run by the former proprietors of the *Washington Square Bar & Grill*, who have taken many of their old clients and become the latest word in power lunching for the media-politico crowd. The moderate-to-expensive California cuisine satisfies.

Murray's, 740 Sutter St adjacent to the *Canterbury Hotel* (☎415/474-6478). Finally a "green" restaurant that's gourmet. The eclectic cooking caters to vegetarians and meat-eaters alike and includes Asian and ethnic-inspired comfort food, emphasizing organic and Bay Area-grown foods. Not cheap, but the creative dishes and warm service satisfy.

Original Joe's, 144 Taylor St at Eddy (☎415/775-4877). Inexpensive to moderate American/Italian restaurant, good for steaks, ribs, salads and the like.

Patio Café, 531 Castro St at 18th (☎415/621-4640). Casual terrace restaurant serving wholesome grills and pastas, and good-value weekend brunches where you can sling back inexpensive cocktails.

Postrio, 545 Post St at Mason (☎415/776-7825). One of the favorite, if slightly overrated, top-notch San Francisco restaurants, thanks to the high-style ambiance and five-star reputation of chef Wolfgang Puck who serves up Californian dishes with Asian and Mediterranean influences. Hang out at the bar if you can't score a dinner reservation.

Slow Club, 2501 Mariposa St at Hampshire, Potrero Hill (☎415/241-9390). Venerable SoMa hangout, serving good, reasonably-priced imaginative cooking and populated by *San Francisco Bay Guardian* writers and other arty types.

Stars, 555 Golden Gate Ave at Van Ness (☎415/861-7827). See and be seen home of the rich and powerful, the food is indisputably good but not within the price range of most mortals. Best to sit at the bar with a martini and some oysters watching San Francisco society glide by.

Swan's Oyster Depot, 1517 Polk St at California (☎415/673-1101). You wouldn't know it by the simple decor, but this is one of the city's best and oldest seafood places – take a seat at the bar (there are no tables) for half a dozen fresh-shucked oysters, washed down with a glass of ice-cold Anchor Steam beer. Open 8am–5pm.

Tadich Grill, 240 California St between Front and Battery (☎415/391-2373). The oldest restaurant in California, this place is wood-paneled and very much a San Francisco institution. Grilled fresh seafood and excellent desserts.

Vertigo, 600 Montgomery St at Washington (☎415/433-7520). The food is Italian/French/Asian (very Californian) and the service is uppity. Built in the base of the Transamerica Pyramid, the interior of the restaurant is more exciting than the expensive grub. Good place to spy smug Financial District types from the safe distance of the excellent bar.

Washington Square Bar and Grill, 1707 Powell St at Union (☎415/982-8123). It may have lost a little of its cachet since the owners sold it and opened *Moose's* across the square (see opposite), but this is still the place to sip smart cocktails at the bar and sample the food, cooked to rich and heavy perfection. See also "Drinking: bars and cafés", p.427.

Zuni Café, 1658 Market St at Gough (☎415/552-2522). Despite the often snotty service and unprepossessing location on Market Street, Zuni has remained a chic place to be seen for the last five years, simply because the food is so damned good. Despite the Southwestern name, you get French/Italian-inspired cuisine for around $30 a head with a glass of wine.

Chinese, Thai and Southeast Asian

Bangkok 16, 3214 16th St between Dolores and Guerrero (☎415/431-5838). Moderately priced Thai restaurant down in the Mission, with a great selection for vegetarians. For meat eaters they do a mean lamb satay.

Borobudur, 700 Post St at Jones (☎415/775-1512). A little pocket of authentic Indonesia just a couple of blocks from Union Square. Eat early if you want to avoid the karaoke.

Brandy Ho's Original Hunan, 217 Columbus Ave at Jackson (☎415/788-7527). Excellent, long-established Hunan restaurant. There's another, neon-clad branch at 450 Broadway, serving same food in starker conditions.

Eliza's, 205 Oak near Gough (☎415/621-4819). Not your average Chinese dive, this place is all stained glass and fresh flowers, serving excellent Chinese food to a knowing Hayes Valley crowd.

Empress of China, 838 Grant Ave at Washington (☎415/434-1345). Without doubt, the poshest place in town to get to grips with Chinese cooking, with an incredible selection of dishes and amazing views over neighboring North Beach. You'll be paying $13–20 for a main course, but if you're in the mood for a blow-out it's quite the place to be decadent.

The Golden Turtle, 2211 Van Ness Ave at Broadway (☎415/441-4419). Upscale Vietnamese restaurant serving delicious, well-priced dishes.

Harbor Village, 4 Embarcadero Center, lobby level, between Clay and Drumm (☎415/781-8833). Downtown's best dim sum, especially popular for Sunday lunch, with standard Cantonese dishes for dinner.

House of Nanking, 919 Kearny St between Jackson and Columbus (☎415/421-1429). Always packed, this hole-in-the-wall serves up some of the best, fastest and cheapest Chinese food downtown. You have to endure lining up outside, tiny tables, bumping elbows with yuppies, and being hurried out, but it's all part of the *Nanking* cult experience. Not to be missed.

Manora's Thai Cuisine, 1600 Folsom St at 12th (☎415/861-6224). Massively popular SoMa hangout, you may have to wait, but it's worth it for the light, spicy and fragrant dishes at around $7–11 each.

New Asia, 722 Pacific Ave between Stockton and Grant (☎415/391-6666). Considering Chinatown is so pressed for space, it's amazing that a place this big survives. It serves some of the most authentic dim sum in town – every day from 8.30am to 3.30pm – with waitresses pushing carts down the aisles, shouting out their wares as they pass.

Oriental Pearl, 760/778 Clay St between Grant and Kearny (☎415/433-1817). Dependably delicious with exemplary service and decent prices. Don't miss the house-made *yee min* noodles with *enoki* mushrooms.

The Pot Sticker, 150 Waverly Place, off Clay St between Stockton and Grant (☎415/397-9985). Extensive menu offering your average Szechuan and Hunan dishes in this inexpensive and touristy Chinatown joint.

Sam Woh, 813 Washington St at Grant (☎415/982-0596). Basic late-night (until 3am) restaurant that attracts the North Beach crowds when the bars turn out. You have to climb dodgy old steps through the kitchen to reach the eating area.

Taiwan Restaurant, 445 Clement St at Sixth Avenue (☎415/387-1789). Stellar Chinese grub in this quick, efficient and inexpensive Richmond favorite.

Thai Stick, 698 Post St at Jones (☎415/928-7730). Popular downtown Thai hangout that offers a wide selection of vegetarian dishes and promises that everything is made without MSG.

Thep-Phanom Restaurant, 400 Waller St at Fillmore (☎415/431-2526). Simple, delicate decor and beautifully prepared Thai dishes make this Lower Haight restaurant seem more expensive than it really is. You'll pay no more than $8 for main course dishes, but you'll have to wait in line.

Tommy Toy's Cuisine Chinoise, 655 Montgomery St at Columbus (☎415/397-4888). The idea is Chinese food presented French-style in opulent surroundings, with steep prices accompanying. You pay more for the gorgeously-appointed dining room than for the flavors.

Tu Lan, 8 Sixth St at Market, (☎415/626-0927). If you can brave the seedy neighborhood, you can stuff your face with fresh Vietnamese food for $4. Open daytime only.

Yuet Lee, 1300 Stockton St at Broadway (☎415/982-6020). Cheap and cheerful Chinese restaurant with a good seafood menu and enthusiastic crowds of diners. Beer only, but you can bring your own wine. Surprisingly good food can be had here as late as 3am.

French

Boulevard, 1 Mission St at Steuart (☎415/543-6084). When you want great French food without the attitude, look no further than this beautiful brasserie-style restaurant in the happening Embarcadero district. Not cheap, but worth every cent; book in advance.

Café Claude, 7 Claude Lane, between Grant and Kearny (☎415/392-3505). More than any of the other imitations in town, this one feels like Paris with its great old furnishings. Go in the evening to find a young, loose crowd listening to jazz. Dinner costs around $20.

Julius' Castle, 1541 Montgomery St at Telegraph Hill (☎415/392-2222). A San Francisco institution for lovers, or just lovers of the romantic, this Telegraph Hill restaurant serves pretty pricey, if delicious food, but hopefully the incredible view of the San Francisco Bay will keep your eyes off the bill – easily $100 for two.

Le Charm, 315 Fifth St between Folsom and Harrison (☎415/546-6128). Good, unpretentious French food in this SoMa bistro ideally placed for the new museums and arts centers. You can park, too.

Pastis, 1015 Battery St at Green (☎415/391-2555). Well-executed dishes served in a stylish but relaxed atmosphere, as good as you'll find in the downtown venues but thankfully not as pricey. The out-of-the-way location is just off Levi's Plaza near Embarcadero.

South Park Café, 108 South Park (☎415/495-7275). Chic SoMa gathering place for aficionados of all things French, especially pastries and good brandy. See also "Drinking: bars and cafés" on p.430.

German

Suppenküche, 601 Hayes at Laguna (☎415/252-9289). Satisfying and delicious German cooking in this loud, lively bar/restaurant decked out like a traditional Bavarian pub. Don't miss the potato pancakes appetizer – it's enough alone for a light supper. See also "Drinking: bars and cafés", p.429.

Greek and Middle Eastern

Helmand, 430 Broadway between Kearny and Montgomery (☎415/362-0641). Excellent, inexpensive Afghani food. Exotic, unique and very popular.

Pasha's, 1516 Broadway at Polk (☎415/885-4477). An extraordinary dining experience. Moroccan and Middle Eastern dishes served while you sit on the floor watching belly dancers gyrate past your table, proffering their cleavage for you to insert dollar bills. Go with a group of rowdy drunks, or not at all.

Socca Restaurant, 5800 Geary Blvd at 22nd Avenue (☎415/379-6720). Inspired Mediterranean and Middle-Eastern cooking in this smart Richmond restaurant that has comfortable booths and fine bar.

Yaya Cuisine, 1220 Ninth Ave at Lincoln (☎415/566-6966). Romantic, candle-lit Middle-Eastern restaurant near Golden Gate Park, with a Californian twist. Good vegetarian selection and overall excellent value.

Indian

Appam, 1261 Folsom St at Ninth (☎415/626-2798). Indian food with a mild, modern slant in this stylish SoMa restaurant. Great atmosphere, and the old Indian method of *Dum Pukht* cooking is employed. Dishes are prepared in large clay pots in an open kitchen where you can watch as nan breads and *kulchas* bake in the tandoori oven.

Gaylord, Ghirardelli Square, 900 North Point at Larkin, Ghirardelli Square (☎415/771-8822). One of the very few Indian restaurants in San Francisco and probably the best, though you should expect to pay around $25 a head for dinner. Still, it's worth it if you're dying for a curry.

Maharani, 1122 Post St at Van Ness (☎415/775-1988). Voted one of the top ten restaurants in the US by the Academy of Restaurant Sciences (whoever they are), this is indeed an intimate place to eat delicious food from traditional low-seated alcoves. For the romantic curry lover.

Scenic India, 532 Valencia St at 16th (☎415/621-7226). Spartan Mission restaurant that serves inexpensive Indian food. Part of the host of Valencia Corridor restaurants that is doing so much for the area.

Zante's, 3489 Mission between 30th St and Cortland, Bernal Heights (☎415/821-3949). This is a weird one, an Indian restaurant that serves pizza – surprisingly tasty.

Italian

Calzone's, 430 Columbus Ave at Vallejo (☎415/397-3600). Busy bar and restaurant right at the heart of North Beach, serving lush pizzas and calzone.

Capp's Corner, 1600 Powell St at Union (☎415/989-2589). Funky, family-style restaurant, where fashionable clients line up for the big portions.

Fior d'Italia, 601 Union St at Stockton (☎415/986-1886). This is the place to go when you're fed up with fancy new-age Italian cooking and posturing and you just want the real thing: very traditional Northern Italian cooking. Great old-timer scene going on at the bar.

Frascati, 1901 Hyde St at Green (☎415/928-1406). Attractive Russian Hill venue for delicious pastas and seafood. Moderately-priced entrees for $12–16.

Gold Spike, 527 Columbus Ave between Green and Union (☎415/986-9747). More like a museum than a restaurant, with enough photographs, mooseheads and war souvenirs to keep you occupied during what can be a long wait for the excellent-value six-course dinner.

Golden Boy, 542 Green St at Columbus (☎415/982-9738). Good venue to sample exotic pizza by the slice. Seven different kinds at $2–3 a slice.

Il Pollaio, 555 Columbus Ave at Green (☎415/362-7727). You'd be hard pushed to spend more than $15 for a blow-out meal in this postage stamp restaurant, where sheer value for money more than makes up for the lack of elbow room.

Kuleto's, 221 Powell St between Geary and O'Farrell (☎415/397-7720). Action-packed downtown hangout with modern Italian cuisine and a very inviting bar. The interior design of this restaurant has won awards.

Little Joe's, 523 Broadway at Columbus (☎415/433-4343). There's always a line, but the inexpensive, enormous portions of well-cooked food in this North Beach institution are well worth waiting for.

North Beach Pizza, 1499 Grant Ave at Union (☎415/433-2444). Good location in one of the best bar-hopping areas in the city. Their low-priced pizza used to be some of the best; sadly it's become inconsistent of late. Adequate for a drink-induced munchie.

Ristorante Ecco, 101 South Park, between Second and Third, Bryant and Brannan (☎415/495-3291). Robust, imaginative cuisine served in this modern SoMa trattoria. Very nice.

Rose Pistola 532 Columbus near Stockton and Green (☎415/399-0499). The latest addition to North Beach's Cal-Ital dining scene, headed by one of SF's hottest chefs. Appealing for the wide range of eclectic tapas and thin-crust pizzas that won't break the bank, and serving until 1am. Highly creative entrees – don't miss the gnocchi in *calamari* bolognese sauce.

Sodini's Green Valley Restaurant, 510 Green St (☎415/291-0499). Good, hearty meals in a basic but busy place full of North Beach families and birthday celebrants. Eat till you drop for around $15.

Vicolo Pizza, 20 Ivy off Franklin at Market (☎415/863-2382). You have probably never eaten pizza as good as this and are unlikely to want to have any other kind afterwards. Popular Hayes Valley venue.

Zinzino, 2355 Chestnut St between Divisadero and Scott (☎415/346-6623). Lively Marina-district bistro decked out like a Roman piazza and serving Italian favorites tinged with San Francisco creativity, at reasonable prices. The wild mushroom lasagne is very good.

Japanese and Korean

Ebisu, 1283 Ninth Ave between Irving and Lincoln (☎415/566-1770). Rated as one of the top sushi bars in town, the fish is fresh and the queue for a seat at the 18-seat sushi bar can be long. Go early to this favorite Richmond restaurant. Around $40 for two, including sake and service.

Hamano Sushi, 1332 Castro St at 24th (☎415/826-0825). Another excellent and popular sushi bar, this one in Noe Valley; dinner for two will set you back around $45 but it's worth it.

Ma Tante Sumi, 4243 18th St at Diamond (☎415/552-6663). Interesting one this: Japanese with a French twist, producing innovative combinations of dishes ranging from the very light to the incredibly rich. A popular Castro dining spot.

Mifune 1737 Post St at Webster (☎415/922-0337). Fast, inexpensive Japanese place, specializing in house-made noodles to eat in or take out.

Moshi Moshi, 2092 Third St (☎415/861-8285). Obscure SoMa restaurant full of people who pride themselves on finding such an out-of-the-way gem. Excellent Japanese, sushi and seafood, moderately priced.

Sushi Bar, 1800 Divisadero at Bush. Bright, inexpensive and quick.

Sushi Bune Restaurant, 389 Geary Blvd between Mission and Powell (☎415/781-5111). Perfect for those who can't resist a gimmick, this place will make your sushi and then float it over to you on a little boat. Hours of fun for the kids, if you can find any that'll eat sushi.

Yoshida Ya, 2909 Webster St at Union (☎415/346-3431). San Francisco has countless sushi bars, but few where you can actually kick off your shoes and eat at low tables on futoned floors (three or more people only). This is just such a place; expect to pay around $25 per head for a good selection of sushi and a few drinks.

LATE NIGHT EATING

For that midnight snack or 3am binge, here are a few last resorts.

North Beach:

Rose Pistola, 532 Columbus near Stockton and Green (☎415/399-0499). Tapas and thin-crusted pizzas. Open until 1am Fri & Sat; until midnight Sun–Thurs.

Yuet Lee, 1300 Stockton St at Broadway (☎415/982-6020). Terrific Chinese seafood until 3am; daily except Tues.

Downtown:

Grubstake, 1525 Pine St at Polk (☎415/673-8268). Burgers and breakfasts until 4am.

Lori's Diner, 336 Mason St at Geary and O'Farrell (☎415/392-8646). Long-standing 24hr diner two blocks from Union Square, selling breakfast, omelets, burgers and sandwiches.

Pine Crest, 401 Geary Blvd at Mason (☎415/885-6407). 24hr diner.

The Marina:

Allstar Pastry & Donuts, 2095 Chestnut St at Steiner (☎415/441-9270). Your basic 24hr donut shop popular with pretty Marina people who get the munchies after the bars and clubs close.

International House of Pancakes, 2299 Lombard St at Pierce (☎415/921-4004). 24hr diner specializing in pancakes, waffles and breakfasts, but serving burgers, shrimp and steaks as well.

The Castro:

Bagdad Café, 2295 Market St at 16th Street (☎415/621-4434). 24hr diner.

Orphan Andy's, 3991 17th St at Market and Castro (☎415/864-9795). 24hr diner.

Sparky's, 242 Church St (☎415/621-6001). 24hr diner.

Mexican and South American

Café do Brasil 104 Seventh St at Mission (☎415/626-6432). Great Brazilian tapas and reasonably-priced dinners.

Cadillac Bar, 1 Minna St between Fourth and Fifth, Mission and Howard (☎415/543-8226). By the standards of most Mexican restaurants, this one is fairly upmarket, and offers live guitar music to help your burritos go down.

Café Marimba, 2317 Chestnut St (☎415/776-1506). Not a bad choice if you're down in the Marina district, which has bloated into a yuppified outdoor mall of chain boutiques and restaurants. *Marimba* tries to replicate authentic Mexican regional cuisine, with excellent salsas, interesting *moles* and bright cocktails.

Cha Cha Cha, 1801 Haight St at Shrader (☎415/386-5758). First-rate Caribbean/Cuban cuisine served in loud, brightly painted surroundings. Great place for swilling oversized margaritas. Open late and always packed.

Chava's Mexican Restaurant, 3245 18th St at Shotwell (☎415/552-9387). Packed-out Mission favorite that serves good, honest grub. Their *huevos rancheros* (served all day) are the perfect hang-over cure for Sunday brunch.

El Balazo, 1654 Haight St at Clayton (☎415/864-8608). Mexican food, healthy style. Have your bur-rito filled with prawns, vegetables, tofu and any other unlikely ingredients. Very popular with the Haight-Ashbury crowd who come to listen to the Spanish guitar music and slug back beers.

El Farolito 2777 Mission St at 24th (☎415/826-4870). Huge, tasty burritos which will last you all day, served in a cafeteria atmosphere.

La Taqueria, 2889 Mission St at 25th (☎415/285-7117). Always busy with locals, which is as good a recommendation as any for its fairly standard Mexican menu. Service is slow, but the food is fresh and delicious.

Mom Is Cooking, 1166 Geneva Ave between Edinburgh and Naples (☎415/585-7000). Small and crowded place out in the foggy Excelsior district. You may have to wait for a table, but it's well worth it for the super-inexpensive fresh Mexican food.

Roosevelt Tamale Parlor, 2817 24th St (☎415/550-9213). For a couple of dollars you couldn't find a better meal in town. Tamales, rice and a beer should set you up for around $6.

Sweet Heat, 3324 Steiner (☎415/474-9191). Healthy Mexican food for a squeamish Marina crowd who are worried about fat and cholesterol.

Vegetarian

Amazing Grace, 216 Church St at Market (☎415/626-6411). Rated highly by local vegetarians, with a standard menu starting at around $5 a dish.

Greens, Building A, Fort Mason Center (☎415/771-6222). A converted army supply warehouse that's now San Francisco's only Zen Buddhist restaurant, serving unusual and delicious macro-biotic and vegetarian food to an eager clientele. Always busy, despite average cost of $40 per head.

Millennium, *Abigail Hotel*, 246 McAllister St (☎415/487-9800). You'd swear it couldn't be done, but this restaurant has managed to make delicious meals for vegans – egg-, dairy- and flesh-free, and predominantly organic to boot. Stylish decor complements the subterranean setting.

Now and Zen Bistro, 1826 Buchanan St between Bush and Sutter (☎415/922-9696). Cozy vegan restaurant in Japantown that serves excellent food, but steer clear of the organic wine.

Raw Living Foods 1224 Ninth Ave at Lincoln across from Golden Gate Park (☎415/665-6519). Only in San Francisco will you find a restaurant where everything served is a hundred percent organic, totally vegan and completely raw (actually, some of it's dehydrated). Much talked about, but you will have to decide for yourself whether it's palatable.

Val 21, 995 Valencia St at 21st (☎415/821-6622). Vegetarian and wholefood finally becomes trendy in this modern Mission hotspot. New York atmosphere with high ceilings and an avant-garde crowd.

Drinking: bars and cafés

San Francisco, while famous for its restaurants, has a huge number of eclectic **drinking** establishments ranging from comfortably scruffy jukebox joints to the chic watering holes of social climbers. At most bars you'll find a wide range of **microbrewed "craft" beers** and interesting imports, and you might come up dry if you're hoping for a Miller Lite. Ever-popular are martinis and cosmopolitans; some bars specialize in one particular cocktail, while most offer a different special each night of the week. Ambiance varies as widely as the liquor – completely red bars, or blue ones, tiki bars with Polynesian thatch huts, jammed meat-markets or low-key neighborhood oases with pool tables in the back. Though spread fairly evenly over the city, happening bars are particularly numerous in North Beach, where they literally line up one after the other. Some of the more colorful (and seedy) are to be found in the Mission district and the Haight, yuppie cruising zones populate the Marina, slick lounges speckle downtown and have begun to spread South of Market, and of course, **gay bars** fill the Castro. According to new California law, there is **no smoking** allowed in any bar unless its sole employees are the owners, though the debate still rages and enforcement has been spotty.

The city is dotted with excellent cafés serving first-rate coffees, teas and soft drinks in addition to beer and wine. More social than utilitarian, people hang out in these generally lively venues to pass time as much as refresh themselves. Other non-drinkers looking for social alternatives to bars are opting for the old English tradition of **afternoon tea** (see p.428). So far it has only taken root in the big hotels, but neighborhood cafés are catching on fast.

Unsurprisingly, the city has many specifically **gay bars** (see p.439), most plentifully in the Castro, Polk Street and the Mission – although few bars are at all threatening for either gay men or lesbians, or women on their own.

Downtown

The Big Four, *Huntington Hotel*, 1075 California St at Taylor. Classy hotel bar, aimed squarely at the sedate set who want a well-made drink in civilized surroundings.

Gordon Biersch Brewery, 2 Harrison St at Embarcadero. Bayfront microbrewery housed in converted Hills Brothers coffee warehouse. Good bar food and some of the best beers in San Francisco bring out downtown's overpaid twentysomethings.

Harry Denton's, 161 Steuart St at Howard. For the after-work Financial District crowd, this is San Francisco's prime place to cruise and be cruised. Fortunately, the fully stocked bar has enough rare

---

ROOFTOP BARS

Carnelian Room, 555 California St at Kearny. The best of the rooftop cocktail lounges, 52 floors up in the Bank of America Building. A truly elegant spot for some smart cocktails; bring smart money.

Equinox, *Hyatt Regency*, The Embarcadero. Good for the novelty value only, this rooftop cocktail lounge attracts crowds of tourists who ascend its dizzy spires just to look at the views. The whole thing revolves, so you get a 360° view of the city without ever leaving your seat. Serious drinkers wouldn't be caught dead in here – have a drink, revolve and leave.

Harry Denton's Starlight Room, *Sir Francis Drake Hotel*, 450 Powell St at Sutter. Dress up and drink martinis. This is a sophisticated grown-up scene with a moneyed crowd who come for the live jazz.

Top of the Mark, *Mark Hopkins Hotel*, California St at Mason. The most famous of the rooftop bars, its reputation surpasses the actual experience of drinking up here, and generally it only attracts tourists and hotel guests who can't be bothered to find anywhere else.

bourbons and West Coast microbrews to make whiling away an evening very pleasant indeed, even if you're not on the prowl. Great interior.

Li Po's Bar, 916 Grant Ave at Jackson. Named after the Chinese poet, *Li Po's* is something of a literary hangout among the Chinatown regulars. Enter through the false cavern front and sit at the very dimly lit bar where Wayne Wang filmed *Chang is Missing*.

The London Wine Bar, 415 Sansome St at Sacramento. Dubiously tagged as "America's first wine bar," this place is a suitably pretentious and expensive locale for the Financial District clones that flock here after work. Open Mon–Fri until 9pm.

Royal Exchange, 301 Sacramento St. The consummate Financial District after-work hangout for the pretty people.

Tonga Room, *Fairmont Hotel*, Powell and Mason streets. Outrageously lavish Polynesian theme bar with waitresses in grass skirts, a native-laden raft floating around the room, and expensive cocktails. Fun if you like the joke and are in the mood for camp hilarity. See also "Live Music", p.434.

North Beach and the northern waterfront

Balboa Café, 3199 Fillmore St at Greenwich. A favorite with the young upmarket singles of the Marina. Very good food, too.

Lost & Found Saloon, 1353 Grant Ave. North Beach's most enticing dive, where your outfit doesn't matter. Live music usually means the place starts rocking around midnight.

Paragon, 3251 Scott St at Francisco. Slick Marina supper club that's more about the music and drinking than eating, though that too is tasty and inexpensive. A smooth crowd jam-packs it on weekends. Recommended.

Perry's, 1944 Union St at Buchanan. Sophisticated meat market, featured in Armistead Maupin's *Tales of the City* as the quintessential breeder bar.

The Saloon, 1232 Grant Ave at Vallejo. This bar has stood for over a hundred years and seen use as a whorehouse and Prohibition speakeasy. Today the old structure creaks nightly as blues bands and crowds of enthusiastic dancers do their thing.

San Francisco Brewing Co, 155 Columbus Ave at Pacific. A must for beer fans who tire quickly of the insipid corporate variety, this North Beach hangout makes its own full-flavored brews on the premises.

Savoy Tivoli, 1434 Grant Ave at Green. Without a doubt, this place is North Beach's most attractively decorated and populated bar, also serving good, reasonably priced food – although the emphasis is definitely on liquid enjoyment.

Tosca Café, 242 Columbus Ave at Broadway. The theme here is opera, in time-worn but still stylish surroundings. Mingle with media people at the bar or slump into a comfy red leather booth and try to talk above the sound-level of the arias.

Vesuvio's, 255 Columbus Ave at Broadway. Legendary North Beach Beat haunt in the 1950s, and still catering to an arty but friendly crowd who prop up the bar into the small hours. Next to City Lights Bookstore, it's a good place to peruse your new purchases over a drink.

Washington Square Bar & Grill, 1707 Powell St at Union. Primarily a restaurant, but worth checking out for the great bar and the chance to spy on the media and literary crowd who have made this their second home.

Civic Center, SoMa and the Mission

Backflip *Phoenix Hotel* 601 Eddy St (formerly *Miss Pearl's Jam House*). The latest cool place to sip cocktails and munch unusual appetizers, this fantastically retro bar overlooks the hotel's pool patio. You'll be amused by the black vinyl-clad waitstaff, the entirely blue, clubby decor and the menagerie of lively patrons.

Blondie's Bar and No Grill 540 Valencia St between 16th and 17th. Specializing in martinis – over forty varieties, including chocolate – and served in a pint glass. Drink yourself silly for around $6, then get cooking to the live swing and straight-ahead jazz on weekends.

Brain Wash Laundromat/Café, 1122 Folsom St at Seventh. Great idea – a café/bar and laundrette where you can have breakfast or a beer while you do your washing. Needless to say it's popular with the young and novelty-conscious. See also "Eating", p.419.

AFTERNOON TEA

One of the nicest ways to finish an afternoon of intense consuming in the downtown stores is to partake of **afternoon tea** in one of the plush Union Square hotels. In true California style, the food is exquisite, and you'll be offered the gamut from cucumber and watercress sandwiches to fresh fruit sorbets and scones with cream.

Garden Court, *Sheraton Palace*, 2 New Montgomery St at Market (☎415/392-8600). The best thing about the recent renovation of this landmark hotel was the restoration of its exquisite lobby, where you can sip fine teas while enjoying the soothing live harp music. Make reservations, it fills up. Wed–Sat 2–4.30pm & Sun 2–3.30pm.

Imperial Tea Court, 1411 Powell St at Broadway (☎415/788-6080). A traditional Chinese tea house, with décor evocative of old Shanghai. Open daily 11am–6.30pm.

King George Hotel, 334 Mason St between Geary and O'Farrell (☎415/781-5050). A Laura Ashley nightmare, where customers nibble at finger sandwiches in mock-British cottage surroundings. Only for Anglophiles and homesick Brits. Tues–Sun 3–6.30pm.

Mark Hopkins, 999 California St (☎415/392-3434). Standard high teas served on lovely Wedgwood china. Mon–Fri 3–5pm.

Neiman Marcus, 150 Stockton St (☎415/362-3900). Tea is served in the glorious *Rotunda* restaurant at the top of the store. Watch the social x-rays nibble fearfully at the calorie-laden food. Daily 2.30–5pm.

Ritz-Carlton, 600 Stockton St (☎415/296-7465). The fanciest of them all, this is the place to slurp tea to the accompaniment of a tinkling harp. Mon–Fri 2.30–4.30pm, Sat & Sun 1–4.30pm.

Café Babar, 994 Guerrero St at 22nd. Hip hangout in the Mission with pool tables, a young, alternative crowd and occasional live music.

Café du Nord, 2170 Market St near Church. One of the first to revive the old tradition of supper clubs, this popular bar is quite the place to experience hot jazz combos over good food, though it's OK just to have a beer at the bar and shoot some pool. See also "Live music", p.433.

Casanova, 527 Valencia St at 16th. Laid-back neighborhood lounge redecorated to resemble an apartment frozen in time – circa 1974. The crowd is local, mellow twenty-to-thirtysomethings who come to converse, down a microbrew and take in tunes on the jukebox.

El Rio, 3158 Mission St near Cesar Chavez. Mixed crowds gather for changing nightly entertainment. All music styles and some great giveaways, like oysters on the half-shell on a Friday. Most popular though, live salsa on a Sunday afternoon that draws a predominantly female crowd. See also "Clubbing", p.431.

Julie's Supper Club, 1123 Folsom St at Seventh. A popular restaurant, but best for sitting at the bar munching good-value Cajun snacks and listening to the free live jazz – if you get in before 9pm, after that it's $5 on weekends. Dancing happens later.

Lilo Lounge 1469 18th at Connecticut. Potrero Hill tiki bar that's a laid-back neighborhood hangout with a young cool clientele.

Paradise Lounge, 1501 Folsom St. Cleverly constructed on two floors, you can suit your mood with a game of pool and a quiet drink upstairs or dance to live music downstairs. See also "Live music", p.433.

The Ramp, 855 China Basin. Way out on the old docks, this is well worth the half-mile trek from downtown (you'll need a car unless you're a seasoned walker) to sit out on the patio and sip beers overlooking the abandoned piers and new boatyards.

Timo's 842 Valencia between 19th and 20th streets. Intimate neighborhood bar where you can get some of the best tapas in the city to go with your Pernod.

The Uptown, 200 Capp St at 17th and Mission. Best of the Mission's dive bars, embracing an eclectic clientele who shoot pool, drink like fiends and fall all over the scruffy leatherette upholstery. Some simply go to watch the ball game on TV. A more bizarre collection of characters would be hard to find. Don't miss it.

Central neighborhoods

Harry's, 2020 Fillmore St at California. A bona fide saloon, this elegantly decorated hangout serves a mixed, unpretentious crowd and makes for a great night's drinking.

Hayes & Vine, 377 Hayes St. Cozy, well-designed spot in trendy Hayes Valley with a truly excellent selection of local and international wines.

Johnny Love's 1500 Broadway at Polk. Straight pick-up scene on an industrial scale. Hormone-driven Young Republicans line up around the block nightly to get a piece of the action.

The Mad Dog in the Fog, 530 Haight St at Steiner. Aptly named by the two lads from Birmingham, England, who own the joint, this is one of the Lower Haight's most loyally patronized bars, with darts, English beer, copies of *The Sun* newspaper and a typical pub menu that includes bangers and mash, hearty ploughman's and the like. Amazingly, it is not the ex-pat English, but the trend-conscious young blades of the Lower Haight who find it so groovy.

Noc Noc, 557 Haight St at Steiner. Decorated like an Egyptian tomb. Draws a fashionable but informal young crowd for new wave music and flasks of hot sake.

The Rat and the Raven, 4054 24th St at Noe. Friendly, hard-drinking neighborhood bar with pool, darts and a superb jukebox. Sunday nights brings out *Simpsons* and *X-Files* fans for communal television watching.

Suppenküche 601 Hayes at Laguna. Of the 28 varieties of beer in this loud, lively bar/restaurant decked out like a traditional Bavarian pub, 23 are German and the rest Belgian. The food is excellent as well. The only bad thing is that since it's located in a residential neighborhood, the place closes early – so get started before 10pm. See also "Eating", p.422.

Golden Gate Park, the beaches and outlying areas

Blue Danube Coffee House, 306 Clement St at Third. Café society alive and well in the suburbs? Not quite, but about as alternative as you'll get in the Richmond.

Boathouse, 1 Harding Park Avenue (on Lake Merced). Popular sports bar, with a superb view of Lake Merced and occasional live music.

Pig & Whistle Pub, 2801 Geary Blvd at Wood. Good range of English and California microbrews, and still the cheapest happy hour in SF – $2 pints of beer served 4–6pm daily. Pool table and dartboards, plus very good pub food.

The Plough and Stars, 116 Clement St at Second Avenue. Irish ex-pat bar with live music seven nights a week starting at 9.15pm. Cover charge Fri & Sat $3–4.

Yancy's Saloon 734 Irving St at Eighth Avenue. Mellow, plant-festooned collegiate bar with free darts and cheap drinks. Across the street from a great oyster house which will call you over from Yancy's when your table is ready.

Cafés

Buena Vista Café, 2765 Hyde St at Beach, Fisherman's Wharf. If you like your coffee with a kick, this is the place for you. Claims to be the home of the world's first Irish coffee, which isn't hard to believe – it's certainly the best in town and the crowds who pack the place are testimony to the generously laced coffee. Good, inexpensive food too, making it a decent stop-off for a sightseeing lunch.

Café Flore, 2298 Market St at Noe. Lively, mostly gay café near the Castro serving great food until 10pm. A popular cruising spot for the locals who come to string a coffee out for hours and be seen reading the latest in hip gay literature. Drown in a sea of newspapers and pretty faces. See also "Gay and lesbian bars", p.439.

Café La Boheme, 3138 24th St at Mission. As the name suggests, a badly dressed crowd, but a staggering range of coffees keeps the Mission's caffeine addicts coming from sunrise until late at night.

Caffè Greco 423 Columbus Ave between Green and Vallejo. One of North Beach's best cafés for people watching with its big windows and outdoor tables. Excellent espresso.

Caffè Trieste, 601 Vallejo St at Grant. Noisy North Beach Italian café, popular with a serious literary crowd who hang out and listen to the opera classics that boom from the jukebox. Saturday lunchtimes are a treat – the family who run it get up and sing. Get there by noon to get a seat.

Mario's Bohemian Cigar Store, 566 Columbus Ave at Union. Small informal North Beach hangout for sipping coffee or slinging beers.

Muddy Waters, 521 Valencia at 16th. The Mission's young and funky come here to wake up or waste an afternoon. Fashionably scruffy.

Picaro, 3120 16th St at Mission. Chic Spanish venue where you can nibble tapas for as little as $2.50 at the bar.

South Park Café, 108 South Park. Chic SoMa rendezvous, where architects and other creative professionals meet their peers to drink in tasteful surroundings. See also "Eating", p.422.

Specialty's Café & Bakery, 101 New Montgomery St at Mission, plus other downtown locations. Not a hangout; just a good place to grab a takeout sandwich on your way to the SF MOMA or Center for the Arts. Huge selection of luscious baked goods, vegetarian and meat sandwiches on housebaked bread, excellent soups, and the usual range of coffees.

Steps of Rome, Columbus at Vallejo. Venerable North Beach late-night café where the taxi drivers congregate. If you're looking for caffeine action after midnight, this is your place.

Nightlife

Compared to Los Angeles, where you need money and attitude in equal amounts, San Francisco's **nightlife** demands little of either. This is no 24-hour city, and the approach to socializing is often surprisingly low-key, with little of the pandering to fads and fashions that goes on elsewhere. The casualness is contagious, and manifest in a **club scene** that, far as it is from the cutting edge of hip, is encouragingly inexpensive compared to other cities. Thirty to forty dollars can buy you a decent night out, including cover charges and a few drinks, and maybe even a taxi home. The **live music** scene is similarly economical – and, frankly, what the city does best. San Franciscans may be relatively unconcerned with fashion, but there are some excellent rock, jazz and folk venues all over town, many entertaining you for no more than the price of a drink. Be sure to always bring a picture ID with you to get past the bouncers.

San Francisco has a great reputation for **opera** and **classical music**; its orchestra and opera company are among the most highly regarded in the country. **Theater** is accessible and much less costly than elsewhere, with discount tickets available, but most of the mainstream downtown venues – barring a couple of exceptions – are mediocre, forever staging Broadway reruns, and you'd do better to take some time to explore the infinitely more interesting fringe circuit.

Cabaret and **comedy** are also lively, and **film**, too, is almost as big an obsession as eating in San Francisco; you may well be surprised by the sheer number of movie theaters – repertory and current release – that flourish in this city.

Clubbing

Still trading on a reputation for hedonism earned decades ago, San Francisco's **nightclubs** in fact trail light years behind those of other large American cities. That said, the compensations are manifold – it is rare to encounter high cover charges, ridiculously priced drinks, feverish posing or long lines, though a few of the cavernous dance clubs South of Market do have lines on weekends. Instead you'll find a diverse range of small to medium-sized, affordable clubs in which leather-clad goths rub shoulders with the bearded and beaded, alongside a number of gay hangouts (listed on p.440) still rocking to the sounds of high-energy funk and Motown. You'll find the occasional place which is up to the minute, playing acid jazz, jungle and the like, but what San Francisco does best is all the old favorites – songs you know the words to; clubbing is more of a party than a pose in this city and much the better for it. The greatest concentration of clubs is in **SoMa**, especially the area around 11th Street and Folsom, though the **Mission** is

similarly well provided with bars and small live music venues – not to mention a couple
of outrageous drag bars – of almost exclusively Latino origin. There are a few places in
North Beach too, so just pick a neighborhood and explore.

Unlike most other cities, where the action never gets going until after midnight,
many San Francisco clubs have to **close** at 2am during the week, so you can usually be
sure of finding things well under way by 11.30pm. At weekends, most places stay open
until 3 or 4am. Very few venues operate any kind of restrictive **admission** policy, and
only on very busy nights are you likely to have to wait.

The clubs

Cat's Alley Club, 1190 Folsom St at Eighth (☎415/431-3332). Perfect for the mature clubber, the
Cat's Alley Club puts on varied entertainment. Live bands and DJs play nightly, everything from
drum-and-bass funk to goth-industrial, hip-hop and acid-jazz, with several women-oriented nights a
week (including standup comedy). Call for the lineup.

Club 181, 181 Eddy St (☎415/673-8181). Dreadful location, smack in the vortex of the Tenderloin,
but take a cab or valet park and check out one of San Francisco's coolest nightspots: three rooms
with dancing to acid-jazz, house, and Seventies funk and disco with a very good-time crowd. Open
Fri & Sat only; free 9–10pm, then $10. Highly recommended.

Club Oz, *Westin St Francis Hotel*, 335 Powell St (☎415/774-0116). Skyline dance room on the 32nd
floor of the hotel draws a young dance-crazy crowd. Worth going just for the view but watch out for
that cover charge: Mon–Thurs $8, Fri & Sat $15, Sun $5.

Covered Wagon Saloon, 917 Folsom St (☎415/974-1585). Definitely one of the better SoMa places
– they serve up a very varied menu of different one-nighters, offering everything from hip-hop to
rockabilly.

DNA Lounge, 375 11th St at Harrison (☎415/626-1409). Club which changes its music style
nightly but draws the same young hipsters. Large dance floor downstairs, and when the dancing
gets too much you can lounge around in comfy sofas on the mezzanine. Cover charge.

DV8, 55 Natoma St between First and Second, Mission and Howard (☎415/957-1730). Huge, ornate
Travolta-style Seventies survivor, this is the closest San Francisco comes to rivalling the big clubs
of New York and Los Angeles, decorated by Keith Haring pop art and playing high-energy funk and
house music. It also has a nice members-only bar that's worth bluffing your way into if you can.
About the only club in town worth dressing up for. Wed–Sat; cover $10.

El Rio, 3158 Mission St at Army (☎415/282-3325). When it isn't staging one of its specials (live salsa
and BBQ on Sunday, DJ dancing Wed, Fri & Sat), this is a great place for a quiet drink and a game
on one of San Francisco's most handsome pool tables. See also "Drinking: bars and cafés", p.428.

The End Up, 401 Sixth St at Harrison (☎415/357-0827). A mostly gay crowd ("Girl Spot Saturdays"
and "Fag Fridays" dance parties) but recently discovered by the weekend clubbers, and a good
place for the hardcore party animal. Famous continuous T-dance starts at 5am Saturday and goes
until 9pm Sunday. See also "Gay and lesbian San Francisco", p.437.

Holy Cow, 1531 Folsom St at 12th (☎415/621-6087). Young college kids try hard to be cool, but a
good rave once it warms up. A huge plastic cow hangs outside, so you can't miss it. Never a cover.
Tues–Sun.

THREE BABES AND A BUS

One excellent way to get the flavor of San Francisco's clubs when you first arrive is to experience the **Three Babes and a Bus** tour (☎415/552-2582) of various hot spots around town. For $35, the three women who organize the tours will drag you around on their bus on a Friday or Saturday night, visiting clubs, which you get into for free, and throwing in the odd drink. In between visits there is much carousing and game-playing on board.

Nickie's, 460 Haight St at Fillmore (☎415/621-6508). This place rocks every night. Whether it's "Grateful Dead Night," African, Latino or Seventies funk, *Nickie's* is for the very lively.

The Palladium, 1031 Kearny St at Columbus (☎415/434-1308). Three dance floors, MTV screens and a teenybopper crowd that can't be persuaded to quit before 6am (Fri & Sat). Good old disco-fun.

Sound Factory, 525 Harrison (☎415/979-8686). Huge multilevel place with three rooms for simultaneous house, hip-hop and Latin dance parties. Saturday nights 9.30pm–4am; cover charge.

Ten15, 1015 Folsom (☎415/431-0700). Another huge club for serious sweating: six rooms with different music in each, especially deep jungle, house, and cool laser light shows. Very popular – you may have to wait in a long line Thurs–Sat. Cover charge.

330 Ritch, 330 Ritch St, South of Market (☎415/541-9574). Low-ceilinged and crowded with slender SoMa types. Serves food until 10pm, then DJs spin funk, soul, disco and British pop music on different nights. On Saturdays there's live jazz and on Wednesdays a live swing band and free swing lessons. Cover charge.

Live music: rock, jazz, blues, and folk

San Francisco's **music scene** reflects the character of the city as a whole: laid back, eclectic, and not a little nostalgic. The options for catching **live music** are wide and the scene is consistently progressive, characterized by the frequent emergence of good young bands. However, San Francisco has never recaptured its crucial Sixties role, and these days is principally renowned as a venue for good R&B, psychedelia, folk and rock standards, as well as country and western and Latin American bands. **Jazz** is very good and not just confined to the city proper: the East Bay in particular is very strong on jazz/funk/blues bands.

Bands are extremely easy to catch. Many restaurants offer live music, so you can eat, drink and dance all at once and often with no cover charge; ordinary neighborhood bars regularly host groups, often for free, and there are any number of good and inexpensive small venues spread out across the city. Few fall into any particular camp, with most varying their bill throughout the week, and it can be hard to specify which of them cater to a certain music style. Many also double as clubs, hosting some kind of disco after the live music has stopped.

What follows is a pretty comprehensive list of established venues, but be sure to check the music press, the best of which is the free *BAM (Bay Area Music)*. Available in most record stores, it carries exhaustive listings of events in the city and Bay Area as a whole.

The large performance venues

Although San Francisco has a couple of major-league concert halls, bear in mind that some of the Bay Area's best large-scale venues, where the big names tend to play, are actually across the bay in Oakland and Berkeley. See the relevant listings later in this chapter.

Great American Music Hall, 859 O'Farrell St at Polk (☎415/885-0750). Civic Center venue, too small for major names but too large for local yokels, and hosting a range of musical styles from balladeers to thrash bands. The lovely interior – it used to be a burlesque house and upscale bordello – makes for a great night out.

The Warfield, 982 Market St at Sixth (☎415/775-7722). *The Warfield* can usually be relied upon to stage major rock crowd-pullers. Chart bands, big-name indie groups and popular old-timers keep the place packed.

Rock, blues, folk and country

Albion, 3139 16th St at Albion (☎415/552-8558). Primarily just a simple Mission neighborhood bar, which hosts local bands on its tiny stage on Sundays. Small, inexpensive and intimate, it's ideal for a night out on the cheap. No cover.

Biscuits and Blues, 401 Mason St at Geary (☎415/292-2583). Primarily a supper club, though the emphasis is on music. Sounds too good to be true, but you can eat great Southern food for around $10 a head and listen to live blues. Call for ticket prices, which range from $3–20.

Bruno's 2389 Mission St at 20th (☎415/550-7455). Swank new jazz bar and restaurant drawing the kind of attractive young crowd who finds it titillating to be in the seedy section of town. Cover charge about $5.

Cocodrie, 1024 Kearny St (☎415/986-6678). Old North Beach club, has changed hands a lot, and now probably books more bands than any other: four a night, seven nights a week. Crowd and quality change daily, from 18-and-over punk shows to world music. Cover charge $3–8.

Hotel Utah, 500 Fourth St at Bryant (☎415/421-8308). Good selection of mainly country bands which you can usually see for free or a very small cover.

Last Day Saloon, 406 Clement St at Fourth (☎415/387-6343). Very lively bar in the Richmond with regular live music including rock, surfer rock, blues and soul. Cover $5.

Lost and Found Saloon, 1353 Grant Ave at Columbus (☎415/397-3751). Informal North Beach hangout with a catch-all selection of music styles.

Lou's, 300 Jefferson St at Taylor (☎415/771-0377). Country/rock and blues bar on Fisherman's Wharf that hosts good local bands. Weekend lunchtimes are a good time to check out the lesser-knowns in relative peace – come nightfall it's madness. No cover before 9pm. See also "Eating", p.420.

Mick's Lounge, 2513 Van Ness Ave (☎415/928-0404). Books local San Francisco bands ranging from rock and funk to Seventies retro and alternative. Cover $4–8.

Paradise Lounge, 308 11th St (☎415/861-6906). Good SoMa venue to see up-and-coming rock bands (usually three per night), or take a break for a game of pool upstairs. See also "Drinking: bars and cafés", p.428.

Plough and Stars, 116 Clement St (☎415/751-1122). In Richmond, this is quite a way from downtown but worth the trip if you're into Irish folk music. Very much the haunt of the Irish ex-pat community. Fri & Sat $3–4 cover charge.

Purple Onion, 140 Columbus Ave at Broadway (☎415/398-8415). Established North Beach venue for hearing a good selection of rock and country.

The Rite Spot, 2099 Folsom St (☎415/552-6066). Informal café where people come to converse and listen to live music of the jazz and original-pop variety. Appetizers and full menu until midnight; no cover.

Saloon, 1232 Grant St at Columbus (☎415/397-3751). Always packed to the gills, this is undeniably North Beach's best spot for some rowdy R&B.

The Up & Down Club, 1151 Folsom St at Eighth (☎415/626-2388). One of the city's best jazz venues, this small club split across two floors serves great drinks and draws a lively attractive crowd out for a good time.

Jazz and Latin American

Bahia Cabana, 1600 Market St at Franklin (☎415/861-4202). Lively bar and supper club with good Brazilian and salsa bands – attracts a skilled dancing crowd who can shake it with a vengeance. 21 and over only. Live music and DJ dancing seven nights a week. Cover charge $7–10.

Bimbo's 365 Club, 1025 Columbus Ave at Chestnut (☎415/474-0365). Varied menu of music styles from jazz to ska, always something worth seeing on the weekly bill. Plush, and fairly expensive.

Café du Nord, 2170 Market St at Church (☎415/861-5016). Excellent, friendly and affordable venue to catch nightly live music while you sample the food on offer or just drink at the bar. Mostly jazz with some mambo and salsa thrown in. Recommended. See also "Drinking: bars and cafés", p.428.

John Lee Hooker's Boom Boom Room, 1601 Fillmore St (☎415/673-8000). Recently opened, this small, intimate bar delivers straight-ahead jazz or classic blues acts nightly; no cover Sun & Tues, otherwise $3 cover weekdays and $7 weekends.

Paragon, 3251 Scott St at Francisco (☎415/922-2456). Smart, cool Marina venue for a fashion-conscious crowd who come to enjoy the nightly jazz, jazz fusion, funk and soul. Recommended.

The Plush Room, *York Hotel*, 940 Sutter St at Hyde (☎415/885-2800). A San Francisco institution, which has successfully revived jazz cabaret in the city and on a good night attracts a very glamorous crowd. Tickets around $20.

Slim's, 333 11th St at Folsom (☎415/522-0333). Slick but reliable showcase for internationally known bands. Not cheap, but a better class of jazz act and a grown-up crowd.

The Tonga Room, *Fairmont Hotel*, 950 Mason St at Powell (☎415/772-5000). An absolute must for fans of the ludicrous, or just the very drunk. The whole place is decked out as a Polynesian village, complete with pond and simulated rainstorms, and a grass-skirted band play terrible jazz and pop covers on a raft in the middle of the water. See also "Drinking: bars and cafés", p.427.

Classical music, opera and dance

Though the San Francisco arts scene has to fight against a reputation for provincialism, this is the only city on the West Coast to boast its own professional **symphony** orchestra, **ballet** and **opera** companies, each of which has a thriving upper-crust social support scene, wining and dining its way through fundraisers and the like. During the summer months, look out for the **free concerts** in Stern Grove (at 19th Avenue and Sloat Boulevard) where the symphony orchestra, opera and ballet give open-air performances for ten successive Sundays (starting in June).

Concert halls

Louise M. Davies Symphony Hall, 201 Van Ness Ave at Hayes (☎415/431-5400). The permanent home of the San Francisco Symphony Orchestra, which offers a year-round season of classical music and sometimes performances by other, often offbeat musical and touring groups. Established in 1909 as a small musical group, the orchestra rose to international prominence in the 1950s when it started touring and recording. Although not quite on par with the New York Philharmonic or Chicago Symphony, they're not far behind and certainly among the top half-dozen US orchestras. They have spent much time in the recording studio with their Danish maestro, Herbert Blomstedt, receiving acclaim for many of their performances, such as the award-winning cycle of Nielsen symphonies. Prices obviously depend on the performance, but are marginally lower than either the opera or ballet, with the least expensive seats going for around $26.

The San Francisco Ballet, in the War Memorial Opera House, 301 Van Ness Ave at Grove (☎415/865-2000). The city's ballet company, the oldest and third largest in the US, puts on an ambitious annual program (Feb–May) of both classical and contemporary dance, and a Christmas production of *Nutcracker*. Founded in 1933, the ballet was the first American company to stage full-length productions of *Swan Lake* and *Nutcracker*. They've won Emmys, broadcast, toured and generally earned themselves a reputation for ambition, which drove them toward bankruptcy in the 1970s. They seemed to be sliding until 1985, when the Icelandic Helgi Tomasson, "premier danseur" of the New York City Ballet, stepped in as artistic director. Since his appointment, the company can seem to do no wrong and some proud San Franciscans consider it "America's premier ballet company." Tickets range from $7 to $110.

War Memorial Opera House, 301 Van Ness Ave at Grove (ticket and schedule information ☎415/864-3330). A night at the opera in San Francisco is no small-time affair. The Opera House, designed by architect Arthur Brown Jr, the creator of City Hall and Coit Tower, makes a very opulent venue for the San Francisco Opera Association which has been performing here since the building opened in 1932. By far the strongest of San Francisco's cultural trio, the Opera Association has won critical acclaim for its performances of the classics as well as lesser known Russian works that other companies prefer not to tackle. The SF Opera carries considerable international weight and pulls in big names like Placido Domingo and Kiri Te Kanawa on a regular basis. Its main season runs from the beginning of September through the end of January, and its opening night is one of the principal social events on the West Coast. In addition, there is also a summer season during June and July. Tickets cost upwards of $20 – for which you do at least get supertitles. Standing room costs a bargain $10–12, and 250 tickets are available (one per person) at 10.30am on the day of performance.

Theater

The majority of the city's **theaters** congregate downtown around the Theater District. Most aren't especially innovative (although a handful of more inventive fringe places are scattered in other parts of town, notably SoMa), but tickets are reasonably cheap – up to $30 a seat – and there's usually good availability. Check out the Sunday *Chronicle*'s Pink Pages to read up on the latest productions around town.

Tickets can be bought direct from the theater box offices, or, using a credit card, through BASS (☎510/762-2277). The TIX Bay Area ticket booth on the Stockton Street side of Union Square regularly has day-of-performance tickets for half price as well as full-price advance sales. (Tues–Thurs 11am–6pm, Fri–Sat 11am–7pm; ☎415/433-7827).

Downtown

American Conservatory Theater, 415 Geary St (☎415/749-2ACT). San Francisco's flagship theater company, the Tony award-winning ACT puts on eight major plays each season. The city's best serious theater venue.

Golden Gate Theater, 1 Taylor St at Market (☎415/551-2000). Originally constructed during the 1920s and recently restored to its former splendor, the Golden Gate is San Francisco's most elegant theater, with marble flooring, rococo ceilings and gilt trimmings. It's a pity that the programs don't live up to the surroundings – generally a mainstream diet of Broadway musicals on their latest rerun, although they occasionally manage to pull a big name out of the bag for a one-man Vegas-type show.

Lorraine Hansberry Theater, 620 Sutter St at Mason (☎415/474-8800). The mainstay of African-American theater in San Francisco. Traditional theater as well as contemporary political pieces and jazz/blues musical revues. Impressive.

The Orpheum, 1192 Market St at Eighth (☎415/474-3800). Showtime, song and dance performances and "light" cabaret-style theater.

Stage Door Theater, 420 Mason St at Post (☎415/749-2228). Attractive, medium-sized turn-of-the-century theater, run by the American Conservatory Theater group.

Theater On The Square, 450 Post St at Mason (☎415/433-9500). Converted Gothic theater with drama, musicals, comedy and mainstream theater pieces.

Elsewhere

Beach Blanket Babylon, *Club Fugazi*, 678 Green St at Powell (☎415/421-4222). One of the few musts for theatergoers in the city, its formality smacks of a Royal Command Performance, but the shows themselves are zany and fast-paced cabarets of jazz singers, dance routines and current political comedy, very slickly put together. Recommended.

Intersection for the Arts, 446 Valencia St at 16th (☎415/626-3311). Well-meaning, community-based group that tackles interesting productions in inadequate facilities.

The Magic Theater, Fort Mason Center, Building D (☎415/441-8822). The busiest and largest company after the ACT, and probably the most exciting, the Magic Theater specializes in the works of contemporary playwrights and emerging new talent; Sam Shepard traditionally premieres his work here.

Mission Cultural Center, 2868 Mission St at 24th (☎415/821-1155). An organization dedicated to preserving and developing Latino culture, staging small but worthy productions using the wealth of talented but underrated performers in San Francisco's Latino community.

Phoenix Theater, 301 Eighth St (☎415/621-4423). Small SoMa playhouse that specializes in readings, one-act plays and sketches.

Theater Artaud, 450 Florida St (☎415/621-7797). Very modern theater in a converted warehouse that tackles the obscure and abstract; visiting performers, both dance and theatrical. Always something interesting.

Theater Rhinoceros, 2926 16th St (☎415/861-5079). San Francisco's only uniquely gay theater group, this company (not surprisingly) tackles productions that confront gay issues, as well as lighter, humorous productions.

Comedy

Comedians have always found a welcoming audience in San Francisco, but in the last few years the alternative **comedy** and **cabaret** scene has been reborn. Some new, excellent venues have opened, and while many may be smartening up beyond the tastes of some, they will undoubtedly be able to draw bigger names to the city.

Few of the comedians are likely to be familiar: as with any cabaret you take your chances, and whether you consider a particular club to be good will depend on who happens to be playing the week you go. You can expect to pay roughly the same kind of cover in most of the clubs ($7–15), and two-drink minimums are common. There are usually two shows per night, the first kicking off around 8pm and a late show starting at around 11pm. For bargains, check the press for "Open Mike" nights when unknowns and members of the audience get up and have a go; there's rarely a cover charge for these evenings and, even if the acts are diabolical, it can be a fun night out.

Comedy venues

Cobb's Comedy Club, The Cannery, 2801 Leavenworth St at Beach (☎415/928-4320). Pricey and usually full of tourists, but the standard of the acts is fairly consistent. Worth a look if everything else is booked up.

Finocchio's, 506 Broadway at Kearny (☎415/982-9388). A San Francisco institution and former Prohibition speakeasy, Finocchio's presents a small cast of female impersonators who run through textbook routines, heavy on the sauciness. At one time it was considered outrageous; these days it's more than a little tame, good for cheap laughs and expensive drinks.

Josie's Cabaret and Juice Joint, 3583 16th St at Noe (☎415/861-7933). A good all-rounder offering a mixed menu of cabaret and comedy during the week, and live music and dancing weekends. The bill changes weekly.

The Punch Line, 444 Battery St at Washington (☎415/397-7573). Frontrunner of the city's "polished" cabaret venues, this place has an intimate, smoky feel that's ideal for downing expensive cocktails and laughing your head off. The club usually hosts the bigger names in the world of stand-up and is always packed.

Film

After eating, watching **films** is the next favorite San Francisco pastime. For one thing it's inexpensive (rarely more than $8, sometimes as little as $4 for a matinee), and secondly there's a staggering assortment of current-release and repertory film houses, with programs that range from the latest general-release films to Hollywood classics, iconoclastic Sixties pieces, and a selection of foreign and art films. Film-going in San Francisco is a pleasure: there are rarely lines, and the cinemas are often beautiful

FILM FESTIVALS

The San Francisco Film Festival, specializing in political and short films you wouldn't normally see, is held at the Kabuki eight-screen cinema, the Castro Theater, and the Pacific Film Archive in Berkeley (see p.471), at the end of April and first week or so of May. Tickets sell extremely fast and you'll need to book well in advance for all but the most obscure movies. If you know you're going to be in town, call ☎415/931-FILM or buy tickets on the Web at *www.sfiff.org*. Just as popular is the **Gay and Lesbian Film Festival**, held in June at the Castro and other theaters. Call ☎415/703-8663 for program and ticket information.

Spanish Revival and Art Deco buildings that are in themselves a delight to behold. For screening times and locations of current run films, call ☎415/777-FILM.

Cinemas

ATA-Artists Television Access, 992 Valencia St at 21st (☎415/824-3890). Nonprofit media center that puts on the city's most challenging barrage of film video and performance art, often with a political or psychosexual bent; or sometimes just trashy entertainment. Screenings Thurs–Sat.

The Castro Theater, 429 Castro St at Market (☎415/621-6120). Perhaps San Francisco's most beautiful movie house, offering a steady stream of reruns, art films, Hollywood classics and (best of all) a Wurlitzer organ played between films by a man who rises up from below the stage.

AMC Kabuki 8, 1881 Post St and Fillmore (☎415/931-9800). Attractive, modern building in the Japan Center complex, where eight screens show mainly current-release movies.

Embarcadero Center Cinemas, One Embarcadero Center, Promenade level (☎415/352-0810). A good choice for American, international and some art films. Five screens, two with digital sound; free parking on weekends and evenings with validation, or just take the BART.

Four Star, 2300 Clement at 23rd Avenue. (☎415/666-3488) Way out in the fog belt, but worth a visit for the interesting mix of Asian, international and American culture films; two screens.

The Lumiere, 1572 California St at Polk (☎415/352-0810). Another opulent Spanish Revival art house, a bit run-down but often with an interesting program of obscure art films as well as a select choice of current-release films. Beware – nighttime parking is nearly impossible so take a cab or Muni bus.

Pacific Film Archive, at the UC Berkeley Art Museum, Durant Ave, Berkeley (☎510/642-1412). For the serious film fan, this is perhaps the best movie theater in California, with seasons of contemporary works from around the world plus revivals of otherwise forgotten classics. The cinema is not in San Francisco, but across the bay in the city of Berkeley (see p.471).

The Red Vic, 1727 Haight St at Cole (☎415/668-3994). Friendly collective, formerly housed in a room full of ancient couches where you could put your feet up, and now moved to smarter premises up the street. Same idea though, showing popular reruns and cult films.

The Roxie, 3117 16th St at Valencia (☎415/863-1087). San Francisco's trendiest, independent rep house situated in the heart of the Mission, showing a steady diet of punk, film noir and political movies.

Gay and lesbian San Francisco

San Francisco's reputation as a city for gay celebration is not new – in fact it could even be outdated. This is still the undoubted gay capital of the world, but despite a high profile, the gay scene hasn't had much to celebrate in the last few years and there's been a definite move from the outrageous to the mainstream. It's unlikely that even AIDS will wipe out the increasing number of gay activists in public office, but it has made them more conservative in approach, if not in policy. The exuberant energy that went into the posturing and parading of the 1970s has taken on a much more sober, down-to-business attitude, and these days you'll find more political activists organizing conferences than drag queens throwing parties.

Certainly, post-AIDS, San Francisco's gay scene is a different way of life altogether. The Seventies were notorious for the bar-and-bathhouse culture and the busy and often anonymous promiscuity which went with it, but this toned down abruptly when AIDS first became a problem in the latter part of the decade. This wasn't a foregone conclusion by any means; many men saw the closure of the bathhouses as an infringement on their civil liberties, rooted in homophobia.

Socially, San Francisco's gay scene has also mellowed, though in what is an increasingly conservative climate in the city generally, gay parties, parades and street fairs still swing better than most. Like any well-organized section of society, the gay scene definitely has its social season, and if you're here in June, you'll coincide with the Gay and Lesbian Film Festival, Gay Pride Week, the Gay Freedom Day Parade and numbers of conferences. Come October, the street fairs are in full swing and Halloween still sees some of the most outrageous carryings-on (see box on p.412). **Lesbian culture** flowered in the 1980s, but today, though women's club nights do exist, the scene is more in evidence in bookstores than bars. Details of gay accommodation, bars and clubs appear below; mention of gay bookstores and theater and film ventures are under the relevant headings earlier in this chapter.

Neighborhoods

Traditionally, the area for gay men has been the **Castro**, together with a few bars and clubs in the **SoMa** area – though gay life these days is much less ghettoized and there are bars and clubs all over town. Rent boys and pimps prowl **Polk Street**, not the safest area at 2am, but neither is it a danger zone if you use common sense. Lesbian interests are more concentrated in the East Bay than the city, although women's activities thrive in the **Mission**.

Gay accommodation

Not surprisingly, San Francisco has several **accommodation** options that cater specifically to gay travelers. Most are geared towards men, although it's unlikely that lesbians would be turned away; see "Women's San Francisco" on p.441, for women-only alternatives. All of the places we've listed below are in San Francisco. In the rest of the Bay

---

CONTACTS AND RESOURCES

AIDS Hotline (☎415/863-2437). 24hr information and counseling.

Bisexual Resources Line (☎415/703-7977). Contacts and voicemail boxes of various bisexual groups.

Dignity, 1329 Seventh Ave (☎415/681-2491). Catholic worship and services.

Gay/Lesbian Legal Referral Services, Box 1983 SF (☎415/621-3900). Inquiries regarding legal problems and legal representation.

Gay Therapy Center, 3393 Market St (☎415/558-8828). Counseling and help with coming out.

Lesbian/Gay Switchboard, Pacific Center, 2712 Telegraph Ave, Berkeley 94705 (☎510/841-6224). 24hr counseling

and advice. Contacts and activities referral service.

Lyric (☎415/863-3636). For gay and lesbian youth 23 and younger, discussion groups, movie nights, camping and sporting events, women's issues.

New Leaf, 1853 Market St at Guerrero (☎415/626-7000). Outpatient mental health on a sliding fee scale.

San Francisco Sex Information, PO Box 881254 (☎415/989-7374). Free, anonymous and accurate information.

SF AIDS Foundation, 25 Van Ness Ave (☎415/864-4376). Referral service providing advice, testing, support groups.

SF Suicide Prevention (☎415/781-0500). What it says, 24 hours a day.

PUBLICATIONS

New clubs and groups spring up all the time, and you should keep an ear to the ground as well as referring to the many free **gay publications**: *The Sentinel*, *Oblivion*, *The Bay Area Reporter* and *Bay Times* all give listings of events, services, clubs and bars in the city and Bay Area. Women should also keep an eye out in bookstores for *On Our Backs* and *Bad Attitude*, two magazines that often have pointers to lesbian organizations in town. Also useful for men and women is the **Lavender Pages**, a telephone-cum-resource book available in gay bookstores. Alternatively, if you don't mind forking out $11, a must-have for every visiting gay man with a sense of humor is *Betty & Pansy's Severe Queer Review*, listing everything from the best place to eat upscale food to the best cruising alleys – in unashamedly explicit detail.

Area, gay travelers (including couples) rarely raise eyebrows, and your sexual orientation shouldn't be an issue.

Andora Inn 2434 Mission St at 21st (☎415/282-0337). Lovingly-restored Victorian manor in the lively Mission district, catering to gays but straight-friendly. Free continental breakfast, plus wine and cheese in the evenings. Recommended. ④.

Archbishop's Mansion, 1000 Fulton St (☎415/563-7872). Grandly camp Alamo Square mansion that was once a school for wayward Catholic boys and is now a really interesting, gay-friendly B&B. Attentive personalized service, a variety of "theme" rooms, the ballroom chandelier from *Gone With the Wind*, and everything from fitness training to image consultancy. A riot. ⑥.

Gough Hayes Hotel, 417 Gough St at Hayes (☎415/431-9131). Bit of a flophouse, but popular with a rowdy crowd. ③.

Inn on Castro, 321 Castro St at Market (☎415/861-0321). A long-standing favorite with visiting gays, this luxury bed and breakfast doesn't come cheap, but is worth the price for the large rooms and good breakfasts. About two minutes' walk from the Castro. ⑤.

Queen Anne Hotel, 1590 Sutter St at Post (☎415/262-2663). Very much a gay hotel with overdone decor, full valet service and complimentary afternoon tea and sherry. ⑥.

24 Henry, 24 Henry St (☎415/864-5686). Intimate guesthouse in a quiet street just off the heart of the Castro. ④.

Twin Peaks Hotel, 2160 Market St at Dolores (☎415/621-9467). Set in the hills above, this is a quieter and prettier location not far from the Castro, even if the rooms are small and short on luxury. ②.

Bars

San Francisco's **gay bars** are many and varied, ranging from cozy cocktail bars to no-holds-barred leather and chain hangouts. In the last few years nearly every single lesbian bar has disappeared, with the notable exception of Lexington Club, a small low-key place with a friendly and sometimes packed crowd in the Mission. Otherwise, if you want exclusively female company you'll have to check out clubs that have lesbian nights. Bear in mind, too, that the increasingly integrated nature of the gay scene means that formerly exclusively male bars now have a sizeable lesbian contingent; indeed, most are perfectly welcoming for straights. Take note that places we've listed as bars may switch on some music later on and transform into a club; we've listed the better ones that do this under "Clubs", see overleaf.

Alta Plaza, 2301 Fillmore at Clay. Catering to the Pacific Heights junior executive crowd. Boys in suits looking for similar.

Badlands, 4121 18th St between Collingworth and Castro. Not quite as cruisy as the *Midnight Sun*, but the lively thirtysomething crowd are not exactly here to read the papers either.

The Café, 2367 Market St at Castro. A Castro institution, this place has gone from being a gay bar to a lesbian bar and is now fifty-fifty. One of the busiest bars in the Castro, there's DJ dancing every night of the week and it's especially packed on weekends.

Café Flore, 2298 Market St at Noe. Very much the in spot before dark. Attractive café, with matching clientele and leafy outdoor area, and no shortage of people eyeing each other up. Very mixed, lots of women. See also "Drinking: bars and cafés" on p.429.

The Castro Station, 456 Castro St at 18th. Noisy disco bar that manages to pack 'em in even in the middle of the day. Very much the die-hard scene of the Seventies, with a fair number in their leather trousers.

El Rio, 3158 Mission St near Army. Mixed crowds gather for changing nightly entertainment.

Harvey's 500 Castro St at 18th. Formerly the Elephant Walk, this newly reincarnated hangout is a lively place drawing a friendly, community-oriented mixed gay and lesbian crowd for socializing. Serves food, too.

Lexington Club 3464 19th St at Lexington. Perhaps San Francisco's only lesbian bar: laid-back, no frills and packed with the pretty as well as the butch. Friendly folks and a good jukebox.

Midnight Sun, 4067 18th St between Castro and Hartford. Young white boys dressed to the nines and cruising like maniacs in this noisy Castro video bar.

The Mint, 1942 Market St at Guerrero. Gay karaoke bar where a mixed crowd goes to live out its fantasies of being Diana Ross, or at least a Supreme.

Moby Dick, 4049 18th St at Hartford. Civilized-looking neighborhood bar by day, gets rowdier by night. Pool tables and TV screens for the shy.

Rawhide, 280 Seventh St at Folsom. If men in chaps are your scene, go no further than this dimly lit SoMa landmark that plays country and western and bluegrass music to a jovial mixed crowd. Definitely recommended.

SF Eagle, 12th and Harrison St. Easily the best known leather bar in San Francisco. Large outdoor area with stage. Best time for a visit is for the $8 Sunday brunch when they have a "beer bust" 3–6pm to raise money for AIDS.

The Stud, 399 Ninth St at Harrison. A favorite dancing spot with a mixed but mostly gay crowd. Variable cover charge depending on the night, and some raucous times and shameless freaking out on the dance floor. A San Francisco institution, highly recommended.

The Swallow, 1750 Polk St between Clay and Washington. This sophisticated piano bar pulls in a well-behaved middle-aged crowd who just want a good drink and some conversation. Not for randy party animals.

Twin Peaks, 401 Castro at Market and 17th. The Castro's first blatantly gay bar, with large windows to make the point. Draws a low-key older crowd who gather for quiet drinks and conversation.

Uncle Bert's Place, 4086 18th St at Castro. Lives up to its name – a cozy neighborhood bar.

Clubs

Many **gay clubs** are simply bars that host various club nights at least once a week. Pleasingly unpretentious, they rank among the city's best, and although a number are purely male affairs, with a few women-only dance parties gaining a solid following in recent years, the majority, particularly those listed below under the heading "Mixed," welcome gay people of both sexes. Because in recent years all the **lesbian bars** seem to have disappeared (with the exception of Lexington Club, see overleaf), women now usually share space with gay bars and host one-night affairs from various venues. The nature of these club nights mean that they change all the time – numbers are listed in the free magazines distributed at bars in the Castro.

Mixed

The Café, 2367 Market St at Castro, upstairs (☎415/861-3846). Always one of the busiest bars in the Castro, there's DJ dancing every night of the week. You may find long lines on weekends. No cover.

The Box, at 715 Harrison St at Third. Very popular, split-level dance club that plays a good selection of funk and house music. Still the hot favorite for dance-serious men and women. Thurs $6.

Club Townsend, 177 Townsend St (☎415/974-6020). Site of long-running gay and lesbian dance parties (Club Q for women, Club Universe and Pleasuredome for men) on Friday, Saturday and Sunday respectively. Call their information line for the latest events.

Club Universe, 177 Townsend at Third (☎415/985-5241). Easily San Francisco's hottest gay dance club, on Saturday nights this large, cavernous space draws mainly a twenty- to thirtysomething crowd (21 and up; ID required) for dancing to progressive house music until 7am. $10.

Come-Unity, 1015 Folsom between Sixth and Seventh streets (no phone). Entirely word-of-mouth advertised, this underground dance party is supposed to be cutting-edge, and attracts a mixed straight and gay crowd. First Wed of the month; cover $7.

The End Up, Sixth St at Harrison (☎415/495-9550). Changes its bill weekly, but Fridays are gay and Saturdays lesbian – always a safe bet when you're stuck for a place to go. See also "Nightlife", p.431.

Mainly for men

Esta Noche, 3079 16th St at Valencia (☎415/861-5757). Discomania Latin-style. Young men and their pursuers dance to a hi-NRG disco beat reminiscent of the Seventies.

Futura, King Street Garage, 174 King St at Third behind *Club Townsend* (☎415/974-6020). On the second and fourth Saturdays of the month, San Francisco's gay Latino contingent gathers to dance to high energy Spanish house music. Quite a scene.

Rawhide, 280 Seventh St at Folsom (☎415/621-1197). Country and western dance hall. Hysterical good fun if you're into square dancing and the like.

The Stud, 399 Ninth St at Harrison (☎415/252-STUD). An oldie but a goodie. Has been popular for years for its energetic, uninhibited dancing and good times.

Mainly for women

Cherry Bar at the *Co-Co Club*, see below. Every third Wednesday, three of San Francisco's most innovative DJ's introduce diverse dance music, including soul, funk and the latest progressive house, to a loyal crowd of all colors. Small and intimate with a low cover.

Co-Co Club, 139 Eighth St at Minna between Mission and Howard (☎415/626-2337). Lesbian-owned, with a new restaurant upstairs, this dyke clearinghouse hosts different events each night of the week, from dance parties to open mike.

Club Q at *Club Townsend*, 177 Townsend St (☎415/974-6020). Lesbian dance party held the first Friday of the month and patronized by a young, ethnically mixed group of women. Always packed.

Girl Spot at *The End Up*, 401 Sixth St at Harrison (☎415/337-4962). The city's most friendly women-only evening where everyone from the toughest dyke to the most fey femme just wants to have a good time. No politics, no posturing, just fun.

Red at *Blondie's Bar and No Grill*, 540 Valencia St (☎415/339-8310). Sunday nights bring out ethnically-diverse lesbians for a hip-house, funky dance party at this fun, non-cruisy small bar.

Junk at *The Stud*, 399 Ninth St at Harrison (☎415/252-STUD). The fourth Saturday of the month attracts spunky, leather and flannel girls ready for anything.

Women's San Francisco

The flip side of San Francisco's gay revolution has in some **women**'s circles led to a separatist culture, and women's resources and services are sometimes lumped together under the lesbian category. While this may be no bad thing, it can be hard to tell which organizations exist irrespective of sexuality. Don't let this stop you from checking out anything that sounds interesting; nobody is going to refuse you either entry or help if you're

---

CONTACTS AND RESOURCES FOR WOMEN

Bay Area Women's Resource Center, 318 Leavenworth St (☎415/474-2400). Services, information and clothing.

Radical Women/Freedom Socialist Party, New Valencia Hall, 1908 Mission St (☎415/864-1278). Socialist feminist organization dedicated to building women's leadership and achieving full equality. Meetings, discussion groups and poetry readings held on various issues: call for details.

Rape Crisis Line (☎415/647-7273). 24hr switchboard.

Women's Building, 3543 18th St (☎415/431-1180). Central stop in the Mission for women's art and political events. A very good place to get information also – the women who staff the building are happy to deal with the most obscure of inquiries.

Women's Needs Center, 2166 Hayes St (☎415/487-5607). Low-cost health care and referral service.

not a lesbian – support is given to anybody who needs it. Similarly women's health care is very well provided for in San Francisco and there are numerous clinics you can go to for routine gynecological and contraceptive services: payment is on a sliding scale according to income, but even if you're flat broke, you won't be refused treatment.

Women's accommodation

Campton Place, 340 Stockton St at Post (☎415/781-5555). Not specifically a women's hotel, but favored by female executives who like the discreet profile and safe, quiet floors. ⑧.

Mary Elizabeth Inn, 1040 Bush St at Jones (☎415/673-6768). Run by the United Methodist Church, so don't expect a swinging dyke scene. However, it is a safe place to stay. ③.

Women's Hotel, 642 Jones St at Post (☎415/775-1711). Comfortable, secure building that is quite safe despite being situated in the unpleasant Tenderloin district. Singles $160 per week, doubles $200. ①.

Shopping

San Francisco is a good place for **shopping**; all the international names are displayed in downtown storefronts, but where the city really excels is in its range of smaller-scale outlets, great for picking up odd and unusual things you wouldn't find at home. The great majority of places are low-key and unpretentious. Not only does this mean slightly lower prices, but it also makes shopping a more pleasant, stress-free activity all round.

If you want to run the gauntlet of designer labels, or just watch the style brigades in all their consumer fury, **Union Square** is the place to aim for. Heart of the city's shopping territory, it has a good selection of big-name and chic stores – expense account stuff admittedly, but good for browsing. For things that you can actually afford, you'll have a less disheartening and more interesting time in neighborhoods such as **Haight-Ashbury** and the **Mission**, where the secondhand, quirky and plain bizarre are in abundance, fascinating to pick through if you're at a loose end or on the lookout for some good American kitsch and unique souvenirs; the Mission, especially, has some marvelous secondhand **clothing** stores. The city in general is home to a small but excellent array of **bookstores**, and its one-off, independent **record stores** are unbeatable for rare birds to add to your collection.

For a real feel for different city neighborhoods, and to escape the tourist hordes, try strolling around the following shopping districts: **Fillmore Street** between Jackson and Ellis for home furnishings, antiques, designer clothes and classier secondhand stores interspersed with lively eateries and popular bars; **Castro Street** from where it intersects Market and 17th to 19th Street, and Market Street from Castro to Church, for gay-oriented bars and boutiques, clubwear and unusual designer clothes and shoes; and **Union Street** (also known as Cow Hollow) from Van Ness to Steiner, for more expensive boutiques and cafés.

Department stores and shopping malls

If you want to pick up a variety of things in a hurry, without having to roam all over town, it's hard to beat the one-stop convenience of **department stores** or, increasingly, **shopping malls**. These have gotten classier and pricier but they're still useful, and can be quite lively.

Macy's Union Square, Stockton and O'Farrell (☎415/397-3333). Probably the city's best-stocked store, and as such a good place for general shopping, even if it's not a patch on its New York counterpart. Nonetheless, brimming with trinkets, and a dangerous place to go with a full wallet. Beautifully presented merchandise beckons from all sides.

Nieman Marcus, 150 Stockton St at O'Farrell (☎415/362-3900). The sheer cheek of the pricing department has earned this store the nickname "Needless Mark-up." Undoubtedly Union Square's most beautiful department store, however, with its classic rotunda, and good for browsing.

Nordstrom, 865 Market St at Powell (☎415/243-8500). Shoppers flock here for the high-quality (and expensive) fashions, as well as a chance to ride on the spiral escalators that climb the four-story atrium.

Sak's Fifth Avenue, 384 Post St at Powell (☎415/986-4300). A scaled-down version of its New York sister store, geared largely to the middle-aged shopaholic, Saks is *the* high-end speciality shopping store.

Shopping malls

Crocker Galleria, 50 Post St at Kearny (☎415/393-1505). A modern, Italianate atrium, this Financial District mall features some very pricey showcase boutiques. It's all very nice for a wander, but expensive.

Embarcadero Center, at Embarcadero BART/Muni station at the foot of California Street (☎415/772-0500). Ugly, six-block shopping complex with 125 stores and a few unremarkable restaurants, distinguished from other anodyne shopping malls only by the occasional work of art and a quite carefully planned layout. Good stores, though they tend to cater to rich yuppies.

Ghirardelli Square, 900 North Point at Larkin (☎415/775-5500). This attractive turn-of-the-century building used to be a chocolate factory, but is now home to 43 stores and five restaurants – the nicest way to drop dollars at the wharf.

Japan Center, Post St at Buchanan (☎415/922-6776). Surprisingly characterless five-acre complex of stores, movie theaters and restaurants with a Japanese theme. A few redeemable antique and art shops.

San Francisco Shopping Center, Fifth and Market streets (☎415/495-5656). A good-looking mall; glass, Italian marble, polished green granite and spiral escalators up and down its eight stories all add to the seductive appeal of spending money with California-style panache. Sumptuous Parisian cakes at *La Nouvelle Patisserie* vie for your attention with Bugs Bunny paraphernalia at the Warner Bros store.

Food and drink

Food faddists will have a field day in San Francisco's many **gourmet stores**, which are on a par with the city's restaurants for culinary quality and diversity. The simplest neighborhood deli will get your taste buds jumping, while the most sophisticated places are enough to make you swoon. Be sure to try such **local specialities** as *Boudin*'s sourdough bread, Gallo salami and Anchor Steam beer. Bear in mind, too, that however overwhelming the food on offer in San Francisco itself may seem, some of the very best places are to be found across the bay in Berkeley. For more basic stocking up there are, of course, **supermarkets** all over the city (Safeway is probably the most widespread name), some of them open 24 hours per day.

Andronico's Market, 1200 Irving St between Funston and 14th Ave (☎415/753-0403); also four locations in Berkeley. The California gourmet's answer to Safeway. Pricey but gorgeous produce: microbrews, good wine, craft breads, fancy cheeses, an olive bar and a pretty good deli. Not the cheapest, but way better quality than your average supermarket.

Boudin, 156 Jefferson St, Fisherman's Wharf (☎415/928-1849). They only make one thing – sourdough bread – but it's the best around. Cafés pushing their dough are scattered all over the city.

California Wine Merchant, 3237 Pierce St at Chestnut (☎415/567-0646). Before you set off for the Wine Country (see p.537), pick up a sample selection at this Marina wine emporium so you know what to look out for.

Casa Lucas, 2934 24th St at Guerrero (☎415/826-4334). Mission store with an astonishing array of exotic fruits and vegetables.

David's, 474 Geary St at Taylor (☎415/771-1600). The consummate Jewish deli, open until 12am. A downtown haven for the after-theater crowd and night owls.

Heart of the City Farmer's Market, United Nations Plaza at Market Street near Civic Center (☎415/558-9455). Huge, friendly certified farmer's market (which means everything is sold by the growers themselves), distinguished from others by catering to the multiethnic inner city clientele at low prices. Mouthwateringly fresh local produce. Wed & Sun 7am–5pm.

Ferry Plaza Farmer's Market, on the Embarcadero in front of the Ferry Building at Market Street. Higher prices accompany the mostly organic produce in this very popular downtown market. Beautiful produce and fine foodstuffs. Sat 8.30am–2pm.

Graffeo Coffee, 733 Columbus Ave at Filbert (☎415/986-2420). Huge sacks of coffee are piled up all around this North Beach store – you can smell the place from half a block away.

Harvest Ranch Market, 2285 Market St at Church (☎415/626-0805). Health-nut heaven. Organic everything.

Liguria Bakery, 1700 Stockton St at Filbert, North Beach (☎415/421-3786). Marvellous old-world Italian bakery, with deliciously fresh *focaccia*.

Molinari's, 373 Columbus Ave (☎415/421-2337). Bustling North Beach Italian deli, jammed to the rafters with goodies.

Pasta Gina, 741 Diamond at 24th in Noe Valley (☎415/921-7576). Fresh pasta and sauces to heat and eat. Everything you need, including wine, for an Italian dinner when you don't want to cook.

Rainbow Grocery, 1745 Folsom St (☎415/863-0620). Progressive politics and organic food in this huge SoMa wholefood store.

Sunrise Deli and Café, 2115 Irving St at 22nd (☎415/664-8210). Speciality Middle Eastern foodstuffs – stuffed vine leaves, *baba ghanoush* and hummus.

Urban Cellars, 3821 24th St at Church (☎415/824-2300). The dipsomaniac's dream – hundreds of wines and exotic spirits taking booze shopping to its zenith.

Bookstores

Although San Francisco does boast some truly excellent **bookstores**, the range of reading material on offer is surprisingly small for a city with such a literary reputation. The established focus for literature has long been in North Beach, in the area around the legendary City Lights Bookstore, but increasingly the best spots, particularly for contemporary creative writing, are to be found in the lower-rent Mission district, which is home to some of the city's more energized – and politicized – bookstores. There are a few **secondhand booksellers** in the city itself, but these can't compare with the diverse bunch across the bay in Oakland and Berkeley. Most bookstores tend to open every day, roughly 10am–8pm, though City Lights is open daily until midnight.

General bookstores

The Booksmith, 1644 Haight St near Cole (☎415/863-8688). Good general bookstore with an excellent stock of counter-cultural titles. Very Haight-Ashbury.

Borders Books and Music, 400 Post St at Powell (☎415/399-1633). Massive, emporium-style bookstore with over 160,000 books to chose from as well as CDs, videos and software. They've thoughtfully included a café.

City Lights Bookstore, 261 Columbus Ave at Broadway (☎415/362-8193). America's first paperback bookstore, and still the city's best, with a range of titles including City Lights' own publications.

Crown Books 1700 Van Ness Ave at Sacramento (☎415/441-7479). San Francisco branch of the nationwide chain, selling new general books at discounted prices.

Tillman Place Bookstore, 8 Tillman Place, off Grant Ave, near Union Square (☎415/392-4668). Downtown's premier general bookstore and certainly one of the oldest, with a beautifully elegant feel.

Specialist and secondhand bookstores

A Different Light, 489 Castro St at 18th (☎415/431-0891). Well-stocked gay bookshop, diverse and popular.

Around the World, 1346 Polk St at Pine (☎415/474-5568). Musty, dusty and a bit of a mess, this is a great place to spend hours poring over first editions, rare books and records.

Books Etc, 538 Castro St at 18th (☎415/621-8631). Stocks the gamut of gay publishing, from psychology to soft-core porn.

Bound Together Anarchist Collective Bookstore, 1369 Haight St (☎415/431-8355). Haight-Ashbury store specializing in radical and progressive publications.

China Books, 2929 24th St (☎415/282-2994). Mission bookstore with books and periodicals from China, and a good number of publications on the history and politics of the Third World.

Columbus Books, 540 Broadway at Union (☎415/986-3872). North Beach store with a good selection of new and used books, and a large guide and travel books section.

Good Vibrations, 1210 Valencia St at 23rd (☎415/974-8980). A comfortable, decidedly un-sleazy place to buy how-to sex books and erotica. So keen is this outfit to promote women's sexuality they even publish their own titles under the Down There Press imprint. Also sells a bewildering diversity of sex toys, condoms and intimate apparel.

Great Expectations, 1512 Haight St at Ashbury (☎415/863-5515). Radical liberal bookstore with hundreds of T-shirts bearing political slogans, some funnier than others.

Modern Times, 888 Valencia St at 20th (☎415/282-9246). Good selection of gay and lesbian literature, many radical feminist publications, and a hefty stock of Latin American literature and progressive political publications. Stages regular readings of authors' works.

Rand McNally Map & Travel Store, 595 Market St at Second (☎415/777-3131). Large store selling travel guides, maps and paraphernalia for the person on the move.

Sierra Club Bookstore, 85 Second St at Mission (☎415/977-5600). Indispensable for the camper or hiker, check in here before you wander off to explore the great wide yonder.

William Stout Architectural Books, 804 Montgomery St at Jackson (☎415/391-6757). One of San Francisco's world-class booksellers, with an excellent range of books on architecture, building, and urban studies.

Record stores

San Francisco's **record stores** are of two types: massive, anodyne warehouses pushing all the latest releases, and impossibly small specialist stores crammed to the rafters with obscure discs. The big places like Tower Records are more or less identical to those throughout the world, though foreign visitors tend to find the prices marginally cheaper than back home. More exciting is the large number of **independent** retailers and **secondhand and collectors'** stores, where you can track down anything you've ever wanted, especially in West Coast jazz or psychedelic rock.

Amoeba Records, 1855 Haight St (☎415/831-1200). Just opened, this big sister to Berkeley's renowned emporium of new and used records is quite possibly the largest retailer in America specializing in used music. A giant trading post, it's stocked to the gills with hard-to-find releases on vinyl and rarities of every stripe. Over 100,000 used CDs too.

Aquarius Records, 3961 24th St at Noe (☎415/647-2272). Small neighborhood store with friendly, knowledgeable staff. Emphasis on indie rock, jazz and blues.

CD & Record Rack, 3987 18th St at Castro (☎415/552-4990). Castro emporium with a brilliant selection of dance music including a few Seventies twelve-inch singles. The accent is definitely on stuff you can dance to.

Discolandia, 2964 24th St at Mission (☎415/826-9446). Join the snake-hipped groovers looking for the latest in salsa and Central American sounds in this Mission outlet.

Groove Merchant Records, 687 Haight St (☎415/252-5766). Very groovy Lower Haight soul and jazz shop.

Jack's Record Cellar, 254 Scott St at Page (☎415/431-3047). The city's best source for American secondhand records – R&B, jazz, country and rock'n'roll. They'll track down rare discs and offer you the chance to listen before you buy.

Musica Latina/American Music Store, 2653 Mission St between 22nd and 23rd streets (☎415/664-5554). Mission store selling music from all over the continent, especially South America.

Rasputin's, 2401 Telegraph Ave. Open until 11pm, and good for jazz, rock and ethnic.

Reckless Records, 1401 Haight St at Masonic (☎415/431-3434). Specializes in independent music, buys and sells new and used.

Record Finder, 258 Noe St at Market (☎415/431-4443). One of the best independents, with a range as broad as it's absorbing. Take a wad and keep spending.

Recycled Records, 1377 Haight St at Masonic (☎415/626-4075). Good all-round store, with a decent selection of music publications, American and imported.

Rooky Ricardo's, 448 Haight St at Fillmore (☎415/864-7526). Albums and singles specializing in Fifties to Seventies soul, funk and jazz. Vinyl only.

Streetlight Records, 3979 24th St (☎415/282-3550). Also at 2350 Market St (☎415/282-8000). A great selection of used records, tapes and CDs. The perfect opportunity to beef up your collection on the cheap.

Tower Records Columbus Avenue and Bay Street, near Fisherman's Wharf (☎415/885-0500). Main San Francisco location of the multinational empire.

Virgin Megastore, 2 Stockton at the corner of Market Street (☎415/397-4525). As the name implies, it's a big shop, claiming to be "the largest music, media and book store in America."

Drugs, beauty products and toiletries

Body Time, 2072 Union St (☎415/922-4076), with outlets at 1932 Fillmore and in the Haight. Though this Bay Area-born company sold the original name to the UK-based Body Shop, they still put out a full range of aromatic natural bath oils, shampoos and skin creams, and will custom scent anything.

Common Scents, 3920 24th St (☎415/826-1019). Essential oils, bath salts as well as hair and skin-care products, stocked in bulk and sold by the ounce. They'll refill your empties.

Embarcadero Center Pharmacy, 1 Embarcadero Center (☎415/788-4511). Prescription drugs and general medical and toiletry supplies. Not open late.

Fairmont Pharmacy, 801 Powell St (☎415/362-3000). Huge pharmacy, perfumery and toiletry supply store that also has a good selection of maps and books on San Francisco.

Mandarin Pharmacy, 895 Washington St (☎415/989-9292). This amiable, well-stocked drugstore is a sanctuary in the bustle of Chinatown.

Skin Zone, 575 Castro St (☎415/626-7933). Every unguent imaginable at very reasonable prices. Look for Skin Zone's own brand for real bargains.

Walgreens, various locations around the city. 24hr pharmacies at 498 Castro St (☎415/861-6276), 3201 Divisadero (☎415/931-6415) and 25 Point Lobos between 42nd and 43rd Ave near Geary (☎415/386-0706). The largest chain pharmacy, selling prescription drugs and general medical supplies, as well as cosmetics and toiletries.

Miscellaneous

In among the **designer clothes** stores and **art galleries** of the Union Square area, a handful of stores sell treasureable objects; though prohibitively expensive, many repay a look-in at least. Check out also the countless **secondhand clothes** stores specializing in period costume, from Twenties gear to leftover hippy garb. Better still, explore the myriad of charitable **thrift stores**, where you can pick up high-quality cast-offs for next to nothing. In trendier shopping areas, such as Fillmore Street, these shops tend to have higher prices, along with niftier goods. We've also pulled together in this section some of the city's **miscellaneous** shops specializing in things you often need desperately but never know where to find.

American Rag Co, 1305 Van Ness Ave at Bush (☎415/474-5214). As secondhand clothing stores go, this one is expensive, but it's probably also superior to most others in San Francisco. Also a good collection of stylish new clothing.

Brooks Cameras, 125 Kearny St at Post (☎415/362-4708). High-quality camera store with full repair department.

Community Thrift, 625 Valencia St at 18th (☎415/861-4910). Gay thrift store in the Mission with clothing, furniture and general junk. All proceeds are ploughed back into local charities and AIDS organizations.

FAO Schwarz, 48 Stockton St at O'Farrell (☎415/394-8700). Mega-toystore on three floors designed to turn children into monsters.

Good Vibrations, 1210 Valencia St at 23rd (☎415/974-8980). Hard to describe with any delicacy. Dildo store, sex toy emporium and a great selection of adult books. Owned and operated by women who have created a safe and friendly atmosphere for women, men, and giddy couples to probe the depths of their sexuality (see p.445).

Gump's, 135 Post St at Kearny (☎415/982-1616). Famous for its jade, oriental rugs and objects cast in crystal, silver and china. Fuel for fantasies rather than genuine consumption.

Headlines, 838 Market St (☎415/989-8240) and 557 Castro St (☎415/626-8061). Good, cheap clothes and huge range of novelty gift items. Fun to browse, even if you don't want to spend any money.

San Francisco Symphony Thrift Store, 2223 Fillmore St (☎415/563-3123). Top-rate vintage clothing store in Pacific Heights, with flamboyant and original pieces going for top dollar.

St Vincent de Paul, 1519 Haight St. Also at 425 Fourth St at Harrison. Queen of the junk stores, St Vinnie's will keep you amused for hours. You could spend money all day and still have change from $50.

Worn Out West, 1850 Castro St at 19th (☎415/431-6020). Gay secondhand cowboy gear – a trip for browsing, and if you're serious about getting some Wild West kit, this is the least expensive place in town to pick out a good pair of boots, stylish Western shirts and chaps.

Listings

American Express 560 California St between Kearny and Montgomery (Mon–Fri 9am–5pm; ☎415/536-2600). Travel Service Office, 455 Market St at First Street (Mon-Fri 8.30am–5.30pm, Sat 9am–2pm). Also at 124 Geary St at Grant near Union Square (Mon-Fri 9am–6pm, Sat 9am–5pm; ☎415/398-8578).

Babysitting Bay Area Child Care (☎415/991-7474).

Car Rental All the major firms have branches in the airport. Here we've listed their offices in town: Alamo, 687 Folsom St (☎415/882-9440); Avis, 675 Post St (☎415/885-5011); Dollar, 364 O'Farrell St (☎415/771-5300); Enterprise, 1133 Van Ness Ave (☎415/441-3369); Hertz, 433 Mason St (☎415/771-2200); Reliable, 349 Mason St (☎415/928-4414).

Children San Francisco is very much a place for adults – more so than, say, LA, where Disneyland and Universal Studios are major attractions – and there aren't many things to occupy young ones. Of the few places that exist (they tend to be more learning-oriented than commercial), the Exploratorium in the Marina District is excellent, as is the Steinhart Aquarium in Golden Gate Park, and the Lawrence Hall of Science in Berkeley will captivate any young mind. For more organized distractions, try the Great America amusement park in Santa Clara, or the animal-themed Marine World/Africa USA in Vallejo, accessible by transbay ferry.

Churches Grace Cathedral on Nob Hill at 1051 Taylor St caters to an Episcopalian (Anglican) congregation, and Catholics can worship at St Mary's Cathedral, 600 California St.

Consulates UK, 1 Sansome St (☎415/981-3030); Ireland, 44 Montgomery St (☎415/392-4214); Australia (for New Zealand as well), 1 Bush St (☎415/362-6160); Netherlands, 1 Maritime Plaza (☎415/981-6454).

Dental Treatment San Francisco Dental Office, 131 Steuart St (☎415/777-5115). 24hr emergency service and comprehensive dental care.

Disabled Visitors Steep hills aside, the Bay Area is generally considered to be one of the most barrier-free cities around, and physically challenged travelers are well catered for. Most public buildings have been modified for disabled access, all BART stations are wheelchair-accessible, and most buses have lowering platforms for wheelchairs – and, usually, understanding drivers. The Center for Independent Living, 2539 Telegraph Ave in Berkeley (☎510/841-4776), has long been one of the most effective disabled people's organizations in the world; they have a variety of counselling services and are generally a useful resource.

Ferries Golden Gate Ferry, commute-hours to Sausalito and Larkspur in Marin County, leaves from the Ferry Building, east end of Market Street (☎415/923-6000); Red and White Fleet has bay cruises from Pier 43^1/$_2$, Fisherman's Wharf (☎415/447-0597); Blue and Gold Fleet bay ferries to Sausalito, Tiburon, Vallejo, and the Alcatraz island tour, from Pier 41 and 39, Fisherman's Wharf (☎415/705-5555).

Hospitals The San Francisco General Hospital, 1001 Potrero Ave (☎415/206-8000 or 206-8111 emergency), has a 24hr emergency walk-in service. Castro-Mission Health Center, 3850 17th St (☎415/487-7500), offers a drop-in medical service with charges on a sliding scale depending on income, and free contraception and pregnancy testing. Davies Medical Center, Castro and Duboce streets (☎415/565-6000) has 24-hr emergency care and a doctors' referral service. The Haight-Ashbury Free Clinic, 558 Clayton St (Mon–Thurs 9am–9pm, Fri 9am–5pm; ☎415/487-5632), provides a general health care service with special services for women and detoxification, by appointment only.

Left Luggage Greyhound, First and Mission St (☎415/495-1555); open daily 6am–8pm.

Legal Advice Lawyer Referral Service (☎415/764-1616).

Passport and Visa Office US Dept of Immigration, 630 Sansome St (☎1-800/755-0777).

Post Office You can collect general delivery mail (bring your ID) from the main post office, 101 Hyde St, in the Civic Center (Mon–Fri 8.30am–5.30pm, Sat 10am–2pm; ☎1-800/275-8777), but letters will only be held for thirty days before being returned to sender, so make sure there's a return address on the envelope. If you're receiving mail at someone else's address, it should include "c/o" and the regular occupant's name; otherwise it too is likely to be returned.

Main Public Library Civic Center, at Fulton and Larkin streets (☎415/557-4400). Mon 10am–6pm, Tues–Thurs 9am–8pm, Fri 11am–5pm, Sat 9am–5pm, Sun noon–5pm.

Sports Advance tickets for all Bay Area sports events are available through the BASS charge-by-phone ticket service (☎510/762-BASS), as well as from the teams themselves. Baseball: the San Francisco Giants play at often cold and foggy Candlestick (now 3COM) Park, south of the city (☎415/467-8000), while Oakland's A's play at the usually sunny Oakland Coliseum (☎510/638-0500). Ticket prices range from $4 for bleacher seats to $125 for a field-side box. Basketball: the Golden State Warriors play at the Oakland Arena (☎510/762-BASS). Football: the fabulous San Francisco 49ers, many-time Super Bowl champions, also appear at 3COM Park (☎415/468-2249). All tickets are priced at $50. Ice hockey: the Bay Area's newest sports team is the San Jose Sharks (☎408/287-7070), based at their own arena in the South Bay.

Tax In San Francisco and the Bay Area the sales tax is 7.5 percent, plus a 0.5 percent "earthquake" tax. Hotel tax will add fourteen percent onto your bill.

Telegrams Western Union, citywide locations. Call ☎1-800/325-6000 to find the nearest.

Travel Agents Council Travel, 530 Bush St (☎415/421-3473); STA Travel, 51 Grant Ave (☎415/391-8407).

Whale-watching The nonprofit Oceanic Society, Building E, Fort Mason Center (☎415/441-1104), runs seven-hour boat trips from the Marina to observe the gray whales on their migration from Alaska to Baja. Incredible, but even the strongest constitutions will need travel sickness pills to survive the choppy seas in the small boat. Trips cost $50 and should be booked in advance.

THE BAY AREA

Of the six million people who make their home in the San Francisco **Bay Area**, only a lucky one in eight lives in the actual city of San Francisco. Everyone else is spread around one of the many smaller cities and suburbs that ring the bay, either down the Peninsula or across one of the two impressively engineered bridges that span the chilly waters of the world's most exquisite natural harbor. There's no doubt about the supporting role these places play in relation to San Francisco – always "The City" – but each has a distinctive character, and contributes to the range of people and landscapes that makes the Bay Area one of the most desirable places in the US to live or to visit.

Across the center steel **Bay Bridge**, eight miles from downtown San Francisco, the **East Bay** is home to the lively, left-leaning cities of **Oakland** and **Berkeley**, which together have some of the best bookstores and restaurants, and most of the live music venues in the greater Bay Area. The weather's generally much sunnier and warmer here too, and it's easy to reach by way of the space-age BART trains that race under the bay. The remainder of the East Bay is filled out by Contra Costa County, which includes the short-lived early state capital of California – the near-ghost town of **Benicia** – as well as the former homes of writers John Muir and Eugene O'Neill.

South of the city, the Peninsula holds some of San Francisco's oldest and most upscale suburbs, spreading down through the computer-rich **Silicon Valley** and into **San Jose** – California's fastest-growing city – though apart from some fancy houses there's not a lot to see. To the west, however, the **beaches** are excellent – sandy, clean and uncrowded – and there's a couple of youth hostels in old lighthouses perched on the edge of the Pacific.

For some of the most beautiful land- and seascapes in California, cross the Golden Gate Bridge or ride a ferry boat across the bay to **Marin County**, a mountainous peninsula that's one-half wealthy suburbia and one-half unspoiled hiking country, with **redwood forests** rising sheer out of the thundering Pacific Ocean. A range of 2500-foot peaks divides the county down the middle, separating the yacht clubs and plush bay-view houses of **Sausalito** and **Tiburon** from the nearly untouched wilderness that runs along the Pacific coast, through Muir Woods and the Point Reyes National Seashore. North of Marin County, at the top of the bay, and still within an hour's drive of San Francisco, the Wine Country regions of the Sonoma and Napa Valleys make an excellent day-trip; they're detailed in "Northern California," beginning on p.535.

The East Bay

The largest and most-traveled bridge in California, the **Bay Bridge** heads east from downtown San Francisco, part graceful suspension bridge and part heavy-duty steel truss. Built in 1933 as an economic booster during the Depression, the bridge is made from enough steel cable to wrap around the earth three times. Completed just seven months before the more famous (and better-loved) Golden Gate, it works a lot harder for a lot less respect: a hundred million vehicles cross the bridge each year, though you'd have to search hard to find a postcard of it. Indeed, its only claim to fame – apart from the much-broadcast videotape of its partial collapse during the 1989 earthquake – is that Treasure Island, where the two halves of the bridge meet, hosted the 1939 World's Fair. During World War II the island became a Navy base, which, pending post-Cold War closures, it remains; just inside the gates there's a small museum (daily 10am–3pm; free) with pictures of the Fair amid maritime memorabilia. The island also offers great views of San Francisco and the Golden Gate.

The Bay Bridge empties into **Oakland**, a hard-working, blue-collar city that is at the heart of the East Bay. The city earns its livelihood from shipping and transportation services, as evidenced by the enormous cranes in the massive Port of Oakland, dominating the horizon like futuristic dinosaurs. Oakland spreads north along wooded foothills to **Berkeley**, an image-conscious university town that looks out across to the Golden Gate and collects a mixed bag of pinstriped Young Republicans, much-pierced dropouts, ageing 1960s radicals, and Nobel prize-winning nuclear physicists in its cafés and bookstores.

Berkeley and Oakland blend together so much as to be virtually the same city, and the hills above them are topped by a twenty-mile string of forested **regional parks**, providing much needed fresh air and quick relief from the concrete grids below. The rest of the East Bay is filled out by Contra Costa County, a huge area that contains some intriguing, historically important waterfront towns – well worth a detour if you're passing through on the way to the Wine Country region of the Napa and Sonoma valleys – as well as some of the Bay Area's most inward-looking suburban sprawl. Curving around the **North Bay** from the heavy-industrial landscape of Richmond, and facing each other across the narrow **Carquinez Strait**, both Benicia and Port Costa were vitally important during California's first twenty years of existence after the 1849 Gold Rush; they're now strikingly sited but little-visited ghost towns. In contrast, standing out from the soulless dormitory communities that fill up the often baking hot **inland valleys**, are the preserved homes of an unlikely pair of influential writers: the naturalist John Muir, who, when not out hiking around Yosemite and the High Sierra, lived most of his life near **Martinez**, and playwright Eugene O'Neill, who wrote many of his angst-ridden works at the foot of **Mount Diablo**, the Bay Area's most impressive peak.

Arrival

You're most likely to be staying in San Francisco when you visit the East Bay, though it is possible and sometimes better value to fly direct to **Oakland Airport**, particularly if you're coming from elsewhere in the US. Domestic airlines which serve the airport include American, Southwest, America West and Delta. It's an easy trip from the airport into town: take the AirBART Shuttle van (every 15min; $2) from outside the terminal direct to the Coliseum BART station, from where you can reach Oakland, Berkeley, or San Francisco. In addition, various privately operated shuttle buses cost from $10.

Oakland's Greyhound **bus station** is in a dubious part of town, alongside the I-980 freeway on San Pablo Avenue at 21st. Amtrak **trains** terminate at Second Street near Jack London Square in Oakland, though it's a better option to get off at Richmond and change there onto BART.

The most enjoyable way to arrive in the East Bay is aboard a Blue and Gold Fleet **ferry** ($4 each way; ☎415/773-1188), which sails every hour from San Francisco's Ferry Building and Pier 39 to Oakland's Jack London Square.

Getting around

The East Bay is linked to San Francisco via the underground BART transbay **subway** (Mon–Fri 4am–midnight, Sat 6am–midnight, Sun 8am–midnight). Three lines run from Daly City through San Francisco and on to downtown Oakland, before diverging to service East Oakland out to Fremont, Berkeley, north to Richmond, and east into Contra Costa County as far as Concord. Fares range from $1.10–4.45, and the cost of each ride is deducted from the total value of the ticket, purchased from machines on the station concourse. If you're relying on BART to get around a lot, buy a **high-value ticket** ($5 or $10) to avoid having to stand in line to buy a new ticket each time you ride. To phone BART from San Francisco dial ☎650/992-2278; from the East Bay ☎510/465-2278.

From East Bay BART stations, pick up a **free transfer** saving you 25¢ on the $1.25 fares of AC Transit (☎510/839-2882), which provides a good **bus service** around the entire East Bay area, especially Oakland and Berkeley. AC Transit also runs buses on a number of routes to Oakland and Berkeley from the Transbay Terminal in San Francisco. These operate all night, and are the only way of getting across the bay by public transit once BART has shut down. You can pick up excellent free maps of both BART and the bus system from any station. A smaller-scale bus company that can also prove useful, the Contra Costa County Connection (☎510/676-7500), runs buses to most of the inland areas, including the John Muir and Eugene O'Neill historic houses.

One of the best ways to get around is by bike; a fine **cycle route** follows Skyline and Grizzly Peak Boulevards along the wooded crest of the hills between Berkeley and Lake Chabot. If you haven't got one, rent touring bikes or mountain bikes from Carl's Bikes (☎510/835-8763), 2416 Telegraph Ave in Oakland, and from Cal Adventures (☎510/642-4000), 2301 Bancroft Way on the UC Berkeley campus. For those interested in **walking tours**, the city of Oakland sponsors free "discovery tours" (☎510/238-3050) of various neighborhoods.

If you're **driving**, allow yourself plenty of time to get there: the East Bay has some of California's worst traffic, with I-80 in particular jam-packed sixteen hours a day.

Information

The **Oakland Visitor Information Booth**, on Broadway between Water Street and Embarcadero Street in Jack London Square (daily 11am–5pm; ☎1-800/262-5526), offers free maps and information, as does the **Berkeley CVB**, 2015 Center St (Mon–Fri 9am–5pm; ☎510/549-7040). The **Berkeley Trip Commute Store** (Mon–Wed & Fri 8.30am–5.30pm, Thurs 9am–6pm; ☎510/644-7665), right beside the visitor center at 2033 Center St, sells passes to all Bay Area transit systems and can help you figure out how to get just about anywhere on public transportation. If you're spending any time at all in the Berkeley area, pick up a copy of *Berkeley Inside/Out* by Don Pitcher (Heyday Books, $12.95), an informative guide that'll tell you everything you ever wanted to know about the town and its inhabitants. For information on hiking or horseriding in the many parks that top the Oakland and Berkeley hills, contact the **East Bay Regional Parks District**, 11500 Skyline Blvd (☎510/562-7275). The widely available (and free) *East Bay Express* has the most comprehensive listings of what's on in the vibrant East Bay music and arts scene. The troubled daily *Oakland Tribune* (50¢) is also worth a look for its coverage of local politics and sporting events.

East Bay accommodation

Surprisingly, it's not a great deal cheaper to stay in the East Bay than in San Francisco, and, in truth, there's little to choose from anyway. **Motels** and **hotels**, at $40–60 a night, are slightly better value for money than their San Francisco equivalents, and there are a couple of **dorm-bed** places for those on a budget. **Bed and breakfast** is a more pleasant option, and there are also a couple of **campgrounds**, though these are hard to reach without a car.

Hotels, motels and B&Bs

Claremont Hotel, 41 Tunnel Rd at Ashby Avenue on the Oakland/Berkeley border (☎510/843-3000). At the top end of the scale, this enormous Victorian palace has panoramic bay view rooms and all-inclusive "weekend breaks." ⑧.

Dean's Bed & Breakfast, 480 Pedestrian Way, Oakland (☎510/652-5024). A hidden and inexpensive room with pool, private entrance and Japanese garden tucked away in Rockridge. Pleasant owner who stays out of your way; reserve in advance. ④.

Durant, 2600 Durant Ave, Berkeley (☎1-800/238-7268 or 510/845-8981). Fairly plain but well worn and comfortable hotel, and very handy for the UC Berkeley campus. ⑥.

East Brother Light Station, 117 Park Place, San Pablo Bay (☎510/233-2385). A handful of rooms in a converted lighthouse, on an island in the middle of the bay. Not a handy base for seeing the sights, this is a retreat and adventure for an evening. Prices include highly rated gourmet dinners as well as breakfast. ⑨.

Elmwood House, 2609 College Ave, Berkeley (☎510/540-5123). Attractive, turn-of-the-century house with B&B rooms, not far from UC Berkeley. ④.

French, 1538 Shattuck Ave, North Berkeley (☎510/548-9930). Small and comfortable hotel, in the heart of Berkeley's Gourmet Ghetto. ⑤.

Golden Bear Motel, 1620 San Pablo Ave, West Berkeley (☎1-800/525-6770 or 510/525-6770). The most pleasant of the many motels in the "flatlands" of West Berkeley, though somewhat out of the way. ③.

Gramma's, 2740 Telegraph Ave, Berkeley (☎510/549-2145). Pleasant, if slightly dull, rooms with fireplaces in a pretty mock-Tudor mansion half a mile south of UC Berkeley. ⑤.

Holiday Inn Bay Bridge, 1800 Powell St, Emeryville (☎510/658-9300). Not outrageously pricey considering the great views to be had from the upper floors. Free parking. ⑥.

Mac, 10 Cottage Ave, Point Richmond (☎510/235-0010). Built in 1907, the recently refurbished *Hotel Mac* boasts luxurious rooms with unbeatable prices. This was supposedly John Rockefeller's favorite place to stay when visiting his Standard Oil enterprise. ⑥.

Marriott, 200 Marina Blvd, Berkeley (☎1-800/228-9290 or 510/548-7920). Comfortable hotel verging on the upscale. Some rooms have a view of the bay. ⑥.

Ramada Inn, 920 University Ave, Berkeley (☎1-800/954-7575 or 510/849-1121). Bargain rooms with live music nightly, mostly blues. Near Berkeley Marina. ③.

Shattuck, 2086 Allston Way, Berkeley (☎510/845-7300). Very central and well-restored hotel, near Berkeley BART. ⑤.

Travelodge, 423 Seventh St, downtown Oakland (☎1-800/255-3050 or 510/451-6316). Spacious rooms, some of which have kitchens, make this a good option for families or groups. ④.

Union Hotel and Gardens, 401 First St, Benicia (☎707/746-0100). A bordello from 1882 until 1950, since converted into a comfortable bed and breakfast with twelve rooms. ⑤.

Waterfront Plaza, 10 Washington St, Oakland (☎1-800/729-3638 or 510/836-3800). Newly redecorated hotel, located on the best stretch of the Oakland waterfront. ⑦.

Hostels

Berkeley YMCA, 2001 Allston Way, Berkeley (☎510/848-6800). Ideal East Bay mixed-sex accommodation a block from the Berkeley BART, with single rooms for $25, including use of gym and swimming pool.

Haste-Channing Summer Visitor Housing, 2424 Channing Ave, Berkeley (☎510/642-4444). Summer-only dorm rooms for $50.

Campgrounds

Chabot Family Campground, off I-580 in East Oakland (☎510/562-2267). Walk-in, tent-only places, with hot showers and lots of good hiking nearby; reserve through Parknet ☎1-800/444-7275 in summer; $20.

Mount Diablo State Park, 20 miles east of Oakland off I-680 in Contra Costa County (☎510/837-2525). RV and tent places; likewise, book through Parknet ☎1-800/444-7275 in summer; $16.

Oakland

A quick trip across the Bay Bridge or on BART brings you to **OAKLAND**, a solidly working-class counterbalance to upwardly mobile San Francisco: the workhorse of the Bay Area, one of the busiest ports on the West Coast, and the western terminal of the rail network. It's not all hard slog, though: the climate is rated the best in the US, often sunny and mild when San Francisco is cold and dreary, and, despite the 1991 fire that ravaged the area, there's great hiking around the redwood- and eucalyptus-covered hills above the city – featuring views of the entire Bay Area.

Oakland has more historical and literary associations than important sights. **Gertrude Stein** and **Jack London** both grew up in the city, at about the same time though in entirely different circumstances – Stein was a stockbroker's daughter, London an orphaned delinquent. The macho and adventurous London is far better remembered – most of the waterfront, where he used to steal oysters and lobsters, is now named in his memory – while Stein is all but ignored. Perhaps this is due to her book, *Everybody's Autobiography*, in which she wrote: "What was the use of me having come from Oakland, it was not natural for me to have come from there yes write about it if I like or anything

OAKLAND

- MacArthur (BART)
- Berkeley
- Mosswood Park
- San Francisco
- W. MACARTHUR BOULEVARD
- MACARTHUR BOULEVARD
- Morcom Rose Garden
- ADELINE STREET
- SAN PABLO AVENUE
- MARKET STREET
- TELEGRAPH AVENUE
- BROADWAY
- GRAND AVENUE
- OAKLAND AVENUE
- PIEDMONT AVENUE
- East Oakland
- WEST GRAND AVENUE
- MANDELA PARKWAY (CYPRESS STREET)
- PERALTA STREET
- 18TH STREET
- Children's Fairyland
- Paramount Theater
- Greyhound Station
- 19th St (BART)
- City Hall
- 14TH STREET
- 12TH STREET
- 12th St (BART)
- Lakeside Park
- BELLEVUE AVENUE
- LAKESHORE AVENUE
- Sailboat House
- 18TH STREET
- HARRISON STREET
- 14TH STREET
- LAKESIDE DRIVE
- Lake Merritt
- PARK BLVD
- Chamber of Commerce
- SEVENTH STREET
- West Oakland (BART)
- Oakland Museum
- Lake Merritt (BART)
- FOOTHILL BLVD
- E. 14TH STREET
- Produce Market
- Amtrak Station
- JEFFERSON ST
- WASHINGTON ST
- EMBARCADERO
- E. EIGHTH ST.
- EMBARCADERO
- East Oakland
- N
- Jack London Square
- Estuary Park
- Inner Harbor
- WEBSTER STREET
- 0   400 yds
- ALAMEDA

ACCOMMODATION
1 Dean's Bed & Breakfast
2 Holiday Inn Bay Bridge
3 Travelodge
4 Waterfront Plaza Hotel

if I like but not there, there is no *there* there" – a quote which has haunted Oakland ever since. The city's businesses have a history of deserting their hometown when the going gets good, and even its football team, the Raiders, defected to Los Angeles for thirteen years before returning in 1995. Nonetheless, the majority of Oaklanders stick with the city, and would argue that there is indeed a *there* there, notably in the small and trendy communities of Rockridge, Piedmont Avenue and the lively Grant Avenue.

Jack London's mildly socialist leanings set a style for the city, and Oakland has been the breeding ground for some of America's most unabashedly revolutionary **political movements** ever since. The 1960s saw the city's fifty-percent black population find a voice through the militant Black Panther movement, and in the 1970s Oakland was again on the nation's front pages, when the Symbionese Liberation Army demanded free food distribution to the city's poor as ransom for kidnapped heiress Patty Hearst. Oakland is still very much its own city, and it's worth taking the time to get a feel for its diversity and dynamism.

Downtown Oakland

Coming by BART from San Francisco, get off at the 12th Street–Civic Center station and you're in **downtown Oakland**, a compact district of spruced-up Victorian store-fronts overlooked by modern hotels and office buildings that has been in the midst of an ambitious program of restoration and redevelopment for over a decade. Fraught with allegations of illegal dealings and incompetent planning, so far the program has been less than a complete success. To make way for the moat-like I-980 freeway – the main route through Oakland since the collapse of the Cypress Freeway in the 1989 earthquake – entire blocks were cleared of houses, some of which were saved and moved to **Preservation Park** at 12th Street and Martin Luther King Jr Way. The late nineteenth-century commercial center along Ninth Street west of Broadway, now tagged **Victorian Row**, underwent a major restoration some years ago, but many of the buildings are still waiting for tenants. By way of contrast stroll a block east of Broadway, between Seventh and Ninth, to Oakland's **Chinatown**, whose bakeries and restaurants are as lively and bustling – if not as picturesque – as those of its more famous cousin across the Bay.

Luckily, not all of downtown Oakland has the look of a permanent building site. The city experienced its greatest period of growth in the early twentieth century, and many of the grand buildings of this era survive a few blocks north along Broadway, centered on the awkwardly imposing 1914 **City Hall** on 14th Street. Two blocks away at 13th and Franklin stands Oakland's most unmistakable landmark, the chateauesque lantern of the **Tribune Tower**, the 1920s-era home of the *Oakland Tribune* newspaper.

Further north, around the 19th Street BART station, are some of the Bay Area's finest early twentieth-century buildings, highlighted by the outstanding Art Deco interior of the 1931 **Paramount Theater** at 2025 Broadway (tours 10am first and third Sat of the month; $1; ☎510/465-6400), which shows Hollywood classics, and hosts occasional concerts and performances. Nearby buildings are equally flamboyant, ranging from the wafer-thin Gothic "flatiron" office tower of the **Cathedral Building** at Broadway and Telegraph, to the Hindu temple-like facade of the magnificent 3500-seat **Fox Oakland** (now closed) on Telegraph at 19th – the largest movie house west of Chicago at the time it was built in 1928 – and, across the street, the 1931 **Floral Depot**, a group of small modern storefronts faced in black-and-blue terra-cotta tiles with shiny silver highlights.

West of Broadway, the area around the Greyhound bus station on San Pablo Avenue is fairly seedy. San Pablo used to be the main route in and out of Oakland before the freeways were built, but many of the roadside businesses are now derelict, especially around the industrial districts of **Emeryville**. Some of the old warehouses have been converted into artists' lofts and studios, though any gentrification there might be is diffused by the scenes on the street, where prostitutes and drug-dealers hang out under the neon signs of the dingy bars and gambling halls such as the *Oaks Card Club*, where "Oaktown" (the local name for Oakland) rapper M.C. Hammer, who once made the city proud, used to work.

Lake Merritt and the Oakland Museum

Five blocks east of Broadway, the eastern third of downtown Oakland comprises **Lake Merritt**, a three-mile-circumference tidal lagoon that was bridged and dammed in the 1860s to become the centerpiece of Oakland's most desirable neighborhood. All that remains of the many fine houses that once circled the lake is the elegant **Camron-Stanford House**, on the southwest shore at 1418 Lakeside Drive, a graceful Italianate mansion whose sumptuous interior is open for visits (Wed 11am–4pm, Sun 1–5pm; $4). The lake is also the nation's oldest wildlife refuge, and migrating flocks of ducks, geese, and herons break their journeys here. **Lakeside Park** lines the north shore, where you can rent canoes and row-boats ($4 per hour), and a range of sailing boats and catamarans

($4–10 per hour) from the **Sailboat House** (summer daily 10am–5pm; winter Fri–Sun 10am–4.30pm; ☎510/238-2196) – provided you can convince the staff you know how to sail. A miniature Mississippi riverboat makes thirty-minute lake **cruises** ($1) on weekend afternoons, and kids will like the puppet shows and pony rides at the **Children's Fairyland** (summer daily 10am–5.30pm; winter Fri–Sun 10am–5.30pm; $3.25), along Grand Avenue on the northwest edge of the park. Every year, on the first weekend in June, the park comes to life during the **Festival at the Lake**, when all of Oakland gets together to enjoy nonstop music and performances from local bands and entertainers.

Two blocks south of the lake, or a block up Oak Street from the Lake Merritt BART station, the **Oakland Museum** (Wed–Sat 10am–5pm, Sun noon–7pm; $5, free Sun after 4pm) is perhaps Oakland's most worthwhile stop, not only for the exhibits but also for the superb modern building in which it's housed, topped by a terraced rooftop sculpture garden that gives great views out over the water and the city. The museum covers many diverse areas: displays on the **ecology** of California, including a simulated walk from the seaside through various natural habitats up to the 14,000-foot summits of the Sierra Nevada mountains; state history, ranging from old mining equipment to the guitar that Berkeley-born Country Joe MacDonald played at the Woodstock festival in 1969; and a broad survey of works by California artists and craftspeople, some highlights of which are pieces of turn-of-the-century **arts and crafts furniture**. You'll also see excellent **photography** by Edward Muybridge, Dorothea Lange, Imogen Cunningham and many others. The museum has a collector's gallery that rents and sells works by California artists.

The waterfront, Alameda, and West Oakland

Half a mile down from Downtown Oakland on AC Transit bus #51, at the foot of Broadway on the Waterfront, **Jack London Square** is Oakland's sole concession to the tourist trade. Also accessible by direct ferry from San Francisco (see "Arrival"; p.450), this somewhat anesthetic complex of harborfront boutiques and restaurants was named after the self-taught writer who grew up pirating shellfish around here, but is about as distant from the spirit of the man as it's possible to get. Jack London's best story, *The Call of the Wild*, was written about his adventures in the Alaskan Yukon, where he carved his initials in a small cabin that has been reconstructed here; another survivor is *Heinhold's First and Last Chance Saloon*, a seedy bar where London spent much of his wayward youth.

If you're not a keen fan of London (and if you are, you'd be better off visiting his Sonoma Valley ranch – see p.546), there are still a few worthwhile things to do here. **The Ebony Museum of Arts** at 30 Alice St on the second floor (Tues–Sun noon–6pm; donation) is worth a visit for its African art and pop American counterculture collectibles. Otherwise, walk a few short blocks inland to the **Produce Marke**t, along Third and Fourth streets, where a couple of good places to eat and drink lurk among the rail tracks (see "Eating" on p.466). This bustling warehouse district has fruit and vegetables by the forklift load, and is at its most lively early in the morning, from about 5am.

AC Transit bus #51 continues from Broadway under the inner harbor to **Alameda**, a quiet and conservative island of middle America dominated by a large, empty naval air station, one of the first to be closed by President Bill Clinton in 1995 – although massive nuclear-powered aircraft carriers still dock here occasionally. Alameda, which has been hit very hard by post-Cold War military cutbacks, was severed from the Oakland mainland as part of a harbor improvement program in 1902. The fine houses along the original shoreline on Clinton Street were part of the summer resort colony that flocked here to the *contra costa* or "opposite shore" from San Francisco, near the now demolished Neptune Beach amusement park. The island has since been much enlarged by dredging and landfill, and 1960s apartment buildings now line the long, narrow shore of **Robert Crown Memorial Beach** along the bay – a quiet, attractive spot.

West Oakland – an industrial district of warehouses, rail tracks, 1960s housing projects and decaying Victorian houses – may be the nearest East Bay BART stop to San Francisco, but it's light years away from that city's prosperity. Despite the obvious poverty, it's quite a safe and settled place, but the only time anyone pays any attention to it is when something dramatic happens; in the double-whammy year of 1989, for example, when Black Panther Huey Newton was gunned down here in a drugs-related revenge attack, and the double-decker I-880 freeway that divided the neighborhood from the rest of the city collapsed in on itself during the earthquake, killing dozens of commuters.

Local people have successfully resisted government plans to rebuild the old concrete eyesore, which is currently being rerouted closer to the harbor; the broad and potentially very attractive **Nelson Mandela Parkway** has replaced it. Otherwise, this remains one of the Bay Area's poorest and most neglected neighborhoods, and apart from a marvelous stock of turn-of-the-century houses there's little here to tempt tourists.

East Oakland

The bulk of Oakland spreads along foothills and flatlands to the east of downtown, in neighborhoods obviously stratified along the main thoroughfares of Foothill and MacArthur boulevards. Gertrude Stein grew up here, though when she returned years later in search of her childhood home it had been torn down and replaced by a dozen Craftsman-style bungalows – the simple 1920s wooden houses that cover most of **East Oakland**, each fronted by a patch of lawn and divided from its neighbor by a narrow concrete driveway.

A quick way out from the gridded streets and sidewalks of the city is to take AC Transit bus #15 from downtown east up into the hills to Joaquin Miller Park, the most easily accessible of Oakland's hilltop parks. It stands on the former grounds of the home of the "Poet of the Sierras", Joaquin Miller, who made his name playing the eccentric frontier American in the literary salons of 1870s London. His poems weren't exactly acclaimed (his greatest poetic achievement was rhyming "teeth" with "Goethe"), although his prose account, *Life Amongst the Modocs*, documenting time spent with the Modoc people near Mount Shasta, does stand the test of time. It was more for his outrageous behavior that he became famous, wearing bizarre clothes and biting debutantes on the ankle.

Perched in the hills at the foot of the park, the pointed towers of the **Mormon Temple** look like missile-launchers designed by the Wizard of Oz – unmissable by day or floodlit night. In December, speakers hidden in the landscaping make it seem as if the plants are singing Christmas carols. Though you can't go inside (unless you're a confirmed Mormon), there are great views out over the entire Bay Area, and a small museum explains the tenets of the faith (daily 9am–9pm; free).

Some twenty miles of tract house suburbs stretch along the bay south to San Jose, and the only vaguely interesting area is around the end of the BART line in **FREMONT**, where the short-lived Essanay movie studios were based. Essanay, the first studios on the West Coast, made over 700 films in three years, including Charlie Chaplin's *The Tramp* in 1914. Not much remains from these pre-Hollywood days, however, and the only real sight is the **Mission San Jose de Guadalupe** on Mission Boulevard south of the I-680 freeway (daily 10am–5pm; donation), which in the best traditions of Hollywood set design was completely rebuilt in Mission style only a few years ago.

North Oakland and Rockridge

The horrific October 1991 **Oakland fire**, which destroyed 3000 homes and killed 26 people, did most of its damage in the high-priced hills of North Oakland. It took the better part of two years, but most of the half-million dollar houses have been rebuilt, and though the lush vegetation that made the area so attractive will never be allowed to grow back, things are pretty much back to normal. Which is to say that these bay-view homes, some of the Bay Area's most valuable real estate, look out across some of its poorest – the neglected flatlands below that in the 1960s were the proving grounds of Black Panthers Bobby Seale and Huey Newton.

Broadway is the dividing line between the two halves of North Oakland, and also gives access (via the handy AC Transit #51 bus) to most of what there is to see and do. The **Oakland Rose Garden**, on Oakland Avenue three blocks east of Broadway (April–Oct daily dawn–dusk; free), repays a look if you come during the day. One of Oakland's most neighborly streets, **Piedmont Avenue**, runs in between, lined by a number of small bookstores and cafés. At the north end of Piedmont Avenue, the **Mountain View Cemetery** was laid out in 1863 by Frederick Law Olmsted (designer of New York's Central Park) and holds the elaborate dynastic tombs of San Francisco's most powerful families – the Crockers, the Bechtels and the Ghirardellis. You can jog or ride a bike around the well-tended grounds, or just wonder at the enormous turtles in the pond.

Back on Broadway, just past College Avenue, Broadway Terrace climbs up along the edge of the fire area to **Lake Temescal** – where you can swim in summer – and continues up on up to the forested ridge at the **Robert Sibley Regional Preserve**. This includes the 1761-foot volcanic cone of Round Top Peak and offers panoramas of the entire Bay Area. Skyline Boulevard runs through the park and is popular with cyclists, who ride the twelve miles south to Lake Chabot or follow Grizzly Peak Boulevard five miles north to Tilden Park through the Berkeley Hills.

Most of the Broadway traffic, and the AC Transit #51 bus, cuts off onto College Avenue through Oakland's most upscale shopping district, **Rockridge**. Spreading for half a mile on either side of the Rockridge BART station, the quirky stores and restaurants here, despite their undeniable yuppie overtones, are some of the best around and make for a pleasant afternoon's wander.

Berkeley

This Berkeley was like no somnolent Siwash out of her own past at all, but more akin to those Far Eastern or Latin American universities you read about, those autonomous culture media where the most beloved of folklores may be brought into doubt, cataclysmic of dissents voiced, suicidal of commitments chosen – the sort that bring governments down.

Thomas Pynchon *The Crying of Lot 49*

More than any other American town, **BERKELEY** conjures up an image of 1960s student dissent. During that era, when university campuses were protesting against the Vietnam War, it was the students of the University of California, Berkeley, who led the charge, gaining a name for themselves as the vanguard of what was increasingly seen as a challenge to the very authority of the state. Full-scale battles were fought almost daily here at one point, on the campus and on the streets of the surrounding town, and there were times when Berkeley looked almost on the brink of revolution itself: students (and others) throwing stones and gas bombs were met with tear-gas volleys and truncheons by National Guard troops under the nominal command of the then-Governor Ronald Reagan. It was, of course, inspired by the mood of the time, and in an increasingly conservative America, Berkeley politics are nowadays decidedly middle-of-the-road. But despite an influx of non-rebellious students, a thriving bedrock of exclusive California cuisine restaurants, and the dismantling of the city's rent control program, something of the progressive legacy does still linger in the many small bookstores and regular political demonstrations, if not on the agenda of the city council.

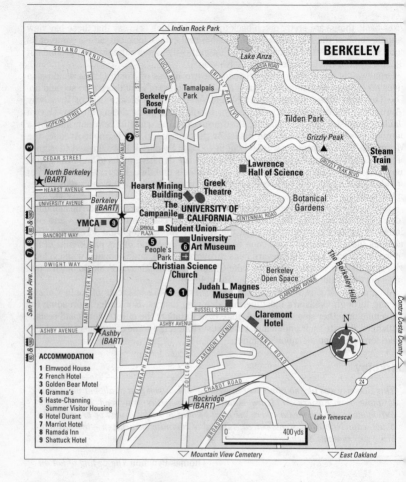

BERKELEY

△ Indian Rock Park

Lake Anza

SOLANO AVENUE

SHASTA ROAD

Tamalpais
Park

Berkeley
Rose
Garden

Tilden Park

Grizzly Peak ▲

Steam
Train

CEDAR STREET

North Berkeley
(BART) ★

Lawrence
Hall of Science

HEARST AVENUE

Hearst Mining
Building

Greek
Theatre

Botanical
Gardens

UNIVERSITY AVENUE

Berkeley
(BART)

The
Campanile

UNIVERSITY OF
CALIFORNIA

CENTENNIAL ROAD

YMCA

Student Union

BANCROFT WAY

SPROUL
PLAZA

University
Art Museum

People's
Park

DWIGHT WAY

Christian Science
Church

Berkeley
Open Space

Judah L. Magnes
Museum

RUSSELL STREET

Claremont
Hotel

ASHBY AVENUE

ASHBY AVENUE

Ashby
(BART) ★

The Berkeley Hills

Contra Costa County

N

ACCOMMODATION
1 Elmwood House
2 French Hotel
3 Golden Bear Motel
4 Gramma's
5 Haste-Channing
  Summer Visitor Housing
6 Hotel Durant
7 Marriot Hotel
8 Ramada Inn
9 Shattuck Hotel

Rockridge
(BART) ★

CHABOT ROAD

BROADWAY

Lake Temescal

24

0   400 yds

▽ Mountain View Cemetery   ▽ East Oakland

The **University of California**, right in the center of town, completely dominates
Berkeley and makes a logical starting point for a visit. Its many grand buildings and
30,000 students give off a definite energy that spills down the raucous stretch of
Telegraph Avenue which runs south from the campus and holds most of the
studenty hangouts, including a dozen or so lively cafés, as well as a number of fine
bookstores. Older students, and a good percentage of the faculty, congregate in the
Northside area, popping down from their woodsy hillside homes to partake of goodies from the "Gourmet Ghetto", a stretch of Shattuck Avenue crammed with restaurants, delis, and bakeries. Of quite distinct character are the flatlands that spread
through **West Berkeley** down to the bay, a poorer but increasingly gentrified district
that mixes old Victorian houses with builder's yards and light industrial premises.
Along the bay itself is the **Berkeley Marina**, where you can rent sailboards and sail-
boats or just watch the sun set behind the Golden Gate.

The University of California

Caught up in the frantic crush of students who pack the **University of California** campus during the semesters, it's nearly impossible to imagine the bucolic learning environment envisaged by its high-minded founders. When the Reverend Henry Durant and other East Coast academics decided to set up shop here in the 1860s, these rolling foothills were still largely given over to dairy herds and wheatfields, the last remnants of the Peralta family's Spanish land-grant rancho which once stretched over most of the East Bay. Construction work on the two campus buildings – imaginatively named North Hall and South Hall – was still going on when the first 200 students, including 22 women, moved here from Oakland in 1873. Since then an increasing number of buildings have been squeezed into the half-mile-square main campus, and the state-funded university has become one of America's most highly respected, with so many Nobel laureates on the faculty that it's said you have to win one just to get a parking permit. Overcrowding aside, the beautifully landscaped campus, stepping down from the eucalyptus-covered Berkeley Hills toward the Golden Gate, is eminently strollable. With maps posted everywhere, you'd have to try hard to get lost – though enthusiastic students will show you around on a free ninety-minute **tour** (Mon–Sat 10am, Sun 1pm; ☎510/642-5215).

A number of footpaths climb the hill from the Berkeley BART station on Shattuck Avenue, but the best way to get a feel for the place is to follow Strawberry Creek from the top of Center Street across the southeast corner of the campus, emerging from the groves of redwood and eucalyptus trees at **Sproul Plaza**. It's the newest and largest public space on campus, enlivened by street musicians playing for quarters on the steps of the **Student Union** building and conga drummers pounding away in the echoing courtyard below. **Sather Gate**, which bridges Strawberry Creek at the north end of Sproul Plaza, marks the entrance to the older part of the campus. Up the hill, past the imposing facade of Wheeler Hall, the 1914 landmark **Campanile** (daily 10am–4.30pm; $1) is modeled after the one in the Piazza San Marco in Venice; take an elevator to the top for a great view of the campus and the entire Bay Area. At the foot of the tower stands red-brick **South Hall**, the sole survivor of the original pair of buildings.

Inside the plain white building next door, the **Bancroft Library** (Mon–Fri 9am–5pm, Sat 1–5pm) displays odds and ends from its exhaustive accumulation of artifacts and documents tracing the history of California, including a faked brass plaque supposedly left by Sir Francis Drake when he claimed all of the West Coast for Queen Elizabeth I. It also contains an internationally important collection of manuscripts and rare books, from Mark Twain to James Joyce – though to see any of these you have to show some academic credentials. Around the corner and down the hill, just inside the arched main entrance to Doe Library, you'll find the **Morrison Reading Room**, a great place to sit for a while and read foreign magazines and newspapers, listen to a CD, or just ease down into one of the many comfy overstuffed chairs and unwind.

Also worth a look if you've got time to kill is the **Museum of Paleontology** in the nearby Earth Sciences Building, which details evolutionary concepts with hundreds of fossils, skeletons, and geological maps displayed along the corridors on the lower floors. From here it's a quick walk to the collection of cafés and restaurants lining Euclid Avenue and Hearst Avenue, and the beginning of Berkeley's Northside (see p.461).

The Hearst family name appears with disturbing regularity around the Berkeley campus, though in most instances this is due not to the notorious newspaper baron William Randolph but to his altruistic mother, Phoebe Apperson Hearst. Besides inviting the entire senior class to her home every spring for a giant picnic, she sponsored the architectural competition that came up with the original campus plan, and donated a good number of the campus buildings, including many that have since been destroyed. One of the finest survivors, the 1907 **Hearst Mining Building** (daily

8am–5pm) on the northeast edge of the campus, conceals a delicate metalwork lobby topped by three glass domes, above ageing exhibits on geology and mining – which is how the Hearst family fortune was originally made, long before scion W.R. took up publishing. Another Hearst legacy is the **Greek Theater**, an open-air amphitheater cut into the Berkeley Hills east of the campus, which hosts a summer season of rock concerts.

Higher up in the hills, above the 80,000-seat Memorial Stadium, the lushly landscaped **Botanical Garden** (daily 9am–5pm; free) defeats on-campus claustrophobia with its thirty acres of plants and cactuses. Near the crest, with great views out over the bay, a full-size fiberglass sculpture of a whale stretches out in front of the space-age **Lawrence Hall of Science** (daily 10am–5pm; $6), an excellent museum and learning center that features earthquake simulations, model dinosaurs and a planetarium, plus hands-on exhibits for kids in the Wizard's Lab. Both the gardens and the Lawrence Hall of Science are accessible on weekdays via the free UC Berkeley Shuttle bus from the campus or the Berkeley BART station.

In the southeast corner of the campus, the **Hearst Museum of Anthropology** in Kroeber Hall (Wed–Sun 10am–4.30pm, Thurs until 9pm; $3, free Thurs) holds a variety of changing exhibits as well as an intriguing display of artifacts made by Ishi, the last surviving Yahi Indian who was found near Mount Lassen in Northern California in 1911. Anthropologist (and father of writer Ursula Le Guin) Alfred Kroeber brought Ishi to the museum (then located on the UC San Francisco campus), where he lived under the scrutiny of scientists and journalists – in effect, in a state of captivity – until his death from tuberculosis a few years later.

The brutally modern, angular concrete of the **University Art Museum** across Bancroft Way (Wed–Sun 11am–5pm, Thurs until 9pm; $6) is in stark contrast to the campus' older buildings. Its skylit, open-plan galleries hold works by Picasso, Cézanne, Rubens and other notables, but the star of the show is the collection of Fifties American

---

BERKELEY'S BOOKSTORES

Berkeley's **bookstores** are as exhaustive as they are exhausting – not surprising for a university town. Perfect for browsing and taking your time, you won't be made to feel guilty or obliged to buy a book you've been poring over for ages.

Black Oak Books, 1491 Shattuck Ave (☎510/486-0698). Huge selection of secondhand and new books for every interest; also holds regular evening readings by internationally acclaimed authors.

Cody's Books, 2454 Telegraph Ave (☎510/845-7852). The flagship of Berkeley booksellers, with an excellent selection of fiction, poetry and literary criticism.

Comics and Comix, 2502 Telegraph Ave (☎510/845-4091). Great selection of comic books, both current and classic.

Easy Going, 1385 Shattuck Ave (☎510/843-3533). The essential bookstore for every traveler. Packed with printed travel paraphernalia, it offers a wide selection of guidebooks and maps for local, countrywide and worldwide exploration.

Moe's Books, 2476 Telegraph Ave (☎510/849-2087). An enormous selection of new and used books on four floors with esoteric surprises in every field of study; for academics, book-collectors and browsers. There's also an excellent art section on the top floor.

Serendipity Books, 1201 University Ave (☎510/841-7455). Damp and disorganized, but with an incredible selection of first edition and out-of-print books. A must for collectors of first editions and obscure fiction and poetry.

Shakespeare and Company, 2499 Telegraph Ave (☎510/841-8916). Crammed with quality secondhand books at reasonable prices. The best place to linger and scour the shelves for finds.

Shambala Booksellers, 2482 Telegraph Ave (☎510/848-8443). Have a transcendental out-of-body experience where eastern and western religious traditions meet in this cozy store near campus.

painter Hans Hofmann's energetic and colorful abstract paintings on the top floor. The museum is renowned for its cutting-edge, changing exhibitions: the main space hosts a range of major shows – such as Robert Mapplethorpe's controversial photographs – while the Matrix Gallery focuses on lesser known, generally local artists. Works on paper are shown downstairs outside the **Pacific Film Archive**, which shares the building, showing new films from around the world that you won't see elsewhere, as well as revivals from its extensive library (see p.471 for details).

Telegraph Avenue and South Berkeley

Downtown Berkeley – basically two department stores, a few banks, a post office, and the City Hall building – lies west of the university campus around the Berkeley BART station on Shattuck Avenue, but the real activity centers on **Telegraph Avenue**, which runs south of the university from Sproul Plaza. This thoroughfare saw some of the worst of the Sixties riots and is still a frenetic bustle, especially the four short blocks closest to the university, which are packed to the gills with cafés and secondhand bookstores. Sidewalk vendors hawk handmade jewelry and brilliantly colored T-shirts, while down-and-outs hustle for spare change and spout psychotic poetry.

People's Park, now a seedy and overgrown plot of land half a block up from Telegraph between Haste Street and Dwight Way, was another battleground in the late Sixties, when organized and spirited resistance to the university's plans to develop the site into dormitories brought out the troops, who shot dead an onlooker by mistake. To many, the fact that the park is still a community-controlled open space (and outdoor dosshouse for Berkeley's homeless legions) symbolizes a small victory in the battle against the Establishment, though it's not a pleasant or even very safe place to hang about, especially after dark. A mural along Haste Street recalls some of the reasons why the battles were fought, in the words of student leader Mario Savio: "There's a time when the operation of the machine becomes so odious, makes you so sick at heart, that you can't take part, you can't even tacitly take part. And you've got to put your bodies upon the gears and upon the wheels, upon the levers, upon all the apparatus, and you've got to make it stop" – ideals that can't help but be undermined by the state of the place these days. Recent efforts by the university to reclaim the space with volleyball and basketball courts were met with short-lived but violent protests: rioters trashed Telegraph Avenue storefronts, and a nineteen-year-old woman was shot dead by police while trying to assassinate the Chancellor.

Directly across Bowditch Street from People's Park stands one of the finest buildings in the Bay Area, Bernard Maybeck's **Christian Science Church**. Built in 1910, it's an eclectic but thoroughly modern structure, laid out in a simple Greek Cross floor plan and spanned by a massive redwood truss with carved Gothic tracery and Byzantine painted decoration. The interior is only open on Sundays for worship and for tours at 11am, but the outside is worth lingering over, its cascade of many gently pitched roofs and porticoes carrying the eye from one handcrafted detail to another. It's a clever building in many ways: while the overall image is one of tradition and craftsmanship, Maybeck also succeeded in inconspicuously incorporating such materials as industrial metal windows, concrete walls and asbestos tiles into the structure – thereby cutting costs.

North Berkeley

North Berkeley, also called "Northside," is a subdued neighborhood of professors and postgraduate students, its steep, twisting streets climbing up the lushly overgrown hills north of the campus. At the foot of the hills, some of the Bay Area's finest restaurants and delis – most famously *Chez Panisse*, started and run by Alice Waters, the acclaimed inventor of California cuisine – have sprung up along Shattuck Avenue to form the so-called "Gourmet Ghetto," a great place to pick up the makings of a tasty al fresco lunch.

Above the Gourmet Ghetto on Euclid Avenue (if you want to avoid the fairly steep walk, take bus #65 from Shattuck Avenue), there are few more pleasant places for a picnic than the **Berkeley Rose Garden** (daily dawn–dusk; free), a terraced amphitheater filled with some three thousand varietal roses and looking out across the bay to San Francisco. Built as part of a WPA job-creation scheme during the Depression, a wooden pergola rings the top, stepping down to a small spring.

Along the crest of the Berkeley Hills, a number of enticing parks give great views over the bay. The largest and highest of them, **Tilden Park**, spreads along the crest of the hills, encompassing some 2065 acres of near wilderness. You can get there from downtown Berkeley via AC Transit bus #65 or #67. Kids can enjoy a ride on the carved wooden horses or a mini-steam train through the redwood trees. In the warm months, don't miss a swim in Lake Anza (lifeguard on duty May–Oct daily 11am–6pm; $3).

Nearer to town at the north end of Shattuck Avenue and close by the shops and cafés along Solano Avenue, the gray basalt knob of **Indian Rock** stands out from the foot of the hills, challenging rock-climbers who hone their skills on its forty-foot vertical faces. (Those who just want to appreciate the extraordinary view can take the steps around its back.) Carved into similarly hard volcanic stone across the street are the mortar holes used by the Olhone to grind acorns into flour. In between, and in stark contrast, stands the rusting hulk of a Cold War-era air-raid siren.

West Berkeley and the waterfront

From downtown Berkeley and the UC campus, **University Avenue** runs downhill toward the bay, lined by increasingly shabby frontages of motels and massage parlors. The liveliest part of this **West Berkeley** area is around the intersection of University and San Pablo Avenues – the pre-freeway main highway north – where a community of recent immigrants from India and Pakistan have set up stores and restaurants that serve some of the best of the Bay Area's rare curries.

The area between San Pablo Avenue and the bay is the oldest part of Berkeley, and a handful of hundred-year-old houses and churches – such as the two white-spired Gothic Revival structures on Hearst Avenue – survive from the time when this district was a separate city, known as Ocean View. The neighborhood also holds remnants of Berkeley's industrial past, and many of the old warehouses and factory premises have been converted into living and working spaces for artists, craftspeople and computer software companies. The newly polished and yuppified stretch of **Fourth Street** between Gilman and University features upscale furniture outlets and quaint gourmet delis, as well as some outstanding restaurants.

The I-80 freeway, and the still-used rail tracks that run alongside it, pretty well manage to cut Berkeley off from its waterfront. The best way to get there is to take AC Transit bus #51, which runs regularly down University Avenue. Once a major hub for the transbay ferry services – to shorten journey times a three-mile-long pier was constructed, much of which still sticks out into the bay – the **Berkeley Marina** is now one of the prime spots on the bay for leisure activities, especially windsurfing and kayaking.

The North Bay and inland valleys

Compared to the urbanized bayfront cities of Oakland and Berkeley, the rest of the East Bay is sparsely populated, and places of interest are few and far between. The **North Bay** is home to some of the Bay Area's heaviest industry – oil refineries and chemical plants dominate the landscape – but also holds a few remarkably unchanged waterfront towns that merit a side trip if you're passing by. Away from the bay, the inland valleys are a whole other world of dry rolling hills dominated by the towering peak of **Mount Diablo**. Dozens of tract house developments have made commuter suburbs out of what were once cattle ranches and farms, but so far the region has been able to absorb the numbers and still feels rural, despite having doubled in population in the past twenty years.

The North Bay

North of Berkeley there's not a whole lot to see or do. In **ALBANY**, Golden Gate Fields has horse-racing from October to June, and El Cerrito's main contribution to world culture was the band Creedence Clearwater Revival, who staged most of their *Born on the Bayou* publicity photographs in the wilds of Tilden Park in the hills above; El Cerrito is still home to one of the best record stores in California, Down Home Music, at 10341 San Pablo Ave. **RICHMOND**, at the top of the bay, was once a boomtown, building ships during World War II at the Kaiser Shipyards, which employed 100,000 workers between 1940 and its closure in 1945. Now it's the proud home of the gigantic Standard Oil refinery, the center of which you drive through before crossing the **Richmond–San Rafael Bridge** ($1) to Marin County. About the only reason to stop in Richmond is that it marks the north end of the BART line, and the adjacent Amtrak station is a better terminal for journeys to and from San Francisco than the end of the line in West Oakland.

Though not really worth a trip in itself, if you're heading from the East Bay to Marin County, **Point Richmond** merits a look. A cozy little town tucked away at the foot of the bridge between the refinery and the bay, its many Victorian houses are rapidly becoming commuter territory for upwardly mobile professionals from San Francisco. Through the narrow tunnel that cuts under the hill stands the most obvious sign of this potential gentrification: "Brickyard Landing," an East Bay docklands development with modern bay-view condos, a private yacht harbor, and a token gesture to the area's industrial past – disused brick kilns, hulking next to the tennis courts on the front lawn. The rest of the waterfront is taken up by the broad and usually deserted strand of **Keller Beach**, which stretches for half a mile along the sometimes windy shoreline.

The Carquinez Straits

At the top of the bay some 25 miles north of Oakland, the land along the Carquinez Straits is a bit off the beaten track, but it's an area of some natural beauty and much historic interest. The still-small towns along the waterfront seem worlds away from the bustle of the rest of the Bay Area, but how long they'll be able to resist the pressure of the expanding commuter belt is anybody's guess. AC Transit bus #74 runs every hour from Richmond BART north to **CROCKETT** at the west end of the narrow straits – a tiny town cut into the steep hillsides above the water that seems entirely dependent upon the massive C&H Sugar factory at its foot, whose giant neon sign lights up the town and the adjacent Carquinez Bridge.

From Crockett the narrow Carquinez Straits Scenic Drive, an excellent cycling route, heads east along the Sacramento river. A turn two miles along drops down to **PORT COSTA**, a small town that was dependent upon ferry traffic across the straits to Benicia until it lost its livelihood when the bridge was built at Crockett. It's still a nice enough place to watch the huge ships pass by on their way to and from the inland ports of Sacramento and Stockton. If you don't have a bike (or a car) you can enjoy the view from the window of an Amtrak train which runs alongside the water from Oakland and Richmond, not stopping until Martinez at the eastern end of the straits, two miles north of the John Muir house (see p.465).

Benicia

On the north side of the Straits, and hard to get to without a car (see "Getting around" p.450), **BENICIA** is the most substantial of the historic waterfront towns, but one that has definitely seen better days. Founded in 1847, it initially rivaled San Francisco as the major Bay Area port and was even the state capital for a time; but despite Benicia's better weather and fine deep-water harbor, San Francisco eventually became the main transportation point for the fortunes of the Gold Rush, and the town very nearly faded away altogether. Examples of Benicia's efforts to become a major city stand poign antly around the very compact downtown area, most conspicuously the 1852 Greek Revival structure that was used as the **first State Capitol** for just thirteen months The building has been restored as a museum (Thurs–Mon 10am–5pm; $2), furnished in the legislative style of the time, complete with top hats on the tables and shining spittoons every few feet.

A walking-tour map of Benicia's many intact Victorian houses and churches is avail able from the **tourist office**, on 601 First St (☎707/745-2120), including on its itinerary the steeply pitched roofs and gingerbread eaves of the **Frisbie-Walsh house** at 235 East L St – a prefabricated Gothic Revival building that was shipped here in pieces from Boston in 1849 (an identical house was put up by General Vallejo as his residence in Sonoma; see p.546). Across the City Hall park, the arched ceiling beams of **St Paul's Episcopal Church** look like an upturned ship's hull; it was built by shipwrights from the Pacific Mail Steamship Company, one of Benicia's many successful nineteenth-century shipyards. Half a dozen former brothels and saloons stand in various stages of decay and restoration along First Street down near the waterfront, from where the world's largest train ferries used to ply the waters between Benicia and Port Costa until 1930.

In recent years Benicia has attracted a number of artists and craftspeople, and you can watch glass-blowers and furniture-makers at work in the **Yuba Complex** at 670 East H St (Mon–Fri 10am–5pm, Sat 10am–4pm). Ceramic artist Judy Chicago and scu pltor Robert Arneson are among those who have worked in the converted studios and modern light industrial parks around the sprawling fortifications of the old **Benicia Arsenal** east of the downtown area, whose thickly walled sandstone buildings formed the main Army storage facility for weapons and ammunition from 1851 up to and includ ing the Korean War. One of the oddest parts of the complex is the **Camel Barn** (Wed–Sun 1–4pm; free), now a museum of local history, but formerly used to house camels that the Army imported in 1856 to transport supplies across the deserts of the Southwestern US. The experiment failed, and the camels were kept here until they were sold off in 1864.

Vallejo and Marine World/Africa USA

Across the Carquinez Bridge from Crockett, the biggest and dullest of the North Bay towns – **VALLEJO** – was, like Benicia, an early capital of California, though it now lacks any sign of its historical significance. In contrast to most of the other Gold Rush era towns that line the Straits, Vallejo remained economically vital, largely because of the massive military presence here at the **Mare Island Naval Shipyard**, a sprawl ing, relentlessly gray complex that covers an area twice the size of Golden Gate Park Closed in late 1997, Mare Island was once Vallejo's largest employer, and its less than glamorous history – the yard built and maintained supply ships and submarines, no carriers or battleships – is recounted in a small **museum** in the old city hall building at 734 Marin St (Tues–Sat 10am–4.30pm; $1.50), where the highlight is a working periscope that looks out across the bay. Though no great thrill, it's worth a quick stop, sited in the center of town right on Hwy-29, the main route from the East Bay to the Wine Country.

The best reason to come to Vallejo, however, is the newly renovated **Marine World/Africa USA** (daily 10am–10pm; $27.95), five miles north of Vallejo off I-80 at the Marine World Parkway (Hwy-37) exit. Operated by a nonprofit educational group, it offers a well above average range of performing sea lions, dolphins, and killer whales kept in approximations of their natural habitats, as well as water-ski stunt shows and several newly constructed roller coasters. It can be a fun day out, especially for children, and it's not bad as these things go: the animals seem very well cared for, their quarters are clean and spacious, and the shows are fun for all but the most jaded. The shark exhibit lets you walk through a transparent tunnel alongside twenty-foot Great Whites, and the tropical butterfly aviary is truly amazing. The best way to get here from San Francisco is on the Blue and Gold Fleet **ferry** from Fisherman's Wharf, which takes an hour each way and costs $15 round trip (☎415/773-1188 for details).

The inland valleys

Most of the inland East Bay area is made up of rolling hills covered by grasslands, slowly yielding to suburban housing developments and office complexes as more and more businesses abandon the pricey real estate of San Francisco. The great peak of **Mount Diablo** that dominates the region is twice as high as any other Bay Area summit, and surrounded by acres of campgrounds and hiking trails; other attractions include two historic homes that serve as memorials to their literate and influential ex-residents, John Muir and Eugene O'Neill.

BART tunnels from Oakland through the Berkeley Hills to the leafy-green stockbroker settlement of **ORINDA**, continuing east through the increasingly hot and dry landscape to the end of the line at **CONCORD**, site of a controversial nuclear weapons depot. A few years ago, a peaceful, civilly disobedient blockade here ended in protester Brian Wilson losing his legs under the wheels of a slow-moving munitions train. The event raised public awareness – before it happened few people knew of the depot's existence – but otherwise it's still business as usual.

From the Pleasant Hill BART station, one stop before the end of the line, Contra Costa County Connection buses leave every thirty minutes for **MARTINEZ**, the seat of county government, passing the preserved home of naturalist **John Muir** (Wed–Sun 10am–4.30pm; $2), just off Hwy-4 two miles south of Martinez. Muir, an articulate, persuasive Scot whose writings and political activism were of vital importance in the preservation of America's wilderness, spent much of his life exploring and writing about the majestic Sierra Nevada mountains, particularly Yosemite. He was also one of the founders of the **Sierra Club** – a wilderness lobby and education organization still active today (see p.000 for more). Anyone familiar with the image of this thin, bearded man wandering the mountains with his knapsack, notebook and packet of tea might be surprised to see his very conventional, upper-class Victorian home, now restored to its appearance when Muir died in 1914. Built by Muir's father-in-law, only those parts of the house Muir added himself reflect much of the personality of the man, not least the massive, rustic fireplace he had built in the East Parlor so he could have a "real mountain campfire." The bulk of Muir's personal belongings and artifacts are displayed in his study on the upper floor, and in the adjacent room an exhibition documents the history of the Sierra Club and Muir's battles to protect America's wilderness.

Behind the bell-towered main house is a large, still productive orchard where Muir cultivated grapes, pears and cherries to earn the money to finance his explorations (you can sample the fruits free of charge, pre-picked by staff gardeners). Beyond the orchard is the 1849 **Martinez Adobe**, homestead of the original Spanish land-grant settlers and now a small **museum** of Mexican colonial culture. The contrast between Mexican and American cultures in early California is fascinating and, as a bonus, the building's two-foot-thick walls keep it refreshingly cool on a typically hot summer day.

At the foot of Mount Diablo, fifteen miles south, playwright **Eugene O'Neill** used the money he got for winning the Nobel Prize for Literature in 1936 to build a home and sanctuary for himself, which he named **Tao House**. It was here, before 1944 when he was struck down with Parkinson's Disease, that he wrote many of his best-known plays: *The Iceman Cometh, A Moon for the Misbegotten* and *Long Day's Journey into Night.* Readings and performances of his works are sometimes given in the house, which is open to visitors, though you must reserve a place on one of the free guided **tours** (Wed–Sun 10am & 12.30pm; ☎925/838-0249). There's no parking on site, so the tours pick you up in the town of **Danville**.

As for **Mount Diablo** itself, it rises up from the rolling ranchlands at its foot to a height of nearly four thousand feet, its summit and flanks preserved within **Mount Diablo State Park** (daily 8am–sunset; parking $5). The main road through the park reaches within three hundred feet of the top, so it's a popular place for an outing and you're unlikely to be alone to enjoy the marvelous view: on a clear day you can see over two hundred miles in every direction. There's no public transportation, though the Sierra Club sometimes organizes day-trips: see Basics, p.46.

Two main entrances lead into the park, both well marked off I-680. The one from the southwest by way of Danville passes by the **ranger station**, where you can pick up a trail map ($1) which lists the best day-hikes. The other runs from the northwest by way of Walnut Creek, and the routes join together five miles from the summit. March and April, when the wildflowers are out, are the best times to come, and since mornings are ideal for getting the clearest view, you should drive to the top first and then head back down to a trailhead for a hike, or to one of the many picnic spots for a leisurely lunch. In summer it can get desperately hot and dry, and parts of the park are closed because of fire danger.

Livermore and Altamont

Fifteen miles southeast of Mount Diablo on the main road out of the Bay Area (I-580), the rolling hills around sleepy **LIVERMORE** are covered with thousands of shining, spinning, high-tech **windmills**, placed here by a private power company to take advantage of the nearly constant winds. The largest wind farm in the world, you'll probably have seen it used in a number of TV ads as a space-age backdrop to hype flashy new cars or sexy perfumes. Though the federal government provides no funding for this non-polluting, renewable source of energy, it spends billions of dollars every year designing and building nuclear weapons and other sinister applications of modern technology at the nearby **Lawrence Livermore Laboratories**, where most of the research and development of the nuclear arsenal takes place. A small **visitor center** (Mon–Fri 9am–4.30pm, Sat & Sun noon–5pm; free) two miles south of I-580 on Greenville Road, holds hands-on exhibits showing off various scientific phenomena and devices.

Up and over the hills to the east, where I-580 joins I-5 for the four-hundred-mile route south through the Central Valley to Los Angeles, stand the remains of **Altamont Speedway**, site of the nightmarish Rolling Stones concert in December 1969. The free concert, which was captured in the film *Gimme Shelter*, was intended to be a sort of second Woodstock, staged in order to counter allegations that the Stones had ripped off their fans during a long US tour. In the event it was a complete disaster: three people died, one of whom was kicked and stabbed to death by the Hell's Angels "security guards" – in full view of the cameras – after pointing a gun at Mick Jagger while he sang *Sympathy for the Devil*. Needless to say, no historical plaque marks the site.

East Bay eating

Official home of **California cuisine** and with some of the best restaurants in the state, Berkeley is an upmarket diner's paradise. But it's also a college town, and you can eat cheaply and well, especially around the southern end of the campus, along and around Telegraph Avenue. The rest of the East Bay is less remarkable, except for when it comes to **plain American** food such as barbecued ribs, grilled steaks or deli sandwiches, for which it's unbeatable.

Budget food: diners and delis

Bette's Ocean View Diner, 1807 Fourth St, Berkeley. Named after the neighborhood, not after the vista, but serving up some of the Bay Area's best breakfasts and lunches. Very popular on weekends, when you may have to wait an hour for a table, so come during the week if possible.

Flint's Barbecue, 3314 San Pablo Ave, Oakland. Open until the early hours of the morning for some of the best ribs and link sausages west of Chicago.

Genova Delicatessen, 5095 Telegraph Ave, Oakland. Friendly deli complete with hanging sausages that serves up superb sandwiches.

Holy Land Kosher Food, 677 Rand Ave, Oakland. Casual diner-style restaurant near the lake serving Israeli food, including excellent falafel, to those who can find it.

Homemade Café, 2454 Sacramento St, Berkeley. Non-traditional California-style Mexican and Jewish food served for breakfast and lunch at shared tables when crowded.

Intermezzo, Telegraph Avenue near Haste. Huge sandwiches on homemade sliced bread, even bigger salads, and great coffee – all very fresh and cheap.

Lois the Pie Queen, 851 60th St at Adeline, Oakland. Famous around the bay for its Southern-style sweet potato and fresh fruit pies, this cozy diner also serves massive, down-home breakfasts and Sunday dinners.

Saul's Deli, 1475 Shattuck Ave, Berkeley. For pastrami, corned beef, kreplach or knishes, this is the place. Great sandwiches and picnic fixings to take away, plus a full range of sit-down evening meals.

Time to Eat, 325 Franklin St, in Oakland's Produce Market. A Chinese bar and café that serves breakfasts from 5am. Cheap beer, plus a pool table at 25¢ per game.

Top Dog, 2534 Durant Ave, Berkeley. Not just a hot dog stand, it stays open late for such assorted goodies as bockwurst, bratwurst, kielbasas, Louisiana Hot Sausages and veggie dogs.

Tropix, 3814 Piedmont Ave, Oakland. Large portions of fruity Jamaican delicacies at reasonable prices with plenty of authentic jerk sauce and thirst-quenching mango juice.

American

Bay Wolf Café, 3853 Piedmont Ave, Oakland (☎510/655-6004). Comfortable restaurant serving grilled meat and fish dishes on an ever-changing, moderately expensive menu.

Café Fanny, 1603 San Pablo, Berkeley (☎510/524-5447). Delicious and relatively cheap breakfasts and lunches in a small and unlikely space with a sparse industrial decor. Owned by Alice Waters, of *Chez Panisse* fame (see below).

Café Rouge, 1782 Fourth St, Berkeley (☎510/525-1440). Fresh California cuisine specializing in delicately prepared organic meats from their own butcher shop. Dinner plates are about $16; lunch is cheaper.

Chez Panisse, 1517 Shattuck Ave, North Berkeley (☎510/548-5525). The first and still the best of the California cuisineries – although at $38 (Mon), $58 (Tues–Thurs) and $68 (Fri & Sat) a head prix-fixe (plus wine), you may prefer to try the comparatively inexpensive café upstairs, especially if you don't have the obligatory three-months-in-advance reservation.

Fatapple's, 1346 Martin Luther King Jr Way, Berkeley (☎510/526-2260). Crowded but pleasant family oriented restaurant with excellent cheap American breakfasts and an assortment of sandwiches and burgers for lunch or dinner.

Gulf Coast Oyster Bar & Specialty Co, 736 Washington St, Oakland (☎510/836-3663). Popular and reasonably priced Cajun-flavored seafood restaurant.

Lalime's, 1329 Gilman, Berkeley (☎510/527-9838). Won't (yet) knock *Chez Panisse* off its pedestal, but increasingly popular with the East Bay chattering classes for generic nouvelle. Reservations mandatory at night; for once à la carte is much better value than the set $30 per meal.

Asian and African

The Blue Nile, 2525 Telegraph Ave, Berkeley (☎510/540-6777). Come with a group to share the giant platters of Ethiopian stewed meats and veggies, eaten by hand with pancake-like injera bread.

Cha-Am, 1543 Shattuck Ave, Berkeley (☎510/848-9664). Climb the stairs to this unlikely-looking, always crowded small restaurant, for deliciously spicy Thai food at bargain prices.

Jade Villa, 800 Broadway, downtown Oakland (☎510/839-1688). For endless dim sum lunches or traditional Cantonese meals, this is one of the best places in Oakland's thriving Chinatown.

Kirala, 2100 Ward St, Berkeley (☎510/549-3486). Many argue that *Kirala* serves the best sushi in the Bay Area. Others argue that it's the best in the world.

Le Cheval, 1007 Clay St, Oakland (☎510/763-8495). You can't beat the tender prawn shish kebabs at this wildly popular Vietnamese restaurant in downtown Oakland. Second location at 344 20th St (☎510/763-3610).

O Chame, 1830 Fourth St, West Berkeley (☎510/841-8783). One of the very best Japanese restaurants in the US, with beautifully prepared sashimi and sushi as well as a full range of authentic Japanese specialties. A treat.

Sala Thai, 807 First St, Benicia (☎707/745-4331). Small-town Thai food can be just as delicious here as in any big city. Check out the enormous fish tank as your feet dangle in foot caves under the tables.

Steve's Barbeque, in the Durant Center, 2521 Durant Ave, Berkeley (☎510/848-6166). Excellent, low- priced Korean food (*kim chee* to die for); other cafés in the center sell Mexican food, healthy sandwiches, deep-fried doughnuts and slices of pizza – not to mention bargain pitchers of beer.

Italian and pizza

Blondie's Pizza, 2340 Telegraph Ave, Berkeley (☎510/548-1129). Delicious takeout New York-style pizza by the slice ($1.75, plus topping) or by the pie; stays open until 2am, and is always crowded.

Café Rustica, 5422 College Ave, Oakland (☎510/654-1601). Intimate adobe-style, upscale eatery for designer pizza with a pesto and sun-dried tomatoes motif. If it's too expensive, try the tapas bar upstairs.

Cheese Board Pizza, 1512 Shattuck Ave, Berkeley (☎510/549-3055). Tiny storefront selling some of the world's best "designer pizza" at very reasonable prices: $2 a slice, with a different topping every day. Worth searching out, but keeps irregular hours; usually Tues–Sat 11.30am–2pm & 4.30–7pm.

Gio's Trattoria, 2220 First St, Livermore (☎510/606-6644). Offers outstanding Italian food in an elegant atmosphere.

Locanda Olmo, 2985 College Ave, Berkeley (☎510/848-5544). Simple but discriminating menu at this tiny, intimate trattoria in the charming Elmwood neighborhood.

Oliveto, 5655 College Ave, Rockridge (☎510/547-5356). Popular sidewalk café, where good-sized Italian sandwiches cost around $6. Upstairs is a pricey but appetizing gourmet Italian restaurant where you can watch the chef and the cooking team in action.

Zachary's Pizza, 5801 College Ave, Rockridge (☎510/655-6385); also at 1853 Solano Ave, North Berkeley (☎510/525-5950). Good salads, and arguably the best pizzas in the East Bay.

Mexican and South American

Café de la Paz, 1600 Shattuck Ave, Berkeley (☎510/843-0662). Located upstairs inside a complex of boutiques, Latin American entrees and tapas are served fresh and sometimes spicy. Don't miss the Brazilian seafood stew.

Juan's Place, 941 Carleton St, West Berkeley (☎510/845-6904). The original Berkeley Mexican restaurant, with great food (tons of it) and an interesting mix of people.

Mario's La Fiesta, 2444 Telegraph Ave at Haste, Berkeley (☎510/540-9123). Always crowded with students and other budget-minded souls who flock here for the heaped portions of good, inexpensive Mexican food.

Picante, 1328 Sixth St at Gilman, West Berkeley (☎510/525-3121). Good, inexpensive tacos with fresh salsa, plus live jazz on weekends.

aqueria **Morelia**, 4481 E 14th St, East Oakland (☎510/535-6030). Excellent burritos and the more nusual but authentic *tortas*.

ce cream and desserts

reyers Grand Ice Cream Parlor, 5925 College Ave, Oakland (☎510/658-0502). Oakland's own ch ice cream, which is distributed through California, is served at this small, slightly dull ockridge café.

enton's Creamery, 4226 Piedmont Ave, N Oakland (☎510/658-7000). A brightly lit 1950s ice ream and sandwich shop, open until 11pm on weeknights, midnight on weekends.

ogurt Park, 2433a Durant Ave, Berkeley (☎510/549-0570). Frozen yogurt a specialty; open until idnight for the student throngs.

pecialty shops and markets

cme Bread, 1601 San Pablo Ave, West Berkeley (☎510/524-1327). Small bakery that supplies ost of Berkeley's better restaurants; the house specialty is delicious sourdough baguettes.

erkeley Bowl, 2777 Shattuck Ave, Berkeley (☎510/841-6346). A converted bowling alley which is ow an enormous produce, bulk and healthfood market. The least expensive grocery in town, with e largest selection of fresh food.

heese Board, 1504 Shattuck Ave, North Berkeley (☎510/549-3183). Collectively owned and perated since 1967, this was one of the first outposts in Berkeley's Gourmet Ghetto and is still ping strong, offering over 200 varieties of cheese and a range of delicious breads. Great pizzas a w doors down, too; see opposite.

a Farine, 6323 College Ave, Rockridge (☎510/654-0338). Small but highly rated French-style bak- ry, with excellent pain au chocolat.

Ionterey Foods, 1550 Hopkins St, North Berkeley (☎510/526-6042). The main supplier of exotic roduce to Berkeley's gourmet restaurants, this boisterous market also has the highest quality esh fruit and vegetables available.

ast Bay drinking: cafés and bars

ne of the best things about visiting the East Bay is the opportunity to enjoy its many **afés**. Concentrated most densely around the UC Berkeley campus, they're on a par ith the best of San Francisco's North Beach for bohemian atmosphere – heady with e smell of coffee, and from dawn to near midnight full of earnest characters wear- g their intellects on their sleeves. If you're not after a caffeine fix, you can gen- rally also get a glass of beer, wine, or fresh fruit juice, though for serious drinking ou'll be better off in one of the many **bars**, particularly in rough-hewn Oakland. rittier versions of what you'd find in San Francisco, they're mostly blue-collar, con- vial, and almost always cheaper. Not surprisingly, Berkeley's bars are brimming ith students and academics.

afés

afé Mediterraneum, 2475 Telegraph Ave, Berkeley (☎510/841-5634). Berkeley's oldest café, raight out of the Beat archives: beards and berets optional, battered paperbacks *de rigeur*.

afé Milano, 2522 Bancroft Way, Berkeley (☎510/644-3100). Airy, arty café across from UC erkeley.

afé Strada, 2300 College Ave, Berkeley (☎510/843-5282). Upmarket, open-air café where art and rchitecture students cross paths with would-be lawyers and chess wizards.

offee Mill, 3363 Grand Ave, Oakland (☎510/465-4224). Spacious room that doubles as an art allery, and often hosts poetry readings.

ompany of Wolves Coffee House, 737 First St, Benicia (☎707/746-0572). Progressive coffee- ouse, with sketch pads on the tables for caffeine-induced doodles.

Mama Bear's, 6536 Telegraph Ave, N Oakland (☎510/428-9684). Mainly a women's bookstore, i doubles as a café and meeting place and has regular readings, often for women only, by lesbian and feminist writers. Open daily 10.30am–7pm, later for readings.

Peet's Coffee and Tea, 2124 Vine St, Berkeley (☎510/841-0564), 3258 Lakeshore Ave, Oaklan (☎510/832-6761), and numerous branches throughout the Bay Area. Originating in Berkeley, *Peet'* has grown from a dedicated cult following to a local market leader, with many charming outlets Widely considered as the standard of extra-strong coffee.

Royal Ground, 6255 College Ave, Oakland (☎510/653-5458). Bright, modern and relaxing spot i the Rockridge area, with outdoor seating. Perfect for a leisurely afternoon with the newspaper.

Bars

Bison Brewing Company, 2598 Telegraph Ave, Berkeley (☎510/841-7734). Eat and drink on the terrace, at great prices, where some of the best Bay Area beers are brewed. Honey Basil ale i highly recommended. Noisy bands on the weekend.

Brennan's, Fourth Street and University, Berkeley (☎510/841-0960). Solidly blue-collar hangou that's a great place for drinking inexpensive beers and watching a game on TV.

Cato's Alehouse, 3891 Piedmont, Oakland (☎510/655-3349). Very local and casual with a goo beer selection. Relax with a couple of beers and a pizza or sandwich.

Heinhold's First and Last Chance Saloon, 56 Jack London Square, Oakland (☎510/839-6761) Authentic waterfront bar that's hardly changed since the turn of the century, when Jack London wa a regular. They still haven't bothered to fix the slanted floor caused by the 1906 earthquake.

Jupiter, 2181 Shattuck Ave, Berkeley (☎510/843-8277). Many types of beer to select from at thi local favorite. Live jazz on weekends, an excellent atmosphere, and an outdoor beer garden.

The Kingfish, 5227 Claremont Ave, Oakland (☎510/655-7373). More like a tumbledown shed tha a bar, selling low-priced pitchers of cold beer to UC Berkeley rugby players and other headbangers

Rickey's Sports Lounge, 15028 Hesperian Blvd, San Leandro, near Bayfair BART (☎510/352 0200). With seven giant-screen TVs and 35 others spread around the cavernous room, this bar-cum restaurant is the place to go to watch sports.

Triple Rock Brewery, 1920 Shattuck Ave, Berkeley (☎510/843-2739). Buzzing, all-American bee bar: the decor is Edward Hopper-era retro, and the beers (brewed on the premises) are highly car bonated to suit the soda-pop palates of the studenty crowd, but it's still fun.

The White Horse, 6560 Telegraph Ave at 66th St, Oakland (☎510/652-3820). Oakland's oldest ga bar – a smallish, friendly place, with mixed nightly dancing for men and women.

Nightlife

Nightlife is where the East Bay really comes into its own. Even more than in San Francisco, dancing to canned music and paying high prices for flashy decor is not the thing to do, which means that discos are virtually non-existent. Instead there are dozens of **live music** venues, covering a range of musical tastes and styles – from small, unpretentious jazz clubs to buzzing R&B venues – of which Oakland's hot spot are unsurpassed. Berkeley's clubs tend more towards folk and world music, with occa sional bouts of hard-core thrash, and the university itself holds two of the best medium sized venues in the entire Bay Area, both of which attract touring big-name stars **Tickets** for most venues are available at their box office or, for a $3 service charge through BASS (☎510/762-2277).

Though not bad by US standards, the East Bay theater scene isn't exactly thriving and shows tend to be politically worthy rather than dramatically innovative. By con trast, the range of **films** is first class, with a dozen movie theaters showing new re leases and Berkeley's Pacific Film Archive, one of the world's finest film libraries, fill ing its screens with obscure but brilliant art flicks.

Check the free *East Bay Express* or the *SF Weekly* for details of who and **what's or** where in the entire East Bay region.

The large performance venues

Berkeley Community Theater, 1930 Allston Way, Berkeley (☎510/845-2308). Jimi Hendrix played here, and the 3500-seat theater still hosts major rock concerts and community events.

Center for Contemporary Music, Mills College, 5000 MacArthur Bvld, Oakland (☎510/430-2191). One of the prime centers in the world for experimental music.

Oakland Coliseum Complex, Coliseum BART, near the airport (☎510/639-7700). Mostly stadium shows, inside the 18,000-seat arena or outdoors in the adjacent 55,000-seat coliseum.

Paramount Theater, 2025 Broadway, downtown Oakland (☎510/465-6400). Beautifully restored Art Deco masterpiece, hosting classical concerts, big-name crooners, ballets and operas. Tickets $6–20. Some nights they play old Hollywood classics for $6.

Zellerbach Hall and the outdoor **Greek Theater** on the UC Berkeley campus (☎510/642-9988). Two of the prime spots for catching touring big names in the Bay Area. Tickets cost $15–25.

Live music venues

Ashkenaz, 1317 San Pablo Ave, Berkeley (☎510/525-5054). World music and dance café. Acts range from modern Afro-beat to the best of the Balkans. Kids and under-21s welcome. Cover $5–8.

Caribee Dance Center, 1408 Webster St, Oakland (☎510/835-4006). For reggae, rockers, calypso, soca, dub, salsa or lambada, this place is hard to beat. Cover $5–10.

Eli's Mile High Club, 3629 Martin Luther King Jr Way, N Oakland (☎510/655-6661). The best of the Bay Area blues clubs. Waitresses balance pitchers of beer on their heads to facilitate a safer passage through the rocking crowds. Cover $5–8.

Freight and Salvage, 1111 Addison St, W Berkeley (☎510/548-1761). Singer-songwriters in a coffeehouse setting. Cover $6–12.

Gilman Street Project, 924 Gilman St, W Berkeley (☎510/525-9926). On the outer edge of the hard-core punk scene. Cover $3–8.

Kimball's East, 4800 Shellmound St, Emeryville (☎510/658-2555). Fairly slick, high-style jazz and dancing venue. Cover $10–25.

Koncepts Cultural Gallery, Oakland (☎510/763-0682). Excellent, ground-breaking jazz organization, hosting a wide variety of different acts at venues around Oakland. Cover $8–25.

La Peña Cultural Center, 3105 Shattuck Ave, Berkeley near Ashby BART (☎510/849-2568). More folk than rock, often politically charged. Cover $3–6.

Starry Plough, 3101 Shattuck Ave, Berkeley (☎510/841-2082). Music ranges from noisy punk to alternative pop to country to traditional Irish folk, and the crowd is just as varied. Doubles as a friendly saloon and restaurant in the afternoon and early evening.

Stork Club, 380 12th St, Oakland (☎510/444-6147). Local alternative bands and experimental musicians play at this downtown Oakland bar with pool table. Doubles as a country and western bar during the day.

Cinemas

Act One and Act Two, 2128 Center St, Berkeley (☎510/548-7200). Foreign films and non-mainstream American ones.

Grand Lake Theater, 3200 Grand Ave (☎510/452-3556). The grand dame of East Bay picture palaces, right on Lake Merritt, showing the best of the current major releases.

Pacific Film Archive, 2621 Durant Ave, Berkeley, in the University Art Museum (☎510/642-1124). For the serious film fan, this is perhaps the best cinema in all California, with seasons of contemporary works from around the world, plus revivals of otherwise forgotten favorites. Two films a night; tickets $5.50 each, $7 for both.

UC Theater, 2036 University Ave, Berkeley, just below Shattuck Ave (☎510/843-6267). Popular revival house, with a huge auditorium and a daily double feature. Tickets $6.50.

Theater

Berkeley Repertory Theater, 2025 Addison St, Berkeley (☎510/845-4700). One of the West Coast's most highly respected theater companies, presenting updated classics and contemporary plays in an intimate modern theater. Tickets $6–25.

Black Repertory Group, 3201 Adeline St, Berkeley near Ashby BART (☎510/652-2120). After years of struggling, this politically conscious company moved into its own specially built home in 1987, since when they've encouraged new talent with great success. Tickets $5–15.

California Shakespeare Festival, Siesta Valley, Orinda (☎510/548-3422). After fifteen seasons in a North Berkeley park, this summer-long outdoor festival was forced to move to a larger home in the East Bay Hills. Tickets $8–30.

Julia Morgan Theater, 2640 College Ave, Berkeley (☎510/845-8542). A variety of touring shows stop off in this cunningly converted old church. Tickets $8–20.

The Peninsula

The city of San Francisco sits at the tip of a five-mile-wide neck of land commonly referred to as the **Peninsula**. Home of old money and new technology, the Peninsula stretches for fifty miles of relentless suburbia south from San Francisco along the bay, past the wealthy enclaves of Hillsborough and Atherton, winding up in the futuristic roadside landscape of the **"Silicon Valley"** near **San Jose**.

There was a time when the region was largely agricultural, but the continuing computer boom – spurred by Stanford University in **Palo Alto** – has replaced orange groves and fig trees with office complexes and parking lots. Surprisingly, however, most of the land along the **coast** – separated from the bayfront sprawl by a ridge of redwood-covered peaks – remains rural and undeveloped; it also contains some excellent **beaches** and a couple of affably down-to-earth communities, all well served by public transportation.

Getting around and information

BART only travels down the Peninsula as far as Daly City, from where you can catch SamTrans (☎1-800/660-4287) buses south to Palo Alto or along the coast to Half Moon Bay. For longer distances, **Caltrain** (☎1-800/660-4287) offers an hourly rail service from its terminal at Fourth and Townsend streets in downtown San Francisco, stopping at most bayside towns between the city and San Jose ($1–5); Greyhound (☎1-800/231-2222) runs regular **buses** along US-101 to and from their San Jose terminal at 70 S Almaden, on the corner of Santa Clara Street. Santa Clara Valley Transit Authority (VTA) (☎408/321-2330) runs buses and modern trolleys around metropolitan San Jose. If you're going to be spending most of your time there, it's possible to fly direct into **San Jose International Airport** (SJO), alarmingly close to downtown San Jose.

Information

The **Palo Alto Chamber of Commerce**, 325 Forest Ave (Mon–Fri 9am–noon & 1–5pm; ☎650/324-3121), has lists of local restaurants and cycle routes; for information on nearby Stanford University, phone ☎650/723-2560. To find out what's on and where, pick up a free copy of the *Palo Alto Weekly*, available at most local shops. At the southern end of the bay, the **San Jose Convention and Visitors' Bureau**, 333 W San Carlos St, Suite 1000 (Mon–Fri 8am–5.30pm, Sat & Sun 11am–5pm; ☎ 1-800/SAN-JOSE or 408/295-9600), is the best bet for tourist information; for local news and events pick up a copy of the excellent *San Jose Mercury* newspaper or the free weekly *Metro*. Along the coast, the **Half Moon Bay Chamber of Commerce**, at 520 Kelly Ave (☎650/726-5202), gives out walking tour maps and information on accommodation.

Peninsula accommodation

Many visitors to San Francisco choose to stay on the Peninsula rather than in the city. Dozens of $60-a-night motels line Hwy-82 – "El Camino Real", the old main highway –

and, with a bit of advanced planning (and a car), sleeping here can save a lot of money. Also, if you're **arriving late** or departing on an early flight from SFO you might want to avail yourself of one of the many airport hotels listed in the box on p.392. Perhaps the best reasons to spend the night down on the Peninsula are its many low-priced, pleasant **hostels**, two of which are housed in old lighthouses right along the Pacific coast. San Jose's hotels cater more to the corporate world than the tourist or traveler, though it's possible to find a decent deal.

Hostels

HI-Hidden Villa, 26807 Moody Rd, Los Altos Hills (☎650/949-8648). Located on an 1800-acre ranch in the foothills above Silicon Valley; closed June–Sept. $13 a night.

HI-Pigeon Point Lighthouse, Hwy-1, just south of Pescadero (☎650/879-0633). Worth planning a trip around, this beautifully sited hostel, fifty miles south of San Francisco, is ideally placed for exploring the redwood forests in the hills above or for watching the wildlife in nearby Año Nuevo State Reserve. Outdoor hot tub. Office hours 7.30–9.30am & 4.30–9.30pm; doors locked at 11pm. Members $12 per night, non-members $15; reservations essential in summer. Private rooms $25 a night.

HI-Point Montara Lighthouse, 16th Street/Hwy-1, Montara (☎650/728-7177). Dorm rooms in a converted 1875 lighthouse, 25 miles south of San Francisco and accessible by bike or SamTrans bus #1L or #1C (Mon–Fri until 5.50pm, Sat until 6.15pm). Outdoor hot tub. Office hours 7.30–9.30am & 4.30–9.30pm; doors locked 11pm. Members $11 per night, non-members $14; reservations essential in summer.

Sanborn Park Hostel, 15808 Sanborn Rd, Saratoga (☎408/741-0166). Comfortable rooms in a beautiful wooded area fifteen minutes outside San Jose. Call from downtown Saratoga and they will arrange to pick you up. $8.50 members; $10.50 non-members.

Motels and Hotels

Best Western Inn, 455 S Second St, San Jose (☎408/298-3500). Right in downtown San Jose, with pool and sauna. ④.

Best Western Stanford Park Hotel, 100 El Camino Real, Menlo Park (☎650/322-1234). Very pleasant first-class hotel near Stanford University. ⑧.

Cardinal Hotel, 235 Hamilton Ave, Palo Alto (☎650/323-5101). Affordable rates and comfortable rooms in the heart of downtown Palo Alto. Some rooms with shared bath. ③.

Comfort Inn, 1215 S First St, San Jose (☎408/280-5300). Basic rooms downtown near the few cafés in the city. ④.

Days Inn Palo Alto, 4238 El Camino Real, Palo Alto (☎1-800/325-2525 or 650/493-4222). A mile from anywhere but the rooms are particularly clean and well kept. ④.

Executive Inn, 3930 Monterey Rd, San Jose (☎408/281-8700). Basic rooms without frills fifteen minutes south of downtown. ⑤.

Hotel California, 2431 Ash St, Palo Alto (☎650/322-7666). Small, central, and reasonable. ④.

Valley Inn, 2155 The Alameda, San Jose (☎408/241-8500). Standard motel not far from the Rosicrucian Museum. ④.

Bed and Breakfast

Cowper Inn, 705 Cowper St, Palo Alto (☎650/327-4475). Restored Victorian with pleasant parlor and attractive rooms close to University Avenue. ④.

Old Thyme Inn, 779 Main St, Half Moon Bay (☎650/726-1616). Half a dozen incredibly quaint rooms, each with private bath, in lovely Victorian house surrounded by luxuriant herb and flower gardens. ⑤.

San Benito House, 356 Main St, Half Moon Bay (☎650/726-3425). Twelve restful B&B rooms in a hundred-year-old building, just a mile from the beach. Excellent restaurant downstairs. ⑤.

Campgrounds

Butano State Park, Pescadero (☎650/879-2040). RV and tent spaces in a beautiful redwood forest; $16.

Half Moon Bay State Beach, Half Moon Bay (☎650/726-8820). Sleep out (illegally but safely) along the beach for free, or in the campground for $16.

South along the Bay

US-101 runs **south** from San Francisco along the bay through over fifty miles of unmitigated sprawl lined by light industrial estates and shopping malls, to San Jose. One place along the freeway worth a visit is the **Coyote Point Museum** (Tues–Sat 10am–5pm, Sun noon–5pm; $3), four miles south of the airport off Poplar Avenue in a large bayfront park, where examples of the natural life of the San Francisco Bay – from tidal insects to birds of prey – are exhibited in engaging and informative displays, enhanced by interactive computers and documentary films.

A more pleasant drive is via **I-280**, one of the newest and most expensive freeways in California, which runs parallel to US-101 but avoids the worst of the bayside mess by cutting through wooded valleys down the center of the Peninsula. Just beyond the San Francisco city limits the road passes through **COLMA**, a unique place made up entirely of cemeteries, which, other than the military burial grounds in the *presidio*, are prohibited within San Francisco. Besides the expected roll call of deceased San Francisco luminaries like Levi Strauss and William Hearst, are a few surprises, such as Wild West gunman Wyatt Earp. If you're interested, contact the Colma Historical Association (☎650/757-1676) for graveyard tour information.

Beyond Colma, the scenery improves quickly as I-280 continues past the **Crystal Springs Reservoir**, an artificial lake which holds the water supply for San Francisco – pumped here all the way from Yosemite. Surrounded by twenty square miles of parkland, hiking trails lead up to the ridge from which San Francisco Bay was first spotted by eighteenth-century Spanish explorers; it now overlooks the airport to the east, but there are good views out over the Pacific coast, two miles distant.

At the south end of the reservoir, just off I-280 on Canada Road in the well-heeled town of **WOODSIDE**, luscious gardens surround the palatial **Filoli Estate** (tours Tues–Thurs 9.30am, 11.30am & 1.30pm; $10; advance reservations required ☎650/364-2880). The 45-room mansion, designed in 1915 in neo-Palladian style by architect Willis Polk, may look familiar – it was used in the TV series *Dynasty* as the Denver home of the Carrington clan. It's the only one of the many huge houses around here that you can visit, although the gardens are what make it worth coming, especially in the spring when everything's in bloom.

Palo Alto and Stanford University

PALO ALTO, just south and three miles east of Woodside between I-280 and US-101, is a small, leafy community, and despite its proximity to Stanford, retains little of the college town vigor of its northern counterpart, Berkeley. In recent years, Palo Alto has become somewhat of a social center for Silicon Valley's *nouveau riche*, as evidenced by the trendy cafés and chic new restaurants that have popped up along its main drag, **University Avenue**. The booming computer industry job market has made more than a few people rich, and this is where many of them come to spend their cash; small houses in the quaint neighborhoods surrounding the downtown area can cost close to a million dollars.

The town doesn't have a lot to offer in terms of sights, but it's a great place for a lazy stroll and a gourmet meal. If you're feeling particularly energetic, or are tired of browsing in overpriced designer furniture stores, try cycling around the town's many well-marked bike routes; a range of bikes is available for $12–25 a day from Action Sports Limited at 401 High St (☎650/328-3180), near the Caltrain station a block west of University Avenue. Be aware, however, that **East Palo Alto**, on the bay side of US-101, has a well-deserved reputation for gang- and drug-related violence, with one of the highest per capita murder rates of any US city. Founded in the 1920s as the utopian

Runnymeade colony, an agricultural, poultry-raising co-operative – the local historical society (☎650/329-0294) can point out the surviving sites. East Palo Alto, where Grateful Dead guitarist Jerry Garcia grew up, is about as far as you can get off the San Francisco tourist trail.

Stanford University, spreading out from the west end of University Avenue, is by contrast one of the tamest places you could hope for. The university is among the best – and most expensive – in the United States, though when it opened in 1891, founded by railroad magnate Leland Stanford in memory of his dead son, it offered free tuition. Ridiculed by East Coast academics, who felt that there was as much need for a second West Coast university (after UC Berkeley) as there was for "an asylum for decayed sea captains in Switzerland," Stanford was defiantly built anyway, in a hybrid of Mission and Romanesque buildings on a huge campus that covers an area larger than the whole of downtown San Francisco.

Stanford, whose reputation as an arch-conservative think-tank was enhanced by Ronald Reagan's offer to donate his video library to the school (Stanford politely declined), hasn't always been an entirely boring place, though you wouldn't know it to walk among the preppy future-lawyers-of-America that seem to comprise the majority of the student body. Ken Kesey came here from Oregon in 1958 on a writing fellowship, working nights as an orderly on the psychiatric ward of one local hospital, and getting paid $75 a day to test experimental drugs (LSD among them) in another. Drawing on both experiences, Kesey wrote *One Flew over the Cuckoo's Nest* in 1960 and quickly became a counter-culture hero.

Approaching from the Palo Alto Caltrain and SamTrans bus station, which acts as a buffer between the town and the university, you enter the campus via a half-mile-long, palm-tree-lined boulevard which deposits you at its heart, the **Quadrangle**, bordered by the phallic **Hoover Tower** and the colorful gold-leaf mosaics of the **Memorial Church**. Free hour-long walking tours of the campus leave from here daily at 11am and 3.15pm, though it's fairly big and best seen by car or bike.

The **Stanford Museum of Art** between "the Quad" and the town was damaged by the 1989 Loma Prieta earthquake and is scheduled to reopen in late 1998. For now, the best reason to come here is to have a look at the distinguished collection of **Rodin sculpture**, including a *Gates of Hell* flanked by a shamed *Adam and Eve*, displayed in an attractive outdoor setting on the museum's south side. Also, if you keep up on the latest trends in subatomic behavior, you won't want to miss the **Stanford Linear Accelerator** (Mon–Fri by appointment only; ☎650/926-3300), a mile west of the central campus on Sand Hill Road, where infinitesimally small particles are crashed into one another at very high speeds to see what happens. For a bird's eye view of the campus (and the rest of the Bay Area) head up one of the **hiking trails** that leads from the gate along Junipero Serra Boulevard at Stanford Avenue to Stanford's giant communications dish atop the foothills to the west of the campus.

San Jose

The fastest-growing major city in America's fastest-growing state, **SAN JOSE** is not strong on identity – despite the Burt Bacharach song – though in area and population it's nearly twice the size of San Francisco. Sitting at the southern end of the Peninsula, located almost exactly in the center of the state, an abundance of cheap land brought developers and businessmen into the area in the 1960s, hoping to draw from the concentration of talent in the commerce-oriented halls of Stanford University. An enormous concentration of the world's technology industry is now located here. Fueled by the success of computer firms such as Apple, Intel and Hewlett-Packard, in the past 25 years San Jose has emerged as the civic heart of **Silicon Valley**, surrounded by miles of faceless high-tech industrial parks where the next generations of computers are designed and crafted.

Ironically, San Jose is one of the oldest settlements in California, though the only sign of that is at the late eighteenth-century **Mission Santa Clara de Asis**, just south of The Alameda (Route 82). On the grounds of the Jesuit-run University of Santa Clara, two miles northwest of the Caltrain station, the **de Saisset Museum** (Tues–Fri 10am–5pm, Sat & Sun 1–5pm; $1) holds a permanent display of objects from the Mission era along with changing shows of contemporary art. Otherwise, there are only a couple of good reasons to subject yourself to San Jose's relentlessly boring cityscape. The main attraction is the **Rosicrucian Museum**, 1342 Naglee Ave (daily 9am–5pm; $6). Languishing in the suburbs, this grand structure contains a brilliant collection of Assyrian and Babylonian artifacts, with displays of mummies, amulets, a replica of a tomb and ancient jewelry. Right downtown, at 145 W San Carlos St, is a more modern magnet, the **Tech Museum of Innovation** (Tues–Sat 10am–5pm, Sun noon–5pm; $6), with hands-on displays of high-tech engineering. Though you shouldn't plan your day around it, if you're in the area, stop by the educational **BFI Recyclery**, 1601 Dixon Landing Rd (☎408/262-1401), just off the 880 freeway in Milpitas, where interactive displays explain various recycling processes and show what happens if we don't use them.

You could also visit the **Winchester Mystery House**, 525 S Winchester Blvd, just off I-280 near Hwy-17 (daily 9.30am–4.30pm; $12.95). Sarah Winchester, heir to the Winchester rifle fortune, was convinced by an occultist upon her husband's death that he had been taken by the spirits of men killed with Winchester rifles. She was told that unless a room was built for each of the spirits and the sound of hammers never ceased, the same fate would befall her. Work on the mansion went on 24 hours per day for the next thirty years, with results that need to be seen to be believed – stairs lead nowhere, windows open onto solid brick, and so on. It is, however, a shameless tourist trap, and you have to run a gauntlet of ghastly gift stores and soda stands to get in or out.

One other Peninsula place might exercise a certain attraction, particularly to those fond of roller coasters, log rides and all-American family fun; **Great America** (summer daily 10am–10pm; winter Sat & Sun 10am–10pm; $28.99). This huge, hundred-acre amusement park on the edge of San Francisco Bay, just off US-101 north of San Jose, is not in the same league as Disneyland, but doesn't suffer from the same crowds and lengthy lines, and the range of high-speed thrills and chills – from the loop-the-looping "Top Gun Jetcoaster" to "Drop Zone," where you free fall for over two hundred feet – are worth the entry fee, especially on weekdays when you may well have the place to yourself.

The coast

The **coastline** of the Peninsula south from San Francisco is in many ways more appealing than inland – relatively undeveloped, with very few buildings, let alone towns, along the 75 miles of coves and beaches that extend down to the resort city of Santa Cruz. Bluffs protect the many nudist beaches from prying eyes and make a popular launching pad for hang-glider pilots, particularly at **Burton Beach** and **Fort Funston**, a mile south of the San Francisco Zoo – also the point where the earthquake-causing San Andreas Fault enters the sea, not to surface again until Point Reyes. Skyline Boulevard follows the coast from here past the repetitious tracts of proverbial ticky-tacky houses that make up Daly City, before heading inland toward Woodside at its intersection with Hwy-1, which continues south along the coast.

San Pedro Point, a popular surfing beach fifteen miles south of the city proper, marks the southern extent of San Francisco's suburban sprawl. The old **Ocean Shore Railroad Depot** here, now a private residence, is one of the few surviving remnants of an ill-advised train line between San Francisco and Santa Cruz. Wiped out during the 1906 earthquake, the line was in any case never more than a third complete. Its few patrons had to transfer back and forth by ferry to connect the stretches of track that were built, the traces of which you can still see scarring the face of the bluffs. The continually eroding cliffs make construction along the coast difficult, as evidenced a mile south by the **Devil's Slide**, where the highway is washed away with some regularity in winter storms. The slide area was also a popular dumping spot for corpses of those who fell foul of rum-runners during Prohibition, and is featured under various names in many of Dashiell Hammett's detective stories.

Just south of the Devil's Slide, the sands of **Gray Whale Cove State Beach** (daily dawn–dusk; $5 parking) are clothing-optional. Despite the name it's not an especially great place to look for migrating gray whales, but the stairway at the bus stop does lead down to a fine strand of sand. Two miles south, the red-roofed buildings of the Montara Lighthouse, set among the windswept Monterey pines at the top of a steep cliff, have been converted into a youth hostel (see p.473). There are a few good places to stop for a drink or a bite to eat in the town of **Moss Beach**, across Hwy-1.

South of the Lighthouse, the **James Fitzgerald Marine Reserve** strings along the shore, a two-mile shelf of flat, slippery rocks that make excellent tidal pools. The ranger often gives guided interpretive walks through the reserve at low tide, the best time to explore. At the south end of the reserve, **Pillar Point** juts out into the Pacific; just to the east, along Hwy-1, fishing boats dock at **Pillar Point Harbor**. Mavericks Beach, just off Pillar Point beyond the enormous communications dish, with the largest waves in North America, attracts some of the world's best (and craziest) surfers when conditions are right – just watching them can be an exhilarating way to spend an hour or so. In the faintly touristy, ramshackle town adjacent to the waterfront, **PRINCETON-BY-THE-SEA**, a couple of bayview restaurants sell freshly caught fish and fries. Further along, the best of the local surfing is just offshore from **Miramar Beach**; after a day in the water or on the beach, the place to head for is the beachfront *Douglass Beach House* (☎650/726-4143) an informal jazz club and beer bar that faces the sands.

Half Moon Bay

HALF MOON BAY, twenty miles south of the city and the only town of any size along the coast between San Francisco and Santa Cruz, takes its name from the crescent-shaped bay formed by Pillar Point. Lined by miles of sandy beaches, the town is surprisingly rural considering its proximity to San Francisco and Silicon Valley, and sports a number of ornate Victorian wooden houses around its center. The oldest of these, at north end of Main Street, was built in 1849 just across a little stone bridge over Pillarcitos Creek. The **Chamber of Commerce** (see p.472 for details) on Hwy-1 has free walking tour maps of the town and information on the two annual festivals for which the place is well known. These are the **Holy Ghost and Pentecost Festival**, a parade and barbecue held on the sixth Sunday after Easter, and the **Pumpkin Festival**, celebrating the harvest of the area's many pumpkin farms, just in time for Halloween when the fields around town are full of families searching for the perfect jack-o'-lantern to greet the hordes of trick-or-treaters. Free, basic campgrounds line the coast in **Half Moon Bay State Park**, half a mile west of the town.

SamTrans bus #1A route ends in Half Moon Bay; to continue south, transfer here to route #90C, which runs every three hours to Waddell Creek, twenty miles south. **San Gregorio State Beach**, ten miles south of Half Moon Bay, is at its best in the spring, after the winter storms, when flotsam architects construct a range of driftwood shelters along the wide beach south of the parking area. On hot summer days, the beach is packed with well-oiled bodies, but the sands around the bluffs to the north are quieter. You can bathe nude at San Gregorio Private Beach, though you pay to park and enter; follow Hwy-1 one mile north of San Gregorio Road and watch for the white gate that marks the turning. Just north of Half Moon Bay, Dunes Beach and Venice Beach are also beautiful expanses of sand and ocean. You can ride a horse along the beaches from the Sea Horse Ranch, Hwy-1 one mile north of Hwy-92 (☎650/726-2362; $20 per hour).

The Butano redwoods and the Año Nuevo State Reserve

If you've got a car and it's not a great day for the beach, head up into the hills above, where the thousands of acres of the **Butano redwood forest** feel at their most ancient and primeval in the greyest, gloomiest weather. About half the land between San Jose and the coast is protected from development in a variety of state and county parks, all of which are virtually deserted despite being within a thirty minute drive of the Silicon Valley sprawl. Any one of a dozen roads heads through endless stands of untouched forest, and even the briefest of walks will take you seemingly miles from any sign of civilization. Hwy-84 climbs up from San Gregorio through the Sam McDonald County Park to the hamlet of **LA HONDA**, from where you can continue on to Palo Alto, or, better, loop back to the coast via Pescadero Road. A mile before you reach the quaint town of **PESCADERO**, Cloverdale Road heads south to **Butano State Park**, where you can hike and camp overlooking the Pacific. Tiny Pescadero itself has one of the best places to eat on the Peninsula – *Duarte's* (see opposite).

Back on Hwy-1, five miles south of Pescadero you can stay the night in the old lighthouse keeper's quarters and soak your bones in a marvelous hot tub at the **HI-Pigeon Point Lighthouse Hostel** (see p.473). If you're here in December or January, continue south another five miles to the **Año Nuevo State Reserve** for a chance to see one of nature's most bizarre spectacles – the mating rituals of the northern elephant seal. These massive, ungainly creatures, fifteen feet long and weighing up to three tons, were once found all along the coast, though they were nearly hunted to extinction by whalers in the last century. During the mating season the beach is literally a seething mass of blubbery bodies, with the trunk-nosed males fighting it out for the right to sire as many as fifty pups in a season. At any time of the year you're likely to see a half dozen or so dozing in the sands. The reserve is also good for bird watching, and in March you might even catch sight of migrating gray whales.

The slowly resurgent Año Nuevo seal population is still carefully protected, and during the breeding season the obligatory guided tours – designed to protect spectators as much as to give the seals some privacy – are often oversubscribed (hourly 8am–4pm; ☎650/879-0227). Otherwise tickets are usually made available to people staying at the *Pigeon Point Hostel*, and SamTrans (☎1-800/660-4287) sometimes runs charter bus tours from the town of **San Mateo** on the bay side of the Peninsula. (See "The Central Coast" for an account of the area from Año Nuevo south to Santa Cruz and Monterey.)

Peninsula eating

The **restaurants** on the Peninsula, particularly in pseudo-ritzy Palo Alto and newly yuppified Burlingame, are increasingly on par with their San Franciscan counterparts, and many, filled with wealthy young computer executives, require dinner reservations every night of the week. The following list concentrates primarily on establishments centrally located in the downtown areas of the various Peninsula cities, with a few others that are worth almost any effort to get to.

Alpine Inn, 3915 Alpine Rd, Woodside (☎650/854-4004). Stagecoach stop turned greasy burger joint in the hills with outdoor picnic tables and an interesting mix of locals and computer guys.

Barbara's Fish Trap, 281 Capistrano Rd, off Hwy-1, Princeton-by-the-Sea (☎650/728-7049). Oceanfront seafood restaurant with good-value fish dinners and an unbeatable view.

Barrio Fiesta, 909 Antoinette Lane, off El Camino Real, S San Francisco (☎650/871-8703). Hard to find amid the shopping sprawl of South City, but well worth it for the huge portions of beautifully presented, delicious Filipino dishes, especially seafood. Full meals cost around $25, but you can snack for a lot less.

Beppo, 643 Emerson St, Palo Alto (☎650/329-0065). To say the food portions are large, the decor eclectic, and the staff wacky would be an understatement. Everything about this place is fun, from the family style Italian meals to the photos of the pope and Frank Sinatra on the walls.

Chateau des Fleurs, 523 Church St, Half Moon Bay (☎650/712-8837). The exquisite flower garden in front welcomes you to this small, reasonably priced French restaurant.

Duarte's, 202 Stage Rd, Pescadero (☎650/879-0464). Platefuls of traditional American food, (especially fish) for around $10 are served in this down-home find connected to a bar full of locals in cowboy hats. Famous for their artichoke soup.

Eulipia, 374 S First St, San Jose (☎408/280-6161). Upscale and stylish spot featuring well-prepared versions of California cuisine staples like grilled fish and fresh pastas. Dinner and drinks will set you back $15–25.

Evvia, 420 Emerson St, Palo Alto (☎650/326-0983). California/Greek lamb and fish dishes with names like "Paidakia Arnisia" and "Arni Kapama" served in a chic, yet cozy and elegant dining room.

Joanie's Cafe, 447 California Ave, Palo Alto (☎650/326-6505). Homestyle breakfasts and lunches in a comfortable neighborhood restaurant.

John's Market, Town and Country Village, Embarcadero at El Camino, Palo Alto (☎650/321-8438). Steer past the high school kids on lunch break to get one of the best (and biggest) deli sandwiches around. Located across the street from Stanford Stadium.

Krung Thai Cuisine, 1699 W San Carlos St, San Jose (☎408/295-5508). Excellent range of satays and delicious, unusual seafood dishes. Start off with a *po-tak* soup of clams and crab legs in citrus broth.

Little Garden, 4127 El Camino Real, Palo Alto (☎650/494-1230). Simple, spicy, well-prepared Vietnamese food – fried chicken on a bed of cabbage, shrimp and hot peppers in peanut sauce – in unpretentious surroundings.

Los Gallos Taqueria, 3726 Florence St, Redwood City (☎650/369-1864). Simply put, they make the best burritos on the Peninsula. Take the Marsh Road exit from Hwy-101 and look for the Marsh Manor shopping center.

Mike's Cafe, Etc., 2680 Middlefield Rd, Palo Alto (☎650/473-6453). Unpretentious neighborhood restaurant hidden behind a hardware store. Excellent fresh salads, pastas, and simple meat dishes are usually brought to your table by Mike himself.

Miyake, 140 University Ave, Palo Alto (☎650/879-0464). Excessively popular restaurant serving decent and extremely cheap sushi to a boisterous crowd. The California Rolls are the best (and biggest) around.

Original Joe's, 301 S First St, San Jose (☎408/292-7030). Grab a stool at the counter or settle into one of the comfy vinyl booths and enjoy a burger and fries or a plate of pasta at this San Jose institution, where $10 goes a long way.

Palermo, 452 University Ave, Palo Alto (☎650/321-9908). Friendly staff and delicious southern Italian pasta dishes served in a lively and cramped dining room.

Peninsula nightlife

For a serious night out on the town, you're better off heading up to San Francisco, though many San Jose residents may try to convince you otherwise. Nevertheless, there are several good **bars and clubs** on the Peninsula – particularly in San Jose, but also in the studenty environs of Palo Alto. If you're in the mood for quiet conversation rather than wild beer drinking, check out one of the **cafes** listed, many of which feature fresh sandwiches and salads along with the requisite microbrewed beers and gourmet coffees.

Agenda, 399 S First St, San Jose (☎408/287-4087). A bar/restaurant/lounge in the popular "SOFA" district, that has some people saying the nightlife is coming alive in San Jose. DJ dancing and live jazz nightly.

Blue Chalk Café, 630 Ramona St, Palo Alto (☎650/326-1020). Yuppies and other young Siliconites have been flocking to this wildly successful bar/pool-hall/restaurant ever since it opened in 1993.

Douglass Beach House, Miramar Beach, two and a half miles north of Half Moon Bay on Hwy-1, go west down Medio Avenue (☎650/726-4143). Two-story country beach house with fireplace and outside deck hosting West Coast jazz performers.

Cactus Club, 417 S First St, San Jose (☎408/491-9300). One of two very good clubs near each other in downtown San Jose, hosting some of the better up-and-coming bands with music ranging from roots reggae to hard-core thrash. Cover $4–8.

Café Matisse, 371 First St, San Jose (☎408/298-7788). Modern art hangs on the walls of this funky artist studio space, which serves fresh coffee and pastries.

Café at Printer's Inc, 320 California Ave, Palo Alto (☎650/323-3347). Good food and coffees served adjacent to Palo Alto's best bookstore.

Caffé Verona, 236 Hamilton Ave, Palo Alto (☎650/326-9942). Relaxing hangout for Palo Alto's intellectual crowd.

The Edge, 260 California Ave, Palo Alto (☎650/324-EDGE). Cheap drinks and low (or no) cover charge make this dance club a lively option. Good live touring bands some nights, when tickets cost $5–10.

FX: The Club, 400 S First St, San Jose (☎408/298-9796). The other good San Jose club, more jazz/hip-hoppy, great for drinking and dancing; 21 and over only. Closed Mon & Tues; free before 10pm, $6 after.

Gordon Biersch Brewery, 640 Emerson St, Palo Alto (☎650/323-7723). Among the first and still the best of the Bay Area's microbrewery-cum-restaurants. Also in SF (see p.426) and in downtown San Jose at 33 E San Fernando St (☎408/294-6785).

M Coffee, 522 Main St, Half Moon Bay (☎650/726-6241). Coffees, teas, sandwiches and ice cream in a small, homely eatery.

Moss Beach Distillery, Beach and Ocean, Moss Beach (☎650/728-0220). If you don't feel like paying out $20 per entree at the popular restaurant, snuggle up under a wool blanket, order a drink and an appetizer, and watch the sunset from the patio overlooking the ocean.

St Michael's Alley, 806 Emerson St, Palo Alto (☎650/326-2530). Small, cozy café for students and locals, serving light breakfasts, lunches, and dinners. Art exhibits on the walls and live music at night.

Marin County

Across the Golden Gate from San Francisco, **Marin County** (pronounced "Ma-RINN") is an unabashed introduction to Californian self-indulgence: an elitist pleasure zone of conspicuous luxury and abundant natural beauty, with sunshine, sandy beaches, high mountains, and thick redwood forests. Often ranked as the wealthiest county in the US, Marin has attracted a sizeable contingent of northern California's wealthiest young professionals, many of whom grew up during the Flower Power years of the 1960s and lend the place its New Age feel and reputation. Though many of the cocaine-and-hot-tub devotees who seemed to populate the swanky waterside towns in the 1970s have traded in their drug habits for mountain bikes, life in Marin still centers around personal pleasure, and the throngs you see hiking and cycling at weekends, not to mention the hundreds of esoteric self-help practitioners – rolfing, rebirthing, and soul-travel therapists fill up the classified ads of the local papers – prove that Marinites work hard to maintain their easy air of physical and mental well-being.

Flashy modern ferry boats, appointed with fully stocked bars, sail across the bay from San Francisco and give a good initial view of the county. As you head past desolate Alcatraz Island, curvaceous **Mount Tamalpais** looms larger until you land at its foot in one of the chic bayside settlements of **Sausalito** or **Tiburon**. **Angel Island**, in the middle of the bay but accessible most easily from Tiburon, provides relief from the excessive style-consciousness of both towns, retaining a wild untouched feeling among the eerie ruins of derelict military fortifications.

Sausalito and Tiburon (and the lifestyles that go with them) are only a small part of Marin. The bulk of the county rests on the slopes of the ridge of peaks that divides the Peninsula down the middle, separating the sophisticated harborside towns in the east from the untrammeled wilderness of the Pacific coast to the west. The **Marin Headlands**, just across the Golden Gate Bridge, hold time-warped old battlements and gun emplacements that once protected San Francisco's harbor from would-be invaders, and now overlook hikers and cyclists enjoying the acres of open space. Along the coastline that stretches north, the broad shore of **Stinson Beach** is the Bay Area's finest and widest stretch of sand, beyond which Hwy-1 clings to the coast past the rural village of **Bolinas** to the seascapes of **Point Reyes**, where Sir Francis Drake landed in 1579 and claimed all of California for England.

Inland, the heights of Mount Tamalpais, and specifically **Muir Woods**, are a magnet to sightseers and nature-lovers, who come to wander through one of the few surviving stands of the native coastal redwood trees. Such trees covered most of Marin before they were chopped down to build and rebuild the dainty wooden houses of San Francisco. The long-vanished lumber mills of the rustic town of **Mill Valley**, overlooking the bay from the slopes of Mount Tam, as it's locally known, bear the guilt for much of this destruction; the oldest town in Marin County is now home to an eclectic bunch of art galleries and cafés. Further north, Marin's largest town, **San Rafael**, is best left alone, though its outskirts contain two of the most unusual attractions in the county: **Frank Lloyd Wright**'s peculiar Civic Center complex and the preserved remnants of an old Chinese fishing village in **China Camp State Park**. The northern reaches of Marin County border the bountiful wine-growing regions of the Sonoma and Napa valleys, detailed in Northern California.

Arrival and getting around

Just getting to Marin County can be a great start to a day out from San Francisco. Golden Gate Transit **ferries** (☎415/923-2000) leave from the Ferry Building on the Embarcadero, crossing the bay past Alcatraz Island to **Sausalito** and **Larkspur**; they run from 5.30am until 8.30pm, approximately every thirty minutes during the rush hour, less often the rest of the day, and every two hours on weekends and holidays. Tickets cost $4.25 one-way to Sausalito, $2.50 to Larkspur Monday to Friday ($4.25 weekends); refreshments are served on board. The more expensive Blue and Gold Fleet ($11 round trip; ☎415/773-1188) sail from Pier 41 at Fisherman's Wharf to **Sausalito** and **Tiburon** – from where the *Angel Island Ferry* ($6 round trip, plus $1 per bicycle; ☎415/435-2131) nips back and forth to **Angel Island State Park** daily in summer, weekends only in the winter. Blue and Gold Fleet provides additional service to Tiburon from the Ferry Building downtown during commute hours ($5.50 one way).

Golden Gate Transit also runs a comprehensive **bus service** around Marin County and across the Golden Gate Bridge from the Transbay Terminal in San Francisco (in Marin County, call ☎415/453-2100), and publishes a helpful and free system map and timetable, including all ferry services. Bus fares range from $1.25 to $4.50, depending on the distance traveled. Basic GGT bus routes run every thirty minutes throughout the day, and once an hour late at night. GGT commuter services, which run only during the morning and evening rush hours, can be the only way to get to some places.

MARIN COUNTY BUS SERVICES ON GOLDEN GATE TRANSIT

#10: San Francisco–Sausalito–Marin City–Mill Valley–Tiburon.

#20: San Francisco–Marin City–Larkspur–San Anselmo–San Rafael.

#24: San Francisco–Ross–San Anselmo–Fairfax; weekdays only.

#50: San Francisco–Sausalito–Marin City–San Rafael–Novato.

#63: Golden Gate Bridge–Sausalito–Marin City–Pan Toll Ranger Station–Stinson Beach; weekends and holidays only.

#65: San Rafael–San Anselmo–Fairfax–Olema–Point Reyes; 9am & 4pm, weekends & holidays only.

SAN FRANCISCO–MARIN COUNTY FERRIES

Because ferry schedules change slightly four times a year, you should use the following **timetable** as an estimate of arrival and departure times. Current schedules are always available from the terminals.

GOLDEN GATE TRANSIT FERRIES (☎415/923-3000)

San Francisco–Larkspur: Mon–Fri depart 6.50am, 7.50am, 8.50am, 10.45am, 12.45pm, 2.45pm, 3.35pm, 4.15pm, 4.50pm, 5.20pm, 6pm, 6.45pm & 8.25pm; Sat, Sun & holidays 10.45am, 12.45pm, 2.45pm, 4.45pm & 6.45pm.

Larkspur–San Francisco: Mon–Fri depart 6am, 7am, 7.30am, 8am, 8.40am, 9.45am, 11.45am, 1.45pm, 3.45pm, 4.25pm, 5.05pm, 5.40pm & 7.35pm; Sat, Sun & holidays 9.45am, 11.45am, 1.45pm, 3.45pm & 5.45pm.

San Francisco–Sausalito: Mon–Fri depart 7.40am, 9.15am, 10.25am, 11.45am, 1.10pm, 2.35pm, 4.10pm, 5.30pm, 6.40pm & 8pm; Sat, Sun & holidays 11.30am, 1pm, 2.30pm, 4pm, 5.30pm & 6.55pm; also May–Sept 8.05pm.

Sausalito–San Francisco: Sat, Sun & holidays depart 7.05am, 8.15am, 11.05am, 12.25pm, 1.55pm, 3.20pm, 4.45pm, 6.05pm & 7.20pm; Sat, Sun & holidays 10.50am, 12.15pm, 1.45pm, 3.15pm, 4.45pm & 6.10pm; also May–Sept 7.30pm.

BLUE AND GOLD FLEET FERRIES (☎415/773-1188)

San Francisco–Sausalito: Mon–Fri depart 11am, 12.15pm, 1.35pm, 2.45pm & 4.50pm; Sat, Sun & holidays 10.40am, 12.25pm, 1.50pm, 3.15pm, 4.45pm & 6.30pm; also May–Sept Fri & Sat 8.25pm.

Sausalito–San Francisco: Mon–Fri depart 11.50am, 1.05pm, 2.15pm, 3.40pm, 5.45pm & 8pm; Sat, Sun & holidays 11.20am, 1.05pm, 2.30pm, 3.55pm, 5.25pm & 7.10pm; also May–Sept Fri & Sat 8.50pm.

San Francisco–Tiburon: Mon–Fri depart 11am, 12.15pm, 1.35pm, 2.45pm, 4.05pm & 4.50pm; Sat, Sun & holidays 10am, noon, 2pm, 4pm, 4.45pm & 6.30pm; also May–Sept Fri & Sat 8.25pm.

Tiburon–San Francisco: Mon–Fri depart 11.25am, 12.40pm, 1.55pm, 3.10pm, 5.25pm & 7.45pm; Sat, Sun & holidays 11.40am, 1.35pm, 3.15pm, 5.15pm & 6.50pm; also May–Sept Fri & Sat 9.10pm.

Also, San Francisco's Muni bus #76 runs hourly from San Francisco direct to the Marin Headlands on Sundays only. Golden Gate Transit bus route #40, the only service available between Marin County and the East Bay, runs from the San Rafael Transit Center to the Del Norte BART station in El Cerrito ($2 each way).

If you'd rather avoid the hassle of bus connections, Gray Line ($30; ☎415/558-9400) offers four-hour **guided bus tours** from the Transbay Terminal in San Francisco, taking in Sausalito and Muir Woods (daily 9am, 10am, 11am, 1.30pm & 2.30pm); the Blue and Gold Fleet ferry also has a boat-and-bus trip to Muir Woods, via Tiburon, for $32 round trip.

One of the best ways to get around Marin is by **bike**, particularly using a mountain bike to cruise the many trails that crisscross the county. If you want to ride on the road, **Sir Francis Drake Highway** – from Larkspur to Point Reyes – makes a good route, though it's best to avoid weekends, when the roads can get clogged up with cars. All ferry services (except Alcatraz) allow bicycles.

Information

Three main on-the-spot sources can provide further information on Marin County: the **Marin County Visitors Bureau**, Marin Center, Avenue of the Flags, San Rafael (Mon–Fri 9am–5pm; ☎415/472-7470), the **Sausalito Chamber of Commerce**, Fourth

Floor, 777 Bridgeway (Tues–Sun 11.30am–4pm; ☎415/332-0505), and the **Mill Valley Chamber of Commerce**, 85 Throckmorton Ave (Mon, Tues, Thurs & Fri 11am–4pm; ☎415/388-9700), in the center of the town.

For information on **hiking** and **camping** in the wilderness and beach areas, depending on where you're heading, contact the Golden Gate National Recreation Area, Building 201, Fort Mason Center (Mon–Fri 9.30am–4.30pm; ☎415/556-0560); Mount Tamalpais State Park, 801 Panoramic Highway, Mill Valley (daily 8.30am–10.30pm; ☎415/388-2070); or the Point Reyes National Seashore, Bear Valley Visitors Center, Point Reyes (Mon–Fri 9am–5pm, Sat & Sun 8am–5pm; ☎415/663-1092). Information on **what's on** in Marin can be found in the widely available local freesheets, such as the down-to-earth *Coastal Post* or the new-agey *Pacific Sun*.

Accommodation

You might prefer simply to dip into Marin County using San Francisco as a base, and if you've got a car or manage to time the bus connections right it's certainly possible, at least for the southernmost parts of the county. However, it can be nicer to take a more leisurely look at Marin, staying over for a couple of nights in some well-chosen spots. Sadly there are few hotels, and those that there are often charge in excess of $100 a night; motels tend to be the same as anywhere, though there are a couple of attractively faded ones along the coast. If you want to stay in a B&B, contact the **Bed and Breakfast Exchange**, 45 Entrata Drive, San Anselmo (☎415/485-1971), which can fix you up with rooms in comfortable private homes all over Marin County from $50 a night for two, ranging from courtyard hideaways on the beach in Tiburon to houseboats in Sausalito. The best bet for budget accommodation is a dorm bed in one of the beautifully situated **hostels** along the western beaches.

Hostels

HI-Marin Headlands, Building 941, Fort Barry, Marin Headlands (closed 9.30am–4.30pm; ☎415/331-2777). Hard to get to unless you're driving – it's near Rodeo Lagoon just off Bunker Road, five miles west of Sausalito – but worth the effort for its setting, in cozy old army barracks just across the Golden Gate Bridge. On Sundays and holidays only, Muni bus #76 from San Francisco stops right outside. Dorm beds $11 a night.

HI-Point Reyes, in the Point Reyes National Seashore (closed 9.30am–4.30pm; ☎415/663-8811). Also hard to reach without your own transportation: just off Limantour Road six miles west of the visitor center and two miles from the beach, it's located in an old ranch house and surrounded by meadows and forests. Dorm beds $12–14 a night.

Motels and hotels

Casa Madrona, 801 Bridgeway, Sausalito (☎1-800/567-9524 or 415/332-0502). Deluxe hideaway tucked into the hills above the bay. ⑦.

Colonial Motel, 1735 Lincoln Ave, San Rafael (☎415/453-9188). Quiet, cheap and friendly motel in a residential neighborhood. ③.

Grand Hotel, 15 Brighton Ave, Bolinas (☎415/868-1757). Budget rooms in a funky, run-down old hotel. ②.

Ocean Court Motel, 18 Arenal St, Stinson Beach (☎415/868-0212). Just a block from the beach, west of Hwy-1. Large simple rooms with kitchens. ⑤.

Stinson Beach Motel, 3416 Shoreline Hwy, Stinson Beach (☎415/868-1712). Basic roadside motel right on Hwy-1, with tiny rooms. Five minutes' walk to the beach. ④.

Bed and breakfast

Blue Heron Inn, 11 Wharf Rd, Bolinas (☎415/868-1102). Lovely double rooms in an unbeatable locale. Breakfast is served at the owner's cozy restaurant, *The Shop Café* at 46 Wharf Rd, which also serves lunch and dinner. ⑤.

Lindisfarne Guest House, Green Gulch Zen Center, Muir Beach (☎415/383-3134). Restful rooms in a meditation retreat set in a secluded valley above Muir Beach. Price includes excellent vegetarian meals. ⑤.

Mountain Home Inn, 810 Panoramic Highway, Mill Valley (☎415/381-9000). Romantically located on Mount Tamalpais' crest, this bed and breakfast offers great views and endless hiking. Some rooms with hot tubs. ⑦.

Pelican Inn, 10 Pacific Way, Muir Beach (☎415/383-6000). Very comfortable rooms in a romantic pseudo-English country inn, with good bar and restaurant downstairs, ten minutes' walk from beautiful Muir Beach. ⑦.

Ten Inverness Way, 10 Inverness Way, Inverness (☎415/669-1648). Quiet and restful, with a hot tub, in small village of good restaurants and bakeries on the fringes of Point Reyes. ⑥.

Campgrounds

China Camp State Park, off N San Pedro Rd, north of San Rafael (☎415/456-0766). Walk-in plots (just 600 ft from the parking lot) overlooking a lovely meadow. First-come-first-camped for $12 a night.

Marin Headlands, just across the Golden Gate Bridge (☎415/331-1540). The best of four campgrounds here is at Kirby Cove (open summer only, and very popular), at the northern foot of the Golden Gate Bridge. Free.

Mount Tamalpais State Park, above Mill Valley (☎415/388-2070). Free plots for backpackers on the slopes of the mountain, and a few rustic cabins ($25 a night), along the coast at Steep Ravine.

Point Reyes National Seashore, forty miles northwest of San Francisco (☎415/663-1092). A wide range of sites for backpackers, near the beach or in the forest.

Samuel Taylor State Park, on Sir Francis Drake Blvd, fifteen miles west of San Rafael (☎415/488-9897). Deluxe, car-accessible plots with hot showers, spread along a river for $14 a night. Don't miss the swimming hole or bat caves. In summer, reserve a place through Parknet ☎1-800/444-7275.

Across the Golden Gate: Marin Headlands and Sausalito

The headlands across the Golden Gate from San Francisco afford some of the most impressive views of the bridge and the city behind. Take the first turn past the bridge, and follow the road up the hill into the **Marin Headlands** section of the Golden Gate National Recreation Area – largely undeveloped land, except for the concrete remains of old forts and gun emplacements standing guard over the entrance to the bay. The coastline here is much more rugged than it is on the San Francisco side, and though it makes a great place for an aimless clifftop scramble or a walk along the beach, it's impossible not to be at least a little sobered by the presence of so many military relics – even if none was ever fired in a war. The oldest of these artillery batteries dates from the Civil War, while the newest was built to protect against a Japanese invasion during World War II, but even though the huge guns have been replaced by picnic tables and brass plaques – one of the concrete bunkers has even been painted to make a trompel'oeil Greek temple – you can't overlook their violent intent. **Battery Wallace**, the largest and most impressive of the artillery sites, is cut through a hillside above the southwestern tip, and the clean-cut military geometry survives to frame views of the Pacific Ocean and the Golden Gate Bridge. If you're interested in such things, come along on the first Sunday of the month and take a guided tour of an abandoned 1950s ballistic missile launchpad, complete with disarmed nuclear missiles. The one non-military sight, the **Point Bonita Lighthouse**, stands at the very end of the Headlands, where it's open for tours on weekends, except during the winter.

Most of what there is to do out here is concentrated half a mile to the north, around the rocky cliffs and islets of the point. Adjacent to the **Marin Headlands Visitor Center** (daily 9.30am–4.30pm; ☎415/331-1540), at the end of the Muni bus #76 route from San Francisco (Sun & holidays only), a wide sandy beach separates the chilly ocean from the marshy warm water of **Rodeo Lagoon**. Swimming is prohibited here, in order to protect the nesting seabirds. Next to the center, the **Marine Mammal Center** rescues and rehabilitates injured and orphaned sea creatures, which you can visit while they recover; there's also a series of displays on the marine ecosystem and a bookstore that sells T-shirts and posters. The largest of the old army officers' quarters in the adjacent **Fort Barry**, half a mile to the east, has been converted into the spacious and homey **Marin Headlands Youth Hostel**, an excellent base for more extended explorations of the inland ridges and valleys.

Sausalito

SAUSALITO, along the bay below US-101, is a pretty, smug little town of exclusive restaurants and pricey boutiques along a picturesque waterfront promenade. Expensive, quirkily designed houses climb the overgrown cliffs above **Bridgeway Avenue**, the main road and bus route through town. Sausalito used to be a fairly gritty community of fishermen and sea-traders, full of bars and bordellos, and despite its upscale modern face it still makes a fun day out from San Francisco by ferry, the boats arriving next to the Sausalito Yacht Club in the center of town. Hang out in one of the waterfront bars and watch the crowds strolling along the esplanade, or climb the stairways above Bridgeway and amble around the leafy hills. If you have sailing experience, split the $130 daily rental fee of a four- to six-person sailboat at Cass's Marine, 1702 Bridgeway (☎415/332-6789).

The old working wharves and warehouses that made Sausalito a haven for smugglers and Prohibition-era rum-runners are long gone; most have been taken over by dull steakhouses such as the *Charthouse*. However, some stretches of it have, for the moment at least, survived the tourist onslaught. Half a mile north of the town center along Bridgeway Avenue, an ad hoc community of exotic barges and houseboats, some of which have been moored here since the 1950s, is being threatened with eviction to make room for yet another luxury marina and bayview office development. In the meantime, many of the boats – one looks like a South Pacific island, another like the Taj Mahal – can be viewed from the marina behind the large brown shed at 2100 Bridgeway that houses the **Bay Model Visitor Center** (Tues–Fri 9am–4pm, Sat & Sun 10am–6pm; free), which features a recently overhauled massive working model of the San Francisco Bay, simulating changing tides and powerful currents.

The Marin County Coast to Bolinas

The **Shoreline Highway**, Hwy-1, cuts off west from US-101 just north of Sausalito, following the old main highway towards Mill Valley (see p.487). The first turn on the left, Tennessee Valley Road, leads up to the less-visited northern expanses of the Golden Gate National Recreation Area. You can take a beautiful three-mile hike from the parking lot at the end of the road, heading down along the secluded and lushly green **Tennessee Valley** to a small beach along a rocky cove, or you can take a guided tour on horseback from Miwok Livery at 701 Tennessee Valley Rd (☎415/383-8048; $30 per hr).

Hwy-1 twists up the canyon to a crest, where **Panoramic Highway** spears off to the right, following the ridge north to Muir Woods and Mount Tamalpais (see p.486); Golden Gate Transit bus #63 to Stinson Beach follows this route every hour on weekends and holidays only. Two miles down from the crest, a small unpaved road cuts off to the left, dropping down to the bottom of the broad canyon to the **Green Gulch Farm and Zen Center** (☎415/383-3134), an organic farm and Buddhist retreat, with an authentic Japanese tea house and a simple but refined prayer hall. On Sunday mornings the center is opened for a public meditation period and an informal discussion of Zen Buddhism, after which you can stroll down to Muir Beach. If you already have some experience of Zen, inquire about the center's Guest Student Program, which enables initiates to stay from three days to several weeks at a time (it costs about $10 a night). If you just want a weekend's retreat, you can also stay overnight in the attached *Lindisfarne Guest House* (⑤), whose rates include meals, and take part as you choose in the communal life. Residents rise well before dawn for meditation and prayer, then work much of the day in the gardens, tending the vegetables that are eventually served in many of the Bay Area's finest restaurants (notably *Green's* in San Francisco – see p.425).

Beyond the Zen Center, the road down from Muir Woods rejoins Hwy-1 at **Muir Beach**, usually uncrowded and beautifully secluded in a semicircular cove. Three miles north, **Steep Ravine** drops sharply down the cliffs to a small beach, past very rustic $30-a-night cabins and a $10-a-night campground, bookable through Mount Tamalpais State Park (see opposite). A mile on is the small and lovely **Red Rocks** nudist beach, down a steep trail from a parking area along the highway. **Stinson Beach**, which is bigger, and more popular despite the rather cold water (it's packed on weekends in summer, when the traffic can be nightmarish), is a mile further. You can rent boogie boards for $8 and wet suits for $10 a day from the Livewater Surf Shop (☎415/868-0333), 3448 Shoreline Hwy, or kayaks for $35–60 per day a bit further down the road at the Stinson Beach Health Club, 3605 Shoreline Hwy (☎415/868-2739).

Bolinas and southern Point Reyes

At the tip of the headland, due west from Stinson Beach, is the village of **BOLINAS**, though you may have a hard time finding it – road signs marking the turn-off from Hwy-1 are removed as soon as they're put up, by locals hoping to keep the place to themselves. The campaign may have backfired, though, since press coverage of the "sign war" has done more to publicize the town than any road sign ever did; to get there, take the first left beyond the estuary and follow the road to the end. Bolinas is completely surrounded by federal property: the Golden Gate National Recreation Area and Point Reyes National Seashore. Even the lagoon was recently declared a National Bird Sanctuary. Known for its leftist hippy culture, the village itself is a small colony of artists, bearded handymen, stray dogs and writers (the late trout-fishing author Richard Brautigan and basketball diarist Jim Carroll among them), and there's not a lot to see – though you can get a feel for the place (and pick up tasty sandwiches and bags of fresh fruit and vegetables) at the Bolinas People's Store in the block-long village center.

Beyond Bolinas there's a rocky beach at the end of Wharf Road west of the village, and **Duxbury Reef Nature Reserve**, half a mile west at the end of Elm Road, is well worth a look for its tidal pools, full of starfish, crabs and sea anemones. Otherwise, Mesa Road heads north from Bolinas past the **Point Reyes Bird Observatory** (☎415/868-0655) – open for informal tours all day, though best visited in the morning. The first bird observatory in the US, this is still an important research and study center. If you time it right you may be able to watch, or even help, the staff as they put colored bands on the birds to keep track of them. Beyond here, the unpaved road leads onto the **Palomarin Trailhead**, the southern access into the Point Reyes National Seashore (see p.489). The best of the many beautiful hikes around the area leads past a number of small lakes and meadows for three miles to **Alamere Falls**, which throughout the winter and spring cascade down the cliffs onto Wildcat Beach. **Bass Lake**, the first along the trail, is a great spot for a swim and is best entered from one of the two rope-swings that hang above its shore.

Mount Tamalpais and Muir Woods

Mount Tamalpais dominates the skyline of the Marin peninsula, hulking over the cool canyons of the rest of the county in a crisp yet voluptuous silhouette and dividing the county into two distinct parts: the wild western slopes above the Pacific coast and the increasingly suburban communities along the calmer bay frontage. Panoramic Highway branches off from Hwy-1 along the crest through the center of **Mount Tamalpais State Park** (☎415/338-2070), which has some thirty miles of hiking trails and many campgrounds, though most of the redwood trees which once covered its slopes have long since been chopped down to form the posts and beams of San Francisco's Victorian houses. One grove of these towering trees does remain, however, protected as the **Muir Woods National Monument** (daily 8am–sunset; $2), a mile down Muir Woods Road from Panoramic Highway. It's a tranquil and majestic spot, with sunlight filtering through the 300ft trees down to the laurel and fern-covered canyon below. The canyon's steep sides are what saved it from Mill Valley's lumbermen, and today it's one of the few first-growth redwood groves between San Francisco and the fantastic forests of Redwood National Park, up the coast near the Oregon border (see p.562).

Its proximity to San Francisco makes Muir Woods a popular target, and the paved trails nearest the parking lot are often packed with bus-tour hordes. However, if you visit during the week, or outside midsummer, it's easy enough to leave the crowds behind, especially if you're willing to head off up the steep trails that climb the canyon sides. Winter is a particularly good time to come, as the streams are gurgling – the main creek flows down to Muir Beach, and salmon have been known to spawn in it – and the forest creatures, including the colonies of ladybugs that spend their winter huddling in the rich undergrowth, are more likely to be seen going about their business. Keep an eye out for the various species of salamanders and newts that thrive in this damp environment; be warned, though, that some are poisonous and will bite if harassed.

One way to avoid the crowds, and the only way to get here on public transportation, is to enter the woods from the top by way of a two-mile hike from the **Pan Toll Ranger Station** (☎415/388-2070) on Panoramic Highway – which is a stop on the Golden Gate Transit #63 bus route. As the state park headquarters, the station has maps and information on hiking and camping, and rangers can suggest hikes to suit your mood and interests. From here the **Pan Toll Road** turns off to the right along the ridge to within a hundred yards of the 2571-foot summit of Mount Tamalpais, where there are breathtaking views of the distant Sierra Nevada, and red-necked turkey vultures listlessly circle.

Mill Valley

From the East Peak of Mount Tamalpais, a quick two-mile hike downhill follows the **Temelpa Trail** through velvety shrubs of chaparral to **MILL VALLEY**, the oldest and most enticing of Marin County's inland towns – also accessible every thirty minutes by Golden Gate Transit bus #10 from San Francisco and Sausalito. Originally a logging center, it was from here that the destruction of the surrounding redwoods was organized, though for many years the town has made a healthy living out of tourism. The **Mill Valley and Mount Tamalpais Scenic Railroad** – according to the blurb, "the crookedest railroad in the world" – was cut into the slopes above the town in 1896, twisting up through nearly three hundred tight curves in under eight miles. The trip proved so popular with tourists that the line was extended down into Muir Woods in 1907, though road-building and fire combined to put an end to the railroad by 1930. You can, however, follow its old route from the end of Summit Avenue in Mill Valley, a popular trip with daredevils on all-terrain bikes, which were, incidentally, invented here.

Though much of Mill Valley's attraction lies in its easy access to hiking and mountain-bike trails up Mount Tam, its compact yet relaxed center has a number of cafés and some surprisingly good shops and galleries. The Book Depot and Cafe is an especially popular bookstore, café and meeting place on Throckmorton and Miller (daily 7am–10pm). Next door, the **Chamber of Commerce** (Mon, Tues, Thurs & Fri 11am–4pm; ☎415/388-9700), has maps and restaurant listings, as well as information on the wide range of local entertainment, including summer plays in the outdoor Mountain Theater and a world-class **film festival** in October.

Tiburon and Angel Island

TIBURON, at the tip of a narrow peninsula three miles east of US-101, is, like Sausalito, a ritzy harborside village to which hundreds of people come each weekend, many of them via direct Blue and Gold Fleet **ferries** from Pier 41 in San Francisco's Fisherman's Wharf. It's a relaxed place, less touristy than Sausalito, and if you're in the mood to take it easy and watch the boats sail across the bay, sitting out on the sunny deck of one of the many cafés and bars can be idyllic. There are few specific sights to look out for, but it's pleasant enough to simply wander around, browsing the galleries and antique shops. The best of these are grouped together in **Ark Row**, at the west end of Main Street, where the quirky buildings are actually old houseboats that were beached here early in the century. On a hill above the town stands **Old St Hilary's Church** (tours Wed & Sun 1–4pm), a Carpenter Gothic beauty that is best seen in the spring, when the surrounding fields are covered with multicolored buckwheat, flax, and paintbrush.

If you're feeling energetic, rent a bicycle from Planeaway Bikes, 1 Blackfield Drive (☎415/383-2123), and cruise around the many plush houses of **Belvedere Island**, just across the Beach Road Bridge from the west end of Main Street, enjoying the fine views of the bay and Golden Gate Bridge. More ambitious cyclists can continue along the waterfront bike path, which winds from the bijou shops and galleries three miles west along undeveloped Richardson Bay frontage to a bird sanctuary at **Greenwood Cove**. The pristine Victorian house here is now the western headquarters of the National Audubon Society and open for tours on Sundays (10am–4pm); a small interpretive center has displays on local and migratory birds and wildlife.

Angel Island

However appealing, the pleasures of Tiburon are soon exhausted, and you'd be well advised to take the hourly Angel Island Ferry ($6 round trip, plus $1 per bicycle; ☎415/435-2131) a mile offshore to the largest island in the San Francisco Bay, ten times the size of Alcatraz. **Angel Island** is now officially a state park, but over the years it's served a variety of purposes, everything from a home for Miwok Native Americans to a World War II prisoner-of-war camp. It's full of ghostly ruins of old military installations, and with oak and eucalyptus trees and sagebrush covering the hills above rocky coves and sandy beaches, feels quite apart from the mainland. The island offers some pleasant biking opportunities: a five-mile road rings the island, and an unpaved track (and a number of hiking trails) leads up to the 800ft hump of **Mount Livermore**, with panoramic views of the Bay Area.

The ferry arrives at **Ayala Cove**, where a small snack bar selling hot dogs and cold drinks provides the only sustenance available on the island – bring a picnic if you plan to spend the day here. The nearby **visitor center** (daily 9am–4pm; ☎415/435-1915), in an old building that was built as a quarantine facility for soldiers returning from the Philippines after the Spanish–American War, has displays on the island's history. Around the point on the northwest corner of the island the **North Garrison**, built in 1905, was the site of a prisoner-of-war camp during World War II, while the larger **East Garrison**, on the bay a half mile beyond, was the major transfer point for soldiers bound for the South Pacific.

Quarry Beach around the point is the best on the island, a clean sandy shore that's protected from the winds blowing in through the Golden Gate; it's also a popular landing spot for kayakers and canoeists who paddle across the bay from Berkeley. **Camping** on Angel Island (☎1-800/444-7275) costs $10 per night ($11 Fri & Sat), well worth the view of San Francisco and the East Bay at night.

Sir Francis Drake Boulevard and Central Marin County

The quickest route to the wilds of the Point Reyes National Seashore, and the only way to get there on public transportation, is by way of **Sir Francis Drake Boulevard**, which cuts across central Marin County through the inland towns of **San Anselmo** and **Fairfax**, reaching the coast thirty miles west at a crescent-shaped bay where, in 1579, Drake landed and claimed all of what he called Nova Albion for England. The route makes an excellent day-long cycling tour, with the reward of good beaches, a youth hostel, and some tasty restaurants at the end of the road.

The Larkspur *Golden Gate Transit* **ferry**, which leaves from the Ferry Building in San Francisco, is the longest and, surprisingly, least expensive of the bay crossings. Primarily a commuter route, it docks at the modern space-frame terminal at Larkspur Landing. The monolithic, red-tile-roofed complex you see on the bayfront a mile east is the maximum-security **San Quentin State Prison**, which houses the state's most violent and notorious criminals, and of which Johnny Cash sang so resonantly "I hate every stone of you." If you arrive by car over the Richmond-San Rafael Bridge, follow road signs off Hwy-101 for the San Quentin Prison **Museum**, Building 106, Dolores Way (Tues–Fri & Sun 11am–3pm, Sat 11.45am–3.15pm; $2).

San Anselmo, Fairfax and Point Reyes Station

SAN ANSELMO, set in a broad valley two miles north of Mount Tam, calls itself "the antiques capital of Northern California" and sports a tiny center of specialty shops, furniture stores and cafés that draws out many San Francisco shoppers on weekends. The ivy-covered **San Francisco Theological Seminary** off Bolinas Avenue, which dominates the town from the hill above, is worth a quick visit for the view and architecture. At serene **Robson-Harrington Park** on Crescent Avenue you can picnic among well-tended gardens, and the very green and leafy **Creek Park** follows the creek that winds through the town center, but otherwise there's not a lot to do but eat and drink – or browse through fine bookstores, such as Oliver's Books, at 645 San Anselmo Ave.

Center Boulevard follows the tree-lined creek west for a mile to **FAIRFAX**, a much less ostentatiously hedonistic community than the harborside towns, though in many ways it still typifies Marin lifestyles, with an array of wholefood stores and bookstores geared to a thoughtfully mellow crowd. From Fairfax, the narrow Bolinas Road twists up and over the mountains to the coast at Stinson Beach, while Sir Francis Drake Boulevard winds through a pastoral landscape of ranch houses hidden away up oak-covered valleys.

Ten miles west of Fairfax along Sir Francis Drake Boulevard, **Samuel Taylor State Park** has excellent camping (see p.484 for details); five miles more brings you to the coastal Hwy-1 and the town of Olema, a mile north of which sits the town of **POINT REYES STATION**, a good place to stop off for a bite to eat or to pick up picnic supplies before heading off to enjoy the wide open spaces of the Point Reyes National Seashore just beyond. Trailhead Rentals, a half-mile from the Point Reyes Visitor Center, at 88 Bear Valley Rd (☎415/663-1958), rents mountain bikes for $24 per day – a great way to get around.

The Point Reyes National Seashore

From Point Reyes Station, Sir Francis Drake Boulevard heads out to the westernmost tip of Marin County at Point Reyes through the **Point Reyes National Seashore**, a near-island of wilderness surrounded on three sides by more than fifty miles of isolated coastline – pine forests and sunny meadows bordered by rocky cliffs and sandy, windswept beaches. This wing-shaped landmass, something of an aberration along the generally straight coastline north of San Francisco, is in fact a rogue piece of the earth's crust that has been drifting slowly and steadily northward along the San Andreas Fault, having started some six million years ago as a suburb of Los Angeles. When the great earthquake of 1906 shattered San Francisco, the land here – the epicenter – shifted over sixteen feet in an instant, though damage was confined to a few skewed cattle fences.

The park's **visitor center** (Mon–Fri 9am–5pm, Sat, Sun & holidays 8am–5pm; ☎415/663-1092) two miles southwest of Point Reyes Station near Olema, just off Hwy-1 on Bear Valley Road, holds engaging displays on the geology and natural history of the region. Rangers can suggest good hiking and cycling routes, and have up-to-date information on the weather, which can change quickly and be cold and windy along the coast even when it's hot and sunny here, three miles inland. They also handle permits and reservations for the various **campgrounds** within the park. Nearby, a replica of a native Miwok village has an authentic religious **roundhouse**, and a popular hike follows the Bear Valley Trail along Coast Creek four miles to **Arch Rock**, a large tunnel in the seaside cliffs that you can walk through at low tide.

North of the visitor center, Limantour Road heads west six miles to the **HI-Point Reyes Hostel** (see p.483), continuing on another two miles to the coast at **Limantour Beach**, one of the best swimming beaches and a good place to watch the seabirds in the adjacent estuary. Bear Valley Road rejoins Sir Francis Drake Boulevard just past Limantour Road, leading north along Tomales Bay through the village of **Inverness**, so-named because the landscape reminded an early settler of his home in the Scottish Highlands. Eight miles west of Inverness, a turn leads down past **Johnson's Oyster Farm** (Tues–Sun 8am–4pm; ☎415/669-1149) – which sells bivalves for around $5 a dozen, less than half the price you'd pay in town – to **Drake's Beach**, the presumed landing spot of Sir Francis in 1579. Appropriately, the coastline here resembles the southern coast of England, often cold, wet and windy, with chalk-white cliffs rising above the wide sandy beach. The main road continues west another four miles to the tip of Point Reyes, where a precariously sited **lighthouse** stands firm against the crashing surf. You can't tour the lighthouse itself, but you can climb the tiring 300 or so steps down the steep cliffs to reach it. Even without making the trek all the way out, the bluffs along here are excellent places to look out for sea lions and, in winter, migrating gray whales.

The northern tip of the Point Reyes seashore, **Tomales Point**, is accessible via Pierce Point Road, which turns off Sir Francis Drake Boulevard two miles north of Inverness. Jutting out into Tomales Bay, it's the least-visited section of the park and a refuge for hefty **tule elk**; it's also a great place to admire the lupines, poppies and other wildflowers that appear in the spring. The best swimming (at least the warmest water) is at **Heart's Desire Beach**, just before the end of the road. Down the bluffs from where the road comes to a dead end, there are excellent tidal pools at rocky **McClure's Beach**. North of Point Reyes Station, Hwy-1 continues along the coast, through Bodega Bay up to Mendocino and the Northern California coast.

San Rafael and Northern Marin County

You may pass through **SAN RAFAEL** on your way north from San Francisco, but there's little worth stopping for. The county seat and the only big city in Marin County, it has none of the woodsy qualities that make the other towns special, though you'll come across a couple of good restaurants and bars along Fourth Street, the main drag. Its one attraction is an old **Franciscan Mission** (daily 11am–4pm; free), in fact a 1949 replica that was built near the site of the 1817 original on Fifth Ave at A Street. The real points of interest, however, are well on the outskirts: the Marin County Civic Center to the north and the little-known China Camp State Park along the bay to the east.

The **Marin County Civic Center** (Mon–Fri 9am–5pm; tours Wed 10.30am; free; ☎415/499-6646), spanning the hills just east of US-101 a mile north of central San Rafael, is a strange, otherworldly complex of administrative offices, plus an excellent performance space that resembles a giant viaduct capped by a bright blue-tiled roof. These buildings were architect **Frank Lloyd Wright**'s one and only government project, and although the huge circus tents and amusement park at the core of the designer's conception were never built, it does have some interesting touches, such as the atrium lobbies that open directly to the outdoors.

From the Civic Center, North San Pedro Road loops around the headlands through **China Camp State Park** (☎415/456-0766), an expansive area of pastures and open spaces that's hard to reach without your own transportation. It takes its name from the intact but long-abandoned Chinese shrimp-fishing village at the far eastern tip of the park, the sole survivor of the many small Chinese communities that once dotted the California coast. The ramshackle buildings, small wooden pier and old boats lying on the sand are pure John Steinbeck; the only recent addition a chain-link fence to protect the site from vandals. On the weekend you can get beer and sandwiches from the old shack at the foot of the pier, but the atmosphere is best during the week at sunset, when there's often no one around at all. There's a **campground** at the northern end of the park, about two miles from the end of the Golden Gate Transit bus #23 route.

Six miles north of San Rafael, the **Lucas Valley Road** turns off west, twisting across Marin to Point Reyes. Although he lives and works here, it was not named after *Star Wars* film-maker George Lucas, whose sprawling **Skywalker Ranch** studios are well hidden off the road. Hwy-37 cuts off east, eight miles north of San Rafael, heading around the top of the bay into the Wine Country of the Sonoma and Napa valleys (see p.537).

Eating

Marin's restaurants are as varied in personality as the people who inhabit the county – homey neighborhood cafés dish out nutritious portions to healthy mountain-bikers, well-appointed waterside restaurants cater to tourists, and gourmet establishments serve delicate concoctions to affluent executives. We have listed the best of the options below.

Bubba's Diner, 566 San Anselmo Ave, San Anselmo (☎415/381-0298). Hip little old-fashioned diner with a friendly and casual atmosphere. Try a delicious biscuit with your meal.

Cactus Café, 393 Miller Ave, Mill Valley (☎415/388-8226). Reasonably priced, small and friendly restaurant serving fun Cal-Mex food flavored with homemade hot sauce.

Dipsea Café, 200 Shoreline Hwy, Mill Valley (☎415/381-0298). Hearty pancakes, omelets, sandwiches and salads, especially good before a day out hiking on Mount Tamalpais. Breakfast and lunch only.

Gatsby's, 39 Caledonia St, Sausalito (☎415/332-4500). Slick pizza parlor a block from the waterfront on the north side of town. Bright new interior comes with an expanded (and more expensive) menu.

Hilda's, 639 San Anselmo Ave, San Anselmo (☎415/457-9266). Great breakfasts and lunches in this down-home, cozy café.

The Lark Creek Inn, 234 Magnolia Ave, Larkspur (☎415/924-7766). The place to go in Marin for fine dining. The contemporary American food at this classy restored Victorian is expensive, but not without reason: the food is exquisite, the service first rate, and the atmosphere charming.

Mikayla, 801 Bridgeway, Sausalito (☎415/331-5888). Mediterranean staples meet California cuisine in this expensive, but highly rated restaurant in the *Casa Madrona* hotel. Romantic views of the harbor and excellent seafood. Huge Sunday brunch buffet.

Mill Valley Market, 12 Corte Madera Ave, Mill Valley (☎415/388-8466). Deliciously large sandwiches and mouth-watering pasta salads that can be enjoyed at the picnic tables in the main plaza across the street.

Mountain Home Inn, 810 Panoramic Hwy, above Mill Valley (☎415/381-9000). A place that's as good for the view as for the food, with broiled meat and fish dishes served up in a rustic lodge on the slopes of Mount Tamalpais.

New Morning Café, 1696 Tiburon Blvd, Tiburon (☎415/435-4315). Lots of healthy wholegrain sandwiches, plus salads and omelets.

Piazza D'Angelo, 22 Miller Ave, Mill Valley (☎415/388-2000). Good salads, tasty pasta and affordable pizzas, served up in a lively but comfortable room right off the downtown plaza.

Rice Table, 1617 Fourth St, San Rafael (☎415/456-1808). From the shrimp chips through the crab pancakes and noodles onto the fried plantain desserts, these fragrant and spicy Indonesian dishes are worth planning a day around. Dinners only, but excellent value at around $15 a head for a very filling meal.

Sam's Anchor Café, 27 Main St, Tiburon (☎415/435-4527). This rough-hewn, amiable waterfront café and bar has been around for more than 75 years. Good burgers, sandwiches and very popular Sunday brunches are best enjoyed on the outdoor deck.

Station House Café, 11180 Hwy-1 (Main Street), Point Reyes Station (☎415/663-1515). Serving three meals daily, this friendly local favorite entices diners from miles around to sample their grilled seafood and great steaks.

Stinson Beach Grill, 3465 Shoreline Hwy, Stinson Beach (☎415/868-2002). Somewhat pricey, but relaxed, with outdoor dining – look out for the bright-blue building right in the heart of town.

Drinking and nightlife

While the Marin County nightlife is never as charged as it gets in San Francisco, almost every town has at least a couple of **cafés** that are open long hours for a jolt of caffeine, and any number of saloon-like **bars** where you'll feel at home immediately. In addition, since most of the honchos of the Bay Area music scene and dozens of lesser-known but no less brilliant session musicians and songwriters live here, Marin's nightclubs are unsurpassed for catching big names in intimate locales.

Cafés

Café Trieste, 1000 Bridgeway, Sausalito (☎415/332-7770). This distant relative of San Francisco's North Beach institution serves good coffee, a wide menu of pastas and salads, and great gelati.

Caledonia Kitchen, 400 Caledonia St, Sausalito (☎415/331-0220). Relaxing, cheery café serving simple sandwiches, fresh pastries, and a variety of salads across from a small park.

Depot Bookstore and Café, 87 Throckmorton Ave, Mill Valley ☎415/383-2665. Lively café in an old train station, sharing space with a bookstore and newsstand. Weekly readings from local and nationally recognized authors.

Fairfix Café, 33 Broadway, Fairfax (☎415/459-6404). Excellent Mediterranean food with occasional evening poetry readings.

Java Rama, 546 San Anselmo Ave, San Anselmo (☎415/453-5282). Specialty coffees and pastries along with modern rock on the stereo attracts a young crowd.

Sweden House, 35 Main St, Tiburon (☎415/435-9767). Great coffee and marvelous pastries on a jetty overlooking the yacht harbor, all for surprisingly reasonable prices.

Bars

Café Amsterdam, 23 Broadway, Fairfax (☎415/256-8020). Live alternative folk rock nightly with an outdoor patio, microbrews, espresso drinks and an extensive menu.

Fourth Street Tavern, 711 Fourth St, San Rafael (☎415/454-4044). Gutsy, no-frills beer bar with free, bluesy music most nights.

Marin Brewing Company, 1809 Larkspur Landing, Larkspur (☎415/461-4677). Lively pub opposite the Larkspur ferry terminal, with half a dozen tasty ales – try the malty Albion Amber or the Marin Hefe Weiss – all brewed on the premises.

No Name Bar, 757 Bridgeway, Sausalito (☎415/332-1392). A smoky ex-haunt of the Beats which hosts live jazz several times per week.

Pelican Inn, Hwy-1, Muir Beach (☎415/383-6000). Fair selection of traditional English and modern Californian ales, plus fish and chips (and rooms to rent in case you overdo it).

Smiley's Schooner Saloon, 41 Wharf Rd, Bolinas (☎415/868-1311). The bartender calls the customers by name at one of the oldest continually operating bars in the state. Basic hotel rooms are available in back for $59–69.

Sweetwater, 153 Throckmorton Ave, Mill Valley (☎415/388-3820). Large, open room full of beer-drinking locals that after dark evolves into Marin's prime live music venue, bringing in some of the biggest names in music, from jazz and blues all-stars to Jefferson Airplane survivors.

travel details

Trains

An Amtrak shuttle bus departs from Transbay Terminal to Oakland depot, from where there is a daily service east to Sacramento and south to Los Angeles and San Diego.

Buses

Greyhound unless specified otherwise.

San Francisco to: Los Angeles (19 daily; 8–12hr; or 1 Green Tortoise weekly; 12hr); Redding (6 daily; 6hr 30min); Reno (7 daily; 6hr); San Diego (8 daily; 12hr); Sacramento (17 daily; 2hr 20min); San Jose (13 daily; 1hr 30min); San Rafael (2 daily; 1hr).

CHAPTER EIGHT

THE GOLD COUNTRY AND LAKE TAHOE

The gold of California is a touchstone which has betrayed the rottenness, the baseness, of mankind. Satan, from one of his elevations, showed mankind the kingdom of California, and they entered into a compact with him at once.

Henry David Thoreau, *Journal*, 1 February 1852

The single most enduring image of California, after surfers and movie stars, is that of the rough and ready 49ers. Not the Steve Young/Joe Montana football-playing variety, but the Argonauts of the Gold Rush of 1849, who came from all over the world to get rich quick in the goldfields of the Sierra Nevada foothills, 150 miles east of San Francisco. The first prospectors on the scene sometimes found large nuggets of solid gold sitting along the river banks. Most, however, worked long hours in the hot sun, wading through fast-flowing, ice-cold rivers to recover trace amounts of the precious metal that had been eroded out of the hard-rock veins of the **Mother Lode**, the name given by miners to the rich source of gold which underlies the heart of the mining district.

The **Gold Country** ranges from the foothills near Yosemite National Park to the deep gorge of the Yuba River two hundred miles north. The heart of the Mother Lode, where gold was first discovered in 1848, is Sutter's Mill in Coloma, forty miles east of **Sacramento**. The largest city in the Gold Country – now the state capital and much the best jumping-off point for the area as a whole – Sacramento was a tiny military outpost and farming community that boomed as a supply town for miners. The mining areas spread to the north and south of Sacramento and preserve distinct identities. The **northern mines** around the twin towns of **Grass Valley** and **Nevada City** were the richest fields, and today retain most of their Gold Rush buildings, although there's been practically no development in the intervening years in a beautiful, near-alpine setting halfway up the towering peaks of the Sierra Nevada mountains. The hot and dusty **southern mines**, on the other hand, became depopulated fast: they were the rowdiest and wildest of all the mines, and it's not too hard to imagine that many of the abandoned towns sprinkled over the area once supported upwards of fifty saloons and gambling parlors, each with its own cast of card sharks and thieves, as immortalized by writers like Bret Harte and Mark Twain.

Most of the mountainous forest along the Sierra crest is preserved as near-pristine wilderness, with excellent hiking, camping and backpacking. There's great skiing in winter around the mountainous rim of **Lake Tahoe** – "Lake of the Sky" to the native Washoe – on the border between California and Nevada, aglow under the bright lights of the nightclubs and casinos that line its southeastern shore. East of the mountains, in the dry Nevada desert, sit the highway towns of **Reno**, famed for low-budget weddings and speedy divorces, and **Carson City**, the Nevada state capital and one-time boomtown of the Comstock silver mines.

RIVER RAFTING IN THE GOLD COUNTRY

Although plenty of people come through the area to see the Gold Rush sights, at least as many come to enjoy the thrills and spills of **whitewater rafting** and kayaking on the various forks of the American, Stanislaus, Tuolumne and Merced rivers, which wind down through the region from the Sierra crest towards Sacramento. Whether you just want to float in a leisurely manner downstream, or fancy careening through five-foot walls of water, contact one of the many river trip operators, among them Ahwahnee (☎1-800/359-9790), CBOC Whitewater Raft Adventures (☎1-800/356-2262), Mother Lode River Trips (☎1-800/427-2387), Oars Inc (☎1-800/346-6277) or Tributary Whitewater Tours (☎916/346-6812). Trips run from late spring through early fall and start at about $70.

Getting around

Hwy-49 runs north to south, linking most of the sights of the Gold Country; two main highways, US-50 and I-80, along with the transcontinental railroad, cross the Sierra Nevada through the heart of the region, and there are frequent Greyhound bus services to most of the major towns. To get a real feel for the Gold Country, however, and to reach the most evocative ghost towns, you'll need a **car**. Also, though it's all very pretty, the region is far too hilly and the roads too narrow to be much good for **cycling**.

SACRAMENTO AND THE CENTRAL MOTHER LODE

Before gold was discovered in 1848, the area around what's now the state capital at Sacramento belonged entirely to one man, John Sutter. He came here from Switzerland in 1839 to farm the flat, marshy lands at the foot of the Sierra Nevada mountains, and the prosperous community he founded became a main stopping place for the few trappers and travelers who made their way inland or across the range of peaks. But it was after the discovery of flakes of gold in the foothills forty miles east that things really took off. Although Sutter tried to keep it a secret, word got out and thousands soon flocked here from all over the world to mine the rich deposits of the Mother Lode.

This area is still very much the center of the Gold Country, though it's richer in history than specific attractions. **Sacramento**, roughly midway between San Francisco and the crest of the Sierra Nevada mountains and well connected by Greyhound and Amtrak and the arterial I-5 highway, is likely to be your first stop, a green open city of wide tree-lined streets centering on grandiose state government buildings and a waterfront quarter restored from the days of the Pony Express. From Sacramento two main routes climb east through the gentle foothills of the Mother Lode: US-50 passes through the old supply town of **Placerville** on its way to Lake Tahoe, and I-80 zooms by **Auburn** over the Donner Pass into Nevada. Both towns have retained enough of their Gold Rush past to merit at least a brief look if you're passing through, and Auburn in particular makes a good base for the more picturesque towns of the northern mines.

Sacramento

California's state capital, **SACRAMENTO**, is not at the top of most travelers' itineraries; indeed, until recently, it had the reputation of being decidedly dull, a suburban enclave of politicians and bureaucrats surrounded by miles of marshes and farmland. However, in the 1990s the town has been undergoing something of a transformation. Flashy

△ Sacramento Airport & Redding

SACRAMENTO

American River
AMERICAN RIVER BIKE TRAIL
RICHARDS
BOULEVARD
LIGHT RAIL SYSTEM

ACCOMMODATION

1 Abigail's
2 Clarion
3 Delta King Hotel
4 Econolodge
5 HI-Sacramento
6 Hyatt Regency
7 Quality Inn
8 Vagabond Inn

N

California State
Railroad Museum
BF Hastings Museum
Discovery
Museum
Huntington
& Hopkins
California
Military Museum
Train Station
Riverboat Dock
OLD
SACRAMENTO
Shopping Mall
Greyhound Station
Crocker
Art Museum
K Street Mall
City Plaza
Old Governor's
Mansion
Capitol Ave
State
Capitol
Capitol
Park
Sutter's Fort
Towe Ford Museum
MIDTOWN
South Side
Park
LIGHT RAIL SYSTEM
BROADWAY
Tower
Theater
Original Tower
Records

San Francisco
Sacramento River
FRONT STREET
JIBOOM STREET

Reno & Nevada
Lake Tahoe & 50
BUSINESS LOOP

0   400 yds

▽ Los Angeles   ▽ Los Angeles

office towers and hotel complexes, catering to the promoters and lobbyists, have
sprung up out of the faceless streetscape, enlivening the grid of leafy, tree-lined blocks,
and multi-million-dollar redevelopment efforts have gone some way toward resurrect-
ing the rowdy, free-for-all spirit of the city's Gold Rush past.

Set at the confluence of the Sacramento and American rivers in the flatlands of the
northern Central Valley, Sacramento was founded in 1839 by a Swiss immigrant, **John
Sutter**, on fifty thousand acres granted to him by the Mexican government. Sutter was a
determined settler, and for ten years worked hard to build the colony into a busy trading
center and cattle ranch, only to be thwarted by the discovery of gold at a nearby sawmill.

<table>
<tr><td colspan="3">ACCOMMODATION PRICE CODES</td></tr>
</table>

All accommodation prices in this book have been coded using the symbols below; prices are for the least expensive **double rooms** in each establishment. For a full explanation see p.36 in Basics. Individual rates rather than price codes are given for **hostels** and whole **apartments**.

① up to $30	④ $60–80	⑦ $130–175
② $30–45	⑤ $80–100	⑧ $175–250
③ $45–60	⑥ $100–130	⑨ $250+

Instead of making his fortune, the gold left Sutter a broken man. His workers quit their jobs to go prospecting, and many thousands more flocked to the goldfields without any respect for Sutter's claims to the land. The small colony was soon overrun: since the ships of the day could sail upriver from the San Francisco Bay, Sacramento quickly became the main supply point for miners bound for the isolated camps in the foothills above. The city prospered, and in 1854 Sacramento was chosen to be the sixth capital of the young state of California, equidistant from the gold mines, the rich farmlands of the Central Valley and the financial center of San Francisco. As the Gold Rush faded, Sacramento remained important as a transportation center, first as the western terminus of the Pony Express and later as the western headquarters of the transcontinental railroad.

Arrival, information and city transportation

At the intersection of the I-5, I-80, US-50 and Hwy-99 freeways, Sacramento is the hub of all the long-distance transportation networks. Sacramento Metro **airport** (☎916/929-5411), twelve miles northwest of downtown, is served by most major domestic airlines, including America West, American, Delta, Southwest and USAir. Air Commuter vans (☎916/424-9640; $10) will take you from the terminals to downtown. **Trains** from Los Angeles, San Francisco and Chicago stop at the Amtrak station at Fourth and I streets, near Old Sacramento, with good Thruway bus links to the main Gold Country towns and the Lake Tahoe area. An almost continuous stream of Greyhound **buses** pull into the bus depot at Seventh and L streets, a block from the K Street Mall.

The **tourist office** at 1421 K St (Mon–Fri 8am–5pm; ☎916/264-7777) has the *Sacramento Visitors' Guide* with maps and listings of accommodation and places to eat and drink in the city, while the **California Division of Tourism** at 801 K St, Suite 1600 (Mon–Fri 8am–5pm; ☎ 1-800/862-2543 or 916/322-2882) holds tons of background and practical information on the rest of the state. For the latest on events and entertainment in Sacramento, pick up the free *Sacramento News & Review*, read "Ticket," the weekend supplement of the *Sacramento Bee* newspaper, or browse the less useful but entertaining and hard-hitting music and style reviews in *Citi:Zen*. The KVMR 99.3FM noncommercial community radio station is also useful (and entertaining).

The city is compact, deadly flat and somewhat **walkable**, though many locals get around (especially along the 25-mile cycle path along the American River to Folsom Lake) by **bike** – rentable from Cycle Depot at 918 Second St in Old Sacramento ($20 per day; ☎916/441-4143). You're unlikely to need it, but there is also a combined **bus and light-rail** transportation system; pick up timetables and route maps from the office at 1400 29th St (Mon–Fri 8am–5pm; ☎916/321-2877). One of the best ways to see the town is on a **river-boat tour**: the paddle-wheel steamboats *Matthew McKinley* and *Spirit of Sacramento* both depart from the L Street, landing in Old Sacramento for varied trips along the Sacramento River ($10–27.50; ☎1-800/433-0263 or 916/552-2932). Should you need to rent a **car**, Enterprise, 1401 16th St at N St (☎916/444-7600) will provide one for under $35 a day, $7 more if you're between 21 and 25.

Accommodation

Sacramento has plenty of reasonably priced places to stay, all within easy walking distance of the center. A number of **motels** cluster around the old Governor's Mansion on the north side of town around 16th and H streets, and dozens more line the highways on the outskirts, particularly Richards Boulevard, just off I–5. **Downtown**, there are a few rather down-at-heel 1930s hotels and flashy new ones springing up every year. There's no good **camping** anywhere within easy reach of Sacramento, though KOA runs the RV-heavy Sacramento Metro site, 3951 Lake Rd (☎1-800/562-2747 or 916/371-6771), four miles west of the center.

Abigail's, 2120 G St (☎1-800/858 1568 or 916/441-5007). Luxurious bed and breakfast in a quiet and appealingly furnished 1912 home. There's a hot tub out in the secluded gardens. ⑥.

Clarion, 700 16th St at H (☎1-800/443-0880 or 916/444-8000). Better than you might expect for a large chain motel, centrally located with excellent facilities and lower weekend rates if you book ahead. ⑤.

Delta King Hotel, 1000 Front St (☎1-800/825-5464 or 916/444-KING). A 1926 paddle-wheel river boat now permanently moored on the water beside Old Sacramento. The rooms fail to justify their "stateroom" description, but nonetheless the vessel makes an enjoyably unusual place to stay. The price rises on weekends. ⑤.

Econo Lodge, 711 16th St (☎1-800/553-2666 or 916/443-6631). Good value across the street from the *Clarion*, with basic rooms and complimentary continental breakfast. ②.

HI-Sacramento, 900 H St (☎916/443-1691). Brand-new hostel in a superb and rambling 1885 mansion right in the center of town. All the usual facilities plus free bike rental, but there's a daytime lockout and 11pm curfew. $13 for members, $16 for others. ①.

Hyatt Regency, 12th and L streets (☎1-800/233-1234 or 916/443-1234). Very flashy, perfect for an expense account stay. Lower prices on weekends. ⑦.

Quality Inn, 818 15th St (☎1-800/228-5151 or 916/444-3980). Refurbished rooms near the old Governor's Mansion, equipped with a pool. ③.

Vagabond Inn, 909 Third St (☎1-800/522-1555 or 916/446-1481). Modern place near the river and Old Sacramento, with a swimming pool and continental breakfast. ④.

The Town

Everything you'd want to see in Sacramento is right around downtown, divided by the I-5 highway into touristy **Old Sacramento** along the river, and the commercial city center along the **K Street Mall**.

The riverfront: Old Sacramento

Sacramento grew up along the riverfront, where the wharves, warehouses, saloons and stores of the city's historic core have been restored and converted into the novelty shops and theme restaurants of **Old Sacramento**, inevitably a major tourist trap but not entirely without appeal. Most of the buildings are original, though some were moved here from nearby in the Sixties to make way for the massive I-5 highway that cuts between the river and the rest of Sacramento, and the area, small though it is, has a period aspect not completely sanitized out of all recognition. The **Information Center** at 1101 Second St (daily 9am–5pm; ☎916/442-7644) has walking tour maps and historical information.

At 113 I Street, between First and Second, is the Huntington & Hopkins hardware store where the **Big Four** – Leland Stanford, Mark Hopkins, Collis P. Huntington and Charles Crocker – first got together to mastermind the Central Pacific and later Southern Pacific railroads (see box overleaf). It's now a **museum** (daily 10am–5pm; free), highlighting the humble beginnings of the men who became some of the richest in the country, with a collection of old woodworking and blacksmith's tools; upstairs there's a low-key homage to the men, with a re-creation of their boardroom and an archive of rail history.

THE BIG FOUR AND CALIFORNIA'S EARLY RAILROADS

For over twenty years from 1861, the **Central Pacific and Southern Pacific Railroads** monopolized transportation and dominated the economy and politics of California and the western US. These companies were the creation of just four men – Leland Stanford, Mark Hopkins, Collis P. Huntington and Charles Crocker – known as the **Big Four**.

For an initial investment of $15,000, the four financiers, along with the railroad designer and engineer Theodore Judah who died before its completion, received federal subsidies of $50,000 per mile of track laid – twice what it actually cost. On top of this, they were granted half the land in a forty-mile strip bordering the railroad: as the network expanded, the Southern Pacific became the largest landowner in the state, owning over twenty percent of California. An unregulated monopoly – caricatured in the liberal press as a grasping **octopus** – the railroad had the power to make or break farmers and manufacturers dependent upon it for the transportation of goods. In the cities, particularly Oakland and Los Angeles, it was able to demand massive concessions from local government as an inducement for rail connections, and by the end of the 1800s the Big Four had extracted and extorted a fortune worth over $200 million each.

The **Discovery Museum of History, Science and Technology**, 101 I St (Mon–Fri noon–5pm, Sat & Sun 10am–5pm; $4), a few steps away, neatly fills in the gaps in California's development before and after the Big Four, though it fails to be as stimulating as the adjacent **California State Railroad Museum** (daily 10am–5pm; $6), which brings together a range of lavishly restored 1860s locomotives with "cowcatcher" front grilles and huge bulbous smokestacks. A number of opulently decked-out passenger cars include the 1929 *St Hyacinthe Pullman* sleeper car, which simulates movement with flashing lights, clanging bells and a gentle rhythmic swaying. The old passenger station and freight depot a block south have also been restored as part of the museum; on summer weekends a refurbished **steam train** (10am–5pm; $6) makes a seven-mile, 45-minute round trip beside the river.

Two smaller museums are really only worth a look if you're desperate to escape the souvenir shops. The **California Military Museum**, 1119 Second St (Tues–Sun 10am–4.30pm; $3) provides an uninspiring chronicle – with documents, weaponry and uniforms – of California's involvement in armed struggles from pre-statehood days to the present day. The **B. F. Hastings Building**, at Second and J streets (daily 10am–5pm; free), is an even less compelling stock of early communications equipment used by companies such as Pony Express and Wells Fargo. Most people only pass through to use the ATMs located inside this 1853 bank building, which also held the first State Supreme Court, the unassuming old chambers of which are sometimes open for public view on the top floor.

There's another museum two blocks south at 216 O St between Second and Third: the **Crocker Art Museum** (Tues–Sun 10am–5pm, Thurs until 9pm; $4.50), which exhibits European paintings collected by Supreme Court judge Edwin Crocker, brother of railroad baron Charles, in an odd complex of Renaissance Revival and modern buildings. More appropriate to its Sacramento setting, however, in the shadow of the massive I-5 and I-80 interchange along the river and two blocks south at 2200 Front St, is the **Towe Ford Museum** (daily 10am–6pm; $5) – the world's most complete collection of antique Ford cars and trucks, from Model Ts and As to classic '57 T-birds and the "woody" station wagons beloved of the Beach Boys.

K Street: the modern center

Running east from the riverfront and the Old Sacramento development, past the Greyhound and Amtrak stations, the **K Street Mall** is the commercial heart of Sacramento, with the downtown end of the modern suburban tramway running

Seals near San Simeon

Golden Gate Bridge

Cable car, with Alcatraz beyond

Houseboat in Sausalito

San Francisco street sign

PREVENT RUNAWAYS
CURB WHEELS
PARK IN GEAR
SET BRAKE

Sacramento

Alamo Square, San Francisco

Muir Woods, Bay Area

San Francisco

Ripening grapes, Sonoma Valley

Totem pole at Lake Tahoe

Lassen Volcanic National Park

through the center of a pedestrianized shopping precinct, amid a growing forest of new office blocks and hotels that tower over Art Deco movie theaters and neon-signed storefronts. K Street dead-ends into the massive new Downtown Plaza shopping complex, and a pedestrian-only tunnel at the west end of the mall leads under Hwy-99 and into Old Sacramento.

Northeast of the mall, at 16th and H, the old **Governor's Mansion** (tours on the hour 10am–5pm; $3) was the elaborate Victorian home of all California governors up to Ronald Reagan; when this white 1874 structure was condemned as a firetrap, he abandoned its high ceilings and narrow staircases in favor of a ranch-style house on the outskirts of town.

The noble dome of the **State Capitol** stands proudly in the middle of a spacious green park two blocks south of the mall, at the geographical center of Sacramento. Restored in the 1970s to its original nineteenth-century elegance, and still the seat of state government, the luxurious building brims over with finely crafted details. Although you're free to walk around, you'll see a lot more if you take one of the free **tours** (daily 9am–5pm; ☎916/324-0333) that leave hourly from room B-27 on the lower ground floor, passing through the old legislative chambers decked out in turn-of-the-century furnishings and fixtures.

Sutter's Fort State Historic Park (daily 10am–5pm; $3), on the east side of town at 27th and L, is a re-creation of Sacramento's original settlement. An adobe house displays relics from the Gold Rush, and on summer weekends local volunteers dress up and pretend they're living in the 1850s. The adjacent **Indian Museum** at 2618 K St (daily 10am–5pm; $3), displays tools, handicrafts and ceremonial objects of the Native Americans of the Central Valley and the Sierra Nevada mountains.

Eating, drinking and nightlife

Dozens of fast-food stands, ice cream shops, and pricey Western-themed **restaurants** fill Old Sacramento, but you'd do better to steer clear of these and search out the places we've listed below – at least four of them are clustered near the junction of Capitol and 20th (a popular area of the city known as **Midtown**), where you'll also find the odd good **bar**. The best venue for slightly off-beat **live music** is *Old Ironsides*, 7041 1901 10th St (☎916/443-9751), while major touring bands usually play at the newly refurbished Crest Theater, 1013 K St (☎916/44-CREST). Arthouse **movies** are shown at Tower Theater at Broadway and 16th (☎916/443-1982).

Café Bernardo, 28th Street and Capitol Avenue (☎916/443-1180). Order huge portions of healthy cheap food from the walk-up counter and eat it in the casual yet chic dining room. Eclectic menu includes stir-fry, penne, grilled polenta, salads and sandwiches. The adjoining *Monkey Bar* serves cocktails until 2am every night.

Café Paris, 2326 K St (☎916/442-2001). Small, down-to-earth beer joint where Sacramento's hipsters congregate to hear local indie bands.

Greta's Café, 1831 Capitol Ave at 19th St (☎916/442-7382). Quality salads, sandwiches, baked goods and fine vegetarian dishes at prices sure to please. Summer Thurs–Sat until 9–10pm; winter daytime only.

Java City, 1800 Capitol Ave at 18th St (☎916/444-5282). It may be a chain, but that doesn't stop people from flocking to this popular midtown spot for great coffee and conversation. Outdoor seating.

Megami, 1010 10th at J Street (☎916/448-4512). A functional, bargain Japanese restaurant with lunch mains and combination sushi plates for under $5. Try the sesame chicken. Mon–Fri only.

New Helvetia Roasters & Bakers, 1215 19th St at Capitol Avenue (☎916/441-1106). An old firehouse that's one of the best of the cafés in town, boasting home-roasted coffee, good cakes and pastries and communal tables inside and out. Open until 11pm most nights, with a mixed clientele but popular with gay men.

Paesano's, 1806 Capitol Ave at 18th Street (☎916/447-8646). Reasonably priced pastas, great oven-baked sandwiches, and delicious pizzas in a comfortable brick-walled dining room.

Paragary's, 1401 28th St at N Street (☎916/457-5737). A broad range of tastes catered for, with good giant-size portions of pasta, and tasty, brick-oven pizzas with unusual toppings. Moderate prices.

River City Brewing Company, 545 Downtown Plaza (☎916/447-2739). Slick modern brew pub at the west end of the shopping mall, usually packed with both diners and drinkers. Unwind with a couple of pints after braving the tourist-heavy Old Town.

Rubicon Brewing Company, 2004 Capitol Ave (☎916/448-7032). One of the more enjoyable and cozy haunts in town, serving the flavorful house-brewed Amber Ale and the wonderfully hoppy India Pale Ale.

The Tower Café, 1518 Broadway at 16th (☎916/441-0222). Nineties version of a Fifties diner, good for burgers, veggie burgers, and late-night caffeine fixes.

Weatherstone Coffee & Trading Co, 812 21st St at H (☎916/443-6340). Sacramento's oldest coffeehouse with garden seating and cool brick interior. A favorite with locals both for its bulging sandwiches and many coffee concoctions. Open until 11pm or later.

The Central Mother Lode

From Sacramento, US-50 and I-80 head east through the heart of the Gold Country, up and over the mountains past Lake Tahoe and into the state of Nevada. The roads closely follow the old stagecoach routes over the Donner Pass, and in the mid-1860s local citizens, seeking to improve dwindling fortunes after the Gold Rush subsided, joined forces with railroad engineer Theodore Judah to finance and build the first railroad crossing of the Sierra Nevada over much the same route – even along much of the same track – as that used by Amtrak today. However, while the area holds much historic interest, its towns aren't nearly as nice as those elsewhere in the Gold Country. Neither Placerville nor Auburn is worth much more than a quick look, though Coloma and Folsom, in between the two highways, have slightly more to offer.

Folsom

In 1995, just as the **FOLSOM** powerhouse was gearing up for the centennial celebration of its pioneering efforts in long-distance electricity transmission, one of the sluice gates on the Folsom Dam gave way, sending millions of gallons of water down the American River towards Sacramento, twenty miles downstream. The levees held but Folsom Lake had to be almost completely drained before repairs could be undertaken. The event sent shockwaves through California's extensive hydroelectric industry and brought a fame to Folsom unknown since Johnny Cash sang of being "stuck in Folsom Prison" after having "shot a man in Reno, just to watch him die." The stone-faced **Folsom State Prison**, two miles north of town on Green Valley Road, has an arts-and-crafts gallery (daily 8am–5pm) selling works by prisoners, who get the proceeds when released. Across the road, a small **museum** (daily 8am–4pm; $1) is filled with grisly photographs and the medical records of murderers and thieves who were hanged for their crimes.

Folsom itself is attractive enough, with a single main street of restored homes and buildings that date from the days of the Pony Express. A reconstruction of the 1860 Wells Fargo office makes an imposing setting for the **Folsom History Museum**, 823 Sutter St (Wed–Sun 11am–4pm; free), whose prized possessions include a working scale model of a steam-powered gold dredge, artifacts from the Chinese community that settled here in the 1850s, and a huge mural depicting the area's main Native American people, the Maidu.

Placerville

PLACERVILLE, forty miles east of Sacramento, takes a perverse delight in having been known originally as Hangtown for its habit of lynching alleged criminals in pairs and stringing them up from a tree in the center of town. Despite these gruesome begin-

EL DORADO WINE COUNTRY

Back in the 1860s, when the now-famous Napa and Sonoma valleys were growing potatoes, **vineyards** flourished in El Dorado county. However, the fields were neglected after the Gold Rush and killed off by phylloxera, only being re-established in 1972. Since then, however, the **wineries** in El Dorado county, around Placerville, have rapidly gained a reputation which belies their diminutive size. Most are low-key affairs where no charge is made for tasting or tours, and you're encouraged to enjoy a bottle out on the verandah. At quiet times you may even be shown around by the winemaker, a far cry from the organized tours and rampant commercialism of Napa and Sonoma.

The differences in altitude and soil types throughout the region lend themselves to a broad range of grape varieties, and the producers here are often criticized as being unfocused. Nonetheless, the wines have notched up a string of gold medals in recent years. Zinfandel and Sauvignon Blanc are big, but it is the Syrah/Merlot blends which attract the attention, and the Barbera (from a Piedmontese grape) is said to be the best in the world.

If you're out for a relaxed day's tasting, avoid the **Passport Weekend**, usually the last weekend in March or the first in April and booked out months in advance (☎1-800/306-3956 or 530/446-6562), when the purchase of said passport entitles you to all manner of foodie extravagances to complement the tastings. Better to pick up the **El Dorado Wine Country Tour** leaflet from the Chamber of Commerce and make your way to Boeger, 1790 Carson Rd (daily 10am–5pm; ☎530/622-8094), less than a mile from the Greyhound stop (see below), where you can sit under an arbor of apples and pears, or Lava Cap, 2221 Fruitridge Rd (daily 11am–5pm; ☎530/621-0175), which in recent years have produced some excellent Chardonnay and Muscat Canelli.

The quality of the local produce – not only grapes, but also apples, pears, peaches, cherries and more – is widely celebrated around the district, especially so during the **Apple Hill Festival** in October when a shuttle bus runs from Placerville to the majority of the orchards and wineries. At other times, you'll have to make your own way – it's not inconceivable to visit a couple of places on foot, given most of the day: the roads are generally quiet and the scenery pleasant.

nings, Placerville has always been more of a market than a mining town, and is now a major crossroads, halfway between Sacramento and Lake Tahoe at the junction of US-50 and Hwy-49. For a time it was the third-largest city in California, and many of the men who went on to become the most powerful in the state got their start here: railroad magnates Mark Hopkins and Collis P. Huntington were local merchants, while car mogul John Studebaker made wheelbarrows for the miners.

The modern town spreads out along the highways in a string of fast-food restaurants, gas stations and motels. The old Main Street, running parallel to US-50, retains some of the Gold Rush architecture, with an effigy dangling by the neck in front of the *Hangman's Tree* bar, which is built over the site where the town's infamous tree once grew. You'll also see many fine old houses scattered among the pine trees in the steep valleys to the north and south of the center. Nearby, one of the best of the Gold Country museums is located in the sprawling El Dorado County Fairgrounds, just north of US-50. This, the **El Dorado County Historical Museum** (Wed–Sat 10am–4pm; free), gives a broad historical overview of the county from the Miwok to the modern day, including logging trains and a mock-up of a general store. For more on the days of the Argonauts, head across US-50 to the **Gold Bug Mine Park**, Bedford Avenue (daily May–Oct 10am–4pm; Nov–April noon–4pm, weather permitting; $2) for a self-guided tour of a typical Mother Lode mine.

Practicalities

Amtrak Thruway **buses** pull up twice daily outside *Buttercup Pantry*, 222 Main St; while Greyhound buses on their way to South Lake Tahoe stop three times a day at 1750

Broadway, a mile and a half east of town. Eldorado Transit buses provide local transit service. Near the Greyhound stop are a number of **motels**, such as the *Hangtown Motel*, 1676 Broadway (☎530/622-0637; ②), and the nicer but slightly pricier *National 9 Inn*, 1500 Broadway (☎530/622-3884; ②). With more money, you're far better off at the *Chichester-McKee House*, 800 Spring St (☎1-800/831-4008 or 530/626-1882; ⑤), a very comfortable and welcoming **B&B** reached by turning north off US-50 onto Hwy-49 at the traffic lights in town.

The El Dorado County **Chamber of Commerce** office, 542 Main St (Mon–Fri 9am–5pm; ☎ 1-800/457-6279 or 530/621-5885), has local information, and can help set up **river rafting** trips in Coloma (see below).

For **eating**, try the local concoction, "Hangtown Fry" (included in the *Penguin Book of American Cookery*), an omelet-like mix-up of bacon, eggs and breaded oysters that you can taste at *Chuck's Pancake House*, 1318 Broadway St (☎530/622-2858). *Sweetie Pies*, at 577 Main St (☎530/642-0128) serves great breakfasts and what could be the best cinnamon rolls on the planet. You can sip coffee, play chess, and listen to local folk and bluegrass inside the musty remnants of an actual gold mine at the bizarre *Placerville Coffee House*, 594 Main St (☎530/295-1481). Not to be missed if you've got a car is *Poor Red's Barbeque*, housed in the old Adams and Co stagecoach office in El Dorado on Hwy-49 three miles south of Placerville, which serves the Gold Country's best barbecued dinners for under $6, with $1 beers and two-fisted margaritas. If none of these appeal, *Lil' Mama D Carlos*, 482 Main St (☎530/626-1612), serves up fine, affordable Italian food.

Coloma

Sights along Hwy-49 north of Placerville are few and far between, but it was here that gold fever began, when on January 24, 1848 James Marshall discovered flakes of gold in the tailrace of a mill he was building for John Sutter along the south fork of the American River at **COLOMA**. By the summer of that year thousands had flocked to the area, and by the following year Coloma was a town of ten thousand – though most left quickly following news of richer strikes elsewhere in the region, and the town all but disappeared within a few years. The few surviving buildings, including the cabin where Marshall lived, have been preserved as the **Marshall Gold Discovery State Historic Park** (daily 8am–dusk; $5 per car).

A reconstruction of **Sutter's Mill** stands along the river, and working demonstrations are often held on weekends at 10am and 1pm. There's a small historical museum across the road, and on a hill overlooking the town a statue marks the spot where Marshall is buried. Marshall never profited from his discovery, in fact it came to haunt him. At first he tried to charge miners for access to what he said was his land along the river (it wasn't), and he spent most of his later years in poverty, claiming supernatural powers had helped him to find gold.

Other supernatural forces are at work in the *Coloma Country Inn* (Tues–Sun; ☎530/622-2217; ⑤), adjacent to the state park on Cold Springs Road, where the ghost of a man tormented by his wife is said to haunt the cellar – now a popular **bar**, with music on weekend nights. If you want to sleep off a night's revelry, **bed and breakfast** is also available.

Auburn and Dutch Flat

If you're heading for the northern mines you might stop off at **AUBURN**, eighteen miles northwest of Coloma at the junction of I-80 and Hwy-49; Greyhound **buses** from Sacramento to Reno stop at 246 Palm Ave and Amtrak Thruway stop outside *Foster's Freeze* on Hwy-49 at Elm Avenue. The outskirts are sprawling and modern, but the Old

Town district just off Hwy-49 has been preserved: a cluster of antique stores and saloons around California's oldest post office and the unmissable red-and-white tower of the 1891 **firehouse**. For a free map and information on places to stay, stop by the **Placer County Visitor Center** north of town at 13464 Lincoln Way (Mon–Fri 9am–5pm, Sat 9am–3pm; ☎ 1-800/427-6463 or 530/887-2111). The **Gold Country Museum**, 1273 High St (Tues–Fri 10am–3.30pm, Sat & Sun 11am–4pm; $1) has the standard displays of guns and mining equipment.

The twenty or so miles of Hwy-49 north of Auburn are a dull but fast stretch of free-way to one of the best parts of the Gold Country – the twin cities of Grass Valley and Nevada City. For an interesting side trip on the way there, or if you're heading for Lake Tahoe, take I-80 from Auburn 27 miles east to the small town of **DUTCH FLAT**, where old tin-roofed cottages are sprinkled among the pine and aspen-covered slopes. Miners here used the profitable but very destructive method of hydraulic mining (see p.511) to get at the gold buried under the surface – with highly visible consequences.

THE NORTHERN MINES

The northern section of the Gold Country includes some of the most spectacularly beautiful scenery in California. Fast-flowing rivers cascade along the bottom of steeply walled canyons, whose slopes are covered in fall with the flaming reds and golds of poplars and sugar maples highlighted against an evergreen background of pine and fir trees. Unlike the freelance placer mines of the south, where wandering prospectors picked nuggets of gold out of the streams and rivers, the gold here was (and is) buried deep underground, and had to be pounded out of hard-rock ore. In spite of that, the northern mines were the most profitable of the Mother Lode – more than half the gold that came out of California came from the mines of **Nevada County**, and most of that from **Grass Valley**'s Empire Mine, now preserved as one of the region's many excellent museums. Just north, the pretty Victorian houses of **Nevada City** make it perhaps the most attractive of all the Gold Rush towns.

A few miles away, at the end of a steep and twisting back road, the scarred landforms of the **Malakoff Diggins** stand as an exotic reminder of the destruction wrought by overzealous miners, who, as gold became harder to find, washed away entire hillsides to get at the precious metal. Hwy-49 winds up further into the mountains from Nevada City, along the Yuba River to the High Sierra hamlet of **Downieville**, at the foot of the towering Sierra Buttes. From here you're within striking distance of the northernmost Gold Rush ghost town of **Johnsville**, which stands in an evocative state of arrested decay in the middle of the forests of **Plumas-Eureka State Park**, on the crest of the Sierra Nevada.

You'll need a **car** to get to any of the outlying sights, but there is public transportation to Grass Valley and Nevada City in the form of four daily Amtrak Thruway buses. Though there are no youth hostels, you'll find a few inexpensive motels and a handful of B&Bs; **camping** is an option too, often in unspoiled sites in gorgeous mountain scenery.

Grass Valley and Nevada City

Twenty-five miles north of Auburn and I-80, the neighboring towns of **GRASS VALLEY** and **NEVADA CITY** were the most prosperous and substantial of the gold- mining towns and are still thriving communities, four miles apart in beautiful surroundings high up in the Sierra Nevada mountains. Together they make one of the better Gold Country destinations, with museums and many balconied, elaborately detailed buildings, staggering up hills and hanging out over steep gorges.

Gold was the lifeblood of the area as recently as the mid-1950s, and although both towns look largely unchanged since the Gold Rush days, they're by no means stuck in the past: the engineering expertise that enabled miners to extract millions of dollars' worth of gold from deep subterranean veins is now being put to work to make electronic equipment for TV studios and freeze-dried food for backpackers. Also, since the 1960s, a number of artists and craftspeople have settled in the old houses in the hills around the towns, lending a vaguely alternative feel that's reflected in the *Community Endeavor* newspaper, the KVMR 89.5FM non-commercial community radio station, and in the friendly throngs that turn out for the annual Bluegrass Festival in the middle of June. Alternative lifestyles don't always accord with more hard-headed businessfolk in the twin towns and there is an understated but distinct tension between the two factions.

Getting around is relatively easy: both towns are very compact, and connected every thirty minutes by the Gold Country Stage minibus (Mon–Fri 8am–5pm, Sat 9.15am–5.30pm; $1 a trip, $2 for a day pass; ☎530/477-0103).

Accommodation

Places to stay don't come cheap, but if you can afford to splurge on a **bed and breakfast**, Nevada City in particular has some excellent options. Otherwise there are a couple of revamped old **Gold Rush hotels**, and a scattering of motels, though be warned that these may be booked up weeks in advance.

Airway Motel, 575 E Broad St, Nevada City (☎530/265-2233). Quiet, 1940s motel with swimming pool, a 10min walk from the center of town. Credit cards are not accepted. ②.

Downey House, 517 W Broad St, Nevada City (☎530/265-2815). Pretty 1870s Victorian home at the top of Broad Street, looking out over the town and surrounding forest. Simple decor and original artwork makes a welcome change from the over-fancy B&B norm. Rates include wine on arrival and full breakfast. ④.

Flume's End, 317 S Pine St, Nevada City (☎530/265-9665). Across the Pine Creek bridge from the center of town, this small inn overlooks a pretty waterfall and features lovely gardens ranged along Deer Creek. ⑤.

Holbrooke Hotel, 212 W Main St, Grass Valley (☎1-800/933-7077 or 530/273-1353). Recently renovated and right in the center of town, this historic hotel, where Mark Twain once stayed, has great rooms and an opulent bar. ④.

Murphy's Inn, 318 Neal St, Grass Valley (☎1-800/875-2488 or 530/273-6873). Cozy rooms – some with fireplaces – in an old Victorian place close to downtown. Great breakfasts. ⑤.

Northern Queen Inn, 400 Railroad Ave, Nevada City (☎530/265-5824). Good-value hotel with a heated pool. Attractive woodland cottages and chalets and simpler rooms. ④.

Shady Rest Motel, 10845 Rough and Ready Hwy, Grass Valley (☎530/273-4232). A little way out of town, but a pleasant walk; good-value weekly rates available. ②.

CAMPING IN NEVADA COUNTY

One of the best ways to get a feel for the day-to-day life of the miners is to "rough it" yourself, camping out in one of the many easily accessible **campgrounds** in the surrounding hills, which you can only reach by car. On Hwy-20 five miles east of Nevada City towards I-80, *Scott's Flat Lake* (☎530/265-5302) is privately operated, has the best facilities and charges $16 a night; seven miles on, *White Cloud* costs $10 a night; much further out, 24 miles east of Nevada City and four north of Hwy-20, *Fuller Lake Campground* is free but has no running water. Along Hwy-49 north of Nevada City there are half a dozen more campgrounds, the most attractive of which, the *Sierra* campground ($10) seven miles beyond Sierra City and *Chapman Creek* ($10) another mile upstream, lie along the Yuba River. For details contact the **ranger station** (☎530/265-4531) in Nevada City on Coyote Street, a quarter of a mile past the tourist office.

Sierra Motel, 816 W Main St, Grass Valley (☎530/273-8133). A bit run-down and not quite central, but cheap. ②.

Swan-Levine House, 328 S Church St, Grass Valley (☎530/272-1873). Accommodation with the artist in mind; the friendly owners also give instruction in printmaking. Attractively decorated, sunny en-suite rooms in an old Victorian hospital. ④.

Grass Valley

Jonathan Richman wasn't the first performer to settle in **GRASS VALLEY**: Lola Montez, an Irish dancer and entertainer who had been the mistress of Ludwig of Bavaria and a friend of Victor Hugo and Franz Liszt, embarked on a highly successful tour of America, playing to packed houses from New York to San Francisco. Her provocative "Spider Dance," in which she wriggled about the stage shaking cork spiders out of her dress, didn't much impress the miners, but she liked the wild lifestyle of the town, gave up dancing and retired to Grass Valley with her pet grizzly bear, which she kept tied up in the front yard.

A few mementos of Lola's life are displayed in the **Grass Valley Museum**, in the Old St Mary's Academy at the corner of Church and Chapel streets (June–Oct Tues–Sun 12.30–3.30pm; Nov–May call for hours; ☎530/273-5509; donation). The town's **tourist office** (Mon–Fri 9.30am–4.30pm, Sat 10am–3pm; ☎ 1-800/655-4667 or 530/273-4667) is housed in a replica of her home, on the south side of town at 248 Mill St. It also has reams of historical information, lists of accommodation, and a walking tour **map** of the

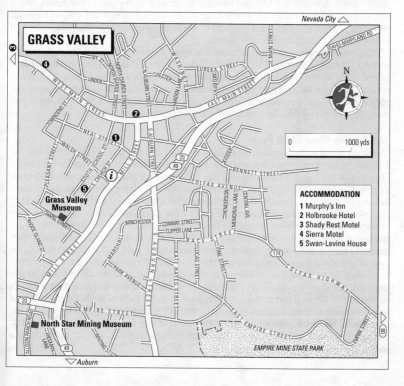

GRASS VALLEY

ACCOMMODATION
1 Murphy's Inn
2 Holbrooke Hotel
3 Shady Rest Motel
4 Sierra Motel
5 Swan-Levine House

town, pointing out the oldest hardware store in California (which, sadly, closed in 1990 and has been converted into a tacky art gallery) among the wooden awnings and storefronts of the gas-lighted business district.

The North Star Mining Museum

Two intriguing museums illustrate the days when Grass Valley was the richest and most important of all the California mining towns. The **North Star Mining Museum** at the south end of Mill Street (May–Sept daily 10am–4pm; donation) is far and away the best of all the Gold Country museums, both for the quality of the exhibits and the knowledge and enthusiasm of the guides. Housed in what used to be the power station for the North Star Mine, the featured exhibit is the giant **Pelton wheel**. Resembling nothing so much as a thirty-foot-diameter bicycle wheel, this was patented in 1878 and became one of the most important inventions to come out of the Gold Country. A hundred or so small iron buckets, each divided into bowl-like scoops, are fixed to the rim of the wheel; a jet of water shot into the center of the buckets is turned around to create a secondary jet, spinning the wheel at a speed of over seventy miles per hour. Many Pelton wheels were used to generate electricity, though the one here drove an air compressor to power the drills and hoists of the mine.

A series of dioramas in the museum describe the day-to-day working life of the miners, three-quarters of whom had emigrated here from the depressed tin mines of Cornwall in England. Besides their expertise at working deep underground, the "Cousin Jacks," as they were called by the non-Cornish miners, introduced the Cornish pump (not to mention the Cornish pastie, a traditional pastry pie) to the mines. Some of these pumps had rods over a mile long, made of lengths of wood spliced together with iron plates – you can see a mock-up of one of these mammoth beasts here, as well as a replica of the old surface mechanism.

The great machines are now at peace, but when they were in action the racket could be heard for miles around. The noisiest offenders were the thundering **stamp mills**, a scaled-down version of which is operated upon request. In a full-size stamp mill, banks of from ten to eighty huge pistons, each weighing upwards of 1500 pounds, mashed and pulverized the gold-bearing quartz ore, freeing up the gold which was then separated from the gravel and dust by a variety of chemical amalgamation processes.

The Empire Mine State Park

The largest and richest gold mine in the state, and also the last to shut down, was the **Empire Mine**, now preserved as a state park a mile southeast of Grass Valley, just off Hwy-174 at the top of Empire Street. The 800-acre park (daily 10am–5pm; $3) is surrounded by pines, amongst which are vast quantities of mining equipment and machinery, much of it only recently re-instated here after having been sold off for scrap after the mine closed in 1956. But in recent years a fair quantity has been bought back or replaced and it is now easy to imagine the din that shook the ground 24 hours a day, or the cages of fifty men descending the now-desolate shaft into the 350 miles of underground tunnels. After more than six million ounces of gold had been recovered, the cost of getting the gold out of the ground exceeded $35 an ounce – the government-controlled price at the time – and production ceased. Most of the mine has been dismantled, but there's a small, very informative **museum** at the entrance with a superb model of the whole underground system, built secretly to help predict the location of lucrative veins of gold. You can get some sense of the mine's prosperity by visiting the owner's house, the **Empire Cottage** at the north end of the park – a stone and brick, vaguely English manor house with a glowing, redwood-paneled interior overlooking a formal garden.

Nevada City

NEVADA CITY, four miles north, may have less to see than Grass Valley, but it's smaller and prettier, with dozens of elaborate Victorian homes set on the winding, narrow, maple tree-lined streets that rise up from Hwy-49. It's the least changed of all the Gold Country towns, and a gem for aimless wandering or following the many steep streets up into the surrounding forest.

A good first stop is at the **tourist office** (Mon–Fri 9am–5pm, Sat 11am–4pm; ☎ 1-800/655-6569 or 530/265-2692) at 132 Main St, a block north of Hwy-49, where you can pick up a free walking-tour **map** of the town. It's hard to select specific highlights, but one place to start is the newly restored, lacy-balconied and bell-towered **Old**

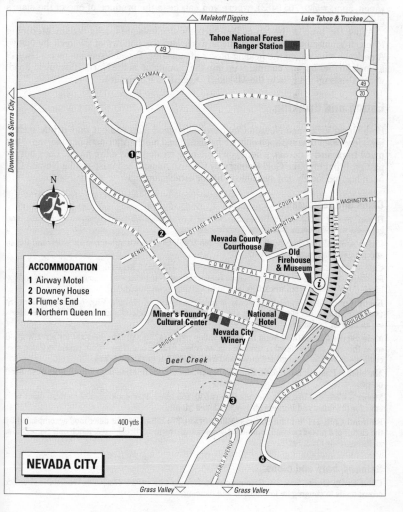

△ Malakoff Diggins

Lake Tahoe & Truckee △

**Tahoe National Forest
Ranger Station**

Downieville & Sierra City ◁

N

ACCOMMODATION
1 Airway Motel
2 Downey House
3 Flume's End
4 Northern Queen Inn

**Nevada County
Courthouse**

**Old
Firehouse
& Museum**

**Miner's Foundry
Cultural Center**

**National
Hotel**

**Nevada City
Winery**

Deer Creek

0   400 yds

NEVADA CITY

Grass Valley ▽   ▽ Grass Valley

Firehouse, 214 Main St, next to the tourist office, which houses a small **museum** (May–Oct daily 11am–4pm; Nov–April Thurs–Sun 11am–4pm; donation) describing the social history of the region. The heart of town is Broad Street, which climbs up from the highway past the 1852 *National Hotel* and a number of antique shops and restaurants, all decked out in Gold Country balconies and wooden awnings. Almost the only exception to the rule of picturesque nostalgia is the Art Deco 1937 **City Hall**, near the top of Broad Street.

The **Miner's Foundry Cultural Center** (daily 9am–5pm; free), perched precariously above the Deer Creek canyon at 325 Spring St, is an old tool foundry converted into a multi-use cultural center, art gallery, performance space and KVMR radio studios. Immediately next door stands the **Nevada City Winery**, 321 Spring St (noon–5pm; ☎530/265-9463), where you can taste the produce of one of the state's oldest vineyards.

Above the town at the top of Pine Street a small plaque marks **Indian Medicine Rock**, a granite boulder with sunbeds worn into the hollows of the rock by Native Americans who valued the healing power of sunshine. Broad Street intersects Hwy-49 a block further on, and continues up into the mountains as the North Bloomfield Road, which twists up the hills to the Malakoff Diggins (see opposite).

Eating and drinking

Both Grass Valley and Nevada City have some good places to **eat and drink**, including a few **cafés** that are open only for breakfast and lunch. After dark head to one of the many **bars and saloons**, where you'll often be treated to free live music. Look out for pasties, brought to the Gold Country by Cornish miners, and crisp-tasting Nevada City beer, brewed locally and available at better establishments.

Cafés and restaurants

Broad Street Books, 426 Broad St, Nevada City (☎530/265-4204). Pastries, light fare, and espresso with wonderful tree-shaded outdoor seating.

Cirino's, 309 Broad St, Nevada City (☎530/265-2246). Good deli sandwiches for lunch and Italian specialties at dinner, plus a full bar.

Café Mekka, 237 Commercial St, Nevada City (☎530/478-1517). Relaxed, fabulously decorated coffee shop – from exposed piping to trompe l'oeil wallpaper – popular with teenagers, trendies and ex-hippies. Open 8am–11pm weekdays, and until 1.30am on weekends.

Earth Song, 135a Argall Way, about a mile southwest of Nevada City, following S Pine St (☎530/265-8025). Excellent gourmet vegetarian café and wholefood supermarket. The café closes for an hour or two in the afternoon.

Main Street Café, 213 W Main St, Grass Valley (☎530/477-6000). The best bet for a really good meal, this casual but refined restaurant has an eclectic range of dishes – from pastas to Cajun specialties – as well as good grilled meats and fresh fish, all at moderate prices.

Marshall's Pasties, 203 Mill St, Grass Valley (☎530/272-2844). Mind-boggling array of fresh filled pasties.

Moore's Café, 216 Broad St, Nevada City (☎530/265-1959). Plain-looking, all-American diner with eggs for breakfast and burgers for lunch. Closed Mon.

Railroad Café, 111 W Main St, Grass Valley (☎530/274-2233). Decent diner food accompanied by the clatter of a model railroad continuously operating overhead. Breakfast & lunch only Sun–Thurs, all three meals Fri & Sat.

Saloons, bars and clubs

Chief Crazy Horse Inn, 230 Commercial St, Nevada City (☎530/273-2650). Where the younger crowd tends to congregate for billiards and dancing.

Friar Tuck's, 111 N Pine St, Nevada City (☎530/265-9093). Somewhat kitsch wine bar, with occasional live folk and jazz music. Also serves fairly expensive meals – try the fondue dinner for around $15.

Gold Exchange Saloon, 158 Mill St, Grass Valley (☎530/272-5509). Lively, unpretentious and unthreatening beer bar and saloon, great for quenching a thirst after a day's hiking, biking or prospecting.

Mad Dogs and Englishmen, 211 Spring St, Nevada City (☎530/265-8173). Pub-like bar with darts, good beer and regular live, danceable blues and rock music. Open until 2am on weekends.

Main Street Café, 215 W Main St, Grass Valley (☎530/477-6000). Wine and cocktail bar next to restaurant, with live music most weekends.

Nevada County and the Malakoff Diggins

Grass Valley, Nevada City and the foothills of **Nevada County** yielded more than half the gold that came out of California. Before the deep, hard-rock mines were established in the late 1860s, there were mining camps spread all over the northern Gold Country with evocative names like "Red Dog" and "You Bet," that disappeared as soon as the easily recovered surface deposits gave out. **ROUGH AND READY**, five miles west of Grass Valley, survives on the tourist trade alone, its visitors coming to take a look at the only mining town ever to secede from the United States, which Rough and Ready did in 1850. The band of veterans who founded the town, fresh from the Mexican–American War, opted to quit the Union in protest against unfair taxation by the federal government, and although they declared their renewed allegiance in time for that summer's Fourth of July celebrations, the conflict was not officially resolved until 1948. Now the place isn't worth visiting; little more than a handful of ramshackle buildings, including a gas station and a general store.

Six miles northwest of Rough and Ready, off the winding Bitney Springs Road, is the **Bridgeport covered bridge**, the largest in the US, spanning the Yuba River: splintery wood shingles disguise the hefty trussed arch structure that's clearly visible from the inside if you walk the 250 feet across. The swimming area underneath offers some relief from a hot summer's day, but don't jump from the bridge – it's further than it looks.

Malakoff Diggins State Park

The waters of the Yuba River are now crisp and clear, but when the bridge was completed in 1862 they were being choked with mud and residue from the many hydraulic mining or **hydraulicking** operations upstream. Hydraulic mining was used here in the late 1850s to get at the trace deposits of gold which were not worth recovering by orthodox methods. It was an unsophisticated way of retrieving the precious metal: giant nozzles or monitors sprayed powerful jets of water against the gold-bearing hillsides, washing away tons of gravel, mud and trees just to recover a few ounces of gold. It also required an elaborate system of flumes and canals to collect the water, which was sprayed at a rate of over thirty thousand gallons a minute. Some of these canals are still used to supply water to local communities. Worst of all, apart from the obvious destruction of the landscape, was the waste it caused, silting up rivers, causing floods, impairing navigation and eventually turning San Francisco Bay muddy brown.

The worst offender, whose excesses caused hydraulic mining to be outlawed in 1884, was the **Malakoff Diggins**, sixteen miles up steep and winding North Bloomfield Road from Nevada City (or reachable via the sixteen-mile Tyler Foote Crossing Road, which turns off Hwy-49 twelve miles northwest of Nevada City), where a canyon more than a mile long, half a mile wide and over six hundred feet deep was carved out of the red and gold earthen slopes. Natural erosion has softened the scars somewhat, sculpting pinnacles and towers into a miniature Grand Canyon now preserved as a 3000-acre **state park** (daily dawn–dusk; $5 per car). Inside the park, old buildings from ghost towns around the Gold Country are being moved to the restored town of **NORTH BLOOMFIELD**, where a small **museum** (June–Aug daily 10am–4pm; Sept–May Sat & Sun only, call ☎530/265-2740 for winter hours) shows a twenty-minute film on hydraulicking, and there's a **campground** ($10 tent sites, $20 cabins) near the eerie cliffs.

Downieville and the High Sierra towns

From Nevada City, Hwy-49 climbs up along the Yuba River gorge into some of the highest and most marvelous scenery in the Gold Country, where waterfalls tumble over sharp, black rocks bordered by tall pines and maple trees. In the middle of this wilderness, an hour's drive from Nevada City, **DOWNIEVILLE**, the most evocatively sited of the Gold Rush towns, spreads out along both banks of the river, crisscrossed by an assortment of narrow bridges. Hwy-49 runs right through the center of town, slowing to a near-stop to negotiate tight curves that have not been widened since the stagecoaches passed through. Thick stone buildings, some enhanced with delicate wooden balconies and porches, others with heavy iron doors and shutters, face on to raised wooden sidewalks, their backs dangling precipitously over the steep banks of the river.

For what is now a peaceful and quiet little hamlet of three hundred people, Downieville seems strangely proud of its fairly nasty history. It has the distinction of being the only mining camp ever to have hanged a woman, Juanita, "a fiery Mexican dancehall girl," who stabbed a miner in self-defense. A restored wooden gallows, last used in 1885, still stands next to the County Jail on the south bank of the river, to mark the ghastly heritage. Across the river and two blocks north, at the end of a row of 1850s storefronts, the **Downieville Museum** (April–Oct daily 10am–5pm; donation) is packed full of odd bits and historical artifacts, including a set of snowshoes for horses and a scaled-down model of a stamp mill, "made by the boys of the shop classes 1947–8." Pick up a walking tour map of the town from the **tourist office** kiosk (☎530/289-3507), next to the firebell tower in the center of town. It can also help out with **accommodation**, which is provided by the *Riverside Inn* (☎530/289-1000; ③) and *Robinson's Motel* (☎530/289-3573; ②), both centrally located on Hwy-49 alongside the Yuba River, and the wonderfully sited *Sierra Shangri-La* (☎530/289-3455; ④) four miles further east, which has B&B rooms and fully-fixtured cottages, the latter available weekly in summer. **Eat and drink** at the family-style *Downieville Diner*, on Main Street (☎530/289-3616).

The full-size original of the county museum stamp mill is maintained in working order at the **Kentucky Mine Museum** (summer Wed–Sun 10am–5pm; closed winter; $1), a mile east of **SIERRA CITY** further up Hwy-49, where a guided tour (11am, 1pm & 3pm; $4) takes you inside a reconstructed miner's cabin, down a mine shaft and gives you a look at various other pieces of equipment used for retrieving the gold-bearing ore. Until the mine was shut down during World War II, the ore was dug out from tunnels under the massive **Sierra Buttes**, the craggy granite peaks that dominate the surrounding landscape.

Sierra City is full of rustic charm, and can be a useful base for visiting the surrounding area, staying at the *Busch & Heringlake Inn* B&B (☎530/862-1501; ④), the *Sierra Chalet Motel* (☎530/862-1110; ②), or, best of the lot, *Buttes Resort*, Hwy-49 (☎530/862-1170; ③), which has self-contained units and suites. There's a **campground** ($10) a mile and a half to the west.

Hwy-49 continues east, passing **SIERRAVILLE** after twenty miles, where you'll find basic facilities, and **Bassetts Junction** where Hwy-89 heads north to Johnsville, ending near US-395, and south to Truckee and the Lake Tahoe area.

Johnsville

JOHNSVILLE, 25 miles north of Bassett Junction, is, after Bodie (see p.281), the best-preserved and most isolated old mining town in California. Surrounded by over seven thousand acres of pine forest and magnificent alpine scenery, it lies at the center of the **Plumas-Eureka State Park** – which has $16 **camping** (reserve through Parknet ☎1-800/444-7275) and miles of hiking trails. Johnsville's huge stamp mill and mine buildings are being restored, and in the meantime a small **museum** (daily 9am–5pm; $2) describes the difficult task of digging for gold in the High Sierra winters.

THE SOUTHERN MINES

Though never as rich or successful as the diggings further north, the camps of the **southern mines** had a reputation for being the liveliest and most uproarious of all the Gold Rush settlements, and inspired most of the popular images of the era: Wild West towns full of gambling halls, saloons and gunfights in the streets. The mining methods here were quite different from those used further north. Instead of digging out gold-bearing ore from deep underground, claims here were more often worked by itinerant, roving prospectors searching for bits of gold washed out of rocks by rivers and streams, known as **placer** gold (from the Spanish word meaning both "sand bar," where much of the gold was found, and, appropriately, "pleasure"). Nuggets were sometimes found sitting on the river banks, though most of the gold had to be laboriously separated from mud and gravel using hand-held pans or larger sluices. It wasn't a particularly lucrative existence: freelance miners roamed the countryside until they found a likely spot, and if and when they struck it rich quickly spent most of the earnings, either in celebration or buying the expensive supplies needed to carry on digging.

The boom towns that sprung up around the richest deposits were abandoned as soon as the gold ran out, but a few slowly decaying ghost towns have managed to survive more or less intact to the present day, hidden among the forests and rolling ranchland. Other sites were buried under the many **reservoirs** – built in the 1960s to provide a stable source of water for the agricultural Central Valley – that cover much of the lower elevations.

During spring the hillsides are covered in fresh green grasses and brightly colored wildflowers, though by the end of summer the hot sun has baked everything a dusty golden brown. Higher up, the free-flowing rivers rush through steep canyons lined by oak trees and cottonwoods, and the ten-thousand-foot granite peaks in the Sierra Nevada mountains above offer excellent skiing in winter, and hiking and camping in the pine and redwood forests all year round. South from Placerville, Hwy-49 passes through **Jackson**, which makes a good base for exploring the many dainty villages scattered around the wine-growing countryside of **Amador County**, continuing on through the mining towns of **Calaveras County**. The center of the southern mining district, then as now, is **Sonora**, a small, prosperous town of ornate Victorian houses set on ridges above steep gorges. Once an arch rival but now a ghost town, neighboring **Columbia** has a carefully restored Main Street that gives an excellent – if slightly contrived – idea of what Gold Rush life might have been like. The gold-mining district actually extended as far south as **Mariposa**, but the mines here were comparatively worthless and little remains to make it worth the trip, except perhaps as a quick stop on the way to Yosemite National Park (see p.312).

You'll need your own **transportation** to see much of the southern Gold Country. Trains steer well clear of the hilly terrain and buses only pass through Mariposa on their way from Fresno and Merced to Yosemite.

Amador County

South from Placerville and US-50, the old mining landscape of **Amador County** has been given over to the vineyards of one of California's up-and-coming **wine-growing** regions, best known for its robust Zinfandel, a full-flavored vintage that thrives in the sun-baked soil. Most of the wineries are located above Hwy-49 in the Shenandoah Valley, near Plymouth on the north edge of the county.

Amador City and Sutter Creek

About thirty miles east of Sacramento, Hwy-16 joins Hwy-49 at **AMADOR CITY**, whose short strip of false-fronted antique shops give it a distinctive, Old West look. The land-mark *Imperial Hotel* at the northern edge dominates the town, its four-foot-thick brick walls standing at a sharp bend in Hwy-49. The hotel has just been done up, with sunny double **rooms** (☎209/267-9172; ⑤), and the **restaurant** on the ground floor is one of the more sophisticated in the Mother Lode, but otherwise there isn't much to the place.

The real appeal of **SUTTER CREEK**, a much larger town two miles south of Amador City, is at first obscured behind the tidy facades of the cloying touristy restaurants and antique shops that line up along Hwy-49 through town. Though there are a number of surprisingly large Victorian wooden houses – many styled after Puritan New England farmhouses – the town lacks the disheveled spontaneity that animates many of the other Gold Rush towns, perhaps because its livelihood was based not on independent prospectors panning for placer gold but on hired hands working underground in the more organized and capital-intensive hard-rock mines. It was a lucrative business for the mine-owners: the Eureka Mine, owned by Hetty Green, at one time the richest woman in the world, operated until 1958, while the Lincoln Mine made enough money for owner Leland Stanford to become a railroad magnate and Governor of California.

Sutter Creek also holds the bulk of Amador County's **accommodation** and **eating** places, with two central and very comfortable B&Bs: *The Foxes*, 77 Main St (☎209/267-5882; ⑥), with well-appointed rooms and claw-foot baths; and the larger, more commu-nally minded *Sutter Creek Inn*, 75 Main St (☎209/267-5606; ④), with no TVs, no phones and no fake Victoriana, but a nice garden with hammocks and a welcoming atmos-phere. The *Bellotti Inn*, 53 Main St (☎209/267-5211; ②), has the cheapest accommoda-tion in town and a decent restaurant serving full meals for $15 and pasta dishes for $7. *Susan's Place*, in the Eureka Street Courtyard, a half-block east of Hwy-49 (Wed–Sun; ☎209/267-0945), serves sandwiches, soups, and salads under a shaded gazebo and, across the street, the *Sutter Creek Coffee Roasting Co.* serves the best coffee in town. For dessert, don't miss the *Sutter Creek Ice Cream Emporium*, 51 Main St, where the friendly owner will play Scott Joplin tunes on the piano while you sip your milkshake.

Jackson

After Sutter Creek, the town of **JACKSON**, four miles south, can seem distinctly blue-collar, mainly because of the huge Georgia Pacific lumber mill that serves as its north-ern gateway. Despite this first impression, Jackson makes a more affordable base for exploring the surrounding countryside. Its well-preserved center of photogenic brick facades makes a fine frame for the beautiful, but architecturally inappropriate 1939 Art Deco front of the **County Courthouse** at the top of the hill, and further along the crest, the **Amador County Museum** at 225 Church St (Wed–Sun 10am–4pm; donation) has displays of all the usual Gold Rush artifacts, but is worth a look most of all for its detailed models of the local hard-rock mines that were in use up until World War II, with shafts over a mile deep. The headframes and some of the mining machinery are still standing a mile north of the museum on Jackson Gate Road, where two sixty-foot diameter **tailing wheels** (8am–dusk; free), which carried away the waste from the Kennedy Mine, are accessible by way of short trails that lead up from a well-signposted parking area. The headframe of the six-thousand-foot shaft, the deepest in North America, stands out at the top of the slope, along Hwy-49. The other major mine in Jackson, the **Argonaut Mine** (of which nothing remains), was the scene of a tragedy in 1922, when 47 men were killed in an underground fire.

The **Amador County Chamber of Commerce** (daily 9am–5pm; ☎ 1-800/649-4988 or 209/223-0350), at the junction of Hwy-49 and Hwy-88, gives away an excellent *Visitors Guide to Amador County*, full of maps and interesting local anecdotes. The best **place to stay** is the friendly, if slightly run-down *National Hotel*, 77 Main St (☎1-800/894-3446 or 209/223-0500; ④), an 1860s hotel with individually decorated rooms, such as the "Bordello Room" with flock wallpaper, a four-poster bed and a claw-foot bath. If the *National* is full, try the *Amador Motel* (☎209/223-0970; ②) on Hwy-49 north of town, or nearby, the *Jackson Holiday Lodge* (☎209/223-0486; ③). *Mel and Faye's Diner* (☎209/223-0835) on Hwy-49 near the town center, is open all day for **breakfasts and burgers**, while *Café Max Swiss Bakery*, 140 Main St (☎209/223-0174), serves pastries and a mean cup of coffee. For **drinking**, the *Pioneer Rex Saloon*, 28 Main St (☎209/223-3859), is the modern equivalent of a Wild West saloon, with cheap beers and all-night poker games behind swinging louvre doors.

Indian Grinding Rock and Volcano
Hwy-88 heads east from Jackson up the Sierra Crest through hills that contain one of the most fitting memorials to the Native Americans who lived here for thousands of years before the Gold Rush all but wiped them out. Nine miles from Jackson, off Hwy-88, a side road passes by the restored remains of an old Miwok settlement at **Indian Grinding Rock State Historic Park** (daily dawn–dusk; $5 per car), where eleven hundred small cups – *Chaw'Se* in Miwok – were carved into the limestone boulders to be used as mortars for grinding acorns into flour. If you look closely from the small elevated platform next to the biggest of the flat rocks, you can just detect the faint outline of some of the 360 petroglyphs. The state has developed the site into an interpretive center and has constructed replicas of Miwok dwellings and religious buildings – interesting, even if they haven't managed to disguise the nails. Descendants of the Miwok gather here during the third week in July for "Big Time," a celebration of the survival of their culture with traditional arts and crafts, and to play a spirited game a bit like soccer. At the entrance to the site, the **Chaw'Se Regional Indian Museum** (Mon–Fri 11am–3pm, Sat & Sun 10am–4pm; free) explores the past and present state of the ten Sierra Nevada Native groups in a building said to simulate a Miwok roundhouse. The full process of producing acorn flour is covered, but modern Miwok life is given scant regard. A **campground** in the surrounding woods costs $14 a pitch and can be booked through Parknet ☎1-800/444-7275.

Named after the crater-like bowl in which it sits, **VOLCANO**, a tiny village a mile and a half north, once boasted over thirty saloons and dance halls – though the town is now little more than a shadow of its Gold Rush self. The densely forested countryside around, however, makes it well worth a visit, especially during spring (particularly mid-March to mid-April) when **Daffodil Hill**, three miles north of Volcano, is carpeted with more than 300,000 of the bobbing heads. Signs directing you there are only displayed when the flowers are in bloom. The sole accommodation in the immediate area is the friendly *St George Hotel* on Main Street (☎209/296-4458; ④), offering bed and breakfast without the comforts of televisions, phones or private bathrooms. Guests congregate in the bar, whose ceiling is covered in dollar bills and whose walls are decked with every office poster and wisecrack bumper sticker imaginable. This is the only place to **eat** in town, too, but it's excellent. From here, a narrow, scenic road follows Sutter Creek twelve miles down a wooded canyon back to the eponymous town.

Highway 88

Hwy-88 heads east beyond the Volcano turn-off to Pioneer where it meets Hwy-26 from Mokelumne Hill (see below). Three miles east, the **Amador Eldorado Forest Ranger Station** (Mon–Fri 8am–4.30pm; ☎209/295-4251) supplies wilderness permits for overnighting in the **Mokelumne Wilderness**, a segment of the Stanislaus and Toiabe National Forests south of Hwy-88 which closely follows the route of many early settlers. The ranger station also has details of camping and hiking in the **Eldorado National Forest**, beautiful in the fall, just before the winter snows turn the Sierra Nevada mountains around the 8500-foot Carson Pass into one of California's best cross-country ski resorts.

The few hotels along Hwy-88 cater almost exclusively to cross-country skiers, leaving summer visitors with little to choose from except the **campgrounds** dotted along the highway. Most are RV-friendly and cost at least $10, but some are free.

Beyond Carson Pass and the mountain meadows around **Lake Kirkwood**, close to the Nevada border, Hwy-88 joins Hwy-89, from where it's a short drive south to **MARKLEEVILLE**, a town of two hundred people on the Sierra Crest. The major attraction here is the **Grover Hot Springs State Park**, four miles west (May to mid-Sept daily 9am–9pm; closed last two weeks in Sept, reduced hours through winter; $4; ☎916/694-2248), with its two concrete tubs – one hot, one tepid – in which the water appears yellow-green due to mineral deposits on the pool bottom. There's a $12-a-night **campground** (reserve through Parknet ☎1-800/444-7275) on site.

Calaveras County

Calaveras County lies across the Mokelumne River, eight miles south of Jackson. You'll find a few good swimming and hiking spots on the north side of the river, along Electra Road, or you can push straight over the bridge, where a barely marked "Historic 49" turn-off loops around through the center of **MOKELUMNE HILL**, perhaps the most evocative – and least touristy – town in the southern Gold Country. Moke Hill, as it's called, was as action-packed in its time as any of the southern Gold Rush towns, but tourism has been slower to take hold here and the town today remains an intriguing concoction of ruined and half-restored buildings. It also has a couple of good **bars**, one on the south side of town in the lobby of the old *Hotel Léger*, 8305 Main St (☎209/286-1401; ④), and another inside the three-story **Odd Fellows Hall** at the north end of Main Street, where the Adams and Co saloon – and adhoc museum (Fri–Sun only) – is one of the few places in the region to retain much of the rowdy spirit of the pioneer years. On a more sober note, the range of names and languages on the headstones of the **Protestant Cemetery**, on a hill a hundred yards west of town, gives a good idea of the mix of people who came from all over the world to the California mines.

San Andreas

After the haunting decay of Moke Hill, **SAN ANDREAS**, eight miles south, hardly seems to warrant a second look: the biggest town for miles, it's now the Calaveras County seat, and has sacrificed historic character for commercial sprawl. What remains of old San Andreas survives along narrow Main Street, on a steep hill just east of the highway, where the 1893 granite and brick County Courthouse has been restored and now houses an interesting collection of Gold Rush memorabilia in the **Calaveras County Museum**, 30 N Main St (daily 10am–4pm; free). Local **nightlife** revolves around the *Black Bart Inn*, 35 Main St (☎209/754-3808; ③) across the street, which hosts bands on weekends. It is named after the gentleman stagecoach robber, **Black Bart**, who was captured and convicted here. Black Bart led a double life: in San Francisco he was a prominent citizen named Charles Bolton, who claimed to be a wealthy mining engineer; in the mining camps he made his name by committing thirty robberies between 1877 and 1883, always addressing his victims as "Sir" and "Madam" and sometimes reciting bits of poetry before escaping with the loot. He was finally discovered after dropping a handkerchief at the scene of a hold-up; police got him by tracing the laundry mark. He spent four years of a six-year sentence in San Quentin, and after his release disappeared without trace.

Angels Camp and Carson Hill

The mining camps of southern Calaveras County were some of the richest in the Gold Country, both for the size of their nuggets and for the imaginations of their residents. The author Bret Harte spent an unhappy few years teaching in and around the mines in the mid-1850s and based his short story, *The Luck of the Roaring Camp*, on his stay in **ANGELS CAMP**, thirty miles south of Jackson. There isn't much to see here these days, though the downtown feels mildly authentic. The saloon in the *Angels Hotel* on Main Street, where the 29-year-old **Mark Twain** was told a tale that inspired him to write his first published short story, the *Celebrated Jumping Frog of Calaveras County*, has been converted into a discount tire store. The unfortunate legacy of the story is the **Jumping Frog Jubilee** held on the third weekend in May each year and attended by thousands of people.

On the north side of town, the **Angels Camp Museum**, 753 Main St (daily 10am–3pm; $1) presents a cornucopia of gold-panning equipment, though this isn't a match for the hangar full of carriages behind the museum.

CARSON HILL, now a ghost town along Hwy-49 four miles south of Angels Camp, boasted the largest single nugget ever unearthed in California: 195 pounds of solid gold that was fifteen inches long and six inches thick, worth $43,000 then and well over a million dollars today.

Murphys

Nine miles east of Angels Camp, up the fairly steep Hwy-4, **MURPHYS'** one and only street is shaded by locust trees and graced by rows of decaying monumental buildings. One of the Gold Country's few surviving wooden water flumes still stands on Murphys' northern edge, while the oldest structure in town now houses the **Oldtimer's Museum** (Fri–Sun 11am–4pm; donation), a small gathering of documents and a wall-full of rifles. If you want to **stay**, head across the street to the old *Murphys Hotel*, 457 Main St (☎1-800/532-7684 or 209/728-3454; ④), which hosted some of the leading lights of the boom days in its rustic double rooms. The **Calaveras Big Trees State Park**, fifteen miles east

---

LIMESTONE CAVERNS IN THE GOLD COUNTRY

Limestone caverns abound in the southern Gold Country. Three have been developed for the public, and any one of them can provide, at the very least, a cool and constant 55°F relief from the sometimes baking-hot summer days. At Vallecito, just south of Hwy-4 and five miles east of Angels Camp on Parrot's Ferry Road, the **Moaning Cavern** (daily 10am–4pm; $7.75) is the largest in California, filled with strange rock formations, 150ft below ground; the human remains on display here greeted gold-seekers who found the cave in 1851. The natural acoustics of the cavern, which caused the low moaning sounds after which it is named, were destroyed by the insertion of the spiral staircase that takes visitors down into its depths (although for $35 you can rappel the 180 feet). **Mercer Caverns** (Sun–Thurs 10am–4.30pm, Fri & Sat 10am–7.30pm; $7), a mile north of Murphys on Sheep Ranch Road, focus on an 800-foot-long gallery of sculpted limestone, which takes the shape of angel's wings and giant flowers; the third cave system, **California Caverns** (daily 10am–4pm; $8), six miles east of San Andreas then two miles south from Mountain Ranch, offers a Wild Cave Expedition ($75): call ☎209/736-2708 for details and times.

($5 per car), covers six thousand acres of gigantic Sequoia trees, threaded with trails. It makes for fine ski touring in winter, with hiking and **camping** ($16; reserve mid-summer through Parknet ☎1-800/444-7275) the rest of the year.

Sonora, Columbia and Jamestown

SONORA, fifteen miles southeast of Angels Camp, is the center of the southern mining district. Now a logging town, set on steep ravines, the town makes a good base for exploring the southern region, with a thriving commercial center that manages to avoid tourist overkill. There's little to see beyond the false-fronted buildings and Victorian houses on the main **Washington Street** and the Gothic **St James Episcopal Church** at its far end, but it's a friendly, animated place, which warrants an afternoon's amble. You can pick up architectural and historical walking-tour **maps** (25¢) from the tourist office desk inside the small **Tuolumne County Museum**, in the old County Jail at 158 W Bradford Ave (Mon–Fri 10am–4pm, Sat 10am–3.30pm; free), which is worth a look for the restored cell block, if not for the collection of old clothes and photographs.

Walking-tour maps are also available from the **Tuolumne County Visitors Bureau**, 55 W Stockton St (June–Aug Mon–Fri 9am–7pm, Sat 10am–6pm, Sun 10am–5pm; Sept–May Mon–Fri 9am–6pm, Sat 10am–6pm; ☎ 1-800/446-1333 or 209/533-4420), a block from Washington Street, and the best source of **information** on the area; for specific details on camping, backpacking or outdoor recreation head for the Sierra Nevada Adventure Co at 173 S Washington St (☎209/532-5621).

The best **place to stay** in Sonora is the *Ryan House*, 153 S Shepherd St (☎209/533-3445; ⑤), a comfortable and welcoming old home set in lovely rose gardens two blocks east of the town center. Other options include the old adobe *Gunn House* at 286 S Washington St (☎209/532-3421; ③), or the good-value *Miner's Motel* (☎209/532-7850; ③) on Hwy-108 half way to Jamestown. For **lunch** try the gourmet sandwiches at *Good Heavens*, 49 N Washington St (☎209/532-3663); after dark make for *Alfredo's*, 123 S Washington St (☎209/532-8332), widely regarded as the best reasonably priced Mexican restaurant in these parts. For a quick and delicious burrito, you can't go wrong at *Garcia's Taqueria*, upstairs at 145 S Washington St (☎209/588-1915), and for great hamburgers, head to the *Diamond Back Grill*, 110 Washington St (☎209/532-6661). Of several **bars** along S Washington Street, *The Brass Rail* at no. 131, and the *Horseshoe Club* at no. 97, are the places to go for a real Wild West atmosphere around the pool and poker tables.

Columbia

Perhaps the most striking introduction to the southern Gold Rush towns is **COLUMBIA**, four miles north of Sonora on Parrots Ferry Road. Now a ghost town, it experienced a brief burst of riches after a Dr Thaddeus Hildreth and his party picked up thirty pounds of gold in just two days in March 1850. Within a month over five thousand miners were working claims limited by local law to ten square feet, and by 1854 Columbia was California's second largest city, with fifteen thousand inhabitants supporting some forty saloons, eight hotels and one school. The town missed becoming the state capital by two votes – just as well, since by 1870 the gold had run out and the town was abandoned, after over two and a half million ounces of gold (worth nearly a billion dollars at today's prices) had been taken out of the surrounding area.

Columbia is preserved as a state historic park, but there is no main gate or entrance fee: the dusty streets and wooden boardwalks are open all the time. Most of the buildings that survive date from the late 1850s, built in brick after fire destroyed the town for a second time. Roughly half of them house historical exhibits – including a dramatized visit to the frontier dentist's office, complete with a two-hundred-proof anesthetic and tape-recorded screams. The rest have been converted into shops, restaurants and saloons, where you can sip a sarsaparilla or eat a Gold Rush hot dog. There's even a **stagecoach ride** ($5) along the old mining trails around the town, which leaves from in front of the Wells Fargo Building. Needless to say it's all a bit contrived, and summer weekends can be nightmarishly crowded, especially on Living History Days when volunteers dress up and act out scenes from the old days. But most of the year the tree-lined streets are empty, and the place as a whole makes for a reasonably effective evocation of Gold Rush life. If you want to **stay**, the *City Hotel* on Main Street (☎1-800/532-1479 or 209/532-1479; ④) is luxurious and central, while a mile south of town the *Columbia Gem Motel*, 22131 Parrots Ferry Rd (☎209/532-4508; ②), offers basic accommodation in rustic cabins. Even cheaper is the *Sonora Hostel*, 11800 Columbia College Drive (☎209/533-2339; ①), where dorm beds on the college campus cost $15.

When you've tired of the town, you might try touring the surrounding trails on **horseback**. The Columbia Riding Stable, inside the park (☎209/532-0663), offers rides of varying duration and difficulty for about $24 per hour.

Jamestown

Three miles south of Sonora on Hwy-49 lies **JAMESTOWN**, a saccharine-sweet little village that serves as the southern gateway to the Gold Country for drivers coming on Hwy-120 from the San Francisco Bay Area. Before 1966, when much of Jamestown burned down in a fire, it was used as location for many well-known Westerns – most famously for the filming of *High Noon*. The train from that movie is now the biggest attraction of **Railtown 1897 State Historic Park**, four blocks east of Main Street – a collection of old steam trains that's open year round, on summer weekends offering trips on restored local railroads ($9). Along with its train collection, Jamestown is one of the few Gold Country towns that still has a **working mine** – the huge open-pit Sonora Mining Corp operation west of town on Hwy-49 – and a number of outfits take visitors on gold-mining expeditions. Among them, Gold Prospecting Expeditions ($30 for 2hr; ☎209/984-4653) gives brief instruction in the arts of panning, sluicing and sniping, kits you out and allows you two hours to pan what you can from its local stream. Main Street is the town's main drag, lined with old balconied Gold Rush **hotels** such as the *National* (☎209/984-3446; ④) and the *Royal* (☎209/984-5271; ③), and with a few good **eating places**. The *Mother Lode Coffee Shop* (☎209/984-3386) is popular with locals, while the more touristy *Smoke Café* (☎209/984-3733) has fairly tame Mexican food and huge margaritas.

Mariposa County and south to Yosemite

Hwy-49 winds south from Sonora through some sixty miles of the sparsely populated, rolling foothills of **Mariposa County**, passing near the remains of the town of **CHINESE CAMP**. It was here that the worst of the Tong Wars between rival factions of Chinese miners took place in 1856, after the Chinese had been excluded from other mining camps in the area by white miners. Racism was rampant in the southern Gold Rush camps, something which also accounts for its most enduring legend, the story of the so-called Robin Hood of the Mother Lode, **Joaquin Murieta**. Very little is actually known of the truth behind the stories of this figure, yet virtually every southern Gold Rush town has some tale to tell of him. A romantic hero, rather than a real one, Murieta was probably a composite of many characters, mostly dispossessed Mexican miners driven to banditry by violent racist abuse at the hands of newly arrived white Americans. In May 1853, the State Legislature hired a man named Harry Love to capture any one of five men named "Joaquin" wanted for cattle theft. Love soon returned with the head of a man pickled in a glass jar, and collected the reward. A year later J.R.

Ridge wrote a story called *The Life and Times of Joaquin Murieta, the Celebrated California Bandit*, mixing together flights of fancy with a few well-placed facts – including the pickled head – and the legend was born.

Hwy-49 continues south right on the fringes of the Gold Country. Branching off it, Hwy-120 passes **Groveland**, a way-station on the San Francisco to Yosemite run. The ranger station (☎209/586-3234) has information on hiking and camping in the nearby Stanislaus National Forest.

Hornitos

The town with the most likely claim to Murieta's patronage is **HORNITOS**, twenty miles west of Bear Valley on the southern edge of the Gold Country. Hornitos, which is Spanish for "little ovens," was named after the oven-shaped tombs in the cemetery at the edge of town and was once a quiet little Mexican pueblo, one of the few in the area founded before the Gold Rush. The population swelled to over fifteen thousand when Mexican miners were exiled from nearby mining camps by white miners who didn't feel like sharing the wealth, and the town became notorious for its saloons, opium dens and gambling halls, a favorite haunt of many an outlaw like Murieta – who, it's claimed, had his own secret escape route out of town via an underground tunnel. Today Hornitos is a heap of substantial ruins grouped around a central plaza.

Mariposa

Hwy-49 continues south to **MARIPOSA**, the county seat and the last major supply stop before Yosemite. The **Mariposa Museum and History Center** (summer daily 10am–4.30pm; rest of year Sat & Sun only, closed Jan; donation), behind the Bank of America off Hwy-49 at the north end of town, has a little bit of everything to do with the Gold Rush – from miners' letters home to ancient bottles of E & J Burke's Guinness Stout – and is well worth a look if you're passing through. From Mariposa, Hwy-140 heads east along the Merced River into Yosemite National Park (see p.312). Along its length, the *Meadows Ranch* café at no. 5029 serves good food all-day.

LAKE TAHOE, RENO AND CARSON CITY

High above the Gold Country, just east of the Sierra ridge, **Lake Tahoe** sits placidly in a dramatic alpine bowl, surrounded by high granite peaks and miles of thickly wooded forest. It's a heavily touristy area; the sandy beaches and surrounding pine-tree wilderness attract thousands of families throughout the summer, and in winter the snow-covered slopes of the nearby peaks are packed with skiers. The eastern third of the lake lies in Nevada and gleams with the neon signs of flashy casinos.

Truckee, 25 miles north of Lake Tahoe, ranges along the Truckee River, which flows out of Lake Tahoe down into the desert of Nevada's Great Basin. It's a main stop on Greyhound and Amtrak cross-country routes, though apart from an influx of skiers in winter is little-visited. **Donner Pass**, just west of town, was named in memory of the pioneer Donner family, many of whom lost their lives when trapped here by heavy winter snows.

Across the border in Nevada, **Reno**, at the eastern foot of the Sierra Nevada, is a downmarket version of Las Vegas, popular with slot-machine junkies and elderly gamblers; others come to take advantage of Nevada's lax marriage and divorce laws. Though far smaller than Reno, **Carson City**, thirty miles south, is the Nevada state capital, with a couple of engaging museums that recount the town's frontier history.

Heading deeper into Nevada in the arid mountains further east, the silver mines of the Comstock Lode, whose wealth paid for the building of much of San Francisco, are buried deep below the tourist center of **Virginia City**.

The two main trans-Sierra highways, I-80 and US-50, head east from Sacramento and are kept open all year round, regardless of snowfall, passing by Truckee and Lake Tahoe respectively. Both places are served by Greyhound, and there are also services from the Nevada cities to the Tahoe casinos, though there's no public transportation between Truckee and the lake.

Lake Tahoe

Fault-formed **LAKE TAHOE** is one of the highest, largest, deepest, cleanest, coldest and most beautiful lakes in the world. More than sixteen hundred feet deep, it is so cold – or so the story goes – that at its depths cowboys who drowned over a century ago have been recovered in perfectly preserved condition, gun holsters and all. It's a place for all seasons, thronged with jet-skiers, boaters and anglers in summer, and equally packed with snowboarders and skiers in winter. When the snows melt, the wilderness areas all around the lake offer excellent hiking.

Its position, straddling the border between California and Nevada, lends the lake a schizophrenic air, the dichotomy most evident at **South Lake Tahoe**, the lakeside's largest community, where ranks of restaurants, modest motels and pine-bound cottages stand cheek by jowl with the high-rise gambling dens of **Stateline**, just across the border. **Tahoe City**, the hub of the lake's northwestern shore, does not escape the tourists, but nevertheless manages to retain a more relaxed small-town attitude. Expensive vacation homes and shabby family oriented mini-resorts line much of the remainder of the lake; in spring and fall, when the snow is either melting or just beginning to appear, it can actually feel quite deserted.

Arrival, information and getting around

One hundred miles east of Sacramento on both US-50 and US-80, Lake Tahoe is well served by Greyhound **buses** and a number of coach tours, mainly catering to weekend gamblers. The five daily Greyhound buses from San Francisco and Sacramento use *Harrah's* casinos in South Lake Tahoe as a terminus: Amtrak Thruway buses stop twice daily on their Sacramento to Carson City run. Tahoe Casino Express buses ($17 one-way; ☎1-800/446-6128 or 702/785-2424) run half-hourly from 9am to 5pm between Reno airport and the *Stateline* casinos, and Gray Line (☎702/331-1147) has daily tours from Reno around the lake, stopping off at Virginia City; their "gambler's special" coach tours leave from San Francisco. If you're **driving**, expect to get here in a little over three hours from San Francisco unless you join the Friday night exodus in which case you can add an hour or two, more in winter when you'll need to carry chains; call the Caltrans road phone (☎1-800/427-7623) to check on road conditions before you depart.

There are booths claiming to be visitor centers all over South Lake Tahoe, but most are just advertising outlets for the casinos or fronts for timeshare agents. Instead, get useful **information**, maps and help with finding a place to stay at the **South Lake Tahoe Chamber of Commerce**, 3066 US-50 (Mon–Sat 8.30am–4.30pm; ☎530/541-5255) just west of El Dorado beach. Just north of Stateline in Nevada, the **Tahoe-Douglas Visitor Center**, 195 Hwy-50 (☎702/588-4591) has thousands of useless brochures but will help with room reservations. The **North Lake Tahoe Chamber of Commerce**, 245 North Lake Blvd in Tahoe City (Mon–Sat 9am–5pm; ☎530/581-6900) is the best bet for information on the North Lake region.

Getting around

STAGE **buses** (☎530/541-6328) run 24 hours a day all over the South Lake Tahoe area, and will take you anywhere within a ten-mile radius for a flat $1.25 fare ($2 buys you an all-day pass). Tahoe Casino Express (☎1-800/446-6128) runs northeast from South Lake Tahoe to Glenbrook then east to Carson City. In the north, TART (roughly 6am to 6pm; $1 flat fare, $2.50 for an all-day pass; ☎1-800/736-6365 or 530/581-6365) runs between Truckee, Tahoe City, Sugar Pine Point State Park and Incline Village. Alternatively, an unlimited day pass on the convenient Tahoe Lake Lapper (☎530/542-5900), which has buses going in both directions around the lake and allows bikes, costs $5. **Car rental**, at about $30 a day, is available through the South Lake Tahoe outlets of all the national chains – Avis (☎1-800/831-2847 or 530/542-5638), Enterprise (☎530/544-7788) and Hertz (☎1-800/654-3131 or 530/544-2327) – as well as slightly cheaper local firms such as Tahoe Rent-a-car (☎530/544-4500). You could also **rent a bicycle** for around $20 a day from any of over a dozen lakeside shops in South Lake Tahoe, among them Anderson Bike Rental, 645 Emerald Bay Rd (☎530/541-0500). In Tahoe City, try Cycle Paths, 1785 West Lake Blvd, two miles south of the "Y" (☎530/581-1171), or Porter's Ski and Sport, 120 N Lake Blvd (☎530/583-2314) right in town.

Accommodation

Most of the hundred or so **motels** that circle the lake are collected together along US-50 in South Lake Tahoe. During the week, except in summer, many have bargain rates, from around $30 for a double; however, these rates can easily double on weekends, so be sure to confirm all prices. If you're having trouble finding a room, the **South Lake Tahoe Visitors' Authority**, 1156 Ski Run Boulevard (☎1-800/AT-TAHOE or 530/583-3494) runs a free **reservation service**.

Tahoe City lacks the range and competition of its southerly neighbor, so you can expect to pay a little more for a room there, although the scarcity of ugly hotels and motels may just make the extra cost worth it. Unlike Las Vegas or Reno, the **casinos** rarely offer good-value accommodation. **Camping** (see box on p.526) is only an option during summer (Tahoe gets upwards of 20ft of snow every winter).

South shore

Caesars Tahoe Resort/Casino, US-50, Stateline, Nevada (☎1-800/648-3353 or 702/588-3515). Deluxe resort and upmarket casino; the best rooms overlook the lake. ⑥.

Doug's Mellow Mountain Retreat, 3787 Forest Ave, S Lake Tahoe (☎530/544-8065). Essentially Doug's home operating as a relaxed, if cramped, hostel with cooking facilities, cheap bike rental and occasional barbecues. Beds are $13 a night and double rooms are available. A mile from the Greyhound stop but Doug will pick you up. ①.

Inn by the Lake, 3300 Lake Tahoe Blvd, S Lake Tahoe (☎1-800/877-1466 or 530/542-0330). Nicely furnished rooms, a heated swimming pool and jacuzzi, free breakfast and use of bicycles make this relaxing spot good value for money. Free shuttle bus to the casinos. ⑤.

Lamplighter Motel, 4143 Cedar Ave, S Lake Tahoe (☎530/544-2936). Just off US-50, near the casinos and the lakeshore. It has a hot tub with views of the skifield behind. ②.

Motel 6, 2375 Lake Tahoe Blvd, S Lake Tahoe (☎530/542-1400). Huge, and one of the better bets for budget accommodation. It's filled during the ski season and in summer, so book early. ③.

Red Carpet Inn, 4100 Lake Tahoe Blvd (Hwy-50), S Lake Tahoe (☎1-800/336-5553 or 530/544-2261). This tacky hotel is about as close as you can get to the casinos without staying in Nevada. Rooms are surprisingly comfortable. ②.

Seven Seas, 4145 Manzanita Ave, S Lake Tahoe (☎530/544-7031). One of the south shore's countless small motels, offering clean, simple rooms and a hot tub. ②.

North shore

Falcon Motor Lodge, Hwy-28, Kings Beach (☎530/546-2583). Ordinary but dependable budget accommodation. ②.

Lake of the Sky Motor Inn, 955 N Lake Blvd, Tahoe City (☎530/583-3305). Justifiably a little more expensive than the *Tahoe City Inn*. ④.

Sunnyside, 1850 W Lake Blvd, Tahoe City (☎530/583-7200 or 822-2754). Large, comfortable mountain lodge right on the lakeshore. Unbeatable views of the lake from many rooms, and a popular restaurant on the ground floor (see p.527). Rates are highest in summer. ⑤.

Tahoe City Inn, 790 N Lake Blvd, Tahoe City (☎1-800/800-TAHO or 530/581-3333). This place can cost as little as $45 midweek off-season. ③.

Tamarack Lodge, 2311 N Lake Blvd, Tahoe City (☎1-888/824-6323 or 530/583-3350). The cheapest lodging near Tahoe City is comfortable and clean. ③.

Travelodge, 455 N Lake Blvd, Tahoe City (☎530/583-3766). The location is unbeatable, right across from the lake in the center of town, but mid-winter and mid-summer, you'll pay for it. Off-season, these well-appointed rooms are a great deal. Lake-view spa and sauna. ③.

South Lake Tahoe and Stateline

Almost all of Tahoe's lakeshore is developed in some way or another, but nowhere is it as concentrated and overbearing as at the contiguous settlements of **SOUTH LAKE TAHOE** and **STATELINE**. The latter is compact, a clutch of gambling houses huddled, as you might expect, along the Nevada–California border. The half-dozen-or-so casinos compete for the attentions of the punters who almost all base themselves in the much larger South Lake Tahoe on the Californian side. At some time during their stay, almost everyone chances their arm at the tables and slot machines, but few come for that purpose alone. Lake Tahoe is primarily an outdoors attraction, as the numerous lakefront sporting paraphernalia outlets will attest, and the time you spend in South Lake Tahoe or Stateline should really be confined to sleeping or eating.

Though many stretches of Lake Tahoe are breathtakingly beautiful, the 75-mile **drive** around the lake can be a bit of a disappointment. A better way to see the lake is to take one of two **paddle-wheel boat** cruises: the *Tahoe Queen*, a restored Mississippi riverboat, sets sail from the end of Ski Run Boulevard in South Lake Tahoe (July–Sept daily 10.30am, 1.05pm & 3.40pm; Oct daily 11am & 2pm; $16; ☎1-800/238-2463 or 530/541-3364); and the *MS Dixie II*, a modern replica, leaves from Zephyr Cove, three miles north of Stateline in Nevada, for a two-hour cruise to Emerald Bay (three departures daily, call for times; ☎702/588-3508; $18).

Perhaps most impressive is the view of the lake from above, either skiing in winter or hiking along the many trails that rim the lake basin (see the "Hiking" box on p.526). The lazy way to get up is on the **Heavenly Valley Tram** (summer daily 10am–9pm; winter times vary depending on ski conditions; $17), a giant ski lift that shuttles tourists up to the 8200-foot summit of the south lake's largest ski resort.

West around the lake

In summer, many enjoyable music and arts events take place at the **Tallac Historic Site** (April–Oct daily 10am–6pm; free), beside Hwy-89 on the western side of the lake two miles northwest of the South Lake Tahoe "Y". Even when there's nothing special going on, the historic site's sumptuous wood-built homes – constructed by wealthy San Franciscans as lakeside vacation retreats in the late 1800s – are well worth a look. You can also see the remains of the lavish casino-hotel erected by Elias "Lucky" Baldwin, which brought the rich and famous to Lake Tahoe's shores until it was destroyed by fire in 1914. Inside the former Baldwin house, the **Tallac Museum** (daily 11am–3pm; free) records the family's impact on the region.

The prettiest part of the lake, however, is along the southwest shore, where **Emerald Bay State Park**, ten miles from South Lake Tahoe (daily dawn–dusk; $5 per vehicle), surrounds a narrow, rock-strewn inlet and the lake's one island, Fanette Island, topped by a small and unused teahouse. In the park, at the end of a mile-long trail from the parking lot is **Vikingsholm**, an authentic reproduction of a Viking castle, believe it or not, built as a summer home in 1929. It is open for half-hourly **tours** (summer daily 10am–4pm; $2). From Vikingsholm, the **Rubicon Trail** runs two miles north along the lakeside to **Rubicon Bay**, flanked by other grand old mansions, dating from the days when Lake Tahoe was accessible only to the most well-heeled of travelers. You can also drive here on Hwy-89 and enter through the **D.L. Bliss State Park** (extremely limited parking $5). The 15,000-square-foot **Ehrman Mansion** here (guided

LAKE TAHOE SKIING

Lake Tahoe has some of the best **downhill skiing** in North America, with some of its larger resorts rivaling their Rocky Mountain counterparts. More than a few Bay Area residents head for the mountains at the first sign of snow and, in a good year, many lifts continue to operate through the end of April. Although skiing is certainly not cheap – the largest ski areas charge close to $50 for the privilege of using their mountain for a single day – many resorts offer decent-value rental/lift ticket/lesson packages or multi-day discounts. **Snowboarding** has of course caught on in a big way, and the same resorts that once scoffed at the sport have now installed massive snow parks with radical half-pipes and jumps. **Cross-country skiing** is also a popular activity, especially among the more fitness-oriented. The following list of ski resorts is not exhaustive, rather it highlights the best options for skiers of varying ability and financial standing. Skis can be rented at the resorts for about $20, snowboards for $30.

DOWNHILL SKIING

Homewood, six miles southwest of Tahoe City on Hwy-89 (☎530/525-2992). Smaller and more relaxed than its massive resorty neighbors, Homewood boasts some surprisingly good skiing, with reasonable prices and unbeatable views of the lake. It's also known for its great tree skiing. Lift tickets go for $35. Beginner package costing $39 includes equipment, lesson, and beginner lift ticket.

Kirkwood Ski Resort, 35 miles south of South Lake Tahoe on Hwy-88 (☎209/258-6000). A bit out of the way if you're staying in Tahoe, but worth the trip as a destination in itself. Located in the El Dorado National Forest, away from any major cities, Kirkwood manages to escape the over-developed feel of many of the Tahoe resorts while still providing some amazing skiing. Lift tickets are $43.

Squaw Valley USA, Squaw Valley Road, halfway between Truckee and Tahoe City (☎1-800/545-4350). Thirty lifts service over 4000 acres of unbeatable terrain at the site of the 1960 Winter Olympics. Squaw can be a bit of a scene, and the resorts are growing like weeds around the base of the mountain, but for sheer variety, it remains unparalleled in Lake Tahoe. Lift tickets are $48.

Sugar Bowl, ten miles west of Truckee at the Soda Springs Norden exit (☎530/426-9000). The closest ski area to San Francisco has twelve lifts and newly expanded terrain. Inexplicably, this excellent mountain is often less crowded than others in the area. Lift tickets cost $42.

CROSS-COUNTRY SKIING

Royal Gorge, in Soda Springs, ten miles west of Truckee (☎530/426-3871). The largest and best of Tahoe's cross-country resorts has 204 miles of groomed trails. $19.50 trail fee, $16.50 rental fee, and $18 for lessons.

Spooner Lake, in Nevada at the intersection of Hwy-50 and Hwy-28 (☎702/887-8844). The closest cross-country resort to South Lake Tahoe has lake views and 63 miles of groomed trails. Trail fees are $15, rentals $15, and lessons $34.

tours daily 10am–4pm on the hour; free), decorated in a happy blend of 1930s opulence and backcountry rustic, is surrounded by extensive lakefront grounds which were used as a location for the movie *Godfather II*.

Tahoe City and around

TAHOE CITY is less developed and more compact than South Lake Tahoe, and a close-knit population of permanent residents coupled with a family-oriented atmosphere give it a relaxed, peaceful disposition. That isn't to say that the city is without excitement or a social scene; well-off twenty- and thirtysomethings from the Bay Area flood the bike paths during the summer, the surrounding ski slopes during the winter, and the town's few bars most weekend nights.

At the western end of town, Hwy-89 meets Hwy-28 at Fanny Bridge, named for the body part that greets drivers as people lean over the edge to view the giant trout in the **Truckee River**. Flow-regulating sluice gates at the mouth of the river are remotely controlled from Reno, but were once operated by a gatekeeper who lived in what is now the **Gatekeeper's Museum** (mid-June to early Sept daily 11am–5pm; May to mid-June & early to late Sept Wed–Sun 11am–5pm; $2), containing a well-presented hodgepodge of artifacts from the last century, and a good collection of native basketware. Nearby, the **Truckee River Bike Trail** begins its three-mile waterside meander west to the River Ranch, which is also the end of a popular river rafting route. **Rafting** down the Truckee is the thing to do on warm summer days, though it's really more of a relaxing social affair than a serious or challenging adventure. Several well-advertised boat rental stands congregate along the river across from the Chevron Station.

A couple of miles south along Hwy-89, 500 yards past the Kaspian picnic grounds, you'd be well advised to **hike** ten minutes up the unmarked trail to the top of **Eagle Rock** (see box overleaf for more ambitious hiking suggestions). The amazing panoramic views that surround you as you look down on the expansive royal-blue lake make this one of the world's greatest picnic spots. Several miles further south along Hwy-89 is **Chamber's Beach**, which, in summer, is as popular for sunning and **swimming** as it is for socializing.

You could also visit **Squaw Valley**, the site of the 1960 Winter Olympics, situated five miles west of Tahoe City off Hwy-89, although the original facilities (except the flame and the Olympic rings) are now swamped by the rampant development which has made this California's largest ski resort (see opposite). Non-skiers might enjoy the $14 cable car ride up to the newly completed High Camp Bath and Tennis Club, where you can ice skate ($19 including cable car, $11 after 5pm), bungee jump, play tennis or swim (same price as skating) at 8200 feet. In the valley below, hiking, horseback riding and mountain biking are all popular summertime activities.

East from Tahoe City are unremarkable settlements, among them Incline Village, a short distance from the eminently missable **Ponderosa Ranch** (April–Oct daily 9.30am–5pm; $8.50) where *Bonanza* was filmed. If you're staying in Tahoe City and have the urge to **gamble** without making the hour drive to Stateline, a couple of appealingly small-scale casinos, including the aptly named *Cal-Neva*, huddle on the north side of the lake just across the Nevada border. One of the best destinations on the northern side of the lake is the **Lake Tahoe Nevada State Park** at Sand Harbor, which has a great beach – though the water is always prohibitively cold – and trails winding up through the backcountry to the Tahoe Rim Trail.

Eating and drinking

Lake Tahoe has few exceptional **restaurants**; average burger and steak places, rustic in decor with raging fireplaces are commonplace. Far better are the **buffets** at the Nevada **casinos**: *Harrah's*, for example, serves a wonderful spread, with good all-you-

HIKING AND CAMPING AROUND LAKE TAHOE

Of the many wonderful hikes in the Lake Tahoe area, only one – the 150-mile **Tahoe Rim Trail** – makes the circuit of the lake, some of it on the Pacific Crest National Scenic Trail which follows the Sierra ridge from Canada to the Mexican border. Most people tackle only a tiny section of it, such as **Kingsbury Grade to Big Meadows** (22 miles), starting off Hwy-207 northwest of South Lake Tahoe and finishing on Hwy-50, south of Lake Tahoe. Many other sections are equally spectacular: ask at the **US Forest Service visitor center**, 870 Emerald Bay Rd (summer Mon–Thurs & Sat–Sun 8am–5.30pm, Fri 8am–7pm; ☎530/573-2674), three miles northwest of the South Lake Tahoe "Y", for recommendations, free maps and brochures.

There are also many **mountain biking** trails around the lake: **Meiss Country**, between Luther Pass and Carson Pass twenty miles south of South Lake Tahoe is one favored area. The three-mile loop of the **Pope-Baldwin Trail** near the south shore is another winner, as is the popular **Marlett Lake/Flume Trail** in the Nevada State Park.

CAMPING

Lake Tahoe's best **campground** is *Campground by the Lake*, on the lakeshore three miles west of Stateline (☎530/542-6096; reserve through Parknet ☎1-800/444-7275; $16.50). Other south shore sites include *Nevada Beach* (☎530/544-5994 reserve through *Biospherics*; 1-800/280-2267; $16) several miles north of Stateline, and there are any number of backcountry sites in the surrounding forest. The **north** has several sites within striking distance of Tahoe City, including *Tahoe State Recreation Area* (☎530/583-3074; reserve through Parknet ☎1-800/444-7275; $14) right in the center, and as crowded as you would expect. A mile and a half east, *Lake Forest* (☎530/581-4017; $10) is cheaper though a way from the beach, and two miles southwest along Hwy-89, there's the large *William Kent* site (☎530/544-5994; reserve through Parknet ☎1-800/444-7275; $12).

Along the western side of the lake, the Tahoe Rim Trail follows the Pacific Crest Trail through the glaciated valleys and granite peaks of the **Desolation Wilderness**. Here, **wilderness permits** are required by all users, though for day users these are self-issued. For overnighters, a quota system operates in summer: fifty percent of these are first-come-first-served on the day of entry from the Forest Service visitor center, the remainder are reservable up to ninety days in advance (☎530/644-6048). Primitive sites include *Bayview* (☎530/544-5994; free). The other wilderness areas around the lake – Granite Chief to the northwest and Mount Rose to the northeast – are used much less and consequently no wilderness permits are needed, though campfire permits are.

can-eat food for low rates. The casinos are also good places to **drink** – roving barmaids bring free cocktails to gamblers – and hold most of the region's entertainment options as well: crooners and comedians mostly, plus small-scale versions of Las Vegas revues. For its size, Tahoe City has a good range of moderately priced places to eat as well as a couple of happening **bars**, all within easy walking distance of each other.

South shore

Carlos Murphy's, 3678 US-50, S Lake Tahoe (☎530/542-1741). Pseudo-Mexican cantina, serving up large platefuls of anodyne Tex-Mex food; come early in the evening for free Happy Hour nachos, cheap margaritas and $1 shots of Jose Cuervo.

Nephele's, 1169 Ski Run Blvd, S Lake Tahoe (☎530/544-8130). Long-standing restaurant at the foot of Heavenly Valley ski resort, with a great selection of moderate to expensive California cuisine: grilled meat, fish and pasta dishes.

Red Hut Waffle Shop, 2479 US-50, S Lake Tahoe (☎530/541-9024). Ever-popular coffee shop, justifiably crowded early winter mornings with carbo-loading skiers.

Sprouts, 3123 US-50, S Lake Tahoe (☎530/541-6969). Almost, but not completely vegetarian, with good organic sandwiches, burritos and smoothies.

Steamers Bar and Grill, 2236 US-50, S Lake Tahoe (☎530/541-8818). Fairly cruisey après-ski hangout that gets especially lively when there's a game on the big-screen TV; the bar food is good value.

Tep's Villa Roma, 3450 Hwy-50, S Lake Tahoe (☎530/541-8227). Long-standing south shore institution that serves large portions of hearty Italian food, including several simple yet tasty vegetarian pasta dishes for about $10.

North shore

Bluewater Brewing Company, Lighthouse Center, Tahoe City (☎530/81-BLUE). Fine microbrews and live music.

Bridgetender, 30 Emerald Bay Rd, Tahoe City (☎530/583-3342). For burgers, sandwiches or just a beer by the rushing Truckee River, make for this wonderfully sited place with heavy wooden tables outdoors and a rustic log-cabin feel inside. The food is better than average and well priced, but the styrofoam beakers aren't pleasant.

Coyote's Mexican Grill, 521 N Lake Blvd, Tahoe City (☎530/583-6653). Great-value burritos and enchiladas in a lively atmosphere.

Lakehouse Pizza, 120 Grove St, Tahoe City (☎530/583-2222). Tahoe's best place for pizza is also a popular spot for cocktails on the lake at sundown. Be prepared to wait in winter.

Pete and Peters, N Lake Blvd, in the center of Tahoe City (☎530/583-2400). Play pool with the locals at this longtime friendly bar.

Pierce Street Annex, in the back of the Lighthouse Center, Tahoe City (☎530/583-5800). The place for drinking and dancing on the north shore. Packed with sunburned skiers or drunk beachgoers, depending on the season.

Rosie's Cafe, 571 N Lake Blvd, Tahoe City (☎530/583-8504). Cozy restaurant with a vaulted ceiling and fireplace, serving delicious grilled meats, fresh sandwiches and filling breakfasts.

Sunnyside, 1850 W Lake Blvd, Tahoe City (☎530/583-7200). If you'd rather not spend $18 for one of their decent entrees, order an appetizer, a burger and a beer and have a seat on the deck overlooking the lake. Friendly atmosphere and very popular.

Truckee and Donner Lake

Just off I-80, along the main transcontinental Amtrak train route, **TRUCKEE**, 25 miles north of Lake Tahoe, makes a refreshing change from the tourist-dependent towns around the lake. A small town, lined up along the north bank of the Truckee River, it retains a fair amount of its late nineteenth-century wooden architecture along the main street, Commercial Row – some of which appeared in Charlie Chaplin's *The Gold Rush* – but is nevertheless more of a stop-off than a destination in its own right, a livelihood dependent on the forestry industry and the railroad. The town's rough, lively edge, however, makes it as good a base as any from which to see the Lake Tahoe area, a fact which hasn't escaped the businesses beginning to exploit the commercial opportunities. There's even public transportation between the two (see below).

Practicalities

Greyhound **buses** from San Francisco stop in Truckee five times a day and are met by TART buses to Tahoe City (daily 6.30am–6.30pm; $1.25; ☎530/581-6365). One Amtrak train and two Thruway buses a day in each direction stop at the station on Commercial Row in the middle of town. Visitor information is available in the lobby, but the **visitor center**, a couple of miles west at 12036 Donner Pass Rd (Mon–Sat 9am–6pm; ☎ 1-800/548-8388 or 530/587-2757), is better. Where Hwy-89 branches north off I-80, a **Forest Service Ranger Station** (Mon–Thurs & Sat 8am–5pm, Fri 8am–6pm; ☎530/587-3558) has details of camping and hiking in the surrounding countryside. To get around, rent a **mountain bike** from Truckee Bike Works, 11400 Donner Pass Rd ($25 a day; ☎530/587-7711), or a **car** from Rent-a-Dent ($25 a day; ☎530/587-6711).

Truckee's cheapest **place to stay** is the *Cottage Hotel*, 10178 Donner Pass Rd (☎530/587-3108; ②), central but a bit shabby. Much nicer is the *Truckee Hotel*, 10007 Bridge St almost opposite the station (☎1-800/659-6921 or 530/587-4444; ④), once decorated in the grand old railroad tradition, now decked out in Victorian B&B style, but with some of the best rooms in town. A number of low-priced **campgrounds** line the Truckee River between the town and Lake Tahoe, off Hwy-89: the closest and largest is *Granite Flat*, a mile and a half from Truckee; others are *Goose Meadows* and *Silver Creek*, four and six miles south respectively (you can contact all three campgrounds on ☎530/587-3558).

Commercial Row has several good **eating places**, especially the diner-style *Coffee And* at no. 10106 (☎530/587-3123), the more expensive, French-style *The Left Bank* at no. 10096 (☎530/587-4694) and *Cafe Meridian* at no. 10118, a refreshingly modern place with a rooftop terrace, good light food, coffee and drinks. Omelets are the specialty at *Squeeze In*, 10060 Donner Pass Rd (☎530/587-9814), which serves breakfast daily from 7am to 2pm. Though the old Bucket of Blood saloons of frontier-lore are long gone, there are a few good places to stop for a **drink**, including the *Bar of America*, downtown at the corner of Hwy-26 and Donner Pass Road (☎530/587-3110), or *The Pastime Club* (☎530/582-9219) across from the train station – both featuring free **live music** most nights.

Donner Lake

Two miles west of Truckee, surrounded by alpine cliffs of silver-gray granite, **Donner Lake** was the site of one of the most gruesome and notorious tragedies of early California, when pioneers trapped by winter snows were forced to eat the bodies of their dead companions (see box).

The horrific tale of the Donner party is recounted in some detail in the small **Emigrant Trail Museum** (summer daily 10am–5pm; rest of year daily 10am–4pm; $2) – just off Donner Pass Road, three miles west of Truckee in **Donner Memorial State Park** – which shows slides and a dramatized video of the events. Outside, the **Pioneer Monument** stands on a plinth as high as the snow was deep that fateful winter – 22 feet. From the museum an easy nature trail winds through the forest past a memorial plaque marking the site where the majority of the Donner Party built their simple cabins. Nearby, on the southeast shore of the lake, there's a $14-a-night summer-only **campground** (reserve through Parknet ☎1-800/444-7275).

THE DONNER PARTY

The **Donner Party**, named after two of the pioneer families among the group of 91 travelers, set off for California in April 1846 from Illinois across the Great Plains, following a short cut recommended by the first traveler's guide to the West Coast (the 1845 *Emigrant's Guide to California and Oregon*) that actually took three weeks longer than the established route. By October they had reached what is now Reno, and decided to rest a week to regain their strength for the arduous crossing of the Sierra Nevada mountains – a delay that proved fatal. When at last they set off, early snowfall blocked their route beyond Donner Lake, and the group were forced to stop and build crude shelters, hoping that the snow would melt and allow them to complete their crossing; it didn't, and they were stuck.

Within a month the pioneers were running out of provisions, and a party of fifteen set out across the mountains to try and reach Sutter's Fort in Sacramento. They struggled through yet another storm and, a month later, two men and five women stumbled into the fort, having survived by eating the bodies of the men who had died. A rescue party set off from Sutter's Fort immediately, only to find more of the same: thirty or so half-crazed survivors, living off the meat of their fellow travelers.

Above Donner Lake the Southern Pacific railroad tracks climb west over the **Donner Pass** through tunnels built by Chinese laborers during the nineteenth century – still one of the main rail routes across the Sierra Nevada. For much of the way the tracks are protected from the usually heavy winter snow by a series of wooden sheds, which you can see from across the valley, where Donner Pass Road snakes up the steep cliffs. Rock-climbers from the nearby Alpine Skills Institute can often be seen honing their talents on the 200-foot granite faces; the institute offers a variety of climbing and mountaineering courses and trips. At the crest the road passes the Soda Springs, Sugar Bowl and Royal Gorge ski areas before rejoining I-80, which runs east from Donner Pass to Reno, Nevada, and west to Sacramento.

Into Nevada: Reno and around

If you don't make it to Las Vegas (see p.239), you can get a feel for the nonstop, neon-lit gambler's lifestyle by stopping in **RENO, Nevada**: "the biggest little city in the world," as it likes to call itself. It's a dirtier downmarket version of Vegas, with miles of gleaming slot machines and poker tables, surrounded by kitsch wedding chapels and quickie divorce courts.

On I-80 at the foot of the Sierra Nevada, thirty miles east of Truckee, Reno is quick and easy to reach, with plenty of places to stay and eat, making it a good – and unique – stop-off. The town itself may not be much to look at, apart from the stream of blazing neon, but its setting is nice enough, with the Truckee River winding through and the snowcapped Sierra peaks as a distant backdrop. When the gambling begins to pall, you can still pass a pleasant afternoon here ambling in the dry desert heat or visiting one of the mildly diverting museums. Reno is also another good place from which to visit Lake Tahoe (see p.521).

Arrival and information

Reno's Cannon International **airport** is served by most major domestic carriers – including American, Delta, United, Southwestern and RenoAir. Local bus #24 makes the twenty-minute journey from the terminals to the casinos in Reno's town center. Greyhound **buses** from San Francisco via Sacramento and Truckee, and from LA via the Owens Valley, use the terminal at 155 Stevenson St also used by KT Services (☎702/945-2282) which operate a daily bus to Las Vegas and Phoenix. The Amtrak California Zephyr **train** from Chicago stops in the center of town on Second Street. To **rent a car**, try Avis (☎1-800/831-2837 or 702/785-2727) or Thrifty (☎1-800/367-2277 or 702/329-0096), both at the airport.

The **visitor center** (daily 9am–5pm; ☎1-800/FOR-RENO) is inside the National Bowling Center at 300 N Center St near the main casinos, identified by the silver geodesic dome. It has maps of the fairly extensive **local bus** services run by RTC/Citifare, whose main depot is across the road.

Accommodation

Inexpensive **accommodation** is plentiful, though if you arrive on a weekend you should book ahead and be prepared for rates to all but double. All the **casinos** offer accommodation, often with discounted rates that are advertised on hard-to-miss billboards.

Camping is an RV experience in Reno; for tent sites head west to the numerous campgrounds around Lake Tahoe (see p.526).

Circus Circus, 500 N Sierra St (☎1-800/648-5010 or 702/329-0711). Generally the cheapest and definitely the largest of the casinos, with over 1600 rooms. ③.

Crest Inn, 525 W Fourth St (☎702/329-0808). Simple motel with few trimmings but low prices. ②.

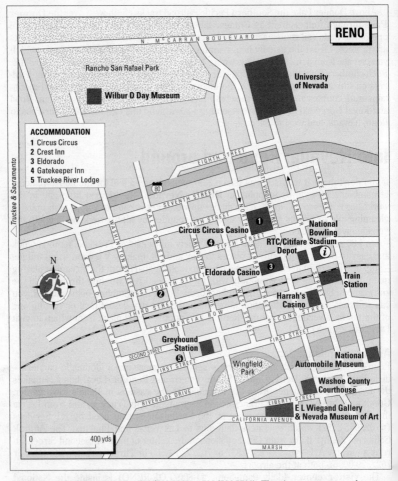

Eldorado, 345 N Virginia St (☎1-800/648-5966 or 702/786-5700). The nicer rooms are on the upper
floors, those lower down are cheaper. ③.

Gatekeeper Inn, 221 W Fifth St (☎1-800/822-3504 or 702/786-3500). Mainstream motel with cable
TV and prices which don't double on weekends. ②.

Truckee River Lodge, 501 W First St (☎1-800/635-8950 or 702/786-8888). Non-smoking hotel with
an emphasis on recreation. It has a fitness center and rents bikes from $20 a day. ②.

The casinos

It may lack the glitz and the glamor (and the unrepentant kitsch) that helps make Vegas
a global draw, but Reno is unchallenged as northern Nevada's number one **gambling**
spot. Almost all of its dozen or so casinos are located within a few minutes' walk of each
other downtown and all of them offer a 24-hour diet of slot machines, blackjack (most
have daily and weekly competitions), craps, keno, roulette and many more ways to win
and lose a fortune.

GETTING MARRIED (AND DIVORCED) IN RENO

If you've come to Reno to get **married**, you and your intended must: be at least eighteen years old and able to prove it; swear that you're not already married; and appear before a judge at the **Washoe County Court**, south of the main casino district at S Virginia and Court streets (daily 8am–midnight; ☎702/328-3275), to obtain a **marriage license** ($35). There is no waiting period or blood test required. Civil services are performed for an additional $25 at the **Commissioner for Civil Marriages**, behind the Courthouse at 195 S Sierra St (☎702/328-3461). If you want something a bit more special, however, wedding chapels all around the city will help you tie the knot: across the street from the courthouse, the Starlight Chapel, 62 Court St (☎702/786-6882) – "No Waiting, Just Drive In" – does the job for around $80, providing a pink chintz parlor full of plastic flowers. Fork out more cash and you get the tux and frock and can invite a few guests. Other chapels include the Park Wedding Chapel, 136 S Virginia St (☎702/323-1770), and Silver Bells Wedding Chapel, 628 N Virginia St (☎1-800/221-9336 or 702/322-0420). If it doesn't work out, you'll have to stay in Nevada for another six weeks before you can get a **divorce**.

Harold's Club, 250 N Virginia St, founded in 1935, was among the first of Nevada's casinos to make gambling a socially acceptable pastime, earning a reputation for giving punters a (comparatively) fair shake. Reno's newest casino, *Silver Legacy*, 407 N Virginia St, is also its first "themed attraction," with over 1700 rooms and a planetarium-style dome under which a makeshift 120-foot mining derrick, appearing to draw raw silver ore out of the ground, spilling cascades of coins – presumably an inducement for you to continue feeding the machines in the hope of a similar deluge.

To gain a modest inkling of the intricacies of the casinos, join the free ninety- minute **Casino Tour**, which leaves every half-hour from the Town Center Mall, 100 N Sierra St (Mon–Fri 9am–1pm, Sat 9am–noon; proof of hotel or motel registration necessary), and takes you behind the scenes at several of the town's biggest gambling dens. The tour includes food, drink and gambling credits. If you miss the tour, most of the casinos run teaching sessions at quieter times.

Reno's museums

A number of museums struggle to lure visitors away from Reno's casinos and wedding chapels. Largest among them is the **National Automobile Museum**, at Mill and Lake streets (daily 9.30am–5.30pm; $7.50), which holds an excellent collection of several hundred vintage and classic cars, some of them artfully arranged along re-created city streets of bygone decades. Art buffs should take a look at the inventive contemporary exhibitions at the **E.L. Weigand Gallery and Nevada Museum of Art**, 160 W Liberty St (Tues–Sat 10am–4pm, Sun noon–4pm; $3). You'll find Reno's most curious trove, however, at the **Wilbur D. May Museum** (summer Tues–Sun 10am–5pm; rest of year Wed–Sun 10am–5pm; around $2 depending on temporary exhibits), which sits on the edge of Rancho San Rafael Park, a mile north of downtown Reno off North Sierra Street. Already heir to the May department store fortunes, Wilbur May made even more money through a stroke of luck just prior to the Depression and later distinguished himself as a traveler, hunter, military aviator and cattle-breeder. The museum outlines his eventful life with several rooms of furnishings, mounted animal heads and plunder from his trips to Africa and South America.

On the other side of US-395, the University of Nevada campus hosts the **Nevada Historical Society Museum**, 1650 N Virginia St (Mon–Sat 10am–5pm; $2), full of items of local interest, especially Native American artifacts, and, next door, the **Fleischmann Planetarium** (Mon–Fri 8am–10pm Sat & Sun 11am–10pm; $5) where, amongst the telescopes and solar system galleries, OMNIMAX style films (2–4 shows daily; ☎702/784-4811) are projected onto a huge dome.

Eating and nightlife

All-you-can-eat-buffets are the order of the day in Reno. Everyone goes out and stuffs themselves to bursting whenever they can drag themselves from the tables. They can be fun, if a little bland, and we list the best of them below along with alternatives.

The Blue Heron, 1091 S Virginia St (☎702/786-4110). Great vegetarian restaurant much favored by locals of all persuasions. Soy burgers and falafel are the staples but there's a wide range, and nightly specials for around $6, posted up to a month ahead on the window.

Café Royale, 236 California Ave (☎702/322-3939). Daytime and evening café with seats outside and a wide range of light snacks and pastries to accompany good coffee.

Circus Circus, 500 Sierra St. The place to go for a buffet meal if your budget is of greater concern than your stomach, with all-you-can-eat lunches for under $5.

Eldorado Casino, Fourth and Virginia. The best of Reno's buffets, serving breakfast, lunch and dinner for a dollar or two more than its counterparts. $5–6 for an excellent lunch.

La Vecchia Varese, 130 West St. Unfussy decor and an excellent, moderately priced selection of gourmet Italian dishes, with several vegetarian choices.

Java Jungle, 246 W First St (☎702/324-5282). Some of the best coffee in town with *biscotti* and magazines to boot, just a couple of blocks from the casinos. Daily until 6pm.

Around Reno: Carson City

US-395 heads south from Reno along the jagged spires of the High Sierra past Mono Lake, Mount Whitney and Death Valley. Just thirty miles south of Reno it briefly becomes Carson Street as it passes through **CARSON CITY**, the state capital of Nevada. It is small compared to Reno, and despite the sprawling mess of fast-food joints, strip malls, and car dealerships that surround the town center, it has a number of elegant buildings, excellent historical museums and a few world-weary casinos, populated mainly by old ladies armed with buckets of nickels which they pour ceaselessly into the "one-arm bandits."

Named, somewhat indirectly, after frontier explorer Kit Carson in 1858, Carson City is still redolent with Wild West history: you'll get a good introduction at the **Nevada State Museum** at 600 N Carson St (daily 8.30am–4.30pm; $3). Housed in a sandstone structure built during the Civil War as the Carson Mint, the museum's exhibits deal with the geology and natural history of the Great Basin desert region, from prehistoric days up through the heyday of the 1860s, when the silver mines of the nearby Comstock Lode were at their peak. Amid the many guns and artifacts, the two best features of the museum are the reconstructed **Ghost Town**, from which a tunnel allows entry down into a full-scale model of an **underground mine**, giving some sense of the cramped and constricted conditions in which miners worked.

Four blocks from the museum on the other side of Carson Street, the impressively restored **State Capitol** (daily 9am–5pm; free), dating from 1871, merits a look for its stylish architecture and the commendable stock of artifacts relating to Nevada's past housed in an upper floor room.

The **Nevada State Railway Museum**, 2180 S Carson St (Wed–Sun 8.30am–4.30pm; $2), just a stone's throw away from the visitor center, displays carefully restored locomotives and carriages, several of them from the long since defunct but fondly remembered Virginia & Truckee Railroad, founded in the nineteenth century.

Further south from Carson City's diminutive center, the **Stewert Indian Culture Center**, 5366 Snyder Ave (daily 9am–4pm; free), occupies one of the eye-catching stone buildings which, until 1980, formed the campus of a Native American boarding school. The first intake of 37 students was enrolled in 1890, part of a federal plan to provide Nevada's Native Americans with a basic education and work skills. The museum actually reveals comparatively little about the school – save for a roomful of trophies won by its numerous victorious sports teams – but has many fine examples of basketry and other crafts.

Practicalities

Greyhound buses stop once a day in each direction between Reno and Los Angeles outside the *Frontier Motel* on N Carson Street. KT Services (☎702/945-2282) also stop by here on their daily journey between Reno and Las Vegas. The twice daily Amtrak Thruway services from Sacramento and South Lake Tahoe stop outside the Nugget casino at the junction of Robinson and Carson streets. The **visitor center**, on the south side of town at 1900 S Carson St (Mon–Sat 9am–5pm; ☎1-800/NEVADA-1 or 702/687-7410), can help with practical details, and give you the *Kit Carson Trail Map*, a leaflet detailing a **walking tour** of the town, taking in the main museums, the state capitol and many of the fine 1870s Victorian wooden houses and churches on the west side.

There are a number of reasonably priced **motels** in town, among them the *Westerner* at 555 N Stewart St (☎702/883-6565; ②) behind the *Nugget* casino, and the more characterful *St Charles Hotel*, 310 S Carson St (☎702/882-1887; ③) almost opposite the State Capitol. If exploring Carson City gives you an appetite, you could try the generous **breakfasts** and **lunches** served at *Heidi's Dutch Mill*, 1020 N Carson St (☎702/882-0486).

Virginia City

Much of the wealth on which Carson City – and indeed San Francisco – was built came from the silver mines of the Comstock Lode, a solid seam of pure silver discovered underneath Mount Hamilton, fourteen miles east of Carson City off US-50, in 1859. Raucous **VIRGINIA CITY** grew up on the steep slopes above the mines, and very soon a young writer named Samuel Clemens made his way west with his older brother, who'd been appointed acting Secretary to the Governor of the Nevada Territory, to see what all the fuss was about. His descriptions of the wild life of the mining camp, and of the desperately hard work men put in to get at the valuable ore, were published years later under his adopted pseudonym, **Mark Twain**. Though Twain also spent some time in the Gold Rush towns of California's Mother Lode on the other side of the Sierra – which by then were all but abandoned – his accounts of Virginia City life, collected in *Roughing It*, give a hilarious, eyewitness account of the hard-drinking life of the frontier miners.

The miners left, but Virginia City still exploits a rich vein, one which runs through the pocketbooks of tour parties bussed up here from Reno. Day-trips seem to consist of a cursory look at the clutch of museums (anyone who has more than two artifacts over fifty years old seems to open a museum), half an hour of camera toting amid the reconstructed Wild West storefronts, and an afternoon tucked away in ersatz honky-tonk bars and Olde-Style gambling halls.

travel details

Trains

Oakland to: Reno (4 daily; 6hr); Sacramento (5 daily; 2hr).

Reno to: Sacramento (4 daily; 5hr); Oakland for San Francisco (4 daily; 7hr 30min); Truckee (4 daily; 55min).

Sacramento to: Reno (4 daily; 5hr); Truckee (4 daily; 3hr) .

Buses

All buses are Greyhound unless otherwise stated.

Reno to: Las Vegas (1 daily; 9hr); Los Angeles (11 daily; 12hr 30min); Sacramento (11 daily; 3hr 30min); San Francisco (11 daily & Amtrak Thruway 2 daily; 5hr).

Reno airport to: Carson City (6 daily No Stress Express; 40min); Stateline (14 daily Tahoe Casino Express; 1hr).

Sacramento to: Auburn (3 daily; 1hr); Truckee (3 daily; 3hr); Placerville (3 daily; 1hr 30min); Reno (6 daily & Amtrak Thruway 3 daily; 3hr 30min); South Lake Tahoe (3 daily; 3hr).

San Francisco to: Auburn (3 daily; 3hr 30min); Reno (4 daily & Amtrak Thruway 2 daily; 5hr); Sacramento (17 daily; 2hr 20min); South Lake Tahoe (11 daily; 6hr); Truckee (3 daily; 5hr).

San Francisco, Pleasant Hill BART to: Sonora (3 daily Calaveras Transit).

South Lake Tahoe to: Placerville (3 daily & Amtrak Thruway 2 daily; 1hr 30min); Sacramento (3 daily & Amtrak Thruway 2 daily; 2hr 10min).

Stockton to: Sonora (3 daily Calaveras Transit; 2hr)

CHAPTER NINE

NORTHERN CALIFORNIA

C alifornia's **northern coast** and **interior** covers around a third of the entire state, a huge area (four hundred miles long and over half as wide) of sparsely populated, densely wooded and almost entirely unspoiled terrain. A massive and eerily silent land of volcanic proclivity, this is California at its most deeply rural; much of the region has more in common with the states of Oregon and Washington further north than with the built-up areas that make up much of Southern California. The majority of settlements are small towns populated by a mixture of die-hard locals, most involved in logging, fishing and farming activities, and ageing hippies who have moved north from San Francisco to work on the marijuana farms of the so-called "Emerald Triangle." For both groups, the uniting factor is the land – and a deep-rooted suspicion of the bigger cities to the south.

As with elsewhere in California, the first inhabitants of the north were Native Americans, whose past has all but been erased, leaving only the odd reservation or crafts museum. Much later, the Russians figured briefly in the region's history when they had a modest nineteenth-century settlement at Fort Ross on the coast, ostensibly to protect their interests in otter hunting and fur trading, though more likely to promote territorial claims. Mexican explorers and maintenance costs that exceeded revenues prevented them from extending their hunting activities further south, and in the 1840s they sold the fort to the Americans. It was the discovery of gold in 1848 that really put the north on the map, and much of the countryside bears the marks of this time, dotted with abandoned mining towns, deserted since the gold ran out. Not a lot has happened since, although in the 1980s New Ageism triggered a kind of future for the region, with low land prices drawing more and more devotees up here to sample the delights of a landscape they see as rich in rural symbolism. More realistically, however, it will probably be the upsurge in weekend homes for the wealthy that will save the region's bacon.

Immediately north of the Bay Area, the **Wine Country** might be your first – indeed your only – taste of Northern California, though it's by no means typical. The two valleys of Napa and Sonoma unfold in around thirty miles of rolling hills and premium real estate, home to the Californian wine barons and San Franciscan weekenders wanting to rough it in comfort. The third, though less significant wine-growing area, **Lake County**, lies to the north of its prosperous counterparts on the other side of Mount St Helena, a mountain that deters most visitors, leaving it blissfully empty and easily affordable. Most people see the Wine Country on a day trip from San Francisco; it is also feasible to take the area in before encountering the grittier territory further north, hooking up to the coast by bus from Santa Rosa.

It's the **coast** which provides the most appealing route through the region, beginning just north of Marin County and continuing for four hundred miles of rugged bluffs and forests as far as the Oregon border. The landscape varies little at first, but given time reveals tangible shifts, from the cutesy seaside homes in **Sonoma County** to the coastal elegance of **Mendocino** and the big logging country further north in **Humboldt**. Trees are the big attraction up here: some thousands of years old and hundreds of feet high, dominating a very sparsely populated landscape swathed in swirling mists. In summer, areas like the **Redwood National Park**, stretching into the most northerly **Del Norte** county, teem with campers and hikers, but out of season it can be idyllic. Although the

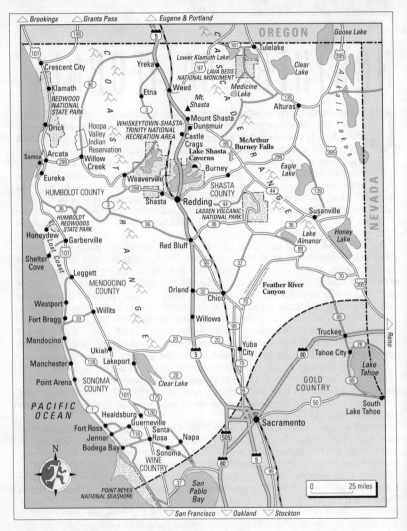

nightlife is rarely swinging, towns like **Eureka** and **Arcata** at the top end of the northern coast make a lively refuge when the great outdoors begins to pall.

The **interior** is more remote still, an enchanting land whose mystery and sheer physical enormity can't help but leave a lasting impression. I-5 neatly divides the region, cutting through the forgettable Sacramento Valley northeast to the **Shasta Cascade**, a mountainous area of isolated towns, massive lakes and a forbidding climate. In winter much of this corner of the state is completely impassable, and the region's commercial activities are centered around the lower, warmer climes of the largest town and transportation hub of **Redding**. Redding is not an especially inviting place – too big to retain any vestige of small-town cordiality, too small to have many of the social amenities of a city – but it is, however, the only feasible base for exploring the outlying regions of the **Whiskeytown-Shasta-Trinity National Recreation Area** and the **Lassen Volcanic National Park**, both massive slabs of wilderness set aside for public use. During the summer months you'll find them packed with camper vans, windsurfers and hikers, but again, outside of peak season you're on your own.

Getting around

Public transportation is sparse all over Northern California, and to enjoy the region you'll need to be independently mobile. Infrequent Greyhound buses run from San Francisco and Sacramento up and down I-5, stopping in Chico, Redding and Mount Shasta, and Hwy-101, stopping in Garberville, Eureka, Arcata and Crescent City – though this does not solve the problem of actually getting around once you've arrived. Frankly, your best bet is a **driving tour**, fixing on a few points. Only the largest of Northern California's towns have any local bus service and for some of the remoter spots you could, perhaps, consider an organized trip, notably Green Tortoise's one-week tours – see p.34 of Basics for details.

THE WINE COUNTRY

San Francisco during the summer can be a shock – persistent fog and cool temperatures dog the city from May to September – but you only need to travel an hour north to find a warm and sunny climate among the rolling hills of the Napa and Sonoma valleys, known jointly as the **Wine Country**. With its cool, oak tree-shaded ravines climbing up along creeks and mineral springs to chaparral-covered ridges, it would be a lovely place to visit even without the vineyards, but as it is, the "wine country" tag dominates almost everything here, including many often overlooked points of historical and literary interest. The Wine Country area doesn't actually yield all that much wine – production is roughly five percent of the California total, most of which is of the Gallo and Paul Masson jug-wine variety and comes from the Central Valley – but what it produces is by far the best in the country. The region has been producing wines since the days of the Spanish missions, and though many of the vines withered during Prohibition, the growers these days manage to turn out premium vintages that satisfy wine snobs around the world. It's a wealthy region, and a smug one, thriving as much on its role as a vacation land for upper-crust San Franciscans as on the wine trade. Designer restaurants (all with massive wine lists) and luxury inns line the narrow roads that, on summer weekends especially, are bumper-to-bumper with wine-tasting tourists.

Wineries are everywhere, and while the sprawling city of **Napa** is quickly done with, the many small towns further up the valley, particularly **St Helena**, have retained

Healdsburg & 101 △   △ Mount St Helena (12)

THE WINE COUNTRY

Petrified Forest ■   ■ Old Faithful Geyser
Calistoga
Ukiah 101
128
Napa Valley
CALISTOGA ROAD
BOTHE-NAPA STATE PARK   ● St Helena
128
Santa Rosa   12   *SUGARLOAF RIDGE STATE PARK*   ● Rutherford
Oakville
SILVERADO TRAIL
ANNADEL STATE PARK   ● Yountville
OAKVILLE GRADE
101   Glen Ellen   *Napa Valley*
Sonoma Valley   *Mayacamas Mountains*   29
JACK LONDON STATE HISTORIC PARK   ARNOLD DRIVE
Napa   121
● Sonoma
Redding
12
Petaluma   116
i
121   29
101   37   80
37
Novato   Vallejo
780
San Pablo Bay
Carquinez Bridge   80
N
0   5 miles
San Rafael
Sacramento
Sebastopol & Bodega Bay
▽ *San Francisco*   *East Bay* ▽

enough of their turn-of-the-century-homestead character to be a welcome relief. **Calistoga**, at the top of the valley, offers the best range of non-wine-related distractions – mostly involving tubs full of hot spring water and soothing massages.

On the western side of the dividing Mayacamas Mountains, the smaller back-road wineries of the **Sonoma Valley** reflect the more down-to-earth nature of the place, which is both more beautiful and less crowded than its neighbor to the east. The town of **Sonoma** itself is by far the most attractive of the Wine Country communities, retaining a number of fine Mission-era structures around its gracious central plaza. **Santa Rosa**, at the north end of the valley, is the region's sole urban center, handy for budget lodgings but otherwise unremarkable.

Arrival and getting around

The Wine Country region spreads north from the top of the San Francisco Bay in two parallel, thirty-mile-long valleys, **Napa** and **Sonoma**, divided by the Mayacamas Mountains. As long as you avoid the rush-hour traffic, it's about an hour's drive from

San Francisco along either of two main routes: through Marin County via the Golden Gate Bridge and US-101, or through the East Bay via the Bay Bridge and I-80.

As the Wine Country's attractions are spread over a fairly broad area, a **car** is pretty much essential. There are other options however: Golden Gate Transit (☎415/923-2000) runs commuter buses all day for the two-hour, $4.50 ride between the city and Santa Rosa; Greyhound (☎1-800/231-2222) has buses to Napa and Sonoma, leaving San Francisco at various times ($11; pick up a free schedule at the Transbay Transit Terminal, First & Mission streets); and from Santa Rosa, Sonoma County Transit (☎707/576-RIDE) buses serve the entire Sonoma Valley on a comprehensive, if less than frequent, schedule. Another option for the car-less is to sign up for a Gray Line **guided bus tour** (☎415/558-9400) from San Francisco. These cost $43, and leave from the Transbay Terminal at 9am, visiting a winery in each valley, stopping for lunch in Yountville and returning to the city at about 6.30pm. To bypass San Francisco altogether, take the Sonoma Airporter (7 daily; 1hr 30min; $20; ☎707/938-4246) from the San Francisco airport directly to Sonoma City Hall.

Blue and Gold Fleet ferries travel from both Pier 39 (three daily; $7.50 one-way ☎415/773-1188) and the Ferry Building (eight daily; $7.50 one-way) in San Francisco to Vallejo, and are met by hourly Napa Valley Transit buses (Mon–Sat; ☎1-800/696-6443) which continue on to the city of Napa and beyond.

The much-hyped **Wine Train** (3hrs; full meal and ticket, $63; ☎1-800/427-4124 or 707/253-2111) runs from Napa up the valley to St Helena, but is more a wining and dining experience than a means of transportation.

Cycling in the Wine Country

If you don't want to drive all day, **cycling** is a great way to get around. You can bring your own bike on Greyhound (though it costs $10, and the bike must be in a box), or rent one locally for around $25. Try: Napa Valley Bike Tours, 4080 Byway East, Napa (☎707/255-3377); St Helena Cyclery, 1156 Main St, St Helena (☎707/963-7736); Getaway Bike Shop, 1117 Lincoln Ave, Calistoga (☎1-800/859-BIKE); or the Sonoma Cyclery, 20093 Broadway, Sonoma (☎707/935-3377).

Both valleys are generally flat, although the peaks in between are steep enough to challenge the hardiest of hill-climbers. If the main roads through the valleys are full of cars, as they are most summer weekends, try the smaller parallel routes: the **Silverado Trail** in Napa Valley and pretty **Arnold Drive** in Sonoma Valley. For the more athletically inclined, the **Oakville Grade** between Oakville in the Napa Valley and Glen Ellen in the Sonoma Valley has challenged the world's finest riders: Coors Classic tours were routed over the grade several years ago. Alternatively, plot your own route with the *Bicycle Rider Directory* (see Contexts. p.618).

A few local firms organize **tours**, providing bikes, helmets, food and sag wagons in case you get worn out. In Calistoga, Getaway Adventures (☎1-800/499-2453) offers trips of varying lengths, and the Napa Valley Cyclery (☎707/255-3377) sets up more leisurely tours – highlighted by gourmet lunches – all over the Napa area. More ambitious (and quite expensive) overnight tours are run most weekends by Backroads Bicycle Tours, 1516 Fifth St, Berkeley (☎510/527-1555).

Ballooning in the Wine Country

The most exciting way to see the region is on one of the widely touted **hot-air balloon rides** over the Napa Valley. These usually lift off at dawn (hot air rises more strongly in the cold morning air) and last ninety magical minutes, winding up with a champagne brunch. The first, and still the best, of the operators is Napa Valley Balloons (☎707/253-2224), who fly out of Yountville. Others include Balloons Above the Valley

(☎707/253-2222) and Sonoma Thunder (☎707/538-7359). The crunch comes when you realize the price – around $160 a head – but it really is worth every cent.

Information

Not surprisingly for such a tourist-dependent area, the Wine Country has a well-developed network of **tourist information** outlets, though the rivalry between the two valleys makes it next to impossible to find out anything about Sonoma when you're in Napa, and vice versa. Both the **Napa Valley Visitors Bureau**, 1310 Napa Town Center off First Street in downtown Napa (daily 9am–5pm; ☎707/226-7459), and the **Sonoma Valley Visitors Bureau**, temporarily at 10 East Spain St (June–Sept daily 9am–7pm; Oct–May daily 9am–5pm; ☎707/996-1090), with the office at 453 First St East scheduled to reopen in winter 1998, should be able to tell you all you need to know about their respective areas. If you're keen on touring the wineries, both the above places sell handy **maps** ($1.50–3) giving the lowdown on the hundreds of producers.

Accommodation

Most people are content to visit the Wine Country as a day trip from San Francisco, visiting a few of the wineries and maybe having a picnic or a meal before heading back to the city. But if you really want to absorb properly what the region has to offer, plan to spend at least one night here, pampering yourself in one of the many (generally pricey) **hotels** and **bed and breakfast inns** that provide the bulk of the area's accommodation options. At peak times rooms of all descriptions get snapped up, so if you have a hard time finding a place, make use of one of the many **accommodation services** here: Bed and Breakfast Inns of Napa Valley (☎707/944-4444); Inns of Sonoma Valley (☎707/996-INNS); Reservations Unlimited (☎707/252-1985); or the Napa Valley Visitors Bureau (☎707/226-7459).

Campers can find a pitch eight miles north of Sonoma at the *Sugar Loaf Ridge State Park*, 2605 Adobe Canyon Rd ($14; ☎707/833-5712); or outside Santa Rosa at the *Spring Lake Regional Park*, Newanga Avenue (May–Sept daily; Oct–April Sat & Sun; $14; ☎707/539-8092).

Hotels and motels

Best Western Hillside Inn, 2901 Fourth St, Santa Rosa (☎707/546-9353). Clean, attractive motel with swimming pool. ③.

Calistoga Inn, 1250 Lincoln Ave, Calistoga (☎707/942-4101). Comfortable rooms, most with private bath, in a landmark building with its own restaurant and microbrewery. ③.

The Chablis Inn, 3360 Solano Ave, Napa (☎707/257-1944). One of the cheaper places in the valley with reasonable rooms, a pool and hot tub. ④.

Comfort Inn, 1865 Lincoln Ave, Calistoga (☎707/942-9400). Quiet, modern motel on the edge of town with heated mineral pool, steam room and sauna. ③.

El Bonita Motel, 195 Main St, St Helena (☎707/963-3216). Old roadside motel recently done up in Art Deco style, with a pool and jacuzzi. ⑤.

El Pueblo Inn, 896 W Napa St, Sonoma (☎707/996-3651). Basic highway motel with a pool. ④.

Jack London Lodge, 13740 Arnold Drive, Glen Ellen (☎707/938-8510). Modern motel near the Jack London State Park, with a good restaurant and pool. ④.

Magliulo's Pensione, 691 Broadway, Sonoma (☎707/996-1031). Cozy accommodation, despite shared bathroom facility. Also has a decent Italian restaurant. ⑤.

Motel 6, 2760 Cleveland Ave, Santa Rosa (☎707/546-1500). A little distant from the main wine areas, but good and cheap. ②

Mount View Hotel, 1457 Lincoln Ave, Calistoga (☎1-800/816-6877 or 707/942-6877). Lively Art Deco-style hotel with nightly jazz and an excellent Cajun restaurant, *Catahoula*, on the ground floor. ⑤.

Nance's Hot Springs 1614 Lincoln Ave, Calistoga (☎707/942-6211). Modest hotel with full spa, perfect for the budget traveler. Funky rooms with kitchenettes. ③.

Triple-S Ranch 4600 Mount Home Ranch Road, Calistoga (☎707/942-6730). Up the hill from Calistoga, in the middle of the wilderness, these unpublicized cozy cabins are clean and affordable. Rustic steakhouse/bar on the premises. Take Hwy-128 north for one mile, turn left on Petrified Forest Road, follow it for five miles to Mount Home Road, turn right and continue one mile. ③.

Vintage Inn, 6541 Washington St, Yountville (☎1-800/351-1133 or 707/944-1112). Huge luxury rooms in a modern hotel complex – all with fireplaces – plus swimming pool and free bike rental. Handy for Yountville's many fine restaurants, and great for romantic getaways. ⑦.

White Sulphur Springs, 3100 White Sulphur Springs Rd, west of St Helena (☎707/963-8588). A relaxing retreat from the tourism of the Napa Valley – simple rooms in a ramshackle 300-acre hillside resort, surrounded by hiking trails, with an outdoor sulphur pool and bike rental. ⑤.

Bed and breakfast

Calistoga Wine Way Inn, 1019 Foothill Blvd, Calistoga (☎1-800/572-0679 or 707/942-0680). Small and friendly B&B with lovely garden and antique-filled rooms, a short walk from the center of town. ⑤.

Churchill Manor 485 Brown St, Napa (☎707/253-7733). Regal nineteenth-century mansion hidden on an unlikely suburban street. Antique furnishings, delicious breakfasts, and free tandem bikes. ⑤.

Cinnamon Bear 1407 Kearney St, St Helena (☎1-888/963-4600 or 707/963-4653). Quirky, sumptuously furnished inn. ⑤.

Gaige House Inn, 13540 Arnold Drive, Glen Ellen (☎1-800/935-0237 or 707/935-0237). Beautifully restored Queen Anne Victorian farmhouse in a quiet and contemporary country setting. No children under twelve permitted. ⑦.

Kenwood Inn 10400 Sonoma Hwy, Kenwood (☎1-800/353-6966 or 707/833-1293). Deluxe, beautiful, and secluded Italian villa-style bed and breakfast. ⑧.

St Helena, 1309 Main St, St Helena (☎1-888/478-4355 or 707/963-4388). Opulently redecorated 1881 inn. ⑦.

Sonoma Hotel, 110 W Spain St, Sonoma (☎1-800/468-6016 or 707/996-2996). Tasteful bed and breakfast in the heart of downtown Sonoma featuring antique-decorated rooms with brass-legged bathtubs. ④.

Thistle Dew Inn, 171 W Spain St, Sonoma (☎1-800/382-7895 or 707/938-2909). Newly and elegantly restored rooms near Sonoma plaza. Features one of the best full breakfasts around and free bike rental. Some rooms with private hot tub. ⑥.

The Napa Valley

A thirty-mile strip of gently landscaped corridors and lush hillsides, the **Napa Valley** looks more like southern France than a near-neighbor of the Pacific Ocean. In spring the valley floor is covered with brilliant wildflowers which mellow into autumnal shades by grape-harvest time. Local Native Americans named the fish-rich river which flows through the valley "Napa," meaning "plenty;" the name was adopted by Spanish missionaries in the early 1800s, but the natives themselves were soon wiped out. The few ranches the Spanish and Mexicans managed to establish were in turn taken over by Yankee traders, and by the 1850s, with California part of the US, the town of Napa had become a thriving river port, sending agricultural goods to San Francisco and serving as a supply point for farmers and ranchers. Before long Napa was bypassed by the railroads and unable to compete with other, deep-water Bay Area ports, but the area's fine climate saved it from oblivion, encouraging a variety of crops including the grape, which spawned the now super-lucrative wine industry.

Napa, Yountville and Oakville

NAPA itself, at the southern end of the valley, is still the local economic linchpin, and the highway sprawl that greets travelers is fair warning of what the rest of the town has to offer. But for a proud courthouse and some intriguingly decrepit old warehouses along the river, there's not much to see, though it's not bad for food, and the **Visitors Bureau** is the most helpful in the whole valley; pick up a detailed winery map.

YOUNTVILLE, the next town north, boasts the highest proportion of **eating places** in the whole region, but other than wineries, has little to offer. Tiny **OAKVILLE**, further north along Hwy-29, is dominated by the massive Robert Mondavi Winery (see box below), and except for the wonderful **Oakville Grocery**, an unmissable deli packed with the finest local and imported foods, does not have much worth seeing.

St Helena

The first town worth a stop – and it's not really much more than a large village – is pretty **ST HELENA**, 22 miles north of Napa. Its main street, Hwy-29, is lined by some of the Wine Country's finest old buildings, most of which have been restored to – or maintained in – prime condition. The town is also at the heart of the greatest concentration of wineries, as well as boasting some unlikely literary attractions.

The **Silverado Museum** (Tues–Sun noon–4pm; free), housed in St Helena's former Public Library building just off Main Street in the center of town, has a collection of

NAPA VALLEY WINERIES

Almost all of the Napa Valley's wineries offer tastings, though comparatively few have tours. There are over one hundred wineries in all, producing wines of a very high standard, so your taste should ultimately determine the ones you visit. The following selections, listed from south to north, are some long-standing favorites, plus a few lesser-known hopefuls. Keep in mind that the intention is for you to get a sense of a winery's product, and perhaps buy some, rather than get drunk on the stuff, so don't expect more than a sip or two of any one sort – though some wineries do sell wines by the glass. If you want to buy a bottle, particularly from the larger producers, you can in fact usually get it cheaper in supermarkets than at the wineries themselves.

The Hess Collection, 4411 Redwood Rd, Napa (☎707/255-1144). A bit off the beaten track, this secluded winery features, in addition to its superior wines, a surprisingly good collection of modern art. Tasting daily 10am–4pm; $2.50.

Domaine Chandon, 1 California Drive, Yountville (☎707/944-2280). Sparkling wines from this progeny of France's Moët & Chandon are known to challenge the authentic champagnes from France. Enormous and modern, this winery and gallery is a standard to be toured by all visiting connoisseurs. Highly regarded but expensive restaurant. Tasting daily 11am–6pm; tours daily 11am–5pm.

Stag's Leap, 5766 Silverado Trail, east of Yountville (☎707/944-2020). The winery that put Napa Valley on the international map by beating a bottle of Chateau Lafitte-Rothschild at a Paris tasting way back in 1976. Still quite highly rated. Tasting daily 10am–4pm; tours by appointment.

Robert Mondavi, 7801 St Helena Highway, Oakville (☎707/963-9611). Long the standard-bearer for Napa Valley wines ("Bob Red" and "Bob White" are house wines at many California restaurants), they have the most informative and least hard-sell tours. Tours and tasting daily 9am–5pm, book ahead in summer. Free half-day tours also available.

Niebaum-Coppola Estate Winery & Vineyards, 1991 St Helena Hwy, Rutherford (☎707/963-9099). Hollywood film director Francis Ford Coppola purchased this Inglenook estate in 1975, which was originally established by Gustav Niebaum in 1879. Memorabilia over eight thousand articles relating to Robert Louis Stevenson, who spent just under a year in the area, honeymooning and recovering from an illness (see p.544). It's claimed to be the second most extensive collection of Stevenson artifacts in the US, though the only thing of interest to any but the most obsessed fan is a scribbled-on manuscript of *Dr Jekyll and Mr Hyde*. The other half of the building is taken up by the **Napa Valley Wine Library** (same hours), a briefly entertaining barrage of photos and clippings relating to the development of local viticulture. On the north side of town, at 1515 Main St, the former residence of Ambrose Bierce has been converted into the **Ambrose Bierce House** bed-and-breakfast inn (☎707/963-3003; ⑤) and houses a very small collection of memorabilia relating to the misanthropic ghost-story writer, who lived here for some fifteen years, before heading off to fight for Pancho Villa in the Mexican Revolution and mysteriously vanishing.

Calistoga
Beyond St Helena, towards the far northern end of the valley, the wineries become prettier and the traffic a little thinner. At the very tip of the valley, nestling at the foot of Mount St Helena, **CALISTOGA** is the most enjoyable of the Napa towns, with a few good wineries, though it's really better known for its mud baths and hot springs – and the mineral water that adorns every Californian supermarket shelf. Sam Brannan, the young Mormon entrepreneur who made a mint out of the Gold Rush, established a resort community here in 1860. In his groundbreaking speech he attempted to assert

---

from Coppola's movie career is on display in the entryway to the massive new wine-tasting room, featuring their signature Rubicon wine. Tasting daily 10am–5pm; $5.

V. Sattui, 1111 White Lane, St Helena (☎707/963-7774). Small family-owned winery right off Hwy 29 with award winning wines – the Riesling and Gamay rouge are particularly good. Sattui wines are only sold at the winery or through the mail. The adjoining gourmet deli has a large selection of cheeses and breads that can be enjoyed with a bottle of wine in the popular tree-shaded picnic grove. Tasting daily 9am–6pm.

Berringer Vineyards, 2000 Main St, St Helena (☎707/963-7115). Napa Valley's most famous piece of architecture, the "Rhine House," modeled on an ancestral German Gothic mansion, graces the cover of many a wine magazine. Expansive lawns and a grand tasting room, heavy on dark wood, make for a regal experience. Tours and tasting daily 9.30am–5pm.

Mumm Napa Valley, 8445 Silverado Trail, Rutherford (☎707/942-3434). Opened in 1986 by G.H. Mumm, France's renowned Champagne house, and Joseph E. Seagram & Sons, the sparkling wines from this beautifully situated winery are good, but the sweeping views of the surrounding valleys are the real reason to visit. The tours are particularly engaging and witty, and the informative guides never lose sight of the primary purpose: fun. Tasting daily 10.30am–6pm; hourly tours 11am–4pm; $3.50.

Conn Creek, 8711 Silverado Trail, St Helena (☎707/963-9100). A truly modern organization whose lightweight stone and steel building is worlds away from the cutesy old-stone image that's the norm in the rest of the valley. Tasting 10am–4pm daily; tours by appointment.

Clos Pégase, 1060 Dunaweal Lane, Calistoga (☎707/942-4981). A flamboyant upstart at the north end of the valley, this high-profile winery emphasizes the links between fine wine and fine art, with a sculpture garden around buildings designed by postmodern architect Michael Graves. Tours daily at 11am and 2pm; tasting daily 10.30am–5pm.

Sterling Vineyards, 1111 Dunweal Lane, Calistoga (☎707/942-3359). Famous for the tram ride from the parking lot bringing visitors for the wine tasting and tour, though the extravagant white mansion itself makes the visit worthwhile. Tasting 10.30am–4.30pm; hourly tours 11am–4pm; $6.

his desire to create the "Saratoga of California," modeled upon the Adirondack gem, but in the event got tongue-tied and coined the town's unique name.

Calistoga's main attraction, then as now, has nothing to do with wines, but rather with another pleasurable activity: soaking in the soothing hot water that bubbles up here from deep inside the earth. A multitude of spas and volcanic mud baths, together with a homey, rather health-conscious atmosphere, beckon jaded city-dwellers and tourists alike; not surprisingly, the crowds are always larger on weekends. The extravagant might enjoy *Dr. Wilkinson's Hot Springs*, 1507 Lincoln Ave (☎707/942-4102; treatments from $40, rooms $69–129 per night) a legendary health spa and hotel whose heated mineral water and volcanic ash tension-relieving treatments have been featured on TV's *Lifestyles of the Rich & Famous*. Or try the elegant but unpretentious *Lavender Hill Spa*, 1015 Foothill Blvd (☎707/942-4495; massages from $40, baths from $55, reserve one week ahead), featuring special mud baths, which consist of "unthick" mud made from volcanic ash and French sea kelp, known to revitalize and relax. If swaddled luxury is not what you're after, a number of more down-to-earth establishments are spread along the mile-long main drag, Lincoln Avenue. *Nance's Hot Springs*, 1614 Lincoln Ave (☎707/942-6211), for example, offers a full mineral rub-down, blanket wrap, steam bath and massage for around $50.

Another sign of Calistoga's lively underground activity is the **Old Faithful Geyser** (daily 9am–6pm; $6), two miles north of town on Tubbs Lane, off Hwy-128, which spurts boiling water sixty feet into the air at forty-minute intervals. The water source was discovered during oil-drilling here in the 1920s, when search equipment struck a force estimated to be up to a thousand pounds per square foot; the equipment was blown away and, despite heroic efforts to control it, the geyser has continued to go off like clockwork ever since. Landowners finally realized that they'd never tame it and turned it into a high-yield tourist attraction.

The **Petrified Forest** (daily 10am–5pm), located five miles west of Calistoga on the steep road over the hills to Santa Rosa, is another local tourist trap. After the entire redwood grove was toppled during an eruption of Mount St Helena some three million years ago, the forest was petrified by the action of the silica-laden volcanic ash as it gradually seeped into the decomposing fibers of the uprooted trees.

Mount St Helena

The clearest sign of the local volcanic unrest is the massive conical mountain that marks the north end of the Napa Valley, **Mount St Helena**, some eight miles north of Calistoga. The 4343-foot summit is worth a climb for its great views – on a very clear day you can see Point Reyes and the Pacific coast to the west, San Francisco to the south, the towering Sierra Nevada to the east and impressive Mount Shasta to the north. It is, however, a long steep climb (ten miles round trip) and you need to set off early in the morning to enjoy it – take plenty of water (and maybe a bottle of wine).

The mountain and most of the surrounding land is protected and preserved as the **Robert Louis Stevenson Park** (daily 8am–sunset; free), though the connection is fairly weak: Stevenson spent his honeymoon here in 1880 in a bunkhouse with Fanny Osborne, recuperating from tuberculosis and exploring the valley – a plaque marks the spot where his bunkhouse once stood. Little else about the park's winding roads and dense shrub growth evokes its former notoriety, though it's a pretty enough place to take a break from the wineries and have a picnic. In Stevenson's novel, *Silverado Squatters*, he describes the highlight of the honeymoon as the day he managed to taste eighteen of local wine baron Jacob Schram's champagnes in one sitting. Quite an extravagance, especially considering that Schramsberg champagne is held in such high esteem that Richard Nixon took a few bottles with him when he went to visit Chairman Mao.

The Sonoma Valley

On looks alone the crescent-shaped **Sonoma Valley** beats Napa hands down. This smaller and altogether more rustic valley curves between oak-covered mountain ranges from Spanish colonial **Sonoma** a few miles north along Hwy-12 to **Glen Ellen**, to end up at the region's main city, **Santa Rosa**. The Sonoma Valley is also known as the "Valley of the Moon," after a Native American legend popularized by long-time resident Jack London that tells how, as you move through the valley, the moon seems to rise several times from behind the various peaks. Many of Sonoma Valley's wineries are smaller and less formal than their Napa Valley counterparts, and as a result Sonoma Valley on the whole has a quieter, more relaxed feel. With fewer visitors, and a large concentration of wineries close to the centrally located Sonoma Plaza, Sonoma is, in fact, a much less stressful alternative to the busy Napa Valley.

Sonoma

Behind a layer of somewhat touristy stores and restaurants, the small town of **SONOMA** retains a good deal of its Spanish and Mexican architecture. Set around a spacious plaza, the town has a welcoming feel that's refreshing after brash Napa, although as a popular retirement spot with a median age of about fifty and a matching

---

SONOMA WINERIES

Fine **wineries** are scattered all over the Sonoma Valley, but there's a good concentration in a well-signposted group a mile east of Sonoma Plaza, down East Napa Street. Some are within walking distance, but often along quirky back-roads, so take a winery map from the tourist office and follow the signs closely. If you're tired of driving around, visit the handy Wine Exchange of Sonoma, 452 First St E (☎1-800/938-1794), a commercial tasting room where for a small fee, you can sample the best wines from all over California.

Bartholomew Park, 1000 Vineyard Lane (☎707/935-9511). A lavish Spanish colonial building, with some great topiary in the gardens and extensive vineyards. The wines are relatively inexpensive, middle-of-the-range vintages that appeal to the pocket and palate alike; if you're looking to buy a case, this one's a safe bet. There's a good little museum, too. Self-guided tours and free tastings daily 10am–4.30pm.

Buena Vista Winery, 18000 Old Winery Rd (☎707/938-1266). Oldest and grandest of the wineries, although the wine itself has a reputation for being pretty mediocre. The tasting room, a restored state historical landmark, features a small art gallery. Tasting daily 10.30am–4.30pm; tours daily at 2pm.

Chateau St Jean, 8555 Sonoma Hwy, Kenwood (☎707/833-4134). Attractive estate with an overwhelming aroma of wine throughout the buildings. Quirky tower to climb from where you can admire the view. Tasting daily 10am–4.30pm.

Gundlach-Bundschu, 2000 Denmark St, Sonoma (☎707/938-5277). Set back about a mile from the main cluster, this winery is highly regarded, having stealthily crept up from the lower ranks of the wine league to the point where it now regularly steals from the big names. The plain, functional building is deceptive – this is premium stuff and definitely not to be overlooked. Tasting daily 11am–4.30pm; tours Sat & Sun only.

Ravenswood, 18701 Gehricke Rd, Sonoma (☎707/938-1960). Noted for their "gutsy, unapologetic" Zinfandel, the tasting room staff at this unpretentious winery are particularly friendly and easygoing. Tastings daily 10am–4.30pm; tours by appointment.

Sebastiani Vineyards, 389 Fourth St E, Sonoma (☎1-800/888-5532 or 707/938-5532). One of California's oldest family wineries, only four blocks from central Sonoma. Free tasting and tours daily 10am–5pm.

pace, it's not exactly bubbling with action. The **visitors bureau** (see p.540), across from the leafy central plaza, has walking-tour plans of the town and excellent maps and guides to the wineries. Sonoma's history is more interesting than its actual sights; what little there is to see will take up no more than an hour.

It's hard to believe now that Sonoma was the site of a key event in West Coast history, but the so-called **Bear Flag Revolt** of 1846 was just that – at least as far as the flag-waving crowds who take over the central square every Fourth of July are concerned. In this much-romanticized episode, American settlers in the region, who had long lived in uneasy peace under the Spanish and, later, Mexican rulers, were threatened with expulsion from California along with all other non-Mexican immigrants. In response, a band of thirty armed settlers – some of whom came from as far away as Sacramento – descended upon the disused and unguarded *presidio* at Sonoma, taking the retired and much-respected commander, Colonel Guadalupe Vallejo, as their prisoner. Ironically, Vallejo had long advocated the American annexation of California and supported the aims of his rebel captors, but he was nonetheless bundled off to Sutter's Fort in Sacramento and held there for the next two months while the militant settlers declared California an independent republic. The Bear Flag, which served as the model for the current state flag, was raised on Sonoma Plaza. A month later the US declared war on Mexico and, without firing a shot took possession of the entire Pacific coast.

In memory of this, there's a monument to the Bear Flag revolutionaries in the middle of the plaza, and across the street to the north, a number of historic buildings and relics in the sprawling **Sonoma State Historic Park** ($2 combined entry to all sites; all daily 10am–5pm). The restored **Mission San Francisco Solano de Sonoma** was the northernmost and last of the California missions, and the only one established while California was under Mexican rule. Half a mile west stands the **General Vallejo Home**, the leader's ornate former residence, dominated by decorated filigree eaves and slender Gothic-revival arched windows. The chalet-style storehouse next door has been turned into a **museum** of artifacts from the general's reign.

To see Sonoma at its unspoiled best, get out of the car and ride across the Valley of the Moon on **horseback**. The Sonoma Cattle Co (☎707/996-8566) offers daily tours, weather permitting, starting at $25.

Glen Ellen and Jack London State Park

While the drive up the valley can be soothing, there's really very little to see north of Sonoma apart from a few small villages and the **Jack London State Park** (daily 9.30am to dusk; $6 per car) – just ten minutes from Sonoma on the London Ranch Road which curves sharply off Hwy-12 close to tiny, charming **GLEN ELLEN** village. Jack London lived here with his wife for the last years of his short, unsettled life, on a 140-acre ranch in the hills above what he described as the "most beautiful, primitive land in California." A series of paths and walking trails leads through densely wooded groves to the lava-stone remains of the **Wolf House**, built for the Londons in 1913 but burned to the ground in an arson attack before they even moved in. London died three years later and is buried on a hill above the trail to the Wolf House. After his death, his widow Charmian built the more formal House of Happy Walls, which today serves as a small **museum** (daily 10am–5pm; free). Photographs and artifacts – including the desk where London cranked out his two thousand words a day – enliven the otherwise dry displays about the writer's life and work.

Santa Rosa

Sixty miles due north of San Francisco on US-101, and about twenty miles from Sonoma, **SANTA ROSA**, the largest town in Sonoma County, sits at the top end of the Sonoma Valley and is more or less the hub of this part of the Wine Country. It's a very different world from the indulgence of other Wine Country towns, however; much of it is given over to shopping centers and roadside malls, and signs downtown ban teenagers from cruising the rarely packed but confusing system of one-way streets.

Probably the most interesting thing about Santa Rosa is that it was the home town of Raymond Chandler's fictional private eye Philip Marlowe; after that it's all downhill. You can kill an hour or two at the **Luther Burbank Home and Gardens**, at the junction of Santa Rosa and Sonoma avenues (April–Sept Wed–Sun 10am–3.30pm; $2). California's best-known horticulturist is remembered here in the house where he lived and in the splendid gardens where he created some of his most unusual hybrids. If you're not into gardening, nip across the street to the **Ripley Museum**, 492 Sonoma Ave (April–Oct Wed–Sun 10am–4pm; $1.50), where you might spend twenty minutes or so in one of the cartoonist Ripley's mediocre "Believe It or Not" chain of museums – Santa Rosa was Ripley's home town.

For **eating**, try *Pepe's*, on Sebastopol Road, corner of Stony Point Road, west of US-101, for the best Mexican in the county (shut Tues).

Wine Country eating and drinking

Culinary satisfaction looms around every corner in the Wine Country, and food quality is at least as high as anywhere in San Francisco. **California cuisine** is almost standard in both valleys, and freshness and innovative presentation are very much the order of the day. **Yountville**, in particular, is little more than a string of high-style restaurants, any of which is up there with the best San Francisco has to offer, with prices to match. **Calistoga**, though more low-key, is a gourmet paradise. **Sonoma**, too, has its share and is strong on Italian food. **Bars** are rare, and nightlife nearly non-existent, perhaps a result of the free booze on offer from the wineries. While a couple of bars are worth a look, most are decidedly locals' hangouts.

Budget food: cafés and takeouts

Bosko's Ristorante, 1364 Lincoln Ave, Calistoga (☎707/942-9088). Standard Italian restaurant preparing good-value, fresh pasta dishes. Cheap and cheerful, and popular with families.

Cafe Citti, 9049 Sonoma Hwy, Kenwood (☎707/833-2690). Small, inexpensive trattoria with great Italian food and an intimate, yet casual atmosphere.

Café Sarafornia, 1413 Lincoln Ave, Calistoga (☎707/942-0555). Famous for delicious and enormous breakfasts and lunches with lines around the block on weekends. Let the owner talk your ear off.

La Casa, 121 E Spain St, Sonoma (☎707/996-3406). Friendly, festive and inexpensive Mexican restaurant just across from Sonoma Mission. Enjoy an enchilada on the sunny outdoor patio.

Checkers Pizza, 1414 Lincoln Ave, Calistoga (☎707/942-9300). Soups, salads, and sandwiches, plus adventurous pizzas and good pasta dishes. Open daily until 10pm.

The Coffee Garden, 421 First St W, Sonoma (☎707/996-6645). 150-year-old adobe converted into a café with small gift shop. Fresh sandwiches served on the back patio.

The Diner, 6476 Washington St, Yountville (☎707/944-2626). Start the day's wine-touring off right, with good strong coffee and brilliant breakfasts where locals and day-trippers mix. Open 8am–3pm for breakfast and lunch, and 5.30–9.30pm for flavorful Mexican dinners. Closed Mon.

Ford's Café, 22900 Broadway, Sonoma (☎707/938-9811). Hearty, working-class American food served to locals in this out-of-the-way diner. The generous breakfasts are worth the trip.

Juanita Juanita, 19114 Arnold Drive, Glen Ellen (☎707/935-3981). A basic Mexican diner offering at least twenty salsas to accompany the sizeable burritos and *tostadas*.

PJ's Café, 1001 Second St, Napa (☎707/224-0607). A Napa institution, open 8am to 10pm every day for pancakes, pasta, pizzas and sandwiches.

The Spot, One mile south of St Helena on Hwy-29 (☎707/963-2844). This tacky roadside diner is conveniently located for lunchtime on the cheap.

Restaurants

Bear Flag Cafe, 18625 Sonoma Hwy, Sonoma (☎707/938-1927). Exceptional European influenced food in an airy and comfortable bistro just outside of downtown Sonoma. All dinners $9.95 before 6pm Tues–Fri.

La Boucane, 1778 Second St, Napa (☎707/253-1177). Mouthwatering chunks of tender meat with traditional but imaginative sauces, plus perfect fish (especially shellfish) and vegetables. Very expensive, dinner only.

Calistoga Inn, 1250 Lincoln Ave, Calistoga (☎707/942-4101). Very good seafood appetizers – spicy Cajun prawns, or crispy crab cakes – plus a wide range of wines, microbrewed beers, excellent desserts and occasional live music. See also "Accommodation", p.540.

Downtown Joe's, 902 Main St at Second, Napa (☎707/258-2337). One of Napa's most popular and lively spots for sandwiches, ribs and pasta, with beer brewed on the premises. Open until midnight with outdoor dining by the river.

Glen Ellen Inn, 13670 Arnold Drive, Glen Ellen (☎707/996-6409). Husband-and-wife team cook and serve slightly pricey gourmet dishes in an intimate, romantic dining room with half a dozen tables. Daily 5.30–9.30pm.

Greystone Restaurant at the Culinary Institute of America, 2555 Main St, St Helena (☎707/967-1010). Mediterranean cuisine served in an elegant ivy-walled mansion just outside of town, with a tastefully wacky Art Deco interior. Reasonable for the delicious large portions.

Mustards, 7399 St Helena Highway (Hwy-29), Yountville (☎707/944-2424). Credited with starting the late-1980s trend toward "grazing" food, emphasizing tapas-like tidbits rather than main meals. Reckon on spending $15–20 a head, and waiting for a table if you come on a weekend.

Pairs, 1420 Main St, St Helena (☎707/963-7566). Tasty Cal-Asian cuisine in a funky yet cozy café setting in the heart of St Helena. The chefs suggest a specific Napa Valley wine to go with every dish. Closed Tues.

Rutherford Grill, 1180 Rutherford Rd, Rutherford (☎707/963-1920). Large portions of basic contemporary American food served in a handsome new dining room. The mashed potatoes should not be missed.

Tra Vigne, 1050 Charter Oak Ave, St Helena (☎707/963-4444). Just north of town, but it feels as if you've been transported to Tuscany. Excellent food and fine wines, served up in a lovely vine-covered courtyard or elegant dining room. They also have a small deli, where you can pick up picnic goodies.

Wappo Bar Bistro, 1226 Washington St, Calistoga (☎707/942-4712). Creative cuisine featuring unheard-of combinations like chile *rellenos* with walnut pomegranate sauce and roasted rabbit with potato gnocchi make this new restaurant a culinary adventure.

Bars

Ana's Cantina, 1205 Main St, St Helena (☎707/963-4921). Long-standing, down-to-earth saloon and Mexican restaurant with billiards and darts tournaments.

Babette's Restaurant & Wine Bar, 464 First St E, Sonoma (☎707/939-8921). The place to see and be seen in Sonoma. Stylish gourmet restaurant serving expensive multi-course meals. Closed Sun & Mon.

Murphy's Irish Pub, 464 First St E, Sonoma (☎707/935-0660). Small bar with an eclectic interior and a few outdoor tables serving basic pub grub and European beers.

Pancha's, 6764 Washington St, Yountville (☎707/944-2125). If wine-tasting becomes boring, try this western-saloon style dive bar.

Santa Rosa Brewing Company, 458 B St, Santa Rosa (☎707/544-4677). Lively brewpub with occasional live music.

Southwest Corner, 529 First St W, Sonoma (☎707/938-2122). Bright new microbrewery with four original beers, good southwestern cuisine and a sunny outdoor patio.

THE NORTHERN COAST

Rugged in the extreme, often foggy, always dangerous and thunderously dramatic, the **Northern Coast** is leagues away from the gentle, sun-drenched beaches of Southern California. The climate, at best moderate, rules out both sunbathing and swimming; sudden groundswells and a strong undertow make even surf play risky, and there is no lifeguard service along any of the beaches. Instead, this is an area to don hiking boots, wrap up warm and explore the enormous forests with their plentiful camping facilities.

The only way to see the coast properly is on the painfully slow but visually magnificent Hwy-1, which hugs the coast for two hundred miles through the wild counties of **Sonoma** and **Mendocino** before turning sharply inland at Legget to join Hwy-101 and **Humboldt County**. The hundred miles of wild coastline it never reaches has become known, appropriately, as the **Lost Coast**. North of here, **redwood forests** swathe the landscape as far as the Oregon border, doubling as raw material for the huge logging industries (the prime source of employment in the area) and the region's prime tourist attraction, most notably in the **Redwood National Park**. **Eureka** and **Arcata** are the main towns here, both easily reached by public transportation, and the principal centers of nightlife and action for the coast as a whole.

You'll need to be fairly independent to **get around** this region: one Amtrak Thruway and two Greyhound buses a day travel the length of US-101, which parallels the coastal highway, but don't link up with the coast until Eureka, far to the north.

The Sonoma Coast and Russian River Valley

Proximity to San Francisco means the **Sonoma Coast** and **Russian River Valley** areas have never been short on weekend visitors. But tourist activity is confined to a few narrow corridors at the height of summer, leaving behind a network of north coast villages and backwater wineries that for most of the year are all but asleep. The coast is colder and lonelier than the villages along the valley, and at some point most people head inland for a change of scene and a break from the pervasive fog. What both areas have in common, however, is a reluctance to change. As wealthy San Franciscans cast their eyes towards the north for potential second-home sites, the California Coastal Commission endeavors to keep the architects at bay, keenly maintaining beach access for all, and most farmers have so far managed to resist the considerable sums offered for their grazing land. For the time being the Sonoma coastal area remains relatively undeveloped, the majority of it state beach, with good access to hiking trails and views.

The Sonoma Coast

BODEGA BAY, about fifty miles north of San Francisco, is the first Sonoma County village you reach on Hwy-1. Pomo and Miwok Indians populated the area peacefully for centuries, until Captain Lt Juan Francisco de la Bodega y Quadra Mollineda anchored his ship in the bay and "discovered" it in 1775. Hitchcock filmed the waterside scenes for *The Birds* here; an unsettling number of them are still squawking down by the harbor. Not so long ago, a depleted fishing industry, a couple of restaurants and some isolated seaside cottages were all there was to Bodega Bay, but in recent years San Franciscans have got wind of its appeal and holiday homes and modern retail developments now crowd the waterside.

If you're traveling the whole coast, Bodega Bay makes a tolerable first stop, especially if you're in the mood for long moody walks and early nights. Of several **places to stay**, the *Bodega Harbor Inn*, 1345 Bodega Ave (☎707/875-3594; ③), is the best value in town, while the extremely comfortable *Bodega Coast Inn*, 521 Hwy-1 (☎1-800/346-6999 or 707/875-2217; ⑤), has lovely rooms with fireplaces. Reservations are pretty much essential in summer and on weekends throughout the year. If you don't have a reservation, the helpful **Sonoma Coast Visitor Center** (☎1-800/905-9050 or 707/875-2868), 850 Hwy-1, has information on room availability throughout the area. There's **camping** at the *Bodega Dunes Campground* (☎707/875-3382), two miles north of the village on Hwy-1 at the base of a windy peninsula known as **Bodega Head**; laid out across sand dunes that end in coastal cliffs behind the beach, it has places for $14 a night. There are hiking and horseriding trails around the dunes behind the beach – though in summer these tend to be packed with picnicking families, and for less crowded routes you should head up the coast. *Breakers Cafe*, 1400 Hwy-1 (☎707/875-2513), serves nouvelle Californian **seafood** plates for around $15.

North of Bodega Bay

North of Bodega Bay, along the **Sonoma Coast State Beach** (actually a series of beaches separated by rocky bluffs) the coastline coarsens and the trails become more dramatic. It's a wonderful stretch to hike – quite possible in a day for an experienced hiker – although the shale formations are often unstable and you must stick to the trails, which are actually quite demanding. Of Sonoma's thirteen miles of beaches, the finest are **Salmon Creek Beach**, a couple of miles north of Bodega Bay and site of the park headquarters and **Goat Rock Beach**, at the top of the coast.

Campgrounds are dotted along the coast (call ☎707/875-3483 for information), but the best **places to stay** are in the tiny village of **JENNER**, which marks the turn-off for the Russian River Valley. Choose between the salubrious cabins and cottages of *The Jenner Inn*, 10400 Hwy-1 (☎1-800/732-2377 or 707/865-2377; ⑤) or the comfortable *River's End Resort* (☎707/865-2484; ⑥). The relatively inexpensive *Salt Point Lodge*, seventeen miles north of town at 23255 Hwy 1 (☎1-800/956-3437 or 707/847-3234; ③), also houses an excellent restaurant featuring seafood and steak dinners for $12–20. The Russian River joins the ocean here, and a massive sand spit at its mouth provides a breeding ground for harbor seals from March to June.

Fort Ross

North of Jenner, the population evaporates and Hwy-1 turns into a slalom course of hairpin bends and steep inclines for twelve miles as far as **Fort Ross State Historic Park** (daily 10am–4.30pm; $6). At the start of the nineteenth century, San Francisco was still the northernmost limit of Spanish occupation in Alta California, and from 1812 to 1841 Russian fur traders quietly settled this part of the coast, clubbing the Californian Sea Otter almost to extinction, building a fort to use as a trading outpost, and growing crops for the Russian stations in Alaska. Officially they posed no territorial claims, but by the time the Spanish had gauged the extent of the settlement, the fort was heavily armed and vigilantly manned with a view to continued eastward expansion. The Russians traded here for thirty years until over-hunting and the failure of their shipbuilding efforts led them to pull out of the region. They sold the fort and chattels to one John Sutter in 1841, who moved them to his holdings in the Sacramento Valley, so all you see is an accomplished reconstruction built using the original techniques.

Among the empty bunkers and storage halls, the most interesting buildings are the Russian Orthodox Chapel and the Commandant's house, with its fine library and wine cellar. At the entrance, a potting shed, which labors under the delusion that it is a **museum**, provides cursory details on the history of the fort, with a few maps and diagrams. Informative formal talks are given at 1pm and 3pm on weekends.

Fort Ross has a small beach and picnicking facilities. You can **camp** here (☎707/847-3286; $12) or in **Salt Point State Park** (☎707/847-3221; $14-16), six miles north on Hwy-1. Just north of Salt Point, the **Kruse Rhododendron State Reserve** is a sanctuary for twenty-foot-high rhododendrons, indigenous to this part of the coast and at their best in early summer. You can drive through, or walk along a short trail. The beaches on this last stretch of the Sonoma coastline are usually deserted, save a few abalone fishermen, driftwood and the seal pups who rest here. Again, they're good for hiking and beachcombing, but stick to the trails.

The Russian River Valley

Hwy-116 begins at Jenner (see opposite) and turns sharply inland, leaving behind the cool fogs of the coast and marking the western entrance to a relatively warm and pastoral area known as the **Russian River Valley**. The tree-lined highway follows the river's course through twenty miles of what appear to be lazy, backwater resorts but in fact are the major stomping grounds for partying weekenders from San Francisco. The fortunes of the valley have come full circle; back in the Twenties and Thirties it was a recreational resort for well-to-do city folk who abandoned the area when newly constructed roads took them elsewhere. Drawn by low rents, city-saturated hippies started arriving in the late Sixties, and the Russian River took on a non-conformist flavor that lingers today. More recently, an injection of affluent Bay Area property seekers, many of them gay, has sustained the region's economy, and the funky mix of loggers, sheep farmers and wealthy weekenders gives it an offbeat cachet that has restored its former popularity.

The road that snakes through the valley is dotted with campgrounds every few miles, most with sites for the asking, although during the first weekend of September when the region hosts the **Russian River Jazz Festival** (☎707/869-3940), things can get a bit tight. The jazz festival is something of a wild weekend around here and a good time to come: bands set up on Johnson's Beach by the river and in the woods for impromptu jamming sessions as well as regular scheduled events. The new mid-June **Russian River Blues Festival** looks set to prove equally popular (call ☎707/869-3930 for details).

Sonoma County Transit (☎707/576-7433) runs a fairly good weekday bus service (though patchy on weekends) between the Russian River resorts and Santa Rosa in the Wine Country, although to see much of the valley, you really need a **car**, or hire a **bike** from Mike's Bike Rental, 16442 Main St, Guerneville ($25 a day; ☎707/869-1106).

Guerneville

The main town of the Russian River valley, **GUERNEVILLE**, has finally come out. No longer disguised by the tourist office as a place where "a mixture of people respect each other's lifestyles," it's quite clearly a **gay resort** and has been for the last fifteen years: a lively retreat popular with tired city-dwellers who come here to unwind. Gay men predominate, except during two **Women's Weekends** (☎707/869-2971) – in early May and late September – when many of the hotels take only women.

If you don't fancy venturing along the valley, there's plenty to keep you busy without leaving town. Weekend visitors flock here for the canoeing, swimming and sunbathing that comprise the bulk of local activities: **Johnson's Beach**, on a placid reach of the river in the center of town, is the prime spot, with canoes ($12 a day), pedal boats ($5 an hour) and tubes ($3 a day). But Guerneville's biggest natural asset is the magnificent **Armstrong Redwoods State Reserve** (☎707/869-2015), two miles north at the top of Armstrong Woods Road ($6 parking) – 700 acres of massive redwood trees, hiking and riding trails and primitive camping sites. Take food and water and don't stray off the trails: the densely forested central grove is quite forbidding and very easy to get lost in. One of the best ways to see it is on horseback; the Armstrong Woods Pack

Station (☎707/887-2939) offers guided horseback tours that range from a half-day trail ride for $45 to a three-day pack trip for $400. A natural amphitheater provides the setting for the **Redwood Forest Theater** which stages dramatic and musical productions during the summer.

The **Chamber of Commerce**, 16200 First St (Mon–Fri 9am–5pm; 24-hr info line ☎707/869-3533), has good free maps of the area, and **accommodation** listings. The friendly **Russian River Region Visitors Bureau**, across the street at 14034 Armstrong Woods Rd (☎1-800/253-8800 or 707/869-9212) can recommend places to stay all over the area. As with most of the valley, B&Bs are the staple; two luxurious choices are the comfortable *Creekside Inn*, 16180 Neely Rd (☎1-800/776-6586 or 707/869-3623; ④), and *Applewood: an Estate Inn*, 13555 Hwy-116 (☎707/869-9093; ⑦), which also features a highly acclaimed gourmet restaurant. *Fife's*, 16467 River Rd (☎1-800/7-FIFES-1 or 707/869-0656; ④), is the original gay resort right by the river, while *The Willows*, 15905 River Rd (☎707/869-2824; ④) is a bit more modest. A dearth of cheap motels (unless you head east to Hwy-101 or the one place in Monte Rio) makes **camping** the economical answer: the *Austin Creek State Recreation Area*, Armstrong Woods Road ($12; ☎707/865-2391), is guaranteed RV-free, while *Johnson's Beach and Resort*, 16241 First St, also has cabins and rooms available ($10; ☎707/869-2022; ②). There are a couple of free primitive sites, and $7 walk-in backcountry sites in the state reserve.

Guerneville has a good selection of reasonably priced, reliable **restaurants**, among them *Brew Moon*, 16248 Main St (☎707/869-0201), which serves tasty barbecued meats

RUSSIAN RIVER VALLEY WINERIES

The Guerneville Chamber of Commerce (see above) issues an excellent *Russian River Wine Road* map, which lists all the **wineries** that spread along the entire course of the Russian River. Unlike their counterparts in Napa and Sonoma, the wineries here neither organize guided tours nor charge for wine-tasting. You can wander around at ease, guzzling as many and as much of the wines as you please. Some of the wines (the Cabernet Sauvignons and Merlots in particular) are of remarkably good quality, if not as well known as their Wine Country rivals. By car, you could easily travel up from the Sonoma Coast and check out a couple of Russian River wineries in a day, although the infectiously slow pace may well detain you longer.

Chateau Souverain, 400 Souverain Rd, Geyserville (☎707/433-8281). A large selection of wines and a café. Tasting daily 10am–6pm.

Dry Creek Vineyard, four miles northwest of Healdsburg at Dry Creek and Lambert Bridge Road (☎707/433-1000). Family owned operation well known for its consistently top-notch wines – particularly the Cabernet Sauvignon and Chardonnay. Picnic facilities. Tastings daily 10.30am–4.30pm.

Hop Kiln, 6050 Westside Rd, Healdsburg (☎707/433-8281). Recently established rustic winery with a traditional atmosphere but not a snobbish attitude. Tastings daily 10am–6pm.

Korbel Champagne Cellars, 13250 River Rd, two miles east of Guerneville (☎707/887-2294). Even if you're not "doing" the wineries, you shouldn't miss this place. The bubbly itself – America's best-selling premium champagne – isn't anything you couldn't find in any supermarket, but the wine and brandy are sold only from the cellars, and are of such notable quality that you'd be crazy not to swing by for a glass or two. The estate where they are produced is lovely, surrounded by hillside gardens covered in blossoming violets, coral bells and hundreds of varieties of roses – perfect for quiet picnics. A new microbrewery and upscale deli have recently opened on the premises.

Topolos at Russian River Vineyards, 5700 Gravenstein Hwy, Forestville, five miles from Guerneville along Hwy-116 (daily 10am–5pm; ☎ 1-800/TOP-OLOS or 707/887-1575). One of the Russian River Valley's most accessible wineries.

on paper plates in addition to cheap breakfasts and good coffees. *Burdon's Restaurant*, 15405 River Rd, is slightly more upscale, with excellent gourmet meat and pasta dishes for around $12. Really, though, it's the **nightlife** that makes Guerneville a worthwhile stop. The *Bullpen*, 16246 First St (☎707/869-3377), is a happening bar with an occasional live act, while the *Russian River Resort* ("Triple R"), 16390 4th St (☎707/869-0691), and *River Business, Inc*, 16225 Main St (☎707/869-3400), both serve alcohol and food and are popular with the gay crowd – though you'd be hard pressed to find a place that isn't in Guerneville.

Monte Rio

The small town of **MONTE RIO**, three miles west along the river from Guerneville, is definitely worth a look: a lovely, crumbling old resort town with big Victorian houses in stages of graceful dilapidation. For years it has been the entrance to the 2500-acre **Bohemian Grove**, a private park that plays host to the San Francisco-based Bohemian Club. A grown-up summer camp, its membership includes a very rich and very powerful male elite – ex-presidents, financiers, politicians and the like. Every year in July they descend for "Bohemian Week" – the greatest men's party on earth, noted for its high jinks and high-priced hookers, away from prying cameras in the seclusion of the woods.

The best of Monte Rio's pricey **places to stay** are the lovely *Rio Villa Beach Resort*, 20292 Hwy-116 (☎707/865-1143; ④) in a beautiful spot on the banks of the Russian River, and the *Highland Dell Inn*, 21050 River Blvd (☎1-800/767-1759 or 707/865-1759; ⑤). You can sleep more cheaply at the *Village Inn* at 20822 River Boulevard (☎1-800/303-2303 or 707/865-2304; ④), with substantial reductions for three-day stays. *Huckleberry Springs Country Inn* (☎1-800/822-2683 or 707/865-2683; ⑥) is a deluxe women's retreat with massages and a spa, just outside of town on Old Beedle Road.

If you're touring the area by car, the lonely, narrow **Cazadero Highway** just to the west makes a nice drive from here, curving north through the wooded valley and leading back to Fort Ross on the coast.

Healdsburg

The peaceful town of **HEALDSBURG** straddles the invisible border between the Wine Country and the Russian River Valley, and as a result, in a quiet way manages to get the best of both worlds. While **Veterans Memorial Beach**, a mile south of the plaza along the banks of the Russian River, is a popular spot for swimming, picnicking, and canoeing in the summertime, there are also some twenty wineries, most of them family owned, within a few miles of the center of town. Romantic bed and breakfasts have sprung up all over the area, including the neighboring village of **GEYSERVILLE**, and although the town's economic well-being is almost exclusively dependent on tourism, it still manages to maintain a relaxed, backcountry feel. The Healdsburg Area **Chamber of Commerce**, 217 Healdsburg Ave (☎1-800/648-9922 or 707/433-6935), provides winery and lodging information.

As might be expected, cheap places to stay are virtually nonexistent in Healdsburg, but if you have the money to spend, the *Madrona Manor*, 1001 Westside Rd (☎1-800/258-4003 or 707/433-4231; ⑦), a luxurious Victorian-style bed and breakfast hidden on a hilltop, with meticulously maintained gardens and a gourmet restaurant, is hard to beat.

Of several gourmet restaurants that circle the plaza, *Bistro Ralph*, 109 Plaza St (☎707/433-1380), with sparse modern decor and well crafted dishes ($15–20 per main course), is your best bet. *Flying Goat Coffee Roastery and Cafe*, just off the main plaza at 324 Center St (☎707/433-9081), is a great place to unwind with a newspaper and good cup of coffee.

The Mendocino coast

The coast of Mendocino County, 150 miles north of San Francisco, is a dramatic exten-sion of the Sonoma coastline – the headlands a bit sharper, the surf a bit rougher, but otherwise more of the same. Despite the efforts of the local chambers of commerce, this remains a remote, almost desolate area, its small former lumbering towns served by limited public transportation. It does thrive, however, as a location spot for the movie industry, having featured in such illustrious titles as *East of Eden*, *Frenchman's Creek*, and more recently, *The Fog*.

This is the place for a quiet getaway weekend – join all the other couples avoiding the crowds in the pricey bed and breakfasts. Inland, there's little to see beyond the small contingent of wineries – stick to the coast where there is at least some sign of life, and content yourself with brisk walks and brooding scenery.

Only Willits, forty miles inland, is served by Greyhound and Amtrak Thruway. From here, the Skunk Trains (see p.556) provide the sole **public transportation** to the main towns of **Mendocino** and **Fort Bragg**, linked to each other by Mendocino Stage and Transit Authority buses (☎707/964-0167), which continue south to the small villages of Navarro and Gualala.

Mendocino

Once you leave Sonoma County, Hwy-1 winds for fifty miles along the wrinkled coast, past the sleepy communities of Gualala and Point Arena – which feature one of the best (and least crowded) surfing spots in the state – before you reach the coast's first viable stop, the decidedly touristy village of **MENDOCINO**. The quaint town sits on a broad-shouldered bluff with waves crashing on three sides; it's hard to find a spot here where you *can't* see the ocean sparkling in the distance. New England-style architecture is abundant, lending Mendocino a down-home, almost cutesy air. Its appearance on the National Register of Historic Places and reputation as something of an artists' colony draw the curious up the coastal highway, and a fairly extensive network of bed and breakfasts, restaurants, and bars are more than happy to cater to their every need.

The Town

Like other small settlements along the coast, Mendocino was originally a lumber port, founded in the late nineteenth century by merchants from Maine who thought the proximity to the redwoods and exposed location made it a good site for sawmill opera-tions. The industry has now vanished, but the large community of artists has spawned craftsy commerce in the form of art galleries, gift shops, and boutique delicatessens.

The **visitor center**, 735 Main St (Mon–Sat 11am–4pm Sun noon–4pm; ☎707/937-5397), is housed in **Ford House**, one of many mansions built by the Maine lumbermen in the style of their home state. The **Kelley House Museum**, 45007 Albion St (daily 1–4pm; ☎707/937-5791), has exhibits detailing the town's role as a center for shipping redwood lumber to the miners during the Gold Rush, and conducts **walking tours** of the town on Saturday mornings at 11am – though you could do it yourself in under an hour, collecting souvenirs from the galleries as you go. Among them, the **Mendocino Art Center**, 45200 Little Lake St (daily 10am–5pm; ☎707/937-5818; free), gives classes and has a gallery showing some good works (if a little heavy on the seascapes) by mainly Mendocino-based artists.

Otherwise there's plenty to occupy you around the town: **hiking** and **cycling** are popular, with bikes available for around $25 a day from Catch a Canoe & Bicycles, Too

(☎1-800/320-2453 or 707/937-0273), just south of Mendocino at the corner of Hwy-1 and Compche-Ukiah Road. At the west end of Main Street, hiking trails lead out into the **Mendocino Headlands**, where you can explore the grassy cliffs and make your way down to the tidepools, next to the breaking waves. The **Russian Gulch State Park** (☎707/937-5804; $6), two miles north of town, has bike trails, beautiful fern glens and waterfalls. Just south of town, hiking and cycling trails weave through the unusual **Van Damme State Park** (☎707/937-5804; $6), which has a **Pygmy Forest** of ancient trees, stunted to waist-height because of poor drainage and soil chemicals. After a day of hiking and shopping, you may want to pamper yourself with a **massage** and a **hot tub** at one of the town's spas. Sweetwater Gardens, 955 Ukiah St (☎1-800/300-4140 or 707/937-4140), offer private hot tubs with saunas for $11.50 per hour and massages for $55 per hour.

Abalone diving is extremely popular along the coast here, particularly just south of town in the small cove beside Van Damme State Park. In an attempt to thwart poaching, the practice is strictly regulated – the tasty gastropods are not available commercially and you can only have four in your possession at any given time. In early October, four-hundred hungry judges pay a substantial fee for the opportunity to help choose the best abalone chef in the annual Abalone Cookoff. The Sub-Surface Progression Dive Center, 18600 Hwy-1 (☎707/964-3793) in Fort Bragg, leads all-inclusive half-day diving expeditions for $50.

Accommodation

Room rates in Mendocino are generally high, but provided you stay away from the chintzy hotels on the waterfront, it is possible to find adequate, reasonably priced hotels on the streets behind. The *Sea Gull Inn*, 44960 Albion St (☎1-888/937-5204 or 707/937-5204; ③), is the best of the affordable options right in the center, though the antique-filled rooms at *The Mendocino Hotel*, 45080 Main St (☎1-800/548-0513 or 707/937-0511; ⑤), are more luxurious. The *Blackberry Inn*, east of Hwy-1, at 44951 Larkin Rd (☎1-800/950-7806 or 707/937-5281; ④) is a bit far from the center of town, but is nonetheless a (relatively) good value. Probably the most romantic place to stay in the whole region is at **ALBION**, a small fishing village ten miles south of Mendocino; the *Albion River Inn*, 3790 N Hwy-1 (☎1-800/479-7944 or 707/937-1919; ⑦), on Hwy-1 just beyond the junction with Hwy-128, perches on the edge of a cliff, and all the rooms except one have ocean views. The inn also has a first-class restaurant, serving pricey, wonderful food.

There's $16 **camping** at Russian Gulch State Park (reserve through Parknet ☎1-800/444-7275), and Van Damme State Park.

Eating, drinking and nightlife

Of Mendocino's **restaurants**, the best is the pricey *Café Beaujolais*, 961 Ukiah St (☎707/937-5614), which specializes in organic California cuisine. For slightly cheaper fair, try the *Mendocino Café*, 10451 Lansing St (☎707/937-2422), serving an eclectic mix of salads, pastas, and sandwiches daily until 9pm. *Tote Féte Bakery*, behind the deli of the same name at 10450 Lansing St (☎707/937-3140; daily until 7pm), produces delicious breads, pastries and muffins, which you can eat outside on the tree-shaded deck.

In mid-July the town hosts the two-week **Mendocino Music Festival**, bringing in blues and jazz bands from all over the state, although the emphasis is largely on classical music and opera. For an earthier experience (and cheaper beer), *Dick's Place*, 45070 Main St, is Mendocino's oldest **bar**, with all the robust conviviality you'd expect from a spit-and-sawdust saloon.

Fort Bragg, Willits and Leggett

FORT BRAGG is very much the blue-collar flipside to its comfortable neighbor. Where Mendocino exists on wholefood and art, Fort Bragg brings you the rib-shack and lumberjack, and sits beneath a perpetual cloud of steam choked out from the lumbermills of the massive Georgia Pacific Corporation, which monopolizes California's logging industry and to which Fort Bragg owes its existence. There was once a fort here, but it was only used for ten years until the 1860s when it was abandoned and the land sold off cheaply. The otherwise attractive **Noyo Harbor** (south of town on Hwy-1) has been crammed full of commercial fishing craft, and the billowing smog does little to add to the charm. Nevertheless, its proximity to the more isolated reaches of the Mendocino Coast, an abundance of budget accommodation and no-nonsense restaurants make it a good alternative to Mendocino.

As for things to do, or even just a convenient way of getting to or from the coast, you can amuse yourself on the **Skunk Trains** operated by the Californian Western Railroad ($21 one-way, $26 round-trip; ☎ 1-800/77-SKUNK or 707/964-6371), which run twice daily from the terminus on Laurel Street forty miles inland to US-101 and the town of Willits. Taking their name from the days when they were powered by gas engines and could be smelt before they were seen, piled up with timber from the redwood forests, the trains now operate almost exclusively for the benefit of tourists – it's good fun to ride in the open observation car as it tunnels through mountains and rumbles across the thirty-odd high bridges on its route through the towering redwoods. **WILLITS**, where the trains end up, is the official county seat thanks only to its location in the center of Mendocino, and is no different from other strip-development, mid-sized American towns – disembark only to get a drink, if at all.

A short drive or bus ride south of Fort Bragg will take you to the **Mendocino Coast Botanical Gardens**, 18220 North Hwy-1 (summer daily 9am–5pm, winter Mon–Fri & Sun 9am–4pm; $5), where you can see more or less every wildflower under the sun spread across 47 acres of prime coastal territory. The coast here is also reputed to be one of California's best areas for **whale-watching**: if you're visiting in November when they pass on their way south to Baja to breed or, better still, in March when they're on their way back to the Arctic, a few patient hours spent on the beach may be rewarded by the sighting of a gray whale. Lost Coast Kayaking (☎707/937-2434; $45) leads two-hour **kayak** trips to the sea caves at Van Damme State Park, or river trips on the Noyo River when sea conditions are particularly rough.

Hwy-1 continues north for another twenty miles of slow road and windswept beach before leaving Mendocino County and the coastline to turn inland and meet Hwy-101 at **LEGGETT**. Redwood country begins in earnest here: there's even a tree you can drive through for $3, though you'd do better to stay on course for the best forests further north.

Practicalities

Fort Bragg's **Chamber of Commerce** (☎1-800/726-2780 or 707/961-6300) is almost directly across the street from the train station at 332 N Main St. Most of the **motels** cluster along Hwy-1 in the center of town, the lowest priced of which is the rather dingy looking *Fort Bragg Motel*, 763 N Main St (☎1-800/253-9972 or 707/964-4787; ②). Other good options include the basic but clean *Ebb Tide Lodge*, 250 S Main St (☎1-800/974-6730 or 707/964-5321; ③), the *Surf Motel*, 1220 S Main St (☎707/964-5361; ④) approaching town from the south, or the more upscale *Grey Whale Inn B&B*, 615 N Main St (☎1-800/382-7244 or 707/964-9800; ⑤), which has great views from its rooms. Arguably the best place to stay in the region is inland, three miles north of Leggett: *Eel River Redwoods Hostel and Bell Glen B&B*, 70400 US-101 (☎707/925-6425; ⑤), boasting luxurious woodland cabins, $12 dorm beds, a sauna, open-air jacuzzi and bar.

Finally, there's **camping** among coastal pines at **MacKerricher State Park** ($14; reserve through Parknet ☎1-800/444-7275), three miles north of Fort Bragg, with a ranch that offers horse rides along the secluded stretch of beach.

Restaurants in Fort Bragg (of which there are plenty) tend to cater for the ravenous carnivore. Both *Jenny's Giant Burger*, a roadside burger joint, 940 N Main St (☎707/964-2235), and the *Redwood Cookhouse*, 118 E Redwood Ave (☎707/964-1517), serve huge tree-felling dinners of steaks, ribs and burgers, and are usually full of men from the mills. Otherwise, *The Restaurant*, at 418 Main St (☎707/964-9800), has great Cajun and Creole fish dishes for around $6; *David's Restaurant & Deli*, 450 S Franklin St (☎707/964-1964), does great lunchtime sandwiches; and vegetarians can take refuge in the hearty Italian offerings at *Headlands Coffee*, 120 East Laurel St (☎707/964-1987). For big breakfasts, try *Egghead's Restaurant*, at 326 N Main St (daily 7am–2pm), which lists 41 different omelets on their menu. If you're feeling thirsty, stop in for one of the "handmade ales" at the *North Coast Brewing Company*, 444 N Main St.

The Humboldt Coast

Of the coastal counties, **Humboldt** is by far the most beautiful – overwhelmingly peaceful in places, in others plain eerie. The coastal highway cuts inland in southern Humboldt County, guaranteeing isolation and lending the region the name of the "Lost Coast." Humboldt is perhaps most renowned for its "Emerald Triangle," as it's known, which produces the majority of California's largest cash crop, **marijuana**. As the Humboldt Coast's fishing and logging industries slide, more and more people have been turning to growing the stuff to make ends meet. In the 1980s the Bush administration took steps to crack down on the business with CAMP (Campaign against Marijuana Planting), sporadically sending out spotter planes to pinpoint the main growing areas. Aggressive law enforcement and a steady stream of crop-poaching has been met with a defiant, booby-trapped and frequently armed protection of crops, and production goes on – the camouflage netting and irrigation pipes you find on sale in most stores clearly do their job.

Apart from considerable areas of clandestine agriculture, the county is almost entirely forestland, vast areas of which are protected in National Parks. The highway rejoins the coast at **Eureka** and **Arcata**, Humboldt's two major towns and both spirited jumping-off points for the **redwoods**, which stretch up the coast with a vengeance to the north of here. These prehistoric giants are the real crowd-pullers in this part of the state, at their best in the **Redwood National Park**, which covers some 58,000 acres of skyscraping forest. Again, **getting around** is going to be your biggest problem. Although Greyhound and Amtrak Thruway buses run the length of the county along US-101, they're hardly a satisfactory way to see the trees, and you'll need a car to make the trip worthwhile. For information on **what's on** in Humboldt, two excellent, free county newspapers, *The Activist* and *North Coast View*, detail the local scene and people, and where to go and what to do in the area. Look out, too, for the campaigning Arcata-based *Econews*, which highlights the ecological plight of northern California's wild country.

Southern Humboldt: Garberville and the "Lost Coast"

The inaccessibility of the Humboldt Coast in the south is ensured by the **Kings Range**, an area of impassable cliffs that shoots up several thousand feet from the ocean, so that even a road as sinuous as Hwy-1 can't negotiate a passage through. To get there you have to travel US-101 through deep redwood territory as far as **GARBERVILLE**, a one-street town with a few good bars that is the center of the cannabis industry and a lively alternative to the wholesome, happy-family nature of much of this part of California. Each week, the local paper runs a "bust-barometer" which charts the week's pot raids, and every August, the town hosts the massive two-day **Reggae on the River** festival. Tickets cost around $75; call ☎707/923-3368 by early May to reserve them.

Practicalities

Amtrak Thruway **buses** stop twice daily outside the *Waterwheel Restaurant* on Redwood Drive, Garberville's main street, while the two daily Greyhound services connecting north to Eureka and south to San Francisco pull in around the corner on Church Street. The town's **Chamber of Commerce** (☎1-800/923-2613 or 707/923-2613) is located at 773 Redwood Drive. For what you get, much of the town's **accommodation** is a bit overpriced. Of a couple you might try, the *Benbow Inn*, 445 Lake Benbow Drive (☎1-800/355-3301 or 707/923-2124; ⑥), is a flash place for such a rural location (former guests include Eleanor Roosevelt and Herbert Hoover); the *Sherwood Forest Motel*, 814 Redwood Drive (☎707/923-2721; ③), is pleasant with a nice pool; and the *Lone Pine Motel*, 912 Redwood Drive (☎707/923-3520; ②), is more affordable, if a lot scruffier. The closest **campground** is three miles south at **Benbow Lake State Recreation Area** (☎707/923-3238; reserve through Parknet ☎1-800/444-7275; $14); if you're independently mobile you can head five miles further south on US-101 to the **Richardson Grove State Park** in Piercy (☎707/247-3318; reserve through Parknet ☎1-800/444-7275; $16).

Even if you don't intend to stay in Garberville, at least stop off to sample some of the town's **restaurants** and **bars**, which turn out some of the best live bluegrass you're likely to hear in the state. Redwood Drive is lined with bars, cafés and restaurants: the *Eel River Café* at no. 801 (☎707/923-3783) is a good bet for breakfast, while the *Woodrose Café* at no. 911 (☎707/923-3191) serves organic lunches, and the *Mateel Café* at no. 478 (☎707/923-2030) serves gourmet dishes and coffee on the terrace. For casual dining or cheap take-out, try *Calico's Deli and Pasta*, 808 Redwood Drive (☎707/923-2253). All the town bars tend to whoop it up in the evening; the noisiest of the lot is probably the *Branding Iron Saloon*, at 744 Redwood Drive, with a small cover for its nightly live music. The *Riverwood Inn* (☎707/943-3333), in nearby Phillipsville is especially renowned for its live bluegrass.

Shelter Cove and the Humboldt Redwoods State Park

From Garberville, via the adjoining village of **Redway**, the Briceland-Whitehorn road winds 23 miles through territory populated by old hippies and New Agers beetling around in battered vehicles, to the **Lost Coast** at **SHELTER COVE**, set in a tiny bay neatly folded between sea cliffs and headlands. First settled in the 1850s when gold was struck inland, its isolated position at the far end of the Kings Range kept the village small until recent years. Now, thanks to a new airstrip, weekenders arrive in their hordes and modern houses are indiscriminately dotted across the headland. Unfortunately, it's the closest real settlement to the **hiking** and **wildlife** explorations of the surrounding wilderness, which remains inhabited only by deer, river otter, mink, black bear, bald eagles and falcons, so you might find yourself using the *Marina Motel*, 461 Machi Rd (☎707/986-7595; ④), as a base. The **Lost Coast Trail** runs along clifftops dotted with primitive **campgrounds** ($9), all near streams and with access to black-sand beaches. Another trail takes you to the top of **Kings Peak**, which at 4086ft, is the highest point on the continental United States shoreline.

The heart of redwood country begins in earnest a few miles north of Garberville along US-101, when you enter the **Humboldt Redwoods State Park** (unrestricted entry): over 53,000 acres of predominantly virgin timber, protected from lumber companies, make this the largest of the redwood parks – though it is the least used. Thanks to the Save-the-Redwoods League, who have been acquiring land privately for the park, it continues to slowly expand year after year. The serpentine **Avenue of the Giants** weaves for 33 miles through trees which block all but a few strands of sunlight. This is the habitat of *sequoia sempervirens*, the coast redwood with ancestors dating back to the days of the dinosaur. John Steinbeck described them as "ambassadors from another time" – and indisputably they're big, some over 350 feet tall, evoking a potent sense of solitude that makes a day of stopping off along the highway time well spent. To explore the deepest and quietest **backcountry** areas of the park, which most visitors neglect to do, head west off the Avenue of the Giants at Mattole Road. Back along the main road, small stalls selling lumber products and refreshments dot the course of the highway, chief among them the **Chimney Tree** (daily 9am–5pm; free), a wonderfully corny gift shop built into the burnt-out base of a still-living redwood. There are three **camp-grounds** ($16; reserve through Parknet; ☎1-800/444-7275) within the park.

The Avenue follows the south fork of the Eel River, eventually rejoining US-101 at **Pepperwood**. Ten miles before this junction, the turn-off to **HONEYDEW** provides a possible respite from the trees in a region thin on even small settlements. A good base from which to explore the northerly Lost Coast, Honeydew is a postage-stamp town popular with marijuana growers who appreciate its remote location – and the two hundred inches of annual rain that sustains the crops.

Any visitors awed by the majesty of the redwood forests can soon be brought back down to earth a few miles north at **SCOTIA**, a one-industry town if ever there was one. In this case it is timber, and the stacks and stacks of logs that line the freeway are actually quite a sight. The Pacific Lumber Company has been here since 1869, but with the decline in the industry and the rise in environmental objections to clear-felling of native forests, the company is throwing itself at the tourist market. Boasting of being "The World's Largest Redwood Mill," it uses half-truths and stretched facts to win you over to the loggers' cause on self-guided **sawmill tours** (Mon–Fri 7.30am–2pm; ☎707/764-2222; free), starting at the **Scotia Museum** on Main Street.

Eureka

Near the top of the north coast of California between the Arcata and Humboldt Bays, **EUREKA**, the largest coastal settlement north of San Francisco, is – despite some rather attractive Victorian mansions – an industrial, gritty and often foggy lumbermill town. It's not, as its name might suggest, a place that will make you think you've struck it rich, but it does make a useful stopover with its proximity to the largest groves of old-growth redwood trees in the world.

Downtown Eureka is fairly short on charm, lit by the neon of motels and generic chain restaurants, and surrounded by rail and shipyards, but the so-called **Old Town**, bounded by C, G, First and Third Streets, at the edge of the bay, is in the process of smartening up. The peeling Victorian buildings and poky bars of the old sailors' district are pretty much rundown – though they do have a certain seedy appeal, along with a handful of lively, mostly Italian restaurants. What few sights there are include the **Carson Mansion**, 143 M St at Second, an opulent Gothic pile built in the 1880s by William Carson, who made and lost fortunes in both timber and oil. It now operates as a private gentleman's club behind its gingerbread facade. Nearby, at 1410 Second St, the one-room **Maritime Museum** (daily 11am–4pm; donation) is chock-full of photos, maps and relics from the days when Eureka was a whaling port.

The collection of Native American applied art at the **Clarke Memorial Museum**, Third and E (Tues–Sat noon–4pm; donation), can't hold a candle to the stuff at the **Indian Art Gallery**, 241 F St (Mon–Sat 10am–4.30pm; free), a rare opportunity for Native American artists to show and market their works in a gallery setting, and an even rarer opportunity to get your hands on some incredibly good, inexpensive silver jewelry. If dragging yourself around town for these low-key sights doesn't appeal, you might prefer the **Eureka Health and Spa**, 601 Fifth St (☎707/445-2992), with its salt-rubs, tranquility tanks and saunas.

A few minutes by car from Eureka across the Samoa bridge, squashed against the Louisiana-Pacific plywood mill, the tiny community of **SAMOA** is a company town that is the site of the last remaining cookhouse in the west. **The Samoa Cookhouse**, (daily 6am–3.30pm & 5–9pm; ☎707/442-1659) was where the lumbermen would come to eat gargantuan meals after a day of felling redwoods, and although the oilskin tablecloths and burly workers have gone, the lumbercamp style remains, with long tables, the most basic of furnishings, and massive portions of red meat.

Practicalities

An abundance of affordable **motels** around the Broadway area at the southern (and noisy) end of town make Eureka bearable for a night or two. Try the *Matador Motel*, 129 Fourth St at C (☎707/443-9751; ②), or the *Downtowner*, 424 Eighth St at E (☎707/443-5061; ③). The *Eagle House Inn*, at 139 2nd St (☎707/444-3344; ③) is a strangely deserted cavernous Victorian relic with surprisingly clean rooms. If you want more than just a bed and a shower, head for *An Elegant Victorian Mansion B&B*, 1406 C St at 14th St (☎707/443-6512; ⑤), which, as the name suggests, recalls the opulence and splendor of a bygone era and offers an architectural tour of the town in a Model "A" Ford. **Campgrounds** line US-101 between Eureka and Arcata; the best is the *KOA* (☎1-800/462-5267 or 707/822-4243), a large site with copious amenities five miles north of town.

Transportation links are good: Greyhound, 1603 Fourth St, connects Eureka to San Francisco in the south and Portland in the north twice daily, while Amtrak Thruway goes from outside *Stanton's Coffee Shop* on Fifth and L streets. For getting around town and up the coast as far as Trinidad, Humboldt Transit, 133 V St (☎707/443-0826), has a weekday service. The Eureka **Chamber of Commerce** is at 2112 Broadway (June–Sept Mon–Fri 9am–7pm, Sat & Sun 10am–4pm; Oct–May Mon–Fri 9am–5pm, Sat & Sun 10am–4pm; ☎1-800/356-6381 or 707/442-3738).

In addition to the *Samoa Cookhouse* (see above), **eating** possibilities include most of the Italian restaurants of the Old Town, notably *Roy's*, 218 D St (☎707/442-4574), where complete meals cost under $15. The *Lost Coast Brewery and Café*, 617 Fourth St at F St (☎707/445-4480), serves large, hearty dishes to a rumbustious crowd of microbrew drinkers and baseball watchers, while the *Humboldt Bay Coffee Company*, 211 F St (☎707/444-3969), is a quieter spot with good coffee, open until around 8pm. For delicious seafood and burgers, you might try *Cafe Waterfront*, 102 F St (☎707/443-9190), where entrees cost around $11. For **entertainment**, the *Rathskeller Pub*, on F St at seventh, hosts blues bands several nights per week, and *Hefe's*, an all-ages club on Fifth Street at F Street, has nightly dancing and live rock music.

Arcata and around

ARCATA, twelve miles up the coast from Eureka, is by far the more appealing of the two places. Beards and birkenstocks are the norm in this small college town, with a large community of rat-race refugees and Sixties throwbacks whose presence is manifest in some raunchy bars and an earthy, mellow pace. The beaches north of town are some of the best on the north coast, white-sanded and windswept, and known for their easy hikeability and random parties.

Arcata itself is centered on a main square of shops and bars, with everything you're likely to want to see and do within easy walking distance. In the middle of the square the statue of President McKinley, originally intended for nearby McKinleyville, fell off the train on the way and stayed put in Arcata. Just east of the town center, **Humboldt State University**, with its nationally known environmental education and natural resource management programs, attracts a decidedly liberal student body, which contributes considerably to Arcata's leftist feel.

At the foot of I Street, the **Arcata Marsh and Wildlife Sanctuary**, a restored former dump on 175 acres of wetland, is a peaceful place where you can lie on the boardwalk in the sun and listen to the birds. The **Interpretive Center** at the foot of South G Street (Mon–Fri 1–5pm, Sat & Sun 10am–4pm; ☎707/826-2359) runs **guided wildlife walks** (Sat 2pm), as does the Audubon Society, which meets at the very end of I St at 8.30am every Saturday morning. For those who don't have time to explore the Redwood National Park, Arcata's own second-growth **community forest**, at 11th and 14th, makes a good alternative – a 600-acre, beautiful spot with manageable trails and ideal picnic areas.

If you're around over Memorial Day weekend, don't miss the three-day **Kinetic Sculpture Race**, a spectacular event in which competitors use human-powered contraptions of their own devising to propel themselves over land, water, dunes and marsh from Arcata to Ferndale.

Practicalities

Greyhound and Amtrak Thruway **buses** pull into the station at 925 E St between Ninth and Tenth, connecting with the Eureka services going north and south; there's also a weekday Humboldt Transit link with Eureka. The small but helpful **Chamber of Commerce**, 1062 G St (Mon–Fri 10am–4pm, Sat 9am–3pm; ☎707/822-3619), has free maps and lists of **accommodation**.

Motels just out of town on US-101 are lower-priced than the increasingly popular bed and breakfasts, if a little less inviting, and can usually be found for under $55 per night. Three blocks from the bus station, the *Arcata Youth Hostel*, 1390 I St (late June–late Aug only; ☎707/822-9995; ①), is easily the best deal in town with beds for $10 a night. You can get reasonable rooms at the *Fairwinds Motel*, 1674 G St (☎707/822-4824; ②), though if you've a bit more money the *Hotel Arcata*, 708 Ninth St (☎1-800/344-1221 or 707/826-0217; ④), on the town's main square, is a very stylish way to get rid of it. Of the B&Bs, try *The Lady Anne*, 902 14th St (☎707/822-2797) ④. There are several **campgrounds** north of Arcata along the coast, but none within easy reach of town unless you've got a car. *Big Lagoon County Park* (☎707/445-7651), fifteen miles north on Hwy-1, has spaces for $12, as does the nearby *Clam Beach County Park* (☎707/445-7651), four miles north of town on US-101.

Dotted around the plaza and tangential streets, Arcata's **bars** set the town apart. The best of the bunch, *Jambalaya* at 915 H St, draws a long-haired crowd for its nightly diet of R&B, jazz and rock bands. *The Humboldt Brewery*, 856 Tenth St (☎707/826-2739), is a working beer factory with its own bar and low-priced restaurant, where you can sample the preferred stronger, darker brews of Northern California. There's also the café at the Finnish County Sauna and Tubs, on the corner of Fifth and J streets, with live acoustic sets at the weekend, chess on Tuesdays, and tubs in the garden for $12 an hour. Good **restaurants** are in shorter supply, though *Wildflower Café and Bakery*, 1604 G St (☎707/822-0360), turns out good, cheap organic meals, and *Abruzzi*, 780 Eighth St (☎707/826-2345), serves top-quality Italian dinners at moderate prices.

Around Arcata

If you've got a car, take time to explore the coastline just north of Arcata along Hwy-101. **Moonstone Beach**, about ten miles north of town, is a vast, sandy strip that, save for the odd beachcomber, remains empty during the day, and by night heats up with guitar-strumming student parties that rage for as long as the bracing climate allows. **Trinidad Harbor**, a few miles further on, is a good stop for a drink, to nose around the small shops or just sit down by the sea wall and watch the fishing boats being tossed about beyond the harbor. **Patrick's Point State Park**, five miles further north, offers reasonably secluded **camping** for $16 (reserve through Parknet ☎1-800/444-7275).

A more adventurous – some would say insane – destination is **Hoopa Valley Indian Reservation**, sixty miles inland. In past years the site of often violent confrontation between Native Americans and whites over fishing territory, Hoopa is now seen by some as the badlands of Humboldt and few take the time to check out the valley. There's a dead, lawless feel about the place, the locals hanging around listlessly outside their caravans or roaring up and down the dirt tracks on their Harley-Davidsons. Even the bar and bingo hall, once the lifeblood of the community, have been closed down as a result of alcohol-induced violence. The nervous will want to move on quickly, but if you're here in the last week in July you should make an effort to catch the All Indian Rodeo, which is held southwest of the village. Otherwise it is enough to visit the **Hoopa Tribal Museum** (Mon–Fri 8am–5pm, Sat 10am–4pm; donation) – full of crafts, baskets and jewelry of the Natinixwe (aka Hupa) and Yurok tribes.

To get to the reservation, take Hwy-299 west out of Arcata for forty miles until you hit **WILLOW CREEK** – self-proclaimed gateway to "**Bigfoot Country**". Reports of giant 350 to 800-pound humanoids wandering the forests of northwestern California have circulated since the late nineteenth century, fueled by long-established Indian legends, though they weren't taken seriously until 1958, when a road maintenance crew found giant footprints in a remote area near Willow Creek. Photos were taken and the Bigfoot story went worldwide, since when there have been more than fifty separate sightings of Bigfoot prints. At the crossroads in Willow Creek stands a huge wooden replica of the prehistoric-looking apeman, who in recent years has added kidnapping to his list of alleged activities. Beside the statue, a small **Chamber of Commerce** (summer daily 9am–4pm; rest of year irregular hours; ☎530/629-2693) has details of Bigfoot's escapades, and information on the **whitewater rafting** that is done on the Smith, Klamath and Trinity rivers near here. Among the numerous rafting companies in the area, two are based in Willow Creek – Aurora River Adventures (☎1-800/562-8475 or 530/629-3843) and Bigfoot Rafting Company (☎1-800/722-2223 or 530/629-2263), both offering trips from $40. Otherwise, the town comprises a handful of grocery stores, diners and cheap motels such as the *Willow Creek Motel*, Hwy-96 (☎530/629-2115; ②). Just north of town, the **Lower Trinity Ranger Station** (summer Mon–Sat 8am–4.30pm; rest of year Mon–Fri 8am–4.30pm; ☎530/629-2118) handles camping and wilderness permits for the immediate surroundings.

The Redwood National and State Parks

Some thirty miles north of Arcata, the small roadside town of **Orick** marks the southernmost end of a contiguous strip of forest jointly managed as the **REDWOOD NATIONAL AND STATE PARKS** (unrestricted access; free), a massive area that stretches up into Del Norte County at the very northernmost point of California, ending at the dull town of **Crescent City**. The fragmented Redwoods National Park and the three state parks which plug the gaps – Prairie Creek Redwoods, Del Norte Coast Redwoods and Jedediah Smith Redwoods – together contain the world's first, third and sixth highest trees; the pride of California's forestland, especially between June and September when every school in the state seems to organize its summer camp here. Increasingly, and despite being designated a World Heritage Site and International Biosphere Reserve, it's becoming a controversial area – campers wake to the sound of chainsaws and huge lumber trucks roaring up and down the highway. Despite this, locals are still dissatisfied and claim that they've lost much of the prime timber they relied on before the days of the parks to make their living.

One word of warning: **bears** and **mountain lions** inhabit this area, and you should heed the warnings in Basics on p.45.

Practicalities

The parks' 58,000 acres divide into distinct areas: **Redwood National Park**, southwest of the **Orick Area**; the **Prairie Creek Redwoods State Park**, south of the riverside town of **Klamath**; and the area in the far north around the **Del Norte** and **Jedediah Smith State Parks**, in the environs of Crescent City in Del Norte County. The park headquarters are in Crescent City, at 1111 Second St (daily 8am–5pm; ☎ 1-800/423-6101 or 707/464-6101), but the **visitor centers** and **ranger stations** throughout the parks are far better for maps and information. Most useful is the **Redwood National Park Information Center** (daily 9am–6pm; ☎707/488-3461), right by the southern entrance.

The two daily Greyhound **buses** that run along US-101 to Crescent City will, if asked, stop (and if you're lucky can be flagged down) along forested stretches of the highway, and there's a twice-daily Redwood Coast Transit service looping out from Crescent City and back, but unless you want to single out a specific area and stay there (not the best way to see the parks), you'll be stuck without a **car**.

As for accommodation, **camping** is your best bet. You can stay at the many primitive and free campgrounds all over the parks; for more comfort, head for the sites we've mentioned in the text below (all $14–16), along with a hostel and a couple of motel recommendations. If you're really desperate, get onto US-101 and look for **motels** around Crescent City.

Orick and Tall Trees Grove

As the southernmost, and therefore most used, entrance to the Redwood National Park, the **Orick** area is always busy. Its major attraction is **Tall Trees Grove**, home of the world's tallest tree – a mightily impressive specimen that stands at some 367 feet. The easiest way to get there, avoiding too much picking amongst the lush undergrowth, is to drive yourself, although you will need to get a free access permit at the visitor center. Some people prefer to hike the 8.5 mile **Redwood Creek Trail** (permit needed) from near Orick: take a right off US-101 onto Bald Hills Road, then, 600 yards along, fork off to the picnic area where the trail starts. The bridge, 1.5 miles away, is passable in summer only. If you can make it from here, a bit further east another trail turns north off Bald Hills Road and winds for half a mile to **Lady Bird Johnson Grove** – a collection of trees dedicated to the former US President LBJ's wife, Lady "Bird" Johnson, a big lover, apparently, of flora and fauna. A mile-long self-guided trail winds through the grove of these giant patriarchs. **Permits** are available from the Information Center.

In **ORICK** itself (actually two miles north of the entrance and ranger station), Lane's Pack Station (☎707/488-5225) offers **horseback trips** through the forests and along the coast. Trips vary from two-hour rides along coastal trails to full weekends in the forest. Several **stores** and **cafés** string north along US-101, where you can pick up supplies and have a sit-down meal. Of several places, the *Palm Cafe*, (☎707/488-3381) serves cheap burgers and sandwiches. You might also stop just up the road at the *Lumberjack* for a game of pool and an ice-cold beer.

Three miles north of Orick, the narrow Davison Road turns coastwards for five miles to **Gold Bluffs Beach** (dawn–dusk) where you can camp. The $5 per vehicle fee also covers **Fern Canyon**, visited on an easy three-quarter-mile trail, its 45-foot walls slippery with mosses, fern and lichen.

Prairie Creek State Park and Klamath

Of the three state parks within the Redwood National Park area, **PRAIRIE CREEK** is the most varied and popular, and while bear and elk roam across all three, it's only here that you can be taken around by the rangers for a **tour** of the wild and damp profusion of a solidly populated redwood forest. Whether you choose to go independently, or opt for an organized tour, main features include the meadows of **Elk Prairie** in front of the **ranger station** (summer daily 8am–6pm; rest of year daily 8am–5pm; ☎707/488-2171), where herds of Roosevelt Elk, massive beasts weighing up to four hundred pounds, roam freely, protected from poachers. Day use is $5 per vehicle but you can park beside the road and wander at will. There's a **campground** on the edge of Elk Prairie, at the hub of a network of trails.

A mile north of the ranger station the magnificent **Big Tree Wayside** redwood, more than three hundred feet tall and, at over 21ft in diameter, the fattest of the coastal redwoods, overlooks the road.

Prairie Creek also has a couple of **restaurants** on the southern approach on US-101. All do a good line in wild boar roasts, elk steaks and the like, as well as a more traditional menu of burgers and breakfasts. *Rolf's Park Café* (☎707/488-3841), on US-101 by the Fern Canyon turn-off, is one of the best, with outdoor seating and German entrees.

Klamath Area

KLAMATH isn't technically part of the Redwood area nor, by most definitions, does it qualify as a town as most of the buildings were washed away when the nearby Klamath River flooded in 1964. Nonetheless, there are spectacular coastal views from trails where the Klamath River meets the ocean, a few decent accommodation options and, for a bit of fun, the **Trees of Mystery** (daily 8am–6pm; $6.50) on US-101, where you'll notice two huge wooden sculptures of Paul Bunyan and Babe, his blue ox. You can climb through, jump over and scoot under the trees – with the exception of the most impressive specimen of all, the **Cathedral Tree**, where nine trees have grown from one root structure to form a spooky circle. Enterprising Californians hold wedding services here throughout the year. The most spectacular scenery in Klamath, however, is not the trees, but the ocean: take Requa Road about three quarters of a mile down to the estuary, to a point known as the **Klamath Overlook**, from where, once the fog has burnt off, there is an awe-inspiring view of the sea and coast. From here, a coastal trail begins and leads for ten miles along some of California's most remote beach, ending at Endert's Beach in Crescent City.

The *Requa Inn*, 451 Requa Rd (☎707/482-8205; ⑤) offers some of the best **accommodation** around. There are the simple cabins at *Woodland Villa*, a mile and a half north of Requa (☎707/482-2081; ②), and small cottages with kitchenettes at *Camp Marigold* (☎1-800/621-8513 or 707/464-6101; ①), one mile south of the Trees of Mystery. The beautifully situated *HI-Redwood National Park Hostel* three miles further along US-101(☎707/482-8265; ①) has dorm beds for $12–14 whether you are a member or not. A couple of miles yet further north is the free, primitive *DeMartin* **campground**.

Crescent City and around

The northernmost outpost of the National Park, the Del Norte and Jedediah Smith state parks sit either side of **CRESCENT CITY**, a woebegone place with little to recommend it other than its proximity to the parks. However, if you've come this far, and are tired of camping and inadequate food supplies, it could save you from despair.

Greyhound **buses** stop at 1125 Northcrest Drive, and the **visitor center** is at 1001 Front St (Mon–Fri 9am–6pm; also June–Oct Sat & Sun 9am–5.30pm; ☎ 1-800/343-8300 or 707/464-3174). Of several passable **motels** on US-101, try *Curly Redwood Lodge*, 701 US-101 S (☎707/464-2137; ②), the *Ocean Way Motel* (☎707/464-9845; ①) further south at no. 1875, or the *Royal Inn Motel*, Front and L streets (☎1-800/752-9610 or 707/464-4113; ②). For **eating**, try the moderately priced Italian food at *Da Lucianna Ristorante*, 575 US-101 (☎707/465-6566), or the seafood and steaks at the *Harbor View Grotto*, 155

Citizens Dock Rd (☎707/464-3815). Considerably cheaper is *Los Compadres*, a Mexican diner on US-101 opposite the marina.

While here, take an hour to visit the **Battery Point Lighthouse** (June–Sept Wed–Sun 10am–4pm; tours sporadically during low tide; $2) reached by a causeway from the western end of town. The oldest working lighthouse on the West Coast, it houses a collection of artifacts from the *Brother Jonathan*, wrecked off Point St George in the 1870s. Because of this loss, the **St George Lighthouse**, the tallest and most expensive in the US, was built six miles north of Crescent City.

Del Norte and Jedediah Smith State Parks

Del Norte Park, seven miles south of Crescent City, is worth visiting less for its redwood forests (you've probably had enough of them by now anyway), than its fantastic beach area and hiking trails, most of which are an easy two miles or so along the coastal ridge where the redwoods meet the sea. From May to July, wild rhododendrons and azaleas shoot up everywhere, laying a floral blanket across the park's floor. **Jedediah Smith Park**, nine miles east of Crescent City, is named after the European explorer who was the first white man to trek overland from the Mississippi to the Pacific in 1828, before being killed by Comanche tribes in 1831. Not surprisingly, his name is everywhere: no less than eighteen separate redwood groves are dedicated to his memory. Sitting squatly on the south fork of the Smith River, the park attracts many people to canoe downstream or, more quietly, sit on the riverbank and fish. Of the hiking trails, the **Stout Grove Trail** is the most popular, leading down to a most imposing Goliath – a twenty-foot diameter redwood.

If you're heading further east and can't face more highway, you could opt for the painfully slow, but scenic route that follows Howland Hill Road from Crescent City through the forest to the **Hiouchi Information Center** (May–Oct 9am–5pm) on Hwy-199, about five miles away. Branching off this are several blissfully short and easy trails (roughly half a mile) which are quieter than the routes through the major parts of the park. You'll also find the Jedediah Smith Redwoods **campground** (reserve through Parknet ☎1-800/444-7275; $14), and **picnicking** facilities at the end of the Howland Hill Road.

THE NORTHERN INTERIOR

As big as Ohio, yet with a population of only 250,000, the **northern interior** of California is about as remote as the state gets. Cut off from the coast by the **Shasta Cascade** range, it's a region dominated by forests, lakes, some fair-sized mountains – and two thirds of the state's precipitation. It's largely uninhabited too, and, for the most part, infrequently visited. This is, of course, the greater part of its appeal, and while it doesn't have the biggest waterfalls, the bluest lakes or the highest mountains, it lacks the congestion that marks many of California's better-known areas. Those who do come stick to a few easily accessible locations, leaving vast miles of the state for the more adventurous to explore.

I-5 leads through the very middle of this near wilderness, forging straight up the **Sacramento Valley** through acres of unspectacular farmland to **Redding**: neatly placed for the best of the northern interior's natural phenomena. Redding isn't much of a place in itself, but makes a useful base from where you can venture out on loop trips a day or so at a time. Most accessible, immediately west and north of Redding, the **Whiskeytown-Shasta-Trinity National Recreation Area** is a series of three lakes and forests set aside for what can be heavily subscribed public use, especially in summer when it's hard to avoid the camper vans, windsurfers, jet-skiers and packs of happy holidaymakers. East of here the **Lassen Volcanic National Park** enjoys its biggest crowds in summer, though the volcanic summits and panoramic slopes make for some increasingly fashionable cross-country skiing territory. The **Plumas National Forest**, which spreads southeast as far as the borders of Nevada and the Gold Country, will hold no surprises: another mountainous cloak of forest with almost repetitive appeal.

By far the most interesting town in the region is the schizophrenic **Mount Shasta**, in the shadow of the 14,000-foot volcano of the same name. Mountaineers and anglers flock here in the summer and co-exist with a hard-core community of alternative lifestylers. When this palls, and you have a yearning for solitude, make for the very northeastern tip of the state and the loneliest of all California's verdant landscapes, the **Modoc National Forest**. Isolation makes the volcanic **Lava Beds National Monument** one of the least visited areas in the state, all the more reason to come and explore the hollow lava tubes and unearthly, arid landscapes.

It's the usual story with **public transportation**: reasonably frequent Greyhound and Amtrak Thruway buses connect San Francisco and Sacramento to Portland via I-5, stopping off at the Sacramento Valley towns and Redding on the way, and trains from Oakland stop in Redding and Chico. But neither route provides anything close to comprehensive access to the area, and if you're going to come here at all it should be in a **car**. Anything worth seeing lies at least five miles from the nearest bus stop. The area is too big and the towns too far apart to make traveling by bus even faintly enjoyable.

The Sacramento Valley

The **Sacramento Valley** lays fair claim to being California's most uninteresting region; a flat, largely agricultural corridor of small, sleepy towns and endless vistas of dull arable land. By far the best thing to do is pass straight through on I-5 – the half-empty, speedy freeway cuts an almost two-hundred mile-long swathe through the region, and you could forge right ahead to the more enticing far north quite painlessly in half a day.

Chico

CHICO, about midway between Sacramento and Redding and some thirty miles east of I-5, is a good stop-off if you don't want to attempt to cover the whole valley from top to bottom in one day, or if you're here to visit Lassen National Volcanic Park (see p.571) and need somewhere to stay. A typical small American college town, its low-key charm lies in its cozy suburban appeal rather than anything you can see or do when you get here. **Chico State University**, which gives the town much of its youthful character, was named "Best Party School in the Country" by *Playboy Magazine* several years ago. Depending on who you talk to, it has been trying to either live up to, or make up for, this reputation ever since.

Arrival, information and getting around

Chico is right on Hwy-99. **Trains** (and Amtrak Thruway buses) stop at the unattended station at Fifth and Orange; while Greyhound buses pull into the depot at 717 Wall St, between Seventh and Eighth.

On the south side of the central Downtown Park Plaza, the **Chamber of Commerce**, 500 Main St at Fifth (Mon–Fri 9am–5.30pm; ☎ 1-800/852-8570 or 530/891-5556), can supply you with a free map as well as lists of accommodation and eating options. To find out **what's on**, consult the free Chico *News & Review*, published every Thursday and available all over town, or tune in to KZFR (90.1 FM) or KCHO (88.9 FM), both broadcasting charmingly slapdash local community radio.

The majority of places you are likely to want to visit are within walking distance of the town center, although you can **rent a bike** for $20 per day from Campus Bicycles right by the plaza at 501 Main St (☎530/345-2081).

Accommodation

Chico has much more in the way of **accommodation** than it does in sights, though for camping you'll need to head to the Plumas National Forest to the east or Lassen National Volcanic Park. Motels are everywhere in town, particularly in the Main Street and Broadway area, and there are a couple of good B&Bs.

Esplanade, 620 The Esplanade (☎530/345-8084). A particularly good value B&B right across from the Bidwell Mansion. The beds are so high you almost need to pole-vault onto them, and tasty breakfasts are served on the back verandah. ④.

L'Abri Inn, 14350 Hwy-99 (☎1-800/489-3319 or 530/893-0824). Five miles north of town, this place comprises three rooms in a ranch-style home with a serene country atmosphere. Enjoy a sumptuous breakfast, then go out and pet the barnyard animals. ④.

Matador, 1934 The Esplanade (☎530/342-7543). A pretty Spanish Revival building ten blocks north of the Plaza; the tasteful rooms have individual tiling. Set around a courtyard, with palms shading one of Chico's largest pools, this is one of the town's best deals. ②.

Thunderbird Lodge, 715 Main St (☎530/343-7911). Decent and low-cost motel two blocks from the Plaza. Some rooms have refrigerators and coffee-makers. ②.

Western Travel Inn, 740 Broadway (☎530/343-3286). About the cheapest downtown motel just two blocks south of the Plaza, with refrigerators in rooms and a pool. ②.

The Town

Short on sights as Chico is, you might try the three-story **Bidwell Mansion** at 525 The Esplanade, the continuation of Main Street (daily, tours on the hour 10am–4pm; $3). Built in 1868 by the town's founder, General Bidwell, it's an attractive enough Victorian building, filled with family paraphernalia visited on 45-minute anecdotal tours. It's reasonably interesting, but **Bidwell Park** (most sections open daylight hours; free) is a more pleasurable place to spend your time. Extending from the center of the town for ten miles to the northeast, this is a tongue of semi-wilderness and oak parkland where, incidentally, the first *Robin Hood* film, starring Errol Flynn, was made. No road runs right through the park, and it is too large to cover on foot, so cycling (see bike rental on p.566) is by far the best way to explore. The most heavily used areas are around the recreation areas at One-mile Dam and Five-mile Dam, both reached off Vallombrosa Avenue, and Cedar Grove, reached off E Eighth Street, but a half-hour stroll into Upper Park will leave most of the regulars behind.

Back in town, vintage American car fans will enjoy **Cruces Classic Auto Sales**, downtown on 720 Main St, a commercial showroom with a walk-through museum showing some of the really rare models that are brought here to be restored. Or visit the **Sierra Nevada Brewing Company**, 1075 E 20th St (☎530/893-3520), which gives free and fairly cursory twenty-minute tours of the plant (Tues–Fri & Sun 2.30pm, Saturday noon–3pm) and the chance to sample each of the ten or so brews on tap for under $5.

Eating and nightlife

Chico also does itself proud when it comes to **food**. Being a California State University town, there are many excellent places aimed at the younger (and poorer) customer, as well as a handful of lively **bars** to while away your evenings. It's noticeably quieter when school's out, but on summer Friday evenings, **free concerts** by talented locals draw the crowds to the Downtown Park Plaza.

Café Sandino, 817 Main St (☎530/894-6515). Small vegetarian café with plenty of low-fat and vegan dishes, and good *tamales* for under $5. Open until 9pm, closed Sun.

Cory's, 230 W Third St (☎530/345-2955). Excellent breakfasts and lunches, featuring sandwiches served on freshly baked bread.

Gashouse Pizza, 1444 Park Ave (☎530/345-6602). Old auto repair shop turned hole-in-the-wall pizza joint that serves far and away the best pizza in town. Open 4.30pm.

Jack's Restaurant, 540 Main St (☎530/343-8383). 24-hr diner, a bit on the greasy side, but good for breakfasts and late-night munchies.

Jasco's California Cafe, 300 Broadway (☎530/899-8075). Salads, sandwiches, and gourmet pizza are all top notch and reasonable. The vegetarian sandwiches are especially delicious. Lunch and dinner only.

LaSalle's, 229 Broadway (☎530/893-1891). The place to consume large quantities of beer, play pool, and listen to live rock bands.

Madison Bear Garden, 316 W Second St (☎530/891-1639). A place for swigging beer with students from the nearby campus. Burgers, buffalo wings and the like are also served.

Riley's, Fifth and Ivy (☎530/343-7459). Catch the ballgame on one of the many TV screens and hang out with the excited students at the most popular bar in Chico.

Sierra Nevada Brewing Company, 1075 E 20th St (☎530/893-3520). The bar food is unexceptional, but the pale ale, porter, stout and seasonal brews are a strong draw. There's usually jazz on Mondays and good local bands some weekends.

Thai Chada, downstairs at 117b W Second St (☎530/342-7121). Authentic, and predominantly vegetarian, Thai cuisine at very reasonable prices, especially at lunchtime. Closed Sun.

Tres Hombres Taco Bar, 100 Broadway (☎530/342-0425). Large restaurant popular with students for the wide selection of margaritas. Reasonably priced burritos, *quesadillas, tostadas,* and tacos in a fun environment. Dinner until 10pm every night, drinks until 2am on weekends. Live jazz Sunday afternoons.

Red Bluff

Strung along the Sacramento Valley around 45 miles north from Chico up Hwy-99, **RED BLUFF** is not a particularly exciting place, and has long since outgrown the small-town friendliness exuded by Chico. Still, it's the one point at which you can pick up **public transportation** heading towards Lassen National Volcanic Park (see p.571), so you may find yourself staying over. There's a reasonable selection of $30-a-night motels along Main Street – among them the *Crystal Motel*, 333 S Main St (☎530/527-1021; ①) – and a handful of diners and burger joints in town. You may consider visiting the **Kelly-Grigs House Museum**, 311 Washington St (Thurs–Sun 1–4pm; donation), where there's an exhibit on Ishi, "the last wild Indian," who appeared out of what is now the Ishi Wilderness in 1911 and was feted until his death in 1916. Pick up more information from the **Chamber of Commerce**, 100 Main St (Mon 8.30am–4pm, Tues–Thurs 8.30am–5pm, Fri 8.30am–4.30pm; ☎530/527-6220).

Redding and around

After the high-flown descriptions of Northern California's isolated beauty and charm, **REDDING's** sprawl of franchise motels and fast-food chains comes as something of a shock to most visitors, and the town doesn't improve with longer acquaintance. But Redding's position, close to both the Whiskeytown-Shasta-Trinity National Recreation Area to the west and the Lassen National Volcanic Park to the east, makes it a premium transit point and the major source of accommodation for those wanting to sample the best of this part of the state without being forced under canvas. It's basically a railroad center, a characterless assembly of cheap lodgings and little else, whose streets only really brighten during midsummer, when the tourists hit.

If conditions don't suit hiking, there's not a lot to do here, other than visit **Shasta** on the outskirts (see p.571). You could kill thirty minutes at the **Redding Museum of Art & History** in Caldwell Park on the banks of the Sacramento (Tues–Sun 10am–5pm; $2), which has a permanent display of Native American artifacts, and rotating contemporary and historical art exhibits. The neighboring **Carter House Natural Science Museum** (Tues–Sun 10am–5pm; $2) is aimed at kids, with hands-on exhibits and a self-guided nature walk through an arboretum. The river bank here forms part of the **Sacramento River Trail**, a pleasant, six-mile loop designed for walkers and cyclists.

Practicalities

Considering its position at the crossroads of northern California, **public transportation** in Redding is woefully inadequate, though the new **Intermodal Transportation Facility**, the terminus for Greyhound, Amtrak, Amtrak Thruway and the local RABA bus system (☎530/241-2877), at least provides a central focus for what there is. As usual, you're not going to get to see much without a car. If you are driving, call Caltrans to check ahead for weather and road conditions (☎1-800/427-7623) and, if necessary, make extra provisions (de-icer, tire chains and so on) in case of snowstorms. Though fiercely hot in summer, the temperature drops forbiddingly in some of the surrounding areas in winter, and what looks like a mild day in Redding could turn out to be blizzard conditions a few miles up the road (and several thousand feet up a mountainside).

The **Redding CVB**, 777 Auditorium Drive (Mon–Fri 8am–5pm; ☎ 1-800/874-7562 or 530/225-4100), can give advice on accommodation in Redding, information on camping in the outlying areas and details on where to rent camping equipment. For information more specifically on the surrounding area, the **Shasta Cascade Wonderland Association** on Wonderland Boulevard, six miles north of town off I-5 (Mon–Sat 9am–6pm, Sun 10am–4pm; ☎ 1-800/474-2782 or 530/275-5555), has a more detailed collection of maps and information, and is staffed by helpful outdoor experts. As a general rule, Lassen National Volcanic Park is for hardier and more experienced hikers, and novices are pointed in the direction of the Whiskeytown-Shasta-Trinity National Recreation Area, where there are warmer climes and easier trails.

△ Mount Shasta

Redding Shopping Center

273

5

229

BENTON DRIVE

MARKET STREET

HILLTOP DRIVE

OLD OREGON TRAIL

Redding Museum of Art and History

Carter House Natural Science Museum

RIVERSIDE DR.

Sacramento River

Burney △ Lava Beds National Monument

Shasta & Weaverville

❶
❸

Thunderbird Lodge

i

299

299

❷

HILLTOP DRIVE

44

Lassen Volcanic National Park

Intermodal Transportation Facility

Downtown Redding Mall

❹

PARK MARINA DRIVE

AIRPORT ROAD

PLACER STREET
GOLD STREET

RAILROAD AVENUE

WEST CYPRESS

EAST CYPRESS

HARTNELL AVENUE

BECHELLI LANE

Sacramento River

273

5

ACCOMMODATION
1 Budget Lodge
2 Palisades Paradise
3 Redding Lodge
4 River Inn

REDDING

0 _____ 1 mile

▽ Sacramento

Motels are concentrated along Redding's main strip, Market Street (Hwy-273), and Pine Street. *Budget Lodge*, 1055 Market St (☎530/243-4231; ②), is a good budget option, while the *Redding Lodge*, 1135 Market St (☎530/243-5141; ②), is slightly more luxurious. For something grander still, try either *River Inn*, close to the river at 1835 Park Marina Drive (☎1-800/995-4341 or 530/241-9500; ③), or *Palisades Paradise*, 1200 Palisades Ave (☎1-800/382-4649; ③), an upscale B&B with a fabulous view of the Trinity mountains to the west.

Restaurants are as ubiquitous as motels, many of them 24-hour, most of them unappealing. Exceptions include *Jack's Grill*, 1743 California St (☎530/241-9705; closed Sun) with fine grilled steak and shrimp and chicken dishes for $10–15. You'll probably have to wait for a table, but you can always go across the road to *Downtown Espresso*, 1545 Placer St at California (☎530/243-4548), attached to the Redding Bookstore and the only place in town where you can get a decent coffee in the evening. In the mornings, good coffee and healthy breakfasts are served at *Hill o' Beans*, 1804 Park Marina Drive (☎530/246-8852), while *The Hatch Cover*, 202 Hemsted Drive (☎530/223-5606), serves tasty steak and seafood from its riverside terrace.

Shasta

Huddling four miles west of Redding, the ghost town of **SHASTA** – not to be confused with Mount Shasta (see p.577) – is more appealing than Redding, though it is mainly residential. A booming gold-mining town when Redding was an insignificant dot on the map, Shasta's fortunes changed when the railroad tracks were laid to Redding. Abandoned since then, it remains today a row of half-ruined brick buildings that were once part of a runaway prosperity, and literally the end of the road for prospectors. All roads from San Francisco, Sacramento and other southerly points terminated at Shasta; beyond, rough and poorly marked trails made it almost impossible to find gold diggings along the Trinity, Salmon and Upper Sacramento Rivers, and diggers contented themselves with the rich pickings in the surrounding area, pushing out the local Native Americans in a brutal territorial quest for good mining land. The **Courthouse**, on the east side of Main Street, has been turned into a museum (Thurs–Mon 10am–5pm; $2), full of mining paraphernalia and paintings of past heroes, though best are the gallows at the back and the prison cells below – a grim reminder of the daily executions that went on here. The miners were largely an unruly lot, and in the main room of the Courthouse a charter lays down some basic rules of conduct:

> *IV Thou shalt neither remember what thy friends do at home on the Sabbath day, lest the remembrance may not compare favorably with what thou doest here.*
> *VII Thou shalt not kill the body by working in the rain, even though thou shalt make enough money to buy psychic attendance. Neither shalt thou destroy thyself by "tight" nor "slewed" nor "high" nor "corned" nor "three sheets to the wind," by drinking smoothly down brandy slings, gin cocktails, whiskey punches, rum toddies and egg nogs.*

From the Miners' Ten Commandments

The **Shasta State Historic Park** (☎530/243-8194; unrestricted entry) straddles Main Street, and is less grand than it sounds. Indistinguishable ruins of brick buildings are identified by plaques as stores and hotels, and the central area, not much bigger than the average garden really, features miscellaneous mining machinery and a picnic area.

Lassen Volcanic National Park

Around forty miles directly east from Redding, the 106,000 acres that make up the pine forests, crystal-green lakes and boiling thermal pools of the **LASSEN VOLCANIC NATIONAL PARK** are one of the most unearthly parts of California. A forbidding climate, which brings up to fifty feet of snowfall each year, keeps the area pretty much uninhabited, with the roads all blocked by snow and (apart from a brief June to October season) completely deserted. It lies at the southerly limit of the Cascades, a low, broad range which stretches six hundred miles north to Mount Garibaldi in British Colombia and is characterized by high volcanoes forming part of the Pacific Circle of Fire. Dominating the park at over 10,000ft is a fine example, **Mount Lassen** itself, which – although quiet in recent years – erupted in 1914, beginning a cycle of outbursts which climaxed in 1915 when the peak blew an enormous mushroom cloud some seven miles skyward, tearing the summit into chunks that landed as far away as Reno. Although eighty years of geothermal inactivity have since made the mountain a safe and fascinating place, scientists predict that of all the Californian volcanoes, Lassen is the likeliest to blow again.

LASSEN VOLCANIC NATIONAL PARK

CARIBOU WILDERNESS

N

2 miles

Widow Lake

Butte Lake

Snag Lake

Juniper Lake

Juniper Lake Primitive

Horseshoe Lake

Cluster Lakes

PACIFIC CREST TRAIL

Summit Lake North
Summit Lake
Summit Lake South

Ranger Station

Emigrant Pass

Warner Valley

Drakesbad Guest Ranch

Boiling Springs Lake

LASSEN NATIONAL FOREST

Crags Overflow
Lost Creek

Hot Rock

Dersert

Kings Creek

Crags Lake

NOBLES EMIGRANT TRAIL

CHAOS CRAGS

Lassen Peak 10457 ft

Bumpass Hell

Mill Creek Falls

Reflection Lake

Manzanita Lake

Lake Helen

LITTLE HOT SPRINGS AREA

Southwest

Ridge Lakes

Sulphur Works

Brokeoff Mountain 9235 ft

LASSEN NATIONAL FOREST

Visitor Center and Museum

Redding (89)

Hat Creek & Burney (89)

Red Bluff & Chico (89)

Chester

Chester

44

Arrival and information

Lassen is always open ($5 per vehicle for seven days, $3 per hiker or biker), but you'll have a job getting in or around without a car. During the winter, when the roads in the park are almost always shut down due to snow, a car won't do you much good either – snowshoes and cross-country skis are popular modes of transportation. The only **public transportation** that even approaches the park is provided by Mount Lassen Motor Transit (Mon–Sat from 8am; ☎530/529-2722) from **Red Bluff**, in the Sacramento Valley (see p.568), but even this only reaches **MINERAL**, some eight miles short of the park's southwestern entrance. From Mineral, Hwy-89 leads through Lassen to the northern entrance at the junction of Hwy-44 and Hwy-89 near Manzanita Lake.

The Park Service has its **headquarters** in Mineral (daily 8am–4.30pm; PO Box 100, Mineral, CA 96063; ☎530/595-4444), where you can get free maps and information (there's a box outside when it's closed), including the *Lassen Park Guide*. The main **visitor center** (summer daily 9am–5pm; ☎530/595-4444 ext 5180) is at Manzanita Lake, just inside the northern entrance, and occupies the same building as the Loomis Museum (see p.575).

Accommodation and eating

The only way to **stay** inside the Lassen park is to camp (see box), but even in August night temperatures can hover around freezing, and many people prefer to stay in one of the resorts and lodges that pepper the surrounding forest. To be sure of a room in the popular summer months, it pays to book well ahead. For **food**, you don't have an

---

CAMPING IN AND AROUND LASSEN

During the few months of the year when conditions are suitable for camping, this is by far the best option. All **developed campgrounds** in the park are listed below and operate on a first-come-first-served basis; not a problem except on midsummer weekends.

Primitive camping requires a free **wilderness permit** obtainable in advance from the park headquarters in Mineral (see above), or in person from the visitor centers and entrance stations. There is no self-registration and chosen sites must be a mile from developed campgrounds and a quarter of a mile from most specific sites of interest. In the surrounding **Lassen National Forest**, camping is permitted anywhere, though you'll need a free permit to operate a cooking stove or to light a fire; these are sometimes refused in the dry summer months. In addition there are a couple of dozen developed sites strung along the highways within thirty miles of Lassen, most charging between $5 and $11.

Juniper Lake ($8; 6800ft). In the far southeastern corner of the park, with good hiking trails nearby and swimming in the lake. Drinking water must be boiled or treated.

Manzanita Lake ($12; 5900ft). By far the largest of the Lassen campgrounds and the only one with a camp store (8am–8pm), firewood for sale ($6), 24-hour showers (bring quarters), and a laundrette. Rangers run interpretive programs from here.

Southwest ($10; 6700ft). Small tent-only campground by the southwest entrance on Hwy-89 with walk-in sites, water and fire rings.

Summit Lake ($10–12; 6700ft). The pick of the Hwy-89 campgrounds, right in the center of the park and at the hub of numerous hiking trails. It's divided into two sections, the northern half equipped with flush toilets, the southern half only vaults. There's swimming in the lake for the brave.

Warner Valley ($10; 5700ft). Off Hwy-89 in the south of the park, this is a beautiful site, but its distance from the road makes it only worth heading for if you're planning extended hiking in the region.

awful lot to choose from. There's a reasonable general store at Manzanita Lake campground (see overleaf), and *Lassen Chalet* has a surprisingly good café (daily 9am–6pm), but beyond that you'll have to go outside the park.

Hat Creek Resort, Hwy-89, Old Station, eleven miles northwest of the northern entrance (☎530/335-7121). A complex of motel units and fancier cabins with kitchens (two-day minimum stay). ③.

Lassen Mineral Lodge, Hwy-36, Mineral (☎530/595-4422). Unspectacular base-rate rooms and considerably more comfortable family ones for just $5 extra. There's a pool, general store, restaurant and bar on site. ③.

Mill Creek Park, Mill Creek Road, off Hwy-44, fourteen miles east of the northern entrance (☎530/474-5384). Set amid pines and cedars, simple cabins with cold-water kitchenettes cost $30, those with hot water and bath are $10 more, and space at the campground is $9. ②.

Padilla's Rim Rock Ranch Resort, 13275 Hwy-89, Old Station (☎530/335-7114). A collection of cabins of varying standards, the best sleeping up to six ($40–60), dotted around a meadow. Closed Nov–March. ②.

Weston House, Red Rock Road, Shingletown, a few miles east of Mineral (☎530/474-3738). One of the nicest B&Bs in all of California, with four elegant rooms beautifully sited on a volcanic ridge with pool and deck, overlooking the Ishi National Wilderness Area. ⑤.

The park

Unlike most other wilderness areas, you don't actually need to get out of the car to appreciate Lassen, as some of the best features are visible from the paved Hwy-89 that traverses the park. A thorough tour should take no more than a few hours. Pick up a copy of the *Road Guide: Lassen Volcanic National Park* ($4) in the visitor center.

HIKING IN LASSEN PARK

For a volcanic landscape, a surprisingly large proportion of the walking trails in the park are predominantly flat, and the heavily glaciated terrain to the east of the main volcanic massif is pleasingly gentle. Rangers will point you toward the **hiking routes** best suited to your ability – the park's generally high elevations will leave all but the most experienced walker short of breath, and you should stick to the shorter trails at least until you're acclimatized. For anything but the most tentative explorations, you should pick up a copy of *Lassen Trails* ($2.50) or the better, color *Hiking Trails of Lassen* ($12.95), which describe the most popular hikes.

Chaos Crags Lake (3.5 miles round trip; 2–3hr; 800ft ascent). From the *Manzanita Lake* campground access road, the path leads gently up through pine and fir forest to the peaceful lake. An adventurous extension climbs a ridge of loose rock to the top of Chaos Crags, affording a view of the whole park.

Lassen Peak (5 miles round trip; 4hr; 2000ft ascent). A fairly strenuous hike from road marker 22 to the highest point in the park. Be prepared with water and warm clothing.

Manzanita Lake (1.5 miles; 1hr; flat). Easy trails on level ground make this one of the most popular short walks in the park.

Nobles Emigrant Trail (2.5 miles; 1–2hr; 200ft ascent). The most accessible and one of the more interesting sections of a trail forged in 1850 starts opposite the Manzanita Lake entrance station and meets Hwy-89 at marker 60. It isn't maintained, but is heavily compacted and easy going.

Paradise Meadows (3 miles round trip; 3hr; 800ft ascent). Starting either at the Hat Creek parking area (marker 42) or marker 27, and passing Terrace Lake on the way, this hike winds up at Paradise Meadows, ablaze with wildflowers in the summer and a marvelous spot to pass an afternoon.

Starting from the northern entrance, the first points of interest along Hwy-89 are **Manzanita Lake** and the **Loomis museum** (summer daily 9am–5pm; free), a memorial to Benjamin Loomis whose documentary photos of the 1914 eruption form the centerpiece of an exhibition strong on local geology – plug domes, composite cones and cinder cones – and flora. An easy trail circles the lake, but so do many of the campers from the nearby campground: an early start is needed for any serious wildlife spotting.

At the halfway point you'll come to **Summit Lake**, a busy camping area set around a beautiful icy lake, from where you can start on the park's most manageable hiking trails. Press on further to the **Devastated Area**, where, in 1914, molten lava from Lassen poured down the valley, denuding the landscape as it went, ripping out every tree and patch of grass. Slowly the earth is recovering its green mantle, but the most vivid impression is still one of complete destruction.

Further south along Hwy-89, you reach the parking area (8000ft up) where the steep five-mile ascent to Lassen Peak begins. Wilderness seekers will have a better time pushing east to the **Juniper Lake** area.

Continuing south, Lassen's indisputable show-stealers are **Bumpass Hell** and **Emerald Lake**, the former – named after a man who lost a leg trying to cross it – a steaming valley of active pools and vents that bubble away at a low rumble all around. It looks dangerous, but the trails are sturdy and easy to manage. Be warned, though, that the crusts over the thermal features are often brittle, and breaking through them could literally land you in very hot water – *never* venture off the trails. The paths around Emerald Lake are spectacular too, in a much quieter fashion; the lake itself resembles a sheet of icy-green glass, perfectly still and clear but for the snow-covered rock mound which rises from its center. Only during summer does the lake approach swimmable temperatures, and if you're visiting outside of July or August you'll have to content yourself with gazing at its mirror-like surface.

Before leaving the park at Mineral, you'll notice the rising steam and acrid smell of **Sulphur Works**, a boiling cauldron of fumaroles and mud pots visible from the road and reached on a 200-yard boardwalk. The far south of the park also contains **Lassen Chalet**, site of some limited skiing facilities.

Whiskeytown-Shasta-Trinity National Recreation Area

Traveling west from Redding through the ghost town of Shasta (see p.571), Hwy-299 is a deserted, often precipitous but enjoyable road that leads after ten miles into the western portion of the **Whiskeytown-Shasta-Trinity National Recreation Area**. Assuming the road's open – it's often blocked off due to bad weather – this huge chunk of land is open for public use daily, year-round. Its series of three impounded lakes – Trinity, Whiskeytown and Shasta – have artificial beaches, forests and camping facilities designed to meet the needs of anyone who has ever fancied themselves as a water-skier, sailor or wilderness hiker. Sadly, during summer it's completely congested, as windsurfers, motorboats, jet skis and recreational vehicles block the narrow routes which serve the lakes. But in the winter when the tourists have all gone, it can be supremely untouched, at least on the surface. In fact there's an extensive system of tunnels, dams and aqueducts directing the plentiful waters of the Sacramento River to California's Central Valley to irrigate cash crops for the huge agribusinesses. The lakes are pretty enough, but residents complain they're not a patch on the wild waters that used to flow from the mountains before the Central Valley Project came along in the 1960s.

Of the three lakes, **Whiskeytown**, just beyond Shasta, is the smallest, easiest to get to, and inevitably the most popular. Ideal for watersports, it hums with the sound of jet skis and powerboats ripping across the still waters. Those who don't spend their holiday in a wet suit can usually be found four-wheel driving and pulling action-man stunts on the primitive roads all around. The best place for **camping** and **hiking** is in the **Brandy Creek** area – a hairy five-mile drive along the narrow J.F. Kennedy Memorial Drive from the main entrance and **Whiskeytown Visitor Information Center** on Hwy-299 (daily 9am–6pm; ☎530/246-1225). There's a small store at the water's edge in Brandy Creek and three campgrounds (mostly $11–14 sites) about a mile behind in the woods.

Northeast on Hwy-3 (off Hwy-299 forty miles west of Whiskeytown), **Trinity Lake** (officially called Clair Engle Lake, but not locally referred to as such) is much quieter, rarely used in summer and in winter primarily a picturesque stop-off for skiers on their way to the **Salmon-Trinity Alps** area beyond, part of the extensive **Salmon Mountains** range. It's very remote around here, and most people only venture this far west to visit the small Gold Rush town of **WEAVERVILLE**, a few miles west along Hwy-299. The distinctive brick buildings, fitted with exterior spiral staircases, were built to withstand fires – indeed, the fire station itself is particularly noteworthy. The main draw, though, is the **Joss House** on Main Street (Thurs–Mon 10am–5pm; $2), a small Taoist temple built in 1874 by indentured Chinese mineworkers. A beautiful shrine, still in use today, it features a three-thousand-year-old altar and can be visited on a poor guided tour.

You can **stay** at the *Weaverville Hotel*, 205 Main St (☎530/623-3121; ②) a century-old, gracefully dilapidated place with large characterful rooms and no phones or TV – register in Brady's sports store next door. Alternatives include the well-lit *49er Motel*, 718 Main St (☎530/623-49ER; ②). The friendly *Motel Trinity* (☎530/623-2129) on Main Street just south of Hwy-3, has rooms for $55 with hot tubs, or $35 without. You can **eat** well-prepared chicken, steaks, and pasta for around $11 at the cozy *La Grange Café*, 315 N Main St (☎530/623-5325), or knock back local microbrews over a hearty meal at the eclectically decorated *Pacific Brewery Restaurant & Bar*, 401 S Main St (☎530/623-3000). Also on Main Street, across from the Joss House, the *New York Saloon* is a great place to mingle with the friendly locals over a glass of beer. For more information, consult the **Chamber of Commerce**, 317 S Main St (summer daily 9am–5pm; rest of year Mon–Fri 9am–5pm; ☎ 1-800/421-7259 or 530/623-6101).

East of the other two, eight miles north of Redding, is **Shasta Lake**. The biggest of the three lakes – larger than the San Francisco Bay – it's marred by the unsightly and enormous **Shasta Dam**, 465ft high and over half a mile long, bang in the middle. Built between 1938 and 1945 as part of the enormous Central Valley irrigation project, the dam backs up the Sacramento, McCloud and Pit rivers to form the lake, the project's northern outpost. The best views are from marked vista points along the approach road (US-151, off I-5), but a more vivid way to experience the sheer enormity of the thing is to drive down to the powerhouse (daily 9am–4pm) and take the **free tour** of the dam and ancillary structures, feeling the power of millions of gallons of water gushing beneath you.

On the north side of the lake, the massive limestone formations of the **Shasta Caverns** (daily tours 10am, noon & 2pm; $14) are the largest in California, jutting above ground and clearly visible from the freeway. The interior, however, is something of a letdown: a fairly standard series of caves and tunnels in which stalactite and stalagmite formations are studded with crystals, flow-stone deposits and miniature waterfalls. The admission price covers the short ferry journey from the ticket booth across an arm of Shasta Lake. From Lake Shasta, I-5 races up towards Mount Shasta, an impressive drive against a staggering backdrop of mountains and lakes.

Mt Shasta ... and Mount Shasta

Lonely as God and as white as a winter moon.

Joaquin Miller, about Mt Shasta

The lone peak of the 14,162-foot **Mt Shasta** dominates the landscape for a hundred miles all around, almost permanently snow-covered, hypnotically beautiful but menacing in its potential for destruction: it last erupted over two hundred years ago, but is still considered an active volcano. Under the enormous bulk of the mountain, the town of **MOUNT SHASTA** has a compact and pleasing center free from the worst excesses of urban sprawl. This, and the energy channels which are said to converge on the mountain, have combined over the last decade to make it California's ascendant hotbed of spiritual activity, a fact not lost on those who prey on the centered, but barely grounded, individuals who flock here, exploiting every weakness in their holistic armor through expensive courses and retreats.

Arrival and information

Merely getting to Mount Shasta is a rewarding journey, easily accomplished on Greyhound **buses** which connect the town with Redding to the south and stop on Commercial Way, a couple of blocks from the very helpful **Visitors' Bureau**, 300 Pine St (Mon–Sat 9am–5pm, Sun 9am–3pm; ☎ 1-800/926-4865 or 530/926-4865). Amtrak trains stop in Dunsmuir, six miles south, in the middle of the night; from there, six daily STAGE buses (☎1-800/24-STAGE or 530/842-8295) stop at the Mount Shasta Shopping Center, next to the Black Bear Diner.

Accommodation

Mount Shasta has no shortage of **accommodation**, and reservations should only be necessary on weekends in the height of summer. **Campgrounds** abound in the surrounding area, but few have full amenities (hot showers are vital when the mercury drops).

Hotels, motels and B&Bs

Alpenrose Cottage Hostel, 204 E Hinckley St (☎530/926-6724). A top-quality independent hostel with a relaxed atmosphere and a great deck for watching the sunset over Mt Shasta immediately behind. There's a fully equipped kitchen, a double room for those who don't fancy the small dorms, and showers which are available to non-guests for $2. Rates are $13 a night, less by the week, and you may even be able to work for your board. Follow N Mount Shasta Boulevard north for a mile and follow the *KOA* signs. ①.

McCloud Guest House, 606 W Colombero Drive, McCloud (☎530/964-3160). Though inconveniently sited twelve miles away in McCloud, you can't go far wrong in this plush B&B set in the former logging company headquarters. Excellent breakfasts, and dinners served. ④.

Dream Inn, 326 Chestnut St (☎530/926-1536). Very central B&B, a block east of Mount Shasta Boulevard, in a Victorian house with all the usual trappings. ④.

Evergreen Lodge, 1312 S Mount Shasta Blvd (☎530/926-2143). Bargain motel a mile south of town with basic rooms (and more expensive ones with kitchenettes), a pool and hot tub. ②.

Mount Shasta Cabins & Cottages, 500 S Mount Shasta Blvd (☎530/926-5396). This organization acts as an agency for a wide range of cabins and houses in and around Mount Shasta, rented by the night but particularly suited for longer stays. Most have kitchenettes, TVs and wood stoves, and drop their rates substantially outside the summer season. ③.

Mount Shasta Ranch B&B, 1008 W A Barr Rd (☎530/926-3870). A stylish ranch house with spacious rooms and a great view of Mt Shasta. ⑤.

Stoney Brook Inn B&B, 309 W Colombero Drive, McCloud (☎1-800/369-6118 or 530/964-2300). Affordable retreat close to the ski park with comfortable rooms and an outdoor hot tub. Double rooms cost $44 with shared bath, $55 without. ②.

Travel Inn, 504 S Mount Shasta Blvd (☎530/926-4617). Decent, clean motel with basic rooms. ②.

Camping

The most picturesque campground in the area is the woodland *Lake Siskiyou Camp Resort* ($18; ☎530/926-2618), four miles west of town on a lake of the same name, where you can picnic, bathe and go boating. More **primitive sites** tend to be free if there is no piped drinking water, though creek water is often available. The most useful of these is the walk-in *Panther Meadows* (7400ft, closed in winter), high up on the mountain at the end of the Everitt Memorial Highway, though *McBride Springs* ($10; 5000ft) being lower down the same road tends to be open for longer. The fully equipped *KOA*, 900 N Mt Shasta Blvd (☎1-800/736-3617 or 530/926-4029), two blocks from downtown, charges $19 per site.

The town and around

Quite rightly, few people come to Mount Shasta for its museums, but in bad weather you might visit the otherwise missable **Sisson Museum**, 1 N Old Stage Rd (June–Aug daily 10am–4pm; Sept–May daily 1–4pm; donation), with a few examples of Native basketware, a fair bit on pioneering life in the region, and some more diverting material on the mountain itself. The brown, rainbow and eastern brook trout in the **fish hatchery** outside (daily 8am–4pm; free) can be fed on food from a vending machine.

A couple of New-Age **bookstores** along N Mount Shasta Boulevard provide the key to some of the town's more offbeat activities: Golden Bough Books at no. 219 (☎1-800/343-8888 or 530/926-3228), and Wings Bookstore at no. 226 (☎1-800/70-WINGS or 530/926-3041), have active bulletin boards and stacks of publications exhorting you to visit a sweatlodge or discover your inner goddess.

Mainly, though, Mount Shasta is full of outfits hoping to help you into the **outdoors**. Competition keeps prices reasonable and the options wide open. Obviously, there are a thousand ways to climb Mt Shasta, and these are covered in the box on p.581. Otherwise, Shasta Mountain Guides, 1938 Hill Rd (☎530/926-3117), arranges jeep trips up the mountain and conducts rock- and ice-climbing courses for all levels from $65. For real thrills, **whitewater rafting trips** on the churning Upper Sacramento are offered by Turtle River Rafting (☎530/926-3223) and River Dancers (☎530/926-3517), both starting at $80 a day. You might even try a three-day, $400 **llama trek** (the beasts only carry your bags, not you) with Rainbow Ridge Ranch (☎530/926-5794). In Weed, Shasta Cycling Adventures, 9404 N Old Stage Rd (☎530/938-3002), leads half-day **mountain bike tours** all over the Mount Shasta area for $30, and full-day tours for $45.

Eating

Aside from a rash of fast-food outlets towards I-5, Mount Shasta's **eating** options are largely health-conscious, with vegetarian dishes featured on almost every menu. Hardy mountain types are amply catered for, too, with plenty of opportunities to stoke up on hearty fare before hitting the mountain heights.

Acacia, 1136 S Mount Shasta Blvd (☎530/926-0250). Homemade pasta, seasoned chicken, and tender veal for about $10, served up in a quaint dining room. Outdoor seating when the weather permits.

The Bagel Café and Natural Bakery, 105 E Alma St (☎530/926-1414). A favorite with Mount Shasta's spiritual community, serving moderately priced soups, sandwiches, great *huevos rancheros* and, of course, bagels.

Lily's, 1013 S Mount Shasta Blvd (☎530/926-3372). Moderately priced and consistently good restaurant serving California cuisine, vegetarian and Mexican dishes. Mains cost $12–15, sandwiches around $6.

Mike and Tony's, 501 S Mount Shasta Blvd (☎530/926-4792). An excellent Italian restaurant with some good wines specializing in homemade raviolis. Dinner only; closed Wed.

Serge's, 531 Chestnut St (☎530/926-1276). Moderately priced and informal French dining at lunchtime and evenings. Several vegetarian plates are featured, and the Sunday brunch is something of a local tradition.

Simply Vegetarian, at the *Stoney Brook Inn*, 309 W Colombero Drive, McCloud (☎530/964-2300). The only fully vegetarian place around, twelve miles away in McCloud. There's a lunchtime soup and organic salad bar, and $8 full dinners, most of them vegan, in the evening. Closed Mon & Tues.

Willy's Bavarian Kitchen, 107 Chestnut St (☎530/926-3636). The pick of the town's restaurants, serving sauerbraten and wiener schnitzel alongside tasty vegetarian dishes inside or on the deck. Wash your dinner down with German beer, local microbrews or fabulous fruit shakes.

Around Mount Shasta

Five miles north of town, the treeless cone of **Black Butte** (2.5 miles; 2–3hr; 1800ft ascent), offers a more modest alternative to climbing Mount Shasta. The switchback trail to this 6325ft volcanic plug dome is hard to find without the leaflet available from the ranger station or Visitors' Bureau.

If you have time, you'd also be well advised to explore the beautiful trails that climb 4000ft up to the 225 million-year-old glacier-polished granite crags at the aptly named **Castle Crags State Park** (☎1-800/444-7275 or 530/235-2684), thirteen miles south of Mount Shasta along I-5. Campgrounds with full amenities are available for $16 per night in the often deserted 6200-acre forested park.

The decade-old **Mt Shasta Ski Park**, near McCloud on Hwy-89, has yet to establish itself on the ski circuit, so its rental charges ($17) and lift tickets ($29) are quite reasonable. **Snowboarding**, on the other hand, has created quite a scene around here – you can rent equipment at House of Ski in Mount Shasta, but the requisite goatee, baggy pants, wrap-around shades and attitude are up to you. In summer, it transforms into some of the best **mountain biking** territory in the region, with marked trails following the ski runs. A pass is $10, and bikes can be rented for $16 a day. There's also an artificial tower for climbing ($8 an hour).

After a day or two trudging around or up Mt Shasta, **Stewart Mineral Springs** (Sun–Thurs 10am–6pm, Fri & Sat 10am–8pm; ☎ 1-800/322-9223 or 530/938-2222; ①) at 4617 Stewart Springs Rd off I-5 just north of Weed provides welcome relief. Individual bathing rooms in a cedar and pine forest glade soothe your aches away for $15, less if you stay in the cabins, dorm units, tepees or campground here.

Yreka

There's little to justify more than an hour or two in quiet, leafy **YREKA** (pronounced "Why-reeka"), fifteen-odd miles north of Weed, but it makes a pleasant break. Most people come here to ride the Yreka Western Railroad, better known as the **Blue Goose** (mid-June to Aug Wed–Sun; late May to mid-June & Sept–Oct Sat & Sun only; ☎1-800/973-5277 or 530/842-4146), a 1915 Baldwin steam engine pulling attractive carriages to and from the nearby historic town of **Montague**; the three-hour excursion costs $9 and includes an hour in Montague – all very agreeable. The **Siskiyou County Museum**, 910 S Main St (summer Tues–Fri 9am–8pm, Sat 9am–5pm; rest of year Tues–Sat 9am–5pm; donation) deserves some attention, particularly the outdoor section (closes 4pm) with its historic buildings – church, houses and shops – transported here from around the county. Finally, there's a paltry collection of gold nuggets in the **County Courthouse**, 311 Fourth St (Mon–Fri 8am–5pm; free).

The **Chamber of Commerce**, inside *Sue's Coffee and Cones* at 117 W Miner St (summer Mon 9am–5pm, Tues–Fri 9am–7.30pm, Sat 10am–6.30pm; rest of year Mon–Fri 9am–5pm; ☎530/842-1649), issues maps for a self-guided **Historic Walking Tour** around Yreka's numerous Victorian homes. It can also help you find **accommodation**, not difficult with dozens of chain motels and the *Thunderbird Lodge*, 526 S Main St (☎1-800/554-4339 or 530/842-4404; ②). The *Heritage Inn*, 306 N Main St (☎530/842-6835; ①), is cheap and surprisingly adequate. **Eating** is best done along the street at *Nature's*

CLIMBING MT SHASTA

Even if you are only passing through the region, you'll be tempted to tackle Mt Shasta. Ambling among the pines of the lower slopes is rewarding enough, but the assault on the summit is the main challenge – and it can be done in a day with basic equipment and some determination.

Every year several deaths occur and numerous injuries are sustained through inexperience and over-ambition. The wise will stick to the routes prescribed by the **Mt Shasta Ranger District Office**, 204 W Alma St (summer daily 8am–4.30pm; rest of year Mon–Fri 8am–4.30pm; ☎530/926-4511), who will insist that you obtain a **wilderness permit** (also self-issued outside the office when closed and at the trailhead) and enter your name in the **voluntary climbers' register** before and after your ascent.

The mountain's isolation creates its own weather, which can change with alarming rapidity. In early summer, when most novice attempts are made, the snow cover is complete and crampons and an ice axe are a requirement to get a good grip; later during the season, as the snow melts, patches of loose ash and cinder appear, making the going more difficult and the chance of rockfall greater. Only at the end of summer, with most of the snow melted, is there a chance of climbing safely without equipment. There are countless equipment rental agencies in town, such as Fifth Season, 300 N Mount Shasta Blvd (☎530/926-3606), which can fit you out with boots ($20 for two–three days), crampons and ice axe ($16 for two–three days) and camping gear ($28 for two–three days), and provide a mountain weather forecast on ☎530/926-5555. House of Ski, 1208 Everitt Memorial Hwy (☎530/926-2359), offers much the same at very competitive rates.

Even for fit, acclimatized climbers **the ascent**, from 7000ft to over 14,000ft, will take eight to ten utterly exhausting hours. The easiest, safest and most popular way up is via **Avalanche Gulch** – just follow the footprints of the person in front of you. Drive up the mountain on the Everitt Memorial Highway to the Bunny Flat trailhead at 7000ft. A gentle hour's walk brings you to **Horse Camp**, 7900ft, a good place to acclimatize and spend the night before your ascent – there's drinking water, toilet facilities and a knowledgeable caretaker who can offer good advice about your impending climb. The return trip is done in four or five hours, depending on the recklessness of your descent: Mt Shasta is a renowned spot for **glissading** – careering down the slopes on a jacket or strong plastic sheet – a sport best left to those proficient in ice-axe arrests, but wonderfully exhilarating nonetheless.

On the lower slopes, keep your eyes skinned for the inedible **watermelon snow**, its bright red appearance caused by a microbe which flourishes here. Most importantly, be prepared for storms on the mountain. Bring extra food, stove fuel, a good, wind resistant shelter, and plenty of warm clothing. And if the weather does take a turn for the worst, don't hesitate to head back down the mountain – high elevation storms sometimes last for days, with little or no visibility.

Kitchen, 412 S Main St (☎530/842-1136; closed Sun), not at the cutesy *Grandma's Restaurant* which has an unfathomable, statewide appeal to elderly Americans whose RVs fill the parking lot. Yreka can be reached by STAGE **bus** (☎1-800/24-STAGE or 530/842-8295) from Mount Shasta and Dunsmuir.

If you're here on a Saturday, fancy a drink and don't mind backtracking a little, head twenty miles south of Yreka along Hwy-3 to charming, turn-of-the-century **ETNA**, home to the Etna Brewery, 131 Callahan St (Sat 1–5pm; ☎530/467-5277), a tiny microbrewery producing just three-hundred barrels a year for local distribution. There are usually four or five of the malty real ales and other beers available to taste, each and every one a beer drinker's dream. While here, check out the Fifties soda fountain in the Scott Valley Drugstore at the top of Main Street. And if you're really struck by the place, you can **camp** for free in the town park on Diggles Street.

Lava Beds National Monument and around

After seeing Mount Shasta you could push on to the **Lava Beds National Monument** in the far northeastern corner of the state. Carved out of the huge **Modoc National Forest**, it's actually a series of volcanic caves and huge black lava flows with a history as violent as the natural forces that created it.

Lava Beds is the most remote and forgotten of California's parks in the heart of Modoc country, a desolate outback where cowboys still ride the range, and where, as the territory of one of the last major battles with the Native Americans, there is still a suspicious relationship between the settlers and the native peoples. Until the 1850s Gold Rush it was home to the Modoc tribe, but after their repeated and bloody confrontations with the miners, the government ordered them into a reservation with the Klamath, their traditional enemy. After only a few months, the Modoc drifted back to their homeland in the lava beds, and in 1872 the army was sent in to return them by

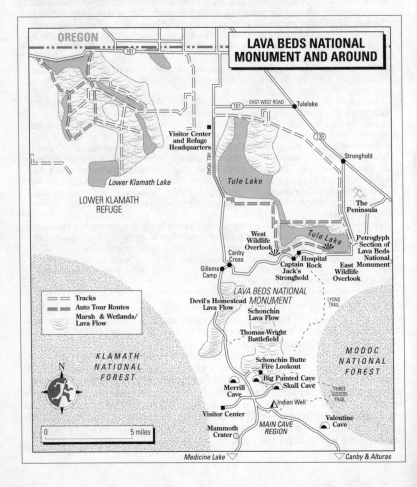

force to the reservation. It was driven back by 52 Modoc warriors under the leadership of one Kientpoos, better known as "Captain Jack," who held back an army of US regulars and volunteers twenty times the size of his for five months, from a stronghold at the northern tip of the park (see p.584).

Eventually Captain Jack was captured and hanged and what was left of the tribe sent off to a reservation in Oklahoma, where most of them died of malaria. Today the lava beds region is inhabited only by the wild deer and three million migrating ducks who attract the trickle of tourists that make it this far.

Yet further north, the **Klamath Basin National Wildlife Refuge** spreads over the border into Oregon, is seemingly choked with birdlife and makes a good side trip.

Practicalities

Lava Beds National Monument ($4 per vehicle for seven days) is 160 miles northeast of Redding, and inaccessible without a **car**. It's a conceivable day-trip from Mount Shasta, two and a half hours away, but is far more rewarding as an overnight, or even two-night, trip. The most tortuous route follows Hwy-89 to Bartle, then passing Medicine Lake (see p.585); the approach via Hwy-139 is easier, but the fastest is from the north, off US-97, and through the Klamath Basin National Wildlife Refuge (see p.585).

Pick up an excellent map of the monument from the **visitor center**, just inside the southwestern entrance (summer daily 8am–6pm; rest of year Sat & Sun 8am–5pm and sporadic weekdays; ☎530/667-2282). Close by, at Indian Wells, is the park's one **campground** ($10 in summer, $6 in winter). All **wilderness camping** throughout the monument is free and no permits are necessary, but campers must pitch at least a mile from any road, trail or camping area, and fifty yards from any cave. Be warned, though, that elevation throughout the park ranges from 4000 to 5700 feet and there's snow and freezing nights for most of the year, which can make camping uncomfortable.

The only **accommodation** center in the area, and the one place to pick up supplies (the monument can only muster a soda machine), is **TULELAKE**, 25 miles north. The near-deserted main street (Hwy-139) holds the *Park Motel* (☎530/667-2913; ②) and the *Ellis Motel* (☎530/667-5242; ②) and a few restaurants. Nearby is the **Modoc Ranger Station** (Mon–Fri 8am–4.30pm; ☎530/667-2248) with general information on the Modoc National Forest.

The monument

A day spent in the **Lava Beds** is akin to exploring the innards of a volcano, scampering down hollow tubes through which molten lava once coursed. The youngest of them were formed 30,000 years ago when volcanic upwellings sent molten, basaltic magma careering across the Modoc Plateau. As the magma came into contact with cool air, it solidified, leaving a flowing molten core feeding the expanding lava field downhill. In time, the magma flow stopped and the molten lava drained out, leaving the world's largest concentration of such hollow tubes. Most remain unexplored, but where the casing has collapsed, access is possible and you are free to scramble through. Some of the caves are so small that you have to crawl along on all fours, while others are an enormous 75 feet in diameter. Some contain Native American **petroglyphs** – not to be confused with the names painted on the cave walls by J.D. Howard, one of the first white men to explore and name the caves.

After being guided, herded, molly-coddled and generally treated as a child in any number of Californian attractions it comes as a surprise to find that at Lava Beds you are free to explore at will. Initially, though, entering the darkness alone can be an unnerving experience, so most people prefer to take the **free guided ranger walks** (daily early June to early Sept). Two-to-three-hour morning walks (9am) leave from the visitor center and explore little-known sections of the monument; afternoon tours (2pm) concentrate on ninety-minute guided cave trips, and in the evening (9pm) rangers lead hour-long campfire talks and slide shows.

If you insist on eschewing ranger guidance, you must abide by a few rules. Don't go alone, wear decent shoes, and take two flashlights each. These are available for loan (free) from the visitor center but – to ensure no one remains underground – they must be returned by closing time. For night explorations (the caves remain open) you'll need your own light source. Hard hats are strongly advised and available for $3.50 at the visitor center.

A car is vital if you're planning to tackle the northern reaches of the park around **Captain Jack's Stronghold**, a natural fortress of craggy lava flows and shallow caves on the shores of the Old Tule Lake. When you get here you'll see how the Modoc managed to hide and move around through the passageways of the hill (which from the outside looks like nothing special). Two **self-guided trails** (one half a mile, the other 1.5 miles) will take you through the fort, pointing out significant spots along the way. Two miles west, the shallow lava bowl of **Hospital Rock** marks the point where one Lt Sherwood, wounded by the Modoc, was unsuccessfully tended in a makeshift field hospital towards the end of the siege on the stronghold.

EXPLORING THE LAVA TUBES

Most of the interest in Lava Beds lies around the visitor center, where the largest concentration of caves can be visited on the short **Cave Loop** access road. For a confidence-building handle on your location in the twenty-five "developed" caves – less than a tenth of the known total – get the *Lava Caves Map* ($4.50) from the visitor center. New ones are discovered all the time, so the possibilities are almost endless, but for the moment, the tried and tested caves below should be enough to be going on with.

Catacomb Cave At over a mile long, this is the longest open tube in the monument, though you need perseverance, a slim body and a cool head to get anywhere near the end. The profusion of interconnecting passageways make it one of the most confusing; keep track of whether you are heading up or downhill.

Fern Cave Full of ferns growing in patches of light where the roof has fallen in, with Native pictographs on the walls.

Labyrinth Striking geological features – lava pillars and lavacicles – and evidence of Native American habitation.

Mushpot Cave Right by the visitor center, this is the most developed of the caves. It provides a good introduction, is lit during center opening hours, and has interpretive panels highlighting key features.

Skull Cave Named for Bighorn skulls found when the cave was discovered by early explorer E.L. Hopkins, this has the largest entrance of any of the lava tubes and contains ice all year round.

Symbol Bridge and **Big Painted Cave** (1.5 mile round trip; almost flat). Two very worthwhile caves adjacent to each other on a trail north of the visitor center. No flashlight is needed though one could come in handy. Some of the best examples of pictographs in the Monument – tentatively dated between 1000AD and 1500AD – show up as different angles of sunlight catch the rocks beside the entrance. Respecting Modoc sensibilities, make two clockwise turns before descending into a large cave, open at both ends (hence the "bridge" name), in which zigzags, squiggles, sunbursts and human figures are picked out in grease and charcoal on pumice-washed background. Make a single anti-clockwise turn on departure for Big Painted Cave, where the pictographs are less impressive. In the mid 1920s J.D. Howard excavated a small tunnel at the very back of the cave to reveal an ice flow in a cavity fifteen feet down: with a flashlight you can scramble down there.

Around the monument

Small volcanic craters, buttes, spatter cones and chimneys dot Lava Beds, but the flows which produced most of the lava tubes came from **Mammoth Crater** on the southern perimeter of the monument, where a short path leads to a viewpoint overlooking the deep conical crater.

Underlying the most recent of Lava Beds' fabulous creations is a bed of basalt, the product of a huge shield volcano with a profile so flat it is barely noticeable. Its core is now filled by the sub-alpine **Medicine Lake**, ten miles southwest of Mammoth Crater. Formerly a Modoc healing center, the only therapies on offer today are fishing and swimming from the $7 **campsites** along the north shore.

More volcanic spectacle lies just west at **Glass Mountain**, made almost entirely of glassy, black obsidian – source of Modoc arrowheads – but covered in fluffy, white pumice quarried for stonewashing jeans. A short and fairly easy trail leads in from the road. Just beyond the monument's northeast corner, a small outlier known as the Petroglyph Section contains **Petroglyph Point**, a three-hundred-yard-long cliff face made of "tuff," volcanic rock formed when lava flows hit Old Tule Lake. The soft rock offers some fine, but cryptic, examples of ancient art: shields, female figures and a series of small circles thought to represent travel. Pick up an interpretive leaflet at the visitor center.

East of the Petroglyphs Section, the road continues to Hwy-139 and the town of **NEWELL**, site of the **Tule Lake Camp**, where 110,000 people of Japanese descent, many of them American citizens, were interned without charge or trial between 1942 and 1946. Many of the camp buildings have been sold off to local farmers, but the wooden-sided police and military barracks remain.

Perhaps the most rewarding excursion from the monument, though, is to the **Klamath Basin National Wildlife Refuge** (open daylight hours), just to the north and spreading into Oregon. One of the last wetlands in California, with swathes of open water and emerging vegetation on the shoreline, it attracts an estimated eighty percent of birds following the Pacific Flyway, the major migration routes from Alaska and northern Canada to Baja California in Mexico. In spring and fall, almost a hundred species are present and the population tops a million. The most accessible reaches are the **Lower Klamath Refuge** and **Tule Lake**, an open body of water surrounded by reeds (*tule* in Modoc). At the northwestern corner of the latter, the **visitor center** (Mon–Fri 8am–4.30pm, Sat & Sun 10am–4pm; ☎530/667-2231) issues free permits for the birdwatching blinds: call ahead to be sure of getting one. Surprisingly, the best way of spotting the wildlife is by driving along designated routes: getting out of the car and walking scares the birds off.

travel details

Trains

Oakland to: Chico (1 daily; 4hr 30min); Redding (1 daily; 5hr 44min).

Buses

Combined Greyhound and Amtrak Thruway schedules.

Arcata to: Crescent City (2 daily; 1hr 30min); Garberville (2 daily; 1hr 30min).

Chico to: Redding (4 daily; 1hr 30min).

Eureka to: Crescent City (2 daily; 1hr 50min); Garberville (2 daily; 1hr 30min).

Mount Shasta to: Yreka (3 daily; 50min).

Redding to: Chico (5 daily; 2hr); Mount Shasta (4 daily; 1hr 30min); Sacramento (7 daily; 4hr); Yreka (3 daily; 2hr 15min).

San Francisco to: Chico (4 daily; 5hr); Redding (5 daily; 6hr); Santa Rosa (2 daily; 1hr 30min).

Santa Rosa to: Arcata (2 daily; 6hr); Crescent City (2 daily; 8hr); Eureka (2 daily; 4hr 40min); Garberville (2 daily; 4hr); Leggett (2 daily; 3hr 30min); Willits (2 daily; 2hr).

PART THREE

THE
CONTEXTS

THE HISTORICAL FRAMEWORK

To many people, California seems one of the least historic places on the planet. Unburdened by the past, it's a land where anything seems possible, whose inhabitants live carefree lives, wholly in and for the present moment. Its very name, appropriately for all its idealized images, is a work of fiction, free from any historical significance. The word first appeared as the name of an island, located "very near to the terrestrial paradise" and inhabited entirely by Amazons "without any men among them," in a popular Spanish picaresque novel of the early 1500s, *Las Sergas de Esplandián* by García de Montalvo.

NATIVE PEOPLES

For thousands of years prior to the arrival of Europeans, the **aboriginal peoples** of California flourished in the naturally abundant land, living fairly peacefully in tribes along the coast and in the deserts and the forested mountains. Anthropologists estimate that nearly half the native population then living within the boundaries of the present-day US were spread throughout what's now California, in small, tribal villages of a few hundred people, each with a clearly defined territory and often its own distinct language. Since there was no political or social organization beyond the immediate level of the tribe, it was not difficult for the colonizing Spaniards to divide and

to conquer, effectively wiping them out – though admittedly more died through epidemics of disease than outright genocide.

Very little remains to mark the existence of the Californian Native Americans: they had no form of written language, relatively undeveloped craft skills, and built next to nothing that would last beyond the change of seasons. About the only surviving signs of the coastal tribes are the piles of seashells and discarded arrowheads that have been found, from which anthropologists have deduced a bit about their cultures. Also, a few examples of **rock art** survive, as at the Chumash Painted Cave, near Santa Barbara on the Central Coast. Similar sorts of petroglyph figures were drawn by the Paiute Native Americans, who lived in the deserts near Death Valley, and by the Miwok from the Sierra Nevada foothills.

DISCOVERY AND EARLY EXPLORATION

The first Europeans to set foot in California were Spanish explorers, intent on extending their colony of New Spain, which under the 1494 Treaty of Tordesillas included all the New World lands west of Brazil and all of North America west of the Rocky Mountains. In 1535, **Hernán Cortéz**, fresh from decimating the Aztecs, headed westward in search of a short cut to Asia, which he believed to be adjacent to Mexico. Though he never reached what's now California, he set up a small colony at the southern tip of the Baja (lower) California peninsula. He thought it was an island, and named it Santa Cruz, writing in his journals that he soon expected to find the imagined island of the Amazons.

The first explorer to use the name California, and to reach what's now the US state, was **Juan Cabrillo**, who sighted San Diego harbor in 1542, and continued north along the coast to the Channel Islands off Santa Barbara. He died there six months later, persistent headwinds having made it impossible to sail any further north. His crew later made it as far north as what is now the state of Oregon, but were unable to find any safe anchorage and returned home starved and half-dead from scurvy. It was fifty years before another Spaniard braved the difficult journey: **Juan de Fuca**'s 1592 voyage caused great excitement when he claimed to have discovered the Northwest Passage, a potentially lucrative trade route across North

America. It has long since turned out that there is no such thing as the Northwest Passage (de Fuca may have discovered the Puget Sound, outside Seattle), but Europeans continued to search for it for the next two hundred years.

The British explorer **Sir Francis Drake** arrived in the *Golden Hind* in 1579, taking a break from his piracy of Spanish vessels in order to make repairs. His landing spot, now called Drake's Bay, near Point Reyes north of San Francisco, had "white bancks and cliffes" that reminded him of Dover. Upon landing, he was met by a band of native Miwoks, who feted him with food and drink and placed a feathered crown upon his head; in return, he claimed all of their lands – which he called Nova Albion (New England) – for Queen Elizabeth, supposedly leaving behind a brass plaque that's now on display in the Bancroft Library at the University of California.

Setting sail from Acapulco in 1602, **Sebastián Vizcaíno**, a Portuguese explorer under contract to Spain, made a more lasting impact than his predecessors, undertaking the most extensive exploration of the coast, and bestowing most of the place names that survive. In order to impress his superiors he exaggerated the value of his discoveries, describing a perfect, sheltered harbor which he named **Monterey** in honor of his patron back in Mexico. Subsequent colonizers based their efforts, 150 years later, upon these fraudulent claims (the windy bay did not live up to Vizcaíno's estimation), and the headquarters of the missions and military and administrative center of the Spanish government remained at Monterey, 100 miles south of San Francisco, for the next 75 years.

COLONIZATION: THE SPANISH AND THE BRITISH

The Spanish occupation of California began in earnest in 1769 as a combination of military expediency (to prevent other powers from gaining a foothold) and Catholic missionary zeal (to convert the heathen Native Americans). Father **Junípero Serra** and a company of three hundred soldiers and clergy set off from Mexico for Monterey, half of them by ship, the other half overland. In June 1770, after establishing a small mission and *presidio* (fort) at San Diego, the expedition arrived at Monterey where another mission and small *presidio* were constructed.

The Spanish continued to build missions all along the coast, ostensibly to Catholicize the Native Americans, which they did with inquisitional obsession. The mission complexes were broadly similar, with a church and cloistered residential structure surrounded by irrigated fields, vineyards, and more extensive ranchlands. The labor of the Native American converts was co-opted: they were put to work making soap and candles, were often beaten and never educated. Objective accounts of the missionaries' treatment of the indigenous peoples are rare, though mission registries record twice as many deaths as they do births, and their cemeteries are packed with Native American dead. Not all of the Native Americans gave up without a fight: many missions suffered from raids, and the now ubiquitous red-tiled roofs were originally a replacement for the earlier thatch to better resist arson attacks.

Most of the mission structures that survive today were built to the designs of Serra's successor, Father **Fermín de Lasuén**, who was in charge of the missions during the period of their greatest growth. By the time of his death in 1804, a chain of twenty one missions, each a long day's walk from its neighbors and linked by the dirt path of *El Camino Real* (The Royal Road), ran from San Diego to San Francisco.

During this time the first towns, called **pueblos**, were established in order to attract settlers to what was still a distant and undesirable territory. The first was laid out in 1777 at San Jose, south of the new mission at San Francisco. Los Angeles, the second *pueblo*, was established in 1781, though neither had more than a hundred inhabitants until well into the 1800s.

One reason for Spain's military presence in California – which consisted of four *presidios* all told, with twelve cannons and only two hundred soldiers – was to prevent the expansion of the small **Russian** colony based in Alaska, mostly trappers collecting beaver and otter pelts in the Northwestern states of Washington and Oregon. The two countries were at peace and relations friendly, and in any case the Spanish *presidios* were in no position to enforce their territorial claims. In fact, they were so short of supplies and ammunition that they had to borrow the gunpowder to fire welcoming salutes whenever the two forces came into contact. Well aware of the Spanish weakness, in 1812 the Russians established an outpost, called **Fort Ross**, sixty miles north of San Francisco. This further undermined Spanish sovereignty over the region, though the Russians abandoned the fort in 1841, selling it to John Sutter (who features prominently in later California history; see p.592).

THE MEXICAN ERA

While Spain, France and England were engaged in the bitter struggles of the Napoleonic Wars, the colonies of New Spain rebelled against imperial neglect, with Mexico finally gaining independence in 1821. The Mexican Republic, or the United States of Mexico as the new country called itself, governed California as a terri-tory, though none of the fifteen distinct administrations it set up – lacking the money to pay for improvements and the soldiers needed to enforce the laws – was ever able to exercise any degree of authority.

The most important effect of the Mexican era was the final **secularization** in 1834, after years of gradual diminution, of the Franciscan missions. As most of the missionaries were Spanish, under Mexican rule they had seen their position steadily eroded by the increasingly wealthy, close-knit families of the *Californios* – Mexican immigrants who'd been granted vast tracts of ranchland. The government's intention was that half of the missions' extensive lands should go to the Indian converts, but this was never carried out, and the few powerful families divided most of it up among themselves.

In many ways this was the most lawless and wantonly wasteful period of California's history, an era described by **Richard Henry Dana** – scion of a distinguished Boston family, who dropped out of Harvard to sail to California – in his 1840 book *Two Years Before the Mast*. Most of the agriculture and cottage industries that had developed under the missionaries disappeared, and it was a point of pride amongst the *Californios* not to do any work that couldn't be done from horseback. Dana's Puritan values led him to heap scorn upon the "idle and thriftless people" who made nothing for themselves. For example, the large herds of cattle that lived on the mission lands were slaughtered for their hides and sold to Yankee traders, who turned the hides into leather which they sold back to the *Californios* at a tidy profit. "In the hands of an enterprising people," he wrote, "what a country this might be."

THE FIRST AMERICANS

Throughout the Mexican and Spanish eras, foreigners were legally banned from settling, and the few who showed up, mostly sick or injured sailors dropped off to regain their health, were often jailed until they proved themselves useful, either as craftsmen or as traders able to supply needed goods. In the late 1820s the first **Americans**, males without exception, began to make their way to California. They tended to fit in with the existing Mexican culture, often marrying into established families and converting to the Catholic faith. The American presence grew slowly but surely as more and more people emigrated, still mostly by way of a three-month sea voyage around Cape Horn. Among these was **Thomas Larkin**, a New England merchant who, in 1832, set up shop in Monterey, and later was instrumental in pointing the disgruntled *Californios* towards the more accommodating US; Larkin's wife Rachel was the first American woman on the West Coast.

The first people to make the four-month journey to California overland – in a covered wagon like in so many Hollywood Westerns – arrived in 1841, having forged a trail over the Sierra Nevada mountains via Truckee Pass, just north of Lake Tahoe. Soon after, hundreds of people each year were following in their tracks. In 1846, however, forty migrants, collectively known as the **Donner Party**, died when they were trapped in the mountains by early winter snowfall. The immense difficulties involved in reaching California, over land and by sea, kept population levels at a minimum, and by 1846 just seven thousand people, not counting Native Americans but including all the Spanish and Mexicans, lived in the entire region.

THE MEXICAN–AMERICAN WAR

From the 1830s onwards – inspired by **Manifest Destiny**, the popular, almost religious belief that the United States was meant to cover the continent from coast to coast – US government policy regarding California was to buy all of Mexico's land north of the Rio Grande, the river that now divides the US and Mexico. President Andrew Jackson was highly suspicious of British designs on the West Coast – he himself had been held as a (fourteen-year-old) prisoner of war during the Revolutionary War of 1776 – and various diplomatic overtures were made to the

Mexican Republic, all of which backfired. In April 1846 Jackson's protégé, President James Polk, offered forty million dollars for all of New Mexico and the California territory, but his simultaneous annexation of the newly independent Republic of Texas – which Mexico still claimed – resulted in the outbreak of war.

Almost all the fighting of the **Mexican–American War** took place in Texas; only one real battle was ever fought on Californian soil, at San Pasqual, northeast of San Diego, where a roving US battalion was surprised by a band of pro-Mexican *Californios*, who killed twenty-two soldiers and wounded another fifteen before withdrawing south into Mexico. Monterey, still the territorial capital, was captured by the US Navy without a shot being fired, and in January 1847, when the rebel *Californios* surrendered to the US forces at Cahuenga, near Los Angeles, the Americans controlled the entire West Coast.

Just before the war began, California had made a brief foray into the field of self-government: the short-lived **Bear Flag Republic**, whose only lasting effect was to create what's still the state flag, a prowling grizzly bear with the words "California Republic" written below. In June 1846, American settlers in the Sonoma Valley took over the local *presidio* – long abandoned by the Mexicans – and declared California independent, which lasted for all of three weeks until the US forces took command.

THE GOLD RUSH

As part of the Treaty of Guadalupe Hidalgo, which formally ended the war in 1848, Mexico ceded all of the *Alta California* territory to the US. Nine days before the signing of the accord, in the distant foothills of the Sierra Nevada mountains, flakes of **gold** were discovered by workmen building a sawmill along the American River at Coloma, though it was months before this momentous conjunction of events became known.

At the time, California's non-Native American population was mostly concentrated in the few small towns along the coastal strip. Early rumors of gold attracted a trickle of prospectors, and, following news of their subsequent success, by the middle of 1849 – eighteen months after the initial find – men were flooding into California from all over, in the most madcap migration in world history. **Sutter's Fort**, a small agricultural community, trading post and stage stop which had been established six years earlier by John Sutter on the banks of the American River, was overrun by miners, who headed up into the nearby foothills to make their fortune. Some did, most didn't, but in any case, within fifteen years most of the gold had been picked clean. The miners moved on or went home and their camps vanished, prompting Mark Twain to write that "in no other land, in modern times, have towns so absolutely died and disappeared as in the old mining regions of California."

STATEHOOD

Following the US takeover after the defeat of Mexico, a **Constitutional Convention** was held at Monterey in the autumn of 1849. The men who attended were not the miners – most of whom were more interested in searching for gold – but those who had been in California for some time (about three years on average). At the time, the Territory of California extended all the way east to Utah, so the main topic of discussion was where to draw the eastern boundary of the intended state. The drawing up of a state constitution was also important, since it was the basis on which California applied for admission to the US. The constitution contained a couple of noteworthy inclusions. To protect the dignity of the manually laboring miners, **slavery** was prohibited; and to attract well-heeled **women** from the East Coast, California was the first state to recognize in legal terms the separate property of a married woman. In 1850, California was admitted to the US as the thirty-first state.

THE INDIAN WARS

Though the US Civil War had little effect on California, many bloody battles were fought throughout the 1850s and 1860s by white settlers and US troops against the various Native American tribes whose lands the immigrants wanted. At first the government tried to move willing tribes to fairly large reservations, but as more settlers moved in the tribes were pushed onto smaller and smaller tracts. The most powerful resistance to the well-armed invaders came in the mountainous northeast of California, where a band of **Modoc** fought a long-running guerrilla war, using their superior knowledge of the terrain to evade the US troops.

Due to a combination of disease and lack of food, as well as deliberate acts of violence, the Native American population was drastically reduced, and by 1870 almost ninety percent had been wiped out. The survivors were concentrated in small, relatively valueless reservations, where their descendants still live: the Cahuila near Palm Springs, the Paiute/Shoshone in the Owens Valley, and the Hupa on the northwest coast continue to reside near their ancestral homelands, and are quite naturally defensive of their privacy.

THE BOOM YEARS: 1870–1900

After the Gold Rush, **San Francisco** boomed into a boisterous frontier town, exploding in population from 500 to 50,000 within five years. Though far removed from the mines themselves, the city was the main landing spot for shipborne Argonauts (as the prospectors were called), and the main supply town. Moreover, it was the place where successful miners went to blow their hard-earned cash on the whisky and women of the **Barbary Coast**, then the raunchiest waterfront in the world, full of brothels, saloons and opium dens. Ten years later, San Francisco enjoyed an even bigger boom as a result of the silver mines of the Comstock Lode in Nevada, owned in the main by San Franciscans, who displayed their wealth by building grand palaces and mansions on Nob Hill – still the city's most exclusive address.

The completion in 1869 of the **transcontinental railroad**, built using imported Chinese laborers, was a major turning point in the settlement of California. Whereas the trip across the country by stagecoach took at least a month, and was subject to scorching hot weather and attacks by hostile natives, the crossing could now be completed in just five days.

In 1875, when the Santa Fe railroad reached Los Angeles (the railroad company having extracted huge bribes from local officials to ensure the budding city wasn't bypassed), there were just ten thousand people living in the whole of **Southern California**, divided equally between San Diego and Los Angeles. A rate war developed between the two rival railroads, and ticket costs dropped to as little as $1 for a one-way ticket from New York. Land speculators placed advertisements in East Coast and European papers, offering cheap land for homesteaders in towns and suburbs all over the West Coast that as often as not existed only on paper. By the end of the nineteenth century, thousands of people, ranging from Midwestern farmers to the East Coast elite, had moved to California to take advantage of the fertile land and mild climate.

MODERN TIMES

The greatest boost to California's fortunes was, of course, the **film industry**, which moved here from the East Coast in 1911, attracted by the temperate climate that enabled films to be shot outdoors year-round, and by the incredibly cheap land that allowed large indoor studios to be built at comparatively little cost. Within three years, movies like D.W. Griffith's *Birth of a Nation* – most of which was filmed along the dry banks of the Los Angeles River – were being cranked out by the hundred.

Hollywood, a suburb of Los Angeles that was the site of many of the early studios, and ever since the buzzword for the entire entertainment industry, has done more to promote the mystique of California as a pleasure garden landscape than any other medium, disseminating images of its glamorous lifestyles around the globe. Los Angeles still dominates the world film industry, and, increasingly, is an international center for the music business as well.

This widespread, idealized image had a magnetic effect during the **Great Depression** of the 1930s, when thousands of people from all over the country descended upon California, which was perceived to be – and for the most part was – immune from the economic downturn which crippled the rest of the US. From the Dust Bowl Midwest, entire families, who came to be known as **Okies**, packed up everything they owned and set off for the farms of the Central Valley, an epic journey captured by John Steinbeck's bestselling novel *The Grapes of Wrath*, in the photographs of Dorothea Lange, and in the baleful tunes of folk singer Woody Guthrie. Some Californians who feared losing their jobs to the incoming Okies formed vigilante groups and, with the complicity of local and state police, set up roadblocks along the main highways to prevent unemployed outsiders from entering the state.

One Depression-era initiative to alleviate the poverty, and to get the economy moving again, were the US government-sponsored

Works Progress Administration (WPA) construction projects, ranging from restoring the California missions to building trails and park facilities, and commissioning art works like the marvellous Social Realist murals in San Francisco's Coit Tower.

Things turned around when **World War II** brought heavy industry to California, as shipyards and aeroplane factories sprang up, providing well-paid employment in wartime factories. After the war, most stayed on, and still today California companies – McDonnell Douglas, Lockheed, Rockwell and General Dynamics, for example – make up the roll call of suppliers to the US military and space programmes. More recently, the "Silicon Valley" area south of San Francisco has been at the forefront of hi-tech developments in the computer industry.

After the war many of the soldiers who'd passed through on their way to the battle-grounds of the South Pacific came back to California and decided to stay on. There was plenty of well-paid work, the US government subsidized house purchases for war veterans and, most importantly, constructed the **freeways** and Interstate highways that enabled land speculators to build new commuter suburbs on land that had been used for farms and citrus orchards.

The **Fifties** brought prosperity to the bulk of middle-class America (typified by President Eisenhower's goal of "two cars in every garage and a chicken in every pot"), and California, particularly San Francisco, became a nexus for alternative artists and writers, spurring an immigration of intellectuals that by the end of the decade had become manifest as the **Beat generation**, pegged "Beatniks," in honor of Sputnik, the Soviet space satellite, by San Francisco columnist Herb Caen.

California remained at the forefront of youth and **social upheavals** into and throughout the **Sixties**. In a series of drug tests carried out at Stanford University – paid for by the CIA, who were interested in developing a "truth drug" for interrogation purposes – unwitting students were dosed with **LSD**. One of the guinea pigs was the writer Ken Kesey, who had just published the highly acclaimed novel *One Flew Over the Cuckoo's Nest*. Kesey quite liked the experience and soon secured a personal supply of the drug (which was as yet still legal) and toured the West Coast to spread the word of

"Acid" In and around San Francisco Kesey and his crew, the Merry Pranksters, turned on huge crowds at **Electric Kool-Aid Acid Tests** – in which LSD was diluted into bowls of the soft drink Kool-Aid – complete with psychedelic light shows and music by the Grateful Dead. The Acid craze reached its height during the **Summer of Love** in 1967, when the entire Haight-Ashbury district of San Francisco seemed populated by barefoot and drugged Flower Children.

Within a year the superficial peace of Flower Power was shattered, as protests mounted against US involvement in the **Vietnam War**; Martin Luther King and Bobby Kennedy, heroes of left-leaning youth, were both gunned down – Kennedy in Los Angeles after winning the California primary of the 1968 presidential election. The militant **Black Panthers**, a group of black radical activists based in Oakland, terrorized a white population that had earlier been supporters of the Civil Rights Movement. By the end of the Sixties the "system," in California especially, seemed to be at breaking point, and the atrocities committed by **Charles Manson** and his "Family" proved what the rest of the US had known all along: that California was full of madmen and murderers.

The antiwar protests, concentrated at the University of California campus in Berkeley, continued through the early **Seventies**. Emerging from the milieu of revolutionary and radical groups, the Symbionese Liberation Army, a small, well-armed and stridently revolutionary group, set about the overthrow of the US, attracting media (and FBI) attention by murdering civil servants, robbing banks and, most famously, kidnapping nineteen-year-old heiress **Patty Hearst**. Amid much media attention Hearst converted to the SLA's cause, changing her name to Tanya and for the next two years – until her capture in 1977 – she went underground, provoking national debate about her motives and beliefs.

After the unrest of the previous decade, the **late Seventies** were decidedly dull. The one interesting phenomenon was the rise of **cults**, among them LA's Scientology Church, megalomaniac L. Ron Hubbard's personality-testing sect; the Moonies, who pestered people at airports and public places all over the coast; and San Francisco's People's Temple, of which over a thousand members died when their leader,

Jim Jones, dosed them with cyanide in a religious service held at their commune in Guyana. The most public and visible of the lot were the followers of the **Bhagwan Shree Rajshneesh**, clothed entirely in shades of red.

Californian **politics**, after Watergate and the end of American involvement in Vietnam, seemed to lose whatever idealistic fervor it might once have had, and popular culture withdrew into self-satisfaction, typified by the smug harmonies of musicians like the Eagles and Jackson Browne. While the Sixties upheavals were overseen by California Governor Ronald Reagan, who was ready and willing to fight the long-haired hippies, the 1970s saw the reign of "Governor Moonbeam" Jerry Brown, under whose leadership California enacted some of the most stringent **anti-pollution** measures in the world – one of which pays environmental activists to expose corporate polluters, offering a 25 percent commission on the multi-million-dollar fines imposed by the courts. The state also actively encouraged the development of renewable forms of energy such as solar and wind power, and protected the entire coastline from despoliation and development. California also decriminalized the possession of under an ounce of **marijuana** (though it remains an offense to grow or sell it), and the harvesting of marijuana in both states continues to account for over $1 billion each year, making it the number-one cash crop in the number-one agricultural region in the US.

The easy-money **Eighties** crash-landed in a tangled mess, with LA junk-bond king Michael Milkin convicted of multi-billion-dollar fraud and the S&L banking scandals enmeshing such high-ranking politicos as California Senator Alan Cranston, and the **Nineties** kicked off with a stagnant property market and rising unemployment.

In **Los Angeles**, the videotaped beating of black motorist Rodney King by uniformed officers of the LA Police Department, and the subsequent acquittal of those officers by the jurors of conservative Simi Valley, sparked off destructive **rioting** in April 1992. State and federal authorities, forced into taking notice of LA's endemic poverty and violence, promised all sorts of new initiatives – with, as yet, few concrete results. The race issue also dominated the year-long trial of black former football star **O.J. Simpson** – accused and finally acquitted of murdering his ex-wife and a male friend – splitting public opinion into directly opposed camps of black and white. The result, when it came, prompted jubilation and disbelief in equal measure.

Such events, coupled with a chain of natural disasters – the wildfires of 1993, followed by the devastating 6.8-scale earthquake and mud slides of January 1994 – have so eroded local morale that for the first time in history a majority of residents would like to move *away from* LA – if they could. Many of those with the means have upped sticks to Oregon, Washington or the desert states to the east. Those who remain fence themselves off in exclusive, security-patrolled compounds, and the 1994 passage of Proposition 187, a state law denying access to health and education services to illegal immigrants, has only served to widen the chasm between rich and poor.

San Francisco, too, has been hit hard: on top of AIDS-related illnesses stretching health services, the area has been hit by a series of natural disasters. An **earthquake** in October 1989 devastated much of the San Francisco Bay Area, followed two years later by a massive **fire** in the Oakland Hills which burned over two thousand homes and killed two dozen people – the third worst fire in US history.

Somehow, despite all this, California still clings on to its aura as something of a promised land. Barring its complete destruction by the **Big One** (the earthquake that's destined one day to drop half of the state into the Pacific and wipe out the rest under massive tidal waves), the state seems set to continue much as it is, as the source of so much of the nation's wealth, with successful Silicon Valley companies like Hewlett Packard, Intel, Oracle, Sun and Netscape in particular, sparking new growth and prosperity.

WILDLIFE

Though popularly imagined as little more than palm trees and golden sand beaches, for sheer range of landscape, California is hard to beat. With glaciated alpine peaks and meadows, desolate desert sand dunes and flat, fertile agricultural plains, it's no wonder that Hollywood film-makers have so often and successfully used California locations to simulate distant and exotic scenes. These diverse landscapes also support an immense variety of plant and animal life, much of which – due to the protection offered by the various state and National Parks, forests and wilderness areas – is both easily accessible and unspoiled by encroaching civilization.

BACKGROUND: LANDSCAPES, GEOLOGY AND EARTHQUAKES

California's landscape has been formed over millions of years through the interaction of all the main geological processes: Ice Age glaciation, erosion, earthquakes and volcanic eruptions. The most impressive results can be seen in **Yosemite National Park**, east of San Francisco, where solid walls of granite have been sliced and shaped into unforgettable cliffs and chasms. In contrast, the sand dunes of **Death Valley** are being constantly shaped and reshaped by the dry desert winds, surrounded by foothills tinted by oxidized mineral deposits into every color of the spectrum.

Earthquakes – which earned Los Angeles the truck driver's nickname "Shakeytown" – are the most powerful expression of the volatile unrest underlying the placid surface. California sits on the Pacific "Ring of Fire," at the junction of two tectonic plates slowly drifting deep within the earth. Besides the occasional earthquake – like the 1906 quake which flattened San Francisco, or the 1994 tremor which collapsed many of LA's freeways – this instability is also the cause of California's many **volcanoes**. Distinguished by their symmetrical, conical shape, almost all of them are now dormant, though Mount Lassen, in Northern California, did erupt in 1914 and 1915, destroying much of the surrounding forest. Along with the boiling mud pools that accompany even the dormant volcanoes, the most attractive features of volcanic regions are the bubbling **hot springs** – pools of water that flow up from deep underground, heated to a sybaritically soothing temperature. Hot springs occur naturally all over the state, and though some have now been developed into luxurious health spas, most remain in their natural condition, where you can soak your bones *au naturel* surrounded by mountain meadows or wide-open deserts. The best of these are listed throughout the Guide.

Though some of the most fantastic **wildlife**, like the grizzly bear – a ten-foot-tall, two-ton giant that still adorns the state flag of California – and the California condor – one of the world's largest birds, with a wingspan of over eight feet – are now extinct in their natural habitats, plenty more are still alive and thriving, like the otters, elephant seals and gray whales seen all along the coast, and the chubby marmots – shy mammals often found sunning themselves on rocks in higher reaches of the mountains. Plant life is equally varied, from the brilliant but short-lived desert wildflowers to the timeless Bristlecone pine trees, which live for thousands of years on the arid peaks of the Great Basin desert.

Below you will find details of the major **ecosystems** of California. The accounts are inevitably brief, as the area encompasses almost 320,000 square miles (ranging from moist coastal forests and the snow-capped Sierra Nevada peaks to Death Valley, 276 feet below sea level with an annual rainfall of two inches), and is inhabited by a multitude of species. Native to California are 54 species of cactus, 123 species of amphibians and reptiles, 260 species of birds, and 27,000–28,000 species of insects. See "Books" for recommendations of more specific habitat guides. Bear in mind, also, that museums all over the state examine and exhibit the natural world in depth, notably Monterey's superb Aquarium – see p.365 for details.

THE OCEAN

The **Pacific Ocean** determines California's climate, keeping the coastal temperatures moderate all year round. During the spring and summer, cold nutrient-rich waters rise or well up to produce cooling banks of fog and abundant crops of phytoplankton (microscopic algae). The algae nourishes creatures such as krill (small shrimps), which in their turn provide baby food for juvenile fish. This food chain provides fodder for millions of nesting **seabirds**, as well as harbor and elephant seals, California **sea lions** and whales. **Gray whales**, the most common species spotted from land, were once almost hunted to the point of extinction, but have returned to the coast in large numbers. During their southward migration to their breeding grounds off Mexico, from December to January, it is easy to spot them from prominent headlands all along the coast, and most harbors have charter services offering whale-watching tours. On their way back to the Arctic Sea, in February and March, the newborn whale pups can sometimes be seen playfully leaping out of the water, or "breaching." Look for the whale's white-plumed spout – once at the surface, it will usually blow several times in succession.

TIDEPOOLS

California's shoreline is composed of three primary ecosystems: tidepools, sandy beach and estuary. To explore the **tidepools**, first consult a local newspaper to see when the low tides (two daily) will occur. Be careful of waves, don't be out too far from the shore when the tide returns, and also watch your step – there are many small lives underfoot. There are miles of beaches with tidepools, some of the best at Pacific Grove near Monterey. Here you will find **sea anemones** (they look like green zinnias), hermit crabs, purple and green shore crabs, red sponges, purple sea urchins, starfish ranging from the size of a dime to the size of a hub cap,

mussels, abalone and chinese-hat limpets – to name a few. You may also see black **oyster-catchers**, their squawking easily heard over the surf, foraging for an unwary, lips-agape mussel. Gulls and black turnstones are also common, and during the summer brown pelicans dive for fish just offshore.

The life of the tidepool party is the **hermit crab**, who protects its soft and vulnerable hindquarters with scavenged shells, usually those of the aptly named black turban snail. Hermit crabs scurry busily around in search of a detritus snack, or scuffle with other hermit crabs over the proprietorship of vacant snail shells.

Pacific Grove is also home to large populations of **sea otters**. Unlike most marine mammals, sea otters keep themselves warm with a thick soft coat rather than blubber. The trade in sea otter pelts brought entrepreneurial Russian and British fur hunters to the West Coast, and by the mid-nineteenth century the otters were virtually extinct. In 1938, a small population was discovered near Big Sur, and with careful protection otters have re-established themselves in the southern part of their range. They are charming creatures with big rubbery noses and Groucho Marx moustaches. With binoculars, it's easy to spot them amongst the bobbing kelp, where they lie on their backs opening sea urchins with a rock, or sleep entwined within a seat belt of kelp which keeps them from floating away. The bulk of the population resides between Monterey Bay and the Channel Islands, but – aside from Pacific Grove – the best places to see them are Point Lobos State Park, the Seventeen-Mile Drive and the Monterey Wharf, where, along with sea lions, they often come to beg for fish.

Many of the **seaweeds** you see growing from the rocks are edible. As one would expect from a Pacific beachfront, there are also **palms** – sea palms, with four-inch-long rubbery stems and flagella-like fronds. Their thick root-like holdfasts provide shelter for small crabs. You will also find giant **kelp** washed up on shore – harvested commercially for use in thickening ice cream.

SANDY BEACHES

The long, golden **sandy beaches** for which California is so famous may look sterile from a distance. However, observe the margin of sand exposed as a gentle wave recedes, and you will see jetstreams of small bubbles emerge from numerous clams and mole crabs. Small shore birds called **sanderlings** race amongst the waves in search of these morsels, and sand dollars are often easy to find along the high tide line.

The most unusual sandy-shore bathing beauties are the **northern elephant seals**, which will tolerate rocky beaches but favor soft sand mattresses for their rotund torsos. The males, or bulls, can reach lengths of over six metres and weigh upwards of four tons; the females, or cows, are petite by comparison – four metres long, and averaging a mere two thousand pounds in weight. They have large eyes, adapted for spotting fish in deep or murky waters; indeed, elephant seals are the deepest diving mammals, capable of staying under water for twenty minutes at a time, reaching depths of over four thousand feet, where the pressure is over a hundred times that at the surface. They have to dive so deeply in order to avoid the attentions of the great white sharks who lurk offshore, for whom they are a favorite meal.

Like otters, elephant seals were decimated by commercial whalers in the mid-nineteenth century for their blubber and hides. By the turn of the century less than a hundred remained, but careful protection has partially restored the California population, which is concentrated on the Channel and Farallon Islands and at Año Nuevo State Park.

Elephant seals only emerge from the ocean to breed or molt; their name comes from the male's long trunk-like proboscis, through which it produces a resonant pinging sound that biologists call "trumpeting," which is how it attracts a mate. The Año Nuevo beach is the best place to observe this ritual. In December and January, the bulls haul themselves out of the water and battle for dominance. The predominant, or alpha, male will do most of the mating, siring as many as fifty young pups, one per mating, in a season. Other males fight it out at the fringes, each managing one or two couplings with the hapless, defenceless females. During this time, the beach is a seething mass of ton upon ton of blubbery seals – flopping sand over their back to keep cool, squabbling with their neighbors while making rude snoring and belching sounds. The adults depart in March but the weaned pups hang around until May.

Different age groups of elephant seals continue to use the beach at different times throughout the summer for molting. Elephant seals are completely unafraid of people, but are huge enough to hurt or even kill you if you get in their way, though you're allowed to get close, except during mating season, when entry into the park is restricted to ranger-guided tours.

ESTUARIES

Throughout California, many **estuarine** or river-mouth habitats have been filled, diked, drained, "improved" with marinas or contaminated by pollutants. Those that survive intact consist of a mixture of mud flats, exposed only at low tide, and salt marsh, together forming a critical wildlife area that provides nurseries for many kinds of invertebrates and fish, and nesting and wintering grounds for many birds. Cord grass, a dominant wetlands plant, produces five to ten times as much oxygen and nutrients per acre as does wheat.

Many interesting creatures live in the thick organic ooze, including the fat **innkeeper**, a revolting-looking pink hot dog of a worm that sociably shares its burrow with a small crab and a fish, polychaete worms, clams and other goodies. Most prominent of estuary birds are the **great blue herons** and **great egrets**. Estuaries are the best place to see wintering shore birds such as dunlin, dowitchers, eastern and western sandpipers and yellowlegs. Peregrine falcons and osprey are also found here.

Important Californian estuaries include Elkhorn Slough, near Monterey, San Francisco Bay and Bolinas Lagoon.

COASTAL BLUFFS

Along the shore, **coastal meadows** are bright with pink and yellow sand verbena, lupines, sea rocket, sea fig and the bright orange **California poppy**, the state flower. Slightly inland, hills are covered with coastal scrub, which consists largely of coyote brush. Coastal canyons contain broadleaf trees such as California laurel, alder, buckeye and oaks – and a tangle of sword ferns, horsetail and cow parsnip.

Common rainy-season canyon inhabitants include four-inch-long banana slugs and rough-skinned newts. In winter, orange and black **Monarch butterflies** inhabit large roosts in a few discreet locales, such as Bolinas, Monterey and Pacific Grove. Coastal thickets also provide homes to weasels, bobcats, gray fox, raccoons, black-tailed deer, California quail and garter snakes. **Tule elk**, a once common member of the deer family, have also been reintroduced to the wild; a good place to view them is on Tomales Point at the Point Reyes National Seashore; see p.489 of the Guide.

RIVER VALLEYS

Like most fertile **river valleys**, the Sacramento and Central (San Joaquin) valleys have both been greatly affected by agriculture. Riparian (streamside) vegetation has been logged, wetlands drained and streams contaminated with agricultural runoff. Despite this, the riparian habitat that does remain is a prime wildlife habitat. Wood ducks, kingfishers, swallows and warblers are common, as are gray fox, raccoon and striped skunks. The Sacramento National Wildlife Refuge has one of the world's largest concentrations of **snow geese** during winter months. Other common winter migrants include Canada geese, green-winged and cinnamon teals, pintail, shovelers and wigeon. These refuges are well worth a visit, but don't be alarmed by large numbers of duck-hunters – the term "refuge" is a misnomer. However, most have tour routes where hunting is prohibited.

Vernal pools are a valley community unique to California. Here, hardpan soils prevent the infiltration of winter rains, creating seasonal ponds. As these ponds slowly evaporate in April and May, sharply defined concentric floral rings come into bloom. The white is meadowfoam, the blue is the violet-like downingia, and the yellow is goldfields. Swallows, meadowlarks, yellowlegs and stilts can also be found. Jepson Prairie Nature Conservancy Reserve is the easiest to visit, south of Sacramento near the small town of Rio Vista.

FORESTS

Perhaps the most notable indigenous features of Californian forests are the wide expanses of **redwood** and **sequoia trees**. It's easy to confuse the coastal species, *Sequoia sempervirens*, or redwood, with the *Sequoiadendron giganteum*, or giant sequoia (pronounced *suk-oy-ah*), as both have the same fibrous reddish-brown bark. Redwoods are the world's tallest trees, sequoias have the greatest base circumference and are the largest single organisms

on earth. Both species can live for over two thousand years, and recent research now indicates a maximum age of 3500 years for the Sequoia. Their longevity is partially due to their bark: rich in tannin, it protects the tree from fungal and insect attack and inhibits fire damage. In fact, fire is beneficial to these trees and necessary for their germination; prescribed fires are set and controlled around them. The wood of these great trees is much sought after for its beauty – near any forest you'll see signs advertising redwood burl furniture – and its resistance to decay (the bark continues to protect the tree for several hundred years after felling).

They are the only surviving members of a family of perhaps forty species of trees which, fossil records show, grew worldwide 175 million years ago. Now just a few pockets remain, and a tremendous battle between environmentalists and loggers is being waged over the remaining acres. These **virgin forests** provide homes to unique creatures such as the spotted owl and marbled murrelet.

Redwoods are a relict species, which means that they flourished in a moister climate during the Arcto-Tertiary (just after the golden age of the dinosaurs), and now occupy a much-reduced range. As the weather patterns changed, redwoods slowly retreated to their current near-coastal haunts. Today, they are found from the border with Oregon to just south of Monterey.

The floor of the redwood forest is a hushed place with little sunlight, the air suffused with a rufous glow from the bark, which gives the trees its name. One of the commonest ground covers in the redwood forest is the redwood sorrel, or oxalis, with its shamrock leaves and tubular pink flowers; ferns are also numerous. Birds are usually high in the canopy and hard to see, but you might hear the double-whistled song of the varied thrush, or the "chickadee" call from the bird of that name. Roosevelt elk, larger than the tule elk, also inhabit the humid northwest forests. Prairie Creek Redwoods State Park, near the border with Oregon, has a large herd.

Sequoias are found on the western slopes of the Sierra Nevada, most notably in Yosemite and Kings Canyon National Parks – though saplings given as state gifts can be found growing to more modest dimensions all over the world.

The sequoia forest tends to be slightly more open than the redwood forest. Juvenile sequoias – say up to a thousand years old – exhibit a slender conical shape which, as the lower branches fall away, ages to the classical heavy-crowned shape with its columnar trunk. For its bulk, its cones are astonishingly small, no bigger than a hen's egg, but they live on the tree for up to thirty years before falling.

THE SIERRA NEVADA

In the late nineteenth century, the environmental movement was founded when John Muir fell in love with the **Sierra Nevada** mountains, which he called the Range of Light. Muir fought a losing battle to save Hetch Hetchy, a valley said to be more beautiful than Yosemite, but in the process the Sierra Club was born and the move to save America's remaining wilderness began.

The Sierra mountains, which run almost the entire length of the state, have a sharp, craggy, freshly glaciated look. Many of the same conifers can be found as in the forests further west, but ponderosa and lodge-pole pines are two of the dominants, and the forests tend to be drier and more open. Lower elevation forests contain incense cedar, sugar pine (which has the longest pine cones – over eighteen inches – in the world) and black oak. The oaks, along with dogwood and willows, produce spectacular autumnal color. The east side is drier and has large groves of aspen, a beautiful white-barked tree with small round leaves that tremble in the wind. **Wildflowers** flourish for a few short months – shooting star, elephant's head and wild onions in early spring, asters and yarrow later in the season.

The dominant campground scoundrels are two sorts of noisy, squawking bird: Steller's jays and Clark's nutcrackers. Black bears, who may make a raid on your campground, pose more danger to iceboxes than humans, but nonetheless you should treat them with caution. The friendly twenty-pound pot-bellied rodents that lounge around at the fringes of your encampment are **marmots**, who probably do more damage than bears: some specialize in chewing on radiator hoses of parked cars.

Other common birds include mountain chickadees, yellow-rumped warblers, white-crowned sparrows and juncos. Deer, golden-mantled ground squirrels and chipmunks are also plentiful.

THE GREAT BASIN

The little-known **Great Basin** stretches from the northernmost section of the state down almost to Death Valley, encompassing all of Nevada and parts of all the other bordering states. It's a land of many shrubs and few streams, and what streams do exist drain into saline lakes rather than the ocean.

Mono Lake, reflecting the 13,000-foot peaks of Yosemite National Park, is a spectacular example. Its salty waters support no fish but lots of algae, brine shrimp and brine flies, the latter two providing a smorgasbord for nesting gulls (the term "seagull" isn't strictly correct – many gulls nest inland) and migrating phalaropes and grebes. Like many Great Basin lakes, Mono Lake has been damaged through diversion of its freshwater feeder streams to provide water for the city of Los Angeles.

Great Basin plants tolerate hot summers, cold winters and little rain. The dominant Great Basin plant is **sagebrush**. Its dusky green leaves are very aromatic, especially after a summer thunderstorm. Other common plants include bitterbrush, desert peach, junipers and piñon pines. Piñon cones contain tasty nuts that were a mainstay of the Paiute diet.

The **sage grouse** is one of the most distinctive Great Basin birds. These turkey-like birds feed on sage during the winter and depend on it for nesting and courtship habitat. In March and April, males gather at dancing grounds called leks, where they puff out small pink balloons on their necks, make soft drumbanging calls, and in general succeed in looking and sounding rather silly. The hens coyly scout out the talent by feigning greater interest in imaginary seeds.

Pronghorns are beautiful tawny-gold antelope seen in many places in the Great Basin. Watch for their twinkling white rumps as you drive.

Other Great Basin denizens include golden eagles, pinyon jays, black-billed magpies, coyotes, feral horses and burros, black-tailed jackrabbits and western rattlesnakes. Large concentrations of waterfowl gather at Tule Lake in northeastern California, where hundreds of wintering **bald eagles** gather in November before the cold really sets in.

THE MOJAVE DESERT

The **Mojave Desert** lies in the southeast corner of the state, near Death Valley. Like the Great Basin, the vegetation here consists primarily of drought-adapted shrubs, one of the commonest of which is Creosote, with its olive-green leaves and puffy yellow flowers. Death Valley is renowned for its early spring wildflower shows. The alluvial fans are covered with desert trumpet, gravel ghost and pebble pincushion. The quantity and timing of rainfall determines when the floral display peaks, but it's usually some time between mid-February and mid-April in the lower elevations, late April to early June higher up.

Besides shrubs, the Mojave has many interesting kinds of **cactus**. These include barrel, cottontop, cholla and beavertail cactus, and many members of the yucca family. Yuccas have stiff, lance-like leaves with sharp tips, a conspicuous representative being the **Joshua tree**, whose twisting arm-like branches are covered with shaggy upward-pointing leaf fronds, which can reach to thirty feet high.

Many Mojave desert animals conserve body moisture by foraging at night, including the kit fox, wood rat and various kinds of mice. The **kangaroo rat**, an appealing animal that hops rather than runs, has specially adapted kidneys that enable it to survive without drinking water. Other desert animals include mammals such as the Mojave ground squirrel, bighorn and coyote; birds like the roadrunner, ash-throated flycatcher, ladder-backed woodpecker, verdin and Lucy's warbler; and reptiles like the Mojave rattlesnake, sidewinder and chuckwalla.

CALIFORNIA
ON FILM

In the early 1910s, attracted by the endless sunshine, the cheap real estate and the rich variety of landscape throughout the state of California, a number of independent movie producers left the East Coast and the strangle-hold monopoly of the Motion Picture Patents Company, and set up shop in a small Los Angeles suburb called Hollywood. Within a decade Hollywood had become the movie capital of the world and Southern California, by default, became the setting for everything from Keystone Cop car chases to low-rent Westerns, not to mention the odd Biblical epic or old-world romance shot on studio lots.

But, as the movie industry grew, Hollywood's films about California – as opposed to those that just happened to be set there – began to take on a special sheen, whether presenting the state as the kind of idyllic El Dorado beloved of the pioneers, or, more commonly, as a state of mind. Much has changed on the long road between John Farrow's **California** (1946), in which Ray Milland leads a wagon train to the Promised Land during the Gold Rush, and Dominic Sena's **Kalifornia** (1993), in which David Duchovny unwittingly invites a serial killer along for the cross-country ride, but both films posit California as the answer to everybody's problems. ("If it wasn't OK there, then it probably wouldn't be OK anywhere" says Duchovny).

Transcendence used to be what California was all about, and it's still a major theme in Californian films. But more and more California – or more specifically Los Angeles – seems to be turning into not an answer, but simply a problem. The City of Dreams is becoming the City of Recurring Nightmares, a locus of vapid consumerism, rampant crime, racial division and millennial anxiety, trembling on the verge of **apocalypse**. Or so the movies tell us.

Hardly surprisingly, the list of movies set in California, and especially Los Angeles, is endless. What follows is a roll-call of the most significant movies, those that make the most original use of Californian locations (from the vertiginous streets of San Francisco, to the breakers of Monterey, from the dust bowls of the Mojave to the storm drains of LA), as well as those that reflect California's navel-gazing fascination with itself.

HOLLYWOOD DOES HOLLYWOOD

The Bad and the Beautiful (Vincente Minnelli 1952). Made just as the studio system was beginning to come apart at the seams, Minnelli's bitter insider tale of the rise and fall of a ruthless Hollywood producer (Kirk Douglas) is told in flashbacks by the star, the writer and the director he launched and subsequently lost.

Ed Wood (Tim Burton 1994). The ragged low-budget fringes of Fifties Hollywood are beautifully re-created in this loving tribute to the much-derided auteur of *Plan Nine from Outer Space* and *Glen or Glenda*. Gorgeously shot in black and white, and with a stunning performance by Martin Landau as ailing Hollywood habitué Bela Lugosi.

Get Shorty (Barry Sonnenfeld 1995). When movie-loving Miami loan shark Chili Palmer (John Travolta) is sent to Hollywood to collect a debt from schlock-horror auteur Harry Zim (Gene Hackman), he sees his chance to pull a fast one on a gang of drug-smuggling mobsters and get his name in lights. Faithfully based on the Elmore Leonard novel.

In a Lonely Place (Nicholas Ray 1950). A glamor-less Hollywood peopled with alcoholic former matinee idols, star-struck hat-check girls and desperate agents forms the cynical background for this devastating doomed romance between Humphrey Bogart's hot-tempered screenwriter and his Beverly Hills neighbor Gloria Grahame.

The Last Action Hero (John McTiernan 1993). One of Arnold Schwarzenegger's rare commercial flops, though needlessly trashed, is a *Purple Rose of Cairo* for the blockbuster crowd, full of Hollywood locations and po-mo jokes about everything from movie phone numbers (all of which have the same prefix) and Ingmar Bergman films.

The Player (Robert Altman 1992). Tim Robbins is perfectly smug as an egocentric studio executive getting away with murder. Peopled with movie stars playing themselves, and packed with movie-biz in-jokes, Altman's tour-de-force is a wickedly accurate depiction of Hollywood's lowered expectations and diminishing returns.

Singin' in the Rain (Stanley Donen & Gene Kelly 1952). The eternally popular, lovingly made song and dance satire about Hollywood's fraught transition from silents to talkies. With great songs, perceptive gags, and the unforgettable title sequence, the film is pure pleasure.

A Star is Born (George Cukor 1954). The best of many versions of this classic Hollywood weepie, in which Judy Garland is given a hand up the ladder by James Mason, an alcoholic former star very much on the way down.

Sunset Boulevard (Billy Wilder 1950). The darkest of the many mirrors Hollywood has held up to itself, Wilder's acerbic classic about an impoverished screenwriter (William Holden) who falls into the clutches of an ageing silent film star (Gloria Swanson) posits Hollywood as a nightmare world of vanity, illusion and decline.

Who Framed Roger Rabbit? (Robert Zemeckis 1988). This eye-popping fusion of live-action and animation imagines a Forties Hollywood in which cartoon characters inhabit the same universe as humans, but only as second class citizens forced to live in the crime-ridden cartoon ghetto of Toontown.

LA CRIME STORIES

American Gigolo (Paul Schrader 1980). LA is at its glossiest and most vacuous in this arty, muted, pulp thriller about a high-class, Armani-clad male prostitute (Richard Gere), framed for murder and searching for grace.

Chinatown (Roman Polanski 1974). One of the most memorable cinematic marriages of story and setting, Polanski's classic neo-noir stars Jack Nicholson as a private eye adrift in the moral desert of late Thirties LA, when real estate was booming, water scarce, and corruption at every level a given.

Double Indemnity (Billy Wilder 1944). The definitive LA noir, in which traveling insurance salesman and all-round fall-guy Fred MacMurray provides us with an incidental tour of Forties LA as he winds himself ever more tightly into Barbara Stanwyck's devastating web of duplicity.

Heat (Michael Mann 1995). The urban architecture of LA has rarely been more beautifully filmed than in this criminally underrated face-off between Robert De Niro's master-thief and Al Pacino's dogged detective which plays out against a stunning Antonioniesque backdrop of shimmering cityscapes, spaghetti-looped freeways, and the runways of LAX.

He Walked By Night (Alfred Werker 1948). This verité-style crime story set in "the fastest growing city in the nation" starts with a random cop-killing in Santa Monica and ends with a manhunt though the 700-mile subterranean city storm drain system, stunningly shot by torch-light by peerless noir cinematographer John Alton.

The Killing of a Chinese Bookie (John Cassavetes 1976). Strange and self-indulgent, but perfectly evoking the sleazy charms of the Sunset Strip, Cassavetes' behavioral crime story about a club-owner (Ben Gazzara) in hock to the mob is just one of his many great LA-based character studies.

LA Confidential (Curtis Hanson 1997). A sizzling epic of police corruption and Tinsel-town sleaze in Fifties Los Angeles – a city swarming with unscrupulous tabloid journalists, venal bureaucrats, racist cops and movie-star-lookalike whores. Superbly done.

The Long Goodbye (Robert Altman 1973). Altman's masterpiece updates Raymond Chandler's shadowy Forties noir to sun-drenched Seventies me-generation LA. Elliot Gould's disheveled Philip Marlowe lives in the Hollywood Hills with a bevy of hippy chicks for neighbors and a bushel of problems that take him from Tijuana to Malibu and back.

Point Blank (John Boorman 1967). Though it begins and ends at Alcatraz, Boorman's virtuoso avant-garde thriller, in which a poker-faced Lee Marvin seeks revenge for an earlier betrayal, is most effective imagining Los Angeles as an impenetrable citadel of concrete and glass built on the wages of corporate crime.

To Live and Die in LA (William Friedkin 1985). The glossiest and flashiest of LA policiers, Friedkin's updating of his *French Connection* formula to the Eighties and the West Coast follows two FBI agents on the trail of a master counterfeiter, and features another of his trademark spectacular car-chases – this time LA-style on a major freeway at rush hour.

APOCALYPTIC LA

Blade Runner (Ridley Scott 1982). This brilliant combination of sci-fi and neo-noir envisions the Los Angeles of 2019 as a depopulated, crime-ridden metropolis of towering skyscrapers, sprawling street-markets, and perpetual darkness, where Harrison Ford's gumshoe tracks renegade replicants through the never-ending acid rain.

Escape from LA (John Carpenter 1996). In Carpenter's alternative vision of the future, Los Angeles has been cut off from the mainland by an earthquake and declared so "ravaged by crime and immorality" that it has been turned into a deportation zone for undesirables. Sent in to uproot insurrection, Kurt Russell battles psychotic plastic surgeons in Beverly Hills and surfs a Tsunami to a showdown in a netherworld Disneyland.

Falling Down (Joel Schumacher 1993). Mad as hell, and unable to tolerate the height-of-summer LA traffic jam in which he finds himself, Michael Douglas abandons his car and goes on the rampage through some of the city's less picturesque neighborhoods, railing at petty injustices and wreaking havoc with every step.

Kiss Me Deadly (Robert Aldrich 1955). Aldrich's no-holds barred apocalypse-noir follows proto-fascist private eye Mike Hammer on a punch-drunk tour of LA in search of a deadly Maguffin – from boarding houses to the mansions of Beverly Hills to a Malibu beach house where, quite literally, all hell breaks loose.

1941 (Steven Spielberg 1979). "This isn't the State of California, this is a state of insanity," yells Robert Stack's General Stillwell as LA prepares for a Japanese invasion at the height of post-Pearl Harbor paranoia. Spielberg's joylessly frantic epic comedy begins with John Belushi crash-landing in Death Valley and ends with a submarine attack on the Santa Monica Pier.

The Rapture (Michael Tolkin 1991). Mimi Rogers plays an LA telephone operator who abandons her hedonistic lifestyle when she hears a fundamentalist group talking about the impending "Rapture," and becomes Born Again, ultimately heading into the desert to await Armageddon. Michael Tolkin's wonderfully literal film takes his premise just as far as it can go, and then some.

Strange Days (Kathryn Bigelow 1995). In this visceral, millennial joy-ride by one of LA's most visionary auteurs, Angelenos party like it's 1999, and Ralph Fiennes' Lenny Nero fiddles while his racially-sundered city burns. Surrogate thrills, in the form of virtual reality tapes of someone else's private heaven or hell, are the illegal drug of choice as the century goes out with a bang.

Terminator 2: Judgment Day (James Cameron 1991). As in Cameron's impressive first *Terminator* (1984), the machines in charge of the future have sent a cyborg back in time to assassinate a future resistance leader. This time, however, the film makes even more memorable use of LA locations, with a thrilling truck chase along the concrete bed of the Los Angeles River and a spectacular visualization of the city's apocalyptic destiny.

They Live (John Carpenter 1988). In this ludicrous but entertaining horror flick, a drifter living in a shanty town pitched on the outskirts of LA discovers a pair of sunglasses which allow him to see that skull-faced aliens in positions of wealth and power are subliminally encouraging the city's rampant consumerism.

Volcano (Mick Jackson 1997). "The coast is toast" and only the canny resourcefulness of Tommy Lee Jones and Anne Heche can save downtown LA from a neon-gold sea of lava emanating from the La Brea Tar Pits and consuming everything in its path like a latter-day Blob.

LA IN THE NINETIES

Boyz 'n' the Hood (John Singleton 1991). Singleton's influential debut film, a sober portrayal of life in South Central LA, highlights the odds against success or even survival in a community riddled with drugs, poverty and violence.

Clueless (Amy Heckerling 1995). As exemplary of LA in the Nineties as *Boyz 'n' the Hood*, Heckerling's Girls in the Mall comedy made a star of Alicia Silverstone, who guides us through the empty heads of shopaholic Beverly Hills High schoolgirls and their Valley-inflected, rich-kid lingo.

The End of Violence (Wim Wenders 1997). Bill Pullman plays a successful schlock-movie producer obsessed with violence who finds redemption after he is nearly murdered himself. Wenders' existential thriller is preposterous and po-faced but he films end-of-the-millennium LA with a hypnotically other-worldly beauty and his typically quizzical outsider's gaze.

The Glass Shield (Charles Burnett 1995). Institutionalized racism in the LAPD is brought under the harsh glare of Charles Burnett, who, with his masterpieces *Killer of Sheep* (1977) and *My Brother's Wedding* (1983), has long been one of the great chroniclers of LA's black urban underclass.

Grand Canyon (Lawrence Kasdan 1992). Danny Glover, Kevin Kline and Steve Martin cross LA's many race and class barriers in this sentimental, self-important, symbol-laden buddy movie that purported to express the everyday horrors of living in the city in the 1990s.

Pulp Fiction (Quentin Tarantino 1994). Tarantino's electrifying roundelay of stories about sudden deaths and second chances is set in a depopulated, down-at-heel Los Angeles of kitsch diners and low-rent motels, store basements and funereal saloons – a deliberately bland backdrop against which his fast-talking hustlers and half-hearted hit-men seem all the more vivid.

Short Cuts (Robert Altman 1993). Transposing the stories of Raymond Carver from Washington to LA, Altman's haunting, bluesy city symphony brilliantly knits together the parallel universes inhabited by a gaggle of suburban Angelenos whose lives are interlinked by small disasters and surprising moments of grace.

Speed (Jan De Bont 1994). In a city in which public transportation is little more than a utopian ideal, and in which bumper-to-bumper traffic clogs the freeways from morning till night, the idea of a city bus primed to explode if its speed drops below 50mph was the perfect LA joke, as well as the excuse for a thrilling travelogue of the city's transit system.

Star Maps (Miguel Arteta 1997). A *telenovela*-esque melodrama of immigrant life on the fringes of Hollywood. Carlos, who has grandiose dreams of movie stardom, is doing time in his father's prostitution ring, standing on street corners ostensibly selling maps to the homes of the stars, in reality selling his body for cash.

Swingers (Doug Liman 1996). Cocktail culture in the Nineties is skewered in this hilarious cult favorite about a couple of dudes who spend their nights in Sunset Boulevard lounges and swing clubs eyeing up the "beautiful babies" and shooting the breeze like Rat-Pack-Era Sinatras.

IF YOU'RE GOING TO SAN FRANCISCO . . .

The Conversation (Francis Ford Coppola 1974). Opening with a mesmerizing sequence of high-tech eavesdropping in Union Square, Coppola's chilling character study of San Francisco surveillance expert Harry Caul (Gene Hackman at his finest) is one of the best films of the paranoid Watergate era.

Dim Sum: A Little Bit of Heart (Wayne Wang 1985). Set among San Francisco's Chinese community, Wayne Wang's appealing comedy-of-manners about assimilation and family ties is a modest and rewarding treat. His earlier sleeper *Chan is Missing* (1982) also shows a Chinatown tourists don't usually see.

Dirty Harry (Don Siegel 1971). Based on the infamous case of the Bay Area Zodiac Killer, Siegel's morally debatable, sequel-spawning, catch-phrase-begetting thriller casts Clint Eastwood in his most famous role as neo-fascist San Francisco cop who'll do anything to get his man and make his day.

Escape from Alcatraz (Don Siegel 1979). Though evocatively portrayed in *The Bird Man of Alcatraz*, *Point Blank*, *The Rock* and many others, this is the ultimate movie about San Francisco's famously unbreachable offshore penitentiary. Starring Clint Eastwood (again) as a most resourceful con.

Greed (Erich von Stroheim 1924). This legendary silent masterpiece about the downfall of Polk Street dentist Doc McTeague was shot mostly on location in the Bay Area, and remains, even in its notoriously truncated version, a wonderful time capsule of working-class San Francisco in the 1920s.

Petulia (Richard Lester 1968). Julie Christie is dazzling in this fragmented puzzle of a movie about a vivacious and unpredictable married woman who has an affair with a divorced doctor (George C. Scott). Set against the wittily-described background of psychedelic-era San Francisco, and superbly shot by Nicolas Roeg, *Petulia* is a forgotten Sixties masterpiece.

Play It Again, Sam (Herbert Ross 1972). A strike in Manhattan led to one of Woody Allen's rare visits to the West Coast, for this hilarious film about a neurotic San Francisco film critic in love with his best friend's wife and obsessed with Humphrey Bogart in *Casablanca*.

The Times of Harvey Milk (Robert Epstein 1984). This powerful and moving documentary about America's first openly gay politician chronicles his career in pre-Aids-era San Francisco and the aftermath of his 1978 assassination.

Vertigo (Alfred Hitchcock 1958). Hitchcock's somber, agonized, twisted, tragic love story is the San Francisco movie nonpareil. From James Stewart's wordless drives around the city to the film's climax at the San Juan Bautista mission, Hitchcock takes us on a mesmerizing tour of a city haunted by its past.

What's up Doc (Peter Bogdanovich 1972). This madcap homage to the heyday of Hollywood screwball comedy stars Ryan O'Neal as a hapless stuffed-shirt musicologist and Barbara Streisand as the kook who drives him around the bend, and features, next to Steve McQueen's *Bullitt*, one of the great vertiginous San Francisco car chases.

"WAY OUT" WEST

Bob & Carol & Ted & Alice (Paul Mazursky 1969). This once-daring, now dated, but still funny zeitgeist satire about wife-swapping and bed-hopping in late Sixties Southern California, starring Natalie Wood, Robert Culp, Elliott Gould and Dyan Cannon as the titular foursome.

Boogie Nights (Paul Thomas Anderson, 1997). Eddie Adams from Torrance meets stroke-movie auteur Jack Horner in a San Fernando Valley nightclub and is reborn as porn-star "Dirk Diggler" in this delirious ode to Seventies excess and Eighties redemption in sexy, swingin' Southern California.

California Suite (Herbert Ross 1978). "It's like paradise, with a lobotomy" snarls Jane Fonda's hard-bitten East Coast journalist when faced with ex-husband Alan Alda's new Californian lifestyle in the best of these four Neil Simon stories about out-of-towners at the Beverly Hills Hotel.

LA Story (Mick Jackson 1991). Steve Martin's sentimental, only-in-LA love story is laced with in-jokes about automobile dependence, health-obsession, and double-decaf lattes, and filmed by British director Jackson with an outsider's tolerant delight.

Modern Romance (Albert Brooks 1981). Brooks – the Woody Allen of the West Coast – stars in this hysterical comedy about a neurotic film editor who dumps his girlfriend and instantly regrets it. Full of early Eighties LA signifiers from Quaaludes to jogging suits to off-Hollywood parties with B-movie stars.

Point Break (Kathryn Bigelow 1991). If any film captures the sun-drenched, free-spirited élan of California, it's this slightly preposterous but thrillingly kinetic crime story starring Patrick Swayze as a bank-robbing, sky-diving New Age surfer dude and Keanu Reeves as his straight-arrow FBI nemesis significantly named Johnny Utah.

Rebel Without a Cause (Nicholas Ray 1955). The seminal LA youth movie in which James Dean, at his most perfectly iconographic as the new kid in town, kicks over the traces at Hollywood High School and falls in with disaffected rich kid Sal Mineo and mixed-up school sweetheart Natalie Wood.

Safe (Todd Haynes 1995). In Haynes' brilliant tale of millennial unease and corporeal paranoia, Julianne Moore plays a San Fernando Valley homemaker with seemingly little inner-life and an opulent outer one, who is diagnosed with environmental sickness and finds refuge at a New Age desert retreat.

Shampoo (Hal Ashby 1975). Great cast in a spot-on adult comedy, which sees LA as a big bed on the eve of the 1968 American Presidential Election. Co-writer Warren Beatty has one of his best roles as an inarticulate, confused, priapic Beverly Hills hairdresser.

Valley Girl (Martha Coolidge 1983). Southern Californian cultures clash in this sweet romance between the eponymous Valley Girl Deborah Foreman and "Hollyweird" punk Nicholas Cage. The *Clueless* of its day.

OFF THE BEATEN TRACK

Bagdad Café (Percy Adlon 1988). Lovable, inspiring fable about a German tourist (the incomparable Marianne Sagebrecht) who arrives at a dusty roadside diner in the Mojave Desert and magically transforms the place with her larger-than-life charm.

The Birds (Alfred Hitchcock 1963). Set in Bodega Bay, just north of San Francisco, Hitchcock's terrifying allegory about a small town besieged by a plague of vicious birds, features indelible bird's-eye views of the Northern Californian coastline.

California (John Farrow 1946). Ray Milland leads a wagon train to the Land of Milk and Honey only to find the land ruled by greed and graft, in this elaborate paean to the pioneer spirit and the founding of the state. Worth seeing for its ecstatic opening montage of Californian vistas and aphorisms about the approaching Promised Land.

Faster, Pussycat! Kill! Kill! (Russ Meyer 1965). Meyer's wonderfully lurid camp action flick unleashes a trio of depraved go-go girls upon an unsuspecting California desert. One of a kind.

Fat City (John Huston 1972). Stacy Keach and Jeff Bridges star in Huston's poignant, evocative, beautifully paced portrait of barflies, has-beens and no-hopers on the small-time boxing circuit in Stockton, Northern California.

One-Eyed Jacks (Marlon Brando 1961). Set, unusually for a western, on the roaring shores of Monterey, where Brando tracks down Karl Malden — the bank-robbing partner who betrayed him five years earlier in Mexico — only to find him reformed and comfortably ensconced as sheriff.

Play Misty for Me (Clint Eastwood 1971). Another Monterey movie, Eastwood's directorial debut, a thriller about the consequences of a DJ's affair with a psychotic fan, was shot in Clint's home town of Carmel, and on his own two hundred acres of Monterey coastland.

Shadow of a Doubt (Alfred Hitchcock 1943). Urbane Uncle Charlie (Joseph Cotten) comes to stay with his sister's Santa Rosa family and seems to be the answer to his bored niece's prayers, until she starts to suspect that he might be a mass murderer. Hitchcock's brilliantly funny and enthralling film is a perfect depiction of life in small-town Northern California.

Three Women (Robert Altman 1977). A fascinating, hypnotic and utterly unique film in which Sissy Spacek and Shelley Duvall, co-workers at a geriatric center in Desert Springs, mysteriously absorb each other's identity. A film brilliantly imbued with the woozy spirit of Southern California.

Zabriskie Point (Michelangelo Antonioni 1970). Though it opens with student sit-ins at UCLA, Antonioni's gorgeous, too often derided homage to Flower Power disaffection is most famous for its Death Valley love-in and the stunningly voluptuous explosion in the desert, that blows the lid off Southern Californian consumerism.

Adrian Curry

CALIFORNIA IN FICTION

While California may be mythologized as the ultimate stimulant for the imagination, it has inspired comparatively few travel writers, an exception being Robert Louis Stevenson, whose lively description of the Napa Valley and Mount St Helena is printed below. In contrast, floods of fiction have poured out of the state, in particular Los Angeles, over the last few decades, not only shaping perceptions of the region, but often redefining the whole course of modern American writing.

The contemporary writers featured here – Amy Tan and T. Coraghessan Boyle – are both concerned with newcomers to the state, Amy Tan with the interaction of an older generation who grew up in China with their sophisticated San Francisco daughters, and T.C. Boyle with the explosion of the Mexican population in LA, and its uneasy impact on the white elite.

ROBERT LOUIS STEVENSON

Robert Louis Stevenson was born in Edinburgh in 1850, and was educated at the academy and university there. He became an ardent traveler, writing *An Inland Voyage* and *Travels with a Donkey* about his journeys through France, where he fell in love with a married American woman, Fanny Osbourne. She obtained her divorce in 1879 and Stevenson, battling with ill-health, sailed to America to marry her. They took their honeymoon in the mountains of San Francisco. The result of this happy period in Stevenson's life is *Silverado Squatters*, a charming if occasionally slight volume about the landscape and characters of the mountains, already inflected with Stevenson's vigorous descriptive powers – and love of a good yarn. In this extract, Stevenson sets the scene of his book, and interestingly prefigures how development will change the area.

THE SILVERADO SQUATTERS

The scene of this little book is on a high mountain. There are, indeed, many higher; there are many of a nobler outline. It is no place of pilgrimage for the summary globe-trotter; but to one who lives upon its sides, Mount Saint Helena soon becomes a centre of interest. It is the Mont Blanc of one section of the Californian Coast Range, none of its near neighbours rising to one-half its altitude. It looks down on much green, intricate country. It feeds in the springtime many splashing brooks. From its summit you must have an excellent lesson of geography: seeing, to the south, San Francisco Bay, with Tamalpais on the one hand and Monte Diablo on the other; to the west and thirty miles away, the open ocean; eastward, across the cornlands and thick tule swamps of Sacramento Valley, to where the Central Pacific railroad begins to climb the sides of the Sierras; and northward, for what I know, the white head of Shasta looking down on Oregon. Three counties, Napa County, Lake County, and Sonoma County, march across its cliffy shoulders. Its naked peak stands nearly four thousand five hundred feet above the sea; its sides are fringed with forest; and the soil, where it is bare, glows warm with cinnabar.

Life in its shadow goes rustically forward. Bucks, and bears, and rattlesnakes, and former mining operations, are the staple of men's talk. Agriculture has only begun to mount above the valley. And though in a few years from now the whole district may be smiling with farms, passing trains shaking the mountain to the heart, many-windowed hotels lighting up the night like factories, and a prosperous city occupying the site of sleepy Calistoga; yet in the meantime, around the foot of that mountain the silence of nature reigns in a great measure unbroken, and the people of hill and valley go sauntering about their business as in the days before the flood.

To reach Mount Saint Helena from San Francisco the traveller has twice to cross the bay: once by the busy Oakland Ferry, and again, after an hour or so of the railway, from Vallejo junction to Vallejo. Thence he takes rail once more to mount the long green strath of Napa Valley.

In all the contractions and expansions of that inland sea, the Bay of San Francisco, there can be few drearier scenes than the Vallejo Ferry. Bald shores and a low, bald islet enclose the sea; through the narrows the tide bubbles, muddy like a river. When we made the passage (bound, although yet we knew it not, for

Silverado) the steamer jumped, and the black buoys were dancing in the jabble; the ocean breeze blew killing chill; and, although the upper sky was still unflecked with vapour, the sea fogs were pouring in from seaward, over the hilltops of Marin County, in one great, shapeless, silver cloud.

South Vallejo is typical of many Californian towns. It was a blunder; the site had proved untenable; and, although it is still such a young place by the scale of Europe, it has already begun to be deserted for its neighbour and namesake, North Vallejo. A long pier, a number of drinking saloons, a hotel of a great size, marshy pools where the frogs keep up their croaking, and even at high noon the entire absence of any human face or voice – these are the marks of South Vallejo. Yet there was a tall building beside the pier, labelled the *Star Flour Mills*; and seagoing, full-rigged ships lay close along shore, waiting for their cargo. Soon these would be plunging round the Horn, soon the flour from the *Star Flour Mills* would be landed on the wharves of Liverpool. For that, too, is one of England's outposts; thither, to this gaunt mill, across the Atlantic and Pacific deeps and round about the icy Horn, this crowd of great, three-masted, deep-sea ships come, bringing nothing, and return with bread.

The Frisby House, for that was the name of the hotel, was a place of fallen fortunes, like the town. It was now given up to labourers, and partly ruinous. At dinner there was the ordinary display of what is called in the west a *two-bit house*: the tablecloth checked red and white, the plague of flies, the wire hencoops over the dishes, the great variety and invariable vileness of the food and the rough coatless men devouring it in silence. In our bedroom, the stove would not burn, though it would smoke; and while one window would not open, the other would not shut. There was a view on a bit of empty road, a few dark houses, a donkey wandering with its shadow on a slope, and a blink of sea, with a tall ship lying anchored in the moonlight. All about that dreary inn frogs sang their ungainly chorus.

Early the next morning we mounted the hill along a wooden footway, bridging one marsh spot after another. Here and there, as we ascended, we passed a house embowered in white roses. More of the bay became apparent,

and soon the blue peak of Tamalpais rose above the green level of the island opposite. It told us we were still but a little way from the city of the Golden Gates, already, at that hour, beginning to awake among the sand-hills. It called to us over the waters as with the voice of a bird. Its stately head, blue as a sapphire on the paler azure of the sky, spoke to us of wider outlooks and the bright Pacific. For Tamalpais stands sentry, like a lighthouse, over the Golden Gates, between the bay and the open ocean, and looks down indifferently on both. Even as we saw and hailed it from Vallejo, seamen, far out at sea, were scanning it with shaded eyes; and, as if to answer to the thought, one of the great ships below began silently to clothe herself with white sails, homeward bound for England.

For some way beyond Vallejo the railway led us through bald green pastures. On the west the rough highlands of Marin shut off the ocean; in the midst, in long, straggling, gleaming arms, the bay died out among the grass; there were few trees and few enclosures; the sun shone wide over open uplands, the displumed hills stood clear against the sky. But by-and-by these hills began to draw nearer on either hand, and first thicket and then wood began to clothe their sides; and soon we were away from all signs of the sea's neighbourhood, mounting an inland, irrigated valley. A great variety of oaks stood, now severally, now in a becoming grove, among the fields and vineyards. The towns were compact, in about equal proportions, of bright, new wooden houses and great and growing forest trees; and the chapel bell on the engine sounded most festally that sunny Sunday, as we drew up at one green town after another, with the townsfolk trooping in their Sunday's best to see the strangers, with the sun sparkling on the clean houses, and great domes of foliage humming overhead in the breeze.

This pleasant Napa valley is, at its north end, blockaded by our mountain. There, at Calistoga, the railroad ceases, and the traveller who intends faring farther, to the Geysers or to the springs in Lake County, must cross the spurs of the mountain by stage. Thus, Mount Saint Helena is not only a summit, but frontier; and, up to the time of writing, it has stayed the progress of the iron horse.

AMY TAN

Amy Tan was born in Oakland in 1952, and first visited China in 1987. Her father, who was educated in Beijing and worked for the United States Information Service after the war, came to America in 1947. Her mother came to the United States in 1949, shortly before the Communists seized control of Shanghai. Amy Tan now lives in San Francisco and New York. Her first work of fiction, *The Joy Luck Club*, explores the nuances of Chinese-American identity through the relationships between four Chinese mothers and their American daughters, each of whom narrate their own stories, rich in detail and atmosphere. Each character's story carries inflections of their cultural identity, which is both a barrier to understanding between the two generations, and a source of shared strength. Here junior chess champion Waverly Jong takes a plunge into San Francisco's Chinatown.

THE JOY LUCK CLUB

My mother imparted her daily truths so she could help my older brothers and me rise above our circumstances. We lived in San Francisco's Chinatown. Like most of the other Chinese children who played in the back alleys of restaurants and curio shops, I didn't think we were poor. My bowl was always full, three five-course meals every day, beginning with a soup full of mysterious things I didn't want to know the names of.

We lived on Waverly Place, in a warm, clean, two-bedroom flat that sat above a small Chinese bakery specializing in steamed pastries and dim sum. In the early morning, when the alley was still quiet, I could smell fragrant red beans as they were cooked down to a pasty sweetness. By daybreak, our flat was heavy with the odor of fried sesame balls and sweet curried chicken crescents. From my bed, I would listen as my father got ready for work, then locked the door behind him, one-two-three clicks.

At the end of our two-block alley was a small sandlot playground with swings and slides well-shined down the middle with use. The play area was bordered by wood-slat benches where old-country people sat cracking roasted watermelon seeds with their golden teeth and scattering the husks to an impatient gathering of gurgling pigeons. The best playground, however, was the dark alley itself. It was crammed with daily mysteries and adventures. My brothers and I would

peer into the medicinal herb shop, watching old Li dole out onto a stiff sheet of white paper the right amount of insect shells, saffron-colored seeds, and pungent leaves for his ailing customers. It was said that he once cured a woman dying of an ancestral curse that had eluded the best of American doctors. Next to the pharmacy was a printer who specialized in gold-embossed wedding invitations and festive red banners.

Farther down the street was Ping Yuen Fish Market. The front window displayed a tank crowded with doomed fish and turtles struggling to gain footing on the slimy green-tiled sides. A hand-written sign informed tourists, "Within this store, is all for food, not for pet." Inside, the butchers with their bloodstained white smocks deftly gutted the fish while customers cried out their orders and shouted, "Give me your freshest," to which the butchers always protested, "All are freshest." On less crowded market days, we would inspect the crates of live frogs and crabs which we were warned not to poke, boxes of dried cuttlefish, and row upon row of iced prawns, squid, and slippery fish. The sanddabs made me shiver each time; their eyes lay on one flattened side and reminded me of my mother's story of a careless girl who ran into a crowded street and was crushed by a cab. "Was smash flat," reported my mother.

At the corner of the alley was Hong Sing's, a four-table café with a recessed stairwell in front that led to a door marked "Tradesmen." My brothers and I believed the bad people emerged from this door at night. Tourists never went to Hong Sing's, since the menu was printed only in Chinese. A Caucasian man with a big camera once posed me and my playmates in front of the restaurant. He had us move to the side of the picture window so the photo would capture the roasted duck with its head dangling from a juice-covered rope. After he took the picture, I told him he should go into Hong Sing's and eat dinner. When he smiled and asked me what they served, I shouted, "Guts and duck's feet and octopus gizzards!" Then I ran off with my friends, shrieking with laughter as we scampered across the alley and hid in the entryway grotto of the China Gem Company, my heart pounding with hope that he would chase us.

My mother named me after the street that we lived on: Waverly Place Jong, my official name for important American documents. But my family called me Meimei, "Little Sister." I was the youngest, the only daughter. Each morning before school, my mother would twist and yank on my thick black hair until she had formed two tightly wound pigtails. One day, as she struggled to weave a hard-toothed comb through my disobedient hair, I had a sly thought.

I asked her, "Ma, what is Chinese torture?" My mother shook her head. A bobby pin was wedged between her lips. She wetted her palm and smoothed the hair above my ear, then pushed the pin in so that it nicked sharply against my scalp.

"Who say this word?" she asked without a trace of knowing how wicked I was being. I shrugged my shoulders and said, "Some boy in my class said Chinese people do Chinese torture."

"Chinese people do many things," she said simply. "Chinese people do business, do medicine, do painting. Not lazy like American people. We do torture. Best torture."

Reproduced by kind permission of The Putnam Publishing Group.

T. CORAGHESSAN BOYLE

PEN/Faulkner Award winner **T. Coraghessan Boyle** was born in Manhattan, but now lives in California; his sixth novel, *The Tortilla Curtain*, is pure LA. Its protagonist, prosperous and peaceable Delaney, lives on the leafy fringes of the city and spins out his nature column "Pilgrim at Topanga Creek", while his dynamic wife Kyra shifts real estate. Meanwhile another pilgrim has come to the creek: Cándido, an illegal Mexican immigrant, who is trying to protect his young pregnant wife América from the natural and unnatural forces around them. The initial violent encounter between the two men precipitates events that both tear at the veneer of Delaney's liberalism, satirized with easy precision by Boyle, and expose the vulnerability of LA's legions of have-nots. In this extract, Delaney's incipient fear of invasion is realized, in an unexpected and dramatic form.

THE TORTILLA CURTAIN

High up in the canyon, nestled in a fan-shaped depression dug out of the side of the western ridge by the action of some long-forgotten stream, lay the subdivision known as Arroyo Blanco Estates. It was a private community,

comprising a golf course, ten tennis courts, a community center and some two hundred and fifty homes, each set on one-point-five acres and strictly conforming to the covenants, conditions and restrictions set forth in the 1973 articles of incorporation. The houses were all of the Spanish Mission style, painted in one of three prescribed shades of white, with orange tile roofs. If you wanted to paint your house sky-blue or Provençal-pink with lime-green shutters, you were perfectly welcome to move into the San Fernando Valley or to Santa Monica or anywhere else you chose, but if you bought into Arroyo Blanco Estates, your house would be white and your roof orange.

Delaney Mossbacher made his home in one of these Spanish Mission houses (floor plan #A227C, Rancho White with Navajo trim), along with his second wife, Kyra, her son, Jordan, her matching Dandie Dinmont terriers, Osbert and Sacheverell, and her Siamese cat, Dame Edith. On this particular morning, the morning that Cándido Rincón began to feel he'd lost control of his wife, Delaney was up at seven, as usual, to drip Kyra's coffee, feed Jordan his fruit, granola and hi-fiber bar and let Osbert and Sacheverell out into the yard to perform their matinal functions. He hadn't forgotten his unfortunate encounter with Cándido four days earlier – the thought of it still made his stomach clench – but the needs and wants and minor irritations of daily life had begun to push it into the background. At the moment, his attention was focused entirely on getting through the morning ritual with his customary speed and efficiency. He was nothing if not efficient.

He made a sort of game of it, counting the steps it took him to shut the windows against the coming day's heat, empty yesterday's coffee grounds into the mulch bucket, transform two kiwis, an orange, apple, banana and a handful of Bing cherries into Jordan's medley of fresh fruit, and set the table for two. He skated across the tile floor to the dishwasher, flung open the cabinets, rocketed the plates and cutlery into position on the big oak table, all the while keeping an eye on the coffee, measuring out two bowls of dog food and juicing the oranges he'd plucked from the tree in the courtyard.

Typically, he stole a moment out in the courtyard to breathe in the cool of the morning and listen to the scrub jays wake up the neighborhood, but today he was in a rush and the only sound that penetrated his consciousness was a strange excited yelp from one of the dogs – they must have found something in the fenced-in yard behind the house, a squirrel or a gopher maybe – and then he was back in the kitchen, squeezing oranges. That was what he did, every morning, regular as clockwork: squeeze oranges. After which he would dash round the house gathering up Jordan's homework, his backpack, lunchbox and baseball cap, while Kyra sipped her coffee and washed down her twelve separate vitamin and mineral supplements with half a glass of fresh-squeezed orange juice. Then it was time to drive Jordan to school, while Kyra applied her makeup, wriggled into a form-fitting skirt with matching jacket and propelled her Lexus over the crest of the canyon and into Woodland Hills, where she was the undisputed volume leader at Mike Bender Realty, Inc. And then, finally, Delaney would head back home, have a cup of herbal tea and two slices of wheat toast, dry, and let the day settle in around him.

Unless there was an accident on the freeway or a road crew out picking up or setting down their ubiquitous plastic cones, he would be back at home and sitting at his desk by nine. This was the moment he lived for, the moment his day really began. Unfailingly, no matter what pressures were brought to bear on him or what emergencies arose, he allotted the next four hours to his writing – four hours during which he could let go of the world around him, his fingers grazing lightly over the keyboard, the green glow of the monitor bathing him in its hypnotic light. He took the phone off the hook, pulled the shades and crept into the womb of language.

There, in the silence of the empty house, Delaney worked out the parameters of his monthly column for *Wide Open Spaces,* a naturalist's observations of the life blooming around him day by day, season by season. He called it "Pilgrim at Topanga Creek" in homage to Annie Dillard, and while he couldn't pretend to her mystical connection to things, or her verbal virtuosity either, he did feel that he stood apart from his fellow men and women, that he saw more deeply and felt more passionately – particularly about nature. And every day, from nine to one, he had the opportunity to prove it.

Of course, some days went better than others. He tried to confine himself to the flora and fauna of Topanga Canyon and the surrounding mountains, but increasingly he found himself brooding over the fate of the pupfish, the Florida manatee and the spotted owl, the ocelot, the pine marten, the panda. And how could he ignore the larger trends – overpopulation, desertification, the depletion of the seas and the forests, global warming and loss of habitat? We were all right in America, sure, but it was crazy to think you could detach yourself from the rest of the world, the world of starvation and loss and the steady relentless degradation of the environment. Five and a half billion people chewing up the resources of the planet like locusts, and only seventy-three California condors left in all the universe.

It gave him pause. It depressed him. There were days when he worked himself into such a state he could barely lift his fingers to the keys, but fortunately the good days outnumbered them, the days when he celebrated his afternoon hikes through the chaparral and into the ravines of the mist-hung mountains, and that was what people wanted – celebration, not lectures, not the strident call to ecologic arms, not the death knell and the weeping and gnashing of environmental teeth. The world was full of bad news. Why contribute more?

The sun had already begun to burn off the haze by the time Jordan scuffed into the kitchen, the cat at his heels. Jordan was six years old, dedicated to Nintendo, superheroes and baseball cards, though as far as Delaney could see he had no interest whatever in the game of baseball beyond possessing the glossy cardboard images of the players. He favored his mother facially and in the amazing lightness of his hair, which was so pale as to be nearly translucent. He might have been big for his age, or maybe he was small – Delaney had nothing to compare him to.

"Kiwi," Jordan said, thumping into his seat at the table, and that was all. Whether this was an expression of approval or distaste, Delaney couldn't tell. From the living room came the electronic voice of the morning news: *Thirty-seven Chinese nationals were drowned early today when a smuggler's ship went aground just east of the Golden Gate Bridge . . .* Outside, beyond the windows, there was another yelp from the dogs.

Jordan began to rotate his spoon in the bowl of fruit, a scrape and clatter accompanied by the moist sounds of mastication. Delaney, his back to the table, was scrubbing the counter in the vicinity of the stove, though any splashes of cooking oil or spatters of sauce must have been purely imaginary since he hadn't actually cooked anything. He scrubbed for the love of scrubbing. "Okay, buckaroo," he called over his shoulder, "you've got two choices today as far as your hi-fiber bar is concerned: Cranberry Nut and Boysenberry Supreme. What'll it be?"

From a mouth laden with kiwi: "Papaya Coconut."

"You got the last one yesterday."

No response.

"So what'll it be?"

Kyra insisted on the full nutritional slate for her son every morning — fresh fruit, granola with skim milk and brewer's yeast, hi-fiber bar. The child needed roughage. Vitamins. Whole grains. And breakfast, for a growing child at least, was the most important meal of the day, the foundation of all that was to come. That was how she felt. And while Delaney recognized a touch of the autocratic and perhaps even fanatic in the regimen, he by and large subscribed to it. He and Kyra had a lot in common, not only temperamentally, but in terms of their beliefs and ideals too — that was what had attracted them to each other in the first place. They were both perfectionists, for one thing. They abhorred clutter. They were joggers, nonsmokers, social drinkers, and if not full-blown vegetarians, people who were conscious of their intake of animal fats. Their memberships included the Sierra Club, Save the Children, the National Wildlife Federation and the Democratic Party. They preferred the contemporary look to Early American or kitsch. In religious matters, they were agnostic.

Delaney's question remained unanswered, but he was used to cajoling Jordan over his breakfast. He tiptoed across the room to hover behind the boy, who was playing with his spoon and chanting something under his breath. "Rookie card, rookie card," Jordan was saying, dipping into his granola without enthusiasm. "No looking now," Delaney warned, seductively tapping a foil-wrapped bar on either side of the boy's thin wilted neck, "right hand or left?"

Jordan reached up with his left hand, as Delaney knew he would, fastening on the Boysenberry Supreme bar just as Kyra, hunched over the weight of two boxes of hand-addressed envelopes — Excelsior, 500 Count — clattered into the kitchen in her heels. She made separate kissing motions in the direction of her husband and son, then slid into her chair, poured herself half a cup of coffee lightened with skim milk — for the calcium — and began sifting purposively through the envelopes.

"Why can't I have Sugar Pops or Honey Nut Cheerios like other kids? Or bacon and eggs?" Jordan pinched his voice. "Mom? Why can't I?"

Kyra gave the stock response — "You're not other kids, that's why" — and Delaney was taken back to his own childhood, a rainy night in the middle of an interminable winter, a plate of liver, onions and boiled potatoes before him.

"I hate granola," Jordan countered, and it was like a Noh play, timeless ritual.

"It's good for you."

"Yeah, sure". Jordan made an exaggerated slurping sound, sucking the milk through his teeth.

"Think of all the little children who have nothing to eat," Kyra said without looking up, and Jordan, sticking to the script, came right back at her: "Let's send them this."

Now she looked up. "Eat," she said, and the drama was over.

"Busy day?" Delaney murmured, setting Kyra's orange juice down beside the newspaper and unscrewing the childproof caps of the sturdy plastic containers that held her twelve separate vitamin and mineral supplements. He did the little things for her — out of love and consideration, sure, but also in acknowledgment of the fact that she was the chief breadwinner here, the one who went off to the office while he stayed home. Which was all right by him. He had none of those juvenile macho hang-ups about role reversal and who wore the pants and all of that — real estate was her life, and he was more than happy to help her with it, so long as he got his four hours a day at the keyboard.

Kyra lifted her eyebrows, but didn't look up. She was tucking what looked to be a small white packet into each of the envelopes in succession. "Busy?" she echoed. "Busy isn't the word for it. I'm presenting two offers this morning, both of them real low-ball, I've got a buyer with cold feet on that Calabasas property — with escrow due to close in eight days — and I'm scheduled for an open house on the Via Escobar place at one . . . is that the dogs I hear? What are they barking at?"

Delaney shrugged. Jordan had shucked the foil from his hi-fiber bar and was drifting toward the TV room with it – which meant he was going to be late for school if Delaney didn't hustle him out of there within the next two minutes. The cat, as yet unfed, rubbed up against Delaney's leg. "I don't know," he said. "They've been yapping since I let them out. Must be a squirrel or something. Or maybe Jack's dog got loose again and he's out there peeing on the fence and driving them into a frenzy."

"Anyway," Kyra went on, "it's going to be hell. And it's Carla Bayer's birthday, so after work a bunch of us – don't you think this is a cute idea?" She held up one of the packets she'd been stuffing the envelopes with. It was a three-by-five seed packet showing a spray of flowers and printed with the legend *Forget-Me-Not, Compliments of Kyra Menaker-Mossbacher, Mike Bender Realty, Inc.*

"Yeah, I guess," he murmured, wiping at an imaginary speck on the counter. This was her way of touching base with her clients. Every month or so, usually in connection with a holiday, she went through her mailing list (consisting of anyone she'd ever sold to or for, whether they'd relocated to Nome, Singapore or Irkutsk or passed on into the Great Chain of Being) and sent a small reminder of her continued existence and willingness to deal. She called it "keeping the avenues open." Delaney reached down to stroke the cat. "But can't one of the secretaries do this sort of thing for you?"

"It's the personal touch that counts – and moves property. How many times do I have to tell you?"

There was a silence, during which Delaney became aware of the cartoon jingle that had replaced the voice of the news in the other room, and then, just as he was clearing Jordan's things from the table and checking the digital display on the microwave for the time – 7:32 – the morning fell apart. Or no: it was torn apart by a startled breathless shriek that rose up from beyond the windows as if out of some primal dream. This was no yip, no yelp, no bark or howl – this was something final and irrevocable, a predatory scream that took the varnish off their souls, and it froze them in place. They listened, horrified, as it rose in pitch until it choked off as suddenly as it had begun.

The aftereffect was electric. Kyra bolted up out of her chair, knocking over her coffee cup and scattering envelopes; the cat darted between Delaney's legs and vanished; Delaney dropped the plate on the floor and groped for the counter like a blind man. And then Jordan was coming through the doorway on staccato feet, his face opened up like a pale nocturnal flower: "Delaney," he gasped, "Delaney, something, something—"

But Delaney was already in motion. He flung open the door and shot through the courtyard, head down, rounding the corner of the house just in time to see a dun-colored blur scaling the six-foot chainlink fence with a tense white form clamped in its jaws. His brain decoded the image: a coyote had somehow managed to get into the enclosure and seize one of the dogs, and there it was, wild nature, up and over the fence as if this were some sort of circus act. Shouting to hear himself, shouting nonsense, Delaney charged across the yard as the remaining dog (Osbert? Sacheverell?) cowered in the corner and the dun blur melded with the buckwheat, chamise and stiff high grass of the wild hillside that gave onto the wild mountains beyond.

He didn't stop to think. In two bounds he was atop the fence and dropping to the other side, absently noting the paw prints in the dust, and then he was tearing headlong through the undergrowth, leaping rocks and shrubs and dodging the spines of the yucca plants clustered like breastworks across the slope. He was running, that was all he knew. Branches raked him like claws. Burrs bit into his ankles. He kept going, pursuing a streak of motion, the odd flash of white: now he saw it, now he didn't. "Hey!" he shouted. "Hey, goddamnit!"

The hillside sloped sharply upward, rising through the colorless scrub to a clump of walnut trees and jagged basalt outcroppings that looked as if they'd poked through the ground overnight. He saw the thing suddenly, the pointed snout and yellow eyes, the high stiff leggy gait as it struggled with its burden, and it was going straight up and into the trees. He shouted again and this time the shout was answered from below. Glancing over his shoulder, he saw that Kyra was coming up the hill with her long jogger's strides, in blouse, skirt and stocking feet. Even at this distance he could recognize the look on her face – the grim set of her jaw, the flaring eyes and clamped mouth that spelled doom for whoever got in her way, whether it was a stranger who'd locked his dog in a car with the windows rolled up or the hapless seller who refused a cash-out bid. She was coming, and that spurred him on. If he could only stay close the coyote would have to drop the dog, it would have to.

By the time he reached the trees his throat was burning. Sweat stung his eyes and his arms were striped with nicks and scratches. There was no sign of the dog and he pushed on through the trees to where the slope fell away to the feet of the next hill beyond it. The brush was thicker here — six feet high and so tightly interlaced it would have taken a machete to get through it in places — and he knew, despite the drumming in his ears and the glandular rush that had him pacing and whirling and clenching and unclenching his fists, that it was looking bad. Real bad. There were a thousand bushes out there — five thousand, ten thousand — and the coyote could be crouched under any one of them.

It was watching him even now, he knew it, watching him out of slit wary eyes as he jerked back and forth, frantically scanning the mute clutter of leaf, branch and thorn, and the thought infuriated him. He shouted again, hoping to flush it out. But the coyote was too smart for him. Ears pinned back, jaws and forepaws stifling its prey, it could lie there, absolutely motionless, for hours. "Osbert!" he called out suddenly, and his voice trailed off into a hopeless bleat. "Sacheverell!"

The poor dog. It couldn't have defended itself from a rabbit. Delaney stood on his toes, strained his neck, poked angrily through the nearest bush. Long low shafts of sunlight fired the leaves in an indifferent display, as they did every morning, and he looked into the illuminated depths of that bush and felt desolate suddenly, empty, cored out with loss and helplessness.

"Osbert!" The sound seemed to erupt from him, as if he couldn't control his vocal cords. "Here, boy! Come!" Then he shouted Sacheverell's name, over and over, but there was no answer except for a distant cry from Kyra, who seemed to be way off to his left now.

All at once he wanted to smash something, tear the bushes out of the ground by their roots. This didn't have to happen. It didn't. If it wasn't for those idiots leaving food out for the coyotes as if they were nothing more than sheep with bushy tails and eyeteeth . . . and he'd warned them, time and again. You can't be heedless of your environment. You can't. Just last week he'd found half a bucket of Kentucky Fried Chicken out back of the Dagolian place — waxy red-and-white-striped cardboard with a portrait of the grinning chicken-killer himself smiling large — and he'd stood up at the bimonthly meeting of the property owners' association to say something about it. They wouldn't even listen. Coyotes, gophers, yellow jackets, rattlesnakes even — they were a pain in the ass, sure, but nature was the least of their problems. It was humans they were worried about. The Salvadorans, the Mexicans, the blacks, the gangbangers and taggers and carjackers they read about in the Metro section over their bran toast and coffee. That's why they'd abandoned the flatlands of the Valley and the hills of the Westside to live up here, outside the city limits, in the midst of all this scenic splendor.

Coyotes? Coyotes were quaint. Little demidogs out there howling at the sunset, another amenity like the oaks, the chaparral and the views. No, all Delaney's neighbors could talk about, back and forth and on and on and on as if it were the key to all existence, was gates. A gate, specifically. To be erected at the main entrance and manned by a twenty-four-hour guard to keep out those very gangbangers, taggers and carjackers they'd come here to escape. Sure. And now poor Osbert — or Sacheverell — was nothing more than breakfast.

The fools. The idiots.

Delaney picked up a stick and began to beat methodically at the bushes.

Reproduced by kind permission of Bloomsbury Publishing Plc and Viking Penguin.

BOOKS

In the following listing, wherever a book is in print, the publisher's name is given in parentheses after the title, in the format: UK publisher; US publisher. Where books are published in only one of these countries, we have specified which one; when the same company publishes the book in both, it appears just once.

TRAVEL AND IMPRESSIONS

Tim Cahill *Jaguars Ripped My Flesh* (Fourth Estate; Vintage). Adventure travel through California and the world, including skin diving with hungry sharks off LA and getting lost and found in Death Valley. Thoughtful and sensitive yet still a thrill a minute.

Jan Morris *Destinations* (OUP, UK). Of the essay on LA in this fine collection of essays written for *Rolling Stone* magazine, Joan Didion said, "A lot of people come here and don't get it. She got it."

Peter Theroux *Translating LA* (Norton). East Coaster-gone-West Theroux tours some of the more interesting neighborhoods which make up his new home. Part history, part observation and part anecdote, it digs deeper than some, but ultimately fails to spark.

Mark Twain *Roughing It* (Penguin; University of California Press). Vivid tales of frontier California, particularly evocative of life in the silver mines of the 1860s Comstock Lode, where Twain got his start as a journalist and story-teller.

John Waters *Crackpot* (Fourth Estate; Random House). Odds and ends from the Pope of Trash, the mind behind cult film *Pink Flamingos*, including a personalized tour of LA.

Edmund White *States of Desire* (Picador; Plume). Part of a cross-country sojourn that includes a rather superficial account of the gay scene in 1970s LA.

Tom Wolfe *The Electric Kool-Aid Acid Test* (Black Swan; Bantam). Take a trip with the Grateful Dead and the Hell's Angels on the magic bus of Ken Kesey and the Merry Pranksters as they travel through the early days of the psychedelic 1960s, on a mission to turn California youth onto LSD.

HISTORY

Walton Bean *California: An Interpretive History* (McGraw-Hill). Blow-by-blow account of the history of California, including all the shady deals and back-room politicking, presented in accessible, anecdotal form.

Daniel Boorstin *The Americas 2: The National Experience* (Random House; Cardinal, US o/p). Heavy going because of the glut of detail, but otherwise an energetic appraisal of the social forces that shaped the modern USA, with several chapters on the settlement of the West.

Carey McWilliams *Southern California: An Island on the Land* (Gibbs Smith, US). The bible of Southern Californian histories, focusing on the key years between the two world wars. Evocatively written and richly detailed.

Kevin Starr *Inventing the Dream* (OUP). One of a series of captivating books – the other two are *Material Dreams* (OUP) and *Americans and the Californian Dream* (OUP, US o/p) studying the phenomenon known as California. Cultural histories written with a novelist's flair.

POLITICAL, SOCIAL AND ETHNIC

Jean Baudrillard *America* (Verso). Scattered thoughts of the trendy French philosopher, whose (very) occasionally brilliant but often overreaching exegesis of American Pop Culture, especially in LA, is undermined by factual inaccuracy.

Mike Davis *City of Quartz: Excavating the Future in Los Angeles* (Vintage). The best modern history of LA bar none, with a wealth of factual and anecdotal information painting a clear picture of a city on the edge of apocalypse.

Joan Didion *Slouching Towards Bethlehem* (Flamingo; Noonday Press). Selected essays from one of California's best journalists, taking a critical look at Sixties California, from the acid culture of San Francisco to a profile of American hero John Wayne. In a similar style, *The White Album* (Farrar Straus & Giroux, UK) traces the West Coast characters and events that shaped the Sixties and Seventies, including The Doors, Charles Manson and the Black Panthers.

Frances Fitzgerald *Cities on a Hill* (Picador; Simon & Schuster). Intelligent and sympathetic exploration of four of the odder corners of American culture, including San Francisco's gay Castro district.

Lynell George *No Crystal Stair* (Verso; Anchor). A perceptive account of life in LA's black community from one of the city's most respected African-American journalists.

Russel Miller *Barefaced Messiah* (Sphere; Holt both o/p). An eye-opening study of the rise and rise of L. Ron Hubbard and his Scientology cult, who have their HQ in LA and their devotees lurking everywhere.

Jay Stevens *Storming Heaven: LSD and the American Dream* (Flamingo; HarperPerennial). An engaging account of psychedelic drugs and their relationship with American society through the Sixties, with an epilogue to bring things up to date with "designer drugs" – Venus, Ecstasy, Vitamin K and others – and the inner space they apparently help some modern Californians chart.

Danny Sugarman *Wonderland Avenue* (Abacus; Bullfinch). Publicist for The Doors and other seminal US rock bands from the late Sixties on, Sugarman delivers a raunchy autobiographical account of sex, drugs, and LA rock'n'roll.

ARCHITECTURE

Reyner Banham *Los Angeles: The Architecture of Four Ecologies* (Penguin). The most lucid account of how LA's history has shaped its present form; the author's enthusiasms are infectious.

Philip Jodidio *Contemporary Californian Architects* (Taschen). This glossy trilingual (English, French and German) book argues that the public and private buildings of Frank Gehry, Eric Owen Moss, Frank Israel and Michael Routundi, among others, are strongly influenced by the state itself. The gorgeous photographs strengthen the case.

Sam Hall Kaplan *LA Lost and Found: An Architectural History of Los Angeles* (Random House, US). The text is informative but dull, though the outstanding photos vividly portray the city's growth and the trends in its design.

Charles Moore *The City Observed: Los Angeles* (Random House, US). The best book to guide you around the diffuse buildings and settings of LA, loaded with maps, illustrations and historical anecdotes.

HOLLYWOOD/THE MOVIES

Kenneth Anger *Hollywood Babylon* (Arrow; Bantam). A vicious yet high-spirited romp through Tinseltown's greatest scandals, although the facts are bent rather too often. A rarer second volume covers more recent times, but was hurriedly put together and shoddily researched.

Peter Bogdanovich *Who the Devil made It* (Random House, US). Acclaimed new book of conversations with the great Hollywood filmmakers.

David Bordwell, Janet Staiger & Kirstin Thompson *The Classical Hollywood Cinema* (Routledge; Columbia UP). Academic handbook aimed at the serious student, but still a generally interesting account of the techniques used in the best-known Hollywood movies up to 1960.

Kevin Brownlow *Hollywood: The Pioneers* (Knopf, US). History of the founding of Hollywood by one of the great historians of the early days of cinema. (Brownlow and David Gill's 1980 TV documentary *Hollywood* is available on video.)

Otto Friedrich *City of Nets* (Headline o/p; University of California Press). A rich and colorful social and cultural history of Hollywood during its golden age in the Forties.

Clayton R. Koppes & Gregory D. Black *Hollywood Goes to War* (University of California Press; I.B Tauris). Masterly examination of the influence of World War II on the film industry – and vice versa.

Barry Norman *Talking Pictures: The Story of Hollywood* (Arrow; NAL-Dutton o/p). The most accessible mainstream outline of the growth of movies in Hollywood, informative and pleasantly irreverent in tone.

Julia Phillips *You'll Never Eat Lunch in This Town Again* (Mandarin; Signet). From the woman who became a Hollywood somebody by co-producing *The Sting*, a diary of drug abuse, spouse abuse and film-business bitching.

SPECIFIC GUIDES

Bicycle Rider Directory (Cycle America, US). Low-cost guide to do-it-yourself bicycle touring around the Bay Area and Napa and Sonoma valleys, with good fold-out route maps.

Jack Erickson *Brewery Adventures in the Wild West* (Redbrick Press, US). A comprehensive list of over a hundred beer-bars and breweries.

Tom Kirkendall & Vicky Spring *Bicycling the Pacific Coast* (Mountaineers Books). Detailed guide to the bike routes all the way along the coast from Mexico up to Canada.

National Audobon Society Nature Guides: *Western Forests; Deserts; Pacific Coast; Wetlands* and others (Random House; Knopf). California has six of the world's seven major ecosystem types, and between them, these immaculately researched and beautifully photographed field guides, though not specific to California, cover the lot.

National Geographic Society *A Field Guide to the Birds of North America* (National Geographic). Self-explanatory – and thoroughly useful.

Peterson Series Field Guides: *A Field Guide to Western Reptiles and Amphibians; A Field Guide to the Insects of America North of Mexico; A Field Guide to Pacific State Wildflowers* (Houghton Mifflin). Excellent general field guides to the flora and fauna of California and the West Coast.

Schaffer *The Pacific Crest Trail (California)* (Atlantic Books). A guide to the southern section of the trail that leads all the way from Mexico to Canada through the Sierra Nevada range.

David & Kay Scott *Traveling and Camping in the National Park Areas: the Western States* (Globe Pequot). How to get around and camp in the West's National Parks, including Yosemite and the Kings Canyon.

Tom Steinstra and Michael Hodson *California Hiking: The Complete Guide* (Foghorn Press, US). Dense 800-page tome detailing over 1000 hikes, from hour-long strolls to the 1700 Californian miles of the Pacific Crest Trail. Unfortunately, the trail notes and maps are limited, and the text is hardly inspirational.

For guidebooks of specific relevance to travelers with **disabilities**, see pp.48–49 of Basics.

Walking the West Series: *Walking Southern California; Walking the California Coast; Walking California's State Parks* and others (HarperReference). Well written and produced paperbacks, each covering over a hundred excellent day walks from two to twenty miles. They're strong on practical details (maps, route descriptions and so on), and boast inspiring prose and historical background. Recommended.

CALIFORNIA IN FICTION

James P. Blaylock *Land of Dreams* (Grafton o/p; Ace Books). A fantastic tale spun out as the twelve-year Solstice comes to a Northern Californian coastal town.

T. Coraghessan Boyle *The Tortilla Curtain* (Bloomsbury; Penguin). Set in LA, this novel boldly borrows its premise – a privileged white man running down a member of the city's ethnic underclass – from Tom Wolfe's *The Bonfire of the Vanities*, and develops its plot with a similar pacey intensity. See p.611 for an extract from the novel.

Ray Bradbury *The Martian Chronicles* (Flamingo; Bantam). Brilliant, lyrical study of colonization, of new worlds and new lands – it's very easy to read the Martian setting as a Californian one. Bradbury's first, and still best, book.

Scott Bradfield *What's Wrong With America* (Picador). Humor and idiosyncratic absurdity combine as Bradfield explores America's malaise through an elderly woman's slide towards mental breakdown. Southern California provides the backdrop and its people the caricatured bit players.

Richard Brautigan Born in Tacoma, Brautigan is more often associated with the California Beat writers of the Fifties and Sixties. His surreal fable-like work seems overtly simple, but is overlaid with cultural references which question the direction the country was traveling in. His most successful book, *Trout Fishing in America* (Vintage; Dell o/p), although designed as a fishing handbook, stealthily creates a disturbing image of contemporary life. Other novels include *A Confederate General from Big Sur* (Houghton Mifflin), *In Watermelon Sugar* (o/p), and he also wrote a fine book of poems, *The Pill Versus the Springhill Mine Disaster* (Dell, US).

Charles Bukowski *Post Office; Women* (Black Sparrow). Three hundred-hangovers-a-year Henry Chinaski (the author, thinly veiled) drinks and screws his way around downbeat LA, firstly as a misfit mailman, then as a moderately successful writer with his own tab at the local liquor store and an endless supply of willing female fans. Savage and quite unique. See also *Factotum* (Black Sparrow), which recounts Chinaski's early days.

James M. Cain *The Five Great Novels of James M. Cain* (Picador, UK); *Double Indemnity; The Postman Always Rings Twice; The Butterfly; Mildred Pierce; Love's Lovely Counterfeit* (all Vintage, US). Haunting stories of smoldering passion told with clipped prose and terse dialogue.

Raymond Carver *What We Talk About When We Talk About Love* (Harvil; Knopf); *Where I'm Calling From: New and Selected Stories* (Harvill; Vintage). Set mostly in the Northwest and Northern California, Carver's deceptively simple eye-level pictures of plain-dealing Americans, concise and sharply observed, are difficult to forget.

Raymond Chandler *Three Novels* (Penguin, UK); *The Raymond Chandler Omnibus* (Random House, US). Essential reading, some of the toughest and greatest LA crime fiction of the Thirties and Forties – including *The Big Sleep*, *The Lady in the Lake*, and *Farewell My Lovely*, to name only the best.

Susan Compo *Life After Death and Other Stories* (Faber). Strange and zany romp through the clubs, clothes and characters of LA's goth scene; completely original in style and scope, and very believable.

Philip K. Dick *A Scanner Darkly* (Voyager; Random House). Of all Dick's erratic but frequently brilliant books, this is the best evocation of California. Set in the mid-1990s, when society is split between the Straights, the Dopers and the Narks, it's a dizzying study of individual identity, authority and drugs. Among the pick of the rest of Dick's vast legacy is *Blade Runner/Do Androids Dream of Electric Sheep?* (Voyager; Ballantine), set (unlike the movie) in San Francisco.

Joan Didion *Run, River* (Vintage, US). Focuses on the Sacramento Valley of the author's childhood and follows its change from agriculture into a highly charged consumer society. In contrast, but just as successfully done, *Play It As It Lays* (Flamingo; Farrar Straus & Giroux) is an electrifying dash through the pills, booze, and self-destruction linked with the LA film world.

Bret Easton Ellis *Less Than Zero* (Picador; Vintage). Numbing but readable tale of wealthy LA teen life. A classic brat-pack tome, with influence and fame far in excess of its worth.

James Ellroy *White Jazz* (Arrow; Fawcett). The final instalment of Ellroy's quartet of LA books exploring, in nail-biting noir style, the mind-set of corrupt LA cops and psychotic criminals over three decades. The series began with *The Black Dahlia* and continued with *The Big Nowhere* and *LA Confidential* (all Arrow; Warner).

Robert Ferringo *The Horse Latitudes* (Pocket Books o/p; Avon). Drug-dealer turned lecturer on Mayan civilization returns to his Newport Beach house after a midnight swim to find his wife has run off – leaving behind a corpse.

F. Scott Fitzgerald *The Last Tycoon* (Penguin; Macmillan). Fitzgerald died before he completed his Hollywood novel, but what remains is executed in glittering prose, with passages of deep poignancy and tenderness, as well as Fitzgerald's trademark conjuring of glamorous decadence. The complex portrait of the brilliant, melancholy film producer Monroe Stahr is peculiarly memorable.

David Freeman *A Hollywood Education* (Michael Joseph o/p; Carrol & Graf). Cumulatively powerful collection of short stories concerning a writer's lot in Hollywood.

James Gardner *Fat City* (University of California Press). A beautifully precise, poignant account of small-time Stockton boxing, following the initiation and fitful progress of a young hopeful and the parallel decline of an old contender. Painfully exact on the confused, murky emotions of its men as their lives stagnate in the heat of the town and the surrounding country. Brilliantly filmed by John Huston, with a script by Gardner himself.

Ursula le Guin *Always Coming Home* (Gollancz; Bantam). Impressive "archeology of the future," describing the lifestyles and culture of a mysterious race living in Northern California.

Dashiell Hammett *The Four Great Novels* (Picador; Vintage); *The Maltese Falcon* (Random House, US). The former is a volume of seminal detective novels starring Sam Spade, the private investigator working out of San Francisco; the latter is probably Hammett's best-known work. See also the absorbing biography of Hammett: Diane Johnson's *Dashiell Hammett: A Life* (Picador; Fawcett).

Joseph Hansen *The Dave Brandstetter Omnibus* (No Exit Press, UK o/p); *Death Claims* (Holt; No Exit Press); *Gravedigger* (Holt; No Exit Press); *Skinflick* (Holt; No Exit Press); *Troublemaker* (Holt; No Exit Press). Entertaining tales of Dave Brandstetter, a gay insurance claims investigator, set against a vivid Southern California backdrop.

Aldous Huxley *Ape and Essence* (Flamingo; I.R. Dee); *After Many a Summer Dies the Swan* (I.R. Dee, US). Huxley spent his last twenty years earning a crust as a Hollywood screenwriter, and both these novels are a product of that time. The first chronicles moral degeneracy and Satanic rituals in post-apocalyptic Southern California; the latter, based on William Randolph Hearst, concerns a rich, pampered figure who surrounds himself with art treasures and dwells on the meaning of life.

Jack Kerouac *Desolation Angels* (Flamingo; Riverhead); *The Dharma Bums* (Penguin).The most influential of the Beat writers on the rampage in California. See also his first novel *On The Road* (Penguin), which has a little of San Francisco and a lot of the rest of the US.

Elmore Leonard *Get Shorty* (Penguin; Bantam). Ice-cool mobster Chili Palmer is a Miami debt collector who follows a client to Hollywood, and finds that the increasing intricacies of his own situation are translating themselves into a movie script.

David Lodge *Changing Places* (Penguin). Thinly disguised autobiographical tale of an English academic who spends a year teaching at UC Berkeley and finds himself bang in the middle of the late Sixties student upheaval.

Jack London *The Call of the Wild* (Penguin); *White Fang and Other Stories* (Penguin); *Martin Eden* (Penguin); *The Iron Heel* (Wordsworth Editions; Dugan). *The Call of the Wild*, a short story about a tame dog discovering the ways of the wilderness while forced to labor pulling sleds across the snow and ice of Alaska's Klondike, made London into the world's best-selling author almost overnight. Afterwards, frustrated by the emptiness of his easy fame and success, the young, self-taught author wrote the semi-autobiographical *Martin Eden*, in which he rails against the cultured veil of polite society. Besides his prolific fiction, London also wrote a number of somewhat sophomoric political essays and socialist tracts; the most effective was *The Iron Heel*, presaging the rise of Fascism.

Ross MacDonald *Black Money* (Allison & Busby; Vintage); *The Blue Hammer* (Allison & Busby; Vintage); *The Zebra-Striped Hearse* (Allison & Busby o/p; Knopf o/p); *The Doomsters*; *The Instant Enemy* (Allison & Busby, US). Following in the footsteps of Sam Spade and Philip Marlowe, private detective Lew Archer looks behind the glitzy masks of Southern California life to reveal the underlying nastiness of creepy sexuality and manipulation. All captivating reads.

Armistead Maupin *Tales of the City*; *Further Tales of the City* (both Black Swan; Harper-Collins); *More Tales of the City* (Corgi; Harper-Collins). Lively and witty soap operas detailing the sexual antics of a select group of archetypal San Francisco characters of the late Seventies and early Eighties. See also *Babycakes* (Black Swan; HarperCollins) and *Significant Others*, which continue the story, though in more depth, and *Sure of You* (last two Black Swan; Harper-Collins) – set several years later and more downbeat, though no less brilliant.

Brian Moore *The Great Victorian Collection* (Flamingo, UK). A professor dreams up a parking lot full of Victoriana, which becomes the biggest tourist attraction of Carmel, California.

Walter Mosely *Devil in a Blue Dress* (Pan; Pocket Books). The book that introduced Easy Rawlins, a black private detective in late-1940s South Central LA, the central character in an excellent portrayal of time and place. Easy gets further into his stride in the subsequent *A Red Death* and *White Butterfly* (both Pan; Pocket Books).

Thomas Pynchon *The Crying of Lot 49* (Vintage; HarperPerennial). Follows the hilarious adventures of techno-freaks and potheads in Sixties California, and reveals the sexy side of stamp-collecting.

Richard Rayner *Los Angeles without a Map* (Flamingo; Apa Productions). An English non-driving journalist goes to LA on a romantic whim and lives out movie fantasies made even more fantastic by the city itself.

Theodore Roszak *Flicker* (Bantam, US). In a tatty LA movie house, Jonathan Gates discovers cinema, "like a bewildered neophyte wandering into the dark womb of an unformed faith." His particular obsession is the director Max Castle – a genius of the silent era who disappeared under mysterious circumstances in the Forties – and it leads Gates into a labyrinthine conspiracy with its roots in medieval heresy. Unlikely, disturbing and immensely readable, *Flicker* deserves to be a Hollywood classic.

Danny Santiago *Famous All over Town* (New American Library, US). Coming-of-age novel set among the street gangs of East LA, vividly depicting life in the Hispanic community.

Vikram Seth *The Golden Gate* (Faber; Vintage). A novel in verse which traces the complex social lives of a group of San Francisco yuppies.

Mona Simpson *Anywhere But Here* (Faber; Vintage). Bizarre and unforgettable saga of a young girl and her ambitious mother as they pursue LA stardom for the daughter.

John Steinbeck *The Grapes of Wrath* (Mandarin; Penguin). The classic account of a migrant family forsaking the Midwest for the Promised Land. For more localized fare, read the light-hearted but crisply observed novella, *Cannery Row*, capturing daily life on the pre-war Monterey waterfront, or the epic *East of Eden* (both Mandarin; Penguin) which updates and resets the Bible in the Salinas Valley and depicts three generations of familial feuding.

Robert Louis Stevenson *The Silverado Squatters* (Everyman; Tuttle). Stevenson vividly describes the splendor of the San Francisco hills and the cast of eccentrics and immigrants that populate them, as well as the strange atmosphere of Silverado itself, a deserted former gold-rush settlement, where the last trace of the mine is "a mound of gravel, some wreck of a wooden aqueduct, and the mouth of a tunnel, like a treasure grotto in a fairy story." For an extract, see p.608.

Amy Tan *The Joy Luck Club* (Mandarin; Ivy). The premise of this novel is that four Chinese women, new arrivals in San Francisco in the 1940s, come together to play mahjong, and tell their stories. They have four daughters, divided between Chinese and American identities, who also tell their stories, from childhood and from their often troubled present. The format of the novel is over-complex so that it often reads like a book of unconnected short stories, but there are passages of brilliant prose, and the evocation of childhood fears and perceptions is wonderful. For an extract, see p.610.

Michael Tolkin *The Player* (Faber; Grove Atlantic). Convincing, multi-layered story of a movie executive using his power and contacts to skirt justice after committing murder.

Nathanael West *Complete Works* (Picador, UK o/p). Includes *The Day of the Locust*, an insightful and caustic tale that is *the* classic satire of early Hollywood.

MEXICAN-SPANISH TERMS

California is bound to its Spanish colonial and Mexican past, a fact manifest in the profusion of Spanish place names, particularly in the south of the state. Today large numbers of people living in California speak Spanish as their first language, so it can be useful to know a few terms. Note that the double-L is pronounced like a "Y" and an "Ñ" sounds like an N and a Y run together.

ABIERTO	open	**MAR**	sea
AGUA	water	**MESA**	high plateau, literally "table"
ALTA, ALTO	high		
ANGELES	angels	**MONTE**	mount(ain)
ARROYO	canyon or gully	**NEVADA**	snowy
AVENIDA	avenue	**NORTE**	north
BUENA, BUENO	good	**OBISPO**	bishop
CALIENTE	hot	**ORO**	gold
CALLE	street, pronounced "ka-ye"	**PARQUE**	park
		PESCADERO	fisherman
CERRADO	closed	**PLAYA**	beach
COSTA	coast	**REY**	king
CRUZ	cross	**RIO**	river
DE	of	**SAN, SANTA, SANTO**	saint
DEL	of the	**SIERRA**	mountain range
DORADO	golden	**SOL**	sun
EL	the	**SUR**	south
ESCONDIDO	hidden	**TAQUERIA**	taco stall or shop
GRANDE	big	**TIENDA**	shop
HERMOSA	beautiful	**TIERRA**	land
JOLLA	jewel, pronounced "hoya"	**TRES**	three
LAS, LOS	the (plural)	**VERDE**	green

For the basics, the most useful Language book on the market is *Mexican Spanish: A Rough Guide Phrasebook* (Rough Guides); £3.50/$5, which covers the essential phrases and expressions, as well as dipping into grammar and providing a fuller vocabulary in dictionary format.

INDEX

direct orders from

		UK£8.99	US$14.95	CAN$19.99
Amsterdam	1-85828-218-7			
Andalucia	1-85828-219-5	9.99	16.95	22.99
Antigua Mini Guide	1-85828-346-9	5.99	9.95	12.99
Australia	1-85828-220-9	13.99	21.95	29.99
Austria	1-85828-325-6	10.99	17.95	23.99
Bali & Lombok	1-85828-134-2	8.99	14.95	19.99
Bangkok Mini Guide	1-85828-345-0	5.99	9.95	12.99
Barcelona	1-85828-221-7	8.99	14.95	19.99
Belgium & Luxembourg	1-85828-222-5	10.99	17.95	23.99
Belize	1-85828-351-5	9.99	16.95	22.99
Berlin	1-85828-327-2	9.99	16.95	22.99
Boston Mini Guide	1-85828-321-3	5.99	9.95	12.99
Brazil	1-85828-223-3	13.99	21.95	29.99
Britain	1-85828-312-4	14.99	23.95	31.99
Brittany & Normandy	1-85828-224-1	9.99	16.95	22.99
Bulgaria	1-85828-183-0	9.99	16.95	22.99
California	1-85828-330-2	11.99	18.95	24.99
Canada	1-85828-311-6	12.99	19.95	25.99
Central America	1-85828-335-3	14.99	23.95	31.99
China	1-85828-225-X	15.99	24.95	32.99
Corfu & the Ionian Islands	1-85828-226-8	8.99	14.95	19.99
Corsica	1-85828-227-6	9.99	16.95	22.99
Costa Rica	1-85828-136-9	9.99	15.95	21.99
Crete	1-85828-316-7	9.99	16.95	22.99
Cyprus	1-85828-182-2	9.99	16.95	22.99
Czech & Slovak Republics	1-85828-317-5	11.99	18.95	24.99
Dublin Mini Guide	1-85828-294-2	5.99	9.95	12.99
Edinburgh Mini Guide	1-85828-295-0	5.99	9.95	12.99
Egypt	1-85828-188-1	10.99	17.95	23.99
Europe 1998	1-85828-289-6	14.99	19.95	25.99
England	1-85828-301-9	12.99	19.95	25.99
First Time Asia	1-85828-332-9	7.99	9.95	12.99
First Time Europe	1-85828-270-5	7.99	9.95	12.99
Florida	1-85828-184-4	10.99	16.95	22.99
France	1-85828-228-4	12.99	19.95	25.99
Germany	1-85828-309-4	14.99	23.95	31.99
Goa	1-85828-275-6	8.99	14.95	19.99
Greece	1-85828-300-0	12.99	19.95	25.99
Greek Islands	1-85828-310-8	10.99	17.95	23.99
Guatemala	1-85828-323-X	9.99	16.95	22.99
Hawaii: Big Island	1-85828-158-X	8.99	12.95	16.99
Hawaii	1-85828-206-3	10.99	16.95	22.99
Holland	1-85828-229-2	10.99	17.95	23.99
Hong Kong & Macau	1-85828-187-3	8.99	14.95	19.99
Hotels & Restos de France 1998	1-85828-306-X	12.99	19.95	25.99
Hungary	1-85828-123-7	8.99	14.95	19.99
India	1-85828-200-4	14.99	23.95	31.99
Ireland	1-85828-179-2	10.99	17.95	23.99
Israel & the Palestinian Territories	1-85828-248-9	12.99	19.95	25.99
Italy	1-85828-167-9	12.99	19.95	25.99
Jamaica	1-85828-230-6	9.99	16.95	22.99
Japan	1-85828-340-X	14.99	23.95	31.99
Jordan	1-85828-350-7	10.99	17.95	23.99
Kenya	1-85828-192-X	11.99	18.95	24.99
Lisbon Mini Guide	1-85828-297-7	5.99	9.95	12.99
London	1-85828-231-4	9.99	15.95	21.99
Madrid Mini Guide	1-85828-353-1	5.99	9.95	12.99
Mallorca & Menorca	1-85828-165-2	8.99	14.95	19.99
Malaysia, Singapore & Brunei	1-85828-232-2	11.99	18.95	24.99
Mexico	1-85828-044-3	10.99	16.95	22.99
Morocco	1-85828-169-5	11.99	18.95	24.99
Moscow	1-85828-322-1	9.99	16.95	22.99
Nepal	1-85828-190-3	10.99	17.95	23.99
New York	1-85828-296-9	9.99	15.95	21.99
New Zealand	1-85828-233-0	12.99	19.95	25.99
Norway	1-85828-234-9	10.99	17.95	23.99

UK orders: 0181 899 4036

around the world

		UK£	US$	CAN$
Pacific Northwest	1-85828-326-4	12.99	19.95	25.99
Paris	1-85828-235-7	8.99	14.95	19.99
Peru	1-85828-142-3	10.99	17.95	23.99
Poland	1-85828-168-7	10.99	17.95	23.99
Portugal	1-85828-313-2	10.99	17.95	23.99
Prague	1-85828-318-3	8.99	14.95	19.99
Provence & the Cote d'Azur	1-85828-127-X	9.99	16.95	22.99
The Pyrenees	1-85828-308-6	10.99	17.95	23.99
Rhodes & the Dodecanese	1-85828-120-2	8.99	14.95	19.99
Romania	1-85828-305-1	10.99	17.95	23.99
San Francisco	1-85828-299-3	8.99	14.95	19.99
Scandinavia	1-85828-236-5	12.99	20.95	27.99
Scotland	1-85828-302-7	9.99	16.95	22.99
Seattle Mini Guide	1-85828-324-8	5.99	9.95	12.99
Sicily	1-85828-178-4	9.99	16.95	22.99
Singapore	1-85828-237-3	8.99	14.95	19.99
South Africa	1-85828-238-1	12.99	19.95	25.99
Southwest USA	1-85828-239-X	10.99	16.95	22.99
Spain	1-85828-240-3	11.99	18.95	24.99
St Petersburg	1-85828-298-5	9.99	16.95	22.99
Sweden	1-85828-241-1	10.99	17.95	23.99
Syria	1-85828-331-0	11.99	18.95	24.99
Thailand	1-85828-140-7	10.99	17.95	24.99
Tunisia	1-85828-139-3	10.99	17.95	24.99
Turkey	1-85828-242-X	12.99	19.95	25.99
Tuscany & Umbria	1-85828-243-8	10.99	17.95	23.99
USA	1-85828-307-8	14.99	19.95	25.99
Venice	1-85828-170-9	8.99	14.95	19.99
Vienna	1-85828-244-6	8.99	14.95	19.99
Vietnam	1-85828-191-1	9.99	15.95	21.99
Wales	1-85828-245-4	10.99	17.95	23.99
Washington DC	1-85828-246-2	8.99	14.95	19.99
West Africa	1-85828-101-6	15.99	24.95	34.99
Zimbabwe & Botswana	1-85828-186-5	11.99	18.95	24.99

Phrasebooks

Czech	1-85828-148-2	3.50	5.00	7.00
Egyptian Arabic	1-85828-319-1	4.00	6.00	8.00
French	1-85828-144-X	3.50	5.00	7.00
German	1-85828-146-6	3.50	5.00	7.00
Greek	1-85828-145-8	3.50	5.00	7.00
Hindi & Urdu	1-85828-252-7	4.00	6.00	8.00
Hungarian	1-85828-304-3	4.00	6.00	8.00
Indonesian	1-85828-250-0	4.00	6.00	8.00
Italian	1-85828-143-1	3.50	5.00	7.00
Japanese	1-85828-303-5	4.00	6.00	8.00
Mandarin Chinese	1-85828-249-7	4.00	6.00	8.00
Mexican Spanish	1-85828-176-8	3.50	5.00	7.00
Portuguese	1-85828-175-X	3.50	5.00	7.00
Polish	1-85828-174-1	3.50	5.00	7.00
Russian	1-85828-251-9	4.00	6.00	8.00
Spanish	1-85828-147-4	3.50	5.00	7.00
Swahili	1-85828-320-5	4.00	6.00	8.00
Thai	1-85828-177-6	3.50	5.00	7.00
Turkish	1-85828-173-3	3.50	5.00	7.00
Vietnamese	1-85828-172-5	3.50	5.00	7.00

Reference

Classical Music	1-85828-113-X	12.99	19.95	25.99
European Football	1-85828-256-X	14.99	23.95	31.99
Internet	1-85828-288-8	5.00	8.00	10.00
Jazz	1-85828-137-7	16.99	24.95	34.99
Millennium	1-85828-314-0	5.00	8.95	11.99
More Women Travel	1-85828-098-2	10.99	16.95	22.99
Opera	1-85828-138-5	16.99	24.95	34.99
Reggae	1-85828-247-0	12.99	19.95	25.99
Rock	1-85828-201-2	17.99	26.95	35.00
World Music	1-85828-017-6	16.99	22.95	29.99

US/International orders: 1-800-253-6476

Stay in touch with us!

ROUGH*NEWS* **is Rough Guides' free newsletter. In three issues a year we give you news, travel issues, music reviews, readers' letters and the latest dispatches from authors on the road.**

I would like to receive ROUGH*NEWS*: please put me on your free mailing list.

NAME . . . .

ADDRESS . . . .

Please clip or photocopy and send to: Rough Guides, 1 Mercer Street, London WC2H 9QJ, England or Rough Guides, 375 Hudson Street, New York, NY 10014, USA.